"If a man empties his purse into his head, no man can take it away from him. An investment in knowledge always pays the best interest."

BENJAMIN FRANKLIN

1999 EDITION

The Complete Car Cost Guide

Credits

President
Kevin Dulsky

Founder
Peter Levy

Managing Editors
Peter Bohr
Steve Gross
Vincent Paul Mendolia
Kristina A. Olson

Editorial Staff
Stephen Landau
Carolyn A. Moyer

Research Director
Charles A. Donaldson

Research Manager
Gloria A. Merck

Sr. Database Analysts
Scott Bennett
Jeani Blom
Marlon Calso
Vu Duong
Lew Morris
Joseph A. Perez
Raj Shah
Ken Takahashi
Brad Taylor
Shane Toy

Database Analysts
Jeff Bryan
John Conde
Jill Jenkins
Antonio Lim
Joe Maille

IT Manager
Timothy H. Denney

Programming
Josh de la Cuesta
Deborah L. Eldridge
Warren Hirakawa
Chris Howard
Chris Mangrum
Donald J. Oates
Roy Seta
Stephen Smith

Public Relations
Pacific Communications Group, LLC

Cover Design
Tollner Design Group

Graphics
Greg Hester

Photo Scanning
Jon Florence

Contributors
Ron Dion
Kylan Frazer
Enrico Gonzales
Naomi Johnston
Martin King
Aimee Leanos
Jeffrey Minton
Linda Sbragia
Brenda Solis
Holly von Mulldorfer
Michael Beebe

Thanks

A special thank you to:

Mr. John Dinkel
Ms. Carol Jaech, Santa Clara County Library System
Mr. Tom Kempner
Mr. Ron Raymond
Mr. Gregory A. Seigler
Mr. Richard Saul Wurman, author of *Information Anxiety*, for his input toward the original design of this book.

Thanks to the public relations, technical, and marketing departments of all the manufacturers whose vehicles are represented in this book for their willingness to provide information and answer questions.

Thanks to the people of the United States Government, Department of Commerce, Department of Energy, and Department of Transportation for their information and support.

Thanks to Linotext.

Thanks to the technical support staff at ACI US for their technical information.

Finally, a special thanks to all of our customers for making this book a success.

Production

This book was designed and produced using Macintosh OS® computer systems, with 4th Dimension® and Print Central™ software. Every page was printed directly onto film negatives. Photos were scanned using Adobe Photoshop® on a Microtek® scanning system.

Library of Congress Catalog Card Number: 98-86850

IntelliChoice, Inc.
471 Division Street
Campbell, California 95008-6922
Phone (408) 866-1400
Fax (408) 866-1470
info@intellichoice.com

Visit IntelliChoice on the World Wide Web at: http://www.intellichoice.com.

Printed and bound in the United States of America.

Ordering Information

Are you in the market for a van, wagon, utility vehicle, or truck? If so, pick up a copy of *The Complete Small Truck Cost Guide.*

Copies of *The Complete Small Truck Cost Guide* and *The Complete Car Cost Guide* may be ordered directly from the publisher.

Orders should be sent to:
IntelliChoice, Inc., 471 Division Street, Campbell, CA 95008-6922

Phone orders may be placed toll-free at 1-800-CAR-BOOK (1-800-227-2665).

Call (408) 866-1400 for current information on pricing and availability of these books or visit us on the World Wide Web at **http://www.intellichoice.com**

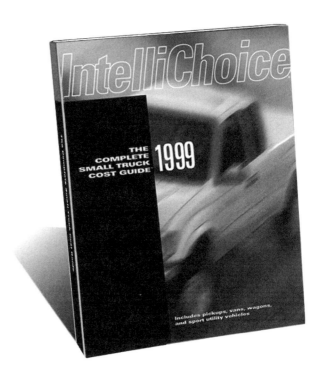

The Complete Small Truck Cost Guide $49*
(ISBN 0-941443-28-0)

The Complete Car Cost Guide $49*
(ISBN 0-941443-27-2)

*Includes shipping and handling cost.

To Our Continuing Readers

We have made changes that may interest our continuing readers. The changes are as follows:

Luxury Tax

Includes the new tax rate of 6% for every dollar over $36,000 of your purchase price.

Fuel Cost

Fuel cost has been changed as follows; $1.02 for unleaded regular, $1.12 for unleaded mid-grade, $1.21 for premium, and $1.05 for diesel.

Sales Tax Rate

The nationwide average for sales tax has been increased from 4.5% to 5%.

Loan Interest Rate

The annual loan interest rate has been reduced from 9.1% to 8.92%.

State Registration Fees

The national average one-time state registration fee has been increased to $13.00.

From the Founder

This is the last edition of *The Complete Car Cost Guide* to be published in this millenium. Next year's edition will focus on 2000 models, and will be published in the year 2000. (I know that the next millenium technically begins in 2001, but that's so anti-climatic compared to 2000).

We keep hearing of the coming great changes to us as individuals and as a society. Perhaps the automobile as we know it will become obsolete in the next millenium, or even in the next century.

But so long as there are individuals who purchase automobiles, and so long as automobiles remain such expensive items relative to most people's incomes, there will be a need to understand and evaluate automobile ownership costs.

Two vehicles with the same purchase price can have very different costs to own and operate. The buyer who knows this could save $500, $1,000, even $5,000 or more.

That's why *The Complete Car Cost Guide* is so useful. This is the only publication that will show you the long-term cost to own and operate any new vehicle you may be considering.

Armed with this information, you can purchase the right vehicle. The advice in this book can also help you purchase that right vehicle at the right price.

So even though the Jetson's "spacemobile" may be in our collective future, you're buying a land-based car in 1999. And if you invest the money that you save this year by choosing your next car wisely, you will be quite wealthy by the time George Jetson becomes your neighbor.

Shop wisely, and enjoy your new car!

Some final thoughts...

I always knew that someday I would be writing this letter, but it is bittersweet and difficult all the same.

This is the last letter that I will write as introduction to *The Complete Car Cost Guide* and as Chief Executive Officer of IntelliChoice, Inc.

Recently, I sold IntelliChoice to PRIMEDIA, Inc. after they made a very attractive offer. I am confident that I found a good home for IntelliChoice, which has been my labor of love for the past 12 years.

It's hard to imagine life without IntelliChoice, but we all must, on occasion, move on to new frontiers.

What I will miss most about IntelliChoice are the people that I've worked with, laughed with, sometimes cried with over the years. The people who have made IntelliChoice such a successful company, such an influential company, such a warm company.

There's Dave Chelemer, Autumn Allen, and Roy Koons, the first three employees. I bet they had no idea the company would grow as it did. Other people who were there at the beginning with encouragement and elbow grease were Bob Oliver and Steve Smith.

An honest thank you is due to my last manager at Apple Computer. If he and I hadn't had the professional differences that we did, I might not have left Apple to start IntelliChoice.

I thank the contributions of several people who were never IntelliChoice employees. Bryce Benjamin and Wayne Oler were always steady in their guidance as Directors. Art Jenkins, Richard Hart, and Gary David always provided professional, wise advice. Peter Bohr, Walter Burns, J.J. Chao, Louis Cooper, John Dinkel, Michael Everitt, Chris Ford,

Carol Jaech, Tom Kempner (and all the other IntelliChoice investors), Michael London, Ron Raymond, Nathan Shedroff, and Richard Saul Wurman all were great supporters who kept the faith when the company was on new and shaky ground.

Then there are the people who put in long years of hard work, most of whom are still loyally and enthusiastically working at IntelliChoice. These people, whom I count as my friends, include Kris Olson, Don Oates, Deb Eldridge, Charles Donaldson, and Tim Denny.

Carolyn Moyer, Benton McMillan-Gordon, Steve Landau, Vu Duong, Josh de la Cuesta, Chris Howard, and Brad Taylor were not there at the beginning, but their efforts over the past few years were key, and allowed me to focus my energy on growing the business.

It was Chris Mangrum's persistence that got IntelliChoice started on the internet back in 1994, and I greatly appreciate Chris' effort.

It's with gratitude and sadness that I reflect on the contributions of Martha Topor, who passed away last year, and Peter Baum, who is miraculously recovering from a massive heart attack as I write these words.

I have a special thank you for Vince Mendolia, who was there through thick and thin, and has seen the highest highs and the lowest lows (especially when I was beating him in our late night, take-a-break quarters matches).

Another special thank you is for Bryce Benjamin. Not only did Bryce provide insight and guidance as a Board member, he provided consistent encouragement. When I needed him most, he was there.

Of course, I've saved the biggest thank-yous for last. Steve Gross is my business partner, my colleague, sometimes my alter ego, my therapist, and most of all my friend. He was with this little experiment from the start, and has provided consistent encouragement and brainpower for the life of the company. He's been my friend since I was 13 years old, and is the only non-blood relative who is truly my son's uncle. To Steve, to whom I can't put my thanks into mere words, all I can say is that I hope (and I'm sure) that we remain close friends forever.

My wife Cheryl supported my ideas from the start. At one point when I was wavering in my commitment to IntelliChoice, she encouraged me to stick it out. She insisted that I was sure to make IntelliChoice a success, that I had the talent to conquer the world. To Cheryl, I love you now and always.

My Mom, my Dad, and my brothers always had confidence in me (Well, Mom and Dad anyway. After all, I'm the "little brother"). I'm thankful that we're even closer today than we ever were.

And that leaves my sweet son Noah. The light of my life, the reason I feel that I'm a blessed person, the reason I start each day with a smile. Noah, you are everything a father could want. I pledge to you now and forever to be the best Dad I can, and to help you, teach you, laugh with you, and be with you as you make the long and sometimes difficult journey to adulthood. The real reason that I sold IntelliChoice was to give us both greater opportunities, and to allow me to spend more time with you.

To you, IntelliChoice customers, thank you for allowing me to serve your needs. I always tried my best to deliver to you more than you expected.

If some of the above sounds melancholy, it reflects the bittersweet nature of saying goodbye. I've never been happier, but I guess you can be sad and happy simultaneously.

Thank you all for your support throughout the years. I wish you health, happiness, and peace.

Sincerely,

Peter S. Levy

Peter S. Levy

TABLE OF CONTENTS

TABLE OF CONTENTS

AUTOEXPLORER™

All prices listed below are based on the manufacturer's retail price and do not include factory or dealer installed options. Actual prices may vary due to rebates and local dealer markups.

Subcompact/Minicompact

	Under $13,000	$13,001-$16,000	$16,001-$21,000	Over $21,000
Acura			Integra GS (C) Integra LS (S, C)	2.3CL (C) 3.0CL (C) Integra GS (S) Integra GS-R (S)
Chevrolet	Metro (H) Metro LSi (S, H)			
Ford	Escort ZX2 Cool (C)	Escort ZX2 Hot (C)		
Honda	Civic CX (H) Civic DX (S, H, C)	Civic EX (C) Civic HX (C) Civic LX (S)	Civic EX (S)	Prelude (C) Prelude Type SH (C)
Hyundai		Tiburon (C) Tiburon FX (C)		
Mitsubishi	Mirage DE (S, C)	Mirage LS (S, C)		
Nissan	Sentra XE (S)	Sentra GXE (S) Sentra SE (S)		
Pontiac	Sunfire SE (S, C)	Sunfire GT (C)		Sunfire GT (CN)
Saturn	SC1 (C)	SC2 (C)		
Subaru		Impreza L AWD (S, C)	Impreza 2.5 RS AWD (C)	
Suzuki	Esteem GL (S) Swift (H)	Esteem GLX (S)		
Toyota				Celica GT (H, CN)
Volkswagen		Beetle GL (H)	Beetle GLS (H) Cabrio (CN)	Cabrio GLS (CN)

Compact

	Under $12,000	$12,001-$16,000	$16,001-$19,000	Over $19,000
Audi				A4 1.8T (S) A4 1.8T Quattro (S-4WD)
BMW				318 ti (H)
Chevrolet	Cavalier (S, C)	Cavalier LS (S) Cavalier RS (C) Cavalier Z24 (C) Prizm (S) Prizm LSi (S)		Cavalier Z24 (CN)
Chrysler			Sebring LX (C)	Sebring JX (CN) Sebring JXi (CN) Sebring LXi (C)
Daewoo	Lanos S (S, H) Lanos SE (S, H) Lanos SX (S, H)	Nubira CDX (S, H 4 Dr) Nubira SX (S, H 4 Dr)		
Dodge	Neon Competition (S, C) Neon Highline (S, C)	Avenger (C)	Avenger ES (C)	

C–Coupe	S–Sedan	H–Hatchback	CN–Convertible	4WD–4 Wheel Drive

All prices listed below are based on the manufacturer's retail price and do not include factory or dealer installed options. Actual prices may vary due to rebates and local dealer markups.

Compact continued

	Under $12,000	$12,001-$16,000	$16,001-$19,000	Over $19,000
Ford	Escort LX (S)	Contour LX (S) Contour SE (S) Escort SE (S)		Contour SVT (S)
Hyundai	Accent GL (S) Accent GS (H) Accent L (H) Elantra (S)	Elantra GLS (S)		
Infiniti				G20 (S) G20t (S)
Kia	Sephia (S) Sephia LS (S)			
Mazda	Protege DX (S)	Protege ES (S) Protege LX (S)		
Mercury	Tracer GS (S)	Tracer LS (S)	Cougar (C) Cougar V-6 (C) Mystique GS (S) Mystique LS (S)	
Nissan		Altima XE (S)	Altima GXE (S) Altima SE (S)	Altima GLE (S)
Oldsmobile			Alero GL (S, C) Alero GX (S, C)	Alero GLS (S, C)
Plymouth	Neon Competition (S, C) Neon Highline (S, C)			
Pontiac		Grand Am SE (C)	Grand Am SE (S) Grand Am SE 1 (S, C) Grand Am SE 2 (S, C)	Grand Am GT (S, C) Grand Am GT1 (S, C)
Saturn	SL (S) SL1 (S)	SL2 (S)		
Subaru				Legacy 2.5 GT AWD (S) Legacy L AWD (S) Legacy Limited AWD (S) Legacy Spt Utility Sedan AWD (S) Legacy Spt Utility Sedan Ltd AWD (S)
Toyota		Corolla CE (S) Corolla LE (S) Corolla VE (S)	Camry Solara SE (C)	Camry Solara SE V6 (C) Camry Solara SLE V6 (C)
Volkswagen		Golf GL (H 4 Dr) Golf Wolfsburg Edition (H 4 Dr) Jetta GL (S) Jetta TDI (S)	Jetta New GL (S) Jetta New GL TDI (S) Jetta New GLS (S) Jetta New GLS TDI (S) Jetta Wolfsburg Edition (S)	Golf GTI VR6 (H) Jetta GLX (S)

Midsize

	Under $18,000	$18,001-$20,000	$20,001-$22,000	Over $22,000
Buick		Century Custom (S)	Century Limited (S) Regal LS (S)	Regal GS (S)

C–Coupe	S–Sedan	H–Hatchback	CN–Convertible	4WD–4 Wheel Drive

All prices listed below are based on the manufacturer's retail price and do not include factory or dealer installed options. Actual prices may vary due to rebates and local dealer markups.

Midsize continued

	Under $18,000	$18,001-$20,000	$20,001-$22,000	Over $22,000
Chevrolet	Malibu (S)	Lumina (S) Lumina LS (S) Malibu LS (S) Monte Carlo LS (C)	Lumina LTZ (S) Monte Carlo Z34 (C)	
Chrysler		Cirrus LXi (S)		
Daewoo	Leganza SE (S) Leganza SX (S)	Leganza CDX (S)		
Dodge	Stratus (S)	Stratus ES (S)		
Ford	Taurus LX (S)	Taurus SE (S)		Taurus SHO (S)
Honda	Accord DX (S)	Accord LX (S, C)	Accord EX (S, C) Accord LX V-6 (S, C)	Accord EX V-6 (S, C)
Hyundai	Sonata (S) Sonata GLS (S)			
Mazda	626 LX (S)	626 ES (S) 626 LX V-6 (S)		626 ES V-6 (S)
Mercury		Sable GS (S) Sable LS (S)		
Mitsubishi	Galant DE (S) Galant ES (S)			Galant GTZ (S) Galant LS (S)
Nissan			Maxima GXE (S)	Maxima GLE (S) Maxima SE (S)
Oldsmobile		Cutlass GL (S) Cutlass GLS (S)	Intrigue GX (S)	Intrigue GL (S) Intrigue GLS (S)
Plymouth	Breeze (S)			
Pontiac		Grand Prix SE (S)	Grand Prix GT (S, C)	Grand Prix GTP (S, C)
Toyota	Camry CE (S)	Camry LE (S)	Camry LE V6 (S)	Camry XLE (S) Camry XLE V6 (S)
Volkswagen			Passat GLS (S)	Passat GLS V6 (S-4WD) Passat GLX V6 (S-4WD)

Large

	Under $22,000	$22,001-$24,000	$24,001-$28,000	Over $28,000
Buick		LeSabre Custom (S)	LeSabre Limited (S)	
Chrysler	Concorde (S)			300M (S) LHS (S)
Dodge	Intrepid (S)	Intrepid ES (S)		
Ford	Crown Victoria (S)	Crown Victoria LX (S)		
Mercury		Grand Marquis GS (S)	Grand Marquis LS (S)	
Oldsmobile		Eighty Eight (S)	Eighty Eight 50th Ann. Edition (S) Eighty Eight LS (S)	
Pontiac		Bonneville SE (S)		Bonneville SSE (S)
Toyota			Avalon XL (S)	Avalon XLS (S)

C–Coupe	S–Sedan	H–Hatchback	CN–Convertible	4WD–4 Wheel Drive

All prices listed below are based on the manufacturer's retail price and do not include factory or dealer installed options. Actual prices may vary due to rebates and local dealer markups.

Near Luxury

	Under $29,000	$29,001-$33,000	$33,001-$35,000	Over $35,000
Acura	3.2TL (S)			
Audi	A4 2.8 (S)	A4 2.8 Quattro (S-4WD)	A6 (S)	A6 Quattro (S-4WD)
BMW	323 i (S) 323 iS (C)		323 iC (CN) 328 i (S) 328 iS (C)	328 iC (CN)
Buick		Park Avenue (S)	Riviera (C)	Park Avenue Ultra (S)
Cadillac			Catera (S)	
Infiniti	I30 (S)	I30 Touring (S)		
Lexus		ES 300 (S)		
Mazda	Millenia (S)	Millenia S (S)		
Mercedes-Benz		C230 Kompressor (S)		C280 (S)
Mitsubishi	Diamante (S)			
Oldsmobile		LSS (S)		
Saab	9-3 (H 4 Dr, H)	9-3 SE (H 4 Dr) 9-5 (S)	9-5 SE (S) 9-5 V6 (S)	9-3 (CN) 9-3 SE (CN) 9-5 SE V6 (S)
Volvo	S70 (S)	S70 GLT (S)	S70 AWD (S) S70 T5 (S)	S80 2.9 (S)

Luxury

	Under $40,000	$40,001-$48,000	$48,001-$65,000	Over $65,000
Acura		3.5RL (S)		
Audi	A6 Avant (4WD)		A8 3.7 (S) A8 4.2 Quattro (S-4WD)	
BMW	528 i (S)	528 iT (W)	540 i (S) 540 iT (W) 740 i (S)	740 iL (S) 750 iL (S)
Cadillac	DeVille (S) Eldorado (C)	DeVille Concours (S) DeVille d'Elegance (S) Eldorado Touring Coupe (C) Seville SLS (S) Seville STS (S)		
Infiniti			Q45 (S) Q45 Touring (S)	
Jaguar			Vanden Plas (S) XJ8 (S) XJ8L (S)	XJR (S) XK8 (CN, C)
Lexus	GS 300 (S)	GS 400 (S) SC 300 (C)	LS 400 (S) SC 400 (C)	
Lincoln	Continental (S) Town Car Executive (S)	Town Car Cartier (S) Town Car Signature (S)		

C–Coupe	S–Sedan	H–Hatchback	CN–Convertible	4WD–4 Wheel Drive

All prices listed below are based on the manufacturer's retail price and do not include factory or dealer installed options. Actual prices may vary due to rebates and local dealer markups.

Luxury continued

	Under $40,000	$40,001-$48,000	$48,001-$65,000	Over $65,000
Mercedes-Benz		CLK 320 (C) CLK 320 Cabriolet (CN) CLK 430 (C) E300 (S) E300 Turbodiesel (S)	C43 (S) E300 AWD (S) E430 (S) S320 Standard Wheelbase (S)	CL500 (C) CL600 (C) S320 (S) S420 (S) S500 (S) S600 (S) SL500 Roadster (CN) SL600 Roadster (CN)
Oldsmobile	Aurora (S)			
Volvo	C70 (C)	C70 (CN) S80 T-6 (S)		

Base Sport

	Under $20,000	$20,001-$24,000	$24,001-$28,000	Over $28,000
Acura		Integra GS-R (C)		
BMW				Z3 2.3 Roadster (CN) Z3 2.8 Coupe (C) Z3 2.8 Roadster (CN)
Chevrolet	Camaro (C)	Camaro (CN) Camaro Z28 (C)	Camaro Z28 (CN)	
Ford	Mustang (C)	Mustang (CN) Mustang GT (C)	Mustang Cobra (C) Mustang GT (CN)	Mustang Cobra (CN)
Mazda	MX-5 Miata (CN)			
Mitsubishi	Eclipse GS (C) Eclipse RS (C)	Eclipse GS-T (C) Eclipse Spyder GS (CN)	3000GT (C) Eclipse GSX Turbo AWD (C) Eclipse Spyder GS-T Turbo (CN)	3000GT SL (C)
Pontiac	Firebird (C)	Firebird Formula (C)	Firebird (CN) Firebird Trans Am (C)	Firebird Trans Am (CN)

Sport

	Under $40,000	$40,001-$42,000	$42,001-$65,000	Over $65,000
Acura				NSX (C) NSX-T (C)
BMW	M3 (C)	Z3 M Coupe (C)	M3 (CN) Z3 M Roadster (CN)	
Chevrolet	Corvette (S 2 Dr, C)		Corvette (CN)	
Dodge				Viper GTS (C) Viper RT/10 (CN)
Mercedes-Benz	SLK2 Kompressor (CN)			
Mitsubishi			3000GT VR-4 (C-4WD)	
Plymouth	Prowler (CN)			
Porsche		Boxster (CN)		911 (C) 911 Cabriolet (CN)

C–Coupe	S–Sedan	H–Hatchback	CN–Convertible	4WD–4 Wheel Drive

THE COMPLETE CAR COST GUIDE

All prices listed below are based on the manufacturer's retail price and do not include factory or dealer installed options. Actual prices may vary due to rebates and local dealer markups.

Wagon

	Under $16,000	$16,001-$19,000	$19,001-$22,000	Over $22,000
Audi				A4 1.8T Avant Quattro (4WD) A4 2.8 Avant Quattro (4WD) A6 Avant (4WD)
BMW				528 iT 540 iT
Daewoo	Nubira CDX Nubira SX			
Ford	Escort SE		Taurus SE	
Hyundai	Elantra Elantra GLS			
Mercedes-Benz				E300 E300 AWD (4WD)
Mercury	Tracer LS		Sable LS	
Saturn	SW1 SW2			
Subaru		Impreza L AWD Impreza Outback AWD Legacy Brighton AWD	Legacy L AWD	Legacy 2.5 GT AWD Legacy Outback AWD Legacy Outback Limited AWD
Suzuki	Esteem GL Esteem GLX			
Volkswagen			Passat GLS Wagon	Passat GLS V6 (4WD) Passat GLX V6 (4WD)
Volvo				V70 V70 AWD V70 GLT V70 R AWD V70 T5 V70 XC AWD

C–Coupe	S–Sedan	H–Hatchback	CN–Convertible	4WD–4 Wheel Drive

INTRODUCTION

An inexpensive car to buy could be expensive to own.

Do you want to get a good value the next time you buy a new car? Of course. Why else would you be reading this book?

What does "good value" mean anyway? Most people think it means choosing a nice-looking, reliable car, and negotiating the lowest possible price for it. So they trek through dealerships comparing car features and prices.

This may be a reasonable sounding approach, but it doesn't have much to do with getting a good value. That's because ultimately a car's value has less to do with its initial price than it does with its cost to own and operate.

You don't believe it? Let's take a closer look. The price you pay to buy a car is not a cost. "Price" and "cost" are related, but there's a distinct difference between them. A car's price is simply an amount of your hard-earned cash that you must exchange to own the car. There's no expense involved at the time of the purchase because, at this point, the car is still worth exactly what you just paid for it. If you paid the dealer $20,000, he or she will have the money, but you

will have something of equal value — the car.

Ah, but as soon as you slip behind the wheel, turn on the stereo, drive home, and park your new car in the driveway hoping to attract envious glances from the neighbors, you'll start to run up a tab. The car will begin to depreciate. It will use fuel. You'll have to pay insurance premiums, state fees and taxes, finance charges, and at some point down the road, repair bills. These are the car's ownership costs. When you want the best value, it's more prudent to consider these costs than just the purchase price.

By the time the typical car is five years old, the cost to own and operate it will exceed its original purchase price. Even more important, similarly priced cars can have very different ownership costs over a five-year period (See Figure 1). An inexpensive car to buy could be an expensive car to own.

That's why it's important to understand ownership costs when you search for the car that will truly be the best value.

Figure 1

Ownership Cost Comparison

■ PURCHASE PRICE   ■ COST AFTER 5 YEARS

HONDA ACCORD LX	PONTIAC GRANDPRIX SE	MERCURY SABLE GS
$20,262 / $25,944	$20,637 / $28,411	$20,361 / $30,852

This graph illustrates how cars with a similar purchase price can have different ownership costs over time. In this example, the Mercury Sable owner will spend about $2,400 more than the Pontiac Grand Prix owner and almost $5,000 more than the Honda Accord owner in the first five years. (Prices are based on "Total Target Price" listed in the Vehicle Charts, beginning on page 1.)

Sources:

IntelliChoice, Inc. is not associated with any automobile manufacturer or supplier. We strive to be completely impartial in our analyses and conclusions. Our primary responsibility is to assist the new car shopper.

The research used to compile the vehicle data and ratings in this book has been done in its entirety by IntelliChoice, Inc. Where appropriate, we make use of information supplied by the United States Government, by automobile manufacturers, and by a variety of industry sources. If you have technical questions about any area of this book, please write to the Director of Research, IntelliChoice, Inc., 471 Division Street, Campbell, California, 95008-6922.

The Complete Car Cost Guide is unlike any other reference source. It's the only one that gives you a complete financial profile of today's new cars and detailed cost projections for five years into the future.

Specifically, this book provides you with:

Detailed ownership costs. Allows you to compare the costs of owning different makes and models so you can choose the best value.

Expected annual costs for five years. Helps you budget your annual expenses.

Expected resale value for five years. Allows you to negotiate a favorable agreement if you plan to lease a car.

Dealer cost and list price. Helps you to negotiate the best possible deal for your new car.

Warranty information. Lets you see how well your car is protected by the manufacturer.

Advice. Gives you tips on selecting options, on choosing a dealer, shopping on the World Wide Web, on maintaining your car's resale value, on financing or leasing your new car, and on selling your old car.

Ratings. Lets you see at a glance which cars deliver the best overall value.

THE COMPLETE CAR COST GUIDE

The Complete Car Cost Guide is an economic guide. It doesn't offer subjective reviews of a car's comfort, handling, or style. It doesn't list braking or zero-to-sixty miles-per-hour performance figures. Nor does it provide the results of government crash tests.

Of course performance, comfort, handling, style, and safety are important factors in buying a new car. But then, if you can't afford to buy and operate the car you want, nothing else really matters, does it?

SECTION ONE

Ownership Costs

OWNERSHIP COSTS

Understanding ownership costs can save you money. Regardless of what you may read in new car reviews or hear in new car ads, it's not possible to know whether a vehicle is a good or a poor value until you learn about all the major ownership costs: depreciation, insurance, financing costs, maintenance, repairs, and more.

For example, a higher-priced car that holds its value over the years may be a bargain compared to a lower-priced car that plunges in value like Christmas tree ornaments on December 26th. In just one year, depreciation could eliminate the apparent initial advantage of the car with the lower purchase price. However, even if the lower-priced vehicle holds its value well, it may still cost a fortune to insure. So which is the better value?

Here's a more specific example. You may be told that a particular vehicle, such as a Suzuki Swift, is very economical because it gets such great gas mileage. Beware! A Swift may get good mileage but, since it rates poorly in insurance, its *overall* economy rates poorly compared to other cars in its class. You cannot determine the overall value of a car, or any savings you may realize in selecting one car over another, without considering all the ownership costs. Information on overall economy is what this book provides.

All the major ownership costs can be divided into two categories: standing costs and running costs. Standing costs, also called fixed costs, are what you pay to own the car whether you ever take it out of the driveway or not. Running costs, also called variable costs, are the expenses you incur as you use the car.

Standing Costs

Standing costs include depreciation, insurance, financing, and various government fees. (We do not factor into our analysis the cost of garaging your car, but if you live in Manhattan or downtown San Francisco, keep in mind that this expense can substantially add to your car's standing cost.)

The good news about standing costs is that they usually decrease with time. Depreciation is less each year, insurance premiums may decline as the value of the car decreases, state fees usually decrease on older cars, and finance charges will be eliminated once you pay off the loan.

The seven major ownership cost categories:

Standing Costs
- Depreciation
- Insurance
- State fees
- Financing

Running Costs
- Fuel
- Repairs
- Maintenance

DEPRECIATION TIPS

Before You Buy

■ Choose a car with low expected depreciation. Let the vehicle charts beginning on page 1 in this book be your guide.

■ Select a popular, highly regarded model, or a car from a prestigious automaker. Avoid offbeat or less well-known makes and models.

■ Choose a car from an automaker that doesn't frequently change body styles. If you are set on buying a vehicle that does have frequent style changes, make sure to buy soon after a change.

■ Select a larger engine if it's an option offered on the car you want. A larger engine generally adds to a car's resale value.

■ Select appropriate features and options for your geographic area. Cars in southern California or Florida are expected to have air conditioning, for instance. High-quality stereo sound systems almost always increase a car's value. And keep in mind that pink cars don't sell well anywhere.

■ Consider buying a convertible. As they say in the car-selling trade, when the top goes down, the price — even the resale price — goes up (Caveat: Keep in mind that other ownership costs may be very high on a convertible.)

■ Find out if the car you're considering has a "sister" model, a near-identical car sold as a different brand or model. If possible, choose the one that holds its value better. For instance, the 1993 Mercury Sable sold for more than its sister, the Ford Taurus, but the Taurus retains a higher percentage of it's value and is, therefore, worth more today. *(See "Saving Money on Corporate Cousins," page 63A.)*

Depreciation

This is the big one — at least for most cars during the first few years they're on the road. In fact, some cars depreciate as much as 20% or more during the first year alone.

Depreciation is the amount something decreases in value over time. Although it's a very real cost, depreciation is tricky because you don't get a monthly bill for it. You don't continually dole out money from your pocket to pay depreciation as you do, for example, every time you visit your mechanic.

But, make no mistake about it; you will pay for depreciation when the time comes to sell your car and buy another one. For instance, let's assume you purchase a car in 1999 for $15,000. If you unload it five years later for $5,000, you'll have spent $10,000 in depreciation to own the car.

The cost of depreciation should be a primary factor in your choice of which car to buy. If you expect to keep the car five years or less, it may be the most important factor.

Not all cars depreciate as much or at the same rate. Often there's a difference between even two- and four-door versions of the same model. And why is this? It's one of life's little mysteries, but here are some likely reasons:

■ **Cars that capture the public's fancy tend to hold their value.**

Many people would like to own a new Mercedes-Benz or Lexus, but few can afford to. So there's strong demand for used cars of these brands, which keeps resale values up.

■ **When the price of a popular model increases, the price of used versions of the same car may also rise.**

The price of a used car is based, in part, upon the price of its new model. Therefore, when the price of a new model has a significant increase relative to other new vehicles, used versions of the same model tend to hold their value.

■ **Import quotas often result in higher prices for popular new cars, and eventually for used cars as well.**

Basic supply and demand suggests that this will increase the prices of these vehicles, both in the new and used markets.

■ **A model change can lower resale value.**

When a model is dropped or completely restyled by a carmaker, cars of that model already on the road are likely to decrease in value more than they would otherwise.

■ **A car's depreciation will vary depending on whether the car accumulates either very high or very low mileage for its age.**

The "normal" annual mileage range is generally considered to be between 10,000 and 15,000 miles.

■ **The "base" model in a lineup usually holds its value better than the higher priced models.**

A "GL," "XLT," "Limited," or some other upmarket edition will usually cost several thousand dollars more than the base edition when new, but its resale value will be little more than the base model's after two or more years.

■ **A vehicle's class is often an indicator of its resale value.**

Subcompacts and luxury vehicles typically hold their values better than compact, midsize, or larger cars. However, if getting the highest resale value is your goal, you're probably better off with a van, sport utility vehicle, or pickup truck. (You may want to consult *The Complete Small Truck Cost Guide* for details on depreciation and other ownership costs of these vehicles.)

DEPRECIATION TIPS

Before You Buy continued

■ Consider buying a slightly used car rather than a brand-new one. (See section "Certified Used Vehicle Programs" on page 33A.)

■ Maybe you shouldn't buy another car at all! (See section "Keeping Your Old Car vs. Buying a New One" on page 75A.)

After You've Bought

■ Keep your car longer. Cars typically depreciate the most during the first three years; after five years, depreciation will be minimal.

■ When it comes time to sell your car, don't trade it in to a dealer. You'll almost always get a higher price — and minimize depreciation — by selling it yourself to a private party.

■ Perhaps most importantly, keep up the mechanical condition and appearance of your car and save all receipts for maintenance work that you've had done on your car. Low mileage "cream puffs," no matter what make or model, will always have plenty of buyers and will command the highest resale value. (See maintenance tips on page 22A.)

Figure 2

Depreciation Comparison

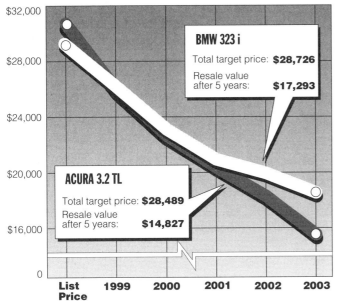

This graph illustrates how two cars with a similar purchase price have vastly different depreciation rates and, therefore, substantially different resale values after 5 years. However, even though one car appears to be a better value than the other, you should not draw that conclusion until you have examined all of the major cost areas.

Before You Buy

■ **Choose your car carefully.** Sports and specialty cars generally have the most costly claims records and are also favorites of thieves. Insurers frown on cars that offer less protection to drivers and passengers during an accident—usually small or midsize imported cars. Insurers are also wary of cars with powerful engines that could get unskilled drivers into trouble; companies often tag as a high-performance vehicle any car that has a turbocharger or a 0-60 m.p.h. acceleration time of under seven or eight seconds. Finally, many insurers would rather avoid cars with price tags of $35,000 or more because of their high replacement cost.

■ **Be aware that many insurers are now reviewing credit ratings of applicants.** Insurance companies believe that a poor credit history may be an even better predictor of future losses than an applicant's driving record. Consequently, insurers are rejecting applicants with bad credit ratings.

■ **Some insurers will offer discounts that can reduce your total insurance premium by 5% to 40%.** Always ask your insurer about the following discounts if you think they might apply to you:

- ■ Low annual mileage or restricted mileage
- ■ Air bags and anti-lock brakes
- ■ Good driver discounts for having no accidents or moving violations in the past three years
- ■ Multi-car discounts for insuring more than one car with the same company
- ■ Completion of driver training courses
- ■ Antitheft devices such as ignition or fuel shut-off devices or alarm systems
- ■ Nonsmoker discounts
- ■ Auto and homeowners coverage with the same company
- ■ Drivers between ages 55 and 65
- ■ Car-pooling to work

Insurance

Ugh—insurance! The only thing worse than paying for it is not having it when you need it.

Insurance is the price you pay to protect yourself, your passengers, and your car against unexpected losses. It's required by law, and if you've ever insured a car, you know it makes up a formidable portion of your total ownership expense. Unlike depreciation, insurance is a very visible expense — your insurance bill is a regular visitor to your mailbox.

Although you pay a single auto insurance premium, you're actually protecting several entities: your car (that's the collision and comprehensive part of your bill), and yourself and others (the bodily injury and property damage parts).

In most cases, where you live and the type of car you own will determine the price of your collision and comprehensive coverage. The price of your bodily injury and property damage coverage (also known as "liability" coverage) depends on your driving record, as well as on who you are, where you live, and how much you drive your car.

Though the price of auto insurance is high, by shopping around, by eliminating coverage you don't need, and by getting no more than necessary on the rest, you may be able to trim your bill by hundreds of dollars.

INSURANCE COVERAGES

TYPE OF COVERAGE	WHAT IT COVERS
Collision	Pays for damages to your vehicle that result from a collision with another vehicle or object.
Comprehensive	Pays for damages to your vehicle other than those caused in a collision (e.g., flood, fire, hail, theft, or vandalism).
Personal Liability	Pays claims against you, and covers the cost of legal defense if your vehicle damages property or injures or kills someone in an accident.
Property Damage	Pays for legal defense and claims if your car damages someone else's property.
Medical Payments	Pays for medical expenses of the driver and passengers of your car in an accident.
Un/Underinsured Motorist	Pays for injuries caused by an uninsured or hit-and-run driver.

Liability Coverage
(about 60% of your premium)

When it comes to insuring yourself against damage or harm to others, you certainly don't want to skimp, leaving yourself vulnerable to a lawsuit that could take away your assets. Most states require you to buy bodily injury and property damage liability coverage. While you may be able to satisfy the law with bodily injury coverage that pays $20,000 for each person you injure, up to $40,000 per accident, and property damage coverage that pays $5,000, these are minimum figures.

Most insurance advisors recommend bodily injury coverage of at least $100,000 a person up to $300,000 an accident, and property damage coverage of $50,000. If your net worth is more than $300,000, you should carry coverage of $200,000 a person and $500,000 an accident, and perhaps an "umbrella" policy that will bolster coverage even further. A $1 million umbrella policy will typically add $120-$150 to your yearly bill.

You also won't want to skimp on uninsured or underinsured motorist coverage. This pays for injuries to your passengers and for expenses health plans don't cover if you are involved in an accident with an uninsured driver. Keep in mind that one in ten drivers across the country has no auto insurance.

On the other hand, don't buy more coverage than your net worth requires. If you don't own a home and you've wiped out your bank account to put a down payment on a new Hyundai, you may not need that $1 million umbrella policy.

Collision and Comprehensive Coverage
(about 40% of your premium)

Many people can also save on other parts of their policy. Collision coverage pays for damages to your car caused by an accident, while comprehensive coverage pays for damage to your car caused by other risks, such as theft or fire. Unlike liability coverage, collision and comprehensive coverage is often subject to a deductible — an amount you must pay before you can collect.

Having a high deductible can save you substantial sums on the collision and comprehensive portion of your total insurance bill. For example, one insurer charges $99 a year more for a policy with a $300 deductible than for one with a $500 deductible. This means you'd pay almost $100 per year to save, at most, $200 if you have an accident. Instead, if you put that $100 in the bank each year, you'd soon have enough to pay the full deductible in the event of a collision.

Because you don't want to collect on minor mishaps and risk raising your premiums, you'll want a high deductible anyway. Collecting $50 beyond a $250 deductible to replace a $300 cracked windshield could prompt the insurer to raise your total premium by several hundred dollars.

INSURANCE TIPS

After You've Bought

■ **Stay clean.** No single factor is more important than your motor vehicle report (MVR) in determining the premiums for your liability coverage. Each time you receive a traffic ticket, you risk increasing your future premiums. In general, you will pay substantially higher premiums if you receive more than one or two tickets during a three-year period. If your state allows you to attend traffic school in exchange for removing a violation from your MVR, take advantage of the option.

■ **Stay a stranger to your insurance company.** Claims, as well as tickets, upset insurers. Don't involve your insurance company in repairing door dings or annoyances like cracked windshields even if you could collect a little something beyond your deductible. Pay for these repairs out of your own pocket. If someone damages your car and you don't live in a no-fault insurance state, try to collect from the other person's insurance company before you involve your own insurer. Obtain a police report that indicates you were not at fault in the accident.

■ **If you own a business, put your car in your company's name.** You may be able to persuade the insurer who writes your business policy to cover the car as a company vehicle at a lower rate than you would receive on a personal policy.

■ **Get married. Insurers prefer drivers between the ages of 30 and 65.** Some insurers give discounts to drivers aged 55-65. But once you're over 70, you are considered risky, as you are if you're under 30. However, insurers generally treat a married person under 30 years old as they would someone in the lower risk 30-65 age group. Marriage, they figure, puts an end to your partying days and keeps you off the streets at night.

INSURANCE TIPS

After You've Bought

continued

■ Every time you receive your insurance bill, review your coverage. Make sure your bill is accurate and that you're receiving all discounts to which you're entitled. If there's been a change in your insurance profile (e.g., you've just turned 30), inform your insurer. If your car is over five years old, consider eliminating your collision coverage.

Other Coverages

Medical coverage pays hospital and doctor fees for the driver and passengers. But if your health insurance already covers these costs, you may not need medical coverage included with your auto insurance.

If you live in a state with no-fault insurance, you may be required to buy personal-injury protection that covers your medical bills. But you may be able to cut some of the costs for this coverage if your heath plan covers you in an auto accident.

There are a number of other minor types of auto insurance, such as towing coverage. If you're a member of an auto club, you may not need the additional towing coverage.

Insurance Symbols

Insurers use a car rating system to determine the premium price for collision and comprehensive coverage.

In many systems, every car is given a rating symbol between 1 and 27; the higher the rating number, the more costly the premium. All things being equal, two identically priced cars will have the same insurance rating.

However, insurance companies often loathe the cars most of us love — luxury and exciting high-performance cars — and these cars may be subject to surcharges. In addition, some cars are more expensive to repair or are more likely to incur extensive damage in a collision. And some cars are more — or less — likely to be stolen; the Highway Data Loss Institute says cars with especially low theft claims are four-door sedans like the Chevrolet Lumina

and station wagons like the Saturn SW, while cars with especially high theft claims include BMW and Mercedes-Benz convertibles. So ratings are adjusted for these risk factors.

Insurance rating figures used in this book are based on "Insurance Symbols," with the rating for a particular vehicle adjusted for any special risk factors.

Shop Around

The insurance business is essentially a gigantic bookmaking operation that bets premiums against the probabilities of having to pay out on an accident or injury claim. Except in a handful of states where bureaucrats set the rates, it's up to each insurer to develop its own probabilities and set its rates accordingly. Rates and underwriting guidelines will reflect what market segments an insurer wishes to target and how efficiently the company is managed.

All of which says, rates for the same driver and car can vary dramatically from company to company. If you live in a state with competitive insurance rates, start shopping by obtaining a quote from one of the major firms in the industry — State Farm, Allstate, Farmers, Nationwide, USAA, and AAA are among the largest. (See Appendix B for the addresses and phone numbers of the ten largest insurance companies.) Then contact an independent agent who can query other companies for you. Compare them all. Use the worksheet (Figure 3) on the next page to compare rates. You'll find that premium prices can differ by as much as 50% for the same coverage.

Figure 3

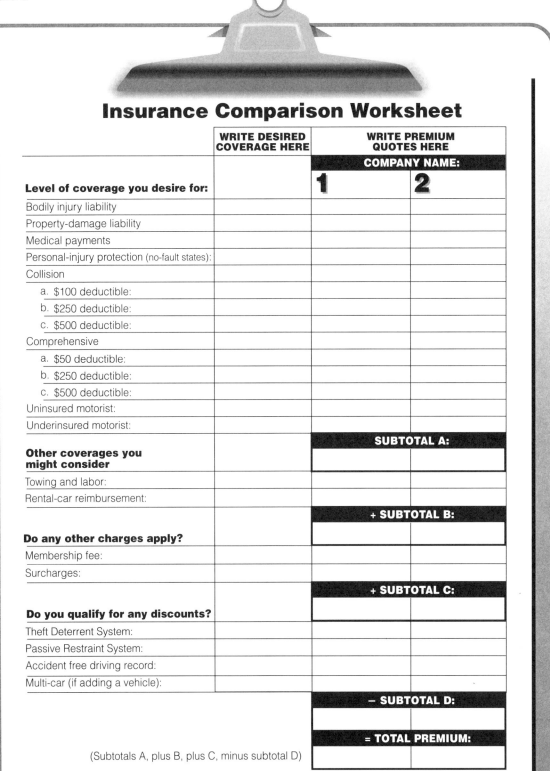

Insurance Comparison Worksheet

Level of coverage you desire for:	WRITE DESIRED COVERAGE HERE	WRITE PREMIUM QUOTES HERE	
		COMPANY NAME:	
		1	**2**
Bodily injury liability			
Property-damage liability			
Medical payments			
Personal-injury protection (no-fault states):			
Collision			
a. $100 deductible:			
b. $250 deductible:			
c. $500 deductible:			
Comprehensive			
a. $50 deductible:			
b. $250 deductible:			
c. $500 deductible:			
Uninsured motorist:			
Underinsured motorist:			
		SUBTOTAL A:	
Other coverages you might consider			
Towing and labor:			
Rental-car reimbursement:			
		+ SUBTOTAL B:	
Do any other charges apply?			
Membership fee:			
Surcharges:			
		+ SUBTOTAL C:	
Do you qualify for any discounts?			
Theft Deterrent System:			
Passive Restraint System:			
Accident free driving record:			
Multi-car (if adding a vehicle):			
		− SUBTOTAL D:	
		= TOTAL PREMIUM:	
(Subtotals A, plus B, plus C, minus subtotal D)			

Luxury Tax

As of 1991, Congress imposed a new tax on expensive vehicles, the so-called "luxury tax." The tax is 6% of a vehicle's price that exceeds $36,000. Thus the buyer of a vehicle with a price tag of $44,000 would have to pay a luxury tax of $480 — that is, 6% of $8,000.

State Fees

The government will have its paw out as soon as you buy your new car. You'll have to pay tax and license, and registration fees. Furthermore, you'll be required to pay taxes and/or fees every year for as long as you own the car.

Some states base their fees on the original price of the car and/or on its age. Others base the fees on the car's weight. Still others have fixed fees.

Finance Costs

It is now time for a *very* brief accounting lesson. When we talk about finance costs, it is important to distinguish between what is actually a cost and what is not.

Let's say you bought a new car for $19,000. You no longer have the money, but you do have a car

of equal value — an asset. If a bank loaned you $19,000 to buy the car, you owe the bank that money, but it still hasn't cost you anything. However, when you borrow money from any lending institution, not only will the lender ask you to pay back the money they loaned you, but they will also charge you interest. The money that they loan you is not a cost — the interest charge is. End of lesson.

Pay Cash or Take Out A Loan?

For most car buyers, the answer to this question is easy: Let me sign those loan docs! If they want a new car, they'll have to borrow to the hilt to get it.

But, what if a buyer has a choice: to pay cash or to take out a loan. Let's say that Debbie Debtor and Kris Cash each buy a $19,000 car, and each has exactly $19,000 in the bank. Kris pays cash for her car. Debbie puts 20% down, finances the $15,200 difference with a 48-month, 9.3% loan, and puts her $15,200 in a bank earning 3.5% interest. She withdraws $339.81 from the bank each month to pay her car payment, which leaves her with a bank balance of $0 after 48 months.

Kris doesn't earn any interest on her money, but didn't pay any either, so she has a net cost of $0. Debbie must pay $380.42 each month in car payments, but she can take out only $339.81 each month from her bank account (or else she would deplete her bank account before 48 months). She has to pay an additional $40.61 per month for 48 months, or a total of $1,949 more than Kris.

Another way to look at it is that Debbie will pay $3,060 in interest over the 48 months, but will earn only $1,111 on her money in the bank, a difference of $1,949. To make matters worse, Debbie will probably pay income tax on the $1,111 that her money earned in the bank.

It used to be that Debbie could deduct her interest payments from her income taxes, which could have made her come out ahead of Kris, but these interest deductions are no longer allowed.

The bottom line: as long as the after-tax interest rate on the car loan is more than the after-tax interest rate that you could earn on your money, paying cash is less expensive than taking a loan.

Sources for Loans

Okay, so paying cash is usually the least expensive way to buy a new vehicle. But in an age when the typical new car carries a price tag of at least $20,000, few people have the requisite pennies in the piggy bank. So what's the best way to borrow the money? You have plenty of options:

■ **Borrow from a dealer.** Convenience is one reason to obtain a loan from a dealer. At some dealers, it typically takes less than 30 minutes to obtain a loan.

Dealers are also more likely than banks to qualify buyers with shaky credit ratings. And the lending arms of Ford, General Motors, and other automakers usually have plans to help customers with special needs. There are "first-time buyer" and "college-graduate" plans for those with no credit ratings. Ford Motor Credit can even set up a flexible payment schedule to accommodate teachers who receive pay checks only nine months out of the year.

But promotional cut-rate financing can be the best reason of all to borrow from a dealer. Ford, for example, recently offered 2.9% and 5.9% financing on some models at a time when prevailing bank rates were around 9 to 10%. Such deals can be true money savers. Don't however, expect manufacturers to offer discount financing on hot-selling models.

And the downside to dealer financing? Dealers obtain loans for their customers through local banks and finance companies, as well as through the automakers' lending arms. Dealers usually add a bit to the interest rate over what they pay for the loan, keeping the difference as profit. Persuasive dealers working with uninformed buyers can make as much off financing a new car as they can on the car sale itself.

■ **Borrow from a bank, credit union, or finance company.**

In contrast to obtaining a loan through a dealer, borrowing from a lending institution tends to be haggle-free. Lending institutions usually offer set, nonnegotiable loan rates. And they're less likely to push credit life insurance—an unnecessary, expensive frill. Compared to banks and finance companies, membership credit unions typically offer the lowest interest rates. Finance companies are often the most expensive.

FINANCE TIPS

■ Compare discount financing to a cash rebate if both are offered. "Buy now and we'll give you $500 cash, or provide a 4.8% loan for four years." Which should you choose? It depends on a lot of factors. Appendix J lets you easily determine which option is more advantageous for you.

■ If you can afford to buy the car outright, do it — it's usually the least expensive way to buy a car.

■ If you take out a loan, put as large a down payment on the vehicle as you can manage. And pay as much per month as you can possibly budget to keep the length of the loan to a minimum. If you can't put at least 20% down and finance the vehicle for four years or less, then you should buy a less expensive vehicle.

■ Be aware that there are several ways to lower monthly payments, but only a lower interest rate or a lower amount borrowed will lower your total interest expense.

■ If you take out a lengthy loan on a car, refer to the vehicle charts in this book and buy one that will retain a high proportion of its value. This will shorten the time you are "upside down."

■ When is an interest rate not an interest rate? When it doesn't include the "hidden" costs of a loan. All interest rates are not comparable. One rate may include a loan origination fee, and expensive "simple" interest, while another may have no loan fee and cheaper "compound" interest. APR (Annual Percentage Rate) is a very specific term that factors in any hidden fees and tells you the rate you will actually pay when all fees are taken into account. It is the "apples-to-apples" comparable rate. Lenders are required by law to tell you the APR of your loan. You should use this rate, and only this rate, in your comparisons.

Figure 4

Interest Expense

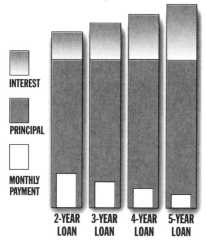

INTEREST

PRINCIPAL

MONTHLY PAYMENT

| 2-YEAR LOAN | 3-YEAR LOAN | 4-YEAR LOAN | 5-YEAR LOAN |

As the length of the loan increases, the interest cost also increases, yet the monthly payment decreases. The principal, however, remains the same regardless of the length of the payment period. The total interest that you pay can be computed by adding up the monthly payments and subtracting the amount that you initially borrowed (loan amount). You can convert the loan amount into a monthly payment using Appendix I.

■ Borrow on a home-equity loan.

Transforming a part of your home's value into a new Mustang has one great advantage: Unlike the interest on a car loan, the interest on a home equity loan is usually tax deductible. If you're in a high tax bracket, you can save as much as 40% on interest costs by buying a car with the proceeds from a home equity loan.

The danger is that your house, not just your car, is on the line if you can't make the payments. Moreover, revolving credit lines based on home equity require you to make payments of only interest, not principal. If you don't have the discipline to pay the principal you could easily end up with a depreciated car worth little or nothing and a huge loan against your house. In addition, start-up costs—including property appraisal, title search, and lender points—can be substantial if you don't already have a home-equity credit line.

■ Borrow on investments or insurance.

If you own a large portfolio of securities, a passbook savings account, a 401(k) savings account, or a cash-value life insurance policy, you may be able to borrow against them at attractive interest rates with flexible — or even no — repayment plans. But with any of these loans, you're hocking some element of your future. If there's a margin call against your security loan, you might be forced to sell your stocks and bonds at a big loss. Or if you died while your insurance-policy loan was outstanding, the proceeds to your family would be reduced by the loan amount.

Striking a Balance: Monthly Payments vs. Interest Expense

Determining the cost of a loan is inherently complex. There is a myriad of terms that affect the final cost of the loan. Through it all, a few simple truths exist:

■ The higher the interest rate, the higher the monthly payment.

■ The more you borrow, the higher the monthly payment.

■ The longer the period of your loan, the lower the monthly payment.

In each of these cases, the cost of the loan will be higher. While the first two points are fairly intuitive, the third point catches a lot of people off guard. A salesperson will frequently attempt to lower your monthly payment, sometimes quite substantially, by stretching out the loan period. But, buyer beware, this will ultimately cost you more. For example, the monthly payment on a $15,000 loan at 8% for five years is $62 less than the same loan over a four-year period. However, the total interest expense is $672 more for the five-year loan versus the four-year loan. This is the cost you pay for the privilege of stretching out your payments for one more year (see Figure 4).

Finding Yourself "Upside Down"

Nowadays, it seems you have to pay as much for a new car as you did a few years ago for a house. But as new-car prices rose dramatically in recent years, lenders found a clever way to allow people to continue to buy new cars — they simply extended the length of loans, thus keeping monthly payments affordable.

In the past, 24-month or 36-month car loans were the norm. But today, 60- and even 72-month loans are common. With the longer loans, however, it takes longer to reach a positive equity position in a car and owe less on it than it's worth. As soon as you drive that shiny new car off the dealer's lot, the car plunges in value — thanks to that ol' devil depreciation. But with a shorter length loan, after a year or so of making payments, your car's value will be worth more than you owe on it. Until then, you're "upside-down," as they say in the auto business.

With longer loans however, you could be upside down for two, three, or four years. It typically takes 40 to 42 months to build equity in a car if you put 20% down and have a 60-month loan. And therein lies the rub: If during that time you want to trade in your car on another one, you'll be in the frustrating situation of owing more on your old car than it's worth, thus making it all the more expensive for you to buy the newer car.

So if you must take a longer loan in order to lower the monthly payments on the car you really want, plan on keeping the car for nearly the life of the loan or more. If you can't keep it that long, be sure to choose a car that holds its resale value well (See Vehicle Charts) because that will reduce the time it takes you to reach a positive equity position.

The Cost of Leasing

In the past few years, leasing has exploded in popularity. Automakers from General Motors to Mercedes-Benz are offering attractive lease programs and inundating their dealers with sales brochures touting all the advantages of leasing. As a result, leasing now accounts for more than a third of all new-car transactions. Leasing has become so popular that many one- to three-year-old pre-owned cars are also leased from dealers.

No question about it, leasing has advantages over buying.

For one thing, you usually don't have to come up with as large a down payment when you lease. With the price of the typical new car these days exceeding $20,000, the usual 20% down payment can amount to a hefty sum. And, if you're in the market for really expensive machinery in the $50,000 to $100,000 range, you're looking at tying up $10,000 to $20,000 in cash just for the down payment.

Aside from the difficulty of coming up with substantial cash to put down, some people don't want to pull their cash resources out of particularly lucrative investments to buy a car.

But perhaps leasing's biggest advantage is that your monthly payments will be lower than if you take out a loan. Here's why: When you buy a $30,000 car, for instance, you make payments based on that price (minus the down payment). But when you lease, the payments are lower because the car won't be yours when the lease is up. In other words, you'll only pay for part of the car. A $30,000 car might still be

To Lease...
Leasing may be right for you if:

■ The manufacturer is subsidizing the lease.

■ You prefer to use your cash for investments other than a car.

■ You would like to have lower monthly payments.

■ You would like to drive a more expensive car for a lower initial cash outlay.

■ You like to drive a new car every two to four years.

■ You want to avoid the hassle of disposing of a used car.

...Or Not to Lease? Leasing may not be right for you if:

- Saving money is a major consideration.

- You usually drive your car more than 12,000 miles a year.

- You are not inclined to take care of your car.

- You think there's any chance you will have to end the lease early.

- You want to modify your car.

worth $14,000 at the end of a 36-month lease. So the leasing company would base your monthly payments on the depreiciated $16,000, not the entire $30,000.

Or, by the same reasoning, you may be able to drive a more expensive leased car than you could afford to buy with a loan. Because you're not paying for the whole car with a lease, but only on the depreciated amount, the monthly lease payment on a $40,000 car could well be the same as a monthly loan payment on a $30,000 car.

But there are still other advantages to leasing. At the end of the lease contract, you can walk away from the car and let the leasing company have the headache of reselling it. If you like to drive a new car every two, three or four years, trading in one leased car for another is very easy.

In some states, you may be able to save on sales taxes with a leased car. When you buy a car, you'll pay a sales tax on the entire sales price up front. But when you lease, you'll pay a sales tax on each monthly payment. And because as we've said before, you'll only be making payments on the depreciated portion of the car, you'll only pay sales tax on the depreciated portion rather than the entire value of the car.

If you use your car for business, you may also be able to deduct more from your taxes on a leased car. When you lease a car and use it only for business, you can write off nearly the entire amount of the lease payment, even on high-priced cars. By contrast, when you buy a car, there are limits on how much you can write off each year. On high-priced cars, it can take eight, ten or more years to fully depreciate the car for tax purposes. The

leased car, especially one with a price tag of $20,000 or more, can give you more sizeable tax deductions if your car is a legitimate business deduction. (Consult a knowledgeable tax accountant.)

No down payment, lower monthly payments, no resale hassles — these are nice advantages but, unfortunately, they don't come free.

As a rule, leasing usually costs more than buying a car outright with cash. Moreover, leasing a car is almost always more expensive than buying it with a loan *(see Figure 5)*. At the end of the lease, you have nothing to show for all those monthly payments except memories and gasoline credit receipts jammed in the glove compartment.

However, there are a few exceptions to the rule. If a manufacturer-subsidized lease offer is available, leasing will be less costly than financing a purchase. Subsidized leases very often have net interest rates several percentage points below the APR for a loan.

Or, if you have some surefire investment that will pay a very high return for your cash, leasing may be less costly. But in these days of 4 or 5% money market rates, few of us have such high paying, risk-free investment opportunities.

Leasing may also be less costly if you can use what cash you have to pay off existing high-interest loans — credit card balances at 16% interest, for example — instead of putting the cash into a new car.

(For tips on finding the best lease deal, see "Shopping for a Lease," page 40A.)

Figure 5

COMPARISON: CASH, LOAN, LEASE

This example illustrates a typical lease and loan arrangement for a mid-priced 1999 sedan. If you pay cash for the car you will end up paying less than if you finance or lease the car for 36 months. This is true even after taking into account any investment income — or "opportunity cost" — that you may earn if you invest the $21,500 and withdraw the lease payments as you need them (or if you finance the car and withdraw the down payment and monthly payments as you need them).

In this example we assume your investment has an after-tax yield of 3.5%. We also assume the lessee will purchase the vehicle at the end of the lease for $10,100 — the predetermined resale value. We assume a 8.92% after-tax interest rate on the loan.

It all boils down to interest rates. The loan costs $1,664 more than buying with cash because the loan interest rate of 8.92% exceeds the investment interest rate of 3.5%. The regular lease costs $4,394 more than paying cash because the lease's base interest rate of over 11% is higher than the investment rate for the cash buy (see the Lease Interest Rate Worksheet, page 41a, figure 8). Even the subvented lease costs $999 more than the cash purchase, since it has a base interest rate of 4.5%.

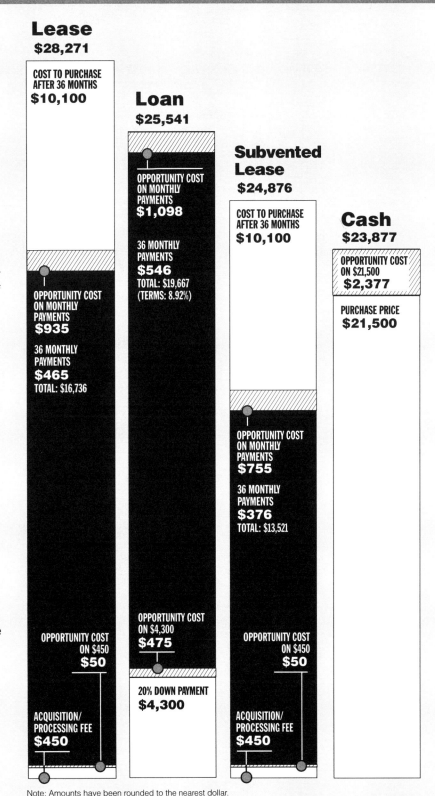

Note: Amounts have been rounded to the nearest dollar.

FUEL TIPS

Before You Buy

■ Buy a fuel-efficient car. Refer to the vehicle charts in this book for fuel-economy ratings.

■ Be aware that buying a car that requires premium fuel will cost you considerably more at the pump. If you drive a car that gets 20 m.p.g. 15,000 miles per year, you will pay an additional $112 per year if premium fuel costs 15 cents per gallon more than regular fuel. The charts in this book indicate which vehicles require premium fuel.

Running Costs

Running costs, or variable costs, are the costs you bear every time you take your car out of your garage. They include fuel, maintenance, and repairs. (Bridge tolls, occasional parking fees, and when you're naughty, traffic tickets are running costs, too. However, they vary too greatly to be considered in this book.)

Running costs tend to increase as a car gets older. But remember that standing costs usually decrease over time. Usually the increase in running costs is outweighed by the decrease in standing costs, so overall, the car is less costly to own and operate when it becomes an old crock — a good reason to hang on to your car for several years after you buy it. For example, after age five or so, the car may require more repairs, but depreciation costs fall to practically nothing.

Fuel Costs

Fuel is the one expense car owners face almost on a daily basis. Of course you can reduce your fuel costs by driving less, though that's often easier said than done.

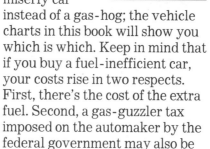

You can also buy a fuel-miserly car instead of a gas-hog; the vehicle charts in this book will show you which is which. Keep in mind that if you buy a fuel-inefficient car, your costs rise in two respects. First, there's the cost of the extra fuel. Second, a gas-guzzler tax imposed on the automaker by the federal government may also be included in the vehicle's purchase price — so you'll end up paying it.

But beyond the type of vehicle you buy, there are other considerations in reducing fuel costs.

Selecting the Proper Octane

Advertising hype about "Lead-Free Super," "Ultra-High Test Unleaded," "Extra-Mile Regular," "Irregular Regular," etc., can make buying gasoline a little confusing. You may begin to feel like a recent cartoon character; faced with all the choices, he tells the gas station attendant, "Just surprise me!"

It's an amusing approach, but not wise. A car's engine develops power because a mixture of gasoline and air is burned in the engine's combustion chambers. If this mixture burns too rapidly, there's an explosion in the combustion chambers. The engine won't fly apart, but the explosion will set up a vibration that you will hear as a "knocking" sound, especially when you accelerate briskly. Inside the engine, the effect is like a hammer blow to the top of the piston. If the blows are severe enough, they can damage the engine.

By matching the engine's octane requirements to a gasoline's octane rating, you'll get a nice, even burn of the gas/air mixture. You can get an idea of your car's octane requirements by looking in your car's owner's manual. Unfortunately, finding the optimum choice of fuel for your car is not quite that simple. An engine's octane requirements can vary according to its age, the outside air temperature, humidity, and altitude. All this means you have to experiment with different grades and brands until you find one that eliminates knocking in your vehicle.

But if your car doesn't knock or ping when you use a regular grade of gasoline, don't waste your money by "treating" your car to a more expensive premium grade. Unless your car's owner's manual specifies premium gasoline or your car's engine knocks on regular gasoline, using premium will not provide any advantages over a less expensive regular grade. It won't give your car more power, and it won't keep the inside of your engine any cleaner. Federal clean air rules now require oil companies to formulate their gasoline with additives and detergents to prevent internal deposits — no matter what the grade of gasoline.

Alternative-Fuel Vehicles

In the fall of 1996, General Motors became the first major automaker since the early 1900s to offer a car specifically built to run on electricity. GM's EV1 coupe is leased — along with garage terminals needed to recharge it — through 25 Saturn dealerships in Los Angeles, San Diego, Phoenix, and Tucson.

The EV1's introduction was just the beginning of a move by many U.S. and foreign automakers to introduce electric-powered vehicles to help meet stricter emissions laws in states like California.

By introducing the two-seat EV1, GM got a head start in learning how to market electric cars to consumers. But other automakers

aren't far behind. Honda introduced a four-passenger hatchback electric vehicle called the EV Plus in 1997; the vehicle is being marketed through California and New York dealers. And these two vehicles have been joined by an electric version of Chevrolet's S-10 pickup and an electric version of Ford's Ranger pickup.

All these vehicles can be purchased by individual motorists. But DaimlerChrysler has also introduced the Epic, a five-passenger electric minivan based on the Plymouth Voyager and Dodge Caravan aimed at fleet-vehicle buyers. Toyota sells its electric RAV4,, and Nissan may soon sell its Altra EV, to fleet buyers. And another fleet vehicle, Ford's Ecostar electric van, has been on the road since 1993; Ecostars have collectively logged more than 250,000 miles.

In addition to emitting no harmful emissions, electric cars are cheaper to operate than gasoline-powered vehicles and require little maintenance.

GM used state-of-the-art technology to make the EV1 more appealing to consumers. Its plastic body, aluminum frame, and use of magnesium parts help counter the weight of its lead-acid batteries.

The two-seater's design is aerodynamically the slickest ever produced by a U.S. automaker. It is peppy (0-to-60 m.p.h. in under nine seconds) and comes with a number of standard features.

But like other alternative-fuel vehicles, electric cars and trucks have drawbacks.

They're expensive; generally priced between $20,000 and $50,000.

After You've Bought

- Buy gas with the proper octane rating for your car.

- Keep your car's engine tuned, and its tires properly inflated and aligned.

- Avoid putting the pedal to the metal; accelerate smoothly instead.

- At highway speeds, it's more fuel-efficient to close the windows and turn on the air conditioner. At speeds over 40 m.p.h., open windows create wind resistance that increases fuel consumption.

- The most fuel-efficient speed range is 35 to 55 m.p.h..

- After starting a cold engine, don't let it idle for more than 30 seconds; instead drive slowly for several miles until the engine temperature warms up.

- If you think you'll be waiting for more than a minute — at a railroad crossing, for instance — turn off the engine.

- If you have a car with a manual transmission, learn the proper shift points.

Fuel Consumption Facts:

■ Misaligned front wheels can increase fuel consumption by 2%.

■ Underinflated tires can increase fuel consumption by 5%.

■ A malfunctioning thermostat in the cooling system can increase fuel consumption by 7%.

■ Worn spark plugs and other ignition components, as well as clogged air filters, can increase fuel consumption by 11%.

■ Altogether, these maladies could increase your fuel costs by a whopping 25%. The point here is obvious — a well-tuned car uses less fuel.

They have a short range before re-quiring a recharge, and within two or three years, the batteries have to be replaced.

However, GM's EV1 and Honda's EV Plus are only available through three-year leases. GM has been leasing the EV1 for $399 a month, including the cost of the home charging terminal. The Honda lease costs $499 a month, plus a one-time fee of $750 or more for the home terminal.

GM claims the EV1 will go 70 to 90 miles before its lead-acid batteries need a recharge, which takes eight to 10 hours. (GM has constructed 165 fast-charge stations in Southern California that drops the time to about three hours).

After three years, EV1's lead-acid batteries will need replacing at a cost of about $1,500 — likely a major reason why GM decided the first EV1s will be leased, not purchased by consumers.

The California Energy Commission and Southern California Edison estimate electric vehicles cost between 1.5¢ to 10.4¢ per mile, depending on whether they're charged overnight at "off-peak" rates or during peak hours.

In May, 1996 the California Energy Commission studied how prices of alternative fuels compared with reformulated premium (92-octane) gasoline, which then was selling for an average of $1.73 a gallon.

To get the same amount of energy from electricity as you would get from the $1.73 gallon of reformulated premium gasoline would cost an average of 54¢,

based on "off-peak" electricity rates. In other words, it would cost you an average of 54¢ in electricity to travel about the same distance as a gallon of 92-octane, reformulated premium gasoline costing $1.73, according to the study.

This year, GM may use nickel metal hydride batteries in the EV1, which can store about three times the energy for about the same battery weight. But, they're considerably more expensive than lead-acid batteries.

Here are some other types of AFVs to consider:

Methanol-powered/ Flexible-fuel vehicles

Popular for fleet and private vehicles, methanol (also known as "wood alcohol") can be used in existing gasoline engines with minor modifications.

The methanol used in most flexible-fuel vehicles is a blend of 85% methanol and 15% unleaded gasoline, known as M85. A vehicle using M85 produces about one-half the smog-forming emissions than a gasoline-powered vehicle.

Ford first produced a flexible-fuel vehicle in 1987 — Crown Victoria LTD models made to run on any combination of methanol and gas. Ford, GM, Chrysler and some foreign automakers now offer flexible-fuel cars, vans, and trucks. The flexible-fuel vehicles generally cost the same or only a little more than gasoline-powered vehicles.

Because it takes about 1.7 gallons of methanol to produce the same amount of energy as a gallon of gasoline, a flexible-fuel car will have a shorter mileage range unless it has a larger fuel tank or uses a greater percentage of unleaded fuel to extend the range.

In the California Energy Commission study, it would cost an average of $1.72 in M85 fuel to go about the same distance as on premium reformulated gasoline costing an average of $1.73 a gallon.

Natural-gas vehicles

Of all the alternative fuels used in commercial cars and trucks, natural gas — either compressed natural gas (CNG) or liquefied natural gas (LNG) — offers the biggest cut in emissions compared to gasoline.

Domestic automakers offer specific car or truck models propelled by compressed or liquefied natural gas. Natural gas vehicles are even more common in Europe.

There also are dual-fuel or bi-fuel vehicles that can run on both natural gas and gasoline, but trunk or cargo space may be reduced because of the space needed for the cylinders to store the natural gas.

The range of a natural gas vehicle depends on its engine size, number of cylinders used and your driving habits, but it's generally less than a gasoline-powered vehicle.

The average natural gas vehicle with three cylinders has a range between 120-180 miles. (However, Honda Civic and Geo Prizm CNG prototypes reportedly can go up to 300 miles).

Refueling sites generally are more plentiful than with other alternative fuels. In California, nearly 200 natural gas fueling stations are available — more than half have full or limited public access. They include facilities at some gasoline service stations under contracts with gas utility companies.

Natural gas vehicles cost about $4,000 more than gasoline-powered models. Gasoline-powered vehicles also can be retrofitted at a cost of $1,500 to $4,000. There also may be rebates or tax credits available on dedicated natural gas vehicles or conversions.

In the California Energy Commission study, it cost an average of 88¢ to go about the same distance on natural gas as a gallon of reformulated premium gasoline selling for an average of $1.73.

Propane

Also known as LPG or liquefied petroleum gas, propane is used in several fleet vehicle operations, including taxis, police cars, school buses and trucks.

Cars and light trucks can be converted to propane for an average cost of $1,000 to $2,000. Dual-fuel gasoline/propane conversions also are possible.

As with natural gas vehicles, the loss of trunk or cargo space is a drawback to propane power. However, because propane burns cleaner than gasoline, spark plug life can exceed 80,000 miles and propane engines can last two or three times longer than gasoline or diesel engines.

Propane generally costs about the same as gasoline.

A program of routine maintenance, including oil changes, tune-ups, radiator flushes, tire pressure checks, and so on, can save you big money in several ways:

■ It will prevent premature breakdowns and budget-busting repairs.

■ It will make your car last longer, so you won't need to buy a new car as often. That means you avoid the costs of depreciation, taxes, and finance charges that come with a new car.

■ When the time comes to sell your car, you'll get a higher price for it.

■ Routine maintenance is required in order to keep your new-car warranty in effect.

■ Routine maintenance may even improve your car's fuel economy.

Before You Buy

■ Many new cars are designed and built to minimize maintenance costs. For instance, many GM cars now feature long-lasting stainless steel mufflers, and distributor-less ignition systems. Use the Vehicle Charts to compare vehicles' overall maintenance costs, as well as costs for tune-ups and brake service.

■ Take advantage of any maintenance warranty offered on your car, but don't choose a car just because it comes with a maintenance warranty. Use the charts to see which vehicles feature this type of warranty.

Maintenance

Automakers do sometimes build cars that should simply have "headache" written on the side. But happily, most modern cars, no matter the make or model, are darned impressive machines — especially if they're given periodic care.

Though new cars are mighty expensive to buy these days, the good news is that they're capable of lasting longer than ever. With frequent oil changes — perhaps the most important maintenance task of all — most modern car engines are capable of going 150,000 miles or more without major repairs. Tires are sometimes warranted for 80,000 miles and exhaust systems for the life of the car. Even minor repairs — tune-ups — are required much less often on modern vehicles. Ford's Contour and Mystique, with the "Duratec" engine, shouldn't need a tune-up for 100,000 miles!

Regular maintenance includes all services required to maintain the car's warranty, services suggested by the manufacturer to ensure trouble-free operation, and other regular service, such as tune-ups and replacing brake pads, exhaust systems, tires, fluids, and filters.

Some Thoughts on Extended Service Intervals

In the old days — the really old days — cars required routine service every few hundred miles.

During the 1960s and 1970s, 3,000-mile oil and lubrication service intervals were the norm. Today, automakers have stretched recommended oil changes to 7,500 miles or more, while chassis components are sealed so they never need lubrication.

There's no question that technology has eliminated or reduced the need for several routine service chores. Electronic ignitions, for instance, have greatly prolonged the life of spark plugs. But when it comes to oil, many mechanics question the whole business of extended service intervals. They still prefer to see the oil changed every 3,000 miles or so; after all, oil is an engine's life blood.

Automaker recommendations can be tricky. In the fine print of the owner's manual, some automakers specify extended intervals for cars used in "normal driving," which they define as high-speed, highway driving. They classify puttering around town or getting stuck in commuter traffic as "severe driving," to which the extended changes don't apply.

Extended service intervals have one drawback: If your mechanic sees your car less often, he has fewer opportunities to spot potential problems, which makes it all the more important for you to inspect your car frequently. But if you're serious about giving your car a long, trouble-free life, change the oil and filter every 3,000 to 5,000 miles. It's worth a few extra dollars in the long run.

Maintenance Warranties

As of this writing, three manufactures offer maintenance warranties on either some or all of their 1999 models: Audi, BMW, and Volkswagen.

Maintenance warranties cover the services required to maintain a new vehicle's overall warranty — typically tune-ups, oil changes, and minor adjustments — and are offered for between one year and four years.

The actual dollar value of a maintenance warranty ranges from nothing (if you don't take advantage of it) to several hundred or a thousand dollars for three years of maintenance. Most of the really costly maintenance services occur after three years, e.g., tire replacement, exhaust system work, etc. That's one of the reasons you'll rarely see maintenance warranties extend much beyond three years.

Keep On Shining

Many a love affair with a vehicle is based on appearances. Today, thanks to automobile "detailers," the affair doesn't necessarily have to dim with age. With a combination of skill, elbow grease, and the right products, a professional detailer can keep a car looking like new almost indefinitely. Of course, if you have the time and the inclination, you can detail your car yourself. But whether you hire a professional or do the job yourself, detailing your car once or twice a year should be part of your routine maintenance program. It isn't an extravagance — it's protection for your considerable investment. An old car that looks new will have the highest resale value.

Repairs

One of the blessings of a new car is a warranty. If something goes kerplunk in the night, at least you won't have to pay to fix it.

As your car gets older you won't have the assurance of a warranty. However, follow the maintenance advice in the preceding section, and you will keep repair costs — even on an old car — to a minimum. Preventive maintenance will prevent costly breakdowns.

Warranties

Every automaker offers a warranty on its new vehicles. So what then is the important difference between automakers' basic warranties? Time. For decades, the traditional warranty was 12 months or 12,000 miles, whichever came first. Today, that warranty has gone the way of 8-track stereos and carburetors.

Among the major automakers from Europe, Japan, Korea, and the U.S., basic bumper-to-bumper warranties now range from as little as two years and 24,000 miles to as long as four years and 60,000 miles. The longest warranties are usually from those that build luxury cars — Acura, BMW, Cadillac, Infiniti, Jaguar, Lexus, Lincoln, Mercedes-Benz, Saab, and Volvo, as examples. Given the high cost of repairs on modern, electronically complex vehicles, and given the fact that more things are likely to go wrong the older a vehicle becomes, often beginning in year three, the extra miles and years of cover-

MAINTENANCE TIPS

After You've Bought

■ The most important tip of all: read your car's owner's manual.

■ Don't skimp on routine maintenance. A regular maintenance program will protect your warranty, save you from costly, unexpected repairs, and will extend the life of your car.

■ Perform a quick inspection of your car every two weeks for problems in the making. (See "The Ten-Minute Technical Inspection" on page 30A.)

■ Be wary of extended service intervals; at minimum, have your car's oil and filter changed every 3,000 to 5,000 miles.

■ Keep all your service receipts; a complete set can increase your car's resale value if it proves your car was well maintained.

REPAIR TIPS

Before You Buy

■ Don't reject a car just because the charts show a high expected repair cost. The cost of repair is often the smallest of the seven major ownership costs, since most cars today are very reliable.

age can be a true money saver.

If you plan to keep your vehicle longer than two years or 24,000 miles — the vast majority of buyers do — compare warranties as you shop.

It's just as important to consider the basic warranty if you lease your new vehicle. If the term of your lease is longer than the vehicle's basic warranty, you may end up paying out of pocket for say, a new transmission, in what is essentially a rental vehicle.

The basic warranty is nearly always transferable to a subsequent owner. So if you want to sell your vehicle after two years and 24,000 miles and there's still a year and 12,000 miles left on the basic warranty, this could be a positive resale feature.

Roadside Help

Automakers and dealers alike have recognized the importance of customer service in the long-term success of their products. And part of their efforts are roadside assistance programs that come with their new cars, often at no extra charge.

Virtually every automaker offers free towing service in the event of a breakdown while the car is still covered by the warranty. And though some offer little more than the free towing, others are far more comprehensive. Oldsmobile, for example, pays for flat-tire repair, replacement of lost keys, and lockouts. The Olds dealer will provide you with courtesy transportation while your car is in the shop. And if there's a breakdown while you're away from home, Olds will pay for your food and

lodging while you wait for repairs. Most roadside assistance programs cease when the car's warranty is up. But Mercedes-Benz will pay for flat-tire repair, lockout service and minor repairs no matter how old the car may be or how many miles it has under its chassis.

Service Bulletins

Manufacturers sometimes issue "service bulletins" for certain problems. A service bulletin can be an authorization to dealers to fix a particular problem on a car for free — even if it is no longer covered by the warranty. Manufacturers do this when a large number of vehicles experience the same problem. Service bulletins are generally not publicized, and are often overlooked. Before you pay for any repairs, you should first check with your dealer's service manager to see if the repair costs are covered by a service bulletin.

Service Contracts (Mechanical Breakdown Insurance)

As a new-car buyer, you'll be confronted with yet another warranty of sorts — an extended service contract. Typically, the dealer will offer the contract to you at the time you buy the car.

No doubt about it, extended service contracts are big business. Nearly half of all new-car buyers purchase these contracts each year. The typical extended service contract backed by an automaker can have a markup of 100% by the automaker to the dealer, plus a 200 to 300% markup by dealer to the car buyer.

WARRANTIES

TYPE OF COVERAGE	WHAT IT COVERS
Basic or Bumper-to-Bumper Warranty	Covers defects in any area of the car, from the front bumper to the tailpipe, and anything in between. Normal wear items, such as brake pads or windshield wipers, are usually not covered, however. Repairs to correct defects will be made at no charge to the vehicle buyer for either parts or labor.
Powertrain Warranty	Covers the engine, transmission, and other parts of the drivetrain only. If an automaker offers a powertrain warranty, it will usually last longer than the basic warranty. Because powertrains are usually very reliable in modern cars, extended powertrain warranties are a nice bonus — but only IF they're in addition to a good basic warranty of at least three years and 36,000 miles.
Corrosion of Rust-Through Warranty	Covers rust perforations caused by natural elements. Surface rust is generally not covered under this warranty.
Emissions Control Warranty	Covers for two years or 24,000 miles virtually any defective component or system that could increase a car's pollutants, from onboard computers to the oil filler cap. This warranty is required by law but is usually meaningless because an automaker's basic warranty also covers such defects. There are, however, two exceptions to these limits. Automakers must warrant catalytic converters and powertrain control modules for eight years or 80,000 miles. And in California only, automakers must warranty a long list of components, from fuel injection systems to spark plugs, for either three years and 50,000 miles or seven years and 70,000 miles, depending on the component.
Specific Component Warranty	Covers batteries and tires under separate warranties by their makers.
	Covers roadside emergencies, such as flat tires or running out of gas. Roadside assistance plans are typically offered as part of the warranty package, and apply as long as the basic warranty is in effect. Some even offer free lodging and meals if your vehicle breaks down on a trip.
Optional Extended Warranty or Service Contract	Extends warranty protection beyond the period of the basic warranty, and is available for an extra charge.

REPAIR TIPS

After You've Bought

■ Keep receipts and document all the services performed on your car. If you can't prove that you've followed the manufacturer's recommended service program, you could invalidate your warranty.

■ Before you pay for a repair, see if the automaker has issued a service bulletin for the problem. Even if your car is no longer under warranty, the repairs may be covered.

■ Cultivate a good relationship with a mechanic. Interview mechanics in your area before you desperately need one.

■ Don't be afraid to switch dealers if your car is under warranty and you're dissatisfied with the service you are getting.

■ Don't be afraid to try an independent mechanic for routine service or, if your car is out of warranty, for repair. They're often less expensive than a dealer's service department.

■ Expect full explanations and estimates of costs before you authorize your mechanic to perform any work.

Extended service contracts can be a rip-off, or they can be a prudent form of budget control by eliminating unexpected repair bills. Whether one is right for you depends upon a) how many miles a year you drive your car; b) how long you plan to keep your car; and c) the length of the new-car basic warranty. If for example, you buy a new car with a three-year/36,000-mile basic warranty and you plan to keep it for five or six years and drive it 90,000 or 100,000 miles, then an extended service contract may be right for you.

But if you plan to keep the car for four years and 48,000 miles, you may be better off to self-insure. Put the money that you would otherwise pay for the contract in the bank; it's there if you need it for a repair during your last year of ownership, and if you don't, the money is still yours when you trade in the car.

If an extended service contract seems right for you, follow these guidelines when you purchase one:

■ **Consider the source.** Not all extended service contracts are backed by the automaker. Dealers may offer contracts backed by independent companies, often at a lower price. But automakers are less likely to disappear.

■ **Consider what's covered.** Some contracts may only cover the powertrain — the engine, transmission and differential. But in modern cars, these items are much less likely to fail than all the electronic doodads and amenities in most new cars. Virtually no contract will cover normal "wear"

items like brake pads. Expect there to be some sort of deductible for each repair as well.

■ **Consider who's to perform the repairs.** A contract backed by a dealer will probably require the repairs to be made at that dealership. A contract backed by an automaker will usually allow you take the car to any of its authorized dealers.

■ **Consider how the bill is to be paid.** Some contracts require you to pay the bill, and you will be reimbursed later. Others provide for direct payment to the repair shop.

■ **Consider the price.** Extended service contracts, like most everything else in buying a new car, are negotiable. There's usually plenty of room to bargain. Try offering half the price quoted by the dealer.

There's a less well-known alternative to dealer-marketed extended service contracts called "mechanical breakdown insurance" or MBI. This insurance is underwritten by insurance companies and is only available through licensed insurance agents. Unlike extended service contracts, MBI policies typically must be approved by a state's department of insurance.

MBI policies are often comprehensive in their coverage. Prices are comparable to, or even less than dealer-offered service contracts. Their prices however, are not negotiable. The policies are sold through insurance agencies. Many credit unions have licensed insurance agents on their staffs who can sell MBI policies.

Numbing the Pain of Car Repairs

For many car owners, a visit to a repair shop is accompanied by all the joy and excitement of heading for the dentist's chair. There are ways to make the visit less painful, however.

If your car is under warranty, you're pretty much married to an authorized dealer for repairs. But if you receive lousy service from say, the Subaru dealer who sold you your Legacy L, there's no reason why you can't high-tail it across town to another authorized Subaru dealer for service. All dealers must honor a manufacturer's warranty whether or not they originally sold the car.

Once your car is out of warranty *(see Warranties section on page 23A)*, you have a couple of other choices. You can take your car to an independent mechanic, or to a specialist who works on only specific components: radiators, brakes, mufflers, and so on.

Independent mechanics and specialists will often charge less than a dealer. But make sure they have a working knowledge of your kind of car, can obtain the correct parts, and have the diagnostic equipment necessary to repair complex electronic gadgets found in so many cars today.

How do you find a competent, trustworthy mechanic? There's a certain amount of trial and error involved. But recommendations from friends or owners of cars like yours are usually your best bet. In addition, mechanics usually know the scoop on other mechanics in town; if you buy a Chevy and

know a good Toyota mechanic, ask him or her to recommend someone who works on Chevys.

Whether you take your car to a dealer, independent, or specialist, be polite. It's a great American pastime to bad-mouth auto mechanics — and unfortunately, some deserve it. But in the long run, a car is only as good as the mechanic who takes care of it. Here are some pointers to help the two of you have a long and happy relationship:

■ A good mechanic may have grease on his overalls, but don't treat him as if he's not intelligent. You can't be a dummy and properly repair complex, modern cars.

■ Follow a trusted mechanic's repair recommendations. A good mechanic will spot potential problems before they occur.

■ Look for ASE (Automotive Service Excellence) certification. ASE certified mechanics have passed rigorous industry tests and continually update their technical knowhow.

■ If you're not sure whether to trust a mechanic, ask to watch while he works on your car. If that's not possible, you should at least expect him to explain the problem in simple language and to show you the defective part while it's still on the car. If he's a good mechanic, he'll appreciate your interest.

■ It's proper business practice for you to receive a written estimate before any work is performed. In some states it's the law. And if you authorize a repair and the mechanic later finds more is involved, he should get your permission to raise the estimate before he does the work.

■ If you don't trust your mechanic and if a quote seems too high, be sure you understand what's involved with the repair. Then before you agree to the repair, telephone one or two other mechanics for quotes so you can compare.

■ When talking to your mechanic, be as specific as possible. "There's a high-pitched squeal that seems to come from the right rear wheel between 50 and 60 m.p.h.," is a lot more helpful than, "The wheel makes funny noises."

■ If you're unhappy about warranty work, don't hesitate to complain to the manufacturer's regional service representative. Your car's owner's manual will usually give an address. If you're unhappy about work you paid for, contact your state's bureau of automotive repair. As a last resort, small claims courts are generally sympathetic to car owners who can present a well-documented case of an auto repair rip-off.

Resolving Complaints

Tears, angry letters, and threats might get your once-friendly dealer to fix your new car right while it's under warranty. But if you're not getting satisfactory repairs from the dealer, follow these steps and you'll probably get better results:

First, write as concisely as possible a letter of complaint to the dealer's general manager or owner. Make sure you do this while the vehicle is still under warranty. Make sure, too, that you keep all your repair records and copies of your correspondence.

Second, if the dealer can't or won't resolve the problem, ask the automaker's "zone representative" to intervene. Ask the dealer for the zone office address; it may also be listed in your vehicle's owner's manual. The zone rep can authorize additional repairs or take other steps to resolve the dispute.

Third, if the zone rep won't help, contact the automaker's owner relations or public relations department. Again, your owner's handbook should list the address. Ask for their suggestions on how you might proceed to get your car fixed to your satisfaction.

Finally, if you believe the defects of your car are serious, and if you would like the automaker to either replace the car with another or give you a refund, you can take action against the automaker under your state's so-called "lemon law."

Lemon Laws

Every state and the District of Columbia has a "lemon law" for consumers to obtain either a refund or a replacement of a new car or light truck if a significant defect isn't repaired after a reasonable number of attempts.

Under most state laws, the buyer can seek a replacement or refund for defects that occur either within the first 12 to 24 months or 12,000 to 24,000 miles, or within the vehicle's warranty period. In about half of the states, the law includes leased vehicles, and used vehicles are included in a handful of states if sold under warranty.

Most of the laws define "defect" as a serious condition that would substantially impair the vehicle's use, value, or safety.

If you suspect you may have a lemon, get a copy of the lemon law from the state where you purchased the vehicle. The state attorney general's office or local Better Business Bureau also may have pamphlets or other information on the law, or may be able to answer any questions you may have about the law.

Generally, state lemon laws require three or four warranty repair attempts or 30 calendar or business days in which the car wasn't in service before consumers can proceed to arbitration. If the defect is considered a serious safety defect (such as steering or brakes), you often can seek relief after only one or two attempted warranty repairs.

Most states require that you notify in writing both the manufacturer and the dealer of your intent to seek a refund or replacement under your state's lemon law. When writing, use certified or registered mail, and keep the return receipt. The dealer or manufacturer generally is given one final attempt to fix the problem. If that attempt fails, you can seek arbitration.

Arbitration also varies by state. Many states have arbitration programs operated or supported by the manufacturers. In some states, the program is operated by the Better Business Bureau or through the National Automobile Dealers Association. About a dozen states operate their own arbitration programs.

In arbitration, both you and the manufacturer have the opportunity to present arguments (in many arbitration programs you have the option to present your case in person or in writing), generally before a single arbitrator or a panel. In most cases, the arbitrator's decision is binding on the manufacturer but not on you. If you're still not satisfied you may take your case to court.

If you win, many states give you the choice of a replacement vehicle or a refund. But in some states, the arbitrator or manufacturer may choose the replacement vehicle, which means you may have to accept a vehicle with about the same miles and remaining warranty as your lemon vehicle.

To document your case, always obtain and save any warranty or other repair orders, service records, and any written communication you sent or received from the dealer or manufacturer. Log any problems that occur with the vehicle, including dates, details of the repairs performed, repair costs, and number of days the vehicle was out of service.

If you have a choice between a state-operated or a manufacturer-run arbitration program, choose the state program. Some consumer groups say state-operated programs are more likely to decide in favor of the consumer.

If You Get Stuck With a Lemon:

You can retain an attorney knowledgeable of your state's lemon law. To get a list of attorneys near you, contact your local or state bar association and ask for a list of attorneys specializing in consumer law or "lemon law." You can also contact the Center for Auto Safety in Washington, D.C. at 202-328-7700.

THE TEN-MINUTE TECHNICAL INSPECTION

Your mechanic may deftly tune your car's engine, but that won't matter a bit if the engine fries itself because you failed to notice that the radiator ran out of coolant. So roll up your sleeves, because now you're going to learn your way around your car. And in the process, you may thwart a costly, irritating, and possibly dangerous breakdown in the making. Here goes:

First, pop open the hood. Do you see the engine? Good. Actually that's quite an accomplishment, what with engines mounted sideways and all the complicated paraphernalia automakers hang on them these days.

Now find the engine dipstick; it's sticking up somewhere along the side of the engine. (If you can't find it, check your owner's manual.) Pull it out, wipe it off, stick it back in, and pull it out again. Does the oil level reach somewhere between the hatch marks on the dipstick? If not, add some. If it needs more than a quart, take the car to your mechanic and find out why it is losing oil.

Now find the radiator or the radiator overflow tank. Take off the cap and look inside. Do you see some colorful liquid that looks like Kool-Aid? If not, add water. Again, if it takes more than a quart, you'd better have your mechanic take a look.

While you're at the radiator, examine all the rubber hoses running from the radiator to the engine. Look at any other hoses in the engine compartment for that matter. Are they cracked, or do they look so brittle that they should be? Are there any bulges, or are they squishy soft? If so, have them replaced. Chances are you'll not find the right size in a provincial gas station when a hose bursts on your next trip out of town.

If your car isn't quite as up to date as today's news, look for a distributor. It's a round thing with thick wires running out of the top. Follow each of the wires to the engine. Are they firmly attached to the distributor at one end, and to the spark plugs at the other? Are the little rubber booties that cover the ends in place? If your car is a new or nearly new model, the distributor and plug wires probably won't be visible, so you can skip this step. Indeed, some of the newest cars don't even have traditional distributors or plug wires.

Next, find the belt (or belts) that run the alternator, air conditioning compressor, and perhaps the radiator cooling fan or other accessories. Make sure it isn't frayed or cracked. Find a spot where it's suspended between two pulleys and push down with your finger; if it gives more than a half inch, it needs tightening.

Now find the battery. If it's a refillable type, take off the caps and check all six cells to see that there's water. If the terminals look like they've grown moss, scrub them with a little baking soda and water. And if you see signs of battery acid on the pan where the battery resides, wash the pan thoroughly and check the battery case for leaks. Acid will eventually eat right through metal.

Now start the engine. Look back under the hood. Do you see the fan whirring? Does the engine settle into a smooth idle, or does it jerk around while it runs? Do you see any leaks from any hoses? Do you hear any ominous sounds? Once the novelty of all this has worn off, stop the engine and shut the hood.

Glance under the car. Your car can hold up to 11 different fluids of one kind or another, and all of them should be in the car, not on the driveway. Examine the exhaust system for rusty holes. If your car has front- wheel drive, glance in back of the front wheels. Do you see a greasy mess behind there? The rubber boots that cover the constant velocity joints may be torn or missing. CV joints are relatively expensive to replace, and the boots protect them from dirt and sand that can ruin them.

Get up, turn on all the lights and walk around the car to see that they work. Don't forget to check the turn signals. Look at the windshield wipers; make sure they're not shredding or you'll have a scratched windshield after the next rain.

Now look at all four tires. Is there plenty of tread? Are the sidewalls cracking? Look especially closely at the front tires for signs of uneven wear. If they're scalloped or worn excessively on one side, either the suspension is tired or there's an alignment problem. Buy a tire gauge for a couple of bucks and check the pressures. Don't forget the spare tire, too. Correct pressures are listed in your owner's manual.

That's it. You've just learned where all the more important fallible things are. Make this inspection a ritual every other week and you'll forestall many expensive repairs.

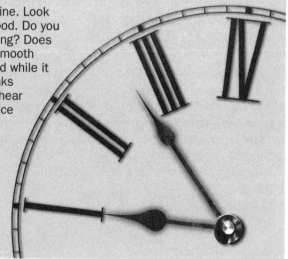

SECTION TWO

Choosing and Buying a Car

CHOOSING AND BUYING A CAR

I t's inevitable. It happens to every car driver. Sooner or later, you'll have fantasies. Fantasies of buying a brand-new car. Fantasies of gazing into the deep, lustrous, unblemished paint of a brand-new car. Fantasies of how you'll look — a sneer on your aristocratic lips, perhaps — as you sit behind the wheel of a brand-new car. Fantasies of not having to worry about repairs and break-downs of a brand-new car. Freedom, power, sex, and elan — a brand-new car can provide it all.

...pop! Hold on. Back to reality for a moment. All this fantasizing can make you forget mundane matters like budget-busting monthly payments or how you're going to get rid of the old clunker you're currently driving.

How Much Can You Afford?

It's a pretty basic question, after all. Unfortunately, few new-car or truck buyers have an accurate answer before they buy because they neglect to consider the ownership costs discussed in the previous section.

Disregarding depreciation for the moment, other ownership costs — insurance, state fees and taxes, fuel, maintenance and repair — can, when averaged out on a monthly basis, easily equal the monthly car payment. As a result, too many buyers end up seeing their dream machine hanging from the hook of a repossesor's tow truck (*see Flat Broke, page 79A*) after finding

they can't afford to actually use the vehicle and make the payments too.

Auto dealers are masters at making a new vehicle SEEM affordable — "Just $299 a month, and this baby is all yours!" But only you, after careful consideration of all the expected costs in addition to the purchase price, can determine if a new car or truck fits comfortably into your budget. Filling out the affordability worksheet (*figure 6, page 34A*) will help you find the answer.

Lenders typically frown on folks who have debt obligations amounting to more than 36% of their gross income. Thus, if your house payments are say, 21% of your gross income and your credit card payments amount to 5%, that leaves no more than 10% for car or truck payments. Financial advisors often recommend keeping vehicle loan or lease payments plus other vehicle operating costs at 10% to 15% of gross income.

Certified Used Vehicle Programs

Yes, you've got your eye on that pristine beauty on the dealer's showroom floor. But before you take that final fateful step, consider buying a slightly used vehicle instead of a brand-new one. That may be odd advice coming from a new-vehicle guide, but it could be worth the price of this book a hundred times over.

As we've shown in Section One, "Ownership Costs," a new car may be very costly to own —

Before you completely surrender yourself to your dream car, resist temptation for a few moments and ask yourself some prudent questions:

■ What's really more important, the kids' college tuition or my dream car?

■ How long do I expect to own the car? If these buying-a-new-car fantasies come infrequently, say once every eight or ten years, then depreciation is less of a factor and you can consider vehicles with a higher rate of depreciation.

■ How well do I tend to maintain a car? If you're the kind to drive 'em and leave 'em, you'd better steer clear of fussy, high-maintenance cars even if you do find them attractive.

■ How many miles a year will I drive? If you pile on the miles, a car with poor fuel economy and high maintenance costs could bankrupt you.

■ How do I drive? If you live in a big city, a fancy car could mean astronomical insurance costs. If you live in the mountains, an underpowered econobox might not get you where you need to go. If you live in sunny Florida, a car with four-wheel drive might be a silly extravagance.

Figure 6

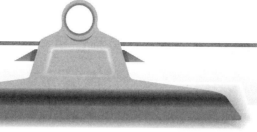

Affordability Worksheet

	WHAT YOU CAN AFFORD 1. Maximum monthly amount you can comfortably afford to buy and operate a vehicle:
	INSURANCE 2. Monthly cost of insurance: (See vehicle charts in this guide for 5-year cost of vehicle you want; divide figure by 60.)
	MAINTENANCE 3. Monthly cost of routine maintenance: (See vehicle charts; though maintenance costs increase in later years, dividing 5-year cost by 60 will give an average monthly cost.)
	REPAIR 4. Monthly cost of repairs: (See vehicle charts; repair costs will rise in later years after vehicle warranty expires. But dividing 5-year cost by 60 will give a reasonable average monthly cost.)
	STATE FEES 5. Monthly cost of state fees: (See vehicle charts; divide figure by 60)
	FUEL 6. Monthly cost of fuel: (See vehicle charts; divide figure by 60) Add items 2-6 together and subtract total from item 1. Enter the result in item 7.
	YOUR PAYMENTS??? 7. Amount remaining that you can afford for a monthly loan or lease payment: (If you plan to lease, this is the maximum lease payment you should consider. If you plan to buy the vehicle with a loan, fill in items 8 through 11.)
	PRICE OF VEHICLE 8. See vehicle charts; enter Total Target Price.)
	DOWN PAYMENT 9. Enter amount of down payment you can make.
	AMOUNT TO BE FINANCED 10. (Subtract item 9 from item 8.)
	MONTHLY PAYMENT 11. See Appendix 1 to determine payments at various terms and interest rates. Compare item 11 to item 7. If you can't find a monthly payment that doesn't exceed item 7, then you'd better consider buying either a less expensive vehicle or one with less expensive ownership costs.

most of all, because of depreciation. If you buy a used vehicle, you can help beat the high cost of depreciation and get more car for your buck at the same time.

Of course, many motorists fear that buying a used vehicle means buying somebody else's troubles. But, several automakers are addressing this concern with innovative factory-certified used-car programs.

Thanks to the spurt in new-car leasing earlier in the decade, dealers are now finding their lots crowded with late-model used cars coming off leases written two or three years ago.

To move all these used vehicles off their lots, dealers are transforming the cars and trucks into cream puffs and then wrapping them in the security blanket of a comprehensive factory warranty. The upshot: You can have the important benefits of a new car at a used-car price.

Consider Volvo's certified used-car program, Volvo Select PreOwned. Volvo models that are five years old or less, and with fewer than 75,000 miles, are eligible for the program. Each car undergoes a 70-point inspection; the dealer repairs anything found amiss. The buyer receives the remainder of the car's four-year/ 50,000-mile new-car warranty plus an additional one-year or 12,000-mile warranty that will be honored at any Volvo dealer. Volvo even throws in free roadside assistance for one year. Under this program, you'll probably save around $10,000 on say, a three-year-old fully-loaded 850 sedan with 25,000 miles on its odometer, compared to a new, similarly equipped S70 sedan.

The Starmark certified used-car program from Mercedes-Benz covers Mercedes models eight years old or less with fewer than 90,000 miles; the reconditioned cars are backed by special warranties ranging from one to three years. Like Volvo, Mercedes offers financing and leasing programs for its certified used cars.

Saturn's program not only includes used Saturn models, but other makes as well. Most makes on a Saturn dealer's lot are eligible if they're five years old or less and carry fewer than 60,000 miles. Saturn dealers also offer their used cars with a three-day, money-back guarantee if the buyer isn't satisfied.

Other manufacturers with certified used-car programs include Acura, BMW, Cadillac, Ford, Honda, Jaguar, Lexus, Nissan, Infiniti, Toyota, and Volkswagen.

What Price Should You Pay?

Wouldn't it be a relief if new-car prices were no more negotiable than a can of tuna at the supermarket? Unfortunately, that's not the nature of the game.

And in many ways it is a game. Unless you've been trained, don't expect to beat the dealer — he or she is a pro, after all. But if you do a little homework, you can arrive at a fair deal for both yourself and the dealer.

Dealer Incentives

The "dealer cost" figures shown in this book are known in the trade as the "dealer invoice" prices. But in reality, dealers usually purchase a car for less than factory invoice *(See page 38A)*. This is because

When negotiating a price, keep in mind that the following three prices are very different:

1. The dealer's cost or price (a.k.a. factory invoice) — the maximum price the dealer paid the factory for the car.
2. The manufacturer's suggested list price.
3. The car's sticker price, which usually differs from the suggested list price, and includes special equipment, options, preparation charges, and other fees.

REBATE TIPS

■ Don't rely on the dealer to inform you of available rebates and incentives. Each issue of *Automotive News*, available at many public libraries, lists current consumer and dealer incentives. If you would like a complete report on a particular vehicle, including current consumer and dealer incentives, you can order the *Just the Facts®️ Report,* as advertised in this book.

■ Don't buy a car just because it comes with a large rebate. A rebate tacked on a poor value doesn't automatically make it a good value. Use the charts in this book to determine the good values, then see which of those have a rebate.

automakers frequently provide so-called "dealer incentives."

All domestic automakers and some foreign automakers give their dealers a "holdback," or a refund of 1 to 3% of the invoice price after the car is sold. Automakers often give "factory-to-dealer" rebates as well. The dealers can either keep the rebates or pass them along to the customer to sweeten a deal. These and other dealer incentives explain why a dealer can sell a car at "cost" and still make a profit.

Knowing the dealer's true cost for a car — that is, the invoice price minus holdbacks and factory-to-dealer rebates does not automatically guarantee that you will get the deal of the century. But, it is an effective weapon to have as part of your negotiating arsenal. Not only will it give you a good indication of how much profit a dealer is trying to make on each sale, but it will also serve as an excellent point from which to begin negotiating. Realistically, you should set your goal on purchasing a new car at the "target price" listed in the vehicle charts starting on page 1. This figure is calculated using the dealer invoice as a base, and factoring in current market conditions to arrive at a price that represents a good deal to you and a fair profit for the dealer.

Customer Incentives

Cash-back rebates have become as much a part of the new-car sales routine as tire-kicking and test drives.

In recent years, manufacturers have added a number of other items to their sales-incentive menu as well. Automakers may

offer a choice of discount financing or a cash rebate, for instance. (See Appendix J.)

You may also want to check out discount leases, where automakers subsidize some of the leasing costs the buyer would otherwise incur. *(See "Shopping for a Lease," page 40A.)*

Dealer "Packs"

Every car on a dealer's lot will have a window sticker showing the manufacturer's suggested retail price. (This sticker is known as a Monroney sticker in the trade.) But a dealer will often add a second window sticker. This can be a gold mine of added profit for a dealer. The sticker may include charges for worthwhile dealer-installed options — an alarm system perhaps. But it may also include goodies such as documentation fees, dealer preparation charges and, most blatant of all, "market value adjustments" (MVA) or "added dealer profit" (ADP).

These extra charges — except for the dealer-installed options that you want on the car, and a reasonable destination charge that covers the manufacturer's cost of delivering the vehicle to the dealer — are profit padders, and you should not have to pay them unless the car is in great demand.

Dealer Advertising Fees

As stated on the previous page, the dealer's cost on a vehicle may be lower than the figure published in this book since manufacturers may offer hidden incentives to their dealers.

On the other hand, the dealer cost may actually be higher than the figure in this book because some dealers are required to pay an advertising fee for each vehicle they sell. This fee is charged by the manufacturer and is used to promote the brand in the dealer's geographic area.

The dealer will tell you that he must sell the vehicle at a price that covers his advertising fees. This is a legitimate fee, but you shouldn't hesitate to ask the salesperson to show you his invoice for the vehicle. If he has been straightforward, he should have no problem unveiling his cost to you.

If you do have a chance to see the invoice, you may find it somewhat complicated *(see "Anatomy of an Invoice", page 38A)*, but the dealer advertising fee should appear on the invoice. If it isn't clear, ask the salesperson to point it out for you.

Make sure you question any charge you do not understand. And always remember to find out if there is a dealer holdback on the vehicle. (This should also appear on the invoice.) If the dealer insists that you cover the cost of his advertising fee, you should make sure that he deducts any holdback offered by the manufacturer. In fact if there is a holdback, it usually more than offsets the advertising fee.

Ultimately, your goal should be to find out what the bottom line cost is to the dealer and try to aggressively negotiate the best deal you can.

Supply and Demand

Keep in mind that a dealer can charge any price the market will bear for a car. In most cases, the "target prices" given in this book will be enough to give the dealer a fair profit and you a fair price.

However, if a car is in great demand and short supply, the dealer may refuse to sell the car for anything less than the manufacturer's retail price. Indeed, if the car is in very great demand, the dealer may even insist on a markup over the MSRP. In this instance, check with dealers outside your local market who may have a better supply of the cars.

By the same token, it will be easier to negotiate a better deal on overstocked cars or models that are not selling well. Dealers who are carrying less popular models that have been sitting on their lots for a long time are stuck with a double-edged liability. Not only are they losing profit on potential sales, but they are paying finance charges and other expenses while they keep the cars. They may be happy to get them off the lot at a bargain price.

No Dicker Stickers

Take-it-or-leave-it price tags have suddenly become all the rage in the auto industry. A handful of enlightened individual dealers across the country, as well as all the dealers of one automaker, have decided to face head-on the traditional notion that the new-car showroom should take on the atmosphere of a third-world bazaar.

General Motors' newest division, Saturn Corporation, took the lead in eliminating the haggling over a car's price at its dealerships.

Individual dealers for other automakers, after noting Saturn's

Figure 7

Anatomy of an Invoice

Your negotiating strategy should focus on the "Factory Invoice," the actual bill from the manufacturer to the dealer. It details the options installed on the particular vehicle, and the various charges and discounts the dealer has incurred on the vehicle.

The invoice is an important buyer's tool for two reasons:

1. It allows the buyer to determine the real price of the vehicle to the dealer, preparing the buyer to negotiate upward from this price, rather than downward from the "Window Sticker" price.

2. While most of the information on the invoice is readily available through services such as the Just-the-Facts™ report (available from IntelliChoice. See the ad in the center of this book, or call 1-800-227-2665), the invoice may contain dealer-cost information that is otherwise difficult to obtain, such as regional factory-to-dealer discounts and "holdbacks."

When you are ready to buy the vehicle, ask to see the Factory Invoice. Many dealers will gladly show it to you because they consider you a serious buyer and realize a sale will be made at a fair price without wasting a lot of their time. Other dealers would rather walk on hot coals than share the invoice with you. If you find that to be the case, find yourself a more accommodating dealer.

Even when you get your hands on a Factory Invoice, you may have a hard time figuring out what the figures mean and what the dealer actually paid for the vehicle. The following is an actual invoice from Ford. To help you interpret an invoice, we've noted the meaningful parts. Factory invoices from other manufacturers will differ from this example, but all invoices contain similar information.

SAMPLE DEALER INVOICE EXPLANATION

1 The Order Code. This matches the Window Sticker.

2 Item Description. This matches the Window Sticker.

3 The List Price. This matches the Window Sticker. Nothing from this point on is included in the Window Sticker.

4 The Invoice Amount. For the vehicle and all its options, the factory charge by line item. This is the largest component of dealer price.

5 This says that the dealer may be getting other discounts above and beyond what's on the invoice, so his cost can be even lower than shown. You cannot easily determine additional discounts and most dealers will not volunteer to tell you. However, you should ask the dealer if there are any other discounts that he is currently receiving. Always negotiate the best price that you can, even if the dealer complains that he is not making any money at that price. Remember, if the dealer makes the deal, you know he is making money.

6 Manufacturers may also offer additional discounts or "Bonus Savings." In 1999 Ford offers, on another model, a bonus discount on leather sport bucket seats of $1,050 list and $893 dealer price. (The example on page 39A lists the bonus savings as $0 because this vehicle doesn't have any additional discounts that qualify for the savings.)

7 The sum of the dealer discounts on the vehicle—$1,391.25 dealer invoice.

8 Believe it or not, the manufacturer charges the dealer for a tank of gas. This figure is a legitimate expense that increases the dealer's cost.

A This is the amount that Mercury is charging this dealer to pay for regional advertising. Essentially, Mercury determines how much to spend on advertising, then charges each vehicle sold in the area a portion of the total advertising dollars. Dealers that sell the most vehicles pay the most for advertising. This figure is a legitimate expense that increases the dealer's cost.

B This figure is the sum of the total invoice plus the regional advertising fee. It is what the dealer may say is his cost, but read on. . .

C This may be the most important number on the invoice. Many manufacturers now include a "holdback" on the invoice. This figure ($848 in this case) is given back to the dealer at the end of the quarter. It lowers the true dealer cost without lowering the Invoice Total (B above). Make sure you deduct this holdback from the Invoice Total to determine actual dealer cost. Mercury allows for a holdback of 3% of the list price of the vehicle not including the destination fee. In this example, $848 is 3% of $28,260. $28,260 comes from subtracting the $605 destination fee from the $28,865 total list price of the vehicle. GM (except Saturn), Ford and Chrysler also have 3% holdbacks, while import holdbacks range from none (Audi, Kia, Land Rover, Lexus, & Porsche), to 2% (Acura, BMW, Honda, Mazda, Mitsubishi, Subaru, Suzuki, & Volkswagen) to 3% (Isuzu, Mercedes-Benz, Volvo & Saab). Others are based off of Invoice (Hyundai, Infiniti, Jaguar, Nissan, & Toyota).

D This invoice is created the moment the vehicle comes off the line at the factory. The dealer is charged for the vehicle at that time, though he may not receive the vehicle for weeks afterward. For that reason, Mercury credits the dealer to compensate him for the interest lost on his money from the time the invoice is created to the time the dealer receives the vehicle. Although this discount reduces the dealer invoice, it is really just a refund of the dealer's financing expense. You should not reduce the dealer's cost by this amount.

E This is the Invoice Total less Holdback and Financing Cost. For your purposes, you should deduct the Holdback, but not the Financing, to determine the dealer's final cost. In this example, the dealer cost would be $25,599.00 (the Invoice Total) less $848.00 (the Holdback), or $24,551.00.

F This figure means nothing unless you are a current or retired employee of Mercury . If so, it is the price that you pay for the car. Mercury will credit the dealer for the difference between this figure and the dealer cost, so the dealer does not lose money on the transaction.

Sample Dealer Invoice

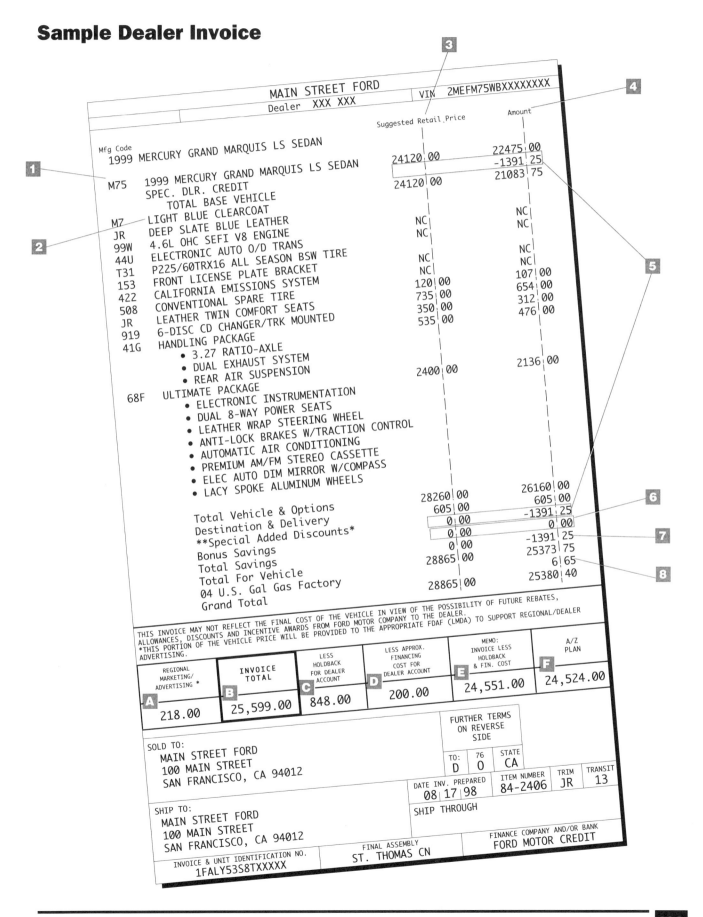

Net Interest Rate — The True Measure of a Lease

Remember, the net interest rate — not to be confused with the base interest rate — is the one true measure of the cost of a lease and the only way to compare leases on an apples-to-apples basis. Unfortunately, this rate is very difficult to obtain from a lessor. To determine the lessor's approximate net interest rate, use the Lease Interest Rate Worksheet, figure 8, or visit the IntelliChoice World Wide Web site at www.intellichoice.com for our leasing calculators and Gold Star Lease evaluations.

success, are also trying no-haggle policies. And surveys have shown that most customers love it.

Instead of boosting the window sticker prices by thousands with the expectation of knocking them down during the grueling negotiating process, the dealers tack on a reasonable profit to the invoice price and refuse to bargain down the price with the customer.

Though no-dicker-stickers eliminate part of the new-car-shopping hassle, they are not however, a panacea for haggle-phobic customers. Even no-dicker-sticker dealers have other ways to line their pockets with your money.

Buyers who wish to trade in their old car to the dealer must still negotiate a price for their trade-in.

Dealer "F&I" (finance and insurance) managers can still pad dealer-provided loan or lease agreements with high or unnecessary extra charges if you let your guard down.

And because dealer overhead can vary depending upon a dealer's location, the no-dicker prices will vary. Car buyers still need to shop around for the best price, even among one-price dealerships.

Worst of all, some dealerships purport to have no-dicker-stickers — but will actually negotiate if you press them. This of course, means their one-price policy is a sham.

Finally, if you really think you can beat the dealer at his own game (few people can), if you enjoy a good haggle, and if you have the time and patience to try, there's still no substitute for hard, astute bargaining at a traditional dealer.

Shopping for a Lease

Although a lease is more complicated than a loan, it's important to remember that, as with a loan, a lease is just a financial transaction and, like the cost of a loan, the cost of a lease is measured by the net interest rate or APR. Leasing is in part more complex because the terminology is different and in part because you are paying for only part of the car.

Many factors influence how much a lease costs and what the monthly payments are. All of the factors are shown on Gold Star Lease evaluations (see pages 46A-47A). However, the three most significant factors influencing cost and monthly payments are purchase price, residual value, and base interest rate (also called the money factor). Never enter into a lease agreement unless you know and are comfortable with all three of these factors.

■ **Purchase Price:** Whether leasing or buying, there is a purchase price for the vehicle. There's absolutely no reason why the price of a vehicle should be higher if you lease rather than buy the car. If the purchase price in a lease is higher than you would pay to buy the car, you're simply paying too much, and the difference is just added profit for the dealer.

Sometimes the purchase price in a manufacturer subsidized lease is actually lower than what you would pay to buy the car. This tends to reduce the depreciation and is a common way for manufac-

Figure 8

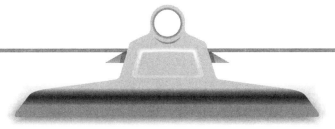

Lease Interest Rate Worksheet

Step	Your Figures	Example Figures *	Explanation
A) Enter your monthly payment	_____	$299.00	This does not include tax, license and extra options.
B) Enter the net capitalized cost	_____	$21,171.00	The offer price of the car minus dealer and manf. discounts and required down payment.
C) Enter the residual amount	_____	$15,035.00	The pre-determined value of the car at end of lease.
D) Enter the lease term in months	_____	36	This is the number of payments that need to be made.
E) Subtract **C** from **B**	_____	$6,136.00	This is the net depreciation for the lease.
F) Divide **E** by **D**	_____	$170.44	This is the depreciation per month.
G) Subtract **F** from **A**	_____	$128.56	This is the interest per month.
H) Add **B** to **C**	_____	$36,206.00	This is a total of cap cost and residual.
I) Divide **G** by **H**	_____	.0035507	This is the money factor used in the lease.
J) Multiply **I** by 24	_____	8.52%	This is the base interest rate in the lease.
K) Multiply acquisition fee by .000044 for 24 mo lease by .000032 for 36 mo lease by .000026 for 48 mo lease	_____	0.00%	$0.00 times .000032
L) Multiply disposition fee by .000036 for 24 mo lease by .000022 for 36 mo lease by .000015 for 48 mo lease	_____	.33%	$150.00 times .000022
M) Add **J**, **K** and **L**	_____	8.85%	This is the approximate net interest rate.

*The figures used in this example were taken from the "Special Lease Incentives" section on page 50A.

LEASING GLOSSARY

Unfortunately, the details of leasing make new-car shopping all the more complex. And the savvy lessee must learn a new vocabulary.

Acquisition Fee. An acquisition fee is a charge for processing a lease and is probably not negotiable. On a shorter term lease, the acquisition fee can have a large impact on the cost of the lease.

Base Interest Rate. This represents the interest paid on the usage of the vehicle during a lease. It is the 'cost' of a lease before factoring in discounts, fees, and penalties and is not directly comparable to the APR for a loan.

Lowering the base interest rate is one of the methods manufacturers use to subsidize leases. The phrase 'money factor' measures the same cost and can be converted into a base interest rate. For example, to convert a money factor of 0.00276 into an approximate base interest rate we would multiply the money factor by 24. The result would be 0.0662 or 6.62%.

Buy at end-of-term interest rate. This is the effective net interest rate for the lease if, at the end of the lease, the car is purchased at the end-of-lease purchase price.

Capitalized (Cap) Cost. This is the total price of the vehicle, in effect, its purchase price. In theory, the cap cost should equal the amount you would pay for the vehicle if you were purchasing the vehicle. When a lease is made, the dealer sells that vehicle to the leasing company (for the cap cost), which then leases the vehicle to you.

Capitalized (Cap) Cost Reduction. This is a fancy name for a cash down payment, money you pay up front that is applied to the final purchase price. A large cap cost reduction will, of course, reduce the monthly payments, but it will also negate one of the big advantages of leasing. However, if you own your present car, you may be able to use it, as a trade-in, to satisfy the cap cost reduction to start the lease. Remember, you must pay sales tax on any cap cost reduction you make.Another source of capital

cost reduction may be dealer or manufacturer participation. Dealers and manufacturers will sometimes lower the cap cost or offer a rebate that reduces the cap cost. A dealer or manufacturer cap cost reduction does lower your total out-of-pocket dollars, unlike a cap cost reduction that you must pay.

Closed and Open End Leases. Most leases offered today are closed-end leases, meaning that the residual value is fixed and stated in the lease contract. The lessee's financial obligations are unaffected by what the vehicle is actually worth when the lease ends. In other words, the lessee assumes no risk for the depreciation of the vehicle.

With an open-end lease, there is still a residual value set at the beginning of the lease. However, if the car is worth less than the residual value at the lease's end, the lessee must pay the difference. In other words, the lessee assumes the risk for depreciation with an open-end lease.

Dealer Participation. This is the amount contributed by the dealer to reduce the final purchase price in the lease contract. Dealer participation can take the form of a rebate or simply a discount. The dealer participation is reflected in the lease contract as a capitalized cost reduction.

Depreciation. The amount by which property loses its value. In automobile leasing, depreciation is the difference between the new car cost and the value of the car at the end of the lease.

Disposition Fee. This is a fee you pay at the end of the lease, to the lessor, that covers the lessor's cost of getting the vehicle ready for sale after you have returned the vehicle. It is often applied against any deposit you made at lease inception.

"Down Payment." See capital cost reduction.

Early Termination. A vehicle's depreciation is highest in the first few months after it leaves the dealer's lot. Since a lessee pays for depreciation in equal monthly payments, lessees who end a lease early have almost always used up more of a car's value than they've paid for. Therefore, lease contracts generally include penalties for early termination. Be aware of these penalties before you sign the lease contract and consider your ability to fulfill the contract.

End-of-Lease Purchase Price. If there is a purchase option in the lease contract or agreement, this will be the agreed upon price for the purchase of the vehicle at the end of the lease-the stated residual value. This price may also include additional fees.

Final Purchase Price. This price is equivalent to the amount you would pay for the vehicle if you were buying or financing rather than leasing. The final purchase price does not include any 'down' payment by the lessee.

Gap Insurance. This covers you against additional losses not covered by your auto insurance in the case of an accident in which the vehicle is totaled. Most auto insurance will cover the actual cash value of the car at the time of its loss. Gap insurance covers the difference (gap) between the actual cash value of the vehicle and what is owed on the lease contract, including early termination fees. Gap insurance is most important in the early years of a lease when the difference between the value of the car and what is owed are greatest. Some manufacturers now include Gap insurance in their leases.

Gold Star Lease. Gold Star Leases represent the best value (lowest cost) leases available today from manufacturers. IntelliChoice evaluates national and regional subsidized leases offered by manufacturers and determines the net interest rate (true cost) of the lease. To qualify as a Gold Star Lease, each lease must satisfy the following two requirements. 1) The net interest rate of the lease must be in the lowest 25% of all evaluated leases. 2) The net interest rate for the lease must be at least two percentage points less than the average credit union loan rate or average bank loan rate, whichever is less. Leases that meet the Gold Star Lease criteria are leases that will cost you the least in terms of real dollars.

Lease Term. This is the duration of the lease. 24 and 36 month leases are the are the most common but you can lease a vehicle for 12, 48, or even 60 months if you choose. Remember that your monthly payment will change depending on the length of the lease.

Lessee. The individual or party signing the lease contract and taking responsibility for the vehicle and lease payments.

LEASING GLOSSARY (Continued)

Lessor. The individual, dealer, business, manufacturer, or financial institution that owns the vehicle.

Independent Lessor. Independent Lessors are usually individual businesses that can provide for the lease of virtually any make or model of vehicle. Independent lessors, like dealers, can write custom leases, including those with different conditions and special mileage considerations.

MSRP. Manufacturer suggested retail price.

Manufacturer Discounts. In some leases, particularly subvented leases, the manufacturer reduces the MSRP which lowers the purchase price of the vehicle, which the lease is based on. This is a form of capitalized cost reduction.

Mileage Allowance. Mileage Allowance. Lease agreements usually establish the average miles per year that the car may be driven during the lease. This is often between 12,000 and 15,000 miles. The lease contract also establishes the amount you'll have to pay for every mile driven over the allowance. This mileage fee is usually 15¢ per mile. You can often purchase additional miles at the start of the lease at a discounted rate. If you're sure you're going to drive more than the number of miles allowed, then your best option is to negotiate for a higher allowance on the lease.

Money Factor. The most common way to express the base interest rate of a lease is as a money factor. If you multiply a money factor by 2400, the result will be equivalent to the base interest rate. The money factor of most leases is known by a dealer's sales staff. The money factor measures the cost of money, just like an interest rate. However, money factors are used almost exclusively in leases, whereas interest rates are used everywhere else.

Monthly Payment. The amount that must be paid each month to satisfy the lease contract. It is common for the monthly payment shown in lease advertisements to exclude applicable taxes, which will add to the amount paid each month.

Net Capitalized Cost. This is the price of the vehicle after deducting any dealer participation, manufacturer discounts, and cap cost reduction ('down' payment) from the MSRP.

Net Interest Rate. This is the total interest rate for the lease. It represents the lease's true cost, similar to an APR for a bank or credit union loan. The lower the net interest rate, the lower the cost of the lease.

Opportunity Cost. The cost of what you didn't do. For instance, if you have the cash to buy a car, the opportunity cost of the purchase is the interest lost on the cash you used for the car. One of the often-cited advantages of leasing is that it frees up your money to invest elsewhere.

Purchase Option. Most closed-end leases grant the lessee an option to purchase the vehicle at the end of the lease. The end-of-lease purchase price is usually the same as the stated residual value. Check your lease contract before signing to ensure that there is a purchase option. The lessor must disclose the purchase option price prior to your signing the lease contract.

Purchase Price. This is the price you would expect to pay for the vehicle if you were financing or buying the vehicle. To determine the purchase price, start with the MSRP and subtract any manufacturer discount and dealer discount you negotiate. Purchase price is a key determinant of the true cost of a lease. Purchase price less your down payment and dealer participation equals the net capitalized cost.

Refundable Deposit. This is a refundable deposit required at lease inception. In some cases it may be used to satisfy the final monthly payment. It is sometimes called a security deposit.

Residual Discount. If the end-of-lease purchase price (stated residual value) is greater than the expected end-of-lease value (expected residual value), the dollar difference represents the value of the vehicle that you will not pay for during the lease.

Residual Penalty. If the end-of-lease purchase price (stated residual value) is less than the expected end-of-lease value (expected residual value), the dollar difference represents the additional value of the vehicle you'll pay for during the lease.

Residual Value, Expected. This is the projected expected value of the vehicle at the end of the lease. Residual value is a measure of the vehicle's expected depreciation.

Residual Value, Stated. The stated residual value is usually the same as the end-of-lease purchase price. The higher the stated residual value of the car, the lower your monthly payments. Stated residual values are often higher or lower than the expected residual value. By adjusting the stated residual value for a car, the lessor can raise or lower the monthly payments and the net interest rate for the lease.

Stated residual value also determines whether you should buy the vehicle at the end of the lease. If at the end of a lease, the vehicle's market value is less than the stated residual value, the lessee would be prudent not to purchase the car. On the other hand, if the actual market value were greater than the predetermined residual, then the lessee could buy the car, sell it, and pocket the difference.

Subvented (Subsidized) Lease. A subvented lease is a lease offered by manufacturers with special incentives to make it more attractive. Special incentives often take the form of a lower base interest rate, higher residual values, and manufacturer discounts. In many cases, a subvented lease will have a lower net interest rate than other leases. Subvented leases are usually only available for a limited time and the terms are not negotiable. Any negotiated change in the terms will result in a different net interest rate.

Total Out-of-Pocket Cost. This is the total of all monthly payments, any lease fees and deposits, and any capital cost reduction (except tax, license, and registration) from lease inception to closure.

Wear and Tear. It's your responsibility to keep the car in good condition. Return the car with a dented fender, bald tires, or a ruined engine because of lack of routine maintenance and you'll be charged for the repairs. Some wear and tear is allowed, of course. But if you aren't inclined to take reasonable care of your car, leasing may not be for you.

New Leasing Rules

In September 1996, the Federal Reserve Board ruled on and passed new leasing disclosure requirements for lessors. These new regulations took effect January, 1998. Until then, dealers were not required to disclose the vehicle price upon which lease payments were based — the so-called "capital cost" or "capitalized cost" of the vehicle. Without knowing the selling price of the vehicle, buyers can't easily tell whether it is cheaper to buy or lease the vehicle. Under the new leasing guidelines, dealers now have to disclose the vehicle's total price. They must also disclose:

- The vehicle's residual value at the end of the lease.

- That the buyer may be responsible for added charges at the end of the lease for what the dealer considers to be abnormal wear and tear.

- That the buyer will face substantial early termination penalties.

The guidelines do not, however, require dealers to disclose the net interest rate.

The new Federal Reserve Board rules also require the use of a standard format lease contract.

turers to lower the net interest (cost) of the lease.

■ **Residual Value:** Just as the purchase price sets the value of the car at the start of the lease, residual value (in a closed-end lease) is the predetermined value of the vehicle at the end of the lease. The difficulty here is forecasting what the car will be worth in 24, 36, or 48 months.

This is key because the difference between the residual value stated in a lease and the purchase price is the amount of depreciation you will pay. If the residual value is set too low, you'll pay for too much depreciation. Sometimes manufacturers will subsidize a lease offer by setting the residual value artificially high. This reduces the depreciation you pay for and lowers the cost of the lease.

■ **Base Interest Rate or Money Factor:** When a salesperson talks about interest rates for leases, they're referring to the base interest rate or money factor. This is a case where smaller is better. The lower the base interest rate, the more likely the true net interest rate will also be lower.

Some worksheets and on-line calculators make reasonable approximations of the net interest rate associated with a lease. However, most approximations

are based primarily on the base interest rate which, for any given lease, can under- or overstate the true net interest rate by as much as three percentage points! A lease with a money factor of 8% could really have a net interest rate as low as 5% or as high as 11%. Unfortunately, the base interest rate doesn't take into account a lot of factors that can significantly impact the total cost of the lease. Nonetheless, if you know the base interest rate is 4%, you're probably getting a reasonable deal. If it's 13%, you're probably paying too much and should consider financing the purchase.

There are many resources to help you with pricing, depreciation, and interest rate information. In the Vehicle Chart section of this book you will find target prices and residual values for virtually every 1999 car. For the most current pricing data you can visit the IntelliChoice web site at www.intellichoice.com. You can also experiment with each of these factors and evaluate their impact on a lease by using the on-line calculators you'll find there.

Subsidized Leases — They Really Do Cost Less

Open a newspaper, turn on the TV, listen to the radio, and you're likely to see or hear about a "great" lease offer. Dealers and manufacturers tout low monthly payments, low down payments, and more, to make you think they're offering a fantastic deal.

Well, sometimes they really are — so much so that it can make good economic sense to lease a car instead of buy it. These subsidized or "subvented" leases are usually offered by the manufacturers and their captive finance companies, such as GMAC, Toyota Motor Credit Corporation, and others.

When a manufacturer subsidizes a lease, it artificially lowers the cost (net interest rate) by doing any or all of the following:

- Lowering the purchase price of the vehicle below the price you would be able to buy it for, resulting in your paying for less depreciation.

- Raising the residual value above what is expected so that you pay for less depreciation.

- Using a low base interest rate to keep the cost of money low.

Not only do you have lower monthly payments with a subsidized lease, you also end up paying much less in interest when compared to a loan. If the net interest rate for a subsidized lease is 3% and the APR for a loan is 9%, it would make sense to lease and save 6% interest per year over the term of the lease.

Gold Star Lease Evaluations

It's almost impossible to tell which leases are subsidized and have low net interest rates and which don't just by looking at an ad. As you can see from our lease ad example *(Figure 10, page 50A)*, there's nothing that identifies the lease as manufacturer subsidized. Unfortunately, not all manufacturer leases are, so the net interest rate for leases varies substantially. The only way to identify which current manufacturer lease offers really are good deals is to look at a Gold Star Lease evaluation *(Figure 9, page 46A)*.

Gold Star Lease evaluations identify the manufacturer leases that have the lowest net interest rates and therefore cost you the least, considering all factors that affect your cost. At present, IntelliChoice is the only company that prepares this information for consumers.

Each month, IntelliChoice evaluates manufacturer lease offers to determine their true net interest rate — remember this is the only number that's directly comparable to the APR for a loan. The lowest cost leases receive a Gold Star Lease Award and are listed on the IntelliChoice web site (www.intellichoice.com).

We already know that the purchase price, residual value, and money factor are three main

Figure 9

Gold Star Lease Evaluation

1999 Saab 9-3 5 Door

$298.94 per month / 39 months
Lease Availability: National, Expires 12/31/98
Total up-front cash required to start lease is $2,048 plus tax, license & registration

Interest Rate Comparisons

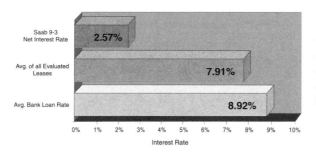

Saab 9-3 5 Door Net Interest Rate	2.57%
Average Bank Loan Rate	8.92%
Average Credit Union Loan Rate	7.94%
Average of all Evaluated Leases	7.91%
Buy at end of Term Interest Rate	2.44%

Gold Star Lease Review

Summary: Because of its low 2.57% net interest rate, IntelliChoice awards the Saab 9-3 5 Door lease, for December 1998, a Gold Star. The lease net interest rate is below the average bank loan rate by 6.35 percentage points. It is 5.34 percentage points below the average of all the evaluated leases this month.

The primary contributing factor to this Gold Star Lease's low net interest rate is the low base interest rate of 1.30% (a function of the money factor). Remember, when leasing a car, you're primarily paying for the vehicle's depreciation that occurs during your lease--the amount of the car that you use. If the total of your monthly payments and down payments is greater than the depreciation over your lease term, then the difference is really interest you're paying.

The Offer

The Bottom Line

Core Factors

Months in Lease:	39
Monthly Payment:	$298.94
Down Payment:	$999.00
End of Lease Purchase Price:	$16,555.30
Net Capitalized Cost:	$27,286.00

Base Interest Rate: 1.30%

The base rate of the lease is a mathematical function based on the above terms. All other things being equal, the lower the base interest rate, the lower your monthly payment. Dealer salespeople usually know either the money factor or the base interest rate.

Vehicle Price Factors

Vehicle MSRP:	$28,285.00	
Manufacturer/Dealer Discounts:	$0.00	
Final Purchase Price:	$28,285.00	
Your Target Purchase Price:	$27,571.79	
Pro-rated Purchase Price Discount:	$295.77	**Purchase Price Discount: 0.44%**

The lease 'sets' the price of the vehicle. If the Final Purchase Price is greater than the price you would pay if you were financing or buying the car, then you are paying too much. The purchase price penalty (or discount) takes into account the financial impact for the purchase price being too high or too low. We pro-rate the penalty or discount because in a lease situation you're not paying for the whole car, just a portion of the car represented by depreciation.

Residual Factor

End of Lease Purchase Price:	$16,555.30	
Expected End of Lease Value:	$16,647.14	
Residual Discount:	$91.84	**Residual Rate Discount: 0.13%**

If the End of Lease Purchase Price is higher than the expected value of the lease, then you will pay for less depreciation than actually occurs. In this case, you will see a Residual Rate Discount. If, however, the End of Lease Purchase Price is lower than the expected value of the vehicle at the end of the lease, then you will pay for more depreciation than actually occurs and there will be a Residual Rate Penalty. If you buy the car at the end of the lease then this factor is zero.

Fees and Deposits

Acquisition Fees:	$450.00	**Acquisition Fee Rate Penalty:**	**0.67%**
Refundable Deposit:	$300.00	**Deposit Rate Penalty:**	**0.04%**
Disposition Fee:	$0.00	**Disposition Rate Penalty:**	**0.00%**

Every fee and deposit adds to the net interest rate. We include refundable fees and deposits in our interest calculations. They can be subtracted from the Total Interest Rate if you don't want them considered.

Mileage Penalty

Free Mileage per Year:	12,000		
Expected Annual Miles:	12,000		
Total Excess Miles:	0		
Excess Mileage Penalty:	$.15		
Total Mileage Charge:	$0.00	**Excess Mileage Rate Penalty:**	**0.00%**

We assume that you will drive 12,000 miles per year. If allowable miles for the lease is less than 12,000 or less per year, then you will have to pay a penalty at the end of the lease.

Maintenance Discount

Free Maintenance Value:	$0.00	**Maintenance Discount:**	**0.00%**

Some automakers offer free scheduled maintenance as a part of a special lease offer for the length of the lease.

Total Net Interest Rate   **Total Net Interest Rate: 2.57%**

Total Net Interest Rate is the sum of all the individual factors that influence the base interest rate of this lease. It is directly comparable to the interest rates offered by financial institutions for the purchase of the vehicle. If the rate is less than what you could obtain through a loan, then leasing costs less than purchasing.

The total out of pocket cost for this lease over 39 months is $13,108. This includes all fees and monthly payments. Taxes, license, registration costs and refundable deposit are not included.

Total lease cost $29,663: This is the sum of all cash costs plus the purchase option price of the vehicle.

Actual Offer Language: $999.00 Down Payment $298.94 a month / 39 months / $450.00 acquisition fee

Subject to credit approval. Delivery must be taken out of dealer inventory by December 31, 1998. Terms apply to a 1999 Saab 9-3 5-door w/ 5-speed manual transmission with sunroof, heated front seats and in-dash CD based on MSRP of $28,285.00 (including destination charge). Lease payment for the 9-3 5-door is $298.94 for 39 months totaling $11,658.66. Option to purchase at lease end for $16,555.30 (including purchase fee) (plus any license and title fees and taxes). The customer is allowed 39,000 miles during the term of this lease. The customer is liable for a mileage charge of $.15 per mile over 39,000 miles and for excess wear and tear. Taxes, insurance, title and registration fees extra. Not to be combined with any other program offer. **Manual transmission. ***Active head restraint front seats only. SEE YOUR PARTICIPATING SAAB DEALER FOR COMPLETE DETAILS ON THIS AND OTHER LEASE AND FINANCE OPTIONS. © 1998 SAAB CARS USA, INC.

components of a lease. Gold Star Lease evaluations are precise because they also detail and explain the impact of each of the following cost areas:

- Fees and deposits
- Purchase price
- Residual value
- Mileage allowance
- Free maintenance offers

Whether or not you're considering a manufacturer lease, it's important to keep each of these cost areas in mind when you're negotiating. For instance, if you can obtain a lower purchase price for the car without lowering the residual value, you'll pay for less depreciation and save yourself real dollars. The same kind of reasoning can be applied to each of the other factors. The less money taken out of your pocket over the term of the lease, the lower the interest rate, and the lower the cost. These cost areas and their impact on the net interest rate are fully described in the sample Gold Star Lease evaluation *(Figure 9, page 46A)*.

If you're thinking about leasing, you can find each month's Gold Star Leases on the IntelliChoice web site or check your local newspaper's automobile section for our Gold Star Lease table.

How to Read a Lease Ad

Whether you plan to lease, get a loan, or pay cash, remember the dealer's ultimate objective is the same: to sell the car. If you lease a car, the dealer is essentially selling it to a finance company. If you pay cash, the dealer is selling the car to you. If you take out a loan, he's selling to you with the lender as lienholder.

Either way, keep in mind that the dealer is selling the car and, whether you plan to lease or buy, he wants his offer to appeal to you as much as possible. It's no surprise that all a lease's detail is in the small print. There you'll often find the purchase price, the down payment required, how many miles you're allowed to drive, and much more.

In Figure 10 *(Page 50A)* we show you how to take apart the fine print of a lease ad so you can understand what you'd be paying for. In most cases, if you use the fine print in the ad, you can calculate an approximate net interest rate for the lease and see how good a deal the lease really is. Our sample ad asks, "Will this make you Smile?" Let's find out.

Determining the Interest Rate

Let's determine the approximate net interest rate for this sample lease offer.

It requires you to fork out $2,000 as a down payment. The manufacturer has already reduced the MSRP by $1,887, so if we deduct the down payment of $2,000, the difference equals the amount being financed in the lease, $21,171. Using our Lease Interest Rate Worksheet *(Figure 8)*, we've used some quick calculations to approximate the net interest rate and filled in the worksheet with the numbers from the lease example. We've left space for you to complete the worksheet with your own figures from any other automobile lease.

The worksheet calculates an approximate net interest rate of 8.85%. (While our computer model actually calculated a net interest rate of 10% — it considers additional factors as shown on Gold Star Lease Evaluations — the worksheet comes close enough for us to be able to adequately assess this lease offer.)

So, does the offer make you smile? Well, at the time this advertisement was run, new car loan rates ranged from about 8 to 11%, so it's likely that this lease wouldn't cost any more or less than buying the car. That's probably worth smiling about. You can take the lease, have lower monthly payments, and drive the car you want, all the time knowing you got a good deal.

Negotiating a Lease

Negotiating a lease can be difficult and confusing. Dealer salespeople have many ways to change different parts of a lease, including the fees, monthly payments, residual value, and even the purchase price of the vehicle. There are a few things you can do to make the leasing process a little easier for yourself. Many of the following suggestions apply to the buying process as well.

1. Know how much you'd want to pay for the car. Even though you're leasing, a purchase price for the car will be part of the

lease contract. That purchase price should be the same price you would pay if you were buying. You can negotiate!

2. Negotiate the price upwards from the dealer cost, not down from the MSRP. (Dealer cost information is available in *Just the Facts* reports on-line or via fax or mail from IntelliChoice.)

3. Don't talk about leasing with a salesperson until you know what car you want and what you want to pay unless you're specifically responding to an advertised lease.

4. If you see a lease offer you like, and the dealership offers you the same car with additional options or features, know that the terms of the lease will be different from what was advertised. The monthly payment might stay the same, but other factors, such as residual value and purchase price, will likely change.

5. When you're negotiating the lease, be prepared to walk away if you don't like the way the negotiation is going or if you're not comfortable with the figures you're presented.

6. Lease contracts are complex documents. Take the time to read all the papers you're asked to sign. Be willing to ask questions. Remember, it's your money!

Leasing really can be a great way to get a new car and it can be financially a better option than buying. But leasing is always more complicated than buying so it's worth the extra effort to be prepared. In the long run, you'll be a little richer and happier.

Before You Negotiate a Lease You Should Know:

■ The price you would pay to buy the car as equipped.

■ The current market value of any vehicle you may trade-in.

■ The approximate residual value for the car you plan on leasing.

Never Sign a Lease Contract Unless:

■ The vehicle purchase price is shown.

■ The residual value and optional purchase price at the end of the lease is shown.

■ The value of your trade-in is properly listed and treated as a cap cost reduction.

■ The lease rate or money factor is shown.

Figure 10

Special Lease Incentives

Understanding the Fine Print

The following are key points taken from a sample lease ad:

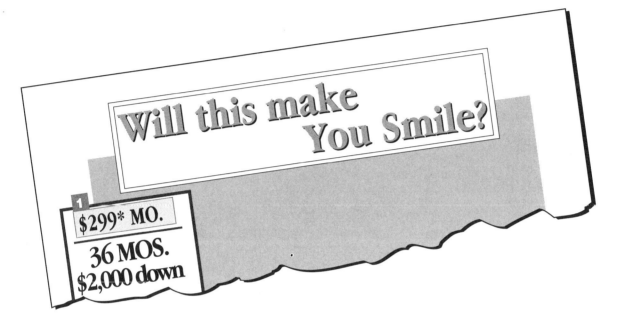

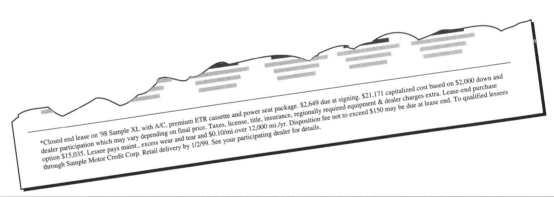

*Closed end lease on '99 Sample XL with A/C, premium ETR cassette and power seat package. $2,649 due at signing. $21,171 capitalized cost based on $ 2,000 down and dealer participation, which may vary. MSRP of $25,058 including destination charge. Monthly payments total $10,764. Your payment may vary depending on final price. Taxes, license, title, insurance, regionally required equipment, & dealer charges extra. Lease-end purchase option $15,035. Lessee pays maint., excess wear and tear, and $0.10/mi. over 12,000 mi./yr. Disposition fee not to exceed $150 may be due at lease end. To qualified lessees through Sample Motor Credit Corp. Retail delivery by 1/2/99. See your participating dealer for details.

Special Lease Incentives (Continued)

LEASING FINE PRINT EXPLANATION

1 $299/mo. This is your monthly payment; however, keep in mind that this figure does not include tax, license, or registration, which will add approximately $20 per month.

2 Closed-end lease. The car's residual, or resale value at the end of the lease is predetermined. Your lease payments will be based in part on the difference between the resale value and the selling price. At the end of the lease term you will have the option of either purchasing the vehicle or simply walking away. This is the most popular type of lease.

3 $2,649 due at signing. You are required to make a down payment of $2,000 (capital cost reduction), plus first month's payment ($299). The refundable security deposit ($350) is a deposit that you will be eligible to recuperate at the end of the lease. All of these charges added up means you'll have to fork out an upfront fee of $2,649 ($2,000 + $299 + $350) plus tax on your $2,000 down payment. And of course that assumes that you take the vehicle equipped as it is. So much for small down payments.

4 $21,171 capitalized cost. This represents the price of the vehicle as it is used in the computation for the base monthly payment. This tells you that the dealer is going to reduce $1,887 from the $25,058 MSRP after you pitch-in your $2,000 down. Effectively, the purchase price of the vehicle is $23,171. According to the charts in this book, the target price for this vehicle is $807.81 more than the lease list price. Therefore, the price used as a basis for this lease is probably very reasonable.

5 Dealer participation which may vary. This tells you that the dealer may not reduce the list price at all, and you'll end up paying more than $299 per month.

6 MSRP of $25,058 including destination charge. The manufacturer's suggested retail price (this lease offer includes Premium ETR Cassette and Power Seat Package). At the time of this printing, the MSRP for this model was $23,538 and the destination charge was $420, which means you are being charged $1,100 for the Premium ETR Cassette and Power Seat Package (incidentally, $1,100 equals the normal retail price for these options).

7 Monthly payments total $10,764. This is the monthly payments multiplied by the number of months in the lease ($299 x 36 = $10,764).

8 Taxes, license, title, insurance, regionally required equipment, & dealer charges extra. You will have to pay for these items even though you do not own the car. You should also keep in mind that there are a variety of features and option packages you may wish to add to the vehicle that will bump up your monthly payments above the advertised price.

9 Lease-end purchase option $15,035. As previously stated, in a closed-end lease, you will have the option at the end of the term to either purchase the vehicle or walk away. The figure $15,035 listed in this ad is the predetermined resale value. This is the price for which the lessor is willing to sell the car to you at the end of the lease. In this example the lessor is using a residual value of 60%.

10 Lessee pays maint., excess wear and tear. This is telling you that it is your responsibility to keep the car in good condition. If you return the car with a problem due to lack of routine maintenance, you may be charged for repairs.

11 $0.10/mi. over 12,000 mi./yr. This tells you that you will be charged an additional 10 cents per mile for each mile you drive over 12,000 miles per year.

12 Disposition fee not to exceed $150 may be due at lease end. A disposition fee is a charge that you will pay at the end of the lease for getting the car ready to be sold. If you were to accept this lease, you are agreeing to pay up to $150 for this charge.

13 To qualified lessees. You will need to have good credit (no major blemishes) in order to qualify for this lease offer.

14 Sample Motor Credit Corp. Offered by this sample manufacturer's captive finance arm. This could indicate it might be a "subvented" or special lease offer.

When is the Best Time to Buy a New Car?

Best Time of Year

The winter months usually present good bargain opportunities. With increased cash outlays for clothing, utility bills, and holiday expenses, auto sales are slow and salespeople are eager to make a sale.

The summer months can also be a good time to shop. This is when sales of the current-year model have slowed down and consumers are waiting for the new model year cars to be introduced.

But be cautious during spring-time! That's when consumers come out of their winter doldrums and car sales increase. Dealers are less inclined to make price concessions while sales are up.

Best Time of Month

The end of the month is the best time to buy a new car. A salesperson prospers by consistently meeting or exceeding his or her monthly quota. To increase a salesperson's incentive, dealers often have contests and offer bonuses for exceeding monthly quotas. As a result, salespeople are more likely to sacrifice a small part of their commission at the end of the month if it will help them meet or exceed a quota.

The Golden Rule of Car Buying

There is one golden rule when it comes to negotiating for a new car: Buying a new car, financing it, and trading in your old car may all occur at the same time, but these are three separate transactions and should be negotiated separately.

Imagine this scenario. A salesman is negotiating with a customer about the price of a new car. Negotiations have come to a standstill because the customer says he can not afford a penny more than $13,000 for a particular car that is priced at $13,200. The dialogue might sound like this:

"What are your current monthly payments?" asks the salesman.

"$275 a month," the customer replies, "and I only have two payments left."

"How about this," says the salesman, "if I can get you into that new car for $275 a month, have we got a deal?"

"That sounds reasonable," answers the customer.

The salesman smiles, "Do you want to trade your car in? I could probably get your monthly payments even lower."

"Well, sure. I'll trade my car in if you can give me a good deal," says the customer.

SIX STEPS TO A GOOD DEAL

Haggling, horse-trading, bartering. Call it what you will. Though some buyers may consider it great sport to try and beat the last penny of profit out of an auto dealer, most consumers hate the hassle.

Consider the sad saga of Mrs. B. Innocently enough, she went to a showroom and announced that she had $10,000 to spend on a modest new car for her college-student daughter. A nice salesman showed her a nice car, and eventually they came to a nice agreement. Or so Mrs. B thought.

After telephoning her daughter with the good news, Mrs. B returned to the dealership the next day, ready to buy. "I'm sorry," said the salesman, "but my sales manager won't let me sell the car for less than $12,000." Yep, it was the old bait and switch — and Mrs. B was furious. "How can they get away with this?" she demanded.

They can and they do. But in today's highly competitive auto market, dealers and automakers are beginning to realize that many car buyers would just as soon face a firing squad as go through the tribulations of negotiating for a new car. Thank goodness the system is beginning to change.

But until then, here are six steps to help you deal with the dealer:

1. Know the car you want and how much you can afford to pay. Experts say your annual income should be at least twice the price of the new car you buy. Check the "AutoExplorer™" section in the front pages of this book. This will give you an idea of all the models offered by each manufacturer in several price ranges. Don't waste everyone's time test-driving and negotiating for a car you can't possibly afford.

2. Be prepared. Review the charts in this book for cars you're interested in. Study the suggested retail prices and dealer's cost for the model and options you want.

Find out about current factory-to-dealer rebates and current factory-to-customer rebates *(See page 35A)*.

If there's a choice between a cash rebate and discount financing, use Appendix J to determine which is best for you.

Add up the dealer's cost for the car and the options you want. Subtract any factory-to-customer rebates (unless you plan to take discount financing) and any factory-to-dealer rebate. Then add in what you think is a fair profit, considering the popularity and availability of the model. Or, simply shoot for the target price suggested in this guide.

3. Qualify the dealer. Call several dealers within a reasonable driving distance and ask each if they have the car on their lot with the options you want. You'll nearly always get a better deal if the dealer doesn't have to trade with another dealer for the car you want.

4. Remember the golden rule of car-buying: First negotiate the price of the car. Then discuss financing. Then discuss the value of your trade-in. Always keep the three transactions separate; salespeople are adept at giving away with one hand and taking a lot more with the other.

For instance, they may talk about monthly payments instead of the car's price; by stretching out the length of a loan — with correspondingly lower monthly payments — they can make an overpriced car seem affordable.

5. Keep cool. The salesperson may try to pressure you — "Are you ready to buy today?" The salesperson may play on your sympathy — "I'll lose my job if I agree to ..." The salesperson may intimidate you — "The dealer cost figures you have are all wrong." Or the salesperson may indicate you have a deal and then turn you over to the sales manager who nixes it; together, they'll work on you to sweeten the deal in their favor.

Through it all, stay confident of your research, and remember the Scout's motto: Be prepared. Be prepared to put down a deposit as soon as you've arrived a fair price, and if you feel mistreated, be prepared to walk out of the dealership.

6) Let the dealer make a buck. Bear in mind that "profit" is not a dirty word, and that no dealer is going to sell you a $10 bill for a buck and remain in business.

Purchase a Vehicle on the World Wide Web

Auto-By-Tel, a popular internet service for new and used car buyers, promises to eliminate the haggling and hassles that are often associated with dealerships. Shoppers submit their requests to Auto-By-Tel and are then contacted by a subscribing dealer who offers them a low, competitive vehicle price.

The salesman checks out the customer's car and says, "How about this, I will buy out the balance of your loan, give you a $2,000 check on top of that to use as a down payment for the new car, and then I'll finance the rest for 60 months at a monthly payment of only $250 — $25 lower than you're currently paying. Now, doesn't that sound terrific?"

Unfortunately, it isn't so terrific. In fact, the customer is going to pay more for his new car than he initially wanted to. The salesman has confused him. $250 a month has the illusion of a good deal because it is less than the customer's current payments. However, upon closer examination we can see what is really happening.

First of all, the salesman offered the customer $2,000 in addition to "buying out" his current loan on the old car. That means the customer receives a total value of $2,550 for his car. $550 will be paid to the title holder of the old car (for the last two payments) and the $2,000 will be applied as a down payment for the new car. If we then calculate the present value of $250 dollars per month over a 60-month term at 11% interest, it works out to be about $11,600. Combining all this together, we find that the customer has agreed to pay the equivalent of $13,600 for his car: $2,000 from the trade-in and $11,600 from the loan. This is $600 more than the customer originally said he'd pay. To add insult to injury, the customer is without a doubt going to get less on his trade-in than if he sells the car himself.

Even though this example is contrived, situations like this

happen every day. Salespeople are experts at this tactic and employ it every chance they get. Even if you know all your facts, it is still easy to get confused. It can be difficult enough trying to negotiate a single transaction with a salesman, but when you try to do all three at once, you are stacking the deck in his favor. Don't even try; keep these three transactions separate.

Cruising For Cars On-Line

You're hip, you're cool, you're a cutting-edge kind of person. Trudging from dealer to dealer and enduring endless sales chatter from a succession of salespersons, sales managers, and deal closers seems pretty lame when you could instead cybershop for a new car.

Shopping for a vehicle on-line is a reality. With a computer, a modem, and access to the Internet's World Wide Web, you can peruse electronic brochures, find critical reviews, research safety data, and obtain that all-important price data on any new vehicle you might desire.

But you can go even further. Within the last couple of years, it's become possible to actually make a deal on-line and have the new car delivered to your driveway without ever setting foot on a dealer's lot.

About 30% of new-car buyers shop on-line now. Experts predict that within the next few years, 40% of auto loans will originate on the internet. If you're ready to experience the future, here's a six-step approach to shopping for a new car on-line:

1. Do your homework. You can't do better than the World Wide Web for basic research on new vehicles. Type in "automobiles" while using a search engine such as Yahoo! or Lycos, and you'll turn up literally tens of thousands of sites. Most of them will be arcane — discussions of European-Japanese automotive trade, for instance — or mere advertisements for products of dubious value.

But you'll also find sites that will be gold mines of useful information that is either free or available for a nominal charge. The free IntelliSearch on IntelliChoice's site is, for example, a good place to start your quest for a new set of wheels. IntelliSearch asks you to give a few important parameters for your new vehicle — its price range, the number of seats, safety equipment you require, and so on. Using these parameters, IntelliSearch will search the more than 800 new car and truck models available in the U.S. for several vehicles that custom fit your specifications.

2. Refine your choices. Once you have a list of new-car candidates, continue your on-line research to narrow your choices to one or two models. Read critical reviews on-line from magazines such as *Road & Track, Automobile,* or *Consumer Reports.* Look at government crash test results. Take a peek in the virtual showrooms of the automakers; General Motors (http://www.GM.com) and Toyota (http://www.Toyota.com) even offer multidimensional interior and exterior views of their models. In the not too distant future, you may be able to take virtual test drives of new cars.

3. Take a real test drive. Of course the virtual-world spin on the computer is no replacement for a real-world test drive. Once you've narrowed your choices through your on-line research to one or two models, it's time to shut down the computer and take a test drive or two at your local dealer. *(See "Test Drive Checklist" on page 71A.)* Be prepared for some sales person to pressure you into buying the vehicle right then. But resist it; don't go into an office to talk about anything. Explain that you're still comparison shopping. Thank the salesperson for their time. Take their card. But don't give them your phone number or address.

You might also find a friend or family member with the kind of vehicle you're considering and test drive their car. Attend an auto show; you won't be able to drive the vehicle, but you will be able to sit in it and examine it closely. Better still, rent the vehicle you might want to buy for a day so you can come to know it well. The rental fee is a small price to pay to avoid buying the wrong car.

4. Obtain pricing data. Now that you've settled on the new vehicle you want, it's time to figure out a target purchase price. Review the vehicle's chart in this book. Study the suggested retail prices and dealer's cost for both the vehicle and its options. Or go back into cyberspace to IntelliChoice's World Wide Web site and order a *Just the Facts* report that will give you all the pricing data for the vehicle you want plus current buyer and dealer incentives *(See "What Price Should You Pay" on page 35A.)*

At IntelliChoice's site, you can also calculate the value of your used-car trade-in, or check out the

How Much Can a Broker Save You?

If you're a good negotiator, you can almost always negotiate a better deal than a broker can offer. A broker has to make money, which means the price you pay the broker will always be more than the price the broker paid the dealer — a price you could probably get on your own. However, if you're not comfortable negotiating, a broker can get you a real bargain.

lowest cost automaker leases with IntelliChoice's AutoLease Evaluation — for free. At other sites, you can even conduct a little comparison shopping for financing and insurance on-line.

5. Obtain price quotes. At this point, you're ready to go back to the dealer and negotiate a purchase. Or if you prefer to continue your adventure into cybershopping, contact dealers on-line. There are several dealer networks on the World Wide Web that will refer you to dealers that sell vehicles on-line. Communicating by telephone, fax, or E-mail, you can work out a deal without ever having to come face-to-face with a salesperson. You may be surprised at the low quotes; dealers know that some of the usual costs involved with selling a new car — advertising, sales commissions — can be much lower when selling on-line.

6. Take delivery of your new car. Some on-line dealers will deliver your new vehicle right to your driveway. Others will want you to pick it up at their dealership. Either way, chances are good that you will have saved time and aggravation by shopping in cyberspace.

Buying Services

There are few things better than getting a new car and, for many, few things worse than the hassle of buying or leasing one.

That's why car shoppers are increasingly turning to auto-buying agents — sometimes referred to as brokers — as a way to sidestep rising sticker prices and flimflam showroom tactics.

Agents or buying services vary widely, and so do their claims on how much you can save. Some claim prices at factory invoice, so much below sticker, or at wholesale prices.

At the top are traditional agents and buying services, which — for a fee generally ranging from $250 to $350, or a set percentage of a car's price — will take your order, find the car you want, take delivery of it, and let you buy it from them.

Because this type of agent becomes the vehicle's first owner, you'll want to make sure there won't be problems with manufacturer warranties. Some dealers don't like agents or buying services and won't deal with them. And in some states and communities — because of warranty and other problems — these kinds of agents or brokers are outlawed.

More common are buying services that don't take possession of the vehicle, but help you decide which car you want, provide detailed information, then negotiate with the dealer on your behalf. You simply show up, buy or lease the car from the dealer at the negotiated price, fill out the usual paperwork, and take possession. These buying services generally charge $100 to $300, depending on the level of service you want.

Other buying services will, for a modest fee, seek bids from a handful of nearby dealers for the vehicle you want. You choose which dealer to use and negotiate a final deal. Other similar services are free — they collect part of their profit from the dealers who join their referral network.

Before signing up with any agent or fee service, contact your local Better Business Bureau to inquire about complaints. Check how long the service has been in business and ask if the agent has a state license and posted a performance bond. Ask the agent or service for customer referrals, and contact them.

Perhaps the most popular buying or leasing services today are the no-fee dealer referrals offered by auto clubs, credit unions, and other financial institutions and wholesale retailers. These services often claim they will refer you to a dealer or dealers that have agreed to sell or lease the car you want at a discounted price.

Unlike other services or agents that charge a fee, you often must know exactly what kind of car and options you want before contacting a no-fee basic buying service. And often, the discounted price isn't as good as with other agents or buying services. And you may still have to do some negotiating if you're trading in your old car or need financing.

You can explore a wide variety of agents and buying services to see what they're offering or gather your own information on the car you want via the Internet.

Many of the major full-service agents, buying services, and even no-charge locator services have Web pages. One way to find them: Point your browser to "vehicle buying services."

Some services can even handle your request via the Internet. You tell the service via e-mail the kind of car you're interested in, and you get back via e-mail information on the vehicle, a sign-up form, or, in some cases, a phone call from a dealer in your area that will quote you a price.

European Delivery

Would you like a free European holiday? One that may include lodging in a swank hotel, a VIP tour of your favorite automaker's factory and maybe even a spin around the factory test track? All you have to do is bring back a souvenir of your journey — a new vehicle.

If you've been planning to buy a new BMW, Mercedes-Benz, Porsche, Saab, or Volvo, you too, can have such an adventure. That's because these European automakers have programs that make an overseas delivery almost as easy as buying a car right off a local dealer's showroom floor. And because all of them offer reduced prices on cars delivered at the factory, the savings can sometimes cover the cost of your European vacation.

The amount you save by taking delivery in Europe varies by automaker and by the model of car you buy. Here are a couple of examples:

Should you have in mind a 1999 Saab 9-3 Coupe with a manual transmission, Saab will quote you an overseas delivery price of $24,370. This price includes shipping, marine insurance, customs duty, port processing charges and inland transport to your local dealer. Saab occasionally offers a special overseas delivery program that even includes free round-trip air fare for two between the U.S. and Sweden.

While you drive your new Saab in Europe, you'll need tourist registration for the car plus liability and collision insurance. A package that includes the European license plates and two week's insurance coverage costs $235. So the total overseas delivery price is $24,605. This compares to a U.S. MSRP of $26,225 including destination charge. Net savings: $1,620.

But if your new car should be something more grand, so too will your savings. If you fancy say, a 1999 Mercedes-Benz S500 sedan, Mercedes will deliver one to you at the factory for $83,150. And this price includes everything —even two week's full insurance coverage and transport to a local dealer. The 1999 S500 carries a U.S. MSRP of $88,095 including a destination charge. Net savings: $4,945.

As with U.S. manufacturer's suggested retail prices, overseas delivery prices are also negotiable. But keep in mind that the automakers allow their dealers substantially less markup on a European delivery car, so your room for haggling will be considerably narrowed. Bear in mind too, that as with any car you purchase off the showroom floor, all the usual local, state, and federal (gas guzzler) taxes will still apply to a car delivered to you in Europe.

So how is it that these automakers can offer lower prices on cars delivered overseas? Primarily because they and their dealers don't have to add in many of their usual costs, especially the interest charges associated with keeping a car in inventory. Each factory-delivered car is paid for before it is built. Moreover, the overseas delivery programs are good public relations. By seeing where your car was designed and built, the automakers hope you'll feel more like part of the "family."

The automakers offering overseas delivery typically have the factory-delivery ritual honed to perfection. At Mercedes for instance, you'll be welcomed at the elegant European Delivery Center in Stuttgart-Sindelfingen, adjacent to the assembly plant. You'll be given a tour of the production facilities, a complimentary meal at the Center's own restaurant, and assistance in planning your driving vacation. For the finale, a Mercedes-Benz technician will hand over the keys to your new wunderwagen, after which you can drive to a first-class hotel in Stuttgart, a castle overlooking the Rhine Valley, or a resort in the Black Forest, where your room and meals will be "on the house" for two nights.

BMW, Porsche, and Volvo offer similar routines, though without the free lodging. But both Saab and Volvo offer reduced rates at hotels throughout Sweden. BMW, Mercedes, and Porsche have special self-guided or group driving tours. In addition, a Volvo technician will acquaint you with your new car on the factory test track.

To order a car for overseas delivery, make arrangements through any BMW, Mercedes-Benz, Porsche, Saab, or Volvo dealer. There are however, a few caveats to keep in mind. If you want — or need — a new car RIGHT NOW, then European delivery isn't for you. Depending on where you drop off your car in Europe for shipping to the States, as well as the moods of various unions, it can take up to three months to receive your car. And not every model from these automakers is available for overseas delivery. For example, BMW's new Z3 sports car is built in the U.S., not in Germany.

The automakers also typically advise you to order your car three months in advance of your trip. And to assure yourself of VIP treatment, avoid arriving at the factory on a weekend, a holiday, or during the summer hiatus; the summer factory shutdowns can last for several weeks during July and August.

Options and Special Features

Options can be a motherlode of profit for dealers and automakers alike. But do you really want a car "loaded" with options, or even one with advanced technical features that come as standard equipment? Some options and features are truly useful and add to a car's resale value. Others end up being expensive maintenance headaches. *(Refer to Figure 11 on pages 60A-61A to help make your choices a little easier.)*

Option Packages and "Value Pricing"

Through the years, automakers have often grouped options together in packages, sometimes providing a discount on the package over the price of the individual options.

Now there's a new twist on this called "value pricing," a marketing strategy that's been getting a lot of attention in recent years. On certain models, and sometimes in certain locations, the automaker equips a value-priced car with all the options that most motorists want anyway — air conditioning, an automatic transmission, AM/FM cassette, as examples. Then the automaker prices the car as low as possible and encourages dealers and customers alike to consider it a "no-dicker" sticker price.

Option packages reduce the manufacturer's production cost, since they have to make fewer variations of each car. It can also save you money if you want those options anyway. On the other hand, you will waste money on these packages if they mean you pay for options you don't want.

To properly evaluate an option package, first determine the options you really want, then add the prices of the individual options and compare them to the total price of the option package.

It's also not uncommon for a dealer to put cars on the lot with accessories and options already installed. "Sorry, you have to buy it as is," the salesperson will tell you. However, if you don't want this car, try custom ordering it if you don't mind waiting. On the other hand, if you're willing to purchase a car that is already on the dealer's lot, you may be able to negotiate a better deal than if you have the car custom ordered.

Special Deals for Disabled Drivers

When you're young and healthy, it's easy to take driving for granted. But what if your legs become impaired some day, and you can't operate the brake or accelerator pedals? What if a back injury prevents you from comfortably sitting in a standard-issue car or truck seat? Or what if your hearing is diminished to the point you can't recognize an approaching emergency vehicle's siren?

As America's population grows increasingly older, auto manufacturers — particularly U.S. manufacturers — are establishing programs to help make driving easier for folks with physical limitations. General Motors, Ford and DaimlerChrysler offer financial assistance to new-car or truck

OPTIONS TIP

■ Don't let the dealer salesperson talk you into options you don't need or want. Rustproofing is rarely needed on today's vehicles, which already come with lengthy rust-through warranties. Nor are dealer fabric treatments.

Figure 11

A Handy Guide To Options And Technical Features

Any option or feature you add will raise the sticker price of a new vehicle but, may not increase the price when it comes time for resale. Just like cars, car options vary in how rapidly they depreciate. For example, $500 spent on air conditioning may add $400 to the vehicle price when it's time to resell, but $500 spent on a leather interior may add little or nothing to the resale price. Some options (e.g., anti-lock brakes) that are clearly beneficial may not be available on a particular model, or might not fit into your budget. When selecting your options, it is important to weigh emotional, safety, and practical aspects along with the economic ones. A car with wisely chosen options will prove to be a better value.

OPTIONS ➤	BENEFITS	DRAWBACKS
Adjustable Shock Absorbers/Ride Control: Shock absorbers that can be adjusted by either the driver or an on-board computer.	Allows you to adjust the ride according to different driving conditions. Sport handling means a firm, more controlled ride, and Touring means a softer, more comfortable ride.	Expensive to buy; expensive to repair; most drivers put on one setting and leave it.
Adjustable Steering Column	Let's driver find ideal position behind wheel—especially important for particularly short or tall drivers. A memory feature is useful for cars with multiple drivers.	None
Air Conditioning	Reduces fatigue in hot weather. Reduces outside noise and window fogging. Adds considerably to resale value of car.	Expensive to buy. Somewhat expensive to maintain. May increase fuel consumption.
All-Wheel Drive	Increases traction; particularly in snow, rain. Improves handling on dry roads.	Adds complexity and weight, which raises car's price and lowers its fuel economy.
Anti-Lock Brakes or ABS: Electronic sensors and computer control prevent the brakes from locking up.	Prevents the car from skidding uncontrollably during a panic stop. Shortens stopping distances in adverse conditions.	Expensive to buy, but is often standard equipment. May require some additional maintenance.
Automatic Transmission	Makes driving easier in stop-and-go traffic and on mountain or hilly roads. Adds to resale value if appropriate for vehicle.	May decrease fuel economy, though not as much as in years past. May decrease acceleration. May decrease resale value if on inappropriate vehicle (sports car).
Cellular Telephone: Hands-free systems are safer, easier to use than a hand-held phone.	Safety: Let's you call police, ambulance, or tow truck without leaving your car.	Monthly and per-call charges can be high.
Central Locking System: Some systems automatically lock the doors when the transmission is shifted into gear, or automatically unlock when the transmission is shifted into park. The best systems have a remote key-fob transmitter to lock or unlock the car from outside.	Convenience and safety: allows you to quickly lock all doors if you feel threatened.	Added cost: may require more maintenance. Keyless-entry fobs are expensive to replace.
Continuously Variable Transmission: An automatic transmission that, instead of using three or four separate gears, uses belts to produce continuously changing speed ratios.	Better fuel economy than with a manual transmission, because it lets the engine work in its most efficient range.	It's a complex technology whose reliability hasn't been proven. May be very expensive to maintain.
Cruise Control	Reduces driver fatigue on long trips, and may help increase fuel economy.	May require some maintenance. May lull driver into inattention.
Digital Instrumentation	Amusing—if you're into video games.	Can be confusing and distracting; also very expensive to repair.
Diesel Engine	Fuel economy.	Slow acceleration; difficult to start in extremely cold weather; unpleasant fumes; fuel sometimes hard to find.
ESP: Electronic Stability Program that uses engine-management and ABS electronics to help prevent the car from sliding sideways on slick surfaces.	Added safety, particularly on icy roads.	Added initial cost; may also require more maintenance.
Four-Wheel Disc Brakes: Cars often have "disc" brakes on the front wheels and "drum brakes on the rear wheels. However, under hard use, disc brakes remain cooler, which means they retain their stopping power longer. Disc brakes on all four wheels are preferable.	Retain stopping power longer; disc brake pads cheaper to replace.	Disc brake pads wear more quickly than drum brake pads.

OPTIONS	➤ BENEFITS	DRAWBACKS
Four-Wheel Steering: At low speeds, the rear wheels turn in the opposite direction to the front wheels; at higher speeds, all four wheels turn in the same direction.	Makes the car generally easier to steer, particularly during parking.	Added initial cost, and possibly added maintenance and repair cost.
Head-up Instrument Display: Projects a car's speedometer reading or other instrument displays onto the windshield in front of the driver.	Lets driver read instrument displays without taking eyes off the road.	Unnecessary gizmo. Essential only for fighter pilots.
Heavy-Duty Cooling System	Necessary for hauling heavy loads in hot weather, especially on a vehicle with air conditioning.	No disadvantages except extra initial cost.
Heavy-Duty Suspension	Necessary for hauling heavy loads.	Rougher ride when not hauling a load.
Integrated Child Seat: A child seat that folds out of the regular adult seat and comes with its own set of seatbelts.	Unlike portable seats, it is always correctly secured.	May reduce comfort for adults sitting on a seat that contains an integrated child seat. May be more expensive than separate child seat.
Larger Engine: Engine size is noted by the number of cylinders, and by "displacement." Displacement can be measured in liters, cubic centimeters, or cubic inches. The more cylinders and the greater the displacement, the larger the engine. Larger engines generally provide more torque and more horsepower.	Quieter and smoother during highway cruising; added power for passing, for mountain travel, and for hauling a trailer.	Slightly higher maintenance costs; possibly higher costs for fuel, insurance, and state registration.
Leather Seating Surfaces	Looks, smells, and feels luxurious; doesn't soil as easy as cloth or velour.	Can be hot in summer, cold in winter: can also be slippery.
Limited-Slip Differential	Improves traction on slippery surfaces; improves handling on dry surfaces.	Not as sophisticated as traction control; not nearly effective as all-wheel drive or four-wheel drive.
Limp-Home: Electronics automatically cut out half the engine's cylinders to create less heat should the cooling system ever fail.	Allows you to continue to drive the car with an overheating engine, without damaging the engine.	None.
Metallic Paint	Provides a richer, deeper—though sometimes flashy—paint job.	Added initial cost; more expensive to repair.
Multiple Valves: All engines have at least two valves for each cylinder. But some have three or four valves for each cylinder. The additional valves allow a more efficient movement of the air/fuel mixture in the combustion chambers so the engine develops more power.	Better acceleration without sacrificing fuel economy.	Added complication; possibly higher repair costs.
Onboard Navigation System: Some use global positioning service system to plot a course on an electronic map. Some use cell phone to connect you to a central command post where you can obtain directions. Some automatically dial for help in an emergency.	Convenience and safety.	Pricey. Not always accurate. May require a monthly fee and may require a cell phone.
Overhead Cam: Some engines have single or double overhead camshafts instead of pushrods to open and close the valves as the engine operates.	Better engine response at high speeds.	None really, except slightly higher manufacturing costs.
Power Mirrors	Easily adjustable so there's no excuse for not using them, which contributes to safety	Added initial cost.
Power Seats	Fun but frivolous. however memory feature useful for cars with multiple drivers.	Added initial cost.
Power Steering, and Power Steering with Variable Assist: At higher speeds, simple power steering can make the steering feel too light. Variable-assist or speed-sensitive steering is a type of power steering that automatically boosts the power assist at low speeds and reduces it at high speeds.	Makes it easier to turn the steering wheel, especially when parking. Necessary for large, heavy vehicles; can increase resale value for those vehicles.	Added initial cost; added maintenance cost.

OPTIONS ➤	BENEFITS	DRAWBACKS
Power Windows	So convenient, it's hard to make due without them. Particularly useful for those who frequently use toll roads.	Added initial cost. More to go wrong, so higher maintenance costs.
Rear Window Defroster	Increases outward vision in icy or humid conditions.	Can crack window if left on in hot weather.
Premium Stereo Sound System/Compact Disc Player	Improves resale value of car. Reduces boredom.	Added initial cost. Makes car a target for theft.
Sunroof/T-Top/Moonroof	Fun. Can increase resale value substantially.	Added wind noise; may reduce interior headroom, and may leak or squeak if moldings deteriorate.
Tinted Windows	Keeps car cooler in sunny weather, thus reducing sun-caused damage to upholstery and dashboard. Reduces load on air conditioner.	Slightly higher initial cost. May be illegal in some areas if tint too dark.
Traction Control: Uses sensors to determine when wheels begin to slip and reduces engine speed/applies brakes to maintain optimum traction.	Allows for smooth acceleration on slippery roads. Worth having if you regularly drive wet, muddy, or icy roads, but not as effective as all-wheel drive.	Expensive, with a lot of mechanical complexity. No benefit under normal driving conditions.
Trip Computer: Calculates fuel consumed, miles remaining to destination, miles traveled. May allow driver to monitor various fluid levels and other engine conditions.	Entertaining	Can be distracting.
Turbocharger/Supercharger: A turbocharger is operated by hot exhaust gases that continually rush out of the engine as it runs. A supercharger is driven by a belt or a shaft from the engine. Both devices force extra air and fuel into the engine's combustion chambers for more power.	Provides the acceleration of a larger engine, without higher fuel consumption.	Requires extra maintenance; often more costly to insure.

buyers who need to equip their vehicles with special features.

Through its GM Mobility Program, established in 1991, General Motors will reimburse a buyer of any new GM vehicle up to $1,000 for what the company calls "mobility adaptive equipment." As with other auto manufacturers' programs, this includes such items as wheelchair lifts, scooter lifts, grab bars, hand straps and hand controls. GM will also reimburse for such things as special seats for buyers with chronic pain, and for alerting devices that aid deaf or hearing-impaired drivers. For instance, one device flashes red lights whenever its microphone detects an approaching emergency vehicle.

Ford will rebate up to $1,000 to disabled buyers of any of its new vehicles who need special equipment. Ford's Mobility Motoring Program, formed in 1992, also offers disabled buyers a free cellular phone if they are willing to pay the monthly services charges and agree to a minimum four-month subscription.

DaimlerChrysler formed its Automobility Program back in 1987. It offers buyers of full-size Ram Vans and Ram Wagons up to $1,000 for adaptive equipment. Buyers of other Chrysler vehicles can receive up to $750.

In addition to these domestic auto manufacturer's programs, Sweden's Volvo has reimbursed buyers of its new cars for special adaptive equipment.

Applications for financial assistance are typically available at dealers or by telephone. Buy your new car or truck, take it to a mobility equipment installer and then submit the application to the auto manufacturer who will reimburse you up to their particular program's limits. If the adap-

tive equipment costs more than the auto manufacturer's limit, you may be able to roll the extra cost into the new vehicle's loan to make it more affordable. To obtain information on GM's program, call (800) 323-9935; on Ford's program, call (800) 952-2248; on DaimlerChrysler's program, call (800) 255-9877; or for Volvo, call (800) 458-1552.

Saving Money on Corporate Cousins

Sometimes things just aren't what they seem to be. That old adage is truer than ever in the automotive world, where a Chevy (Cavalier) can be a Pontiac (Sunfire) and a Ford (Taurus) can be a Mercury (Sable). Corporate "cousins" or "twins" are the auto industry's terms for virtually identical models that carry different nameplates. And with a little study of automotive family trees, you may save money on your next car.

Here's how: First, you may be able to save money up front — at the time you buy. Consider corporate cousins Toyota Camry and Lexus ES 300. Lexus is the luxury division of Toyota, and the two models share the same chassis and many components. They also carry a strong family resemblance, with nearly identical styling. Yet the ES 300 has a base price of $30,905 while a top-of-the-line Camry XLE V-6 goes for $24,998.

And what does the Lexus deliver for the nearly $6,000 difference? A longer warranty, a few extra features (more horsepower, leather upholstery, as examples), top-rated dealer service and the prestige of the Lexus name. For some buyers,

Safety Features Every Vehicle Should Have

- Deformable crash structure
- Collapsible steering column
- Easy to fasten and release, three-point seat belts
- Automatic seatbelt tensioners
- Adjustable seatbelt shoulder mount
- Driver's air bag
- Front passenger's air bag
- Adjustable or fixed head restraint properly positioned to prevent whiplash
- Jam-resistant door latches
- Side door anti-intrusion beams
- Roll bar (convertible vehicles)
- Anti-lock brakes
- Legible instruments
- Easily operated controls and switches
- Clear field of vision to all sides
- Day/night rearview mirror
- Dual side mirrors
- Center high-mounted brake light
- Adequate heat/defrost system
- Electric rear-window defroster
- Comfortable but firmly-padded seats
- Light, bright exterior color
- Adjustable steering wheel

Optional Safety Features

- Rear window wiper
- Headlight washing system
- All-wheel drive
- Traction control/Electronic stablity program
- Halogen headlights
- Power mirrors and locks
- Full-size spare tire
- Cellular telephone
- Side air bags

Corporate Cousins

Mnfr	Model	Sister Car Names
Acura	CL	Honda Accord Coupe
Acura	SLX	Isuzu Trooper
Audi	A6	Volkswagen Passat
Buick	Century	Oldsmobile Intrigue, Pontiac Gran Prix, Buick Regal, Chevrolet Monte Carlo/Lumina
Buick	LeSabre	Pontiac Bonneville, Oldsmobile Eighty Eight/LSS/Regency
Buick	Park Avenue	Oldsmobile Aurora, Buick Riviera
Buick	Regal	Pontiac Grand Prix, Oldsmobile Intrigue, Chevrolet Lumina/Monte Carlo, Buick Century
Buick	Riviera	Oldsmobile Aurora, Buick Park Avenue
Cadillac	Seville	Cadillac Eldorado
Cadillac	Eldorado	Cadillac Seville
Chevrolet	Astro	GMC Safari
Chevrolet	Blazer	Oldsmobile Bravada, GMC Jimmy/Envoy
Chevrolet	C 3500 Fleetside Crew Cab	GM C Sierra C 3500 Crew Cab
Chevrolet	C Trucks	GMC Sierra C Trucks
Chevrolet	Camaro	Pontiac Firebird
Chevrolet	Cavalier	Pontiac Sunfire
Chevrolet	Chevy Van	Savana Cargo Van
Chevrolet	Express Van	GMC Savana
Chevrolet	K 3500 Fleetside Crew Cab	GMC Sierra K 3500 Crew Cab
Chevrolet	K Trucks	GMC Sierra K Trucks
Chevrolet	Lumina	Pontiac Grand Prix, Oldsmobile Intrigue, Buick Regal/Century, Chevrolet Monte Carlo
Chevrolet	Malibu	Oldsmobile Cutlass
Chevrolet	Metro 2dr hatchback	Suzuki Swift 2dr hatchback
Chevrolet	Monte Carlo	Pontiac Grand Prix, Oldsmobile Intrigue, Buick Regal/Century, Chevrolet Lumina
Chevrolet	Prizm	Toyota Corolla
Chevrolet	S-10	GMC Sonoma, Isuzu Hombre
Chevrolet	Suburban C & K	GMC Suburban C & K
Chevrolet	Tahoe	GMC Yukon
Chevrolet	Tracker	Suzuki Sidekick
Chevrolet	Venture	Oldsmobile Silhouette, Pontiac Trans Sport
Chrysler	Cirrus	Dodge Stratus, Plymouth Breeze
Chrysler	Concorde	Dodge Intrepid
Chrysler	Sebring(except Convertible)	Dodge Avenger, Mitsubishi Galant
Chrysler	Town & Country LX, LXi	Plymouth Grand Voyager, Dodge Grand Caravan
Chrysler	Town & Country SX	Plymouth Voyager, Dodge Caravan
Dodge	Avenger	Chrysler Sebring(except Convertible), Mitsubishi Galant
Dodge	Caravan	Plymouth Voyager, Chrysler Town & Country SX
Dodge	Grand Caravan	Plymouth Grand Voyager, Chrysler Town & Country LX, LXi
Dodge	Intrepid	Chrysler Concorde
Dodge	Neon	Plymouth Neon
Dodge	Stratus	Chrysler Cirrus, Plymouth Breeze
Eagle	Talon	Mitsubishi Eclipse
Ford	Contour	Mercury Mystique
Ford	Crown Victoria	Mercury Grand Marquis
Ford	Escort	Mercury Tracer
Ford	Expedition	Lincoln Navigator
Ford	Explorer	Mercury Mountaineer
Ford	Ranger	Mazda B Trucks
Ford	Taurus	Mercury Sable
GMC Trucks	C Sierra Trucks	Chevrolet C Trucks
GMC Trucks	Jimmy/Envoy	Oldsmobile Bravada, Chevrolet Blazer
GMC Trucks	K Sierra Trucks	Chevrolet K Trucks

Mnfr	Model	Sister Car Names
GMC Trucks	Safari	Chevrolet Astro
GMC Trucks	Savana	Chevrolet Express Van
GMC Trucks	Savana Cargo Van	Chevrolet Van
GMC Trucks	Sierra C 3500 Crew Cab	Chevrolet C 3500 Fleetside Crew Cab
GMC Trucks	Sierra K 3500 Crew Cab	Chevrolet K 3500 Fleetside Crew Cab
GMC Trucks	Sonoma	Chevrolet S-10, Isuzu Hombre
GMC Trucks	Suburban C & K	Chevrolet Suburban C & K
GMC Trucks	Yukon	Chevrolet Tahoe
Honda	Accord Coupe	Acura CL
Honda	Odyssey	Isuzu Oasis
Honda	Passport	Isuzu Rodeo
Infiniti	I30	Nissan Maxima
Infiniti	QX4	Nissan Pathfinder
Isuzu	Hombre	Chevrolet S-10, GMC Sonoma
Isuzu	Oasis	Honda Odyssey
Isuzu	Rodeo	Honda Passport
Isuzu	Trooper	Acura SLX
Lexus	ES 300	Toyota Camry/Avalon
Lexus	LX 450/470	Toyota Land Cruiser
Lincoln	Navigator	Ford Expedition
Mazda	B Trucks	Ford Ranger
Mercury	Grand Marquis	Ford Crown Victoria
Mercury	Mountaineer	Ford Explorer
Mercury	Mystique	Ford Contour
Mercury	Sable	Ford Taurus
Mercury	Tracer	Ford Escort
Mercury	Villager	Nissan Quest
Mitsubishi	Eclipse	Eagle Talon
Mitsubishi	Galant	Chrysler Sebring(except Convertible), Dodge Avenger
Nissan	200SX	Nissan Sentra
Nissan	Maxima	Infiniti I30
Nissan	Pathfinder	Infiniti QX4
Nissan	Quest	Mercury Villager
Nissan	Sentra	Nissan 200SX
Oldsmobile	Achieva	Pontiac Grand Am
Oldsmobile	Aurora	Buick Riviera/Park Avenue
Oldsmobile	Bravada	GMC Jimmy/Envoy, Chevrolet Blazer
Oldsmobile	Cutlass	Chevrolet Malibu
Oldsmobile	Eighty Eight	Pontiac Bonneville, Buick LeSabre, Oldsmobile LSS/Regency
Oldsmobile	Intrigue	Pontiac Grand Prix,, Buick Regal/Century, Chevrolet Monte Carlo/Lumina
Oldsmobile	LSS	Oldsmobile Eighty Eight/Regency, Pontiac Bonneville, Buick LeSabre
Oldsmobile	Regency	Buick Le Sabre, Oldsmobile LSS/Eighty Eight, Pontiac Bonneville
Oldsmobile	Silhouette	Chevrolet Venture, Pontiac Trans Sport
Plymouth	Breeze	Dodge Stratus, Chrysler Cirrus
Plymouth	Grand Voyager	Dodge Grand Caravan, Chrysler Town & Country
Plymouth	Neon	Dodge Neon
Plymouth	Voyager	Dodge Caravan
Plymouth	Voyager	Dodge Carvan, Chrysler Town & Country LX
Pontiac	Bonneville	Oldsmobile Eighty Eight/LSS/Regency, Buick LeSabre
Pontiac	Firebird	Chevrolet Camaro
Pontiac	Grand Am	Oldsmobile Achieva
Pontiac	Grand Prix	Chevrolet Lumina/Monte Carlo, Oldsmobile Intrigue, Buick Regal/Century
Pontiac	Sunfire	Chevrolet Cavalier
Pontiac	Trans Sport	Chevrolet Venture, Oldsmobile Silhouette
Suzuki	Sidekick	Geo Tracker
Suzuki	Swift 2dr hatchback	Geo Metro 2dr hatchback
Toyota	Avalon	Camry, Lexus ES 300
Toyota	Camry	Avalon, Lexus ES 300
Toyota	Corolla	Geo Prizm
Toyota	Land Cruiser	Lexus LX 450/470

💡 **SAFETY TIPS**

- When you choose a car, make sure that from the driver's seat you can see and recognize safety hazards approaching from all directions. Any part of the car that obstructs your view, such as headrests, front or back roof pillars, large areas of reflection, or poorly placed rear-deck brake lights, poses a potential danger. And don't forget to consider the placement of passengers and cargo.

- When you're sitting in the dealer showroom checking out your dream car, don't forget to try out the car's seatbelt system. Can you easily reach the belt from your driving position, pull it across your body in one motion, and snap it in place without having to search for the buckle? Does the lap belt fit snugly across your pelvis (not your stomach), and does the shoulder belt fit snugly across your torso and over your collar bone without riding up on your neck? Check to see if the shoulder mounting is adjustable, to provide you with the most comfortable fit. Reach down and see if the seatbelt release is easy to find and operate, and that the belt retracts smoothly to its original position. If the seatbelt system fails any of these tests, you may not use it consistently, and because seatbelts are so important, you're better off looking at another car.

these differences justify the Lexus price premium. But others will just as soon save the six grand — plus the extra taxes and finances charges — and settle for the Toyota, a car that's nearly as good.

You can also save money at the back end — when you turn in the car — because corporate cousins can also have different resale values several years down the road. For instance, a 1993 Mercury Sable originally cost more than its corporate cousin, a 1993 Ford Taurus. But the Ford's trade-in value is now slightly higher than the Mercury's. Thus the Sable cost its buyer a little more at both ends of the deal.

So before you buy, find out if the car you fancy has a corporate cousin (*see page 64A for a list of corporate cousins*). Then check out their respective charts in this Guide and weigh their purchase prices, features, warranties and expected resale values.

Choosing Safety

Ponder this for a moment: According to the National Highway Traffic Safety Administration (NHTSA), two out of three motorists are involved in an accident at some time that injures someone in the car.

Other statistics show that every motorist can expect to be in an automobile crash once every 10 years. And for about one out of 20, it will cause serious injury.

With numbers like this, it's no wonder that more new-car buyers have found the safety religion. Today, safety ranks right up there with price, quality, and reliability.

Anatomy of a Crash

NHTSA research shows that the major causes of injury inside the car during a collision are, in descending order, the steering wheel, the instrument panel, the doors, the windshield, the front roof pillar, the glove box area, the roof edges, and the roof itself. It's not surprising then, that front-seat passengers are more likely to be injured than rear-seat passengers who are protected by the padding of the front seat backs.

NHTSA data also shows that 51% of deaths occur in head-on impacts, 27% in side impacts, and only 4% in rear impacts. Rollovers are particularly lethal because they are more likely to eject unrestrained passengers from the car than other types of collisions. And fatality rates are 25 times higher for ejected passengers than for those who remain in the car.

The objectives of safety features are 1) to keep the occupants inside the vehicle; 2) to keep them from banging around inside; 3) to absorb some of the forces of impact rather than transfer it to the occupants; or 4) to help prevent a collision from happening in the first place.

NHTSA's book of Federal Motor Vehicle Safety Standards And Regulations is chock-a-block with good intentions. And for 1999, many important mandated safety features — including center-mounted brake lights and air bags for both the driver and front-seat passenger — are standard on all cars. However, other safety features — anti-lock brakes, for example — aren't required by law and are available at the automaker's discretion.

In other words, there is still plenty of variation in the safety features of 1999 models, despite all the rules and regulations. Here are the important features that should be on your safety wish list:

Seatbelts

A three-point seatbelt is a belt with three attachment points: one on the side pillar and one on each side of the driver's or passenger's hips.

The three-point belt is superior to the older lap-only seatbelt for a couple of reasons. Not only do three-point belts reduce the likelihood of the wearer hitting the steering wheel, windshield or other interior surfaces, but they spread the crash forces over more of the body and reduce the strain of the lap belt on the lower body. All 1998 passenger cars are required to have some form of three-point seatbelts for both front- AND rear-seat occupants.

Above all, a seatbelt must be comfortable when it's snug up against the body. If it's not comfortable, it's tempting not to wear it. And if it's not snug, it may not provide the protection it should. In fact, slackened seat belts may INCREASE the risk of injury.

For these reasons, some 1999 cars have belt adjusters and belt tensioners. The former is a simple slide device that allows the shoulder belt anchor on the car's pillar to be moved up and down to accommodate occupants of various heights and body builds. It's not rocket-science, and it's a wonder all cars don't have them.

The latter device is a little more high-tech and is typically found on upscale cars like all or some models of Acuras, Audis, BMWs, Lexus', Mercedes', Saabs, and Volvos. The tensioners automatically tighten the belts around the occupants in the first milliseconds of a crash so there's absolutely no slack in the belts.

Air Bags

Air bags have taken quite a rap in recent months — a bum rap in the view of most safety experts.

Automakers began installing air bags in relatively large numbers in 1990, first in the steering wheel to protect the driver and later in the dash to protect the front-seat passenger. For 1999, NHTSA has mandated that every new car have these dual air bags.

Despite that fact that some children and adults have been injured or killed by deploying air bags, there's still no doubt that air bags are an important safety feature *(see Air Bag Facts and Myths, page 67A-68A)*. But it's a question of policy that has led air bags to become objects of suspicion — or even fear — among many motorists.

The most important safety feature in any car is a three-point seatbelt. When properly secured, seatbelts alone reduce the risk of fatal injury to drivers and front-seat occupants by 45 percent and the risk of moderate-to-critical injury by 50 percent.

Unlike air bags, seatbelts protect in all kinds of accidents, including frontal impacts, side impacts, rear impact and roll-overs. Steering-wheel or dash-mounted air bags are only effective in frontal impacts — accidents that account for only about half of all highway fatalities. That's why, to be fully protected, it's vital to wear a seatbelt even in cars with air bags. And that's why air bags are considered "supplemental" or additional restraints to the primary retraints, the seatbelts. (The little "SRS" logo on the steering wheel in cars equipped with air bags stands for "Supplemental Restraint System.")

Air Bag Facts & Myths

Myth: Air bags are dangerous.
Fact: Air bags have saved many more people from death than they've killed. According to a recent tally, air bags were blamed in the deaths of 91 adults and children. But they've saved nearly 2,000 lives. Air bags can be dangerous to some, but they've saved nearly 20 lives for each one they've killed.

Myth: Air bags are the most important safety device in a vehicle.
Fact: Seatbelts are the most important safety device. Most air bags protect only in frontal collisions. Seatbelts protect in frontal, rear and side impacts, as well as in roll-overs. Most of the people killed by air bags were not wearing seatbelts, were not wearing seatbelts correctly or in the case of children, were in rear-facing infant seats that had been placed in the front passenger seat.

Myth: Passenger-side air bags should be deactivated in vehicles that carry kids.
Fact: That's true only if the vehicle has no rear seat, such as a pickup truck or sports car. And that's why some vehicles have key-operated deactivation switches. Otherwise, children up to the age of 12 should always ride in the rear seat, properly buckled into the seat or an infant seat.

Myth: Short people and the elderly will be harmed or killed by air bags.
Fact: Short people and the elderly are at greatest risk if they sit too close to an air bag and aren't wearing a seatbelt. These people should push their seats back as far as possible (for short drivers, pedal extenders can help — see Air Bag Precautions, page 69A). As a rule, if a person sits at least 12 inches from the bag and is belted, they will be safe from a deploying air bag. Wearing a seatbelt is important because it prevents the person from being propelled forward just when the air bag is inflating at its maximum speed.

Air Bag Facts & Myths

Myth: Air bags aren't necessary if you always wear a seatbelt.

Fact: Seatbelts, even those with automatic tensioners, allow some occupant movement during a crash as the belt pulls tightly around the reel. In a very serious crash, the belt may stretch enough to allow the front-seat occupant to hit the steering wheel or dash. The air bag serves as a cushion between people's heads and faces.

Myth: Air bags are frequently set off by a minor fender bender or even go off "all by themselves" when no collision is involved.

Fact: There have been very rare instances when air bags have spontaneously deployed, sometimes when the car was parked and no one was in the car. But air bags have proven to be very reliable. In one study, the National Highway Traffic Safety Adminstration investigated 1,200 accidents and found that in every case air bags deployed when they were supposed to. Air bags are triggered by sophisticated sensors after the vehicle has an impact at speeds of 11 to 14 m.p.h. or more. An air bag won't deploy during minor bumps.

Myth: The sound of an air bag going off causes deafness.

Fact: The noise of a deploying air bag — much like a shotgun blast — may pose a slight risk to some individuals. But the sounds involved in a crash severe enough to deploy an air bag are often more harmful.

But some stupid schnooks refuse to wear their seatbelts — about 40% of all American drivers and occupants, despite laws in 49 states that require people to buckle up (New Hampshire, whose motto ironically is "Live Free or Die," is the one exception). So early on in the air bag game, NHTSA decided that air bags should protect unbelted folks in frontal collisions as well as those responsible citizens who always buckle up.

Unfortunately, it takes a more powerful air bag to protect an unbelted person than a belted one, especially a large American male. To protect them, an air bag needs to burst out of the steering wheel or dash at nearly 200 mph, and that's what NHTSA mandated.

Now that it's been shown that these powerful air bags can harm or kill children or frail adults, NHTSA has relaxed its rules to allow automakers to install "de-powered" or "second-generation" air bags that are 20% to 35% less powerful in 1999 models. These bags, which deploy with less force, are still powerful enough to protect people who wear their seatbelts, but should provide less chance of harm to children and to the elderly.

You can check the vehicle charts in this guide to see which vehicles have de-powered air bags.

There is some evidence that passenger-side air bags that deploy vertically up the windshield are safer than air bags that release horizontally toward the passenger. Among the automakers with models that use vertical-deploying air bags are Ford, Honda and Nissan.

In the future, you can expect to see a wide variety of air bags. There will ultimately be "smart" air bags that deploy at different speeds, depending upon the circumstances — whether a person is sitting close to the steering wheel or further away from it, for instance. Smart air bags may also be able to calculate the size of the occupant and vary its force accordingly.

Even in 1999, some automakers have come up with variations on the standard driver and passenger, air bags. Several manufacturers — BMW, Ford, General Motors, Lexus, Cadillac, Mercedes-Benz, Saab, Volkswagen and Volvo, among them — have introduced air bags mounted in the doors or the sides of the seats to protect in side impacts.

BMW, Mercedes-Benz and Volvo are also bringing to the market in 1999 a curtain-style, roof mounted air bags designed to prevent the driver's head from smashing into the pillar between the windshield and the driver's side windows.

Car Size

Once upon a time, before NHTSA, air bags, three-point seat belts, and all the rest, if you wanted the safest car you went out and bought the biggest car you could find and depended on its mass to protect you.

Well, the laws of physics haven't changed. Modern technology may have made small cars safer, but if you're going to be involved in a crash, your survival odds are still higher in a large car.

In one recent study by the Insurance Institute for Highway Safety (IIHS), insurance-company injury claims showed that among the 17 cars with the highest number of claims, 15 of the cars were small. Two were midsize, and not one was large. Conversely, among the nine cars with the lowest number of injury claims, seven were large cars, two were midsize and not one was small.

The big break in the death rate seems to come with cars that have a wheelbase of just over 100 inches (that's considered a midsize car). According to IIHS data, cars with wheelbases of 105 inches or more have 1.4 deaths or less per 10,000 registered vehicles, while cars with 104-inch wheelbases or less have 2.1 or more deaths per 10,000 registered vehicles.

Structural Crashworthiness

Large car or small, there are differences in injury rates between cars in the same size range.

Automakers build two important structures into a car to protect the occupants. The first is a collapsible energy-absorbing structure designed to crush in a controlled manner, absorbing the energy of the crash and increasing the time it takes for the car to come to a stop. The second structure is a reinforced, protective cabin that surrounds the car's occupants and protects them from injury by keeping the exterior impact from reaching them.

Each year NHTSA crash tests popular models into a fixed barrier at 35 m.p.h.. The tests measure the crash's impact on the driver and passenger dummies' heads, chests, and thighbones, using all the car's standard safety equipment. And the results, even among different models in the same size class, do indeed vary greatly. You can get information on NHTSA's crash tests by calling 1-800-424-9393 or on the Internet (www.NHTSA.dot.gov).

The IIHS also publishes periodic reports, assembled from claims data collected from the institute's sponsoring insurance companies, that show injury frequencies for popular models. For more information, or for a copy of the institute's pamphlet "Shopping For A Safer Car," write IIHS Publications, P.O. Box 1420, Arlington, VA 22210.

Side Impact Protection

For 1999, all cars must meet federal requirements for beefed-up doors and side structures. The standard calls for a car to withstand a broadside hit by another vehicle traveling 33.5 m.p.h.. Most automakers are meeting this requirement by adding stronger steel beams beneath the body panels.

Side impacts are second only to head-on collisions as the most serious traffic accidents. If a model meets the standard, you and your passengers will have better protection for your chest and pelvic areas during a collision.

For 1999 several automakers, will offer side-impact air bags on some or all of their models. (See Air Bags, page 67A)

Head Restraints

Of course, these are popularly known as "head rests," a terrible misnomer. Their purpose is not to give your head a place to rest, but to prevent it from snapping back sharply in a rear-end collision.

Though all cars must have front-seat head restraints, not all head restraints are alike. There are two basic kinds, adjustable and fixed. Adjustable head restraints are fine — if they're adjusted high enough (about ear level) and far enough forward to hit the occupant's head, not his or her neck. Problem is, few people take the time to adjust their head restraints.

Air Bag Precautions

For infants: Never put infants in rear-facing child seats in the front seat of a car. The child seat should be properly buckled in the rear seat. Some vehicles without rear seats have air bag deactivation switches for use with child safety seats.

For children: Children up to the age of 12 should also sit in the vehicle's rear seat, properly buckled with a seatbelt. If a child must ride in the front seat, the seat should be pushed back as far as it will go.

For drivers: The driver should also sit as far back from the steering wheel as possible, properly buckled. Drivers should not steer with a hand at the 12 o'clock position. In that position, a deploying air bag could injure the driver's arm. The driver should grasp the right and left sides of the wheel instead, at the 9 o'cock and 3 o'clock positions. This leaves room for the air bag to inflate.

For short drivers: Short drivers should install pedal extenders that will allow them to sit further back from the steering wheel. Call the National Mobility Equipment Dealers Association at (813) 932-8566 for the name of a nearby dealer.

Don't Forget the Kids

If you have a family, there are several additional safety features you will want to look for when choosing a car.

■ You want the driver to be able to lock automatic windows so children can't play with them. For the same reason, you want child-proof door locks, so small children cannot open rear doors from the inside.

■ Also, small, wide-angle "child-view" mirrors are available that snap on to the regular rearview mirror, and allow you to keep tabs on the kids in the back seat without taking your eyes far from the road.

■ Built-in Child Seats — Chrysler pioneered the idea of built-in child restraint seat in its vans. The seat folds out from the regular, adult seat, and comes complete with its own seatbelts. It's recommended for kids weighing 20 to 45 pounds.

The fixed type, like those found in Volvos, are always high enough, and are probably the best kind for most people. Look too, for head restraints in the rear seats.

Anti-lock Brakes (ABS)

Slam on the brakes during an emergency, and chances are your car will become Mr. Toad's wild ride as it skids down the road, especially if it's rain-slicked or icy. Locking up the wheels — or skidding — is dangerous because it not only increases the distance before the car stops, but because the driver loses the ability to steer.

An ABS system pumps the brakes automatically, many times a second, to prevent lockup and help to maintain control. On dry pavement, ABS doesn't substantially shorten stopping distances. But on wet or slippery surfaces, ABS can help a great deal — if a driver knows how to use it. Drivers are traditionally taught to pump the brakes on slippery roads to avoid a skid. But with ABS, firm and continuous pressure — not pumping — is required to activate the ABS feature.

■ **Dos and Don'ts of ABS.** Like air bags, anti-lock brakes (ABS) have had their share of controversy. Some studies have shown that vehicles equipped with ABS don't have better safety records than those vehicles not equipped with ABS; indeed, some have shown their records to be worse. But safety officials suspect the problem is not with ABS itself, but with drivers who don't know how to use ABS correctly. To this end, the National Safety Council has the following recommendations:

■ **Don't be alarmed by mechanical noises or pedal pulsations when applying ABS brakes.** ABS is only activated under hard braking.

Pulsations, and sometimes noises, are normal and indicate the ABS is working correctly. Don't pump the brakes in an effort to avoid locking up the wheels. ABS automatically pumps the brakes, much faster than the driver ever could.

■ **Don't forget to steer.** The main advantage of ABS is that it prevents the wheels from locking up, which helps to keep the vehicle from going into an uncontrollable skid. Thus ABS allows you to maintaining steering control during emergency braking, but only if you continue to steer.

■ **Do keep your foot on the brake pedal.** Maintain firm and continuous pressure on the brake pedal when braking, even if the pedal pulsates.

■ **Do know the difference between between four-wheel and two- or rear-wheel ABS.** Most cars and many trucks have four-wheel ABS. But some light trucks have only rear-wheel ABS; with rear-wheel ABS, the front wheels can still lock up during hard braking. If this happens, you should ease up on the brake pedal with just enough pressure to allow the front wheels to roll again so you can steer.

■ **Do practice driving with ABS.** Find an empty parking lot or open area and practice emergency stops so that you can become accustomed to the feel — the normal pulsations — of ABS when it activates.

■ **Do allow enough distance to stop.** ABS doesn't necessarily allow you stop in a shorter distance; it primarily helps you to maintain directional control. Just because your car or truck is equipped with ABS doesn't mean you can take more chances.

Daytime Running Lights

Studies have shown that using headlights during the day can prevent some car-to-car crashes because of a vehicle's enhanced

TEST DRIVE CHECKLIST

The price may be right. The size may be right. And your significant other may just love the styling. But if you slide behind the wheel and find that you can't get comfortable, or that the seatbelt slices across your neck, or that you can't reach important controls, then the car isn't for you. Discovering such fatal flaws is why the test drive is so important. If you test drive several vehicles, it may be hard to recall the plusses and minuses of each at the end of the day when it comes time to make the big decision. Here's a scorecard that can help. Jot down a "+" or " " beside each item. Make photocopies of this page and fill one out for every vehicle you test drive.

1) Exterior Inspection

☐ **Styling**
Does it please you?

☐ **Overall size**
Too big, too small or just right?

☐ **Trunk**
Is it large enough for your needs, and does it seem easy to load?

☐ **Build quality**
Does the exterior seem well finished?

2) On The Road

☐ **Acceleration from rest**
Does the vehicle move away smartly?

☐ **Acceleration from speed**
Does the engine have enough passing and hill — climbing power?

☐ **Transmission**
Does it shift from gear to gear smoothly?

☐ **Brakes**
Do they stop the vehicle quickly and in a straight line?

☐ **Ride**
Is it comfortable on different surfaces without being either soft and mushy or too harsh?

☐ **Handling**
During quick lane changes or hard cornering, does the body lean excessively?

☐ **Steering**
Does it seem quick and precise?

☐ **Noise**
Is there excessive wind, engine, or tire noise at high speeds?

☐ **Heat/air conditioning**
Do they seem up to the job?

☐ **Audio system**
Is the sound pleasing and the radio reception good?

☐ **Build quality**
Are there any rattles or squeaks as you travel over poor road surfaces?

3) Interior Inspection

☐ **Doors**
Are they easy to open?

☐ **Entry/exit**
Can you get in and out of the cabin easily?

☐ **Seats, front and rear**
Are they comfortable and supportive?

☐ **Room, front and rear**
Is there enough leg room and head room?

☐ **Instruments/controls**
Can you see and reach all of them easily?

☐ **Seatbelts**
Can they be adjusted to fit you well?

☐ **Visibility**
Are there any potentially dangerous blind spots?

☐ **Styling**
Is the interior attractive?

☐ **Build quality**
Does everything seem well assembled?

visibility when its lights are on. For 1999, some automakers are equipping a few of their models with daytime running lights, automatically activated when the ignition switch is turned on. They include GM brand cars, Saab, Suzuki, Volkswagen, and Volvo.

Traction Control/ All-Wheel Drive

Traction control does for acceleration what ABS does for deceleration. Traction control and all-wheel-drive are pricey features. But they provide more control, and hence an extra margin of safety, on wet or icy roads.

Proper Ergonomics

A car's sound system may reproduce music that's the next best thing to a live performance, but if the system's controls are so tiny that you need bifocals to find them, they're a detriment to safety.

All of a car s switches, controls and instruments should be easy to see and easy to use.

Child Safety Seats

They may squirm, wriggle, kick and scream, but young kids have be buckled into child safety seats. Every state has laws on its books that require it. And with good reason: When properly used, the seats reduce the risk of death in a crash by 69 percent for infants and by 47 percent for toddlers.

The guidelines for selecting the right restraints are quite simple. Infants up to one year of age and weighing up to 20 pounds should always be placed in a rear-facing safety seat. Older children are best protected in a forward-facing child seat with its own harness.

Children who have reached 40 pounds and 40 inches in height should be moved to a booster seat to help the adult safety belt fit correctly. Only when your child is large enough so that the adult safety belt system in the vehicle fits the child correctly can you forget about safety seats. That means the lap belt should fit low over the child's upper thighs and the shoulder belt should rest on the child's shoulder — not across the neck or face.

And the message that safety experts make over and over again is that all child safety seats should be placed in the vehicle's rear seat. Small children are safest in back for two reasons. First, the front seat provides additional impact protection during a front-end collision. Second, activated passenger-side air bags pose a significant risk to young kids. If the new vehicle you fancy doesn't have a rear seat, then select one that has a switch to deactivate the passenger-side air bag. Many 1999 pickup trucks and sports cars without rear seats will have these switches.

Here are some other child safety seat tips:

■ Make sure the child seat is properly secured; there's not much point in using a child seat if the seat itself isn't buckled into the vehicle. Follow the seat manufacuter's instructions and your vehicle's owner's manual for instructions specific to your vehicle. Seat belts that lock only in emergencies may need a locking clip to hold child seats correctly.

■ Make sure the child seat harness is snug and stays on the

child's shoulders, and that the shoulder straps are in the appropriate slots.

■ Call the Auto Safety Hotline (800) 424-9393 to find out if your child seat has ever been recalled.

■ Consider buying a vehicle with built-in child safety seats. Some cars and vans, like DaimlerChrysler's minivans and Toyota's Corolla, have integrated child seats that allow you to skip any concerns about whether the child seat will fit your car or whether the seat is properly secured to your car.

Taking Delivery Of Your New Car

Whew, you did it! It took hours of haggling. But you and the dealer have finally come to terms on your new car.

You bargained hard to get what you consider a fair price for the car and its optional equipment. You even managed to get the dealer to give you a reasonable price in trade for that old jalopy you've been driving. And the nice salesman quoted you a competitive interest rate on dealer-arranged financing.

Why, you can practically feel the keys to your new dream car dropping into the palm of your hand. All that's left to do is a quick trip to the dealer's finance and insurance (F&I) office to wrap up a little paperwork. Time to relax, right?

Wrong — not unless you want to risk spending more than you bargained for.

The dealer's F&I person is often a master salesperson as well.

In a few strokes of the pen, he or she can turn a good deal for you into a bonanza for the dealer.

For instance, the F&I person can add on an extended warranty for "just a few dollars a month." Or he can tack on credit life, accident and health insurance designed to pay off the car should you die or become disabled; it's often expensive, and most people already have disability and life insurance anyway.

So before you sign the paperwork and drive your new car off the dealer's lot — in most states, the car then becomes all yours- consider these points:

Read the stupid paperwork!
Don't take anybody's word for it; take the time to read before you sign. Make sure all the blanks are filled. Make sure you're paying what you agreed to pay in your negotiations. Make sure you're not paying for anything you didn't agree to buy. If you see any discrepancies or have any questions, speak up. Make sure you have copies of all the documents. Remember, it's your money.

Inspect the car. Once the wheels hit the public street, the new car no longer belongs to the dealer. And if you discover anything wrong with the car, you can bet that the dealer will fix it faster if the problem holds up the closing of the sale. Make sure the optional equipment you paid for is on the car. Inspect the body and paint for damage; after you've driven the car away, the dealer can claim you caused the damage. Check the odometer to be sure it reads no more than a couple of hundred miles; if it reads more, find out why.

Buyer's Remorse: No Cooling Off Period

Keep in mind there is no "cooling off" period on car sales (Saturn is the exception to this). The 72-hour cooling-off law, during which time you can change your mind about your purchase, in most states applies only to salespersons who come to you — such as door-to-door insurance or magazine peddlers.

You certainly won't get your money back once you've signed the final paperwork and driven away in the car. And even if you haven't signed the final paperwork or taken possession of the new car, the dealer isn't required to return any deposit you made if you cancel a sales contract just because you have a case of buyer's remorse.

Preventing Theft

Just because you expect to buy an inexpensive sedan or an ordinary pickup truck, don't kid yourself into thinking thieves won't have any interest in swiping it. According to the National Insurance Crime Bureau (NICB) — an organization funded by insurance companies to gather data on theft — common vehicles are also the most commonly stolen vehicles.

That's because vehicles are often stolen so they can be stripped of their parts; there's a ready market for parts from such popluar vehicles as Honda Civics or Toyota pickups. Or thieves will ship stolen vehicles out of the country for resale, or they'll switch vehicle identification numbers and sell them as used cars in this country. Stolen vehicles are also commonly used as transportation in drug runs or as getaway cars in robberies.

Which isn't to say that sports cars or luxury vehicles are safe from brigands. In raw numbers, there aren't as many of them stolen because there aren't as many of them in the total vehicle population. But relative to the numbers of them on the road, they do have high theft-claim frequencies.

In fact, about the only vehicle that isn't a target for thieves is a station wagon, according to NICB data. So unless you plan on parking a station wagon in your driveway, you should consider taking precautions against theft. Not only will precautions lend you some peace of mind, but anti-theft devices may help you land a reduction in the premium for your comprehensive insurance coverage.

Short of surrounding your vehicle with Scud missles, there's no way you can absolutely prevent a determined thief from absconding with your new car or truck. Given time, skill and perhaps a flatbed truck, a thief can foil most any anti-theft device. Still, taking precautions can cause a thief to pass on stealing your vehicle in favor of searching out an easier target.

The NICB advocates a "layered" approach to anti-theft protection, consisting of four layers. The more layers you use, the more difficult your vehicle will be to steal.

Layer No. 1: Common Sense. Removing the keys from the car, closing the windows and locking the doors every time you leave your car or truck — plus parking in well-lighted areas — are the simplest and most cost-effective ways to prevent theft. Cost: None.

Layer No. 2: Visible or Audible deterrents. Audible alarms are typically equipped with motion or impact sensors that trigger a loud siren. Cost: $150 to $1,000.

Steering column collars prevent thieves from hot-wiring the vehicle. Cost: $100 to $200.

Steering wheel locks are metal bars that prevent the steering wheel from turning. Cost: $25 to $100.

Tire locks or a steel boot prevent the vehicle from being driven. Cost: $80 to $200.

Etching the windows with the vehicle's identification number makes it difficult for the thief to resell the vehicle. Cost: up to $100.

Layer No. 3: Immobilizing Systems. Kill switches inhibit the flow of electricity or fuel to the engine unless a hidden switch is activated. Cost: $10 to $125.

Ignition-key systems that contain coded computer chips or radio frequencies prevent the engine from being started unless the right "smart" key is inserted in the ignition. These systems are standard equipment on several 1999 vehicles, including models from BMW, Mercedes-Benz and General Motors.

Layer No. 4: Tracking Devices. Most tracking devices are electronic transmitters hidden in the vehicle that emit signals to police or monitoring stations that help them locate the vehicle when it is reported to be stolen. Cost: $400 to $1,500. there may be a monthly charge as well.

With layers No. 3 and 4, it;s also a good idea to use some sort of visible deterrent — a decal — or audible deterrent — a siren — that makes it obvious to the thief that the vehicle is protected. Otherwise, the thief might break into the vehicle, get frustrated when it won't start and vandalize the vehicle.

Keeping Your Old Car vs. Buying a New One

OK, you've done your homework. You've studied the charts in this book, compared your choices, and now you are ready to buy a new car. All you need to do is get rid of your old clunker and purchase the car of your dreams. Hold on for just a minute.

You probably have a list of reasons to buy a new car. Reasons that might include the newest safety features, modern styling, or perhaps you need a larger vehicle to fit your growing family. These are just a few; the list goes on and on. Still, with all the good reasons to buy a new car, there is a very compelling one to consider holding on to the old car: Cost!

Taking a purely left-brain, economic approach, keeping your old car could save you thousands of dollars.

It is true that older cars generally cost more to maintain, and are more likely to break down, resulting in an expensive and aggravating repair. But before you push the panic button, let's look at the economics.

For example, let's assume you own a 1994 Ford Taurus LX and you are faced with the decision of buying a new one or keeping the old one. How do the numbers stack up? Figure 12 shows a comparison of the projected five-year ownership costs for your 1994 Taurus LX to a new 1999 model. (This example is based on the assumption that you drive the national average of 14,000 miles per year.)

Figure 12

Projected Five-year Comparison

FORD TAURUS LX

COST AREAS	1999 MODEL	1994 MODEL
Depreciation	$11,638	$3,740
Financing	3,930	0
Insurance	6,606	5,362
State Fees	804	304
Fuel	3,387	3,042
Maintenance	3,228	6,816
Repair	1,000	1,655
TOTAL	**$30,593**	**$20,919**
DIFFERENCE		$9,674

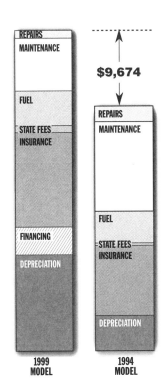

$9,674

1999 MODEL

1994 MODEL

Why is there a difference in expected ownership costs? For one thing, your used car will depreciate at a much slower rate than the new one. Cars depreciate the fastest in the first few years. Therefore, your 1994 Taurus LX has already been through its highest depreciation. You can see from the example that the 1999 car will depreciate $7,898 more than the 1994 edition over the next five years.

Your insurance rates are likely to be lower on a used model. The example shows a $1,244 cost advantage for the used car. You may even consider raising the deductible on the collision portion of your premium, or dropping collision entirely, lowering your insurance payments even more.

And then there are finance charges. Chances are you have paid back your loan or are close to making that last payment. The prospect of four or five years of paying loan interest may put a dent in your budget planning.

As for various annual taxes and license fees, again the used car will cost approximately $500 less over five years, depending on the state you live in.

Fuel costs are also slightly higher for the 1999 model, resulting in an advantage for the used car.

What about maintenance and repair costs for the used car? These are the cost areas that show a dramatic advantage for the new car. The expected maintenance and repair cost for the 1994 model is $4,243 more than the expected five-year cost for the 1999 model.

However, when you tally up all of the expected costs, if you decide to keep your old car for another five years you will save $9,674 ($30,593 minus $20,919).

A Heap of Trouble

Now, in the preceding example we're dealing with a vehicle that's not terribly ancient — one that's just a few years old and with much less than 100,000 miles on the clock. But there comes a point when every vehicle is just plain pooped, when it becomes more trouble than it's worth.

And when will the typical car or truck reach that point? Not too many years ago, the furthest reach of a vehicle's useful life was 100,000 miles. By then, if the mechanicals weren't worn out, then the body and chassis would be a conglomeration of squeaks, rattles and rust. But not today. Many modern vehicles can breeze right past that 100,000-mile mark with not a great deal more than a tune-up and maybe a new fuel pump or timing chain. And thanks to plastic body panels and factory rust-proofing methods, the tin worm is much less of a pest.

Still, as the miles pile on, repairs become inevitable. Here are some examples of components and the mileages at which they typically need replacement:

■ Alternator, 125,000 miles

■ Axle boot, 100,000 miles

■ Brake rotors, 90,000 miles

■ Brake drums, 150,000 miles

■ Brake calipers, 150,000 miles

- Catalytic converter, 125,000 miles
- Clutch, 75,000 miles
- EGR valve, 60,000 miles
- Fuel pump, 100,000 miles
- Headlamp, 60,000 miles
- Muffler, 60,000 miles
- Oxygen sensor, 60,000 miles
- Radiator fan, 150,000 miles
- Sealed front bearings, 125,000 miles
- Shock absorbers, 50,000 miles
- Starter, 100,000 miles
- Tie rods, 150,000 miles
- Timing belt, 60,000 miles
- Timing chain, 100,000 miles
- Water pump, 120,000 miles

From this list, you can see that repairs seem to cluster around the 50,000-75,000-mile mark, the 100,000-mile mark and the 120,000-150,000-mile mark. But the earlier repairs — headlamps, EGR valves, etc. — tend to be considerably less costly than later repairs — water pumps, catalytic converters and so on. Moreover, by 150,000 miles, paint and upholstery usually become rather ragged as well. And to top it all off, by 125,000 or 150,000 miles, the components that needed replacement at 60,000 miles may need replacement for a second time!

From the perspective of pure economics, it's unwise to trade in a relatively young vehicle because it needs several hundred dollars worth of repairs. But it also may be financially foolish to throw thousands of dollars into a car or truck that's on its last legs.

Unloading Your Old Car

Finally, you've considered all of the advantages and disadvantages of keeping your old car, and you have concluded that your best option is to buy a new one. So what should you do about that old lump you're now driving?

The easiest solution would be to trade it in on the new car — no ads to write, no waiting by the phone for replies, and no worries about smog or safety certificates (in many states, the seller's responsibility).

Of course, you pay for this convenience. The dealer has to make a fair profit on any transaction, and if he takes your old car in trade, he's got to be able to turn around and sell it for more than he or she paid you. So the dealer will probably offer you the "wholesale price." But, if you sold the car yourself, you could probably get a figure between the dealer wholesale price and the dealer's full "retail price."

To Fix or Not to Fix

Whether you trade it or sell it yourself, you'll have to make an honest assessment of the old heap and what it needs in the way of repairs.

Keep in mind that a car in decent shape will be easier to sell and will command a higher price. It probably won't make sense to rebuild an old car's engine for $2,000—you'll never recoup the money. But if relatively inexpensive items aren't working, fix them — things like mufflers, the radio, or the speedometer.

A Marketing Plan

As anyone on Madison Avenue will tell you, a successful sale involves the right packaging, the right advertising and the right price. Once you've made any worthwhile repairs to your old heap, it's time to turn your attention to its cosmetics. It's amazing, but the vast majority of buyers will overlook mechanical ills, sometimes major ones, if the paint shines and interior seems fresh. And conversely, a vehicle in good mechanical shape but with a ratty appearance will turn off most buyers. So by all means, have your old vehicle cleaned up, whether you've decided to sell it yourself or trade it in to a dealer. It's worth the extra $100 or $150 for a detailing job because a good-looking car or truck will not only fetch a higher price, it'll sell faster.

When you've transformed the old buggy into a "meticulously maintained" vehicle, you'll need to attach a price to it. Even if you want to trade it to a dealer, you'll want to know if the dealer is offering you a fair price. But keep in mind those two prices mentioned earlier, wholesale and retail. Even if your vehicle is in fine shape, the dealer may have to perform some work before he can put the car or truck on his lot — say, a safety check or a set of new tires. It can cost a dealer $1500 or more to get a vehicle ready for a certified-used car or truck program. He'll also have to advertise the vehicle, pay his sales personnel and cover overhead costs. On top of all that, he needs to make a profit on the deal. If the vehicle isn't one he's likely to keep on his used-car lot because it's too much of a clunker or it doesn't fit the mix at his dealership (a Yugo at a Cadillac dealer), he'll have to wholesale it. The wholesaler will have to make a profit, and the dealer who finally ends up with the vehicle will have to make a profit. All this tends to drive down the price the dealer can offer you for your old heap. Thus, he'll offer you a "wholesale," "trade-in" or "low-book" price.

At the other end of the price spectrum, there's the "full retail" or "high-book" price. That's usually the price the dealer will ask for a used car or truck — one that includes all the reconditioning and in many cases, a warranty. Should you decide to sell your old vehicle yourself, you should ask a price somewhere in between low and high book if it is in decent shape.

Ah, but where do you find these prices? First, get a feel for your local market. Look in your local newspaper's classifieds to see how similar cars are priced. Or pick up a local edition of "The Recycler" or "Auto Trader" at a convenience store. The so-called "book" prices usually come from either the Kelly Blue Book or the NADA Used Car Guide; often banks or credit unions will have these books on hand. Or you can hit the World Wide Web. There are many sites that give used-car pricing, including IntelliChoice's site (www. intellichoice.com). The best sites will ask you to get specific about your car or truck, including its condition, mileage and equipment. Mileage especially, can make a big difference in its value. A four-year-old Honda Accord Sedan EX-V6, for instance, with only 25,000 miles on the odometer will be worth around $1,800 more than the same car with 45,000 miles.

Getting a fix on your old vehicle's value will help you decide whether to trade it or sell it yourself. If your old car or truck isn't worth much, you'll probably decide it isn't worth the trouble to sell it yourself, and you'll be willing to take what you can from the dealer. Or you might consider donating it to a charitable organization and taking a tax-write-off. Many charities, including children's homes, religious groups and the American Red Cross, are eager to accept old vehicles. They'll usually come and fetch it, and will provide you with a receipt, though they'll let you fill in the vehicle's value — high book value, if you think it's fair. Make a photocopy of the appropriate page from one of the price guides, or print out a hard copy from one of the Web sites for your tax records. If you're in a high tax bracket, it may be worthwhile to donate your old vehicle.

But even if your car or truck is worth a tidy sum, you may want to trade to a dealer. In many states, sales tax is figured on the difference between the trade and the new-car cost, not the full purchase price of the new car. With this tax saving, it may be to your advantage to make the trade even though the dealer offers you low book price. If you decide to trade, remember the Golden Rule of Car Buying *(page 52A):* keep your negotiations for your new car separate from those for your old car. Otherwise, what the dealer givith for your old car, he may taketh from (a price reduction) on the new car.

If you decide to sell the car yourself, the next step is to write an enticing ad. Include the brand name, the year, the model and any important features — such as an automatic transmssion or air conditioning. Mention the condition of the car. If the miles are low for the car's age, you may want to mention that too. And if there's space in the ad, note the car's color. Always include a price, even if you're willing to bargain.

Now just sit back and let the calls come in. When someone makes you an acceptable offer, always ask for cash or a bank check. Never take a personal check.

Flat Broke

You buy or lease a new car or truck and then disaster hits. Your company downsizes and you're laid off. Or you file for a divorce. Or you're faced with an illness and monstrous medical bills. Or it could be any of life's other calamities that makes it impossible for you to continue to make the lease or loan payment on your vehicle.

Chances are, you'll find that bailing out of your payments will be more difficult than you imagined. Even if you let your car or truck be repossessed by the creditor, your obligation to make good on the lease or the loan won't necessarily end. Once back in the creditor's possession, the vehicle will usually go to auction and the proceeds will be applied to your debt. But auction bids are invariably low, and you'll end up with a "deficiency balance" — the difference between the loan or lease payoff balance and the auction price, plus any towing, storage and fix-up costs to get the car or truck ready for auction.

Deficiency balances are likely to be higher on a lease contract than on a loan because you won't have been building equity in the vehicle.

Unless you're considered "judgment-proof" — somebody who has no assets and is unemployed or is employed in a very low-paying job — the creditor will sue, put a lien on your assets or garnish your wages to satisfy the deficiency balance. But should you find yourself unable to make your payments, there are ways to avoid repossession and minimize your losses, though none of them is without pain:

■ **Sell your car or truck.** A buyer could either take over your payments or pay you a lump sum — hopefully, one large enough to pay off what you owe. And who would want to take over your payments? People who have bad credit ratings and can't get a loan, or who don't have cash for a down payment on a loan. But clear such a plan with your creditor first; the creditor may want the person who takes over the payments to sign a contract.

You could also retain the note on the car, but have the buyer make the payments to you, which you then turn over to the creditor. The danger is that the buyer has the car, but you're still responsible for the loan or lease should the buyer default.

In either case, you must act quickly. Creditors will often repossess a car within 60 days of a missed payment.

■ **Attempt a settlement.** If you can demonstrate that you're

really in the financial dumpster and can muster up some cash — not likely if you really are in the dumpster — the creditor might accept a 70-90 percent settlement. Being ill and having your house in foreclosure may be enough grounds for a settlement. But you should demonstrate that lenderon your car or truck isn't in a unique losing position — that is, that you're trying to settle your debts with all your creditors. Credit counseling services can often help by arranging a debt-resolution program.

■ **Trade in your vehicle for a less expensive one.** This is an easy route to take, but it's not without pitfalls. The dealer will give you low book value on your car or truck. The difference between the trade-in value and the loan or lease payoff can be rolled into a new loan on a less expensive car if the dealer is cooperative. Though your monthly payments will be lower, you will essentially be paying say, $15,000 for a $10,000 vehicle. That means you'll be way upside-down in the new, cheaper car, and at some point you'll still have to deal with it.

■ **Declare bankruptcy.** A Chapter 7 bankruptcy will discharge you of any deficiency balance owed on your vehicle. You may be able to keep the car if you can "reaffirm the collateral" — the vehicle — in the bankruptcy. That is, if the bankruptcy discharges other debt — unsecured credit-card debt, for instance — you may find that you can continue to make payments on the car or truck. Of course, a bankruptcy will have serious consequences on your credit-worthiness for years to come and isn't to be taken lightly.

Annotated Vehicle Charts

ANNOTATED VEHICLE CHARTS

This section will give you an in-depth explanation of every aspect of the vehicle charts in this book. On pages 84A-90A you will find a sample vehicle chart divided into distinct sections: vehicle description; warranty and maintenance; purchase price; and ownership costs.

The text on pages 91A-98A explains the formulas used and the assumptions made to calculate the ownership costs for every vehicle included in this book.

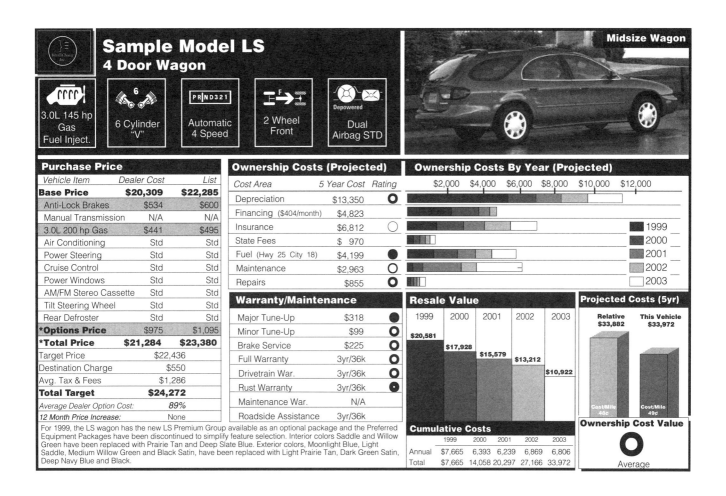

Sample Model LS
4 Door Wagon

Midsize Wagon

3.0L 145 hp Gas Fuel Inject. | 6 Cylinder "V" | Automatic 4 Speed | 2 Wheel Front | Dual Airbag STD

Purchase Price

Vehicle Item	Dealer Cost	List
Base Price	**$20,309**	**$22,285**
Anti-Lock Brakes	$534	$600
Manual Transmission	N/A	N/A
3.0L 200 hp Gas	$441	$495
Air Conditioning	Std	Std
Power Steering	Std	Std
Cruise Control	Std	Std
Power Windows	Std	Std
AM/FM Stereo Cassette	Std	Std
Tilt Steering Wheel	Std	Std
Rear Defroster	Std	Std
*Options Price	$975	$1,095
*Total Price	**$21,284**	**$23,380**
Target Price	$22,436	
Destination Charge	$550	
Avg. Tax & Fees	$1,286	
Total Target	**$24,272**	
Average Dealer Option Cost:	89%	
12 Month Price Increase:	None	

For 1999, the LS wagon has the new LS Premium Group available as an optional package and the Preferred Equipment Packages have been discontinued to simplify feature selection. Interior colors Saddle and Willow Green have been replaced with Prairie Tan and Deep Slate Blue. Exterior colors, Moonlight Blue, Light Saddle, Medium Willow Green and Black Satin, have been replaced with Light Prairie Tan, Dark Green Satin, Deep Navy Blue and Black.

Ownership Costs (Projected)

Cost Area	5 Year Cost	Rating
Depreciation	$13,350	◐
Financing ($404/month)	$4,823	
Insurance	$6,812	○
State Fees	$ 970	
Fuel (Hwy 25 City 18)	$4,199	●
Maintenance	$2,963	◐
Repairs	$855	◐

Warranty/Maintenance

Major Tune-Up	$318	●
Minor Tune-Up	$99	◐
Brake Service	$225	◐
Full Warranty	3yr/36k	◐
Drivetrain War.	3yr/36k	◐
Rust Warranty	3yr/36k	◐
Maintenance War.	N/A	
Roadside Assistance	3yr/36k	

Ownership Costs By Year (Projected)

$2,000 $4,000 $6,000 $8,000 $10,000 $12,000

■ 1999
■ 2000
■ 2001
□ 2002
□ 2003

Resale Value

1999	2000	2001	2002	2003
$20,581	$17,928	$15,579	$13,212	$10,922

Cumulative Costs

	1999	2000	2001	2002	2003
Annual	$7,665	6,393	6,239	6,869	6,806
Total	$7,665	14,058	20,297	27,166	33,972

Projected Costs (5yr)

Relative $33,882 | This Vehicle $33,972

Cost/Mile 48¢ | Cost/Mile 49¢

Ownership Cost Value

○ Average

It is very important for a new car buyer to distinguish between *price* and *cost*. The consumer who compares vehicles based only on purchase price is using a set of criteria that can be misleading. The true cost of owning a car is not the money you exchange for the "pink slip," the true cost is what you pay after you drive your new car off the dealer's lot. This cost includes depreciation, interest payments, insurance, state fees, fuel, maintenance, and repairs. Therefore, when you shop and compare new cars, use the purchase price to find the cars that fit your budget, and use the expected ownership costs to determine the car that is the best value.

Vehicle Description

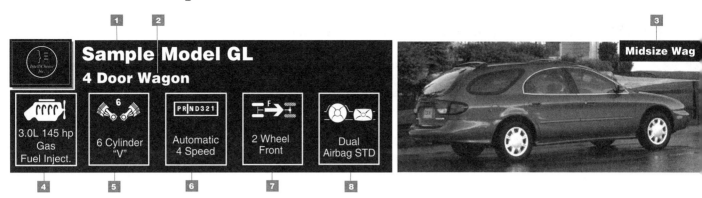

1 The brand and model name of the vehicle.

2 The number of doors and body style of the vehicle, defined as follows:

Convertible	An open-topped vehicle.
Coupe	Usually 2-door and bucket seat design, including a traditional hood and trunk.
Hatchback	(Also known as fastback or liftback) A sloping design from the rear window backward (often a very steep slope). The rear window and rear trunk lid are often one piece.
Sedan	(Also known as hardtop or notchback) Usually a 4-door design, including a traditional hood and trunk.
Wagon	Usually square rear end with rear cargo door that provides for expanded cargo area behind the seats.

3 The vehicle class, defined as follows:

Compact	Total interior volume between 100 and 109 cubic feet.
Large	Total interior volume greater than 120 cubic feet.
Large Wagon	Total interior volume greater than 160 cubic feet.
Near Luxury	Base model priced from $24,000 to $36,000, and not a "Base Sport" or "Sport."
Luxury	Priced over $36,000, and not a "Base Sport" or "Sport."
Midsize	Total interior volume between 110 and 119 cubic feet.
Midsize Wagon	Total interior volume between 130 and 159 cubic feet.
Minicompact	Total interior volume less than 85 cubic feet.
Base Sport	A performance oriented car differentiated from "Sport" by price and/or market position.
Sport	A performance oriented car.
Small Wagon	Total interior volume less than 130 cubic feet.
Subcompact	Total interior volume between 85 and 99 cubic feet.

4 The engine type/engine aspiration.

Gas	Standard piston powered engine.
Turbo	Turbo charged piston engine.
Diesel	Diesel design piston engine requiring diesel fuel.
Turbo Diesel	Turbo charged diesel design piston engine.
Fuel Injection	A pump/injector method of metering fuel.
Turbo Rotary	Turbo charged Wankel engine.

5 Cylinders

In-line	Cylinders are in a straight line.
Opposing	Cylinders are in two rows facing each other.
V-shaped	Cylinders are in two rows that form a V.

6 Transmission

Manual 5-speed, Manual 6-speed, Automatic 3-speed, Automatic 4-speed, Automatic 5-speed, Continuosly Variable Automatic.

7 Drive

Front Wheel Drive	Front wheels deliver power.
Rear Wheel Drive	Rear wheels deliver power.
4 WD On-Demand	All-wheel drive that the driver manually engages (a.k.a. Part-time) and disengages.
4 WD Full-Time (a.k.a. AWD)	All-wheel drive that automatically delivers power to wheels as needed.

8 Restraint system

Dual Airbags Std	Driver and passenger airbags are standard.
Dual Side Impact Airbags Std	Driver and passenger side impact airbags are standard. May be located in the front and/or rear of the vehicle.

Note: "Depowered" airbags are indicated in the chart where applicable.

Warranty and Maintenance

Warranty/Maintenance Info		
Major Tune-Up	$204	○
Minor Tune-Up	$74	○
Brake Service	$195	◉
Overall Warranty	3yr/50k	○
Drivetrain Warranty	5 yrs/60k	◉
Rust Warranty	3 yrs/50k	○
Maintenance Warranty	3 yrs/50k	●
Roadside Assistance	3yrs/36K	

NOTE: For all items in this section, the rating symbol compares the expected dollar expense for the specific vehicle against the average expected dollar expense for vehicles of the same class. Parts prices are manufacturer labeled, while labor rates are the national average for the brand.

1 The average cost of a major tune-up (minor tune-up, distributor cap and rotor replacement, fuel filter and PCV valve replacement, ignition cable set replacement, and ignition system inspection).

2 The average cost of a minor tune-up (replacing the air cleaner and spark plugs, inspecting the distributor cap, rotor, and ignition wires, checking compression, and adjusting the ignition timing and idle speed).

3 The average cost of brake service (replacing the pads on disk brakes, or shoes on drum brakes, on all four wheels, and checking, bleeding, and adjusting the brake system).

4 The overall warranty on the vehicle. The full warranty typically covers parts and labor for any factory-installed part that is defective in material or workmanship under normal use. This typically excludes tires, emission system parts (covered by a separate warranty), expendable maintenance items, glass breakage, and air conditioning lubricant.

5 Coverage on the engine, transaxle, transmission, and axle and drive components. For some manufacturers, this warranty applies to the original purchaser only. In other cases, the coverage changes if the car is sold.

6 Rust-through coverage. This applies to perforation only, generally meaning complete rust-through in a sheet metal panel. Surface corrosion resulting from stone chips or paint scratches are typically not covered.

7 Maintenance Warranty. With this coverage, all routine services and oil changes will be paid for when the work is performed at an authorized dealer (includes wiper blades, brake pads, light bulbs, wheel alignments, and other wear items).

8 Roadside Assistance. The length of time and mileage for which the manufacturer will provide a toll-free 800 number and free towing in the event of a breakdown. Many manufacturers provide additional services as part of their roadside assistance plan. To determine all the components of a roadside assistance plan for a particular vehicle, ask your dealer.

Purchase Price

Vehicle Item	Dealer Cost	List
Base Price	**$9,216**	**$10,320**
ABS Brakes	Std	Std
Auto 3 Speed Trans.	$417	$490
2.3 L Eng.	$561 **	$660
Air Conditioning	$574	$675
Power Steering	Std	Std
Cruise Control	$149	$175
Rear Defroster	N/A	N/A
AM/FM w/Cass.	Dlr	Dlr
Tilt Wheel	$106	$125
Power Windows	$242	$285
***Options Price**	*$417*	*$490*
***Total Price**	**$9,633**	**$10,810**
Target Price		$10,200
Destination Charge		$400
Avg. Tax & Fees		$679
Luxury/Gas Guzzler Tax		$1,000
Total Target $		**$12,279**
Average Dealer Option Cost:	91%	
12 Month Price Increase:	6%	

1 The-left hand column identifies specific vehicle items. Each line represents a different item, such as the Base Price and various options.

2 Dealer Cost is the dealer's factory invoiced cost for each item. It is the price paid by the dealer, not including any manufacturer's incentive or holdback.

3 **List price.** This is the manufacturer's suggested retail price for the particular vehicle item.

4 The feature list. The list includes the most popular major features/options in use today. If a feature does not have a price listed next to it, it will have one of the following designations:

Dlr	Dealer Installed Equipment
N/A	Not available on this model
N/C	No Charge
Pkg	Available as part of a package of options
Std	Standard equipment for this model
N/R	Pricing not available a time of printing
Grp	Available only with another option
—	Optional, pricing not available

5 Total Price is the sum of the base vehicle price plus the options price.

6 The Target Price is the price that you can reasonably expect to negotiate for the vehicle as configured; however, it is not necessarily the lowest price you may find. It includes an average acceptable mark-up for the dealer, which varies from model to model based on market conditions. Recent market conditions have been included in the Target Prices shown.

7 The destination charge is usually the same anywhere in the country, but may vary in some locations.

8 Forty seven out of fifty states have a sales tax on vehicles, which ranges from 1.5% to 7.25%. We have used an average tax rate of 5%, based on the price of the specific vehicle shown. Furthermore, most states have annual registration fees, which are often paid to the dealer at the time of delivery. An average figure is used here based on the price of the specific vehicle. You can refer to Figure 15 on page 98A to determine the applicable fees for your state.

9 **Luxury Tax:** The Federal Government imposes a tax on a vehicle that has a maximum loaded weight of 6,000 pounds or less, and is over $36,000. The buyer must pay 6% on the portion of a vehicle's price, including destination fee and gas guzzler tax, that exceeds $36,000. For example, the buyer of a vehicle with a selling price of $44,000 would have to pay a luxury tax of $480 — that is 6% of $8,000.

Gas Guzzler Tax: A Federal tax based on a vehicle's fuel economy. For each vehicle the government determines an "harmonic" average considering city and highway mileage figures. Here is the tax breakdown by fuel economy:

Miles Per Gallon	Tax
At Least 22.5	$0
At Least 21.5 but less than 22.5	$1,000
At Least 20.5 but less than 21.5	$1,300
At Least 19.5 but less than 20.5	$1,700
At Least 18.5 but less than 19.5	$2,100
At Least 17.5 but less than 18.5	$2,600
At Least 16.5 but less than 17.5	$3,000
At Least 15.5 but less than 16.5	$3,700
At Least 14.5 but less than 15.5	$4,500
At Least 13.5 but less than 14.5	$5,400
At Least 12.5 but less than 13.5	$6,400
Less than 12.5	$7,700

10 The Total Target is the grand total price that you can reasonably expect to pay for the vehicle as configured. It is the sum of the Target Price, plus all taxes, destination fees, and registration fees.

11 The Average Dealer Option Cost is the average percent of list price that the dealer pays for options. You can use this to estimate the dealer's cost for any option not specifically shown in the chart. For example, if the Average Dealer Option Cost shown is 91%, and the suggested retail price of leather seats is $400, then the dealer's cost for the leather seats is about .91 x $400, or $364. This is shown as "N/A" on vehicles that have no available manufacturer-installed options. This field is not shown if the vehicle has Luxury/Gas Guzzler tax.

12 The 12 Month Price Increase is the amount in price that this model has risen from its introduction list price in 1998 compared to its introduction list price in 1999. Prices have been adjusted to account for features that were options on the 1998 models, but are standard equipment on the 1999 model. For instance, if a passenger-side air bag was a $500 option in 1998, but is standard on the 1999 edition, then that $500 is added to the base price of the 1998 edition before calculating the price increase. Conversely, if the price of a vehicle decreased in 1999, it is shown as "None." On the other hand, if there was no comparable model offered in 1998, it is shown as N/A.

Purchase Price (Feature Shading)

Shading - All features shaded in the Vehicle Price section of the vehicle charts are included in the total price of the vehicle, as well as in all ownership cost calculations. In an effort to make true "apples-to-apples" comparisons, we attempt to include the same equipment on same class vehicles. (It would be unfair to evaluate one car with a manual transmission and another in the same class with an automatic transmission.

The choice of shaded features differs by class as listed below. Using the most recent available information, we have shaded the most popular features equipped in two-thirds or more of the vehicles sold in each class. For instance, in recent model years, over 90% of all midsize vehicles were equipped with cruise control, while less than 50% of subcompact models had this feature. Therefore, we shade cruise control for the midsize class, but not for subcompacts.

Optional engines are shaded and included in the analysis based on horsepower and engine size. For each vehicle class, we establish a "target" horsepower and engine size based on the average horsepower and size of engines on all models in the class weighted by the number of vehicles actually sold. Using the desirability methodology explained below, we strive to choose an engine that meets the target for the class.

Desirability and Price - Our quest for "apples-to-apples" comparisons is challenged by the way manufacturers equip vehicles. For example, an automatic transmission and a V-6 engine may be mutually exclusive in a vehicle that "ought" to have both selected. Or they may be purchased together, but only within a $4,000 option package.

For this reason, we assign each equipment item a numerical desirability rating, based on our assessment of how important each feature is. We look at every possible way that a vehicle can be equipped with some or all of the equipment we want to include, and we compute the total desirability and total cost of each scenario. We choose the lowest cost way to equip the vehicle with the highest desirability scenario.

In the first example above, the V-6 engine may have a desirability rating of five, while the automatic transmission has a rating of three. If everything else including price is equal, the scenario that includes the V-6 engine would have a desirability rating of two points higher than the automatic transmission scenario, so we would choose the V-6 scenario.

To compare scenarios with different total desirability ratings,we assign a value of $1,100 to each desirability point.

Using the same example, let's further assume that the scenario with the V-6 engine has a total desirability rating of 13, and a total cost of $4,000, and that the automatic transmission scenario has a total desirability rating of 11, and a cost of $2,800. Solely for the purpose of making a choice, we add two desirability points and $2,200 to the transmission scenario, raising its desirability to 13, and its cost to $5,000 ($2,800 plus $2,200). We still choose the V-6 scenario because its 13 desirability points cost $4,000, while the transmission scenario's 13 points cost $5,000.

Please note that we are not changing the actual desirability or the actual price of the transmission scenario. We are just using a price of $1,100 per desirability point to allow us to compare scenarios with different prices and desirability ratings. Were we to have chosen the transmission scenario, it would still cost $2,800, and still have a desirability rating of 11.

In some cases it is necessary to add options to the vehicle that do not appear in the charts. For example, there may be a case where an engine with a high desirability and low cost requires the purchase of a $100 engine heater. Even including the additional $100, the scenario is still the most desirable with the lowest cost. We therefore choose this scenario and reflect the $100 in the chart as "Other Options Cost" or as part of another chart item marked with a triple asterisk (***) to let you know there is additional equipment required. When we do this, we list the additional equipment in Appendix E.

Required Packages - Sometimes manufacturers require the buyer to purchase one of a selection of option packages. The vehicle cannot be purchased without one of these packages. More often than not, a "base" package (which is typically no cost) is available; however, the equipment offered in that package may not yield a high desirability vehicle. We choose the required package based on the desirability and price method described above.

In certain circumstances, a package may prove to be too costly to be selected in this manner. In those instances where, after careful analysis, we strongly feel that the desirability of the vehicle outweighs the potential impact on the price; we will insure that the higher level package is selected.

Base Sport
Sport

Anti-Lock Brakes
Air Conditioning
Power Steering
Cruise Control
AM/FM Stereo Cassette
Steering Wheel, Tilt
Power Windows

Minicompact
Subcompact

Air Conditioning
Power Steering
AM/FM Stereo Cassette
Rear Defroster

Near Luxury
Luxury

Anti-Lock Brakes
Automatic Transmission
Air Conditioning
Power Steering
Cruise Control
AM/FM Stereo Cassette
Steering Wheel, Tilt
Power Windows
Rear Defroster

Small Wagon

Automatic Transmission
Air Conditioning
Power Steering
AM/FM Stereo Cassette
Steering Wheel, Tilt
Rear Defroster

Midsize/Large
Midsize/Large Wagon

Anti-Lock Brakes
Automatic Transmission
Air Conditioning
Power Steering
Cruise Control
AM/FM Stereo Cassette
Steering Wheel, Tilt
Power Windows
Rear Defroster

Compact

Automatic Transmission
Air Conditioning
Power Steering
AM/FM Stereo Cassette
Steering Wheel, Tilt
Rear Defroster

Ownership Costs

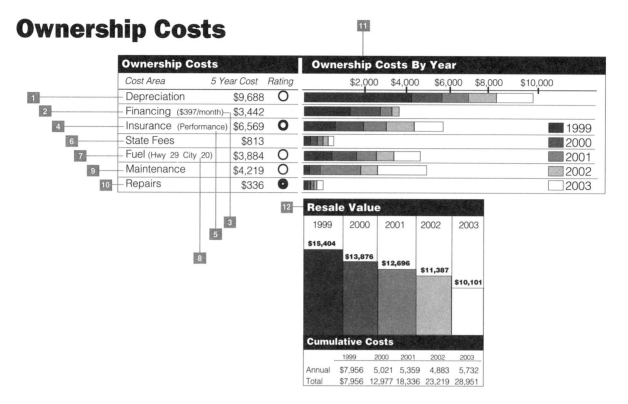

Ownership Costs		
Cost Area	5 Year Cost	Rating
Depreciation	$9,688	○
Financing ($397/month)	$3,442	
Insurance (Performance)	$6,569	○
State Fees	$813	
Fuel (Hwy 29 City 20)	$3,884	○
Maintenance	$4,219	○
Repairs	$336	◉

Ownership Costs By Year

$2,000 $4,000 $6,000 $8,000 $10,000

■ 1999
■ 2000
■ 2001
▨ 2002
□ 2003

Resale Value

1999	2000	2001	2002	2003
$15,404	$13,876	$12,696	$11,387	$10,101

Cumulative Costs

	1999	2000	2001	2002	2003
Annual	$7,956	5,021	5,359	4,883	5,732
Total	$7,956	12,977	18,336	23,219	28,951

NOTE: The rating symbols compare the expected figure for the specific vehicle against the average expected figure for vehicles of the same class and price range. The fuel rating symbol compares the vehicle against vehicles of the same class and similar transmission (automatic or manual).

1 The total cost of depreciation over five years. *(See page 91A)*

2 The total cost of financing over five full years. Financing cost includes the interest on a loan, but not the principal. *(See Page 93A)*

3 The monthly payment. *(See page 93A)*

4 The total cost of insurance over five years. *(See page 92A)*

5 The insurance rating for this vehicle. If a surcharge applies, the rating is shown as "Performance." The charge is also reflected in the premium. If a rating is estimated, it is followed by "[Est]."

6 The total cost of state fees over five years. *(See page 93A)*

7 The total cost of fuel over five years *(See page 93A)*. The rating symbol compares this vehicle equipped with the chosen engine and transmission against vehicles of the same class and similar transmission (automatic or manual).

8 The EPA reported miles per gallon figures for the specific vehicle. "Hwy" refers to highway driving. If a figure is estimated, it is indicated by "[Est]." If premium gasoline is required, it is indicated by "Prem."

9 The total cost of maintenance over five years. *(See page 94A)*

10 The total cost of repair over five years. *(See page 95A)*

11 **Ownership Costs By Year**. In this graph, each cost area is represented by a horizontal bar that shows the total of that cost over a five-year period. The bar is broken up into different shaded sections, with each section representing one year between 1999 and 2003. For example, look at the depreciation bar in the sample chart. The bar consists of five shaded segments that extend to $9,688. This is the total amount of depreciation for this vehicle over the next five years. However, if you want to be more specific, you can measure the distance of a shaded segment to find out the depreciation for a single year. For instance, note that the shade representing 2000 extends from about $4,200 to $5,800. The difference between these two figures, $1,600, is the amount of depreciation for 2000. (In some cost areas, most often "Repairs," it can be difficult to distinguish where one shade ends and the next begins. However, since shorter bars always mean less cost compared to longer ones, it is a positive sign when shaded segments are extremely close together.)

12 **Resale value.** The bar graph illustrates the vehicle's expected resale value over time. This graph allows you to determine what this vehicle is likely to be worth at annual intervals during the five-year period.

Why are there no rating symbols for "Financing" and "State Fees?"

Because these two costs are *mathematically derived* from the purchase price of the car, using our economic assumptions. If two cars have the exact same purchase price, they will have the exact same finance charge and state fees, so there is no point in comparing these areas. On the other hand, these two cars could have very different depreciation, insurance, fuel, repair, and maintenance costs.

Ownership Cost Rating: A Measurement of Value

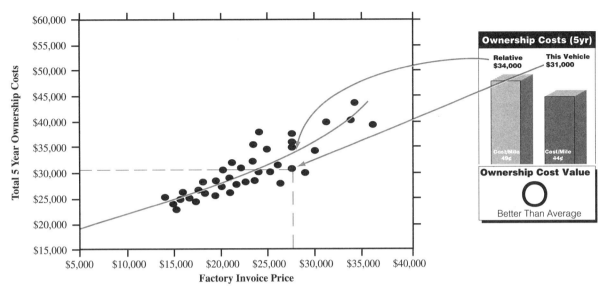

The above graph charts the invoice price and ownership cost of each vehicle in the represented class. The vehicles with better than average ownership cost/invoice price correlations are the best values, and are represented by the dots below the curve. Vehicles with worse than average or poor values, appear above the curve.

One way to view the graph is to draw a vertical line through any invoice price. You may see several dots that fall on this line — each of which is a vehicle with a similar invoice price. However, notice the difference in ownership costs represented by the vertical position of the dot. Two different vehicles with the same invoice price can have thousands of dollars difference in ownership costs. This is what separates "good values" from "poor values."

Throughout this book, we discuss the importance of ownership costs, and investigate each of the seven individual ownership cost areas. The Ownership Cost Rating is where the areas are all "added up," and we determine how good a value an individual model is.

In automobile economic terms, a "good value" is a vehicle whose cost to own and operate is less than expected. The lower the cost to own and operate compared to what is expected, the better the value.

But how do we know what is a vehicle's "expected cost"?

For each vehicle in the class, we plot the vehicle's invoice price against its total five-year cost to own and operate. Each dot on the above chart represents a specific vehicle. Generally, we find that as the invoice price increases, the cost to own and operate increases. This is why the dots on the graph tend to rise upward and to the right. This phenomenon also makes intuitive sense - as the invoice price rises, financing costs tend to rise, as do insurance, depreciation, taxes, and most other ownership costs.

This is an important concept. It's normal for ownership costs to rise as invoice price rises. Therefore, we can't just establish one "average" ownership cost number for each class, since vehicles in the class have different invoice prices. (This is why the "Relative" shown on each chart is different for vehicles in the same vehicle class.)

Using statistical techniques, we "connect the dots" to form a curve that defines, for this vehicle class, the relationship between invoice price and ownership costs. This curve is our "expected cost" curve. The curve defines, for any vehicle in the class, the five year ownership cost that we would expect to see at each possible invoice price.

If every vehicle in the class were an average value, then all the dots would fall exactly on the curve. However, it's rare that any dot is exactly on the curve. Some dots are a little higher or lower, and some are a lot higher or lower. The dots that are a little lower are better than average values, while the dots that are a lot lower are excellent values (A dot that is a lot lower than the curve has ownership costs much lower than expected for a vehicle of its invoice price). Conversely, a dot a little higher than the curve is a poorer than average value, while a dot that is much higher than the curve is a poor value.

Value is a relative term, not an absolute term. It is performing better than the logical expectation.

For a non-car example, look at Noah, age five years, who is 43" tall. Is he tall? Well, not in an absolute sense. All the adults around him are taller, naturally. But, when his height is plotted against other children his age, he's taller than most. So he is tall in a relative sense. He's not tall, but he's tall for his age.

So is a Mercedes Benz E320 expensive to own and operate? Certainly in an absolute sense. Most other vehicles cost less. But, when its cost to own and operate is plotted against vehicles with comparable invoice prices, the Mercedes costs less. So the E320 is not expensive to own and operate - it is a good value. The Mercedes does not have low ownership costs, but it has low ownership costs for its invoice price.

Figure 13

OWNERSHIP COSTS (ASSUMPTIONS)

Ownership Period	5 years
Annual Inflation	2.3%
Annual Mileage	14,000 miles
Dealer Cost/Manufacturer Suggested List Price/Destination Fees	As reported by manufacturers. Actual dealer cost may be somewhat lower than listed dealer cost due to manufacturer allowances.
Target Purchase Price	Based on dealer cost of an individual model with options shown and shaded. Varies by individual model based on market conditions. Target price is always more than dealer cost, usually below list price, but sometimes higher.
Luxury/Gas Guzzler taxes:	Luxury tax rate at 6% for every dollar over $36,000 that went into affect on January 1, 1999. For Gas Guzzler tax amounts see page 86A.
State Sales/Use tax/ State Registration fees	5% sales tax is used as a nationwide average; 1% initial state registration fee based on MSRP and destination charge. Additionally, there is a one-time $13 fee. Refer to Figure 15 on page 98A to determine the exact figure for your state.
Resale Value	There is a large range in used car prices, ranging from a low "wholesale auction" price, to a high "private party" transaction price. Prices here are assumed to be closer to the private party price. Each individual vehicle will tend to follow a pattern set by earlier models, by brand, by model group, by vehicle class, by vehicle price range, and by area of the country.
Insurance	Principal operator is under age 65; lives in a suburban/urban community; all drivers have more than six years experience with no chargeable accidents; vehicle is for personal use, with the following coverages (subject to inflation): Collision $500 Deductible Comprehensive $500 Deductible Personal liability $100,000/$300,000 Medical $25,000 Property $50,000 Uninsured driver $25,000/$50,000
Finance Costs	20% down payment on a 60 month loan. Annual interest rate of 8.92%.
State Fees	1% of MSRP and destination in the first year, reduced by .1% in each successive year, plus $13 one-time fee. Refer to Figure 15 on page 98A to determine the exact figure for your state.
Fuel	U.S. Government EPA mileage figures. Mileage is 60% highway driving, 40% city. Fuel cost per gallon is $1.02 for unleaded regular, $1.12 for unleaded mid-grade, $1.21 for premium, and $1.05 for diesel (subject to inflation).
Repairs	Cost of a $0 deductible extended service contract that will pay for repairs for 5 years or at least 70,000 miles. Figures used are actual prices from nationally available service contract providers.
Maintenance	Services performed generally at manufacturer's suggested intervals where stated. Other services done at selected intervals. (See page 94A) Cost per service is based upon industry-standard service times and national labor rate averages by brand. Parts prices are based on manufacturer's suggested list price where available (subject to inflation).

OWNERSHIP COST DERIVATION

The following pages describe the methods used, as well as the basic assumptions made for each ownership cost area shown in the vehicle charts.

Depreciation

The vehicle charts show, for each new vehicle, the projected annual and cumulative amount of depreciation over five years. A rating symbol gives you an easy way to compare one car's depreciation to all other cars of a similar class and price. Additionally, the charts have a resale section that shows the expected resale value of the car each year over the next five years.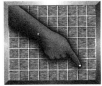

Depreciation and resale value are two measures of the same element. A car's purchase price less depreciation equals a car's resale value. By the same token, a car's purchase price less its resale value equals its depreciation.

We project the future resale value of a car on the basis of several factors. We assume that the vehicle will be purchased at the Total Target Price, which is the total "out-the-door" price that the buyer can expect to pay. This price includes state and local taxes, destination fees, and luxury car and/or gas guzzler taxes if applicable. We then factor in the historical depreciation for that specific car model. We also consider depreciation trends by brand, by model group, vehicle category, and price. For example, to forecast the expected resale value of a 1999 Nissan Maxima, we consider the resale value history of previous Maximas, of other Nissan models, of midsize class cars, and of other cars in the same price range. When actual history is lacking for the exact model, we rely more on these other areas. To this statistical method, we add our own economic, industry, and model-specific expectations to determine the expected resale value for that particular vehicle.

Depreciation is determined by a car's resale value, and can vary somewhat depending on where you're selling the car, who you're selling it to, optional equipment, and the condition and mileage of the car. We assume values for the Western United States (other regions of the country may be a few to several percentage points lower), and that your car is sold to a private buyer. Furthermore, in our resale value/depreciation calculations, we include the cost of optional equipment (the shaded options in the vehicle charts). Additionally, we assume that the car is in good, but not mint, condition, and that you've driven it approximately 14,000 miles per year.

Depreciation is determined by a car's resale value, and can vary somewhat depending on where you're selling the car, who you're selling it to, optional equipment, and the condition and mileage of the car.

It's almost always true that an older car will cost less to insure than a newer car of the same model. However, over time, inflation makes the insurance premium increase faster than the age of the car makes it decrease, so the overall cost goes up.

Insurance

The insurance premiums used in the charts are derived from information provided by the Insurance Service Office and from the insurance industry. There are, however, a few variables that need to be considered when determining the premium. The  premium is based on the engine/transmission combination that is selected in the ownership cost analysis. (See page 85A to find out how the engine and transmission are selected.)

The charts show, based on the assumed coverages and deductibles, how much you can expect to spend on insurance over five years. The cost figures let you easily compare the cost of insuring different cars in the same class and price range.

Many personal, geographic, and political factors determine your exact insurance premium. We assume that you're under age 65. You have a good driving record, drive about 14,000 miles per year, and have no inexperienced drivers in your household.

Insurance rates vary tremendously depending on where you live. We assume that you live in a suburban area in a state with average insurance rates. You can refer to Figure 13 on page 94A to adjust the insurance figures to match your state's figures.

You may be wondering why the annual insurance premium shown in the vehicle charts goes up every year, especially since you may know that it generally costs less to insure a used car than a new one. It's almost always true that an older car will cost less to insure than a newer car of the same model. However, over time, inflation makes the premium increase faster than the age of the car makes it decrease, so the overall cost goes up.

Of all car costs, insurance is the most variable. Your actual rates will probably differ somewhat from those found in *The Complete Car Cost Guide*. However, when comparing cars, the difference between our projections and your actual rates will be consistent from car to car. If you need more precise information, we recommend that you call a local insurance agent to determine the actual insurance costs for each automobile that you consider.

Finance Costs

The vehicle charts show the total interest charges you can expect to pay for the car over five years. They also show your monthly car payment if you purchase the car at the "target purchase price."

There is no rating symbol for finance costs. This is because these costs do not depend on the car you buy, but are related to the purchase price. If two different cars are purchased for the same amount, they will have the same finance cost.

Our financial projections are based on the latest economic information. We assume that you will put down 20% immediately and take a 60 month, 8.92% loan.

·If you're considering a loan with terms other than these, you can use Appendix I to determine your monthly payment.

Even if you pay cash for your car instead of borrowing money to pay for it, you should factor a finance cost into the cost of ownership. The reason for this is that if you didn't invest the money in the car, it could be in the bank earning interest.

State Fees

The charts show the amount you can expect to pay in state taxes and registration fees over five years. Our state fee calcula-tions assume initial state fees of 1% of the current MSRP and destination  charge of the vehicle, reduced by .1% in each successive year.

Registration fees and taxes vary by state. You can use Figure 15 on page 98A to determine the exact fee structure for your state.

Fuel

The vehicle charts show EPA (U.S. Environmental Protection Agency) fuel mileage figures for both "highway" and "city" driv-ing. If automatic transmission is standard or is a shaded option, the fuel figures are for automatic transmission;  otherwise, the figures are based on manual transmission. The charts also show the amount you can expect to pay in fuel expenses over a five-year period. A rating symbol gives you an easy way to compare this vehicle's fuel ex-pense against all other vehicles of a similar class and price.

To determine actual fuel costs, we assume that vehicles will perform closer to the "highway" mileage figure. We assume that fuel will cost $1.02 per gallon for unleaded regular, $1.12 for un-leaded mid-grade, $1.21 for unleaded premium, and $1.05 for diesel. Additionally, we assume that fuel costs will increase by the rate of inflation and that you will drive 14,000 miles per year.

Maintenance

The vehicle charts show the amount you can expect to pay for routine maintenance expenses over five years. A rating symbol gives you an easy way to compare a particular car's maintenance costs against all other  cars of a similar class and price. The charts also show average costs to perform the standard maintenance services of a major tune-up, a minor tune-up, and a standard brake service.

We include the following services in determining our maintenance cost figures:

- Oil changes
- Major tune-ups
- Minor tune-ups
- Basic brake service
- Basic clutch service
- Basic automatic transmission service
- Alignments
- Front bearing service
- Cooling system maintenance
- Shock absorber service
- Muffler replacement
- Hoses and belts (including timing belt)
- Fluids and filters
- Tires
- Batteries
- Headlamp replacement
- Regular inspections
- EGR Valve (s)

We assume that services take place at an authorized dealer location, using standard flat labor times, an average hourly labor rate for each individual brand, and manufacturer's suggested retail prices for parts, where available. You can often get better prices than these. (We use them for consistency from car to car.)

We generally factor in a manufacturer suggested mileage or time interval to perform a particular service. If the manufacturer does not specify, we apply our own intervals for particular services. We assume that most trips are longer than five miles ("normal" driving conditions).

Repairs

The vehicle charts project the amount you can expect to pay for repair expenses over five years or at least 70,000 miles. A rating symbol helps you easily compare one car's expected repair costs against all  other cars in the same class. The charts also show manufacturers' warranties for full coverage, drivetrain coverage, rust coverage, maintenance coverage, and roadside assistance coverage. Repair costs in the charts take into account all of these manufacturer warranties.

To determine the cost projection, we take advantage of service contract pricing. Conceptually, a service contract is an insurance policy protecting against repair costs. In exchange for your "premium," the service contract provider agrees to pay for any needed repairs. (See page 24A for a more detailed description of service contracts.) To provide this service profitably, the service contract provider has to make sure that, on average, the actual cost of repairs on the vehicle is less than the premium price. Service contract providers take great pains in pricing their products low enough to stay competitive, yet high enough to make a profit.

Therefore, we can expect that the service contract price is an excellent estimate of likely repair costs (in fact, their price is somewhat higher than the likely repair costs, allowing for a reasonable profit).

Whether or not you purchase a service contract, you can use the service contract price to estimate the cost of repairs.

We utilize pricing from several separate service contract providers to determine the repair costs shown in this book. The plans used from all providers are for five years or at least 70,000 miles, and are $0 deductible plans, meaning you pay nothing during the plan period other than the initial premium. Although the repair figure shown is based on service contract prices, the figure is <u>less</u> than what you would probably pay for a service contract. It is more reflective of what you will actually pay for repairs.

It's important to separate hype from reality when considering how a car's expected repair incidence will influence your decision on which car to buy.

At one time, there were vast differences in relative reliability among vehicles. Today, most any new vehicle you purchase is likely to be highly reliable. Other than minor state fees, the expected cost of repairs in the first five years will be less than any other cost associated with your new car! That's right, and it's true even for the vehicles with the highest expected repair cost. The cost of depreciation, insurance, interest, fuel, and maintenance will all be considerably higher than the cost of repairs.

Therefore, you are likely to jump to the wrong economic conclusion if you purchase a car because you heard it's "very reliable," or avoid a car because you heard it's a "lemon."

Figure 13

INSURANCE FACTORS

	Rank	Index
Alabama	32	.83
Alaska	9	1.20
Arizona	16	1.07
Arkansas	38	.77
California	8	1.22
Colorado	13	1.10
Connecticutt	5	1.37
Deleware	12	1.11
District	6	1.37
Florida	18	1.03
Georgia	25	.91
Hawaii	2	1.48
Idaho	47	.70
Illinois	27	.89
Indiana	35	.80
Iowa	50	.64
Kansas	46	.72
Kentucky	30	.84
Lousiana	10	1.18
Maine	40	.76
Maryland	17	1.04
Massachusetts	4	1.38
Michigan	14	1.08
Minnesota	26	.90
Misissippi	28	.88
Missouri	34	.82
Montana	42	.75
Nebraska	48	.68
Nevada	11	1.17
New Hampshire	22	.97
New Jersey	1	1.50
New Mexico	19	1.00
New York	7	1.35
North Carolina	45	.72
North Dakota	51	.61
Ohio	43	.75
Oklahoma	33	.83
Oregon	29	.87
Pennsylvania	20	.99
Rhode Island	3	1.42
South Carolina	24	.94
South Dakota	49	.66
Tennessee	37	.79
Texas	15	1.08
Utah	31	.83
Vermont	36	.79
Virginia	39	.77
Washington	21	.98
West Virginia	23	.95
Wisconsin	41	.76
Wyoming	44	.73

NATIONAL AVERAGE 1

Insurance Adjustment Table

To calculate the total five-year insurance cost for each vehicle listed in the "Vehicle Charts", we use a national average. To be more precise, the Insurance Factors table (Figure 13) will allow you to adjust the total insurance cost listed in the vehicle charts for the state in which you live. To make this adjustment, simply find your state on the chart and then multiply its Index by the total insurance cost shown in the vehicle charts. The figures in the left column (Rank) shows the highest insurance rate (1-New Jersey) to the lowest (51-North Dakota).

Remember that insurance rates can vary greatly, even within a state. For an exact insurance rate, you should contact an insurance agent. We recommend that you get quotes from several different agents before you actually buy your insurance.

*Source: National Association of Insurance Commissioners, 1995.

Mileage Adjustment Table

To calculate the total five-year fuel cost for each vehicle listed in the charts, we assume that the vehicle is driven 14,000 miles per year, and that the price of gasoline may range from $1.02 to $1.21 per gallon, depending on the type of fuel. If your annual mileage differs from our assumptions, or if you expect to pay more (or less) for gas, then this table (Figure 14) allows you to adjust the total fuel cost for any vehicle in which you are interested. To make this adjustment, first find your annual mileage in the left-hand column. Then, find the column that corresponds with the price you pay for a gallon of gasoline. Finally, multiply the number (factor) shown in this column by the total fuel cost shown in the vehicle charts.

Use the mileage table below if your vehicle uses unleaded regular fuel.

Figure 14

ANNUAL MILEAGE	FUEL PRICE PER GALLON									
	$1.00	$1.05	$1.10	$1.15	$1.20	$1.25	$1.30	$1.40	$1.50	$1.60
4,000	0.24	0.25	0.26	0.27	0.28	0.30	0.31	0.33	0.35	0.38
6,000	0.35	0.37	0.39	0.41	0.43	0.44	0.46	0.50	0.53	0.57
8,000	0.47	0.50	0.52	0.54	0.57	0.59	0.61	0.66	0.71	0.76
10,000	0.59	0.62	0.65	0.68	0.71	0.74	0.77	0.83	0.89	0.94
12,000	0.71	0.74	0.78	0.81	0.85	0.89	0.92	0.99	1.06	1.13
14,000	0.83	0.87	0.91	0.95	0.99	1.03	1.07	1.16	1.24	1.32
16,000	0.94	0.99	1.04	1.09	1.13	1.18	1.23	1.32	1.42	1.51
18,000	1.06	1.12	1.17	1.22	1.28	1.33	1.38	1.49	1.59	1.70
20,000	1.18	1.24	1.30	1.36	1.42	1.48	1.53	1.65	1.77	1.89
22,000	1.30	1.36	1.43	1.49	1.56	1.62	1.69	1.82	1.95	2.08
24,000	1.42	1.49	1.56	1.63	1.70	1.77	1.84	1.98	2.13	2.27
26,000	1.53	1.61	1.69	1.77	1.84	1.92	2.00	2.15	2.30	2.46
28,000	1.65	1.74	1.82	1.90	1.98	2.07	2.15	2.31	2.48	2.64
30,000	1.77	1.86	1.95	2.04	2.13	2.21	2.30	2.48	2.66	2.83
35,000	2.07	2.17	2.27	2.38	2.48	2.58	2.69	2.89	3.10	3.31
40,000	2.36	2.48	2.60	2.72	2.83	2.95	3.07	3.31	3.54	3.78
45,000	2.66	2.79	2.92	3.05	3.19	3.32	3.45	3.72	3.98	4.25
50,000	2.95	3.10	3.25	3.39	3.54	3.69	3.84	4.13	4.43	4.72
55,000	3.25	3.41	3.57	3.73	3.90	4.06	4.22	4.55	4.87	5.19
60,000	3.54	3.72	3.90	4.07	4.25	4.43	4.60	4.96	5.31	5.67
65,000	3.84	4.03	4.22	4.41	4.60	4.80	4.99	5.37	5.76	6.14
70,000	4.13	4.34	4.55	4.75	4.96	5.17	5.37	5.79	6.20	6.61
75,000	4.43	4.65	4.87	5.09	5.31	5.53	5.76	6.20	6.64	7.08
80,000	4.72	4.96	5.19	5.43	5.67	5.90	6.14	6.61	7.08	7.56
85,000	5.02	5.27	5.52	5.77	6.02	6.27	6.52	7.02	7.53	8.03
90,000	5.31	5.58	5.84	6.11	6.38	6.64	6.91	7.44	7.97	8.50
95,000	5.61	5.89	6.17	6.45	6.73	7.01	7.29	7.85	8.41	8.97
100,000	5.90	6.20	6.49	6.79	7.08	7.38	7.67	8.26	8.85	9.45

Figure 15 State Fees, Regulations, and Insurance Information

| State | Taxes | | | Registration Fees | | | Insurance | | |
	Sales/Use Tax Rate	Based on	Additional Local Tax	Fixed Fee	By Value[1]	By Weight[2]	Competitive	No Fault	Minimum Financial Responsibility
Alabama	2.00%	Net of Trade-in	Yes	$15.00	$0.00	$0.00	Somewhat	No	20/40/10
Alaska	0.00%		Yes	$5.00	$0.00	$34.00	Somewhat	No	50/100/25
Arizona	5.00%	Net of Trade-in	Yes	$4.00	$0.00	$0.00	Yes	No	15/30/10
Arkansas	4.63%	Net of Trade-in	Yes	$5.00	$0.00	$17.00	Yes	No	25/50/15
California	7.25%	Full Value	Yes	$22.00	$300.00	$0.00	Somewhat	No	15/30/05
Colorado	3.00%	Net of Trade-in	Yes	$6.50	$0.00	$11.00	Yes	Yes	25/50/15
Connecticut	6.00%	Net of Trade-in	No	$25.00	$0.00	$0.00	Somewhat	No	20/40/10
DC	6.00%	Full Value	No	$20.00	$0.00	$65.00	Somewhat	No	10/20/05
Delaware	2.75%	Net of Trade-in	No	$15.00	$0.00	$0.00	Somewhat	Yes	15/30/10
Florida	6.00%	Net of Trade-in	Yes	$29.95	$0.00	$34.60	Yes	Yes	10/20/10
Georgia	4.00%	Net of Trade-in	Yes	$18.00	$0.00	$0.00	Somewhat	No	10/20/05
Hawaii	4.00%	Net of Trade-in	Yes	$20.00	$0.00	$22.50	Somewhat	Yes	25/25/10
Idaho	5.00%	Net of Trade-in	No	$8.00	$0.00	$0.00	Yes	No	25/50/15
Illinois	6.25%	Net of Trade-in	Yes	$13.00	$0.00	$0.00	Yes	No	20/40/15
Indiana	5.00%	Net of Trade-in	No	$5.00	$0.00	$12.75	Somewhat	No	25/50/10
Iowa	5.00%	Net of Trade-in	No	$15.00	$150.00	$12.00	Somewhat	No	20/40/15
Kansas	4.90%	Net of Trade-in	Yes	$7.00	$0.00	$27.25	Somewhat	Yes	25/50/10
Kentucky	5.40%	Full Value	No	$6.00	$0.00	$0.00	Yes	Yes	25/50/10
Louisiana	4.00%	Net of Trade-in	Yes	$24.00	$0.00	$15.00	Somewhat	No	10/20/10
Maine	6.00%	Net of Trade-in	No	$15.00	$0.00	$23.00	Yes	No	20/40/10
Maryland	5.00%	Full Value	No	$20.00	$0.00	$35.00	Somewhat	No	20/40/10
Massachusetts	5.00%	Net of Trade-in	No	$50.00	$0.00	$0.00	No	Yes	20/40/05
Michigan	6.00%	Full Value	No	$11.00	$0.00	$0.00	Somewhat	Yes	20/40/10
Minnesota	6.50%	Net of Trade-in	No	$2.00	$192.50	$0.00	Yes	Yes	30/60/10
Mississippi	7.00%	Net of Trade-in	Yes	$4.00	$0.00	$0.00	Somewhat	No	10/20/05
Missouri	4.23%	Net of Trade-in	Yes	$8.50	$0.00	$30.93[†]	Yes	No	25/50/10
Montana	1.50%	Full Value	Yes	$5.00	$0.00	$15.25	Yes	No	25/50/10
Nebraska	5.00%	Net of Trade-in	Yes	$10.00	$0.00	$0.00	Somewhat	No	25/50/25
Nevada	6.50%	Unique Trade Credit	Yes	$20.00	$0.00	$33.00	Somewhat	No	15/30/10
New Hampshire	0.00%		No	$20.00	$0.00	$19.20	Somewhat	No	25/50/25
New Jersey	6.00%	Net of Trade-in	No	$20.00	$0.00	$62.50	Somewhat	Yes	15/30/05
New Mexico	3.00%	Net of Trade-in	No	$4.50	$0.00	$30.00	Somewhat	No	25/50/10
New York	4.00%	Net of Trade-in	Yes	$5.00	$0.00	$25.80	Somewhat	Yes	25/50/10
North Carolina	3.00%	Net of Trade-in	Yes	$35.00	$0.00	$0.00	Somewhat	No	25/50/15
North Dakota	5.00%	Net of Trade-in	No	$5.00	$0.00	$50.00	Somewhat	Yes	25/50/25
Ohio	5.00%	Net of Trade-in	Yes	$5.00	$0.00	$22.25	Yes	No	12.5/25/7.5
Oklahoma	3.25%	Full Value	Yes	$11.00	$192.50	$0.00	Somewhat	No	10/20/10
Oregon	0.00%		No	$10.00	$0.00	$31.50	Yes	No	25/50/10
Pennsylvania	6.00%	Net of Trade-in	Yes	$22.50	$0.00	$36.00	Somewhat	No	15/30/05
Rhode Island	7.00%	Net of Trade-in	No	$25.00	$0.00	$30.00	Yes	No	25/50/10
South Carolina	5.00%	Net of Trade-in	Yes	$5.00	$0.00	$12.00	Somewhat	No	15/30/10
South Dakota	3.00%	Net of Trade-in	No	$5.00	$0.00	$30.00	Yes	No	25/50/25
Tennessee	6.00%	Net of Trade-in	Yes	$8.00	$0.00	$23.00	Somewhat	No	15/30/10
Texas	6.25%	Net of Trade-in	No	$13.00	$0.00	$58.80	Somewhat	No	20/40/15
Utah	5.875%	Net of Trade-in	Yes	$6.00	$0.00	$24.50	Yes	Yes	15/30/05
Vermont	6.00%	Net of Trade-in	No	$10.00	$0.00	$43.00	Yes	No	20/40/10
Virginia	3.00%	Full Value	Yes	$10.00	$0.00	$26.50	Somewhat	No	25/50/20
Washington	7.90%	Net of Trade-in	Yes	$5.25	$330.00	$30.60	Somewhat	No	25/50/10
West Virginia	5.00%	Net of Trade-in	No	$5.00	$0.00	$30.00	Somewhat	No	20/40/10
Wisconsin	5.00%	Net of Trade-in	Yes	$21.00	$0.00	$45.00	Yes	No	25/50/10
Wyoming	4.00%	Net of Trade-in	Yes	$6.00	$0.00	$15.00	No	No	25/50/20

[1] Fee based on a $15,000 vehicle. [†] Fee based on an average taxable horsepower of 31.
[2] Fee based on 3,000 pound vehicle weight.

Best Overall Values

Subcompact/Minicompact

Under $14,000

Honda Civic CX/DX/HX Series
2 & 4 Door Coupes, Sedans Hatchbacks

Saturn SC1
2 and 3 Door Coupe

2 Door Coupe Model Shown

Pontiac Sunfire SE
4 Door Sedan

Over $14,000

Honda Civic LX/EX Series
2 & 4 Door Coupes & Sedans

Saturn SC2
2 and 3 Door Coupe

Toyota Celica GT
2 Door Liftback

This appendix shows the best economic values for vehicles in the above class and price ranges. The best value does not mean the lowest cost to own, but rather the best relationship between cost to own and the price to buy (see page 89A for more details). Note that we've only pictured one member of a model family per class and price range even though multiple vehicles in that family may also be a Best Overall Value of the Year. All BOVY winners are designated in the vehicle charts.
Convertibles and diesel equipped models have been excluded.

BEST OVERALL VALUES OF THE YEAR

Compact

Under $15,000

Saturn SL Series
4 Door Sedans

LE Model Shown

Toyota Corolla CE and VE
4 Door Sedans

Mazda Protégé DX
4 Door Sedan

Over $15,000

Audi A4 1.8T/1.8T Quattro
4 Door Sedans

Infiniti G20/G20t
4 Door Sedans

Nissan Altima SE
4 Door Sedan

This appendix shows the best economic values for vehicles in the above class and price ranges. The best value does not mean the lowest cost to own, but rather the best relationship between cost to own and the price to buy (see page 89A for more details). Note that we've only pictured one member of a model family per class and price range even though multiple vehicles in that family may also be a Best Overall Value of the Year. All BOVY winners are designated in the vehicle charts. Convertibles and diesel equipped models have been excluded.

Midsize

Under $19,500

Honda Accord DX/LX
2 & 4 Door Coupe & Sedans

Toyota Camry CE
4 Door Sedan

Pontiac Gran Prix SE
4 Door Sedan

Over $19,500

Honda Accord EX
4 Door Sedan

Nissan Maxima GLE
4 Door Sedan

Pontiac Grand Prix GT
4 Door Sedan

This appendix shows the best economic values for vehicles in the above class and price ranges. The best value does not mean the lowest cost to own, but rather the best relationship between cost to own and the price to buy (see page 89A for more details). Note that we've only pictured one member of a model family per class and price range even though multiple vehicles in that family may also be a Best Overall Value of the Year. All BOVY winners are designated in the vehicle charts.
Convertibles and diesel equipped models have been excluded.

Large

Toyota Avalon XLS
4 Door Sedan

Pontiac Bonneville SSE
4 Door Sedan

LS Model Shown

Mercury Grand Marquis GS
4 Door Sedan

This appendix shows the best economic values for vehicles in the above class and price ranges. The best value does not mean the lowest cost to own, but rather the best relationship between cost to own and the price to buy (see page 89A for more details). Note that we've only pictured one member of a model family per class and price range even though multiple vehicles in that family may also be a Best Overall Value of the Year. All BOVY winners are designated in the vehicle charts.
Convertibles and diesel equipped models have been excluded.

Near Luxury

BMW 323i
4 Door Sedan

Mercedes-Benz C230 Kompressor
4 Door Sedan

Mercedes-Benz C280
4 Door Sedan

Lexus ES 300
4 Door Sedan

This appendix shows the best economic values for vehicles in the above class and price ranges. The best value does not mean the lowest cost to own, but rather the best relationship between cost to own and the price to buy (see page 89A for more details). Note that we've only pictured one member of a model family per class and price range even though multiple vehicles in that family may also be a Best Overall Value of the Year. All BOVY winners are designated in the vehicle charts.
Convertibles and diesel equipped models have been excluded.

BEST OVERALL VALUES OF THE YEAR

Luxury

Mercedes-Benz E320
Wagon & AWD Sedan

Mercedes-Benz S320 Standard Wheelbase
4 Door Sedan

BMW 528i
4 Door Sedan

This appendix shows the best economic values for vehicles in the above class and price ranges. The best value does not mean the lowest cost to own, but rather the best relationship between cost to own and the price to buy (see page 89A for more details). Note that we've only pictured one member of a model family per class and price range even though multiple vehicles in that family may also be a Best Overall Value of the Year. All BOVY winners are designated in the vehicle charts. Convertibles and diesel equipped models have been excluded.

Base Sport

Chevrolet Camaro
2 Door Convertible

Mitsubishi Eclipse Spyder GS
2 Door Convertible

BMW Z3 2.3 Roadster
2 Door Convertible

Pontiac Firebird
2 Door Convertible

This appendix shows the best economic values in vehicles in the above class and price ranges. The best value does not mean the lowest cost to own, but rather the best relationship between cost to own and the price to buy (see page 89A for more details). Note that we've only pictured one member of a model family per class and price range even though multiple vehicles in that family may also be a Best Overall Value of the Year. All BOVY winners are designated in the vehicle charts.
Diesel equipped models have been excluded.

Sport

BMW M3
2 Door Convertible

BMW Z3 M Roadster
2 Door Convertible

Chevrolet Corvette
2 Door Coupe

This appendix shows the best economic values in vehicles in the above class and price ranges. The best value does not mean the lowest cost to own, but rather the best relationship between cost to own and the price to buy (see page 89A for more details). Note that we've only pictured one member of a model family per class and price range even though multiple vehicles in that family may also be a Best Overall Value of the Year. All BOVY winners are designated in the vehicle charts.
Diesel equipped models have been excluded.

Small Wagon

Saturn SW Series
4 Door Wagons

Audi A4 1.8T Avant Quattro
4 Door Wagon

This appendix shows the best economic values for vehicles in the above class and price ranges. The best value does not mean the lowest cost to own, but rather the best relationship between cost to own and the price to buy (see page 89A for more details). Note that we've only pictured one member of a model family per class and price range even though multiple vehicles in that family may also be a Best Overall Value of the Year. All BOVY winners are designated in the vehicle charts.
Diesel equipped models have been excluded.

Midsize/Large Wagon

V6 Model Shown

Volkswagen Passat GLS
4 Door Wagon

Subaru Legacy Outback AWD
4 Door Wagon

This appendix shows the best economic values for vehicles in the above class and price ranges. The best value does not mean the lowest cost to own, but rather the best relationship between cost to own and the price to buy (see page 89A for more details). Note that we've only pictured one member of a model family per class and price range even though multiple vehicles in that family may also be a Best Overall Value of the Year. All BOVY winners are designated in the vehicle charts.
Diesel equipped models have been excluded.

Best Car Value Under $20,000

Honda Civic DX
4 Door Sedan

This appendix shows the best economic values for vehicles in the above class and price ranges. The best value does not mean the lowest cost to own, but rather the best relationship between cost to own and the price to buy (see page 89A for more details). Note that we've only pictured one member of a model family per class and price range even though multiple vehicles in that family may also be a Best Overall Value of the Year. All BOVY winners are designated in the vehicle charts. Diesel equipped models have been excluded.

BEST OVERALL VALUES OF THE YEAR

BEST OVERALL VALUES OF THE YEAR

Best Car Value Over $20,000

Mercedes-Benz E320
Wagon

This appendix shows the best economic values for vehicles in the above class and price ranges. The best value does not mean the lowest cost to own, but rather the best relationship between cost to own and the price to buy (see page 89A for more details). Note that we've only pictured one member of a model family per class and price range even though multiple vehicles in that family may also be a Best Overall Value of the Year. All BOVY winners are designated in the vehicle charts. Diesel equipped models have been excluded.

SECTION FIVE
Vehicle Charts

Acura 2.3CL
2 Door Coupe

 2.3L 150 hp Gas Fuel Inject.

 4 Cylinder In-Line

 Manual 5 Speed

 2 Wheel Front

 Dual Airbags Std

Purchase Price

Car Item	Dealer Cost	List
Base Price	**$20,873**	**$23,100**
Anti-Lock Brakes	Std	Std
Automatic 4 Speed	$723	$800
Optional Engine	N/A	N/A
Auto Climate Control	Std	Std
Power Steering	Std	Std
Cruise Control	Std	Std
Power Windows	Std	Std
AM/FM Stereo CD	Std	Std
Steering Wheel, Tilt	Std	Std
Rear Defroster	Std	Std
*Options Price	$0	$0
*Total Price	**$20,873**	**$23,100**
Target Price	$22,288	
Destination Charge	$455	
Avg. Tax & Fees	$1,272	
Total Target $	**$24,015**	
Average Dealer Option Cost:	**90%**	
12 Month Price Increase:	4%	

The 2.3CL coupe features new standard equipment for this year, including the leather-trimmed interior that was previously only available with the optional Premium Package. Other new standard features for this model include a HomeLink universal transmitter and a trunk-mounted cargo net. The CL series was the first Acura model to be designed and engineered entirely in the United States. This vehicle is now manufactured exclusively in East Liberty, Ohio.

Ownership Costs (Projected)

Cost Area	5 Year Cost	Rating
Depreciation		⊖
Financing ($398/month)	$4,672	
Insurance	$8,313	○
State Fees	$955	
Fuel (Hwy 31 City 24)	$2,692	○
Maintenance	$3,225	◉
Repairs	$580	○

Warranty/Maintenance Info

Major Tune-Up (60K mile int.)	$299	◉
Minor Tune-Up (30K mile int.)	$104	◉
Brake Service	$306	●
Overall Warranty	4 yr/50k	○
Drivetrain Warranty	4 yr/50k	○
Rust Warranty	5 yr/unlim. mi	○
Maintenance Warranty	N/A	
Roadside Assistance	4 yr/50k	

Ownership Costs By Year (Projected)

$2,000 $4,000 $6,000 $8,000 $10,000

Insufficient Depreciation Information

■ 1999
■ 2000
■ 2001
□ 2002
□ 2003

Resale Value

Insufficient Information

Projected Costs (5yr)

Insufficient Information

Cumulative Costs

	1999	2000	2001	2002	2003
Annual	*Insufficient Information*				
Total	*Insufficient Information*				

Ownership Cost Value

⊖

Insufficient Information

Acura 3.0CL
2 Door Coupe

Subcompact

 3.0L 200 hp Gas Fuel Inject.

 6 Cylinder "V"

 Automatic 4 Speed

 2 Wheel Front

Dual Airbags Std

Purchase Price

Car Item	Dealer Cost	List
Base Price	**$23,629**	**$26,150**
Anti-Lock Brakes	Std	Std
Manual Transmission	N/A	N/A
Optional Engine	N/A	N/A
Auto Climate Control	Std	Std
Power Steering	Std	Std
Cruise Control	Std	Std
Power Windows	Std	Std
AM/FM Stereo CD	Std	Std
Steering Wheel, Tilt	Std	Std
Rear Defroster	Std	Std
*Options Price	$0	$0
*Total Price	**$23,629**	**$26,150**
Target Price	$25,307	
Destination Charge	$455	
Avg. Tax & Fees	$1,438	
Total Target $	**$27,200**	
Average Dealer Option Cost:	**N/A**	
12 Month Price Increase:	3%	

The 3.0CL coupe features upgrades such as a standard Acura/Bose six speaker sound system, featuring an in-dash CD player and a 100 watt amplifier. Additional standard upgrades include heated front seats and heated outside rearview mirrors. Seating enhancements include an eight-way power driver's seat that includes power recline and walk-in features with auto-position and fast-forward. The engine powering the 3.0CL is the first Acura V6 to be manufactured in the United States.

Ownership Costs (Projected)

Cost Area	5 Year Cost	Rating
Depreciation		⊖
Financing ($451/month)	$5,292	
Insurance	$8,865	○
State Fees	$1,077	
Fuel (Hwy 28 City 20)	$3,097	●
Maintenance	$3,381	◉
Repairs	$580	○

Warranty/Maintenance Info

Major Tune-Up (60K mile int.)	$247	○
Minor Tune-Up (30K mile int.)	$131	●
Brake Service	$306	●
Overall Warranty	4 yr/50k	○
Drivetrain Warranty	4 yr/50k	○
Rust Warranty	5 yr/unlim. mi	○
Maintenance Warranty	N/A	
Roadside Assistance	4 yr/50k	

Ownership Costs By Year (Projected)

$2,000 $4,000 $6,000 $8,000 $10,000

Insufficient Depreciation Information

■ 1999
■ 2000
■ 2001
□ 2002
□ 2003

Resale Value

Insufficient Information

Projected Costs (5yr)

Insufficient Information

Cumulative Costs

	1999	2000	2001	2002	2003
Annual	*Insufficient Information*				
Total	*Insufficient Information*				

Ownership Cost Value

⊖

Insufficient Information

 Poor
 Worse Than Average
 Average
 Better Than Average
 Excellent
 Insufficient Information

Refer to *Section 3: Annotated Vehicle Charts* for an explanation of these charts.

1

Acura Integra LS
2 Door Coupe

Subcompact

1.8L 140 hp Gas Fuel Inject.

4 Cylinder In-Line

1 3 5 / 2 4 R Manual 5 Speed

2 Wheel Front

Dual Airbags Std

GS-R Model Shown

Purchase Price

Car Item	Dealer Cost	List
Base Price	**$17,155**	**$19,200**
Anti-Lock Brakes	Std	Std
Automatic 4 Speed	$715	$800
Optional Engine	N/A	N/A
Air Conditioning	Std	Std
Power Steering	Std	Std
Cruise Control	Std	Std
Power Windows	Std	Std
AM/FM Stereo Cass/CD	Std	Std
Steering Wheel, Tilt	Std	Std
Rear Defroster	Std	Std
*Options Price	$0	$0
*Total Price	**$17,155**	**$19,200**
Target Price	$18,090	
Destination Charge	$455	
Avg. Tax & Fees	$1,045	
Total Target $	**$19,590**	
Average Dealer Option Cost:	**89%**	
12 Month Price Increase:	None	

For 1999, the Integra LS coupe sports new standard equipment such as 15 inch alloy wheels and a leather-wrapped steering wheel and shift knob. In addition, a power moonroof is also standard. Both the Type R and the RS have been dropped from the Integra lineup, making the LS the new base model. The suspension has been refined this year in order to improve handling. Additionally, two new exterior colors are now being offered on the LS: Clover Green and Taffeta White.

Ownership Costs (Projected)

Cost Area	5 Year Cost	Rating
Depreciation	$7,519	◔
Financing ($325/month)	$3,811	
Insurance	$10,182	●
State Fees	$800	
Fuel (Hwy 32 City 25)	$2,597	◎
Maintenance	$3,104	◎
Repairs	$551	◎

Warranty/Maintenance Info

Major Tune-Up (60K mile int.)	$318	●
Minor Tune-Up (30K mile int.)	$130	●
Brake Service	$286	◉
Overall Warranty	4 yr/50k	◎
Drivetrain Warranty	4 yr/50k	◎
Rust Warranty	5 yr/unlim. mi	◎
Maintenance Warranty	N/A	
Roadside Assistance	4 yr/50k	

Ownership Costs By Year (Projected)

$2,000 $4,000 $6,000 $8,000 $10,000 $12,000

- ■ 1999
- ■ 2000
- ■ 2001
- ▨ 2002
- □ 2003

Resale Value

1999	2000	2001	2002	2003
$17,886	$16,348	$14,968	$13,539	$12,071

Cumulative Costs

	1999	2000	2001	2002	2003
Annual	$5,677	$5,323	$5,165	$5,683	$6,716
Total	$5,677	$11,000	$16,165	$21,848	$28,564

Projected Costs (5yr)

Relative $28,976	This Car $28,564
Cost/Mile 41¢	Cost/Mile 41¢

Ownership Cost Value

◯ Average

Acura Integra GS
2 Door Coupe

Subcompact

1.8L 140 hp Gas Fuel Inject.

4 Cylinder In-Line

1 3 5 / 2 4 R Manual 5 Speed

2 Wheel Front

Dual Airbags Std

GS-R Model Shown

Purchase Price

Car Item	Dealer Cost	List
Base Price	**$18,629**	**$20,850**
Anti-Lock Brakes	Std	Std
Automatic 4 Speed	$715	$800
Optional Engine	N/A	N/A
Air Conditioning	Std	Std
Power Steering	Std	Std
Cruise Control	Std	Std
Power Windows	Std	Std
AM/FM Stereo Cass/CD	Std	Std
Steering Wheel, Tilt	Std	Std
Rear Defroster	Std	Std
*Options Price	$0	$0
*Total Price	**$18,629**	**$20,850**
Target Price	$19,671	
Destination Charge	$455	
Avg. Tax & Fees	$1,132	
Total Target $	**$21,258**	
Average Dealer Option Cost:	**89%**	
12 Month Price Increase:	None	

The Integra GS coupe upgrades the base LS model by featuring both a rear spoiler and leather-trimmed seats as standard equipment. Additionally, the GS also features an improved stabilizer bar equipped with ball joints instead of the rubber bushings used on the LS. Clover Green is now also being made available on the GS as a new exterior color. All manual-equipped Integra models also feature a short-stroke shift linkage system, a design often compared to that in the Acura NSX.

Ownership Costs (Projected)

Cost Area	5 Year Cost	Rating
Depreciation	$8,977	◎
Financing ($352/month)	$4,135	
Insurance	$10,589	●
State Fees	$865	
Fuel (Hwy 32 City 25)	$2,597	◎
Maintenance	$3,104	◎
Repairs	$551	◎

Warranty/Maintenance Info

Major Tune-Up (60K mile int.)	$318	●
Minor Tune-Up (30K mile int.)	$130	●
Brake Service	$286	◉
Overall Warranty	4 yr/50k	◎
Drivetrain Warranty	4 yr/50k	◎
Rust Warranty	5 yr/unlim. mi	◎
Maintenance Warranty	N/A	
Roadside Assistance	4 yr/50k	

Ownership Costs By Year (Projected)

$2,000 $4,000 $6,000 $8,000 $10,000 $12,000

- ■ 1999
- ■ 2000
- ■ 2001
- ▨ 2002
- □ 2003

Resale Value

1999	2000	2001	2002	2003
$18,171	$16,609	$15,206	$13,762	$12,281

Cumulative Costs

	1999	2000	2001	2002	2003
Annual	$7,264	$5,531	$5,350	$5,834	$6,839
Total	$7,264	$12,795	$18,145	$23,979	$30,818

Projected Costs (5yr)

Relative $30,638	This Car $30,818
Cost/Mile 44¢	Cost/Mile 44¢

Ownership Cost Value

◎ Average

2

* Includes shaded options
** Other purchase requirements apply
*** Price includes other options

● Poor   ◉ Worse Than Average   ◎ Average   ◔ Better Than Average   ◯ Excellent   ⊖ Insufficient Information

Refer to *Section 3: Annotated Vehicle Charts* for an explanation of these charts.

Acura Integra GS-R
2 Door Coupe

Base Sport

| 1.8L 170 hp Gas Fuel Inject. | 4 Cylinder In-Line | Manual 5 Speed | 2 Wheel Front | Dual Airbags Std |

Purchase Price

Car Item	Dealer Cost	List
Base Price	**$19,746**	**$22,100**
Anti-Lock Brakes	Std	Std
Automatic Transmission	N/A	N/A
Optional Engine	N/A	N/A
Air Conditioning	Std	Std
Power Steering	Std	Std
Cruise Control	Std	Std
Power Windows	Std	Std
AM/FM Stereo Cass/CD	Std	Std
Steering Wheel, Tilt	Std	Std
Rear Defroster	Std	Std
*Options Price	$0	$0
*Total Price	**$19,746**	**$22,100**
Target Price	$20,872	
Destination Charge	$455	
Avg. Tax & Fees	$1,199	
Total Target $	**$22,526**	
Average Dealer Option Cost:	**N/A**	
12 Month Price Increase:	4%	

For 1999, the Integra GS-R coupe adds a leather-trimmed interior to its list of standard features. A new exterior color, Taffeta White, has also been made available on this model. Winner of last year's Best Overall Value Award in its class, this model sports the same VTEC system first introduced in the Acura NSX. This system, working in conjunction with a dual-stage intake manifold, allows both high-end horsepower and low-end torque to be achieved without compromising either.

Ownership Costs (Projected)

Cost Area	5 Year Cost	Rating
Depreciation	$9,805	◐
Financing ($373/month)	$4,382	
Insurance (Performance)	$13,195	●
State Fees	$915	
Fuel (Hwy 31 City 25 -Prem.)	$3,136	○
Maintenance	$3,104	◐
Repairs	$551	○

Warranty/Maintenance Info

Major Tune-Up (60K mile int.)	$318	◐
Minor Tune-Up (30K mile int.)	$130	○
Brake Service	$286	◐
Overall Warranty	4 yr/50k	○
Drivetrain Warranty	4 yr/50k	○
Rust Warranty	5 yr/unlim. mi	○
Maintenance Warranty	N/A	
Roadside Assistance	4 yr/50k	

Ownership Costs By Year (Projected)

$2,000 $4,000 $6,000 $8,000 $10,000 $12,000 $14,000

■ 1999
■ 2000
■ 2001
□ 2002
□ 2003

Resale Value

1999	2000	2001	2002	2003
$20,123	$18,123	$16,362	$14,596	$12,721

Cumulative Costs

	1999	2000	2001	2002	2003
Annual	$7,277	$6,663	$6,398	$6,841	$7,910
Total	$7,277	$13,940	$20,338	$27,179	$35,089

Projected Costs (5yr)

Relative $34,242	This Car $35,089
Cost/Mile 49¢	Cost/Mile 50¢

Ownership Cost Value

◉ Worse Than Average

Acura Integra LS
4 Door Sedan

Subcompact

| 1.8L 140 hp Gas Fuel Inject. | 4 Cylinder In-Line | Manual 5 Speed | 2 Wheel Front | Dual Airbags Std |

Purchase Price

Car Item	Dealer Cost	List
Base Price	**$17,870**	**$20,000**
Anti-Lock Brakes	Std	Std
Automatic 4 Speed	$715	$800
Optional Engine	N/A	N/A
Air Conditioning	Std	Std
Power Steering	Std	Std
Cruise Control	Std	Std
Power Windows	Std	Std
AM/FM Stereo Cass/CD	Std	Std
Steering Wheel, Tilt	Std	Std
Rear Defroster	Std	Std
*Options Price	$0	$0
*Total Price	**$17,870**	**$20,000**
Target Price	$18,856	
Destination Charge	$455	
Avg. Tax & Fees	$1,087	
Total Target $	**$20,398**	
Average Dealer Option Cost:	89%	
12 Month Price Increase:	None	

The Integra LS becomes the base model sedan this year as a result of the RS being dropped from the Integra lineup. New standard equipment not previously featured on this model includes larger diameter 15 inch alloy wheels and both a leather-wrapped steering wheel and shift knob. The sedans come equipped with a diversity antenna system, compared to a power antenna on the coupes. Additionally, two new exterior colors are now being offered on the LS: Clover Green and Taffeta White.

Ownership Costs (Projected)

Cost Area	5 Year Cost	Rating
Depreciation	$8,485	○
Financing ($338/month)	$3,968	
Insurance	$9,775	●
State Fees	$832	
Fuel (Hwy 32 City 25)	$2,597	○
Maintenance	$3,068	○
Repairs	$551	○

Warranty/Maintenance Info

Major Tune-Up (60K mile int.)	$318	●
Minor Tune-Up (30K mile int.)	$130	●
Brake Service	$286	◉
Overall Warranty	4 yr/50k	○
Drivetrain Warranty	4 yr/50k	○
Rust Warranty	5 yr/unlim. mi	○
Maintenance Warranty	N/A	
Roadside Assistance	4 yr/50k	

Ownership Costs By Year (Projected)

$2,000 $4,000 $6,000 $8,000 $10,000

■ 1999
■ 2000
■ 2001
□ 2002
□ 2003

Resale Value

1999	2000	2001	2002	2003
$17,879	$16,293	$14,870	$13,408	$11,913

Cumulative Costs

	1999	2000	2001	2002	2003
Annual	$6,476	$5,342	$5,166	$5,658	$6,634
Total	$6,476	$11,818	$16,984	$22,642	$29,276

Projected Costs (5yr)

Relative $29,779	This Car $29,276
Cost/Mile 43¢	Cost/Mile 42¢

Ownership Cost Value

○ Better Than Average

---

* Includes shaded options

** Other purchase requirements apply

*** Price includes other options

 Poor   Worse Than Average   Average   Better Than Average   Excellent   Insufficient Information

Refer to *Section 3: Annotated Vehicle Charts* for an explanation of these charts.

3

Acura Integra GS
4 Door Sedan

| 1.8L 140 hp Gas Fuel Inject. | 4 Cylinder In-Line | Manual 5 Speed | 2 Wheel Front | Dual Airbags Std |

LS Model Shown

Purchase Price

Car Item	Dealer Cost	List
Base Price	**$19,121**	**$21,400**
Anti-Lock Brakes	Std	Std
Automatic 4 Speed	$715	$800
Optional Engine	N/A	N/A
Air Conditioning	Std	Std
Power Steering	Std	Std
Cruise Control	Std	Std
Power Windows	Std	Std
AM/FM Stereo Cass/CD	Std	Std
Steering Wheel, Tilt	Std	Std
Rear Defroster	Std	Std
*Options Price	$0	$0
*Total Price	**$19,121**	**$21,400**
Target Price	$20,199	
Destination Charge	$455	
Avg. Tax & Fees	$1,161	
Total Target $	**$21,815**	
Average Dealer Option Cost:	**89%**	
12 Month Price Increase:	None	

The Integra GS sedan upgrades the LS by featuring leather-trimmed seats as standard equipment. Clover Green is now also being made available this year on the GS as a new exterior color. Features not available on the coupe that come standard on all sedans include shoulder belt height adjustment and a remote trunk release. This third-generation Integra often finds its strongest market among young well-educated people and can be typically found in the parking lots of high-tech companies.

Ownership Costs (Projected)

Cost Area	5 Year Cost	Rating
Depreciation	$9,683	◯
Financing ($362/month)	$4,244	
Insurance	$10,182	●
State Fees	$888	
Fuel (Hwy 32 City 25)	$2,597	◯
Maintenance	$3,068	◯
Repairs	$551	◯

Warranty/Maintenance Info

Major Tune-Up (60K mile int.)	$318	◑
Minor Tune-Up (30K mile int.)	$130	◑
Brake Service	$286	◑
Overall Warranty	4 yr/50k	◯
Drivetrain Warranty	4 yr/50k	◯
Rust Warranty	5 yr/unlim. mi	◯
Maintenance Warranty	N/A	
Roadside Assistance	4 yr/50k	

Ownership Costs By Year (Projected)

$2,000 $4,000 $6,000 $8,000 $10,000 $12,000

■ 1999
■ 2000
■ 2001
▨ 2002
□ 2003

Resale Value

1999	2000	2001	2002	2003
$18,371	$16,713	$15,221	$13,690	$12,132

Cumulative Costs

	1999	2000	2001	2002	2003
Annual	$7,586	$5,583	$5,384	$5,856	$6,804
Total	$7,586	$13,169	$18,553	$24,409	$31,213

Projected Costs (5yr)

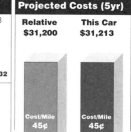

Relative	This Car
$31,200	$31,213
Cost/Mile 45¢	Cost/Mile 45¢

Ownership Cost Value

◯ Average

Acura Integra GS-R
4 Door Sedan

Subcompact

| 1.8L 170 hp Gas Fuel Inject. | 4 Cylinder In-Line | Manual 5 Speed | 2 Wheel Front | Dual Airbags Std |

LS Model Shown

Purchase Price

Car Item	Dealer Cost	List
Base Price	**$20,014**	**$22,400**
Anti-Lock Brakes	Std	Std
Automatic Transmission	N/A	N/A
Optional Engine	N/A	N/A
Air Conditioning	Std	Std
Power Steering	Std	Std
Cruise Control	Std	Std
Power Windows	Std	Std
AM/FM Stereo Cass/CD	Std	Std
Steering Wheel, Tilt	Std	Std
Rear Defroster	Std	Std
*Options Price	$0	$0
*Total Price	**$20,014**	**$22,400**
Target Price	$21,160	
Destination Charge	$455	
Avg. Tax & Fees	$1,215	
Total Target $	**$22,830**	
Average Dealer Option Cost:	**N/A**	
12 Month Price Increase:	4%	

The Integra GS-R sedan adds a leather-trimmed interior to its list of standard features for this year. A new exterior color, Taffeta White, has also been made available on this model. The GS-R sedan is the only trim line that includes the interior upgrade of a woodgrain console. The transmission of the GS-R differs from that used in both the LS and GS models in several key areas; closer ratios and different gear synchronizers are designed to handle the larger engine of the GS-R.

Ownership Costs (Projected)

Cost Area	5 Year Cost	Rating
Depreciation	$10,240	◯
Financing ($378/month)	$4,441	
Insurance	$10,589	●
State Fees	$928	
Fuel (Hwy 31 City 25 -Prem.)	$3,136	◯
Maintenance	$3,068	◯
Repairs	$551	◯

Warranty/Maintenance Info

Major Tune-Up (60K mile int.)	$318	◑
Minor Tune-Up (30K mile int.)	$130	◑
Brake Service	$286	◑
Overall Warranty	4 yr/50k	◯
Drivetrain Warranty	4 yr/50k	◯
Rust Warranty	5 yr/unlim. mi	◯
Maintenance Warranty	N/A	
Roadside Assistance	4 yr/50k	

Ownership Costs By Year (Projected)

$2,000 $4,000 $6,000 $8,000 $10,000 $12,000

■ 1999
■ 2000
■ 2001
▨ 2002
□ 2003

Resale Value

1999	2000	2001	2002	2003
$19,947	$17,996	$16,218	$14,414	$12,590

Cumulative Costs

	1999	2000	2001	2002	2003
Annual	$7,283	$6,123	$5,909	$6,355	$7,283
Total	$7,283	$13,406	$19,315	$25,670	$32,953

Projected Costs (5yr)

Relative	This Car
$32,226	$32,953
Cost/Mile 46¢	Cost/Mile 47¢

Ownership Cost Value

◯ Average

4

● Poor ◑ Worse Than Average ◯ Average ◯ Better Than Average ◯ Excellent ⊖ Insufficient Information

Refer to *Section 3: Annotated Vehicle Charts* for an explanation of these charts.

Acura NSX-T
2 Door Coupe

 3.2L 290 hp Gas Fuel Inject. | 6 Cylinder "V" | Manual 6 Speed | 2 Wheel Rear | Dual Airbags Std

Purchase Price

Car Item	Dealer Cost	List
Base Price	**$76,850**	**$88,000**
Anti-Lock Brakes	Std	Std
Automatic 4 Speed	N/C	N/C
3.0L 252 hp Gas	N/C	**N/C
Auto Climate Control	Std	Std
Power Steering	Std	Std
Cruise Control	Std	Std
Power Windows	Std	Std
AM/FM Stereo Cassette	Std	Std
Steering Wheel, Tilt	Std	Std
Rear Defroster	Std	Std
*Options Price	$0	$0
*Total Price	**$76,850**	**$88,000**
Target Price	$83,212	
Destination Charge	$745	
Avg. Tax & Fees	$4,678	
Luxury Tax	$2,877	
Total Target $	**$91,512**	
12 Month Price Increase:	None	

For 1999, the NSX-T has no major changes. Less than 500 will be imported in the U.S. for the 1999 model year. The NSX-T is a mid-engine two seat aluminum-bodied sports car with a one-piece removable roof panel. The roof panel is also made of aluminum, for light weight. The chassis also features all-aluminum construction to reduce weight. For security, an anti-theft vehicle immobilizer system disables the vehicle in the event of tampering, even with the top removed.

Ownership Costs (Projected)

Cost Area	5 Year Cost	Rating
Depreciation	$40,466	◍
Financing ($1,517/month)	$17,803	
Insurance (Performance)	$18,204	◉
State Fees	$3,562	
Fuel (Hwy 24 City 17 -Prem.)	$4,303	◉
Maintenance	$4,270	◉
Repairs	$1,435	◍

Warranty/Maintenance Info

Major Tune-Up (60K mile int.)	$317	◉
Minor Tune-Up (30K mile int.)	$176	◉
Brake Service	$446	●
Overall Warranty	4 yr/50k	◍
Drivetrain Warranty	4 yr/50k	◍
Rust Warranty	5 yr/unlim. mi	◍
Maintenance Warranty	N/A	
Roadside Assistance	4 yr/50k	

Ownership Costs By Year (Projected)

$5 $10 $15 $20 $25 $30 $35 $40 $45 (x1,000)

■ 1999
■ 2000
▨ 2001
▨ 2002
□ 2003

Resale Value

1999	2000	2001	2002	2003
$75,968	$69,270	$63,023	$56,983	$51,046

Projected Costs (5yr)

Relative $89,930	This Car $90,044
Cost/Mile $1.28	Cost/Mile $1.29

Cumulative Costs

	1999	2000	2001	2002	2003
Annual	$26,823	$16,884	$15,538	$15,344	$15,455
Total	$26,823	$43,707	$59,245	$74,589	$90,044

Ownership Cost Value

◯ Average

Acura NSX
2 Door Coupe

Sport

 3.2L 290 hp Gas Fuel Inject. | 6 Cylinder "V" | Manual 6 Speed | 2 Wheel Rear | Dual Airbags Std

Purchase Price

Car Item	Dealer Cost	List
Base Price	**$73,357**	**$84,000**
Anti-Lock Brakes	Std	Std
Automatic 4 Speed	N/C	N/C
3.0L 252 hp Gas	N/C	**N/C
Auto Climate Control	Std	Std
Power Steering	Std	Std
Cruise Control	Std	Std
Power Windows	Std	Std
AM/FM Stereo Cassette	Std	Std
Steering Wheel, Tilt	Std	Std
Rear Defroster	Std	Std
*Options Price	$0	$0
*Total Price	**$73,357**	**$84,000**
Target Price	$79,430	
Destination Charge	$745	
Avg. Tax & Fees	$4,468	
Luxury Tax	$2,651	
Total Target $	**$87,294**	
12 Month Price Increase:	None	

For 1999, the NSX is a carryover from last year. The aluminum-bodied NSX is painstakingly handcrafted in a special manufacturing facility in Japan. Less than 500 will be imported in the U.S. for the 1999 model year. The only factory option is the SportShift automatic transmission. The SportShift transmission features a unique steering column-mounted electronic shifter. Standard NSX amenities include leather seats, an automatic climate control system and power windows and locks.

Ownership Costs (Projected)

Cost Area	5 Year Cost	Rating
Depreciation	$39,494	◉
Financing ($1,447/month)	$16,982	
Insurance (Performance)	$18,204	◉
State Fees	$3,402	
Fuel (Hwy 24 City 17 -Prem.)	$4,303	◉
Maintenance	$4,270	●
Repairs	$1,435	◍

Warranty/Maintenance Info

Major Tune-Up (60K mile int.)	$317	◉
Minor Tune-Up (30K mile int.)	$176	◉
Brake Service	$446	●
Overall Warranty	4 yr/50k	◍
Drivetrain Warranty	4 yr/50k	◍
Rust Warranty	5 yr/unlim. mi	◍
Maintenance Warranty	N/A	
Roadside Assistance	4 yr/50k	

Ownership Costs By Year (Projected)

$5 $10 $15 $20 $25 $30 $35 $40 (x1,000)

■ 1999
■ 2000
▨ 2001
▨ 2002
□ 2003

Resale Value

1999	2000	2001	2002	2003
$71,561	$65,186	$59,241	$53,480	$47,800

Projected Costs (5yr)

Relative $88,276	This Car $88,091
Cost/Mile $1.26	Cost/Mile $1.26

Cumulative Costs

	1999	2000	2001	2002	2003
Annual	$26,694	$16,298	$15,034	$14,930	$15,135
Total	$26,694	$42,992	$58,026	$72,956	$88,091

Ownership Cost Value

◯ Average

---

* Includes shaded options

** Other purchase requirements apply

*** Price includes other options

 Poor Worse Than Average Average Better Than Average ◯ Excellent ⊖ Insufficient Information

Refer to *Section 3: Annotated Vehicle Charts* for an explanation of these charts.

5

Acura 3.5RL
4 Door Sedan

Luxury

3.5L 210 hp Gas Fuel Inject.	6 Cylinder "V"	PRND321 Automatic 4 Speed	2 Wheel Front	Dual Front/Side Airbags Std

Purchase Price

Car Item	Dealer Cost	List
Base Price	**$36,579**	**$41,900**
Anti-Lock Brakes	Std	Std
Manual Transmission	N/A	N/A
Optional Engine	N/A	N/A
Auto Climate Control	Std	Std
Power Steering	Std	Std
Cruise Control	Std	Std
Power Windows	Std	Std
AM/FM Stereo Cassette	Std	Std
St Whl, Tilt/Scope/Mem	Std	Std
Rear Defroster	Std	Std
*Options Price	$0	$0
*Total Price	**$36,579**	**$41,900**
Target Price	$39,418	
Destination Charge	$455	
Avg. Tax & Fees	$2,231	
Luxury Tax	$232	
Total Target $	**$42,336**	
12 Month Price Increase:	2%	

The 3.5RL features new standard equipment for this year including a six disc CD changer, an automatic day/night rearview mirror and a HomeLink universal transmitter. The major safety enhancement on the RL is the addition of driver and front passenger side airbags. The only factory-installed option is the satellite-linked Acura Navigation System, which pinpoints the vehicle's precise location and provides both audio and visual cues to direct the driver to their desired destination.

Ownership Costs (Projected)

Cost Area	5 Year Cost	Rating
Depreciation	$19,790	◐
Financing ($702/month)	$8,236	
Insurance	$9,135	◯
State Fees	$1,707	
Fuel (Hwy 24 City 18 -Prem.)	$4,187	◐
Maintenance	$3,192	◉
Repairs	$675	◯

Warranty/Maintenance Info

Major Tune-Up (60K mile int.)	$241	◯
Minor Tune-Up (30K mile int.)	$142	◯
Brake Service	$286	◯
Overall Warranty	4 yr/50k	◯
Drivetrain Warranty	4 yr/50k	◯
Rust Warranty	5 yr/unlim. mi	◯
Maintenance Warranty	N/A	
Roadside Assistance	4 yr/50k	

Ownership Costs By Year (Projected)

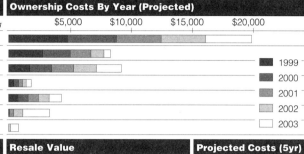

	$5,000	$10,000	$15,000	$20,000

1999
2000
2001
2002
2003

Resale Value

1999	2000	2001	2002	2003
$37,505	$33,463	$29,774	$26,161	$22,546

Cumulative Costs

	1999	2000	2001	2002	2003
Annual	$10,638	$9,359	$8,718	$8,642	$9,565
Total	$10,638	$19,997	$28,715	$37,357	$46,922

Projected Costs (5yr)

Relative	This Car
$48,225	$46,922
Cost/Mile 69¢	Cost/Mile 67¢

Ownership Cost Value

◯

Better Than Average

Acura 3.2TL
4 Door Sedan

Near Luxury

3.2L 225 hp Gas Fuel Inject.	6 Cylinder "V"	PRND321 Automatic 4 Speed	2 Wheel Front	Dual Airbags Std

Purchase Price

Car Item	Dealer Cost	List
Base Price	**$24,973**	**$27,950**
Anti-Lock Brakes	Std	Std
Manual Transmission	N/A	N/A
Optional Engine	N/A	N/A
Auto Climate Control	Std	Std
Power Steering	Std	Std
Cruise Control	Std	Std
Power Windows	Std	Std
AM/FM Stereo Cass/CD	Std	Std
Steering Wheel, Tilt	Std	Std
Rear Defroster	Std	Std
*Options Price	$0	$0
*Total Price	**$24,973**	**$27,950**
Target Price	$26,523	
Destination Charge	$455	
Avg. Tax & Fees	$1,511	
Total Target $	**$28,489**	
Average Dealer Option Cost:	**89%**	
12 Month Price Increase:	None	

The 3.2TL arrives this year with several new features. The most notable is an optional navigation system. This system includes a six inch LCD screen with picture-to-picture capability via satellite, and displays a map with detailed navigation instructions. Along with reduced noise and vibration, the 1999 TL features standard traction control and an air filtration system that traps dust and pollen. Other features include a remote keyless entry and antilock brakes.

Ownership Costs (Projected)

Cost Area	5 Year Cost	Rating
Depreciation	$13,662	◉
Financing ($472/month)	$5,543	
Insurance (Performance)	$10,267	◉
State Fees	$1,149	
Fuel (Hwy 27 City 19 -Prem.)	$3,838	◯
Maintenance	$3,159	◯
Repairs	$585	◯

Warranty/Maintenance Info

Major Tune-Up (60K mile int.)	$238	◯
Minor Tune-Up (30K mile int.)	$135	◯
Brake Service	$287	◉
Overall Warranty	4 yr/50k	◯
Drivetrain Warranty	4 yr/50k	◯
Rust Warranty	5 yr/unlim. mi	◯
Maintenance Warranty	N/A	
Roadside Assistance	4 yr/50k	

Ownership Costs By Year (Projected)

	$2,000	$4,000	$6,000	$8,000	$10,000	$12,000	$14,000

1999
2000
2001
2002
2003

Resale Value

1999	2000	2001	2002	2003
$26,824	$23,593	$20,667	$17,773	$14,827

Cumulative Costs

	1999	2000	2001	2002	2003
Annual	$6,567	$7,833	$7,429	$7,728	$8,646
Total	$6,567	$14,400	$21,829	$29,557	$38,203

Projected Costs (5yr)

Relative	This Car
$37,347	$38,203
Cost/Mile 53¢	Cost/Mile 55¢

Ownership Cost Value

◉

Worse Than Average

6

*Includes shaded options

** Other purchase requirements apply

*** Price includes other options

● Poor	◉ Worse Than Average	◐ Average	◯ Better Than Average	◯ Excellent	⊖ Insufficient Information

Refer to *Section 3: Annotated Vehicle Charts* for an explanation of these charts.

Audi A4 1.8T
4 Door Sedan

Compact

 1.8L 150 hp Turbo Gas Fuel Inject.
 4 Cylinder In-Line
 Manual 5 Speed
 2 Wheel Front
Dual Front/Side Airbags Std

Purchase Price

Car Item	Dealer Cost	List
Base Price	$20,942	$23,790
Anti-Lock Brakes	Std	Std
Automatic 5 Speed	$1,025	$1,075
Optional Engine	N/A	N/A
Auto Climate Control	Std	Std
Power Steering	Std	Std
Cruise Control	Std	Std
Power Windows	Std	Std
AM/FM Stereo Cassette	Std	Std
Steering Wheel, Tilt	Std	Std
Rear Defroster	Std	Std
*Options Price	$1,025	$1,075
*Total Price	$21,967	$24,865
Target Price	$23,849	
Destination Charge	$500	
Avg. Tax & Fees	$1,363	
Total Target $	$25,712	
Average Dealer Option Cost:	88%	
12 Month Price Increase:	None	

Ownership Costs (Projected)

Cost Area	5 Year Cost	Rating
Depreciation	$10,088	◒
Financing ($426/month)	$5,002	
Insurance	$8,093	◐
State Fees	$1,028	
Fuel (Hwy 31 City 21 -Prem.)	$3,406	◐
Maintenance	$2,394	◯
Repairs	$1,440	●

Warranty/Maintenance Info

Major Tune-Up (60K mile int.)	$254	◐
Minor Tune-Up (30K mile int.)	$145	●
Brake Service	$291	●
Overall Warranty	3 yr/50k	◐
Drivetrain Warranty	3 yr/50k	◐
Rust Warranty	10 yr/unlim. mi	◯
Maintenance Warranty	3 yr/50k	◯
Roadside Assistance	3 yr/unlim. mi	

Ownership Costs By Year (Projected)

$2,000 $4,000 $6,000 $8,000 $10,000 $12,000

Legend: 1999, 2000, 2001, 2002, 2003

Resale Value

1999	2000	2001	2002	2003
$24,253	$21,438	$19,218	$17,304	$15,624

Cumulative Costs

	1999	2000	2001	2002	2003
Annual	$5,620	$6,670	$5,755	$6,541	$6,865
Total	$5,620	$12,290	$18,045	$24,586	$31,451

Projected Costs (5yr)

Relative	This Car
$34,172	$31,451
Cost/Mile 49¢	Cost/Mile 45¢

Ownership Cost Value

◯ Excellent

The 1999 A4 1.8T sedan is equipped with FrontTrak front wheel drive with Electronic Differential Locks (EDL). EDL detects and limits wheelspin and redistributes drive torque for available traction. Standard safety features for the A4 1.8T include pretensioning seatbelts with automatic locking retractors for front and rear seats, and front and side airbags for both the driver and front seat passenger. Lockable front headrests are also added for this year.

Audi A4 1.8T Quattro
4 Door Sedan

Compact

 1.8L 150 hp Turbo Gas Fuel Inject.
 4 Cylinder In-Line
 Manual 5 Speed
 4 Wheel Full-Time
Dual Front/Side Airbags Std

2WD Model Shown

Purchase Price

Car Item	Dealer Cost	List
Base Price	$22,592	$25,440
Anti-Lock Brakes	Std	Std
Automatic 5 Speed	$1,025	$1,075
Optional Engine	N/A	N/A
Auto Climate Control	Std	Std
Power Steering	Std	Std
Cruise Control	Std	Std
Power Windows	Std	Std
AM/FM Stereo Cassette	Std	Std
Steering Wheel, Tilt	Std	Std
Rear Defroster	Std	Std
*Options Price	$1,025	$1,075
*Total Price	$23,617	$26,515
Target Price	$25,642	
Destination Charge	$500	
Avg. Tax & Fees	$1,459	
Total Target $	$27,601	
Average Dealer Option Cost:	88%	
12 Month Price Increase:	None	

Ownership Costs (Projected)

Cost Area	5 Year Cost	Rating
Depreciation	$10,503	◯
Financing ($458/month)	$5,369	
Insurance	$8,313	◐
State Fees	$1,093	
Fuel (Hwy 27 City 18 -Prem.)	$3,942	●
Maintenance	$2,407	◯
Repairs	$1,690	●

Warranty/Maintenance Info

Major Tune-Up (60K mile int.)	$266	●
Minor Tune-Up (30K mile int.)	$145	●
Brake Service	$291	●
Overall Warranty	3 yr/50k	◐
Drivetrain Warranty	3 yr/50k	◐
Rust Warranty	10 yr/unlim. mi	◯
Maintenance Warranty	3 yr/50k	◯
Roadside Assistance	3 yr/unlim. mi	

Ownership Costs By Year (Projected)

$2,000 $4,000 $6,000 $8,000 $10,000 $12,000

Legend: 1999, 2000, 2001, 2002, 2003

Resale Value

1999	2000	2001	2002	2003
$26,029	$23,115	$20,813	$18,833	$17,098

Cumulative Costs

	1999	2000	2001	2002	2003
Annual	$6,018	$7,032	$6,077	$6,932	$7,258
Total	$6,018	$13,050	$19,127	$26,059	$33,317

Projected Costs (5yr)

Relative	This Car
$36,133	$33,317
Cost/Mile 52¢	Cost/Mile 48¢

Ownership Cost Value

◯ Excellent

The A4 1.8T Quattro sedan features full-time all-wheel drive. It is available with either a five speed manual or five speed automatic transmission. The automatic transmission includes steering wheel- mounted Tiptronic controls to make shifting easier. An optional Sport Package is available on all A4 models and includes a sport suspension with firmer shock settings, a larger rear sway bar, 16 inch wheels and tires and a three spoke leather-wrapped steering wheel.

---

* Includes shaded options

** Other purchase requirements apply

*** Price includes other options

 Poor   Worse Than Average   Average   Better Than Average ◯ Excellent ⊖ Insufficient Information

7

Refer to *Section 3: Annotated Vehicle Charts* for an explanation of these charts.

Audi A4 2.8
4 Door Sedan

Near Luxury

2.8L 190 hp Gas Fuel Inject.	6 Cylinder "V"	Manual 5 Speed	2 Wheel Front	Dual Front/Side Airbags Std	

Purchase Price

Car Item	Dealer Cost	List
Base Price	**$24,944**	**$28,390**
Anti-Lock Brakes	Std	Std
Automatic 5 Speed	$1,025	$1,075
Optional Engine	N/A	N/A
Auto Climate Control	Std	Std
Power Steering	Std	Std
Cruise Control	Std	Std
Power Windows	Std	Std
AM/FM Stereo Cassette	Std	Std
Steering Wheel, Tilt	Std	Std
Rear Defroster	Std	Std
*Options Price	**$1,025**	**$1,075**
*Total Price	**$25,969**	**$29,465**
Target Price	$28,176	
Destination Charge	$500	
Avg. Tax & Fees	$1,603	
Total Target $	**$30,279**	
Average Dealer Option Cost:	**88%**	
12 Month Price Increase:	1%	

For 1999, the A4 2.8 sedan comes standard with a V6 engine and an all-speed traction control system called ASR (anti-slip regulation). Improvements for 1999 include a larger right outside mirror, lockable front headrests and last but not least, an improved center console cup holder. There are three different interior appearances available, which Audi refers to as Atmospheres; each Atmosphere offers different color choices and a different type of wood applique.

Ownership Costs (Projected)

Cost Area	5 Year Cost	Rating
Depreciation	$13,357	○
Financing ($502/month)	$5,890	
Insurance	$8,865	◒
State Fees	$1,213	
Fuel (Hwy 29 City 18 -Prem.)	$3,806	○
Maintenance	$3,023	◒
Repairs	$1,360	●

Warranty/Maintenance Info

Major Tune-Up (60K mile int.)	$304	◉
Minor Tune-Up (30K mile int.)	$145	○
Brake Service	$275	◉
Overall Warranty	3 yr/50k	○
Drivetrain Warranty	3 yr/50k	○
Rust Warranty	10 yr/unlim. mi	○
Maintenance Warranty	3 yr/50k	○
Roadside Assistance	3 yr/unlim. mi	

Ownership Costs By Year (Projected)

Legend: 1999, 2000, 2001, 2002, 2003

Resale Value

1999	2000	2001	2002	2003
$28,745	$25,464	$22,552	$19,732	$16,922

Cumulative Costs

	1999	2000	2001	2002	2003
Annual	$6,266	$7,652	$6,901	$7,934	$8,761
Total	$6,266	$13,918	$20,819	$28,753	$37,514

Projected Costs (5yr)

Relative $37,852	This Car $37,514
Cost/Mile 54¢	Cost/Mile 54¢

Ownership Cost Value

○ Better Than Average

Audi A4 2.8 Quattro
4 Door Sedan

Near Luxury

2.8L 190 hp Gas Fuel Inject.	6 Cylinder "V"	Manual 5 Speed	4 Wheel Full-Time	Dual Front/Side Airbags Std	

Purchase Price

Car Item	Dealer Cost	List
Base Price	**$26,594**	**$30,040**
Anti-Lock Brakes	Std	Std
Automatic 5 Speed	$1,025	$1,075
Optional Engine	N/A	N/A
Auto Climate Control	Std	Std
Power Steering	Std	Std
Cruise Control	Std	Std
Power Windows	Std	Std
AM/FM Stereo Cassette	Std	Std
Steering Wheel, Tilt	Std	Std
Rear Defroster	Std	Std
*Options Price	**$1,025**	**$1,075**
*Total Price	**$27,619**	**$31,115**
Target Price	$29,975	
Destination Charge	$500	
Avg. Tax & Fees	$1,700	
Total Target $	**$32,175**	
Average Dealer Option Cost:	**88%**	
12 Month Price Increase:	1%	

The 1999 A4 2.8 Quattro sedan is equipped with a full-time all-wheel drive system and a Torsen center differential. This also includes an Electronic Differential Lock (EDL) system, which functions as an electronic traction assist for the front and rear differentials. The optional Sport Package includes a lowered sport suspension, firmer shock settings, larger rear sway bar, 16 inch wheels and tires, and a three spoke leather-wrapped steering wheel.

Ownership Costs (Projected)

Cost Area	5 Year Cost	Rating
Depreciation	$13,786	○
Financing ($533/month)	$6,260	
Insurance	$8,865	◒
State Fees	$1,278	
Fuel (Hwy 27 City 17 -Prem.)	$4,058	○
Maintenance	$3,037	◒
Repairs	$1,610	●

Warranty/Maintenance Info

Major Tune-Up (60K mile int.)	$316	◉
Minor Tune-Up (30K mile int.)	$145	○
Brake Service	$275	◉
Overall Warranty	3 yr/50k	○
Drivetrain Warranty	3 yr/50k	○
Rust Warranty	10 yr/unlim. mi	○
Maintenance Warranty	3 yr/50k	○
Roadside Assistance	3 yr/unlim. mi	

Ownership Costs By Year (Projected)

Legend: 1999, 2000, 2001, 2002, 2003

Resale Value

1999	2000	2001	2002	2003
$30,302	$26,990	$24,055	$21,213	$18,389

Cumulative Costs

	1999	2000	2001	2002	2003
Annual	$6,794	$7,849	$7,063	$8,180	$9,008
Total	$6,794	$14,643	$21,706	$29,886	$38,894

Projected Costs (5yr)

Relative $38,845	This Car $38,894
Cost/Mile 55¢	Cost/Mile 56¢

Ownership Cost Value

○ Average

8

 ● Poor   ◉ Worse Than Average ◒ Average ○ Better Than Average ○ Excellent ⊖ Insufficient Information

Refer to *Section 3: Annotated Vehicle Charts* for an explanation of these charts.

Audi A4 1.8T Avant Quattro
4 Door Wagon

Small Wagon

1.8L 150 hp Turbo Gas Fuel Inject.	4 Cylinder In-Line	Manual 5 Speed	4 Wheel Full-Time	Dual Front/Side Airbags Std

Purchase Price

Car Item	Dealer Cost	List
Base Price	**$23,462**	**$26,440**
Anti-Lock Brakes	Std	Std
Automatic 5 Speed	$1,025	$1,075
Optional Engine	N/A	N/A
Auto Climate Control	Std	Std
Power Steering	Std	Std
Cruise Control	Std	Std
Power Windows	Std	Std
AM/FM Stereo Cassette	Std	Std
Steering Wheel, Tilt	Std	Std
Rear Defroster	Std	Std
*Options Price	$1,025	$1,075
*Total Price	$24,487	$27,515
Target Price	$26,621	
Destination Charge	$500	
Avg. Tax & Fees	$1,513	
Total Target $	**$28,634**	
Average Dealer Option Cost:	88%	
12 Month Price Increase:	None	

Ownership Costs (Projected)

Cost Area	5 Year Cost	Rating
Depreciation	$10,982	◯
Financing ($475/month)	$5,571	◯
Insurance	$8,556	◉
State Fees	$1,133	
Fuel (Hwy 27 City 18 -Prem.)	$3,942	⊙
Maintenance	$2,407	◯
Repairs	$1,690	●

Warranty/Maintenance Info

Major Tune-Up (60K mile int.)	$266	◯
Minor Tune-Up (30K mile int.)	$145	●
Brake Service	$291	●
Overall Warranty	3 yr/50k	◯
Drivetrain Warranty	3 yr/50k	◯
Rust Warranty	10 yr/unlim. mi	◯
Maintenance Warranty	3 yr/50k	◯
Roadside Assistance	3 yr/unlim. mi	

The A4 1.8T Avant Quattro is a new model addition for 1999. The front wheel drive A4 Avant has been discontinued. This is the first year that the A4 Avant Quattro has been available with the 1.8L turbocharged five valve per cylinder engine. Standard features include a fully automatic climate control system, central locking, and new for 1999, a remote keyless entry system. Front side airbags are standard as well as front driver and passenger airbags.

Ownership Costs By Year (Projected)

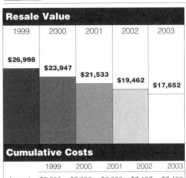

$2,000 $4,000 $6,000 $8,000 $10,000 $12,000

■ 1999
■ 2000
■ 2001
■ 2002
□ 2003

Resale Value

1999	2000	2001	2002	2003
$26,998	$23,947	$21,533	$19,462	$17,652

Cumulative Costs

	1999	2000	2001	2002	2003
Annual	$6,206	$7,282	$6,286	$7,107	$7,400
Total	$6,206	$13,488	$19,774	$26,881	$34,281

Projected Costs (5yr)

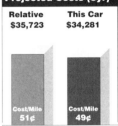

Relative	This Car
$35,723	$34,281
Cost/Mile 51¢	Cost/Mile 49¢

Ownership Cost Value

◯ Excellent

Audi A4 2.8 Avant Quattro
4 Door Wagon

Small Wagon

2.8L 190 hp Gas Fuel Inject.	6 Cylinder "V"	Manual 5 Speed	4 Wheel Full-Time	Dual Front/Side Airbags Std

Purchase Price

Car Item	Dealer Cost	List
Base Price	**$27,464**	**$31,040**
Anti-Lock Brakes	Std	Std
Automatic 5 Speed	$1,025	$1,075
Optional Engine	N/A	N/A
Auto Climate Control	Std	Std
Power Steering	Std	Std
Cruise Control	Std	Std
Power Windows	Std	Std
AM/FM Stereo Cassette	Std	Std
Steering Wheel, Tilt	Std	Std
Rear Defroster	Std	Std
*Options Price	$1,025	$1,075
*Total Price	$28,489	$32,115
Target Price	$30,955	
Destination Charge	$500	
Avg. Tax & Fees	$1,754	
Total Target $	**$33,209**	
Average Dealer Option Cost:	88%	
12 Month Price Increase:	None	

Ownership Costs (Projected)

Cost Area	5 Year Cost	Rating
Depreciation	$14,199	◯
Financing ($550/month)	$6,460	◯
Insurance	$9,135	◯
State Fees	$1,318	
Fuel (Hwy 27 City 17 -Prem.)	$4,058	⊙
Maintenance	$3,037	◯
Repairs	$1,610	●

Warranty/Maintenance Info

Major Tune-Up (60K mile int.)	$316	●
Minor Tune-Up (30K mile int.)	$145	●
Brake Service	$275	⊙
Overall Warranty	3 yr/50k	◯
Drivetrain Warranty	3 yr/50k	◯
Rust Warranty	10 yr/unlim. mi	◯
Maintenance Warranty	3 yr/50k	◯
Roadside Assistance	3 yr/unlim. mi	

For 1999, the A4 2.8 Avant Quattro wagon shares most of the same standard features and options with the A4 2.8 Quattro sedan. The central locking system unlocks the doors and turns on lights in the event of airbag deployment. This system can also operate the fuel filler door, power windows and interior lights. Standard equipment includes a remote keyless entry system and dual front and side-impact airbags. Available options include leather seating, a Sport Package and special pearlescent paint.

Ownership Costs By Year (Projected)

$5,000 $10,000 $15,000

■ 1999
■ 2000
■ 2001
■ 2002
□ 2003

Resale Value

1999	2000	2001	2002	2003
$30,887	$27,604	$24,631	$21,766	$19,010

Cumulative Costs

	1999	2000	2001	2002	2003
Annual	$7,373	$7,937	$7,205	$8,291	$9,011
Total	$7,373	$15,310	$22,515	$30,806	$39,817

Projected Costs (5yr)

Relative	This Car
$39,108	$39,817
Cost/Mile 56¢	Cost/Mile 57¢

Ownership Cost Value

◉ Average

 Poor Worse Than Average Average Better Than Average Excellent Insufficient Information

Refer to *Section 3: Annotated Vehicle Charts* for an explanation of these charts.

Audi A6
4 Door Sedan

Near Luxury

| 2.8L 200 hp Gas Fuel Inject. | 6 Cylinder "V" | Automatic 5 Speed | 2 Wheel Front | Dual Front/Side Airbags Std |

Purchase Price

Car Item	Dealer Cost	List
Base Price	**$29,697**	**$33,750**
Anti-Lock Brakes	Std	Std
Manual Transmission	N/A	N/A
Optional Engine	N/A	N/A
Auto Climate Control	Std	Std
Power Steering	Std	Std
Cruise Control	Std	Std
Power Windows	Std	Std
AM/FM Stereo Cassette	Std	Std
Steering Wheel, Tilt	Std	Std
Rear Defroster	Std	Std
*Options Price	$0	$0
*Total Price	$29,697	$33,750
Target Price	$32,412	
Destination Charge	$500	
Avg. Tax & Fees	$1,837	
Total Target $	**$34,749**	
Average Dealer Option Cost:	87%	
12 Month Price Increase:	None	

Ownership Costs (Projected)

Cost Area	5 Year Cost	Rating
Depreciation	$15,847	◉
Financing ($576/month)	$6,761	
Insurance	$8,556	○
State Fees	$1,384	
Fuel (Hwy 27 City 17 -Prem.)	$4,058	○
Maintenance	$3,388	◉
Repairs	$1,465	◉

Warranty/Maintenance Info

Major Tune-Up (60K mile int.)	$448	●	
Minor Tune-Up (30K mile int.)	$145	○	
Brake Service	$321	●	
Overall Warranty	3 yr/50k	○	
Drivetrain Warranty	3 yr/50k	○	
Rust Warranty	10 yr/unlim. mi	○	
Maintenance Warranty	3 yr/50k	○	
Roadside Assistance	3 yr/unlim. mi		

The A6 sedan, featuring FrontTrak front wheel drive, arrives this year with 30 valve 200 hp engine technology and many comfort features. Standard features include power windows with pinch protection, cruise control, antilock brakes, a power central locking system and second generation driver and passenger front and side airbags. Lockable front headrests are new for this year. An optional Enhanced Security Package offers two side airbags for the rear passengers.

Ownership Costs By Year (Projected)

$5,000 $10,000 $15,000 $20,000

■ 1999
■ 2000
■ 2001
□ 2002
□ 2003

Resale Value

1999	2000	2001	2002	2003
$31,825	$28,247	$25,052	$21,963	$18,902

Projected Costs (5yr)

Relative $40,376	This Car $41,459
Cost/Mile 58¢	Cost/Mile 59¢

Cumulative Costs

	1999	2000	2001	2002	2003
Annual	$7,983	$8,216	$7,386	$8,416	$9,458
Total	$7,983	$16,199	$23,585	$32,001	$41,459

Ownership Cost Value

◉

Worse Than Average

Audi A6 Quattro
4 Door Sedan

Near Luxury

| 2.8L 200 hp Gas Fuel Inject. | 6 Cylinder "V" | Automatic 5 Speed | 4 Wheel Full-Time | Dual Front/Side Airbags Std |

 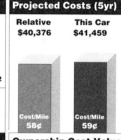

Purchase Price

Car Item	Dealer Cost	List
Base Price	**$31,347**	**$35,400**
Anti-Lock Brakes	Std	Std
Manual Transmission	N/A	N/A
Optional Engine	N/A	N/A
Auto Climate Control	Std	Std
Power Steering	Std	Std
Cruise Control	Std	Std
Power Windows	Std	Std
AM/FM Stereo Cassette	Std	Std
Steering Wheel, Tilt	Std	Std
Rear Defroster	Std	Std
*Options Price	$0	$0
*Total Price	$31,347	$35,400
Target Price	$34,229	
Destination Charge	$500	
Avg. Tax & Fees	$1,935	
Total Target $	**$36,664**	
Average Dealer Option Cost:	87%	
12 Month Price Increase:	None	

Ownership Costs (Projected)

Cost Area	5 Year Cost	Rating
Depreciation	$16,302	○
Financing ($608/month)	$7,132	
Insurance	$8,865	○
State Fees	$1,448	
Fuel (Hwy 26 City 17 -Prem.)	$4,134	◉
Maintenance	$3,395	◉
Repairs	$1,765	◉

Warranty/Maintenance Info

Major Tune-Up (60K mile int.)	$454	●	
Minor Tune-Up (30K mile int.)	$145	○	
Brake Service	$321	●	
Overall Warranty	3 yr/50k	○	
Drivetrain Warranty	3 yr/50k	○	
Rust Warranty	10 yr/unlim. mi	○	
Maintenance Warranty	3 yr/50k	○	
Roadside Assistance	3 yr/unlim. mi		

The A6 Quattro all-wheel drive sedan arrives this year with 30 valve 200 hp engine technology. The permanently engaged Quattro system, designed to improve handling and traction, requires no buttons to push and is transparent to the driver. Standard equipment includes an antilock braking system, power windows, cruise control, a power central locking system and both front and side airbags for front passengers. The optional Enhanced Security Package offers two side airbags for rear passengers.

Ownership Costs By Year (Projected)

$5,000 $10,000 $15,000 $20,000

■ 1999
■ 2000
■ 2001
□ 2002
□ 2003

Resale Value

1999	2000	2001	2002	2003
$33,449	$29,826	$26,586	$23,458	$20,362

Projected Costs (5yr)

Relative $41,813	This Car $43,041
Cost/Mile 60¢	Cost/Mile 61¢

Cumulative Costs

	1999	2000	2001	2002	2003
Annual	$8,490	$8,453	$7,598	$8,727	$9,773
Total	$8,490	$16,943	$24,541	$33,268	$43,041

Ownership Cost Value

◉

Worse Than Average

10

* Includes shaded options
** Other purchase requirements apply
*** Price includes other options

 Poor   Worse Than Average   Average   Better Than Average Excellent   Insufficient Information

Refer to *Section 3: Annotated Vehicle Charts* for an explanation of these charts.

Audi A6 Avant
4 Door Wagon

Luxury

 2.8L 200 hp Gas Fuel Inject.
 6 Cylinder "V"
 Automatic 5 Speed
 4 Wheel Full-Time
Dual Front/Side Airbags Std

Purchase Price

Car Item	Dealer Cost	List
Base Price	**$32,391**	**$36,600**
Anti-Lock Brakes	Std	Std
Manual Transmission	N/A	N/A
Optional Engine	N/A	N/A
Auto Climate Control	Std	Std
Power Steering	Std	Std
Cruise Control	Std	Std
Power Windows	Std	Std
AM/FM Stereo Cassette	Std	Std
Steering Wheel, Tilt	Std	Std
Rear Defroster	Std	Std
*Options Price	$0	$0
*Total Price	**$32,391**	**$36,600**
Target Price	$35,417	
Destination Charge	$500	
Avg. Tax & Fees	$2,000	
Total Target $	**$37,917**	
Average Dealer Option Cost:	**87%**	
12 Month Price Increase:	2%	

The A6 Avant wagon with Quattro all-wheel drive arrives this year with 30 valve 200 hp engine technology. Equipped with standard features such as power windows, cruise control and a central locking system, this wagon offers versatility. The optional removable third rear seat can be folded against the side or against the second seat, or removed entirely. With front and side airbags standard for front passengers, the optional Enhanced Security Package offers two side airbags for rear passengers.

Ownership Costs (Projected)

Cost Area	5 Year Cost	Rating
Depreciation	$16,149	◯
Financing ($629/month)	$7,377	
Insurance	$8,865	◯
State Fees	$1,498	
Fuel (Hwy 26 City 17 -Prem.)	$4,134	◯
Maintenance	$3,395	●
Repairs	$1,765	◉

Warranty/Maintenance Info

Major Tune-Up (60K mile int.)	$454	●
Minor Tune-Up (30K mile int.)	$145	◯
Brake Service	$321	●
Overall Warranty	3 yr/50k	◯
Drivetrain Warranty	3 yr/50k	◯
Rust Warranty	10 yr/unlim. mi	◯
Maintenance Warranty	3 yr/50k	◯
Roadside Assistance	3 yr/unlim. mi	

Ownership Costs By Year (Projected)

$5,000 $10,000 $15,000 $20,000

- 1999
- 2000
- 2001
- 2002
- 2003

Resale Value

1999	2000	2001	2002	2003
$35,415	$31,638	$28,253	$24,991	$21,768

Cumulative Costs

	1999	2000	2001	2002	2003
Annual	$7,872	$8,686	$7,803	$8,902	$9,920
Total	$7,872	$16,558	$24,361	$33,263	$43,183

Projected Costs (5yr)

Relative $43,756	This Car $43,183
Cost/Mile 63¢	Cost/Mile 62¢

Ownership Cost Value

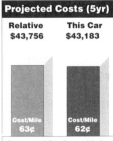

◯ Better Than Average

Audi A8 3.7
4 Door Sedan

Luxury

 3.7L 230 hp Gas Fuel Inject.
 8 Cylinder "V"
 Automatic 5 Speed
 2 Wheel Front
Dual Front/Side Airbags Std

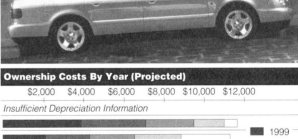

Purchase Price

Car Item	Dealer Cost	List
Base Price	**$50,183**	**$57,400**
Anti-Lock Brakes	Std	Std
Manual Transmission	N/A	N/A
Optional Engine	N/A	N/A
Auto Climate Control	Std	Std
Power Steering	Std	Std
Cruise Control	Std	Std
Power Windows	Std	Std
AM/FM Stereo Cassette	Std	Std
St Whl, Tilt/Scope/Mem	Std	Std
Rear Defroster	Std	Std
*Options Price	$0	$0
*Total Price	**$50,183**	**$57,400**
Target Price	$54,981	
Destination Charge	$500	
Avg. Tax & Fees	$3,089	
Luxury Tax	$1,169	
Total Target $	**$59,739**	
12 Month Price Increase:	None	

With minor changes for this year, the 1999 A8 3.7 offers many safety features, including driver and front passenger second generation airbags with dual threshold deployment and occupant detection and front and rear side airbags. Also standard are front passenger side and rear safety belts with ALR (automatic locking retractors, a ratcheting mechanism for conveniently securing a child seat), an emergency warning triangle located in the trunk and a first aid kit located in rear center armrest.

Ownership Costs (Projected)

Cost Area	5 Year Cost	Rating
Depreciation		⊖
Financing ($990/month)	$11,622	
Insurance	$11,266	◯
State Fees	$2,328	
Fuel (Hwy 26 City 17 -Prem.)	$4,134	◯
Maintenance	$3,510	●
Repairs	$1,830	◉

Warranty/Maintenance Info

Major Tune-Up (60K mile int.)	$323	◉
Minor Tune-Up (30K mile int.)	$156	◉
Brake Service	$363	●
Overall Warranty	3 yr/50k	◯
Drivetrain Warranty	3 yr/50k	◯
Rust Warranty	10 yr/unlim. mi	◯
Maintenance Warranty	3 yr/50k	◯
Roadside Assistance	3 yr/unlim. mi	

Ownership Costs By Year (Projected)

$2,000 $4,000 $6,000 $8,000 $10,000 $12,000

Insufficient Depreciation Information

- 1999
- 2000
- 2001
- 2002
- 2003

Resale Value

Insufficient

Information

Cumulative Costs

	1999	2000	2001	2002	2003
Annual	*Insufficient Information*				
Total	*Insufficient Information*				

Projected Costs (5yr)

Insufficient

Information

Ownership Cost Value

⊖

Insufficient Information

● Poor ◉ Worse Than Average ◯ Average ◯ Better Than Average ◯ Excellent ⊖ Insufficient Information

11

Refer to *Section 3: Annotated Vehicle Charts* for an explanation of these charts.

Audi A8 4.2 Quattro
4 Door Sedan

 4.2L 300 hp Gas Fuel Inject.
 8 Cylinder "V"
 Automatic 5 Speed
 4 Wheel Full-Time
Dual Front/Side Airbags Std

Purchase Price

Car Item	Dealer Cost	List
Base Price	**$56,795**	**$65,000**
Anti-Lock Brakes	Std	Std
Manual Transmission	N/A	N/A
Optional Engine	N/A	N/A
Auto Climate Control	Std	Std
Power Steering	Std	Std
Cruise Control	Std	Std
Power Windows	Std	Std
AM/FM Stereo Cassette	Std	Std
St Whl, Tilt/Scope/Mem	Std	Std
Rear Defroster	Std	Std
***Options Price**	**$0**	**$0**
***Total Price**	**$56,795**	**$65,000**
Target Price	$62,232	
Destination Charge	$500	
Avg. Tax & Fees	$3,491	
Luxury Tax	$1,604	
Total Target $	**$67,827**	
12 Month Price Increase:	None	

Ownership Costs (Projected)

Cost Area	5 Year Cost	Rating
Depreciation		⊖
Financing ($1,124/month)	$13,196	
Insurance (Performance)	$14,809	◉
State Fees	$2,634	
Fuel (Hwy 25 City 17 -Prem.)	$4,216	◎
Maintenance	$3,510	●
Repairs	$2,075	●

Warranty/Maintenance Info

Major Tune-Up (60K mile int.)	$323	◉
Minor Tune-Up (30K mile int.)	$156	◉
Brake Service	$363	●
Overall Warranty	3 yr/50k	◎
Drivetrain Warranty	3 yr/50k	◎
Rust Warranty	10 yr/unlim. mi	○
Maintenance Warranty	3 yr/50k	○
Roadside Assistance	3 yr/unlim. mi	

Ownership Costs By Year (Projected)

$5,000 $10,000 $15,000

Insufficient Depreciation Information

- 1999
- 2000
- 2001
- 2002
- 2003

Resale Value

Insufficient Information

Projected Costs (5yr)

Insufficient Information

Cumulative Costs

	1999	2000	2001	2002	2003
Annual		*Insufficient Information*			
Total		*Insufficient Information*			

Ownership Cost Value

⊖

Insufficient Information

The A8 4.2 Quattro sedan arrives this year with notable options. The Cold Weather Package features a heated steering wheel, heated front and rear seats and a ski sack. The Warm Weather Package consists of solar cells in the sunroof that power ventilation fans to cool the interior when the vehicle is parked in the sun, an electric sunshade for the rear window and manual sunshades for the rear side windows. Premium leather/Alcantara interior trim is also available.

BMW 318 ti
2 Door Hatchback

 1.9L 138 hp Gas Fuel Inject.
4 Cylinder In-Line
Manual 5 Speed
 2 Wheel Rear
 Dual Airbags Std

Purchase Price

Car Item	Dealer Cost	List
Base Price	**$21,100**	**$23,300**
Anti-Lock Brakes	Std	Std
Automatic 4 Speed	$925	$975
Optional Engine	N/A	N/A
Air Conditioning	Std	Std
Power Steering	Std	Std
Cruise Control	$395	$475
Power Windows	Std	Std
AM/FM Stereo Cassette	Std	Std
Steering Wheel, Tilt	N/A	N/A
Rear Defroster	Std	Std
***Options Price**	**$925**	**$975**
***Total Price**	**$22,025**	**$24,275**
Target Price	$23,633	
Destination Charge	$570	
Avg. Tax & Fees	$1,350	
Total Target $	**$25,553**	
Average Dealer Option Cost:	**85%**	
12 Month Price Increase:	9%	

Ownership Costs (Projected)

Cost Area	5 Year Cost	Rating
Depreciation	$12,018	◎
Financing ($424/month)	$4,970	
Insurance	$9,911	●
State Fees	$1,007	
Fuel (Hwy 31 City 23 -Prem.)	$3,258	◎
Maintenance	$1,851	○
Repairs	$1,375	●

Warranty/Maintenance Info

Major Tune-Up (35K mile int.)	$228	◎
Minor Tune-Up (18K mile int.)	$115	◉
Brake Service	$227	◎
Overall Warranty	4 yr/50k	◎
Drivetrain Warranty	4 yr/50k	◎
Rust Warranty	6 yr/unlim. mi	◎
Maintenance Warranty	3 yr/36k	○
Roadside Assistance	4 yr/50k	

Ownership Costs By Year (Projected)

$2,000 $4,000 $6,000 $8,000 $10,000 $12,000 $14,000

- 1999
- 2000
- 2001
- 2002
- 2003

Resale Value

1999	2000	2001	2002	2003
$21,390	$19,234	$17,309	$15,406	$13,535

Projected Costs (5yr)

Relative	This Car
$34,240	$34,390

Cost/Mile 49¢ | Cost/Mile 49¢

Cumulative Costs

	1999	2000	2001	2002	2003
Annual	$8,626	$6,325	$6,067	$6,732	$6,640
Total	$8,626	$14,951	$21,018	$27,750	$34,390

Ownership Cost Value

○

Average

For 1999, the 318ti hatchback now includes the Sport Package as standard equipment and includes a standard sport suspension, alloy wheels, high-performance tires and sport bucket seats. All-season traction control, a central locking system and a theft deterrent system are also standard equipment. The BMW Scheduled Maintenance Program, which includes all factory recommended periodic maintenance for the first three years or 36,000 miles, is available at no extra cost.

12

* Includes shaded options
** Other purchase requirements apply
*** Price includes other options

 Poor
 Worse Than Average
 Average
 Better Than Average
 Excellent
 Insufficient Information

Refer to *Section 3: Annotated Vehicle Charts* for an explanation of these charts.

BMW 323 iS
2 Door Coupe

Near Luxury

2.5L 168 hp Gas Fuel Inject.	6 Cylinder In-Line	Manual 5 Speed	2 Wheel Rear	Dual Front/Side Airbags Std

Purchase Price

Car Item	Dealer Cost	List
Base Price	**$25,330**	**$28,700**
Anti-Lock Brakes	Std	Std
Automatic 4 Speed	$925	$975
Optional Engine	N/A	N/A
Auto Climate Control	Std	Std
Power Steering	Std	Std
Cruise Control	Std	Std
Power Windows	Std	Std
AM/FM Stereo Cassette	Std	Std
Steering Wheel, Tilt	Std	Std
Rear Defroster	Std	Std
***Options Price**	**$925**	**$975**
***Total Price**	**$26,255**	**$29,675**
Target Price	$28,474	
Destination Charge	$570	
Avg. Tax & Fees	$1,622	
Total Target $	**$30,666**	
Average Dealer Option Cost:	**84%**	
12 Month Price Increase:	None	

For 1999, the 323iS coupe continues with minimal changes from last year's model. A rear spoiler and power glass moonroof are available as options. Also available is a combination keyless entry/theft deterrent system. The optional Sport Package includes fog lamps, alloy wheels and low-profile tires. Additional options include an onboard navigation system and a Harman/Kardon sound system. For 1999, a new five speed automatic overdrive transmission is available.

Ownership Costs (Projected)

Cost Area	5 Year Cost	Rating
Depreciation	$13,202	◯
Financing ($508/month)	$5,966	
Insurance	$10,996	●
State Fees	$1,222	
Fuel (Hwy 27 City 19 -Prem.)	$3,838	◯
Maintenance	$1,562	◯
Repairs	$1,375	◯

Warranty/Maintenance Info

Major Tune-Up (35K mile int.)	$202	◯
Minor Tune-Up (18K mile int.)	$135	◯
Brake Service	$237	◯
Overall Warranty	4 yr/50k	◯
Drivetrain Warranty	4 yr/50k	◯
Rust Warranty	6 yr/unlim. mi	◯
Maintenance Warranty	3 yr/36k	◯
Roadside Assistance	4 yr/50k	

Ownership Costs By Year (Projected)

$2,000 $4,000 $6,000 $8,000 $10,000 $12,000 $14,000

Legend: 1999, 2000, 2001, 2002, 2003

Resale Value

1999	2000	2001	2002	2003
$27,308	$24,624	$22,241	$19,883	$17,464

Cumulative Costs

	1999	2000	2001	2002	2003
Annual	$8,530	$7,501	$7,084	$7,422	$7,624
Total	$8,530	$16,031	$23,115	$30,537	$38,161

Projected Costs (5yr)

Relative $38,010	This Car $38,161
Cost/Mile 54¢	Cost/Mile 55¢

Ownership Cost Value

◯ Average

BMW 323 iC
2 Door Convertible

Near Luxury

2.5L 168 hp Gas Fuel Inject.	6 Cylinder In-Line	Manual 5 Speed	2 Wheel Rear	Dual Front/Side Airbags Std

Purchase Price

Car Item	Dealer Cost	List
Base Price	**$30,580**	**$34,700**
Anti-Lock Brakes	Std	Std
Automatic 4 Speed	$925	$975
Optional Engine	N/A	N/A
Auto Climate Control	Std	Std
Power Steering	Std	Std
Cruise Control	Std	Std
Power Windows	Std	Std
AM/FM Stereo Cassette	Std	Std
Steering Wheel, Tilt	Std	Std
Rear Defroster	Std	Std
***Options Price**	**$925**	**$975**
***Total Price**	**$31,505**	**$35,675**
Target Price	$34,392	
Destination Charge	$570	
Avg. Tax & Fees	$1,948	
Total Target $	**$36,910**	
Average Dealer Option Cost:	**84%**	
12 Month Price Increase:	None	

For 1999, the 323iC convertible remains mostly unchanged from last year's model. Options include an automatically deploying Rollover Protection System and a keyless entry/theft deterrent system. Additional options include a Premium Package that includes a power convertible roof, and a Sport Package that includes alloy wheels, front fog lamps and upgraded tires. For 1999, a new five speed automatic overdrive transmission is also available.

Ownership Costs (Projected)

Cost Area	5 Year Cost	Rating
Depreciation	$15,038	◯
Financing ($612/month)	$7,181	
Insurance	$12,220	●
State Fees	$1,462	
Fuel (Hwy 27 City 19 -Prem.)	$3,838	◯
Maintenance	$1,562	◯
Repairs	$1,375	◯

Warranty/Maintenance Info

Major Tune-Up (35K mile int.)	$202	◯
Minor Tune-Up (18K mile int.)	$135	◯
Brake Service	$237	◯
Overall Warranty	4 yr/50k	◯
Drivetrain Warranty	4 yr/50k	◯
Rust Warranty	6 yr/unlim. mi	◯
Maintenance Warranty	3 yr/36k	◯
Roadside Assistance	4 yr/50k	

Ownership Costs By Year (Projected)

$5,000 $10,000 $15,000 $20,000

Legend: 1999, 2000, 2001, 2002, 2003

Resale Value

1999	2000	2001	2002	2003
$33,719	$30,477	$27,576	$24,734	$21,872

Cumulative Costs

	1999	2000	2001	2002	2003
Annual	$9,070	$8,687	$8,145	$8,357	$8,417
Total	$9,070	$17,757	$25,902	$34,259	$42,676

Projected Costs (5yr)

Relative $41,961	This Car $42,676
Cost/Mile 60¢	Cost/Mile 61¢

Ownership Cost Value

◯ Average

---

* Includes shaded options
** Other purchase requirements apply
*** Price includes other options

 Poor   Worse Than Average   Average   Better Than Average   Excellent   Insufficient Information

13

Refer to *Section 3: Annotated Vehicle Charts* for an explanation of these charts.

BMW 323 i
4 Door Sedan

Near Luxury

 2.5L 170 hp Gas Fuel Inject.
 6 Cylinder In-Line
 Manual 5 Speed
 2 Wheel Rear
Dual Front/Side Airbags Std

Purchase Price

Car Item	Dealer Cost	List
Base Price	**$23,530**	**$26,400**
Anti-Lock Brakes	Std	Std
Automatic 5 Speed	$1,140	$1,200
Optional Engine	N/A	N/A
Auto Climate Control	Std	Std
Power Steering	Std	Std
Cruise Control	Pkg	Pkg
Power Windows	Std	Std
AM/FM Stereo Cassette	Std	Std
Steering Wheel, Tilt	Std	Std
Rear Defroster	Std	Std
*Options Price	$1,140	$1,200
*Total Price	**$24,670**	**$27,600**
Target Price	$26,637	
Destination Charge	$570	
Avg. Tax & Fees	$1,519	
Total Target $	**$28,726**	
Average Dealer Option Cost:	87%	
12 Month Price Increase:	None	

For 1999, the 323i sedan features an all-new body style, a revised aluminum block engine that allows the vehicle to receive LEV (Low Emissions Vehicle) status, and new lighter aluminum suspension components. Also available this year is a new five speed automatic overdrive transmission. Additional options include a power glass moonroof, onboard navigation system, Harman/Kardon sound system and xenon low-beam headlamps. Optional packages include a Premium Package and Sport Package.

Ownership Costs (Projected)

Cost Area	5 Year Cost	Rating
Depreciation	$11,433	◒
Financing ($476/month)	$5,589	
Insurance	$8,757	◉
State Fees	$1,140	
Fuel (Hwy 28 City 19 -Prem.)	$3,767	○
Maintenance	$1,597	○
Repairs	$1,375	◉

Warranty/Maintenance Info

Major Tune-Up (35K mile int.)	$202	○
Minor Tune-Up (18K mile int.)	$135	○
Brake Service	$234	◉
Overall Warranty	4 yr/50k	○
Drivetrain Warranty	4 yr/50k	○
Rust Warranty	6 yr/unlim. mi	○
Maintenance Warranty	3 yr/36k	◔
Roadside Assistance	4 yr/50k	

Ownership Costs By Year (Projected)

$2,000 $4,000 $6,000 $8,000 $10,000 $12,000

■ 1999
■ 2000
■ 2001
▨ 2002
□ 2003

Resale Value

1999	2000	2001	2002	2003
$26,205	$23,760	$21,612	$19,483	$17,293

Cumulative Costs

	1999	2000	2001	2002	2003
Annual	$7,105	$6,688	$6,292	$6,691	$6,882
Total	$7,105	$13,793	$20,085	$26,776	$33,658

Projected Costs (5yr)

Relative $37,208	This Car $33,658
Cost/Mile 53¢	Cost/Mile 48¢

Ownership Cost Value

○ Excellent

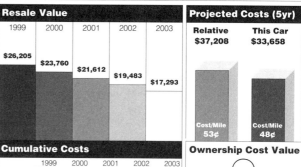

BMW 328 iS
2 Door Coupe

Near Luxury

 2.8L 190 hp Gas Fuel Inject.
 6 Cylinder In-Line
 Manual 5 Speed
 2 Wheel Rear
 Dual Front/Side Airbags Std

Purchase Price

Car Item	Dealer Cost	List
Base Price	**$29,265**	**$33,200**
Anti-Lock Brakes	Std	Std
Automatic 4 Speed	$925	$975
Optional Engine	N/A	N/A
Auto Climate Control	Std	Std
Power Steering	Std	Std
Cruise Control	Std	Std
Power Windows	Std	Std
AM/FM Stereo Cassette	Std	Std
Steering Wheel, Tilt	Std	Std
Rear Defroster	Std	Std
*Options Price	$925	$975
*Total Price	**$30,190**	**$34,175**
Target Price	$32,904	
Destination Charge	$570	
Avg. Tax & Fees	$1,866	
Total Target $	**$35,340**	
Average Dealer Option Cost:	84%	
12 Month Price Increase:	None	

For 1999, the 328iS coupe continues with minimal changes from last year's model. A new five speed automatic overdrive transmission is available this year. A power glass moonroof and rear spoiler are available as options. Also available is an optional keyless entry system, which includes a theft deterrent system. Additional options include an onboard navigation system and a Harman/Kardon sound system. The optional Sport Package includes fog lamps, alloy wheels and low-profile tires.

Ownership Costs (Projected)

Cost Area	5 Year Cost	Rating
Depreciation	$14,441	○
Financing ($586/month)	$6,874	
Insurance	$12,220	●
State Fees	$1,402	
Fuel (Hwy 27 City 20 -Prem.)	$3,745	○
Maintenance	$1,562	○
Repairs	$1,375	◉

Warranty/Maintenance Info

Major Tune-Up (35K mile int.)	$202	○
Minor Tune-Up (18K mile int.)	$135	○
Brake Service	$237	◉
Overall Warranty	4 yr/50k	○
Drivetrain Warranty	4 yr/50k	○
Rust Warranty	6 yr/unlim. mi	○
Maintenance Warranty	3 yr/36k	◔
Roadside Assistance	4 yr/50k	

Ownership Costs By Year (Projected)

$5,000 $10,000 $15,000

■ 1999
■ 2000
■ 2001
▨ 2002
□ 2003

Resale Value

1999	2000	2001	2002	2003
$31,543	$28,622	$26,027	$23,482	$20,899

Cumulative Costs

	1999	2000	2001	2002	2003
Annual	$9,539	$8,250	$7,746	$7,990	$8,094
Total	$9,539	$17,789	$25,535	$33,525	$41,619

Projected Costs (5yr)

Relative $40,785	This Car $41,619
Cost/Mile 58¢	Cost/Mile 59¢

Ownership Cost Value

◉ Average

14

* Includes shaded options
** Other purchase requirements apply
*** Price includes other options

● Poor	◉ Worse Than Average	◒ Average	○ Better Than Average	○ Excellent	⊖ Insufficient Information

Refer to *Section 3: Annotated Vehicle Charts* for an explanation of these charts.

BMW 328 iC
2 Door Convertible

Near Luxury

- 2.8L 190 hp Gas Fuel Inject.
- 6 Cylinder In-Line
- Manual 5 Speed
- 2 Wheel Rear
- Dual Front/Side Airbags Std

Purchase Price

Car Item	Dealer Cost	List
Base Price	**$36,530**	**$41,500**
Anti-Lock Brakes	Std	Std
Automatic 4 Speed	$925	$975
Optional Engine	N/A	N/A
Auto Climate Control	Std	Std
Power Steering	Std	Std
Cruise Control	Std	Std
Power Windows	Std	Std
AM/FM Stereo Cassette	Std	Std
Steering Wheel, Tilt	Std	Std
Rear Defroster	Std	Std
*Options Price	$925	$975
*Total Price	**$37,455**	**$42,475**
Target Price	$41,184	
Destination Charge	$570	
Avg. Tax & Fees	$2,322	
Luxury Tax	$345	
Total Target $	**$44,421**	
12 Month Price Increase:	None	

Ownership Costs (Projected)

Cost Area	5 Year Cost	Rating
Depreciation	$17,424	◯
Financing ($736/month)	$8,642	
Insurance	$12,828	◉
State Fees	$1,733	
Fuel (Hwy 27 City 20 -Prem.)	$3,745	◯
Maintenance	$1,562	◯
Repairs	$1,375	◉

Warranty/Maintenance Info

Major Tune-Up (35K mile int.)	$202		◯
Minor Tune-Up (18K mile int.)	$135		◯
Brake Service	$237		◉
Overall Warranty	4 yr/50k		◯
Drivetrain Warranty	4 yr/50k		◯
Rust Warranty	6 yr/unlim. mi		◯
Maintenance Warranty	3 yr/36k		◯
Roadside Assistance	4 yr/50k		

Ownership Costs By Year (Projected)

Scale: $5,000 — $10,000 — $15,000 — $20,000

- 1999
- 2000
- 2001
- 2002
- 2003

Resale Value

1999	2000	2001	2002	2003
$41,109	$37,243	$33,753	$30,368	$26,997

Cumulative Costs

	1999	2000	2001	2002	2003
Annual	$9,852	$9,876	$9,193	$9,243	$9,145
Total	$9,852	$19,728	$28,921	$38,164	$47,309

Projected Costs (5yr)

Relative	This Car
$48,841	$47,309
Cost/Mile 70¢	Cost/Mile 68¢

Ownership Cost Value

◯ Better Than Average

For 1999, the 328iC convertible remains mostly unchanged from last year's model. A new five speed automatic overdrive transmission is available this year. Options include a combination keyless entry/theft deterrent system and an automatically deploying Rollover Protection System. Additional options for 1999 include a Sport Package, which includes front fog lamps, alloy wheels and upgraded tires, and a Premium Package, which includes a power convertible roof.

BMW 328 i
4 Door Sedan

Near Luxury

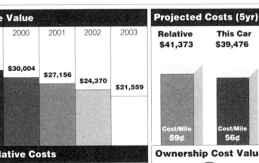

- 2.8L 193 hp Gas Fuel Inject.
- 6 Cylinder In-Line
- Manual 5 Speed
- 2 Wheel Rear
- Dual Front/Side Airbags Std

Purchase Price

Car Item	Dealer Cost	List
Base Price	**$29,725**	**$33,400**
Anti-Lock Brakes	Std	Std
Automatic 5 Speed	$1,140	$1,200
Optional Engine	N/A	N/A
Auto Climate Control	Std	Std
Power Steering	Std	Std
Cruise Control	Std	Std
Power Windows	Std	Std
AM/FM Stereo Cassette	Std	Std
Steering Wheel, Tilt	Std	Std
Rear Defroster	Std	Std
*Options Price	$1,140	$1,200
*Total Price	**$30,865**	**$34,600**
Target Price	$33,583	
Destination Charge	$570	
Avg. Tax & Fees	$1,902	
Total Target $	**$36,055**	
Average Dealer Option Cost:	**87%**	
12 Month Price Increase:	None	

Ownership Costs (Projected)

Cost Area	5 Year Cost	Rating
Depreciation	$14,496	◯
Financing ($598/month)	$7,014	
Insurance	$9,775	◯
State Fees	$1,420	
Fuel (Hwy 27 City 19 -Prem.)	$3,838	◯
Maintenance	$1,558	◯
Repairs	$1,375	◯

Warranty/Maintenance Info

Major Tune-Up (35K mile int.)	$202		◯
Minor Tune-Up (18K mile int.)	$135		◯
Brake Service	$234		◯
Overall Warranty	4 yr/50k		◯
Drivetrain Warranty	4 yr/50k		◯
Rust Warranty	6 yr/unlim. mi		◯
Maintenance Warranty	3 yr/36k		◯
Roadside Assistance	4 yr/50k		

Ownership Costs By Year (Projected)

Scale: $5,000 — $10,000 — $15,000

- 1999
- 2000
- 2001
- 2002
- 2003

Resale Value

1999	2000	2001	2002	2003
$33,187	$30,004	$27,156	$24,370	$21,559

Cumulative Costs

	1999	2000	2001	2002	2003
Annual	$8,213	$8,095	$7,560	$7,767	$7,841
Total	$8,213	$16,308	$23,868	$31,635	$39,476

Projected Costs (5yr)

Relative	This Car
$41,373	$39,476
Cost/Mile 59¢	Cost/Mile 56¢

Ownership Cost Value

◯ Excellent

For 1999, the 328i sedan receives many refinements including a new aluminum block engine (allowing the vehicle to receive Low Emissions Vehicle status), a revised body style with new headlamp and taillamp treatments, and new aluminum suspension components. A new five speed automatic overdrive transmission is available this year. An onboard navigation system, xenon low-beam headlamps and a power glass moonroof are available as options, as well as leather seats and a split folding rear seat.

---

* Includes shaded options

** Other purchase requirements apply

*** Price includes other options

● Poor | ◉ Worse Than Average | ◯ Average | ◯ Better Than Average | ◯ Excellent | ⊖ Insufficient Information

15

Refer to *Section 3: Annotated Vehicle Charts* for an explanation of these charts.

BMW M3
2 Door Convertible

Sport

3.2L 240 hp Gas Fuel Inject.	6 Cylinder In-Line	Manual 5 Speed
2 Wheel Rear	Dual Front/Side Airbags Std	

Purchase Price

Car Item	Dealer Cost	List
Base Price	**$40,375**	**$45,900**
Anti-Lock Brakes	Std	Std
Automatic 5 Speed	$1,115	$1,200
Optional Engine	N/A	N/A
Auto Climate Control	Std	Std
Power Steering	Std	Std
Cruise Control	$395	$475
Power Windows	Std	Std
AM/FM Stereo Cassette	Std	Std
Steering Wheel, Tilt	N/A	N/A
Rear Defroster	Std	Std
*Options Price	$395	$475
*Total Price	**$40,770**	**$46,375**
Target Price	$45,059	
Destination Charge	$570	
Avg. Tax & Fees	$2,535	
Luxury Tax	$578	
Total Target $	**$48,742**	
12 Month Price Increase:	None	

The M3 convertible is distinguished by its power-operated triple layer convertible top. Other exclusive convertible features include a Rollover Protection System and an available removable hard top. Motivation is provided via a 3.2L inline-six DOHC engine with 240 hp. For convenience, a five speed automatic transmission with three shift modes is optional. Safety features include dual front seat side-impact airbags and a four wheel antilock braking system with all-speed traction control.

Ownership Costs (Projected)

Cost Area	5 Year Cost	Rating
Depreciation	$17,669	◉
Financing ($808/month)	$9,484	
Insurance (Performance)	$15,394	●
State Fees	$1,892	
Fuel (Hwy 26 City 19 -Prem.)	$3,914	○
Maintenance	$2,078	○
Repairs	$1,680	◐

Warranty/Maintenance Info

Major Tune-Up (35K mile int.)	$202	○
Minor Tune-Up (18K mile int.)	$135	○
Brake Service	$314	◉
Overall Warranty	4 yr/50k	○
Drivetrain Warranty	4 yr/50k	○
Rust Warranty	6 yr/unlim. mi	○
Maintenance Warranty	3 yr/36k	○
Roadside Assistance	4 yr/50k	

Ownership Costs By Year (Projected)

Legend: 1999, 2000, 2001, 2002, 2003

Resale Value

1999	2000	2001	2002	2003
$44,591	$40,820	$37,451	$34,237	$31,073

Projected Costs (5yr)

Relative $57,331	This Car $52,111
Cost/Mile 82¢	Cost/Mile 74¢

Cumulative Costs

	1999	2000	2001	2002	2003
Annual	$11,539	$10,583	$9,824	$10,346	$9,819
Total	$11,539	$22,122	$31,946	$42,292	$52,111

Ownership Cost Value
○ Excellent

BMW M3
2 Door Coupe

Sport

3.2L 240 hp Gas Fuel Inject.	6 Cylinder In-Line	Manual 5 Speed
2 Wheel Rear	Dual Front/Side Airbags Std	

Purchase Price

Car Item	Dealer Cost	List
Base Price	**$34,955**	**$39,700**
Anti-Lock Brakes	Std	Std
Automatic Transmission	N/A	N/A
Optional Engine	N/A	N/A
Auto Climate Control	Std	Std
Power Steering	Std	Std
Cruise Control	$395	$475
Power Windows	Std	Std
AM/FM Stereo Cassette	Std	Std
Steering Wheel, Tilt	N/A	N/A
Rear Defroster	Std	Std
*Options Price	$395	$475
*Total Price	**$35,350**	**$40,175**
Target Price	$38,818	
Destination Charge	$570	
Avg. Tax & Fees	$2,192	
Luxury Tax	$203	
Total Target $	**$41,783**	
12 Month Price Increase:	None	

The M3 coupe features a 3.2L inline-six DOHC engine with 240 hp, an exclusive M-tuned sport suspension system and 17 inch alloy wheels (with M Contour II design wheels available as a no-charge option). Standard amenities include all-speed traction control, 12-way manually adjustable sport seats and dual front seat side-impact airbags. The flagship of the 3-series line, the M3 boasts outstanding performance, as evidenced by a 0 to 60 time of just 5.7 seconds with the five speed transmission.

Ownership Costs (Projected)

Cost Area	5 Year Cost	Rating
Depreciation	$15,097	◉
Financing ($693/month)	$8,128	
Insurance (Performance)	$16,035	●
State Fees	$1,642	
Fuel (Hwy 26 City 19 -Prem.)	$3,914	○
Maintenance	$2,095	○
Repairs	$1,680	◐

Warranty/Maintenance Info

Major Tune-Up (35K mile int.)	$202	○
Minor Tune-Up (18K mile int.)	$135	○
Brake Service	$314	◉
Overall Warranty	4 yr/50k	○
Drivetrain Warranty	4 yr/50k	○
Rust Warranty	6 yr/unlim. mi	○
Maintenance Warranty	3 yr/36k	○
Roadside Assistance	4 yr/50k	

Ownership Costs By Year (Projected)

Legend: 1999, 2000, 2001, 2002, 2003

Resale Value

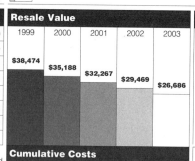

1999	2000	2001	2002	2003
$38,474	$35,188	$32,267	$29,469	$26,686

Projected Costs (5yr)

Relative $49,466	This Car $48,592
Cost/Mile 71¢	Cost/Mile 69¢

Cumulative Costs

	1999	2000	2001	2002	2003
Annual	$10,298	$9,794	$9,174	$9,857	$9,469
Total	$10,298	$20,092	$29,266	$39,123	$48,592

Ownership Cost Value
○ Better Than Average

16

* Includes shaded options
** Other purchase requirements apply
*** Price includes other options

 ● Poor ◐ Worse Than Average ◉ Average ○ Better Than Average ○ Excellent ⊖ Insufficient Information

Refer to *Section 3: Annotated Vehicle Charts* for an explanation of these charts.

BMW 528 i
4 Door Sedan

Luxury

2.8L 193 hp Gas Fuel Inject.	6 Cylinder In-Line
Manual 5 Speed	2 Wheel Rear
Dual Front/Side Airbags Std	

Purchase Price

Car Item	Dealer Cost	List
Base Price	**$34,665**	**$38,900**
Anti-Lock Brakes	Std	Std
Automatic 4 Speed	$925	$975
Optional Engine	N/A	N/A
Auto Climate Control	Std	Std
Power Steering	Std	Std
Cruise Control	Std	Std
Power Windows	Std	Std
AM/FM Stereo Cassette	Std	Std
St Whl, Tilt/Scope/Mem	Std	Std
Rear Defroster	Std	Std
*Options Price	$925	$975
*Total Price	**$35,590**	**$39,875**
Target Price	$38,675	
Destination Charge	$570	
Avg. Tax & Fees	$2,183	
Luxury Tax	$195	
Total Target $	**$41,623**	
12 Month Price Increase:	None	

The 1999 528i sedan arrives in the new model year sporting several changes to its standard and optional equipment lists. A new Sport-Premium Package combines the popular features of the Sport and Premium Packages into one. Appealing new features include a car and key memory system that allows individual users to tailor electronic functions to their own priorities and tastes, an infrared-reflecting windshield and a new aluminum cylinder block for the standard 193 hp six cylinder engine.

Ownership Costs (Projected)

Cost Area	5 Year Cost	Rating
Depreciation	$15,366	◒
Financing ($690/month)	$8,099	◒
Insurance	$9,911	◉
State Fees	$1,631	
Fuel (Hwy 26 City 18 - Prem.)	$4,017	○
Maintenance	$1,642	◒
Repairs	$1,571	◉

Warranty/Maintenance Info

Major Tune-Up (35K mile int.)	$202	○
Minor Tune-Up (18K mile int.)	$135	○
Brake Service	$249	◉
Overall Warranty	4 yr/50k	○
Drivetrain Warranty	4 yr/50k	○
Rust Warranty	6 yr/unlim. mi	○
Maintenance Warranty	3 yr/36k	○
Roadside Assistance	4 yr/50k	

Ownership Costs By Year (Projected)

Legend: 1999, 2000, 2001, 2002, 2003

Resale Value

1999	2000	2001	2002	2003
$37,269	$34,181	$31,469	$28,854	$26,257

Cumulative Costs

	1999	2000	2001	2002	2003
Annual	$10,179	$8,408	$7,754	$7,987	$7,909
Total	$10,179	$18,587	$26,341	$34,328	$42,237

Projected Costs (5yr)

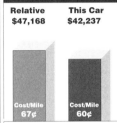

Relative	This Car
$47,168	$42,237
Cost/Mile 67¢	Cost/Mile 60¢

Ownership Cost Value
○ Excellent

BMW 528 i T
4 Door Wagon

Luxury

2.8L 193 hp Gas Fuel Inject.	6 Cylinder In-Line
Manual 5 Speed	2 Wheel Rear
Dual Front/Side Airbags Std	

Purchase Price

Car Item	Dealer Cost	List
Base Price	**$36,255**	**$40,700**
Anti-Lock Brakes	Std	Std
Automatic 4 Speed	$925	$975
Optional Engine	N/A	N/A
Auto Climate Control	Std	Std
Power Steering	Std	Std
Cruise Control	Std	Std
Power Windows	Std	Std
AM/FM Stereo Cassette	Std	Std
St Whl, Tilt/Scope/Mem	Std	Std
Rear Defroster	Std	Std
*Options Price	$925	$975
*Total Price	**$37,180**	**$41,675**
Target Price	$40,475	
Destination Charge	$570	
Avg. Tax & Fees	$2,282	
Luxury Tax	$303	
Total Target $	**$43,630**	
12 Month Price Increase:	N/A	

The 528iT wagon debuts in 1999 as a new model in the 5-series line. The wagon is based on the 528i sedan. Options include a Rear Seat Package with a retractable luggage net, rear window sun blinds and a unique retractable loading floor. A Park Distance Control System, featuring an ultrasonic warning device for maneuvering in tight places, is available. An optional Sport-Premium Package includes 17 inch wheels, Montana Leather interior and a multi-function M-Sport steering wheel.

Ownership Costs (Projected)

Cost Area	5 Year Cost	Rating
Depreciation	$17,045	◒
Financing ($723/month)	$8,487	◒
Insurance	$10,297	◉
State Fees	$1,702	
Fuel (Hwy 26 City 18 - Prem.)	$4,017	○
Maintenance	$1,642	◒
Repairs	$1,571	◉

Warranty/Maintenance Info

Major Tune-Up (35K mile int.)	$202	○
Minor Tune-Up (18K mile int.)	$135	○
Brake Service	$249	◉
Overall Warranty	4 yr/50k	○
Drivetrain Warranty	4 yr/50k	○
Rust Warranty	6 yr/unlim. mi	○
Maintenance Warranty	3 yr/36k	○
Roadside Assistance	4 yr/50k	

Ownership Costs By Year (Projected)

Legend: 1999, 2000, 2001, 2002, 2003

Resale Value

1999	2000	2001	2002	2003
$38,953	$35,525	$32,470	$29,520	$26,585

Cumulative Costs

	1999	2000	2001	2002	2003
Annual	$10,726	$8,946	$8,268	$8,465	$8,356
Total	$10,726	$19,672	$27,940	$36,405	$44,761

Projected Costs (5yr)

Relative	This Car
$48,867	$44,761
Cost/Mile 70¢	Cost/Mile 64¢

Ownership Cost Value
○ Excellent

---

* Includes shaded options
** Other purchase requirements apply
*** Price includes other options

| Poor | Worse Than Average | Average | Better Than Average | Excellent | Insufficient Information |

17

Refer to Section 3: Annotated Vehicle Charts for an explanation of these charts.

BMW 540 i
4 Door Sedan

Luxury

4.4L 282 hp Gas Fuel Inject.	8 Cylinder "V"	Automatic 5 Speed	2 Wheel Rear	Dual Front/Side Airbags Std

Purchase Price

Car Item	Dealer Cost	List
Base Price	**$44,925**	**$51,100**
Anti-Lock Brakes	Std	Std
Automatic 5 Speed	Pkg	Pkg
Optional Engine	N/A	N/A
Auto Climate Control	Std	Std
Power Steering	Std	Std
Cruise Control	Std	Std
Power Windows	Std	Std
AM/FM Stereo Cassette	Std	Std
St Whl, Tilt/Scope/Mem	Std	Std
Rear Defroster	Std	Std
*Options Price	$0	$0
*Total Price	$44,925	$51,100
Target Price	$49,358	
Destination Charge	$570	
Avg. Tax & Fees	$2,777	
Luxury Tax	$836	
Total Target $	**$53,541**	
12 Month Price Increase:	1%	

The 540i sedan continues in 1999 boasting several key enhancements. Most notable is the introduction of VANOS, a variable valve timing system, and other refinements which help the 540i achieve Low Emissions Vehicle (LEV) status. New engineering options include a Park Distance Control System and xenon headlamps. A new car and key memory system allows individual users to tailor functions to their own tastes. Other changes include option package revisions and a new infrared-reflecting windshield.

Ownership Costs (Projected)

Cost Area	5 Year Cost	Rating
Depreciation	$21,644	◯
Financing ($887/month)	$10,415	
Insurance (Performance)	$14,083	◉
State Fees	$2,080	
Fuel (Hwy 21 City 15 -Prem.)	$4,899	●
Maintenance	$1,806	◯
Repairs	$1,571	◯

Warranty/Maintenance Info

Major Tune-Up (35K mile int.)	$210	◯
Minor Tune-Up (18K mile int.)	$169	◉
Brake Service	$256	◯
Overall Warranty	4 yr/50k	◯
Drivetrain Warranty	4 yr/50k	◯
Rust Warranty	6 yr/unlim. mi	◯
Maintenance Warranty	3 yr/36k	◯
Roadside Assistance	4 yr/50k	

Ownership Costs By Year (Projected)

Legend: 1999, 2000, 2001, 2002, 2003

Resale Value

1999	2000	2001	2002	2003
$47,452	$43,140	$39,262	$35,541	$31,897

Cumulative Costs

	1999	2000	2001	2002	2003
Annual	$13,779	$11,358	$10,509	$10,645	$10,206
Total	$13,779	$25,137	$35,646	$46,291	$56,497

Projected Costs (5yr)

Relative	This Car
$57,168	$56,497
Cost/Mile 82¢	Cost/Mile 81¢

Ownership Cost Value

◯ Average

BMW 540 i T
4 Door Wagon

Luxury

4.4L 282 hp Gas Fuel Inject.	8 Cylinder "V"	Automatic 5 Speed	2 Wheel Rear	Dual Front/Side Airbags Std

Purchase Price

Car Item	Dealer Cost	List
Base Price	**$47,005**	**$53,480**
Anti-Lock Brakes	Std	Std
Manual Transmission	N/A	N/A
Optional Engine	N/A	N/A
Auto Climate Control	Std	Std
Power Steering	Std	Std
Cruise Control	Std	Std
Power Windows	Std	Std
AM/FM Stereo Cassette	Std	Std
St Whl, Tilt/Scope/Mem	Std	Std
Rear Defroster	Std	Std
*Options Price	$0	$0
*Total Price	$47,005	$53,480
Target Price	$51,646	
Destination Charge	$570	
Avg. Tax & Fees	$2,904	
Luxury Tax	$973	
Total Target $	**$56,093**	
12 Month Price Increase:	N/A	

The 540iT wagon arrives in 1999 as an addition to the 5-series lineup. Based upon the 540i sedan, the wagon includes features such as a fold-down rear seat, a self-leveling rear suspension system and a luggage compartment cover. Montana Leather interior appointments and burl walnut interior trim are standard equipment, as well as front seat side-impact airbags. Option Packages include a Sport Package with 17 inch alloy wheels, a sport suspension system, and Shadowline exterior trim.

Ownership Costs (Projected)

Cost Area	5 Year Cost	Rating
Depreciation	$23,741	◯
Financing ($930/month)	$10,912	
Insurance (Performance)	$13,519	◉
State Fees	$2,174	
Fuel (Hwy 21 City 15 -Prem.)	$4,899	●
Maintenance	$1,806	◯
Repairs	$1,571	◯

Warranty/Maintenance Info

Major Tune-Up (35K mile int.)	$210	◯
Minor Tune-Up (18K mile int.)	$169	◉
Brake Service	$256	◯
Overall Warranty	4 yr/50k	◯
Drivetrain Warranty	4 yr/50k	◯
Rust Warranty	6 yr/unlim. mi	◯
Maintenance Warranty	3 yr/36k	◯
Roadside Assistance	4 yr/50k	

Ownership Costs By Year (Projected)

Legend: 1999, 2000, 2001, 2002, 2003

Resale Value

1999	2000	2001	2002	2003
$49,770	$44,985	$40,642	$36,458	$32,352

Cumulative Costs

	1999	2000	2001	2002	2003
Annual	$14,098	$11,879	$10,983	$11,073	$10,588
Total	$14,098	$25,977	$36,960	$48,033	$58,621

Projected Costs (5yr)

Relative	This Car
$59,404	$58,621
Cost/Mile 85¢	Cost/Mile 84¢

Ownership Cost Value

◯ Better Than Average

18

* Includes shaded options
** Other purchase requirements apply
*** Price includes other options

 ● Poor   ◉ Worse Than Average   ◯ Average   ◯ Better Than Average   ◯ Excellent   ⊖ Insufficient Information

Refer to *Section 3: Annotated Vehicle Charts* for an explanation of these charts.

BMW 740 i
4 Door Sedan

 4.4L 282 hp Gas Fuel Inject.

 8 Cylinder "V"

 Automatic 5 Speed

 2 Wheel Rear

Dual Front/Side Airbags Std

Purchase Price

Car Item	Dealer Cost	List
Base Price	**$55,465**	**$62,400**
Anti-Lock Brakes	Std	Std
Automatic 5 Speed	Pkg	Pkg
Optional Engine	N/A	N/A
Air Conditioning	Std	Std
Power Steering	Std	Std
Cruise Control	Std	Std
Power Windows	Std	Std
AM/FM Stereo Cassette	Std	Std
St Whl, Pwr Tilt w/Mem	Std	Std
Rear Defroster	Std	Std
*Options Price	$0	$0
*Total Price	**$55,465**	**$62,400**
Target Price	$60,336	
Destination Charge	$570	
Avg. Tax & Fees	$3,384	
Luxury Tax	$1,494	
Total Target $	**$65,784**	
12 Month Price Increase:	2%	

For 1999, the 740i sedan receives minor revisions. Exterior revisions consist of a redesigned front fascia, new side indicator lights and a new trunklid molding. A new Sport Package option is now available. It includes 18 inch alloy wheels, a performance axle and torque converter, and sport suspension. The five speed Steptronic automatic transmission complements the Sport Package and enhances performance. For additional safety, rear side-impact airbags are offered as an option.

Ownership Costs (Projected)

Cost Area	5 Year Cost	Rating
Depreciation	$29,248	◐
Financing ($1,090/month)	$12,798	
Insurance (Performance)	$12,822	◐
State Fees	$2,533	
Fuel (Hwy 21 City 15 -Prem.)	$4,899	●
Maintenance	$1,890	○
Repairs	$1,675	◐

Warranty/Maintenance Info

Major Tune-Up (35K mile int.)	$283	◐
Minor Tune-Up (18K mile int.)	$189	●
Brake Service	$274	◐
Overall Warranty	4 yr/50k	○
Drivetrain Warranty	4 yr/50k	○
Rust Warranty	6 yr/unlim. mi	○
Maintenance Warranty	3 yr/36k	○
Roadside Assistance	4 yr/50k	

Ownership Costs By Year (Projected)

$5,000 $10,000 $15,000 $20,000 $25,000 $30,000

■ 1999
■ 2000
■ 2001
□ 2002
□ 2003

Resale Value

1999	2000	2001	2002	2003
$58,992	$52,818	$47,168	$41,765	$36,536

Cumulative Costs

	1999	2000	2001	2002	2003
Annual	$15,163	$13,734	$12,689	$12,427	$11,852
Total	$15,163	$28,897	$41,586	$54,013	$65,865

Projected Costs (5yr)

Relative	This Car
$68,533	$65,865
Cost/Mile 98¢	Cost/Mile 94¢

Ownership Cost Value

○

Better Than Average

BMW 740 iL
4 Door Sedan

Luxury

 4.4L 282 hp Gas Fuel Inject.

 8 Cylinder "V"

 Automatic 5 Speed

 2 Wheel Rear

Dual Front/Side Airbags Std

Purchase Price

Car Item	Dealer Cost	List
Base Price	**$58,305**	**$66,400**
Anti-Lock Brakes	Std	Std
Manual Transmission	N/A	N/A
Optional Engine	N/A	N/A
Air Conditioning	Std	Std
Power Steering	Std	Std
Cruise Control	Std	Std
Power Windows	Std	Std
AM/FM Stereo Cassette	Std	Std
St Whl, Pwr Tilt w/Mem	Std	Std
Rear Defroster	Std	Std
*Options Price	$0	$0
*Total Price	**$58,305**	**$66,400**
Target Price	$64,075	
Destination Charge	$570	
Avg. Tax & Fees	$3,592	
Luxury Tax	$1,719	
Total Target $	**$69,956**	
12 Month Price Increase:	2%	

For 1999, the 740iL sedan receives minor revisions. A refreshed front-end design, new side indicator lights and a new trunklid molding are some of the updated exterior elements. The engine has been tuned to meet Low Emission Vehicle (LEV) standards. In addition, both the door handles and the road surface next to the doors are now illuminated to enhance nighttime entry and exit. The 740iL includes 16-way dual power seats. The optional Park Distance Control offers assistance in parking maneuvers.

Ownership Costs (Projected)

Cost Area	5 Year Cost	Rating
Depreciation	$31,416	◐
Financing ($1,160/month)	$13,610	
Insurance (Performance)	$12,822	◐
State Fees	$2,693	
Fuel (Hwy 23 City 17 -Prem.)	$4,402	◐
Maintenance	$1,890	○
Repairs	$1,675	◐

Warranty/Maintenance Info

Major Tune-Up (35K mile int.)	$283	◐
Minor Tune-Up (18K mile int.)	$189	●
Brake Service	$274	◐
Overall Warranty	4 yr/50k	○
Drivetrain Warranty	4 yr/50k	○
Rust Warranty	6 yr/unlim. mi	○
Maintenance Warranty	3 yr/36k	○
Roadside Assistance	4 yr/50k	

Ownership Costs By Year (Projected)

$5 $10 $15 $20 $25 $30 $35 (x1,000)

■ 1999
■ 2000
■ 2001
□ 2002
□ 2003

Resale Value

1999	2000	2001	2002	2003
$62,322	$55,782	$49,796	$44,074	$38,540

Cumulative Costs

	1999	2000	2001	2002	2003
Annual	$16,225	$14,263	$13,126	$12,778	$12,116
Total	$16,225	$30,488	$43,614	$56,392	$68,508

Projected Costs (5yr)

Relative	This Car
$71,609	$68,508
Cost/Mile $1.02	Cost/Mile 98¢

Ownership Cost Value

○

Better Than Average

 Poor
 Worse Than Average
 Average
 Better Than Average
Excellent
⊖ Insufficient Information

19

Refer to *Section 3: Annotated Vehicle Charts* for an explanation of these charts.

BMW 750 iL
4 Door Sedan

Luxury

5.4L 322 hp Gas Fuel Inject.	12 Cylinder "V"	Automatic 5 Speed
2 Wheel Rear	Dual Front/Side Airbags Std	

Purchase Price

Car Item	Dealer Cost	List
Base Price	**$80,780**	**$92,100**
Anti-Lock Brakes	Std	Std
Manual Transmission	N/A	N/A
Optional Engine	N/A	N/A
Air Conditioning	Std	Std
Power Steering	Std	Std
Cruise Control	Std	Std
Power Windows	Std	Std
AM/FM Stereo Cass/CD	Std	Std
St Whl, Pwr Tilt w/Mem	Std	Std
Rear Defroster	Std	Std
***Options Price**	$0	$0
***Total Price**	**$80,780**	**$92,100**
Target Price	$88,795	
Destination Charge	$570	
Avg. Tax & Fees	$5,038	
Luxury/Gas Guzzler Tax	$5,004	
Total Target $	**$99,407**	
12 Month Price Increase:	1%	

For 1999, the 750iL sedan receives minor revisions. Exterior changes include a refreshed front-end design, new side indicator lights and a new trunklid molding. In addition, a navigation system and five speed Steptronic automatic transmission are now standard features. The 750iL upgrades the 740iL with numerous luxury amenities such as a heated steering wheel and rear seats and full Nappa leather upholstery. Available options include break-resistant glass and side-impact rear airbags.

Ownership Costs (Projected)

Cost Area	5 Year Cost	Rating
Depreciation	$52,469	◐
Financing ($1,648/month)	$19,339	
Insurance (Performance)	$15,604	◉
State Fees	$3,720	
Fuel (Hwy 20 City 13 -Prem.)	$5,388	●
Maintenance	$3,439	●
Repairs	$1,675	◐

Warranty/Maintenance Info

		Rating
Major Tune-Up (35K mile int.)	$896	●
Minor Tune-Up (18K mile int.)	$354	●
Brake Service	$297	◉
Overall Warranty	4 yr/50k	○
Drivetrain Warranty	4 yr/50k	○
Rust Warranty	6 yr/unlim. mi	○
Maintenance Warranty	3 yr/36k	○
Roadside Assistance	4 yr/50k	○

Ownership Costs By Year (Projected)

$5 $10 $15 $20 $25 $30 $35 $40 $45 $50 $55 (x1,000)

- 1999
- 2000
- 2001
- 2002
- 2003

Resale Value

1999	2000	2001	2002	2003
$78,760	$69,998	$61,919	$54,266	$46,938

Cumulative Costs

	1999	2000	2001	2002	2003
Annual	$32,159	$19,033	$18,025	$16,610	$15,807
Total	$32,159	$51,192	$69,217	$85,827	$101,634

Projected Costs (5yr)

Relative	This Car
$96,157	$101,634
Cost/Mile $1.37	Cost/Mile $1.45

Ownership Cost Value

◉ Worse Than Average

BMW Z3 2.3 Roadster
2 Door Convertible

Base Sport

2.3L 170 hp Gas Fuel Inject.	6 Cylinder In-Line	Manual 5 Speed
2 Wheel Rear	Dual Front/Side Airbags Std	

Purchase Price

Car Item	Dealer Cost	List
Base Price	**$26,555**	**$29,950**
Anti-Lock Brakes	Std	Std
Automatic 4 Speed	$925	$975
Optional Engine	N/A	N/A
Air Conditioning	Std	Std
Power Steering	Std	Std
Cruise Control	$395	$475
Power Windows	Std	Std
AM/FM Stereo Cassette	Std	Std
Steering Wheel, Tilt	N/A	N/A
Rear Defroster	N/A	N/A
***Options Price**	$395	$475
***Total Price**	**$26,950**	**$30,425**
Target Price	$29,447	
Destination Charge	$570	
Avg. Tax & Fees	$1,674	
Total Target $	**$31,691**	
Average Dealer Option Cost:	**84%**	
12 Month Price Increase:	2%	

The 1999 Z3 2.3 roadster receives a new 2.3L inline six cylinder engine generating 170 hp and 181 lb-ft of torque. The 2.3 roadster is now equipped with side-impact airbags for added safety. The available automatic transmission features Adaptive Transmission Control, which analyzes driving style and adapts to it. New this year are an optional removable hard top, single disc in-dash CD player and cross-spoke alloy wheels. Leather seating and a power convertible top are also optional.

Ownership Costs (Projected)

Cost Area	5 Year Cost	Rating
Depreciation	$13,237	○
Financing ($525/month)	$6,165	
Insurance (Performance)	$12,260	◉
State Fees	$1,253	
Fuel (Hwy 27 City 20 -Prem.)	$3,745	◉
Maintenance	$1,870	○
Repairs	$1,375	●

Warranty/Maintenance Info

		Rating
Major Tune-Up (35K mile int.)	$202	○
Minor Tune-Up (18K mile int.)	$148	◉
Brake Service	$259	○
Overall Warranty	4 yr/50k	○
Drivetrain Warranty	4 yr/50k	○
Rust Warranty	6 yr/unlim. mi	○
Maintenance Warranty	3 yr/36k	○
Roadside Assistance	4 yr/50k	

Ownership Costs By Year (Projected)

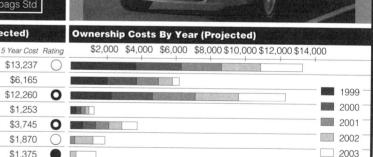

$2,000 $4,000 $6,000 $8,000 $10,000 $12,000 $14,000

- 1999
- 2000
- 2001
- 2002
- 2003

Resale Value

1999	2000	2001	2002	2003
$27,946	$25,311	$22,990	$20,742	$18,454

Cumulative Costs

	1999	2000	2001	2002	2003
Annual	$9,217	$7,742	$7,303	$7,933	$7,709
Total	$9,217	$16,959	$24,262	$32,195	$39,904

Projected Costs (5yr)

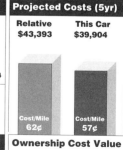

Relative	This Car
$43,393	$39,904
Cost/Mile 62¢	Cost/Mile 57¢

Ownership Cost Value

○ Excellent

BMW Z3 2.8 Coupe
2 Door Coupe

 2.8L 189 hp Gas Fuel Inject.
 6 Cylinder In-Line
 Manual 5 Speed
 2 Wheel Rear
Dual Front/Side Airbags Std

Base Sport

Purchase Price

Car Item	Dealer Cost	List
Base Price	**$31,895**	**$36,200**
Anti-Lock Brakes	Std	Std
Automatic 4 Speed	$925	$975
Optional Engine	N/A	N/A
Air Conditioning	Std	Std
Power Steering	Std	Std
Cruise Control	Std	Std
Power Windows	Std	Std
AM/FM Stereo Cassette	Std	Std
Steering Wheel, Tilt	N/A	N/A
Rear Defroster	Std	Std
*Options Price	$0	$0
*Total Price	**$31,895**	**$36,200**
Target Price	$35,369	
Destination Charge	$570	
Avg. Tax & Fees	$1,998	
Total Target $	**$37,937**	
Average Dealer Option Cost:	**85%**	
12 Month Price Increase:	N/A	

The new Z3 2.8 coupe makes its debut in 1999 with a daring new design. By adding a hard top onto the Z3 roadster body, the Z3 coupe is 200% stiffer than the Z3 roadster. The coupe is equipped with a 2.8L engine that produces 189 hp and 203 lb-ft of torque. Standard on the 2.8 coupe are sport seats, traction control, leather upholstery and a Harman/Kardon sound system. Available options include a power tilt moonroof, automatic transmission and single disc in-dash CD player.

Ownership Costs (Projected)

Cost Area	5 Year Cost	Rating
Depreciation		⊖
Financing ($629/month)	$7,380	
Insurance (Performance)	$13,111	◐
State Fees	$1,484	
Fuel (Hwy 26 City 19 -Prem.)	$3,914	◉
Maintenance	$1,870	○
Repairs	$1,375	●

Warranty/Maintenance Info

Major Tune-Up (35K mile int.)	$202	○
Minor Tune-Up (18K mile int.)	$148	◐
Brake Service	$259	◐
Overall Warranty	4 yr/50k	○
Drivetrain Warranty	4 yr/50k	○
Rust Warranty	6 yr/unlim. mi	○
Maintenance Warranty	3 yr/36k	○
Roadside Assistance	4 yr/50k	

Ownership Costs By Year (Projected)

$2,000 $4,000 $6,000 $8,000 $10,000 $12,000 $14,000

Insufficient Depreciation Information

1999 / 2000 / 2001 / 2002 / 2003

Resale Value

Insufficient Information

Projected Costs (5yr)

Insufficient Information

Cumulative Costs

	1999	2000	2001	2002	2003
Annual	*Insufficient Information*				
Total	*Insufficient Information*				

Ownership Cost Value

⊖ Insufficient Information

BMW Z3 2.8 Roadster
2 Door Convertible

 2.8L 189 hp Gas Fuel Inject.
6 Cylinder In-Line
Manual 5 Speed
 2 Wheel Rear
Dual Front/Side Airbags Std

Base Sport

Purchase Price

Car Item	Dealer Cost	List
Base Price	**$31,895**	**$36,200**
Anti-Lock Brakes	Std	Std
Automatic 4 Speed	$925	$975
Optional Engine	N/A	N/A
Air Conditioning	Std	Std
Power Steering	Std	Std
Cruise Control	Std	Std
Power Windows	Std	Std
AM/FM Stereo Cassette	Std	Std
Steering Wheel, Tilt	N/A	N/A
Rear Defroster	N/A	N/A
*Options Price	$0	$0
*Total Price	**$31,895**	**$36,200**
Target Price	$35,249	
Destination Charge	$570	
Avg. Tax & Fees	$1,993	
Total Target $	**$37,812**	
Average Dealer Option Cost:	**84%**	
12 Month Price Increase:	1%	

The 1999 Z3 2.8 roadster now features standard side-impact airbags, an option in 1998. The 2.8L engine produces 189 hp and 203 lb-ft of torque for added power. Now available are an optional removable hard top, single disc in-dash CD player and the popular BMW cross-spoke alloy wheels. The 2.8 roadster can be ordered with an optional power top for added convenience. The 2.8 features a nine speaker Harman/Kardon sound system, traction control and leather bucket seats.

Ownership Costs (Projected)

Cost Area	5 Year Cost	Rating
Depreciation	$15,795	○
Financing ($627/month)	$7,356	
Insurance (Performance)	$13,111	◐
State Fees	$1,484	
Fuel (Hwy 26 City 19 -Prem.)	$3,914	◉
Maintenance	$1,870	○
Repairs	$1,375	●

Warranty/Maintenance Info

Major Tune-Up (35K mile int.)	$202	○
Minor Tune-Up (18K mile int.)	$148	◐
Brake Service	$259	◐
Overall Warranty	4 yr/50k	○
Drivetrain Warranty	4 yr/50k	○
Rust Warranty	6 yr/unlim. mi	○
Maintenance Warranty	3 yr/36k	○
Roadside Assistance	4 yr/50k	

Ownership Costs By Year (Projected)

$5,000 $10,000 $15,000 $20,000

1999 / 2000 / 2001 / 2002 / 2003

Resale Value

1999	2000	2001	2002	2003
$33,057	$29,988	$27,265	$24,644	$22,017

Projected Costs (5yr)

Relative $47,503	This Car $44,906
Cost/Mile 68¢	Cost/Mile 64¢

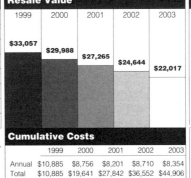

Cumulative Costs

	1999	2000	2001	2002	2003
Annual	$10,885	$8,756	$8,201	$8,710	$8,354
Total	$10,885	$19,641	$27,842	$36,552	$44,906

Ownership Cost Value

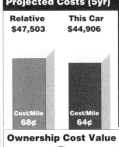
○ Excellent

 ● Poor
 ◉ Worse Than Average
 ◐ Average
 ○ Better Than Average
 ○ Excellent
 ⊖ Insufficient Information

21

Refer to *Section 3: Annotated Vehicle Charts* for an explanation of these charts.

BMW Z3 M Coupe
2 Door Coupe

Sport

| 3.2L 240 hp Gas Fuel Inject. | 6 Cylinder In-Line | Manual 5 Speed | 2 Wheel Rear | Dual Front/Side Airbags Std |

Purchase Price

Car Item	Dealer Cost	List
Base Price	**$36,795**	**$41,800**
Anti-Lock Brakes	Std	Std
Automatic Transmission	N/A	N/A
Optional Engine	N/A	N/A
Air Conditioning	Std	Std
Power Steering	Std	Std
Cruise Control	Std	Std
Power Windows	Std	Std
AM/FM Stereo Cassette	Std	Std
Steering Wheel, Tilt	N/A	N/A
Rear Defroster	Std	Std
*Options Price	$0	$0
*Total Price	**$36,795**	**$41,800**
Target Price	$41,078	
Destination Charge	$570	
Avg. Tax & Fees	$2,311	
Luxury Tax	$339	
Total Target $	**$44,298**	
12 Month Price Increase:	N/A	

The new Z3 M coupe enters the 1999 model year with bold styling enhancements. Based on the Z3 roadster, the hard top gives the coupe a 200% stiffer frame. The stiffer body, 240 hp engine and heavy duty suspension provide improved performance and handling. The M coupe comes well-equipped with dual power leather sport seats, power windows, power locks and a Harman/Kardon sound system. The few options on the M coupe include a power tilt moonroof and an in-dash CD player.

Ownership Costs (Projected)

Cost Area	5 Year Cost	Rating
Depreciation		⊖
Financing ($734/month)	$8,617	
Insurance (Performance)	$13,685	◐
State Fees	$1,708	
Fuel (Hwy 26 City 19 -Prem.)	$3,914	○
Maintenance	$1,960	◔
Repairs	$1,375	●

Warranty/Maintenance Info

Major Tune-Up (35K mile int.)	$202	○
Minor Tune-Up (18K mile int.)	$148	○
Brake Service	$259	○
Overall Warranty	4 yr/50k	○
Drivetrain Warranty	4 yr/50k	○
Rust Warranty	6 yr/unlim. mi	○
Maintenance Warranty	3 yr/36k	◔
Roadside Assistance	4 yr/50k	

Ownership Costs By Year (Projected)

$2,000 $4,000 $6,000 $8,000 $10,000 $12,000 $14,000

Insufficient Depreciation Information

■	1999
■	2000
▨	2001
▨	2002
□	2003

Resale Value

Insufficient

Information

Cumulative Costs

	1999	2000	2001	2002	2003
Annual	*Insufficient Information*				
Total	*Insufficient Information*				

Projected Costs (5yr)

Insufficient

Information

Ownership Cost Value

⊖

Insufficient Information

BMW Z3 M Roadster
2 Door Convertible

Sport

| 3.2L 240 hp Gas Fuel Inject. | 6 Cylinder In-Line | Manual 5 Speed | 2 Wheel Rear | Dual Front/Side Airbags Std |

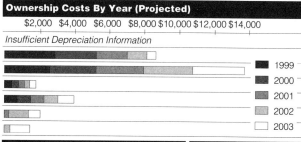

Purchase Price

Car Item	Dealer Cost	List
Base Price	**$37,575**	**$42,700**
Anti-Lock Brakes	Std	Std
Automatic Transmission	N/A	N/A
Optional Engine	N/A	N/A
Air Conditioning	Std	Std
Power Steering	Std	Std
Cruise Control	Std	Std
Power Windows	Std	Std
AM/FM Stereo Cassette	Std	Std
Steering Wheel, Tilt	N/A	N/A
Rear Defroster	N/A	N/A
*Options Price	$0	$0
*Total Price	**$37,575**	**$42,700**
Target Price	$41,995	
Destination Charge	$570	
Avg. Tax & Fees	$2,361	
Luxury Tax	$394	
Total Target $	**$45,320**	
12 Month Price Increase:	1%	

The Z3 M roadster is for individuals who desire performance with the open-air feeling of a drop top. The M roadster features a 3.2L inline six cylinder engine that generates 240 hp and 236 lb-ft of torque. For added convenience, a power convertible top that can be lowered with the push of a button is standard equipment. The M roadster offers a removable hard top and a CD player as options. Heated sport seats and power windows and side mirrors are all standard.

Ownership Costs (Projected)

Cost Area	5 Year Cost	Rating
Depreciation	$18,714	○
Financing ($751/month)	$8,817	
Insurance (Performance)	$13,685	◐
State Fees	$1,744	
Fuel (Hwy 26 City 19 -Prem.)	$3,914	○
Maintenance	$1,999	◔
Repairs	$1,375	●

Warranty/Maintenance Info

Major Tune-Up (35K mile int.)	$202	○
Minor Tune-Up (18K mile int.)	$148	○
Brake Service	$264	○
Overall Warranty	4 yr/50k	○
Drivetrain Warranty	4 yr/50k	○
Rust Warranty	6 yr/unlim. mi	○
Maintenance Warranty	3 yr/36k	◔
Roadside Assistance	4 yr/50k	

Ownership Costs By Year (Projected)

$5,000 $10,000 $15,000 $20,000

■	1999
■	2000
▨	2001
▨	2002
□	2003

Resale Value

1999	2000	2001	2002	2003
$39,129	$35,638	$32,528	$29,553	$26,606

Projected Costs (5yr)

Relative $52,788	This Car $50,249
Cost/Mile 75¢	Cost/Mile 72¢

Cumulative Costs

	1999	2000	2001	2002	2003
Annual	$12,991	$9,751	$9,056	$9,548	$8,903
Total	$12,991	$22,742	$31,798	$41,346	$50,249

Ownership Cost Value

○

Excellent

22

* Includes shaded options
** Other purchase requirements apply
*** Price includes other options

 Poor   Worse Than Average   Average   Better Than Average   Excellent   Insufficient Information

Refer to *Section 3: Annotated Vehicle Charts* for an explanation of these charts.

Buick Century Custom
4 Door Sedan

Midsize

3.1L 160 hp Gas Fuel Inject.

6 Cylinder "V"

Automatic 4 Speed

2 Wheel Front

Dual Airbags Std

Purchase Price

Car Item	Dealer Cost	List
Base Price	**$17,555**	**$18,775**
Anti-Lock Brakes	Std	Std
Manual Transmission	N/A	N/A
Optional Engine	N/A	N/A
Air Conditioning	Std	Std
Power Steering	Std	Std
Cruise Control	$194	$225
Power Windows	Std	Std
AM/FM Stereo Cassette	$168	$195
Steering Wheel, Tilt	Std	Std
1SA Package	N/C	N/C
***Options Price**	**$362**	**$420**
***Total Price**	**$17,917**	**$19,195**
Target Price	$18,669	
Destination Charge	$560	
Avg. Tax & Fees	$1,076	
Total Target $	**$20,305**	
Average Dealer Option Cost:	*86%*	
12 Month Price Increase:	3%	

The 1999 Century Custom sedan remains mostly unchanged from last year. New standard features include a tire inflation monitor and traction control. More new features include a Concert Sound III system that comes equipped with an amplifier and a diversity antenna. Also new are memory locks that allow the driver to program the locks to open or close when the transmission is moved in and out of park. Available options include an Astroroof and steering wheel radio controls.

Ownership Costs (Projected)

Cost Area	5 Year Cost	Rating
Depreciation	$10,245	◯
Financing ($337/month)	$3,951	
Insurance	$6,852	◯
State Fees	$804	
Fuel (Hwy 29 City 20)	$3,041	◯
Maintenance	$3,235	◯
Repairs	$700	◯

Warranty/Maintenance Info

Major Tune-Up (100K mile int.)	$225	◯
Minor Tune-Up (30K mile int.)	$132	◉
Brake Service	$248	◯
Overall Warranty	3 yr/36k	◯
Drivetrain Warranty	3 yr/36k	◯
Rust Warranty	6 yr/100k	◯
Maintenance Warranty	N/A	
Roadside Assistance	3 yr/36k	

Ownership Costs By Year (Projected)

1999, 2000, 2001, 2002, 2003

Resale Value

1999	2000	2001	2002	2003
$17,584	$15,482	$13,672	$11,832	$10,060

Cumulative Costs

	1999	2000	2001	2002	2003
Annual	$6,191	$5,363	$5,191	$5,360	$6,723
Total	$6,191	$11,554	$16,745	$22,105	$28,828

Projected Costs (5yr)

Relative	This Car
$29,375	$28,828
Cost/Mile 42¢	Cost/Mile 41¢

Ownership Cost Value

◯ Better Than Average

Buick Century Limited
4 Door Sedan

Midsize

3.1L 160 hp Gas Fuel Inject.

6 Cylinder "V"

Automatic 4 Speed

2 Wheel Front

Dual Airbags Std

Purchase Price

Car Item	Dealer Cost	List
Base Price	**$18,433**	**$20,145**
Anti-Lock Brakes	Std	Std
Manual Transmission	N/A	N/A
Optional Engine	N/A	N/A
Air Conditioning	Std	Std
Power Steering	Std	Std
Cruise Control	$194	$225
Power Windows	Std	Std
AM/FM Stereo Cassette	$168	$195
Steering Wheel, Tilt	Std	Std
1SD Package	N/C	N/C
***Options Price**	**$362**	**$420**
***Total Price**	**$18,795**	**$20,565**
Target Price	$19,866	
Destination Charge	$560	
Avg. Tax & Fees	$1,143	
Total Target $	**$21,569**	
Average Dealer Option Cost:	*86%*	
12 Month Price Increase:	3%	

The 1999 Century Limited sedan comes equipped with all of the same new standard features as those of the Custom model. A new enhanced antilock braking system and outside dimming mirrors have been added for 1999. Also newly available is the optional OnStar Communication System, which provides emergency services, navigation and travel support. This service requires a mobile phone and includes a monthly service fee. The exterior pearlcoat paint color Auburn Nightmist has been added this year.

Ownership Costs (Projected)

Cost Area	5 Year Cost	Rating
Depreciation	$11,186	◉
Financing ($358/month)	$4,195	
Insurance	$7,140	◯
State Fees	$858	
Fuel (Hwy 29 City 20)	$3,041	◯
Maintenance	$3,235	◯
Repairs	$700	◯

Warranty/Maintenance Info

Major Tune-Up (100K mile int.)	$225	◯
Minor Tune-Up (30K mile int.)	$132	◉
Brake Service	$248	◯
Overall Warranty	3 yr/36k	◯
Drivetrain Warranty	3 yr/36k	◯
Rust Warranty	6 yr/100k	◯
Maintenance Warranty	N/A	
Roadside Assistance	3 yr/36k	

Ownership Costs By Year (Projected)

1999, 2000, 2001, 2002, 2003

Resale Value

1999	2000	2001	2002	2003
$18,566	$16,288	$14,311	$12,309	$10,383

Cumulative Costs

	1999	2000	2001	2002	2003
Annual	$6,625	$5,674	$5,476	$5,623	$6,957
Total	$6,625	$12,299	$17,775	$23,398	$30,355

Projected Costs (5yr)

Relative	This Car
$30,266	$30,355
Cost/Mile 43¢	Cost/Mile 43¢

Ownership Cost Value

◯ Average

---

* Includes shaded options

** Other purchase requirements apply

*** Price includes other options

● Poor   ◉ Worse Than Average   ◯ Average   ◯ Better Than Average   ◯ Excellent   ⊖ Insufficient Information

23

Refer to *Section 3: Annotated Vehicle Charts* for an explanation of these charts.

Buick LeSabre Custom
4 Door Sedan

| 3.8L 205 hp Gas Fuel Inject. | 6 Cylinder "V" | Automatic 4 Speed | 2 Wheel Front | Dual Airbags Std |

Limited Model Shown

Large

Purchase Price

Car Item	Dealer Cost	List
Base Price	**$20,793**	**$22,725**
Anti-Lock Brakes	Std	Std
Manual Transmission	N/A	N/A
Optional Engine	N/A	N/A
Air Conditioning	Std	Std
Power Steering	Std	Std
Cruise Control	Std	Std
Power Windows	Std	Std
AM/FM Stereo Cassette	$168	$195
Steering Wheel, Tilt	Std	Std
1SA Package	N/C	N/C
***Options Price**	$168	$195
***Total Price**	**$20,961**	**$22,920**
Target Price	$21,969	
Destination Charge	$615	
Avg. Tax & Fees	$1,264	
Total Target $	**$23,848**	
Average Dealer Option Cost:	**86%**	
12 Month Price Increase:	1%	

Mostly unchanged for 1999, the LeSabre Custom sedan enters this model year celebrating its 40th anniversary. A new feature is a memory door lock system that allows the driver to program the locks to open or close when the transmission is moved in and out of park. The optional Gran Touring Package includes magnetic variable-assist power steering, 16 inch aluminum wheels and automatic leveling control. The LeSabre was a 1998 BOVY (Best Overall Value Award) winner in the Large class category.

Ownership Costs (Projected)

Cost Area	5 Year Cost	Rating
Depreciation	$12,060	◐
Financing ($395/month)	$4,639	
Insurance	$7,140	◯
State Fees	$954	
Fuel (Hwy 30 City 19)	$3,070	◯
Maintenance	$2,997	◐
Repairs	$895	◐

Warranty/Maintenance Info

Major Tune-Up (100K mile int.)	$251	◐
Minor Tune-Up (30K mile int.)	$100	◐
Brake Service	$271	◐
Overall Warranty	3 yr/36k	◐
Drivetrain Warranty	3 yr/36k	◐
Rust Warranty	6 yr/100k	◯
Maintenance Warranty	N/A	
Roadside Assistance	3 yr/36k	

Ownership Costs By Year (Projected)

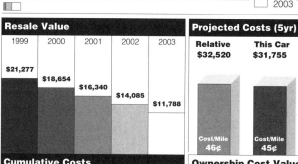

$2,000 $4,000 $6,000 $8,000 $10,000 $12,000 $14,000

■ 1999 ■ 2000 ■ 2001 ◱ 2002 ☐ 2003

Resale Value

1999	2000	2001	2002	2003
$21,277	$18,654	$16,340	$14,085	$11,788

Cumulative Costs

	1999	2000	2001	2002	2003
Annual	$6,372	$6,170	$5,903	$6,059	$7,251
Total	$6,372	$12,542	$18,445	$24,504	$31,755

Projected Costs (5yr)

Relative	This Car
$32,520	$31,755
Cost/Mile 46¢	Cost/Mile 45¢

Ownership Cost Value

◯ Excellent

Buick LeSabre Limited
4 Door Sedan

| 3.8L 205 hp Gas Fuel Inject. | 6 Cylinder "V" | Automatic 4 Speed | 2 Wheel Front | Dual Airbags Std |

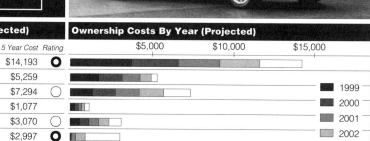

Large

Purchase Price

Car Item	Dealer Cost	List
Base Price	**$23,781**	**$25,990**
Anti-Lock Brakes	Std	Std
Manual Transmission	N/A	N/A
Optional Engine	N/A	N/A
Air Conditioning	Std	Std
Power Steering	Std	Std
Cruise Control	Std	Std
Power Windows	Std	Std
AM/FM Stereo Cassette	Std	Std
Steering Wheel, Tilt	Std	Std
1SD Package	N/C	N/C
***Options Price**	$0	$0
***Total Price**	**$23,781**	**$25,990**
Target Price	$24,984	
Destination Charge	$615	
Avg. Tax & Fees	$1,431	
Total Target $	**$27,030**	
Average Dealer Option Cost:	**86%**	
12 Month Price Increase:	1%	

Mostly unchanged for 1999, the LeSabre Limited sedan is manufactured in Flint, Michigan and is an upgrade of the Custom model. Available as a dealer option is the OnStar Communication System (which requires a cellular phone). It provides assistance such as automatic emergency service notification when the airbags deploy, as well as navigation and travel support. A notable maintenance feature is an oil life monitor that tells you when it's time to change the oil.

Ownership Costs (Projected)

Cost Area	5 Year Cost	Rating
Depreciation	$14,193	◐
Financing ($448/month)	$5,259	
Insurance	$7,294	◯
State Fees	$1,077	
Fuel (Hwy 30 City 19)	$3,070	◯
Maintenance	$2,997	◐
Repairs	$895	◐

Warranty/Maintenance Info

Major Tune-Up (100K mile int.)	$251	◐
Minor Tune-Up (30K mile int.)	$100	◐
Brake Service	$271	◐
Overall Warranty	3 yr/36k	◐
Drivetrain Warranty	3 yr/36k	◐
Rust Warranty	6 yr/100k	◯
Maintenance Warranty	N/A	
Roadside Assistance	3 yr/36k	

Ownership Costs By Year (Projected)

$5,000 $10,000 $15,000

■ 1999 ■ 2000 ■ 2001 ◱ 2002 ☐ 2003

Resale Value

1999	2000	2001	2002	2003
$23,229	$20,368	$17,825	$15,348	$12,837

Cumulative Costs

	1999	2000	2001	2002	2003
Annual	$7,872	$6,636	$6,316	$6,415	$7,546
Total	$7,872	$14,508	$20,824	$27,239	$34,785

Projected Costs (5yr)

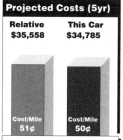

Relative	This Car
$35,558	$34,785
Cost/Mile 51¢	Cost/Mile 50¢

Ownership Cost Value

◯ Better Than Average

24

* Includes shaded options
** Other purchase requirements apply
*** Price includes other options

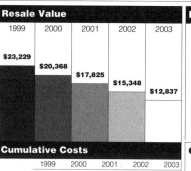

● Poor ◉ Worse Than Average ◐ Average ◯ Better Than Average ◯ Excellent ⊖ Insufficient Information

Refer to *Section 3: Annotated Vehicle Charts* for an explanation of these charts.

Buick Park Avenue
4 Door Sedan

 3.8L 205 hp Gas Fuel Inject.

 6 Cylinder "V"

 Automatic 4 Speed

 2 Wheel Front

 Dual Airbags Std

Purchase Price

Car Item	Dealer Cost	List
Base Price	**$28,173**	**$31,130**
Anti-Lock Brakes	Std	Std
Manual Transmission	N/A	N/A
Optional Engine	N/A	N/A
Auto Climate Control	Std	Std
Power Steering	Std	Std
Cruise Control	Std	Std
Power Windows	Std	Std
AM/FM Stereo Cassette	Std	Std
Steering Wheel, Tilt	Std	Std
1SA Package	N/C	N/C
***Options Price**	**$0**	**$0**
***Total Price**	**$28,173**	**$31,130**
Target Price	$29,290	
Destination Charge	$670	
Avg. Tax & Fees	$1,679	
Total Target $	**$31,639**	
Average Dealer Option Cost:	***86%***	
12 Month Price Increase:	*1%*	

Ownership Costs (Projected)

Cost Area	5 Year Cost	Rating
Depreciation	$16,031	◉
Financing ($524/month)	$6,156	
Insurance	$7,643	○
State Fees	$1,285	
Fuel (Hwy 28 City 19)	$3,176	○
Maintenance	$2,212	○
Repairs	$1,045	○

Warranty/Maintenance Info

Major Tune-Up (100K mile int.)	$250	○
Minor Tune-Up (30K mile int.)	$119	○
Brake Service	$238	○
Overall Warranty	3 yr/36k	○
Drivetrain Warranty	3 yr/36k	○
Rust Warranty	6 yr/100k	○
Maintenance Warranty	N/A	
Roadside Assistance	3 yr/36k	

Ownership Costs By Year (Projected)

$5,000 $10,000 $15,000 $20,000

- 1999
- 2000
- 2001
- 2002
- 2003

Resale Value

1999	2000	2001	2002	2003
$27,409	$24,158	$21,260	$18,437	$15,608

Projected Costs (5yr)

Relative	This Car
$39,223	$37,548
Cost/Mile 56¢	Cost/Mile 54¢

Cumulative Costs

	1999	2000	2001	2002	2003
Annual	$8,746	$7,409	$7,009	$7,056	$7,328
Total	$8,746	$16,155	$23,164	$30,220	$37,548

Ownership Cost Value

○ Excellent

For the 1999 model year the Park Avenue returns with an optional dealer-installed OnStar Communication System. Combined with satellite technology and a voice-activated cellular telephone, it links the driver to a communications center, where advisors are available to provide assistance such as travel directions and roadside assistance. The EyeCue heads-up display projects information onto the windshield such as vehicle speed, turn signal indicators and special check gauges.

Buick Park Avenue Ultra
4 Door Sedan

Near Luxury

 3.8L 240 hp Suprchrged Fuel Inject.

  6 Cylinder "V"

 Automatic 4 Speed

 2 Wheel Front

 Dual Airbags Std

Purchase Price

Car Item	Dealer Cost	List
Base Price	**$32,603**	**$36,025**
Anti-Lock Brakes	Std	Std
Manual Transmission	N/A	N/A
Optional Engine	N/A	N/A
Auto Climate Control	Std	Std
Power Steering	Std	Std
Cruise Control	Std	Std
Power Windows	Std	Std
AM/FM Stereo Cass/CD	Std	Std
Steering Wheel, Tilt	Std	Std
1SE Package	N/C	N/C
***Options Price**	**$0**	**$0**
***Total Price**	**$32,603**	**$36,025**
Target Price	$33,984	
Destination Charge	$670	
Avg. Tax & Fees	$1,939	
Total Target $	**$36,593**	
Average Dealer Option Cost:	***86%***	
12 Month Price Increase:	*1%*	

Ownership Costs (Projected)

Cost Area	5 Year Cost	Rating
Depreciation	$20,335	●
Financing ($607/month)	$7,120	
Insurance	$7,837	○
State Fees	$1,481	
Fuel (Hwy 27 City 18 -Prem.)	$3,942	◑
Maintenance	$2,202	○
Repairs	$1,210	◑

Warranty/Maintenance Info

Major Tune-Up (100K mile int.)	$249	○
Minor Tune-Up (30K mile int.)	$119	○
Brake Service	$238	○
Overall Warranty	3 yr/36k	○
Drivetrain Warranty	3 yr/36k	○
Rust Warranty	6 yr/100k	○
Maintenance Warranty	N/A	
Roadside Assistance	3 yr/36k	

Ownership Costs By Year (Projected)

$5,000 $10,000 $15,000 $20,000 $25,000

- 1999
- 2000
- 2001
- 2002
- 2003

Resale Value

1999	2000	2001	2002	2003
$29,495	$25,863	$22,599	$19,423	$16,258

Projected Costs (5yr)

Relative	This Car
$43,038	$44,127
Cost/Mile 61¢	Cost/Mile 63¢

Cumulative Costs

	1999	2000	2001	2002	2003
Annual	$12,173	$8,287	$7,830	$7,831	$8,006
Total	$12,173	$20,460	$28,290	$36,121	$44,127

Ownership Cost Value

◉ Worse Than Average

For the 1999 model year the Park Avenue Ultra returns with an optional dealer-installed OnStar Communication System. Using satellite technology and a voice-activated cellular phone, it links the driver to a communications center, where advisors are available to provide emergency services and travel directions. The EyeCue heads-up display projects vehicle speed and various indicators onto the windshield. An electronic vehicle status information display is also standard.

● Poor   ◉ Worse Than Average   ◐ Average   ○ Better Than Average   ○ Excellent   ⊖ Insufficient Information

25

Refer to *Section 3: Annotated Vehicle Charts* for an explanation of these charts.

Buick Regal LS
4 Door Sedan

Midsize

 3.8L 200 hp Gas Fuel Inject.

 6 Cylinder "V"

 Automatic 4 Speed

 2 Wheel Front

Depowered Dual Airbags Std

Purchase Price

Car Item	Dealer Cost	List
Base Price	**$19,850**	**$21,695**
Anti-Lock Brakes	Std	Std
Manual Transmission	N/A	N/A
Optional Engine	N/A	N/A
Air Conditioning	Std	Std
Power Steering	Std	Std
Cruise Control	Std	Std
Power Windows	Std	Std
AM/FM Stereo Cassette	Std	Std
Steering Wheel, Tilt	Std	Std
1SA Package	N/C	N/C
***Options Price**	**$0**	**$0**
***Total Price**	**$19,850**	**$21,695**
Target Price	$20,787	
Destination Charge	$560	
Avg. Tax & Fees	$1,197	
Total Target $	**$22,544**	
Average Dealer Option Cost:	**86%**	
12 Month Price Increase:	4%	

The Regal LS sedan has many new amenities for 1999. Some of these standard features include a new tire inflation monitor, an in-glass rear window antenna and Concert Sound II speaker system. For 1999 the 3.8L engine in the Regal LS receives an increase in power, resulting in 200 hp and 225 lb-ft of torque. Optional equipment includes 15 inch aluminum alloy wheels, an outside electrochromic rearview mirror and a Monsoon Premium audio system.

Ownership Costs (Projected)

Cost Area	5 Year Cost	Rating
Depreciation	$10,758	◐
Financing ($374/month)	$4,385	
Insurance	$7,140	○
State Fees	$904	
Fuel (Hwy 30 City 19)	$3,070	◐
Maintenance	$3,618	◉
Repairs	$820	◐

Warranty/Maintenance Info

Major Tune-Up (100K mile int.)	$255	◐
Minor Tune-Up (30K mile int.)	$132	◉
Brake Service	$250	◐
Overall Warranty	3 yr/36k	◐
Drivetrain Warranty	3 yr/36k	◐
Rust Warranty	6 yr/100k	○
Maintenance Warranty	N/A	
Roadside Assistance	3 yr/36k	

Ownership Costs By Year (Projected)

$2,000 $4,000 $6,000 $8,000 $10,000 $12,000

■ 1999
■ 2000
■ 2001
□ 2002
□ 2003

Resale Value

1999	2000	2001	2002	2003
$20,225	$17,874	$15,828	$13,767	$11,786

Cumulative Costs

	1999	2000	2001	2002	2003
Annual	$6,022	$5,816	$5,616	$5,753	$7,488
Total	$6,022	$11,838	$17,454	$23,207	$30,695

Projected Costs (5yr)

Relative $31,439	This Car $30,695
Cost/Mile 45¢	Cost/Mile 44¢

Ownership Cost Value

○ Better Than Average

Buick Regal GS
4 Door Sedan

Midsize

 3.8L 240 hp Suprchrged Fuel Inject.

 6 Cylinder "V"

 Automatic 4 Speed

 2 Wheel Front

Depowered Dual Airbags Std

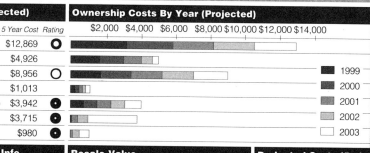

Purchase Price

Car Item	Dealer Cost	List
Base Price	**$22,321**	**$24,395**
Anti-Lock Brakes	Std	Std
Manual Transmission	N/A	N/A
Optional Engine	N/A	N/A
Air Conditioning	Std	Std
Power Steering	Std	Std
Cruise Control	Std	Std
Power Windows	Std	Std
AM/FM Stereo Cassette	Std	Std
Steering Wheel, Tilt	Std	Std
1SD Package	N/C	N/C
***Options Price**	**$0**	**$0**
***Total Price**	**$22,321**	**$24,395**
Target Price	$23,422	
Destination Charge	$560	
Avg. Tax & Fees	$1,342	
Total Target $	**$25,324**	
Average Dealer Option Cost:	**86%**	
12 Month Price Increase:	3%	

The 1999 Regal GS sedan has all the same new features as the Regal LS. Standard on the GS sedan is a 3.8L supercharged engine and an enhanced full-range traction control system with antilock brakes. More new standard amenities include programmable perimeter lighting and an improved sportier suspension. Optional features include the OnStar Communication System, an Astroroof and radio steering wheel controls. Auburn Nightmist Pearl has been added as a new exterior color.

Ownership Costs (Projected)

Cost Area	5 Year Cost	Rating
Depreciation	$12,869	◐
Financing ($420/month)	$4,926	
Insurance (Performance)	$8,956	○
State Fees	$1,013	
Fuel (Hwy 27 City 18 -Prem.)	$3,942	◉
Maintenance	$3,715	◉
Repairs	$980	◉

Warranty/Maintenance Info

Major Tune-Up (100K mile int.)	$255	◐
Minor Tune-Up (30K mile int.)	$132	◉
Brake Service	$250	◐
Overall Warranty	3 yr/36k	◐
Drivetrain Warranty	3 yr/36k	◐
Rust Warranty	6 yr/100k	○
Maintenance Warranty	N/A	
Roadside Assistance	3 yr/36k	

Ownership Costs By Year (Projected)

$2,000 $4,000 $6,000 $8,000 $10,000 $12,000 $14,000

■ 1999
■ 2000
■ 2001
□ 2002
□ 2003

Resale Value

1999	2000	2001	2002	2003
$22,121	$19,451	$17,093	$14,731	$12,455

Cumulative Costs

	1999	2000	2001	2002	2003
Annual	$7,631	$6,834	$6,622	$6,798	$8,515
Total	$7,631	$14,465	$21,087	$27,885	$36,400

Projected Costs (5yr)

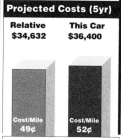

Relative $34,632	This Car $36,400
Cost/Mile 49¢	Cost/Mile 52¢

Ownership Cost Value

◉ Worse Than Average

Poor	Worse Than Average	Average	Better Than Average	Excellent	⊖ Insufficient Information

Refer to *Section 3: Annotated Vehicle Charts* for an explanation of these charts.

Buick Riviera
2 Door Coupe

Near Luxury

3.8L 240 hp Suprchrged Fuel Inject.	6 Cylinder "V"	Automatic 4 Speed	2 Wheel Front	Dual Airbags Std

Purchase Price

Car Item	Dealer Cost	List
Base Price	**$30,269**	**$33,820**
Anti-Lock Brakes	Std	Std
Manual Transmission	N/A	N/A
Optional Engine	N/A	N/A
Auto Climate Control	Std	Std
Power Steering	Std	Std
Cruise Control	Std	Std
Power Windows	Std	Std
AM/FM Stereo Cass/CD	Std	Std
Steering Wheel, Tilt	Std	Std
1SE Package	$1,152	$1,340
***Options Price**	**$1,152**	**$1,340**
***Total Price**	**$31,421**	**$35,160**
Target Price	$31,865	
Destination Charge	$670	
Avg. Tax & Fees	$1,835	
Total Target $	**$34,370**	
Average Dealer Option Cost:	**86%**	
12 Month Price Increase:	**4%**	

The Riviera is offering several key features for 1999. The most notable is the OnStar Communication System, available as a dealer option. It links the driver to a communications center where advisors are available to provide assistance for emergency services, roadside assistance and theft detection. In addition to standard full-range traction control for slippery surfaces, the Riviera also includes a programmable remote keyless entry system featuring perimeter lighting and delayed locking.

Ownership Costs (Projected)

Cost Area	5 Year Cost	Rating
Depreciation	$18,248	◑
Financing ($570/month)	$6,685	
Insurance (Performance)	$9,918	○
State Fees	$1,446	
Fuel (Hwy 27 City 18 -Prem.)	$3,942	○
Maintenance	$3,214	○
Repairs	$1,150	○

Warranty/Maintenance Info

Major Tune-Up (100K mile int.)	$250	○
Minor Tune-Up (30K mile int.)	$156	◑
Brake Service	$263	○
Overall Warranty	3 yr/36k	○
Drivetrain Warranty	3 yr/36k	○
Rust Warranty	6 yr/100k	○
Maintenance Warranty	N/A	
Roadside Assistance	3 yr/36k	

Ownership Costs By Year (Projected)

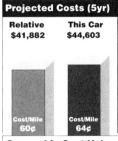

1999, 2000, 2001, 2002, 2003

Resale Value

1999	2000	2001	2002	2003
$29,453	$25,802	$22,514	$19,313	$16,122

Cumulative Costs

	1999	2000	2001	2002	2003
Annual	$10,234	$8,585	$8,234	$8,220	$9,330
Total	$10,234	$18,819	$27,053	$35,273	$44,603

Projected Costs (5yr)

Relative	This Car
$41,882	$44,603
Cost/Mile 60¢	Cost/Mile 64¢

Ownership Cost Value

● Poor

Cadillac Catera
4 Door Sedan

Near Luxury

3.0L 200 hp Gas Fuel Inject.	6 Cylinder "V"	Automatic 4 Speed	2 Wheel Rear	Dual Airbags Std

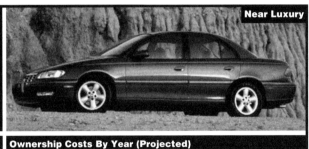

Purchase Price

Car Item	Dealer Cost	List
Base Price	**$31,772**	**$34,180**
Anti-Lock Brakes	Std	Std
Manual Transmission	N/A	N/A
Optional Engine	N/A	N/A
Air Conditioning	Std	Std
Power Steering	Std	Std
Cruise Control	Std	Std
Power Windows	Std	Std
AM/FM Stereo Cassette	Std	Std
Steering Wheel, Tilt	Std	Std
Rear Defroster	Std	Std
***Options Price**	**$0**	**$0**
***Total Price**	**$31,772**	**$34,180**
Target Price	$33,107	
Destination Charge	$640	
Avg. Tax & Fees	$1,880	
Total Target $	**$35,627**	
Average Dealer Option Cost:	**80%**	
12 Month Price Increase:	**14%**	

The 1999 Catera sedan is offered with the optional OnStar Communication System. Combined with a Global Positioning Satellite receiver and cellular phone, it features services such as automatic airbag deployment notification, as well as advisors that provide roadside assistance 24 hours a day. Standard Catera equipment includes second generation dual front airbags, five-point adjustable seatbelts, a road ice warning indicator, rear defroster and programmable door locks.

Ownership Costs (Projected)

Cost Area	5 Year Cost	Rating
Depreciation		⊖
Financing ($591/month)	$6,931	
Insurance	$9,524	○
State Fees	$1,406	
Fuel (Hwy 24 City 18 -Prem.)	$4,187	●
Maintenance	$2,618	○
Repairs	$975	○

Warranty/Maintenance Info

Major Tune-Up (100K mile int.)	$502	●
Minor Tune-Up (30K mile int.)	$99	○
Brake Service	$284	◑
Overall Warranty	4 yr/50k	○
Drivetrain Warranty	4 yr/50k	○
Rust Warranty	6 yr/100k	○
Maintenance Warranty	N/A	
Roadside Assistance	4 yr/50k	

Ownership Costs By Year (Projected)

Insufficient Depreciation Information

1999, 2000, 2001, 2002, 2003

Resale Value

Insufficient Information

Cumulative Costs

	1999	2000	2001	2002	2003
Annual	Insufficient Information				
Total	Insufficient Information				

Projected Costs (5yr)

Insufficient Information

Ownership Cost Value

⊖ Insufficient Information

---

* Includes shaded options

** Other purchase requirements apply

*** Price includes other options

 Poor Worse Than Average Average Better Than Average Excellent Insufficient Information

27

Refer to *Section 3: Annotated Vehicle Charts* for an explanation of these charts.

© 1999 by IntelliChoice, Inc. (408) 866-1400 http://www.intellichoice.com All Rights Reserved. Reproduction Prohibited.

Cadillac DeVille
4 Door Sedan

Luxury

 4.6L 275 hp Gas Fuel Inject.
 8 Cylinder "V"
 PRND321 Automatic 4 Speed
 2 Wheel Front
 Dual Front/Side Airbags Std

Purchase Price

Car Item	Dealer Cost	List
Base Price	**$35,501**	**$38,630**
Anti-Lock Brakes	Std	Std
Manual Transmission	N/A	N/A
Optional Engine	N/A	N/A
Auto Climate Control	Std	Std
Power Steering	Std	Std
Cruise Control	Std	Std
Power Windows	Std	Std
AM/FM Stereo Cassette	Std	Std
Steering Wheel, Tilt	Std	Std
Rear Defroster	Std	Std
*Options Price	$0	$0
*Total Price	**$35,501**	**$38,630**
Target Price	$37,505	
Destination Charge	$670	
Avg. Tax & Fees	$2,124	
Luxury Tax	$131	
Total Target $	**$40,430**	
12 Month Price Increase:	2%	

For 1999, the DeVille is a carryover from last year's model. Improvements to the DeVille include an audible theft deterrent system and an electronic compass as standard equipment. The DeVille features a 275 hp Northstar engine that does not require scheduled maintenance for 100,000 miles. Options include leather seating, StabiliTrak for improved driving control and a premium 11 speaker stereo with cassette, CD and RDS that allows the radio to receive digital data along with the normal signal.

Ownership Costs (Projected)

Cost Area	5 Year Cost	Rating
Depreciation	$21,137	●
Financing ($670/month)	$7,865	
Insurance (Performance)	$9,226	O
State Fees	$1,585	
Fuel (Hwy 26 City 17 -Prem.)	$4,134	O
Maintenance	$2,478	O
Repairs	$1,040	O

Warranty/Maintenance Info

Major Tune-Up (100K mile int.)	$309	●
Minor Tune-Up (30K mile int.)	$89	O
Brake Service	$247	O
Overall Warranty	4 yr/50k	O
Drivetrain Warranty	4 yr/50k	O
Rust Warranty	6 yr/100k	O
Maintenance Warranty	N/A	
Roadside Assistance	4 yr/50k	

Ownership Costs By Year (Projected)

Legend: 1999, 2000, 2001, 2002, 2003

Resale Value

1999	2000	2001	2002	2003
$33,702	$29,725	$26,151	$22,698	$19,293

Cumulative Costs

	1999	2000	2001	2002	2003
Annual	$12,386	$9,172	$8,505	$8,340	$9,061
Total	$12,386	$21,558	$30,063	$38,403	$47,464

Projected Costs (5yr)

Relative	This Car
$47,073	$47,464
Cost/Mile 67¢	Cost/Mile 68¢

Ownership Cost Value

O Average

Cadillac DeVille d'Elegance
4 Door Sedan

Luxury

Concours Model Shown

 4.6L 275 hp Gas Fuel Inject.
 8 Cylinder "V"
 PRND321 Automatic 4 Speed
 2 Wheel Front
Dual Front/Side Airbags Std

Purchase Price

Car Item	Dealer Cost	List
Base Price	**$39,253**	**$42,730**
Anti-Lock Brakes	Std	Std
Manual Transmission	N/A	N/A
Optional Engine	N/A	N/A
Auto Climate Control	Std	Std
Power Steering	Std	Std
Cruise Control	Std	Std
Power Windows	Std	Std
AM/FM Stereo Cass/CD	Std	Std
Steering Wheel, Tilt	Std	Std
Rear Defroster	Std	Std
*Options Price	$0	$0
*Total Price	**$39,253**	**$42,730**
Target Price	$41,445	
Destination Charge	$670	
Avg. Tax & Fees	$2,342	
Luxury Tax	$367	
Total Target $	**$44,824**	
12 Month Price Increase:	3%	

For 1999, the DeVille d'Elegance can be ordered with new massaging lumbar seats, operated via the same button as the lumbar control. The massage feature can run continuously for ten minutes per cycle. StabiliTrak is offered as an option to provide improved driver control on all surfaces at all speeds. Standard d'Elegance features include an audible theft deterrent system, 11 speaker AM/FM stereo with cassette and CD, and dual power seats with leather upholstery.

Ownership Costs (Projected)

Cost Area	5 Year Cost	Rating
Depreciation	$24,442	●
Financing ($743/month)	$8,719	
Insurance (Performance)	$9,463	O
State Fees	$1,749	
Fuel (Hwy 26 City 17 -Prem.)	$4,134	O
Maintenance	$2,478	O
Repairs	$1,040	O

Warranty/Maintenance Info

Major Tune-Up (100K mile int.)	$309	●
Minor Tune-Up (30K mile int.)	$89	O
Brake Service	$247	O
Overall Warranty	4 yr/50k	O
Drivetrain Warranty	4 yr/50k	O
Rust Warranty	6 yr/100k	O
Maintenance Warranty	N/A	
Roadside Assistance	4 yr/50k	

Ownership Costs By Year (Projected)

Legend: 1999, 2000, 2001, 2002, 2003

Resale Value

1999	2000	2001	2002	2003
$36,250	$31,878	$27,927	$24,122	$20,382

Cumulative Costs

	1999	2000	2001	2002	2003
Annual	$14,607	$9,886	$9,138	$8,883	$9,511
Total	$14,607	$24,493	$33,631	$42,514	$52,025

Projected Costs (5yr)

Relative	This Car
$51,084	$52,025
Cost/Mile 73¢	Cost/Mile 74¢

Ownership Cost Value

O Average

28

* Includes shaded options
** Other purchase requirements apply
*** Price includes other options

● Poor ◑ Worse Than Average ◐ Average O Better Than Average ○ Excellent ⊖ Insufficient Information

Refer to *Section 3: Annotated Vehicle Charts* for an explanation of these charts.

Cadillac DeVille Concours
4 Door Sedan

Luxury

 4.6L 300 hp Gas Fuel Inject.
 8 Cylinder "V"
 Automatic 4 Speed
 2 Wheel Front
 Dual Front/Side Airbags Std

Purchase Price

Car Item	Dealer Cost	List
Base Price	**$39,710**	**$43,230**
Anti-Lock Brakes	Std	Std
Manual Transmission	N/A	N/A
Optional Engine	N/A	N/A
Auto Climate Control	Std	Std
Power Steering	Std	Std
Cruise Control	Std	Std
Power Windows	Std	Std
AM/FM Stereo Cass/CD	Std	Std
Steering Wheel, Tilt	Std	Std
Rear Defroster	Std	Std
*Options Price	$0	$0
*Total Price	$39,710	$43,230
Target Price	$41,942	
Destination Charge	$670	
Avg. Tax & Fees	$2,370	
Luxury Tax	$397	
Total Target $	**$45,379**	
12 Month Price Increase:	2%	

The 1999 DeVille Concours is equipped with a 300 hp Northstar V8 and StabiliTrak to provide powerful acceleration and agile handling. The Concours is now available with massaging lumbar seats that gently massage back muscles. The Concours is equipped with leather upholstery, an 11 speaker AM/FM stereo with CD and cassette and an audible theft deterrent system. Optional equipment includes a power sliding sunroof, chrome wheels and RDS, which allows the radio to receive digital data.

Ownership Costs (Projected)

Cost Area	5 Year Cost	Rating
Depreciation	$24,281	●
Financing ($752/month)	$8,828	
Insurance (Performance)	$9,858	○
State Fees	$1,768	
Fuel (Hwy 26 City 17 -Prem.)	$4,134	◔
Maintenance	$2,478	○
Repairs	$1,040	○

Warranty/Maintenance Info

Major Tune-Up (100K mile int.)	$309	●
Minor Tune-Up (30K mile int.)	$89	◔
Brake Service	$247	○
Overall Warranty	4 yr/50k	○
Drivetrain Warranty	4 yr/50k	○
Rust Warranty	6 yr/100k	○
Maintenance Warranty	N/A	
Roadside Assistance	4 yr/50k	

Ownership Costs By Year (Projected)

$5,000 $10,000 $15,000 $20,000 $25,000

1999, 2000, 2001, 2002, 2003

Resale Value

1999	2000	2001	2002	2003
$37,376	$32,896	$28,842	$24,936	$21,098

Cumulative Costs

	1999	2000	2001	2002	2003
Annual	$14,154	$10,105	$9,347	$9,081	$9,700
Total	$14,154	$24,259	$33,606	$42,687	$52,387

Projected Costs (5yr)

Relative $51,574	This Car $52,387
Cost/Mile 74¢	Cost/Mile 75¢

Ownership Cost Value

○ Average

Cadillac Eldorado
2 Door Coupe

Luxury

 4.6L 275 hp Gas Fuel Inject.
 8 Cylinder "V"
 Automatic 4 Speed
 2 Wheel Front
 Dual Airbags Std

Purchase Price

Car Item	Dealer Cost	List
Base Price	**$36,055**	**$39,235**
Anti-Lock Brakes	Std	Std
Manual Transmission	N/A	N/A
Optional Engine	N/A	N/A
Auto Climate Control	Std	Std
Power Steering	Std	Std
Cruise Control	Std	Std
Power Windows	Std	Std
AM/FM Stereo Cass/CD	Std	Std
Steering Wheel, Tilt	Std	Std
Rear Defroster	Std	Std
*Options Price	$0	$0
*Total Price	$36,055	$39,235
Target Price	$37,979	
Destination Charge	$670	
Avg. Tax & Fees	$2,151	
Luxury Tax	$159	
Total Target $	**$40,959**	
12 Month Price Increase:	2%	

The 1999 Eldorado coupe features minor improvements. The Eldorado now comes with an audible theft deterrent system and an electronic compass. New exterior colors include Cashmere, Parisian Blue and Sterling Silver. Oatmeal replaces Cappuccino Cream as an interior color. The Eldorado is equipped with a 275 hp Northstar V8 that requires no tuneups for 100,000 miles. Optional features include an 11 speaker AM/FM stereo with cassette and CD, leather upholstery and power sunroof.

Ownership Costs (Projected)

Cost Area	5 Year Cost	Rating
Depreciation	$20,730	○
Financing ($679/month)	$7,968	
Insurance (Performance)	$10,331	○
State Fees	$1,608	
Fuel (Hwy 26 City 17 -Prem.)	$4,134	◔
Maintenance	$2,407	○
Repairs	$1,100	○

Warranty/Maintenance Info

Major Tune-Up (100K mile int.)	$309	●
Minor Tune-Up (30K mile int.)	$89	◔
Brake Service	$247	○
Overall Warranty	4 yr/50k	○
Drivetrain Warranty	4 yr/50k	○
Rust Warranty	6 yr/100k	○
Maintenance Warranty	N/A	
Roadside Assistance	4 yr/50k	

Ownership Costs By Year (Projected)

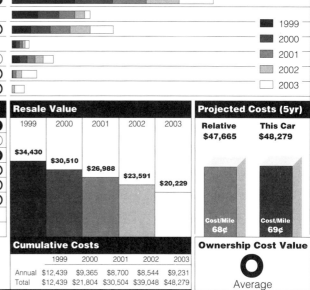

$5,000 $10,000 $15,000 $20,000 $25,000

1999, 2000, 2001, 2002, 2003

Resale Value

1999	2000	2001	2002	2003
$34,430	$30,510	$26,988	$23,591	$20,229

Cumulative Costs

	1999	2000	2001	2002	2003
Annual	$12,439	$9,365	$8,700	$8,544	$9,231
Total	$12,439	$21,804	$30,504	$39,048	$48,279

Projected Costs (5yr)

Relative $47,665	This Car $48,279
Cost/Mile 68¢	Cost/Mile 69¢

Ownership Cost Value

○ Average

---

* Includes shaded options
** Other purchase requirements apply
*** Price includes other options

 Poor
 Worse Than Average
 Average
 Better Than Average
 Excellent
 Insufficient Information

29

Refer to *Section 3: Annotated Vehicle Charts* for an explanation of these charts.

Cadillac Eldorado Touring Coupe
2 Door Coupe

Luxury

 4.6L 300 hp Gas Fuel Inject.
 8 Cylinder "V"
 Automatic 4 Speed
 2 Wheel Front
Dual Airbags Std

Purchase Price

Car Item	Dealer Cost	List
Base Price	**$39,953**	**$43,495**
Anti-Lock Brakes	Std	Std
Manual Transmission	N/A	N/A
Optional Engine	N/A	N/A
Auto Climate Control	Std	Std
Power Steering	Std	Std
Cruise Control	Std	Std
Power Windows	Std	Std
AM/FM Stereo Cass/CD	Std	Std
Steering Wheel, Tilt	Std	Std
Rear Defroster	Std	Std
*Options Price	$0	$0
*Total Price	**$39,953**	**$43,495**
Target Price	$42,206	
Destination Charge	$670	
Avg. Tax & Fees	$2,384	
Luxury Tax	$413	
Total Target $	**$45,673**	
12 Month Price Increase:	2%	

The 1999 Eldorado Touring coupe is designed to appeal to the performance-minded, with a 300 hp Northstar V8 and StabiliTrak as standard equipment. The Touring version is outfitted with a premium Bose sound system including AM/FM stereo, cassette, CD and RDS. RDS technology allows the radio to receive digital data along with the standard signal. Commuters can hear traffic announcements or emergency information. The optional massaging lumbar seats massage back muscles to improve blood flow.

Ownership Costs (Projected)

Cost Area	5 Year Cost	Rating
Depreciation	$23,977	◉
Financing ($757/month)	$8,885	
Insurance (Performance)	$10,331	○
State Fees	$1,779	
Fuel (Hwy 26 City 17 -Prem.)	$4,134	◔
Maintenance	$2,604	◑
Repairs	$1,100	○

Warranty/Maintenance Info

Major Tune-Up (100K mile int.)	$309	◉
Minor Tune-Up (30K mile int.)	$89	○
Brake Service	$247	◑
Overall Warranty	4 yr/50k	○
Drivetrain Warranty	4 yr/50k	○
Rust Warranty	6 yr/100k	○
Maintenance Warranty	N/A	
Roadside Assistance	4 yr/50k	

Ownership Costs By Year (Projected)

$5,000 $10,000 $15,000 $20,000 $25,000

■ 1999
■ 2000
■ 2001
□ 2002
□ 2003

Resale Value

1999	2000	2001	2002	2003
$38,328	**$33,760**	**$29,619**	**$25,623**	**$21,696**

Cumulative Costs

	1999	2000	2001	2002	2003
Annual	$13,609	$10,304	$9,542	$9,490	$9,866
Total	$13,609	$23,913	$33,455	$42,945	$52,811

Projected Costs (5yr)

Relative $51,834	This Car $52,811
Cost/Mile 74¢	Cost/Mile 75¢

Ownership Cost Value

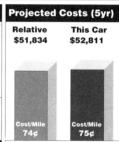

Average

Cadillac Seville SLS
4 Door Sedan

Luxury

 4.6L 275 hp Gas Fuel Inject.
 8 Cylinder "V"
 Automatic 4 Speed
 2 Wheel Front
 Dual Front/Side Airbags Std

Purchase Price

Car Item	Dealer Cost	List
Base Price	**$39,825**	**$43,355**
Anti-Lock Brakes	Std	Std
Manual Transmission	N/A	N/A
Optional Engine	N/A	N/A
Auto Climate Control	Std	Std
Power Steering	Std	Std
Cruise Control	Std	Std
Power Windows	Std	Std
AM/FM Stereo Cass/CD	Std	Std
Steering Wheel, Tilt	N/A	N/A
Rear Defroster	Std	Std
*Options Price	$0	$0
*Total Price	**$39,825**	**$43,355**
Target Price	$41,917	
Destination Charge	$670	
Avg. Tax & Fees	$2,369	
Luxury Tax	$395	
Total Target $	**$45,351**	
12 Month Price Increase:	2%	

The 1999 Seville SLS is offered with a 275 hp Northstar system DOHC V8, StabiliTrak and all-speed traction control. StabiliTrak has a yaw control system that helps the driver maintain control in bad weather or during emergency maneuvers. Also standard is a continuously variable road-sensing suspension that optimizes ride and handling on all types of roads. A Convenience Package, Personalization Package and Adaptive Seat Package are also available.

Ownership Costs (Projected)

Cost Area	5 Year Cost	Rating
Depreciation	$23,286	○
Financing ($752/month)	$8,822	
Insurance (Performance)	$9,918	○
State Fees	$1,773	
Fuel (Hwy 26 City 17 -Prem.)	$4,134	◔
Maintenance	$2,442	○
Repairs	$1,100	○

Warranty/Maintenance Info

Major Tune-Up (100K mile int.)	$309	◉
Minor Tune-Up (30K mile int.)	$89	○
Brake Service	$247	○
Overall Warranty	4 yr/50k	○
Drivetrain Warranty	4 yr/50k	○
Rust Warranty	6 yr/100k	○
Maintenance Warranty	N/A	
Roadside Assistance	4 yr/50k	

Ownership Costs By Year (Projected)

$5,000 $10,000 $15,000 $20,000 $25,000

■ 1999
■ 2000
■ 2001
■ 2002
□ 2003

Resale Value

1999	2000	2001	2002	2003
$39,695	**$34,859**	**$30,462**	**$26,227**	**$22,065**

Cumulative Costs

	1999	2000	2001	2002	2003
Annual	$11,818	$10,473	$9,701	$9,471	$10,012
Total	$11,818	$22,291	$31,992	$41,463	$51,475

Projected Costs (5yr)

Relative $51,697	This Car $51,475
Cost/Mile 74¢	Cost/Mile 74¢

Ownership Cost Value

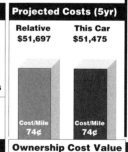

Average

30

* Includes shaded options
** Other purchase requirements apply
*** Price includes other options

 Poor
 Worse Than Average
 Average
 Better Than Average
 Excellent
 Insufficient Information

Refer to *Section 3: Annotated Vehicle Charts* for an explanation of these charts.

Cadillac Seville STS
4 Door Sedan

 4.6L 300 hp Gas Fuel Inject.
 8 Cylinder "V"
 Automatic 4 Speed
 2 Wheel Front
 Dual Front/Side Airbags Std

Purchase Price

Car Item	Dealer Cost	List
Base Price	**$43,938**	**$47,850**
Anti-Lock Brakes	Std	Std
Manual Transmission	N/A	N/A
Optional Engine	N/A	N/A
Auto Climate Control	Std	Std
Power Steering	Std	Std
Cruise Control	Std	Std
Power Windows	Std	Std
AM/FM Stereo Cass/CD	Std	Std
St Whl, Power Scope/Tilt	Std	Std
Rear Defroster	Std	Std
***Options Price**	$0	$0
***Total Price**	**$43,938**	**$47,850**
Target Price	$46,316	
Destination Charge	$670	
Avg. Tax & Fees	$2,612	
Luxury Tax	$659	
Total Target $	**$50,257**	
12 Month Price Increase:	2%	

The 1999 Seville STS is offered with a 300 hp Northstar system DOHC V8, StabiliTrak, all-speed traction control and antilock brakes. The STS also features massaging lumbar seats as an option. A single tap on the power lumbar switch produces a continuous roller motion that can be interrupted or repeated at any time while driving. It is designed to relax muscle tension, improve driver comfort and reduce fatigue. The STS also features the optional OnStar mobile communications system.

Ownership Costs (Projected)

Cost Area	5 Year Cost	Rating
Depreciation	$26,449	◉
Financing ($833/month)	$9,778	◑
Insurance (Performance)	$10,625	○
State Fees	$1,954	
Fuel (Hwy 26 City 17 -Prem.)	$4,134	◎
Maintenance	$2,442	○
Repairs	$1,100	○

Warranty/Maintenance Info

Major Tune-Up (100K mile int.)	$309	◉
Minor Tune-Up (30K mile int.)	$89	◎
Brake Service	$247	○
Overall Warranty	4 yr/50k	○
Drivetrain Warranty	4 yr/50k	○
Rust Warranty	6 yr/100k	○
Maintenance Warranty	N/A	
Roadside Assistance	4 yr/50k	○

Ownership Costs By Year (Projected)

$5,000 $10,000 $15,000 $20,000 $25,000 $30,000

■ 1999
■ 2000
■ 2001
■ 2002
□ 2003

Resale Value

1999	2000	2001	2002	2003
$43,562	$38,162	$33,224	$28,467	$23,808

Projected Costs (5yr)

Relative $56,108	This Car $56,483
Cost/Mile 80¢	Cost/Mile 81¢

Cumulative Costs

	1999	2000	2001	2002	2003
Annual	$13,361	$11,479	$10,618	$10,295	$10,730
Total	$13,361	$24,840	$35,458	$45,753	$56,483

Ownership Cost Value

○ Average

Chevrolet Camaro
2 Door Coupe

 3.8L 200 hp Gas Fuel Inject.
 6 Cylinder "V"
 Manual 5 Speed
 2 Wheel Rear
 Dual Airbags Std

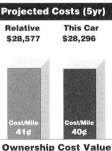

Purchase Price

Car Item	Dealer Cost	List
Base Price	**$15,212**	**$16,625**
Anti-Lock Brakes	Std	Std
Automatic 4 Speed	$725	$815
Optional Engine	N/A	N/A
Air Conditioning	Std	Std
Power Steering	Std	Std
Cruise/Speed Control	Inc	Inc
Power Windows	Inc	Inc
AM/FM Stereo Cassette	Std	Std
Steering Wheel, Tilt	Std	Std
1SC Package	$1,109	$1,246
***Options Price**	**$1,109**	**$1,246**
***Total Price**	**$16,321**	**$17,871**
Target Price	$16,613	
Destination Charge	$535	
Avg. Tax & Fees	$969	
Total Target $	**$18,117**	
Average Dealer Option Cost:	*89%*	
12 Month Price Increase:	None	

For 1999, the Camaro coupe receives engine enhancements that include electronic throttle control, engine oil-life monitoring and an optional Zexel Torsen differential. New colors added include Hugger Orange, Light Pewter and Bright Blue. The coupe is available with an optional leather interior and Monsoon premium radio. The Sport Appearance Package includes a rear spoiler and aluminum wheels. Acceleration Slip Regulation (traction control) improves control on most slippery surfaces.

Ownership Costs (Projected)

Cost Area	5 Year Cost	Rating
Depreciation	$8,410	○
Financing ($300/month)	$3,524	◎
Insurance	$9,083	●
State Fees	$749	
Fuel (Hwy 30 City 19)	$3,070	○
Maintenance	$2,720	○
Repairs	$740	○

Warranty/Maintenance Info

Major Tune-Up (100K mile int.)	$269	○
Minor Tune-Up (30K mile int.)	$137	○
Brake Service	$287	○
Overall Warranty	3 yr/36k	○
Drivetrain Warranty	3 yr/36k	○
Rust Warranty	6 yr/100k	○
Maintenance Warranty	N/A	
Roadside Assistance	3 yr/36k	

Ownership Costs By Year (Projected)

$2,000 $4,000 $6,000 $8,000 $10,000

■ 1999
■ 2000
■ 2001
■ 2002
□ 2003

Resale Value

1999	2000	2001	2002	2003
$16,146	$14,384	$12,864	$11,338	$9,707

Projected Costs (5yr)

Relative $28,577	This Car $28,296
Cost/Mile 41¢	Cost/Mile 40¢

Cumulative Costs

	1999	2000	2001	2002	2003
Annual	$5,714	$5,335	$5,148	$6,244	$5,855
Total	$5,714	$11,049	$16,197	$22,441	$28,296

Ownership Cost Value

○ Better Than Average

---

* Includes shaded options
** Other purchase requirements apply
*** Price includes other options

 ● Poor
 ◉ Worse Than Average
 ◎ Average
 ○ Better Than Average
 ○ Excellent
 ⊖ Insufficient Information

31

Refer to *Section 3: Annotated Vehicle Charts* for an explanation of these charts.

Chevrolet Camaro Z28
2 Door Coupe

Base Sport

 5.7L 305 hp Gas Fuel Inject. | 8 Cylinder "V" | Automatic 4 Speed | 2 Wheel Rear | Dual Airbags Std

Purchase Price

Car Item	Dealer Cost	List
Base Price	**$19,096**	**$20,870**
Anti-Lock Brakes	Std	Std
Manual 6 Speed	N/C	N/C
Optional Engine	N/A	N/A
Air Conditioning	Std	Std
Power Steering	Std	Std
Cruise/Speed Control	Inc	Inc
Power Windows	Inc	Inc
AM/FM Stereo Cassette	Std	Std
Steering Wheel, Tilt	Std	Std
1SE Package	$1,416	$1,591
***Options Price**	**$1,416**	**$1,591**
***Total Price**	**$20,512**	**$22,461**
Target Price	$21,077	
Destination Charge	$535	
Avg. Tax & Fees	$1,216	
Total Target $	**$22,828**	
Average Dealer Option Cost:	**89%**	
12 Month Price Increase:	**2%**	

For the 1999 Camaro Z28 coupe, the V8 system is calibrated to allow for some wheel slip during acceleration in tandem with the optional Acceleration Slip Regulation system. A six speed manual transmission is available as a no-cost option. An optional SS Performance/Appearance Package adds increased horsepower, a unique hood and 17 inch wheels and tires. A removable glass roof, keyless remote entry, chrome wheels and leather interior are optional. A Monsoon audio system (without CD) is standard.

Ownership Costs (Projected)

Cost Area	5 Year Cost	Rating
Depreciation	$10,823	◔
Financing ($378/month)	$4,441	
Insurance (Performance)	$12,728	●
State Fees	$933	
Fuel (Hwy 28 City 19 -Prem.)	$3,767	◔
Maintenance	$3,980	●
Repairs	$880	◔

Warranty/Maintenance Info

Major Tune-Up (100K mile int.)	$519	●
Minor Tune-Up (30K mile int.)	$208	●
Brake Service	$287	◔
Overall Warranty	3 yr/36k	◔
Drivetrain Warranty	3 yr/36k	◔
Rust Warranty	6 yr/100k	○
Maintenance Warranty	N/A	
Roadside Assistance	3 yr/36k	◔

Ownership Costs By Year (Projected)

$2,000 $4,000 $6,000 $8,000 $10,000 $12,000 $14,000

Legend: ■ 1999 ■ 2000 ■ 2001 ▨ 2002 □ 2003

Resale Value

1999	2000	2001	2002	2003
$19,796	$17,675	$15,809	$13,953	$12,005

Cumulative Costs

	1999	2000	2001	2002	2003
Annual	$7,963	$6,838	$6,683	$8,686	$7,383
Total	$7,963	$14,801	$21,484	$30,170	$37,553

Projected Costs (5yr)

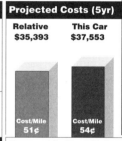

Relative $35,393	This Car $37,553
Cost/Mile 51¢	Cost/Mile 54¢

Ownership Cost Value

● Poor

Chevrolet Camaro
2 Door Convertible

Base Sport

 3.8L 200 hp Gas Fuel Inject. | 6 Cylinder "V" | Manual 5 Speed | 2 Wheel Rear | Dual Airbags Std

Purchase Price

Car Item	Dealer Cost	List
Base Price	**$20,244**	**$22,125**
Anti-Lock Brakes	Std	Std
Automatic 4 Speed	$725	$815
Optional Engine	N/A	N/A
Air Conditioning	Std	Std
Power Steering	Std	Std
Cruise/Speed Control	Inc	Inc
Power Windows	Inc	Inc
AM/FM Stereo Cassette	Std	Std
Steering Wheel, Tilt	Std	Std
1SB Package	$1,176	$1,321
***Options Price**	**$1,176**	**$1,321**
***Total Price**	**$21,420**	**$23,446**
Target Price	$21,841	
Destination Charge	$535	
Avg. Tax & Fees	$1,260	
Total Target $	**$23,636**	
Average Dealer Option Cost:	**89%**	
12 Month Price Increase:	**None**	

For 1999, the Camaro convertible features new engine enhancements that include electronic throttle control, engine oil-life monitoring and an optional Zexel Torsen differential. Standard on convertible models is a power-operated top with a glass rear window. An optional Performance Handling Package is available on the convertible that features a limited-slip differential, dual exhaust and sport steering ratio. Three new exterior colors are available: Hugger Orange, Light Pewter and Bright Blue.

Ownership Costs (Projected)

Cost Area	5 Year Cost	Rating
Depreciation	$11,144	◔
Financing ($392/month)	$4,597	
Insurance	$10,182	●
State Fees	$973	
Fuel (Hwy 30 City 19)	$3,070	○
Maintenance	$2,720	○
Repairs	$740	○

Warranty/Maintenance Info

Major Tune-Up (100K mile int.)	$269	○
Minor Tune-Up (30K mile int.)	$137	○
Brake Service	$287	◔
Overall Warranty	3 yr/36k	◔
Drivetrain Warranty	3 yr/36k	◔
Rust Warranty	6 yr/100k	○
Maintenance Warranty	N/A	
Roadside Assistance	3 yr/36k	◔

Ownership Costs By Year (Projected)

$2,000 $4,000 $6,000 $8,000 $10,000 $12,000

Legend: ■ 1999 ■ 2000 ■ 2001 ▨ 2002 □ 2003

Resale Value

1999	2000	2001	2002	2003
$20,353	$18,209	$16,324	$14,453	$12,492

Cumulative Costs

	1999	2000	2001	2002	2003
Annual	$7,656	$6,278	$5,998	$6,994	$6,500
Total	$7,656	$13,934	$19,932	$26,926	$33,426

Projected Costs (5yr)

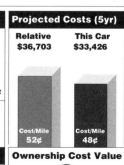

Relative $36,703	This Car $33,426
Cost/Mile 52¢	Cost/Mile 48¢

Ownership Cost Value

○ Excellent

32

| Poor | Worse Than Average | Average | ○ Better Than Average | ○ Excellent | Insufficient Information |

Refer to *Section 3: Annotated Vehicle Charts* for an explanation of these charts.

Chevrolet Camaro Z28
2 Door Convertible

5.7L 305 hp Gas Fuel Inject.	8 Cylinder "V"
Automatic 4 Speed	2 Wheel Rear
Dual Airbags Std	

Purchase Price

Car Item	Dealer Cost	List
Base Price	**$25,483**	**$27,850**
Anti-Lock Brakes	Std	Std
Manual 6 Speed	N/C	N/C
Optional Engine	N/A	N/A
Air Conditioning	Std	Std
Power Steering	Std	Std
Cruise/Speed Control	Inc	Inc
Power Windows	Inc	Inc
AM/FM Stereo Cassette	Std	Std
Steering Wheel, Tilt	Std	Std
1SC Package	N/C	N/C
*Options Price	$0	$0
*Total Price	$25,483	$27,850
Target Price	$26,263	
Destination Charge	$535	
Avg. Tax & Fees	$1,503	
Total Target $	**$28,301**	
Average Dealer Option Cost:	**89%**	
12 Month Price Increase:	1%	

For the 1999 Camaro Z28 convertible, the Monsoon audio sound system (without CD) is now standard. Other standard features include a power convertible top with a glass rear window and integrated rear defroster. Fog lamps, remote keyless entry and a PASS-Key II theft deterrent system are all standard. Optional equipment includes a leather interior, SS Package and Sport Appearance Package. Hugger Orange, Light Pewter and Bright Blue are three new exterior colors available this year.

Ownership Costs (Projected)

Cost Area	5 Year Cost	Rating
Depreciation	$13,775	◉
Financing ($469/month)	$5,506	
Insurance (Performance)	$13,745	●
State Fees	$1,148	
Fuel (Hwy 28 City 19 -Prem.)	$3,767	◉
Maintenance	$3,980	●
Repairs	$880	◉

Warranty/Maintenance Info

Major Tune-Up (100K mile int.)	$519	●
Minor Tune-Up (30K mile int.)	$208	●
Brake Service	$287	◉
Overall Warranty	3 yr/36k	◉
Drivetrain Warranty	3 yr/36k	◉
Rust Warranty	6 yr/100k	○
Maintenance Warranty	N/A	
Roadside Assistance	3 yr/36k	

Ownership Costs By Year (Projected)

$2,000 $4,000 $6,000 $8,000 $10,000 $12,000 $14,000

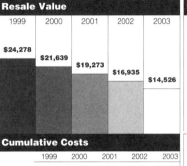

- 1999
- 2000
- 2001
- 2002
- 2003

Resale Value

1999	2000	2001	2002	2003
$24,278	$21,639	$19,273	$16,935	$14,526

Cumulative Costs

	1999	2000	2001	2002	2003
Annual	$9,563	$7,896	$7,650	$9,553	$8,139
Total	$9,563	$17,459	$25,109	$34,662	$42,801

Projected Costs (5yr)

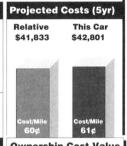

Relative	This Car
$41,833	$42,801
Cost/Mile 60¢	Cost/Mile 61¢

Ownership Cost Value

◉

Average

Chevrolet Cavalier
2 Door Coupe

2.2L 115 hp Gas Fuel Inject.	4 Cylinder In-Line
Manual 5 Speed	2 Wheel Front
Dual Airbags Std	

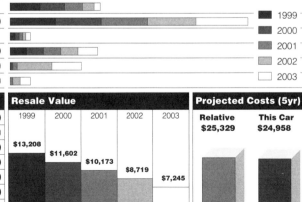

Purchase Price

Car Item	Dealer Cost	List
Base Price	**$11,099**	**$11,871**
Anti-Lock Brakes	Std	Std
Automatic 3 Speed	$540	$600
Optional Engine	N/A	N/A
Air Conditioning	$716	$795
Power Steering	Std	Std
Cruise/Speed Control	Inc	Inc
Power Windows	N/A	N/A
AM/FM Stereo Cassette	$149	$165
Steering Wheel, Tilt	Inc	Inc
1SC Package	$891	$990
*Options Price	$2,296	$2,550
*Total Price	$13,395	$14,421
Target Price	$13,747	
Destination Charge	$510	
Avg. Tax & Fees	$804	
Total Target $	**$15,061**	
Average Dealer Option Cost:	**90%**	
12 Month Price Increase:	2%	

For 1999, the Cavalier coupe is equipped with four wheel antilock brakes, a four speaker AM/FM stereo, a PASSlock theft deterrent system and daytime running lamps. An optional premium four speaker AM/FM stereo with CD includes auto tone control and speed-compensated volume. The Preferred Equipment Package, available as an option, includes power mirrors, cruise control and tilt steering wheel. A power sliding sunroof, automatic transmission and air conditioning are available as options.

Ownership Costs (Projected)

Cost Area	5 Year Cost	Rating
Depreciation	$7,816	◉
Financing ($250/month)	$2,930	
Insurance	$7,837	●
State Fees	$610	
Fuel (Hwy 29 City 23)	$2,847	◉
Maintenance	$2,308	○
Repairs	$610	○

Warranty/Maintenance Info

Major Tune-Up (100K mile int.)	$248	◉
Minor Tune-Up (30K mile int.)	$72	○
Brake Service	$199	◉
Overall Warranty	3 yr/36k	◉
Drivetrain Warranty	3 yr/36k	◉
Rust Warranty	6 yr/100k	○
Maintenance Warranty	N/A	
Roadside Assistance	3 yr/36k	

Ownership Costs By Year (Projected)

$2,000 $4,000 $6,000 $8,000

- 1999
- 2000
- 2001
- 2002
- 2003

Resale Value

1999	2000	2001	2002	2003
$13,208	$11,602	$10,173	$8,719	$7,245

Cumulative Costs

	1999	2000	2001	2002	2003
Annual	$5,078	$4,693	$4,517	$5,515	$5,155
Total	$5,078	$9,771	$14,288	$19,803	$24,958

Projected Costs (5yr)

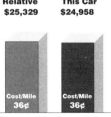

Relative	This Car
$25,329	$24,958
Cost/Mile 36¢	Cost/Mile 36¢

Ownership Cost Value

○

Better Than Average

● Poor	Worse Than Average	◉ Average
○ Better Than Average	○ Excellent	⊖ Insufficient Information

Refer to *Section 3: Annotated Vehicle Charts* for an explanation of these charts.

Chevrolet Cavalier RS
2 Door Coupe

Compact

 2.2L 115 hp Gas Fuel Inject.
 4 Cylinder In-Line
 Manual 5 Speed
 2 Wheel Front
 Dual Airbags Std

Purchase Price

Car Item	Dealer Cost	List
Base Price	**$12,277**	**$13,131**
Anti-Lock Brakes	Std	Std
Automatic 4 Speed	$702	$780
Optional Engine	N/A	N/A
Air Conditioning	$716	$795
Power Steering	Std	Std
Cruise Control	Std	Std
Power Windows	Pkg	Pkg
AM/FM Stereo Cassette	$149	$165
Steering Wheel, Tilt	Std	Std
1SD Package	N/C	N/C
*Options Price	$1,567	$1,740
*Total Price	**$13,844**	**$14,871**
Target Price	$14,214	
Destination Charge	$510	
Avg. Tax & Fees	$830	
Total Target $	**$15,554**	
Average Dealer Option Cost:	90%	
12 Month Price Increase:	2%	

Ownership Costs (Projected)

Cost Area	5 Year Cost	Rating
Depreciation	$8,216	◐
Financing ($258/month)	$3,026	
Insurance	$7,837	●
State Fees	$628	
Fuel (Hwy 31 City 23)	$2,748	○
Maintenance	$2,372	○
Repairs	$610	○

Warranty/Maintenance Info

Major Tune-Up (100K mile int.)	$248	○
Minor Tune-Up (30K mile int.)	$72	○
Brake Service	$199	○
Overall Warranty	3 yr/36k	○
Drivetrain Warranty	3 yr/36k	○
Rust Warranty	6 yr/100k	○
Maintenance Warranty	N/A	
Roadside Assistance	3 yr/36k	

Ownership Costs By Year (Projected)

$2,000 $4,000 $6,000 $8,000 $10,000

■ 1999
■ 2000
■ 2001
■ 2002
□ 2003

Resale Value

1999	2000	2001	2002	2003
$13,493	$11,838	$10,361	$8,858	$7,338

Projected Costs (5yr)

Relative $25,736	This Car $25,437
Cost/Mile 37¢	Cost/Mile 36¢

Cumulative Costs

	1999	2000	2001	2002	2003
Annual	$5,305	$4,754	$4,569	$5,623	$5,186
Total	$5,305	$10,059	$14,628	$20,251	$25,437

Ownership Cost Value

○ Better Than Average

For 1999, the Cavalier RS coupe has new badging and a body-colored grille. Standard equipment includes electronic cruise control, tilt wheel, four wheel antilock brakes and a PASSlock theft deterrent system. The exterior of the RS features a rear decklid spoiler, 15 inch bolt-on full wheel covers and Rally Sport badging on the rear quarter panels. Optional features include air conditioning, a power sliding sunroof, 15 inch aluminum wheels, an AM/FM stereo with CD and power windows and locks.

Chevrolet Cavalier Z24
2 Door Coupe

Compact

 2.4L 150 hp Gas Fuel Inject.
 4 Cylinder In-Line
 Manual 5 Speed
 2 Wheel Front
 Dual Airbags Std

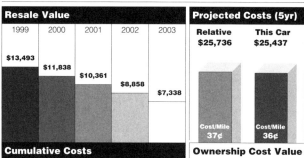

Purchase Price

Car Item	Dealer Cost	List
Base Price	**$14,933**	**$15,971**
Anti-Lock Brakes	Std	Std
Automatic 4 Speed	$702	$780
Optional Engine	N/A	N/A
Air Conditioning	Std	Std
Power Steering	Std	Std
Cruise Control	Std	Std
Power Windows	Std	Std
AM/FM Stereo Cassette	Std	Std
Steering Wheel, Tilt	Std	Std
1SA Package	N/C	N/C
*Options Price	$702	$780
*Total Price	**$15,635**	**$16,751**
Target Price	$16,074	
Destination Charge	$510	
Avg. Tax & Fees	$932	
Total Target $	**$17,516**	
Average Dealer Option Cost:	90%	
12 Month Price Increase:	2%	

Ownership Costs (Projected)

Cost Area	5 Year Cost	Rating
Depreciation	$9,735	◐
Financing ($290/month)	$3,408	
Insurance	$8,500	●
State Fees	$704	
Fuel (Hwy 30 City 22)	$2,855	○
Maintenance	$2,467	○
Repairs	$610	○

Warranty/Maintenance Info

Major Tune-Up (100K mile int.)	$205	○
Minor Tune-Up (30K mile int.)	$72	○
Brake Service	$199	○
Overall Warranty	3 yr/36k	○
Drivetrain Warranty	3 yr/36k	○
Rust Warranty	6 yr/100k	○
Maintenance Warranty	N/A	
Roadside Assistance	3 yr/36k	

Ownership Costs By Year (Projected)

$2,000 $4,000 $6,000 $8,000 $10,000

■ 1999
■ 2000
■ 2001
■ 2002
□ 2003

Resale Value

1999	2000	2001	2002	2003
$14,235	$12,512	$10,964	$9,383	$7,781

Projected Costs (5yr)

Relative $27,423	This Car $28,279
Cost/Mile 39¢	Cost/Mile 40¢

Cumulative Costs

	1999	2000	2001	2002	2003
Annual	$6,821	$5,096	$4,890	$6,008	$5,464
Total	$6,821	$11,917	$16,807	$22,815	$28,279

Ownership Cost Value

◉ Worse Than Average

For 1999, the Cavalier Z24 coupe offers sport cloth seating with Scotchgard, Z24 body-color front and rear fascias and fog lamps. The Z24 also offers an AM/FM stereo with cassette, power windows and locks, air conditioning and electronic cruise control as standard equipment. Safety features include four wheel antilock brakes, second generation dual front airbags, daytime running lamps and traction control when equipped with the automatic transmission.

34

* Includes shaded options
** Other purchase requirements apply
*** Price includes other options

 Poor
Worse Than Average
 Average
Better Than Average
Excellent
 Insufficient Information

Refer to *Section 3: Annotated Vehicle Charts* for an explanation of these charts.

Chevrolet Cavalier Z24
2 Door Convertible

Compact

 2.4L 150 hp Gas Fuel Inject.
 4 Cylinder In-Line
 Manual 5 Speed
 2 Wheel Front
 Dual Airbags Std

Purchase Price

Car Item	Dealer Cost	List
Base Price	**$18,299**	**$19,571**
Anti-Lock Brakes	Std	Std
Automatic 4 Speed	$702	$780
Optional Engine	N/A	N/A
Air Conditioning	Std	Std
Power Steering	Std	Std
Cruise Control	Std	Std
Power Windows	Std	Std
AM/FM Stereo Cassette	Std	Std
Steering Wheel, Tilt	Std	Std
1SA Package	N/C	N/C
*Options Price	$702	$780
*Total Price	**$19,001**	**$20,351**
Target Price	$19,477	
Destination Charge	$510	
Avg. Tax & Fees	$1,121	
Total Target $	**$21,108**	
Average Dealer Option Cost:	90%	
12 Month Price Increase:	1%	

Ownership Costs (Projected)

Cost Area	5 Year Cost	Rating
Depreciation	$11,213	●
Financing ($350/month)	$4,106	
Insurance	$9,365	●
State Fees	$848	
Fuel (Hwy 30 City 22)	$2,855	◐
Maintenance	$2,382	○
Repairs	$610	○

Warranty/Maintenance Info

Major Tune-Up (100K mile int.)	$205	○
Minor Tune-Up (30K mile int.)	$72	○
Brake Service	$199	○
Overall Warranty	3 yr/36k	○
Drivetrain Warranty	3 yr/36k	○
Rust Warranty	6 yr/100k	○
Maintenance Warranty	N/A	
Roadside Assistance	3 yr/36k	

Ownership Costs By Year (Projected)

$2,000 $4,000 $6,000 $8,000 $10,000 $12,000

■ 1999
■ 2000
■ 2001
■ 2002
□ 2003

Resale Value

1999	2000	2001	2002	2003
$18,010	$15,837	$13,860	$11,877	$9,895

Projected Costs (5yr)

Relative $30,858	This Car $31,379
Cost/Mile 44¢	Cost/Mile 45¢

Cumulative Costs

	1999	2000	2001	2002	2003
Annual	$7,076	$5,941	$5,665	$6,618	$6,079
Total	$7,076	$13,017	$18,682	$25,300	$31,379

Ownership Cost Value

◯ Average

For 1999, the Cavalier Z24 convertible offers a power convertible top with a single-latch logic stick lever. The rear window is glass and comes with an electric defogger. The Z24 convertible features air conditioning, remote keyless entry and power windows and locks. The exterior offers fog lamps, a rear spoiler, 15 inch cast aluminum wheels and Z24 body-color front and rear fascias. Standard safety features include dual front airbags, four wheel antilock brakes and daytime running lamps.

Chevrolet Cavalier
4 Door Sedan

Compact

 2.2L 115 hp Gas Fuel Inject.
 4 Cylinder In-Line
 Manual 5 Speed
 2 Wheel Front
Dual Airbags Std

Purchase Price

Car Item	Dealer Cost	List
Base Price	**$11,193**	**$11,971**
Anti-Lock Brakes	Std	Std
Automatic 3 Speed	$540	$600
Optional Engine	N/A	N/A
Air Conditioning	$716	$795
Power Steering	Std	Std
Cruise Control	N/A	N/A
Power Windows	N/A	N/A
AM/FM Stereo Cassette	$149	$165
Steering Wheel, Tilt	N/A	N/A
1SA Package	N/C	N/C
*Options Price	$1,405	$1,560
*Total Price	**$12,598**	**$13,531**
Target Price	$12,926	
Destination Charge	$510	
Avg. Tax & Fees	$758	
Total Target $	**$14,194**	
Average Dealer Option Cost:	90%	
12 Month Price Increase:	1%	

Ownership Costs (Projected)

Cost Area	5 Year Cost	Rating
Depreciation	$7,369	○
Financing ($235/month)	$2,762	
Insurance	$7,140	○
State Fees	$573	
Fuel (Hwy 29 City 23)	$2,847	○
Maintenance	$2,308	○
Repairs	$610	○

Warranty/Maintenance Info

Major Tune-Up (100K mile int.)	$248	○
Minor Tune-Up (30K mile int.)	$72	○
Brake Service	$199	○
Overall Warranty	3 yr/36k	○
Drivetrain Warranty	3 yr/36k	○
Rust Warranty	6 yr/100k	○
Maintenance Warranty	N/A	
Roadside Assistance	3 yr/36k	

Ownership Costs By Year (Projected)

$2,000 $4,000 $6,000 $8,000

■ 1999
■ 2000
■ 2001
■ 2002
□ 2003

Resale Value

1999	2000	2001	2002	2003
$12,439	$10,927	$9,589	$8,218	$6,825

Projected Costs (5yr)

Relative $24,621	This Car $23,609
Cost/Mile 35¢	Cost/Mile 34¢

Cumulative Costs

	1999	2000	2001	2002	2003
Annual	$4,781	$4,409	$4,244	$5,260	$4,915
Total	$4,781	$9,190	$13,434	$18,694	$23,609

Ownership Cost Value

◯ Excellent

For 1999, the Cavalier sedan is available with two new exterior colors: Medium Green Metallic and Sandrift Metallic. New this year, a bi-fuel engine is available as an option and can run on either gasoline or compressed natural gas. The Cavalier sedan has standard four wheel antilock brakes, daytime running lamps, a five speed manual transmission and PASSlock theft deterrent system. Options include air conditioning, three or four speed automatic transmission and an AM/FM stereo with cassette.

---

* Includes shaded options
** Other purchase requirements apply
*** Price includes other options

● Poor ◉ Worse Than Average ◯ Average ◯ Better Than Average ◯ Excellent ⊖ Insufficient Information

35

Refer to *Section 3: Annotated Vehicle Charts* for an explanation of these charts.

Chevrolet Cavalier LS
4 Door Sedan

Compact

2.2L 115 hp Gas Fuel Inject.	4 Cylinder In-Line	Automatic 4 Speed	2 Wheel Front	Dual Airbags Std

Purchase Price

Car Item	Dealer Cost	List
Base Price	**$13,474**	**$14,411**
Anti-Lock Brakes	Std	Std
Manual Transmission	N/A	N/A
2.4L 150 hp Gas	$405	$450
Air Conditioning	Std	Std
Power Steering	Std	Std
Cruise Control	Std	Std
Power Windows	Pkg	Pkg
AM/FM Stereo Cassette	Std	Std
Steering Wheel, Tilt	Std	Std
1SA Package	N/C	N/C
*Options Price	$405	$450
*Total Price	$13,879	$14,861
Target Price	$14,255	
Destination Charge	$510	
Avg. Tax & Fees	$831	
Total Target $	**$15,596**	
Average Dealer Option Cost:	90%	
12 Month Price Increase:	1%	

For 1999, the Cavalier LS sedan comes standard with air conditioning, electronic cruise control, AM/FM stereo with cassette and a four speed automatic transmission. Safety features include second generation dual front airbags, four wheel antilock brakes, daytime running lamps and traction control. Optional equipment includes power windows, power locks, power outside mirrors and remote keyless entry. The optional 150 hp 2.4L engine does not need scheduled maintenance for 100,000 miles.

Ownership Costs (Projected)

Cost Area	5 Year Cost	Rating
Depreciation	$8,383	◉
Financing ($259/month)	$3,034	
Insurance	$7,463	◉
State Fees	$628	
Fuel (Hwy 30 City 22)	$2,855	◉
Maintenance	$2,574	○
Repairs	$610	○

Warranty/Maintenance Info

Major Tune-Up (100K mile int.)	$205	○
Minor Tune-Up (30K mile int.)	$72	○
Brake Service	$199	○
Overall Warranty	3 yr/36k	◉
Drivetrain Warranty	3 yr/36k	◉
Rust Warranty	6 yr/100k	○
Maintenance Warranty	N/A	
Roadside Assistance	3 yr/36k	

Ownership Costs By Year (Projected)

$2,000 $4,000 $6,000 $8,000 $10,000

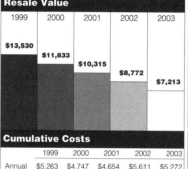

- ■ 1999
- ■ 2000
- ■ 2001
- ▨ 2002
- ☐ 2003

Resale Value

1999	2000	2001	2002	2003
$13,530	$11,833	$10,315	$8,772	$7,213

Cumulative Costs

	1999	2000	2001	2002	2003
Annual	$5,263	$4,747	$4,654	$5,611	$5,272
Total	$5,263	$10,010	$14,664	$20,275	$25,547

Projected Costs (5yr)

Relative	This Car
$25,768	$25,547
Cost/Mile 37¢	Cost/Mile 36¢

Ownership Cost Value

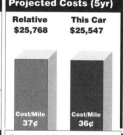

Average

Chevrolet Corvette
2 Door Hardtop

Sport

5.7L 345 hp Gas Fuel Inject.	8 Cylinder "V"	Manual 6 Speed	2 Wheel Rear	Dual Airbags Std

Purchase Price

Car Item	Dealer Cost	List
Base Price	**$33,422**	**$38,197**
Anti-Lock Brakes	Std	Std
Automatic Transmission	N/A	N/A
Optional Engine	N/A	N/A
Air Conditioning	Std	Std
Power Steering	Std	Std
Cruise Control	Std	Std
Power Windows	Std	Std
AM/FM Stereo Cassette	Std	Std
Steering Wheel, Tilt	Std	Std
1SA Package	N/C	N/C
*Options Price	$0	$0
*Total Price	$33,422	$38,197
Target Price	$37,074	
Destination Charge	$580	
Avg. Tax & Fees	$2,095	
Luxury Tax	$99	
Total Target $	**$39,848**	
12 Month Price Increase:	N/A	

For 1999, the Corvette hardtop provides a new entry for Corvette customers seeking less standard equipment. Equipped with a six speed manual transmission, remote trunk release and cloth/vinyl bucket seats, it features minimal standard equipment. The Z19 Performance Package enhances hardtop performance by eliminating the 126 mph engine speed limiter and adding an upgraded suspension, wider wheels and Z-rated performance tires. The available options include a CD changer and six-way driver seat.

Ownership Costs (Projected)

Cost Area	5 Year Cost	Rating
Depreciation	$14,024	○
Financing ($660/month)	$7,751	
Insurance (Performance)	$14,825	◐
State Fees	$1,564	
Fuel (Hwy 28 City 18 -Prem.)	$3,871	○
Maintenance	$3,705	◐
Repairs	$1,360	○

Warranty/Maintenance Info

Major Tune-Up (100K mile int.)	$329	◐
Minor Tune-Up (30K mile int.)	$125	○
Brake Service	$319	○
Overall Warranty	3 yr/36k	○
Drivetrain Warranty	3 yr/36k	○
Rust Warranty	6 yr/100k	○
Maintenance Warranty	N/A	
Roadside Assistance	3 yr/36k	

Ownership Costs By Year (Projected)

$5,000 $10,000 $15,000

- ■ 1999
- ■ 2000
- ■ 2001
- ▨ 2002
- ☐ 2003

Resale Value

1999	2000	2001	2002	2003
$35,798	$33,026	$30,579	$28,213	$25,824

Cumulative Costs

	1999	2000	2001	2002	2003
Annual	$10,682	$8,973	$8,495	$10,294	$8,656
Total	$10,682	$19,655	$28,150	$38,444	$47,100

Projected Costs (5yr)

Relative	This Car
$46,482	$47,100
Cost/Mile 66¢	Cost/Mile 67¢

Ownership Cost Value

Poor

Chevrolet Corvette
2 Door Coupe

Sport

5.7L 345 hp Gas Fuel Inject.

8 Cylinder "V"

Automatic 4 Speed

2 Wheel Rear

Dual Airbags Std

Purchase Price

Car Item	Dealer Cost	List
Base Price	**$33,767**	**$38,591**
Anti-Lock Brakes	Std	Std
Manual 6 Speed	$701	$815
Optional Engine	N/A	N/A
Air Conditioning	Std	Std
Power Steering	Std	Std
Cruise Control	Std	Std
Power Windows	Std	Std
AM/FM Stereo Cassette	Std	Std
Steering Wheel, Tilt	Std	Std
1SA Package	N/C	N/C
*Options Price	$701	$815
*Total Price	**$34,468**	**$39,406**
Target Price	$38,254	
Destination Charge	$580	
Avg. Tax & Fees	$2,161	
Luxury Tax	$170	
Total Target $	**$41,165**	
12 Month Price Increase:	2%	

Ownership Costs (Projected)

Cost Area	5 Year Cost	Rating
Depreciation	$14,358	◯
Financing ($682/month)	$8,007	
Insurance (Performance)	$14,825	◉
State Fees	$1,613	
Fuel (Hwy 28 City 18 -Prem.)	$3,871	◯
Maintenance	$3,705	◉
Repairs	$1,360	◯

Warranty/Maintenance Info

Major Tune-Up (100K mile int.)	$329	◉
Minor Tune-Up (30K mile int.)	$125	◯
Brake Service	$319	◯
Overall Warranty	3 yr/36k	◯
Drivetrain Warranty	3 yr/36k	◯
Rust Warranty	6 yr/100k	◯
Maintenance Warranty	N/A	
Roadside Assistance	3 yr/36k	

Ownership Costs By Year (Projected)

$5,000 $10,000 $15,000

■ 1999
■ 2000
■ 2001
□ 2002
□ 2003

Resale Value

1999	2000	2001	2002	2003
$36,788	$34,017	$31,568	$29,198	$26,807

Cumulative Costs

	1999	2000	2001	2002	2003
Annual	$11,108	$9,054	$8,560	$10,340	$8,677
Total	$11,108	$20,162	$28,722	$39,062	$47,739

Projected Costs (5yr)

Relative	This Car
$48,113	$47,739
Cost/Mile 69¢	Cost/Mile 68¢

Ownership Cost Value

◯ Better Than Average

For 1999, the Corvette coupe is available with an optional six speed manual transmission, custom sport magnesium wheels and a Performance Handling Package. Standard interior features include leather bucket seats, power windows with express down and power door locks. The exterior features a removable roof panel, an aluminized stainless-steel exhaust system and one new exterior color. Standard safety features include daytime running lamps, a rear window defroster and heated outside mirrors.

Chevrolet Corvette
2 Door Convertible

Sport

5.7L 345 hp Gas Fuel Inject.

8 Cylinder "V"

Automatic 4 Speed

2 Wheel Rear

Dual Airbags Std

Purchase Price

Car Item	Dealer Cost	List
Base Price	**$39,374**	**$44,999**
Anti-Lock Brakes	Std	Std
Manual 6 Speed	$701	$815
Optional Engine	N/A	N/A
Air Conditioning	Std	Std
Power Steering	Std	Std
Cruise Control	Std	Std
Power Windows	Std	Std
AM/FM Stereo Cassette	Std	Std
Steering Wheel, Tilt	Std	Std
1SA Package	N/C	N/C
*Options Price	$701	$815
*Total Price	**$40,075**	**$45,814**
Target Price	$45,639	
Destination Charge	$580	
Avg. Tax & Fees	$2,557	
Luxury Tax	$613	
Total Target $	**$49,389**	
12 Month Price Increase:	None	

Ownership Costs (Projected)

Cost Area	5 Year Cost	Rating
Depreciation	$19,492	◯
Financing ($819/month)	$9,608	
Insurance (Performance)	$16,250	◉
State Fees	$1,869	
Fuel (Hwy 28 City 18 -Prem.)	$3,871	◯
Maintenance	$3,705	◉
Repairs	$1,360	◯

Warranty/Maintenance Info

Major Tune-Up (100K mile int.)	$329	◉
Minor Tune-Up (30K mile int.)	$125	◯
Brake Service	$319	◯
Overall Warranty	3 yr/36k	◯
Drivetrain Warranty	3 yr/36k	◯
Rust Warranty	6 yr/100k	◯
Maintenance Warranty	N/A	
Roadside Assistance	3 yr/36k	

Ownership Costs By Year (Projected)

$5,000 $10,000 $15,000 $20,000

■ 1999
■ 2000
■ 2001
□ 2002
□ 2003

Resale Value

1999	2000	2001	2002	2003
$38,758	$36,264	$34,092	$32,005	$29,897

Cumulative Costs

	1999	2000	2001	2002	2003
Annual	$18,241	$9,554	$8,949	$10,604	$8,807
Total	$18,241	$27,795	$36,744	$47,348	$56,155

Projected Costs (5yr)

Relative	This Car
$56,366	$56,155
Cost/Mile 81¢	Cost/Mile 80¢

Ownership Cost Value

◯ Average

For 1999, standard features on the Corvette convertible include a manual convertible top with a heated rear window, dual power outside mirrors and daytime running lamps. Available option packages include the Memory Package and the Performance Handling Package. Optional safety features include dual halogen fog lamps, heated outside mirrors and Extended Mobility tires, designed to allow driving for up to 200 miles without air pressure in a tire.

● Poor ◉ Worse Than Average ◑ Average ◯ Better Than Average ◯ Excellent ⊖ Insufficient Information

37

Refer to *Section 3: Annotated Vehicle Charts* for an explanation of these charts.

Chevrolet Lumina
4 Door Sedan

Midsize

3.1L 160 hp Gas Fuel Inject.	6 Cylinder "V"
Automatic 4 Speed	2 Wheel Front
Dual Airbags Std	

Purchase Price

Car Item	Dealer Cost	List
Base Price	**$16,644**	**$18,190**
Anti-Lock Brakes	$512	$575
Manual Transmission	N/A	N/A
Optional Engine	N/A	N/A
Air Conditioning	Std	Std
Power Steering	Std	Std
Cruise Control	Std	Std
Power Windows	Std	Std
AM/FM Stereo Cassette	Inc	Inc
Steering Wheel, Tilt	Std	Std
1SF Package	$182	$205
***Options Price**	**$694**	**$780**
***Total Price**	**$17,338**	**$18,970**
Target Price	$18,157	
Destination Charge	$560	
Avg. Tax & Fees	$1,050	
Total Target $	**$19,767**	
Average Dealer Option Cost:	**89%**	
12 Month Price Increase:	*1%*	

The Lumina sedan continues in 1999 with few changes. A new exterior color arrives, Nightmist Medium Auburn. Luminas produced after November 2, 1998 will receive additional standard features. These include a rear window defogger, cruise/speed control, power windows and option package revisions. Popular options include a remote keyless entry system, custom cloth 60/40 split bench seating, a four wheel antilock braking system and 16 inch aluminum wheels.

Ownership Costs (Projected)

Cost Area	5 Year Cost	Rating
Depreciation	$10,982	◉
Financing ($328/month)	$3,846	
Insurance	$6,852	○
State Fees	$794	
Fuel (Hwy 29 City 20)	$3,041	○
Maintenance	$3,423	○
Repairs	$745	○

Warranty/Maintenance Info

Major Tune-Up (100K mile int.)	$264	○
Minor Tune-Up (30K mile int.)	$145	●
Brake Service	$238	○
Overall Warranty	3 yr/36k	○
Drivetrain Warranty	3 yr/36k	○
Rust Warranty	6 yr/100k	○
Maintenance Warranty	N/A	
Roadside Assistance	3 yr/36k	

Ownership Costs By Year (Projected)

$2,000 $4,000 $6,000 $8,000 $10,000 $12,000

- 1999
- 2000
- 2001
- 2002
- 2003

Resale Value

1999	2000	2001	2002	2003
$16,016	$14,017	$12,291	$10,514	$8,785

Cumulative Costs

	1999	2000	2001	2002	2003
Annual	$7,183	$5,229	$5,092	$6,529	$5,650
Total	$7,183	$12,412	$17,504	$24,033	$29,683

Projected Costs (5yr)

Relative	This Car
$28,831	$29,683
Cost/Mile 41¢	Cost/Mile 42¢

Ownership Cost Value

○ Average

Chevrolet Lumina LS
4 Door Sedan

Midsize

3.1L 160 hp Gas Fuel Inject.	6 Cylinder "V"
Automatic 4 Speed	2 Wheel Front
Dual Airbags Std	

Purchase Price

Car Item	Dealer Cost	List
Base Price	**$18,227**	**$19,920**
Anti-Lock Brakes	Std	Std
Manual Transmission	N/A	N/A
Optional Engine	N/A	N/A
Air Conditioning	Std	Std
Power Steering	Std	Std
Cruise Control	Std	Std
Power Windows	Std	Std
AM/FM Stereo Cassette	Std	Std
Steering Wheel, Tilt	Std	Std
1SG Package	N/C	N/C
***Options Price**	**$0**	**$0**
***Total Price**	**$18,227**	**$19,920**
Target Price	$19,111	
Destination Charge	$560	
Avg. Tax & Fees	$1,103	
Total Target $	**$20,774**	
Average Dealer Option Cost:	**89%**	
12 Month Price Increase:	*1%*	

The Lumina LS arrives in 1999 featuring minor changes including Nightmist Medium Auburn, a new exterior color. Valuable standard equipment includes air conditioning, 16 inch aluminum wheels with touring tires, a cassette stereo system with speed-compensated volume and automatic tone control, and a four wheel antilock braking system. The LS Value option package includes a remote keyless entry system, floor mats and driver and front passenger temperature controls, among other items.

Ownership Costs (Projected)

Cost Area	5 Year Cost	Rating
Depreciation	$11,876	◉
Financing ($344/month)	$4,041	
Insurance	$6,852	○
State Fees	$832	
Fuel (Hwy 29 City 20)	$3,041	○
Maintenance	$3,449	○
Repairs	$745	○

Warranty/Maintenance Info

Major Tune-Up (100K mile int.)	$255	○
Minor Tune-Up (30K mile int.)	$145	●
Brake Service	$238	○
Overall Warranty	3 yr/36k	○
Drivetrain Warranty	3 yr/36k	○
Rust Warranty	6 yr/100k	○
Maintenance Warranty	N/A	
Roadside Assistance	3 yr/36k	

Ownership Costs By Year (Projected)

$2,000 $4,000 $6,000 $8,000 $10,000 $12,000

- 1999
- 2000
- 2001
- 2002
- 2003

Resale Value

1999	2000	2001	2002	2003
$16,605	$14,493	$12,648	$10,751	$8,898

Cumulative Costs

	1999	2000	2001	2002	2003
Annual	$7,677	$5,404	$5,259	$6,707	$5,789
Total	$7,677	$13,081	$18,340	$25,047	$30,836

Projected Costs (5yr)

Relative	This Car
$29,681	$30,836
Cost/Mile 42¢	Cost/Mile 44¢

Ownership Cost Value

○ Average

38

● Poor	◉ Worse Than Average
○ Average	○ Better Than Average
○ Excellent	⊖ Insufficient Information

Refer to *Section 3: Annotated Vehicle Charts* for an explanation of these charts.

Chevrolet Lumina LTZ
4 Door Sedan

Midsize

3.8L 200 hp Gas Fuel Inject.	6 Cylinder "V"
Automatic 4 Speed	2 Wheel Front
Dual Airbags Std	

Purchase Price

Car Item	Dealer Cost	List
Base Price	**$18,629**	**$20,360**
Anti-Lock Brakes	Std	Std
Manual Transmission	N/A	N/A
Optional Engine	N/A	N/A
Air Conditioning	Std	Std
Power Steering	Std	Std
Cruise Control	Std	Std
Power Windows	Std	Std
AM/FM Stereo Cassette	Std	Std
Steering Wheel, Tilt	Std	Std
1SC Package	N/C	N/C
***Options Price**	**$0**	**$0**
***Total Price**	**$18,629**	**$20,360**
Target Price	$19,539	
Destination Charge	$560	
Avg. Tax & Fees	$1,126	
Total Target $	**$21,225**	
Average Dealer Option Cost:	**89%**	
12 Month Price Increase:	1%	

Ownership Costs (Projected)

Cost Area	5 Year Cost	Rating
Depreciation	$11,727	●
Financing ($352/month)	$4,128	
Insurance	$7,140	○
State Fees	$849	
Fuel (Hwy 30 City 19)	$3,070	○
Maintenance	$3,345	◉
Repairs	$745	◉

Warranty/Maintenance Info

Major Tune-Up (100K mile int.)	$240	○
Minor Tune-Up (30K mile int.)	$145	●
Brake Service	$272	◉
Overall Warranty	3 yr/36k	○
Drivetrain Warranty	3 yr/36k	○
Rust Warranty	6 yr/100k	○
Maintenance Warranty	N/A	
Roadside Assistance	3 yr/36k	

The Lumina LTZ arrives in showrooms in 1999 boasting several key enhancements to its performance sedan image. These revisions include bucket seats with LTZ embroidered on the seat backs, 16 inch machine-faced aluminum wheels with touring tires, and a ride and handling suspension system, all standard. A 3800 V6 200 hp engine is also standard, along with four wheel antilock brakes. Driver and passenger temperature controls and steering wheel radio controls remain popular options.

Ownership Costs By Year (Projected)

$2,000 $4,000 $6,000 $8,000 $10,000 $12,000

■ 1999
■ 2000
■ 2001
□ 2002
□ 2003

Resale Value

1999	2000	2001	2002	2003
$17,091	$15,001	$13,184	$11,317	$9,498

Cumulative Costs

	1999	2000	2001	2002	2003
Annual	$7,736	$5,472	$5,315	$6,792	$5,689
Total	$7,736	$13,208	$18,523	$25,315	$31,004

Projected Costs (5yr)

Relative	This Car
$30,091	$31,004
Cost/Mile 43¢	Cost/Mile 44¢

Ownership Cost Value

○ Average

Chevrolet Malibu
4 Door Sedan

Midsize

2.4L 150 hp Gas Fuel Inject.	4 Cylinder In-Line
Automatic 4 Speed	2 Wheel Front
Dual Airbags Std	

Purchase Price

Car Item	Dealer Cost	List
Base Price	**$14,594**	**$15,950**
Anti-Lock Brakes	Std	Std
Manual Transmission	N/A	N/A
3.1L 150 hp Gas	$536	$595
Air Conditioning	Std	Std
Power Steering	Std	Std
Cruise Control	$203	$225
Power Windows	Inc	Inc
AM/FM Stereo Cassette	$198	$220
Steering Wheel, Tilt	Std	Std
1SB Package	$666	$740
***Options Price**	**$1,603**	**$1,780**
***Total Price**	**$16,197**	**$17,730**
Target Price	$16,933	
Destination Charge	$535	
Avg. Tax & Fees	$982	
Total Target $	**$18,450**	
Average Dealer Option Cost:	**90%**	
12 Month Price Increase:	2%	

Ownership Costs (Projected)

Cost Area	5 Year Cost	Rating
Depreciation	$9,171	○
Financing ($306/month)	$3,589	
Insurance	$7,463	◉
State Fees	$744	
Fuel (Hwy 29 City 20)	$3,041	○
Maintenance	$3,650	◉
Repairs	$705	○

Warranty/Maintenance Info

Major Tune-Up (100K mile int.)	$216	○
Minor Tune-Up (30K mile int.)	$114	○
Brake Service	$187	○
Overall Warranty	3 yr/36k	○
Drivetrain Warranty	3 yr/36k	○
Rust Warranty	6 yr/100k	○
Maintenance Warranty	N/A	
Roadside Assistance	3 yr/36k	

The Malibu continues this year with only minor revisions. Most notable include a Solar-Ray tinted windshield that uses thicker glass to help reduce road noise. Medium Bronzemist Metallic is added as a new exterior color. Value-added features include second generation driver and front passenger airbags, a stainless steel exhaust system and four wheel antilock brakes. Additional creature comforts include air conditioning, a four speed automatic transmission and P215/60R15 touring tires.

Ownership Costs By Year (Projected)

$2,000 $4,000 $6,000 $8,000 $10,000

■ 1999
■ 2000
■ 2001
□ 2002
□ 2003

Resale Value

1999	2000	2001	2002	2003
$16,081	$14,198	$12,580	$10,908	$9,279

Cumulative Costs

	1999	2000	2001	2002	2003
Annual	$5,819	$5,149	$5,013	$6,848	$5,534
Total	$5,819	$10,968	$15,981	$22,829	$28,363

Projected Costs (5yr)

Relative	This Car
$27,858	$28,363
Cost/Mile 40¢	Cost/Mile 41¢

Ownership Cost Value

○ Average

---

* Includes shaded options

** Other purchase requirements apply

*** Price includes other options

● Poor	◉ Worse Than Average	○ Average	○ Better Than Average	○ Excellent	⊖ Insufficient Information

39

Refer to *Section 3: Annotated Vehicle Charts* for an explanation of these charts.

Chevrolet Malibu LS
4 Door Sedan

Midsize

 3.1L 150 hp Gas Fuel Inject.

 6 Cylinder "V"

 PRND321 Automatic 4 Speed

 2 Wheel Front

 Dual Airbags Std

Purchase Price

Car Item	Dealer Cost	List
Base Price	**$17,303**	**$18,910**
Anti-Lock Brakes	Std	Std
Manual Transmission	N/A	N/A
Optional Engine	N/A	N/A
Air Conditioning	Std	Std
Power Steering	Std	Std
Cruise Control	Std	Std
Power Windows	Std	Std
AM/FM Stereo Cassette	Std	Std
Steering Wheel, Tilt	Std	Std
1SA Package	N/C	N/C
*Options Price	$0	$0
*Total Price	**$17,303**	**$18,910**
Target Price	$18,127	
Destination Charge	$535	
Avg. Tax & Fees	$1,047	
Total Target $	**$19,709**	
Average Dealer Option Cost:	**90%**	
12 Month Price Increase:	2%	

Ownership Costs (Projected)

Cost Area	5 Year Cost	Rating
Depreciation	$10,633	◐
Financing ($327/month)	$3,835	
Insurance	$7,643	◐
State Fees	$791	
Fuel (Hwy 29 City 20)	$3,041	○
Maintenance	$3,590	◉
Repairs	$705	○

Warranty/Maintenance Info

Major Tune-Up (100K mile int.)	$209	○
Minor Tune-Up (30K mile int.)	$114	○
Brake Service	$187	○
Overall Warranty	3 yr/36k	○
Drivetrain Warranty	3 yr/36k	○
Rust Warranty	6 yr/100k	○
Maintenance Warranty	N/A	
Roadside Assistance	3 yr/36k	

The Malibu LS arrives this model year with few changes, including Medium Bronzemist Metallic, a new exterior color, and thicker Solar-Ray tinted windshield glass designed to reduce exterior road noise. The Malibu LS is distinguished by additional premium feature enhancements. These include standard power windows, a remote keyless entry system, cruise control and a six-way power driver's seat. Limited options include leather seating surfaces, a power glass sunroof and CD player.

Ownership Costs By Year (Projected)

$2,000 $4,000 $6,000 $8,000 $10,000 $12,000

■ 1999 ■ 2000 ■ 2001 ▨ 2002 ☐ 2003

Resale Value

1999	2000	2001	2002	2003
$16,523	$14,478	$12,700	$10,868	$9,076

Cumulative Costs

	1999	2000	2001	2002	2003
Annual	$6,765	$5,426	$5,271	$7,087	$5,689
Total	$6,765	$12,191	$17,462	$24,549	$30,238

Projected Costs (5yr)

Relative $28,799	This Car $30,238
Cost/Mile 41¢	Cost/Mile 43¢

Ownership Cost Value

● Worse Than Average

Chevrolet Metro
2 Door Hatchback

Subcompact

 1.0L 55 hp Gas Fuel Inject.

 3 Cylinder In-Line

 1 3 5 / 2 4 R Manual 5 Speed

 2 Wheel Front

 Dual Airbags Std

Purchase Price

Car Item	Dealer Cost	List
Base Price	**$8,471**	**$8,993**
Anti-Lock Brakes	$503	$565
Automatic Transmission	N/A	N/A
Optional Engine	N/A	N/A
Air Conditioning	$699	$785
Power Steering	N/A	N/A
Cruise Control	N/A	N/A
Power Windows	N/A	N/A
AM/FM Stereo Cassette	$490	$550
Steering Wheel, Tilt	N/A	N/A
1SA Package	N/C	N/C
*Options Price	$1,189	$1,335
*Total Price	**$9,660**	**$10,328**
Target Price	$9,860	
Destination Charge	$380	
Avg. Tax & Fees	$581	
Total Target $	**$10,821**	
Average Dealer Option Cost:	**89%**	
12 Month Price Increase:	4%	

Ownership Costs (Projected)

Cost Area	5 Year Cost	Rating
Depreciation	$6,283	◉
Financing ($179/month)	$2,105	
Insurance	$7,837	●
State Fees	$441	
Fuel (Hwy 47 City 41)	$1,684	○
Maintenance	$3,016	○
Repairs	$555	○

Warranty/Maintenance Info

Major Tune-Up (100K mile int.)	$444	●
Minor Tune-Up (30K mile int.)	$78	○
Brake Service	$267	◉
Overall Warranty	3 yr/36k	○
Drivetrain Warranty	3 yr/36k	○
Rust Warranty	6 yr/100k	○
Maintenance Warranty	N/A	
Roadside Assistance	3 yr/36k	

The 1999 Metro coupe enters the model year with two new metallic colors: Dark Green and Silver. For added safety, the base coupe features daytime running lamps, second generation dual front airbags and a reinforced safety cage. Standard amenities include dual manual side mirrors, Scotchgard protection and a folding rear seat. The Metro coupe is equipped with a 1.0L engine mated to a five speed manual transmission to provide the highest fuel mileage of all Chevrolet vehicles.

Ownership Costs By Year (Projected)

$2,000 $4,000 $6,000 $8,000

■ 1999 ■ 2000 ■ 2001 ▨ 2002 ☐ 2003

Resale Value

1999	2000	2001	2002	2003
$8,977	$7,799	$6,767	$5,678	$4,538

Cumulative Costs

	1999	2000	2001	2002	2003
Annual	$4,525	$3,773	$3,839	$4,816	$4,968
Total	$4,525	$8,298	$12,137	$16,953	$21,921

Projected Costs (5yr)

Relative $20,965	This Car $21,921
Cost/Mile 30¢	Cost/Mile 31¢

Ownership Cost Value

○ Average

 40

* Includes shaded options
** Other purchase requirements apply
*** Price includes other options

● Poor ◉ Worse Than Average ○ Average ○ Better Than Average ○ Excellent ⊖ Insufficient Information

Refer to *Section 3: Annotated Vehicle Charts* for an explanation of these charts.

Chevrolet Metro LSi
2 Door Hatchback

| 1.3L 79 hp Gas Fuel Inject. | 4 Cylinder In-Line | Manual 5 Speed | 2 Wheel Front | Dual Airbags Std |

Purchase Price

Car Item	Dealer Cost	List
Base Price	**$9,124**	**$9,790**
Anti-Lock Brakes	$503	$565
Automatic 3 Speed	$530	$595
Optional Engine	N/A	N/A
Air Conditioning	$699	$785
Power Steering	N/A	N/A
Cruise Control	N/A	N/A
Power Windows	N/A	N/A
AM/FM Stereo Cassette	$490	$550
Steering Wheel, Tilt	N/A	N/A
1SD Package	N/C	N/C
*Options Price	$1,189	$1,335
*Total Price	$10,313	$11,125
Target Price	$10,513	
Destination Charge	$380	
Avg. Tax & Fees	$618	
Total Target $	**$11,511**	
Average Dealer Option Cost:	89%	
12 Month Price Increase:	4%	

Ownership Costs (Projected)

Cost Area	5 Year Cost	Rating
Depreciation	$6,619	◕
Financing ($191/month)	$2,240	
Insurance	$8,045	●
State Fees	$474	
Fuel (Hwy 43 City 39)	$1,811	○
Maintenance	$3,094	◎
Repairs	$555	◎

Ownership Costs By Year (Projected)

	$2,000	$4,000	$6,000	$8,000	$10,000

- 1999
- 2000
- 2001
- 2002
- 2003

Warranty/Maintenance Info

Major Tune-Up (100K mile int.)	$325	◕
Minor Tune-Up (30K mile int.)	$95	◎
Brake Service	$267	◕
Overall Warranty	3 yr/36k	◎
Drivetrain Warranty	3 yr/36k	◎
Rust Warranty	6 yr/100k	○
Maintenance Warranty	N/A	
Roadside Assistance	3 yr/36k	

Resale Value

1999	2000	2001	2002	2003
$9,563	$8,320	$7,227	$6,082	$4,892

Cumulative Costs

	1999	2000	2001	2002	2003
Annual	$4,747	$3,949	$4,032	$4,964	$5,146
Total	$4,747	$8,696	$12,728	$17,692	$22,838

Projected Costs (5yr)

Relative $21,633	This Car $22,838
Cost/Mile 31¢	Cost/Mile 33¢

Ownership Cost Value

◎ Average

The 1999 Metro LSi coupe is available in two new exterior colors: Dark Green Metallic and Silver Metallic. The LSi is equipped with a larger 1.3L engine with a distributorless ignition, which eliminates the need for periodic engine timing adjustments. Standard equipment includes daytime running lamps, body-colored bumpers and seven spoke painted wheel covers. Air conditioning, a three speed automatic transmission, AM/FM stereo with cassette and four wheel antilock brakes are available options.

Chevrolet Metro LSi
4 Door Sedan

| 1.3L 79 hp Gas Fuel Inject. | 4 Cylinder In-Line | Manual 5 Speed | 2 Wheel Front | Dual Airbags Std |

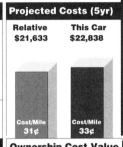

Purchase Price

Car Item	Dealer Cost	List
Base Price	**$9,695**	**$10,402**
Anti-Lock Brakes	$503	$565
Automatic 3 Speed	$530	$595
Optional Engine	N/A	N/A
Air Conditioning	$699	$785
Power Steering	$258	$290
Cruise Control	N/A	N/A
Power Windows	N/A	N/A
AM/FM Stereo Cassette	$490	$550
Steering Wheel, Tilt	N/A	N/A
1SA Package	N/C	N/C
*Options Price	$1,447	$1,625
*Total Price	$11,142	$12,027
Target Price	$11,342	
Destination Charge	$380	
Avg. Tax & Fees	$664	
Total Target $	**$12,386**	
Average Dealer Option Cost:	89%	
12 Month Price Increase:	3%	

Ownership Costs (Projected)

Cost Area	5 Year Cost	Rating
Depreciation	$6,639	◎
Financing ($205/month)	$2,410	
Insurance	$8,045	●
State Fees	$509	
Fuel (Hwy 43 City 39)	$1,811	○
Maintenance	$3,094	◎
Repairs	$555	◎

Ownership Costs By Year (Projected)

	$2,000	$4,000	$6,000	$8,000	$10,000

- 1999
- 2000
- 2001
- 2002
- 2003

Warranty/Maintenance Info

Major Tune-Up (100K mile int.)	$325	◕
Minor Tune-Up (30K mile int.)	$95	◎
Brake Service	$267	◕
Overall Warranty	3 yr/36k	◎
Drivetrain Warranty	3 yr/36k	◎
Rust Warranty	6 yr/100k	○
Maintenance Warranty	N/A	
Roadside Assistance	3 yr/36k	

Resale Value

1999	2000	2001	2002	2003
$10,474	$9,209	$8,100	$6,943	$5,747

Cumulative Costs

	1999	2000	2001	2002	2003
Annual	$4,778	$4,026	$4,090	$5,004	$5,165
Total	$4,778	$8,804	$12,894	$17,898	$23,063

Projected Costs (5yr)

Relative $22,490	This Car $23,063
Cost/Mile 32¢	Cost/Mile 33¢

Ownership Cost Value

◎ Average

The 1999 Metro LSi sedan introduces two new exterior colors: Dark Green Metallic and Silver Metallic. The LSi sedan features daytime running lamps, dual manual side mirrors and composite halogen headlamps, not normally found in cars in this class. The LSi sedan is equipped with a larger 1.3L engine and five speed manual transmission. A three speed automatic transmission can be ordered for added convenience. Options include air conditioning, AM/FM stereo and a Convenience Package.

| ● Poor | ◕ Worse Than Average | ◎ Average | ○ Better Than Average | ○ Excellent | ⊖ Insufficient Information |

Refer to Section 3: Annotated Vehicle Charts for an explanation of these charts.

Chevrolet Monte Carlo LS
2 Door Coupe

 3.1L 160 hp Gas Fuel Inject.
 6 Cylinder "V"
 Automatic 4 Speed
 2 Wheel Front
 Dual Airbags Std

Purchase Price

Car Item	Dealer Cost	List
Base Price	**$16,937**	**$18,510**
Anti-Lock Brakes	Std	Std
Manual Transmission	N/A	N/A
Optional Engine	N/A	N/A
Air Conditioning	Std	Std
Power Steering	Std	Std
Cruise Control	Std	Std
Power Windows	Std	Std
AM/FM Stereo Cassette	Std	Std
Steering Wheel, Tilt	Std	Std
1SC Package	N/C	N/C
*Options Price	$0	$0
*Total Price	**$16,937**	**$18,510**
Target Price	$17,560	
Destination Charge	$560	
Avg. Tax & Fees	$1,019	
Total Target $	**$19,139**	
Average Dealer Option Cost:	**89%**	
12 Month Price Increase:	2%	

Ownership Costs (Projected)

Cost Area	5 Year Cost	Rating
Depreciation	$9,634	◐
Financing ($317/month)	$3,723	
Insurance	$7,294	◐
State Fees	$776	
Fuel (Hwy 29 City 20)	$3,041	◐
Maintenance	$3,423	◐
Repairs	$755	◐

Ownership Costs By Year (Projected)

$2,000 $4,000 $6,000 $8,000 $10,000

■ 1999
■ 2000
■ 2001
□ 2002
□ 2003

Warranty/Maintenance Info

Major Tune-Up (100K mile int.)	$264	◐
Minor Tune-Up (30K mile int.)	$145	●
Brake Service	$238	◐
Overall Warranty	3 yr/36k	◐
Drivetrain Warranty	3 yr/36k	◐
Rust Warranty	6 yr/100k	○
Maintenance Warranty	N/A	
Roadside Assistance	3 yr/36k	

Resale Value

1999	2000	2001	2002	2003
$16,985	$14,936	$13,151	$11,308	$9,505

Projected Costs (5yr)

Relative $28,474	This Car $28,646
Cost/Mile 41¢	Cost/Mile 41¢

Cumulative Costs

	1999	2000	2001	2002	2003
Annual	$5,624	$5,327	$5,213	$6,670	$5,812
Total	$5,624	$10,951	$16,164	$22,834	$28,646

Ownership Cost Value
◐ Average

The 1999 Monte Carlo LS features an electric rear window defogger and cruise control as standard equipment. Medium Auburn Nightmist Metallic replaces Deep Purple Metallic as an exterior color. The LS model features two different seating options for the front seats. One can either order a 60/40 split bench seat to increase seating to six, or two front bucket seats for seating for five. Optional amenities include a power sliding moonroof, premium stereo with CD and leather seating surfaces.

Chevrolet Monte Carlo Z34
2 Door Coupe

 3.8L 200 hp Gas Fuel Inject.
 6 Cylinder "V"
 Automatic 4 Speed
 2 Wheel Front
Dual Airbags Std

Purchase Price

Car Item	Dealer Cost	List
Base Price	**$18,790**	**$20,535**
Anti-Lock Brakes	Std	Std
Manual Transmission	N/A	N/A
Optional Engine	N/A	N/A
Air Conditioning	Std	Std
Power Steering	Std	Std
Cruise Control	Std	Std
Power Windows	Std	Std
AM/FM Stereo Cassette	Std	Std
Steering Wheel, Tilt	Std	Std
1SB Package	N/C	N/C
*Options Price	$0	$0
*Total Price	**$18,790**	**$20,535**
Target Price	$19,506	
Destination Charge	$560	
Avg. Tax & Fees	$1,127	
Total Target $	**$21,193**	
Average Dealer Option Cost:	**89%**	
12 Month Price Increase:	None	

Ownership Costs (Projected)

Cost Area	5 Year Cost	Rating
Depreciation	$10,960	◉
Financing ($351/month)	$4,123	
Insurance	$7,643	○
State Fees	$858	
Fuel (Hwy 30 City 19)	$3,070	◐
Maintenance	$3,345	◐
Repairs	$755	◐

Ownership Costs By Year (Projected)

$2,000 $4,000 $6,000 $8,000 $10,000 $12,000

■ 1999
■ 2000
■ 2001
■ 2002
□ 2003

Warranty/Maintenance Info

Major Tune-Up (100K mile int.)	$240	○
Minor Tune-Up (30K mile int.)	$145	●
Brake Service	$272	◉
Overall Warranty	3 yr/36k	○
Drivetrain Warranty	3 yr/36k	○
Rust Warranty	6 yr/100k	○
Maintenance Warranty	N/A	
Roadside Assistance	3 yr/36k	

Resale Value

1999	2000	2001	2002	2003
$18,369	$16,147	$14,194	$12,191	$10,233

Projected Costs (5yr)

Relative $30,260	This Car $30,754
Cost/Mile 43¢	Cost/Mile 44¢

Cumulative Costs

	1999	2000	2001	2002	2003
Annual	$6,522	$5,702	$5,555	$7,037	$5,938
Total	$6,522	$12,224	$17,779	$24,816	$30,754

Ownership Cost Value
○ Average

The 1999 Monte Carlo Z34 is the performance version of the LS model. The Z34 uses the larger 3800 Series II V6, producing 200 hp and 225 lb-ft of torque. The Z34 is equipped with standard four wheel antilock disc brakes and grippy P225/60R16 Goodyear Eagle RS-A performance tires. Optional amenities include a power sliding moonroof, premium stereo with CD, leather seating and a rear deck spoiler. Daytime running lamps and dual front airbags are standard safety features.

42

* Includes shaded options
** Other purchase requirements apply
*** Price includes other options

● Poor ◉ Worse Than Average ◐ Average ○ Better Than Average ○ Excellent ⊖ Insufficient Information

Refer to *Section 3: Annotated Vehicle Charts* for an explanation of these charts.

Chevrolet Prizm
4 Door Sedan

Compact

1.8L 120 hp Gas Fuel Inject.

4 Cylinder In-Line

Manual 5 Speed

2 Wheel Front

Dual Airbags Std

Purchase Price

Car Item	Dealer Cost	List
Base Price	$11,679	$12,268
Anti-Lock Brakes	$555	$645
Automatic 3 Speed	$426	$495
Optional Engine	N/A	N/A
Air Conditioning	$684	$795
Power Steering	Std	Std
Cruise Control	$159	$185
Power Windows	$258	$300
AM/FM Stereo Cassette	$477	$555
Steering Wheel, Tilt	$69	$80
1SA Package	N/C	N/C
*Options Price	$1,656	$1,925
*Total Price	$13,335	$14,193
Target Price	$13,701	
Destination Charge	$430	
Avg. Tax & Fees	$795	
Total Target $	$14,926	
Average Dealer Option Cost:	86%	
12 Month Price Increase:	None	

For 1999, the Prizm sedan now has power windows as an available option. The Prizm's suspension now includes front and rear stabilizer bars. Wider P185/65R14 all-season tires are optional. Safety equipment includes dual airbags, daytime running lamps with automatic headlamp control and optional side airbags. New colors for 1999 include Dark Blue-Green Metallic, Dark Beige Metallic, Dark Carmine Red Metallic and Silver Metallic. A power sliding sunroof is optional.

Ownership Costs (Projected)

Cost Area	5 Year Cost	Rating
Depreciation	$8,153	◉
Financing ($247/month)	$2,904	
Insurance	$7,837	◉
State Fees	$598	
Fuel (Hwy 33 City 28)	$2,427	○
Maintenance	$3,331	◉
Repairs	$610	○

Warranty/Maintenance Info

Major Tune-Up (100K mile int.)	$240	◎
Minor Tune-Up (30K mile int.)	$75	○
Brake Service	$231	◎
Overall Warranty	3 yr/36k	◎
Drivetrain Warranty	3 yr/36k	◎
Rust Warranty	6 yr/100k	○
Maintenance Warranty	N/A	
Roadside Assistance	3 yr/36k	

Ownership Costs By Year (Projected)

$2,000 $4,000 $6,000 $8,000 $10,000

1999 / 2000 / 2001 / 2002 / 2003

Resale Value

1999	2000	2001	2002	2003
$12,699	$11,129	$9,719	$8,263	$6,773

Cumulative Costs

	1999	2000	2001	2002	2003
Annual	$5,360	$4,566	$4,593	$5,710	$5,631
Total	$5,360	$9,926	$14,519	$20,229	$25,860

Projected Costs (5yr)

Relative	This Car
$25,275	$25,860
Cost/Mile 36¢	Cost/Mile 37¢

Ownership Cost Value

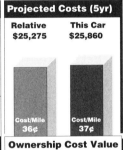

Average

Chevrolet Prizm LSi
4 Door Sedan

Compact

1.8L 120 hp Gas Fuel Inject.

4 Cylinder In-Line

Manual 5 Speed

2 Wheel Front

Dual Airbags Std

Purchase Price

Car Item	Dealer Cost	List
Base Price	$13,682	$14,839
Anti-Lock Brakes	$555	$645
Automatic 3 Speed	$426	$495
Optional Engine	N/A	N/A
Air Conditioning	Std	Std
Power Steering	Std	Std
Cruise Control	Std	Std
Power Windows	$258	$300
AM/FM Stereo Cassette	Std	Std
Steering Wheel, Tilt	$69	$80
1SE Package	N/C	N/C
*Options Price	$495	$575
*Total Price	$14,177	$15,414
Target Price	$14,622	
Destination Charge	$430	
Avg. Tax & Fees	$848	
Total Target $	$15,900	
Average Dealer Option Cost:	86%	
12 Month Price Increase:	1%	

The 1999 Prizm LSi sedan returns with few changes to its interior and exterior. With the standard 120 hp 1.8L engine, three transmissions are available. Safety equipment on the LSi includes dual airbags, adjustable seatbelts, daytime running lamps with automatic headlamp control and child safety locks. Side airbags are optional. The LSi offers the same equipment as the base model, adding a remote keyless entry system with illumination, speed control and carpeted floor mats.

Ownership Costs (Projected)

Cost Area	5 Year Cost	Rating
Depreciation	$9,247	●
Financing ($264/month)	$3,094	
Insurance	$7,837	◉
State Fees	$647	
Fuel (Hwy 33 City 28)	$2,427	○
Maintenance	$3,331	◉
Repairs	$610	○

Warranty/Maintenance Info

Major Tune-Up (100K mile int.)	$240	◎
Minor Tune-Up (30K mile int.)	$75	○
Brake Service	$231	◎
Overall Warranty	3 yr/36k	◎
Drivetrain Warranty	3 yr/36k	◎
Rust Warranty	6 yr/100k	○
Maintenance Warranty	N/A	
Roadside Assistance	3 yr/36k	

Ownership Costs By Year (Projected)

$2,000 $4,000 $6,000 $8,000 $10,000

1999 / 2000 / 2001 / 2002 / 2003

Resale Value

1999	2000	2001	2002	2003
$13,357	$11,576	$9,965	$8,321	$6,653

Cumulative Costs

	1999	2000	2001	2002	2003
Annual	$5,753	$4,840	$4,843	$5,932	$5,825
Total	$5,753	$10,593	$15,436	$21,368	$27,193

Projected Costs (5yr)

Relative	This Car
$26,042	$27,193
Cost/Mile 37¢	Cost/Mile 39¢

Ownership Cost Value

Worse Than Average

---

* Includes shaded options
** Other purchase requirements apply
*** Price includes other options

● Poor   ◉ Worse Than Average   ◎ Average   ○ Better Than Average   ○ Excellent   ⊖ Insufficient Information

43

Refer to Section 3: Annotated Vehicle Charts for an explanation of these charts.

©1999 by IntelliChoice, Inc. (408) 866-1400 http://www.intellichoice.com All Rights Reserved. Reproduction Prohibited.

Chrysler Cirrus LXi
4 Door Sedan

Midsize

 2.5L 168 hp Gas Fuel Inject.   6 Cylinder "V"   Automatic 4 Speed   2 Wheel Front   Dual Airbags Std

Purchase Price

Car Item	Dealer Cost	List
Base Price	**$17,799**	**$19,460**
Anti-Lock Brakes	Std	Std
Manual Transmission	N/A	N/A
Optional Engine	N/A	N/A
Air Conditioning	Std	Std
Power Steering	Std	Std
Cruise Control	Std	Std
Power Windows	Std	Std
AM/FM Stereo Cassette	Std	Std
Steering Wheel, Tilt	Std	Std
26K Package	N/C	N/C
*Options Price	$0	$0
*Total Price	$17,799	$19,460
Target Price	$18,370	
Destination Charge	$535	
Avg. Tax & Fees	$1,064	
Total Target $	**$19,969**	
Average Dealer Option Cost:	85%	
12 Month Price Increase:	None	

The Cirrus LXi arrives this model year highlighted by several improvements. Among the changes are revised suspension tuning to increase ride comfort, restyled exterior emblems, a new Sentry Key theft deterrent system, and revised wheel designs. Other improvements include improved interior quietness, revised instrument cluster graphics and two new exterior colors: Inferno Red and Light Cypress Green. Leather seating is a no-charge option, and includes an eight-way power driver's seat.

Ownership Costs (Projected)

Cost Area	5 Year Cost	Rating
Depreciation	$10,599	◐
Financing ($331/month)	$3,884	
Insurance	$7,643	◐
State Fees	$813	
Fuel (Hwy 27 City 19)	$3,236	◉
Maintenance	$3,233	◐
Repairs	$1,056	●

Warranty/Maintenance Info

Major Tune-Up (60K mile int.)	$416	●
Minor Tune-Up (30K mile int.)	$166	●
Brake Service	$242	◐
Overall Warranty	3 yr/36k	◐
Drivetrain Warranty	3 yr/36k	◐
Rust Warranty	5 yr/100k	○
Maintenance Warranty	N/A	
Roadside Assistance	3 yr/36k	

Ownership Costs By Year (Projected)

$2,000 $4,000 $6,000 $8,000 $10,000 $12,000

■ 1999
■ 2000
■ 2001
■ 2002
□ 2003

Resale Value

1999	2000	2001	2002	2003
$17,255	$15,053	$13,149	$11,223	$9,370

Cumulative Costs

	1999	2000	2001	2002	2003
Annual	$6,353	$5,641	$5,617	$6,313	$6,540
Total	$6,353	$11,994	$17,611	$23,924	$30,464

Projected Costs (5yr)

Relative $29,261	This Car $30,464
Cost/Mile 42¢	Cost/Mile 44¢

Ownership Cost Value

○ Average

Chrysler Concorde
4 Door Sedan

Large

 2.7L 200 hp Gas Fuel Inject.   6 Cylinder "V"   Automatic 4 Speed   2 Wheel Front   Dual Airbags Std

Purchase Price

Car Item	Dealer Cost	List
Base Price	**$19,763**	**$21,565**
Anti-Lock Brakes	$534	**$600
Manual Transmission	N/A	N/A
3.2L 225 hp Gas	$445	**$500
Air Conditioning	Std	Std
Power Steering	Std	Std
Cruise Control	Std	Std
Power Windows	Std	Std
AM/FM Stereo Cassette	Std	Std
Steering Wheel, Tilt	Std	Std
22C Package	N/C	N/C
*Options Price	$0	$0
*Total Price	$19,763	$21,565
Target Price	$20,635	
Destination Charge	$550	
Avg. Tax & Fees	$1,187	
Total Target $	**$22,372**	
Average Dealer Option Cost:	89%	
12 Month Price Increase:	1%	

The 1999 Concorde is available as a single model with two optional packages: the LX and the LXi. The LX option includes a cloth interior, eight-way power dual fronts seats, automatic climate control and a 2.7L engine. The LXi Package includes the features of the LX Package with the addition of a 3.2L engine, antilock brakes, traction control and leather seating. Standard Concorde features include air conditioning, AM/FM cassette, speed control, power driver's seat and power windows.

Ownership Costs (Projected)

Cost Area	5 Year Cost	Rating
Depreciation	$11,734	◐
Financing ($371/month)	$4,354	
Insurance	$7,463	○
State Fees	$898	
Fuel (Hwy 30 City 21)	$2,920	○
Maintenance	$2,893	◐
Repairs	$1,165	◉

Warranty/Maintenance Info

Major Tune-Up (60K mile int.)	$203	◐
Minor Tune-Up (30K mile int.)	$101	◐
Brake Service	$253	◐
Overall Warranty	3 yr/36k	◐
Drivetrain Warranty	3 yr/36k	◐
Rust Warranty	5 yr/100k	○
Maintenance Warranty	N/A	
Roadside Assistance	3 yr/36k	

Ownership Costs By Year (Projected)

$2,000 $4,000 $6,000 $8,000 $10,000 $12,000

■ 1999
■ 2000
■ 2001
■ 2002
□ 2003

Resale Value

1999	2000	2001	2002	2003
$19,962	$17,389	$15,118	$12,902	$10,638

Cumulative Costs

	1999	2000	2001	2002	2003
Annual	$6,135	$6,063	$5,936	$6,734	$6,559
Total	$6,135	$12,198	$18,134	$24,868	$31,427

Projected Costs (5yr)

Relative $31,682	This Car $31,427
Cost/Mile 45¢	Cost/Mile 45¢

Ownership Cost Value

○ Average

44

* Includes shaded options
** Other purchase requirements apply
*** Price includes other options

● Poor ◉ Worse Than Average ◐ Average ○ Better Than Average ○ Excellent ⊖ Insufficient Information

Refer to *Section 3: Annotated Vehicle Charts* for an explanation of these charts.

Chrysler 300M
4 Door Sedan

 3.5L 253 hp Gas Fuel Inject.
 6 Cylinder "V"
 Automatic 4 Speed
 2 Wheel Front
 Dual Airbags Std

Purchase Price

Car Item	Dealer Cost	List
Base Price	**$25,942**	**$28,300**
Anti-Lock Brakes	Std	Std
Manual Transmission	N/A	N/A
Optional Engine	N/A	N/A
Auto Climate Control	Std	Std
Power Steering	Std	Std
Cruise Control	Std	Std
Power Windows	Std	Std
AM/FM Stereo Cass/CD	Std	Std
Steering Wheel, Tilt	Std	Std
Rear Defroster	Std	Std
*Options Price	$0	$0
*Total Price	$25,942	$28,300
Target Price	$27,374	
Destination Charge	$595	
Avg. Tax & Fees	$1,561	
Total Target $	**$29,530**	
Average Dealer Option Cost:	89%	
12 Month Price Increase:	N/A	

Ownership Costs (Projected)

Cost Area	5 Year Cost	Rating
Depreciation		⊖
Financing ($489/month)	$5,744	
Insurance (Performance)	$9,654	○
State Fees	$1,168	
Fuel (Hwy 27 City 18)	$3,322	◉
Maintenance	$3,629	◉
Repairs	$1,269	●

Warranty/Maintenance Info

Major Tune-Up (60K mile int.)	$230	○
Minor Tune-Up (30K mile int.)	$114	○
Brake Service	$253	○
Overall Warranty	3 yr/36k	○
Drivetrain Warranty	3 yr/36k	○
Rust Warranty	5 yr/100k	○
Maintenance Warranty	N/A	
Roadside Assistance	3 yr/36k	

For the 1999 model year, Chrysler introduces the all-new 300M. Representing the image of Chrysler's letter series cars of the past, the 300M delivers 253 hp and 255 lb-ft of torque. The 3.5L V6 is coupled with an automatic transmission featuring the AutoStick feature. The 300M is equipped with a premium Infinity I sound system, automatic climate control, leather seating surfaces and heated seats. Remote keyless entry, traction control and antilock brakes are also standard.

Ownership Costs By Year (Projected)

$2,000　$4,000　$6,000　$8,000　$10,000

Insufficient Depreciation Information

- ■ 1999
- ■ 2000
- ■ 2001
- ■ 2002
- □ 2003

Resale Value

Insufficient Information

Projected Costs (5yr)

Insufficient Information

Cumulative Costs

	1999	2000	2001	2002	2003
Annual		*Insufficient Information*			
Total		*Insufficient Information*			

Ownership Cost Value

⊖

Insufficient Information

Chrysler LHS
4 Door Sedan

 3.5L 253 hp Gas Fuel Inject.
 6 Cylinder "V"
 Automatic 4 Speed
 2 Wheel Front
 Dual Airbags Std

Purchase Price

Car Item	Dealer Cost	List
Base Price	**$26,041**	**$28,400**
Anti-Lock Brakes	Std	Std
Manual Transmission	N/A	N/A
Optional Engine	N/A	N/A
Auto Climate Control	Std	Std
Power Steering	Std	Std
Cruise Control	Std	Std
Power Windows	Std	Std
AM/FM Stereo Cass/CD	Std	Std
Steering Wheel, Tilt	Std	Std
Rear Defroster	Std	Std
*Options Price	$0	$0
*Total Price	$26,041	$28,400
Target Price	$27,560	
Destination Charge	$595	
Avg. Tax & Fees	$1,570	
Total Target $	**$29,725**	
Average Dealer Option Cost:	89%	
12 Month Price Increase:	N/A	

Ownership Costs (Projected)

Cost Area	5 Year Cost	Rating
Depreciation	$16,779	◉
Financing ($493/month)	$5,782	
Insurance (Performance)	$9,654	○
State Fees	$1,173	
Fuel (Hwy 27 City 18)	$3,322	◉
Maintenance	$4,020	●
Repairs	$1,269	●

Warranty/Maintenance Info

Major Tune-Up (60K mile int.)	$230	○
Minor Tune-Up (30K mile int.)	$114	○
Brake Service	$253	○
Overall Warranty	3 yr/36k	○
Drivetrain Warranty	3 yr/36k	○
Rust Warranty	5 yr/100k	○
Maintenance Warranty	N/A	
Roadside Assistance	3 yr/36k	

For the 1999 model year, the LHS returns completely redesigned. Representing Chrysler's statement of luxury and performance, the LHS features a 3.5L V6 with 253 hp and 255 lb-ft of torque. The LHS features many standard luxury amenities. The LHS is equipped with an Infinity I sound system, automatic climate control, leather seats and a rear seat pass-through feature. Options include a power moonroof, Cold Weather Group and an Infinity II 320 watt sound system with 11 speakers.

Ownership Costs By Year (Projected)

$5,000　$10,000　$15,000　$20,000

- ■ 1999
- ■ 2000
- ■ 2001
- ■ 2002
- □ 2003

Resale Value

1999	2000	2001	2002	2003
$25,097	$21,782	$18,792	$15,879	$12,946

Projected Costs (5yr)

Relative	This Car
$39,075	$41,999
Cost/Mile 56¢	Cost/Mile 60¢

Cumulative Costs

	1999	2000	2001	2002	2003
Annual	$9,402	$7,768	$7,613	$8,720	$8,496
Total	$9,402	$17,170	$24,783	$33,503	$41,999

Ownership Cost Value

◐

Worse Than Average

---

* Includes shaded options
** Other purchase requirements apply
*** Price includes other options

● Poor	◉ Worse Than Average	◐ Average
○ Better Than Average	○ Excellent	⊖ Insufficient Information

Refer to *Section 3: Annotated Vehicle Charts* for an explanation of these charts.

Chrysler Sebring LX
2 Door Coupe

Compact

2.0L 140 hp Gas Fuel Inject.	4 Cylinder In-Line	Manual 5 Speed	2 Wheel Front	Dual Airbags Std

LXi Model Shown

Purchase Price

Car Item	Dealer Cost	List
Base Price	**$15,840**	**$17,225**
Anti-Lock Brakes	$534	**$600
Automatic 4 Speed	$619	$695
2.5L 163 hp Gas	$601	$675
Air Conditioning	Std	Std
Power Steering	Std	Std
Cruise/Speed Control	Inc	Inc
Windows, Power	Inc	Inc
AM/FM Stereo Cassette	Std	Std
Steering Wheel, Tilt	Std	Std
24H Package	$832	$935
*Options Price	$2,052	$2,305
*Total Price	$17,892	$19,530
Target Price	$18,442	
Destination Charge	$535	
Avg. Tax & Fees	$1,068	
Total Target $	**$20,045**	
Average Dealer Option Cost:	89%	
12 Month Price Increase:	2%	

The Sebring coupe continues into the new model year featuring detail changes. Most notable are two new exterior colors, Shark Blue and Plum, and the addition of a second key fob to the remote keyless entry system. More sporting appeal is obtained by selecting the optional 2.5L V6 engine, which includes an upgraded suspension and 16 inch wheels and tires. Other popular options, grouped into a package, include power windows and locks, cruise control and four wheel disc brakes.

Ownership Costs (Projected)

Cost Area	5 Year Cost	Rating
Depreciation	$9,154	◐
Financing ($332/month)	$3,899	
Insurance	$8,500	◉
State Fees	$816	
Fuel (Hwy 27 City 19)	$3,236	●
Maintenance	$3,436	◉
Repairs	$1,114	●

Warranty/Maintenance Info

Major Tune-Up (60K mile int.)	$452	●
Minor Tune-Up (30K mile int.)	$170	●
Brake Service	$284	●
Overall Warranty	3 yr/36k	◐
Drivetrain Warranty	3 yr/36k	◐
Rust Warranty	5 yr/100k	○
Maintenance Warranty	N/A	
Roadside Assistance	3 yr/36k	

Ownership Costs By Year (Projected)

Legend: 1999, 2000, 2001, 2002, 2003

Resale Value

1999	2000	2001	2002	2003
$17,303	$15,520	$13,956	$12,412	$10,891

Cumulative Costs

	1999	2000	2001	2002	2003
Annual	$6,551	$5,395	$5,480	$6,278	$6,451
Total	$6,551	$11,946	$17,426	$23,704	$30,155

Projected Costs (5yr)

Relative	This Car
$29,688	$30,155
Cost/Mile 42¢	Cost/Mile 43¢

Ownership Cost Value

○ Average

Chrysler Sebring LXi
2 Door Coupe

Compact

2.5L 163 hp Gas Fuel Inject.	6 Cylinder "V"	Automatic 4 Speed	2 Wheel Front	Dual Airbags Std

Purchase Price

Car Item	Dealer Cost	List
Base Price	**$19,489**	**$21,325**
Anti-Lock Brakes	$534	$600
Manual Transmission	N/A	N/A
Optional Engine	N/A	N/A
Air Conditioning	Std	Std
Power Steering	Std	Std
Cruise Control	Std	Std
Power Windows	Std	Std
AM/FM Stereo Cass/CD	Std	Std
Steering Wheel, Tilt	Std	Std
24K Package	N/C	N/C
*Options Price	$0	$0
*Total Price	$19,489	$21,325
Target Price	$20,137	
Destination Charge	$535	
Avg. Tax & Fees	$1,162	
Total Target $	**$21,834**	
Average Dealer Option Cost:	89%	
12 Month Price Increase:	2%	

The Sebring LXi coupe arrives this year sporting appearance refinements. Among these are new body-color mirrors and body-color wheels for models equipped with either White or Caffe Latte exterior colors. Also, a second key fob has been added to the standard remote keyless entry system. Added value is achieved with the Quick Order Package 24K, which includes a six-way power driver's seat and leather seating surfaces, all for no extra charge.

Ownership Costs (Projected)

Cost Area	5 Year Cost	Rating
Depreciation	$10,722	◐
Financing ($362/month)	$4,248	
Insurance	$8,556	◉
State Fees	$888	
Fuel (Hwy 27 City 19)	$3,236	●
Maintenance	$3,674	●
Repairs	$1,114	●

Warranty/Maintenance Info

Major Tune-Up (60K mile int.)	$452	●
Minor Tune-Up (30K mile int.)	$170	●
Brake Service	$284	●
Overall Warranty	3 yr/36k	◐
Drivetrain Warranty	3 yr/36k	◐
Rust Warranty	5 yr/100k	○
Maintenance Warranty	N/A	
Roadside Assistance	3 yr/36k	

Ownership Costs By Year (Projected)

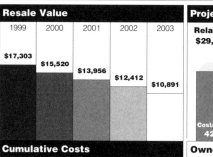

Legend: 1999, 2000, 2001, 2002, 2003

Resale Value

1999	2000	2001	2002	2003
$18,651	$16,570	$14,720	$12,897	$11,112

Cumulative Costs

	1999	2000	2001	2002	2003
Annual	$7,138	$5,816	$5,863	$6,866	$6,755
Total	$7,138	$12,954	$18,817	$25,683	$32,438

Projected Costs (5yr)

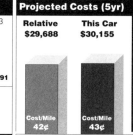

Relative	This Car
$31,385	$32,438
Cost/Mile 45¢	Cost/Mile 46¢

Ownership Cost Value

◉ Worse Than Average

---

* Includes shaded options
** Other purchase requirements apply
*** Price includes other options

● Poor	◉ Worse Than Average	○ Average	○ Better Than Average	○ Excellent	⊖ Insufficient Information

Refer to *Section 3: Annotated Vehicle Charts* for an explanation of these charts.

Chrysler Sebring JX
2 Door Convertible

 2.5L 168 hp Gas Fuel Inject. | 6 Cylinder "V" | Automatic 4 Speed | 2 Wheel Front | Dual Airbags Std

Purchase Price

Car Item	Dealer Cost	List
Base Price	**$21,923**	**$23,970**
Anti-Lock Brakes	Std	Std
Manual Transmission	N/A	N/A
Optional Engine	N/A	N/A
Air Conditioning	Std	Std
Power Steering	Std	Std
Cruise Control	Std	Std
Power Windows	Std	Std
AM/FM Stereo Cassette	Std	Std
Steering Wheel, Tilt	Std	Std
26B Package	N/C	N/C
*Options Price	$0	$0
*Total Price	$21,923	$23,970
Target Price	$22,808	
Destination Charge	$535	
Avg. Tax & Fees	$1,308	
Total Target $	**$24,651**	
Average Dealer Option Cost:	**89%**	
12 Month Price Increase:	12%	

The Sebring JX convertible continues this year featuring major equipment changes. A 2.5L V6 engine is now standard, along with many other previously optional items. These include a remote keyless entry system, a power driver's seat, speed control and speed-sensitive power door locks. The Smokers Package is gone, and stereo system offerings have been simplified, with a standard AM/FM cassette system with CD changer controls. A six disc in-dash mounted CD changer is optional.

Ownership Costs (Projected)

Cost Area	5 Year Cost	Rating
Depreciation	$12,483	◐
Financing ($409/month)	$4,795	
Insurance	$8,045	◐
State Fees	$994	
Fuel (Hwy 27 City 19)	$3,236	●
Maintenance	$3,462	⊙
Repairs	$1,114	●

Warranty/Maintenance Info

Major Tune-Up (60K mile int.)	$422	●
Minor Tune-Up (30K mile int.)	$154	●
Brake Service	$300	●
Overall Warranty	3 yr/36k	◐
Drivetrain Warranty	3 yr/36k	◐
Rust Warranty	5 yr/100k	○
Maintenance Warranty	N/A	
Roadside Assistance	3 yr/36k	

Ownership Costs By Year (Projected)

$2,000 $4,000 $6,000 $8,000 $10,000 $12,000 $14,000

- 1999
- 2000
- 2001
- 2002
- 2003

Resale Value

1999	2000	2001	2002	2003
$20,822	$18,423	$16,282	$14,194	$12,168

Cumulative Costs

	1999	2000	2001	2002	2003
Annual	$7,899	$6,209	$6,166	$6,944	$6,911
Total	$7,899	$14,108	$20,274	$27,218	$34,129

Projected Costs (5yr)

Relative $34,121	This Car $34,129
Cost/Mile 49¢	Cost/Mile 49¢

Ownership Cost Value

◐ Average

Chrysler Sebring JXi
2 Door Convertible

 2.5L 168 hp Gas Fuel Inject. | 6 Cylinder "V" | Automatic 4 Speed | 2 Wheel Front | Dual Airbags Std

JX Model Shown

Purchase Price

Car Item	Dealer Cost	List
Base Price	**$23,984**	**$26,285**
Anti-Lock Brakes	Std	Std
Manual Transmission	N/A	N/A
Optional Engine	N/A	N/A
Air Conditioning	Std	Std
Power Steering	Std	Std
Cruise Control	Std	Std
Power Windows	Std	Std
AM/FM Stereo Cassette	Std	Std
Steering Wheel, Tilt	Std	Std
26D Package	N/C	N/C
*Options Price	$0	$0
*Total Price	$23,984	$26,285
Target Price	$24,995	
Destination Charge	$535	
Avg. Tax & Fees	$1,430	
Total Target $	**$26,960**	
Average Dealer Option Cost:	**89%**	
12 Month Price Increase:	2%	

The Sebring JXi convertible arrives this year with detail improvements. Most noteworthy are simplified stereo sound system offerings and two new exterior colors: Light Cypress Green and Inferno Red. Standard luxury features include a leather-trimmed interior, four wheel antilock brakes and an Infinity stereo sound system. The optional Limited Package includes perforated luxury leather seats, chrome wheels, rose Zebrano woodgrain interior accents and unique interior color schemes.

Ownership Costs (Projected)

Cost Area	5 Year Cost	Rating
Depreciation	$14,209	⊙
Financing ($447/month)	$5,245	
Insurance	$8,313	○
State Fees	$1,086	
Fuel (Hwy 27 City 19)	$3,236	●
Maintenance	$3,560	⊙
Repairs	$1,114	●

Warranty/Maintenance Info

Major Tune-Up (60K mile int.)	$422	●
Minor Tune-Up (30K mile int.)	$154	●
Brake Service	$300	●
Overall Warranty	3 yr/36k	◐
Drivetrain Warranty	3 yr/36k	◐
Rust Warranty	5 yr/100k	○
Maintenance Warranty	N/A	
Roadside Assistance	3 yr/36k	

Ownership Costs By Year (Projected)

$5,000 $10,000 $15,000

- 1999
- 2000
- 2001
- 2002
- 2003

Resale Value

1999	2000	2001	2002	2003
$22,938	$20,141	$17,609	$15,144	$12,751

Cumulative Costs

	1999	2000	2001	2002	2003
Annual	$8,319	$6,803	$6,723	$7,549	$7,369
Total	$8,319	$15,122	$21,845	$29,394	$36,763

Projected Costs (5yr)

Relative $36,580	This Car $36,763
Cost/Mile 52¢	Cost/Mile 53¢

Ownership Cost Value

○ Average

---

* Includes shaded options

** Other purchase requirements apply

*** Price includes other options

 Poor | Worse Than Average | Average | Better Than Average | ○ Excellent | ⊖ Insufficient Information

Refer to *Section 3: Annotated Vehicle Charts* for an explanation of these charts.

Daewoo Lanos S
2 Door Hatchback

Compact

1.6L 105 hp Gas Fuel Inject.	4 Cylinder In-Line	Manual 5 Speed	2 Wheel Front	Dual Airbags Std

Purchase Price

Car Item	Dealer Cost	List
Base Price	**$7,437**	**$8,749**
Anti-Lock Brakes	N/A	N/A
Automatic 4 Speed	$680	$800
Optional Engine	N/A	N/A
Air Conditioning	$595	$700
Power Steering	Std	Std
Cruise Control	N/A	N/A
Power Windows	N/A	N/A
AM/FM Stereo Cassette	Std	Std
Steering Wheel, Tilt	N/A	N/A
Rear Defroster	Std	Std
***Options Price**	$1,275	$1,500
***Total Price**	**$8,712**	**$10,249**
Target Price	$10,249	
Destination Charge	$250	
Avg. Tax & Fees	$590	
Total Target $	**$11,089**	
Average Dealer Option Cost:	**85%**	
12 Month Price Increase:	N/A	

The entry level Lanos S hatchback comes standard with power-assisted steering, power brakes, tinted windows and security code protection for the stereo. Daewoo has instituted a one price haggle-free pricing policy and also offers free maintenance for the first three years or 36,000 miles of ownership. All Daewoo models also come with Daewoo Priority Assistance, which provides 24 hour, 365 day emergency roadside assistance for the first three years or 36,000 miles of ownership.

Ownership Costs (Projected)

Cost Area	5 Year Cost	Rating
Depreciation		⊖
Financing ($184/month)	$2,157	
Insurance	$6,852	◉
State Fees	$432	
Fuel (Hwy 33 City 23)	$2,660	○
Maintenance		⊖
Repairs	$965	●

Warranty/Maintenance Info

Major Tune-Up (60K mile int.)		⊖
Minor Tune-Up (30K mile int.)		⊖
Brake Service		⊖
Overall Warranty	3 yr/36k	◓
Drivetrain Warranty	3 yr/36k	◓
Rust Warranty	3 yr/36k	◉
Maintenance Warranty	3 yr/36k	○
Roadside Assistance	3 yr/36k	

Ownership Costs By Year (Projected)

$2,000 — $4,000 — $6,000 — $8,000

Insufficient Depreciation Information

Insufficient Maintenance Information

Legend: 1999, 2000, 2001, 2002, 2003

Resale Value

Insufficient Information

Projected Costs (5yr)

Insufficient Information

Cumulative Costs

	1999	2000	2001	2002	2003
Annual	*Insufficient Information*				
Total	*Insufficient Information*				

Ownership Cost Value

⊖

Insufficient Information

Daewoo Lanos SE
2 Door Hatchback

Compact

1.6L 105 hp Gas Fuel Inject.	4 Cylinder In-Line	Manual 5 Speed	2 Wheel Front	Dual Airbags Std

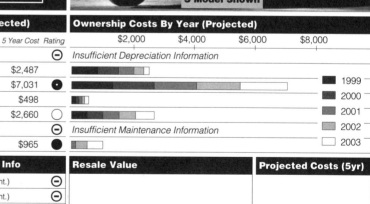

S Model Shown

Purchase Price

Car Item	Dealer Cost	List
Base Price	**$8,798**	**$10,350**
Anti-Lock Brakes	$425	$500
Automatic 4 Speed	$680	$800
Optional Engine	N/A	N/A
Air Conditioning	$595	$700
Power Steering	Std	Std
Cruise Control	N/A	N/A
Power Windows	Std	Std
AM/FM Stereo Cassette	Std	Std
Steering Wheel, Tilt	N/A	N/A
Rear Defroster	Std	Std
***Options Price**	$1,275	$1,500
***Total Price**	**$10,073**	**$11,850**
Target Price	$11,850	
Destination Charge	$250	
Avg. Tax & Fees	$679	
Total Target $	**$12,779**	
Average Dealer Option Cost:	**85%**	
12 Month Price Increase:	N/A	

The Lanos SE hatchback is the mid-level hatchback model for the Lanos. As such, it offers a higher level of standard equipment that includes power windows, power door locks and an anti-theft system with keyless remote entry. Optional equipment that is not available on the Lanos S consists of dual power outside mirrors (with the driver's side heated) and an antilock braking system. Other options available are air conditioning and a four speed automatic transmission.

Ownership Costs (Projected)

Cost Area	5 Year Cost	Rating
Depreciation		⊖
Financing ($212/month)	$2,487	
Insurance	$7,031	◉
State Fees	$498	
Fuel (Hwy 33 City 23)	$2,660	○
Maintenance		⊖
Repairs	$965	●

Warranty/Maintenance Info

Major Tune-Up (60K mile int.)		⊖
Minor Tune-Up (30K mile int.)		⊖
Brake Service		⊖
Overall Warranty	3 yr/36k	◓
Drivetrain Warranty	3 yr/36k	◓
Rust Warranty	3 yr/36k	◉
Maintenance Warranty	3 yr/36k	○
Roadside Assistance	3 yr/36k	

Ownership Costs By Year (Projected)

$2,000 — $4,000 — $6,000 — $8,000

Insufficient Depreciation Information

Insufficient Maintenance Information

Legend: 1999, 2000, 2001, 2002, 2003

Resale Value

Insufficient Information

Projected Costs (5yr)

Insufficient Information

Cumulative Costs

	1999	2000	2001	2002	2003
Annual	*Insufficient Information*				
Total	*Insufficient Information*				

Ownership Cost Value

⊖

Insufficient Information

48

* Includes shaded options

** Other purchase requirements apply

*** Price includes other options

 ● Poor

 ◉ Worse Than Average

 ○ Average

 ○ Better Than Average

 ○ Excellent

⊖ Insufficient Information

Refer to *Section 3: Annotated Vehicle Charts* for an explanation of these charts.

Daewoo Lanos SX
2 Door Hatchback

 1.6L 105 hp Gas Fuel Inject.

 4 Cylinder In-Line

 Manual 5 Speed

 2 Wheel Front

 Dual Airbags Std

Compact

S Model Shown

Purchase Price

Car Item	Dealer Cost	List
Base Price	**$9,706**	**$11,419**
Anti-Lock Brakes	$425	$500
Automatic 4 Speed	$680	$800
Optional Engine	N/A	N/A
Air Conditioning	Std	Std
Power Steering	Std	Std
Cruise Control	N/A	N/A
Power Windows	Std	Std
AM/FM Stereo Cass/CD	Std	Std
Steering Wheel, Tilt	Std	Std
Rear Defroster	Std	Std
***Options Price**	**$680**	**$800**
***Total Price**	**$10,386**	**$12,219**
Target Price	$12,219	
Destination Charge	$250	
Avg. Tax & Fees	$699	
Total Target $	**$13,168**	
Average Dealer Option Cost:	85%	
12 Month Price Increase:	N/A	

Ownership Costs (Projected)

Cost Area	5 Year Cost	Rating
Depreciation		⊖
Financing ($218/month)	$2,562	
Insurance	$7,175	◉
State Fees	$512	
Fuel (Hwy 33 City 23)	$2,660	○
Maintenance		⊖
Repairs	$965	●

Warranty/Maintenance Info

Major Tune-Up (60K mile int.)		⊖
Minor Tune-Up (30K mile int.)		⊖
Brake Service		⊖
Overall Warranty	3 yr/36k	O
Drivetrain Warranty	3 yr/36k	O
Rust Warranty	3 yr/36k	◉
Maintenance Warranty	3 yr/36k	○
Roadside Assistance	3 yr/36k	

Ownership Costs By Year (Projected)

$2,000 $4,000 $6,000 $8,000

Insufficient Depreciation Information

■ 1999
■ 2000
■ 2001
■ 2002
□ 2003

Insufficient Maintenance Information

Resale Value

Insufficient

Information

Projected Costs (5yr)

Insufficient

Information

Cumulative Costs

	1999	2000	2001	2002	2003
Annual	Insufficient Information				
Total	Insufficient Information				

Ownership Cost Value

⊖

Insufficient Information

The Lanos SX hatchback is the top of the line Lanos hatchback model. In addition to the standard equipment on the Lanos SE, the Lanos SX also includes air conditioning, an AM/FM/CD/cassette stereo system, alloy wheels, fog lamps and a tilt steering wheel as standard equipment. Only Lanos SX models are available with an optional power tilt and slide sunroof. All maintenance, including oil changes, is free for the first three years or 36,000 miles of ownership.

Daewoo Lanos S
4 Door Sedan

1.6L 105 hp Gas Fuel Inject.

 4 Cylinder In-Line

 Manual 5 Speed

 2 Wheel Front

Dual Airbags Std

Compact

Purchase Price

Car Item	Dealer Cost	List
Base Price	**$8,032**	**$9,449**
Anti-Lock Brakes	N/A	N/A
Automatic 4 Speed	$680	$800
Optional Engine	N/A	N/A
Air Conditioning	$595	$700
Power Steering	Std	Std
Cruise Control	N/A	N/A
Power Windows	N/A	N/A
AM/FM Stereo Cassette	Std	Std
Steering Wheel, Tilt	N/A	N/A
Rear Defroster	Std	Std
***Options Price**	**$1,275**	**$1,500**
***Total Price**	**$9,307**	**$10,949**
Target Price	$10,949	
Destination Charge	$250	
Avg. Tax & Fees	$629	
Total Target $	**$11,828**	
Average Dealer Option Cost:	85%	
12 Month Price Increase:	N/A	

Ownership Costs (Projected)

Cost Area	5 Year Cost	Rating
Depreciation		⊖
Financing ($196/month)	$2,302	
Insurance	$6,852	◉
State Fees	$461	
Fuel (Hwy 33 City 23)	$2,660	○
Maintenance		⊖
Repairs	$965	●

Warranty/Maintenance Info

Major Tune-Up (60K mile int.)		⊖
Minor Tune-Up (30K mile int.)		⊖
Brake Service		⊖
Overall Warranty	3 yr/36k	O
Drivetrain Warranty	3 yr/36k	O
Rust Warranty	3 yr/36k	◉
Maintenance Warranty	3 yr/36k	○
Roadside Assistance	3 yr/36k	

Ownership Costs By Year (Projected)

$2,000 $4,000 $6,000 $8,000

Insufficient Depreciation Information

■ 1999
■ 2000
■ 2001
■ 2002
□ 2003

Insufficient Maintenance Information

Resale Value

Insufficient

Information

Projected Costs (5yr)

Insufficient

Information

Cumulative Costs

	1999	2000	2001	2002	2003
Annual	Insufficient Information				
Total	Insufficient Information				

Ownership Cost Value

⊖

Insufficient Information

The 1999 Lanos S sedan is a new name in the American automobile market. The Lanos models are Daewoo's entry-level vehicles. Daewoo has a non-negotiable, haggle-free pricing policy and offers free regular scheduled maintenance for the first three years or 36,000 miles of ownership. All Daewoo models also come with Daewoo Priority Assistance, which provides 24 hour, 365 day emergency roadside assistance for the first three years or 36,000 miles of ownership.

---

* Includes shaded options

** Other purchase requirements apply

*** Price includes other options

● Poor   ◉ Worse Than Average   ◐ Average   ○ Better Than Average   ○ Excellent   ⊖ Insufficient Information

49

Refer to *Section 3: Annotated Vehicle Charts* for an explanation of these charts.

Daewoo Lanos SE
4 Door Sedan

 1.6L 105 hp Gas Fuel Inject. 4 Cylinder In-Line Manual 5 Speed 2 Wheel Front | Dual Airbags Std

S Model Shown

Purchase Price

Car Item	Dealer Cost	List
Base Price	**$9,053**	**$10,650**
Anti-Lock Brakes	$425	$500
Automatic 4 Speed	$680	$800
Optional Engine	N/A	N/A
Air Conditioning	$595	$700
Power Steering	Std	Std
Cruise Control	N/A	N/A
Power Windows	Std	Std
AM/FM Stereo Cassette	Std	Std
Steering Wheel, Tilt	N/A	N/A
Rear Defroster	Std	Std
*Options Price	**$1,275**	**$1,500**
*Total Price	**$10,328**	**$12,150**
Target Price	$12,150	
Destination Charge	$250	
Avg. Tax & Fees	$695	
Total Target $	**$13,095**	
Average Dealer Option Cost:	*85%*	
12 Month Price Increase:	N/A	

Ownership Costs (Projected)

Cost Area	5 Year Cost	Rating
Depreciation		⊖
Financing ($217/month)	$2,548	
Insurance	$6,889	◉
State Fees	$509	
Fuel (Hwy 33 City 23)	$2,660	○
Maintenance		⊖
Repairs	$965	●

Warranty/Maintenance Info

Major Tune-Up (60K mile int.)		⊖
Minor Tune-Up (30K mile int.)		⊖
Brake Service		⊖
Overall Warranty	3 yr/36k	○
Drivetrain Warranty	3 yr/36k	○
Rust Warranty	3 yr/36k	◉
Maintenance Warranty	3 yr/36k	○
Roadside Assistance	3 yr/36k	

Ownership Costs By Year (Projected)

| $2,000 | $4,000 | $6,000 | $8,000 |

Insufficient Depreciation Information

■ 1999
■ 2000
■ 2001
■ 2002
□ 2003

Insufficient Maintenance Information

Resale Value

Insufficient

Information

Projected Costs (5yr)

Insufficient

Information

Cumulative Costs

	1999	2000	2001	2002	2003
Annual	*Insufficient Information*				
Total	*Insufficient Information*				

Ownership Cost Value

⊖

Insufficient Information

The mid-level Lanos SE sedan offers additional standard features over the Lanos S model. Additional standard equipment includes power windows, power door locks and an anti-theft system with keyless remote entry. Available optional equipment, not available on the Lanos S, includes dual power outside mirrors (with the driver's side heated) and an antilock braking system. Other options available include air conditioning and a four speed automatic transmission.

Daewoo Lanos SX
4 Door Sedan

 1.6L 105 hp Gas Fuel Inject. 4 Cylinder In-Line Manual 5 Speed 2 Wheel Front | Dual Airbags Std

S Model Shown

Purchase Price

Car Item	Dealer Cost	List
Base Price	**$9,961**	**$11,719**
Anti-Lock Brakes	$425	$500
Automatic 4 Speed	$680	$800
Optional Engine	N/A	N/A
Air Conditioning	Std	Std
Power Steering	Std	Std
Cruise Control	N/A	N/A
Power Windows	Std	Std
AM/FM Stereo Cass/CD	Std	Std
Steering Wheel, Tilt	Std	Std
Rear Defroster	Std	Std
*Options Price	**$680**	**$800**
*Total Price	**$10,641**	**$12,519**
Target Price	$12,519	
Destination Charge	$250	
Avg. Tax & Fees	$716	
Total Target $	**$13,485**	
Average Dealer Option Cost:	*85%*	
12 Month Price Increase:	N/A	

Ownership Costs (Projected)

Cost Area	5 Year Cost	Rating
Depreciation		⊖
Financing ($224/month)	$2,624	
Insurance	$7,031	◉
State Fees	$524	
Fuel (Hwy 33 City 23)	$2,660	○
Maintenance		⊖
Repairs	$965	●

Warranty/Maintenance Info

Major Tune-Up (60K mile int.)		⊖
Minor Tune-Up (30K mile int.)		⊖
Brake Service		⊖
Overall Warranty	3 yr/36k	○
Drivetrain Warranty	3 yr/36k	○
Rust Warranty	3 yr/36k	◉
Maintenance Warranty	3 yr/36k	○
Roadside Assistance	3 yr/36k	

Ownership Costs By Year (Projected)

| $2,000 | $4,000 | $6,000 | $8,000 |

Insufficient Depreciation Information

■ 1999
■ 2000
■ 2001
■ 2002
□ 2003

Insufficient Maintenance Information

Resale Value

Insufficient

Information

Projected Costs (5yr)

Insufficient

Information

Cumulative Costs

	1999	2000	2001	2002	2003
Annual	*Insufficient Information*				
Total	*Insufficient Information*				

Ownership Cost Value

⊖

Insufficient Information

The Lanos SX sedan is the top of the line Lanos sedan model. In addition to the standard equipment on the Lanos SE, the Lanos SX also includes air conditioning, an AM/FM/CD/cassette stereo system, alloy wheels, fog lamps and a tilt steering wheel as standard equipment. Only Lanos SX models are available with an optional power tilt and slide sunroof. All maintenance, including oil changes, is free for the first three years or 36,000 miles of ownership.

50

* Includes shaded options

** Other purchase requirements apply

*** Price includes other options

| ● Poor | ◉ Worse Than Average | ○ Average | ○ Better Than Average | ○ Excellent | ⊖ Insufficient Information |

Refer to *Section 3: Annotated Vehicle Charts* for an explanation of these charts.

Daewoo Leganza SE
4 Door Sedan

2.2L 131 hp Gas Fuel Inject.	4 Cylinder In-Line	Manual 5 Speed	2 Wheel Front	Dual Airbags Std

Purchase Price

Car Item	Dealer Cost	List
Base Price	**$12,359**	**$14,540**
Anti-Lock Brakes	Std	Std
Automatic 4 Speed	$680	$800
Optional Engine	N/A	N/A
Air Conditioning	Std	Std
Power Steering	Std	Std
Cruise Control	N/A	N/A
Power Windows	Std	Std
AM/FM Stereo Cassette	Std	Std
Steering Wheel, Tilt	Std	Std
Rear Defroster	Std	Std
***Options Price**	**$680**	**$800**
***Total Price**	**$13,039**	**$15,340**
Target Price	$15,340	
Destination Charge	$250	
Avg. Tax & Fees	$871	
Total Target $	**$16,461**	
Average Dealer Option Cost:	**85%**	
12 Month Price Increase:	N/A	

The 1999 Leganza SE sedan is a brand-new model being introduced to the U.S. auto market. The Leganza SE comes very well equipped with a comprehensive list of standard features such as power windows and locks, air conditioning and remote keyless entry system. All Daewoos come with Daewoo Priority Assistance (24 hour roadside assistance) and a three year/36,000 mile scheduled maintenance program that includes free oil changes. All Daewoos are sold with a one price no-haggle policy.

Ownership Costs (Projected)

Cost Area	5 Year Cost	Rating
Depreciation		⊖
Financing ($273/month)	$3,202	
Insurance	$7,031	O
State Fees	$637	
Fuel (Hwy 28 City 20)	$3,097	O
Maintenance		⊖
Repairs	$965	◉

Warranty/Maintenance Info

Major Tune-Up (60K mile int.)		⊖
Minor Tune-Up (30K mile int.)		⊖
Brake Service		⊖
Overall Warranty	3 yr/36k	O
Drivetrain Warranty	3 yr/36k	O
Rust Warranty	3 yr/36k	◉
Maintenance Warranty	3 yr/36k	○
Roadside Assistance	3 yr/36k	

Ownership Costs By Year (Projected)

$2,000 $4,000 $6,000 $8,000

Insufficient Depreciation Information

Insufficient Maintenance Information

■ 1999
■ 2000
▨ 2001
▨ 2002
□ 2003

Resale Value

Insufficient Information

Projected Costs (5yr)

Insufficient Information

Cumulative Costs

	1999	2000	2001	2002	2003
Annual	*Insufficient Information*				
Total	*Insufficient Information*				

Ownership Cost Value

⊖

Insufficient Information

Midsize

Daewoo Leganza SX
4 Door Sedan

2.2L 131 hp Gas Fuel Inject.	4 Cylinder In-Line	Automatic 4 Speed	2 Wheel Front	Dual Airbags Std

SE Model Shown

Purchase Price

Car Item	Dealer Cost	List
Base Price	**$14,161**	**$16,660**
Anti-Lock Brakes	Std	Std
Manual Transmission	N/A	N/A
Optional Engine	N/A	N/A
Air Conditioning	Std	Std
Power Steering	Std	Std
Cruise Control	Std	Std
Power Windows	Std	Std
AM/FM Stereo Cass/CD	Std	Std
Steering Wheel, Tilt	Std	Std
Rear Defroster	Std	Std
***Options Price**	**$0**	**$0**
***Total Price**	**$14,161**	**$16,660**
Target Price	$16,660	
Destination Charge	$250	
Avg. Tax & Fees	$943	
Total Target $	**$17,853**	
Average Dealer Option Cost:	**85%**	
12 Month Price Increase:	N/A	

The Leganza SX sedan comes standard with tinted glass, dual power heated mirrors and security code protection for the stereo system. Leather seating surfaces, a CD player, cruise control and an automatic transmission are additional standard features compared to the Leganza SE. Options include a power tilt and slide sunroof and alloy wheels. The Leganza comes with 24 hour Daewoo Priority Assistance and a three year/36,000 mile scheduled maintenance program.

Ownership Costs (Projected)

Cost Area	5 Year Cost	Rating
Depreciation		⊖
Financing ($296/month)	$3,474	
Insurance	$7,334	O
State Fees	$688	
Fuel (Hwy 28 City 20)	$3,097	O
Maintenance		⊖
Repairs	$965	◉

Warranty/Maintenance Info

Major Tune-Up (60K mile int.)		⊖
Minor Tune-Up (30K mile int.)		⊖
Brake Service		⊖
Overall Warranty	3 yr/36k	O
Drivetrain Warranty	3 yr/36k	O
Rust Warranty	3 yr/36k	◉
Maintenance Warranty	3 yr/36k	○
Roadside Assistance	3 yr/36k	

Ownership Costs By Year (Projected)

$2,000 $4,000 $6,000 $8,000

Insufficient Depreciation Information

Insufficient Maintenance Information

■ 1999
■ 2000
▨ 2001
▨ 2002
□ 2003

Resale Value

Insufficient Information

Projected Costs (5yr)

Insufficient Information

Cumulative Costs

	1999	2000	2001	2002	2003
Annual	*Insufficient Information*				
Total	*Insufficient Information*				

Ownership Cost Value

⊖

Insufficient Information

---

* Includes shaded options

** Other purchase requirements apply

*** Price includes other options

 Poor   Worse Than Average   Average   Better Than Average   Excellent   Insufficient Information

Refer to *Section 3: Annotated Vehicle Charts* for an explanation of these charts.

Daewoo Leganza CDX
4 Door Sedan

2.2L 131 hp Gas Fuel Inject.	4 Cylinder In-Line	Automatic 4 Speed	2 Wheel Front	Dual Airbags Std

Midsize

SE Model Shown

Purchase Price

Car Item	Dealer Cost	List
Base Price	**$15,861**	**$18,660**
Anti-Lock Brakes	Std	Std
Manual Transmission	N/A	N/A
Optional Engine	N/A	N/A
Auto Climate Control	Std	Std
Power Steering	Std	Std
Cruise Control	Std	Std
Power Windows	Std	Std
AM/FM Stereo Cass/CD	Std	Std
Steering Wheel, Tilt	Std	Std
Rear Defroster	Std	Std
*Options Price	$0	$0
*Total Price	**$15,861**	**$18,660**
Target Price	$18,660	
Destination Charge	$250	
Avg. Tax & Fees	$1,053	
Total Target $	**$19,963**	
Average Dealer Option Cost:	**N/A**	
12 Month Price Increase:	N/A	

The top of the line Leganza CDX comes standard with a leather interior, an anti-theft system with remote keyless entry and an AM/FM/CD/cassette stereo. Standard features only available on the Leganza CDX include a power driver's seat, automatic climate control and simulated wood grain interior appliques. The Leganza CDX also comes standard with cruise control and a power tilt/slide sunroof. In fact, the only option available on the Leganza CDX is a CD changer with DSP graphic equalizer.

Ownership Costs (Projected)

Cost Area	5 Year Cost	Rating
Depreciation		⊖
Financing ($331/month)	$3,883	
Insurance	$7,334	◐
State Fees	$768	
Fuel (Hwy 28 City 20)	$3,097	◐
Maintenance		⊖
Repairs	$965	◉

Warranty/Maintenance Info

Major Tune-Up (60K mile int.)		⊖
Minor Tune-Up (30K mile int.)		⊖
Brake Service		⊖
Overall Warranty	3 yr/36k	◐
Drivetrain Warranty	3 yr/36k	◐
Rust Warranty	3 yr/36k	◉
Maintenance Warranty	3 yr/36k	○
Roadside Assistance	3 yr/36k	

Ownership Costs By Year (Projected)

$2,000 $4,000 $6,000 $8,000

Insufficient Depreciation Information

Insufficient Maintenance Information

■ 1999
■ 2000
■ 2001
■ 2002
□ 2003

Resale Value

Insufficient

Information

Projected Costs (5yr)

Insufficient

Information

Cumulative Costs

	1999	2000	2001	2002	2003
Annual		Insufficient Information			
Total		Insufficient Information			

Ownership Cost Value

⊖

Insufficient Information

Daewoo Nubira SX
4 Door Hatchback

2.0L 128 hp Gas Fuel Inject.	4 Cylinder In-Line	Manual 5 Speed	2 Wheel Front	Dual Airbags Std

Compact

Purchase Price

Car Item	Dealer Cost	List
Base Price	**$10,413**	**$12,250**
Anti-Lock Brakes	$425	$500
Automatic 4 Speed	$680	$800
Optional Engine	N/A	N/A
Air Conditioning	Std	Std
Power Steering	Std	Std
Cruise Control	N/A	N/A
Power Windows	Std	Std
AM/FM Stereo Cassette	Std	Std
Steering Wheel, Tilt	Std	Std
Rear Defroster	Std	Std
*Options Price	$680	$800
*Total Price	**$11,093**	**$13,050**
Target Price	$13,050	
Destination Charge	$250	
Avg. Tax & Fees	$745	
Total Target $	**$14,045**	
Average Dealer Option Cost:	**85%**	
12 Month Price Increase:	N/A	

The Nubira SX hatchback, along with all SX models, comes standard with air conditioning, power windows, power door locks and power remote outside heated mirrors. Additional standard equipment includes and anti-theft system with remote keyless entry, front seatbelt shoulder height adjustment and an AM/FM stereo system with cassette. Available options include antilock brakes and a four speed automatic transmission. The hatchback models are eight inches shorter than the sedan models.

Ownership Costs (Projected)

Cost Area	5 Year Cost	Rating
Depreciation		⊖
Financing ($233/month)	$2,732	
Insurance	$6,755	◐
State Fees	$545	
Fuel (Hwy 0 City 0)		⊖
Maintenance		⊖
Repairs		⊖

Warranty/Maintenance Info

Major Tune-Up (60K mile int.)		⊖
Minor Tune-Up (30K mile int.)		⊖
Brake Service		⊖
Overall Warranty	3 yr/36k	◐
Drivetrain Warranty	3 yr/36k	◐
Rust Warranty	3 yr/36k	◉
Maintenance Warranty	3 yr/36k	○
Roadside Assistance	3 yr/36k	

Ownership Costs By Year (Projected)

$2,000 $4,000 $6,000 $8,000

Insufficient Depreciation Information

Insufficient Fuel Information

Insufficient Maintenance Information

Insufficient Repair Information

■ 1999
■ 2000
■ 2001
■ 2002
□ 2003

Resale Value

Insufficient

Information

Projected Costs (5yr)

Insufficient

Information

Cumulative Costs

	1999	2000	2001	2002	2003
Annual		Insufficient Information			
Total		Insufficient Information			

Ownership Cost Value

⊖

Insufficient Information

52

* Includes shaded options

** Other purchase requirements apply

*** Price includes other options

 Poor   Worse Than Average   Average   Better Than Average   Excellent ⊖ Insufficient Information

Refer to *Section 3: Annotated Vehicle Charts* for an explanation of these charts.

Daewoo Nubira CDX
4 Door Hatchback

 2.0L 128 hp Gas Fuel Inject.

 4 Cylinder In-Line

 Manual 5 Speed

 2 Wheel Front

 Dual Airbags Std

Compact

SX Model Shown

Purchase Price

Car Item	Dealer Cost	List
Base Price	**$11,526**	**$13,560**
Anti-Lock Brakes	Std	Std
Automatic 4 Speed	$680	$800
Optional Engine	N/A	N/A
Air Conditioning	Std	Std
Power Steering	Std	Std
Cruise Control	Std	Std
Power Windows	Std	Std
AM/FM Stereo Cass/CD	Std	Std
Steering Wheel, Tilt	Std	Std
Rear Defroster	Std	Std
*Options Price	$680	$800
*Total Price	$12,206	$14,360
Target Price	$14,360	
Destination Charge	$250	
Avg. Tax & Fees	$816	
Total Target $	**$15,426**	
Average Dealer Option Cost:	85%	
12 Month Price Increase:	N/A	

New to the American market is the 1999 Nubria CDX hatchback, which features standard air conditioning, front fog lamps and a 60/40 split folding rear seat. With the rear seat folded down, the Nubira hatchback has 30.4 cubic feet of cargo space. The Nubira CDX models feature additional standard equipment upgrades including a stereo system with cassette and CD player, antilock brakes, cruise control and alloy wheels. Additionally, an automatic transmission is available.

Ownership Costs (Projected)

Cost Area	5 Year Cost	Rating
Depreciation		⊖
Financing ($256/month)	$3,001	
Insurance	$6,889	O
State Fees	$597	
Fuel (Hwy 0 City 0)		⊖
Maintenance		⊖
Repairs		⊖

Warranty/Maintenance Info

Major Tune-Up (60K mile int.)		⊖
Minor Tune-Up (30K mile int.)		⊖
Brake Service		⊖
Overall Warranty	3 yr/36k	O
Drivetrain Warranty	3 yr/36k	O
Rust Warranty	3 yr/36k	⊙
Maintenance Warranty	3 yr/36k	○
Roadside Assistance	3 yr/36k	

Ownership Costs By Year (Projected)

$2,000 $4,000 $6,000 $8,000

Insufficient Depreciation Information

■ 1999
■ 2000
■ 2001
□ 2002
□ 2003

Insufficient Fuel Information

Insufficient Maintenance Information

Insufficient Repair Information

Resale Value

Insufficient

Information

Projected Costs (5yr)

Insufficient

Information

Cumulative Costs

	1999	2000	2001	2002	2003
Annual		Insufficient Information			
Total		Insufficient Information			

Ownership Cost Value

⊖

Insufficient Information

Daewoo Nubira SX
4 Door Sedan

 2.0L 128 hp Gas Fuel Inject.

 4 Cylinder In-Line

 Manual 5 Speed

 2 Wheel Front

Dual Airbags Std

Compact

Purchase Price

Car Item	Dealer Cost	List
Base Price	**$10,413**	**$12,250**
Anti-Lock Brakes	$425	$500
Automatic 4 Speed	$680	$800
Optional Engine	N/A	N/A
Air Conditioning	Std	Std
Power Steering	Std	Std
Cruise Control	N/A	N/A
Power Windows	Std	Std
AM/FM Stereo Cassette	Std	Std
Steering Wheel, Tilt	Std	Std
Rear Defroster	Std	Std
*Options Price	$680	$800
*Total Price	$11,093	$13,050
Target Price	$13,050	
Destination Charge	$250	
Avg. Tax & Fees	$745	
Total Target $	**$14,045**	
Average Dealer Option Cost:	85%	
12 Month Price Increase:	N/A	

The Nubira SX sedan is a new entry into the American car market. All Daewoo vehicles come with a three-year/36,000 mile maintenance program that includes no-charge service for all scheduled maintenance, such as oil changes and tuneups. The Nubira, like all Daewoos, is sold at factory-owned outlets that practice a one price, no-haggle pricing policy. The only options available on the SX model include a four speed automatic transmission and a four wheel antilock braking system.

Ownership Costs (Projected)

Cost Area	5 Year Cost	Rating
Depreciation		⊖
Financing ($233/month)	$2,732	
Insurance	$6,755	O
State Fees	$545	
Fuel (Hwy 30 City 22)	$2,855	O
Maintenance		⊖
Repairs	$965	⊙

Warranty/Maintenance Info

Major Tune-Up (60K mile int.)		⊖
Minor Tune-Up (30K mile int.)		⊖
Brake Service		⊖
Overall Warranty	3 yr/36k	O
Drivetrain Warranty	3 yr/36k	O
Rust Warranty	3 yr/36k	⊙
Maintenance Warranty	3 yr/36k	○
Roadside Assistance	3 yr/36k	

Ownership Costs By Year (Projected)

$2,000 $4,000 $6,000 $8,000

Insufficient Depreciation Information

■ 1999
■ 2000
■ 2001
□ 2002
□ 2003

Insufficient Maintenance Information

Resale Value

Insufficient

Information

Projected Costs (5yr)

Insufficient

Information

Cumulative Costs

	1999	2000	2001	2002	2003
Annual		Insufficient Information			
Total		Insufficient Information			

Ownership Cost Value

⊖

Insufficient Information

---

* Includes shaded options

** Other purchase requirements apply

*** Price includes other options

● Poor ⊙ Worse Than Average O Average ○ Better Than Average ○ Excellent ⊖ Insufficient Information

53

Refer to *Section 3: Annotated Vehicle Charts* for an explanation of these charts.

Daewoo Nubira CDX
4 Door Sedan

Compact

 2.0L 128 hp Gas Fuel Inject. 4 Cylinder In-Line Manual 5 Speed 2 Wheel Front Dual Airbags Std

SX Model Shown

Purchase Price

Car Item	Dealer Cost	List
Base Price	**$11,526**	**$13,560**
Anti-Lock Brakes	Std	Std
Automatic 4 Speed	$680	$800
Optional Engine	N/A	N/A
Air Conditioning	Std	Std
Power Steering	Std	Std
Cruise Control	Std	Std
Power Windows	Std	Std
AM/FM Stereo Cass/CD	Std	Std
Steering Wheel, Tilt	Std	Std
Rear Defroster	Std	Std
*Options Price	$680	$800
*Total Price	**$12,206**	**$14,360**
Target Price	$14,360	
Destination Charge	$250	
Avg. Tax & Fees	$816	
Total Target $	**$15,426**	
Average Dealer Option Cost:	85%	
12 Month Price Increase:	N/A	

The Nubira CDX sedan features a high level of standard equipment and a three-year/36,000 mile maintenance program that includes no-charge service for all scheduled maintenance. All Daewoos also come with a 24 hour, 365 day emergency roadside service plan called Daewoo Priority Assistance. The Daewoo Priority Assistance plan is available for the first three years or 36,000 miles of ownership. Nubira CDX models are available with an optional power sunroof and leather seating.

Ownership Costs (Projected)

Cost Area	5 Year Cost	Rating
Depreciation		⊖
Financing ($256/month)	$3,001	
Insurance	$6,755	O
State Fees	$597	
Fuel (Hwy 0 City 0)		⊖
Maintenance		⊖
Repairs		⊖

Warranty/Maintenance Info

Major Tune-Up (60K mile int.)		⊖
Minor Tune-Up (30K mile int.)		⊖
Brake Service		⊖
Overall Warranty	3 yr/36k	O
Drivetrain Warranty	3 yr/36k	O
Rust Warranty	3 yr/36k	◉
Maintenance Warranty	3 yr/36k	○
Roadside Assistance	3 yr/36k	

Ownership Costs By Year (Projected)

$2,000 $4,000 $6,000 $8,000

Insufficient Depreciation Information

■ 1999
■ 2000
■ 2001
□ 2002
□ 2003

Insufficient Fuel Information
Insufficient Maintenance Information
Insufficient Repair Information

Resale Value

Insufficient Information

Projected Costs (5yr)

Insufficient Information

Cumulative Costs

	1999	2000	2001	2002	2003
Annual	*Insufficient Information*				
Total	*Insufficient Information*				

Ownership Cost Value

⊖

Insufficient Information

Daewoo Nubira SX
4 Door Wagon

Small Wagon

 2.0L 128 hp Gas Fuel Inject. 4 Cylinder In-Line Manual 5 Speed 2 Wheel Front Dual Airbags Std

Nubira

Purchase Price

Car Item	Dealer Cost	List
Base Price	**$10,923**	**$12,850**
Anti-Lock Brakes	$425	$500
Automatic 4 Speed	$680	$800
Optional Engine	N/A	N/A
Air Conditioning	Std	Std
Power Steering	Std	Std
Cruise Control	N/A	N/A
Power Windows	Std	Std
AM/FM Stereo Cassette	Std	Std
Steering Wheel, Tilt	Std	Std
Rear Defroster	Std	Std
*Options Price	$680	$800
*Total Price	**$11,603**	**$13,650**
Target Price	$13,650	
Destination Charge	$250	
Avg. Tax & Fees	$778	
Total Target $	**$14,678**	
Average Dealer Option Cost:	85%	
12 Month Price Increase:	N/A	

The Nubira SX wagon is only two inches longer than the sedan and has 65 cubic feet of cargo space with the rear seat folded down. All Nubira models feature standard safety equipment such as dual front airbags, front fog lamps and three-point front seat belts with shoulder adjustment. Nubira SX models also come standard with four wheel power disc brakes, power steering and a tilt steering column. Nubria wagons feature a wide hatch and a low liftover height to make loading and unloading easier.

Ownership Costs (Projected)

Cost Area	5 Year Cost	Rating
Depreciation		⊖
Financing ($243/month)	$2,856	
Insurance	$6,889	O
State Fees	$568	
Fuel (Hwy 0 City 0)		⊖
Maintenance		⊖
Repairs		⊖

Warranty/Maintenance Info

Major Tune-Up (60K mile int.)		⊖
Minor Tune-Up (30K mile int.)		⊖
Brake Service		⊖
Overall Warranty	3 yr/36k	O
Drivetrain Warranty	3 yr/36k	O
Rust Warranty	3 yr/36k	◉
Maintenance Warranty	3 yr/36k	○
Roadside Assistance	3 yr/36k	

Ownership Costs By Year (Projected)

$2,000 $4,000 $6,000 $8,000

Insufficient Depreciation Information

■ 1999
■ 2000
■ 2001
□ 2002
□ 2003

Insufficient Fuel Information
Insufficient Maintenance Information
Insufficient Repair Information

Resale Value

Insufficient Information

Projected Costs (5yr)

Insufficient Information

Cumulative Costs

	1999	2000	2001	2002	2003
Annual	*Insufficient Information*				
Total	*Insufficient Information*				

Ownership Cost Value

⊖

Insufficient Information

---

* Includes shaded options
** Other purchase requirements apply
*** Price includes other options

 Poor
 Worse Than Average
 Average
 Better Than Average
 Excellent
 Insufficient Information

Refer to *Section 3: Annotated Vehicle Charts* for an explanation of these charts.

Daewoo Nubira CDX
4 Door Wagon

Small Wagon

SX Model Shown

 2.0L 128 hp Gas Fuel Inject.   4 Cylinder In-Line   Manual 5 Speed   2 Wheel Front   Dual Airbags Std

Purchase Price

Car Item	Dealer Cost	List
Base Price	**$12,036**	**$14,160**
Anti-Lock Brakes	Std	Std
Automatic 4 Speed	$680	$800
Optional Engine	N/A	N/A
Air Conditioning	Std	Std
Power Steering	Std	Std
Cruise Control	Std	Std
Power Windows	Std	Std
AM/FM Stereo Cass/CD	Std	Std
Steering Wheel, Tilt	Std	Std
Rear Defroster	Std	Std
***Options Price**	**$680**	**$800**
***Total Price**	**$12,716**	**$14,960**
Target Price	$14,960	
Destination Charge	$250	
Avg. Tax & Fees	$849	
Total Target $	**$16,059**	
Average Dealer Option Cost:	**85%**	
12 Month Price Increase:	N/A	

New to the American market in 1999, the Nubira CDX wagon includes standard tinted glass, splash guards and front fog lamps. Other standard equipment includes reclining front seats, shoulder height adjustment for the front seat belts and an AM/FM/CD/cassette stereo. The stereo system features a security code protection system that locks the stereo until the correct code is entered. The Nubira wagon also features a luggage rack, air conditioning and power steering.

Ownership Costs (Projected)

Cost Area	5 Year Cost	Rating
Depreciation		⊖
Financing ($266/month)	$3,124	
Insurance	$7,031	◎
State Fees	$621	
Fuel (Hwy 0 City 0)		⊖
Maintenance		⊖
Repairs		⊖

Warranty/Maintenance Info

Major Tune-Up (60K mile int.)		⊖
Minor Tune-Up (30K mile int.)		⊖
Brake Service		⊖
Overall Warranty	3 yr/36k	◎
Drivetrain Warranty	3 yr/36k	◎
Rust Warranty	3 yr/36k	◉
Maintenance Warranty	3 yr/36k	○
Roadside Assistance	3 yr/36k	

Ownership Costs By Year (Projected)

$2,000 $4,000 $6,000 $8,000

Insufficient Depreciation Information

Insufficient Fuel Information

Insufficient Maintenance Information

Insufficient Repair Information

■ 1999
■ 2000
■ 2001
□ 2002
□ 2003

Resale Value

Insufficient

Information

Projected Costs (5yr)

Insufficient

Information

Cumulative Costs

	1999	2000	2001	2002	2003
Annual	*Insufficient Information*				
Total	*Insufficient Information*				

Ownership Cost Value

⊖

Insufficient Information

Dodge Avenger
2 Door Coupe

Compact

 2.0L 140 hp Gas Fuel Inject.   4 Cylinder In-Line Manual 5 Speed   2 Wheel Front   Dual Airbags Std

Purchase Price

Car Item	Dealer Cost	List
Base Price	**$14,134**	**$15,370**
Anti-Lock Brakes	$534	**$600
Automatic 4 Speed	$619	$695
2.5L 163 hp Gas	$601	$675
Air Conditioning	Inc	Inc
Power Steering	Std	Std
Cruise/Speed Control	Inc	Inc
Windows, Power	Inc	Inc
AM/FM Stereo Cassette	Std	Std
Steering Wheel, Tilt	Std	Std
24S Package	$2,038	$2,290
***Options Price**	**$3,258**	**$3,660**
***Total Price**	**$17,392**	**$19,030**
Target Price	$17,783	
Destination Charge	$535	
Avg. Tax & Fees	$1,033	
Total Target $	**$19,351**	
Average Dealer Option Cost:	**89%**	
12 Month Price Increase:	3%	

For the 1999 Avenger, changes include new 16 inch wheel covers and tires. In addition, the remote keyless entry system includes a security alarm and additional second key fob. The optional V6 engine includes dual exhaust and upgraded suspension. The Sport Package includes amenities such as air conditioning, 16 inch aluminum wheels and a rear spoiler. The unique standard Avenger seating system allows the six-way manually adjustable driver seat to retain memory of its last position.

Ownership Costs (Projected)

Cost Area	5 Year Cost	Rating
Depreciation	$8,441	○
Financing ($321/month)	$3,764	
Insurance	$8,500	◉
State Fees	$796	
Fuel (Hwy 27 City 19)	$3,236	●
Maintenance	$3,387	◉
Repairs	$1,005	●

Warranty/Maintenance Info

Major Tune-Up (60K mile int.)	$467	●
Minor Tune-Up (30K mile int.)	$183	●
Brake Service	$295	●
Overall Warranty	3 yr/36k	○
Drivetrain Warranty	3 yr/36k	○
Rust Warranty	5 yr/100k	○
Maintenance Warranty	N/A	
Roadside Assistance	3 yr/36k	

Ownership Costs By Year (Projected)

$2,000 $4,000 $6,000 $8,000 $10,000

■ 1999
■ 2000
■ 2001
□ 2002
□ 2003

Resale Value

1999	2000	2001	2002	2003
$17,009	$15,328	$13,855	$12,377	$10,910

Projected Costs (5yr)

Relative	This Car
$29,173	**$29,129**
Cost/Mile 42¢	Cost/Mile 42¢

Cumulative Costs

	1999	2000	2001	2002	2003
Annual	$6,100	$5,250	$5,275	$6,188	$6,316
Total	$6,100	$11,350	$16,625	$22,813	$29,129

Ownership Cost Value

○

Average

● Poor   ◉ Worse Than Average   ○ Average   ◎ Better Than Average   ○ Excellent   ⊖ Insufficient Information

55

Refer to *Section 3: Annotated Vehicle Charts* for an explanation of these charts.

Dodge Avenger ES
2 Door Coupe

2.0L 140 hp Gas Fuel Inject.	4 Cylinder In-Line
Manual 5 Speed	2 Wheel Front
Dual Airbags Std	

Compact

Base Model Shown

Purchase Price

Car Item	Dealer Cost	List
Base Price	**$16,159**	**$17,645**
Anti-Lock Brakes	$534	$600
Automatic 4 Speed	$619	$695
2.5L 163 hp Gas	$543	$610
Air Conditioning	Std	Std
Power Steering	Std	Std
Cruise Control	Std	Std
Power Windows	Pkg	Pkg
AM/FM Stereo Cassette	Std	Std
Steering Wheel, Tilt	Std	Std
Rear Defroster	Std	Std
*Options Price	$1,162	$1,305
*Total Price	**$17,321**	**$18,950**
Target Price	$17,726	
Destination Charge	$535	
Avg. Tax & Fees	$1,030	
Total Target $	**$19,291**	
Average Dealer Option Cost:	89%	
12 Month Price Increase:	2%	

Ownership Costs (Projected)

Cost Area	5 Year Cost	Rating
Depreciation	$9,497	◓
Financing ($320/month)	$3,752	
Insurance	$8,500	◉
State Fees	$792	
Fuel (Hwy 27 City 19)	$3,236	●
Maintenance	$3,639	●
Repairs	$1,005	●

Warranty/Maintenance Info

Major Tune-Up (60K mile int.)	$467	●
Minor Tune-Up (30K mile int.)	$183	●
Brake Service	$295	●
Overall Warranty	3 yr/36k	◓
Drivetrain Warranty	3 yr/36k	◓
Rust Warranty	5 yr/100k	○
Maintenance Warranty	N/A	
Roadside Assistance	3 yr/36k	

For the 1999 Avenger ES, leather seats and a power driver's seat are added to the optional package. New exterior colors include Plum and Shark Blue. The ES upgrades the features of the base model with air conditioning, floor mats, fog lamps, rear spoiler and four wheel disc brakes. A HomeLink universal transmitter is mounted on the driver's sun visor and can be programmed to activate three remote devices. The optional V6 engine includes dual bright exhaust tips and an improved suspension.

Ownership Costs By Year (Projected)

$2,000	$4,000	$6,000	$8,000	$10,000

- 1999
- 2000
- 2001
- 2002
- 2003

Resale Value

1999	2000	2001	2002	2003
$16,643	$14,781	$13,118	$11,454	$9,794

Cumulative Costs

	1999	2000	2001	2002	2003
Annual	$6,401	$5,427	$5,462	$6,623	$6,508
Total	$6,401	$11,828	$17,290	$23,913	$30,421

Projected Costs (5yr)

Relative $29,100	This Car $30,421
Cost/Mile 42¢	Cost/Mile 43¢

Ownership Cost Value

● Poor

Dodge Intrepid
4 Door Sedan

2.7L 200 hp Gas Fuel Inject.	6 Cylinder "V"
Automatic 4 Speed	2 Wheel Front
Dual Airbags Std	

Large

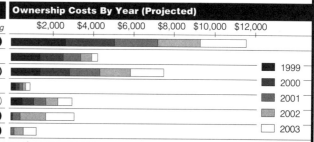

ES Model Shown

Purchase Price

Car Item	Dealer Cost	List
Base Price	**$18,232**	**$19,890**
Anti-Lock Brakes	$534	$600
Manual Transmission	N/A	N/A
Optional Engine	N/A	N/A
Air Conditioning	Std	Std
Power Steering	Std	Std
Cruise Control	Std	Std
Power Windows	Std	Std
AM/FM Stereo Cassette	Std	Std
Steering Wheel, Tilt	Std	Std
22C Package	N/C	N/C
*Options Price	$534	$600
*Total Price	**$18,766**	**$20,490**
Target Price	$19,774	
Destination Charge	$550	
Avg. Tax & Fees	$1,138	
Total Target $	**$21,462**	
Average Dealer Option Cost:	89%	
12 Month Price Increase:	1%	

Ownership Costs (Projected)

Cost Area	5 Year Cost	Rating
Depreciation	$11,497	◓
Financing ($356/month)	$4,175	
Insurance	$7,463	◓
State Fees	$853	
Fuel (Hwy 30 City 21)	$2,920	○
Maintenance	$3,027	◓
Repairs	$1,165	◉

Warranty/Maintenance Info

Major Tune-Up (60K mile int.)	$214	○
Minor Tune-Up (30K mile int.)	$110	○
Brake Service	$261	○
Overall Warranty	3 yr/36k	○
Drivetrain Warranty	3 yr/36k	○
Rust Warranty	5 yr/100k	○
Maintenance Warranty	N/A	
Roadside Assistance	3 yr/36k	

For 1999, the Intrepid returns with minor revisions from the previous year. A new Sentry Key engine immobilizer is included with the anti-theft alarm. The Intrepid offers an optional 50/50 cloth bench seat for more seating flexibility. A new exterior color, Light Cypress Green, has been added for 1999. Available packages offered are a 16 inch Wheel Package and Cold Weather Package. For comfort, an eight-way power driver's seat and a premium stereo with CD are available.

Ownership Costs By Year (Projected)

$2,000	$4,000	$6,000	$8,000	$10,000	$12,000

- 1999
- 2000
- 2001
- 2002
- 2003

Resale Value

1999	2000	2001	2002	2003
$18,783	$16,354	$14,213	$12,118	$9,965

Cumulative Costs

	1999	2000	2001	2002	2003
Annual	$6,333	$5,860	$5,785	$6,615	$6,507
Total	$6,333	$12,193	$17,978	$24,593	$31,100

Projected Costs (5yr)

Relative $31,191	This Car $31,100
Cost/Mile 45¢	Cost/Mile 44¢

Ownership Cost Value

○ Average

56

* Includes shaded options
** Other purchase requirements apply
*** Price includes other options

● Poor	◉ Worse Than Average	◓ Average	○ Better Than Average	○ Excellent	⊖ Insufficient Information

Refer to *Section 3: Annotated Vehicle Charts* for an explanation of these charts.

Dodge Intrepid ES
4 Door Sedan

Large

 3.2L 225 hp Gas Fuel Inject.
 6 Cylinder "V"
 Automatic 4 Speed
 2 Wheel Front
Dual Airbags Std

Purchase Price

Car Item	Dealer Cost	List
Base Price	**$20,680**	**$22,640**
Anti-Lock Brakes	Std	Std
Manual Transmission	N/A	N/A
Optional Engine	N/A	N/A
Air Conditioning	Std	Std
Power Steering	Std	Std
Cruise Control	Std	Std
Power Windows	Std	Std
AM/FM Stereo Cassette	Std	Std
Steering Wheel, Tilt	Std	Std
24L Package	N/C	N/C
*Options Price	$0	$0
*Total Price	**$20,680**	**$22,640**
Target Price	$21,852	
Destination Charge	$550	
Avg. Tax & Fees	$1,253	
Total Target $	**$23,655**	
Average Dealer Option Cost:	**89%**	
12 Month Price Increase:	1%	

Ownership Costs (Projected)

Cost Area	5 Year Cost	Rating
Depreciation	$13,317	◑
Financing ($392/month)	$4,602	
Insurance (Performance)	$9,172	◒
State Fees	$941	
Fuel (Hwy 28 City 18)	$3,263	◒
Maintenance	$3,152	◒
Repairs	$1,165	◑

Warranty/Maintenance Info

Major Tune-Up (60K mile int.)	$241	◒
Minor Tune-Up (30K mile int.)	$110	◒
Brake Service	$261	◒
Overall Warranty	3 yr/36k	◒
Drivetrain Warranty	3 yr/36k	◒
Rust Warranty	5 yr/100k	○
Maintenance Warranty	N/A	
Roadside Assistance	3 yr/36k	

For 1999, the Intrepid ES returns with minor revisions from the previous year. Seton Softee leather seating replaces Wanderer leather. The Intrepid ES also is equipped with the AutoStick system that allows the driver to change gears with a flick of the shifter and without using a clutch pedal. A 60/40 split folding rear seat and eight-way power driver's seat are both standard features. Eight-way dual power seats are included with the optional premium leather bucket seats.

Ownership Costs By Year (Projected)

$2,000 $4,000 $6,000 $8,000 $10,000 $12,000 $14,000

- 1999
- 2000
- 2001
- 2002
- 2003

Resale Value

1999	2000	2001	2002	2003
$19,668	$17,111	$14,845	$12,619	$10,338

Cumulative Costs

	1999	2000	2001	2002	2003
Annual	$8,199	$6,527	$6,426	$7,263	$7,198
Total	$8,199	$14,726	$21,152	$28,415	$35,613

Projected Costs (5yr)

Relative	This Car
$32,299	$35,613
Cost/Mile 46¢	Cost/Mile 51¢

Ownership Cost Value
● Poor

Dodge Neon Competition
2 Door Coupe

Compact

 2.0L 150 hp Gas Fuel Inject.
 4 Cylinder In-Line
Manual 5 Speed
 2 Wheel Front
Dual Airbags Std

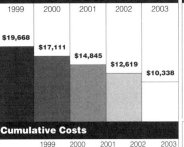

Purchase Price

Car Item	Dealer Cost	List
Base Price	**$10,750**	**$11,375**
Anti-Lock Brakes	N/A	N/A
Automatic Transmission	N/A	N/A
Optional Engine	N/A	N/A
Air Conditioning	$890	$1,000
Power Steering	Std	Std
Cruise Control	N/A	N/A
Power Windows	N/A	N/A
AM/FM Stereo Cassette	N/A	N/A
Steering Wheel, Tilt	N/A	N/A
23A Package	$1,914	***$2,080
*Options Price	$2,804	$3,080
*Total Price	**$13,554**	**$14,455**
Target Price	$13,921	
Destination Charge	$500	
Avg. Tax & Fees	$812	
Total Target $	**$15,233**	
Average Dealer Option Cost:	**91%**	
12 Month Price Increase:	4%	

Ownership Costs (Projected)

Cost Area	5 Year Cost	Rating
Depreciation	$8,338	◑
Financing ($252/month)	$2,963	
Insurance	$7,643	●
State Fees	$613	
Fuel (Hwy 39 City 28)	$2,218	○
Maintenance	$2,720	○
Repairs	$745	◉

Warranty/Maintenance Info

Major Tune-Up (60K mile int.)	$229	○
Minor Tune-Up (30K mile int.)	$100	○
Brake Service	$256	◑
Overall Warranty	3 yr/36k	○
Drivetrain Warranty	3 yr/36k	○
Rust Warranty	5 yr/100k	○
Maintenance Warranty	N/A	
Roadside Assistance	3 yr/36k	

For 1999, the Neon Competition coupe features four wheel disc brakes, body-color door handles, a high-speed engine controller, power bulge hood and cloth low-back bucket seats. Also included with the coupe are a leather-wrapped steering wheel and shift knob, firm-feel power steering, Competition suspension and aluminum wheels with performance tires. Options include air conditioning, a rear window defroster and AM/FM cassette radio with CD changer controls.

Ownership Costs By Year (Projected)

$2,000 $4,000 $6,000 $8,000 $10,000

- 1999
- 2000
- 2001
- 2002
- 2003

Resale Value

1999	2000	2001	2002	2003
$12,564	$11,027	$9,670	$8,289	$6,895

Cumulative Costs

	1999	2000	2001	2002	2003
Annual	$5,751	$4,475	$4,421	$5,262	$5,331
Total	$5,751	$10,226	$14,647	$19,909	$25,240

Projected Costs (5yr)

Relative	This Car
$25,472	$25,240
Cost/Mile 36¢	Cost/Mile 36¢

Ownership Cost Value
○ Average

---

* Includes shaded options

** Other purchase requirements apply

*** Price includes other options

● Poor ◉ Worse Than Average ◒ Average ○ Better Than Average ◯ Excellent ⊖ Insufficient Information

Refer to *Section 3: Annotated Vehicle Charts* for an explanation of these charts.

Dodge Neon Highline
2 Door Coupe

Compact

 2.0L 132 hp Gas Fuel Inject. | 4 Cylinder In-Line | Manual 5 Speed | 2 Wheel Front | Dual Airbags Std

Competition Model Shown

Purchase Price

Car Item	Dealer Cost	List
Base Price	**$10,653**	**$11,520**
Anti-Lock Brakes	$503	**$565
Automatic 3 Speed	$534	$600
2.0L 150 hp Gas	N/C	**N/C
Air Conditioning	$890	$1,000
Power Steering	Std	Std
Cruise Control	Pkg	Pkg
Power Windows	$236	**$265
AM/FM Stereo CD	$352	**$395
Steering Wheel, Tilt	Pkg	Pkg
22D Package	N/C	N/C
*Options Price	$1,424	$1,600
Total Price	**$12,077**	**$13,120**
Target Price	$12,430	
Destination Charge	$550	
Avg. Tax & Fees	$734	
Total Target $	**$13,714**	
Average Dealer Option Cost:	**89%**	
12 Month Price Increase:	3%	

Ownership Costs (Projected)

Cost Area	5 Year Cost	Rating
Depreciation	$7,788	●
Financing ($227/month)	$2,667	
Insurance	$7,837	●
State Fees	$560	
Fuel (Hwy 32 City 23)	$2,702	○
Maintenance	$2,698	○
Repairs	$745	○

Warranty/Maintenance Info

Major Tune-Up (60K mile int.)	$229	○
Minor Tune-Up (30K mile int.)	$100	○
Brake Service	$236	○
Overall Warranty	3 yr/36k	○
Drivetrain Warranty	3 yr/36k	○
Rust Warranty	5 yr/100k	○
Maintenance Warranty	N/A	
Roadside Assistance	3 yr/36k	

For 1999, the Neon Highline coupe has many available options. The optional Light Group includes illuminated visor vanity mirrors, a rear view mirror with built-in reading lights, an underhood lamp, an ignition switch lamp and glovebox lamp. The Value/Fun Group consists of the Power Convenience Group, AM/FM radio with cassette and CD changer controls, power sunroof and power front windows. Quick Order Packages, Sport or R/T Packages and the Value Group are also available.

Ownership Costs By Year (Projected)

$2,000 — $4,000 — $6,000 — $8,000

■ 1999
■ 2000
■ 2001
■ 2002
□ 2003

Resale Value

1999	2000	2001	2002	2003
$11,402	$9,922	$8,618	$7,283	$5,926

Cumulative Costs

	1999	2000	2001	2002	2003
Annual	$5,409	$4,458	$4,432	$5,285	$5,413
Total	$5,409	$9,867	$14,299	$19,584	$24,997

Projected Costs (5yr)

Relative	This Car
$24,168	$24,997
Cost/Mile 35¢	Cost/Mile 36¢

Ownership Cost Value
●
Worse Than Average

Dodge Neon Competition
4 Door Sedan

Compact

 2.0L 132 hp Gas Fuel Inject. | 4 Cylinder In-Line | Manual 5 Speed | 2 Wheel Front | Dual Airbags Std

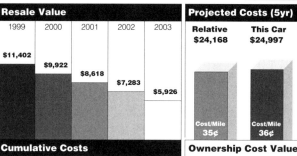

Purchase Price

Car Item	Dealer Cost	List
Base Price	**$10,796**	**$11,425**
Anti-Lock Brakes	N/A	N/A
Automatic Transmission	N/A	N/A
Optional Engine	N/A	N/A
Air Conditioning	$890	$1,000
Power Steering	Std	Std
Cruise Control	N/A	N/A
Power Windows	N/A	N/A
AM/FM Stereo Cassette	N/A	N/A
Steering Wheel, Tilt	N/A	N/A
25A Package	$1,895	***$2,060
*Options Price	$2,785	$3,060
Total Price	**$13,581**	**$14,485**
Target Price	$13,949	
Destination Charge	$500	
Avg. Tax & Fees	$813	
Total Target $	**$15,262**	
Average Dealer Option Cost:	**91%**	
12 Month Price Increase:	3%	

Ownership Costs (Projected)

Cost Area	5 Year Cost	Rating
Depreciation	$8,441	●
Financing ($253/month)	$2,970	
Insurance	$7,463	●
State Fees	$613	
Fuel (Hwy 39 City 28)	$2,218	○
Maintenance	$2,720	○
Repairs	$745	○

Warranty/Maintenance Info

Major Tune-Up (60K mile int.)	$229	○
Minor Tune-Up (30K mile int.)	$100	○
Brake Service	$256	●
Overall Warranty	3 yr/36k	○
Drivetrain Warranty	3 yr/36k	○
Rust Warranty	5 yr/100k	○
Maintenance Warranty	N/A	
Roadside Assistance	3 yr/36k	

For the 1999 Neon Competition sedan, selected options are available. These include air conditioning, a rear window defroster and AM/FM radio with cassette and CD changer controls. The Competition Group consists of four wheel disc brakes, body-color door handles, a high-speed engine controller, cloth low-back bucket seats and leather-wrapped steering wheel and shift knob. Also included in the package are Competition suspension, tachometer, 14 inch aluminum wheels and performance tires.

Ownership Costs By Year (Projected)

$2,000 — $4,000 — $6,000 — $8,000 — $10,000

■ 1999
■ 2000
■ 2001
■ 2002
□ 2003

Resale Value

1999	2000	2001	2002	2003
$12,562	$11,009	$9,634	$8,237	$6,821

Cumulative Costs

	1999	2000	2001	2002	2003
Annual	$5,750	$4,458	$4,404	$5,242	$5,316
Total	$5,750	$10,208	$14,612	$19,854	$25,170

Projected Costs (5yr)

Relative	This Car
$25,497	$25,170
Cost/Mile 36¢	Cost/Mile 36¢

Ownership Cost Value
○
Better Than Average

58

* Includes shaded options
** Other purchase requirements apply
*** Price includes other options

● Poor   ◖ Worse Than Average   ○ Average   ○ Better Than Average   ○ Excellent   ⊖ Insufficient Information

Refer to *Section 3: Annotated Vehicle Charts* for an explanation of these charts.

Dodge Neon Highline
4 Door Sedan

Compact

 2.0L 132 hp Gas Fuel Inject.
 4 Cylinder In-Line
 Manual 5 Speed
 2 Wheel Front
 Dual Airbags Std

Competition Model Shown

Purchase Price

Car Item	Dealer Cost	List
Base Price	**$10,833**	**$11,720**
Anti-Lock Brakes	$458	**$515
Automatic 3 Speed	$534	$600
2.0L 150 hp Gas	N/C	**N/C
Air Conditioning	$890	$1,000
Power Steering	Std	Std
Cruise Control	Pkg	Pkg
Power Windows	$236	**$265
AM/FM Stereo Cass/CD	$254	**$285
Steering Wheel, Tilt	Pkg	Pkg
22D Package	N/C	N/C
*Options Price	$1,424	$1,600
*Total Price	**$12,257**	**$13,320**
Target Price	$12,618	
Destination Charge	$550	
Avg. Tax & Fees	$745	
Total Target $	**$13,913**	
Average Dealer Option Cost:	**89%**	
12 Month Price Increase:	3%	

For the 1999 Neon Highline sedan, both Sport and R/T Quick Order Packages are available. The Highline Sport Quick Order Package includes air conditioning, passenger assist handles, bright sport badging, fog lamps and power bulge hood. The package also includes cloth low-back bucket seats, trunklid spoiler, tachometer and premium wheel covers. Other enhancing options include the Light Group, the Deluxe Convenience Group and the Power Convenience Group (including power locks and mirrors).

Ownership Costs (Projected)

Cost Area	5 Year Cost	Rating
Depreciation	$8,070	●
Financing ($231/month)	$2,707	
Insurance	$7,463	◉
State Fees	$568	
Fuel (Hwy 32 City 23)	$2,702	○
Maintenance	$2,698	○
Repairs	$745	○

Warranty/Maintenance Info

Major Tune-Up (60K mile int.)	$229	○
Minor Tune-Up (30K mile int.)	$100	○
Brake Service	$236	○
Overall Warranty	3 yr/36k	○
Drivetrain Warranty	3 yr/36k	○
Rust Warranty	5 yr/100k	○
Maintenance Warranty	N/A	
Roadside Assistance	3 yr/36k	

Ownership Costs By Year (Projected)

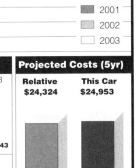

$2,000 $4,000 $6,000 $8,000 $10,000

Legend: 1999, 2000, 2001, 2002, 2003

Resale Value

1999	2000	2001	2002	2003
$11,533	$10,002	$8,644	$7,254	$5,843

Cumulative Costs

	1999	2000	2001	2002	2003
Annual	$5,421	$4,449	$4,421	$5,270	$5,392
Total	$5,421	$9,870	$14,291	$19,561	$24,953

Projected Costs (5yr)

Relative	This Car
$24,324	$24,953
Cost/Mile 35¢	Cost/Mile 36¢

Ownership Cost Value

○ Average

Dodge Stratus
4 Door Sedan

Midsize

 2.0L 132 hp Gas Fuel Inject.
 4 Cylinder In-Line
 Manual 5 Speed
 2 Wheel Front
Dual Airbags Std

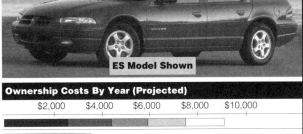
ES Model Shown

Purchase Price

Car Item	Dealer Cost	List
Base Price	**$14,039**	**$15,280**
Anti-Lock Brakes	$503	$565
Automatic 4 Speed	$935	$1,050
2.4L 150 hp Gas	$401	$450
Air Conditioning	Std	Std
Power Steering	Std	Std
Cruise/Speed Control	Inc	Inc
Power Windows	Inc	Inc
AM/FM Stereo Cassette	Std	Std
Steering Wheel, Tilt	Std	Std
21B Package	N/C	N/C
*Options Price	$1,839	$2,065
*Total Price	**$15,878**	**$17,345**
Target Price	$16,546	
Destination Charge	$535	
Avg. Tax & Fees	$961	
Total Target $	**$18,042**	
Average Dealer Option Cost:	**89%**	
12 Month Price Increase:	2%	

The Stratus continues this new model year with a few detail changes, the most notable being the inclusion of the B Package as a no-charge option, a $760 (list) value. This package includes front and rear floor mats, speed-sensitive power door locks, power heated exterior rearview mirrors, a driver's seat height adjuster and power windows. Other changes for 1999 include a more subdued Scroll interior fabric, white-faced gauges and a new design pattern for the standard wheel covers.

Ownership Costs (Projected)

Cost Area	5 Year Cost	Rating
Depreciation	$9,080	○
Financing ($299/month)	$3,510	
Insurance	$7,294	○
State Fees	$728	
Fuel (Hwy 30 City 21)	$2,920	○
Maintenance	$2,724	○
Repairs	$1,056	●

Warranty/Maintenance Info

Major Tune-Up (60K mile int.)	$260	○
Minor Tune-Up (30K mile int.)	$99	○
Brake Service	$226	○
Overall Warranty	3 yr/36k	○
Drivetrain Warranty	3 yr/36k	○
Rust Warranty	5 yr/100k	○
Maintenance Warranty	N/A	
Roadside Assistance	3 yr/36k	

Ownership Costs By Year (Projected)

$2,000 $4,000 $6,000 $8,000 $10,000

Legend: 1999, 2000, 2001, 2002, 2003

Resale Value

1999	2000	2001	2002	2003
$15,412	$13,593	$12,056	$10,480	$8,962

Cumulative Costs

	1999	2000	2001	2002	2003
Annual	$5,993	$5,003	$4,870	$5,706	$5,740
Total	$5,993	$10,996	$15,866	$21,572	$27,312

Projected Costs (5yr)

Relative	This Car
$27,610	$27,312
Cost/Mile 39¢	Cost/Mile 39¢

Ownership Cost Value

○ Average

Dodge Stratus ES
4 Door Sedan

Midsize

 2.5L 168 hp Gas Fuel Inject.
 6 Cylinder "V"
 Automatic 4 Speed
 2 Wheel Front
Dual Airbags Std

Purchase Price

Car Item	Dealer Cost	List
Base Price	**$17,314**	**$18,960**
Anti-Lock Brakes	Std	Std
Manual Transmission	N/A	N/A
Optional Engine	N/A	N/A
Air Conditioning	Std	Std
Power Steering	Std	Std
Cruise Control	Std	Std
Power Windows	Std	Std
AM/FM Stereo Cassette	Std	Std
Steering Wheel, Tilt	Std	Std
26R Package	N/C	N/C
*Options Price	$0	$0
*Total Price	$17,314	$18,960
Target Price	$18,099	
Destination Charge	$535	
Avg. Tax & Fees	$1,047	
Total Target $	**$19,681**	
Average Dealer Option Cost:	**89%**	
12 Month Price Increase:	**4%**	

The Stratus ES arrives this year with key detail improvements. The 2.5L V6 engine and four speed AutoStick automatic transmission are now standard, as well as four wheel disc brakes with an antilock braking system. Appearance enhancements are achieved with the addition of white-faced gauges and a new 15 inch five spoke aluminum wheel design. Other changes include better sound deadening, several new colors, and a new Sentry Key vehicle immobilizer included with the optional Security Group.

Ownership Costs (Projected)

Cost Area	5 Year Cost	Rating
Depreciation	$10,604	◐
Financing ($326/month)	$3,828	
Insurance	$7,643	◐
State Fees	$792	
Fuel (Hwy 27 City 19)	$3,236	◉
Maintenance	$3,336	◐
Repairs	$1,056	●

Warranty/Maintenance Info

Major Tune-Up (60K mile int.)	$431	●
Minor Tune-Up (30K mile int.)	$181	●
Brake Service	$250	◐
Overall Warranty	3 yr/36k	◐
Drivetrain Warranty	3 yr/36k	◐
Rust Warranty	5 yr/100k	○
Maintenance Warranty	N/A	
Roadside Assistance	3 yr/36k	◐

Ownership Costs By Year (Projected)

$2,000 $4,000 $6,000 $8,000 $10,000 $12,000

■ 1999
■ 2000
■ 2001
□ 2002
□ 2003

Resale Value

1999	2000	2001	2002	2003
$16,362	$14,322	$12,573	$10,793	$9,077

Cumulative Costs

	1999	2000	2001	2002	2003
Annual	$6,934	$5,458	$5,478	$6,192	$6,433
Total	$6,934	$12,392	$17,870	$24,062	$30,495

Projected Costs (5yr)

Relative $28,809	This Car $30,495
Cost/Mile 41¢	Cost/Mile 44¢

Ownership Cost Value

◉ Worse Than Average

Dodge Viper RT/10
2 Door Convertible

Sport

 8.0L 450 hp Gas Fuel Inject.
10 Cylinder "V"
Manual 6 Speed
 2 Wheel Rear
 Dual Airbags Std

GTS Model Shown

Purchase Price

Car Item	Dealer Cost	List
Base Price	**$59,038**	**$65,725**
Anti-Lock Brakes	N/A	N/A
Automatic Transmission	N/A	N/A
Optional Engine	N/A	N/A
Air Conditioning	Std	Std
Power Steering	Std	Std
Cruise Control	N/A	N/A
Power Windows	Std	Std
AM/FM Stereo CD	Std	Std
Steering Wheel, Tilt	Std	Std
21A Package	N/C	N/C
*Options Price	$0	$0
*Total Price	$59,038	$65,725
Target Price	$65,299	
Destination Charge	$700	
Avg. Tax & Fees	$3,813	
Luxury/Gas Guzzler Tax	$5,722	
Total Target $	**$75,534**	
12 Month Price Increase:	**None**	

For 1999, the Viper RT/10 roadster receives new 18 inch wheels shod with Michelin performance tires. In addition, power mirrors and satin-finish aluminum interior trim are standard. New Cognac Connolly leather is available. Standard features include power windows and door latches, adjustable foot pedals and reclining leather bucket seats. The RT/10 is also available with a removable body-color hard top. For safety, dual depowered airbags with a passenger airbag cut-off switch are standard.

Ownership Costs (Projected)

Cost Area	5 Year Cost	Rating
Depreciation	$31,232	◐
Financing ($1,252/month)	$14,693	
Insurance (Perf.) [Est.]	$17,959	◉
State Fees	$2,670	
Fuel (Hwy 21 City 12 -Prem.)	$5,491	●
Maintenance	$3,306	◐
Repairs	$3,200	●

Warranty/Maintenance Info

Major Tune-Up (60K mile int.)	$346	◉
Minor Tune-Up (30K mile int.)	$182	◉
Brake Service	$437	●
Overall Warranty	3 yr/36k	◐
Drivetrain Warranty	3 yr/36k	◐
Rust Warranty	5 yr/100k	○
Maintenance Warranty	N/A	
Roadside Assistance	3 yr/36k	◐

Ownership Costs By Year (Projected)

$5 $10 $15 $20 $25 $30 $35 (x1,000)

■ 1999
■ 2000
■ 2001
■ 2002
□ 2003

Resale Value

1999	2000	2001	2002	2003
$61,824	$57,011	$52,624	$48,424	$44,302

Cumulative Costs

	1999	2000	2001	2002	2003
Annual	$23,882	$14,109	$13,476	$13,795	$13,290
Total	$23,882	$37,991	$51,467	$65,262	$78,552

Projected Costs (5yr)

Relative $78,129	This Car $78,552
Cost/Mile $1.12	Cost/Mile $1.12

Ownership Cost Value

◉ Worse Than Average

60

* Includes shaded options
** Other purchase requirements apply
*** Price includes other options

● Poor
◉ Worse Than Average
◐ Average
○ Better Than Average
○ Excellent
⊖ Insufficient Information

Refer to *Section 3: Annotated Vehicle Charts* for an explanation of these charts.

Dodge Viper GTS
2 Door Coupe

 8.0L 450 hp Gas Fuel Inject.

10 Cylinder "V"

 Manual 6 Speed

 2 Wheel Rear

Dual Airbags Std

Purchase Price

Car Item	Dealer Cost	List
Base Price	**$61,238**	**$68,225**
Anti-Lock Brakes	N/A	N/A
Automatic Transmission	N/A	N/A
Optional Engine	N/A	N/A
Air Conditioning	Std	Std
Power Steering	Std	Std
Cruise Control	N/A	N/A
Power Windows	Std	Std
AM/FM Stereo CD	Std	Std
Steering Wheel, Tilt	Std	Std
21A Package	N/C	N/C
*Options Price	$0	$0
***Total Price**	**$61,238**	**$68,225**
Target Price	$67,994	
Destination Charge	$700	
Avg. Tax & Fees	$3,960	
Luxury/Gas Guzzler Tax	$5,884	
Total Target $	**$78,538**	
12 Month Price Increase:	None	

For 1999, the Viper GTS receives new 18 inch wheels shod with Michelin performance tires. New Cognac Connolly leather is also available. Additional standard features include power mirrors and satin-finish aluminum interior trim. The GTS upgrades the RT/10 with a rear defroster, racing-style fuel filler cover, dual overhead courtesy lights and six speaker sound system. For safety, dual depowered airbags with a passenger airbag cut-off switch are standard.

Ownership Costs (Projected)

Cost Area	5 Year Cost	Rating
Depreciation	$31,856	○
Financing ($1,302/month)	$15,279	
Insurance (Perf.) [Est.]	$17,959	◉
State Fees	$2,769	
Fuel (Hwy 21 City 12 -Prem.)	$5,491	●
Maintenance	$3,306	○
Repairs	$3,200	●

Warranty/Maintenance Info

Major Tune-Up (60K mile int.)	$346	●
Minor Tune-Up (30K mile int.)	$182	◉
Brake Service	$437	●
Overall Warranty	3 yr/36k	○
Drivetrain Warranty	3 yr/36k	○
Rust Warranty	5 yr/100k	○
Maintenance Warranty	N/A	
Roadside Assistance	3 yr/36k	

Ownership Costs By Year (Projected)

Legend: 1999, 2000, 2001, 2002, 2003

Resale Value

1999	2000	2001	2002	2003
$64,487	$59,595	$55,139	$50,867	$46,682

Cumulative Costs

	1999	2000	2001	2002	2003
Annual	$24,447	$14,372	$13,685	$13,961	$13,396
Total	$24,447	$38,819	$52,504	$66,465	$79,861

Projected Costs (5yr)

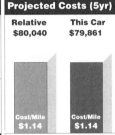

Relative	This Car
$80,040	$79,861
Cost/Mile $1.14	Cost/Mile $1.14

Ownership Cost Value

○ Average

Ford Contour LX
4 Door Sedan

2.0L 125 hp Gas Fuel Inject.

 4 Cylinder In-Line

 Manual 5 Speed

 2 Wheel Front

Dual Airbags Std

Purchase Price

Car Item	Dealer Cost	List
Base Price	**$13,524**	**$14,460**
Anti-Lock Brakes	$445	$500
Automatic 4 Speed	$725	$815
2.0L 125 hp CNG	$232	**$260
Air Conditioning	Std	Std
Power Steering	Std	Std
Cruise Control	$191	$215
Power Windows	N/A	N/A
AM/FM Stereo Cassette	$165	$185
Steering Wheel, Tilt	Std	Std
Rear Defroster	$169	$190
*Options Price	$1,059	$1,190
***Total Price**	**$14,583**	**$15,650**
Target Price	$15,082	
Destination Charge	$535	
Avg. Tax & Fees	$878	
Total Target $	**$16,495**	
Average Dealer Option Cost:	89%	
12 Month Price Increase:	None	

For 1999, the Contour LX sedan includes a revised instrument panel, increased rear leg room and is available in two new paint colors, Tropic Green Metallic and Medium Steel Blue Metallic. The integrated child seat is no longer available. Standard features include second generation airbags, air conditioning, an air filtration system and tilt steering column. Options include a rear 60/40 split fold-down bench seat, AM/FM stereo with cassette, remote keyless entry system and antilock brakes.

Ownership Costs (Projected)

Cost Area	5 Year Cost	Rating
Depreciation	$9,477	◉
Financing ($273/month)	$3,209	
Insurance	$7,294	○
State Fees	$660	
Fuel (Hwy 31 City 23)	$2,748	○
Maintenance	$3,111	○
Repairs	$755	○

Warranty/Maintenance Info

Major Tune-Up (100K mile int.)	$192	○
Minor Tune-Up (30K mile int.)	$82	○
Brake Service	$210	○
Overall Warranty	3 yr/36k	○
Drivetrain Warranty	3 yr/36k	○
Rust Warranty	5 yr/unlim. mi	○
Maintenance Warranty	N/A	
Roadside Assistance	3 yr/36k	

Ownership Costs By Year (Projected)

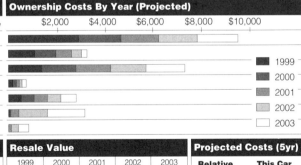

Legend: 1999, 2000, 2001, 2002, 2003

Resale Value

1999	2000	2001	2002	2003
$13,554	$11,786	$10,207	$8,615	$7,018

Cumulative Costs

	1999	2000	2001	2002	2003
Annual	$6,153	$4,823	$4,817	$5,662	$5,799
Total	$6,153	$10,976	$15,793	$21,455	$27,254

Projected Costs (5yr)

 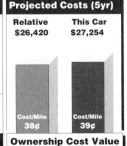

Relative	This Car
$26,420	$27,254
Cost/Mile 38¢	Cost/Mile 39¢

Ownership Cost Value

◉ Worse Than Average

---

* Includes shaded options

** Other purchase requirements apply

*** Price includes other options

 Poor
 Worse Than Average
 Average
 Better Than Average
 Excellent
 Insufficient Information

Refer to Section 3: Annotated Vehicle Charts for an explanation of these charts.

Ford Contour SE
4 Door Sedan

Compact

2.0L 125 hp Gas Fuel Inject.	4 Cylinder In-Line
Manual 5 Speed	2 Wheel Front
Dual Airbags Std	

Purchase Price

Car Item	Dealer Cost	List
Base Price	**$14,565**	**$15,955**
Anti-Lock Brakes	$445	$500
Automatic 4 Speed	$725	$815
2.0L 125 hp CNG	$232	**$260
Air Conditioning	Std	Std
Power Steering	Std	Std
Cruise Control	Std	Std
Power Windows	Std	Std
AM/FM Stereo Cassette	Std	Std
Steering Wheel, Tilt	Std	Std
Rear Defroster	Std	Std
*Options Price	$725	$815
Total Price	**$15,290**	**$16,770**
Target Price	$15,873	
Destination Charge	$535	
Avg. Tax & Fees	$924	
Total Target $	**$17,332**	
Average Dealer Option Cost:	**89%**	
12 Month Price Increase:	None	

Ownership Costs (Projected)

Cost Area	5 Year Cost	Rating
Depreciation	$9,889	●
Financing ($287/month)	$3,371	
Insurance	$7,334	◐
State Fees	$705	
Fuel (Hwy 31 City 23)	$2,748	◐
Maintenance	$3,111	◐
Repairs	$755	◐

Warranty/Maintenance Info

Major Tune-Up (100K mile int.)	$192	○
Minor Tune-Up (30K mile int.)	$82	◐
Brake Service	$210	◐
Overall Warranty	3 yr/36k	◐
Drivetrain Warranty	3 yr/36k	◐
Rust Warranty	5 yr/unlim. mi	○
Maintenance Warranty	N/A	
Roadside Assistance	3 yr/36k	

For 1999, the Contour SE sedan includes increased rear leg room and a revised instrument panel. The integrated child seat is no longer available. Standard features include second generation airbags, power windows and door locks and an AM/FM stereo with cassette. An optional SE Sport Group is available on the SE; it includes a more powerful 2.5L V6 engine, 15 inch aluminum wheels and rear wing spoiler. An optional all-speed traction control system is also available.

Ownership Costs By Year (Projected)

Legend: 1999, 2000, 2001, 2002, 2003

Resale Value

1999	2000	2001	2002	2003
$14,531	$12,615	$10,895	$9,169	$7,443

Cumulative Costs

	1999	2000	2001	2002	2003
Annual	$6,087	$5,034	$5,008	$5,833	$5,951
Total	$6,087	$11,121	$16,129	$21,962	$27,913

Projected Costs (5yr)

Relative $27,090	This Car $27,913
Cost/Mile 39¢	Cost/Mile 40¢

Ownership Cost Value

○ Average

Ford Contour SVT
4 Door Sedan

Compact

2.5L 200 hp Gas Fuel Inject.	6 Cylinder "V"
Manual 5 Speed	2 Wheel Front
Dual Airbags Std	

Purchase Price

Car Item	Dealer Cost	List
Base Price	**$20,537**	**$22,665**
Anti-Lock Brakes	Std	Std
Automatic Transmission	N/A	N/A
Optional Engine	N/A	N/A
Air Conditioning	Std	Std
Power Steering	Std	Std
Cruise Control	Std	Std
Power Windows	Std	Std
AM/FM Stereo Cassette	Std	Std
Steering Wheel, Tilt	Std	Std
Rear Defroster	Std	Std
*Options Price	$0	$0
Total Price	**$20,537**	**$22,665**
Target Price	$21,491	
Destination Charge	$535	
Avg. Tax & Fees	$1,236	
Total Target $	**$23,262**	
Average Dealer Option Cost:	**89%**	
12 Month Price Increase:	1%	

Ownership Costs (Projected)

Cost Area	5 Year Cost	Rating
Depreciation	$13,970	●
Financing ($386/month)	$4,525	
Insurance (Performance)	$9,712	◉
State Fees	$941	
Fuel (Hwy 29 City 20)	$3,041	◐
Maintenance	$3,341	◉
Repairs	$755	◐

Warranty/Maintenance Info

Major Tune-Up (100K mile int.)	$305	●
Minor Tune-Up (30K mile int.)	$99	◐
Brake Service	$204	◐
Overall Warranty	3 yr/36k	◐
Drivetrain Warranty	3 yr/36k	◐
Rust Warranty	5 yr/unlim. mi	○
Maintenance Warranty	N/A	
Roadside Assistance	3 yr/36k	

The Contour SVT sedan was developed by the Ford Special Vehicle Team (SVT) from the Contour SE. The SVT team concentrated on refinements to the engine, suspension and exhaust. The SVT features a 200 hp high-output 2.5L engine and sport suspension. Also included on the SVT are leather sport bucket seats, 16 inch aluminum wheels, performance tires and rocker panel moldings with side body cladding. A power moonroof and AM/FM stereo with CD player are no-charge options.

Ownership Costs By Year (Projected)

Legend: 1999, 2000, 2001, 2002, 2003

Resale Value

1999	2000	2001	2002	2003
$19,084	$16,443	$14,031	$11,644	$9,292

Cumulative Costs

	1999	2000	2001	2002	2003
Annual	$8,426	$6,653	$6,468	$7,686	$7,052
Total	$8,426	$15,079	$21,547	$29,233	$36,285

Projected Costs (5yr)

Relative $32,541	This Car $36,285
Cost/Mile 46¢	Cost/Mile 52¢

Ownership Cost Value

● Poor

62

* Includes shaded options
** Other purchase requirements apply
*** Price includes other options

Legend:
- ● Poor
- ◉ Worse Than Average
- ◐ Average
- ○ Better Than Average
- ○ Excellent
- ⊖ Insufficient Information

Refer to *Section 3: Annotated Vehicle Charts* for an explanation of these charts.

Ford Crown Victoria
4 Door Sedan

 4.6L 200 hp Gas Fuel Inject.

 8 Cylinder "V"

 Automatic 4 Speed

 2 Wheel Rear

 Dual Airbags Std

Purchase Price

Car Item	Dealer Cost	List
Base Price	**$20,438**	**$21,905**
Anti-Lock Brakes	Std	Std
Manual Transmission	N/A	N/A
4.6L 178 hp CNG	$5,487	**$6,165
Air Conditioning	Std	Std
Power Steering	Std	Std
Cruise Control	Std	Std
Power Windows	Std	Std
AM/FM Stereo Cassette	Std	Std
Steering Wheel, Tilt	Std	Std
Rear Defroster	Std	Std
*Options Price	$0	$0
*Total Price	**$20,438**	**$21,905**
Target Price	$21,241	
Destination Charge	$605	
Avg. Tax & Fees	$1,221	
Total Target $	**$23,067**	
Average Dealer Option Cost:	89%	
12 Month Price Increase:	1%	

Ownership Costs (Projected)

Cost Area	5 Year Cost	Rating
Depreciation	$11,347	○
Financing ($382/month)	$4,487	
Insurance	$7,140	○
State Fees	$914	
Fuel (Hwy 24 City 17)	$3,628	◉
Maintenance	$2,950	○
Repairs	$905	○

Warranty/Maintenance Info

Major Tune-Up (100K mile int.)	$284	◉
Minor Tune-Up (30K mile int.)	$100	○
Brake Service	$253	○
Overall Warranty	3 yr/36k	○
Drivetrain Warranty	3 yr/36k	○
Rust Warranty	5 yr/unlim. mi	○
Maintenance Warranty	N/A	
Roadside Assistance	3 yr/36k	

For 1999, the Crown Victoria now includes standard antilock brakes, an AM/FM stereo cassette and updated paint colors. Also new this year, all-speed traction control is now a freestanding option. Standard features include a SecuriLock anti-theft system and 16 inch wheels with wheel covers. The Handling and Performance Package is available as an option and includes revised suspension, low-profile tires with aluminum wheels, rear air suspension, dual exhaust and a 3.27 rear axle ratio.

Ownership Costs By Year (Projected)

$2,000 $4,000 $6,000 $8,000 $10,000 $12,000

■ 1999
■ 2000
■ 2001
□ 2002
□ 2003

Resale Value

1999	2000	2001	2002	2003
$20,565	$18,117	$15,967	$13,869	$11,720

Cumulative Costs

	1999	2000	2001	2002	2003
Annual	$6,351	$6,057	$5,971	$6,315	$6,677
Total	$6,351	$12,408	$18,379	$24,694	$31,371

Projected Costs (5yr)

Relative	This Car
$32,121	$31,371
Cost/Mile 46¢	Cost/Mile 45¢

Ownership Cost Value

○ Better Than Average

Ford Crown Victoria LX
4 Door Sedan

Large

 4.6L 200 hp Gas Fuel Inject.

 8 Cylinder "V"

 Automatic 4 Speed

 2 Wheel Rear

 Dual Airbags Std

Purchase Price

Car Item	Dealer Cost	List
Base Price	**$22,277**	**$23,925**
Anti-Lock Brakes	Std	Std
Manual Transmission	N/A	N/A
4.6L 178 hp CNG	$5,487	**$6,165
Air Conditioning	Std	Std
Power Steering	Std	Std
Cruise Control	Std	Std
Power Windows	Std	Std
AM/FM Stereo Cassette	Std	Std
Steering Wheel, Tilt	Std	Std
Rear Defroster	Std	Std
*Options Price	$0	$0
*Total Price	**$22,277**	**$23,925**
Target Price	$23,190	
Destination Charge	$605	
Avg. Tax & Fees	$1,329	
Total Target $	**$25,124**	
Average Dealer Option Cost:	89%	
12 Month Price Increase:	None	

Ownership Costs (Projected)

Cost Area	5 Year Cost	Rating
Depreciation	$13,079	○
Financing ($416/month)	$4,887	
Insurance	$7,140	○
State Fees	$994	
Fuel (Hwy 24 City 17)	$3,628	◉
Maintenance	$2,950	○
Repairs	$905	○

Warranty/Maintenance Info

Major Tune-Up (100K mile int.)	$284	◉
Minor Tune-Up (30K mile int.)	$100	○
Brake Service	$253	○
Overall Warranty	3 yr/36k	○
Drivetrain Warranty	3 yr/36k	○
Rust Warranty	5 yr/unlim. mi	○
Maintenance Warranty	N/A	
Roadside Assistance	3 yr/36k	

For 1999, the Crown Victoria LX is carried over from last year and now includes standard antilock brakes and updated paint colors. Also new, optional leather seating surfaces are added to the Comfort Plus Group and all-speed traction control is now a freestanding option. Standard features include a remote keyless entry system, cassette player and six-way power driver's seat. Options include a premium audio system, CD player, universal garage door opener and a Handling and Performance Package.

Ownership Costs By Year (Projected)

$2,000 $4,000 $6,000 $8,000 $10,000 $12,000 $14,000

■ 1999
■ 2000
■ 2001
□ 2002
□ 2003

Resale Value

1999	2000	2001	2002	2003
$21,276	$18,727	$16,478	$14,284	$12,045

Cumulative Costs

	1999	2000	2001	2002	2003
Annual	$7,853	$6,286	$6,169	$6,477	$6,798
Total	$7,853	$14,139	$20,308	$26,785	$33,583

Projected Costs (5yr)

Relative	This Car
$33,751	$33,583
Cost/Mile 48¢	Cost/Mile 48¢

Ownership Cost Value

○ Average

 ● Poor
 ◉ Worse Than Average
 ○ Average
 ○ Better Than Average
 ○ Excellent
⊖ Insufficient Information

63

Refer to *Section 3: Annotated Vehicle Charts* for an explanation of these charts.

Ford Escort ZX2 Cool
2 Door Coupe

Subcompact

2.0L 130 hp Gas Fuel Inject.	4 Cylinder In-Line	Manual 5 Speed	2 Wheel Front	Depowered Dual Airbags Std

Purchase Price

Car Item	Dealer Cost	List
Base Price	**$10,865**	**$11,610**
Anti-Lock Brakes	$356	$400
Automatic 4 Speed	$725	$815
Optional Engine	N/A	N/A
Air Conditioning	$708	$795
Power Steering	Std	Std
Cruise Control	N/A	N/A
Power Windows	N/A	N/A
AM/FM Stereo Cassette	$165	**$185
Steering Wheel, Tilt	N/A	N/A
Rear Defroster	$169	$190
*Options Price	$877	$985
*Total Price	$11,742	$12,595
Target Price	$12,069	
Destination Charge	$415	
Avg. Tax & Fees	$705	
Total Target $	**$13,189**	
Average Dealer Option Cost:	**89%**	
12 Month Price Increase:	None	

The 1999 Escort ZX2 Cool is equipped with many standard features. These features include dual depowered airbags, a coin holder, cassette storage integrated with the center console, a separate clock and a new storage bin. Additional standard features include a battery saver that turns off interior lights after ten minutes and a self-adjusting clutch linkage. Optional features include an antilock braking system, all-door remote entry with anti-theft alarm, and air conditioning.

Ownership Costs (Projected)

Cost Area	5 Year Cost	Rating
Depreciation	$6,745	◯
Financing ($219/month)	$2,566	
Insurance	$7,643	●
State Fees	$533	
Fuel (Hwy 33 City 25)	$2,556	◉
Maintenance	$3,517	◉
Repairs	$755	◉

Warranty/Maintenance Info

Major Tune-Up (100K mile int.)	$212	◯
Minor Tune-Up (30K mile int.)	$67	◯
Brake Service	$261	◉
Overall Warranty	3 yr/36k	◉
Drivetrain Warranty	3 yr/36k	◉
Rust Warranty	5 yr/unlim. mi	◯
Maintenance Warranty	N/A	
Roadside Assistance	3 yr/36k	

Ownership Costs By Year (Projected)

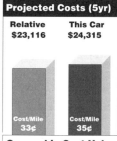

- 1999
- 2000
- 2001
- 2002
- 2003

Resale Value

1999	2000	2001	2002	2003
$11,516	$10,153	$8,954	$7,714	$6,444

Cumulative Costs

	1999	2000	2001	2002	2003
Annual	$4,665	$4,241	$4,498	$5,243	$5,668
Total	$4,665	$8,906	$13,404	$18,647	$24,315

Projected Costs (5yr)

Relative	This Car
$23,116	$24,315
Cost/Mile 33¢	Cost/Mile 35¢

Ownership Cost Value

◯ Average

Ford Escort ZX2 Hot
2 Door Coupe

Subcompact

2.0L 130 hp Gas Fuel Inject.	4 Cylinder In-Line	Manual 5 Speed	2 Wheel Front	Depowered Dual Airbags Std

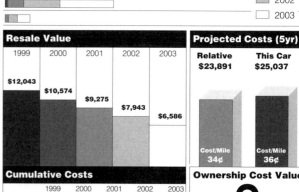

Cool Model Shown

Purchase Price

Car Item	Dealer Cost	List
Base Price	**$12,394**	**$13,290**
Anti-Lock Brakes	$356	$400
Automatic 4 Speed	$725	$815
Optional Engine	N/A	N/A
Air Conditioning	Std	Std
Power Steering	Std	Std
Cruise Control	Pkg	Pkg
Power Windows	Pkg	Pkg
AM/FM Stereo Cassette	$85	$95
Steering Wheel, Tilt	Pkg	Pkg
Rear Defroster	Std	Std
*Options Price	$85	$95
*Total Price	$12,479	$13,385
Target Price	$12,839	
Destination Charge	$415	
Avg. Tax & Fees	$747	
Total Target $	**$14,001**	
Average Dealer Option Cost:	**89%**	
12 Month Price Increase:	1%	

The 1999 Escort ZX2 Hot is equipped with many standard features, including an AM/FM cassette stereo with premium speakers, air conditioning, all-door keyless remote entry system with panic alarm and rear window defroster. Battery rundown protection and dual power mirrors are also standard. Option packages are also available for this model. These packages include the Comfort Group, Power Group and the Sport Group. The ZX2 Hot is targeted mainly to younger, more affluent female drivers.

Ownership Costs (Projected)

Cost Area	5 Year Cost	Rating
Depreciation	$7,415	◉
Financing ($232/month)	$2,723	
Insurance	$7,506	●
State Fees	$565	
Fuel (Hwy 33 City 25)	$2,556	◯
Maintenance	$3,517	◉
Repairs	$755	◉

Warranty/Maintenance Info

Major Tune-Up (100K mile int.)	$212	◯
Minor Tune-Up (30K mile int.)	$67	◯
Brake Service	$261	◉
Overall Warranty	3 yr/36k	◉
Drivetrain Warranty	3 yr/36k	◉
Rust Warranty	5 yr/unlim. mi	◯
Maintenance Warranty	N/A	
Roadside Assistance	3 yr/36k	

Ownership Costs By Year (Projected)

- 1999
- 2000
- 2001
- 2002
- 2003

Resale Value

1999	2000	2001	2002	2003
$12,043	$10,574	$9,275	$7,943	$6,586

Cumulative Costs

	1999	2000	2001	2002	2003
Annual	$4,985	$4,371	$4,608	$5,334	$5,739
Total	$4,985	$9,356	$13,964	$19,298	$25,037

Projected Costs (5yr)

Relative	This Car
$23,891	$25,037
Cost/Mile 34¢	Cost/Mile 36¢

Ownership Cost Value

◯ Average

64

* Includes shaded options
** Other purchase requirements apply
*** Price includes other options

● Poor ◉ Worse Than Average ◯ Average ◯ Better Than Average ◯ Excellent ⊖ Insufficient Information

Refer to Section 3: Annotated Vehicle Charts for an explanation of these charts.

Ford Escort LX
4 Door Sedan

Compact

2.0L 110 hp Gas Fuel Inject.	4 Cylinder In-Line	Manual 5 Speed	2 Wheel Front	Dual Airbags Std

Purchase Price

Car Item	Dealer Cost	List
Base Price	**$10,724**	**$11,455**
Anti-Lock Brakes	$356	$400
Automatic 4 Speed	$725	$815
Optional Engine	N/A	N/A
Air Conditioning	$708	$795
Power Steering	Std	Std
Cruise Control	N/A	N/A
Power Windows	N/A	N/A
AM/FM Stereo Cassette	$165	**$185
Steering Wheel, Tilt	N/A	N/A
Rear Defroster	$169	$190
*Options Price	$1,602	$1,800
*Total Price	**$12,326**	**$13,255**
Target Price	$12,672	
Destination Charge	$415	
Avg. Tax & Fees	$739	
Total Target $	**$13,826**	
Average Dealer Option Cost:	**89%**	
12 Month Price Increase:	2%	

For 1999, the Escort LX sedan offers many of the same optional features as the SE models. These options include front and rear floor mats, an antilock braking system, a Smokers Package and engine block heater. Standard sedan features include height-adjustable front shoulder belts, a 12 volt power outlet, solar-tinted glass and full trunk trim. Child safety rear door locks, front and rear stabilizer bars, rear seat heating ducts and power steering are also standard.

Ownership Costs (Projected)

Cost Area	5 Year Cost	Rating
Depreciation	$7,219	◯
Financing ($229/month)	$2,689	
Insurance	$7,463	◉
State Fees	$560	
Fuel (Hwy 34 City 25)	$2,515	◯
Maintenance	$3,777	●
Repairs	$730	◯

Warranty/Maintenance Info

Major Tune-Up (100K mile int.)	$212	◯
Minor Tune-Up (30K mile int.)	$67	◯
Brake Service	$261	◉
Overall Warranty	3 yr/36k	◯
Drivetrain Warranty	3 yr/36k	◯
Rust Warranty	5 yr/unlim. mi	◯
Maintenance Warranty	N/A	
Roadside Assistance	3 yr/36k	

Ownership Costs By Year (Projected)

$2,000 $4,000 $6,000 $8,000

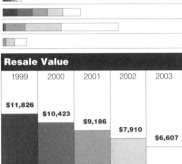

■ 1999
■ 2000
■ 2001
▨ 2002
□ 2003

Resale Value

1999	2000	2001	2002	2003
$11,826	$10,423	$9,186	$7,910	$6,607

Cumulative Costs

	1999	2000	2001	2002	2003
Annual	$4,999	$4,279	$4,645	$5,244	$5,786
Total	$4,999	$9,278	$13,923	$19,167	$24,953

Projected Costs (5yr)

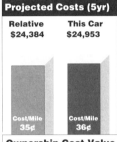

Relative	This Car
$24,384	$24,953
Cost/Mile 35¢	Cost/Mile 36¢

Ownership Cost Value

◯
Average

Ford Escort SE
4 Door Sedan

Compact

2.0L 110 hp Gas Fuel Inject.	4 Cylinder In-Line	Manual 5 Speed	2 Wheel Front	Dual Airbags Std

Purchase Price

Car Item	Dealer Cost	List
Base Price	**$12,071**	**$12,935**
Anti-Lock Brakes	$356	$400
Automatic 4 Speed	$725	$815
Optional Engine	N/A	N/A
Air Conditioning	Std	Std
Power Steering	Std	Std
Cruise Control	Pkg	Pkg
Power Windows	Pkg	Pkg
AM/FM Stereo Cass/CD	$263	$295
Steering Wheel, Tilt	Pkg	Pkg
Rear Defroster	Std	Std
*Options Price	$988	$1,110
*Total Price	**$13,059**	**$14,045**
Target Price	$13,437	
Destination Charge	$415	
Avg. Tax & Fees	$781	
Total Target $	**$14,633**	
Average Dealer Option Cost:	**89%**	
12 Month Price Increase:	3%	

Unique standard features for the 1999 Escort SE sedan are now available. These features include an AM/FM cassette stereo with premium speakers, full trunk trim, air conditioning, all-door remote entry system (with perimeter anti-theft) and rear window defroster. Option packages are also available, such as the SE Comfort Group, SE Power Group and the SE Sport Group. Optional features include an antilock brake system, Smokers Package and front and rear floor mats.

Ownership Costs (Projected)

Cost Area	5 Year Cost	Rating
Depreciation	$8,108	◉
Financing ($243/month)	$2,847	
Insurance	$7,506	◉
State Fees	$592	
Fuel (Hwy 34 City 25)	$2,515	◯
Maintenance	$3,777	●
Repairs	$730	◯

Warranty/Maintenance Info

Major Tune-Up (100K mile int.)	$212	◯
Minor Tune-Up (30K mile int.)	$67	◯
Brake Service	$261	◉
Overall Warranty	3 yr/36k	◯
Drivetrain Warranty	3 yr/36k	◯
Rust Warranty	5 yr/unlim. mi	◯
Maintenance Warranty	N/A	
Roadside Assistance	3 yr/36k	

Ownership Costs By Year (Projected)

$2,000 $4,000 $6,000 $8,000 $10,000

■ 1999
■ 2000
■ 2001
▨ 2002
□ 2003

Resale Value

1999	2000	2001	2002	2003
$12,416	$10,835	$9,426	$7,987	$6,525

Cumulative Costs

	1999	2000	2001	2002	2003
Annual	$5,285	$4,516	$4,865	$5,442	$5,967
Total	$5,285	$9,801	$14,666	$20,108	$26,075

Projected Costs (5yr)

Relative	This Car
$25,028	$26,075
Cost/Mile 36¢	Cost/Mile 37¢

Ownership Cost Value

◉
Worse Than Average

Ford Escort SE
4 Door Wagon

Small Wagon

2.0L 110 hp Gas Fuel Inject.	4 Cylinder In-Line	Manual 5 Speed	2 Wheel Front	Dual Airbags Std

Purchase Price

Car Item	Dealer Cost	List
Base Price	**$13,163**	**$14,135**
Anti-Lock Brakes	$356	$400
Automatic 4 Speed	$725	$815
Optional Engine	N/A	N/A
Air Conditioning	Std	Std
Power Steering	Std	Std
Cruise Control	Pkg	Pkg
Power Windows	Pkg	Pkg
AM/FM Stereo Cassette	Std	Std
Steering Wheel, Tilt	Pkg	Pkg
Rear Defroster	Std	Std
*Options Price	**$725**	**$815**
*Total Price	**$13,888**	**$14,950**
Target Price	$14,302	
Destination Charge	$415	
Avg. Tax & Fees	$829	
Total Target $	**$15,546**	
Average Dealer Option Cost:	**89%**	
12 Month Price Increase:	3%	

Unique standard features are introduced for the 1999 Escort SE wagon. Features not available on the other four Escort models but standard for the SE wagon include a cargo area cover, luggage rack and rear window wiper/washer. Option packages are also available, such as the SE Comfort Group, SE Power Group and SE Sport Group. A variety of optional equipment is also available, including an antilock braking system, Smokers Package, front and rear floor mats and engine block heater.

Ownership Costs (Projected)

Cost Area	5 Year Cost	Rating
Depreciation	$8,772	◕
Financing ($258/month)	$3,023	
Insurance	$7,688	◕
State Fees	$628	
Fuel (Hwy 34 City 25)	$2,515	○
Maintenance	$3,764	◕
Repairs	$730	○

Warranty/Maintenance Info

Major Tune-Up	(100K mile int.)	$212	○
Minor Tune-Up	(30K mile int.)	$67	○
Brake Service		$261	◕
Overall Warranty		3 yr/36k	○
Drivetrain Warranty		3 yr/36k	○
Rust Warranty		5 yr/unlim. mi	○
Maintenance Warranty		N/A	
Roadside Assistance		3 yr/36k	

Ownership Costs By Year (Projected)

$2,000 $4,000 $6,000 $8,000 $10,000

- 1999
- 2000
- 2001
- 2002
- 2003

Resale Value

1999	2000	2001	2002	2003
$12,987	$11,320	$9,830	$8,313	$6,774

Cumulative Costs

	1999	2000	2001	2002	2003
Annual	$5,731	$4,694	$5,026	$5,574	$6,095
Total	$5,731	$10,425	$15,451	$21,025	$27,120

Projected Costs (5yr)

Relative $26,442	This Car $27,120
Cost/Mile 38¢	Cost/Mile 39¢

Ownership Cost Value

○ Average

Ford Mustang
2 Door Coupe

Base Sport

3.8L 190 hp Gas Fuel Inject.	6 Cylinder "V"	Manual 5 Speed	2 Wheel Rear	Dual Airbags Std

Purchase Price

Car Item	Dealer Cost	List
Base Price	**$15,103**	**$16,470**
Anti-Lock Brakes	$445	$500
Automatic 4 Speed	$725	$815
Optional Engine	N/A	N/A
Air Conditioning	Std	Std
Power Steering	Std	Std
Cruise Control	Pkg	Pkg
Power Windows	Std	Std
AM/FM Stereo Cassette	Std	Std
Steering Wheel, Tilt	Std	Std
Other Options Cost	$490	$550
*Options Price	**$935**	**$1,050**
*Total Price	**$16,038**	**$17,520**
Target Price	$16,687	
Destination Charge	$525	
Avg. Tax & Fees	$968	
Total Target $	**$18,180**	
Average Dealer Option Cost:	**89%**	
12 Month Price Increase:	3%	

Celebrating its 35th anniversary, the Mustang coupe has many new enhancements. The most notable comes as a 27% increase in power for the 3.8L engine, now up to 190 hp with 220 lb-ft torque. More enhancements include standard 15 inch cast aluminum wheels, optional all-speed traction control and optional six-way power driver's seat. Exterior enhancements include a restyled hood scoop, front/rear fascias, grille and headlamps and taillamps. The base model will have 35th Anniversary badging.

Ownership Costs (Projected)

Cost Area	5 Year Cost	Rating
Depreciation	$8,278	○
Financing ($301/month)	$3,537	
Insurance	$9,365	●
State Fees	$733	
Fuel (Hwy 29 City 20)	$3,041	○
Maintenance	$2,638	○
Repairs	$799	○

Warranty/Maintenance Info

Major Tune-Up	(100K mile int.)	$362	◕
Minor Tune-Up	(30K mile int.)	$105	○
Brake Service		$252	○
Overall Warranty		3 yr/36k	○
Drivetrain Warranty		3 yr/36k	○
Rust Warranty		5 yr/unlim. mi	○
Maintenance Warranty		N/A	
Roadside Assistance		3 yr/36k	

Ownership Costs By Year (Projected)

$2,000 $4,000 $6,000 $8,000 $10,000

- 1999
- 2000
- 2001
- 2002
- 2003

Resale Value

1999	2000	2001	2002	2003
$16,839	$14,931	$13,277	$11,635	$9,902

Cumulative Costs

	1999	2000	2001	2002	2003
Annual	$5,135	$5,533	$5,406	$6,140	$6,177
Total	$5,135	$10,668	$16,074	$22,214	$28,391

Projected Costs (5yr)

Relative $28,071	This Car $28,391
Cost/Mile 40¢	Cost/Mile 41¢

Ownership Cost Value

○ Average

66

* Includes shaded options

** Other purchase requirements apply

*** Price includes other options

● Poor	◕ Worse Than Average	◒ Average	○ Better Than Average	○ Excellent	⊖ Insufficient Information

Refer to *Section 3: Annotated Vehicle Charts* for an explanation of these charts.

Ford Mustang GT
2 Door Coupe

4.6L 260 hp Gas Fuel Inject.	8 Cylinder "V"	Manual 5 Speed	2 Wheel Rear	Dual Airbags Std

Base Sport

Base Model Shown

Purchase Price

Car Item	Dealer Cost	List
Base Price	**$19,019**	**$20,870**
Anti-Lock Brakes	Std	Std
Automatic 4 Speed	$725	$815
Optional Engine	N/A	N/A
Air Conditioning	Std	Std
Power Steering	Std	Std
Cruise Control	Pkg	Pkg
Power Windows	Std	Std
AM/FM Stereo Cassette	Std	Std
Steering Wheel, Tilt	Std	Std
Other Options Cost	$490	$550
*Options Price	**$490**	**$550**
*Total Price	**$19,509**	**$21,420**
Target Price	$20,376	
Destination Charge	$525	
Avg. Tax & Fees	$1,173	
Total Target $	**$22,074**	
Average Dealer Option Cost:	**89%**	
12 Month Price Increase:	2%	

Ownership Costs (Projected)

Cost Area	5 Year Cost	Rating
Depreciation	$10,419	◐
Financing ($366/month)	$4,295	◐
Insurance (Performance)	$13,236	●
State Fees	$892	○
Fuel (Hwy 24 City 17)	$3,628	●
Maintenance	$2,702	○
Repairs	$799	○

Warranty/Maintenance Info

Major Tune-Up (100K mile int.)	$324	○
Minor Tune-Up (30K mile int.)	$127	○
Brake Service	$252	○
Overall Warranty	3 yr/36k	○
Drivetrain Warranty	3 yr/36k	○
Rust Warranty	5 yr/unlim. mi	○
Maintenance Warranty	N/A	
Roadside Assistance	3 yr/36k	

Ownership Costs By Year (Projected)

$2,000 $4,000 $6,000 $8,000 $10,000 $12,000 $14,000

- 1999
- 2000
- 2001
- 2002
- 2003

Resale Value

1999	2000	2001	2002	2003
$20,414	$18,035	$15,922	$13,830	$11,655

Cumulative Costs

	1999	2000	2001	2002	2003
Annual	$6,602	$7,121	$6,972	$7,707	$7,569
Total	$6,602	$13,723	$20,695	$28,402	$35,971

Projected Costs (5yr)

Relative $33,877	This Car $35,971
Cost/Mile 48¢	Cost/Mile 51¢

Ownership Cost Value

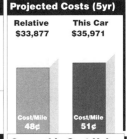

● Poor

The 1999 Mustang GT coupe includes all the same new features and the base model Mustang coupe. The most notable new feature of the Mustang GT is the standard power four wheel disc antilock braking system. The next notable enhancement is an 11% increase in power for the 4.6L engine, now up to 260 hp and 302 lb-ft of torque. New additional enhancements for the Mustang GT include 16 inch forged aluminum wheels, optional 17 inch forged aluminum wheels and standard two-tone cloth seats.

Ford Mustang Cobra
2 Door Coupe

4.6L 305 hp Gas Fuel Inject.	8 Cylinder "V"	Manual 5 Speed	2 Wheel Rear	Dual Airbags Std

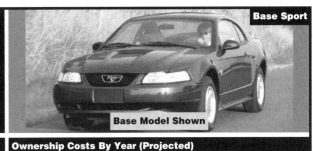

Base Sport

Base Model Shown

Purchase Price

Car Item	Dealer Cost	List
Base Price	**$24,893**	**$27,470**
Anti-Lock Brakes	Std	Std
Automatic Transmission	N/A	N/A
Optional Engine	N/A	N/A
Air Conditioning	Std	Std
Power Steering	Std	Std
Cruise Control	Std	Std
Power Windows	Std	Std
AM/FM Stereo Cassette	Std	Std
Steering Wheel, Tilt	Std	Std
Rear Defroster	Std	Std
*Options Price	**$0**	**$0**
*Total Price	**$24,893**	**$27,470**
Target Price	$26,449	
Destination Charge	$525	
Avg. Tax & Fees	$1,507	
Total Target $	**$28,481**	
Average Dealer Option Cost:	**89%**	
12 Month Price Increase:	N/A	

Ownership Costs (Projected)

Cost Area	5 Year Cost	Rating
Depreciation	$12,448	○
Financing ($472/month)	$5,540	◐
Insurance (Perf.) [Est.]	$14,809	●
State Fees	$1,133	○
Fuel (Hwy 26 City 17 -Prem.)	$4,134	◉
Maintenance	$2,985	○
Repairs	$931	○

Warranty/Maintenance Info

Major Tune-Up (100K mile int.)	$324	○
Minor Tune-Up (30K mile int.)	$127	○
Brake Service	$252	○
Overall Warranty	3 yr/36k	○
Drivetrain Warranty	3 yr/36k	○
Rust Warranty	5 yr/unlim. mi	○
Maintenance Warranty	N/A	
Roadside Assistance	3 yr/36k	

Ownership Costs By Year (Projected)

$5,000 $10,000 $15,000

- 1999
- 2000
- 2001
- 2002
- 2003

Resale Value

1999	2000	2001	2002	2003
$25,771	$23,112	$20,742	$18,416	$16,033

Cumulative Costs

	1999	2000	2001	2002	2003
Annual	$8,533	$8,205	$7,968	$8,907	$8,368
Total	$8,533	$16,738	$24,706	$33,613	$41,981

Projected Costs (5yr)

Relative $41,162	This Car $41,981
Cost/Mile 59¢	Cost/Mile 60¢

Ownership Cost Value

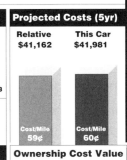

○ Average

The Mustang Cobra coupe includes all the same new features and the base model Mustang coupe. Celebrating the Mustang coupe's 35th anniversary, the Mustang Cobra is built by Ford's Special Vehicle Team (SVT) and has many new enhancements for 1999. New standard features for this year are leather sport bucket seats, a theft deterrent system and an AM/FM cassette audio system. Exterior enhancements include a restyled hood scoop, front/rear fascias, grille and headlamps and taillamps.

Poor	Worse Than Average	Average	Better Than Average	Excellent	Insufficient Information

67

Refer to *Section 3: Annotated Vehicle Charts* for an explanation of these charts.

Ford Mustang
2 Door Convertible

Base Sport

| 3.8L 190 hp Gas Fuel Inject. | 6 Cylinder "V" | Manual 5 Speed | 2 Wheel Rear | Dual Airbags Std |

GT Model Shown

Purchase Price

Car Item	Dealer Cost	List
Base Price	**$19,197**	**$21,070**
Anti-Lock Brakes	$445	$500
Automatic 4 Speed	$725	$815
Optional Engine	N/A	N/A
Air Conditioning	Std	Std
Power Steering	Std	Std
Cruise Control	Pkg	Pkg
Power Windows	Std	Std
AM/FM Stereo Cassette	Std	Std
Steering Wheel, Tilt	Std	Std
Other Options Cost	$490	$550
*Options Price	**$935**	**$1,050**
*Total Price	**$20,132**	**$22,120**
Target Price	$21,032	
Destination Charge	$525	
Avg. Tax & Fees	$1,209	
Total Target $	**$22,766**	
Average Dealer Option Cost:	**89%**	
12 Month Price Increase:	3%	

The 1999 Mustang convertible includes all the same new features as the Mustang coupe. In addition to these new features the convertible has improved rigidity due to a new box section brace. More new enhancements for this model year include an improved turning diameter by as much a three feet and a new standard rear axle ratio of 3.27 on all models. Interior highlights such as the Pony design embroidered on the upper front seat backs and a new analog cluster with new graphics are also new.

Ownership Costs (Projected)

Cost Area	5 Year Cost	Rating
Depreciation	$10,808	◉
Financing ($377/month)	$4,429	
Insurance	$10,589	●
State Fees	$919	
Fuel (Hwy 29 City 20)	$3,041	○
Maintenance	$2,638	○
Repairs	$799	◉

Warranty/Maintenance Info

Major Tune-Up (100K mile int.)	$362	●
Minor Tune-Up (30K mile int.)	$105	○
Brake Service	$252	◉
Overall Warranty	3 yr/36k	◉
Drivetrain Warranty	3 yr/36k	◉
Rust Warranty	5 yr/unlim. mi	○
Maintenance Warranty	N/A	
Roadside Assistance	3 yr/36k	

Ownership Costs By Year (Projected)

$2,000 $4,000 $6,000 $8,000 $10,000 $12,000

■ 1999
■ 2000
■ 2001
□ 2002
□ 2003

Resale Value

1999	2000	2001	2002	2003
$20,427	$18,098	$16,049	$14,039	$11,958

Cumulative Costs

	1999	2000	2001	2002	2003
Annual	$6,716	$6,481	$6,267	$6,908	$6,851
Total	$6,716	$13,197	$19,464	$26,372	$33,223

Projected Costs (5yr)

Relative	This Car
$34,828	$33,223
Cost/Mile 50¢	Cost/Mile 47¢

Ownership Cost Value

○ Excellent

Ford Mustang GT
2 Door Convertible

Base Sport

| 4.6L 260 hp Gas Fuel Inject. | 8 Cylinder "V" | Manual 5 Speed | 2 Wheel Rear | Dual Airbags Std |

Purchase Price

Car Item	Dealer Cost	List
Base Price	**$22,579**	**$24,870**
Anti-Lock Brakes	Std	Std
Automatic 4 Speed	$725	$815
Optional Engine	N/A	N/A
Air Conditioning	Std	Std
Power Steering	Std	Std
Cruise Control	Pkg	Pkg
Power Windows	Std	Std
AM/FM Stereo Cassette	Std	Std
Steering Wheel, Tilt	Std	Std
Other Options Cost	$490	$550
*Options Price	**$490**	**$550**
*Total Price	**$23,069**	**$25,420**
Target Price	$24,174	
Destination Charge	$525	
Avg. Tax & Fees	$1,383	
Total Target $	**$26,082**	
Average Dealer Option Cost:	**89%**	
12 Month Price Increase:	2%	

The 1999 Mustang GT convertible includes all the same new enhancements as the Mustang GT coupe and the base model convertible. In addition to these enhancements come the new exterior color Electric Green Clearcoat Metallic and three new interior colors: Dark Charcoal, Medium Parchment and Oxford White. Another change for this year is the addition of an optional Smokers Package. Improved steering and braking are also part of this year's refinements to the Mustang.

Ownership Costs (Projected)

Cost Area	5 Year Cost	Rating
Depreciation	$12,170	◉
Financing ($432/month)	$5,075	
Insurance (Performance)	$14,509	●
State Fees	$1,052	
Fuel (Hwy 24 City 17)	$3,628	●
Maintenance	$2,702	○
Repairs	$799	◉

Warranty/Maintenance Info

Major Tune-Up (100K mile int.)	$324	◉
Minor Tune-Up (30K mile int.)	$127	○
Brake Service	$252	◉
Overall Warranty	3 yr/36k	◉
Drivetrain Warranty	3 yr/36k	◉
Rust Warranty	5 yr/unlim. mi	○
Maintenance Warranty	N/A	
Roadside Assistance	3 yr/36k	

Ownership Costs By Year (Projected)

$5,000 $10,000 $15,000

■ 1999
■ 2000
■ 2001
□ 2002
□ 2003

Resale Value

1999	2000	2001	2002	2003
$23,490	$20,878	$18,549	$16,261	$13,912

Cumulative Costs

	1999	2000	2001	2002	2003
Annual	$8,081	$7,854	$7,635	$8,295	$8,070
Total	$8,081	$15,935	$23,570	$31,865	$39,935

Projected Costs (5yr)

Relative	This Car
$38,929	$39,935
Cost/Mile 56¢	Cost/Mile 57¢

Ownership Cost Value

● Worse Than Average

Ford Mustang Cobra
2 Door Convertible

4.6L 305 hp Gas Fuel Inject. | 8 Cylinder "V" | Manual 5 Speed | 2 Wheel Rear | Dual Airbags Std

Base Sport

GT Model Shown

Purchase Price

Car Item	Dealer Cost	List
Base Price	**$28,453**	**$31,470**
Anti-Lock Brakes	Std	Std
Automatic Transmission	N/A	N/A
Optional Engine	N/A	N/A
Air Conditioning	Std	Std
Power Steering	Std	Std
Cruise Control	Std	Std
Power Windows	Std	Std
AM/FM Stereo Cassette	Std	Std
Steering Wheel, Tilt	Std	Std
Rear Defroster	Std	Std
*Options Price	$0	$0
*Total Price	**$28,453**	**$31,470**
Target Price	$30,346	
Destination Charge	$525	
Avg. Tax & Fees	$1,722	
Total Target $	**$32,593**	
Average Dealer Option Cost:	**89%**	
12 Month Price Increase:	N/A	

The 1999 Mustang Cobra convertible includes all the same new features as the Mustang Cobra coupe. In addition to these new features, the convertible has improved rigidity due to a new box section brace. More new enhancements for this model year include an improved turning diameter by as much a three feet and a new standard rear axle ratio of 3.27 on all models. Improved steering and braking are also part of this year's refinements to the Mustang.

Ownership Costs (Projected)

Cost Area	5 Year Cost	Rating
Depreciation	$13,949	◯
Financing ($540/month)	$6,341	
Insurance (Perf.) [Est.]	$16,254	●
State Fees	$1,293	
Fuel (Hwy 26 City 17 -Prem.)	$4,134	◉
Maintenance	$2,985	◯
Repairs	$931	◯

Warranty/Maintenance Info

Major Tune-Up (100K mile int.)	$324	◯
Minor Tune-Up (30K mile int.)	$127	◯
Brake Service	$252	◯
Overall Warranty	3 yr/36k	◯
Drivetrain Warranty	3 yr/36k	◯
Rust Warranty	5 yr/unlim. mi	◯
Maintenance Warranty	N/A	
Roadside Assistance	3 yr/36k	

Ownership Costs By Year (Projected)

$5,000 — $10,000 — $15,000 — $20,000

1999 / 2000 / 2001 / 2002 / 2003

Resale Value

1999	2000	2001	2002	2003
$29,852	$26,773	$24,020	$21,345	$18,644

Cumulative Costs

	1999	2000	2001	2002	2003
Annual	$9,152	$9,164	$8,837	$9,683	$9,051
Total	$9,152	$18,316	$27,153	$36,836	$45,887

Projected Costs (5yr)

Relative $44,829	This Car $45,887
Cost/Mile 64¢	Cost/Mile 66¢

Ownership Cost Value

◯ Average

Ford Taurus LX
4 Door Sedan

3.0L 145 hp Gas Fuel Inject. | 6 Cylinder "V" | Automatic 4 Speed | 2 Wheel Front | Dual Airbags Std

Midsize

Purchase Price

Car Item	Dealer Cost	List
Base Price	**$16,110**	**$17,445**
Anti-Lock Brakes	$534	$600
Manual Transmission	N/A	N/A
3.0L 200 hp Gas	$441	$495
Air Conditioning	Std	Std
Power Steering	Std	Std
Cruise Control	$191	$215
Power Windows	Std	Std
AM/FM Stereo Cassette	$165	$185
Steering Wheel, Tilt	Std	Std
Other Options Cost	$245	$275
*Options Price	$1,576	$1,770
*Total Price	**$17,686**	**$19,215**
Target Price	$18,581	
Destination Charge	$550	
Avg. Tax & Fees	$1,072	
Total Target $	**$20,203**	
Average Dealer Option Cost:	**89%**	
12 Month Price Increase:	None	

For 1999, the Taurus LX features the Light Group and cruise control as optional equipment. Additional options include front and rear floor mats, power door locks and an antilock braking system. Standard interior amenities include cloth bench seats, air conditioning and power windows. Standard safety features for the LX include variable intermittent windshield wipers, a rear defroster and child safety locks. Two new exterior colors for 1999 are Tropic Green and Graphite Blue.

Ownership Costs (Projected)

Cost Area	5 Year Cost	Rating
Depreciation	$11,638	◉
Financing ($335/month)	$3,930	
Insurance	$6,606	◯
State Fees	$804	
Fuel (Hwy 26 City 18)	$3,387	●
Maintenance	$3,228	◯
Repairs	$1,000	◉

Warranty/Maintenance Info

Major Tune-Up (100K mile int.)	$256	◯
Minor Tune-Up (30K mile int.)	$108	◯
Brake Service	$220	◯
Overall Warranty	3 yr/36k	◯
Drivetrain Warranty	3 yr/36k	◯
Rust Warranty	5 yr/unlim. mi	◯
Maintenance Warranty	N/A	
Roadside Assistance	3 yr/36k	

Ownership Costs By Year (Projected)

$2,000 $4,000 $6,000 $8,000 $10,000 $12,000

1999 / 2000 / 2001 / 2002 / 2003

Resale Value

1999	2000	2001	2002	2003
$16,139	$14,045	$12,230	$10,372	$8,565

Cumulative Costs

	1999	2000	2001	2002	2003
Annual	$7,549	$5,373	$5,328	$6,296	$6,047
Total	$7,549	$12,922	$18,250	$24,546	$30,593

Projected Costs (5yr)

Relative $29,154	This Car $30,593
Cost/Mile 42¢	Cost/Mile 44¢

Ownership Cost Value

◉ Worse Than Average

---

* Includes shaded options

** Other purchase requirements apply

*** Price includes other options

 Poor   Worse Than Average   Average ◯ Better Than Average Excellent ⊖ Insufficient Information

69

Refer to *Section 3: Annotated Vehicle Charts* for an explanation of these charts.

Ford Taurus SE
4 Door Sedan

Midsize

 3.0L 145 hp Gas Fuel Inject.
 6 Cylinder "V"
 Automatic 4 Speed
 2 Wheel Front
Dual Airbags Std

Purchase Price

Car Item	Dealer Cost	List
Base Price	**$16,826**	**$18,445**
Anti-Lock Brakes	$534	$600
Manual Transmission	N/A	N/A
3.0L 200 hp Gas	$441	$495
Air Conditioning	Std	Std
Power Steering	Std	Std
Cruise Control	Std	Std
Power Windows	Std	Std
AM/FM Stereo Cassette	Std	Std
Steering Wheel, Tilt	Std	Std
Rear Defroster	Std	Std
*Options Price	$975	$1,095
*Total Price	**$17,801**	**$19,540**
Target Price	$18,749	
Destination Charge	$550	
Avg. Tax & Fees	$1,082	
Total Target $	**$20,381**	
Average Dealer Option Cost:	89%	
12 Month Price Increase:	None	

Ownership Costs (Projected)

Cost Area	5 Year Cost	Rating
Depreciation	$11,731	●
Financing ($338/month)	$3,965	
Insurance	$6,723	○
State Fees	$818	
Fuel (Hwy 26 City 18)	$3,387	●
Maintenance	$3,228	◐
Repairs	$1,000	◉

Warranty/Maintenance Info

Major Tune-Up (100K mile int.)	$256	◐
Minor Tune-Up (30K mile int.)	$108	◐
Brake Service	$220	◐
Overall Warranty	3 yr/36k	◐
Drivetrain Warranty	3 yr/36k	◐
Rust Warranty	5 yr/unlim. mi	○
Maintenance Warranty	N/A	
Roadside Assistance	3 yr/36k	

The 1999 Taurus SE features optional packages including the Sport Group and Comfort Group. The Sport Group features a 3.0L V6 Duratec engine, a rear spoiler, a SecuriLock theft deterrent system and five spoke aluminum wheels. Standard SE interior features include air conditioning and power windows and door locks. A power moonroof, leather seating and a cellular phone are available as optional equipment. Antilock brakes and dual heated outside mirrors are available as optional safety features.

Ownership Costs By Year (Projected)

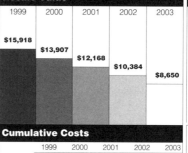

$2,000 $4,000 $6,000 $8,000 $10,000 $12,000

■ 1999　■ 2000　■ 2001　□ 2002　□ 2003

Resale Value

1999	2000	2001	2002	2003
$15,918	$13,907	$12,168	$10,384	$8,650

Cumulative Costs

	1999	2000	2001	2002	2003
Annual	$7,984	$5,326	$5,287	$6,254	$6,001
Total	$7,984	$13,310	$18,597	$24,851	$30,852

Projected Costs (5yr)

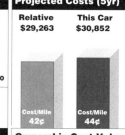

Relative $29,263	This Car $30,852
Cost/Mile 42¢	Cost/Mile 44¢

Ownership Cost Value

Worse Than Average

Ford Taurus SHO
4 Door Sedan

Midsize

 3.4L 235 hp Gas Fuel Inject.
 8 Cylinder "V"
 Automatic 4 Speed
 2 Wheel Front
 Dual Airbags Std

Purchase Price

Car Item	Dealer Cost	List
Base Price	**$26,220**	**$29,000**
Anti-Lock Brakes	Std	Std
Manual Transmission	N/A	N/A
Optional Engine	N/A	N/A
Auto Climate Control	Std	Std
Power Steering	Std	Std
Cruise Control	Std	Std
Power Windows	Std	Std
AM/FM Stereo Cassette	N/A	N/A
Steering Wheel, Tilt	Std	Std
Rear Defroster	Std	Std
*Options Price	$0	$0
*Total Price	**$26,220**	**$29,000**
Target Price	$27,905	
Destination Charge	$550	
Avg. Tax & Fees	$1,589	
Total Target $	**$30,044**	
Average Dealer Option Cost:	89%	
12 Month Price Increase:	None	

Ownership Costs (Projected)

Cost Area	5 Year Cost	Rating
Depreciation	$19,555	●
Financing ($498/month)	$5,844	
Insurance (Performance)	$8,956	○
State Fees	$1,195	
Fuel (Hwy 25 City 16 -Prem.)	$4,346	●
Maintenance	$2,899	○
Repairs	$1,045	●

Warranty/Maintenance Info

Major Tune-Up (100K mile int.)	$257	◐
Minor Tune-Up (30K mile int.)	$108	◐
Brake Service	$244	◐
Overall Warranty	3 yr/36k	◐
Drivetrain Warranty	3 yr/36k	◐
Rust Warranty	5 yr/unlim. mi	○
Maintenance Warranty	N/A	
Roadside Assistance	3 yr/36k	

The 1999 Taurus SHO features leather sport bucket seats, embroidered SHO floor mats and dual power seats as standard interior features. Exterior features include a power moonroof, a rear spoiler, dual exhaust and five spoke chrome aluminum wheels. A Mach audio system and CD changer are also standard equipment. Safety features include an antilock braking system and heated outside mirrors. Two new exterior colors for 1999 are Tropic Green and Graphite Blue.

Ownership Costs By Year (Projected)

$5,000 $10,000 $15,000 $20,000

■ 1999　■ 2000　■ 2001　□ 2002　□ 2003

Resale Value

1999	2000	2001	2002	2003
$22,451	$19,197	$16,266	$13,328	$10,489

Cumulative Costs

	1999	2000	2001	2002	2003
Annual	$12,457	$7,794	$7,580	$7,858	$8,150
Total	$12,457	$20,251	$27,831	$35,689	$43,839

Projected Costs (5yr)

Relative $40,934	This Car $43,839
Cost/Mile 58¢	Cost/Mile 63¢

Ownership Cost Value

Poor

70

* Includes shaded options
** Other purchase requirements apply
*** Price includes other options

 Poor　 Worse Than Average　 Average　 Better Than Average　Excellent　 Insufficient Information

Refer to *Section 3: Annotated Vehicle Charts* for an explanation of these charts.

Ford Taurus SE
4 Door Wagon

Midsize Wagon

 3.0L 145 hp Gas Fuel Inject.
 6 Cylinder "V"
 Automatic 4 Speed
 2 Wheel Front
 Dual Airbags Std (Depowered)

Purchase Price

Car Item	Dealer Cost	List
Base Price	**$17,716**	**$19,445**
Anti-Lock Brakes	$534	$600
Manual Transmission	N/A	N/A
3.0L 200 hp Gas	$441	$495
Air Conditioning	Std	Std
Power Steering	Std	Std
Cruise Control	Std	Std
Power Windows	Std	Std
AM/FM Stereo Cassette	Std	Std
Steering Wheel, Tilt	Std	Std
Rear Defroster	Std	Std
*Options Price	$975	$1,095
*Total Price	**$18,691**	**$20,540**
Target Price	$19,708	
Destination Charge	$550	
Avg. Tax & Fees	$1,136	
Total Target $	**$21,394**	
Average Dealer Option Cost:	**89%**	
12 Month Price Increase:	None	

Ownership Costs (Projected)

Cost Area	5 Year Cost	Rating
Depreciation	$12,081	◉
Financing ($355/month)	$4,162	
Insurance	$6,852	○
State Fees	$858	
Fuel (Hwy 26 City 18)	$3,387	◉
Maintenance	$3,228	○
Repairs	$1,000	◉

Warranty/Maintenance Info

Major Tune-Up (100K mile int.)	$256	◉
Minor Tune-Up (30K mile int.)	$108	◉
Brake Service	$220	◉
Overall Warranty	3 yr/36k	◉
Drivetrain Warranty	3 yr/36k	◉
Rust Warranty	5 yr/unlim. mi	○
Maintenance Warranty	N/A	
Roadside Assistance	3 yr/36k	

Ownership Costs By Year (Projected)

$2,000 $4,000 $6,000 $8,000 $10,000 $12,000 $14,000

■ 1999
■ 2000
■ 2001
□ 2002
□ 2003

Resale Value

1999	2000	2001	2002	2003
$17,363	$15,145	$13,208	$11,232	$9,313

Projected Costs (5yr)

Relative	This Car
$30,702	$31,568
Cost/Mile 44¢	Cost/Mile 45¢

Cumulative Costs

	1999	2000	2001	2002	2003
Annual	$7,654	$5,621	$5,559	$6,505	$6,229
Total	$7,654	$13,275	$18,834	$25,339	$31,568

Ownership Cost Value

◉ Worse Than Average

The 1999 Taurus SE wagon is available with an optional 3.0L 200 hp Duratec engine. Standard wagon features include air conditioning, a luggage rack and four wheel disc brakes. Additional luxury items include cruise control, power door locks and power windows. Optional packages include the Wagon Group, the Light Group and the Comfort Group. The Wagon Group includes a cargo area cover and a cargo net. Two new exterior colors for 1999 are Tropic Green and Graphite Blue.

Honda Accord LX
2 Door Coupe

Midsize

EX V-6 Shown

 2.3L 150 hp Gas Fuel Inject.
 4 Cylinder In-Line
 Manual 5 Speed
 2 Wheel Front
 Dual Airbags Std

Purchase Price

Car Item	Dealer Cost	List
Base Price	**$16,362**	**$18,390**
Anti-Lock Brakes	N/A	N/A
Automatic 4 Speed	$711	$800
2.3L 148 hp Gas	N/C	N/C
Air Conditioning	Std	Std
Power Steering	Std	Std
Cruise Control	Std	Std
Power Windows	Std	Std
AM/FM Stereo Cassette	Std	Std
Steering Wheel, Tilt	Std	Std
Rear Defroster	Std	Std
*Options Price	$711	$800
*Total Price	**$17,073**	**$19,190**
Target Price	$18,200	
Destination Charge	$415	
Avg. Tax & Fees	$1,047	
Total Target $	**$19,662**	
Average Dealer Option Cost:	**89%**	
12 Month Price Increase:	1%	

Ownership Costs (Projected)

Cost Area	5 Year Cost	Rating
Depreciation	$7,617	○
Financing ($326/month)	$3,826	
Insurance	$8,265	◉
State Fees	$797	
Fuel (Hwy 30 City 23)	$2,796	○
Maintenance	$2,644	○
Repairs	$475	○

Warranty/Maintenance Info

Major Tune-Up (60K mile int.)	$281	◉
Minor Tune-Up (30K mile int.)	$94	○
Brake Service	$255	◉
Overall Warranty	3 yr/36k	◉
Drivetrain Warranty	3 yr/36k	◉
Rust Warranty	5 yr/unlim. mi	○
Maintenance Warranty	N/A	
Roadside Assistance	N/A	

Ownership Costs By Year (Projected)

$2,000 $4,000 $6,000 $8,000 $10,000

■ 1999
■ 2000
■ 2001
□ 2002
□ 2003

Resale Value

1999	2000	2001	2002	2003
$18,729	$16,929	$15,360	$13,699	$12,045

Projected Costs (5yr)

Relative	This Car
$28,593	$26,420
Cost/Mile 41¢	Cost/Mile 38¢

Cumulative Costs

	1999	2000	2001	2002	2003
Annual	$4,582	$5,251	$5,029	$5,426	$6,132
Total	$4,582	$9,833	$14,862	$20,288	$26,420

Ownership Cost Value

○ Excellent

For 1999, the Accord LX coupe now features foldaway exterior mirrors. The coupe's appearance features distinctive styling compared to the sedan. The standard air conditioning system includes micron air filtration. The Ultra Low Emission Vehicle (ULEV) designation with automatic transmission is offered in California and in parts of the Northeast. The ULEV's engine output is reduced to 148 hp. Available accessories include a CD player, a rear sunshade and a security system.

---

* Includes shaded options

** Other purchase requirements apply

*** Price includes other options

● Poor ◉ Worse Than Average ◐ Average ○ Better Than Average ○ Excellent ⊖ Insufficient Information

71

Refer to *Section 3: Annotated Vehicle Charts* for an explanation of these charts.

Honda Accord EX
2 Door Coupe

▲ Midsize

| 2.3L 150 hp Gas Fuel Inject. | 4 Cylinder In-Line | Manual 5 Speed | 2 Wheel Front | Dual Airbags Std |

Purchase Price

Car Item	Dealer Cost	List
Base Price	**$18,592**	**$20,900**
Anti-Lock Brakes	Std	Std
Automatic 4 Speed	$711	$800
2.3L 148 hp Gas	N/C	**N/C
Air Conditioning	Std	Std
Power Steering	Std	Std
Cruise Control	Std	Std
Power Windows	Std	Std
AM/FM Stereo CD	Std	Std
Steering Wheel, Tilt	Std	Std
Rear Defroster	Std	Std
*Options Price	$711	$800
*Total Price	$19,303	$21,700
Target Price	$20,628	
Destination Charge	$415	
Avg. Tax & Fees	$1,181	
Total Target $	**$22,224**	
Average Dealer Option Cost:	**89%**	
12 Month Price Increase:	None	

For 1999, the Accord EX coupe has minor revisions such as foldaway exterior mirrors. The EX comes with a keyless remote entry system, security system, power moonroof and premium stereo with CD player. The Ultra Low Emission Vehicle (ULEV) designation requires an automatic transmission. The ULEV is only available in California and in part of the Northeast region. The optional leather interior package includes an eight-way power driver's seat and leather-trimmed seats.

Ownership Costs (Projected)

Cost Area	5 Year Cost	Rating
Depreciation	$9,313	◔
Financing ($368/month)	$4,324	
Insurance	$8,500	◉
State Fees	$898	
Fuel (Hwy 30 City 23)	$2,796	◔
Maintenance	$2,686	◔
Repairs	$475	◔

Warranty/Maintenance Info

Major Tune-Up (60K mile int.)	$281	◉
Minor Tune-Up (30K mile int.)	$94	◔
Brake Service	$294	●
Overall Warranty	3 yr/36k	◒
Drivetrain Warranty	3 yr/36k	◒
Rust Warranty	5 yr/unlim. mi	◔
Maintenance Warranty	N/A	
Roadside Assistance	N/A	

Ownership Costs By Year (Projected)

$2,000 $4,000 $6,000 $8,000 $10,000

Legend: 1999, 2000, 2001, 2002, 2003

Resale Value

1999	2000	2001	2002	2003
$20,405	$18,394	$16,620	$14,759	$12,911

Cumulative Costs

	1999	2000	2001	2002	2003
Annual	$5,707	$5,669	$5,404	$5,799	$6,413
Total	$5,707	$11,376	$16,780	$22,579	$28,992

Projected Costs (5yr)

Relative	This Car
$30,817	$28,992
Cost/Mile 44¢	Cost/Mile 41¢

Ownership Cost Value

◯ Excellent

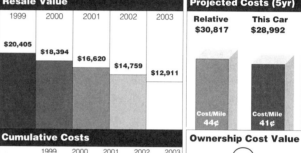

Honda Accord LX V-6
2 Door Coupe

Midsize

| 3.0L 200 hp Gas Fuel Inject. | 6 Cylinder "V" | Automatic 4 Speed | 2 Wheel Front | Dual Airbags Std |

EX Model Shown

Purchase Price

Car Item	Dealer Cost	List
Base Price	**$19,303**	**$21,700**
Anti-Lock Brakes	Std	Std
Manual Transmission	N/A	N/A
Optional Engine	N/A	N/A
Air Conditioning	Std	Std
Power Steering	Std	Std
Cruise Control	Std	Std
Power Windows	Std	Std
AM/FM Stereo Cassette	Std	Std
Steering Wheel, Tilt	Std	Std
Rear Defroster	Std	Std
*Options Price	$0	$0
*Total Price	$19,303	$21,700
Target Price	$20,644	
Destination Charge	$415	
Avg. Tax & Fees	$1,182	
Total Target $	**$22,241**	
Average Dealer Option Cost:	**N/A**	
12 Month Price Increase:	1%	

For 1999, the Accord LX V6 coupe has minor revisions such as foldaway exterior mirrors. Output for the standard V6 engine is 200 hp with 195 lb-ft torque, mated to the standard four speed automatic transmission. The LX V6 upgrades the DX with an eight-way power driver's seat and auto-off headlamps. Available accessories include alloy wheels, wood interior trim, a security system and a cargo net. The first scheduled tuneup is at 105,000 miles, reducing maintenance costs.

Ownership Costs (Projected)

Cost Area	5 Year Cost	Rating
Depreciation	$9,991	◯
Financing ($369/month)	$4,327	
Insurance	$8,500	◉
State Fees	$898	
Fuel (Hwy 28 City 20)	$3,097	◯
Maintenance	$2,873	◯
Repairs	$475	◔

Warranty/Maintenance Info

Major Tune-Up (60K mile int.)	$239	◯
Minor Tune-Up (30K mile int.)	$112	◯
Brake Service	$294	●
Overall Warranty	3 yr/36k	◯
Drivetrain Warranty	3 yr/36k	◯
Rust Warranty	5 yr/unlim. mi	◯
Maintenance Warranty	N/A	
Roadside Assistance	N/A	

Ownership Costs By Year (Projected)

$2,000 $4,000 $6,000 $8,000 $10,000

Legend: 1999, 2000, 2001, 2002, 2003

Resale Value

1999	2000	2001	2002	2003
$20,621	$18,385	$16,388	$14,312	$12,250

Cumulative Costs

	1999	2000	2001	2002	2003
Annual	$5,568	$5,956	$5,708	$6,240	$6,689
Total	$5,568	$11,524	$17,232	$23,472	$30,161

Projected Costs (5yr)

Relative	This Car
$30,817	$30,161
Cost/Mile 44¢	Cost/Mile 43¢

Ownership Cost Value

◯ Better Than Average

72

Honda Accord EX V-6
2 Door Coupe

Midsize

 3.0L 200 hp Gas Fuel Inject.
 6 Cylinder "V"
 Automatic 4 Speed
 2 Wheel Front
Dual Airbags Std

Purchase Price

Car Item	Dealer Cost	List
Base Price	**$21,614**	**$24,300**
Anti-Lock Brakes	Std	Std
Manual Transmission	N/A	N/A
Optional Engine	N/A	N/A
Auto Climate Control	Std	Std
Power Steering	Std	Std
Cruise Control	Std	Std
Power Windows	Std	Std
AM/FM Stereo CD	Std	Std
Steering Wheel, Tilt	Std	Std
Rear Defroster	Std	Std
*Options Price	$0	$0
***Total Price**	**$21,614**	**$24,300**
Target Price	$23,175	
Destination Charge	$415	
Avg. Tax & Fees	$1,322	
Total Target $	**$24,912**	
Average Dealer Option Cost:	N/A	
12 Month Price Increase:	1%	

Ownership Costs (Projected)

Cost Area	5 Year Cost	Rating
Depreciation	$11,781	◐
Financing ($413/month)	$4,847	
Insurance	$9,083	◉
State Fees	$1,001	
Fuel (Hwy 28 City 20)	$3,097	◐
Maintenance	$2,873	◐
Repairs	$475	○

Warranty/Maintenance Info

Major Tune-Up (60K mile int.)	$239	○
Minor Tune-Up (30K mile int.)	$112	○
Brake Service	$294	●
Overall Warranty	3 yr/36k	◐
Drivetrain Warranty	3 yr/36k	◐
Rust Warranty	5 yr/unlim. mi	○
Maintenance Warranty	N/A	
Roadside Assistance	N/A	

For 1999, the Accord EX V6 coupe now features foldaway exterior mirrors. The top of the line EX V6 features 16 inch alloy wheels, steering wheel-mounted radio controls and a leather interior as standard equipment. A HomeLink transmitter system, power moonroof and automatic climate control are also standard. The retained accessory power retains power for ten minutes to operate the windows and sunroof. The Accord EX V6 coupe features a stronger body and larger interior than the past coupe models.

Ownership Costs By Year (Projected)

$2,000 $4,000 $6,000 $8,000 $10,000 $12,000

1999 · 2000 · 2001 · 2002 · 2003

Resale Value

1999	2000	2001	2002	2003
$22,222	$19,801	$17,624	$15,367	$13,131

Cumulative Costs

	1999	2000	2001	2002	2003
Annual	$6,952	$6,421	$6,134	$6,626	$7,024
Total	$6,952	$13,373	$19,507	$26,133	$33,157

Projected Costs (5yr)

Relative	This Car
$33,655	$33,157
Cost/Mile 48¢	Cost/Mile 47¢

Ownership Cost Value

◐ Average

Honda Accord DX
4 Door Sedan

Midsize

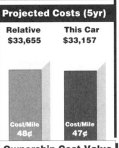

 2.3L 135 hp Gas Fuel Inject.
4 Cylinder In-Line
 Manual 5 Speed
 2 Wheel Front
Dual Airbags Std

LX Model Shown

Purchase Price

Car Item	Dealer Cost	List
Base Price	**$13,527**	**$15,200**
Anti-Lock Brakes	N/A	N/A
Automatic 4 Speed	$711	$800
Optional Engine	N/A	N/A
Air Conditioning	Dlr	Dlr
Power Steering	Std	Std
Cruise Control	N/A	N/A
Power Windows	N/A	N/A
AM/FM Stereo Cassette	Std	Std
Steering Wheel, Tilt	Std	Std
Rear Defroster	Std	Std
*Options Price	$711	$800
***Total Price**	**$14,238**	**$16,000**
Target Price	$15,130	
Destination Charge	$415	
Avg. Tax & Fees	$877	
Total Target $	**$16,422**	
Average Dealer Option Cost:	88%	
12 Month Price Increase:	1%	

Ownership Costs (Projected)

Cost Area	5 Year Cost	Rating
Depreciation	$5,594	○
Financing ($272/month)	$3,195	
Insurance	$7,294	◐
State Fees	$669	
Fuel (Hwy 29 City 22)	$2,906	○
Maintenance	$2,579	○
Repairs	$475	○

Warranty/Maintenance Info

Major Tune-Up (60K mile int.)	$281	◉
Minor Tune-Up (30K mile int.)	$94	○
Brake Service	$255	●
Overall Warranty	3 yr/36k	◐
Drivetrain Warranty	3 yr/36k	◐
Rust Warranty	5 yr/unlim. mi	○
Maintenance Warranty	N/A	
Roadside Assistance	N/A	

For 1999, the Accord DX sedan receives new seat fabric. The DX comes standard with an AM/FM cassette stereo, tilt steering wheel and rear defroster. The fold-down rear seat adds versatility and extra cargo space. Available accessories include wood interior trim, a leather-wrapped steering wheel and alloy wheels. Air conditioning and an automatic transmission are the main factory options available for this model. Safety features include dual airbags and child safety locks.

Ownership Costs By Year (Projected)

$2,000 $4,000 $6,000 $8,000

1999 · 2000 · 2001 · 2002 · 2003

Resale Value

1999	2000	2001	2002	2003
$15,616	$14,036	$12,885	$11,798	$10,828

Cumulative Costs

	1999	2000	2001	2002	2003
Annual	$4,044	$4,661	$4,283	$4,506	$5,218
Total	$4,044	$8,705	$12,988	$17,494	$22,712

Projected Costs (5yr)

Relative	This Car
$26,498	$22,712
Cost/Mile 38¢	Cost/Mile 32¢

Ownership Cost Value

○ Excellent

---

* Includes shaded options

** Other purchase requirements apply

*** Price includes other options

● Poor   ◉ Worse Than Average   ◐ Average   ○ Better Than Average   ○ Excellent   ⊖ Insufficient Information

Refer to Section 3: Annotated Vehicle Charts for an explanation of these charts.

73

Honda Accord LX
4 Door Sedan

 2.3L 150 hp Gas Fuel Inject. | 4 Cylinder In-Line | 1 3 5 / 2 4 R Manual 5 Speed | 2 Wheel Front | Dual Airbags Std

Midsize

1999 Overall Value

Purchase Price

Car Item	Dealer Cost	List
Base Price	**$16,362**	**$18,390**
Anti-Lock Brakes	$533	$600
Automatic 4 Speed	$711	$800
2.3L 148 hp Gas	N/C	**N/C
Air Conditioning	Std	Std
Power Steering	Std	Std
Cruise Control	Std	Std
Power Windows	Std	Std
AM/FM Stereo Cassette	Std	Std
Steering Wheel, Tilt	Std	Std
Rear Defroster	Std	Std
*Options Price	$1,244	$1,400
*Total Price	$17,606	$19,790
Target Price	$18,769	
Destination Charge	$415	
Avg. Tax & Fees	$1,078	
Total Target $	**$20,262**	
Average Dealer Option Cost:	89%	
12 Month Price Increase:	1%	

For 1999, the Accord LX sedan has minor revisions, such as foldaway exterior mirrors and new seat fabric. The LX trim adds power windows and door locks, cruise control and air conditioning. To meet stringent emission requirements, the LX can be equipped with an Ultra Low Emission Vehicle (ULEV) engine mated to an automatic transmission. The ULEV is only available in California and in parts of the Northeast region. The optional antilock braking system requires an automatic transmission.

Ownership Costs (Projected)

Cost Area	5 Year Cost	Rating
Depreciation	$7,623	◒
Financing ($336/month)	$3,942	
Insurance	$7,643	◯
State Fees	$821	
Fuel (Hwy 30 City 23)	$2,796	◒
Maintenance	$2,644	◒
Repairs	$475	◒

Warranty/Maintenance Info

Major Tune-Up (60K mile int.)	$281	◉
Minor Tune-Up (30K mile int.)	$94	◒
Brake Service	$255	◉
Overall Warranty	3 yr/36k	◯
Drivetrain Warranty	3 yr/36k	◯
Rust Warranty	5 yr/unlim. mi	◯
Maintenance Warranty	N/A	
Roadside Assistance	N/A	

Ownership Costs By Year (Projected)

$2,000 $4,000 $6,000 $8,000

Legend: 1999, 2000, 2001, 2002, 2003

Resale Value

1999	2000	2001	2002	2003
$19,218	$17,046	$15,411	$13,930	$12,639

Cumulative Costs

	1999	2000	2001	2002	2003
Annual	$4,620	$5,539	$5,000	$5,138	$5,647
Total	$4,620	$10,159	$15,159	$20,297	$25,944

Projected Costs (5yr)

Relative	This Car
$29,079	$25,944
Cost/Mile 42¢	Cost/Mile 37¢

Ownership Cost Value

◯ Excellent

Honda Accord EX
4 Door Sedan

 2.3L 150 hp Gas Fuel Inject. | 4 Cylinder In-Line | 1 3 5 / 2 4 R Manual 5 Speed | 2 Wheel Front | Dual Airbags Std

Midsize

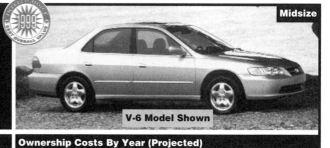

1999 Overall Value

V-6 Model Shown

Purchase Price

Car Item	Dealer Cost	List
Base Price	**$18,592**	**$20,900**
Anti-Lock Brakes	Std	Std
Automatic 4 Speed	$711	$800
2.3L 148 hp Gas	N/C	N/C
Air Conditioning	Std	Std
Power Steering	Std	Std
Cruise Control	Std	Std
Power Windows	Std	Std
AM/FM Stereo CD	Std	Std
Steering Wheel, Tilt	Std	Std
Rear Defroster	Std	Std
*Options Price	$711	$800
*Total Price	$19,303	$21,700
Target Price	$20,628	
Destination Charge	$415	
Avg. Tax & Fees	$1,181	
Total Target $	**$22,224**	
Average Dealer Option Cost:	89%	
12 Month Price Increase:	None	

For 1999, the Accord EX sedan features foldaway exterior mirrors and new seat fabric. The EX comes with all the standard equipment found on the LX model, as well as a keyless remote entry system, security system, power moonroof and premium stereo with CD player. The EX gets a VTEC version of the same engine found in the DX, boosting output to 150 hp. Leather seats, an eight-way power driver's seat and wood trim are available with the optional leather interior package.

Ownership Costs (Projected)

Cost Area	5 Year Cost	Rating
Depreciation	$9,068	◯
Financing ($368/month)	$4,324	
Insurance	$8,045	◯
State Fees	$898	
Fuel (Hwy 30 City 23)	$2,796	◒
Maintenance	$2,673	◒
Repairs	$475	◒

Warranty/Maintenance Info

Major Tune-Up (60K mile int.)	$281	◉
Minor Tune-Up (30K mile int.)	$94	◒
Brake Service	$282	●
Overall Warranty	3 yr/36k	◯
Drivetrain Warranty	3 yr/36k	◯
Rust Warranty	5 yr/unlim. mi	◯
Maintenance Warranty	N/A	
Roadside Assistance	N/A	

Ownership Costs By Year (Projected)

$2,000 $4,000 $6,000 $8,000 $10,000

Legend: 1999, 2000, 2001, 2002, 2003

Resale Value

1999	2000	2001	2002	2003
$20,719	$18,677	$16,881	$15,009	$13,156

Cumulative Costs

	1999	2000	2001	2002	2003
Annual	$5,306	$5,611	$5,335	$5,704	$6,323
Total	$5,306	$10,917	$16,252	$21,956	$28,279

Projected Costs (5yr)

Relative	This Car
$30,817	$28,279
Cost/Mile 44¢	Cost/Mile 40¢

Ownership Cost Value

◯ Excellent

74

* Includes shaded options
** Other purchase requirements apply
*** Price includes other options

| ● Poor | ◉ Worse Than Average | ◯ Average | ◯ Better Than Average | ◯ Excellent | ⊖ Insufficient Information |

Refer to *Section 3: Annotated Vehicle Charts* for an explanation of these charts.

Honda Accord LX V-6
4 Door Sedan

 3.0L 200 hp Gas Fuel Inject.
 6 Cylinder "V"
 Automatic 4 Speed
 2 Wheel Front
 Dual Airbags Std

Midsize

Base Model Shown

Purchase Price

Car Item	Dealer Cost	List
Base Price	**$19,303**	**$21,700**
Anti-Lock Brakes	Std	Std
Manual Transmission	N/A	N/A
Optional Engine	N/A	N/A
Air Conditioning	Std	Std
Power Steering	Std	Std
Cruise Control	Std	Std
Power Windows	Std	Std
AM/FM Stereo Cassette	Std	Std
Steering Wheel, Tilt	Std	Std
Rear Defroster	Std	Std
*Options Price	$0	$0
*Total Price	$19,303	$21,700
Target Price	$20,644	
Destination Charge	$415	
Avg. Tax & Fees	$1,182	
Total Target $	**$22,241**	
Average Dealer Option Cost:	85%	
12 Month Price Increase:	1%	

For 1999, the Accord LX V6 sedan now features foldaway exterior mirrors and new seat fabric. Output for the LX's 3.0L V6 engine is 200 hp with 195 lb-ft of torque. The V6 engine is only available with a four speed automatic transmission. Standard equipment includes an eight-way power driver's seat, power door locks and power windows. The LX V6 trim adds a four wheel antilock braking system. The first tuneup is scheduled at 105,000 miles, which reduces maintenance costs.

Ownership Costs (Projected)

Cost Area	5 Year Cost	Rating
Depreciation	$9,805	○
Financing ($369/month)	$4,327	
Insurance	$8,045	◉
State Fees	$898	
Fuel (Hwy 28 City 20)	$3,097	◉
Maintenance	$2,860	○
Repairs	$475	○

Warranty/Maintenance Info

Major Tune-Up (60K mile int.)	$239	○
Minor Tune-Up (30K mile int.)	$112	○
Brake Service	$282	●
Overall Warranty	3 yr/36k	○
Drivetrain Warranty	3 yr/36k	○
Rust Warranty	5 yr/unlim. mi	○
Maintenance Warranty	N/A	
Roadside Assistance	N/A	

Ownership Costs By Year (Projected)

$2,000 $4,000 $6,000 $8,000 $10,000

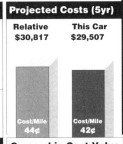

1999 / 2000 / 2001 / 2002 / 2003

Resale Value

1999	2000	2001	2002	2003
$19,403	$17,527	$15,884	$14,155	$12,436

Cumulative Costs

	1999	2000	2001	2002	2003
Annual	$6,699	$5,507	$5,263	$5,787	$6,251
Total	$6,699	$12,206	$17,469	$23,256	$29,507

Projected Costs (5yr)

Relative	This Car
$30,817	$29,507

Cost/Mile 44¢ | Cost/Mile 42¢

Ownership Cost Value

○ Excellent

Honda Accord EX V-6
4 Door Sedan

 3.0L 200 hp Gas Fuel Inject.
 6 Cylinder "V"
 Automatic 4 Speed
 2 Wheel Front / Dual Airbags Std

Midsize

Purchase Price

Car Item	Dealer Cost	List
Base Price	**$21,614**	**$24,300**
Anti-Lock Brakes	Std	Std
Manual Transmission	N/A	N/A
Optional Engine	N/A	N/A
Auto Climate Control	Std	Std
Power Steering	Std	Std
Cruise Control	Std	Std
Power Windows	Std	Std
AM/FM Stereo CD	Std	Std
Steering Wheel, Tilt	Std	Std
Rear Defroster	Std	Std
*Options Price	$0	$0
*Total Price	$21,614	$24,300
Target Price	$23,175	
Destination Charge	$415	
Avg. Tax & Fees	$1,322	
Total Target $	**$24,912**	
Average Dealer Option Cost:	85%	
12 Month Price Increase:	1%	

For 1999, the Accord EX V6 sedan features foldaway exterior mirrors. The EX V6 upgrades the LX V6 with automatic climate control, aluminum alloy wheels, a power moonroof, auto-off headlamps and a leather interior. Exclusive EX V6 equipment includes steering wheel-mounted audio controls and a HomeLink transmitter system. The standard theft deterrent system includes keyless remote entry. The retained accessory power retains power for ten minutes to operate the windows and sunroof.

Ownership Costs (Projected)

Cost Area	5 Year Cost	Rating
Depreciation	$11,531	○
Financing ($413/month)	$4,847	
Insurance	$8,500	◉
State Fees	$1,001	
Fuel (Hwy 28 City 21)	$3,026	○
Maintenance	$2,860	○
Repairs	$475	○

Warranty/Maintenance Info

Major Tune-Up (60K mile int.)	$239	○
Minor Tune-Up (30K mile int.)	$112	○
Brake Service	$282	●
Overall Warranty	3 yr/36k	○
Drivetrain Warranty	3 yr/36k	○
Rust Warranty	5 yr/unlim. mi	○
Maintenance Warranty	N/A	
Roadside Assistance	N/A	

Ownership Costs By Year (Projected)

$2,000 $4,000 $6,000 $8,000 $10,000 $12,000

1999 / 2000 / 2001 / 2002 / 2003

Resale Value

1999	2000	2001	2002	2003
$21,458	$19,297	$17,377	$15,372	$13,381

Cumulative Costs

	1999	2000	2001	2002	2003
Annual	$7,591	$6,033	$5,746	$6,228	$6,642
Total	$7,591	$13,624	$19,370	$25,598	$32,240

Projected Costs (5yr)

Relative	This Car
$33,655	$32,240

Cost/Mile 48¢ | Cost/Mile 46¢

Ownership Cost Value

○ Excellent

Honda Civic Si
2 Door Coupe

 1.6L 160 hp Gas Fuel Inject.  4 Cylinder In-Line Manual 5 Speed 2 Wheel Front   Dual Airbags Std

Purchase Price

Car Item	Dealer Cost	List
Base Price	**N/R**	**N/R**
Anti-Lock Brakes	N/A	N/A
Automatic Transmission	N/A	N/A
Optional Engine	N/A	N/A
Air Conditioning	Std	Std
Power Steering	Std	Std
Cruise Control	Std	Std
Power Windows	Std	Std
AM/FM Stereo CD	Std	Std
Steering Wheel, Tilt	Std	Std
Rear Defroster	Std	Std
*Options Price	N/R	N/R
*Total Price	**N/R**	**N/R**
Target Price	N/R	
Destination Charge	N/R	
Avg. Tax & Fees	N/R	
Total Target $	**N/R**	
Average Dealer Option Cost:	**85%**	
12 Month Price Increase:	N/A	

Ownership Costs (Projected)

Cost Area	5 Year Cost	Rating
Depreciation		⊖
Financing ($0/month)		
Insurance Rating N/R		⊖
State Fees		
Fuel (Hwy 31 City 26)	$2,596	◯
Maintenance	$2,764	◯
Repairs	$475	◯

Warranty/Maintenance Info

Major Tune-Up (60K mile int.)	$264	◯
Minor Tune-Up (30K mile int.)	$85	◯
Brake Service	$277	◉
Overall Warranty	3 yr/36k	◯
Drivetrain Warranty	3 yr/36k	◯
Rust Warranty	5 yr/unlim. mi	◯
Maintenance Warranty	N/A	
Roadside Assistance	N/A	

Ownership Costs By Year (Projected)

$1,000 $2,000 $3,000

Insufficient Depreciation Information
Insufficient Financing Information
Insufficient Insurance Information
Insufficient State Fee Information

■ 1999
■ 2000
■ 2001
■ 2002
□ 2003

Resale Value

Insufficient Information

Projected Costs (5yr)

Insufficient Information

Cumulative Costs

	1999	2000	2001	2002	2003
Annual	*Insufficient Information*				
Total	*Insufficient Information*				

Ownership Cost Value

⊖

Insufficient Information

New for 1999, the Civic Si coupe has been reincarnated with performance in mind. The Si coupe is equipped with a 1.6L VTEC engine with 160 hp, higher than any other Civic model. In addition, four wheel disc brakes, low-profile tires and 15 inch alloy wheels are standard. The suspension is upgraded with thicker front and rear stabilizer bars and Honda's Progressive Valve (HPV) shock absorbers. Available options include fog lamps, a security system, a moonroof visor and fog lamps.

Honda Civic DX
2 Door Coupe

 1.6L 106 hp Gas Fuel Inject. 4 Cylinder In-Line Manual 5 Speed 2 Wheel Front   Dual Airbags Std

EX Model Shown

Purchase Price

Car Item	Dealer Cost	List
Base Price	**$11,370**	**$12,580**
Anti-Lock Brakes	N/A	N/A
Automatic 4 Speed	$722	$800
Optional Engine	N/A	N/A
Air Conditioning	Dlr	Dlr
Power Steering	Std	Std
Cruise Control	N/A	N/A
Power Windows	N/A	N/A
AM/FM Stereo Cassette	Dlr	Dlr
Steering Wheel, Tilt	Std	Std
Rear Defroster	Std	Std
*Options Price	$0	$0
*Total Price	**$11,370**	**$12,580**
Target Price	$12,014	
Destination Charge	$415	
Avg. Tax & Fees	$702	
Total Target $	**$13,131**	
Average Dealer Option Cost:	**90%**	
12 Month Price Increase:	None	

Ownership Costs (Projected)

Cost Area	5 Year Cost	Rating
Depreciation	$3,539	◯
Financing ($218/month)	$2,555	
Insurance	$7,837	●
State Fees	$533	
Fuel (Hwy 37 City 32)	$2,146	◯
Maintenance	$2,495	◯
Repairs	$475	◯

Warranty/Maintenance Info

Major Tune-Up (60K mile int.)	$264	◯
Minor Tune-Up (30K mile int.)	$85	◯
Brake Service	$262	◯
Overall Warranty	3 yr/36k	◯
Drivetrain Warranty	3 yr/36k	◯
Rust Warranty	5 yr/unlim. mi	◯
Maintenance Warranty	N/A	
Roadside Assistance	N/A	

Ownership Costs By Year (Projected)

$2,000 $4,000 $6,000 $8,000

■ 1999
■ 2000
■ 2001
■ 2002
□ 2003

Resale Value

1999	2000	2001	2002	2003
$12,456	$11,544	$10,880	$10,235	$9,592

Projected Costs (5yr)

Relative	This Car
$22,727	$19,580
Cost/Mile 32¢	Cost/Mile 28¢

Cumulative Costs

	1999	2000	2001	2002	2003
Annual	$3,621	$3,743	$3,574	$3,900	$4,742
Total	$3,621	$7,364	$10,938	$14,838	$19,580

Ownership Cost Value

◯

Excellent

For 1999, the Civic DX coupe features new front and rear styling that adds a sportier look. A 60/40 split folding rear seat with a locking feature is standard. Standard features include tilt steering, dual vanity mirrors, cup holders and a trunk/hatch open indicator light. The DX delivers EPA estimated mileage of 32 mpg city and 37 mpg highway when equipped with a five speed manual transmission. Dealer installed options include a theft deterrent system, cassette player and CD player.

76

* Includes shaded options
** Other purchase requirements apply
*** Price includes other options

● Poor	◉ Worse Than Average	◯ Average
◯ Better Than Average	◯ Excellent	⊖ Insufficient Information

Refer to *Section 3: Annotated Vehicle Charts* for an explanation of these charts.

Honda Civic HX — 2 Door Coupe

 1.6L 115 hp Gas Fuel Inject. 4 Cylinder In-Line Manual 5 Speed 2 Wheel Front Dual Airbags Std

EX Model Shown

Purchase Price

Car Item	Dealer Cost	List
Base Price	**$12,110**	**$13,400**
Anti-Lock Brakes	N/A	N/A
Automatic Transmission	$902	$1,000
Optional Engine	N/A	N/A
Air Conditioning	Dlr	Dlr
Power Steering	Std	Std
Cruise Control	N/A	N/A
Power Windows	Std	Std
AM/FM Stereo Cassette	Dlr	Dlr
Steering Wheel, Tilt	Std	Std
Rear Defroster	Std	Std
*Options Price	$0	$0
*Total Price	$12,110	$13,400
Target Price	$12,807	
Destination Charge	$415	
Avg. Tax & Fees	$746	
Total Target $	**$13,968**	
Average Dealer Option Cost:	90%	
12 Month Price Increase:	None	

Ownership Costs (Projected)

Cost Area	5 Year Cost	Rating
Depreciation	$4,019	○
Financing ($232/month)	$2,718	○
Insurance	$7,837	●
State Fees	$566	
Fuel (Hwy 43 City 35)	$1,897	○
Maintenance	$2,495	○
Repairs	$475	○

Warranty/Maintenance Info

Major Tune-Up (60K mile int.)	$264	◉
Minor Tune-Up (30K mile int.)	$85	○
Brake Service	$262	◉
Overall Warranty	3 yr/36k	◉
Drivetrain Warranty	3 yr/36k	◉
Rust Warranty	5 yr/unlim. mi	○
Maintenance Warranty	N/A	
Roadside Assistance	N/A	

For 1999, the Civic HX coupe features new front and rear styling that adds a sportier look. The HX includes power windows and door locks, a center console armrest with storage and cargo area lighting. The HX is also available with a Continuously Variable Transmission (CVT), featuring the performance and economy of a manual transmission. When equipped with the CVT, the HX gets an estimated 34 mpg city and 38 mpg highway, compared to the standard manual transmission's 35 city and 43 highway.

Ownership Costs By Year (Projected)

$2,000 — $4,000 — $6,000 — $8,000

1999 / 2000 / 2001 / 2002 / 2003

Resale Value

1999	2000	2001	2002	2003
$13,241	$12,188	$11,408	$10,669	$9,949

Projected Costs (5yr)

Relative	This Car
$23,502	$20,007
Cost/Mile 34¢	Cost/Mile 29¢

Cumulative Costs

	1999	2000	2001	2002	2003
Annual	$3,688	$3,888	$3,681	$3,970	$4,780
Total	$3,688	$7,576	$11,257	$15,227	$20,007

Ownership Cost Value

○ Excellent

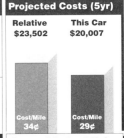

Honda Civic EX — 2 Door Coupe

Subcompact

1.6L 127 hp Gas Fuel Inject. 4 Cylinder In-Line Manual 5 Speed 2 Wheel Front Dual Airbags Std

Purchase Price

Car Item	Dealer Cost	List
Base Price	**$13,959**	**$15,450**
Anti-Lock Brakes	$541	**$600
Automatic 4 Speed	$722	$800
Optional Engine	N/A	N/A
Air Conditioning	Std	Std
Power Steering	Std	Std
Cruise Control	Std	Std
Power Windows	Std	Std
AM/FM Stereo CD	Std	Std
Steering Wheel, Tilt	Std	Std
Rear Defroster	Std	Std
*Options Price	$0	$0
*Total Price	$13,959	$15,450
Target Price	$14,793	
Destination Charge	$415	
Avg. Tax & Fees	$856	
Total Target $	**$16,064**	
Average Dealer Option Cost:	90%	
12 Month Price Increase:	1%	

Ownership Costs (Projected)

Cost Area	5 Year Cost	Rating
Depreciation	$5,793	○
Financing ($266/month)	$3,124	○
Insurance	$8,265	●
State Fees	$648	
Fuel (Hwy 35 City 29)	$2,313	◉
Maintenance	$2,495	○
Repairs	$475	○

Warranty/Maintenance Info

Major Tune-Up (60K mile int.)	$264	◉
Minor Tune-Up (30K mile int.)	$85	○
Brake Service	$262	◉
Overall Warranty	3 yr/36k	◉
Drivetrain Warranty	3 yr/36k	◉
Rust Warranty	5 yr/unlim. mi	○
Maintenance Warranty	N/A	
Roadside Assistance	N/A	

For 1999, the Civic EX coupe features new front and rear styling that adds a sportier look. The EX upgrades the HX with air conditioning, keyless remote entry, power moonroof, map lights and cruise control. The optional antilock braking system is available only with the optional automatic transmission. The automatic transmission features Honda's Grade Logic Control, which provides control when driving up or down steep grades. A moonroof visor and a rear spoiler are available accessories.

Ownership Costs By Year (Projected)

$2,000 — $4,000 — $6,000 — $8,000 — $10,000

1999 / 2000 / 2001 / 2002 / 2003

Resale Value

1999	2000	2001	2002	2003
$14,793	$13,611	$12,564	$11,448	$10,271

Projected Costs (5yr)

Relative	This Car
$25,469	$23,113
Cost/Mile 36¢	Cost/Mile 33¢

Cumulative Costs

	1999	2000	2001	2002	2003
Annual	$4,553	$4,313	$4,216	$4,586	$5,445
Total	$4,553	$8,866	$13,082	$17,668	$23,113

Ownership Cost Value

○ Excellent

---

* Includes shaded options

** Other purchase requirements apply

*** Price includes other options

 Poor Worse Than Average Average Better Than Average Excellent Insufficient Information

Refer to *Section 3: Annotated Vehicle Charts* for an explanation of these charts.

Honda Civic CX
2 Door Hatchback

Subcompact

| 1.6L 106 hp Gas Fuel Inject. | 4 Cylinder In-Line | Manual 5 Speed | 2 Wheel Front | Dual Airbags Std |

DX Model Shown

Purchase Price

Car Item	Dealer Cost	List
Base Price	**$10,063**	**$10,650**
Anti-Lock Brakes	N/A	N/A
Automatic 4 Speed	$943	$1,000
Optional Engine	N/A	N/A
Air Conditioning	Dlr	Dlr
Power Steering	N/C	**N/C
Cruise Control	N/A	N/A
Power Windows	N/A	N/A
AM/FM Stereo Cassette	Dlr	Dlr
Steering Wheel, Tilt	Std	Std
Rear Defroster	Std	Std
*Options Price	$0	$0
*Total Price	$10,063	$10,650
Target Price	$10,381	
Destination Charge	$415	
Avg. Tax & Fees	$610	
Total Target $	**$11,406**	
Average Dealer Option Cost:	93%	
12 Month Price Increase:	None	

For 1999, the Civic CX hatchback receives minor revisions such as easy-to-use electronic controls for heating and air conditioning, and amber instrument illumination. This base model is equipped with a 50/50 split folding rear seat, dual remote mirrors, rear roofline spoiler and AM/FM high-power stereo. Available dealer installed options include air conditioning, a theft deterrent system and a CD player. Power steering is available with the optional four speed automatic transmission.

Ownership Costs (Projected)

Cost Area	5 Year Cost	Rating
Depreciation	$3,197	○
Financing ($189/month)	$2,219	
Insurance	$7,463	●
State Fees	$456	
Fuel (Hwy 37 City 32)	$2,146	○
Maintenance	$2,495	○
Repairs	$475	○

Warranty/Maintenance Info

Major Tune-Up (60K mile int.)	$264	○
Minor Tune-Up (30K mile int.)	$85	○
Brake Service	$262	○
Overall Warranty	3 yr/36k	○
Drivetrain Warranty	3 yr/36k	○
Rust Warranty	5 yr/unlim. mi	○
Maintenance Warranty	N/A	
Roadside Assistance	N/A	

Ownership Costs By Year (Projected)

$2,000 $4,000 $6,000 $8,000

■ 1999
■ 2000
■ 2001
□ 2002
□ 2003

Resale Value

1999	2000	2001	2002	2003
$10,843	$10,007	$9,405	$8,810	$8,209

Projected Costs (5yr)

Relative	This Car
$21,377	$18,451
Cost/Mile 31¢	Cost/Mile 26¢

Cumulative Costs

	1999	2000	2001	2002	2003
Annual	$3,305	$3,484	$3,353	$3,715	$4,594
Total	$3,305	$6,789	$10,142	$13,857	$18,451

Ownership Cost Value

○ Excellent

Honda Civic DX
2 Door Hatchback

Subcompact

| 1.6L 106 hp Gas Fuel Inject. | 4 Cylinder In-Line | Manual 5 Speed | 2 Wheel Front | Dual Airbags Std |

Purchase Price

Car Item	Dealer Cost	List
Base Price	**$10,937**	**$12,100**
Anti-Lock Brakes	N/A	N/A
Automatic 4 Speed	$722	$800
Optional Engine	N/A	N/A
Air Conditioning	Dlr	Dlr
Power Steering	Std	Std
Cruise Control	N/A	N/A
Power Windows	N/A	N/A
AM/FM Stereo Cassette	Dlr	Dlr
Steering Wheel, Tilt	Std	Std
Rear Defroster	Std	Std
*Options Price	$0	$0
*Total Price	$10,937	$12,100
Target Price	$11,551	
Destination Charge	$415	
Avg. Tax & Fees	$676	
Total Target $	**$12,642**	
Average Dealer Option Cost:	90%	
12 Month Price Increase:	None	

For 1999, the Civic DX hatchback adds a rear window wiper/washer, a removable cargo area cover, low-fuel indicator light and a convenient seatback storage pocket. A body-colored rear roofline spoiler is also standard. The DX hatchback comes equipped with an AM/FM stereo with digital clock. Available dealer-installed options include a front center console with armrest, cassette player, alloy wheels and floor mats. This hatchback has a cargo volume of 18.1 cubic feet with seats folded down.

Ownership Costs (Projected)

Cost Area	5 Year Cost	Rating
Depreciation	$3,501	○
Financing ($210/month)	$2,459	
Insurance	$7,643	●
State Fees	$514	
Fuel (Hwy 37 City 32)	$2,146	○
Maintenance	$2,495	○
Repairs	$475	○

Warranty/Maintenance Info

Major Tune-Up (60K mile int.)	$264	○
Minor Tune-Up (30K mile int.)	$85	○
Brake Service	$262	○
Overall Warranty	3 yr/36k	○
Drivetrain Warranty	3 yr/36k	○
Rust Warranty	5 yr/unlim. mi	○
Maintenance Warranty	N/A	
Roadside Assistance	N/A	

Ownership Costs By Year (Projected)

$2,000 $4,000 $6,000 $8,000

■ 1999
■ 2000
■ 2001
□ 2002
□ 2003

Resale Value

1999	2000	2001	2002	2003
$11,998	$11,088	$10,426	$9,782	$9,141

Projected Costs (5yr)

Relative	This Car
$22,277	$19,233
Cost/Mile 32¢	Cost/Mile 27¢

Cumulative Costs

	1999	2000	2001	2002	2003
Annual	$3,516	$3,672	$3,510	$3,843	$4,692
Total	$3,516	$7,188	$10,698	$14,541	$19,233

Ownership Cost Value

○ Excellent

78

* Includes shaded options
** Other purchase requirements apply
*** Price includes other options

● Poor   ◐ Worse Than Average   ○ Average   ○ Better Than Average   ○ Excellent   ⊖ Insufficient Information

Refer to *Section 3: Annotated Vehicle Charts* for an explanation of these charts.

Honda Civic DX
4 Door Sedan

1.6L 106 hp Gas Fuel Inject.	4 Cylinder In-Line	Manual 5 Speed	2 Wheel Front	Dual Airbags Std

EX Model Shown

Purchase Price

Car Item	Dealer Cost	List
Base Price	**$11,555**	**$12,785**
Anti-Lock Brakes	N/A	N/A
Automatic 4 Speed	$722	$800
Optional Engine	N/A	N/A
Air Conditioning	Dlr	Dlr
Power Steering	Std	Std
Cruise Control	N/A	N/A
Power Windows	N/A	N/A
AM/FM Stereo Cassette	Dlr	Dlr
Steering Wheel, Tilt	Std	Std
Rear Defroster	Std	Std
*Options Price	$0	$0
*Total Price	$11,555	$12,785
Target Price	$12,212	
Destination Charge	$415	
Avg. Tax & Fees	$713	
Total Target $	**$13,340**	
Average Dealer Option Cost:	90%	
12 Month Price Increase:	None	

For 1999, the Civic DX sedan features new front and rear styling that adds a sportier look. The instrument panel now features easy-to-use electronic controls for heating and air conditioning, with amber illumination for improved visibility. Standard features on the DX include a 60/40 split fold-down rear seatback, tilt steering, remote trunk release with trunk-open indicator light and a rear window defroster with timer. Available options include a CD changer, rear wing spoiler and fog lamps.

Ownership Costs (Projected)

Cost Area	5 Year Cost	Rating
Depreciation	$3,689	○
Financing ($221/month)	$2,596	
Insurance	$7,294	◉
State Fees	$541	
Fuel (Hwy 37 City 32)	$2,146	○
Maintenance	$2,495	○
Repairs	$475	○

Warranty/Maintenance Info

Major Tune-Up (60K mile int.)	$264	○
Minor Tune-Up (30K mile int.)	$85	○
Brake Service	$262	○
Overall Warranty	3 yr/36k	○
Drivetrain Warranty	3 yr/36k	○
Rust Warranty	5 yr/unlim. mi	○
Maintenance Warranty	N/A	
Roadside Assistance	N/A	

Ownership Costs By Year (Projected)

Legend: 1999, 2000, 2001, 2002, 2003

Resale Value

1999	2000	2001	2002	2003
$12,652	$11,695	$10,994	$10,318	$9,651

Cumulative Costs

	1999	2000	2001	2002	2003
Annual	$3,546	$3,695	$3,513	$3,826	$4,656
Total	$3,546	$7,241	$10,754	$14,580	$19,236

Projected Costs (5yr)

Relative	This Car
$22,920	$19,236
Cost/Mile 33¢	Cost/Mile 27¢

Ownership Cost Value

○ Excellent

Honda Civic LX
4 Door Sedan

1.6L 106 hp Gas Fuel Inject.	4 Cylinder In-Line	Manual 5 Speed	2 Wheel Front	Dual Airbags Std

EX Model Shown

Purchase Price

Car Item	Dealer Cost	List
Base Price	**$13,133**	**$14,830**
Anti-Lock Brakes	N/A	N/A
Automatic 4 Speed	$722	$800
Optional Engine	N/A	N/A
Air Conditioning	Std	Std
Power Steering	Std	Std
Cruise Control	Std	Std
Power Windows	Std	Std
AM/FM Stereo Cassette	Dlr	Dlr
Steering Wheel, Tilt	Std	Std
Rear Defroster	Std	Std
*Options Price	$0	$0
*Total Price	$13,133	$14,830
Target Price	$13,964	
Destination Charge	$415	
Avg. Tax & Fees	$812	
Total Target $	**$15,191**	
Average Dealer Option Cost:	90%	
12 Month Price Increase:	1%	

For 1999, the Civic LX sedan features new front and rear styling that adds a sportier look. The instrument panel now features easy-to-use electronic controls for heating and air conditioning, with amber illumination for improved visibility. The LX comes equipped with extras such as air conditioning, power windows and door locks, cruise control and a tachometer. Available dealer-installed options include fog lamps, a rear wing spoiler, a keyless remote entry system and a theft deterrent system.

Ownership Costs (Projected)

Cost Area	5 Year Cost	Rating
Depreciation	$5,286	○
Financing ($252/month)	$2,955	
Insurance	$7,463	◉
State Fees	$622	
Fuel (Hwy 37 City 32)	$2,146	○
Maintenance	$2,495	○
Repairs	$475	○

Warranty/Maintenance Info

Major Tune-Up (60K mile int.)	$264	○
Minor Tune-Up (30K mile int.)	$85	○
Brake Service	$262	○
Overall Warranty	3 yr/36k	○
Drivetrain Warranty	3 yr/36k	○
Rust Warranty	5 yr/unlim. mi	○
Maintenance Warranty	N/A	
Roadside Assistance	N/A	

Ownership Costs By Year (Projected)

Legend: 1999, 2000, 2001, 2002, 2003

Resale Value

1999	2000	2001	2002	2003
$14,114	$13,007	$12,038	$11,001	$9,905

Cumulative Costs

	1999	2000	2001	2002	2003
Annual	$4,110	$3,995	$3,905	$4,283	$5,149
Total	$4,110	$8,105	$12,010	$16,293	$21,442

Projected Costs (5yr)

Relative	This Car
$24,585	$21,442
Cost/Mile 35¢	Cost/Mile 31¢

Ownership Cost Value

○ Excellent

---

* Includes shaded options

** Other purchase requirements apply

*** Price includes other options

 Poor   Worse Than Average   Average   Better Than Average   Excellent   Insufficient Information

Refer to Section 3: Annotated Vehicle Charts for an explanation of these charts.

Honda Civic EX
4 Door Sedan

Subcompact

1.6L 127 hp Gas Fuel Inject.	4 Cylinder In-Line	Manual 5 Speed	2 Wheel Front	Dual Airbags Std

Purchase Price

Car Item	Dealer Cost	List
Base Price	**$15,114**	**$16,730**
Anti-Lock Brakes	Std	Std
Automatic 4 Speed	$722	$800
Optional Engine	N/A	N/A
Air Conditioning	Std	Std
Power Steering	Std	Std
Cruise Control	Std	Std
Power Windows	Std	Std
AM/FM Stereo CD	Std	Std
Steering Wheel, Tilt	Std	Std
Rear Defroster	Std	Std
*Options Price	$0	$0
*Total Price	$15,114	$16,730
Target Price	$16,038	
Destination Charge	$415	
Avg. Tax & Fees	$924	
Total Target $	**$17,377**	
Average Dealer Option Cost:	**90%**	
12 Month Price Increase:	2%	

Ownership Costs (Projected)

Cost Area	5 Year Cost	Rating
Depreciation	$6,921	◯
Financing ($288/month)	$3,381	
Insurance	$7,837	◉
State Fees	$698	
Fuel (Hwy 35 City 29)	$2,313	◯
Maintenance	$2,495	◯
Repairs	$475	◯

Ownership Costs By Year (Projected)

$2,000 $4,000 $6,000 $8,000

Legend: 1999, 2000, 2001, 2002, 2003

Warranty/Maintenance Info

Major Tune-Up (60K mile int.)	$264	◯
Minor Tune-Up (30K mile int.)	$85	◯
Brake Service	$262	◯
Overall Warranty	3 yr/36k	◯
Drivetrain Warranty	3 yr/36k	◯
Rust Warranty	5 yr/unlim. mi	◯
Maintenance Warranty	N/A	
Roadside Assistance	N/A	

Resale Value

1999	2000	2001	2002	2003
$15,406	$14,111	$12,954	$11,733	$10,456

Projected Costs (5yr)

Relative	This Car
$26,721	$24,120
Cost/Mile 38¢	Cost/Mile 34¢

Cumulative Costs

	1999	2000	2001	2002	2003
Annual	$5,270	$4,424	$4,304	$4,647	$5,475
Total	$5,270	$9,694	$13,998	$18,645	$24,120

Ownership Cost Value

◯ Excellent

For 1999, the top of the line Civic EX sedan features new front and rear styling that adds a sportier look. The instrument panel now features easy-to-use electronic controls for heating and air conditioning, with amber illumination for improved visibility. In addition to the LX's amenities, the EX includes map lights, a power moonroof with tilt feature and a remote entry system. Dealer-installed options include a sunroof visor, a theft deterrent system and a CD changer.

Honda Prelude
2 Door Coupe

Subcompact

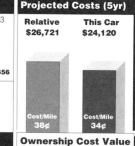

Type SH Shown

2.2L 200 hp Gas Fuel Inject.	4 Cylinder In-Line	Manual 5 Speed	2 Wheel Front	Dual Airbags Std

Purchase Price

Car Item	Dealer Cost	List
Base Price	**$20,937**	**$23,450**
Anti-Lock Brakes	Std	Std
Automatic 4 Speed	$892	$1,000
Optional Engine	N/A	N/A
Air Conditioning	Std	Std
Power Steering	Std	Std
Cruise Control	Std	Std
Power Windows	Std	Std
AM/FM Stereo CD	Std	Std
Steering Wheel, Tilt	Std	Std
Rear Defroster	Std	Std
*Options Price	$0	$0
*Total Price	$20,937	$23,450
Target Price	$21,836	
Destination Charge	$415	
Avg. Tax & Fees	$1,253	
Total Target $	**$23,504**	
Average Dealer Option Cost:	**89%**	
12 Month Price Increase:	1%	

Ownership Costs (Projected)

Cost Area	5 Year Cost	Rating
Depreciation	$9,405	◯
Financing ($390/month)	$4,572	
Insurance (Performance)	$11,730	●
State Fees	$968	
Fuel (Hwy 27 City 22 -Prem.)	$3,583	●
Maintenance	$3,188	◯
Repairs	$475	◯

Ownership Costs By Year (Projected)

$2,000 $4,000 $6,000 $8,000 $10,000 $12,000

Legend: 1999, 2000, 2001, 2002, 2003

Warranty/Maintenance Info

Major Tune-Up (60K mile int.)	$311	●
Minor Tune-Up (30K mile int.)	$108	●
Brake Service	$268	●
Overall Warranty	3 yr/36k	◯
Drivetrain Warranty	3 yr/36k	◯
Rust Warranty	5 yr/unlim. mi	◯
Maintenance Warranty	N/A	
Roadside Assistance	N/A	

Resale Value

1999	2000	2001	2002	2003
$22,244	$20,108	$18,140	$16,133	$14,099

Projected Costs (5yr)

Relative	This Car
$33,299	$33,921
Cost/Mile 48¢	Cost/Mile 48¢

Cumulative Costs

	1999	2000	2001	2002	2003
Annual	$6,017	$6,663	$6,496	$6,903	$7,842
Total	$6,017	$12,680	$19,176	$26,079	$33,921

Ownership Cost Value

◯ Average

For 1999, the Prelude receives a boost in power from the 2.2L VTEC engine. It now produces 200 hp with the manual transmission and 195 hp with the four speed automatic. A keyless entry system is now standard for 1999. A micron air filter has been added to the standard air conditioning system and a new mesh style grille has been added. The Prelude comes fully equipped with luxury amenities including power windows and locks, a power moonroof and an AM/FM stereo with CD player.

80

* Includes shaded options
** Other purchase requirements apply
*** Price includes other options

 ● Poor
 ◉ Worse Than Average
 ◯ Average
Better Than Average
Excellent
 ⊖ Insufficient Information

Refer to *Section 3: Annotated Vehicle Charts* for an explanation of these charts.

Honda Prelude Type SH
2 Door Coupe

Subcompact

2.2L 200 hp Gas Fuel Inject.	4 Cylinder In-Line	Manual 5 Speed	2 Wheel Front	Dual Airbags Std

Purchase Price

Car Item	Dealer Cost	List
Base Price	**$23,167**	**$25,950**
Anti-Lock Brakes	Std	Std
Automatic Transmission	N/A	N/A
Optional Engine	N/A	N/A
Air Conditioning	Std	Std
Power Steering	Std	Std
Cruise Control	Std	Std
Power Windows	Std	Std
AM/FM Stereo CD	Std	Std
Steering Wheel, Tilt	Std	Std
Rear Defroster	Std	Std
*Options Price	$0	$0
*Total Price	**$23,167**	**$25,950**
Target Price	$24,199	
Destination Charge	$415	
Avg. Tax & Fees	$1,385	
Total Target $	**$25,999**	
Average Dealer Option Cost:	**N/A**	
12 Month Price Increase:	1%	

Ownership Costs (Projected)

Cost Area	5 Year Cost	Rating
Depreciation	$11,506	◐
Financing ($431/month)	$5,057	
Insurance (Performance)	$12,218	●
State Fees	$1,068	
Fuel (Hwy 27 City 22 -Prem.)	$3,583	●
Maintenance	$3,177	◐
Repairs	$475	○

Warranty/Maintenance Info

Major Tune-Up (60K mile int.)	$311	●
Minor Tune-Up (30K mile int.)	$108	◉
Brake Service	$268	◉
Overall Warranty	3 yr/36k	◐
Drivetrain Warranty	3 yr/36k	◐
Rust Warranty	5 yr/unlim. mi	○
Maintenance Warranty	N/A	
Roadside Assistance	N/A	

The 1999 Prelude Type SH enters this model year with a boost in power from the 2.2L VTEC engine. The VTEC engine now generates 200 hp, compared to 195 hp in the previous year. The Type SH is equipped with an Active Torque Transfer System (ATTS) that reduces understeer by adjusting power to the front wheels during cornering. The Prelude Type SH comes fully equipped with amenities including power windows, locks and moonroof. The rear decklid is also outfitted with a spoiler.

Ownership Costs By Year (Projected)

$2,000 $4,000 $6,000 $8,000 $10,000 $12,000 $14,000

- 1999
- 2000
- 2001
- 2002
- 2003

Resale Value

1999	2000	2001	2002	2003
$22,718	$20,565	$18,577	$16,550	$14,493

Cumulative Costs

	1999	2000	2001	2002	2003
Annual	$8,321	$6,932	$6,733	$7,104	$7,994
Total	$8,321	$15,253	$21,986	$29,090	$37,084

Projected Costs (5yr)

Relative $35,936	This Car $37,084
Cost/Mile 51¢	Cost/Mile 53¢

Ownership Cost Value

◐ Average

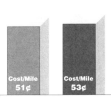

Hyundai Accent L
2 Door Hatchback

Compact

GS Model Shown

1.5L 92 hp Gas Fuel Inject.	4 Cylinder In-Line	Manual 5 Speed	2 Wheel Front	Dual Airbags Std

Purchase Price

Car Item	Dealer Cost	List
Base Price	**$8,610**	**$8,999**
Anti-Lock Brakes	N/A	N/A
Automatic Transmission	N/A	N/A
Optional Engine	N/A	N/A
Air Conditioning	N/A	N/A
Power Steering	N/A	N/A
Cruise Control	N/A	N/A
Power Windows	N/A	N/A
AM/FM Stereo Cassette	Std	Std
Steering Wheel, Tilt	N/A	N/A
Rear Defroster	Std	Std
*Options Price	$0	$0
*Total Price	**$8,610**	**$8,999**
Target Price	$8,818	
Destination Charge	$435	
Avg. Tax & Fees	$523	
Total Target $	**$9,776**	
Average Dealer Option Cost:	**68%**	
12 Month Price Increase:	None	

Ownership Costs (Projected)

Cost Area	5 Year Cost	Rating
Depreciation	$6,141	●
Financing ($162/month)	$1,902	
Insurance	$7,643	●
State Fees	$390	
Fuel (Hwy 37 City 28)	$2,281	○
Maintenance	$2,643	○
Repairs	$680	○

Warranty/Maintenance Info

Major Tune-Up (60K mile int.)	$224	○
Minor Tune-Up (30K mile int.)	$98	○
Brake Service	$208	○
Overall Warranty	5 yr/60k	○
Drivetrain Warranty	10 yr/100k	○
Rust Warranty	5 yr/100k	○
Maintenance Warranty	N/A	
Roadside Assistance	5 yr/unlim. mi	

The Accent L hatchback coupe arrives this year as the base model of the hatchback series. There are several options offered including a rear spoiler, trunk cargo net, mud guards and carpeted floor mats. Also available are a security system, sports rack and driver's door keyless entry. Some of the standard features on the Accent L are dual airbags, AM/FM stereo with cassette and a five speed manual transmission, along with the Hyundai Advantage warranty and roadside assistance program.

Ownership Costs By Year (Projected)

$2,000 $4,000 $6,000 $8,000

- 1999
- 2000
- 2001
- 2002
- 2003

Resale Value

1999	2000	2001	2002	2003
$7,900	$6,753	$5,762	$4,719	$3,635

Cumulative Costs

	1999	2000	2001	2002	2003
Annual	$4,552	$3,752	$3,669	$4,498	$5,209
Total	$4,552	$8,304	$11,973	$16,471	$21,680

Projected Costs (5yr)

Relative $21,370	This Car $21,680
Cost/Mile 31¢	Cost/Mile 31¢

Ownership Cost Value

◐ Average

---

* Includes shaded options

** Other purchase requirements apply

*** Price includes other options

● Poor	◉ Worse Than Average	◐ Average	○ Better Than Average	○ Excellent	⊖ Insufficient Information

Refer to *Section 3: Annotated Vehicle Charts* for an explanation of these charts.

HYUNDAI

Hyundai Accent GS
2 Door Hatchback

| 1.5L 92 hp Gas Fuel Inject. | 4 Cylinder In-Line | Manual 5 Speed | 2 Wheel Front | Dual Airbags Std |

Purchase Price

Car Item	Dealer Cost	List
Base Price	**$9,265**	**$9,899**
Anti-Lock Brakes	N/A	N/A
Automatic 4 Speed	$732	$800
Optional Engine	N/A	N/A
Air Conditioning	Pkg	Pkg
Power Steering	Std	Std
Cruise Control	N/A	N/A
Power Windows	Pkg	Pkg
AM/FM Stereo Cassette	Std	Std
Steering Wheel, Tilt	N/A	N/A
1/AA Package	N/C	N/C
*Options Price	**$732**	**$800**
*Total Price	**$9,997**	**$10,699**
Target Price	$10,267	
Destination Charge	$435	
Avg. Tax & Fees	$606	
Total Target $	**$11,308**	
Average Dealer Option Cost:	84%	
12 Month Price Increase:	None	

Ownership Costs (Projected)

Cost Area	5 Year Cost	Rating
Depreciation	$7,034	●
Financing ($187/month)	$2,199	
Insurance	$7,837	●
State Fees	$458	
Fuel (Hwy 36 City 26)	$2,396	○
Maintenance	$2,660	○
Repairs	$680	○

Warranty/Maintenance Info

Major Tune-Up (60K mile int.)	$224	○
Minor Tune-Up (30K mile int.)	$98	◐
Brake Service	$208	○
Overall Warranty	5 yr/60k	◔
Drivetrain Warranty	10 yr/100k	◔
Rust Warranty	5 yr/100k	○
Maintenance Warranty	N/A	
Roadside Assistance	5 yr/unlim. mi	

Ownership Costs By Year (Projected)

Legend: 1999, 2000, 2001, 2002, 2003

Resale Value

1999	2000	2001	2002	2003
$8,791	$7,581	$6,527	$5,421	$4,274

Cumulative Costs

	1999	2000	2001	2002	2003
Annual	$5,370	$3,972	$3,869	$4,693	$5,360
Total	$5,370	$9,342	$13,211	$17,904	$23,264

Projected Costs (5yr)

Relative	This Car
$22,445	$23,264
Cost/Mile 32¢	Cost/Mile 33¢

Ownership Cost Value

Worse Than Average

The Accent GS hatchback coupe arrives this year offering a standard five speed manual transmission or optional four speed automatic. Upgraded from the L hatchback coupe, the GS offers additional standard and optional features. To upgrade its amenities, Package #3 includes a manual pop-up moonroof with sunshade, AM/FM ETR stereo with CD and air conditioning. The GS also features the Hyundai Advantage warranty and roadside assistance program. The GSi model is no longer available.

 HYUNDAI

Hyundai Accent GL
4 Door Sedan

Compact

| 1.5L 92 hp Gas Fuel Inject. | 4 Cylinder In-Line | Manual 5 Speed | 2 Wheel Front | Dual Airbags Std |

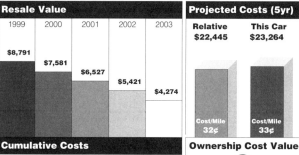

1998 Model Shown

Purchase Price

Car Item	Dealer Cost	List
Base Price	**$9,265**	**$9,899**
Anti-Lock Brakes	N/A	N/A
Automatic 4 Speed	$732	$800
Optional Engine	N/A	N/A
Air Conditioning	Pkg	Pkg
Power Steering	Std	Std
Cruise Control	N/A	N/A
Power Windows	N/A	N/A
AM/FM Stereo Cassette	Std	Std
Steering Wheel, Tilt	N/A	N/A
1/AA Package	N/C	N/C
*Options Price	**$732**	**$800**
*Total Price	**$9,997**	**$10,699**
Target Price	$10,267	
Destination Charge	$435	
Avg. Tax & Fees	$606	
Total Target $	**$11,308**	
Average Dealer Option Cost:	81%	
12 Month Price Increase:	None	

Ownership Costs (Projected)

Cost Area	5 Year Cost	Rating
Depreciation	$6,970	◐
Financing ($187/month)	$2,199	
Insurance	$7,837	●
State Fees	$458	
Fuel (Hwy 36 City 26)	$2,396	○
Maintenance	$2,660	○
Repairs	$680	○

Warranty/Maintenance Info

Major Tune-Up (60K mile int.)	$224	○
Minor Tune-Up (30K mile int.)	$98	◐
Brake Service	$208	○
Overall Warranty	5 yr/60k	◔
Drivetrain Warranty	10 yr/100k	◔
Rust Warranty	5 yr/100k	○
Maintenance Warranty	N/A	
Roadside Assistance	5 yr/unlim. mi	

Ownership Costs By Year (Projected)

Legend: 1999, 2000, 2001, 2002, 2003

Resale Value

1999	2000	2001	2002	2003
$8,886	$7,667	$6,604	$5,491	$4,338

Cumulative Costs

	1999	2000	2001	2002	2003
Annual	$5,275	$3,981	$3,878	$4,700	$5,366
Total	$5,275	$9,256	$13,134	$17,834	$23,200

Projected Costs (5yr)

Relative	This Car
$22,445	$23,200
Cost/Mile 32¢	Cost/Mile 33¢

Ownership Cost Value

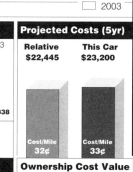

Worse Than Average

The Accent GL sedan arrives this year with a standard five speed manual transmission or optional four speed automatic. The GL sedan offers additional standard features over the L model, including power steering, tinted glass, dual airbags, remote trunk release and AM/FM stereo cassette radio. Air conditioning, a security system with driver's door keyless entry and mud guards are available optional features. The Accent also features the Hyundai Advantage warranty and roadside assistance program.

82

* Includes shaded options

** Other purchase requirements apply

*** Price includes other options

 ● Poor   ◐ Worse Than Average   ○ Average   Better Than Average   Excellent   ⊖ Insufficient Information

Refer to *Section 3: Annotated Vehicle Charts* for an explanation of these charts.

Hyundai Elantra GL
4 Door Sedan

Compact

 2.0L 140 hp Gas Fuel Inject.
 4 Cylinder In-Line
 Manual 5 Speed
 2 Wheel Front
 Dual Airbags Std

Purchase Price

Car Item	Dealer Cost	List
Base Price	**$10,643**	**$11,499**
Anti-Lock Brakes	N/A	N/A
Automatic 4 Speed	$732	$800
Optional Engine	N/A	N/A
Air Conditioning	Std	Std
Power Steering	Std	Std
Cruise Control	Pkg	Pkg
Power Windows	N/A	N/A
AM/FM Stereo Cassette	Std	Std
Steering Wheel, Tilt	Std	Std
01/AA Package	N/C	N/C
*Options Price	$732	$800
*Total Price	**$11,375**	**$12,299**
Target Price	$11,651	
Destination Charge	$435	
Avg. Tax & Fees	$684	
Total Target $	**$12,770**	
Average Dealer Option Cost:	**78%**	
12 Month Price Increase:	None	

The Elantra GL sedan has new styling for the 1999 model year. Also new for this year are a more powerful 2.0L 140 hp engine, improved controls and seat fabrics as well as standard air conditioning. Option Package #3 includes cruise control and an AM/FM stereo with CD player. A security system, mud guards and sports rack are separate optional features. The Elantra GL also features the Hyundai Advantage warranty and roadside assistance program.

Ownership Costs (Projected)

Cost Area	5 Year Cost	Rating
Depreciation	$7,951	●
Financing ($212/month)	$2,484	
Insurance	$8,045	●
State Fees	$522	
Fuel (Hwy 31 City 22)	$2,806	○
Maintenance	$2,906	○
Repairs	$715	○

Warranty/Maintenance Info

Major Tune-Up (60K mile int.)	$214	○
Minor Tune-Up (30K mile int.)	$99	◑
Brake Service	$201	○
Overall Warranty	5 yr/60k	○
Drivetrain Warranty	10 yr/100k	○
Rust Warranty	5 yr/100k	○
Maintenance Warranty	N/A	
Roadside Assistance	5 yr/unlim. mi	

Ownership Costs By Year (Projected)

$2,000 $4,000 $6,000 $8,000 $10,000

- 1999
- 2000
- 2001
- 2002
- 2003

Resale Value

1999	2000	2001	2002	2003
$9,680	$8,382	$7,240	$6,049	$4,819

Cumulative Costs

	1999	2000	2001	2002	2003
Annual	$6,174	$4,274	$4,154	$4,959	$5,868
Total	$6,174	$10,448	$14,602	$19,561	$25,429

Projected Costs (5yr)

Relative	This Car
$23,572	$25,429
Cost/Mile 34¢	Cost/Mile 36¢

Ownership Cost Value
● Poor

Hyundai Elantra GLS
4 Door Sedan

Compact

 2.0L 140 hp Gas Fuel Inject.
 4 Cylinder In-Line
 Manual 5 Speed
 2 Wheel Front · Dual Airbags Std

GL Model Shown

Purchase Price

Car Item	Dealer Cost	List
Base Price	**$11,555**	**$12,749**
Anti-Lock Brakes	Pkg	Pkg
Automatic 4 Speed	$686	$750
Optional Engine	N/A	N/A
Air Conditioning	Std	Std
Power Steering	Std	Std
Cruise Control	Pkg	Pkg
Windows, Power	Std	Std
AM/FM Stereo Cassette	Std	Std
Steering Wheel, Tilt	Std	Std
01/AA Package	N/C	N/C
*Options Price	$686	$750
*Total Price	**$12,241**	**$13,499**
Target Price	$12,570	
Destination Charge	$435	
Avg. Tax & Fees	$737	
Total Target $	**$13,742**	
Average Dealer Option Cost:	**83%**	
12 Month Price Increase:	None	

With only a slight increase of $200 compared to last year's price, the Elantra GLS sedan offers more new features. New for this year are a more powerful 2.0L 140 hp engine, improved controls and seat fabrics as well as standard air conditioning. The GLS sedan is also available with a four speed automatic transmission and many optional packages. Additional separate options are also available, including a security system with driver's door keyless entry, sports rack and mud guards.

Ownership Costs (Projected)

Cost Area	5 Year Cost	Rating
Depreciation	$8,554	●
Financing ($228/month)	$2,673	
Insurance	$8,265	●
State Fees	$570	
Fuel (Hwy 31 City 22)	$2,806	○
Maintenance	$2,843	○
Repairs	$715	○

Warranty/Maintenance Info

Major Tune-Up (60K mile int.)	$214	○
Minor Tune-Up (30K mile int.)	$99	◑
Brake Service	$142	○
Overall Warranty	5 yr/60k	○
Drivetrain Warranty	10 yr/100k	○
Rust Warranty	5 yr/100k	○
Maintenance Warranty	N/A	
Roadside Assistance	5 yr/unlim. mi	

Ownership Costs By Year (Projected)

$2,000 $4,000 $6,000 $8,000 $10,000

- 1999
- 2000
- 2001
- 2002
- 2003

Resale Value

1999	2000	2001	2002	2003
$10,333	$8,961	$7,747	$6,486	$5,188

Cumulative Costs

	1999	2000	2001	2002	2003
Annual	$6,611	$4,453	$4,318	$5,045	$5,999
Total	$6,611	$11,064	$15,382	$20,427	$26,426

Projected Costs (5yr)

Relative	This Car
$24,310	$26,426
Cost/Mile 35¢	Cost/Mile 38¢

Ownership Cost Value
● Poor

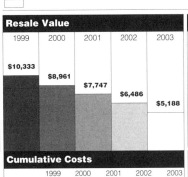

* Includes shaded options
** Other purchase requirements apply
*** Price includes other options

● Poor   ◑ Worse Than Average   ○ Average   ○ Better Than Average   ○ Excellent   ⊖ Insufficient Information

Refer to *Section 3: Annotated Vehicle Charts* for an explanation of these charts.

83

Hyundai Elantra GL
4 Door Wagon

Small Wagon

 2.0L 140 hp Gas Fuel Inject. | 4 Cylinder In-Line | Manual 5 Speed | 2 Wheel Front | Dual Airbags Std

Purchase Price

Car Item	Dealer Cost	List
Base Price	**$11,477**	**$12,399**
Anti-Lock Brakes	N/A	N/A
Automatic 4 Speed	$732	$800
Optional Engine	N/A	N/A
Air Conditioning	Std	Std
Power Steering	Std	Std
Cruise Control	Pkg	Pkg
Power Windows	N/A	N/A
AM/FM Stereo Cassette	Std	Std
Steering Wheel, Tilt	Std	Std
01/AA Package	N/C	N/C
*Options Price	$732	$800
*Total Price	**$12,209**	**$13,199**
Target Price	$12,511	
Destination Charge	$435	
Avg. Tax & Fees	$732	
Total Target $	**$13,678**	
Average Dealer Option Cost:	80%	
12 Month Price Increase:	None	

At a suggested retail price virtually unchanged from last year, the Elantra GL wagon is offering more standard features. New for this year are a more powerful 2.0L 140 hp engine, improved controls and seat fabrics as well as standard air conditioning. The GL wagon is also available with a four speed automatic transmission. Available packages include such features as cruise control and an AM/FM stereo with CD player. Roof rack rails and mud guards are optional features.

Ownership Costs (Projected)

Cost Area	5 Year Cost	Rating
Depreciation	$8,413	●
Financing ($227/month)	$2,661	
Insurance	$8,045	●
State Fees	$558	
Fuel (Hwy 30 City 21)	$2,920	○
Maintenance	$2,906	○
Repairs	$715	○

Warranty/Maintenance Info

Major Tune-Up (60K mile int.)	$214	○
Minor Tune-Up (30K mile int.)	$99	○
Brake Service	$201	○
Overall Warranty	5 yr/60k	○
Drivetrain Warranty	10 yr/100k	○
Rust Warranty	5 yr/100k	○
Maintenance Warranty	N/A	
Roadside Assistance	5 yr/unlim. mi	

Ownership Costs By Year (Projected)

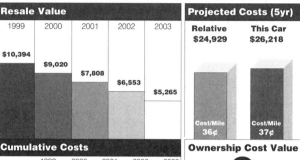

$2,000 $4,000 $6,000 $8,000 $10,000

1999 / 2000 / 2001 / 2002 / 2003

Resale Value

1999	2000	2001	2002	2003
$10,394	$9,020	$7,808	$6,553	$5,265

Cumulative Costs

	1999	2000	2001	2002	2003
Annual	$6,459	$4,429	$4,290	$5,076	$5,964
Total	$6,459	$10,888	$15,178	$20,254	$26,218

Projected Costs (5yr)

Relative $24,929	This Car $26,218
Cost/Mile 36¢	Cost/Mile 37¢

Ownership Cost Value

Worse Than Average

Hyundai Elantra GLS
4 Door Wagon

Small Wagon

2.0L 140 hp Gas Fuel Inject. | 4 Cylinder In-Line | Automatic 4 Speed | 2 Wheel Front | Dual Airbags Std

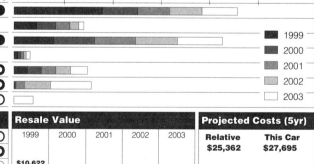

GL Model Shown

Purchase Price

Car Item	Dealer Cost	List
Base Price	**$12,688**	**$13,999**
Anti-Lock Brakes	Pkg	Pkg
Manual Transmission	N/A	N/A
Optional Engine	N/A	N/A
Air Conditioning	Std	Std
Power Steering	Std	Std
Cruise Control	Pkg	Pkg
Windows, Power	Std	Std
AM/FM Stereo Cassette	Std	Std
Steering Wheel, Tilt	Std	Std
01/AA Package	N/C	N/C
*Options Price	$0	$0
*Total Price	**$12,688**	**$13,999**
Target Price	$13,037	
Destination Charge	$435	
Avg. Tax & Fees	$763	
Total Target $	**$14,235**	
Average Dealer Option Cost:	82%	
12 Month Price Increase:	None	

With no price change compared to last year, the GLS wagon is back again with more standard features. New for this year are a more powerful 2.0L 140 hp engine, improved controls and seat fabrics and standard air conditioning. The GLS wagon is only available with a four speed automatic transmission. Three option packages are available. Selected options are also available, including roof rack rails, mud guards and a security system with driver's door keyless entry.

Ownership Costs (Projected)

Cost Area	5 Year Cost	Rating
Depreciation	$9,123	●
Financing ($236/month)	$2,770	
Insurance	$8,500	●
State Fees	$590	
Fuel (Hwy 30 City 21)	$2,920	○
Maintenance	$3,077	○
Repairs	$715	○

Warranty/Maintenance Info

Major Tune-Up (60K mile int.)	$214	○
Minor Tune-Up (30K mile int.)	$99	○
Brake Service	$142	○
Overall Warranty	5 yr/60k	○
Drivetrain Warranty	10 yr/100k	○
Rust Warranty	5 yr/100k	○
Maintenance Warranty	N/A	
Roadside Assistance	5 yr/unlim. mi	

Ownership Costs By Year (Projected)

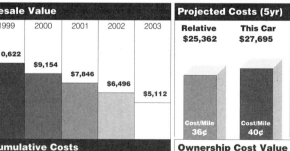

$2,000 $4,000 $6,000 $8,000 $10,000

1999 / 2000 / 2001 / 2002 / 2003

Resale Value

1999	2000	2001	2002	2003
$10,622	$9,154	$7,846	$6,496	$5,112

Cumulative Costs

	1999	2000	2001	2002	2003
Annual	$6,920	$4,649	$4,620	$5,221	$6,285
Total	$6,920	$11,569	$16,189	$21,410	$27,695

Projected Costs (5yr)

Relative $25,362	This Car $27,695
Cost/Mile 36¢	Cost/Mile 40¢

Ownership Cost Value

Poor

 Poor | Worse Than Average | Average | Better Than Average | Excellent | Insufficient Information

Refer to *Section 3: Annotated Vehicle Charts* for an explanation of these charts.

Hyundai Sonata
4 Door Sedan

2.4L 149 hp Gas Fuel Inject.	4 Cylinder In-Line	Manual 5 Speed	2 Wheel Front	Dual Front/Side Airbags Std

Purchase Price

Car Item	Dealer Cost	List
Base Price	**$13,805**	**$14,999**
Anti-Lock Brakes	N/A	N/A
Automatic 4 Speed	$799	$800
Optional Engine	N/A	N/A
Air Conditioning	Std	Std
Power Steering	Std	Std
Cruise Control	Pkg	Pkg
Power Windows	Std	Std
AM/FM Stereo Cassette	Std	Std
Steering Wheel, Tilt	Std	Std
01/AA Package	$208	***$250
*Options Price	$1,007	$1,050
*Total Price	$14,812	$16,049
Target Price	$15,307	
Destination Charge	$435	
Avg. Tax & Fees	$886	
Total Target $	**$16,628**	
Average Dealer Option Cost:	89%	
12 Month Price Increase:	None	

Ownership Costs (Projected)

Cost Area	5 Year Cost	Rating
Depreciation	$9,543	◉
Financing ($276/month)	$3,235	
Insurance	$7,140	O
State Fees	$672	
Fuel (Hwy 28 City 21)	$3,026	O
Maintenance	$2,835	O
Repairs	$935	◉

Warranty/Maintenance Info

Major Tune-Up (60K mile int.)	$183	O
Minor Tune-Up (30K mile int.)	$96	O
Brake Service	$205	O
Overall Warranty	5 yr/60k	
Drivetrain Warranty	10 yr/100k	
Rust Warranty	5 yr/100k	O
Maintenance Warranty	N/A	
Roadside Assistance	5 yr/unlim. mi	

The Sonata is all-new for 1999. A redesigned body, new engine and suspension and advanced safety features are just some of the changes made for this year. A new 2.4L 4 cylinder engine developing 149 hp is standard on the base Sonata. The Passenger Presence Detection System disables both front passenger airbags when a load of less then 60 lbs (33 for the side airbag) is in the passenger seat. Power windows, mirrors and door locks are now standard on the base Sonata.

Ownership Costs By Year (Projected)

$2,000 $4,000 $6,000 $8,000 $10,000

- ■ 1999
- ■ 2000
- ▨ 2001
- ▨ 2002
- □ 2003

Resale Value

1999	2000	2001	2002	2003
$13,456	$11,697	$10,194	$8,625	$7,085

Cumulative Costs

	1999	2000	2001	2002	2003
Annual	$6,418	$4,841	$4,558	$5,359	$6,210
Total	$6,418	$11,259	$15,817	$21,176	$27,386

Projected Costs (5yr)

Relative $26,856	This Car $27,386
Cost/Mile 38¢	Cost/Mile 39¢

Ownership Cost Value

O Average

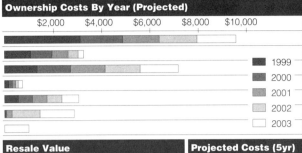

Hyundai Sonata GLS
4 Door Sedan

Midsize

Base Model Shown

2.5L 170 hp Gas Fuel Inject.	6 Cylinder "V"	Manual 5 Speed	2 Wheel Front	Dual Front/Side Airbags Std

Purchase Price

Car Item	Dealer Cost	List
Base Price	**$15,116**	**$16,999**
Anti-Lock Brakes	Pkg	Pkg
Automatic 4 Speed	$799	$800
Optional Engine	N/A	N/A
Air Conditioning	Std	Std
Power Steering	Std	Std
Cruise/Speed Control	Std	Std
Power Windows	Std	Std
AM/FM Stereo CD	Std	Std
Steering Wheel, Tilt	Std	Std
01/AA Package	N/C	N/C
*Options Price	$799	$800
*Total Price	$15,915	$17,799
Target Price	$16,530	
Destination Charge	$435	
Avg. Tax & Fees	$958	
Total Target $	**$17,923**	
Average Dealer Option Cost:	87%	
12 Month Price Increase:	None	

Ownership Costs (Projected)

Cost Area	5 Year Cost	Rating
Depreciation	$10,066	◉
Financing ($297/month)	$3,486	
Insurance	$7,463	O
State Fees	$742	
Fuel (Hwy 28 City 20)	$3,097	O
Maintenance	$3,114	O
Repairs	$935	◉

Warranty/Maintenance Info

Major Tune-Up (60K mile int.)	$278	O
Minor Tune-Up (30K mile int.)	$121	O
Brake Service	$192	O
Overall Warranty	5 yr/60k	O
Drivetrain Warranty	10 yr/100k	O
Rust Warranty	5 yr/100k	O
Maintenance Warranty	N/A	
Roadside Assistance	5 yr/unlim. mi	

For 1999, the Sonata GLS has been completely redesigned. A restyled exterior and new engine and transmission are just some of the updates. The GLS receives a new all-aluminum 2.5L V6 engine developing 170 hp. The optional automatic transmission features fuzzy logic technology, adapting the transmission's performance to the driver's preferences. The Passenger Presence Detection System disables both front passenger airbags when a weight of less then 60 lbs (33 for the side airbag) is detected.

Ownership Costs By Year (Projected)

$2,000 $4,000 $6,000 $8,000 $10,000 $12,000

- ■ 1999
- ■ 2000
- ▨ 2001
- ▨ 2002
- □ 2003

Resale Value

1999	2000	2001	2002	2003
$14,952	$12,996	$11,306	$9,562	$7,857

Cumulative Costs

	1999	2000	2001	2002	2003
Annual	$6,396	$5,203	$4,917	$5,672	$6,715
Total	$6,396	$11,599	$16,516	$22,188	$28,903

Projected Costs (5yr)

Relative $27,639	This Car $28,903
Cost/Mile 39¢	Cost/Mile 41¢

Ownership Cost Value

◉ Worse Than Average

---

* Includes shaded options

** Other purchase requirements apply

*** Price includes other options

● Poor	◉ Worse Than Average	O Average	O Better Than Average	○ Excellent	⊖ Insufficient Information

85

Refer to *Section 3: Annotated Vehicle Charts* for an explanation of these charts.

Hyundai Tiburon
2 Door Coupe

Subcompact

| 2.0L 140 hp Gas Fuel Inject. | 4 Cylinder In-Line | Manual 5 Speed | 2 Wheel Front | Dual Airbags Std |

Purchase Price

Car Item	Dealer Cost	List
Base Price	**$12,446**	**$13,599**
Anti-Lock Brakes	N/A	N/A
Automatic 4 Speed	$725	$800
Optional Engine	N/A	N/A
Air Conditioning	Pkg	Pkg
Power Steering	Std	Std
Cruise Control	N/A	N/A
Windows, Power	Std	Std
AM/FM Stereo Cassette	Std	Std
Steering Wheel, Tilt	Std	Std
01/AA Package	N/C	N/C
***Options Price**	**$0**	**$0**
***Total Price**	**$12,446**	**$13,599**
Target Price	$12,774	
Destination Charge	$435	
Avg. Tax & Fees	$747	
Total Target $	**$13,956**	
Average Dealer Option Cost:	79%	
12 Month Price Increase:	None	

The Tiburon arrives this year with minor refinements, with option package revisions constituting the majority of the changes. The most popular options are now grouped into simple packages. The Tiburon features many standard items that are typically found on an option list, including power windows, an AM/FM/cassette sound system and a rear window defroster. Aluminum wheels, a rear spoiler, and a power tilt/slide sunroof remain popular options, along with a four speed automatic transmission.

Ownership Costs (Projected)

Cost Area	5 Year Cost	Rating
Depreciation	$8,249	●
Financing ($231/month)	$2,716	
Insurance	$8,045	●
State Fees	$573	
Fuel (Hwy 31 City 23)	$2,748	◐
Maintenance	$2,818	○
Repairs	$755	◉

Warranty/Maintenance Info

Major Tune-Up (60K mile int.)	$195	○
Minor Tune-Up (30K mile int.)	$99	◉
Brake Service	$149	○
Overall Warranty	5 yr/60k	○
Drivetrain Warranty	10 yr/100k	○
Rust Warranty	5 yr/100k	○
Maintenance Warranty	N/A	
Roadside Assistance	5 yr/unlim. mi	

Ownership Costs By Year (Projected)

$2,000 $4,000 $6,000 $8,000 $10,000

■ 1999
■ 2000
▨ 2001
▧ 2002
□ 2003

Resale Value

1999	2000	2001	2002	2003
$11,377	$9,840	$8,482	$7,101	$5,707

Cumulative Costs

	1999	2000	2001	2002	2003
Annual	$5,743	$4,577	$4,416	$5,153	$6,015
Total	$5,743	$10,320	$14,736	$19,889	$25,904

Projected Costs (5yr)

Relative	This Car
$23,856	$25,904
Cost/Mile 34¢	Cost/Mile 37¢

Ownership Cost Value

●

Worse Than Average

Hyundai Tiburon FX
2 Door Coupe

Subcompact

| 2.0L 140 hp Gas Fuel Inject. | 4 Cylinder In-Line | Manual 5 Speed | 2 Wheel Front | Dual Airbags Std |

Base Model Shown

Purchase Price

Car Item	Dealer Cost	List
Base Price	**$13,326**	**$14,899**
Anti-Lock Brakes	Pkg	Pkg
Automatic 4 Speed	$725	$800
Optional Engine	N/A	N/A
Air Conditioning	Pkg	Pkg
Power Steering	Std	Std
Cruise Control	Pkg	Pkg
Windows, Power	Std	Std
AM/FM Stereo Cassette	Std	Std
Steering Wheel, Tilt	Std	Std
01/AA Package	N/C	N/C
***Options Price**	**$0**	**$0**
***Total Price**	**$13,326**	**$14,899**
Target Price	$13,717	
Destination Charge	$435	
Avg. Tax & Fees	$803	
Total Target $	**$14,955**	
Average Dealer Option Cost:	84%	
12 Month Price Increase:	None	

The Tiburon FX continues into the 1999 model year sporting revisions to its option packages, making option selection simpler. Value-added standard features include power windows and door locks, aluminum wheels and a rear spoiler. A four wheel antilock braking system remains optional. A major enhancement this year is the new Hyundai Advantage program, which includes bumper-to-bumper coverage for 5 years or 60,000 miles and powertrain coverage for 10 years or 100,000 miles.

Ownership Costs (Projected)

Cost Area	5 Year Cost	Rating
Depreciation	$8,873	●
Financing ($248/month)	$2,910	
Insurance	$8,500	●
State Fees	$626	
Fuel (Hwy 29 City 22)	$2,906	◉
Maintenance	$2,871	○
Repairs	$755	◉

Warranty/Maintenance Info

Major Tune-Up (60K mile int.)	$195	○
Minor Tune-Up (30K mile int.)	$99	◉
Brake Service	$122	○
Overall Warranty	5 yr/60k	○
Drivetrain Warranty	10 yr/100k	○
Rust Warranty	5 yr/100k	○
Maintenance Warranty	N/A	
Roadside Assistance	5 yr/unlim. mi	

Ownership Costs By Year (Projected)

$2,000 $4,000 $6,000 $8,000 $10,000

■ 1999
■ 2000
▨ 2001
▧ 2002
□ 2003

Resale Value

1999	2000	2001	2002	2003
$12,306	$10,620	$9,121	$7,606	$6,082

Cumulative Costs

	1999	2000	2001	2002	2003
Annual	$6,009	$4,912	$4,731	$5,499	$6,290
Total	$6,009	$10,921	$15,652	$21,151	$27,441

Projected Costs (5yr)

Relative	This Car
$24,791	$27,441
Cost/Mile 35¢	Cost/Mile 39¢

Ownership Cost Value

●

Worse Than Average

86

* Includes shaded options
** Other purchase requirements apply
*** Price includes other options

 Poor
 Worse Than Average
Average ○
Better Than Average ○
Excellent ○
⊖ Insufficient Information

Refer to *Section 3: Annotated Vehicle Charts* for an explanation of these charts.

Infiniti G20
4 Door Sedan

Compact

| 2.0L 140 hp Gas Fuel Inject. | 4 Cylinder In-Line | 1 3 5 / 2 4 R Manual 5 Speed | 2 Wheel Front | Dual Front/Side Airbags Std |

Purchase Price

Car Item	Dealer Cost	List
Base Price	**$19,056**	**$20,995**
Anti-Lock Brakes	Std	Std
Automatic 4 Speed	N/C	N/C
Optional Engine	N/A	N/A
Auto Climate Control	Inc	Inc
Power Steering	Std	Std
Cruise Control	Std	Std
Power Windows	Std	Std
AM/FM Stereo Cass/CD	Std	Std
Steering Wheel, Tilt	Std	Std
Other Options Cost	$1,124	$1,500
*Options Price	**$1,124**	**$1,500**
*Total Price	**$20,180**	**$22,495**
Target Price	$21,243	
Destination Charge	$495	
Avg. Tax & Fees	$1,221	
Total Target $	**$22,959**	
Average Dealer Option Cost:	**81%**	
12 Month Price Increase:	N/A	

Ownership Costs (Projected)

Cost Area	5 Year Cost	Rating
Depreciation	$11,447	◉
Financing ($381/month)	$4,466	
Insurance	$7,886	◯
State Fees	$933	
Fuel (Hwy 28 City 22)	$2,962	◉
Maintenance	$2,067	◯
Repairs	$605	◯

Warranty/Maintenance Info

Major Tune-Up (60K mile int.)	$281	◉
Minor Tune-Up (30K mile int.)	$127	●
Brake Service	$237	◉
Overall Warranty	4 yr/60k	◯
Drivetrain Warranty	6 yr/70k	◯
Rust Warranty	7 yr/unlim. mi	◯
Maintenance Warranty	N/A	
Roadside Assistance	4 yr/unlim. mi	

Ownership Costs By Year (Projected)

$2,000 $4,000 $6,000 $8,000 $10,000 $12,000

- 1999
- 2000
- 2001
- 2002
- 2003

Resale Value

1999	2000	2001	2002	2003
$19,023	$17,007	$15,185	$13,352	$11,512

Projected Costs (5yr)

Relative $32,143	This Car $30,366
Cost/Mile 46¢	Cost/Mile 43¢

Cumulative Costs

	1999	2000	2001	2002	2003
Annual	$7,797	$5,636	$5,407	$5,379	$6,147
Total	$7,797	$13,433	$18,840	$24,219	$30,366

Ownership Cost Value

◯ Excellent

For 1999, the G20 is reintroduced to the Infiniti lineup. Standard interior features include cloth bucket seats, a tilt steering wheel and an AM/FM Bose stereo with cassette and CD player. The only optional features on the G20 include a four speed automatic transmission, a Leather and Convenience Package and Seat Package. The Seat Package features heated front seats and heated outside rearview mirrors and is only available with the four speed automatic transmission.

Infiniti G20t
4 Door Sedan

Compact

| 2.0L 140 hp Gas Fuel Inject. | 4 Cylinder In-Line | 1 3 5 / 2 4 R Manual 5 Speed | 2 Wheel Front | Dual Front/Side Airbags Std |

Purchase Price

Car Item	Dealer Cost	List
Base Price	**$20,187**	**$22,495**
Anti-Lock Brakes	Std	Std
Automatic 4 Speed	$718	$800
Optional Engine	N/A	N/A
Auto Climate Control	Std	Std
Power Steering	Std	Std
Cruise Control	Std	Std
Power Windows	Std	Std
AM/FM Stereo Cass/CD	Std	Std
Steering Wheel, Tilt	Std	Std
Rear Defroster	Std	Std
*Options Price	**$718**	**$800**
*Total Price	**$20,905**	**$23,295**
Target Price	$22,026	
Destination Charge	$495	
Avg. Tax & Fees	$1,264	
Total Target $	**$23,785**	
Average Dealer Option Cost:	**83%**	
12 Month Price Increase:	N/A	

Ownership Costs (Projected)

Cost Area	5 Year Cost	Rating
Depreciation	$12,102	◉
Financing ($394/month)	$4,626	
Insurance	$7,886	◯
State Fees	$965	
Fuel (Hwy 28 City 22)	$2,962	◉
Maintenance	$2,020	◯
Repairs	$605	◯

Warranty/Maintenance Info

Major Tune-Up (60K mile int.)	$281	◉
Minor Tune-Up (30K mile int.)	$127	●
Brake Service	$237	◉
Overall Warranty	4 yr/60k	◯
Drivetrain Warranty	6 yr/70k	◯
Rust Warranty	7 yr/unlim. mi	◯
Maintenance Warranty	N/A	
Roadside Assistance	4 yr/unlim. mi	

Ownership Costs By Year (Projected)

$2,000 $4,000 $6,000 $8,000 $10,000 $12,000 $14,000

- 1999
- 2000
- 2001
- 2002
- 2003

Resale Value

1999	2000	2001	2002	2003
$19,403	$17,330	$15,454	$13,570	$11,683

Projected Costs (5yr)

Relative $32,955	This Car $31,166
Cost/Mile 47¢	Cost/Mile 45¢

Cumulative Costs

	1999	2000	2001	2002	2003
Annual	$8,305	$5,744	$5,500	$5,410	$6,207
Total	$8,305	$14,049	$19,549	$24,959	$31,166

Ownership Cost Value

◯ Excellent

For 1999, Infiniti is reintroducing the G20t to its lineup. Luxury amenities on the G20t include automatic climate control, a sport cloth interior, cruise control and a leather-wrapped steering wheel and shift knob. Integrated fog lamps, a rear decklid spoiler and a limited-slip differential are also standard. A power glass moonroof, four speed automatic transmission, Leather and Convenience Package and Seat Package are the only available options on the G20t.

---

* Includes shaded options

** Other purchase requirements apply

*** Price includes other options

 Poor Worse Than Average ◯ Average ◯ Better Than Average ◯ Excellent ⊖ Insufficient Information

87

Refer to *Section 3: Annotated Vehicle Charts* for an explanation of these charts.

Infiniti I30
4 Door Sedan

Near Luxury

 3.0L 190 hp Gas Fuel Inject.   6 Cylinder "V"   Automatic 4 Speed   2 Wheel Front   Dual Front/Side Airbags Std

Purchase Price

Car Item	Dealer Cost	List
Base Price	**$25,935**	**$28,900**
Anti-Lock Brakes	Std	Std
Manual Transmission	N/A	N/A
Optional Engine	N/A	N/A
Auto Climate Control	Std	Std
Power Steering	Std	Std
Cruise Control	Std	Std
Power Windows	Std	Std
AM/FM Stereo Cass/CD	Std	Std
Steering Wheel, Tilt	Std	Std
Rear Defroster	Std	Std
*Options Price	$0	$0
*Total Price	$25,935	$28,900
Target Price	$27,123	
Destination Charge	$495	
Avg. Tax & Fees	$1,550	
Total Target $	**$29,168**	
Average Dealer Option Cost:	80%	
12 Month Price Increase:	None	

The I30 sedan is now in its fourth model year, and sports minor changes. A redesign is scheduled to arrive for the 2000 model year. A six disc CD changer, power tinted glass sunroof and an integrated HomeLink universal transmitter are available options. Safety features include dual front depowered airbags, side airbags and a vehicle security system with remote keyless entry and an ignition immobilizer. A new two-tone exterior color will be available in March of 1999.

Ownership Costs (Projected)

Cost Area	5 Year Cost	Rating
Depreciation	$15,442	◉
Financing ($483/month)	$5,673	
Insurance	$9,524	◉
State Fees	$1,189	
Fuel (Hwy 28 City 21)	$3,026	○
Maintenance	$2,328	○
Repairs	$605	○

Warranty/Maintenance Info

Major Tune-Up (60K mile int.)	$188	○
Minor Tune-Up (30K mile int.)	$131	○
Brake Service	$240	○
Overall Warranty	4 yr/60k	○
Drivetrain Warranty	6 yr/70k	○
Rust Warranty	7 yr/unlim. mi	○
Maintenance Warranty	N/A	
Roadside Assistance	4 yr/unlim. mi	

Ownership Costs By Year (Projected)

1999, 2000, 2001, 2002, 2003

Resale Value

1999	2000	2001	2002	2003
$24,472	$21,526	$18,904	$16,332	$13,726

Cumulative Costs

	1999	2000	2001	2002	2003
Annual	$9,354	$7,288	$7,022	$6,727	$7,396
Total	$9,354	$16,642	$23,664	$30,391	$37,787

Projected Costs (5yr)

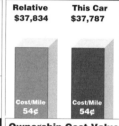

Relative	This Car
$37,834	$37,787
Cost/Mile 54¢	Cost/Mile 54¢

Ownership Cost Value

○ Better Than Average

Infiniti I30 Touring
4 Door Sedan

Near Luxury

 3.0L 190 hp Gas Fuel Inject.   6 Cylinder "V"   Manual 5 Speed   2 Wheel Front Dual Front/Side Airbags Std

Purchase Price

Car Item	Dealer Cost	List
Base Price	**$27,681**	**$31,200**
Anti-Lock Brakes	Std	Std
Automatic 4 Speed	$887	$1,000
Optional Engine	N/A	N/A
Auto Climate Control	Std	Std
Power Steering	Std	Std
Cruise Control	Std	Std
Power Windows	Std	Std
AM/FM Stereo Cass/CD	Std	Std
Steering Wheel, Tilt	Std	Std
Rear Defroster	Std	Std
*Options Price	$887	$1,000
*Total Price	$28,568	$32,200
Target Price	$29,957	
Destination Charge	$495	
Avg. Tax & Fees	$1,710	
Total Target $	**$32,162**	
Average Dealer Option Cost:	80%	
12 Month Price Increase:	None	

The I30 touring sedan features a rear spoiler with an integrated center brake light, a sport-tuned suspension and a viscous limited-slip differential. The interior is equipped with leather upholstery, eight-way power driver and four-way power passenger seats and a black performance steering wheel. The I30 touring sedan features performance 16 inch cast alloy wheels with 215/55R16 tires and a five speed manual transmission. A security system is also standard.

Ownership Costs (Projected)

Cost Area	5 Year Cost	Rating
Depreciation	$17,447	◉
Financing ($533/month)	$6,257	
Insurance	$9,524	◉
State Fees	$1,321	
Fuel (Hwy 28 City 21)	$3,026	○
Maintenance	$2,077	○
Repairs	$605	○

Warranty/Maintenance Info

Major Tune-Up (60K mile int.)	$188	○
Minor Tune-Up (30K mile int.)	$131	○
Brake Service	$240	○
Overall Warranty	4 yr/60k	○
Drivetrain Warranty	6 yr/70k	○
Rust Warranty	7 yr/unlim. mi	○
Maintenance Warranty	N/A	
Roadside Assistance	4 yr/unlim. mi	

Ownership Costs By Year (Projected)

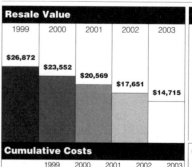

1999, 2000, 2001, 2002, 2003

Resale Value

1999	2000	2001	2002	2003
$26,872	$23,552	$20,569	$17,651	$14,715

Cumulative Costs

	1999	2000	2001	2002	2003
Annual	$10,179	$7,852	$7,361	$7,270	$7,595
Total	$10,179	$18,031	$25,392	$32,662	$40,257

Projected Costs (5yr)

Relative	This Car
$39,506	$40,257
Cost/Mile 56¢	Cost/Mile 58¢

Ownership Cost Value

○ Average

88

Infiniti Q45
4 Door Sedan

 4.1L 266 hp Gas Fuel Inject.

 8 Cylinder "V"

 PRND321 Automatic 4 Speed

 2 Wheel Rear

 Dual Front/Side Airbags Std

Luxury

Purchase Price

Car Item	Dealer Cost	List
Base Price	**$43,255**	**$48,200**
Anti-Lock Brakes	Std	Std
Manual Transmission	N/A	N/A
Optional Engine	N/A	N/A
Auto Climate Control	Std	Std
Power Steering	Std	Std
Cruise Control	Std	Std
Power Windows	Std	Std
AM/FM Stereo Cass/CD	Std	Std
St Whl, Power Scope/Tilt	Std	Std
Rear Defroster	Std	Std
*Options Price	$0	$0
***Total Price**	**$43,255**	**$48,200**
Target Price	$45,730	
Destination Charge	$495	
Avg. Tax & Fees	$2,580	
Luxury Tax	$614	
Total Target $	**$49,419**	
12 Month Price Increase:	1%	

Ownership Costs (Projected)

Cost Area	5 Year Cost	Rating
Depreciation	$28,083	●
Financing ($819/month)	$9,614	
Insurance (Performance)	$11,893	◒
State Fees	$1,961	
Fuel (Hwy 24 City 17 -Prem.)	$4,303	◒
Maintenance	$2,683	◒
Repairs	$750	○

Warranty/Maintenance Info

Major Tune-Up (60K mile int.)	$291	◒
Minor Tune-Up (30K mile int.)	$249	●
Brake Service	$266	◒
Overall Warranty	4 yr/60k	○
Drivetrain Warranty	6 yr/70k	○
Rust Warranty	7 yr/unlim. mi	○
Maintenance Warranty	N/A	
Roadside Assistance	4 yr/unlim. mi	

The Q45 receives revised front and rear styling including xenon headlamps with crystalline lenses, a slightly smaller grille and refashioned rear combination lamps. New exterior colors are Hunter Green, Titanium, and the debut of the two-tone Aspen White Pearl and Platinum Frost. Interior refinements include the reintroduction of an analog clock, a power-operated sunshade and revised audio faceplate. Options available include a six disc CD changer, heated seats and the Infiniti Communicator.

Ownership Costs By Year (Projected)

$5,000 $10,000 $15,000 $20,000 $25,000 $30,000

■ 1999
■ 2000
■ 2001
□ 2002
□ 2003

Resale Value

1999	2000	2001	2002	2003
$41,041	$35,708	$30,799	$26,032	$21,336

Projected Costs (5yr)

Relative	This Car
$55,374	$59,287
Cost/Mile 79¢	Cost/Mile 85¢

Cumulative Costs

	1999	2000	2001	2002	2003
Annual	$15,263	$11,648	$11,123	$10,336	$10,917
Total	$15,263	$26,911	$38,034	$48,370	$59,287

Ownership Cost Value

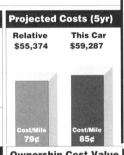

Worse Than Average

Infiniti Q45 Touring
4 Door Sedan

 4.1L 266 hp Gas Fuel Inject.

 8 Cylinder "V"

 PRND321 Automatic 4 Speed

 2 Wheel Rear

 Dual Front/Side Airbags Std

Luxury

Purchase Price

Car Item	Dealer Cost	List
Base Price	**$44,271**	**$49,900**
Anti-Lock Brakes	Std	Std
Manual Transmission	N/A	N/A
Optional Engine	N/A	N/A
Auto Climate Control	Std	Std
Power Steering	Std	Std
Cruise Control	Std	Std
Power Windows	Std	Std
AM/FM Stereo Cass/CD	Std	Std
St Whl, Power Scope/Tilt	Std	Std
Rear Defroster	Std	Std
*Options Price	$0	$0
***Total Price**	**$44,271**	**$49,900**
Target Price	$46,874	
Destination Charge	$495	
Avg. Tax & Fees	$2,649	
Luxury Tax	$682	
Total Target $	**$50,700**	
12 Month Price Increase:	None	

Ownership Costs (Projected)

Cost Area	5 Year Cost	Rating
Depreciation	$28,807	●
Financing ($840/month)	$9,863	
Insurance (Performance)	$11,893	◒
State Fees	$2,029	
Fuel (Hwy 24 City 17 -Prem.)	$4,303	◒
Maintenance	$3,073	●
Repairs	$750	○

Warranty/Maintenance Info

Major Tune-Up (60K mile int.)	$291	◒
Minor Tune-Up (30K mile int.)	$249	●
Brake Service	$266	◒
Overall Warranty	4 yr/60k	○
Drivetrain Warranty	6 yr/70k	○
Rust Warranty	7 yr/unlim. mi	○
Maintenance Warranty	N/A	
Roadside Assistance	4 yr/unlim. mi	

For 1999, Infiniti offers the Q45 Touring model to appeal to the performance-oriented driver. Along with the many standard features shared with the base Q45, the Touring model adds five spoke 17 inch performance alloy wheels, P225/50R17 V-rated tires, a performance steering wheel and electronically-controlled suspension with driver selectable settings. The few options available include a six disc CD changer, heated seats and the Infiniti Communicator.

Ownership Costs By Year (Projected)

$5,000 $10,000 $15,000 $20,000 $25,000 $30,000

■ 1999
■ 2000
■ 2001
□ 2002
□ 2003

Resale Value

1999	2000	2001	2002	2003
$42,445	$36,890	$31,762	$26,790	$21,893

Projected Costs (5yr)

Relative	This Car
$56,465	$60,718
Cost/Mile 81¢	Cost/Mile 87¢

Cumulative Costs

	1999	2000	2001	2002	2003
Annual	$15,242	$11,955	$11,406	$10,975	$11,140
Total	$15,242	$27,197	$38,603	$49,578	$60,718

Ownership Cost Value

Worse Than Average

---

* Includes shaded options

** Other purchase requirements apply

*** Price includes other options

● Poor ◒ Worse Than Average ◒ Average ○ Better Than Average ○ Excellent ⊝ Insufficient Information

89

Refer to *Section 3: Annotated Vehicle Charts* for an explanation of these charts.

©1999 by IntelliChoice, Inc. (408) 866-1400 http://www.intellichoice.com All Rights Reserved. Reproduction Prohibited.

Jaguar Vanden Plas
4 Door Sedan

4.0L 290 hp Gas Fuel Inject.	8 Cylinder "V"	Automatic 5 Speed	2 Wheel Rear	Dual Front/Side Airbags Std

Luxury

Purchase Price

Car Item	Dealer Cost	List
Base Price	**$56,172**	**$64,300**
Anti-Lock Brakes	Std	Std
Manual Transmission	N/A	N/A
Optional Engine	N/A	N/A
Auto Climate Control	Std	Std
Power Steering	Std	Std
Cruise Control	Std	Std
Power Windows	Std	Std
AM/FM Stereo Cassette	Std	Std
St Whl, Tilt/Scope/Mem	Std	Std
Rear Defroster	Std	Std
*Options Price	$0	$0
*Total Price	**$56,172**	**$64,300**
Target Price	$60,818	
Destination Charge	$580	
Avg. Tax & Fees	$3,425	
Luxury Tax	$1,524	
Total Target $	**$66,347**	
12 Month Price Increase:	1%	

The luxurious Vanden Plas is built on the same long-wheelbase platform as the XJ8 L. Alpine and Emerald are new exterior colors available for 1999. Standard items on the Vanden Plas include a premium Autolux Connolly leather interior with walnut picnic trays, lambswool footwell carpeting and inlaid burl walnut trim. Traction control and heated front and rear seats are included in the optional All-Weather Package. Automatic Stability Control (ASC) reduces wheelspin on slippery roads.

Ownership Costs (Projected)

Cost Area	5 Year Cost	Rating
Depreciation	$40,061	●
Financing ($1,100/month)	$12,907	
Insurance (Performance)	$13,356	◐
State Fees	$2,608	
Fuel (Hwy 24 City 17 -Prem.)	$4,303	◐
Maintenance	$3,204	●
Repairs	$3,640	●

Warranty/Maintenance Info

Major Tune-Up (60K mile int.)	$229	◯
Minor Tune-Up (30K mile int.)	$140	◯
Brake Service	$266	◯
Overall Warranty	4 yr/50k	◯
Drivetrain Warranty	4 yr/50k	◯
Rust Warranty	6 yr/unlim. mi	◯
Maintenance Warranty	N/A	
Roadside Assistance	4 yr/50k	

Ownership Costs By Year (Projected)

$5 $10 $15 $20 $25 $30 $35 $40 $45 (x1,000)

■ 1999
■ 2000
■ 2001
■ 2002
□ 2003

Resale Value

1999	2000	2001	2002	2003
$54,199	$46,577	$39,537	$32,800	$26,286

Cumulative Costs

	1999	2000	2001	2002	2003
Annual	$20,600	$15,255	$14,171	$14,185	$15,868
Total	$20,600	$35,855	$50,026	$64,211	$80,079

Projected Costs (5yr)

Relative $69,299	This Car $80,079
Cost/Mile 99¢	Cost/Mile $1.14

Ownership Cost Value

● Poor

Jaguar XJ8
4 Door Sedan

4.0L 290 hp Gas Fuel Inject.	8 Cylinder "V"	Automatic 5 Speed	2 Wheel Rear	Dual Front/Side Airbags Std

Luxury

Purchase Price

Car Item	Dealer Cost	List
Base Price	**$48,222**	**$55,200**
Anti-Lock Brakes	Std	Std
Manual Transmission	N/A	N/A
Optional Engine	N/A	N/A
Auto Climate Control	Std	Std
Power Steering	Std	Std
Cruise Control	Std	Std
Power Windows	Std	Std
AM/FM Stereo Cassette	Std	Std
St Whl, Tilt/Scope/Mem	Std	Std
Rear Defroster	Std	Std
*Options Price	$0	$0
*Total Price	**$48,222**	**$55,200**
Target Price	$52,211	
Destination Charge	$580	
Avg. Tax & Fees	$2,947	
Luxury Tax	$1,007	
Total Target $	**$56,745**	
12 Month Price Increase:	1%	

For 1999, the XJ8 benefits from minor mechanical revisions such as dual-tipped platinum spark plugs and revised cruise control, electronic throttle and engine management systems. Alpine is a new exterior color for 1999. The service maintenance schedule is increased to 100,000 miles for spark plug replacement, with oil change intervals of 10,000 miles under normal driving conditions. In addition, the ZF automatic transmission does not require fluid changes.

Ownership Costs (Projected)

Cost Area	5 Year Cost	Rating
Depreciation	$31,969	●
Financing ($941/month)	$11,039	
Insurance (Performance)	$12,871	◐
State Fees	$2,244	
Fuel (Hwy 24 City 17 -Prem.)	$4,303	◐
Maintenance	$3,453	●
Repairs	$3,640	●

Warranty/Maintenance Info

Major Tune-Up (60K mile int.)	$229	◯
Minor Tune-Up (30K mile int.)	$140	◯
Brake Service	$266	◯
Overall Warranty	4 yr/50k	◯
Drivetrain Warranty	4 yr/50k	◯
Rust Warranty	6 yr/unlim. mi	◯
Maintenance Warranty	N/A	
Roadside Assistance	4 yr/50k	

Ownership Costs By Year (Projected)

$5 $10 $15 $20 $25 $30 $35 (x1,000)

■ 1999
■ 2000
■ 2001
■ 2002
□ 2003

Resale Value

1999	2000	2001	2002	2003
$49,647	$42,864	$36,604	$30,602	$24,776

Cumulative Costs

	1999	2000	2001	2002	2003
Annual	$14,733	$13,724	$12,956	$13,044	$15,064
Total	$14,733	$28,457	$41,413	$54,457	$69,521

Projected Costs (5yr)

Relative $60,714	This Car $69,521
Cost/Mile 87¢	Cost/Mile 99¢

Ownership Cost Value

● Poor

90

* Includes shaded options
** Other purchase requirements apply
*** Price includes other options

● Poor	◐ Worse Than Average	◑ Average	◯ Better Than Average	◯ Excellent	⊖ Insufficient Information

Refer to *Section 3: Annotated Vehicle Charts* for an explanation of these charts.

Jaguar XJ8L
4 Door Sedan

 4.0L 290 hp Gas Fuel Inject.
 8 Cylinder "V"
 Automatic 5 Speed
 2 Wheel Rear
Dual Front/Side Airbags Std

Luxury

Purchase Price

Car Item	Dealer Cost	List
Base Price	**$52,634**	**$60,250**
Anti-Lock Brakes	Std	Std
Manual Transmission	N/A	N/A
Optional Engine	N/A	N/A
Auto Climate Control	Std	Std
Power Steering	Std	Std
Cruise Control	Std	Std
Power Windows	Std	Std
AM/FM Stereo Cassette	Std	Std
St Whl, Tilt/Scope/Mem	Std	Std
Rear Defroster	Std	Std
*Options Price	$0	$0
*Total Price	**$52,634**	**$60,250**
Target Price	$56,988	
Destination Charge	$580	
Avg. Tax & Fees	$3,212	
Luxury Tax	$1,294	
Total Target $	**$62,074**	
12 Month Price Increase:	1%	

The 1999 XJ8 L wheelbase is about five inches longer than the base XJ8. For 1999, the XJ8 benefits from minor mechanical revisions such as dual-tipped platinum spark plugs and revised cruise control, electronic throttle and engine management systems. The XJ8 L is also available with an optional All-Weather Package that includes traction control and heated front and seats. A 240 watt Harman/Kardon audio system with CD changer is an optional upgrade.

Ownership Costs (Projected)

Cost Area	5 Year Cost	Rating
Depreciation	$36,780	●
Financing ($1,029/month)	$12,075	
Insurance (Performance)	$13,356	○
State Fees	$2,446	
Fuel (Hwy 24 City 17 -Prem.)	$4,303	○
Maintenance	$3,453	●
Repairs	$3,640	●

Warranty/Maintenance Info

Major Tune-Up (60K mile int.)	$229	○
Minor Tune-Up (30K mile int.)	$140	○
Brake Service	$266	◉
Overall Warranty	4 yr/50k	○
Drivetrain Warranty	4 yr/50k	○
Rust Warranty	6 yr/unlim. mi	○
Maintenance Warranty	N/A	
Roadside Assistance	4 yr/50k	

Ownership Costs By Year (Projected)

$5 $10 $15 $20 $25 $30 $35 $40 (x1,000)

- 1999
- 2000
- 2001
- 2002
- 2003

Resale Value

1999	2000	2001	2002	2003
$51,711	$44,499	$37,842	$31,469	$25,294

Projected Costs (5yr)

Relative	This Car
$65,473	$76,053
Cost/Mile 94¢	Cost/Mile $1.09

Cumulative Costs

	1999	2000	2001	2002	2003
Annual	$18,492	$14,579	$13,705	$13,684	$15,593
Total	$18,492	$33,071	$46,776	$60,460	$76,053

Ownership Cost Value
● Poor

Jaguar XJR
4 Door Sedan

 4.0L 370 hp Suprchrged Fuel Inject.
 8 Cylinder "V"
 Automatic 5 Speed
 2 Wheel Rear
Dual Front/Side Airbags Std

Luxury

Purchase Price

Car Item	Dealer Cost	List
Base Price	**$59,798**	**$68,450**
Anti-Lock Brakes	Std	Std
Manual Transmission	N/A	N/A
Optional Engine	N/A	N/A
Auto Climate Control	Std	Std
Power Steering	Std	Std
Cruise Control	Std	Std
Power Windows	Std	Std
AM/FM Stereo CD	Std	Std
St Whl, Tilt/Scope/Mem	Std	Std
Rear Defroster	Std	Std
*Options Price	$0	$0
*Total Price	**$59,798**	**$68,450**
Target Price	$64,744	
Destination Charge	$580	
Avg. Tax & Fees	$3,688	
Luxury/Gas Guzzler Tax	$2,819	
Total Target $	**$71,831**	
12 Month Price Increase:	2%	

The XJR luxury sport sedan comes equipped with a supercharged and intercooled 370 hp engine and sport-tuned suspension. For 1999, front disc brakes have been increased from 12 to 12.8 inches and a burl walnut interior replaces stained bird's-eye maple. The XJR features 18 inch alloy wheels, a 240 watt Harman/Kardon audio system with CD autochanger and the All-Weather Package, all of which are optional on other models. The five speed automatic transmission features Normal and Sport shift modes.

Ownership Costs (Projected)

Cost Area	5 Year Cost	Rating
Depreciation	$41,489	●
Financing ($1,191/month)	$13,974	
Insurance (Performance)	$13,356	○
State Fees	$2,773	
Fuel (Hwy 22 City 16 -Prem.)	$4,637	◉
Maintenance	$3,971	●
Repairs	$3,760	●

Warranty/Maintenance Info

Major Tune-Up (60K mile int.)	$229	○
Minor Tune-Up (30K mile int.)	$140	○
Brake Service	$266	◉
Overall Warranty	4 yr/50k	○
Drivetrain Warranty	4 yr/50k	○
Rust Warranty	6 yr/unlim. mi	○
Maintenance Warranty	N/A	
Roadside Assistance	4 yr/50k	

Ownership Costs By Year (Projected)

$5 $10 $15 $20 $25 $30 $35 $40 $45 (x1,000)

- 1999
- 2000
- 2001
- 2002
- 2003

Resale Value

1999	2000	2001	2002	2003
$58,500	$50,784	$43,669	$36,884	$30,342

Projected Costs (5yr)

Relative	This Car
$73,229	$83,960
Cost/Mile $1.05	Cost/Mile $1.20

Cumulative Costs

	1999	2000	2001	2002	2003
Annual	$22,250	$15,746	$14,687	$15,017	$16,260
Total	$22,250	$37,996	$52,683	$67,700	$83,960

Ownership Cost Value
● Poor

---

* Includes shaded options

** Other purchase requirements apply

*** Price includes other options

● Poor   ◉ Worse Than Average   ◑ Average   ○ Better Than Average   ◯ Excellent   ⊖ Insufficient Information

91

Refer to *Section 3: Annotated Vehicle Charts* for an explanation of these charts.

Jaguar XK8
2 Door Coupe

 4.0L 290 hp Gas Fuel Inject.
 8 Cylinder "V"
 Automatic 5 Speed
 2 Wheel Rear
 Dual Airbags Std

Luxury

Purchase Price

Car Item	Dealer Cost	List
Base Price	**$57,440**	**$65,750**
Anti-Lock Brakes	Std	Std
Manual Transmission	N/A	N/A
Optional Engine	N/A	N/A
Auto Climate Control	Std	Std
Power Steering	Std	Std
Cruise Control	Std	Std
Power Windows	Std	Std
AM/FM Stereo Cassette	Std	Std
St Whl, Tilt/Scope/Mem	Std	Std
Rear Defroster	Std	Std
*Options Price	$0	$0
*Total Price	**$57,440**	**$65,750**
Target Price	$62,441	
Destination Charge	$580	
Avg. Tax & Fees	$3,512	
Luxury Tax	$1,621	
Total Target $	**$68,154**	
12 Month Price Increase:	1%	

Ownership Costs (Projected)

Cost Area	5 Year Cost	Rating
Depreciation		⊖
Financing ($1,130/month)	$13,258	
Insurance (Performance)	$14,809	◉
State Fees	$2,666	
Fuel (Hwy 25 City 17 -Prem.)	$4,216	◯
Maintenance	$4,069	●
Repairs	$3,640	●

Warranty/Maintenance Info

Major Tune-Up (60K mile int.)	$229		◯
Minor Tune-Up (30K mile int.)	$140		◯
Brake Service	$250		◯
Overall Warranty	4 yr/50k		◯
Drivetrain Warranty	4 yr/50k		◯
Rust Warranty	6 yr/unlim. mi		◯
Maintenance Warranty	N/A		
Roadside Assistance	4 yr/50k		

Ownership Costs By Year (Projected)

$5,000 $10,000 $15,000

Insufficient Depreciation Information

1999, 2000, 2001, 2002, 2003

Resale Value

Insufficient Information

Projected Costs (5yr)

Insufficient Information

Cumulative Costs

	1999	2000	2001	2002	2003
Annual	*Insufficient Information*				
Total	*Insufficient Information*				

Ownership Cost Value

⊖

Insufficient Information

For 1999, the XK8 coupe benefits from minor mechanical upgrades such as revised electronic throttle, cruise control and engine management systems. Phoenix is a new exterior color for 1999. The audio system accommodates an integrated telephone keypad. The audio and dealer-installed cellular phone controls are mounted on the steering wheel. Headlamp washers, traction control and heated front seats are included with the optional All-Weather Package. Chrome plated alloy wheels are also available.

Jaguar XK8
2 Door Convertible

 4.0L 290 hp Gas Fuel Inject.
 8 Cylinder "V"
 Automatic 5 Speed
 2 Wheel Rear
Dual Airbags Std

Luxury

Purchase Price

Car Item	Dealer Cost	List
Base Price	**$61,808**	**$70,750**
Anti-Lock Brakes	Std	Std
Manual Transmission	N/A	N/A
Optional Engine	N/A	N/A
Auto Climate Control	Std	Std
Power Steering	Std	Std
Cruise Control	Std	Std
Power Windows	Std	Std
AM/FM Stereo Cassette	Std	Std
St Whl, Tilt/Scope/Mem	Std	Std
Rear Defroster	Std	Std
*Options Price	$0	$0
*Total Price	**$61,808**	**$70,750**
Target Price	$67,189	
Destination Charge	$580	
Avg. Tax & Fees	$3,776	
Luxury Tax	$1,906	
Total Target $	**$73,451**	
12 Month Price Increase:	1%	

Ownership Costs (Projected)

Cost Area	5 Year Cost	Rating
Depreciation		⊖
Financing ($1,218/month)	$14,289	
Insurance (Performance)	$15,531	◉
State Fees	$2,866	
Fuel (Hwy 24 City 17 -Prem.)	$4,303	◯
Maintenance	$4,069	●
Repairs	$3,640	●

Warranty/Maintenance Info

Major Tune-Up (60K mile int.)	$229		◯
Minor Tune-Up (30K mile int.)	$140		◯
Brake Service	$250		◯
Overall Warranty	4 yr/50k		◯
Drivetrain Warranty	4 yr/50k		◯
Rust Warranty	6 yr/unlim. mi		◯
Maintenance Warranty	N/A		
Roadside Assistance	4 yr/50k		

Ownership Costs By Year (Projected)

$5,000 $10,000 $15,000 $20,000

Insufficient Depreciation Information

1999, 2000, 2001, 2002, 2003

Resale Value

Insufficient Information

Projected Costs (5yr)

Insufficient Information

Cumulative Costs

	1999	2000	2001	2002	2003
Annual	*Insufficient Information*				
Total	*Insufficient Information*				

Ownership Cost Value

⊖

Insufficient Information

For 1999, the XK8 convertible benefits from minor mechanical upgrades such as revised electronic throttle, cruise control and engine management systems. Phoenix and Alpine are new exterior colors. In addition, a Beige convertible top color is also new. The convertible features a one-button, auto-latching top mechanism that can raise and lower the top while the car travels at up to 10 mph. The optional All-Weather Package includes headlamp washers, traction control and heated seats.

92

* Includes shaded options

** Other purchase requirements apply

*** Price includes other options

● Poor   ◉ Worse Than Average   ◯ Average   ◯ Better Than Average   ◯ Excellent   ⊖ Insufficient Information

Refer to *Section 3: Annotated Vehicle Charts* for an explanation of these charts.

Kia Sephia
4 Door Sedan

Compact

 1.8L 125 hp Gas Fuel Inject. | 4 Cylinder In-Line | Manual 5 Speed | 2 Wheel Front | Dual Airbags Std

Purchase Price

Car Item	Dealer Cost	List
Base Price	**$8,996**	**$9,995**
Anti-Lock Brakes	N/A	N/A
Automatic 4 Speed	$860	$975
Optional Engine	N/A	N/A
Air Conditioning	$745	$900
Power Steering	$224	$260
Cruise Control	N/A	N/A
Power Windows	N/A	N/A
AM/FM Stereo Cassette	$250	$320
Steering Wheel, Tilt	N/A	N/A
Rear Defroster	Std	Std
*Options Price	$2,079	$2,455
*Total Price	$11,075	$12,450
Target Price	$11,470	
Destination Charge	$450	
Avg. Tax & Fees	$678	
Total Target $	**$12,598**	
Average Dealer Option Cost:	83%	
12 Month Price Increase:	None	

A four-door compact sedan from Korea, the Sephia arrives this year with many comfort features. Standard items include dual airbags, a rear window defroster and a stainless steel muffler designed for corrosion resistance and sound reduction. The Sephia features a 125 hp engine and is available with an optional automatic transmission. Other options include air conditioning, power steering, body side moldings, an AM/FM stereo with CD, rear spoiler and floor mats.

Ownership Costs (Projected)

Cost Area	5 Year Cost	Rating
Depreciation	$7,118	●
Financing ($209/month)	$2,451	
Insurance	$7,837	●
State Fees	$528	
Fuel (Hwy 31 City 23)	$2,748	○
Maintenance	$3,949	●
Repairs	$640	○

Warranty/Maintenance Info

Major Tune-Up (60K mile int.)	$215	○
Minor Tune-Up (30K mile int.)	$89	○
Brake Service	$141	◔
Overall Warranty	3 yr/36k	
Drivetrain Warranty	5 yr/60k	◔
Rust Warranty	5 yr/100k	○
Maintenance Warranty	N/A	
Roadside Assistance	3 yr/36k	

Ownership Costs By Year (Projected)

$2,000 $4,000 $6,000 $8,000

■ 1999
■ 2000
■ 2001
□ 2002
□ 2003

Resale Value

1999	2000	2001	2002	2003
$10,851	$9,432	$8,163	$6,844	$5,480

Cumulative Costs

	1999	2000	2001	2002	2003
Annual	$4,771	$4,336	$4,332	$5,435	$6,397
Total	$4,771	$9,107	$13,439	$18,874	$25,271

Projected Costs (5yr)

Relative	This Car
$23,322	$25,271
Cost/Mile 33¢	Cost/Mile 36¢

Ownership Cost Value
● Poor

Kia Sephia LS
4 Door Sedan

Compact

 1.8L 125 hp Gas Fuel Inject. | 4 Cylinder In-Line | Manual 5 Speed | 2 Wheel Front | Dual Airbags Std

Base Model Shown

Purchase Price

Car Item	Dealer Cost	List
Base Price	**$9,791**	**$10,995**
Anti-Lock Brakes	$745	$800
Automatic 4 Speed	$860	$975
Optional Engine	N/A	N/A
Air Conditioning	$745	$900
Power Steering	Std	Std
Cruise Control	Pkg	Pkg
Power Windows	Pkg	Pkg
AM/FM Stereo CD	$375	$475
Steering Wheel, Tilt	Std	Std
Rear Defroster	Std	Std
*Options Price	$1,980	$2,350
*Total Price	$11,771	$13,345
Target Price	$12,212	
Destination Charge	$450	
Avg. Tax & Fees	$721	
Total Target $	**$13,383**	
Average Dealer Option Cost:	85%	
12 Month Price Increase:	None	

The Sephia LS, a Korean import, has many standard and optional features. In addition to the standard equipment on the base model, the LS adds power steering, a split folding rear seat, rear seat heater ducts, full wheel covers and a tilt steering column. An optional automatic transmission and Power Package are also available. The Power Package includes cruise control, power door locks and air conditioning. Antilock brakes are available only on the LS.

Ownership Costs (Projected)

Cost Area	5 Year Cost	Rating
Depreciation	$7,625	●
Financing ($222/month)	$2,602	
Insurance	$7,837	●
State Fees	$565	
Fuel (Hwy 31 City 23)	$2,748	○
Maintenance	$3,949	●
Repairs	$640	○

Warranty/Maintenance Info

Major Tune-Up (60K mile int.)	$215	○
Minor Tune-Up (30K mile int.)	$89	○
Brake Service	$141	◔
Overall Warranty	3 yr/36k	○
Drivetrain Warranty	5 yr/60k	◔
Rust Warranty	5 yr/100k	○
Maintenance Warranty	N/A	
Roadside Assistance	3 yr/36k	

Ownership Costs By Year (Projected)

$2,000 $4,000 $6,000 $8,000

■ 1999
■ 2000
■ 2001
□ 2002
□ 2003

Resale Value

1999	2000	2001	2002	2003
$11,541	$10,013	$8,640	$7,219	$5,758

Cumulative Costs

	1999	2000	2001	2002	2003
Annual	$4,926	$4,495	$4,474	$5,564	$6,507
Total	$4,926	$9,421	$13,895	$19,459	$25,966

Projected Costs (5yr)

Relative	This Car
$23,907	$25,966
Cost/Mile 34¢	Cost/Mile 37¢

Ownership Cost Value
● Poor

---

* Includes shaded options
** Other purchase requirements apply
*** Price includes other options

 Poor | Worse Than Average | Average | Better Than Average | Excellent | ⊖ Insufficient Information

93

Refer to *Section 3: Annotated Vehicle Charts* for an explanation of these charts.

Lexus ES 300
4 Door Sedan

Near Luxury

 3.0L 210 hp Gas Fuel Inject.

 6 Cylinder "V"

PR|ND321 Automatic 4 Speed

 2 Wheel Front

 Dual Front/Side Airbags Std

Purchase Price

Car Item	Dealer Cost	List
Base Price	**$26,844**	**$30,905**
Anti-Lock Brakes	Std	Std
Manual Transmission	N/A	N/A
Optional Engine	N/A	N/A
Auto Climate Control	Std	Std
Power Steering	Std	Std
Cruise Control	Std	Std
Power Windows	Std	Std
AM/FM Stereo Cassette	Std	Std
Steering Wheel, Tilt	Std	Std
Rear Defroster	Std	Std
*Options Price	$0	$0
*Total Price	**$26,844**	**$30,905**
Target Price	$29,386	
Destination Charge	$495	
Avg. Tax & Fees	$1,672	
Total Target $	**$31,553**	
Average Dealer Option Cost:	**80%**	
12 Month Price Increase:	None	

Ownership Costs (Projected)

Cost Area	5 Year Cost	Rating
Depreciation	$13,348	O
Financing ($523/month)	$6,138	O
Insurance	$8,313	O
State Fees	$1,269	
Fuel (Hwy 26 City 19)	$3,299	◉
Maintenance	$2,788	O
Repairs	$645	O

Warranty/Maintenance Info

Major Tune-Up (60K mile int.)	$314	●
Minor Tune-Up (30K mile int.)	$169	●
Brake Service	$216	O
Overall Warranty	4 yr/50k	O
Drivetrain Warranty	6 yr/70k	O
Rust Warranty	6 yr/unlim. mi	O
Maintenance Warranty	1 yr/13k	O
Roadside Assistance	4 yr/unlim. mi	

Ownership Costs By Year (Projected)

$2,000 $4,000 $6,000 $8,000 $10,000 $12,000 $14,000

- 1999
- 2000
- 2001
- 2002
- 2003

Resale Value

1999	2000	2001	2002	2003
$29,653	$26,538	$23,742	$20,993	$18,205

Cumulative Costs

	1999	2000	2001	2002	2003
Annual	$6,562	$7,429	$6,900	$7,134	$7,775
Total	$6,562	$13,991	$20,891	$28,025	$35,800

Projected Costs (5yr)

Relative	This Car
$38,354	$35,800
Cost/Mile 55¢	Cost/Mile 51¢

Ownership Cost Value

O Excellent

The 1999 ES 300 offers state of the art safety technology among entry-level luxury cars. The most notable feature is Vehicle Skid Control, which integrates the sensors and electronics of the antilock braking and traction control systems to help reduce vehicle skid caused by understeer or oversteer conditions. Traction control, which provides secure handling in snowy conditions, and daytime running lamps are also standard. A Lexus fixed mobile cellular telephone is one of the dealer options.

Lexus GS 300
4 Door Sedan

Luxury

 3.0L 225 hp Gas Fuel Inject.

 6 Cylinder In-Line

PR|ND4321 Automatic 5 Speed

 2 Wheel Rear

 Dual Front/Side Airbags Std (Depowered)

Purchase Price

Car Item	Dealer Cost	List
Base Price	**$32,403**	**$37,305**
Anti-Lock Brakes	Std	Std
Manual Transmission	N/A	N/A
Optional Engine	N/A	N/A
Auto Climate Control	Std	Std
Power Steering	Std	Std
Cruise Control	Std	Std
Power Windows	Std	Std
AM/FM Stereo Cassette	Std	Std
Steering Wheel, Tilt	Std	Std
Rear Defroster	Std	Std
*Options Price	$0	$0
*Total Price	**$32,403**	**$37,305**
Target Price	$35,709	
Destination Charge	$495	
Avg. Tax & Fees	$2,020	
Luxury Tax	$12	
Total Target $	**$38,236**	
12 Month Price Increase:	1%	

Ownership Costs (Projected)

Cost Area	5 Year Cost	Rating
Depreciation	$16,929	O
Financing ($634/month)	$7,439	
Insurance	$9,911	O
State Fees	$1,525	
Fuel (Hwy 25 City 20 -Prem.)	$3,902	O
Maintenance	$3,030	◉
Repairs	$660	O

Warranty/Maintenance Info

Major Tune-Up (60K mile int.)	$303	O
Minor Tune-Up (30K mile int.)	$239	●
Brake Service	$221	O
Overall Warranty	4 yr/50k	O
Drivetrain Warranty	6 yr/70k	O
Rust Warranty	6 yr/unlim. mi	O
Maintenance Warranty	1 yr/13k	O
Roadside Assistance	4 yr/unlim. mi	

Ownership Costs By Year (Projected)

$5,000 $10,000 $15,000 $20,000

- 1999
- 2000
- 2001
- 2002
- 2003

Resale Value

1999	2000	2001	2002	2003
$32,317	$29,307	$26,621	$23,981	$21,307

Cumulative Costs

	1999	2000	2001	2002	2003
Annual	$11,504	$8,167	$7,627	$7,671	$8,427
Total	$11,504	$19,671	$27,298	$34,969	$43,396

Projected Costs (5yr)

Relative	This Car
$43,769	$43,396
Cost/Mile 63¢	Cost/Mile 62¢

Ownership Cost Value

◉ Average

The GS 300 sedan enters this model year with a full list of standard features, including daytime running lamps, second generation depowered airbags and a five speed electronically controlled automatic transmission with intelligence (ECT-i). For 1999, the GS 300 qualifies as a TLEV (transitional low emissions) vehicle. An optional navigation system is available, which can track the vehicle's location and plot the best route on an electronic map display.

94

* Includes shaded options
** Other purchase requirements apply
*** Price includes other options

 ● Poor

 ◉ Worse Than Average

 O Average

 O Better Than Average

 O Excellent

⊖ Insufficient Information

Refer to *Section 3: Annotated Vehicle Charts* for an explanation of these charts.

Lexus GS 400
4 Door Sedan

 4.0L 300 hp Gas Fuel Inject. | 8 Cylinder "V" | Automatic 5 Speed | 2 Wheel Rear | Dual Front/Side Airbags Std

Luxury

Purchase Price

Car Item	Dealer Cost	List
Base Price	**$39,066**	**$45,505**
Anti-Lock Brakes	Std	Std
Manual Transmission	N/A	N/A
Optional Engine	N/A	N/A
Auto Climate Control	Std	Std
Power Steering	Std	Std
Cruise Control	Std	Std
Power Windows	Std	Std
AM/FM Stereo Cassette	Std	Std
Steering Wheel, Tilt	Std	Std
Rear Defroster	Std	Std
*Options Price	$0	$0
*Total Price	$39,066	$45,505
Target Price	$43,516	
Destination Charge	$495	
Avg. Tax & Fees	$2,453	
Luxury Tax	$481	
Total Target $	**$46,945**	
12 Month Price Increase:	2%	

The GS 400 sedan is upgraded from the GS 300 and includes the same list of features. A new Premium Package has been added this year, which includes leather seats, a six disc CD changer and high-intensity discharge headlamps. Also included with this package are memory seat, mirror and steering adjustments for two separate drivers. The standard Vehicle Skid Control system engages ABS and traction control when it senses understeer or oversteer conditions.

Ownership Costs (Projected)

Cost Area	5 Year Cost	Rating
Depreciation	$20,864	◐
Financing ($778/month)	$9,133	
Insurance (Performance)	$12,871	◉
State Fees	$1,853	
Fuel (Hwy 24 City 17 -Prem.)	$4,303	◐
Maintenance	$3,266	●
Repairs	$695	○

Warranty/Maintenance Info

Major Tune-Up (60K mile int.)	$218	○
Minor Tune-Up (30K mile int.)	$108	○
Brake Service	$231	○
Overall Warranty	4 yr/50k	○
Drivetrain Warranty	6 yr/70k	○
Rust Warranty	6 yr/unlim. mi	○
Maintenance Warranty	1 yr/13k	○
Roadside Assistance	4 yr/unlim. mi	

Ownership Costs By Year (Projected)

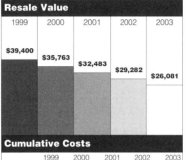

$5,000 $10,000 $15,000 $20,000 $25,000

■ 1999
▨ 2000
▨ 2001
▨ 2002
□ 2003

Resale Value

1999	2000	2001	2002	2003
$39,400	$35,763	$32,483	$29,282	$26,081

Cumulative Costs

	1999	2000	2001	2002	2003
Annual	$14,432	$9,995	$9,176	$9,542	$9,842
Total	$14,432	$24,427	$33,603	$43,145	$52,987

Projected Costs (5yr)

Relative	This Car
$50,884	$52,987
Cost/Mile 73¢	Cost/Mile 76¢

Ownership Cost Value

◉ Worse Than Average

Lexus LS 400
4 Door Sedan

 4.0L 290 hp Gas Fuel Inject. | 8 Cylinder "V" | Automatic 5 Speed | 2 Wheel Rear | Dual Front/Side Airbags Std

Luxury

Purchase Price

Car Item	Dealer Cost	List
Base Price	**$45,478**	**$53,605**
Anti-Lock Brakes	Std	Std
Manual Transmission	N/A	N/A
Optional Engine	N/A	N/A
Auto Climate Control	Std	Std
Power Steering	Std	Std
Cruise Control	Std	Std
Power Windows	Std	Std
AM/FM Stereo Cassette	Std	Std
St Whl, Pwr Tilt w/Mem	Std	Std
Rear Defroster	Std	Std
*Options Price	$0	$0
*Total Price	$45,478	$53,605
Target Price	$50,555	
Destination Charge	$495	
Avg. Tax & Fees	$2,851	
Luxury Tax	$903	
Total Target $	**$54,804**	
12 Month Price Increase:	1%	

For 1999, the LS 400 is powered with a new-generation V8 engine featuring VVT-i (intelligent variable valve timing). The optional navigation system utilizes a hard-disk map database for most major metropolitan areas, eliminating the need to insert separate CD ROMs for different areas. The multi-function key system is equipped with a transponder chip and utilizes a rolling code to thwart computerized scanners. The LS 400 climate control system is equipped with dual-zone temperature controls.

Ownership Costs (Projected)

Cost Area	5 Year Cost	Rating
Depreciation	$26,005	◐
Financing ($908/month)	$10,662	
Insurance (Performance)	$13,356	◉
State Fees	$2,178	
Fuel (Hwy 25 City 18 -Prem.)	$4,099	◐
Maintenance	$2,534	○
Repairs	$695	○

Warranty/Maintenance Info

Major Tune-Up (60K mile int.)	$193	○
Minor Tune-Up (30K mile int.)	$98	○
Brake Service	$294	◉
Overall Warranty	4 yr/50k	○
Drivetrain Warranty	6 yr/70k	○
Rust Warranty	6 yr/unlim. mi	○
Maintenance Warranty	1 yr/13k	○
Roadside Assistance	4 yr/unlim. mi	

Ownership Costs By Year (Projected)

$5,000 $10,000 $15,000 $20,000 $25,000 $30,000

■ 1999
▨ 2000
▨ 2001
▨ 2002
□ 2003

Resale Value

1999	2000	2001	2002	2003
$49,412	$43,869	$38,739	$33,741	$28,799

Cumulative Costs

	1999	2000	2001	2002	2003
Annual	$12,932	$12,451	$11,440	$11,424	$11,282
Total	$12,932	$25,383	$36,823	$48,247	$59,529

Projected Costs (5yr)

Relative	This Car
$57,762	$59,529
Cost/Mile 83¢	Cost/Mile 85¢

Ownership Cost Value

◉ Worse Than Average

---

* Includes shaded options
** Other purchase requirements apply
*** Price includes other options

● Poor | ◉ Worse Than Average | ◐ Average | ○ Better Than Average | ○ Excellent | ⊖ Insufficient Information

95

Refer to *Section 3: Annotated Vehicle Charts* for an explanation of these charts.

©1999 by IntelliChoice, Inc. (408) 866-1400 http://www.intellichoice.com All Rights Reserved. Reproduction Prohibited.

Lexus SC 300
2 Door Coupe

 3.0L 225 hp Gas Fuel Inject.
 6 Cylinder In-Line
Automatic 4 Speed
 2 Wheel Rear
 Dual Airbags Std

Purchase Price

Car Item	Dealer Cost	List
Base Price	**$37,267**	**$42,905**
Anti-Lock Brakes	Std	Std
Manual Transmission	N/A	N/A
Optional Engine	N/A	N/A
Auto Climate Control	Std	Std
Power Steering	Std	Std
Cruise Control	Std	Std
Power Windows	Std	Std
AM/FM Stereo Cassette	Std	Std
Steering Wheel, Tilt	Std	Std
Rear Defroster	Std	Std
*Options Price	$0	$0
*Total Price	**$37,267**	**$42,905**
Target Price	$40,531	
Destination Charge	$495	
Avg. Tax & Fees	$2,293	
Luxury Tax	$302	
Total Target $	**$43,621**	
12 Month Price Increase:	5%	

The SC 300 coupe is manufactured and imported from Motomachi, Japan. The SC 300 has several changes for the 1999 model year. These include a standard in-dash CD changer with Automatic Sound Levelizer technology, daytime running lamps, larger brakes, three new exterior colors and optional perforated leather seats. The SC 300 also comes equipped with second generation depowered airbags and front seat belt pretensioners. Options include a moonroof and Lexus/Nakamichi audiophile sound system.

Ownership Costs (Projected)

Cost Area	5 Year Cost	Rating
Depreciation	$18,869	○
Financing ($723/month)	$8,486	
Insurance (Performance)	$12,356	◉
State Fees	$1,749	
Fuel (Hwy 24 City 19 -Prem.)	$4,083	○
Maintenance	$3,148	◉
Repairs	$660	○

Warranty/Maintenance Info

Major Tune-Up (60K mile int.)	$305	◉
Minor Tune-Up (30K mile int.)	$232	●
Brake Service	$228	○
Overall Warranty	4 yr/50k	○
Drivetrain Warranty	6 yr/70k	○
Rust Warranty	6 yr/unlim. mi	○
Maintenance Warranty	1 yr/13k	○
Roadside Assistance	4 yr/unlim. mi	

Ownership Costs By Year (Projected)

$5,000 $10,000 $15,000 $20,000

1999 / 2000 / 2001 / 2002 / 2003

Resale Value

1999	2000	2001	2002	2003
$40,548	$36,309	$32,418	$28,590	$24,752

Cumulative Costs

	1999	2000	2001	2002	2003
Annual	$9,572	$10,248	$9,604	$9,899	$10,028
Total	$9,572	$19,820	$29,424	$39,323	$49,351

Projected Costs (5yr)

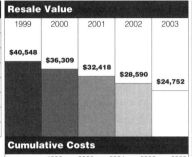

Relative	This Car
$48,960	$49,351
Cost/Mile 70¢	Cost/Mile 71¢

Ownership Cost Value

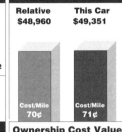

Average

Lexus SC 400
2 Door Coupe

Luxury

 4.0L 290 hp Gas Fuel Inject.
 8 Cylinder "V"
Automatic 5 Speed
 2 Wheel Rear
 Dual Airbags Std

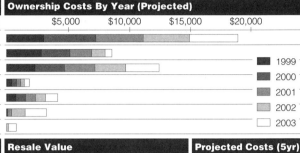

Purchase Price

Car Item	Dealer Cost	List
Base Price	**$47,393**	**$55,205**
Anti-Lock Brakes	Std	Std
Manual Transmission	N/A	N/A
Optional Engine	N/A	N/A
Auto Climate Control	Std	Std
Power Steering	Std	Std
Cruise Control	Std	Std
Power Windows	Std	Std
AM/FM Stereo Cassette	Std	Std
St Whl, Tilt/Scope/Mem	Std	Std
Rear Defroster	Std	Std
*Options Price	$0	$0
*Total Price	**$47,393**	**$55,205**
Target Price	$51,901	
Destination Charge	$495	
Avg. Tax & Fees	$2,928	
Luxury Tax	$984	
Total Target $	**$56,308**	
12 Month Price Increase:	5%	

The SC 400 coupe is upgraded from the SC 300 and includes the same new features. Upgrades on the SC 400 include a 4.0L 290 hp V8 engine, perforated leather seating and a five speed automatic transmission. Included with the standard theft deterrent system is an engine immobilizer, activated by an electronic chip integrated into the ignition key. The SC 400 also features the two-driver Lexus Memory System, which controls the steering wheel, driver's seat and electrochromic mirrors.

Ownership Costs (Projected)

Cost Area	5 Year Cost	Rating
Depreciation	$28,337	○
Financing ($933/month)	$10,955	
Insurance (Performance)	$14,083	◉
State Fees	$2,241	
Fuel (Hwy 25 City 18 -Prem.)	$4,099	○
Maintenance	$3,262	●
Repairs	$695	○

Warranty/Maintenance Info

Major Tune-Up (60K mile int.)	$220	○
Minor Tune-Up (30K mile int.)	$142	○
Brake Service	$228	○
Overall Warranty	4 yr/50k	○
Drivetrain Warranty	6 yr/70k	○
Rust Warranty	6 yr/unlim. mi	○
Maintenance Warranty	1 yr/13k	○
Roadside Assistance	4 yr/unlim. mi	

Ownership Costs By Year (Projected)

$5,000 $10,000 $15,000 $20,000 $25,000 $30,000

1999 / 2000 / 2001 / 2002 / 2003

Resale Value

1999	2000	2001	2002	2003
$48,347	$42,902	$37,843	$32,895	$27,971

Cumulative Costs

	1999	2000	2001	2002	2003
Annual	$15,755	$12,589	$11,638	$11,797	$11,892
Total	$15,755	$28,344	$39,982	$51,779	$63,671

Projected Costs (5yr)

Relative	This Car
$59,822	$63,671
Cost/Mile 85¢	Cost/Mile 91¢

Ownership Cost Value

Worse Than Average

96

● Poor Worse Than Average ◐ Average ○ Better Than Average ○ Excellent ⊖ Insufficient Information

Refer to *Section 3: Annotated Vehicle Charts* for an explanation of these charts.

Lincoln Continental
4 Door Sedan

4.6L 260 hp Gas Fuel Inject.	8 Cylinder "V"	Automatic 4 Speed	2 Wheel Front	Dual Front/Side Airbags Std

Luxury

Purchase Price

Car Item	Dealer Cost	List
Base Price	**$34,955**	**$38,325**
Anti-Lock Brakes	Std	Std
Manual Transmission	N/A	N/A
Optional Engine	N/A	N/A
Auto Climate Control	Std	Std
Power Steering	Std	Std
Cruise Control	Std	Std
Power Windows	Std	Std
AM/FM Stereo Cassette	Std	Std
Steering Wheel, Tilt	Std	Std
Rear Defroster	Std	Std
*Options Price	$0	$0
*Total Price	**$34,955**	**$38,325**
Target Price	$36,953	
Destination Charge	$670	
Avg. Tax & Fees	$2,096	
Luxury Tax	$97	
Total Target $	**$39,816**	
12 Month Price Increase:	1%	

For 1999, the Continental receives exterior and interior enhancements that include standard front seat side-impact airbags, new ten spoke brushed aluminum wheels and new optional six spoke chrome wheels. The Driver Select System, Luxury Appearance Package, Personal Security Package and RESCU Package are optional. A power moonroof, CD changer and Alpine sound system are additional options. The Continental can be equipped as either a five or six passenger automobile.

Ownership Costs (Projected)

Cost Area	5 Year Cost	Rating
Depreciation	$24,490	●
Financing ($660/month)	$7,746	
Insurance (Performance)	$9,226	○
State Fees	$1,573	
Fuel (Hwy 25 City 17 -Prem.)	$4,216	○
Maintenance	$2,389	○
Repairs	$1,135	○

Warranty/Maintenance Info

Major Tune-Up (100K mile int.)	$294	○
Minor Tune-Up (30K mile int.)	$88	○
Brake Service	$192	○
Overall Warranty	4 yr/50k	○
Drivetrain Warranty	4 yr/50k	○
Rust Warranty	5 yr/unlim. mi	○
Maintenance Warranty	N/A	
Roadside Assistance	4 yr/50k	

Ownership Costs By Year (Projected)

$5,000 $10,000 $15,000 $20,000 $25,000

1999, 2000, 2001, 2002, 2003

Resale Value

1999	2000	2001	2002	2003
$32,430	$27,762	$23,506	$19,389	$15,326

Cumulative Costs

	1999	2000	2001	2002	2003
Annual	$13,016	$9,846	$9,243	$8,972	$9,697
Total	$13,016	$22,862	$32,105	$41,077	$50,774

Projected Costs (5yr)

Relative	This Car
$46,490	**$50,774**
Cost/Mile 66¢	Cost/Mile 73¢

Ownership Cost Value

● Worse Than Average

Lincoln Town Car Executive
4 Door Sedan

4.6L 205 hp Gas Fuel Inject.	8 Cylinder "V"	Automatic 4 Speed	2 Wheel Rear	Dual Front/Side Airbags Std

Luxury

Cartier Model Shown

Purchase Price

Car Item	Dealer Cost	List
Base Price	**$34,955**	**$38,325**
Anti-Lock Brakes	Std	Std
Manual Transmission	N/A	N/A
Optional Engine	N/A	N/A
Auto Climate Control	Std	Std
Power Steering	Std	Std
Cruise Control	Std	Std
Power Windows	Std	Std
AM/FM Stereo Cassette	Std	Std
Steering Wheel, Tilt	Std	Std
Rear Defroster	Std	Std
*Options Price	$0	$0
*Total Price	**$34,955**	**$38,325**
Target Price	$36,953	
Destination Charge	$670	
Avg. Tax & Fees	$2,096	
Luxury Tax	$97	
Total Target $	**$39,816**	
12 Month Price Increase:	1%	

The Town Car Executive Series boasts several enhancements for this year. The standard leather seating package is improved with eight-way power adjustments, a front center armrest with storage and a rear armrest with cup holders. Two-tone paint is a new option, and color choices and combinations are improved, as are interior graphics. Most notable, however, is the addition of front seat side-impact airbags, which compliment the already standard antilock brakes and all-speed traction control.

Ownership Costs (Projected)

Cost Area	5 Year Cost	Rating
Depreciation	$22,858	●
Financing ($660/month)	$7,746	
Insurance	$8,045	○
State Fees	$1,573	
Fuel (Hwy 24 City 17)	$3,628	○
Maintenance	$2,443	○
Repairs	$895	○

Warranty/Maintenance Info

Major Tune-Up (100K mile int.)	$361	●
Minor Tune-Up (30K mile int.)	$89	○
Brake Service	$201	○
Overall Warranty	4 yr/50k	○
Drivetrain Warranty	4 yr/50k	○
Rust Warranty	5 yr/unlim. mi	○
Maintenance Warranty	N/A	
Roadside Assistance	4 yr/50k	

Ownership Costs By Year (Projected)

$5,000 $10,000 $15,000 $20,000 $25,000

1999, 2000, 2001, 2002, 2003

Resale Value

1999	2000	2001	2002	2003
$33,078	$28,679	$24,677	$20,798	$16,958

Cumulative Costs

	1999	2000	2001	2002	2003
Annual	$12,030	$9,232	$8,642	$8,323	$8,961
Total	$12,030	$21,262	$29,904	$38,227	$47,188

Projected Costs (5yr)

Relative	This Car
$46,490	**$47,188**
Cost/Mile 66¢	Cost/Mile 67¢

Ownership Cost Value

○ Average

---

* Includes shaded options

** Other purchase requirements apply

*** Price includes other options

● Poor	◐ Worse Than Average	◑ Average	○ Better Than Average	○ Excellent	⊖ Insufficient Information

97

Refer to *Section 3: Annotated Vehicle Charts* for an explanation of these charts.

Lincoln Town Car Signature
4 Door Sedan

| 4.6L 205 hp Gas Fuel Inject. | 8 Cylinder "V" | Automatic 4 Speed | 2 Wheel Rear | Dual Front/Side Airbags Std |

Luxury

Cartier Model Shown

Purchase Price

Car Item	Dealer Cost	List
Base Price	**$36,735**	**$40,325**
Anti-Lock Brakes	Std	Std
Manual Transmission	N/A	N/A
Optional Engine	N/A	N/A
Auto Climate Control	Std	Std
Power Steering	Std	Std
Cruise Control	Std	Std
Power Windows	Std	Std
AM/FM Stereo Cassette	Std	Std
Steering Wheel, Tilt	Std	Std
Rear Defroster	Std	Std
*Options Price	$0	$0
*Total Price	**$36,735**	**$40,325**
Target Price	$38,895	
Destination Charge	$670	
Avg. Tax & Fees	$2,203	
Luxury Tax	$214	
Total Target $	**$41,982**	
12 Month Price Increase:	2%	

Ownership Costs (Projected)

Cost Area	5 Year Cost	Rating
Depreciation	$24,114	●
Financing ($696/month)	$8,167	●
Insurance	$8,265	○
State Fees	$1,653	
Fuel (Hwy 24 City 17)	$3,628	◉
Maintenance	$2,443	○
Repairs	$895	○

Warranty/Maintenance Info

Major Tune-Up (100K mile int.)	$361	●
Minor Tune-Up (30K mile int.)	$89	○
Brake Service	$201	○
Overall Warranty	4 yr/50k	○
Drivetrain Warranty	4 yr/50k	○
Rust Warranty	5 yr/unlim. mi	○
Maintenance Warranty	N/A	
Roadside Assistance	4 yr/50k	

Ownership Costs By Year (Projected)

$5,000 $10,000 $15,000 $20,000 $25,000

■ 1999
■ 2000
■ 2001
□ 2002
□ 2003

Resale Value

1999	2000	2001	2002	2003
$34,676	$30,088	$25,909	$21,862	$17,868

Cumulative Costs

	1999	2000	2001	2002	2003
Annual	$12,803	$9,598	$8,966	$8,605	$9,193
Total	$12,803	$22,401	$31,367	$39,972	$49,165

Projected Costs (5yr)

Relative	This Car
$48,391	$49,165
Cost/Mile 69¢	Cost/Mile 70¢

Ownership Cost Value

○ Average

This year the Town Car Signature Series receives the important safety-related advance of standard side-impact airbags. Other changes include new color combinations, including a two-tone option, various interior appearance enhancements, and an Alpine audio system. This new system features digital signal processing, a 145 watt amplifier and upgraded speakers. The Touring Sedan Package includes monotone appearance items, unique wheels, perforated leather seating and specific suspension tuning.

Lincoln Town Car Cartier
4 Door Sedan

| 4.6L 220 hp Gas Fuel Inject. | 8 Cylinder "V" | Automatic 4 Speed | 2 Wheel Rear | Dual Front/Side Airbags Std |

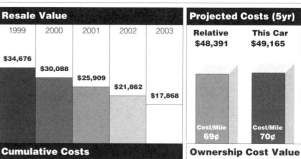

Luxury

Purchase Price

Car Item	Dealer Cost	List
Base Price	**$38,960**	**$42,825**
Anti-Lock Brakes	Std	Std
Manual Transmission	N/A	N/A
Optional Engine	N/A	N/A
Auto Climate Control	Std	Std
Power Steering	Std	Std
Cruise Control	Std	Std
Power Windows	Std	Std
AM/FM Stereo Cassette	Std	Std
Steering Wheel, Tilt	Std	Std
Rear Defroster	Std	Std
*Options Price	$0	$0
*Total Price	**$38,960**	**$42,825**
Target Price	$41,329	
Destination Charge	$670	
Avg. Tax & Fees	$2,338	
Luxury Tax	$360	
Total Target $	**$44,697**	
12 Month Price Increase:	2%	

Ownership Costs (Projected)

Cost Area	5 Year Cost	Rating
Depreciation	$26,250	●
Financing ($741/month)	$8,696	●
Insurance	$8,265	○
State Fees	$1,752	
Fuel (Hwy 24 City 17)	$3,628	◉
Maintenance	$2,443	○
Repairs	$895	○

Warranty/Maintenance Info

Major Tune-Up (100K mile int.)	$361	●
Minor Tune-Up (30K mile int.)	$89	○
Brake Service	$201	○
Overall Warranty	4 yr/50k	○
Drivetrain Warranty	4 yr/50k	○
Rust Warranty	5 yr/unlim. mi	○
Maintenance Warranty	N/A	
Roadside Assistance	4 yr/50k	

Ownership Costs By Year (Projected)

$5,000 $10,000 $15,000 $20,000 $25,000 $30,000

■ 1999
■ 2000
■ 2001
□ 2002
□ 2003

Resale Value

1999	2000	2001	2002	2003
$36,352	$31,477	$27,020	$22,701	$18,447

Cumulative Costs

	1999	2000	2001	2002	2003
Annual	$14,047	$10,053	$9,373	$8,963	$9,493
Total	$14,047	$24,100	$33,473	$42,436	$51,929

Projected Costs (5yr)

Relative	This Car
$50,771	$51,929
Cost/Mile 73¢	Cost/Mile 74¢

Ownership Cost Value

○ Average

The Town Car Cartier Series continues this year with several key changes. Among these are the addition of front seat side-impact airbags, various new colors and interior enhancements and a new Alpine audio system with digital signal processing. Features exclusive to the Cartier include unique gold badging, chrome aluminum wheels and premium leather seating. For even more luxury enhancement, a Premium Package is available, which includes a CD changer and a power moonroof.

98

* Includes shaded options
** Other purchase requirements apply
*** Price includes other options

| ● Poor | ◉ Worse Than Average | ○ Average | ○ Better Than Average | ○ Excellent | ⊖ Insufficient Information |

Refer to *Section 3: Annotated Vehicle Charts* for an explanation of these charts.

Mazda 626 LX
4 Door Sedan

 2.0L 125 hp Gas Fuel Inject.

 4 Cylinder In-Line

 Manual 5 Speed

 2 Wheel Front

 Dual Airbags Std

Purchase Price

Car Item	Dealer Cost	List
Base Price	$15,961	$17,665
Anti-Lock Brakes	$468	$550
Automatic 4 Speed	$696	$800
Optional Engine	N/A	N/A
Air Conditioning	Std	Std
Power Steering	Std	Std
Cruise Control	Std	Std
Power Windows	Std	Std
AM/FM Stereo CD	Std	Std
Steering Wheel, Tilt	Std	Std
Rear Defroster	Std	Std
*Options Price	$1,164	$1,350
*Total Price	$17,125	$19,015
Target Price	$17,827	
Destination Charge	$450	
Avg. Tax & Fees	$1,030	
Total Target $	$19,307	
Average Dealer Option Cost:	83%	
12 Month Price Increase:	None	

The 626 LX sedan comes equipped with many standard features such as a remote keyless entry system, luxury cloth seating, an AM/FM/CD stereo system and a power antenna. More standard features for the 626 LX include variable intermittent wipers and illuminated visor vanity mirrors. The optional moonroof now includes a storage compartment and map lights. The 626 series has been classified as a domestic model since 1993 with 75% domestic content, and is manufactured in Flat Rock, Michigan.

Ownership Costs (Projected)

Cost Area	5 Year Cost	Rating
Depreciation	$10,165	◐
Financing ($320/month)	$3,756	
Insurance	$8,265	⊙
State Fees	$792	
Fuel (Hwy 29 City 22)	$2,906	○
Maintenance	$3,051	○
Repairs	$915	◐

Warranty/Maintenance Info

Major Tune-Up (60K mile int.)	$269	◐
Minor Tune-Up (30K mile int.)	$93	○
Brake Service	$162	○
Overall Warranty	3 yr/50k	◐
Drivetrain Warranty	3 yr/50k	◐
Rust Warranty	5 yr/unlim. mi	○
Maintenance Warranty	N/A	
Roadside Assistance	3 yr/50k	

Ownership Costs By Year (Projected)

$2,000 $4,000 $6,000 $8,000 $10,000 $12,000

■ 1999
■ 2000
■ 2001
□ 2002
□ 2003

Resale Value

1999	2000	2001	2002	2003
$16,325	$14,358	$12,651	$10,880	$9,142

Cumulative Costs

	1999	2000	2001	2002	2003
Annual	$6,628	$5,421	$5,047	$5,977	$6,777
Total	$6,628	$12,049	$17,096	$23,073	$29,850

Projected Costs (5yr)

Relative	This Car
$28,639	$29,850
Cost/Mile 41¢	Cost/Mile 43¢

Ownership Cost Value

⊙

Worse Than Average

Mazda 626 LX V-6
4 Door Sedan

Midsize

 2.5L 170 hp Gas Fuel Inject.

 6 Cylinder "V"

 Manual 5 Speed

 2 Wheel Front

 Dual Airbags Std

Base Model Shown

Purchase Price

Car Item	Dealer Cost	List
Base Price	$17,222	$19,065
Anti-Lock Brakes	$595	$700
Automatic 4 Speed	$696	$800
Optional Engine	N/A	N/A
Air Conditioning	Std	Std
Power Steering	Std	Std
Cruise Control	Std	Std
Power Windows	Std	Std
AM/FM Stereo CD	Std	Std
Steering Wheel, Tilt	Std	Std
Rear Defroster	Std	Std
*Options Price	$1,291	$1,500
*Total Price	$18,513	$20,565
Target Price	$19,290	
Destination Charge	$450	
Avg. Tax & Fees	$1,111	
Total Target $	$20,851	
Average Dealer Option Cost:	83%	
12 Month Price Increase:	None	

The 626 LX V6 sedan has all of the same features as the 626 LX. The most significant upgrade is a 2.5L V6 170 hp engine and four wheel disc brakes. 626 LX V6 features include fade-out interior lighting, power windows and door locks, oscillating center vent louvers and auto-off headlamps. Antilock brakes with an integrated traction control system are optional, as is a Luxury Package, which includes a Bose sound system, power driver's seat, power moonroof and theft deterrent system.

Ownership Costs (Projected)

Cost Area	5 Year Cost	Rating
Depreciation	$11,078	◐
Financing ($346/month)	$4,056	
Insurance	$8,757	⊙
State Fees	$853	
Fuel (Hwy 26 City 20 -Prem.)	$3,821	⊙
Maintenance	$3,898	●
Repairs	$915	◐

Warranty/Maintenance Info

Major Tune-Up (60K mile int.)	$328	●
Minor Tune-Up (30K mile int.)	$122	◐
Brake Service	$166	○
Overall Warranty	3 yr/50k	◐
Drivetrain Warranty	3 yr/50k	◐
Rust Warranty	5 yr/unlim. mi	○
Maintenance Warranty	N/A	
Roadside Assistance	3 yr/50k	

Ownership Costs By Year (Projected)

$2,000 $4,000 $6,000 $8,000 $10,000 $12,000

■ 1999
■ 2000
■ 2001
□ 2002
□ 2003

Resale Value

1999	2000	2001	2002	2003
$17,289	$15,243	$13,453	$11,598	$9,773

Cumulative Costs

	1999	2000	2001	2002	2003
Annual	$7,594	$5,874	$5,517	$6,460	$7,933
Total	$7,594	$13,468	$18,985	$25,445	$33,378

Projected Costs (5yr)

Relative	This Car
$29,971	$33,378
Cost/Mile 43¢	Cost/Mile 48¢

Ownership Cost Value

●

Poor

● Poor ⊙ Worse Than Average ◐ Average ○ Better Than Average ○ Excellent ⊖ Insufficient Information

Refer to *Section 3: Annotated Vehicle Charts* for an explanation of these charts.

Mazda 626 ES
4 Door Sedan

Midsize

 2.0L 125 hp Gas Fuel Inject.
 4 Cylinder In-Line
 PRND321 Automatic 4 Speed
 2 Wheel Front
 Depowered Dual Airbags Std

Purchase Price

Car Item	Dealer Cost	List
Base Price	**$17,654**	**$19,545**
Anti-Lock Brakes	$468	$550
Manual Transmission	N/A	N/A
Optional Engine	N/A	N/A
Air Conditioning	Std	Std
Power Steering	Std	Std
Cruise Control	Std	Std
Power Windows	Std	Std
AM/FM Stereo CD	Std	Std
Steering Wheel, Tilt	Std	Std
Rear Defroster	Std	Std
*Options Price	$468	$550
*Total Price	**$18,122**	**$20,095**
Target Price	$18,884	
Destination Charge	$450	
Avg. Tax & Fees	$1,088	
Total Target $	**$20,422**	
Average Dealer Option Cost:	82%	
12 Month Price Increase:	N/A	

New for 1999 is the 626 ES sedan. The 626 ES sedan replaces the 626 DX. The ES comes equipped with a leather-trimmed interior and shares the same 2.0L 4 cylinder 125 hp engine with the 626 LX. The ES comes equipped with a remote keyless entry system, oscillating center vent louvers and a power antenna. More standard features include woodgrain appliques, variable intermittent wipers and illuminated visor vanity mirrors, as well as an AM/FM/CD stereo system.

Ownership Costs (Projected)

Cost Area	5 Year Cost	Rating
Depreciation	$10,720	◐
Financing ($339/month)	$3,973	◐
Insurance	$8,265	◉
State Fees	$834	
Fuel (Hwy 29 City 22)	$2,906	○
Maintenance	$3,320	○
Repairs	$915	○

Warranty/Maintenance Info

Major Tune-Up (60K mile int.)	$272	◐
Minor Tune-Up (30K mile int.)	$93	○
Brake Service	$162	○
Overall Warranty	3 yr/50k	◐
Drivetrain Warranty	3 yr/50k	◐
Rust Warranty	5 yr/unlim. mi	○
Maintenance Warranty	N/A	
Roadside Assistance	3 yr/50k	

Ownership Costs By Year (Projected)

$2,000 $4,000 $6,000 $8,000 $10,000 $12,000

■ 1999
■ 2000
■ 2001
■ 2002
□ 2003

Resale Value

1999	2000	2001	2002	2003
$17,089	$15,066	$13,306	$11,485	$9,702

Cumulative Costs

	1999	2000	2001	2002	2003
Annual	$7,062	$5,547	$5,283	$6,063	$6,978
Total	$7,062	$12,609	$17,892	$23,955	$30,933

Projected Costs (5yr)

Relative	This Car
$29,576	$30,933
Cost/Mile 42¢	Cost/Mile 44¢

Ownership Cost Value

●

Worse Than Average

Mazda 626 ES V-6
4 Door Sedan

Midsize

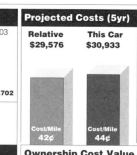
Base Model Shown

2.5L 170 hp Gas Fuel Inject.
 6 Cylinder "V"
 1 3 5 / 2 4 R Manual 5 Speed
 2 Wheel Front
Depowered Dual Airbags Std

Purchase Price

Car Item	Dealer Cost	List
Base Price	**$20,087**	**$22,245**
Anti-Lock Brakes	$595	$700
Automatic 4 Speed	$696	$800
Optional Engine	N/A	N/A
Air Conditioning	Std	Std
Power Steering	Std	Std
Cruise Control	Std	Std
Power Windows	Std	Std
AM/FM Stereo CD	Std	Std
Steering Wheel, Tilt	Std	Std
Rear Defroster	Std	Std
*Options Price	$1,291	$1,500
*Total Price	**$21,378**	**$23,745**
Target Price	$22,322	
Destination Charge	$450	
Avg. Tax & Fees	$1,280	
Total Target $	**$24,052**	
Average Dealer Option Cost:	86%	
12 Month Price Increase:	None	

The 626 ES V6 sedan is the top of the line for the 626 series. The 626 ES V6 has all the same new standard features as the ES model. The 626 ES V6 shares the same 2.5L V6 170 hp engine and four wheel disc brakes with the 626 LX V6. The fully-equipped ES V6 sports lockable alloy wheels, an anti-theft system, a power driver's seat and power moonroof. An upgraded Bose sound system is also standard. Four wheel antilock brakes with an integrated traction control system are optional.

Ownership Costs (Projected)

Cost Area	5 Year Cost	Rating
Depreciation	$13,391	●
Financing ($399/month)	$4,679	◐
Insurance	$8,556	◉
State Fees	$981	
Fuel (Hwy 26 City 20 -Prem.)	$3,821	◉
Maintenance	$3,898	●
Repairs	$915	○

Warranty/Maintenance Info

Major Tune-Up (60K mile int.)	$328	●
Minor Tune-Up (30K mile int.)	$122	◐
Brake Service	$166	○
Overall Warranty	3 yr/50k	◐
Drivetrain Warranty	3 yr/50k	◐
Rust Warranty	5 yr/unlim. mi	○
Maintenance Warranty	N/A	
Roadside Assistance	3 yr/50k	

Ownership Costs By Year (Projected)

$2,000 $4,000 $6,000 $8,000 $10,000 $12,000 $14,000

■ 1999
■ 2000
■ 2001
■ 2002
□ 2003

Resale Value

1999	2000	2001	2002	2003
$19,388	$17,022	$14,925	$12,771	$10,661

Cumulative Costs

	1999	2000	2001	2002	2003
Annual	$8,901	$6,356	$5,939	$6,821	$8,224
Total	$8,901	$15,257	$21,196	$28,017	$36,241

Projected Costs (5yr)

Relative	This Car
$33,340	$36,241
Cost/Mile 48¢	Cost/Mile 52¢

Ownership Cost Value

●

Poor

100

* Includes shaded options
** Other purchase requirements apply
*** Price includes other options

● Poor   ◉ Worse Than Average   ○ Average   ○ Better Than Average   ○ Excellent   ⊖ Insufficient Information

Refer to *Section 3: Annotated Vehicle Charts* for an explanation of these charts.

Mazda Millenia
4 Door Sedan

2.5L 170 hp Gas Fuel Inject.	6 Cylinder "V"	Automatic 4 Speed	2 Wheel Front	Dual Airbags Std

Near Luxury

S Model Shown

Purchase Price

Car Item	Dealer Cost	List
Base Price	**$24,019**	**$26,545**
Anti-Lock Brakes	Std	Std
Manual Transmission	N/A	N/A
Optional Engine	N/A	N/A
Auto Climate Control	Std	Std
Power Steering	Std	Std
Cruise Control	Std	Std
Power Windows	Std	Std
AM/FM Stereo Cass/CD	Std	Std
St Whl, Pwr Tilt w/Mem	Std	Std
Rear Defroster	Std	Std
*Options Price	$0	$0
*Total Price	**$24,019**	**$26,545**
Target Price	$24,985	
Destination Charge	$450	
Avg. Tax & Fees	$1,428	
Total Target $	**$26,863**	
Average Dealer Option Cost:	85%	
12 Month Price Increase:	None	

Mazda's luxury flagship Millenia is manufactured and imported from Hiroshima, Japan. The most notable change for 1999 is an MSRP decrease of $2,450. Also new is a change from 15 inch wheels to standard 215/55VR16 tires and 16 inch alloy wheels. More changes include a redesigned grille and revised front turn lamps and rear combination lamps, as well as depowered airbags. The Millenia features automatic climate control, an AM/FM/CD stereo and a power tilt steering wheel with memory.

Ownership Costs (Projected)

Cost Area	5 Year Cost	Rating
Depreciation	$15,103	●
Financing ($445/month)	$5,226	
Insurance	$8,865	◐
State Fees	$1,093	
Fuel (Hwy 27 City 20 -Prem.)	$3,745	○
Maintenance	$5,403	●
Repairs	$950	○

Warranty/Maintenance Info

Major Tune-Up (60K mile int.)	$424	●
Minor Tune-Up (30K mile int.)	$144	○
Brake Service	$222	○
Overall Warranty	3 yr/50k	○
Drivetrain Warranty	3 yr/50k	○
Rust Warranty	5 yr/unlim. mi	○
Maintenance Warranty	N/A	
Roadside Assistance	3 yr/50k	

Ownership Costs By Year (Projected)

$5,000 $10,000 $15,000 $20,000

1999 / 2000 / 2001 / 2002 / 2003

Resale Value

1999	2000	2001	2002	2003
$21,918	$19,153	$16,692	$14,254	$11,760

Cumulative Costs

	1999	2000	2001	2002	2003
Annual	$9,439	$6,976	$6,654	$7,044	$10,272
Total	$9,439	$16,415	$23,069	$30,113	$40,385

Projected Costs (5yr)

Relative $36,931	This Car $40,385
Cost/Mile 53¢	Cost/Mile 58¢

Ownership Cost Value

● Poor

Mazda Millenia S
4 Door Sedan

2.3L 210 hp Suprchrged Fuel Inject.	6 Cylinder "V"	Automatic 4 Speed	2 Wheel Front	Dual Airbags Std

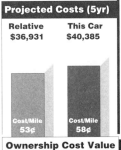

Near Luxury

Purchase Price

Car Item	Dealer Cost	List
Base Price	**$28,084**	**$31,045**
Anti-Lock Brakes	Std	Std
Manual Transmission	N/A	N/A
Optional Engine	N/A	N/A
Auto Climate Control	Std	Std
Power Steering	Std	Std
Cruise Control	Std	Std
Power Windows	Std	Std
AM/FM Stereo Cass/CD	Std	Std
St Whl, Pwr Tilt w/Mem	Std	Std
Rear Defroster	Std	Std
*Options Price	$0	$0
*Total Price	**$28,084**	**$31,045**
Target Price	$29,290	
Destination Charge	$450	
Avg. Tax & Fees	$1,666	
Total Target $	**$31,406**	
Average Dealer Option Cost:	84%	
12 Month Price Increase:	None	

The Millenia S sedan comes equipped with most of the same changes as the base Millenia. The repricing of the Millenia S is reflected in an MSRP decrease of $5,500. New for 1999 is a change from 16 inch wheels to standard 215/50R17 tires and 17 inch alloy wheels. New interior enhancements include chrome trim on the shift lever, handbrake lever and door handles, and woodgrain trim around the power window switches. A power moonroof and traction control system are standard on the Millenia S.

Ownership Costs (Projected)

Cost Area	5 Year Cost	Rating
Depreciation	$17,655	●
Financing ($521/month)	$6,109	
Insurance	$9,135	○
State Fees	$1,272	
Fuel (Hwy 28 City 20 -Prem.)	$3,674	○
Maintenance	$5,696	●
Repairs	$950	○

Warranty/Maintenance Info

Major Tune-Up (60K mile int.)	$232	○
Minor Tune-Up (30K mile int.)	$134	○
Brake Service	$222	○
Overall Warranty	3 yr/50k	○
Drivetrain Warranty	3 yr/50k	○
Rust Warranty	5 yr/unlim. mi	○
Maintenance Warranty	N/A	
Roadside Assistance	3 yr/50k	

Ownership Costs By Year (Projected)

$5,000 $10,000 $15,000 $20,000

1999 / 2000 / 2001 / 2002 / 2003

Resale Value

1999	2000	2001	2002	2003
$25,200	$22,095	$19,303	$16,550	$13,751

Cumulative Costs

	1999	2000	2001	2002	2003
Annual	$11,084	$7,638	$7,336	$7,571	$10,862
Total	$11,084	$18,722	$26,058	$33,629	$44,491

Projected Costs (5yr)

Relative $39,161	This Car $44,491
Cost/Mile 56¢	Cost/Mile 64¢

Ownership Cost Value

● Poor

---

* Includes shaded options

** Other purchase requirements apply

*** Price includes other options

● Poor	◐ Worse Than Average	○ Average	○ Better Than Average	○ Excellent	⊖ Insufficient Information

Refer to *Section 3: Annotated Vehicle Charts* for an explanation of these charts.

101

Mazda MX-5 Miata
2 Door Convertible

Base Sport

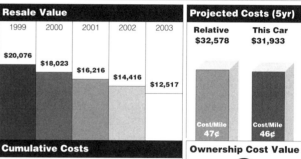

1.8L 140 hp Gas Fuel Inject.	4 Cylinder In-Line	Manual 5 Speed	2 Wheel Rear	Dual Airbags Std (Depowered)

Purchase Price

Car Item	Dealer Cost	List
Base Price	**$17,965**	**$19,770**
Anti-Lock Brakes	$468	**$550
Automatic 4 Speed	$739	**$850
Optional Engine	N/A	N/A
Air Conditioning	$720	$900
Power Steering	Inc	Inc
Cruise Control	Pkg	Pkg
Power Windows	Inc	Inc
AM/FM Stereo CD	Std	Std
Steering Wheel, Tilt	N/A	N/A
Rear Defroster	Std	Std
*Options Price	$720	$900
*Total Price	**$18,685**	**$20,670**
Target Price	$19,626	
Destination Charge	$450	
Avg. Tax & Fees	$1,127	
Total Target $	**$21,203**	
Average Dealer Option Cost:	*83%*	
12 Month Price Increase:	N/A	

The 1999 Miata has a more powerful, yet more efficient, engine than its predecessor. Extensive computer modeling was used to increase the bending and torsional rigidity of the Miata, while keeping its weight low. The interior has been restyled and trunk room has increased. The exterior has exposed oval headlamps and a larger grille opening. There are five option packages to choose from: a Power Steering Package, Touring Package, Popular Equipment Package, Leather Package, and Sports Package.

Ownership Costs (Projected)

Cost Area	5 Year Cost	Rating
Depreciation	$8,686	◯
Financing ($351/month)	$4,126	
Insurance (Performance)	$11,263	◉
State Fees	$858	
Fuel (Hwy 29 City 25)	$2,743	◯
Maintenance	$3,712	●
Repairs	$545	◯

Warranty/Maintenance Info

Major Tune-Up (60K mile int.)	$219	◯
Minor Tune-Up (30K mile int.)	$90	◯
Brake Service	$170	◯
Overall Warranty	3 yr/50k	◉
Drivetrain Warranty	3 yr/50k	◉
Rust Warranty	5 yr/unlim. mi	◯
Maintenance Warranty	N/A	
Roadside Assistance	3 yr/50k	

Ownership Costs By Year (Projected)

$2,000 $4,000 $6,000 $8,000 $10,000 $12,000

- 1999
- 2000
- 2001
- 2002
- 2003

Resale Value

1999	2000	2001	2002	2003
$20,076	$18,023	$16,216	$14,416	$12,517

Cumulative Costs

	1999	2000	2001	2002	2003
Annual	$5,456	$6,178	$5,804	$6,989	$7,506
Total	$5,456	$11,634	$17,438	$24,427	$31,933

Projected Costs (5yr)

Relative	This Car
$32,578	$31,933
Cost/Mile 47¢	Cost/Mile 46¢

Ownership Cost Value

◯ Better Than Average

Mazda Protege DX
4 Door Sedan

Compact

1.6L 105 hp Gas Fuel Inject.	4 Cylinder In-Line	Manual 5 Speed	2 Wheel Front	Dual Airbags Std (Depowered)

Purchase Price

Car Item	Dealer Cost	List
Base Price	**$11,335**	**$11,970**
Anti-Lock Brakes	N/A	N/A
Automatic 4 Speed	$720	$800
Optional Engine	N/A	N/A
Air Conditioning	Pkg	Pkg
Power Steering	Std	Std
Cruise Control	N/A	N/A
Power Windows	N/A	N/A
AM/FM Stereo CD	Pkg	Pkg
Steering Wheel, Tilt	Std	Std
Rear Defroster	Std	Std
*Options Price	$720	$800
*Total Price	**$12,055**	**$12,770**
Target Price	$12,450	
Destination Charge	$450	
Avg. Tax & Fees	$726	
Total Target $	**$13,626**	
Average Dealer Option Cost:	*85%*	
12 Month Price Increase:	None	

The redesigned 1999 Protege DX sedan has a completely new look with interior, exterior and engineering changes. Some of the interior changes include standard depowered airbags and 60/40 split fold-down rear seatbacks. Exterior changes include jeweled headlamp reflectors, a chrome-accented grille and color-keyed bumpers. The most significant engineering changes are under the hood, with a new 1.6L 4 cylinder engine with 105 hp and 107 lb-ft of torque.

Ownership Costs (Projected)

Cost Area	5 Year Cost	Rating
Depreciation	$6,473	◯
Financing ($226/month)	$2,651	
Insurance	$6,852	◯
State Fees	$542	
Fuel (Hwy 33 City 26)	$2,509	◯
Maintenance	$3,428	◉
Repairs	$560	◯

Warranty/Maintenance Info

Major Tune-Up (60K mile int.)	$256	◉
Minor Tune-Up (30K mile int.)	$93	◯
Brake Service	$124	◯
Overall Warranty	3 yr/50k	◉
Drivetrain Warranty	3 yr/50k	◉
Rust Warranty	5 yr/unlim. mi	◯
Maintenance Warranty	N/A	
Roadside Assistance	3 yr/50k	

Ownership Costs By Year (Projected)

$2,000 $4,000 $6,000 $8,000

- 1999
- 2000
- 2001
- 2002
- 2003

Resale Value

1999	2000	2001	2002	2003
$11,557	$10,378	$9,352	$8,273	$7,153

Cumulative Costs

	1999	2000	2001	2002	2003
Annual	$4,931	$3,918	$3,728	$4,890	$5,548
Total	$4,931	$8,849	$12,577	$17,467	$23,015

Projected Costs (5yr)

Relative	This Car
$24,150	$23,015
Cost/Mile 35¢	Cost/Mile 33¢

Ownership Cost Value

◯ Excellent

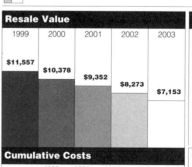

102

* Includes shaded options
** Other purchase requirements apply
*** Price includes other options

 ● Poor — ◉ Worse Than Average — ◯ Average — ◯ Better Than Average — ◯ Excellent — ⊖ Insufficient Information

Refer to *Section 3: Annotated Vehicle Charts* for an explanation of these charts.

Mazda Protege LX
4 Door Sedan

Compact

DX Model Shown

Engine	Cylinders	Transmission	Drive	Airbags
1.6L 105 hp Gas Fuel Inject.	4 Cylinder In-Line	Manual 5 Speed	2 Wheel Front	Dual Airbags Std

Purchase Price

Car Item	Dealer Cost	List
Base Price	**$12,163**	**$13,130**
Anti-Lock Brakes	Pkg	Pkg
Automatic 4 Speed	$720	$800
Optional Engine	N/A	N/A
Air Conditioning	Pkg	Pkg
Power Steering	Std	Std
Cruise Control	Std	Std
Power Windows	Std	Std
AM/FM Stereo CD	Std	Std
Steering Wheel, Tilt	Std	Std
Rear Defroster	Std	Std
*Options Price	$720	$800
*Total Price	**$12,883**	**$13,930**
Target Price	$13,383	
Destination Charge	$450	
Avg. Tax & Fees	$779	
Total Target $	**$14,612**	
Average Dealer Option Cost:	83%	
12 Month Price Increase:	None	

The 1999 Protege LX sedan is equipped with the same enhancements as the DX model. Engineering changes to the Protege include Triple-H body construction for added side-impact and offset crash protection. Changes have also been made to the four speed automatic transmission, which is now lighter and smoother shifting. The new LX Premium Package includes a moonroof, remote keyless entry system and antilock brakes. Also new is the LX Comfort Package, which includes air conditioning and floor mats.

Ownership Costs (Projected)

Cost Area	5 Year Cost	Rating
Depreciation	$7,145	◐
Financing ($242/month)	$2,843	
Insurance	$6,852	◐
State Fees	$588	
Fuel (Hwy 33 City 26)	$2,509	○
Maintenance	$3,428	●
Repairs	$560	○

Warranty/Maintenance Info

Major Tune-Up (60K mile int.)	$256	◐
Minor Tune-Up (30K mile int.)	$93	○
Brake Service	$124	○
Overall Warranty	3 yr/50k	◐
Drivetrain Warranty	3 yr/50k	◐
Rust Warranty	5 yr/unlim. mi	○
Maintenance Warranty	N/A	
Roadside Assistance	3 yr/50k	

Ownership Costs By Year (Projected)

Legend: 1999, 2000, 2001, 2002, 2003

Resale Value

1999	2000	2001	2002	2003
$12,416	$11,096	$9,932	$8,720	$7,467

Cumulative Costs

	1999	2000	2001	2002	2003
Annual	$5,135	$4,122	$3,915	$5,056	$5,697
Total	$5,135	$9,257	$13,172	$18,228	$23,925

Projected Costs (5yr)

Relative	This Car
$24,872	$23,925
Cost/Mile 36¢	Cost/Mile 34¢

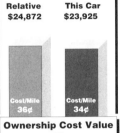

Ownership Cost Value
○ Excellent

Mazda Protege ES
4 Door Sedan

Compact

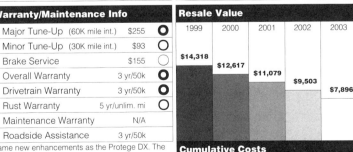

DX Model Shown

Engine	Cylinders	Transmission	Drive	Airbags
1.8L 122 hp Gas Fuel Inject.	4 Cylinder In-Line	Manual 5 Speed	2 Wheel Front	Dual Airbags Std

Purchase Price

Car Item	Dealer Cost	List
Base Price	**$13,670**	**$14,925**
Anti-Lock Brakes	Pkg	Pkg
Automatic 4 Speed	$720	$800
Optional Engine	N/A	N/A
Air Conditioning	Std	Std
Power Steering	Std	Std
Cruise Control	Std	Std
Power Windows	Std	Std
AM/FM Stereo CD	Std	Std
Steering Wheel, Tilt	Std	Std
Rear Defroster	Std	Std
*Options Price	$720	$800
*Total Price	**$14,390**	**$15,725**
Target Price	$14,992	
Destination Charge	$450	
Avg. Tax & Fees	$870	
Total Target $	**$16,312**	
Average Dealer Option Cost:	84%	
12 Month Price Increase:	None	

The 1999 Protege ES sedan comes equipped with all the same new enhancements as the Protege DX. The ES is upgraded with a new 1.8L 4 cylinder engine with 122 hp and 120 lb-ft of torque. Additional standard upgrades include 15 inch alloy wheels, air conditioning and power four wheel disc brakes. New 195/55R15 84V all-season tires have also been added. The optional ES Premium Package includes a moonroof, an antilock braking system and floor mats.

Ownership Costs (Projected)

Cost Area	5 Year Cost	Rating
Depreciation	$8,416	◐
Financing ($270/month)	$3,173	
Insurance	$7,140	◐
State Fees	$660	
Fuel (Hwy 29 City 24)	$2,792	◐
Maintenance	$3,631	●
Repairs	$560	○

Warranty/Maintenance Info

Major Tune-Up (60K mile int.)	$255	◐
Minor Tune-Up (30K mile int.)	$93	○
Brake Service	$155	○
Overall Warranty	3 yr/50k	◐
Drivetrain Warranty	3 yr/50k	◐
Rust Warranty	5 yr/unlim. mi	○
Maintenance Warranty	N/A	
Roadside Assistance	3 yr/50k	

Ownership Costs By Year (Projected)

Legend: 1999, 2000, 2001, 2002, 2003

Resale Value

1999	2000	2001	2002	2003
$14,318	$12,617	$11,079	$9,503	$7,896

Cumulative Costs

	1999	2000	2001	2002	2003
Annual	$5,172	$4,723	$4,484	$5,768	$6,225
Total	$5,172	$9,895	$14,379	$20,147	$26,372

Projected Costs (5yr)

Relative	This Car
$26,240	$26,372
Cost/Mile 37¢	Cost/Mile 38¢

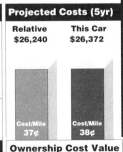

Ownership Cost Value
◐ Average

---

* Includes shaded options

** Other purchase requirements apply

*** Price includes other options

● Poor	◖ Worse Than Average	◐ Average	○ Better Than Average	○ Excellent	⊖ Insufficient Information

103

Refer to *Section 3: Annotated Vehicle Charts* for an explanation of these charts.

Mercedes-Benz C230 Kompressor
4 Door Sedan

Near Luxury

2.3L 185 hp Suprchrged Fuel Inject.	4 Cylinder In-Line	Automatic 5 Speed	2 Wheel Rear	Dual Front/Side Airbags Std

Purchase Price

Car Item	Dealer Cost	List
Base Price	**$27,140**	**$31,200**
Anti-Lock Brakes	Std	Std
Manual Transmission	N/A	N/A
Optional Engine	N/A	N/A
Air Conditioning	Std	Std
Power Steering	Std	Std
Cruise Control	Std	Std
Power Windows	Std	Std
AM/FM Stereo Cassette	Std	Std
Steering Wheel, Scope	$109	$125
Rear Defroster	Std	Std
*Options Price	$109	$125
*Total Price	**$27,249**	**$31,325**
Target Price	$29,829	
Destination Charge	$595	
Avg. Tax & Fees	$1,701	
Total Target $	**$32,125**	
Average Dealer Option Cost:	**86%**	
12 Month Price Increase:	2%	

For 1999, the C230 Kompressor sedan is introduced, replacing the previous C230. Standard features include the same 185 hp supercharged 2.3L engine found in the SLK, a five speed automatic transmission and power windows with driver and passenger side express down. Also standard are automatic climate control, a 10-way power driver's seat and an eight speaker premium sound system with cassette. Electrically heated front seats, a leather interior and power glass sunroof are available as options.

Ownership Costs (Projected)

Cost Area	5 Year Cost	Rating
Depreciation	$12,030	◯
Financing ($532/month)	$6,249	
Insurance	$8,556	◯
State Fees	$1,289	
Fuel (Hwy 29 City 21 -Prem.)	$3,524	◯
Maintenance	$1,657	◯
Repairs	$1,755	◉

Warranty/Maintenance Info

Major Tune-Up (60K mile int.)	$186	◯
Minor Tune-Up (30K mile int.)	$131	◯
Brake Service	$225	◯
Overall Warranty	4 yr/50k	◯
Drivetrain Warranty	4 yr/50k	◯
Rust Warranty	4 yr/50k	◉
Maintenance Warranty	N/A	
Roadside Assistance	unlim. mi	

Ownership Costs By Year (Projected)

$2,000 $4,000 $6,000 $8,000 $10,000 $12,000 $14,000

■ 1999
■ 2000
■ 2001
■ 2002
□ 2003

Resale Value

1999	2000	2001	2002	2003
$30,464	$27,062	$24,416	$22,153	$20,095

Cumulative Costs

	1999	2000	2001	2002	2003
Annual	$6,452	$7,836	$6,831	$6,866	$7,075
Total	$6,452	$14,288	$21,119	$27,985	$35,060

Projected Costs (5yr)

Relative $38,606	This Car $35,060
Cost/Mile 55¢	Cost/Mile 50¢

Ownership Cost Value

◯ Excellent

Mercedes-Benz C280
4 Door Sedan

Near Luxury

2.8L 194 hp Gas Fuel Inject.	6 Cylinder "V"	Automatic 5 Speed	2 Wheel Rear	Dual Front/Side Airbags Std

Purchase Price

Car Item	Dealer Cost	List
Base Price	**$30,970**	**$35,600**
Anti-Lock Brakes	Std	Std
Manual Transmission	N/A	N/A
Optional Engine	N/A	N/A
Auto Climate Control	Std	Std
Power Steering	Std	Std
Cruise Control	Std	Std
Power Windows	Std	Std
AM/FM Stereo Cassette	Std	Std
Steering Wheel, Scope	$109	$125
Rear Defroster	Std	Std
*Options Price	$109	$125
*Total Price	**$31,079**	**$35,725**
Target Price	$34,059	
Destination Charge	$595	
Avg. Tax & Fees	$1,935	
Total Target $	**$36,589**	
Average Dealer Option Cost:	**86%**	
12 Month Price Increase:	1%	

For 1999, the C280 sedan includes side curtain airbags, cruise control, traction control, a 10-way power driver's seat and a first aid kit. Options include metallic paint, integrated cellular telephone, rain-sensing windshield wipers and a headlamp washer system. An optional Sport Package includes 16 inch alloy wheels, sport-tuned suspension, leather sport bucket seats and ivory-colored instrument faces. Sport badging and a telescopic steering column are also included in the Sport Package.

Ownership Costs (Projected)

Cost Area	5 Year Cost	Rating
Depreciation	$13,850	◯
Financing ($606/month)	$7,118	
Insurance	$8,865	◯
State Fees	$1,466	
Fuel (Hwy 27 City 21 -Prem.)	$3,660	◯
Maintenance	$1,744	◯
Repairs	$1,300	◉

Warranty/Maintenance Info

Major Tune-Up (60K mile int.)	$203	◯
Minor Tune-Up (30K mile int.)	$137	◉
Brake Service	$225	◯
Overall Warranty	4 yr/50k	◯
Drivetrain Warranty	4 yr/50k	◯
Rust Warranty	4 yr/50k	◉
Maintenance Warranty	N/A	
Roadside Assistance	unlim. mi	

Ownership Costs By Year (Projected)

$2,000 $4,000 $6,000 $8,000 $10,000 $12,000 $14,000

■ 1999
■ 2000
■ 2001
■ 2002
□ 2003

Resale Value

1999	2000	2001	2002	2003
$34,824	$31,488	$28,515	$25,625	$22,739

Cumulative Costs

	1999	2000	2001	2002	2003
Annual	$6,980	$8,137	$7,473	$7,616	$7,797
Total	$6,980	$15,117	$22,590	$30,206	$38,003

Projected Costs (5yr)

Relative $41,566	This Car $38,003
Cost/Mile 59¢	Cost/Mile 54¢

Ownership Cost Value

◯ Excellent

104

 Poor
 Worse Than Average
 Average
 Better Than Average
◯ Excellent
⊖ Insufficient Information

Refer to *Section 3: Annotated Vehicle Charts* for an explanation of these charts.

Mercedes-Benz C43
4 Door Sedan

4.3L 302 hp Gas Fuel Inject.	8 Cylinder "V"
Automatic 5 Speed	2 Wheel Rear
Dual Front/Side Airbags Std	

Purchase Price

Car Item	Dealer Cost	List
Base Price	**$46,110**	**$53,000**
Anti-Lock Brakes	Std	Std
Manual Transmission	N/A	N/A
Optional Engine	N/A	N/A
Auto Climate Control	Std	Std
Power Steering	Std	Std
Cruise Control	Std	Std
Power Windows	Std	Std
AM/FM Stereo Cassette	Std	Std
Steering Wheel, Scope	Std	Std
Rear Defroster	Std	Std
*Options Price	$0	$0
*Total Price	$46,110	$53,000
Target Price	$51,176	
Destination Charge	$595	
Avg. Tax & Fees	$2,879	
Luxury Tax	$946	
Total Target $	**$55,596**	
12 Month Price Increase:	None	

For 1999 the high-performance C43 sedan includes side airbags. Standard C43 features include a power glass sunroof, distinctive AMG-designed exterior enhancements, sport-tuned suspension, Electronic Stability Program (ESP) and electrically heated multi-contour driver and passenger seats. The C43 is also equipped with 17 inch alloy wheels, low-profile tires, large disc brakes and a Bose premium sound system. Metallic paint is available as an option.

Ownership Costs (Projected)

Cost Area	5 Year Cost	Rating
Depreciation	$22,248	◯
Financing ($922/month)	$10,815	
Insurance (Performance)	$12,871	◯
State Fees	$2,157	
Fuel (Hwy 23 City 18 -Prem.)	$4,283	◯
Maintenance	$2,789	◯
Repairs	$1,300	◯

Warranty/Maintenance Info

Major Tune-Up (60K mile int.)	$258	◯
Minor Tune-Up (30K mile int.)	$188	●
Brake Service	$544	●
Overall Warranty	4 yr/50k	◯
Drivetrain Warranty	4 yr/50k	◯
Rust Warranty	4 yr/50k	◉
Maintenance Warranty	N/A	
Roadside Assistance	unlim. mi	

Ownership Costs By Year (Projected)

$5,000 $10,000 $15,000 $20,000 $25,000

- 1999
- 2000
- 2001
- 2002
- 2003

Resale Value

1999	2000	2001	2002	2003
$49,551	$45,109	$41,079	$37,183	$33,348

Projected Costs (5yr)

Relative $58,442	This Car $56,465
Cost/Mile 83¢	Cost/Mile 81¢

Cumulative Costs

	1999	2000	2001	2002	2003
Annual	$13,575	$11,329	$10,467	$10,940	$10,154
Total	$13,575	$24,904	$35,371	$46,311	$56,465

Ownership Cost Value

◯ Better Than Average

Mercedes-Benz CLK 320
2 Door Coupe

3.2L 215 hp Gas Fuel Inject.	6 Cylinder "V"
Automatic 5 Speed	2 Wheel Rear
Dual Front/Side Airbags Std	

Purchase Price

Car Item	Dealer Cost	List
Base Price	**$35,320**	**$40,600**
Anti-Lock Brakes	Std	Std
Manual Transmission	N/A	N/A
Optional Engine	N/A	N/A
Air Conditioning	Std	Std
Power Steering	Std	Std
Cruise Control	Std	Std
Power Windows	Std	Std
AM/FM Stereo Cassette	Std	Std
Steering Wheel, Tilt	Std	Std
Rear Defroster	Std	Std
*Options Price	$0	$0
*Total Price	$35,320	$40,600
Target Price	$39,045	
Destination Charge	$595	
Avg. Tax & Fees	$2,209	
Luxury Tax	$218	
Total Target $	**$42,067**	
12 Month Price Increase:	N/A	

For 1999, the CLK 320 now comes standard with Brake Assist, which detects an emergency stop by sensing how quickly the brake pedal is pressed and then applies full braking force. An Electronic Stability Program (ESP) is available, designed to keep the vehicle from going into a spin or slide. Three option packages are available as well as a CD player and multi-contour driver and passenger seats. Standard safety features include antilock brakes and dual front and door-mounted side airbags.

Ownership Costs (Projected)

Cost Area	5 Year Cost	Rating
Depreciation		⊖
Financing ($697/month)	$8,184	
Insurance (Performance)	$12,356	◉
State Fees	$1,661	
Fuel (Hwy 29 City 21 -Prem.)	$3,524	◯
Maintenance	$2,062	◯
Repairs	$1,320	◯

Warranty/Maintenance Info

Major Tune-Up (60K mile int.)	$304	◯
Minor Tune-Up (30K mile int.)	$150	◯
Brake Service	$270	◯
Overall Warranty	4 yr/50k	◯
Drivetrain Warranty	4 yr/50k	◯
Rust Warranty	4 yr/50k	◉
Maintenance Warranty	N/A	
Roadside Assistance	unlim. mi	

Ownership Costs By Year (Projected)

$2,000 $4,000 $6,000 $8,000 $10,000 $12,000 $14,000

Insufficient Depreciation Information

- 1999
- 2000
- 2001
- 2002
- 2003

Resale Value

Insufficient Information

Projected Costs (5yr)

Insufficient Information

Cumulative Costs

	1999	2000	2001	2002	2003
Annual	*Insufficient Information*				
Total	*Insufficient Information*				

Ownership Cost Value

⊖ Insufficient Information

 ● Poor   ◉ Worse Than Average   ◯ Average   ◯ Better Than Average   ◯ Excellent   ⊖ Insufficient Information

Refer to *Section 3: Annotated Vehicle Charts* for an explanation of these charts.

Mercedes-Benz CLK 430
2 Door Coupe

Luxury

4.3L 275 hp Gas Fuel Inject.	8 Cylinder "V"
Automatic 5 Speed	2 Wheel Rear
Dual Front/Side Airbags Std	

Purchase Price

Car Item	Dealer Cost	List
Base Price	**$41,670**	**$47,900**
Anti-Lock Brakes	Std	Std
Manual Transmission	N/A	N/A
Optional Engine	N/A	N/A
Air Conditioning	Std	Std
Power Steering	Std	Std
Cruise Control	Std	Std
Power Windows	Std	Std
AM/FM Stereo Cassette	Std	Std
Steering Wheel, Tilt	Std	Std
Rear Defroster	Std	Std
*Options Price	$0	$0
*Total Price	**$41,670**	**$47,900**
Target Price	$46,414	
Destination Charge	$595	
Avg. Tax & Fees	$2,613	
Luxury Tax	$661	
Total Target $	**$50,283**	
12 Month Price Increase:	N/A	

The CLK 430 is an all-new addition to the CLK model lineup. The CLK 430 features a 275 hp V8 engine. Other standard features include 17 inch wheels and tires, and an Electronic Stability Program (ESP) that helps maintain vehicle control through turns and curves. All CLKs come with the Mercedes Flexible Service System that monitors driving habits to provide more precise service intervals. Three option packages are available as well as optional multi-contour driver and passenger seats.

Ownership Costs (Projected)

Cost Area	5 Year Cost	Rating
Depreciation		⊖
Financing ($833/month)	$9,782	
Insurance (Performance)	$13,356	◉
State Fees	$1,952	
Fuel (Hwy 25 City 18 -Prem.)	$4,099	◯
Maintenance	$2,380	◯
Repairs	$1,320	◯

Warranty/Maintenance Info

Major Tune-Up (60K mile int.)	$308	◉
Minor Tune-Up (30K mile int.)	$150	◯
Brake Service	$270	◯
Overall Warranty	4 yr/50k	◯
Drivetrain Warranty	4 yr/50k	◯
Rust Warranty	4 yr/50k	◉
Maintenance Warranty	N/A	
Roadside Assistance	unlim. mi	

Ownership Costs By Year (Projected)

$2,000 $4,000 $6,000 $8,000 $10,000 $12,000 $14,000

Insufficient Depreciation Information

■ 1999
■ 2000
■ 2001
□ 2002
□ 2003

Resale Value

Insufficient

Information

Projected Costs (5yr)

Insufficient

Information

Cumulative Costs

	1999	2000	2001	2002	2003
Annual	Insufficient Information				
Total	Insufficient Information				

Ownership Cost Value

⊖

Insufficient Information

Mercedes-Benz CLK 320 Cabriolet
2 Door Convertible

Luxury

3.2L 215 hp Gas Fuel Inject.	6 Cylinder "V"
Automatic 5 Speed	2 Wheel Rear
Dual Front/Side Airbags Std	

Purchase Price

Car Item	Dealer Cost	List
Base Price	**$41,060**	**$47,200**
Anti-Lock Brakes	Std	Std
Manual Transmission	N/A	N/A
Optional Engine	N/A	N/A
Air Conditioning	Std	Std
Power Steering	Std	Std
Cruise Control	Std	Std
Power Windows	Std	Std
AM/FM Stereo Cassette	Std	Std
Steering Wheel, Tilt	Std	Std
Rear Defroster	Std	Std
*Options Price	$0	$0
*Total Price	**$41,060**	**$47,200**
Target Price	$45,702	
Destination Charge	$595	
Avg. Tax & Fees	$2,574	
Luxury Tax	$618	
Total Target $	**$49,489**	
12 Month Price Increase:	N/A	

The CLK 320 Cabriolet is a new model for 1999. Safety features include a rollbar system and rear head restraints that extend to maximum height in a split second if onboard sensors detect an impending rollover. The standard Brake Assist system detects an emergency stop by sensing how quickly the brake pedal is pressed and then applies full braking force. An optional Electronic Stability Program (ESP) is available, designed to keep the vehicle from going into a spin or slide.

Ownership Costs (Projected)

Cost Area	5 Year Cost	Rating
Depreciation		⊖
Financing ($820/month)	$9,629	
Insurance	$10,685	◯
State Fees	$1,925	
Fuel (Hwy 28 City 19 -Prem.)	$3,767	◯
Maintenance	$2,062	◯
Repairs	$1,320	◯

Warranty/Maintenance Info

Major Tune-Up (60K mile int.)	$304	◯
Minor Tune-Up (30K mile int.)	$150	◯
Brake Service	$270	◯
Overall Warranty	4 yr/50k	◯
Drivetrain Warranty	4 yr/50k	◯
Rust Warranty	4 yr/50k	◉
Maintenance Warranty	N/A	
Roadside Assistance	unlim. mi	

Ownership Costs By Year (Projected)

$2,000 $4,000 $6,000 $8,000 $10,000 $12,000

Insufficient Depreciation Information

■ 1999
■ 2000
■ 2001
□ 2002
□ 2003

Resale Value

Insufficient

Information

Projected Costs (5yr)

Insufficient

Information

Cumulative Costs

	1999	2000	2001	2002	2003
Annual	Insufficient Information				
Total	Insufficient Information				

Ownership Cost Value

⊖

Insufficient Information

106

* Includes shaded options

** Other purchase requirements apply

*** Price includes other options

 Poor   Worse Than Average   Average   Better Than Average   Excellent   Insufficient Information

Refer to *Section 3: Annotated Vehicle Charts* for an explanation of these charts.

Mercedes-Benz E300 Turbodiesel
4 Door Sedan

Luxury

3.0L 174 hp Turbo Dsl Fuel Inject.	6 Cylinder In-Line
Automatic 5 Speed	2 Wheel Rear
Dual Front/Side Airbags Std	

Purchase Price

Car Item	Dealer Cost	List
Base Price	**$36,890**	**$42,400**
Anti-Lock Brakes	Std	Std
Manual Transmission	N/A	N/A
Optional Engine	N/A	N/A
Auto Climate Control	Std	Std
Power Steering	Std	Std
Cruise Control	Std	Std
Power Windows	Std	Std
AM/FM Stereo Cassette	Std	Std
St Whl, Pwr Scope w/Mem	Std	Std
Rear Defroster	Std	Std
*Options Price	$0	$0
*Total Price	**$36,890**	**$42,400**
Target Price	$40,856	
Destination Charge	$595	
Avg. Tax & Fees	$2,308	
Luxury Tax	$327	
Total Target $	**$44,086**	
12 Month Price Increase:	1%	

For 1999, the E300 Turbodiesel now includes leather inserts for the seats, head protection curtain airbags and wood trim on the shift gate. The E300 comes standard with Automatic Slip Control (ASP) and a five speed driver-adaptive transmission that senses driving style and shifts accordingly. The E300 is also equipped with antilock brakes. An Electronic Stability Program (ESP), Bose audio system with speed-sensitive volume adjustment, power sunroof and full leather interior are optional.

Ownership Costs (Projected)

Cost Area	5 Year Cost	Rating
Depreciation	$17,605	◐
Financing ($731/month)	$8,576	
Insurance	$9,135	◐
State Fees	$1,733	
Fuel (Hwy 36 City 26)	$2,466	○
Maintenance	$2,014	○
Repairs	$1,835	●

Warranty/Maintenance Info

Major Tune-Up (60K mile int.)	$138	○
Minor Tune-Up (30K mile int.)	$89	○
Brake Service	$241	○
Overall Warranty	4 yr/50k	○
Drivetrain Warranty	4 yr/50k	○
Rust Warranty	4 yr/50k	●
Maintenance Warranty	N/A	
Roadside Assistance	unlim. mi	

Ownership Costs By Year (Projected)

$5,000	$10,000	$15,000	$20,000

Legend: 1999, 2000, 2001, 2002, 2003

Resale Value

1999	2000	2001	2002	2003
$40,890	$36,942	$33,375	$29,916	$26,481

Cumulative Costs

	1999	2000	2001	2002	2003
Annual	$8,806	$9,051	$8,206	$8,595	$8,706
Total	$8,806	$17,857	$26,063	$34,658	$43,364

Projected Costs (5yr)

Relative	This Car
$48,557	$43,364
Cost/Mile 69¢	Cost/Mile 62¢

Ownership Cost Value
○ Excellent

Mercedes-Benz E320
4 Door Sedan

Luxury

AWD Model Shown

3.2L 221 hp Gas Fuel Inject.	6 Cylinder "V"
Automatic 5 Speed	2 Wheel Rear
Dual Front/Side Airbags Std	

Purchase Price

Car Item	Dealer Cost	List
Base Price	**$40,190**	**$46,200**
Anti-Lock Brakes	Std	Std
Manual Transmission	N/A	N/A
Optional Engine	N/A	N/A
Auto Climate Control	Std	Std
Power Steering	Std	Std
Cruise Control	Std	Std
Power Windows	Std	Std
AM/FM Stereo Cassette	Std	Std
St Whl, Pwr Scope w/Mem	Std	Std
Rear Defroster	Std	Std
*Options Price	$0	$0
*Total Price	**$40,190**	**$46,200**
Target Price	$44,687	
Destination Charge	$595	
Avg. Tax & Fees	$2,519	
Luxury Tax	$557	
Total Target $	**$48,358**	
12 Month Price Increase:	2%	

The E320 sedan comes standard with leather upholstery, 10-way power front seats and dual front and side airbags. The central locking system with remote transmitter is integrated with SmartKey to selectively unlock the driver door and fuel filler door. The SmartKey transmitter can also operate the power windows or activate the anti-theft alarm system or optional sunroof. A Bose audio system with speed-sensitive volume adjustment, power sunroof and Electronic Stability Program (ESP) are optional.

Ownership Costs (Projected)

Cost Area	5 Year Cost	Rating
Depreciation	$17,598	○
Financing ($802/month)	$9,407	
Insurance (Performance)	$11,429	◉
State Fees	$1,885	
Fuel (Hwy 30 City 21 -Prem.)	$3,462	○
Maintenance	$2,131	○
Repairs	$1,615	◉

Warranty/Maintenance Info

Major Tune-Up (60K mile int.)	$293	◉
Minor Tune-Up (30K mile int.)	$101	○
Brake Service	$241	○
Overall Warranty	4 yr/50k	○
Drivetrain Warranty	4 yr/50k	○
Rust Warranty	4 yr/50k	●
Maintenance Warranty	N/A	
Roadside Assistance	unlim. mi	

Ownership Costs By Year (Projected)

$5,000	$10,000	$15,000	$20,000

Legend: 1999, 2000, 2001, 2002, 2003

Resale Value

1999	2000	2001	2002	2003
$45,414	$41,347	$37,698	$34,196	$30,760

Cumulative Costs

	1999	2000	2001	2002	2003
Annual	$9,495	$10,063	$9,146	$9,379	$9,444
Total	$9,495	$19,558	$28,704	$38,083	$47,527

Projected Costs (5yr)

Relative	This Car
$52,088	$47,527
Cost/Mile 74¢	Cost/Mile 68¢

Ownership Cost Value
○ Excellent

---

* Includes shaded options

** Other purchase requirements apply

*** Price includes other options

 Poor   Worse Than Average   Average   Better Than Average   Excellent   Insufficient Information

Refer to *Section 3: Annotated Vehicle Charts* for an explanation of these charts.

©1999 by IntelliChoice, Inc. (408) 866-1400 http://www.intellichoice.com All Rights Reserved. Reproduction Prohibited.

Mercedes-Benz E320 AWD
4 Door Sedan

3.2L 221 hp Gas Fuel Inject. | 6 Cylinder "V" | Automatic 5 Speed | 4 Wheel Full-Time | Dual Front/Side Airbags Std

Luxury

Purchase Price

Car Item	Dealer Cost	List
Base Price	**$42,620**	**$48,990**
Anti-Lock Brakes	Std	Std
Manual Transmission	N/A	N/A
Optional Engine	N/A	N/A
Auto Climate Control	Std	Std
Power Steering	Std	Std
Cruise Control	Std	Std
Power Windows	Std	Std
AM/FM Stereo Cassette	Std	Std
St Whl, Pwr Scope w/Mem	Std	Std
Rear Defroster	Std	Std
*Options Price	$0	$0
*Total Price	$42,620	$48,990
Target Price	$47,490	
Destination Charge	$595	
Avg. Tax & Fees	$2,673	
Luxury Tax	$725	
Total Target $	**$51,483**	
12 Month Price Increase:	2%	

Ownership Costs (Projected)

Cost Area	5 Year Cost	Rating
Depreciation	$19,506	◯
Financing ($853/month)	$10,016	
Insurance	$9,524	◯
State Fees	$1,997	
Fuel (Hwy 28 City 20 -Prem.)	$3,674	◯
Maintenance	$2,131	◯
Repairs	$1,755	●

Warranty/Maintenance Info

Major Tune-Up (60K mile int.)	$293	◑
Minor Tune-Up (30K mile int.)	$101	◯
Brake Service	$241	◯
Overall Warranty	4 yr/50k	◯
Drivetrain Warranty	4 yr/50k	◯
Rust Warranty	4 yr/50k	◉
Maintenance Warranty	N/A	
Roadside Assistance	unlim. mi	

Ownership Costs By Year (Projected)

$5,000 $10,000 $15,000 $20,000

Legend: 1999, 2000, 2001, 2002, 2003

Resale Value

1999	2000	2001	2002	2003
$47,840	$43,441	$39,482	$35,684	$31,977

Projected Costs (5yr)

Relative $54,693	This Car $48,603
Cost/Mile 78¢	Cost/Mile 69¢

Cumulative Costs

	1999	2000	2001	2002	2003
Annual	$10,106	$10,257	$9,266	$9,461	$9,513
Total	$10,106	$20,363	$29,629	$39,090	$48,603

Ownership Cost Value

◯ Excellent

The E320 AWD is the all-wheel drive version of the E320 sedan. The 4MATIC transmission comes standard with Automatic Slip Control (ASC), which senses drive wheel slip and individually brakes the slipping wheel or reduces engine power to regain control. The standard automatic climate control features dual temperature and airflow controls, an electrostatic dust filter, activated charcoal filter with smog sensor, sun sensor and a REST mode that can warm the interior while the engine is off.

Mercedes-Benz E320
4 Door Wagon

3.2L 221 hp Gas Fuel Inject. | 6 Cylinder "V" | Automatic 5 Speed | 2 Wheel Rear | Dual Front/Side Airbags Std

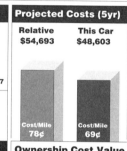

Luxury

Purchase Price

Car Item	Dealer Cost	List
Base Price	**$41,060**	**$47,200**
Anti-Lock Brakes	Std	Std
Manual Transmission	N/A	N/A
Optional Engine	N/A	N/A
Auto Climate Control	Std	Std
Power Steering	Std	Std
Cruise Control	Std	Std
Power Windows	Std	Std
AM/FM Stereo Cassette	Std	Std
St Whl, Pwr Scope w/Mem	Std	Std
Rear Defroster	Std	Std
*Options Price	$0	$0
*Total Price	$41,060	$47,200
Target Price	$45,702	
Destination Charge	$595	
Avg. Tax & Fees	$2,574	
Luxury Tax	$618	
Total Target $	**$49,489**	
12 Month Price Increase:	2%	

Ownership Costs (Projected)

Cost Area	5 Year Cost	Rating
Depreciation	$18,328	◯
Financing ($820/month)	$9,629	
Insurance	$9,524	◯
State Fees	$1,925	
Fuel (Hwy 28 City 20 -Prem.)	$3,674	◯
Maintenance	$2,163	◯
Repairs	$1,615	◉

Warranty/Maintenance Info

Major Tune-Up (60K mile int.)	$293	◉
Minor Tune-Up (30K mile int.)	$101	◯
Brake Service	$270	◉
Overall Warranty	4 yr/50k	◯
Drivetrain Warranty	4 yr/50k	◯
Rust Warranty	4 yr/50k	◉
Maintenance Warranty	N/A	
Roadside Assistance	unlim. mi	

Ownership Costs By Year (Projected)

$5,000 $10,000 $15,000 $20,000

Legend: 1999, 2000, 2001, 2002, 2003

Resale Value

1999	2000	2001	2002	2003
$46,515	$42,267	$38,448	$34,772	$31,161

Projected Costs (5yr)

Relative $53,020	This Car $46,858
Cost/Mile 76¢	Cost/Mile 67¢

Cumulative Costs

	1999	2000	2001	2002	2003
Annual	$9,287	$9,983	$9,031	$9,274	$9,283
Total	$9,287	$19,270	$28,301	$37,575	$46,858

Ownership Cost Value

◯ Excellent

The E320 wagon has seating for seven with the standard third row rear-facing seat. The tailgate is equipped with a pneumatic tailgate closing mechanism to minimize effort. The wagon has a load-sensing system that helps keep the vehicle level when loaded with cargo. The rear wiper automatically turns on when the front wipers are on and reverse gear is engaged. Optional features include a power sunroof, full leather upholstery, electrically heated front seats and a integrated luggage rack.

108

* Includes shaded options
** Other purchase requirements apply
*** Price includes other options

● Poor | ◑ Worse Than Average | ◯ Average | ◯ Better Than Average | ◯ Excellent | ⊖ Insufficient Information

Refer to *Section 3: Annotated Vehicle Charts* for an explanation of these charts.

Mercedes-Benz E320 AWD
4 Door Wagon

3.2L 221 hp Gas Fuel Inject.	6 Cylinder "V"	Automatic 5 Speed	4 Wheel Full-Time	Dual Front/Side Airbags Std

Luxury

Purchase Price

Car Item	Dealer Cost	List
Base Price	**$43,490**	**$49,990**
Anti-Lock Brakes	Std	Std
Manual Transmission	N/A	N/A
Optional Engine	N/A	N/A
Auto Climate Control	Std	Std
Power Steering	Std	Std
Cruise Control	Std	Std
Power Windows	Std	Std
AM/FM Stereo Cassette	Std	Std
St Whl, Pwr Scope w/Mem	Std	Std
Rear Defroster	Std	Std
*Options Price	$0	$0
*Total Price	**$43,490**	**$49,990**
Target Price	$48,460	
Destination Charge	$595	
Avg. Tax & Fees	$2,726	
Luxury Tax	$783	
Total Target $	**$52,564**	
12 Month Price Increase:	2%	

The E320 AWD wagon has all-wheel drive with normal 35/65 front/rear torque split. This system includes four wheel Automatic Slip Control (ASC), which detects wheel slip and applies individual brakes as needed, continually balancing the torque split to ensure power is sent to the wheels with traction. In addition, the wagon is equipped with a rear axle level control that senses cargo load and adjusts to keep the vehicle level. Optional features include a power sunroof and leather interior.

Ownership Costs (Projected)

Cost Area	5 Year Cost	Rating
Depreciation	$20,202	◎
Financing ($871/month)	$10,226	
Insurance	$9,524	◎
State Fees	$2,037	
Fuel (Hwy 26 City 20 -Prem.)	$3,821	◎
Maintenance	$2,163	◎
Repairs	$1,755	●

Warranty/Maintenance Info

Major Tune-Up (60K mile int.)	$293	◉
Minor Tune-Up (30K mile int.)	$101	◎
Brake Service	$270	◉
Overall Warranty	4 yr/50k	◎
Drivetrain Warranty	4 yr/50k	◎
Rust Warranty	4 yr/50k	◉
Maintenance Warranty	N/A	
Roadside Assistance	unlim. mi	

Ownership Costs By Year (Projected)

$5,000 $10,000 $15,000 $20,000 $25,000

■ 1999
■ 2000
▨ 2001
▧ 2002
□ 2003

Resale Value

1999	2000	2001	2002	2003
$49,083	$44,511	$40,354	$36,327	$32,362

Cumulative Costs

	1999	2000	2001	2002	2003
Annual	$10,053	$10,526	$9,545	$9,787	$9,817
Total	$10,053	$20,579	$30,124	$39,911	$49,728

Projected Costs (5yr)

Relative $55,627	This Car $49,728
Cost/Mile 79¢	Cost/Mile 71¢

Ownership Cost Value

○ Excellent

Mercedes-Benz E430
4 Door Sedan

4.3L 275 hp Gas Fuel Inject.	8 Cylinder "V"	Automatic 5 Speed	2 Wheel Rear	Dual Front/Side Airbags Std

Luxury

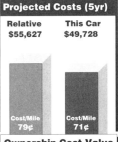

Purchase Price

Car Item	Dealer Cost	List
Base Price	**$44,630**	**$51,300**
Anti-Lock Brakes	Std	Std
Manual Transmission	N/A	N/A
Optional Engine	N/A	N/A
Auto Climate Control	Std	Std
Power Steering	Std	Std
Cruise Control	Std	Std
Power Windows	Std	Std
AM/FM Stereo Cassette	N/A	N/A
St Whl, Pwr Scope w/Mem	Std	Std
Rear Defroster	Std	Std
*Options Price	$0	$0
*Total Price	**$44,630**	**$51,300**
Target Price	$49,730	
Destination Charge	$595	
Avg. Tax & Fees	$2,797	
Luxury Tax	$860	
Total Target $	**$53,982**	
12 Month Price Increase:	1%	

The E430 sedan is the only E-class model with a 275 hp V8 engine. The E430 is equipped with leather upholstery, Electronic Stability Program (ESP), ASR traction control, a Bose eight speaker audio system with speed-sensitive volume adjustment, and driver-adaptive five speed automatic transmission. The optional Sport Package offers five spoke alloy wheels with 45-series performance tires, aerodynamically sculpted lower bodywork and projector beam fog lamps.

Ownership Costs (Projected)

Cost Area	5 Year Cost	Rating
Depreciation	$20,709	◎
Financing ($895/month)	$10,502	
Insurance (Performance)	$12,389	◉
State Fees	$2,088	
Fuel (Hwy 26 City 19 -Prem.)	$3,914	◎
Maintenance	$2,221	◎
Repairs	$1,615	◉

Warranty/Maintenance Info

Major Tune-Up (60K mile int.)	$316	◉
Minor Tune-Up (30K mile int.)	$139	◎
Brake Service	$239	◎
Overall Warranty	4 yr/50k	◎
Drivetrain Warranty	4 yr/50k	◎
Rust Warranty	4 yr/50k	◉
Maintenance Warranty	N/A	
Roadside Assistance	unlim. mi	

Ownership Costs By Year (Projected)

$5,000 $10,000 $15,000 $20,000 $25,000

■ 1999
■ 2000
▨ 2001
▧ 2002
□ 2003

Resale Value

1999	2000	2001	2002	2003
$48,587	$44,340	$40,528	$36,864	$33,273

Cumulative Costs

	1999	2000	2001	2002	2003
Annual	$12,639	$10,867	$9,896	$10,005	$10,030
Total	$12,639	$23,506	$33,402	$43,407	$53,437

Projected Costs (5yr)

Relative $56,851	This Car $53,437
Cost/Mile 81¢	Cost/Mile 76¢

Ownership Cost Value

○ Better Than Average

---

* Includes shaded options

** Other purchase requirements apply

*** Price includes other options

● Poor	◉ Worse Than Average	◎ Average	○ Better Than Average	○ Excellent	⊖ Insufficient Information

109

Refer to *Section 3: Annotated Vehicle Charts* for an explanation of these charts.

Mercedes-Benz S320 Standard Wheelbase
4 Door Sedan

Luxury

 3.2L 228 hp Gas Fuel Inject.   6 Cylinder In-Line   Automatic 5 Speed   2 Wheel Rear   Dual Front/Side Airbags Std

Purchase Price

Car Item	Dealer Cost	List
Base Price	**$56,330**	**$64,750**
Anti-Lock Brakes	Std	Std
Manual Transmission	N/A	N/A
Optional Engine	N/A	N/A
Auto Climate Control	Std	Std
Power Steering	Std	Std
Cruise Control	Std	Std
Power Windows	Std	Std
AM/FM Stereo Cassette	Std	Std
Steering Wheel, Tilt	Std	Std
Rear Defroster	Std	Std
*Options Price	$0	$0
*Total Price	**$56,330**	**$64,750**
Target Price	$62,025	
Destination Charge	$595	
Avg. Tax & Fees	$3,484	
Luxury Tax	$1,597	
Total Target $	**$67,701**	
12 Month Price Increase:	1%	

Ownership Costs (Projected)

Cost Area	5 Year Cost	Rating
Depreciation	$27,374	○
Financing ($1,122/month)	$13,170	○
Insurance	$10,685	○
State Fees	$2,626	
Fuel (Hwy 24 City 17 -Prem.)	$4,303	◉
Maintenance	$2,006	◯
Repairs	$1,755	◉

Warranty/Maintenance Info

Major Tune-Up (60K mile int.)	$254	○
Minor Tune-Up (30K mile int.)	$175	●
Brake Service	$269	○
Overall Warranty	4 yr/50k	○
Drivetrain Warranty	4 yr/50k	○
Rust Warranty	4 yr/50k	◉
Maintenance Warranty	N/A	
Roadside Assistance	unlim. mi	

The S320 standard wheelbase features leather upholstery, a leather-trimmed steering wheel and shift knob, Calyptus wood trim on doors, dash and console, 12-way power front seats with three position memory and a remote illuminated entry system. Optional equipment includes xenon high-intensity discharge headlamps, heated headlamp washers with wipers, heated front seats and an electric rear-window sunshade. Safety equipment includes driver and front passenger front and side-impact airbags.

Ownership Costs By Year (Projected)

$5,000 $10,000 $15,000 $20,000 $25,000 $30,000

■ 1999
■ 2000
■ 2001
☐ 2002
☐ 2003

Resale Value

1999	2000	2001	2002	2003
$60,014	$54,578	$49,633	$44,910	$40,327

Cumulative Costs

	1999	2000	2001	2002	2003
Annual	$15,717	$12,650	$11,471	$11,145	$10,936
Total	$15,717	$28,367	$39,838	$50,983	$61,919

Projected Costs (5yr)

Relative	This Car
$69,470	$61,919
Cost/Mile 99¢	Cost/Mile 88¢

Ownership Cost Value

○ Excellent

Mercedes-Benz S320
4 Door Sedan

Luxury

 3.2L 228 hp Gas Fuel Inject.   6 Cylinder In-Line   Automatic 5 Speed   2 Wheel Rear   Dual Front/Side Airbags Std

Standard Wheelbase Shown

Purchase Price

Car Item	Dealer Cost	List
Base Price	**$59,160**	**$68,000**
Anti-Lock Brakes	Std	Std
Manual Transmission	N/A	N/A
Optional Engine	N/A	N/A
Auto Climate Control	Std	Std
Power Steering	Std	Std
Cruise Control	Std	Std
Power Windows	Std	Std
AM/FM Stereo Cass/CD	Std	Std
Steering Wheel, Tilt	Std	Std
Rear Defroster	Std	Std
*Options Price	$0	$0
*Total Price	**$59,160**	**$68,000**
Target Price	$65,140	
Destination Charge	$595	
Avg. Tax & Fees	$3,657	
Luxury Tax	$1,784	
Total Target $	**$71,176**	
12 Month Price Increase:	1%	

Ownership Costs (Projected)

Cost Area	5 Year Cost	Rating
Depreciation	$30,213	○
Financing ($1,180/month)	$13,848	○
Insurance	$10,685	○
State Fees	$2,757	
Fuel (Hwy 24 City 17 -Prem.)	$4,303	◉
Maintenance	$2,006	◯
Repairs	$1,755	◉

Warranty/Maintenance Info

Major Tune-Up (60K mile int.)	$254	○
Minor Tune-Up (30K mile int.)	$175	●
Brake Service	$269	○
Overall Warranty	4 yr/50k	○
Drivetrain Warranty	4 yr/50k	○
Rust Warranty	4 yr/50k	◉
Maintenance Warranty	N/A	
Roadside Assistance	unlim. mi	

The S320 is available in an extended wheelbase version. Standard equipment is the same as that of the standard wheelbase S320, including leather upholstery, wood trim, power steering with memory and an 11 speaker Bose sound system. Also standard is the BabySmart system, which automatically deactivates the passenger front airbag when a BabySmart-compatible child seat is properly installed. Options include a Parktronic electronic audio-visual parking system and multi-contour front seats.

Ownership Costs By Year (Projected)

$5 $10 $15 $20 $25 $30 $35 (x1,000)

■ 1999
■ 2000
■ 2001
☐ 2002
☐ 2003

Resale Value

1999	2000	2001	2002	2003
$61,946	$56,168	$50,898	$45,852	$40,963

Cumulative Costs

	1999	2000	2001	2002	2003
Annual	$17,523	$13,208	$11,962	$11,580	$11,294
Total	$17,523	$30,731	$42,693	$54,273	$65,567

Projected Costs (5yr)

Relative	This Car
$72,537	$65,567
Cost/Mile $1.04	Cost/Mile 94¢

Ownership Cost Value

○ Excellent

---

 * Includes shaded options
** Other purchase requirements apply
*** Price includes other options

 Poor   ◉ Worse Than Average   Average   Better Than Average   Excellent   ⊖ Insufficient Information

Refer to *Section 3: Annotated Vehicle Charts* for an explanation of these charts.

Mercedes-Benz S420
4 Door Sedan

Luxury

4.2L 275 hp Gas Fuel Inject.	8 Cylinder "V"
Automatic 5 Speed	2 Wheel Rear
Dual Front/Side Airbags Std	

Purchase Price

Car Item	Dealer Cost	List
Base Price	**$64,290**	**$73,900**
Anti-Lock Brakes	Std	Std
Manual Transmission	N/A	N/A
Optional Engine	N/A	N/A
Auto Climate Control	Std	Std
Power Steering	Std	Std
Cruise Control	Std	Std
Power Windows	Std	Std
AM/FM Stereo Cass/CD	Std	Std
Steering Wheel, Tilt	Std	Std
Rear Defroster	Std	Std
*Options Price	$0	$0
*Total Price	**$64,290**	**$73,900**
Target Price	$70,789	
Destination Charge	$595	
Avg. Tax & Fees	$4,029	
Luxury/Gas Guzzler Tax	$3,501	
Total Target $	**$78,914**	
12 Month Price Increase:	None	

The S420 sedan features a 275 hp V8 engine and burl walnut interior trim. Standard equipment includes a remote illuminated entry system, an electronically coded key that disables the engine computer whenever the key is removed from the ignition, and driver and front passenger front and side-impact airbags. Rear cabin dual-zone climate control, heated front seats, automatic rear-axle level control and an Electronic Stability Program (ESP) are available options.

Ownership Costs (Projected)

Cost Area	5 Year Cost	Rating
Depreciation	$35,934	◯
Financing ($1,308/month)	$15,352	
Insurance	$11,266	◯
State Fees	$2,992	
Fuel (Hwy 22 City 15 -Prem.)	$4,784	◉
Maintenance	$1,940	◯
Repairs	$1,831	◉

Warranty/Maintenance Info

Major Tune-Up (60K mile int.)	$213	◯
Minor Tune-Up (30K mile int.)	$124	◯
Brake Service	$292	◉
Overall Warranty	4 yr/50k	◯
Drivetrain Warranty	4 yr/50k	◯
Rust Warranty	4 yr/50k	◉
Maintenance Warranty	N/A	
Roadside Assistance	unlim. mi	

Ownership Costs By Year (Projected)

$5 $10 $15 $20 $25 $30 $35 $40 (x1,000)

- 1999
- 2000
- 2001
- 2002
- 2003

Resale Value

1999	2000	2001	2002	2003
$66,150	$59,777	$53,947	$48,370	$42,980

Cumulative Costs

	1999	2000	2001	2002	2003
Annual	$21,832	$14,485	$13,017	$12,623	$12,142
Total	$21,832	$36,317	$49,334	$61,957	$74,099

Projected Costs (5yr)

Relative	This Car
$78,111	$74,099
Cost/Mile $1.12	Cost/Mile $1.06

Ownership Cost Value

◯ Better Than Average

Mercedes-Benz CL500
2 Door Coupe

Luxury

5.0L 315 hp Gas Fuel Inject.	8 Cylinder "V"
Automatic 5 Speed	2 Wheel Rear
Dual Front/Side Airbags Std	

Purchase Price

Car Item	Dealer Cost	List
Base Price	**$79,950**	**$91,900**
Anti-Lock Brakes	Std	Std
Manual Transmission	N/A	N/A
Optional Engine	N/A	N/A
Air Conditioning	Std	Std
Power Steering	Std	Std
Cruise Control	Std	Std
Power Windows	Std	Std
AM/FM Stereo Cass/CD	Std	Std
Steering Wheel, Tilt	Std	Std
Rear Defroster	Std	Std
*Options Price	$0	$0
*Total Price	**$79,950**	**$91,900**
Target Price	$88,735	
Destination Charge	$595	
Avg. Tax & Fees	$5,016	
Luxury/Gas Guzzler Tax	$4,578	
Total Target $	**$98,924**	
12 Month Price Increase:	None	

For 1999, the CL 500 returns with minimal changes. The CL 500 features Nappa leather upholstery, xenon high-intensity discharge headlamps and a Bose Beta sound system. Safety features include the Adaptive Damping System (ADS) and Electronic Stability Program (ESP). Other key safety systems include Parktronic, an audio-visual warning system that calculates the vehicle's distance from nearby objects, and BabySmart, an automatic passenger airbag deactivation device.

Ownership Costs (Projected)

Cost Area	5 Year Cost	Rating
Depreciation	$40,577	◯
Financing ($1,640/month)	$19,245	
Insurance (Performance)	$15,604	◉
State Fees	$3,712	
Fuel (Hwy 22 City 15 -Prem.)	$4,784	◉
Maintenance	$1,870	◯
Repairs	$1,895	●

Warranty/Maintenance Info

Major Tune-Up (60K mile int.)	$213	◯
Minor Tune-Up (30K mile int.)	$124	◯
Brake Service	$292	◉
Overall Warranty	4 yr/50k	◯
Drivetrain Warranty	4 yr/50k	◯
Rust Warranty	4 yr/50k	◉
Maintenance Warranty	N/A	
Roadside Assistance	unlim. mi	

Ownership Costs By Year (Projected)

$5 $10 $15 $20 $25 $30 $35 $40 $45 (x1,000)

- 1999
- 2000
- 2001
- 2002
- 2003

Resale Value

1999	2000	2001	2002	2003
$86,040	$78,425	$71,416	$64,757	$58,347

Cumulative Costs

	1999	2000	2001	2002	2003
Annual	$24,282	$17,811	$16,010	$15,243	$14,341
Total	$24,282	$42,093	$58,103	$73,346	$87,687

Projected Costs (5yr)

Relative	This Car
$95,244	$87,687
Cost/Mile $1.36	Cost/Mile $1.25

Ownership Cost Value

◯ Better Than Average

 Poor   Worse Than Average   Average   Better Than Average   Excellent   Insufficient Information

111

Refer to *Section 3: Annotated Vehicle Charts* for an explanation of these charts.

Mercedes-Benz S500
4 Door Sedan

Luxury

5.0L 315 hp Gas Fuel Inject.	8 Cylinder "V"
Automatic 5 Speed	2 Wheel Rear
Dual Front/Side Airbags Std	

S600 Model Shown

Purchase Price

Car Item	Dealer Cost	List
Base Price	**$76,120**	**$87,500**
Anti-Lock Brakes	Std	Std
Manual Transmission	N/A	N/A
Optional Engine	N/A	N/A
Auto Climate Control	Std	Std
Power Steering	Std	Std
Cruise Control	Std	Std
Power Windows	Std	Std
AM/FM Stereo Cass/CD	Std	Std
Steering Wheel, Tilt	Std	Std
Rear Defroster	Std	Std
*Options Price	$0	$0
*Total Price	$76,120	$87,500
Target Price	$83,816	
Destination Charge	$595	
Avg. Tax & Fees	$4,769	
Luxury/Gas Guzzler Tax	$4,707	
Total Target $	**$93,887**	
12 Month Price Increase:	None	

The S500 sedan is equipped with a 315 hp V8, coupled with a driver-adaptive five speed automatic transmission. Other standard equipment includes xenon high-intensity discharge headlamps, heated front and rear seats, burl walnut trim and an automatic rear-axle level control. Options include rear cabin dual-zone climate control, electric rear window sunshade, multi-contour front seats, an Electronic Stability Program (ESP) and Parktronic electronic audio-visual parking assistance system.

Ownership Costs (Projected)

Cost Area	5 Year Cost	Rating
Depreciation	$44,718	◐
Financing ($1,556/month)	$18,265	
Insurance (Performance)	$15,604	◉
State Fees	$3,538	
Fuel (Hwy 21 City 15 -Prem.)	$4,899	●
Maintenance	$1,870	○
Repairs	$1,831	◉

Ownership Costs By Year (Projected)

$5 $10 $15 $20 $25 $30 $35 $40 $45 (x1,000)

- 1999
- 2000
- 2001
- 2002
- 2003

Warranty/Maintenance Info

Major Tune-Up (60K mile int.)	$213	○
Minor Tune-Up (30K mile int.)	$124	○
Brake Service	$292	◉
Overall Warranty	4 yr/50k	○
Drivetrain Warranty	4 yr/50k	○
Rust Warranty	4 yr/50k	◉
Maintenance Warranty	N/A	
Roadside Assistance	unlim. mi	

Resale Value

1999	2000	2001	2002	2003
$77,154	$69,475	$62,409	$55,661	$49,169

Cumulative Costs

	1999	2000	2001	2002	2003
Annual	$27,777	$17,587	$15,853	$15,182	$14,326
Total	$27,777	$45,364	$61,217	$76,399	$90,725

Projected Costs (5yr)

Relative	This Car
$91,037	$90,725
Cost/Mile $1.30	Cost/Mile $1.30

Ownership Cost Value

○ Average

Mercedes-Benz CL600
2 Door Coupe

Luxury

6.0L 389 hp Gas Fuel Inject.	12 Cylinder "V"
Automatic 5 Speed	2 Wheel Rear
Dual Front/Side Airbags Std	

CL500 Model Shown

Purchase Price

Car Item	Dealer Cost	List
Base Price	**$119,450**	**$137,300**
Anti-Lock Brakes	Std	Std
Manual Transmission	N/A	N/A
Optional Engine	N/A	N/A
Air Conditioning	Std	Std
Power Steering	Std	Std
Cruise Control	Std	Std
Power Windows	Std	Std
AM/FM Stereo Cass/CD	Std	Std
Steering Wheel, Tilt	Std	Std
Rear Defroster	Std	Std
*Options Price	$0	$0
*Total Price	$119,450	$137,300
Target Price	$132,575	
Destination Charge	$595	
Avg. Tax & Fees	$7,502	
Luxury/Gas Guzzler Tax	$8,586	
Total Target $	**$149,258**	
12 Month Price Increase:	1%	

The 1999 CL 600 features a 389 hp V12 with 420 lb-ft of torque. The CL 600 includes many upper-level amenities including multi-tone Nappa leather, multi-contour power front seats with power adjustable head restraints and a walnut-trimmed interior. The CL 600 also includes an integrated six disc CD changer as well as an integrated docking portable cellular phone. An electric rear window sunshade, Adaptive Damping System (ADS) and Electronic Stability Program (ESP) are also standard.

Ownership Costs (Projected)

Cost Area	5 Year Cost	Rating
Depreciation	$78,366	◐
Financing ($2,474/month)	$29,037	
Insurance (Performance)	$16,254	◉
State Fees	$5,528	
Fuel (Hwy 19 City 13 -Prem.)	$5,529	●
Maintenance	$2,185	○
Repairs	$1,895	●

Ownership Costs By Year (Projected)

$5 $10 $15 $20 $25 $30 $35 $40 $45 $50 $55 $60 $65 $70 $75 $80 (x1,000)

- 1999
- 2000
- 2001
- 2002
- 2003

Warranty/Maintenance Info

Major Tune-Up (60K mile int.)	$283	◉
Minor Tune-Up (30K mile int.)	$191	◉
Brake Service	$292	◉
Overall Warranty	4 yr/50k	○
Drivetrain Warranty	4 yr/50k	○
Rust Warranty	4 yr/50k	◉
Maintenance Warranty	N/A	
Roadside Assistance	unlim. mi	

Resale Value

1999	2000	2001	2002	2003
$119,213	$106,124	$93,857	$82,135	$70,892

Cumulative Costs

	1999	2000	2001	2002	2003
Annual	$45,485	$26,666	$24,019	$22,188	$20,436
Total	$45,485	$72,151	$96,170	$118,358	$138,794

Projected Costs (5yr)

Relative	This Car
$139,241	$138,794
Cost/Mile $1.99	Cost/Mile $1.98

Ownership Cost Value

○ Average

 ● Poor ◉ Worse Than Average ○ Average ○ Better Than Average ○ Excellent ⊖ Insufficient Information

Refer to *Section 3: Annotated Vehicle Charts* for an explanation of these charts.

Mercedes-Benz S600
4 Door Sedan

Luxury

6.0L 389 hp Gas Fuel Inject.	12 Cylinder "V"	Automatic 5 Speed	2 Wheel Rear	Dual Front/Side Airbags Std

Purchase Price

Car Item	Dealer Cost	List
Base Price	**$116,800**	**$134,250**
Anti-Lock Brakes	Std	Std
Manual Transmission	N/A	N/A
Optional Engine	N/A	N/A
Air Conditioning	Std	Std
Power Steering	Std	Std
Cruise Control	Std	Std
Power Windows	Std	Std
AM/FM Stereo Cass/CD	Std	Std
Steering Wheel, Tilt	Std	Std
Rear Defroster	Std	Std
*Options Price	$0	$0
*Total Price	**$116,800**	**$134,250**
Target Price	$128,606	
Destination Charge	$595	
Avg. Tax & Fees	$7,310	
Luxury/Gas Guzzler Tax	$8,772	
Total Target $	**$145,283**	
12 Month Price Increase:	2%	

The S600 features a 389 hp V12, resulting in a 0 to 60 time of 6.3 seconds. Each seat is covered with glove-soft Nappa leather. Leather is also hand-fitted to the dash, steering wheel, door panels, sun visors and rear shelf. Suede covers the headliner and roof pillars. Burl walnut trim accents the notched shift gate as well as the leather-trimmed shift knob, steering wheel and door panels. A four-place seating package and Parktronic parking assistance system are available options.

Ownership Costs (Projected)

Cost Area	5 Year Cost	Rating
Depreciation	$79,209	◉
Financing ($2,408/month)	$28,263	
Insurance (Performance)	$16,254	◉
State Fees	$5,407	
Fuel (Hwy 19 City 13 -Prem.)	$5,529	●
Maintenance	$2,185	○
Repairs	$1,755	◐

Warranty/Maintenance Info

Major Tune-Up (60K mile int.)	$283	◐
Minor Tune-Up (30K mile int.)	$191	●
Brake Service	$292	◉
Overall Warranty	4 yr/50k	○
Drivetrain Warranty	4 yr/50k	○
Rust Warranty	4 yr/50k	◉
Maintenance Warranty	N/A	
Roadside Assistance	unlim. mi	

Ownership Costs By Year (Projected)

$5 $10 $15 $20 $25 $30 $35 $40 $45 $50 $55 $60 $65 $70 $75 $80 (x1,000)

- 1999
- 2000
- 2001
- 2002
- 2003

Resale Value

1999	2000	2001	2002	2003
$113,629	$100,747	$88,685	$77,155	$66,074

Cumulative Costs

	1999	2000	2001	2002	2003
Annual	$46,801	$26,218	$23,630	$21,839	$20,114
Total	$46,801	$73,019	$96,649	$118,488	$138,602

Projected Costs (5yr)

Relative	This Car
$136,254	$138,602
Cost/Mile $1.95	Cost/Mile $1.98

Ownership Cost Value

◐ Average

    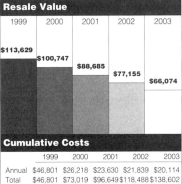

Mercedes-Benz SLK230 Kompressor
2 Door Convertible

Sport

2.3L 185 hp Suprchrged Fuel Inject.	4 Cylinder In-Line	Manual 5 Speed	2 Wheel Rear	Dual Front/Side Airbags Std

Purchase Price

Car Item	Dealer Cost	List
Base Price	**$34,800**	**$40,000**
Anti-Lock Brakes	Std	Std
Automatic 5 Speed	$783	$900
Optional Engine	N/A	N/A
Auto Climate Control	Std	Std
Power Steering	Std	Std
Cruise Control	Std	Std
Power Windows	Std	Std
AM/FM Stereo Cassette	Std	Std
Steering Wheel, Tilt	Std	Std
Rear Defroster	Std	Std
*Options Price	$0	$0
*Total Price	**$34,800**	**$40,000**
Target Price	$39,007	
Destination Charge	$595	
Avg. Tax & Fees	$2,201	
Luxury Tax	$216	
Total Target $	**$42,019**	
12 Month Price Increase:	None	

For 1999, the SLK introduces a new five speed manual transmission and an optional Sport Package to enhance its sporty appearance. The AMG-designed Sport Package includes larger 17 inch wheels and enhances the SLK's shape with styled lower body paneling. In addition, a new generation stereo uses fiber-optic technology and has integrated controls for the optional portable cellular phone. The automatic retractable hard top transforms the SLK from coupe to roadster in less than 30 seconds.

Ownership Costs (Projected)

Cost Area	5 Year Cost	Rating
Depreciation		⊖
Financing ($696/month)	$8,175	
Insurance (Performance)	$14,959	◉
State Fees	$1,637	
Fuel (Hwy 30 City 21 -Prem.)	$3,462	○
Maintenance	$1,982	○
Repairs	$1,651	◉

Warranty/Maintenance Info

Major Tune-Up (60K mile int.)	$231	○
Minor Tune-Up (30K mile int.)	$141	○
Brake Service	$246	○
Overall Warranty	4 yr/50k	○
Drivetrain Warranty	4 yr/50k	○
Rust Warranty	4 yr/50k	◉
Maintenance Warranty	N/A	
Roadside Assistance	unlim. mi	

Ownership Costs By Year (Projected)

$5,000 $10,000 $15,000

Insufficient Depreciation Information

- 1999
- 2000
- 2001
- 2002
- 2003

Resale Value

Insufficient Information

Cumulative Costs

	1999	2000	2001	2002	2003
Annual	Insufficient Information				
Total	Insufficient Information				

Projected Costs (5yr)

Insufficient Information

Ownership Cost Value

⊖ Insufficient Information

● Poor ◉ Worse Than Average ◐ Average ○ Better Than Average ○ Excellent ⊖ Insufficient Information

113

Refer to *Section 3: Annotated Vehicle Charts* for an explanation of these charts.

Mercedes-Benz SL500 Roadster
2 Door Convertible

Luxury

 5.0L 302 hp Gas Fuel Inject.
 8 Cylinder "V"
 Automatic 5 Speed
 2 Wheel Rear
 Dual Front/Side Airbags Std

Purchase Price

Car Item	Dealer Cost	List
Base Price	**$70,560**	**$81,100**
Anti-Lock Brakes	Std	Std
Manual Transmission	N/A	N/A
Optional Engine	N/A	N/A
Auto Climate Control	Std	Std
Power Steering	Std	Std
Cruise Control	Std	Std
Power Windows	Std	Std
AM/FM Stereo Cassette	Std	Std
Steering Wheel, Tilt	Std	Std
Rear Defroster	Std	Std
*Options Price	$0	$0
*Total Price	**$70,560**	**$81,100**
Target Price	$77,692	
Destination Charge	$595	
Avg. Tax & Fees	$4,398	
Luxury/Gas Guzzler Tax	$3,597	
Total Target $	**$86,282**	
12 Month Price Increase:	2%	

Ownership Costs (Projected)

Cost Area	5 Year Cost	Rating
Depreciation	$34,718	◯
Financing ($1,430/month)	$16,785	
Insurance (Performance)	$18,204	◉
State Fees	$3,281	
Fuel (Hwy 23 City 16 -Prem.)	$4,531	◉
Maintenance	$2,547	◯
Repairs	$1,831	◉

Warranty/Maintenance Info

Major Tune-Up (60K mile int.)	$262	◯
Minor Tune-Up (30K mile int.)	$191	●
Brake Service	$318	●
Overall Warranty	4 yr/50k	◯
Drivetrain Warranty	4 yr/50k	◯
Rust Warranty	4 yr/50k	◉
Maintenance Warranty	N/A	
Roadside Assistance	unlim. mi	

Ownership Costs By Year (Projected)

$5 $10 $15 $20 $25 $30 $35 (x1,000)

legend: 1999, 2000, 2001, 2002, 2003

Resale Value

1999	2000	2001	2002	2003
$75,552	$68,997	$62,964	$57,186	$51,564

Cumulative Costs

	1999	2000	2001	2002	2003
Annual	$21,633	$16,432	$15,031	$14,804	$13,998
Total	$21,633	$38,065	$53,096	$67,900	$81,898

Projected Costs (5yr)

Relative $84,950	This Car $81,898
Cost/Mile $1.21	Cost/Mile $1.17

Ownership Cost Value

◯ Better Than Average

The SL500 receives an all-new engine for 1999. The new engine utilizes twin spark plug/three valve technology and innovative casting techniques to achieve low emissions and greater low-end and midrange torque. The new V8 meets Ultra Low Emission Vehicle standards and is certified as a California Low Emissions vehicle. A new rear tailpipe gives the SL500 a more throaty exhaust note. An automatic roll bar, Brake Assist and Electronic Stability Program (ESP) are standard safety features.

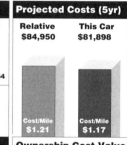

Mercedes-Benz SL600 Roadster
2 Door Convertible

Luxury

 6.0L 389 hp Gas Fuel Inject.
 12 Cylinder "V"
 Automatic 5 Speed
 2 Wheel Rear / Dual Front/Side Airbags Std

Purchase Price

Car Item	Dealer Cost	List
Base Price	**$110,400**	**$126,900**
Anti-Lock Brakes	Std	Std
Manual Transmission	N/A	N/A
Optional Engine	N/A	N/A
Auto Climate Control	Std	Std
Power Steering	Std	Std
Cruise Control	Std	Std
Power Windows	Std	Std
AM/FM Stereo Cassette	Std	Std
Steering Wheel, Tilt	Std	Std
Rear Defroster	Std	Std
*Options Price	$0	$0
*Total Price	**$110,400**	**$126,900**
Target Price	$121,560	
Destination Charge	$595	
Avg. Tax & Fees	$6,902	
Luxury/Gas Guzzler Tax	$7,925	
Total Target $	**$136,982**	
12 Month Price Increase:	2%	

Ownership Costs (Projected)

Cost Area	5 Year Cost	Rating
Depreciation	$67,660	◯
Financing ($2,271/month)	$26,649	
Insurance (Performance)	$18,204	◉
State Fees	$5,112	
Fuel (Hwy 19 City 13 -Prem.)	$5,529	●
Maintenance	$3,009	◉
Repairs	$1,755	◯

Warranty/Maintenance Info

Major Tune-Up (60K mile int.)	$283	◯
Minor Tune-Up (30K mile int.)	$184	●
Brake Service	$318	●
Overall Warranty	4 yr/50k	◯
Drivetrain Warranty	4 yr/50k	◯
Rust Warranty	4 yr/50k	◉
Maintenance Warranty	N/A	
Roadside Assistance	unlim. mi	

Ownership Costs By Year (Projected)

$5 $10 $15 $20 $25 $30 $35 $40 $45 $50 $55 $60 $65 $70 (x1,000)

legend: 1999, 2000, 2001, 2002, 2003

Resale Value

1999	2000	2001	2002	2003
$113,414	$101,581	$90,442	$79,720	$69,322

Cumulative Costs

	1999	2000	2001	2002	2003
Annual	$38,467	$25,038	$22,698	$21,548	$20,168
Total	$38,467	$63,505	$86,203	$107,751	$127,919

Projected Costs (5yr)

Relative $129,062	This Car $127,919
Cost/Mile $1.84	Cost/Mile $1.83

Ownership Cost Value

◯ Average

For 1999, the SL600 receives new SLK-style side mirrors, body-color door handles and side moldings, new taillamps, and a new rear valance panel and tailpipe design. The SL600 features an adaptive damping system, xenon headlamps, heated seats and a CD changer. A Panorama glass hard top, made from heat-reflecting tinted glass, is optional and replaces the standard body-colored aluminum hard top when ordered. The SL600 also comes standard with a canvas soft top and automatic roll bar.

114

* Includes shaded options
** Other purchase requirements apply
*** Price includes other options

 ● Poor
 ◉ Worse Than Average
 ◯ Average
 ◯ Better Than Average
◯ Excellent
⊖ Insufficient Information

Refer to *Section 3: Annotated Vehicle Charts* for an explanation of these charts.

Mercury Cougar
2 Door Coupe

Compact

Engine	Cylinder	Transmission	Drive	Airbags
2.0L 125 hp Gas Fuel Inject.	4 Cylinder In-Line	Manual 5 Speed	2 Wheel Front	Dual Airbags Std

Purchase Price

Car Item	Dealer Cost	List
Base Price	**$14,814**	**$16,195**
Anti-Lock Brakes	$445	$500
Automatic Transmission	N/A	N/A
Optional Engine	N/A	N/A
Air Conditioning	Std	Std
Power Steering	Std	Std
Cruise Control	Pkg	Pkg
Power Windows	Std	Std
AM/FM Stereo Cassette	Std	Std
Steering Wheel, Tilt	Std	Std
Rear Defroster	Std	Std
*Options Price	$0	$0
*Total Price	**$14,814**	**$16,195**
Target Price	$15,412	
Destination Charge	$400	
Avg. Tax & Fees	$891	
Total Target $	**$16,703**	
Average Dealer Option Cost:	**89%**	
12 Month Price Increase:	N/A	

Ownership Costs (Projected)

Cost Area	5 Year Cost	Rating
Depreciation		⊖
Financing ($277/month)	$3,249	
Insurance	$7,643	◉
State Fees	$677	
Fuel (Hwy 34 City 24)	$2,566	◯
Maintenance		⊖
Repairs	$825	◉

Warranty/Maintenance Info

Major Tune-Up (60K mile int.)		⊖
Minor Tune-Up (30K mile int.)		⊖
Brake Service		⊖
Overall Warranty	3 yr/36k	O
Drivetrain Warranty	3 yr/36k	O
Rust Warranty	5 yr/unlim. mi	O
Maintenance Warranty	N/A	
Roadside Assistance	3 yr/36k	

Ownership Costs By Year (Projected)

$2,000 $4,000 $6,000 $8,000

Insufficient Depreciation Information

■ 1999
■ 2000
■ 2001
□ 2002
□ 2003

Insufficient Maintenance Information

Resale Value

Insufficient Information

Projected Costs (5yr)

Insufficient Information

Cumulative Costs

	1999	2000	2001	2002	2003
Annual	Insufficient Information				
Total	Insufficient Information				

Ownership Cost Value

⊖

Insufficient Information

The 1999 Cougar sports coupe has been completely redesigned. Side airbags are now available, and in combination with dual front airbags, occupant safety is greatly increased. Standard Cougar equipment includes a passive theft deterrent system, power height-adjustable driver's seat and 15 inch aluminum wheels. The optional Convenience Group includes cruise control, a remote keyless illuminated entry system and rear wiper. Available options include a CD changer, rear spoiler and power sunroof.

Mercury Cougar V-6
2 Door Coupe

Compact

Engine	Cylinder	Transmission	Drive	Airbags
2.5L 170 hp Gas Fuel Inject.	6 Cylinder "V"	Manual 5 Speed	2 Wheel Front	Dual Airbags Std

Base Model Shown

Purchase Price

Car Item	Dealer Cost	List
Base Price	**$15,259**	**$16,695**
Anti-Lock Brakes	$445	$500
Automatic 4 Speed	$725	$815
Optional Engine	N/A	N/A
Air Conditioning	Std	Std
Power Steering	Std	Std
Cruise Control	Pkg	Pkg
Power Windows	Std	Std
AM/FM Stereo Cassette	Std	Std
Steering Wheel, Tilt	Std	Std
Rear Defroster	Std	Std
*Options Price	$725	$815
*Total Price	**$15,984**	**$17,510**
Target Price	$16,640	
Destination Charge	$400	
Avg. Tax & Fees	$959	
Total Target $	**$17,999**	
Average Dealer Option Cost:	**89%**	
12 Month Price Increase:	N/A	

Ownership Costs (Projected)

Cost Area	5 Year Cost	Rating
Depreciation		⊖
Financing ($298/month)	$3,501	
Insurance	$7,837	◉
State Fees	$728	
Fuel (Hwy 29 City 20)	$3,041	O
Maintenance		⊖
Repairs	$825	◉

Warranty/Maintenance Info

Major Tune-Up (60K mile int.)		⊖
Minor Tune-Up (30K mile int.)		⊖
Brake Service		⊖
Overall Warranty	3 yr/36k	O
Drivetrain Warranty	3 yr/36k	O
Rust Warranty	5 yr/unlim. mi	O
Maintenance Warranty	N/A	
Roadside Assistance	3 yr/36k	

Ownership Costs By Year (Projected)

$2,000 $4,000 $6,000 $8,000

Insufficient Depreciation Information

■ 1999
■ 2000
■ 2001
□ 2002
□ 2003

Insufficient Maintenance Information

Resale Value

Insufficient Information

Projected Costs (5yr)

Insufficient Information

Cumulative Costs

	1999	2000	2001	2002	2003
Annual	Insufficient Information				
Total	Insufficient Information				

Ownership Cost Value

⊖

Insufficient Information

For 1999, the Cougar V6 coupe offers a completely redesigned interior and exterior. A side airbag supplemental restraint system is available in combination with standard dual airbags. Standard equipment includes four wheel disc brakes, a rear spoiler and fog lamps. Leather bucket seats, power driver's seat, traction control and polished aluminum wheels are optional features. The optional Convenience Group includes a keyless remote entry system, rear wiper, Light Group and premium sound system.

---

* Includes shaded options

** Other purchase requirements apply

*** Price includes other options

 Poor Worse Than Average Average Better Than Average Excellent Insufficient Information

115

Refer to Section 3: Annotated Vehicle Charts for an explanation of these charts.

©1999 by IntelliChoice, Inc. (408) 866-1400 http://www.intellichoice.com All Rights Reserved. Reproduction Prohibited.

Mercury Grand Marquis GS
4 Door Sedan

Large

4.6L 200 hp Gas Fuel Inject.	8 Cylinder "V"	Automatic 4 Speed	2 Wheel Rear	Dual Airbags Std

LS Model Shown

Purchase Price

Car Item	Dealer Cost	List
Base Price	**$20,746**	**$22,220**
Anti-Lock Brakes	$534	$600
Manual Transmission	N/A	N/A
Optional Engine	N/A	N/A
Air Conditioning	Std	Std
Power Steering	Std	Std
Cruise Control	Std	Std
Power Windows	Std	Std
AM/FM Stereo Cassette	Std	Std
Steering Wheel, Tilt	Std	Std
Rear Defroster	Std	Std
***Options Price**	**$534**	**$600**
***Total Price**	**$21,280**	**$22,820**
Target Price	$22,179	
Destination Charge	$605	
Avg. Tax & Fees	$1,272	
Total Target $	**$24,056**	
Average Dealer Option Cost:	**89%**	
12 Month Price Increase:	2%	

Ownership Costs (Projected)

Cost Area	5 Year Cost	Rating
Depreciation	$11,847	◯
Financing ($399/month)	$4,679	
Insurance	$7,140	◯
State Fees	$950	
Fuel (Hwy 24 City 17)	$3,628	◉
Maintenance	$2,778	◯
Repairs	$875	◯

Ownership Costs By Year (Projected)

$2,000 $4,000 $6,000 $8,000 $10,000 $12,000

Legend: 1999, 2000, 2001, 2002, 2003

Warranty/Maintenance Info

Major Tune-Up (100K mile int.)	$271	◉
Minor Tune-Up (30K mile int.)	$91	◯
Brake Service	$236	◯
Overall Warranty	3 yr/36k	◯
Drivetrain Warranty	3 yr/36k	◯
Rust Warranty	5 yr/unlim. mi	◯
Maintenance Warranty	N/A	
Roadside Assistance	3 yr/36k	

Resale Value

1999	2000	2001	2002	2003
$21,087	$18,621	$16,458	$14,357	$12,209

Projected Costs (5yr)

Relative	This Car
$32,788	**$31,897**
Cost/Mile 47¢	Cost/Mile 46¢

Cumulative Costs

	1999	2000	2001	2002	2003
Annual	$6,892	$6,136	$5,993	$6,299	$6,577
Total	$6,892	$13,028	$19,021	$25,320	$31,897

Ownership Cost Value
◯ Excellent

For the 1999 Grand Marquis GS, optional antilock brakes are now available separately or with traction control. A SecuriLock theft deterrent system, floor mats, remote trunk release, illuminated entry system and cruise control are standard features on GS. Engine output increases to 215 hp with the optional Handling Package, which includes dual exhaust, a 3.27:1 rear axle ratio, upgraded front and rear stabilizer bars and rear air springs. The optional CD player replaces the cassette.

Mercury Grand Marquis LS
4 Door Sedan

Large

4.6L 200 hp Gas Fuel Inject.	8 Cylinder "V"	Automatic 4 Speed	2 Wheel Rear	Dual Airbags Std

Purchase Price

Car Item	Dealer Cost	List
Base Price	**$22,475**	**$24,120**
Anti-Lock Brakes	$534	$600
Manual Transmission	N/A	N/A
Optional Engine	N/A	N/A
Air Conditioning	Std	Std
Power Steering	Std	Std
Cruise Control	Std	Std
Power Windows	Std	Std
AM/FM Stereo Cassette	Std	Std
Steering Wheel, Tilt	Std	Std
Rear Defroster	Std	Std
***Options Price**	**$534**	**$600**
***Total Price**	**$23,009**	**$24,720**
Target Price	$24,020	
Destination Charge	$605	
Avg. Tax & Fees	$1,374	
Total Target $	**$25,999**	
Average Dealer Option Cost:	**89%**	
12 Month Price Increase:	1%	

Ownership Costs (Projected)

Cost Area	5 Year Cost	Rating
Depreciation	$13,453	◐
Financing ($431/month)	$5,057	
Insurance	$7,294	◯
State Fees	$1,026	
Fuel (Hwy 24 City 17)	$3,628	◉
Maintenance	$2,778	◯
Repairs	$875	◯

Ownership Costs By Year (Projected)

$2,000 $4,000 $6,000 $8,000 $10,000 $12,000 $14,000

Legend: 1999, 2000, 2001, 2002, 2003

Warranty/Maintenance Info

Major Tune-Up (100K mile int.)	$271	◉
Minor Tune-Up (30K mile int.)	$91	◯
Brake Service	$236	◯
Overall Warranty	3 yr/36k	◯
Drivetrain Warranty	3 yr/36k	◯
Rust Warranty	5 yr/unlim. mi	◯
Maintenance Warranty	N/A	
Roadside Assistance	3 yr/36k	

Resale Value

1999	2000	2001	2002	2003
$22,009	$19,394	$17,085	$14,836	$12,546

Projected Costs (5yr)

Relative	This Car
$34,578	**$34,111**
Cost/Mile 49¢	Cost/Mile 49¢

Cumulative Costs

	1999	2000	2001	2002	2003
Annual	$8,089	$6,436	$6,264	$6,542	$6,780
Total	$8,089	$14,525	$20,789	$27,331	$34,111

Ownership Cost Value
◐ Average

For the 1999 Grand Marquis LS, optional antilock brakes are now available separately or with traction control. LS standard equipment includes the Luxury Light Group and a remote keyless entry system. Engine output increases to 215 hp with the optional Handling Package, which includes dual exhaust, a 3.27:1 rear axle ratio, upgraded front and rear stabilizer bars and rear air springs. Electronic instrumentation is available with automatic climate control.

---

* Includes shaded options
** Other purchase requirements apply
*** Price includes other options

 ● Poor
 ◉ Worse Than Average
● ◑ Average
◯ Better Than Average
◯ Excellent
⊖ Insufficient Information

Refer to *Section 3: Annotated Vehicle Charts* for an explanation of these charts.

Mercury Mystique GS
4 Door Sedan

2.0L 125 hp Gas Fuel Inject.	4 Cylinder In-Line	Manual 5 Speed	2 Wheel Front	Dual Airbags Std (Depowered)

Purchase Price

Car Item	Dealer Cost	List
Base Price	**$14,972**	**$16,390**
Anti-Lock Brakes	$445	$500
Automatic 4 Speed	$725	$815
Optional Engine	N/A	N/A
Air Conditioning	Std	Std
Power Steering	Std	Std
Cruise Control	Std	Std
Power Windows	Std	Std
AM/FM Stereo Cassette	$120	$135
Steering Wheel, Tilt	Std	Std
Rear Defroster	Std	Std
*Options Price	$845	$950
*Total Price	**$15,817**	**$17,340**
Target Price	$16,383	
Destination Charge	$535	
Avg. Tax & Fees	$953	
Total Target $	**$17,871**	
Average Dealer Option Cost:	*89%*	
12 Month Price Increase:	7%	

Ownership Costs (Projected)

Cost Area	5 Year Cost	Rating
Depreciation	$10,851	●
Financing ($296/month)	$3,477	
Insurance	$7,463	◑
State Fees	$728	
Fuel (Hwy 34 City 24)	$2,566	○
Maintenance	$3,058	◑
Repairs	$755	◑

Warranty/Maintenance Info

Major Tune-Up (100K mile int.)	$181	○
Minor Tune-Up (30K mile int.)	$75	○
Brake Service	$197	○
Overall Warranty	3 yr/36k	◑
Drivetrain Warranty	3 yr/36k	◑
Rust Warranty	5 yr/unlim. mi	○
Maintenance Warranty	N/A	
Roadside Assistance	3 yr/36k	

Ownership Costs By Year (Projected)

$2,000 $4,000 $6,000 $8,000 $10,000 $12,000

- 1999
- 2000
- 2001
- 2002
- 2003

Resale Value

1999	2000	2001	2002	2003
$14,538	$12,506	$10,678	$8,846	$7,020

Cumulative Costs

	1999	2000	2001	2002	2003
Annual	$6,651	$5,173	$5,173	$5,894	$6,007
Total	$6,651	$11,824	$16,997	$22,891	$28,898

Projected Costs (5yr)

Relative	This Car
$27,600	$28,898
Cost/Mile 39¢	Cost/Mile 41¢

Ownership Cost Value

● Poor

The Mystique GS continues this year with a few minor changes. Among these are two new colors, Tropic Green and Medium Steel Blue. For additional appearance enhancement, the optional GS Sport Group features a rear spoiler, leather-wrapped shift knob and steering wheel, fog lamps, and Sport logos on the floor mats and the exterior. Various other popular options include a power moonroof, remote keyless entry, a premium CD stereo sound system and an antilock braking system.

Mercury Mystique LS
4 Door Sedan

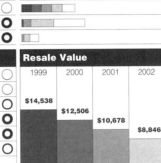

GS Model Shown

2.5L 170 hp Gas Fuel Inject.	6 Cylinder "V"	Manual 5 Speed	2 Wheel Front	Dual Airbags Std (Depowered)

Purchase Price

Car Item	Dealer Cost	List
Base Price	**$16,178**	**$17,745**
Anti-Lock Brakes	$445	$500
Automatic 4 Speed	$725	$815
Optional Engine	N/A	N/A
Air Conditioning	Std	Std
Power Steering	Std	Std
Cruise Control	Std	Std
Power Windows	Std	Std
AM/FM Stereo Cassette	$120	$135
Steering Wheel, Tilt	Std	Std
Rear Defroster	Std	Std
*Options Price	$845	$950
*Total Price	**$17,023**	**$18,695**
Target Price	$17,651	
Destination Charge	$535	
Avg. Tax & Fees	$1,023	
Total Target $	**$19,209**	
Average Dealer Option Cost:	*89%*	
12 Month Price Increase:	3%	

Ownership Costs (Projected)

Cost Area	5 Year Cost	Rating
Depreciation	$11,649	●
Financing ($318/month)	$3,737	
Insurance	$7,506	◑
State Fees	$782	
Fuel (Hwy 29 City 20)	$3,041	◑
Maintenance	$3,096	◑
Repairs	$755	◑

Warranty/Maintenance Info

Major Tune-Up (100K mile int.)	$279	◉
Minor Tune-Up (30K mile int.)	$81	○
Brake Service	$197	○
Overall Warranty	3 yr/36k	◑
Drivetrain Warranty	3 yr/36k	◑
Rust Warranty	5 yr/unlim. mi	○
Maintenance Warranty	N/A	
Roadside Assistance	3 yr/36k	

Ownership Costs By Year (Projected)

$2,000 $4,000 $6,000 $8,000 $10,000 $12,000

- 1999
- 2000
- 2001
- 2002
- 2003

Resale Value

1999	2000	2001	2002	2003
$15,530	$13,379	$11,434	$9,490	$7,560

Cumulative Costs

	1999	2000	2001	2002	2003
Annual	$7,198	$5,480	$5,466	$6,213	$6,209
Total	$7,198	$12,678	$18,144	$24,357	$30,566

Projected Costs (5yr)

Relative	This Car
$28,797	$30,566
Cost/Mile 41¢	Cost/Mile 44¢

Ownership Cost Value

● Poor

The Mystique LS arrives this year with only minor enhancements, including several new color choices. Heralded as the premium Mystique model, the LS features many luxury items as standard equipment. Most notable are leather seating surfaces with a six-way power driver's seat, polished alloy wheels and a remote keyless entry system. For added performance, a 170 hp 2.5L Duratec V6 engine is standard, along with performance-tuned suspension and steering, and larger P205/60R15 tires.

---

* Includes shaded options
** Other purchase requirements apply
*** Price includes other options

 Poor   Worse Than Average   Average   Better Than Average   Excellent   Insufficient Information

117

Refer to *Section 3: Annotated Vehicle Charts* for an explanation of these charts.

Mercury Sable GS
4 Door Sedan

 3.0L 145 hp Gas Fuel Inject.
 6 Cylinder "V"
 Automatic 4 Speed
 2 Wheel Front
 Dual Airbags Std

Midsize

Purchase Price

Car Item	Dealer Cost	List
Base Price	**$16,846**	**$18,445**
Anti-Lock Brakes	$534	$600
Manual Transmission	N/A	N/A
3.0L 200 hp Gas	$494	$555
Air Conditioning	Std	Std
Power Steering	Std	Std
Cruise Control	Std	Std
Power Windows	Std	Std
AM/FM Stereo Cassette	Std	Std
Steering Wheel, Tilt	Std	Std
Rear Defroster	Std	Std
***Options Price**	$1,028	$1,155
***Total Price**	**$17,874**	**$19,600**
Target Price	$18,728	
Destination Charge	$550	
Avg. Tax & Fees	$1,083	
Total Target $	**$20,361**	
Average Dealer Option Cost:	89%	
12 Month Price Increase:	None	

For 1999, the Sable GS sedan includes more luxurious seats and a significant price reduction from last year. The integrated child seat option has been discontinued for 1999. Standard features include second generation airbags, air conditioning, a tilt steering column and AM/FM full logic stereo with cassette and four speakers. A 200 hp 24 valve Duratec V6 engine, antilock brakes, remote keyless entry system and bright aluminum wheels are available as options.

Ownership Costs (Projected)

Cost Area	5 Year Cost	Rating
Depreciation	$11,922	●
Financing ($338/month)	$3,961	
Insurance	$6,723	○
State Fees	$819	
Fuel (Hwy 26 City 18)	$3,387	●
Maintenance	$3,040	○
Repairs	$1,000	◉

Warranty/Maintenance Info

Major Tune-Up (100K mile int.)	$245	○
Minor Tune-Up (30K mile int.)	$98	○
Brake Service	$206	○
Overall Warranty	3 yr/36k	○
Drivetrain Warranty	3 yr/36k	○
Rust Warranty	5 yr/unlim. mi	○
Maintenance Warranty	N/A	
Roadside Assistance	3 yr/36k	

Ownership Costs By Year (Projected)

$2,000 $4,000 $6,000 $8,000 $10,000 $12,000

- 1999
- 2000
- 2001
- 2002
- 2003

Resale Value

1999	2000	2001	2002	2003
$16,706	$14,436	$12,446	$10,416	$8,439

Cumulative Costs

	1999	2000	2001	2002	2003
Annual	$7,176	$5,584	$5,502	$6,444	$6,146
Total	$7,176	$12,760	$18,262	$24,706	$30,852

Projected Costs (5yr)

Relative	This Car
$29,334	$30,852
Cost/Mile 42¢	Cost/Mile 44¢

Ownership Cost Value

◉ Worse Than Average

Mercury Sable LS
4 Door Sedan

 3.0L 145 hp Gas Fuel Inject.
 6 Cylinder "V"
 Automatic 4 Speed
 2 Wheel Front
 Dual Airbags Std

Midsize

GS Model Shown

Purchase Price

Car Item	Dealer Cost	List
Base Price	**$17,825**	**$19,545**
Anti-Lock Brakes	$534	$600
Manual Transmission	N/A	N/A
3.0L 200 hp Gas	$494	$555
Air Conditioning	Std	Std
Power Steering	Std	Std
Cruise Control	Std	Std
Power Windows	Std	Std
AM/FM Stereo Cassette	Std	Std
Steering Wheel, Tilt	Std	Std
Rear Defroster	Std	Std
***Options Price**	$1,028	$1,155
***Total Price**	**$18,853**	**$20,700**
Target Price	$19,775	
Destination Charge	$550	
Avg. Tax & Fees	$1,141	
Total Target $	**$21,466**	
Average Dealer Option Cost:	89%	
12 Month Price Increase:	None	

For 1999, the Sable LS sedan includes a price reduction and more luxurious seats. Also new for 1999 are hard map pockets and an available power passenger seat; leather seating surfaces are available as a no-charge option with the LS Premium Group. In addition, new 16 inch chrome wheels are also available. The integrated child seat option has been discontinued for 1999. Additional standard features include second generation airbags, air conditioning and a tilt steering column.

Ownership Costs (Projected)

Cost Area	5 Year Cost	Rating
Depreciation	$12,767	●
Financing ($356/month)	$4,175	
Insurance	$6,852	○
State Fees	$864	
Fuel (Hwy 26 City 18)	$3,387	●
Maintenance	$3,040	○
Repairs	$1,000	◉

Warranty/Maintenance Info

Major Tune-Up (100K mile int.)	$245	○
Minor Tune-Up (30K mile int.)	$98	○
Brake Service	$206	○
Overall Warranty	3 yr/36k	○
Drivetrain Warranty	3 yr/36k	○
Rust Warranty	5 yr/unlim. mi	○
Maintenance Warranty	N/A	
Roadside Assistance	3 yr/36k	

Ownership Costs By Year (Projected)

$2,000 $4,000 $6,000 $8,000 $10,000 $12,000 $14,000

- 1999
- 2000
- 2001
- 2002
- 2003

Resale Value

1999	2000	2001	2002	2003
$16,509	$14,354	$12,481	$10,563	$8,699

Cumulative Costs

	1999	2000	2001	2002	2003
Annual	$8,587	$5,563	$5,464	$6,394	$6,077
Total	$8,587	$14,150	$19,614	$26,008	$32,085

Projected Costs (5yr)

Relative	This Car
$30,327	$32,085
Cost/Mile 43¢	Cost/Mile 46¢

Ownership Cost Value

◉ Worse Than Average

---

* Includes shaded options
** Other purchase requirements apply
*** Price includes other options

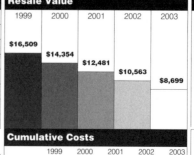

- ● Poor
- ◉ Worse Than Average
- ◐ Average
- ○ Better Than Average
- ○ Excellent
- ⊖ Insufficient Information

Refer to *Section 3: Annotated Vehicle Charts* for an explanation of these charts.

Mercury Sable LS
4 Door Wagon

 3.0L 145 hp Gas Fuel Inject. 6 Cylinder "V" PRND321 Automatic 4 Speed 2 Wheel Front Depowered Dual Airbags Std

Midsize Wagon

1998 Model Shown

Purchase Price

Car Item	Dealer Cost	List
Base Price	**$18,804**	**$20,645**
Anti-Lock Brakes	$534	$600
Manual Transmission	N/A	N/A
3.0L 200 hp Gas	$494	$555
Air Conditioning	Std	Std
Power Steering	Std	Std
Cruise Control	Std	Std
Power Windows	Std	Std
AM/FM Stereo Cassette	Std	Std
Steering Wheel, Tilt	Std	Std
Rear Defroster	Std	Std
*Options Price	$1,028	$1,155
***Total Price**	**$19,832**	**$21,800**
Target Price	$20,824	
Destination Charge	$550	
Avg. Tax & Fees	$1,199	
Total Target $	**$22,573**	
Average Dealer Option Cost:	89%	
12 Month Price Increase:	None	

Ownership Costs (Projected)

Cost Area	5 Year Cost	Rating
Depreciation	$13,107	●
Financing ($374/month)	$4,392	
Insurance	$6,852	○
State Fees	$907	
Fuel (Hwy 26 City 18)	$3,387	◉
Maintenance	$3,040	○
Repairs	$1,000	◉

Warranty/Maintenance Info

Major Tune-Up (100K mile int.)	$245	○
Minor Tune-Up (30K mile int.)	$98	○
Brake Service	$206	○
Overall Warranty	3 yr/36k	◉
Drivetrain Warranty	3 yr/36k	◉
Rust Warranty	5 yr/unlim. mi	○
Maintenance Warranty	N/A	
Roadside Assistance	3 yr/36k	

For 1999, the Sable LS wagon includes more luxurious seats and has an available power passenger seat. The integrated child seat option has been discontinued for 1999. New for 1999, leather seating surfaces are available as a no-charge option with the LS Premium Group. Additional standard features include second generation airbags, a luggage rack, air conditioning and a tilt steering column. Antilock brakes and a rear-facing third rear seat are available as options.

Ownership Costs By Year (Projected)

$2,000 $4,000 $6,000 $8,000 $10,000 $12,000 $14,000

■ 1999
■ 2000
■ 2001
□ 2002
□ 2003

Resale Value

1999	2000	2001	2002	2003
$18,614	$16,108	$13,890	$11,644	$9,466

Cumulative Costs

	1999	2000	2001	2002	2003
Annual	$7,673	$5,983	$5,863	$6,758	$6,408
Total	$7,673	$13,656	$19,519	$26,277	$32,685

Projected Costs (5yr)

Relative $32,073	This Car $32,685
Cost/Mile 46¢	Cost/Mile 47¢

Ownership Cost Value
○ Average

Mercury Tracer GS
4 Door Sedan

 2.0L 110 hp Gas Fuel Inject. 4 Cylinder In-Line 135 24R Manual 5 Speed 2 Wheel Front Dual Airbags Std

Compact

LS Model Shown

Purchase Price

Car Item	Dealer Cost	List
Base Price	**$10,792**	**$11,530**
Anti-Lock Brakes	$356	$400
Automatic 4 Speed	$725	$815
Optional Engine	N/A	N/A
Air Conditioning	$708	$795
Power Steering	Std	Std
Cruise Control	N/A	N/A
Power Windows	N/A	N/A
AM/FM Stereo Cassette	$165	**$185
Steering Wheel, Tilt	N/A	N/A
Rear Defroster	$169	$190
*Options Price	$1,602	$1,800
***Total Price**	**$12,394**	**$13,330**
Target Price	$12,689	
Destination Charge	$415	
Avg. Tax & Fees	$740	
Total Target $	**$13,844**	
Average Dealer Option Cost:	89%	
12 Month Price Increase:	2%	

Ownership Costs (Projected)

Cost Area	5 Year Cost	Rating
Depreciation	$7,092	○
Financing ($229/month)	$2,694	
Insurance	$7,463	◉
State Fees	$562	
Fuel (Hwy 34 City 25)	$2,515	○
Maintenance	$3,550	◉
Repairs	$730	○

Warranty/Maintenance Info

Major Tune-Up (100K mile int.)	$200	○
Minor Tune-Up (30K mile int.)	$62	○
Brake Service	$243	○
Overall Warranty	3 yr/36k	◉
Drivetrain Warranty	3 yr/36k	◉
Rust Warranty	5 yr/unlim. mi	○
Maintenance Warranty	N/A	
Roadside Assistance	N/A	

For 1999, the Tracer GS comes with dual front airbags, solar-tinted glass and an AM/FM stereo with four premium speakers as standard equipment. For added safety, antilock brakes are available as an option. The Tracer GS can be ordered with optional air conditioning, AM/FM stereo with cassette and a four speed automatic transmission. The Trio Appearance Group enhances the Tracer's exterior style with a rear spoiler, chromed bolt-on wheel covers and Trio badging.

Ownership Costs By Year (Projected)

$2,000 $4,000 $6,000 $8,000

■ 1999
■ 2000
■ 2001
□ 2002
□ 2003

Resale Value

1999	2000	2001	2002	2003
$11,972	$10,562	$9,324	$8,050	$6,752

Cumulative Costs

	1999	2000	2001	2002	2003
Annual	$4,872	$4,288	$4,595	$5,190	$5,661
Total	$4,872	$9,160	$13,755	$18,945	$24,606

Projected Costs (5yr)

Relative $24,443	This Car $24,606
Cost/Mile 35¢	Cost/Mile 35¢

Ownership Cost Value
○ Average

---

* Includes shaded options
** Other purchase requirements apply
*** Price includes other options

● Poor ◉ Worse Than Average ○ Average ◐ Better Than Average ○ Excellent ⊖ Insufficient Information

119

Refer to *Section 3: Annotated Vehicle Charts* for an explanation of these charts.

Ford / Mercury / Lincoln

Mercury Tracer LS
4 Door Sedan

Compact

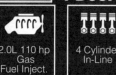 2.0L 110 hp Gas Fuel Inject.
 4 Cylinder In-Line
Manual 5 Speed
 2 Wheel Front
 Dual Airbags Std

Purchase Price

Car Item	Dealer Cost	List
Base Price	**$12,194**	**$13,070**
Anti-Lock Brakes	$356	$400
Automatic 4 Speed	$725	$815
Optional Engine	N/A	N/A
Air Conditioning	Std	Std
Power Steering	Std	Std
Cruise Control	Pkg	Pkg
Power Windows	Pkg	Pkg
AM/FM Stereo Cassette	Std	Std
Steering Wheel, Tilt	Pkg	Pkg
Rear Defroster	Std	Std
*Options Price	$725	$815
*Total Price	$12,919	$13,885
Target Price	$13,236	
Destination Charge	$415	
Avg. Tax & Fees	$770	
Total Target $	**$14,421**	
Average Dealer Option Cost:	**89%**	
12 Month Price Increase:	3%	

For 1999, the Tracer LS comes with an AM/FM stereo with cassette, air conditioning, dual power outside mirrors, and a remote keyless entry system. The LS model can be upgraded with power windows, power locks and a premium sound system including a trunk-mounted six disc CD changer. A four speed automatic transmission and four wheel antilock brakes are available as optional equipment. Available option groups include The LS Comfort Group and Sport Group to enhance interior and exterior appearance.

Ownership Costs (Projected)

Cost Area	5 Year Cost	Rating
Depreciation	$7,921	◉
Financing ($239/month)	$2,805	
Insurance	$7,506	◉
State Fees	$585	
Fuel (Hwy 34 City 25)	$2,515	○
Maintenance	$3,550	◉
Repairs	$730	○

Warranty/Maintenance Info

Major Tune-Up (100K mile int.) $200		○
Minor Tune-Up (30K mile int.) $62		○
Brake Service $243		○
Overall Warranty 3 yr/36k		○
Drivetrain Warranty 3 yr/36k		○
Rust Warranty 5 yr/unlim. mi		○
Maintenance Warranty N/A		
Roadside Assistance N/A		

Ownership Costs By Year (Projected)

$2,000 $4,000 $6,000 $8,000

Legend: 1999, 2000, 2001, 2002, 2003

Resale Value

1999	2000	2001	2002	2003
$12,169	$10,641	$9,288	$7,904	$6,500

Cumulative Costs

	1999	2000	2001	2002	2003
Annual	$5,304	$4,451	$4,745	$5,327	$5,785
Total	$5,304	$9,755	$14,500	$19,827	$25,612

Projected Costs (5yr)

Relative	This Car
$24,904	$25,612
Cost/Mile 36¢	Cost/Mile 37¢

Ownership Cost Value

○ Average

 Mercury / Lincoln

Mercury Tracer LS
4 Door Wagon

Small Wagon

 2.0L 110 hp Gas Fuel Inject.
4 Cylinder In-Line
Manual 5 Speed
 2 Wheel Front
 Dual Airbags Std

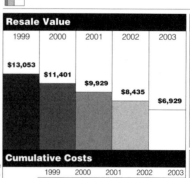

Purchase Price

Car Item	Dealer Cost	List
Base Price	**$13,290**	**$14,275**
Anti-Lock Brakes	$356	$400
Automatic 4 Speed	$725	$815
Optional Engine	N/A	N/A
Air Conditioning	Std	Std
Power Steering	Std	Std
Cruise Control	Pkg	Pkg
Power Windows	Std	Std
AM/FM Stereo Cassette	Std	Std
Steering Wheel, Tilt	Pkg	Pkg
Rear Defroster	Std	Std
*Options Price	$725	$815
*Total Price	$14,015	$15,090
Target Price	$14,370	
Destination Charge	$415	
Avg. Tax & Fees	$833	
Total Target $	**$15,618**	
Average Dealer Option Cost:	**89%**	
12 Month Price Increase:	None	

For 1999, the Tracer LS wagon now includes a remote keyless entry system, a four speaker AM/FM stereo with cassette and air conditioning as standard equipment. The LS Sport Group adds to the appearance of the Tracer with 15 inch aluminum wheels, fog lamps and sport badging. Power windows, power locks and leather sport bucket seats are optional for the LS wagon. The Standard Wagon Group includes a removable cargo cover, deluxe luggage rack and a rear window wiper/washer.

Ownership Costs (Projected)

Cost Area	5 Year Cost	Rating
Depreciation	$8,689	◉
Financing ($259/month)	$3,038	
Insurance	$7,688	◉
State Fees	$634	
Fuel (Hwy 34 City 25)	$2,515	○
Maintenance	$3,538	◉
Repairs	$730	○

Warranty/Maintenance Info

Major Tune-Up (100K mile int.) $200		○
Minor Tune-Up (30K mile int.) $62		○
Brake Service $243		○
Overall Warranty 3 yr/36k		○
Drivetrain Warranty 3 yr/36k		○
Rust Warranty 5 yr/unlim. mi		○
Maintenance Warranty N/A		
Roadside Assistance N/A		

Ownership Costs By Year (Projected)

$2,000 $4,000 $6,000 $8,000 $10,000

Legend: 1999, 2000, 2001, 2002, 2003

Resale Value

1999	2000	2001	2002	2003
$13,053	$11,401	$9,929	$8,435	$6,929

Cumulative Costs

	1999	2000	2001	2002	2003
Annual	$5,743	$4,685	$4,959	$5,502	$5,943
Total	$5,743	$10,428	$15,387	$20,889	$26,832

Projected Costs (5yr)

Relative	This Car
$26,555	$26,832
Cost/Mile 38¢	Cost/Mile 38¢

Ownership Cost Value

○ Better Than Average

● Poor	◉ Worse Than Average	○ Average	○ Better Than Average	○ Excellent	⊖ Insufficient Information

Refer to *Section 3: Annotated Vehicle Charts* for an explanation of these charts.

Mitsubishi 3000GT
2 Door Coupe

 3.0L 161 hp Gas Fuel Inject.
 6 Cylinder "V"
 1 3 5 / 2 4 R Manual 5 Speed
 2 Wheel Front
 Dual Airbags Std

Base Sport

VR-4 Model Shown

Purchase Price

Car Item	Dealer Cost	List
Base Price	**$22,395**	**$25,450**
Anti-Lock Brakes	N/A	N/A
Automatic 4 Speed	$814	$920
Optional Engine	N/A	N/A
Air Conditioning	Std	Std
Power Steering	Std	Std
Cruise Control	Std	Std
Power Windows	Std	Std
AM/FM Stereo Cassette	Std	Std
Steering Wheel, Tilt	Std	Std
Rear Defroster	Std	Std
*Options Price	$0	$0
*Total Price	**$22,395**	**$25,450**
Target Price	$23,719	
Destination Charge	$470	
Avg. Tax & Fees	$1,361	
Total Target $	**$25,550**	
Average Dealer Option Cost:	**80%**	
12 Month Price Increase:	None	

The 1999 3000GT carries over this year with few changes. The 3000GT features a 3.0L V6 that generates 161 hp and 185 lb-ft of torque. The optional four speed automatic transmission is electronically controlled with selectable economy or power modes depending on driver preference. The 3000GT comes fully equipped with luxury features such as power windows and locks, remote keyless entry, speed-sensitive intermittent wipers and a HomeLink transmitter mounted on the sun visor.

Ownership Costs (Projected)

Cost Area	5 Year Cost	Rating
Depreciation	$12,530	●
Financing ($424/month)	$4,970	
Insurance	$9,775	●
State Fees	$1,049	
Fuel (Hwy 25 City 19)	$3,368	◐
Maintenance	$4,066	●
Repairs	$901	●

Warranty/Maintenance Info

Major Tune-Up (60K mile int.)	$355	●
Minor Tune-Up (30K mile int.)	$221	●
Brake Service	$278	○
Overall Warranty	3 yr/36k	○
Drivetrain Warranty	5 yr/60k	◯
Rust Warranty	7 yr/100k	◯
Maintenance Warranty	N/A	
Roadside Assistance	3 yr/36k	

Ownership Costs By Year (Projected)

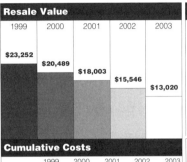

$2,000 $4,000 $6,000 $8,000 $10,000 $12,000 $14,000

- 1999
- 2000
- 2001
- 2002
- 2003

Resale Value

1999	2000	2001	2002	2003
$23,252	$20,489	$18,003	$15,546	$13,020

Cumulative Costs

	1999	2000	2001	2002	2003
Annual	$6,799	$7,000	$6,848	$8,159	$7,853
Total	$6,799	$13,799	$20,647	$28,806	$36,659

Projected Costs (5yr)

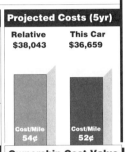

Relative	This Car
$38,043	$36,659
Cost/Mile 54¢	Cost/Mile 52¢

Ownership Cost Value

Better Than Average

Mitsubishi 3000GT SL
2 Door Coupe

 3.0L 218 hp Gas Fuel Inject.
 6 Cylinder "V"
 1 3 5 / 2 4 R Manual 5 Speed
 2 Wheel Front
 Dual Airbags Std

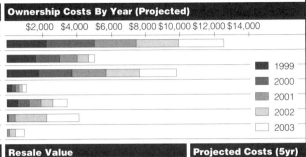

Base Sport

VR-4 Model Shown

Purchase Price

Car Item	Dealer Cost	List
Base Price	**$29,394**	**$33,400**
Anti-Lock Brakes	---	---
Automatic 4 Speed	$781	$890
Optional Engine	N/A	N/A
Air Conditioning	Std	Std
Power Steering	Std	Std
Cruise Control	Std	Std
Power Windows	Std	Std
AM/FM Stereo Cass/CD	Std	Std
Steering Wheel, Tilt	Std	Std
Rear Defroster	Std	Std
*Options Price	$0	$0
*Total Price	**$29,394**	**$33,400**
Target Price	$31,320	
Destination Charge	$470	
Avg. Tax & Fees	$1,783	
Total Target $	**$33,573**	
Average Dealer Option Cost:	**79%**	
12 Month Price Increase:	None	

The 1999 3000GT SL enters this model year with minimal changes. The 3000GT SL offers a more powerful 3.0L DOHC engine that produces 218 hp and 205 lb-ft of torque. The engine is mated to a five speed manual transmission that is geared to optimize power delivery. The optional four speed automatic transmission is electronically controlled and allows the driver to choose economy or power modes. The 3000GT SL comes fully equipped with luxury features including a power moonroof.

Ownership Costs (Projected)

Cost Area	5 Year Cost	Rating
Depreciation	$18,845	●
Financing ($556/month)	$6,531	
Insurance (Performance)	$13,928	●
State Fees	$1,368	
Fuel (Hwy 24 City 19)	$3,443	◐
Maintenance	$4,102	●
Repairs	$901	●

Warranty/Maintenance Info

Major Tune-Up (60K mile int.)	$382	◐
Minor Tune-Up (30K mile int.)	$221	●
Brake Service	$278	○
Overall Warranty	3 yr/36k	○
Drivetrain Warranty	5 yr/60k	◯
Rust Warranty	7 yr/100k	◯
Maintenance Warranty	N/A	
Roadside Assistance	3 yr/36k	

Ownership Costs By Year (Projected)

$5,000 $10,000 $15,000 $20,000

- 1999
- 2000
- 2001
- 2002
- 2003

Resale Value

1999	2000	2001	2002	2003
$27,696	$24,221	$21,043	$17,912	$14,728

Cumulative Costs

	1999	2000	2001	2002	2003
Annual	$11,795	$9,042	$8,771	$9,924	$9,587
Total	$11,795	$20,837	$29,608	$39,532	$49,119

Projected Costs (5yr)

Relative	This Car
$45,645	$49,119
Cost/Mile 65¢	Cost/Mile 70¢

Ownership Cost Value

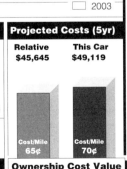

Poor

 Poor   Worse Than Average   Average   Better Than Average   ◯ Excellent   ⊖ Insufficient Information

121

Refer to *Section 3: Annotated Vehicle Charts* for an explanation of these charts.

Mitsubishi 3000GT VR-4
2 Door Coupe

Sport

 3.0L 320 hp Turbo Gas Fuel Inject.
 6 Cylinder "V"
 Manual 6 Speed
 4 Wheel Full-Time
 Dual Airbags Std

Purchase Price

Car Item	Dealer Cost	List
Base Price	**$39,249**	**$44,600**
Anti-Lock Brakes	Std	Std
Automatic Transmission	N/A	N/A
Optional Engine	N/A	N/A
Auto Climate Control	Std	Std
Power Steering	Std	Std
Cruise Control	Std	Std
Power Windows	Std	Std
AM/FM Stereo Cass/CD	Std	Std
Steering Wheel, Tilt	Std	Std
Rear Defroster	Std	Std
*Options Price	$0	$0
*Total Price	**$39,249**	**$44,600**
Target Price	$42,174	
Destination Charge	$470	
Avg. Tax & Fees	$2,383	
Luxury Tax	$399	
Total Target $	**$45,426**	
12 Month Price Increase:	None	

Ownership Costs (Projected)

Cost Area	5 Year Cost	Rating
Depreciation	$26,858	●
Financing ($753/month)	$8,838	
Insurance (Performance)	$16,035	●
State Fees	$1,816	
Fuel (Hwy 24 City 18 -Prem.)	$4,187	◉
Maintenance	$4,657	●
Repairs	$1,250	○

Warranty/Maintenance Info

Major Tune-Up (60K mile int.)	$400	●
Minor Tune-Up (30K mile int.)	$221	●
Brake Service	$278	○
Overall Warranty	3 yr/36k	◉
Drivetrain Warranty	5 yr/60k	○
Rust Warranty	7 yr/100k	○
Maintenance Warranty	N/A	
Roadside Assistance	3 yr/36k	

Ownership Costs By Year (Projected)

Scale: $5,000 $10,000 $15,000 $20,000 $25,000 $30,000

Legend: ■ 1999 ■ 2000 ■ 2001 ■ 2002 □ 2003

Resale Value

1999	2000	2001	2002	2003
$33,709	$29,665	$25,933	$22,269	$18,568

Cumulative Costs

	1999	2000	2001	2002	2003
Annual	$19,075	$10,905	$10,512	$12,014	$11,136
Total	$19,075	$29,980	$40,492	$52,506	$63,642

Projected Costs (5yr)

Relative $55,202	This Car $63,642
Cost/Mile 79¢	Cost/Mile 91¢

Ownership Cost Value

● Poor

The 1999 3000GT VR-4 is the upscale version of the model line. The 3000GT VR-4 features all-wheel drive for better handling. The VR-4 features a twin-turbo 3.0L DOHC 24 valve V6 engine that generates 320 hp and 315 lb-ft of torque. To deliver all this power, the VR-4 is equipped with a six speed manual transmission that is geared to optimize engine power. Standard features include power windows and locks, remote keyless entry, a HomeLink transmitter and a power moonroof.

Mitsubishi Diamante
4 Door Sedan

Near Luxury

 3.5L 210 hp Gas Fuel Inject.
 6 Cylinder "V"
 Automatic 4 Speed
 2 Wheel Front
 Dual Airbags Std

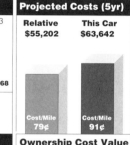

1998 ES Model Shown

Purchase Price

Car Item	Dealer Cost	List
Base Price	**$24,205**	**$27,199**
Anti-Lock Brakes	Std	Std
Manual Transmission	N/A	N/A
Optional Engine	N/A	N/A
Auto Climate Control	Std	Std
Power Steering	Std	Std
Cruise Control	Std	Std
Power Windows	Std	Std
AM/FM Stereo Cassette	Std	Std
Steering Wheel, Tilt	Std	Std
Rear Defroster	Std	Std
*Options Price	$0	$0
*Total Price	**$24,205**	**$27,199**
Target Price	$25,628	
Destination Charge	$470	
Avg. Tax & Fees	$1,464	
Total Target $	**$27,562**	
Average Dealer Option Cost:	81%	
12 Month Price Increase:	None	

Ownership Costs (Projected)

Cost Area	5 Year Cost	Rating
Depreciation	$15,559	●
Financing ($457/month)	$5,362	
Insurance	$8,093	○
State Fees	$1,120	
Fuel (Hwy 24 City 18 -Prem.)	$4,187	●
Maintenance	$3,994	●
Repairs	$720	○

Warranty/Maintenance Info

Major Tune-Up (60K mile int.)	$437	●
Minor Tune-Up (30K mile int.)	$202	●
Brake Service	$282	◉
Overall Warranty	3 yr/36k	○
Drivetrain Warranty	5 yr/60k	○
Rust Warranty	7 yr/100k	○
Maintenance Warranty	N/A	
Roadside Assistance	3 yr/36k	

Ownership Costs By Year (Projected)

Scale: $5,000 $10,000 $15,000 $20,000

Legend: ■ 1999 ■ 2000 ■ 2001 ■ 2002 □ 2003

Resale Value

1999	2000	2001	2002	2003
$22,569	$19,691	$17,121	$14,585	$12,003

Cumulative Costs

	1999	2000	2001	2002	2003
Annual	$9,481	$7,070	$6,910	$7,787	$7,787
Total	$9,481	$16,551	$23,461	$31,248	$39,035

Projected Costs (5yr)

Relative $37,007	This Car $39,035
Cost/Mile 53¢	Cost/Mile 56¢

Ownership Cost Value

◉ Worse Than Average

The 1999 Diamante sedan now comes as a single model, replacing last year's ES and LS versions. The Diamante's automatic transmission includes driver-adaptive neural network electronics. The Diamante is comprehensively equipped, including retained accessory power, solar-tinted glass, a keyless remote entry system and automatic climate control. The available Premium Package includes alloy wheels, leather-trimmed seating, a power driver's seat and power sunroof.

122

* Includes shaded options
** Other purchase requirements apply
*** Price includes other options

● Poor	◉ Worse Than Average	○ Average	○ Better Than Average	○ Excellent	⊖ Insufficient Information

Refer to Section 3: Annotated Vehicle Charts for an explanation of these charts.

Mitsubishi Eclipse RS
2 Door Coupe

Base Sport

GS Model Shown

Engine	Cylinders	Transmission	Drive	Airbags
2.0L 140 hp Gas Fuel Inject.	4 Cylinder In-Line	Manual 5 Speed	2 Wheel Front	Dual Airbags Std

Purchase Price

Car Item	Dealer Cost	List
Base Price	**$14,175**	**$15,750**
Anti-Lock Brakes	N/A	N/A
Automatic 4 Speed	$650	$730
Optional Engine	N/A	N/A
Air Conditioning	$705	$860
Power Steering	Std	Std
Cruise Control	Pkg	Pkg
Power Windows	Inc	Inc
AM/FM Stereo CD	Std	Std
Steering Wheel, Tilt	Std	Std
Other Options Cost	$1,873	$2,289
*Options Price	$2,578	$3,149
*Total Price	**$16,753**	**$18,899**
Target Price	$17,362	
Destination Charge	$435	
Avg. Tax & Fees	$1,007	
Total Target $	**$18,804**	
Average Dealer Option Cost:	82%	
12 Month Price Increase:	None	

Ownership Costs (Projected)

Cost Area	5 Year Cost	Rating
Depreciation	$7,921	◯
Financing ($312/month)	$3,658	
Insurance	$8,757	●
State Fees	$786	
Fuel (Hwy 33 City 22)	$2,718	◯
Maintenance	$2,900	◉
Repairs	$605	◯

Warranty/Maintenance Info

Major Tune-Up (60K mile int.)	$227	◯
Minor Tune-Up (30K mile int.)	$98	◯
Brake Service	$290	◉
Overall Warranty	3 yr/36k	◉
Drivetrain Warranty	5 yr/60k	◯
Rust Warranty	7 yr/100k	◯
Maintenance Warranty	N/A	
Roadside Assistance	3 yr/36k	

For 1999, the Eclipse RS features color-keyed bumpers, full wheel covers and a rear defroster. Inside there is a full console and an AM/FM stereo with cassette and CD. An optional Preferred Equipment Package including air conditioning, alloy wheels, a cargo cover and a rear spoiler is available. Also optional is a Power Package for windows, door locks and cruise control. Options include air conditioning, a CD changer and a power sunroof. All Eclipse models are manufactured in Normal, Illinois.

Ownership Costs By Year (Projected)

Legend: ■ 1999 ■ 2000 ■ 2001 □ 2002 □ 2003

Resale Value

1999	2000	2001	2002	2003
$17,667	$15,800	$14,187	$12,582	$10,883

Projected Costs (5yr)

Relative	This Car
$29,338	$27,345
Cost/Mile 42¢	Cost/Mile 39¢

Cumulative Costs

	1999	2000	2001	2002	2003
Annual	$4,805	$5,352	$5,134	$5,994	$6,060
Total	$4,805	$10,157	$15,291	$21,285	$27,345

Ownership Cost Value

◯ Excellent

Mitsubishi Eclipse GS
2 Door Coupe

Base Sport

Engine	Cylinders	Transmission	Drive	Airbags
2.0L 140 hp Gas Fuel Inject.	4 Cylinder In-Line	Manual 5 Speed	2 Wheel Front	Dual Airbags Std

Purchase Price

Car Item	Dealer Cost	List
Base Price	**$16,111**	**$17,910**
Anti-Lock Brakes	N/A	N/A
Automatic 4 Speed	$649	$720
Optional Engine	N/A	N/A
Air Conditioning	Pkg	Pkg
Power Steering	Std	Std
Cruise Control	Pkg	Pkg
Power Windows	Inc	Inc
AM/FM Stereo Cassette	Std	Std
Steering Wheel, Tilt	Std	Std
Rear Defroster	Std	Std
*Options Price	$0	$0
*Total Price	**$16,111**	**$17,910**
Target Price	$16,687	
Destination Charge	$435	
Avg. Tax & Fees	$966	
Total Target $	**$18,088**	
Average Dealer Option Cost:	89%	
12 Month Price Increase:	None	

Ownership Costs (Projected)

Cost Area	5 Year Cost	Rating
Depreciation	$8,015	◉
Financing ($300/month)	$3,519	
Insurance	$9,365	●
State Fees	$746	
Fuel (Hwy 33 City 22)	$2,718	◯
Maintenance	$3,027	◉
Repairs	$605	◯

Warranty/Maintenance Info

Major Tune-Up (60K mile int.)	$227	◯
Minor Tune-Up (30K mile int.)	$98	◯
Brake Service	$269	◉
Overall Warranty	3 yr/36k	◉
Drivetrain Warranty	5 yr/60k	◯
Rust Warranty	7 yr/100k	◯
Maintenance Warranty	N/A	
Roadside Assistance	3 yr/36k	

For 1999, the Eclipse GS now features an optional Sports Value Package, which includes unique 16 inch alloy wheels, a high-profile spoiler, chrome exhaust, white-faced gauges, leather seats and AM/FM stereo with cassette and CD. The standard GS is identified by its 16 inch wheels, four wheel power disc brakes, rear stabilizer bar, low-profile rear spoiler, side cladding, four wheel disc brakes and fog lamps. A three-channel HomeLink universal transmitter is built into the driver's sun visor.

Ownership Costs By Year (Projected)

Legend: ■ 1999 ■ 2000 ■ 2001 □ 2002 □ 2003

Resale Value

1999	2000	2001	2002	2003
$16,330	$14,607	$13,128	$11,653	$10,073

Projected Costs (5yr)

Relative	This Car
$28,202	$27,995
Cost/Mile 40¢	Cost/Mile 40¢

Cumulative Costs

	1999	2000	2001	2002	2003
Annual	$5,485	$5,280	$5,085	$6,090	$6,055
Total	$5,485	$10,765	$15,850	$21,940	$27,995

Ownership Cost Value

◯ Better Than Average

---

* Includes shaded options

** Other purchase requirements apply

*** Price includes other options

● Poor	◉ Worse Than Average	◯ Average	◯ Better Than Average	◯ Excellent	⊖ Insufficient Information

123

Refer to *Section 3: Annotated Vehicle Charts* for an explanation of these charts.

Mitsubishi Eclipse GS-T
2 Door Coupe

Base Sport

 2.0L 210 hp Turbo Gas Fuel Inject. | 4 Cylinder In-Line | Manual 5 Speed | 2 Wheel Front | Dual Airbags Std

Purchase Price

Car Item	Dealer Cost	List
Base Price	**$20,889**	**$23,210**
Anti-Lock Brakes	$587	$716
Automatic 4 Speed	$785	$880
Optional Engine	N/A	N/A
Air Conditioning	Std	Std
Power Steering	Std	Std
Cruise Control	Std	Std
Power Windows	Std	Std
AM/FM Stereo Cass/CD	Std	Std
Steering Wheel, Tilt	Std	Std
Rear Defroster	Std	Std
*Options Price	$587	$716
*Total Price	**$21,476**	**$23,926**
Target Price	$22,317	
Destination Charge	$435	
Avg. Tax & Fees	$1,281	
Total Target $	**$24,033**	
Average Dealer Option Cost:	**80%**	
12 Month Price Increase:	6%	

The 1999 Eclipse GS-T is at the upper end of the Eclipse lineup. Available this year are chrome-plated 16 inch alloy wheels. Sport seats and other standard equipment such as cruise control and power windows and locks identify the GS-T, as does a premium eight speaker sound system with cassette and CD player. The turbocharged and intercooled engine is capable of producing 210 hp. Optional equipment includes leather seating, a power sunroof, an antilock braking system and a ten disc CD changer.

Ownership Costs (Projected)

Cost Area	5 Year Cost	Rating
Depreciation	$12,073	◉
Financing ($398/month)	$4,675	
Insurance (Performance)	$12,389	●
State Fees	$988	
Fuel (Hwy 30 City 23 -Prem.)	$3,316	○
Maintenance	$2,987	O
Repairs	$735	O

Warranty/Maintenance Info

Major Tune-Up (60K mile int.)	$230	○
Minor Tune-Up (30K mile int.)	$98	○
Brake Service	$269	O
Overall Warranty	3 yr/36k	O
Drivetrain Warranty	5 yr/60k	○
Rust Warranty	7 yr/100k	○
Maintenance Warranty	N/A	
Roadside Assistance	3 yr/36k	

Ownership Costs By Year (Projected)

$2,000 $4,000 $6,000 $8,000 $10,000 $12,000 $14,000

- 1999
- 2000
- 2001
- 2002
- 2003

Resale Value

1999	2000	2001	2002	2003
$20,863	$18,440	$16,289	$14,164	$11,960

Cumulative Costs

	1999	2000	2001	2002	2003
Annual	$8,041	$7,061	$6,787	$7,726	$7,547
Total	$8,041	$15,102	$21,889	$29,615	$37,162

Projected Costs (5yr)

Relative	This Car
$36,782	$37,162
Cost/Mile 53¢	Cost/Mile 53¢

Ownership Cost Value

O
Average

Mitsubishi Eclipse GSX Turbo AWD
2 Door Coupe

Base Sport

 2.0L 210 hp Turbo Gas Fuel Inject. | 4 Cylinder In-Line | Manual 5 Speed | 4 Wheel Full-Time | Dual Airbags Std

Purchase Price

Car Item	Dealer Cost	List
Base Price	**$23,626**	**$26,550**
Anti-Lock Brakes	Std	Std
Automatic 4 Speed	$774	$870
Optional Engine	N/A	N/A
Air Conditioning	Std	Std
Power Steering	Std	Std
Cruise Control	Std	Std
Power Windows	Std	Std
AM/FM Stereo Cass/CD	Std	Std
Steering Wheel, Tilt	Std	Std
Rear Defroster	Std	Std
*Options Price	$0	$0
*Total Price	**$23,626**	**$26,550**
Target Price	$24,620	
Destination Charge	$435	
Avg. Tax & Fees	$1,410	
Total Target $	**$26,465**	
Average Dealer Option Cost:	**79%**	
12 Month Price Increase:	2%	

The Eclipse GSX is the only Eclipse with full-time AWD and a limited-slip rear differential. Standard equipment for 1999 includes a power glass sunroof, leather seats, a power driver's seat, an alarm system and a remote keyless entry system. Other standard equipment includes antilock brakes, cruise control, power windows and locks and a premium eight speaker sound system with cassette and CD. Optional equipment on the GSX includes a ten disc CD changer and a four speed automatic transmission.

Ownership Costs (Projected)

Cost Area	5 Year Cost	Rating
Depreciation	$13,364	●
Financing ($439/month)	$5,148	
Insurance (Performance)	$12,822	●
State Fees	$1,093	
Fuel (Hwy 28 City 21 -Prem.)	$3,590	O
Maintenance	$3,176	O
Repairs	$925	◉

Warranty/Maintenance Info

Major Tune-Up (60K mile int.)	$230	○
Minor Tune-Up (30K mile int.)	$98	○
Brake Service	$269	O
Overall Warranty	3 yr/36k	O
Drivetrain Warranty	5 yr/60k	○
Rust Warranty	7 yr/100k	○
Maintenance Warranty	N/A	
Roadside Assistance	3 yr/36k	

Ownership Costs By Year (Projected)

$2,000 $4,000 $6,000 $8,000 $10,000 $12,000 $14,000

- 1999
- 2000
- 2001
- 2002
- 2003

Resale Value

1999	2000	2001	2002	2003
$22,569	$19,999	$17,703	$15,441	$13,101

Cumulative Costs

	1999	2000	2001	2002	2003
Annual	$9,090	$7,500	$7,220	$8,350	$7,958
Total	$9,090	$16,590	$23,810	$32,160	$40,118

Projected Costs (5yr)

Relative	This Car
$39,636	$40,118
Cost/Mile 57¢	Cost/Mile 57¢

Ownership Cost Value

O
Average

124

 Poor | Worse Than Average | Average | Better Than Average | Excellent | Insufficient Information

Refer to *Section 3: Annotated Vehicle Charts* for an explanation of these charts.

Mitsubishi Eclipse Spyder GS
2 Door Convertible

Base Sport

2.4L 141 hp Gas Fuel Inject.	4 Cylinder In-Line	Manual 5 Speed	2 Wheel Front	Dual Airbags Std

Purchase Price

Car Item	Dealer Cost	List
Base Price	**$19,535**	**$21,710**
Anti-Lock Brakes	N/A	N/A
Automatic 4 Speed	$651	$720
Optional Engine	N/A	N/A
Air Conditioning	Std	Std
Power Steering	Std	Std
Cruise Control	Pkg	Pkg
Power Windows	Std	Std
AM/FM Stereo CD	Std	Std
Steering Wheel, Tilt	Std	Std
Other Options Cost	$567	$691
***Options Price**	**$567**	**$691**
***Total Price**	**$20,102**	**$22,401**
Target Price	$20,872	
Destination Charge	$435	
Avg. Tax & Fees	$1,200	
Total Target $	**$22,507**	
Average Dealer Option Cost:	**79%**	
12 Month Price Increase:	2%	

The 1999 Eclipse Spyder GS is the base convertible model. The Spyder convertibles are the first production convertibles to be built in the U.S. by a Japanese manufacturer. Standard equipment includes air conditioning, AM/FM stereo with CD and wheel locks. The Spyder GS includes a power cloth top, a vinyl boot and a glass rear window with an electric defroster. The optional Appearance Package includes a spoiler, 16 inch alloy wheels, chrome exhaust and fog lamps.

Ownership Costs (Projected)

Cost Area	5 Year Cost	Rating
Depreciation	$9,914	◐
Financing ($373/month)	$4,379	
Insurance	$9,775	●
State Fees	$927	
Fuel (Hwy 30 City 22)	$2,855	○
Maintenance	$2,834	○
Repairs	$605	○

Warranty/Maintenance Info

Major Tune-Up (60K mile int.)	$230	○
Minor Tune-Up (30K mile int.)	$98	○
Brake Service	$269	◐
Overall Warranty	3 yr/36k	◐
Drivetrain Warranty	5 yr/60k	
Rust Warranty	7 yr/100k	○
Maintenance Warranty	N/A	
Roadside Assistance	3 yr/36k	

Ownership Costs By Year (Projected)

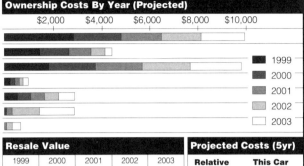

Legend: 1999, 2000, 2001, 2002, 2003

Resale Value

1999	2000	2001	2002	2003
$19,608	$17,656	$15,976	$14,322	$12,593

Projected Costs (5yr)

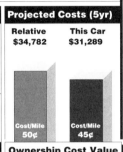

Relative	This Car
$34,782	$31,289
Cost/Mile 50¢	Cost/Mile 45¢

Cumulative Costs

	1999	2000	2001	2002	2003
Annual	$7,067	$5,894	$5,610	$6,352	$6,366
Total	$7,067	$12,961	$18,571	$24,923	$31,289

Ownership Cost Value

○ Excellent

Mitsubishi Eclipse Spyder GS-T Turbo
2 Door Convertible

Base Sport

Base Model Shown

2.0L 210 hp Turbo Gas Fuel Inject.	4 Cylinder In-Line	Manual 5 Speed	2 Wheel Front	Dual Airbags Std

Purchase Price

Car Item	Dealer Cost	List
Base Price	**$24,258**	**$26,960**
Anti-Lock Brakes	$587	$716
Automatic 4 Speed	$778	$860
Optional Engine	N/A	N/A
Air Conditioning	Std	Std
Power Steering	Std	Std
Cruise Control	Std	Std
Power Windows	Std	Std
AM/FM Stereo Cass/CD	Std	Std
Steering Wheel, Tilt	Std	Std
Rear Defroster	Std	Std
***Options Price**	**$587**	**$716**
***Total Price**	**$24,845**	**$27,676**
Target Price	$25,873	
Destination Charge	$435	
Avg. Tax & Fees	$1,478	
Total Target $	**$27,786**	
Average Dealer Option Cost:	**80%**	
12 Month Price Increase:	1%	

The 1999 Eclipse Spyder GS-T is equipped with a turbocharged engine producing 210 hp. Interior features on the Spyder GS-T include leather-trimmed seats, steering wheel and shift knob and a premium AM/FM stereo with cassette and CD player, eight speakers and a separate amplifier. Also standard are a power cloth top, security alarm and keyless entry system. Options include ABS, a ten disc CD changer and a four speed automatic transmission. Chrome-plated 16 inch alloy wheels are also available.

Ownership Costs (Projected)

Cost Area	5 Year Cost	Rating
Depreciation	$13,597	●
Financing ($461/month)	$5,405	
Insurance (Performance)	$12,822	●
State Fees	$1,138	
Fuel (Hwy 30 City 23 -Prem.)	$3,316	○
Maintenance	$3,058	◐
Repairs	$735	◐

Warranty/Maintenance Info

Major Tune-Up (60K mile int.)	$230	○
Minor Tune-Up (30K mile int.)	$98	○
Brake Service	$269	◐
Overall Warranty	3 yr/36k	◐
Drivetrain Warranty	5 yr/60k	○
Rust Warranty	7 yr/100k	○
Maintenance Warranty	N/A	
Roadside Assistance	3 yr/36k	

Ownership Costs By Year (Projected)

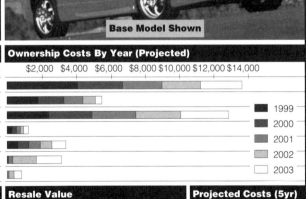

Legend: 1999, 2000, 2001, 2002, 2003

Resale Value

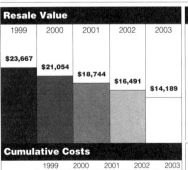

1999	2000	2001	2002	2003
$23,667	$21,054	$18,744	$16,491	$14,189

Projected Costs (5yr)

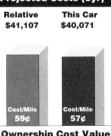

Relative	This Car
$41,107	$40,071
Cost/Mile 59¢	Cost/Mile 57¢

Cumulative Costs

	1999	2000	2001	2002	2003
Annual	$9,358	$7,571	$7,214	$8,134	$7,794
Total	$9,358	$16,929	$24,143	$32,277	$40,071

Ownership Cost Value

○ Better Than Average

---

* Includes shaded options

** Other purchase requirements apply

*** Price includes other options

Poor	Worse Than Average	Average
Better Than Average	Excellent	Insufficient Information

Refer to *Section 3: Annotated Vehicle Charts* for an explanation of these charts.

Mitsubishi Galant DE
4 Door Sedan

Midsize

ES Model Shown

- 2.4L 145 hp Gas Fuel Inject.
- 4 Cylinder In-Line
- Automatic 4 Speed
- 2 Wheel Front
- Dual Airbags Std

Purchase Price

Car Item	Dealer Cost	List
Base Price	**$15,461**	**$16,990**
Anti-Lock Brakes	N/A	N/A
Manual Transmission	N/A	N/A
Optional Engine	N/A	N/A
Air Conditioning	Std	Std
Power Steering	Std	Std
Cruise Control	N/A	N/A
Power Windows	Std	Std
AM/FM Stereo Cassette	Std	Std
Steering Wheel, Tilt	Std	Std
Rear Defroster	Std	Std
*Options Price	$0	$0
*Total Price	**$15,461**	**$16,990**
Target Price	$16,146	
Destination Charge	$435	
Avg. Tax & Fees	$933	
Total Target $	**$17,514**	
Average Dealer Option Cost:	72%	
12 Month Price Increase:	None	

The entry-level Galant DE sedan has a redesigned interior and exterior for 1999. The redesigned Galant is longer, wider and taller than last year's model. Many new added standard features include power door locks, headlamps with a 30 second delay, power windows with 30 second retained power and a 12 volt power outlet. Another new feature on the Galant is the standard four-speed automatic transmission with an adaptive program that adjusts to individual driving styles.

Ownership Costs (Projected)

Cost Area	5 Year Cost	Rating
Depreciation	$7,889	◯
Financing ($290/month)	$3,407	
Insurance	$7,463	◉
State Fees	$710	
Fuel (Hwy 28 City 21)	$3,026	◯
Maintenance	$3,394	◯
Repairs	$636	◯

Warranty/Maintenance Info

Major Tune-Up (60K mile int.)	$296	●
Minor Tune-Up (30K mile int.)	$117	◯
Brake Service	$282	●
Overall Warranty	3 yr/36k	◯
Drivetrain Warranty	5 yr/60k	◯
Rust Warranty	7 yr/100k	◯
Maintenance Warranty	N/A	
Roadside Assistance	3 yr/36k	

Ownership Costs By Year (Projected)

Scale: $2,000 – $8,000

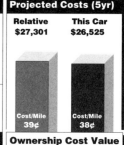

Legend: 1999, 2000, 2001, 2002, 2003

Resale Value

1999	2000	2001	2002	2003
$15,202	$13,657	$12,356	$10,981	$9,625

Cumulative Costs

	1999	2000	2001	2002	2003
Annual	$5,688	$4,751	$4,734	$5,588	$5,764
Total	$5,688	$10,439	$15,173	$20,761	$26,525

Projected Costs (5yr)

Relative	This Car
$27,301	$26,525
Cost/Mile 39¢	Cost/Mile 38¢

Ownership Cost Value

◯ Better Than Average

Mitsubishi Galant ES
4 Door Sedan

Midsize

- 2.4L 145 hp Gas Fuel Inject.
- 4 Cylinder In-Line
- Automatic 4 Speed
- 2 Wheel Front
- Dual Airbags Std

Purchase Price

Car Item	Dealer Cost	List
Base Price	**$16,191**	**$17,990**
Anti-Lock Brakes	Inc	Inc
Manual Transmission	N/A	N/A
3.0L 195 hp Gas	$1,800	$2,000
Air Conditioning	Std	Std
Power Steering	Std	Std
Cruise Control	Std	Std
Power Windows	Std	Std
AM/FM Stereo Cassette	Std	Std
Steering Wheel, Tilt	Std	Std
Rear Defroster	Std	Std
*Options Price	$1,800	$2,000
*Total Price	**$17,991**	**$19,990**
Target Price	$18,832	
Destination Charge	$435	
Avg. Tax & Fees	$1,084	
Total Target $	**$20,351**	
Average Dealer Option Cost:	85%	
12 Month Price Increase:	2%	

The Galant ES includes all the same standard features as the Galant DE. Upgraded features include front fog lamps, interior wood appliques and cruise control. A new 3.0L V6 engine with added horsepower and torque is available on the ES with the new four speed driver-adaptive automatic transmission. Safety features making their debut this year are driver and passenger side-impact airbags, available on the ES with the Premium Package, and standard on the LS and GTZ models.

Ownership Costs (Projected)

Cost Area	5 Year Cost	Rating
Depreciation	$9,127	◯
Financing ($337/month)	$3,958	
Insurance	$7,837	◯
State Fees	$830	
Fuel (Hwy 27 City 20)	$3,156	◯
Maintenance	$3,409	◯
Repairs	$636	◯

Warranty/Maintenance Info

Major Tune-Up (60K mile int.)	$301	●
Minor Tune-Up (30K mile int.)	$121	◯
Brake Service	$278	●
Overall Warranty	3 yr/36k	◯
Drivetrain Warranty	5 yr/60k	◯
Rust Warranty	7 yr/100k	◯
Maintenance Warranty	N/A	
Roadside Assistance	3 yr/36k	

Ownership Costs By Year (Projected)

Scale: $2,000 – $10,000

Legend: 1999, 2000, 2001, 2002, 2003

Resale Value

1999	2000	2001	2002	2003
$18,175	$16,268	$14,618	$12,905	$11,224

Cumulative Costs

	1999	2000	2001	2002	2003
Annual	$5,866	$5,393	$5,329	$6,120	$6,245
Total	$5,866	$11,259	$16,588	$22,708	$28,953

Projected Costs (5yr)

Relative	This Car
$29,447	$28,953
Cost/Mile 42¢	Cost/Mile 41¢

Ownership Cost Value

◯ Better Than Average

126

* Includes shaded options
** Other purchase requirements apply
*** Price includes other options

Legend:
- ● Poor
- ◉ Worse Than Average
- ◯ Average
- ◯ Better Than Average
- ◯ Excellent
- ⊖ Insufficient Information

Refer to *Section 3: Annotated Vehicle Charts* for an explanation of these charts.

Mitsubishi Galant LS
4 Door Sedan

Midsize

3.0L 195 hp Gas Fuel Inject.	6 Cylinder "V"	Automatic 4 Speed	2 Wheel Front	Dual Front/Side Airbags Std

ES Model Shown

Purchase Price

Car Item	Dealer Cost	List
Base Price	**$21,583**	**$24,250**
Anti-Lock Brakes	Std	Std
Manual Transmission	N/A	N/A
Optional Engine	N/A	N/A
Air Conditioning	Std	Std
Power Steering	Std	Std
Cruise Control	Std	Std
Power Windows	Std	Std
AM/FM Stereo Cassette	Std	Std
Steering Wheel, Tilt	Std	Std
Rear Defroster	Std	Std
*Options Price	$0	$0
*Total Price	**$21,583**	**$24,250**
Target Price	$22,732	
Destination Charge	$435	
Avg. Tax & Fees	$1,303	
Total Target $	**$24,470**	
Average Dealer Option Cost:	69%	
12 Month Price Increase:	None	

Ownership Costs (Projected)

Cost Area	5 Year Cost	Rating
Depreciation	$12,843	●
Financing ($406/month)	$4,760	
Insurance	$8,313	◐
State Fees	$1,000	
Fuel (Hwy 27 City 20)	$3,156	◐
Maintenance	$3,469	◐
Repairs	$636	◐

Warranty/Maintenance Info

Major Tune-Up (60K mile int.)	$301	◉
Minor Tune-Up (30K mile int.)	$121	◐
Brake Service	$278	●
Overall Warranty	3 yr/36k	◐
Drivetrain Warranty	5 yr/60k	○
Rust Warranty	7 yr/100k	○
Maintenance Warranty	N/A	
Roadside Assistance	3 yr/36k	

Ownership Costs By Year (Projected)

$2,000 $4,000 $6,000 $8,000 $10,000 $12,000 $14,000

- 1999
- 2000
- 2001
- 2002
- 2003

Resale Value

1999	2000	2001	2002	2003
$19,495	$17,373	$15,497	$13,551	$11,627

Projected Costs (5yr)

Relative $33,613	This Car $34,177
Cost/Mile 48¢	Cost/Mile 49¢

Cumulative Costs

	1999	2000	2001	2002	2003
Annual	$9,071	$5,960	$5,850	$6,645	$6,651
Total	$9,071	$15,031	$20,881	$27,526	$34,177

Ownership Cost Value

○ Average

The Galant LS sedan is the luxury version of the Galant. The LS sedan is upgraded from the ES sedan with standard features such as an eight-way power driver's seat, body side cladding, leather seating, chrome grille and 16 inch alloy wheels. A new 3.0L V6 engine with added horsepower and torque is standard on the LS, along with the new four-speed automatic transmission. Also standard are power four wheel disc brakes with ABS. An upgraded sound system with a separate amplifier is also standard.

Mitsubishi Galant GTZ
4 Door Sedan

Midsize

3.0L 195 hp Gas Fuel Inject.	6 Cylinder "V"	Automatic 4 Speed	2 Wheel Front	Dual Front/Side Airbags Std

Purchase Price

Car Item	Dealer Cost	List
Base Price	**$21,672**	**$24,350**
Anti-Lock Brakes	Std	Std
Manual Transmission	N/A	N/A
Optional Engine	N/A	N/A
Air Conditioning	Std	Std
Power Steering	Std	Std
Cruise Control	Std	Std
Power Windows	Std	Std
AM/FM Stereo Cassette	Std	Std
Steering Wheel, Tilt	Std	Std
Rear Defroster	Std	Std
*Options Price	$0	$0
*Total Price	**$21,672**	**$24,350**
Target Price	$22,828	
Destination Charge	$435	
Avg. Tax & Fees	$1,308	
Total Target $	**$24,571**	
Average Dealer Option Cost:	69%	
12 Month Price Increase:	N/A	

Ownership Costs (Projected)

Cost Area	5 Year Cost	Rating
Depreciation	$12,698	●
Financing ($407/month)	$4,780	
Insurance	$7,688	◐
State Fees	$1,004	
Fuel (Hwy 27 City 20)	$3,156	◐
Maintenance	$3,469	◐
Repairs	$636	◐

Warranty/Maintenance Info

Major Tune-Up (60K mile int.)	$301	◉
Minor Tune-Up (30K mile int.)	$121	◐
Brake Service	$278	●
Overall Warranty	3 yr/36k	◐
Drivetrain Warranty	5 yr/60k	○
Rust Warranty	7 yr/100k	○
Maintenance Warranty	N/A	
Roadside Assistance	3 yr/36k	

Ownership Costs By Year (Projected)

$2,000 $4,000 $6,000 $8,000 $10,000 $12,000 $14,000

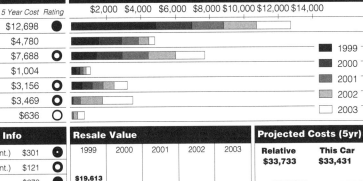

- 1999
- 2000
- 2001
- 2002
- 2003

Resale Value

1999	2000	2001	2002	2003
$19,613	$17,522	$15,678	$13,765	$11,873

Projected Costs (5yr)

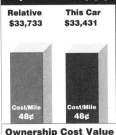

Relative $33,733	This Car $33,431
Cost/Mile 48¢	Cost/Mile 48¢

Cumulative Costs

	1999	2000	2001	2002	2003
Annual	$8,943	$5,814	$5,698	$6,486	$6,490
Total	$8,943	$14,757	$20,455	$26,941	$33,431

Ownership Cost Value

○ Average

The new Galant GTZ sports sedan is being introduced this year. The GTZ sedan includes similar standard features as those found on the LS. Upgrades on the GTZ include features such as a rear spoiler, color-keyed grille, white-faced instruments and a sport-tuned suspension. Mitsubishi's 3.0L V6 engine with added horsepower and torque is standard. Safety features making their debut this year on the Galant are driver and passenger side-impact airbags, also standard on the GTZ.

 ● Poor   ◉ Worse Than Average   ○ Average   ○ Better Than Average   ○ Excellent   ⊖ Insufficient Information

127

Refer to *Section 3: Annotated Vehicle Charts* for an explanation of these charts.

Mitsubishi Mirage DE
2 Door Coupe

Subcompact

1.5L 92 hp Gas Fuel Inject.	4 Cylinder In-Line	Manual 5 Speed
2 Wheel Front	Dual Airbags Std	

LS Model Shown

Purchase Price

Car Item	Dealer Cost	List
Base Price	**$10,252**	**$11,150**
Anti-Lock Brakes	N/A	N/A
Automatic 4 Speed	$701	$760
Optional Engine	N/A	N/A
Air Conditioning	$720	$880
Power Steering	Std	Std
Cruise Control	N/A	N/A
Power Windows	N/A	N/A
AM/FM Stereo Cassette	$247	$352
Steering Wheel, Tilt	Pkg	Pkg
Rear Defroster	Std	Std
***Options Price**	**$967**	**$1,232**
***Total Price**	**$11,219**	**$12,382**
Target Price	$11,700	
Destination Charge	$425	
Avg. Tax & Fees	$687	
Total Target $	**$12,812**	
Average Dealer Option Cost:	*81%*	
12 Month Price Increase:	*3%*	

Ownership Costs (Projected)

Cost Area	5 Year Cost	Rating
Depreciation	$6,608	◔
Financing ($212/month)	$2,494	
Insurance	$8,265	●
State Fees	$525	
Fuel (Hwy 40 City 33)	$2,027	○
Maintenance	$3,820	●
Repairs	$605	◔

Warranty/Maintenance Info

Major Tune-Up (60K mile int.)	$274	◔
Minor Tune-Up (30K mile int.)	$101	◔
Brake Service	$287	◉
Overall Warranty	3 yr/36k	◔
Drivetrain Warranty	5 yr/60k	○
Rust Warranty	7 yr/100k	○
Maintenance Warranty	N/A	
Roadside Assistance	3 yr/36k	

Ownership Costs By Year (Projected)

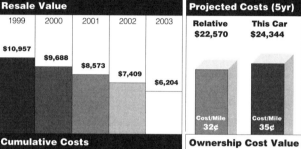

Legend: 1999, 2000, 2001, 2002, 2003

Resale Value

1999	2000	2001	2002	2003
$10,957	$9,688	$8,573	$7,409	$6,204

Cumulative Costs

	1999	2000	2001	2002	2003
Annual	$4,837	$4,143	$4,444	$5,075	$5,845
Total	$4,837	$8,980	$13,424	$18,499	$24,344

Projected Costs (5yr)

Relative	This Car
$22,570	$24,344
Cost/Mile 32¢	Cost/Mile 35¢

Ownership Cost Value

◉ Worse Than Average

For 1999, the Mirage DE coupe remains unchanged. Standard equipment includes front bucket seats, an electric rear window defroster and a day/night rearview mirror. Safety features include tinted glass, side-impact door beams and height-adjustable driver and front passenger shoulder belts. Available as an option is a Preferred Equipment Package that includes an AM/FM stereo with cassette, height-adjustable driver's seat, tilt steering wheel and a center console with armrest.

Mitsubishi Mirage LS
2 Door Coupe

Subcompact

1.8L 113 hp Gas Fuel Inject.	4 Cylinder In-Line	Manual 5 Speed
2 Wheel Front	Dual Airbags Std	

Purchase Price

Car Item	Dealer Cost	List
Base Price	**$13,255**	**$14,600**
Anti-Lock Brakes	$600	$732
Automatic 4 Speed	$690	$750
Optional Engine	N/A	N/A
Air Conditioning	Std	Std
Power Steering	Std	Std
Cruise Control	Pkg	Pkg
Power Windows	Pkg	Pkg
AM/FM Stereo CD	Std	Std
Steering Wheel, Tilt	Std	Std
Rear Defroster	Std	Std
***Options Price**	**$0**	**$0**
***Total Price**	**$13,255**	**$14,600**
Target Price	$13,855	
Destination Charge	$425	
Avg. Tax & Fees	$806	
Total Target $	**$15,086**	
Average Dealer Option Cost:	*83%*	
12 Month Price Increase:	*2%*	

Ownership Costs (Projected)

Cost Area	5 Year Cost	Rating
Depreciation	$8,971	●
Financing ($250/month)	$2,935	
Insurance	$8,757	●
State Fees	$613	
Fuel (Hwy 36 City 28)	$2,314	◔
Maintenance	$3,787	●
Repairs	$605	◔

Warranty/Maintenance Info

Major Tune-Up (60K mile int.)	$245	◔
Minor Tune-Up (30K mile int.)	$101	◔
Brake Service	$287	◉
Overall Warranty	3 yr/36k	◔
Drivetrain Warranty	5 yr/60k	○
Rust Warranty	7 yr/100k	○
Maintenance Warranty	N/A	
Roadside Assistance	3 yr/36k	

Ownership Costs By Year (Projected)

Legend: 1999, 2000, 2001, 2002, 2003

Resale Value

1999	2000	2001	2002	2003
$11,791	$10,285	$8,937	$7,545	$6,115

Cumulative Costs

	1999	2000	2001	2002	2003
Annual	$6,598	$4,674	$4,942	$5,556	$6,212
Total	$6,598	$11,272	$16,214	$21,770	$27,982

Projected Costs (5yr)

Relative	This Car
$24,715	$27,982
Cost/Mile 35¢	Cost/Mile 40¢

Ownership Cost Value

● Poor

The 1999 Mirage LS coupe includes such features as a heavy duty starter and battery, an AM/FM stereo with CD player and power-assisted steering as standard equipment. Standard exterior features on the LS include a rear spoiler, side air dams, alloy wheels and halogen headlamps. Air conditioning, sport bucket seats and a height-adjustable steering column and driver's seat are standard interior features. A power sunroof and color-keyed power mirrors are available as optional equipment.

128

* Includes shaded options
** Other purchase requirements apply
*** Price includes other options

 ● Poor
 ◉ Worse Than Average
Average
 ○ Better Than Average
Excellent
 ⊖ Insufficient Information

Refer to *Section 3: Annotated Vehicle Charts* for an explanation of these charts.

Mitsubishi Mirage DE
4 Door Sedan

Subcompact

 1.5L 92 hp Gas Fuel Inject.

 4 Cylinder In-Line

 Manual 5 Speed

 2 Wheel Front

Dual Airbags Std

Purchase Price

Car Item	Dealer Cost	List
Base Price	**$11,327**	**$12,450**
Anti-Lock Brakes	N/A	N/A
Automatic 4 Speed	$630	$690
Optional Engine	N/A	N/A
Air Conditioning	Pkg	Pkg
Power Steering	Std	Std
Cruise Control	N/A	N/A
Power Windows	N/A	N/A
AM/FM Stereo Cassette	Pkg	Pkg
Steering Wheel, Tilt	Pkg	Pkg
Rear Defroster	Std	Std
*Options Price	**$0**	**$0**
*Total Price	**$11,327**	**$12,450**
Target Price	$11,816	
Destination Charge	$425	
Avg. Tax & Fees	$693	
Total Target $	**$12,934**	
Average Dealer Option Cost:	83%	
12 Month Price Increase:	1%	

The 1999 Mirage DE sedan includes standard interior features such as a rear window defroster, dual slide-out cup holders, remote releases for the fuel door and trunklid and a full-length center console with storage. Available as an option is a Comfort and Convenience Package that includes a tilt steering wheel, a split folding rear seat, a driver's seat height control, air conditioning and intermittent wipers. Other options available on the DE sedan include mudguards and a cargo net.

Ownership Costs (Projected)

Cost Area	5 Year Cost	Rating
Depreciation	$6,938	◐
Financing ($214/month)	$2,516	
Insurance	$8,045	●
State Fees	$528	
Fuel (Hwy 40 City 33)	$2,027	○
Maintenance	$3,820	●
Repairs	$605	◐

Warranty/Maintenance Info

Major Tune-Up (60K mile int.)	$274	◐
Minor Tune-Up (30K mile int.)	$101	◐
Brake Service	$287	◉
Overall Warranty	3 yr/36k	◐
Drivetrain Warranty	5 yr/60k	○
Rust Warranty	7 yr/100k	○
Maintenance Warranty	N/A	
Roadside Assistance	3 yr/36k	

Ownership Costs By Year (Projected)

$2,000 $4,000 $6,000 $8,000 $10,000

■ 1999
■ 2000
■ 2001
▨ 2002
□ 2003

Resale Value

1999	2000	2001	2002	2003
$10,797	$9,519	$8,393	$7,215	$5,996

Cumulative Costs

	1999	2000	2001	2002	2003
Annual	$5,086	$4,116	$4,416	$5,047	$5,814
Total	$5,086	$9,202	$13,618	$18,665	$24,479

Projected Costs (5yr)

Relative $22,683	This Car $24,479
Cost/Mile 32¢	Cost/Mile 35¢

Ownership Cost Value

◉ Worse Than Average

Mitsubishi Mirage LS
4 Door Sedan

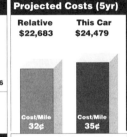

Subcompact

DE Model Shown

1.8L 113 hp Gas Fuel Inject.

 4 Cylinder In-Line

 Manual 5 Speed

 2 Wheel Front

Dual Airbags Std

Purchase Price

Car Item	Dealer Cost	List
Base Price	**$12,192**	**$13,400**
Anti-Lock Brakes	$600	$732
Automatic 4 Speed	$629	$690
Optional Engine	N/A	N/A
Air Conditioning	Pkg	Pkg
Power Steering	Std	Std
Cruise Control	Pkg	Pkg
Power Windows	Pkg	Pkg
AM/FM Stereo Cassette	Pkg	Pkg
Steering Wheel, Tilt	Std	Std
Rear Defroster	Std	Std
*Options Price	**$0**	**$0**
*Total Price	**$12,192**	**$13,400**
Target Price	$12,728	
Destination Charge	$425	
Avg. Tax & Fees	$743	
Total Target $	**$13,896**	
Average Dealer Option Cost:	85%	
12 Month Price Increase:	1%	

The 1999 Mirage LS sedan is available with an LS Value Package that includes cruise control, power windows and door locks, color-keyed mirrors, air conditioning and variable intermittent wipers. Standard safety features include child safety locks for the rear doors and height-adjustable driver and front passenger shoulder belts. Available as an option is a Premium Package that includes a power sunroof and 14 inch alloy wheels. Other options include mudguards, wheel locks and a CD player.

Ownership Costs (Projected)

Cost Area	5 Year Cost	Rating
Depreciation	$7,709	◉
Financing ($230/month)	$2,703	
Insurance	$8,500	●
State Fees	$566	
Fuel (Hwy 36 City 28)	$2,314	○
Maintenance	$3,765	●
Repairs	$605	○

Warranty/Maintenance Info

Major Tune-Up (60K mile int.)	$245	○
Minor Tune-Up (30K mile int.)	$101	○
Brake Service	$287	◉
Overall Warranty	3 yr/36k	○
Drivetrain Warranty	5 yr/60k	○
Rust Warranty	7 yr/100k	○
Maintenance Warranty	N/A	
Roadside Assistance	3 yr/36k	

Ownership Costs By Year (Projected)

$2,000 $4,000 $6,000 $8,000 $10,000

■ 1999
■ 2000
■ 2001
▨ 2002
□ 2003

Resale Value

1999	2000	2001	2002	2003
$10,764	$9,541	$8,471	$7,349	$6,187

Cumulative Costs

	1999	2000	2001	2002	2003
Annual	$6,295	$4,266	$4,556	$5,173	$5,872
Total	$6,295	$10,561	$15,117	$20,290	$26,162

Projected Costs (5yr)

Relative $23,588	This Car $26,162
Cost/Mile 34¢	Cost/Mile 37¢

Ownership Cost Value

● Poor

● Poor   ◉ Worse Than Average   ◐ Average   ○ Better Than Average   ○ Excellent   ⊖ Insufficient Information

Refer to *Section 3: Annotated Vehicle Charts* for an explanation of these charts.

Nissan Altima XE
4 Door Sedan

| 2.4L 150 hp Gas Fuel Inject. | 4 Cylinder In-Line | Manual 5 Speed | 2 Wheel Front | Dual Airbags Std |

SE Model Shown

Purchase Price

Car Item	Dealer Cost	List
Base Price	**$14,402**	**$14,990**
Anti-Lock Brakes	$454	**$499
Automatic 4 Speed	$769	$800
Optional Engine	N/A	N/A
Air Conditioning	Pkg	Pkg
Power Steering	Std	Std
Cruise Control	Pkg	Pkg
Power Windows	Std	Std
AM/FM Stereo Cassette	Pkg	Pkg
Steering Wheel, Tilt	Std	Std
Rear Defroster	Std	Std
*Options Price	$769	$800
*Total Price	$15,171	$15,790
Target Price	$15,419	
Destination Charge	$490	
Avg. Tax & Fees	$892	
Total Target $	**$16,801**	
Average Dealer Option Cost:	87%	
12 Month Price Increase:	None	

The XE is a carryover of last year's completely redesigned Altima. Sound and speaker quality have been improved for the 1999 model year. An XE Option Package is available that includes air conditioning, an AM/FM/cassette stereo and cruise control. Power windows, a tilt steering column and intermittent wipers are standard on the XE. Standard safety features include second generation depowered dual front airbags, rear child safety locks and side-impact door beams.

Ownership Costs (Projected)

Cost Area	5 Year Cost	Rating
Depreciation	$8,225	◐
Financing ($278/month)	$3,269	
Insurance	$8,265	◉
State Fees	$665	
Fuel (Hwy 30 City 22)	$2,855	◐
Maintenance	$2,413	○
Repairs	$470	○

Warranty/Maintenance Info

Major Tune-Up (60K mile int.)	$232	◐
Minor Tune-Up (30K mile int.)	$100	◐
Brake Service	$232	◐
Overall Warranty	3 yr/36k	◐
Drivetrain Warranty	5 yr/60k	○
Rust Warranty	5 yr/60k	◐
Maintenance Warranty	N/A	
Roadside Assistance	N/A	

Ownership Costs By Year (Projected)

Legend: 1999, 2000, 2001, 2002, 2003

Resale Value

1999	2000	2001	2002	2003
$14,230	$12,713	$11,367	$9,985	$8,576

Cumulative Costs

	1999	2000	2001	2002	2003
Annual	$6,008	$4,797	$4,707	$4,957	$5,693
Total	$6,008	$10,805	$15,512	$20,469	$26,162

Projected Costs (5yr)

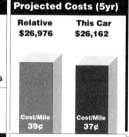

Relative	This Car
$26,976	$26,162
Cost/Mile 39¢	Cost/Mile 37¢

Ownership Cost Value

○ Better Than Average

Nissan Altima GXE
4 Door Sedan

Compact

| 2.4L 150 hp Gas Fuel Inject. | 4 Cylinder In-Line | Manual 5 Speed | 2 Wheel Front | Dual Airbags Std |

Purchase Price

Car Item	Dealer Cost	List
Base Price	**$15,798**	**$17,190**
Anti-Lock Brakes	$454	$499
Automatic 4 Speed	$734	$800
Optional Engine	N/A	N/A
Air Conditioning	Std	Std
Power Steering	Std	Std
Cruise Control	Std	Std
Power Windows	Std	Std
AM/FM Stereo CD	Std	Std
Steering Wheel, Tilt	Std	Std
Rear Defroster	Std	Std
*Options Price	$734	$800
*Total Price	$16,532	$17,990
Target Price	$17,117	
Destination Charge	$490	
Avg. Tax & Fees	$990	
Total Target $	**$18,597**	
Average Dealer Option Cost:	84%	
12 Month Price Increase:	None	

The Altima GXE features upgraded seat cloth and door trim as well as wood-tone interior trim. The GXE model adds a standard AM/FM/CD stereo, 60/40 split fold-down rear seat and power door locks. Also standard are air conditioning, cruise control, variable intermittent wipers and an illuminated entry/exit system. An optional GXE Security and Convenience Package is available that includes AM/FM/cassette/CD stereo, remote keyless entry, a vehicle security system and power diversity antenna.

Ownership Costs (Projected)

Cost Area	5 Year Cost	Rating
Depreciation	$9,488	◉
Financing ($308/month)	$3,619	
Insurance	$8,265	◉
State Fees	$752	
Fuel (Hwy 30 City 22)	$2,855	◐
Maintenance	$2,413	○
Repairs	$470	○

Warranty/Maintenance Info

Major Tune-Up (60K mile int.)	$232	◐
Minor Tune-Up (30K mile int.)	$100	◐
Brake Service	$232	◐
Overall Warranty	3 yr/36k	◐
Drivetrain Warranty	5 yr/60k	○
Rust Warranty	5 yr/60k	◐
Maintenance Warranty	N/A	
Roadside Assistance	N/A	

Ownership Costs By Year (Projected)

Legend: 1999, 2000, 2001, 2002, 2003

Resale Value

1999	2000	2001	2002	2003
$15,801	$14,012	$12,401	$10,764	$9,109

Cumulative Costs

	1999	2000	2001	2002	2003
Annual	$6,374	$5,184	$5,062	$5,273	$5,969
Total	$6,374	$11,558	$16,620	$21,893	$27,862

Projected Costs (5yr)

Relative	This Car
$28,304	$27,862
Cost/Mile 40¢	Cost/Mile 40¢

Ownership Cost Value

○ Better Than Average

130

● Poor   ◉ Worse Than Average   ◐ Average   ○ Better Than Average   ○ Excellent   ⊖ Insufficient Information

Refer to *Section 3: Annotated Vehicle Charts* for an explanation of these charts.

Nissan Altima SE
4 Door Sedan

 2.4L 150 hp Gas Fuel Inject.
 4 Cylinder In-Line
 Manual 5 Speed
 2 Wheel Front
 Dual Airbags Std

Purchase Price

Car Item	Dealer Cost	List
Base Price	$16,798	$18,490
Anti-Lock Brakes	$454	$499
Automatic 4 Speed	$728	$800
Optional Engine	N/A	N/A
Air Conditioning	Std	Std
Power Steering	Std	Std
Cruise Control	Std	Std
Power Windows	Std	Std
AM/FM Stereo Cass/CD	Std	Std
Steering Wheel, Tilt	Std	Std
Rear Defroster	Std	Std
*Options Price	$728	$800
*Total Price	$17,526	$19,290
Target Price	$18,186	
Destination Charge	$490	
Avg. Tax & Fees	$1,051	
Total Target $	$19,727	
Average Dealer Option Cost:	87%	
12 Month Price Increase:	None	

The SE is the sporty version of the Altima and comes standard with a sport-tuned suspension and rear spoiler, and is the only Altima with white-faced gauges. The SE is also the only version that comes standard with four wheel disc brakes, fog lamps and P205/60R15 tires. Additional standard equipment includes remote keyless entry, a vehicle security system and leather-wrapped steering wheel and shift knob (manual transmission models only). A four speed automatic transmission is optional.

Ownership Costs (Projected)

Cost Area	5 Year Cost	Rating
Depreciation	$9,866	●
Financing ($327/month)	$3,837	
Insurance	$8,093	●
State Fees	$804	
Fuel (Hwy 30 City 22)	$2,855	◐
Maintenance	$2,332	○
Repairs	$470	○

Warranty/Maintenance Info

Major Tune-Up (60K mile int.)	$232	◐
Minor Tune-Up (30K mile int.)	$100	◐
Brake Service	$192	◐
Overall Warranty	3 yr/36k	◐
Drivetrain Warranty	5 yr/60k	○
Rust Warranty	5 yr/60k	◐
Maintenance Warranty	N/A	
Roadside Assistance	N/A	

Ownership Costs By Year (Projected)

$2,000 $4,000 $6,000 $8,000 $10,000

■ 1999
■ 2000
■ 2001
■ 2002
□ 2003

Resale Value

1999	2000	2001	2002	2003
$16,966	$15,063	$13,345	$11,608	$9,861

Cumulative Costs

	1999	2000	2001	2002	2003
Annual	$6,393	$5,337	$5,190	$5,294	$6,043
Total	$6,393	$11,730	$16,920	$22,214	$28,257

Projected Costs (5yr)

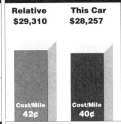

Relative	This Car
$29,310	$28,257
Cost/Mile 42¢	Cost/Mile 40¢

Ownership Cost Value

○ Excellent

Nissan Altima GLE
4 Door Sedan

Compact

 2.4L 150 hp Gas Fuel Inject.
 4 Cylinder In-Line
 Automatic 4 Speed
 2 Wheel Front
Dual Airbags Std

GXE Model Shown

Purchase Price

Car Item	Dealer Cost	List
Base Price	$18,161	$19,990
Anti-Lock Brakes	$454	$499
Manual Transmission	N/A	N/A
Optional Engine	N/A	N/A
Air Conditioning	Std	Std
Power Steering	Std	Std
Cruise Control	Std	Std
Power Windows	Std	Std
AM/FM Stereo Cass/CD	Std	Std
Steering Wheel, Tilt	Std	Std
Rear Defroster	Std	Std
*Options Price	$0	$0
*Total Price	$18,161	$19,990
Target Price	$18,862	
Destination Charge	$490	
Avg. Tax & Fees	$1,089	
Total Target $	$20,441	
Average Dealer Option Cost:	83%	
12 Month Price Increase:	1%	

The GLE is the top of the line Altima and includes a standard leather interior, four speed automatic transmission and 15 inch aluminum alloy wheels. The alloy wheels are an addition to the standard equipment list for 1999. Additional standard equipment includes a remote keyless entry, a vehicle security system and leather-wrapped steering wheel. An eight-way power driver's seat with lumbar support adjustment is also standard. Blue Dusk and Titanium Frost are two new available exterior colors.

Ownership Costs (Projected)

Cost Area	5 Year Cost	Rating
Depreciation	$10,596	●
Financing ($339/month)	$3,976	
Insurance	$8,093	●
State Fees	$832	
Fuel (Hwy 30 City 22)	$2,855	◐
Maintenance	$2,781	◐
Repairs	$470	○

Warranty/Maintenance Info

Major Tune-Up (60K mile int.)	$232	◐
Minor Tune-Up (30K mile int.)	$100	◐
Brake Service	$232	◐
Overall Warranty	3 yr/36k	◐
Drivetrain Warranty	5 yr/60k	○
Rust Warranty	5 yr/60k	◐
Maintenance Warranty	N/A	
Roadside Assistance	N/A	

Ownership Costs By Year (Projected)

$2,000 $4,000 $6,000 $8,000 $10,000 $12,000

■ 1999
■ 2000
■ 2001
■ 2002
□ 2003

Resale Value

1999	2000	2001	2002	2003
$17,123	$15,174	$13,414	$11,635	$9,845

Cumulative Costs

	1999	2000	2001	2002	2003
Annual	$7,004	$5,427	$5,447	$5,440	$6,285
Total	$7,004	$12,431	$17,878	$23,318	$29,603

Projected Costs (5yr)

Relative	This Car
$29,968	$29,603
Cost/Mile 43¢	Cost/Mile 42¢

Ownership Cost Value

◐ Better Than Average

Nissan Maxima GXE
4 Door Sedan

| 3.0L 190 hp Gas Fuel Inject. | 6 Cylinder "V" | Manual 5 Speed | 2 Wheel Front | Dual Airbags Std |

Midsize

Purchase Price

Car Item	Dealer Cost	List
Base Price	**$19,658**	**$21,499**
Anti-Lock Brakes	$454	$499
Automatic 4 Speed	$1,357	$1,750
Optional Engine	N/A	N/A
Air Conditioning	Std	Std
Power Steering	Std	Std
Cruise Control	Std	Std
Power Windows	Std	Std
AM/FM Stereo Cassette	Std	Std
Steering Wheel, Tilt	Std	Std
Rear Defroster	Std	Std
*Options Price	$1,811	$2,249
*Total Price	**$21,469**	**$23,748**
Target Price	$22,088	
Destination Charge	$490	
Avg. Tax & Fees	$1,271	
Total Target $	**$23,849**	
Average Dealer Option Cost:	77%	
12 Month Price Increase:	None	

Ownership Costs (Projected)

Cost Area	5 Year Cost	Rating
Depreciation	$11,402	◐
Financing ($395/month)	$4,639	
Insurance	$8,757	◉
State Fees	$982	
Fuel (Hwy 28 City 21)	$3,026	○
Maintenance	$2,704	○
Repairs	$621	○

Warranty/Maintenance Info

Major Tune-Up (60K mile int.)	$144	○
Minor Tune-Up (30K mile int.)	$105	○
Brake Service	$192	○
Overall Warranty	3 yr/36k	◐
Drivetrain Warranty	5 yr/60k	○
Rust Warranty	5 yr/60k	◐
Maintenance Warranty	N/A	
Roadside Assistance	N/A	

Ownership Costs By Year (Projected)

$2,000 $4,000 $6,000 $8,000 $10,000 $12,000

- Depreciation
- Financing
- Insurance
- State Fees
- Fuel
- Maintenance
- Repairs

■ 1999
■ 2000
■ 2001
□ 2002
□ 2003

Resale Value

1999	2000	2001	2002	2003
$21,492	$19,013	$16,823	$14,602	$12,447

Projected Costs (5yr)

Relative	This Car
$33,461	$32,131
Cost/Mile 48¢	Cost/Mile 46¢

Cumulative Costs

	1999	2000	2001	2002	2003
Annual	$6,466	$6,339	$6,059	$6,241	$7,026
Total	$6,466	$12,805	$18,864	$25,105	$32,131

Ownership Cost Value

○ Excellent

The 1999 Maxima GXE includes standard features such as cruise control, a tilt steering column and power windows, door locks and side mirrors. Optional equipment on the GXE includes antilock brakes, a premium AM/FM stereo with cassette and CD, an automatic transmission and a power sunroof. The Security and Convenience Package features luxury amenities such as an eight-way power driver's seat, a power trunk release, a remote keyless entry system and variable intermittent windshield wipers.

Nissan Maxima SE
4 Door Sedan

| 3.0L 190 hp Gas Fuel Inject. | 6 Cylinder "V" | Manual 5 Speed | 2 Wheel Front | Dual Airbags Std |

Midsize

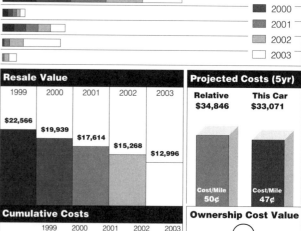

Purchase Price

Car Item	Dealer Cost	List
Base Price	**$21,118**	**$23,499**
Anti-Lock Brakes	$454	$499
Automatic 4 Speed	$899	$1,000
Optional Engine	N/A	N/A
Air Conditioning	Std	Std
Power Steering	Std	Std
Cruise Control	Std	Std
Power Windows	Std	Std
AM/FM Stereo Cassette	Std	Std
Steering Wheel, Tilt	Std	Std
Rear Defroster	Std	Std
*Options Price	$1,353	$1,499
*Total Price	**$22,471**	**$24,998**
Target Price	$23,148	
Destination Charge	$490	
Avg. Tax & Fees	$1,332	
Total Target $	**$24,970**	
Average Dealer Option Cost:	87%	
12 Month Price Increase:	None	

Ownership Costs (Projected)

Cost Area	5 Year Cost	Rating
Depreciation	$11,974	○
Financing ($414/month)	$4,858	
Insurance	$8,757	◉
State Fees	$1,032	
Fuel (Hwy 28 City 21)	$3,026	○
Maintenance	$2,803	○
Repairs	$621	○

Warranty/Maintenance Info

Major Tune-Up (60K mile int.)	$144	○
Minor Tune-Up (30K mile int.)	$105	○
Brake Service	$192	○
Overall Warranty	3 yr/36k	◐
Drivetrain Warranty	5 yr/60k	○
Rust Warranty	5 yr/60k	◐
Maintenance Warranty	N/A	
Roadside Assistance	N/A	

Ownership Costs By Year (Projected)

$2,000 $4,000 $6,000 $8,000 $10,000 $12,000

■ 1999
■ 2000
■ 2001
□ 2002
□ 2003

Resale Value

1999	2000	2001	2002	2003
$22,566	$19,939	$17,614	$15,268	$12,996

Projected Costs (5yr)

Relative	This Car
$34,846	$33,071
Cost/Mile 50¢	Cost/Mile 47¢

Cumulative Costs

	1999	2000	2001	2002	2003
Annual	$6,600	$6,558	$6,249	$6,502	$7,162
Total	$6,600	$13,158	$19,407	$25,909	$33,071

Ownership Cost Value

○ Excellent

The 1999 Maxima SE sports standard features that include a rear spoiler, sport-tuned suspension, 16 inch aluminum alloy wheels and front fog lamps. The SE interior features black-on-white analog gauges, a leather-wrapped steering wheel and leather-wrapped shift knob. Optional equipment includes an AM/FM/CD Bose stereo system and antilock brakes. Optional packages include the Security and Convenience Package, the Deluxe Seating Package and Leather Trim Package.

132

* Includes shaded options

** Other purchase requirements apply

*** Price includes other options

 ● Poor   Worse Than Average   Average   Better Than Average   ○ Excellent   ⊖ Insufficient Information

Refer to *Section 3: Annotated Vehicle Charts* for an explanation of these charts.

Nissan Maxima GLE
4 Door Sedan

Midsize

 3.0L 190 hp Gas Fuel Inject.
 6 Cylinder "V"
 Automatic 4 Speed
 2 Wheel Front
 Dual Airbags Std

Purchase Price

Car Item	Dealer Cost	List
Base Price	$24,174	$26,899
Anti-Lock Brakes	$454	$499
Manual Transmission	N/A	N/A
Optional Engine	N/A	N/A
Air Conditioning	Std	Std
Power Steering	Std	Std
Cruise Control	Std	Std
Power Windows	Std	Std
AM/FM Stereo Cassette	Std	Std
Steering Wheel, Tilt	Std	Std
Rear Defroster	Std	Std
*Options Price	$454	$499
*Total Price	$24,628	$27,398
Target Price	$25,408	
Destination Charge	$490	
Avg. Tax & Fees	$1,457	
Total Target $	$27,355	
Average Dealer Option Cost:	85%	
12 Month Price Increase:	None	

Ownership Costs (Projected)

Cost Area	5 Year Cost	Rating
Depreciation	$14,125	◉
Financing ($453/month)	$5,322	
Insurance	$8,556	◉
State Fees	$1,128	
Fuel (Hwy 28 City 21)	$3,026	○
Maintenance	$3,019	○
Repairs	$621	○

Ownership Costs By Year (Projected)

$5,000 $10,000 $15,000

1999 / 2000 / 2001 / 2002 / 2003

Warranty/Maintenance Info

Major Tune-Up (60K mile int.)	$144	○
Minor Tune-Up (30K mile int.)	$105	○
Brake Service	$192	○
Overall Warranty	3 yr/36k	◉
Drivetrain Warranty	5 yr/60k	○
Rust Warranty	5 yr/60k	◉
Maintenance Warranty	N/A	
Roadside Assistance	N/A	

Resale Value

1999	2000	2001	2002	2003
$23,051	$20,361	$17,975	$15,566	$13,230

Projected Costs (5yr)

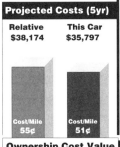

Relative	This Car
$38,174	$35,797
Cost/Mile 55¢	Cost/Mile 51¢

Cumulative Costs

	1999	2000	2001	2002	2003
Annual	$8,643	$6,732	$6,539	$6,502	$7,381
Total	$8,643	$15,375	$21,914	$28,416	$35,797

Ownership Cost Value

Excellent

The 1999 Maxima GLE is equipped with an optional Deluxe Seating Package that includes front side-impact airbags, heated front seats, heated outside mirrors, washer fluid warning light and a heavy duty battery. Standard interior convenience features on the GLE include simulated woodgrain trim, leather seating surfaces, an eight-way power driver's seat and automatic climate control. A power sunroof, antilock braking system and traction control are the only additional optional features.

Nissan Sentra XE
4 Door Sedan

Subcompact

 1.6L 115 hp Gas Fuel Inject.
 4 Cylinder In-Line
 Manual 5 Speed
 2 Wheel Front
 Dual Airbags Std

SE Model Shown

Purchase Price

Car Item	Dealer Cost	List
Base Price	$11,097	$11,799
Anti-Lock Brakes	N/A	N/A
Automatic 4 Speed	$725	$800
Optional Engine	N/A	N/A
Air Conditioning	Dlr	Dlr
Power Steering	Std	Std
Cruise Control	N/A	N/A
Power Windows	N/A	N/A
AM/FM Stereo Cassette	Dlr	Dlr
Steering Wheel, Tilt	Std	Std
Rear Defroster	Std	Std
*Options Price	$0	$0
*Total Price	$11,097	$11,799
Target Price	$11,419	
Destination Charge	$490	
Avg. Tax & Fees	$672	
Total Target $	$12,581	
Average Dealer Option Cost:	83%	
12 Month Price Increase:	None	

Ownership Costs (Projected)

Cost Area	5 Year Cost	Rating
Depreciation	$6,503	○
Financing ($209/month)	$2,448	
Insurance	$7,837	●
State Fees	$505	
Fuel (Hwy 39 City 29)	$2,181	○
Maintenance	$2,129	○
Repairs	$490	○

Ownership Costs By Year (Projected)

$2,000 $4,000 $6,000 $8,000

1999 / 2000 / 2001 / 2002 / 2003

Warranty/Maintenance Info

Major Tune-Up (60K mile int.)	$227	○
Minor Tune-Up (30K mile int.)	$100	○
Brake Service	$227	○
Overall Warranty	3 yr/36k	○
Drivetrain Warranty	5 yr/60k	○
Rust Warranty	5 yr/60k	○
Maintenance Warranty	N/A	
Roadside Assistance	N/A	

Resale Value

1999	2000	2001	2002	2003
$10,807	$9,538	$8,429	$7,271	$6,078

Projected Costs (5yr)

Relative	This Car
$22,443	$22,093
Cost/Mile 32¢	Cost/Mile 32¢

Cumulative Costs

	1999	2000	2001	2002	2003
Annual	$4,683	$4,070	$4,051	$4,303	$4,986
Total	$4,683	$8,753	$12,804	$17,107	$22,093

Ownership Cost Value

Average

For 1999, the Sentra XE receives a minor facelift that includes new headlamp treatment, a new grille and a new front fascia. The XE includes a rear stabilizer bar, full wheel covers, two speed intermittent wipers, body-colored bumpers and remote trunk and fuel filler door releases. Available options include an automatic transmission and the XE Option Package with AM/FM cassette, air conditioning, rear spoiler and floor mats. Standard safety features include dual airbags and side-impact beams.

---

* Includes shaded options

** Other purchase requirements apply

*** Price includes other options

 Poor   Worse Than Average   Average   Better Than Average   Excellent   Insufficient Information

133

Refer to *Section 3: Annotated Vehicle Charts* for an explanation of these charts.

Nissan Sentra GXE
4 Door Sedan

Subcompact

 1.6L 115 hp Gas Fuel Inject.
 4 Cylinder In-Line
 Manual 5 Speed
 2 Wheel Front
 Dual Airbags Std

Purchase Price

Car Item	Dealer Cost	List
Base Price	**$12,880**	**$14,199**
Anti-Lock Brakes	$454	$499
Automatic 4 Speed	$725	$800
Optional Engine	N/A	N/A
Air Conditioning	Std	Std
Power Steering	Std	Std
Cruise Control	Std	Std
Power Windows	Std	Std
AM/FM Stereo Cassette	Std	Std
Steering Wheel, Tilt	Std	Std
Rear Defroster	Std	Std
*Options Price	$0	$0
*Total Price	**$12,880**	**$14,199**
Target Price	$13,332	
Destination Charge	$490	
Avg. Tax & Fees	$782	
Total Target $	**$14,604**	
Average Dealer Option Cost:	79%	
12 Month Price Increase:	None	

Ownership Costs (Projected)

Cost Area	5 Year Cost	Rating
Depreciation	$7,761	◉
Financing ($242/month)	$2,842	
Insurance	$7,837	●
State Fees	$601	
Fuel (Hwy 39 City 29)	$2,181	○
Maintenance	$2,129	○
Repairs	$490	○

Warranty/Maintenance Info

Major Tune-Up (60K mile int.)	$227	○
Minor Tune-Up (30K mile int.)	$100	○
Brake Service	$227	○
Overall Warranty	3 yr/36k	○
Drivetrain Warranty	5 yr/60k	○
Rust Warranty	5 yr/60k	○
Maintenance Warranty	N/A	
Roadside Assistance	N/A	

Ownership Costs By Year (Projected)

Legend: 1999, 2000, 2001, 2002, 2003

Resale Value

1999	2000	2001	2002	2003
$12,208	$10,776	$9,505	$8,191	$6,843

Projected Costs (5yr)

Relative	This Car
$24,316	$23,841
Cost/Mile 35¢	Cost/Mile 34¢

Cumulative Costs

	1999	2000	2001	2002	2003
Annual	$5,462	$4,363	$4,315	$4,527	$5,174
Total	$5,462	$9,825	$14,140	$18,667	$23,841

Ownership Cost Value

○ Better Than Average

For 1999, the Sentra GXE receives a minor facelift that includes new headlamp treatment, a new grille and a new front fascia. The new Limited Edition option package includes an AM/FM radio with CD, a remote keyless entry system, alloy wheels, sport seats, tachometer, front stabilizer bar and body-colored mirrors and moldings. GXE standard features include dual power outside mirrors, power windows and locks. Additional convenience features include cruise control and a split folding rear seat.

Nissan Sentra SE
4 Door Sedan

Subcompact

 2.0L 140 hp Gas Fuel Inject.
 4 Cylinder In-Line
 Manual 5 Speed
 2 Wheel Front
 Dual Airbags Std

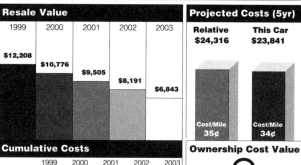

Purchase Price

Car Item	Dealer Cost	List
Base Price	**$13,787**	**$15,199**
Anti-Lock Brakes	$454	$499
Automatic 4 Speed	$725	$800
Optional Engine	N/A	N/A
Air Conditioning	Std	Std
Power Steering	Std	Std
Cruise Control	Std	Std
Power Windows	Std	Std
AM/FM Stereo Cassette	Std	Std
Steering Wheel, Tilt	Std	Std
Rear Defroster	Std	Std
*Options Price	$0	$0
*Total Price	**$13,787**	**$15,199**
Target Price	$14,279	
Destination Charge	$490	
Avg. Tax & Fees	$835	
Total Target $	**$15,604**	
Average Dealer Option Cost:	86%	
12 Month Price Increase:	None	

Ownership Costs (Projected)

Cost Area	5 Year Cost	Rating
Depreciation	$8,308	◉
Financing ($259/month)	$3,036	
Insurance	$7,886	◉
State Fees	$641	
Fuel (Hwy 31 City 23)	$2,748	○
Maintenance	$2,252	○
Repairs	$490	○

Warranty/Maintenance Info

Major Tune-Up (60K mile int.)	$238	○
Minor Tune-Up (30K mile int.)	$100	○
Brake Service	$180	○
Overall Warranty	3 yr/36k	○
Drivetrain Warranty	5 yr/60k	○
Rust Warranty	5 yr/60k	○
Maintenance Warranty	N/A	
Roadside Assistance	N/A	

Ownership Costs By Year (Projected)

Legend: 1999, 2000, 2001, 2002, 2003

Resale Value

1999	2000	2001	2002	2003
$12,544	$11,135	$9,892	$8,609	$7,296

Projected Costs (5yr)

Relative	This Car
$25,285	$25,361
Cost/Mile 36¢	Cost/Mile 36¢

Cumulative Costs

	1999	2000	2001	2002	2003
Annual	$6,319	$4,523	$4,457	$4,711	$5,351
Total	$6,319	$10,842	$15,299	$20,010	$25,361

Ownership Cost Value

○ Average

For 1999, the Sentra SE receives a minor facelift that includes new headlamp treatment, a new grille and a new front fascia. The SE is equipped with 2.0L engine and sport-tuned suspension. The instrument panel features white-on-black reversible gauges. The SE's sporty appearance is enhanced with 15 inch aluminum wheels, low-profile tires, a front air dam, rear spoiler and fog lamps. An SE Option Package is available and includes a premium radio and security system.

134

* Includes shaded options
** Other purchase requirements apply
*** Price includes other options

● Poor ◉ Worse Than Average ○ Average ○ Better Than Average ○ Excellent ⊖ Insufficient Information

Refer to Section 3: Annotated Vehicle Charts for an explanation of these charts.

Oldsmobile Alero GX
2 Door Coupe

2.4L 150 hp Gas Fuel Inject.	4 Cylinder In-Line	Automatic 4 Speed	2 Wheel Front	Dual Airbags Std

Purchase Price

Car Item	Dealer Cost	List
Base Price	**$15,264**	**$16,325**
Anti-Lock Brakes	Std	Std
Manual Transmission	N/A	N/A
Optional Engine	N/A	N/A
Air Conditioning	Std	Std
Power Steering	Std	Std
Cruise Control	$200	$225
Power Windows	N/A	N/A
AM/FM Stereo Cassette	$196	$220
Steering Wheel, Tilt	Std	Std
1SA Package	N/C	N/C
*Options Price	$196	$220
*Total Price	**$15,460**	**$16,545**
Target Price	$16,040	
Destination Charge	$525	
Avg. Tax & Fees	$929	
Total Target $	**$17,494**	
Average Dealer Option Cost:	**89%**	
12 Month Price Increase:	N/A	

The Alero GX coupe is available with standard four wheel antilock brakes, programmable power door locks, daytime running lamps with auto light control and a passive theft deterrent system. The coupe features rear seats that blend with the side panels to provide extra arm and elbow room. The Alero features unibody safety cage construction as well as dual airbags and side-impact beams for added protection. Optional equipment includes cruise control and driver's seat power height adjustment.

Ownership Costs (Projected)

Cost Area	5 Year Cost	Rating
Depreciation		⊖
Financing ($290/month)	$3,404	
Insurance	$7,688	◉
State Fees	$696	
Fuel (Hwy 30 City 22)	$2,855	◯
Maintenance		⊖
Repairs	$830	◉

Warranty/Maintenance Info

Major Tune-Up (100K mile int.)	$161	◯
Minor Tune-Up (30K mile int.)	$80	◯
Brake Service		⊖
Overall Warranty	3 yr/36k	◯
Drivetrain Warranty	3 yr/36k	◯
Rust Warranty	6 yr/100k	◯
Maintenance Warranty	N/A	
Roadside Assistance	3 yr/36k	

Ownership Costs By Year (Projected)

$2,000 $4,000 $6,000 $8,000

Insufficient Depreciation Information

■ 1999
■ 2000
■ 2001
■ 2002
□ 2003

Insufficient Maintenance Information

Resale Value

Insufficient Information

Projected Costs (5yr)

Insufficient Information

Cumulative Costs

	1999	2000	2001	2002	2003
Annual		*Insufficient Information*			
Total		*Insufficient Information*			

Ownership Cost Value

⊖

Insufficient Information

Oldsmobile Alero GL
2 Door Coupe

Compact

2.4L 150 hp Gas Fuel Inject.	4 Cylinder In-Line	Automatic 4 Speed	2 Wheel Front	Dual Airbags Std

Purchase Price

Car Item	Dealer Cost	List
Base Price	**$17,069**	**$18,655**
Anti-Lock Brakes	Std	Std
Manual Transmission	N/A	N/A
3.4L 170 hp Gas	Pkg	Pkg
Air Conditioning	Std	Std
Power Steering	Std	Std
Cruise Control	Std	Std
Power Windows	Std	Std
AM/FM Stereo Cassette	Std	Std
Steering Wheel, Tilt	Std	Std
1SB Package	N/C	N/C
*Options Price	$0	$0
*Total Price	**$17,069**	**$18,655**
Target Price	$17,788	
Destination Charge	$525	
Avg. Tax & Fees	$1,029	
Total Target $	**$19,342**	
Average Dealer Option Cost:	**89%**	
12 Month Price Increase:	N/A	

The Alero GL coupe is available with standard front fog lamps, 15 inch alloy wheels, driver's seat power height adjustment and an AM/FM cassette stereo with six speakers. The coupe features rear seats that blend with the side panels to provide extra arm and elbow room. The Alero features unibody safety cage construction as well as dual airbags and side-impact beams for added protection. Optional equipment includes 16 inch painted alloy wheels, six-way power seats and a leather interior.

Ownership Costs (Projected)

Cost Area	5 Year Cost	Rating
Depreciation		⊖
Financing ($321/month)	$3,764	
Insurance	$7,886	◉
State Fees	$780	
Fuel (Hwy 30 City 22)	$2,855	◯
Maintenance		⊖
Repairs	$830	◉

Warranty/Maintenance Info

Major Tune-Up (100K mile int.)	$161	◯
Minor Tune-Up (30K mile int.)	$80	◯
Brake Service		⊖
Overall Warranty	3 yr/36k	◯
Drivetrain Warranty	3 yr/36k	◯
Rust Warranty	6 yr/100k	◯
Maintenance Warranty	N/A	
Roadside Assistance	3 yr/36k	

Ownership Costs By Year (Projected)

$2,000 $4,000 $6,000 $8,000

Insufficient Depreciation Information

■ 1999
■ 2000
■ 2001
■ 2002
□ 2003

Insufficient Maintenance Information

Resale Value

Insufficient Information

Projected Costs (5yr)

Insufficient Information

Cumulative Costs

	1999	2000	2001	2002	2003
Annual		*Insufficient Information*			
Total		*Insufficient Information*			

Ownership Cost Value

⊖

Insufficient Information

 Includes shaded options

** Other purchase requirements apply

*** Price includes other options

 Poor

 Worse Than Average

 Average

 Better Than Average

◯ Excellent

⊖ Insufficient Information

135

Refer to *Section 3: Annotated Vehicle Charts* for an explanation of these charts.

Oldsmobile Alero GLS
2 Door Coupe

Compact

 3.4L 170 hp Gas Fuel Inject.
 6 Cylinder "V"
 Automatic 4 Speed
 2 Wheel Front
 Dual Airbags Std

Purchase Price

Car Item	Dealer Cost	List
Base Price	**$18,892**	**$20,875**
Anti-Lock Brakes	Std	Std
Manual Transmission	N/A	N/A
Optional Engine	N/A	N/A
Air Conditioning	Std	Std
Power Steering	Std	Std
Cruise Control	Std	Std
Power Windows	Std	Std
AM/FM Stereo Cass/CD	Std	Std
Steering Wheel, Tilt	Std	Std
1SA Package	N/C	N/C
*Options Price	$0	$0
*Total Price	$18,892	$20,875
Target Price	$19,748	
Destination Charge	$525	
Avg. Tax & Fees	$1,139	
Total Target $	**$21,412**	
Average Dealer Option Cost:	89%	
12 Month Price Increase:	N/A	

The Alero GLS coupe is the only trim level that is available with optional performance suspension and performance tires. Additional options include a power sunroof and a premium sound system. Standard equipment includes a 3.4L V6 engine, four wheel ABS, hydraulic engine mounts, a tire inflation monitoring system, remote keyless entry and a leather-wrapped steering wheel and shift knob. The coupe features rear seats that blend with the side panels to provide extra arm and elbow room.

Ownership Costs (Projected)

Cost Area	5 Year Cost	Rating
Depreciation		⊖
Financing ($355/month)	$4,166	
Insurance	$8,313	◉
State Fees	$869	
Fuel (Hwy 28 City 20)	$3,097	◉
Maintenance		⊖
Repairs	$830	◉

Warranty/Maintenance Info

Major Tune-Up (100K mile int.)	$214	○
Minor Tune-Up (30K mile int.)	$105	○
Brake Service		⊖
Overall Warranty	3 yr/36k	○
Drivetrain Warranty	3 yr/36k	○
Rust Warranty	6 yr/100k	○
Maintenance Warranty	N/A	
Roadside Assistance	3 yr/36k	

Ownership Costs By Year (Projected)

Insufficient Depreciation Information

Insufficient Maintenance Information

Legend: ■ 1999 ■ 2000 ▨ 2001 ▧ 2002 ☐ 2003

Resale Value
Insufficient Information

Projected Costs (5yr)
Insufficient Information

Cumulative Costs

	1999	2000	2001	2002	2003
Annual	Insufficient Information				
Total	Insufficient Information				

Ownership Cost Value
⊖ Insufficient Information

Oldsmobile Alero GX
4 Door Sedan

Compact

 2.4L 150 hp Gas Fuel Inject.
 4 Cylinder In-Line
 Automatic 4 Speed
 2 Wheel Front
 Dual Airbags Std

Purchase Price

Car Item	Dealer Cost	List
Base Price	**$15,264**	**$16,325**
Anti-Lock Brakes	Std	Std
Manual Transmission	N/A	N/A
Optional Engine	N/A	N/A
Air Conditioning	Std	Std
Power Steering	Std	Std
Cruise Control	$200	$225
Power Windows	N/A	N/A
AM/FM Stereo Cassette	$196	$220
Steering Wheel, Tilt	Std	Std
1SA Package	N/C	N/C
*Options Price	$196	$220
*Total Price	$15,460	$16,545
Target Price	$16,040	
Destination Charge	$525	
Avg. Tax & Fees	$929	
Total Target $	**$17,494**	
Average Dealer Option Cost:	89%	
12 Month Price Increase:	N/A	

The Alero GX sedan is available with a standard 2.4L DOHC 4 cylinder engine coupled with a four speed automatic transmission. Exterior design elements include crystalline headlamp and taillamp lenses, low-mounted dual air intakes and fluted side sculpting. The interior features an import-style parking brake lever, a short-throw gearshift and high seat cushions. Standard equipment includes second generation airbags, traction control, remote keyless entry and all-speed traction control.

Ownership Costs (Projected)

Cost Area	5 Year Cost	Rating
Depreciation		⊖
Financing ($290/month)	$3,404	
Insurance	$7,334	○
State Fees	$696	
Fuel (Hwy 30 City 22)	$2,855	○
Maintenance		⊖
Repairs	$830	◉

Warranty/Maintenance Info

Major Tune-Up (100K mile int.)	$161	○
Minor Tune-Up (30K mile int.)	$80	○
Brake Service		⊖
Overall Warranty	3 yr/36k	○
Drivetrain Warranty	3 yr/36k	○
Rust Warranty	6 yr/100k	○
Maintenance Warranty	N/A	
Roadside Assistance	3 yr/36k	

Ownership Costs By Year (Projected)

Insufficient Depreciation Information

Insufficient Maintenance Information

Legend: ■ 1999 ■ 2000 ▨ 2001 ▧ 2002 ☐ 2003

Resale Value
Insufficient Information

Projected Costs (5yr)
Insufficient Information

Cumulative Costs

	1999	2000	2001	2002	2003
Annual	Insufficient Information				
Total	Insufficient Information				

Ownership Cost Value
⊖ Insufficient Information

---

* Includes shaded options
** Other purchase requirements apply
*** Price includes other options

 Poor Worse Than Average Average Better Than Average Excellent Insufficient Information

Refer to *Section 3: Annotated Vehicle Charts* for an explanation of these charts.

Oldsmobile Alero GL
4 Door Sedan

2.4L 150 hp Gas Fuel Inject.	4 Cylinder In-Line	Automatic 4 Speed	2 Wheel Front	Dual Airbags Std

GLS Model Shown

Purchase Price

Car Item	Dealer Cost	List
Base Price	**$16,671**	**$18,220**
Anti-Lock Brakes	Std	Std
Manual Transmission	N/A	N/A
3.4L 170 hp Gas	Pkg	Pkg
Air Conditioning	Std	Std
Power Steering	Std	Std
Cruise Control	Std	Std
Power Windows	Std	Std
AM/FM Stereo Cassette	Std	Std
Steering Wheel, Tilt	Std	Std
1SA Package	N/C	N/C
***Options Price**	**$0**	**$0**
***Total Price**	**$16,671**	**$18,220**
Target Price	$17,368	
Destination Charge	$525	
Avg. Tax & Fees	$1,005	
Total Target $	**$18,898**	
Average Dealer Option Cost:	**89%**	
12 Month Price Increase:	N/A	

Ownership Costs (Projected)

Cost Area	5 Year Cost	Rating
Depreciation		⊖
Financing ($313/month)	$3,676	
Insurance	$7,506	◯
State Fees	$762	
Fuel (Hwy 30 City 22)	$2,855	◯
Maintenance		⊖
Repairs	$830	◉

Warranty/Maintenance Info

Major Tune-Up (100K mile int.)	$161	◯
Minor Tune-Up (30K mile int.)	$80	◯
Brake Service		⊖
Overall Warranty	3 yr/36k	◯
Drivetrain Warranty	3 yr/36k	◯
Rust Warranty	6 yr/100k	◯
Maintenance Warranty	N/A	
Roadside Assistance	3 yr/36k	

Ownership Costs By Year (Projected)

Insufficient Depreciation Information

Insufficient Maintenance Information

Legend: 1999, 2000, 2001, 2002, 2003

Resale Value

Insufficient Information

Projected Costs (5yr)

Insufficient Information

Cumulative Costs

	1999	2000	2001	2002	2003
Annual	*Insufficient Information*				
Total	*Insufficient Information*				

Ownership Cost Value

⊖

Insufficient Information

The Alero GL sedan comes standard with a tire inflation monitoring system that warns the driver when one tire's pressure is less than the others by more than 10 psi. Exterior design elements include crystalline headlamp and taillamp lenses, low-mounted dual air intakes and fluted side sculpting. The center console stack is wrapped toward the driver to minimize the reach to radio and climate control switches. A rear spoiler and AM/FM/CD/cassette are among the available options.

Oldsmobile Alero GLS
4 Door Sedan

3.4L 170 hp Gas Fuel Inject.	6 Cylinder "V"	Automatic 4 Speed	2 Wheel Front	Dual Airbags Std

Purchase Price

Car Item	Dealer Cost	List
Base Price	**$18,892**	**$20,875**
Anti-Lock Brakes	Std	Std
Manual Transmission	N/A	N/A
Optional Engine	N/A	N/A
Air Conditioning	Std	Std
Power Steering	Std	Std
Cruise Control	Std	Std
Power Windows	Std	Std
AM/FM Stereo Cass/CD	Std	Std
Steering Wheel, Tilt	Std	Std
1SA Package	N/C	N/C
***Options Price**	**$0**	**$0**
***Total Price**	**$18,892**	**$20,875**
Target Price	$19,748	
Destination Charge	$525	
Avg. Tax & Fees	$1,139	
Total Target $	**$21,412**	
Average Dealer Option Cost:	**89%**	
12 Month Price Increase:	N/A	

Ownership Costs (Projected)

Cost Area	5 Year Cost	Rating
Depreciation		⊖
Financing ($355/month)	$4,166	
Insurance	$7,886	◯
State Fees	$869	
Fuel (Hwy 28 City 20)	$3,097	◉
Maintenance		⊖
Repairs	$830	◉

Warranty/Maintenance Info

Major Tune-Up (100K mile int.)	$214	◯
Minor Tune-Up (30K mile int.)	$105	◯
Brake Service		⊖
Overall Warranty	3 yr/36k	◯
Drivetrain Warranty	3 yr/36k	◯
Rust Warranty	6 yr/100k	◯
Maintenance Warranty	N/A	
Roadside Assistance	3 yr/36k	

Ownership Costs By Year (Projected)

Insufficient Depreciation Information

Insufficient Maintenance Information

Legend: 1999, 2000, 2001, 2002, 2003

Resale Value

Insufficient Information

Projected Costs (5yr)

Insufficient Information

Cumulative Costs

	1999	2000	2001	2002	2003
Annual	*Insufficient Information*				
Total	*Insufficient Information*				

Ownership Cost Value

⊖

Insufficient Information

The Alero GLS sedan includes a standard 3.4L V6 engine. Split-folding rear seats, a leather interior, leather-wrapped steering wheel and shift knob, remote keyless entry and front fog lamps are all standard. The Alero features unibody safety cage construction as well as dual airbags and side-impact door beams for added protection. The interior features an import-style parking brake lever, short-throw gearshift and high seat cushions. A power sunroof and premium sound system are optional.

---

* Includes shaded options

** Other purchase requirements apply

*** Price includes other options

 Poor   Worse Than Average   Average   Better Than Average   Excellent   ⊖ Insufficient Information

Refer to *Section 3: Annotated Vehicle Charts* for an explanation of these charts.

 137

Oldsmobile Aurora
4 Door Sedan

Luxury

 4.0L 250 hp Gas Fuel Inject.
 8 Cylinder "V"
Automatic 4 Speed
2 Wheel Front
Dual Airbags Std

Purchase Price

Car Item	Dealer Cost	List
Base Price	**$32,787**	**$36,229**
Anti-Lock Brakes	Std	Std
Manual Transmission	N/A	N/A
Optional Engine	N/A	N/A
Air Conditioning	Std	Std
Power Steering	Std	Std
Cruise Control	Std	Std
Power Windows	Std	Std
AM/FM Stereo Cass/CD	Std	Std
Steering Wheel, Tilt	Std	Std
Rear Defroster	Std	Std
*Options Price	$0	$0
*Total Price	**$32,787**	**$36,229**
Target Price	$33,367	
Destination Charge	$670	
Avg. Tax & Fees	$1,914	
Total Target $	**$35,951**	
Average Dealer Option Cost:	89%	
12 Month Price Increase:	1%	

With no significant exterior or interior alterations for this year, the 1999 Aurora sedan still offers security and safety. Hydraulic engine mounts have been increased for improved engine stability, and four new exterior colors are available. Standard amenities include a PASS-Key II vehicle security system, full-range traction control and HomeLink universal transmitter. The Aurora also features retained accessory power, a trip computer, genuine wood trim and a remote keyless entry system.

Ownership Costs (Projected)

Cost Area	5 Year Cost	Rating
Depreciation	$20,653	●
Financing ($596/month)	$6,994	
Insurance (Performance)	$9,654	○
State Fees	$1,488	
Fuel (Hwy 26 City 17 -Prem.)	$4,134	○
Maintenance	$3,137	◉
Repairs	$1,065	○

Warranty/Maintenance Info

Major Tune-Up (100K mile int.)	$314	◉
Minor Tune-Up (30K mile int.)	$150	○
Brake Service	$263	○
Overall Warranty	4 yr/50k	○
Drivetrain Warranty	4 yr/50k	○
Rust Warranty	6 yr/100k	○
Maintenance Warranty	N/A	
Roadside Assistance	4 yr/50k	

Ownership Costs By Year (Projected)

1999, 2000, 2001, 2002, 2003

Resale Value

1999	2000	2001	2002	2003
$30,067	$26,032	$22,377	$18,826	$15,298

Cumulative Costs

	1999	2000	2001	2002	2003
Annual	$11,303	$9,051	$8,489	$8,453	$9,829
Total	$11,303	$20,354	$28,843	$37,296	$47,125

Projected Costs (5yr)

Relative $44,178	This Car $47,125
Cost/Mile 63¢	Cost/Mile 67¢

Ownership Cost Value
●
Worse Than Average

Oldsmobile Cutlass GL
4 Door Sedan

Midsize

3.1L 150 hp Gas Fuel Inject.
 6 Cylinder "V"
Automatic 4 Speed
2 Wheel Front
Dual Airbags Std

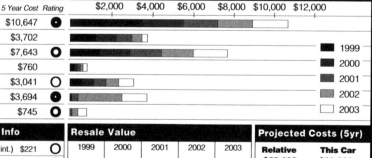

GLS Model Shown

Purchase Price

Car Item	Dealer Cost	List
Base Price	**$16,575**	**$18,115**
Anti-Lock Brakes	Std	Std
Manual Transmission	N/A	N/A
Optional Engine	N/A	N/A
Air Conditioning	Std	Std
Power Steering	Std	Std
Cruise Control	Std	Std
Power Windows	Pkg	Pkg
AM/FM Stereo Cassette	Std	Std
Steering Wheel, Tilt	Std	Std
1SA Package	N/C	N/C
*Options Price	$0	$0
*Total Price	**$16,575**	**$18,115**
Target Price	$17,483	
Destination Charge	$535	
Avg. Tax & Fees	$1,011	
Total Target $	**$19,029**	
Average Dealer Option Cost:	89%	
12 Month Price Increase:	2%	

For 1999, the Cutlass GL features a new Gold Package to enhance the exterior of the vehicle. Bronze Mist and Dark Cherry are two new exterior colors added this year. The GL features the PASSlock II security system that disables the powertrain if any attempt is made to start the vehicle without the proper key. A Convenience Package is available, which upgrades the GL with power windows and locks, dual power outside mirrors, a keyless entry system and cargo net.

Ownership Costs (Projected)

Cost Area	5 Year Cost	Rating
Depreciation	$10,647	◉
Financing ($315/month)	$3,702	
Insurance	$7,643	○
State Fees	$760	
Fuel (Hwy 29 City 20)	$3,041	○
Maintenance	$3,694	◉
Repairs	$745	○

Warranty/Maintenance Info

Major Tune-Up (100K mile int.)	$221	○
Minor Tune-Up (30K mile int.)	$118	○
Brake Service	$190	○
Overall Warranty	3 yr/36k	○
Drivetrain Warranty	3 yr/36k	○
Rust Warranty	6 yr/100k	○
Maintenance Warranty	N/A	
Roadside Assistance	3 yr/36k	

Ownership Costs By Year (Projected)

1999, 2000, 2001, 2002, 2003

Resale Value

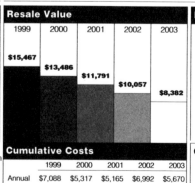

1999	2000	2001	2002	2003
$15,467	$13,486	$11,791	$10,057	$8,382

Cumulative Costs

	1999	2000	2001	2002	2003
Annual	$7,088	$5,317	$5,165	$6,992	$5,670
Total	$7,088	$12,405	$17,570	$24,562	$30,232

Projected Costs (5yr)

Relative $28,166	This Car $30,232
Cost/Mile 40¢	Cost/Mile 43¢

Ownership Cost Value
●
Poor

138

Oldsmobile Cutlass GLS
4 Door Sedan

Midsize

 3.1L 150 hp Gas Fuel Inject.
 6 Cylinder "V"
 Automatic 4 Speed
 2 Wheel Front
 Dual Airbags Std

Purchase Price

Car Item	Dealer Cost	List
Base Price	**$18,039**	**$19,715**
Anti-Lock Brakes	Std	Std
Manual Transmission	N/A	N/A
Optional Engine	N/A	N/A
Air Conditioning	Std	Std
Power Steering	Std	Std
Cruise Control	Std	Std
Power Windows	Std	Std
AM/FM Stereo Cassette	Std	Std
Steering Wheel, Tilt	Std	Std
1SA Package	N/C	N/C
*Options Price	$0	$0
*Total Price	$18,039	$19,715
Target Price	$19,056	
Destination Charge	$535	
Avg. Tax & Fees	$1,098	
Total Target $	**$20,689**	
Average Dealer Option Cost:	89%	
12 Month Price Increase:	1%	

The 1999 Cutlass GLS is the upscale model of the Cutlass line. The GLS features a full assortment of luxury amenities including leather seating, power windows and door locks, remote keyless entry and automatic headlamp control. The GLS features the PASSlock II security system that disables the powertrain if any attempt is made to start the vehicle without the proper key. Options available include a power moonroof, six-way power driver's seat, Gold Package and premium AM/FM/CD cassette stereo.

Ownership Costs (Projected)

Cost Area	5 Year Cost	Rating
Depreciation	$11,545	◐
Financing ($343/month)	$4,025	
Insurance	$7,643	◐
State Fees	$824	
Fuel (Hwy 29 City 20)	$3,041	◐
Maintenance	$3,694	●
Repairs	$745	◐

Warranty/Maintenance Info

Major Tune-Up (100K mile int.)	$221	◐
Minor Tune-Up (30K mile int.)	$118	◐
Brake Service	$190	○
Overall Warranty	3 yr/36k	◐
Drivetrain Warranty	3 yr/36k	◐
Rust Warranty	6 yr/100k	○
Maintenance Warranty	N/A	
Roadside Assistance	3 yr/36k	

Ownership Costs By Year (Projected)

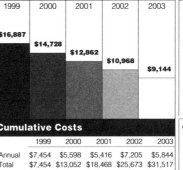

1999, 2000, 2001, 2002, 2003

Resale Value

1999	2000	2001	2002	2003
$16,887	$14,728	$12,862	$10,968	$9,144

Cumulative Costs

	1999	2000	2001	2002	2003
Annual	$7,454	$5,598	$5,416	$7,205	$5,844
Total	$7,454	$13,052	$18,468	$25,673	$31,517

Projected Costs (5yr)

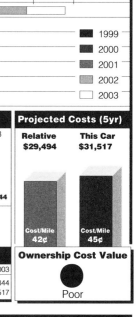

Relative	This Car
$29,494	$31,517
Cost/Mile 42¢	Cost/Mile 45¢

Ownership Cost Value

● Poor

Oldsmobile Eighty Eight
4 Door Sedan

Large

 3.8L 205 hp Gas Fuel Inject.
 6 Cylinder "V"
 Automatic 4 Speed
 2 Wheel Front
 Dual Airbags Std

Purchase Price

Car Item	Dealer Cost	List
Base Price	**$21,082**	**$23,555**
Anti-Lock Brakes	Std	Std
Manual Transmission	N/A	N/A
Optional Engine	N/A	N/A
Air Conditioning	Std	Std
Power Steering	Std	Std
Cruise Control	Std	Std
Power Windows	Std	Std
AM/FM Stereo Cassette	Std	Std
Steering Wheel, Tilt	Std	Std
1SA Package	N/C	N/C
*Options Price	$0	$0
*Total Price	$21,082	$23,555
Target Price	$22,111	
Destination Charge	$615	
Avg. Tax & Fees	$1,278	
Total Target $	**$24,004**	
Average Dealer Option Cost:	86%	
12 Month Price Increase:	3%	

The 1999 Eighty Eight offers a spacious and well appointed interior. Convenience surrounds the driver with features such as air conditioning, power windows and locks, cruise control and an eight-way power driver's seat. The Eighty Eight features the 3800 Series II V6 engine, producing 205 hp and providing ample acceleration and passing power. Champagne and Evergreen have been added as exterior colors. Options include keyless entry, a premium stereo with cassette and CD and aluminum wheels.

Ownership Costs (Projected)

Cost Area	5 Year Cost	Rating
Depreciation	$13,001	●
Financing ($398/month)	$4,670	
Insurance	$7,140	○
State Fees	$980	
Fuel (Hwy 29 City 19)	$3,121	◐
Maintenance	$2,997	◐
Repairs	$1,005	◐

Warranty/Maintenance Info

Major Tune-Up (100K mile int.)	$251	◐
Minor Tune-Up (30K mile int.)	$100	○
Brake Service	$271	◐
Overall Warranty	3 yr/36k	◐
Drivetrain Warranty	3 yr/36k	◐
Rust Warranty	6 yr/100k	○
Maintenance Warranty	N/A	
Roadside Assistance	3 yr/36k	

Ownership Costs By Year (Projected)

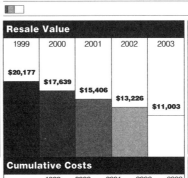

1999, 2000, 2001, 2002, 2003

Resale Value

1999	2000	2001	2002	2003
$20,177	$17,639	$15,406	$13,226	$11,003

Cumulative Costs

	1999	2000	2001	2002	2003
Annual	$7,656	$6,109	$5,859	$6,045	$7,245
Total	$7,656	$13,765	$19,624	$25,669	$32,914

Projected Costs (5yr)

Relative	This Car
$32,619	$32,914
Cost/Mile 47¢	Cost/Mile 47¢

Ownership Cost Value

○ Average

---

* Includes shaded options

** Other purchase requirements apply

*** Price includes other options

● Poor   ◉ Worse Than Average   ◐ Average   ○ Better Than Average   ○ Excellent   ⊖ Insufficient Information

Refer to *Section 3: Annotated Vehicle Charts* for an explanation of these charts.

Oldsmobile Eighty Eight LS
4 Door Sedan

3.8L 205 hp Gas Fuel Inject.	6 Cylinder "V"	Automatic 4 Speed	2 Wheel Front	Dual Airbags Std

Large

Base Model Shown

Purchase Price

Car Item	Dealer Cost	List
Base Price	**$22,469**	**$25,105**
Anti-Lock Brakes	Std	Std
Manual Transmission	N/A	N/A
Optional Engine	N/A	N/A
Air Conditioning	Std	Std
Power Steering	Std	Std
Cruise Control	Std	Std
Power Windows	Std	Std
AM/FM Stereo Cassette	Std	Std
Steering Wheel, Tilt	Std	Std
1SA Package	N/C	N/C
***Options Price**	**$0**	**$0**
***Total Price**	**$22,469**	**$25,105**
Target Price	$23,591	
Destination Charge	$615	
Avg. Tax & Fees	$1,359	
Total Target $	**$25,565**	
Average Dealer Option Cost:	**86%**	
12 Month Price Increase:	4%	

The 1999 Eighty Eight LS is a large sedan, well appointed with luxury amenities. The LS comes with an eight-way power adjustable driver's seat, power windows and locks with a remote keyless entry system, Twilight Sentinel headlamp control and antilock brakes. The optional Value Package upgrades the LS with aluminum alloy wheels, an automatic load leveling system and a premium stereo with cassette and CD. Leather upholstery can be ordered to enhance the interior of the LS.

Ownership Costs (Projected)

Cost Area	5 Year Cost	Rating
Depreciation	$14,320	●
Financing ($424/month)	$4,974	
Insurance	$7,140	○
State Fees	$1,041	
Fuel (Hwy 29 City 19)	$3,121	○
Maintenance	$2,984	○
Repairs	$1,005	○

Warranty/Maintenance Info

Major Tune-Up (100K mile int.)	$251	○
Minor Tune-Up (30K mile int.)	$100	○
Brake Service	$271	○
Overall Warranty	3 yr/36k	○
Drivetrain Warranty	3 yr/36k	○
Rust Warranty	6 yr/100k	○
Maintenance Warranty	N/A	
Roadside Assistance	3 yr/36k	

Ownership Costs By Year (Projected)

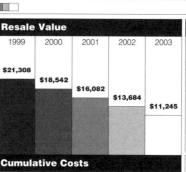

Legend: 1999, 2000, 2001, 2002, 2003

Resale Value

1999	2000	2001	2002	2003
$21,308	$18,542	$16,082	$13,684	$11,245

Cumulative Costs

	1999	2000	2001	2002	2003
Annual	$8,204	$6,434	$6,162	$6,301	$7,484
Total	$8,204	$14,638	$20,800	$27,101	$34,585

Projected Costs (5yr)

Relative $33,958	This Car $34,585
Cost/Mile 49¢	Cost/Mile 49¢

Ownership Cost Value

Worse Than Average

Oldsmobile Eighty Eight 50th Anniversary Edition
4 Door Sedan

3.8L 205 hp Gas Fuel Inject.	6 Cylinder "V"	Automatic 4 Speed	2 Wheel Front	Dual Airbags Std

Large

Base Model Shown

Purchase Price

Car Item	Dealer Cost	List
Base Price	**$24,478**	**$27,350**
Anti-Lock Brakes	Std	Std
Manual Transmission	N/A	N/A
Optional Engine	N/A	N/A
Air Conditioning	Std	Std
Power Steering	Std	Std
Cruise Control	Std	Std
Power Windows	Std	Std
AM/FM Stereo Cass/CD	Std	Std
Steering Wheel, Tilt	Std	Std
1SA Package	N/C	N/C
***Options Price**	**$0**	**$0**
***Total Price**	**$24,478**	**$27,350**
Target Price	$25,741	
Destination Charge	$615	
Avg. Tax & Fees	$1,479	
Total Target $	**$27,835**	
Average Dealer Option Cost:	**86%**	
12 Month Price Increase:	N/A	

1999 marks the 50th anniversary of the Eighty Eight sedan. To celebrate, a 50th Anniversary Edition has been created for this year only. Many luxury options are offered as standard equipment on this Anniversary Edition. These include leather seating, eight-way power seats for both driver and passenger, a premium stereo with cassette and CD and aluminum alloy wheels. Additional standard features include an overhead roof console and memory controls for both the driver's seat and mirrors.

Ownership Costs (Projected)

Cost Area	5 Year Cost	Rating
Depreciation	$16,280	●
Financing ($461/month)	$5,415	
Insurance	$7,463	○
State Fees	$1,133	
Fuel (Hwy 29 City 19)	$3,121	○
Maintenance	$2,984	○
Repairs	$1,005	○

Warranty/Maintenance Info

Major Tune-Up (100K mile int.)	$251	○
Minor Tune-Up (30K mile int.)	$100	○
Brake Service	$271	○
Overall Warranty	3 yr/36k	○
Drivetrain Warranty	3 yr/36k	○
Rust Warranty	6 yr/100k	○
Maintenance Warranty	N/A	
Roadside Assistance	3 yr/36k	

Ownership Costs By Year (Projected)

Legend: 1999, 2000, 2001, 2002, 2003

Resale Value

1999	2000	2001	2002	2003
$22,600	$19,569	$16,858	$14,221	$11,555

Cumulative Costs

	1999	2000	2001	2002	2003
Annual	$9,417	$6,905	$6,587	$6,679	$7,813
Total	$9,417	$16,322	$22,909	$29,588	$37,401

Projected Costs (5yr)

Relative $36,540	This Car $37,401
Cost/Mile 52¢	Cost/Mile 53¢

Ownership Cost Value

Worse Than Average

140

* Includes shaded options
** Other purchase requirements apply
*** Price includes other options

 Poor Worse Than Average Average Better Than Average Excellent ⊖ Insufficient Information

Refer to *Section 3: Annotated Vehicle Charts* for an explanation of these charts.

Oldsmobile LSS
4 Door Sedan

Near Luxury

3.8L 205 hp Gas Fuel Inject.	6 Cylinder "V"	Automatic 4 Speed	2 Wheel Front	Dual Airbags Std

Purchase Price

Car Item	Dealer Cost	List
Base Price	**$26,049**	**$29,105**
Anti-Lock Brakes	Std	Std
Manual Transmission	N/A	N/A
3.8L 240 hp Suprchrg	$912	$1,060
Air Conditioning	Std	Std
Power Steering	Std	Std
Cruise Control	Std	Std
Power Windows	Std	Std
AM/FM Stereo Cass/CD	Std	Std
Steering Wheel, Tilt	Std	Std
1SA Package	N/C	N/C
*Options Price	$0	$0
*Total Price	**$26,049**	**$29,105**
Target Price	$27,426	
Destination Charge	$615	
Avg. Tax & Fees	$1,572	
Total Target $	**$29,613**	
Average Dealer Option Cost:	86%	
12 Month Price Increase:	4%	

The LSS enters this model year with only a few minor refinements. Two new exterior colors are added: Champagne and Evergreen. The LSS comes standard with a 205 hp V6, but a 240 hp supercharged V6 has also been made available if more performance is desired. The LSS comes equipped with luxury amenities including a premium stereo with cassette and CD, keyless remote entry and dual-zone climate control. The only options include a power sliding moonroof, the supercharged V6 engine and chrome wheels.

Ownership Costs (Projected)

Cost Area	5 Year Cost	Rating
Depreciation	$17,010	●
Financing ($491/month)	$5,760	
Insurance	$7,643	○
State Fees	$1,201	
Fuel (Hwy 29 City 19)	$3,121	○
Maintenance	$3,022	○
Repairs	$1,005	○

Warranty/Maintenance Info

Major Tune-Up (100K mile int.)	$251	○
Minor Tune-Up (30K mile int.)	$100	○
Brake Service	$271	●
Overall Warranty	3 yr/36k	○
Drivetrain Warranty	3 yr/36k	○
Rust Warranty	6 yr/100k	○
Maintenance Warranty	N/A	
Roadside Assistance	3 yr/36k	

Ownership Costs By Year (Projected)

$5,000 $10,000 $15,000 $20,000

- 1999
- 2000
- 2001
- 2002
- 2003

Resale Value

1999	2000	2001	2002	2003
$23,339	$20,389	$17,771	$15,202	$12,603

Cumulative Costs

	1999	2000	2001	2002	2003
Annual	$10,624	$6,969	$6,615	$6,743	$7,811
Total	$10,624	$17,593	$24,208	$30,951	$38,762

Projected Costs (5yr)

Relative	This Car
$37,896	$38,762
Cost/Mile 54¢	Cost/Mile 55¢

Ownership Cost Value

○ Average

Oldsmobile Intrigue GX
4 Door Sedan

Midsize

3.8L 205 hp Gas Fuel Inject.	6 Cylinder "V"	Automatic 4 Speed	2 Wheel Front	Dual Airbags Std

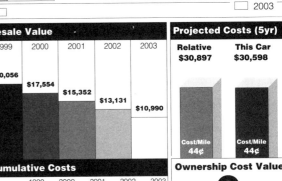

GLS Model Shown

Purchase Price

Car Item	Dealer Cost	List
Base Price	**$19,375**	**$21,175**
Anti-Lock Brakes	Std	Std
Manual Transmission	N/A	N/A
3.5L 215 hp Gas	$352	$395
Air Conditioning	Std	Std
Power Steering	Std	Std
Cruise Control	Std	Std
Power Windows	Std	Std
AM/FM Stereo Cassette	Std	Std
Steering Wheel, Tilt	Std	Std
1SA Package	N/C	N/C
*Options Price	$0	$0
*Total Price	**$19,375**	**$21,175**
Target Price	$20,335	
Destination Charge	$560	
Avg. Tax & Fees	$1,170	
Total Target $	**$22,065**	
Average Dealer Option Cost:	89%	
12 Month Price Increase:	N/A	

The 1999 Intrigue GX replaces last year's base Intrigue. New for 1999 is a 3.5L V6 engine that generates 215 hp and 230 lb-ft of torque, available as an option. Safety features on the GX include four wheel antilock brakes, traction assist and dual airbags. Air conditioning, a four speed automatic transmission, an AM/FM stereo with cassette and a diversity antenna system are all standard. Optional amenities include a power sliding moonroof, power driver's seat and premium sound system.

Ownership Costs (Projected)

Cost Area	5 Year Cost	Rating
Depreciation	$11,075	○
Financing ($366/month)	$4,293	
Insurance	$7,140	○
State Fees	$882	
Fuel (Hwy 30 City 19)	$3,070	○
Maintenance	$3,273	○
Repairs	$865	○

Warranty/Maintenance Info

Major Tune-Up (100K mile int.)	$255	○
Minor Tune-Up (30K mile int.)	$132	◉
Brake Service	$248	○
Overall Warranty	3 yr/36k	○
Drivetrain Warranty	3 yr/36k	○
Rust Warranty	6 yr/100k	○
Maintenance Warranty	N/A	
Roadside Assistance	3 yr/36k	

Ownership Costs By Year (Projected)

$2,000 $4,000 $6,000 $8,000 $10,000 $12,000

- 1999
- 2000
- 2001
- 2002
- 2003

Resale Value

1999	2000	2001	2002	2003
$20,056	$17,554	$15,352	$13,131	$10,990

Cumulative Costs

	1999	2000	2001	2002	2003
Annual	$5,675	$5,937	$5,756	$5,955	$7,275
Total	$5,675	$11,612	$17,368	$23,323	$30,598

Projected Costs (5yr)

Relative	This Car
$30,897	$30,598
Cost/Mile 44¢	Cost/Mile 44¢

Ownership Cost Value

○ Average

 Poor   Worse Than Average   Average   Better Than Average   Excellent   Insufficient Information

Refer to *Section 3: Annotated Vehicle Charts* for an explanation of these charts.

Oldsmobile Intrigue GL
4 Door Sedan

Midsize

 3.8L 205 hp Gas Fuel Inject. | 6 Cylinder "V" | Automatic 4 Speed | 2 Wheel Front | Dual Airbags Std

Purchase Price

Car Item	Dealer Cost	List
Base Price	**$20,656**	**$22,575**
Anti-Lock Brakes	Std	Std
Manual Transmission	N/A	N/A
3.5L 215 hp Gas	$352	$395
Auto Climate Control	Std	Std
Power Steering	Std	Std
Cruise Control	Std	Std
Power Windows	Std	Std
AM/FM Stereo Cassette	Std	Std
Steering Wheel, Tilt	Std	Std
1SB Package	$129	***$145
***Options Price**	**$481**	**$540**
***Total Price**	**$21,137**	**$23,115**
Target Price	$22,211	
Destination Charge	$560	
Avg. Tax & Fees	$1,275	
Total Target $	**$24,046**	
Average Dealer Option Cost:	**89%**	
12 Month Price Increase:	2%	

The 1999 Intrigue GL features new badging on the front fenders and the Oldsmobile script on the rear decklid. Automatic dual-zone climate control, an electronically controlled four speed automatic transmission, an AM/FM stereo with cassette and a diversity antenna system are all standard. An available new 3.5L V6 engine that generates 215 hp and 230 lb-ft of torque is new for 1999. A full-function traction control system is included with the new engine for added stability.

Ownership Costs (Projected)

Cost Area	5 Year Cost	Rating
Depreciation	$12,320	◓
Financing ($399/month)	$4,677	
Insurance	$7,294	◯
State Fees	$960	
Fuel (Hwy 27 City 19)	$3,236	●
Maintenance	$3,260	◔
Repairs	$865	◔

Warranty/Maintenance Info

Major Tune-Up (100K mile int.)	$225	◔
Minor Tune-Up (30K mile int.)	$132	◓
Brake Service	$248	◔
Overall Warranty	3 yr/36k	◔
Drivetrain Warranty	3 yr/36k	◔
Rust Warranty	6 yr/100k	◔
Maintenance Warranty	N/A	
Roadside Assistance	3 yr/36k	

Ownership Costs By Year (Projected)

$2,000 $4,000 $6,000 $8,000 $10,000 $12,000 $14,000

Legend: 1999, 2000, 2001, 2002, 2003

Resale Value

1999	2000	2001	2002	2003
$21,749	$18,990	$16,545	$14,091	$11,726

Cumulative Costs

	1999	2000	2001	2002	2003
Annual	$6,174	$6,379	$6,158	$6,318	$7,583
Total	$6,174	$12,553	$18,711	$25,029	$32,612

Projected Costs (5yr)

Relative $33,025	This Car $32,612
Cost/Mile 47¢	Cost/Mile 47¢

Ownership Cost Value
◯ Average

Oldsmobile Intrigue GLS
4 Door Sedan

Midsize

3.5L 215 hp Gas Fuel Inject. | 6 Cylinder "V" | Automatic 4 Speed | 2 Wheel Front | Dual Airbags Std

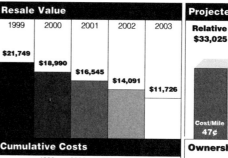

Purchase Price

Car Item	Dealer Cost	List
Base Price	**$22,825**	**$24,945**
Anti-Lock Brakes	Std	Std
Manual Transmission	N/A	N/A
Optional Engine	N/A	N/A
Auto Climate Control	Std	Std
Power Steering	Std	Std
Cruise Control	Std	Std
Power Windows	Std	Std
AM/FM Stereo Cass/CD	Std	Std
Steering Wheel, Tilt	Std	Std
1SC Package	N/C	N/C
***Options Price**	**$0**	**$0**
***Total Price**	**$22,825**	**$24,945**
Target Price	$24,027	
Destination Charge	$560	
Avg. Tax & Fees	$1,374	
Total Target $	**$25,961**	
Average Dealer Option Cost:	**89%**	
12 Month Price Increase:	3%	

The 1999 Intrigue GLS is the upscale model of the line. The GLS come fully equipped with luxury amenities including automatic dual-zone climate control, an electronically controlled four speed automatic transmission, an AM/FM stereo with cassette and a diversity antenna system are standard. The GLS features the new, more powerful 3.5L V6 engine that generates 215 hp and 230 lb-ft of torque. Optional on the GLS are a Bose sound system, 12 disc CD changer, power sliding moonroof and a rear decklid spoiler.

Ownership Costs (Projected)

Cost Area	5 Year Cost	Rating
Depreciation	$14,106	●
Financing ($430/month)	$5,051	
Insurance	$7,463	◯
State Fees	$1,034	
Fuel (Hwy 27 City 19)	$3,236	●
Maintenance	$3,260	◔
Repairs	$865	◔

Warranty/Maintenance Info

Major Tune-Up (100K mile int.)	$225	◔
Minor Tune-Up (30K mile int.)	$132	◓
Brake Service	$248	◔
Overall Warranty	3 yr/36k	◔
Drivetrain Warranty	3 yr/36k	◔
Rust Warranty	6 yr/100k	◔
Maintenance Warranty	N/A	
Roadside Assistance	3 yr/36k	◔

Ownership Costs By Year (Projected)

$5,000 $10,000 $15,000

Legend: 1999, 2000, 2001, 2002, 2003

Resale Value

1999	2000	2001	2002	2003
$23,129	$20,044	$17,281	$14,521	$11,855

Cumulative Costs

	1999	2000	2001	2002	2003
Annual	$6,887	$6,858	$6,602	$6,720	$7,948
Total	$6,887	$13,745	$20,347	$27,067	$35,015

Projected Costs (5yr)

Relative $35,360	This Car $35,015
Cost/Mile 51¢	Cost/Mile 50¢

Ownership Cost Value
◯ Average

---

* Includes shaded options
** Other purchase requirements apply
*** Price includes other options

 ● Poor | ◓ Worse Than Average | ◯ Average | Better Than Average | ◯ Excellent | ⊖ Insufficient Information

Refer to *Section 3: Annotated Vehicle Charts* for an explanation of these charts.

Plymouth Breeze
4 Door Sedan

Midsize

 2.0L 132 hp Gas Fuel Inject.
 4 Cylinder In-Line
 Manual 5 Speed
 2 Wheel Front
 Dual Airbags Std

Purchase Price

Car Item	Dealer Cost	List
Base Price	**$13,743**	**$14,975**
Anti-Lock Brakes	$503	$565
Automatic 4 Speed	$935	$1,050
2.4L 150 hp Gas	$401	$450
Air Conditioning	Std	Std
Power Steering	Std	Std
Cruise/Speed Control	Inc	Inc
Power Windows	Inc	Inc
AM/FM Stereo Cassette	$160	$180
Steering Wheel, Tilt	Std	Std
22B Package	N/C	N/C
***Options Price**	**$1,598**	**$1,795**
***Total Price**	**$15,341**	**$16,770**
Target Price	$15,909	
Destination Charge	$535	
Avg. Tax & Fees	$926	
Total Target $	**$17,370**	
Average Dealer Option Cost:	**89%**	
12 Month Price Increase:	2%	

For the 1999 Breeze, the Quick Order B Package is now offered at no charge. The B Package includes power windows, locks and mirrors, driver's seat height adjuster and rear floor mats. Also for 1999, the Breeze's suspension has been redesigned to improve ride comfort, Inferno Red and Light Cypress Green are new exterior colors and the standard wheel covers have been redesigned. Optional features include antilock brakes, three different stereo systems and a power moonroof.

Ownership Costs (Projected)

Cost Area	5 Year Cost	Rating
Depreciation	$8,967	◐
Financing ($288/month)	$3,379	
Insurance	$6,990	◐
State Fees	$705	
Fuel (Hwy 31 City 22)	$2,806	○
Maintenance	$3,234	◐
Repairs	$920	◐

Warranty/Maintenance Info

Major Tune-Up (60K mile int.)	$257	◐
Minor Tune-Up (30K mile int.)	$97	◐
Brake Service	$224	◐
Overall Warranty	3 yr/36k	◐
Drivetrain Warranty	3 yr/36k	◐
Rust Warranty	5 yr/100k	○
Maintenance Warranty	N/A	
Roadside Assistance	3 yr/36k	

Ownership Costs By Year (Projected)

$2,000 $4,000 $6,000 $8,000 $10,000

■ 1999
■ 2000
■ 2001
■ 2002
□ 2003

Resale Value

1999	2000	2001	2002	2003
$14,915	$13,115	$11,574	$9,971	$8,403

Cumulative Costs

	1999	2000	2001	2002	2003
Annual	$5,688	$4,862	$4,826	$5,565	$6,060
Total	$5,688	$10,550	$15,376	$20,941	$27,001

Projected Costs (5yr)

Relative $27,216	This Car $27,001
Cost/Mile 39¢	Cost/Mile 39¢

Ownership Cost Value
◐ Average

Plymouth Neon Competition
2 Door Coupe

Compact

 2.0L 150 hp Gas Fuel Inject.
 4 Cylinder In-Line
 Manual 5 Speed
 2 Wheel Front
Dual Airbags Std

Purchase Price

Car Item	Dealer Cost	List
Base Price	**$10,612**	**$11,225**
Anti-Lock Brakes	N/A	N/A
Automatic Transmission	N/A	N/A
Optional Engine	N/A	N/A
Air Conditioning	$890	$1,000
Power Steering	Std	Std
Cruise Control	N/A	N/A
Power Windows	N/A	N/A
AM/FM Stereo Cass/CD	$552	$620
Steering Wheel, Tilt	N/A	N/A
23A Package	$1,914	***$2,080
***Options Price**	**$3,356**	**$3,700**
***Total Price**	**$13,968**	**$14,925**
Target Price	$14,290	
Destination Charge	$500	
Avg. Tax & Fees	$833	
Total Target $	**$15,623**	
Average Dealer Option Cost:	**90%**	
12 Month Price Increase:	2%	

The Neon Competition coupe is equipped with key features including standard second generation driver and passenger airbags. Quick Order Package 23A includes four wheel disc brakes, aluminum wheels, a performance-tuned engine controller, power bulge hood and leather-wrapped steering wheel. Firm-feel power steering, a tachometer and Competition suspension are also included in this package. Additional options include air conditioning and a rear window defroster.

Ownership Costs (Projected)

Cost Area	5 Year Cost	Rating
Depreciation	$8,416	◉
Financing ($259/month)	$3,038	
Insurance	$7,643	●
State Fees	$630	
Fuel (Hwy 39 City 28)	$2,218	○
Maintenance	$2,771	○
Repairs	$745	◐

Warranty/Maintenance Info

Major Tune-Up (60K mile int.)	$226	○
Minor Tune-Up (30K mile int.)	$98	○
Brake Service	$254	◉
Overall Warranty	3 yr/36k	○
Drivetrain Warranty	3 yr/36k	○
Rust Warranty	5 yr/100k	○
Maintenance Warranty	N/A	
Roadside Assistance	3 yr/36k	

Ownership Costs By Year (Projected)

$2,000 $4,000 $6,000 $8,000 $10,000

■ 1999
■ 2000
■ 2001
■ 2002
□ 2003

Resale Value

1999	2000	2001	2002	2003
$13,073	$11,481	$10,074	$8,646	$7,207

Cumulative Costs

	1999	2000	2001	2002	2003
Annual	$5,661	$4,555	$4,485	$5,395	$5,365
Total	$5,661	$10,216	$14,701	$20,096	$25,461

Projected Costs (5yr)

Relative $25,850	This Car $25,461
Cost/Mile 37¢	Cost/Mile 36¢

Ownership Cost Value
○ Better Than Average

---

* Includes shaded options

** Other purchase requirements apply

*** Price includes other options

● Poor   Worse Than Average   Average   Better Than Average   ○ Excellent   ⊖ Insufficient Information

143

Refer to *Section 3: Annotated Vehicle Charts* for an explanation of these charts.

Plymouth Neon Highline
2 Door Coupe

2.0L 132 hp Gas Fuel Inject.	4 Cylinder In-Line	Manual 5 Speed	2 Wheel Front	Dual Airbags Std

Compact

Competition Model Shown

Purchase Price

Car Item	Dealer Cost	List
Base Price	**$10,653**	**$11,520**
Anti-Lock Brakes	$503	**$565
Automatic 3 Speed	Inc	Inc
2.0L 150 hp Gas	N/C	N/C
Air Conditioning	Inc	Inc
Power Steering	Std	Std
Cruise Control	Pkg	Pkg
Power Windows	$236	**$265
AM/FM Stereo CD	$352	**$395
Steering Wheel, Tilt	Pkg	Pkg
24G Package	$1,157	$1,300
*Options Price	$1,157	$1,300
*Total Price	$11,810	$12,820
Target Price	$12,102	
Destination Charge	$550	
Avg. Tax & Fees	$716	
Total Target $	$13,368	
Average Dealer Option Cost:	89%	
12 Month Price Increase:	3%	

The Neon Highline coupe is equipped with key features including standard second generation driver and passenger airbags. Expresso Quick Order Packages 23G or 24G include air conditioning, fog lamps, a power bulge hood and cloth low-back seats. A rear spoiler, tachometer and assist handles are also among the features included. Additional Neon options include a keyless entry system, antilock brakes, Deluxe Convenience Group, Light Group and Power Group.

Ownership Costs (Projected)

Cost Area	5 Year Cost	Rating
Depreciation	$7,581	●
Financing ($222/month)	$2,600	
Insurance	$7,837	●
State Fees	$548	
Fuel (Hwy 32 City 23)	$2,702	○
Maintenance	$2,668	○
Repairs	$745	◉

Warranty/Maintenance Info

Major Tune-Up (60K mile int.)	$226	○
Minor Tune-Up (30K mile int.)	$98	○
Brake Service	$233	○
Overall Warranty	3 yr/36k	○
Drivetrain Warranty	3 yr/36k	○
Rust Warranty	5 yr/100k	○
Maintenance Warranty	N/A	
Roadside Assistance	3 yr/36k	

Ownership Costs By Year (Projected)

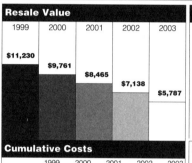

Legend: ■ 1999, ■ 2000, ■ 2001, ▨ 2002, ☐ 2003

Resale Value

1999	2000	2001	2002	2003
$11,230	$9,761	$8,465	$7,138	$5,787

Cumulative Costs

	1999	2000	2001	2002	2003
Annual	$5,209	$4,425	$4,404	$5,259	$5,384
Total	$5,209	$9,634	$14,038	$19,297	$24,681

Projected Costs (5yr)

Relative	This Car
$23,940	$24,681
Cost/Mile 34¢	Cost/Mile 35¢

Ownership Cost Value

● Worse Than Average

Plymouth Neon Competition
4 Door Sedan

2.0L 132 hp Gas Fuel Inject.	4 Cylinder In-Line	Manual 5 Speed	2 Wheel Front	Dual Airbags Std

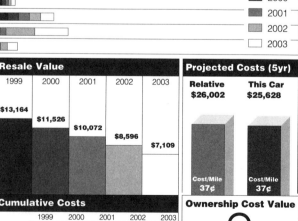

Compact

Highline Model Shown

Purchase Price

Car Item	Dealer Cost	List
Base Price	**$10,796**	**$11,425**
Anti-Lock Brakes	N/A	N/A
Automatic Transmission	N/A	N/A
Optional Engine	N/A	N/A
Air Conditioning	$890	$1,000
Power Steering	Std	Std
Cruise Control	N/A	N/A
Power Windows	N/A	N/A
AM/FM Stereo Cass/CD	$552	$620
Steering Wheel, Tilt	N/A	N/A
25A Package	$1,895	***$2,060
*Options Price	$3,337	$3,680
*Total Price	$14,133	$15,105
Target Price	$14,460	
Destination Charge	$500	
Avg. Tax & Fees	$842	
Total Target $	$15,802	
Average Dealer Option Cost:	90%	
12 Month Price Increase:	3%	

The Neon Competition sedan is equipped with key features including standard second generation driver and passenger airbags. Quick Order Package 25A includes four wheel disc brakes, aluminum wheels, a performance-tuned engine controller, power bulge hood and leather-wrapped steering wheel. Firm-feel power steering, a tachometer and Competition suspension are also included in this package. Additional selected options include air conditioning and a rear defroster.

Ownership Costs (Projected)

Cost Area	5 Year Cost	Rating
Depreciation	$8,693	◉
Financing ($262/month)	$3,075	
Insurance	$7,463	◉
State Fees	$637	
Fuel (Hwy 39 City 28)	$2,218	○
Maintenance	$2,797	○
Repairs	$745	◉

Warranty/Maintenance Info

Major Tune-Up (60K mile int.)	$226	○
Minor Tune-Up (30K mile int.)	$98	○
Brake Service	$254	◉
Overall Warranty	3 yr/36k	○
Drivetrain Warranty	3 yr/36k	○
Rust Warranty	5 yr/100k	○
Maintenance Warranty	N/A	
Roadside Assistance	3 yr/36k	

Ownership Costs By Year (Projected)

Legend: ■ 1999, ■ 2000, ■ 2001, ▨ 2002, ☐ 2003

Resale Value

1999	2000	2001	2002	2003
$13,164	$11,526	$10,072	$8,596	$7,109

Cumulative Costs

	1999	2000	2001	2002	2003
Annual	$5,729	$4,577	$4,506	$5,438	$5,378
Total	$5,729	$10,306	$14,812	$20,250	$25,628

Projected Costs (5yr)

Relative	This Car
$26,002	$25,628
Cost/Mile 37¢	Cost/Mile 37¢

Ownership Cost Value

○ Better Than Average

144

 Poor
 Worse Than Average
 Average
 Better Than Average
 Excellent
 Insufficient Information

Refer to *Section 3: Annotated Vehicle Charts* for an explanation of these charts.

Plymouth Neon Highline
4 Door Sedan

Compact

 2.0L 132 hp Gas Fuel Inject.

 4 Cylinder In-Line

 Manual 5 Speed

 2 Wheel Front

 Dual Airbags Std

Purchase Price

Car Item	Dealer Cost	List
Base Price	**$10,833**	**$11,720**
Anti-Lock Brakes	$503	**$565
Automatic 3 Speed	Inc	Inc
2.0L 150 hp Gas	N/C	**N/C
Air Conditioning	Inc	Inc
Power Steering	Std	Std
Cruise Control	Pkg	Pkg
Windows, Power	Inc	Inc
AM/FM Stereo Cass/CD	Inc	Inc
Steering Wheel, Tilt	Pkg	Pkg
22H Package	$1,905	$2,140
*Options Price	$1,905	$2,140
Total Price	**$12,738**	**$13,860**
Target Price	$13,057	
Destination Charge	$550	
Avg. Tax & Fees	$769	
Total Target $	**$14,376**	
Average Dealer Option Cost:	**89%**	
12 Month Price Increase:	3%	

The Neon Highline sedan is equipped with key features including standard second generation driver and passenger airbags. Expresso and Style Quick Order Packages are now available. Additional options include a remote keyless entry system, antilock brakes, Deluxe Convenience Group (including speed control, tilt steering wheel and a tachometer), Light Group (including illuminated visors and map lights) and Power Group (power door locks and mirrors).

Ownership Costs (Projected)

Cost Area	5 Year Cost	Rating
Depreciation	$8,184	●
Financing ($238/month)	$2,796	
Insurance	$7,463	◉
State Fees	$589	
Fuel (Hwy 32 City 23)	$2,702	○
Maintenance	$2,668	○
Repairs	$745	◉

Warranty/Maintenance Info

Major Tune-Up (60K mile int.)	$226	○
Minor Tune-Up (30K mile int.)	$98	○
Brake Service	$233	○
Overall Warranty	3 yr/36k	○
Drivetrain Warranty	3 yr/36k	○
Rust Warranty	5 yr/100k	○
Maintenance Warranty	N/A	
Roadside Assistance	3 yr/36k	

Ownership Costs By Year (Projected)

$2,000 $4,000 $6,000 $8,000 $10,000

■ 1999
■ 2000
■ 2001
□ 2002
□ 2003

Resale Value

1999	2000	2001	2002	2003
$12,082	$10,495	$9,084	$7,647	$6,192

Cumulative Costs

	1999	2000	2001	2002	2003
Annual	$5,371	$4,534	$4,492	$5,324	$5,426
Total	$5,371	$9,905	$14,397	$19,721	$25,147

Projected Costs (5yr)

Relative $24,744	This Car $25,147
Cost/Mile 35¢	Cost/Mile 36¢

Ownership Cost Value
○ Average

Plymouth Prowler
2 Door Convertible

Sport

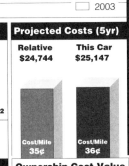

 3.5L 253 hp Gas Fuel Inject.

 6 Cylinder "V"

 Automatic 4 Speed

 2 Wheel Rear

 Dual Airbags Std

Purchase Price

Car Item	Dealer Cost	List
Base Price	**$36,773**	**$39,300**
Anti-Lock Brakes	N/A	N/A
Manual Transmission	N/A	N/A
Optional Engine	N/A	N/A
Air Conditioning	Std	Std
Power Steering	Std	Std
Cruise Control	Std	Std
Power Windows	Std	Std
AM/FM Stereo Cass/CD	Std	Std
Steering Wheel, Tilt	Std	Std
21A Package	N/C	N/C
*Options Price	$0	$0
Total Price	**$36,773**	**$39,300**
Target Price	$51,879	
Destination Charge	$700	
Avg. Tax & Fees	$2,779	
Luxury Tax	$995	
Total Target $	**$56,353**	
12 Month Price Increase:	N/A	

For 1999, production of the Prowler roadster will resume in Detroit, Michigan. Limited production of this two seat roadster will begin with 2,500 units. New for the Prowler is a lighter 3.5L aluminum V6 engine with 39 more horsepower, now up to 253. Other new features include a power driver's side express down window, depowered airbags and a key-operated passenger airbag deactivation switch. Also new is the addition of the exterior paint colors Prowler Yellow, Prowler Black and Prowler Red.

Ownership Costs (Projected)

Cost Area	5 Year Cost	Rating
Depreciation		⊖
Financing ($934/month)	$10,962	
Insurance (Performance)	$14,416	◉
State Fees	$1,613	
Fuel (Hwy 23 City 17 -Prem.)	$4,402	◉
Maintenance		⊖
Repairs	$3,200	●

Warranty/Maintenance Info

Major Tune-Up (60K mile int.)		⊖
Minor Tune-Up (30K mile int.)		⊖
Brake Service		⊖
Overall Warranty	3 yr/36k	○
Drivetrain Warranty	3 yr/36k	○
Rust Warranty	5 yr/100k	○
Maintenance Warranty	N/A	
Roadside Assistance	3 yr/36k	

Ownership Costs By Year (Projected)

$5,000 $10,000 $15,000

Insufficient Depreciation Information

Insufficient Maintenance Information

■ 1999
■ 2000
■ 2001
□ 2002
□ 2003

Resale Value
Insufficient Information

Projected Costs (5yr)
Insufficient Information

Cumulative Costs

	1999	2000	2001	2002	2003
Annual	Insufficient Information				
Total	Insufficient Information				

Ownership Cost Value
⊖ Insufficient Information

---

* Includes shaded options
** Other purchase requirements apply
*** Price includes other options

● Poor ◉ Worse Than Average ○ Average ○ Better Than Average ○ Excellent ⊖ Insufficient Information

145

Refer to *Section 3: Annotated Vehicle Charts* for an explanation of these charts.

©1999 by IntelliChoice, Inc. (408) 866-1400 http://www.intellichoice.com All Rights Reserved. Reproduction Prohibited.

Pontiac Bonneville SE
4 Door Sedan

Large

 3.8L 205 hp Gas Fuel Inject.   6 Cylinder "V"   Automatic 4 Speed   2 Wheel Front   Dual Airbags Std

Purchase Price

Car Item	Dealer Cost	List
Base Price	**$20,935**	**$22,880**
Anti-Lock Brakes	Std	Std
Manual Transmission	N/A	N/A
Optional Engine	N/A	N/A
Air Conditioning	Std	Std
Power Steering	Std	Std
Cruise Control	Std	Std
Power Windows	Std	Std
AM/FM Stereo Cassette	$196	$220
Steering Wheel, Tilt	Std	Std
1SA Package	N/C	N/C
*Options Price	$196	$220
*Total Price	**$21,131**	**$23,100**
Target Price	$22,149	
Destination Charge	$615	
Avg. Tax & Fees	$1,274	
Total Target $	**$24,038**	
Average Dealer Option Cost:	**89%**	
12 Month Price Increase:	2%	

The Bonneville SE is now available with the OnStar Communication System that integrates advanced vehicle electronics with the Global Positioning System (GPS) and a hands-free phone to provide roadside assistance, travel route support and emergency services. The Bonneville SE has added Galaxy Silver Metallic and Dark Bronzemist Metallic as new exterior colors. Standard on the SE is an electronic load-leveling system to keep the vehicle at the correct height no matter what the cargo load.

Ownership Costs (Projected)

Cost Area	5 Year Cost	Rating
Depreciation	$12,605	◐
Financing ($398/month)	$4,676	
Insurance	$7,140	○
State Fees	$961	
Fuel (Hwy 28 City 19)	$3,176	◐
Maintenance	$2,901	◐
Repairs	$989	◐

Warranty/Maintenance Info

Major Tune-Up (100K mile int.)	$240	◐
Minor Tune-Up (30K mile int.)	$94	○
Brake Service	$262	◐
Overall Warranty	3 yr/36k	◐
Drivetrain Warranty	3 yr/36k	◐
Rust Warranty	6 yr/100k	○
Maintenance Warranty	N/A	
Roadside Assistance	3 yr/36k	

Ownership Costs By Year (Projected)

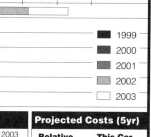

$2,000 $4,000 $6,000 $8,000 $10,000 $12,000 $14,000

Legend: ■ 1999 ■ 2000 ■ 2001 ▨ 2002 ▢ 2003

Resale Value

1999	2000	2001	2002	2003
$20,481	$17,980	$15,777	$13,629	$11,433

Cumulative Costs

	1999	2000	2001	2002	2003
Annual	$7,394	$6,080	$5,824	$5,992	$7,158
Total	$7,394	$13,474	$19,298	$25,290	$32,448

Projected Costs (5yr)

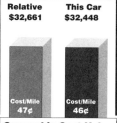

Relative	This Car
$32,661	$32,448
Cost/Mile 47¢	Cost/Mile 46¢

Ownership Cost Value

◐ Average

Pontiac Bonneville SSE
4 Door Sedan

Large

 3.8L 205 hp Gas Fuel Inject.   6 Cylinder "V"   Automatic 4 Speed   2 Wheel Front   Dual Airbags Std

Purchase Price

Car Item	Dealer Cost	List
Base Price	**$27,340**	**$29,880**
Anti-Lock Brakes	Std	Std
Manual Transmission	N/A	N/A
3.8L 240 hp Suprchrg	Pkg	Pkg
Auto Climate Control	Std	Std
Power Steering	Std	Std
Cruise Control	Std	Std
Power Windows	Std	Std
AM/FM Stereo CD	Std	Std
Steering Wheel, Tilt	Std	Std
1SA Package	N/C	N/C
*Options Price	$0	$0
*Total Price	**$27,340**	**$29,880**
Target Price	$28,807	
Destination Charge	$615	
Avg. Tax & Fees	$1,642	
Total Target $	**$31,064**	
Average Dealer Option Cost:	**89%**	
12 Month Price Increase:	2%	

The Bonneville SSE is now offered with a standard EyeCue heads-up display, an option in 1998. A customized Bose eight speaker premium sound system has been designed to match the acoustic environment of the SSE to balance the delivery of music. For individuals who want more performance, the optional SSEi Package offers a supercharged V6 engine that generates 240 hp and 280 lb-ft of torque. It comes with the 4T65-E four speed automatic transmission with driver-selectable shift modes.

Ownership Costs (Projected)

Cost Area	5 Year Cost	Rating
Depreciation	$18,304	●
Financing ($515/month)	$6,043	
Insurance	$7,506	○
State Fees	$1,232	
Fuel (Hwy 28 City 19)	$3,176	◐
Maintenance	$2,940	◐
Repairs	$989	◐

Warranty/Maintenance Info

Major Tune-Up (100K mile int.)	$240	◐
Minor Tune-Up (30K mile int.)	$94	○
Brake Service	$262	◐
Overall Warranty	3 yr/36k	◐
Drivetrain Warranty	3 yr/36k	◐
Rust Warranty	6 yr/100k	○
Maintenance Warranty	N/A	
Roadside Assistance	3 yr/36k	

Ownership Costs By Year (Projected)

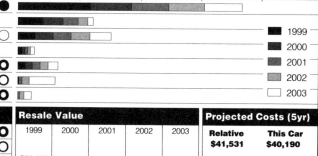

$5,000 $10,000 $15,000 $20,000

Legend: ■ 1999 ■ 2000 ■ 2001 ▨ 2002 ▢ 2003

Resale Value

1999	2000	2001	2002	2003
$25,115	$21,736	$18,689	$15,732	$12,760

Cumulative Costs

	1999	2000	2001	2002	2003
Annual	$10,388	$7,468	$7,078	$7,140	$8,116
Total	$10,388	$17,856	$24,934	$32,074	$40,190

Projected Costs (5yr)

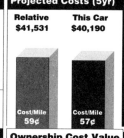

Relative	This Car
$41,531	$40,190
Cost/Mile 59¢	Cost/Mile 57¢

Ownership Cost Value

○ Excellent

146

* Includes shaded options
** Other purchase requirements apply
*** Price includes other options

Legend:
● Poor   ◉ Worse Than Average   ◐ Average   ○ Better Than Average   ○ Excellent   ⊖ Insufficient Information

Refer to *Section 3: Annotated Vehicle Charts* for an explanation of these charts.

©1999 by IntelliChoice, Inc. (408) 866-1400 http://www.intellichoice.com All Rights Reserved. Reproduction Prohibited.

Pontiac Firebird
2 Door Coupe

Base Sport

3.8L 200 hp Gas Fuel Inject.

6 Cylinder "V"

Manual 5 Speed

2 Wheel Rear

Dual Airbags Std

Purchase Price

Car Item	Dealer Cost	List
Base Price	**$16,621**	**$18,165**
Anti-Lock Brakes	Std	Std
Manual 5 Speed	($725)	($815)
Optional Engine	N/A	N/A
Air Conditioning	Std	Std
Power Steering	Std	Std
Cruise Control	Std	Std
Power Windows	Pkg	Pkg
AM/FM Stereo CD	$383	**$430
Steering Wheel, Tilt	Std	Std
1SA Package	N/C	N/C
*Options Price	($725)	($815)
*Total Price	$15,896	$17,350
Target Price	$16,392	
Destination Charge	$535	
Avg. Tax & Fees	$954	
Total Target $	**$17,881**	
Average Dealer Option Cost:	**89%**	
12 Month Price Increase:	1%	

For 1999, the Firebird coupe's fuel tank capacity has increased to 16.8 gallons and the oil monitoring system that determines when an oil change is required is standard. Two new exterior colors are added this year: Pewter and Medium Blue. A limited-slip differential is included with the V6 and the 3800 Performance Package. A six-way power driver's seat and removable locking hatch roof are optional, as is traction control. The Security Package includes a keyless remote entry system and alarm.

Ownership Costs (Projected)

Cost Area	5 Year Cost	Rating
Depreciation	$9,021	◉
Financing ($296/month)	$3,478	
Insurance	$9,365	●
State Fees	$728	
Fuel (Hwy 30 City 19)	$3,070	○
Maintenance	$2,691	○
Repairs	$755	○

Warranty/Maintenance Info

Major Tune-Up (100K mile int.)	$264	○
Minor Tune-Up (30K mile int.)	$134	○
Brake Service	$284	○
Overall Warranty	3 yr/36k	○
Drivetrain Warranty	3 yr/36k	○
Rust Warranty	6 yr/100k	○
Maintenance Warranty	N/A	
Roadside Assistance	3 yr/36k	

Ownership Costs By Year (Projected)

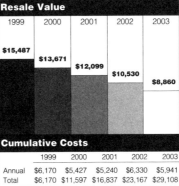

- 1999
- 2000
- 2001
- 2002
- 2003

Resale Value

1999	2000	2001	2002	2003
$15,487	$13,671	$12,099	$10,530	$8,860

Cumulative Costs

	1999	2000	2001	2002	2003
Annual	$6,170	$5,427	$5,240	$6,330	$5,941
Total	$6,170	$11,597	$16,837	$23,167	$29,108

Projected Costs (5yr)

Relative	This Car
$27,815	$29,108
Cost/Mile 40¢	Cost/Mile 42¢

Ownership Cost Value

Worse Than Average

Pontiac Firebird Formula
2 Door Coupe

Base Sport

5.7L 305 hp Gas Fuel Inject.

8 Cylinder "V"

Automatic 4 Speed

2 Wheel Rear

Dual Airbags Std

Purchase Price

Car Item	Dealer Cost	List
Base Price	**$21,104**	**$23,065**
Anti-Lock Brakes	Std	Std
Manual 6 Speed	N/C	N/C
Optional Engine	N/A	N/A
Air Conditioning	Std	Std
Power Steering	Std	Std
Cruise Control	Std	Std
Power Windows	Std	Std
AM/FM Stereo CD	Std	Std
Steering Wheel, Tilt	Std	Std
1SA Package	N/C	N/C
*Options Price	$0	$0
*Total Price	$21,104	$23,065
Target Price	$21,823	
Destination Charge	$535	
Avg. Tax & Fees	$1,255	
Total Target $	**$23,613**	
Average Dealer Option Cost:	**89%**	
12 Month Price Increase:	1%	

For 1999, the Firebird Formula's fuel tank capacity has increased to 16.8 gallons and the oil monitoring system that determines when an oil change is required is standard. The AutoCross Package upgrades the suspension system, and the Ram Air WS6 Package is now equipped with dual exhaust outlets. With the Ram Air Package, the 5.7L V8 engine's power output is increased to 320 hp. A six-way power driver's seat and T-bar roof are optional features. A power steering oil cooler is also available.

Ownership Costs (Projected)

Cost Area	5 Year Cost	Rating
Depreciation	$12,155	●
Financing ($391/month)	$4,593	
Insurance (Performance)	$12,728	●
State Fees	$957	
Fuel (Hwy 28 City 19 -Prem.)	$3,767	○
Maintenance	$3,121	○
Repairs	$755	○

Warranty/Maintenance Info

Major Tune-Up (100K mile int.)	$513	●
Minor Tune-Up (30K mile int.)	$203	●
Brake Service	$284	○
Overall Warranty	3 yr/36k	○
Drivetrain Warranty	3 yr/36k	○
Rust Warranty	6 yr/100k	○
Maintenance Warranty	N/A	
Roadside Assistance	3 yr/36k	

Ownership Costs By Year (Projected)

- 1999
- 2000
- 2001
- 2002
- 2003

Resale Value

1999	2000	2001	2002	2003
$20,556	$18,063	$15,859	$13,690	$11,458

Cumulative Costs

	1999	2000	2001	2002	2003
Annual	$8,046	$7,257	$7,034	$8,139	$7,601
Total	$8,046	$15,303	$22,337	$30,476	$38,077

Projected Costs (5yr)

Relative	This Car
$36,254	$38,077
Cost/Mile 52¢	Cost/Mile 54¢

Ownership Cost Value

Worse Than Average

 Poor   Worse Than Average   ○ Average   Better Than Average   ○ Excellent   ⊖ Insufficient Information

147

Refer to *Section 3: Annotated Vehicle Charts* for an explanation of these charts.

Pontiac Firebird Trans Am
2 Door Coupe

Base Sport

 5.7L 305 hp Gas Fuel Inject.
 8 Cylinder "V"
 Automatic 4 Speed
 2 Wheel Rear
 Dual Airbags Std

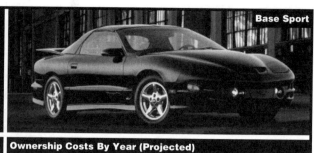

Purchase Price

Car Item	Dealer Cost	List
Base Price	**$23,950**	**$26,175**
Anti-Lock Brakes	Std	Std
Manual 6 Speed	N/C	N/C
Optional Engine	N/A	N/A
Air Conditioning	Std	Std
Power Steering	Std	Std
Cruise Control	Std	Std
Power Windows	Std	Std
AM/FM Stereo CD	Std	Std
Steering Wheel, Tilt	Std	Std
1SA Package	N/C	N/C
*Options Price	$0	$0
*Total Price	**$23,950**	**$26,175**
Target Price	$24,808	
Destination Charge	$535	
Avg. Tax & Fees	$1,420	
Total Target $	**$26,763**	
Average Dealer Option Cost:	***89%***	
12 Month Price Increase:	1%	

For 1999, the Trans Am's fuel tank capacity has increased to 16.8 gallons and the oil monitoring system that determines when an oil change is required is standard. The Ram Air WS6 Package is now equipped with dual exhaust outlets. With the Ram Air Package, the 5.7L V8 engine's power output is increased to 320 hp. Electronic traction control and a power steering oil cooler are available. The optional six speed transmission is now available with a Hurst shifter.

Ownership Costs (Projected)

Cost Area	5 Year Cost	Rating
Depreciation	$13,636	◉
Financing ($444/month)	$5,207	
Insurance (Performance)	$12,728	●
State Fees	$1,081	
Fuel (Hwy 28 City 19 -Prem.)	$3,767	○
Maintenance	$4,073	◉
Repairs	$931	◉

Warranty/Maintenance Info

Major Tune-Up (100K mile int.)	$513	
Minor Tune-Up (30K mile int.)	$203	
Brake Service	$284	○
Overall Warranty	3 yr/36k	○
Drivetrain Warranty	3 yr/36k	○
Rust Warranty	6 yr/100k	○
Maintenance Warranty	N/A	
Roadside Assistance	3 yr/36k	

Ownership Costs By Year (Projected)

$2,000 $4,000 $6,000 $8,000 $10,000 $12,000 $14,000

- 1999
- 2000
- 2001
- 2002
- 2003

Resale Value

1999	2000	2001	2002	2003
$23,618	$20,753	$18,186	$15,681	$13,127

Cumulative Costs

	1999	2000	2001	2002	2003
Annual	$8,373	$7,826	$7,574	$9,598	$8,053
Total	$8,373	$16,199	$23,773	$33,371	$41,424

Projected Costs (5yr)

Relative $40,038	This Car $41,424
Cost/Mile 57¢	Cost/Mile 59¢

Ownership Cost Value

◉ Worse Than Average

Pontiac Firebird
2 Door Convertible

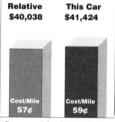

Base Sport

 3.8L 200 hp Gas Fuel Inject.
 6 Cylinder "V"
 Manual 5 Speed
 2 Wheel Rear
 Dual Airbags Std

Trans Am Model Shown

Purchase Price

Car Item	Dealer Cost	List
Base Price	**$22,678**	**$24,785**
Anti-Lock Brakes	Std	Std
Automatic 4 Speed	$725	$815
Optional Engine	N/A	N/A
Air Conditioning	Std	Std
Power Steering	Std	Std
Cruise Control	Std	Std
Power Windows	Std	Std
AM/FM Stereo CD	Std	Std
Steering Wheel, Tilt	Std	Std
1SA Package	N/C	N/C
*Options Price	$0	$0
*Total Price	**$22,678**	**$24,785**
Target Price	$23,472	
Destination Charge	$535	
Avg. Tax & Fees	$1,346	
Total Target $	**$25,353**	
Average Dealer Option Cost:	***89%***	
12 Month Price Increase:	2%	

For 1999, the Firebird convertible's fuel tank capacity has increased to 16.8 gallons and the oil monitoring system that determines when an oil change is required is standard. The Firebird convertible features a power convertible top. A six-way power driver's seat is standard. The available Security Package includes a keyless remote entry system and theft deterrent system. The V6 engine with the 3800 Performance Package includes a Torsen II rear differential. Traction control is now available.

Ownership Costs (Projected)

Cost Area	5 Year Cost	Rating
Depreciation	$12,508	○
Financing ($420/month)	$4,931	
Insurance	$10,589	●
State Fees	$1,026	
Fuel (Hwy 30 City 19)	$3,070	○
Maintenance	$2,691	○
Repairs	$755	○

Warranty/Maintenance Info

Major Tune-Up (100K mile int.)	$264	○
Minor Tune-Up (30K mile int.)	$134	○
Brake Service	$284	○
Overall Warranty	3 yr/36k	○
Drivetrain Warranty	3 yr/36k	○
Rust Warranty	6 yr/100k	○
Maintenance Warranty	N/A	
Roadside Assistance	3 yr/36k	

Ownership Costs By Year (Projected)

$2,000 $4,000 $6,000 $8,000 $10,000 $12,000 $14,000

- 1999
- 2000
- 2001
- 2002
- 2003

Resale Value

1999	2000	2001	2002	2003
$22,845	$20,114	$17,677	$15,289	$12,845

Cumulative Costs

	1999	2000	2001	2002	2003
Annual	$7,086	$7,048	$6,710	$7,641	$7,085
Total	$7,086	$14,134	$20,844	$28,485	$35,570

Projected Costs (5yr)

Relative $38,419	This Car $35,570
Cost/Mile 55¢	Cost/Mile 51¢

Ownership Cost Value

○ Excellent

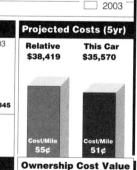

148

● Poor	◉ Worse Than Average	○ Average	○ Better Than Average	○ Excellent	⊖ Insufficient Information

Refer to *Section 3: Annotated Vehicle Charts* for an explanation of these charts.

Pontiac Firebird Trans Am
2 Door Convertible

Base Sport

5.7L 305 hp Gas Fuel Inject.	8 Cylinder "V"	Automatic 4 Speed	2 Wheel Rear	Dual Airbags Std

Purchase Price

Car Item	Dealer Cost	List
Base Price	**$27,674**	**$30,245**
Anti-Lock Brakes	Std	Std
Manual 6 Speed	N/C	N/C
Optional Engine	N/A	N/A
Air Conditioning	Std	Std
Power Steering	Std	Std
Cruise Control	Std	Std
Power Windows	Std	Std
AM/FM Stereo CD	Std	Std
Steering Wheel, Tilt	Std	Std
1SA Package	N/C	N/C
*Options Price	$0	$0
*Total Price	**$27,674**	**$30,245**
Target Price	$28,728	
Destination Charge	$535	
Avg. Tax & Fees	$1,638	
Total Target $	**$30,901**	
Average Dealer Option Cost:	**89%**	
12 Month Price Increase:	2%	

For 1999, the Trans Am convertible's fuel tank capacity has increased to 16.8 gallons and the oil monitoring system that determines when an oil change is required is standard. The Ram Air WS6 Package is now equipped with dual exhaust outlets, and increases the 5.7L V8 engine's power output to 320 hp. The optional six speed transmission is now available with a Hurst shifter. Electronic traction control and a power steering oil cooler are also available.

Ownership Costs (Projected)

Cost Area	5 Year Cost	Rating
Depreciation	$14,649	◐
Financing ($512/month)	$6,011	◐
Insurance (Performance)	$15,275	●
State Fees	$1,244	◐
Fuel (Hwy 28 City 19 -Prem.)	$3,767	◐
Maintenance	$4,073	●
Repairs	$931	◑

Warranty/Maintenance Info

Major Tune-Up (100K mile int.)	$513	●
Minor Tune-Up (30K mile int.)	$203	●
Brake Service	$284	◐
Overall Warranty	3 yr/36k	◐
Drivetrain Warranty	3 yr/36k	◐
Rust Warranty	6 yr/100k	○
Maintenance Warranty	N/A	
Roadside Assistance	3 yr/36k	

Ownership Costs By Year (Projected)

$5,000 — $10,000 — $15,000 — $20,000

■ 1999
■ 2000
■ 2001
■ 2002
□ 2003

Resale Value

1999	2000	2001	2002	2003
$28,490	$25,151	$22,138	$19,207	$16,252

Cumulative Costs

	1999	2000	2001	2002	2003
Annual	$8,440	$9,056	$8,728	$10,678	$9,049
Total	$8,440	$17,496	$26,224	$36,902	$45,951

Projected Costs (5yr)

Relative	This Car
$44,105	**$45,951**
Cost/Mile 63¢	Cost/Mile 66¢

Ownership Cost Value

◉

Worse Than Average

Pontiac Grand Am SE
2 Door Coupe

Compact

2.4L 150 hp Gas Fuel Inject.	4 Cylinder In-Line	Automatic 4 Speed	2 Wheel Front	Dual Airbags Std

Purchase Price

Car Item	Dealer Cost	List
Base Price	**$14,521**	**$15,870**
Anti-Lock Brakes	Std	Std
Manual Transmission	N/A	N/A
Optional Engine	N/A	N/A
Air Conditioning	Std	Std
Power Steering	Std	Std
Cruise Control	$209	$235
Power Windows	N/A	N/A
AM/FM Stereo Cassette	$174	$195
Steering Wheel, Tilt	Std	Std
1SA Package	N/C	N/C
*Options Price	$174	$195
*Total Price	**$14,695**	**$16,065**
Target Price	$15,469	
Destination Charge	$525	
Avg. Tax & Fees	$899	
Total Target $	**$16,893**	
Average Dealer Option Cost:	**89%**	
12 Month Price Increase:	4%	

The 1999 Grand Am SE coupe features a completely redesigned interior and exterior. New features include a wheelbase increased by 3.6 inches and rear cornering lamps for extra illumination when backing up. Standard safety features on the SE include daytime running lamps, an antilock braking system, a rear defroster and battery rundown protection. A rear spoiler, an engine block heater, cruise control and an AM/FM stereo with cassette and CD are available as optional equipment.

Ownership Costs (Projected)

Cost Area	5 Year Cost	Rating
Depreciation	$8,390	○
Financing ($280/month)	$3,286	◐
Insurance	$7,837	◑
State Fees	$677	◐
Fuel (Hwy 30 City 22)	$2,855	◐
Maintenance	$2,459	○
Repairs	$720	○

Warranty/Maintenance Info

Major Tune-Up (100K mile int.)	$160	○
Minor Tune-Up (30K mile int.)	$76	○
Brake Service	$197	○
Overall Warranty	3 yr/36k	◐
Drivetrain Warranty	3 yr/36k	◐
Rust Warranty	6 yr/100k	○
Maintenance Warranty	N/A	
Roadside Assistance	3 yr/36k	

Ownership Costs By Year (Projected)

$2,000 — $4,000 — $6,000 — $8,000 — $10,000

■ 1999
■ 2000
■ 2001
■ 2002
□ 2003

Resale Value

1999	2000	2001	2002	2003
$14,363	$12,772	$11,364	$9,938	$8,503

Cumulative Costs

	1999	2000	2001	2002	2003
Annual	$5,894	$4,794	$4,701	$5,434	$5,401
Total	$5,894	$10,688	$15,389	$20,823	$26,224

Projected Costs (5yr)

Relative	This Car
$26,525	**$26,224**
Cost/Mile 38¢	Cost/Mile 37¢

Ownership Cost Value

○

Average

● Poor ◉ Worse Than Average ◑ Average ◐ Better Than Average ○ Excellent ⊖ Insufficient Information

Refer to *Section 3: Annotated Vehicle Charts* for an explanation of these charts.

Pontiac Grand Am SE 1
2 Door Coupe

Compact

 2.4L 150 hp Gas Fuel Inject.　 4 Cylinder In-Line　 PRND321 Automatic 4 Speed　 2 Wheel Front　 Dual Airbags Std

Base Model Shown

Purchase Price

Car Item	Dealer Cost	List
Base Price	**$15,802**	**$17,270**
Anti-Lock Brakes	Std	Std
Manual Transmission	N/A	N/A
3.4L 170 hp Gas	$530	$595
Air Conditioning	Std	Std
Power Steering	Std	Std
Cruise Control	Std	Std
Power Windows	Std	Std
AM/FM Stereo Cassette	Std	Std
Steering Wheel, Tilt	Std	Std
1SB Package	N/C	N/C
*Options Price	$0	$0
*Total Price	$15,802	$17,270
Target Price	$16,655	
Destination Charge	$525	
Avg. Tax & Fees	$964	
Total Target $	**$18,144**	
Average Dealer Option Cost:	**89%**	
12 Month Price Increase:	None	

The 1999 Grand Am SE1 coupe features a redesigned interior and exterior. Also new, the optional 3.4L V6 engine now produces 170 hp while achieving nearly the same fuel economy as its predecessor. The SE1 features five spoke aluminum wheels, dual power exterior mirrors, a power driver's seat height adjuster and a split folding rear seat as standard equipment. Optional features include a power glass sunroof, a keyless remote entry system and an AM/FM stereo with CD.

Ownership Costs (Projected)

Cost Area	5 Year Cost	Rating
Depreciation	$9,007	○
Financing ($301/month)	$3,530	○
Insurance	$7,837	●
State Fees	$725	○
Fuel (Hwy 30 City 22)	$2,855	O
Maintenance	$2,459	○
Repairs	$720	O

Warranty/Maintenance Info

Major Tune-Up (100K mile int.)	$160	○
Minor Tune-Up (30K mile int.)	$76	○
Brake Service	$197	O
Overall Warranty	3 yr/36k	O
Drivetrain Warranty	3 yr/36k	O
Rust Warranty	6 yr/100k	O
Maintenance Warranty	N/A	
Roadside Assistance	3 yr/36k	

Ownership Costs By Year (Projected)

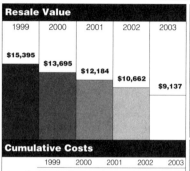

$2,000　$4,000　$6,000　$8,000　$10,000

■ 1999
■ 2000
■ 2001
□ 2002
□ 2003

Resale Value

1999	2000	2001	2002	2003
$15,395	$13,695	$12,184	$10,662	$9,137

Cumulative Costs

	1999	2000	2001	2002	2003
Annual	$6,208	$4,981	$4,864	$5,571	$5,509
Total	$6,208	$11,189	$16,053	$21,624	$27,133

Projected Costs (5yr)

Relative	This Car
$27,585	$27,133
Cost/Mile 39¢	Cost/Mile 39¢

Ownership Cost Value

○

Better Than Average

Pontiac Grand Am SE 2
2 Door Coupe

Compact

 3.4L 170 hp Gas Fuel Inject.　 6 Cylinder "V"　 PRND321 Automatic 4 Speed　 2 Wheel Front　 Dual Airbags Std

Base Model Shown

Purchase Price

Car Item	Dealer Cost	List
Base Price	**$17,175**	**$18,770**
Anti-Lock Brakes	Std	Std
Manual Transmission	N/A	N/A
2.4L 150 hp Gas	($530)	($595)
Air Conditioning	Std	Std
Power Steering	Std	Std
Cruise Control	Std	Std
Power Windows	Std	Std
AM/FM Stereo CD	Std	Std
Steering Wheel, Tilt	Std	Std
1SC Package	N/C	N/C
*Options Price	($530)	($595)
*Total Price	$16,645	$18,175
Target Price	$17,565	
Destination Charge	$525	
Avg. Tax & Fees	$1,014	
Total Target $	**$19,104**	
Average Dealer Option Cost:	**89%**	
12 Month Price Increase:	N/A	

For 1999, the Grand Am SE2 coupe features a completely redesigned interior and exterior. Some new standard features include rear cornering lamps, a longer wheelbase and a larger 3.4L engine producing 170 hp. The interior features standard amenities such as power windows and door locks, a CD player, a high-performance speaker system and a keyless remote entry system. A power glass moonroof, six-way power driver's seat adjuster and leather seating are optional.

Ownership Costs (Projected)

Cost Area	5 Year Cost	Rating
Depreciation	$9,491	○
Financing ($317/month)	$3,715	○
Insurance	$7,837	●
State Fees	$761	○
Fuel (Hwy 30 City 22)	$2,855	O
Maintenance	$2,570	○
Repairs	$720	O

Warranty/Maintenance Info

Major Tune-Up (100K mile int.)	$160	○
Minor Tune-Up (30K mile int.)	$76	○
Brake Service	$197	O
Overall Warranty	3 yr/36k	O
Drivetrain Warranty	3 yr/36k	O
Rust Warranty	6 yr/100k	O
Maintenance Warranty	N/A	
Roadside Assistance	3 yr/36k	

Ownership Costs By Year (Projected)

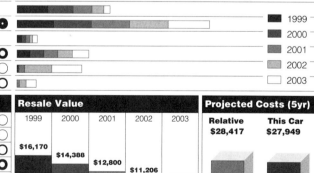

$2,000　$4,000　$6,000　$8,000　$10,000

■ 1999
■ 2000
■ 2001
□ 2002
□ 2003

Resale Value

1999	2000	2001	2002	2003
$16,170	$14,388	$12,800	$11,206	$9,613

Cumulative Costs

	1999	2000	2001	2002	2003
Annual	$6,465	$5,122	$4,987	$5,784	$5,591
Total	$6,465	$11,587	$16,574	$22,358	$27,949

Projected Costs (5yr)

Relative	This Car
$28,417	$27,949
Cost/Mile 41¢	Cost/Mile 40¢

Ownership Cost Value

○

Better Than Average

Pontiac Grand Am GT
2 Door Coupe

Compact

 3.4L 175 hp Gas Fuel Inject.
 6 Cylinder "V"
 Automatic 4 Speed
 2 Wheel Front
Depowered Dual Airbags Std

Purchase Price

Car Item	Dealer Cost	List
Base Price	**$17,449**	**$19,070**
Anti-Lock Brakes	Std	Std
Manual Transmission	N/A	N/A
Optional Engine	N/A	N/A
Air Conditioning	Std	Std
Power Steering	Std	Std
Cruise Control	Std	Std
Power Windows	Std	Std
AM/FM Stereo Cassette	Std	Std
Steering Wheel, Tilt	Std	Std
1SA Package	N/C	N/C
*Options Price	**$0**	**$0**
*Total Price	**$17,449**	**$19,070**
Target Price	$18,421	
Destination Charge	$525	
Avg. Tax & Fees	$1,062	
Total Target $	**$20,008**	
Average Dealer Option Cost:	**89%**	
12 Month Price Increase:	11%	

The 1999 Grand Am GT coupe features a completely redesigned interior and exterior. Key refinements for the GT coupe include a wider front fascia, a larger air dam opening and a redesigned grille for improved airflow. In addition, the 3.4L engine now produces 175 hp and torque is increased to 205 lb-ft. The list of luxury amenities on the GT includes air conditioning, programmable door locks, battery rundown protection and an AM/FM stereo with cassette.

Ownership Costs (Projected)

Cost Area	5 Year Cost	Rating
Depreciation	$10,627	◐
Financing ($332/month)	$3,893	
Insurance	$8,265	◉
State Fees	$797	
Fuel (Hwy 28 City 20)	$3,097	◉
Maintenance	$2,732	○
Repairs	$720	○

Warranty/Maintenance Info

Major Tune-Up (100K mile int.)	$212	○
Minor Tune-Up (30K mile int.)	$99	○
Brake Service	$215	○
Overall Warranty	3 yr/36k	○
Drivetrain Warranty	3 yr/36k	○
Rust Warranty	6 yr/100k	○
Maintenance Warranty	N/A	
Roadside Assistance	3 yr/36k	

Ownership Costs By Year (Projected)

$2,000 $4,000 $6,000 $8,000 $10,000 $12,000

■ 1999 ■ 2000 ■ 2001 ■ 2002 □ 2003

Resale Value

1999	2000	2001	2002	2003
$16,488	$14,564	$12,839	$11,107	$9,381

Cumulative Costs

	1999	2000	2001	2002	2003
Annual	$7,250	$5,454	$5,327	$6,229	$5,871
Total	$7,250	$12,704	$18,031	$24,260	$30,131

Projected Costs (5yr)

Relative	This Car
$29,231	$30,131
Cost/Mile 42¢	Cost/Mile 43¢

Ownership Cost Value
◉ Worse Than Average

Pontiac Grand Am GT 1
2 Door Coupe

Compact

 3.4L 175 hp Gas Fuel Inject.
 6 Cylinder "V"
 Automatic 4 Speed
 2 Wheel Front
Depowered Dual Airbags Std

Base Model Shown

Purchase Price

Car Item	Dealer Cost	List
Base Price	**$18,822**	**$20,570**
Anti-Lock Brakes	Std	Std
Manual Transmission	N/A	N/A
Optional Engine	N/A	N/A
Air Conditioning	Std	Std
Power Steering	Std	Std
Cruise Control	Std	Std
Power Windows	Std	Std
AM/FM Stereo CD	Std	Std
Steering Wheel, Tilt	Std	Std
1SB Package	N/C	N/C
*Options Price	**$0**	**$0**
*Total Price	**$18,822**	**$20,570**
Target Price	$19,898	
Destination Charge	$525	
Avg. Tax & Fees	$1,143	
Total Target $	**$21,566**	
Average Dealer Option Cost:	**89%**	
12 Month Price Increase:	N/A	

Redesigned for 1999, the Grand Am GT1 coupe is equipped with standard equipment upgrades such as a six-way power driver's seat, a power moonroof and a high-performance AM/FM stereo with CD. Exterior changes include a wider front fascia, a larger air dam opening and a redesigned grille for improved airflow. The 3.4L engine now produces 175 hp and torque is increased to 205 lb-ft. For added safety, four wheel antilock disc brakes and daytime running lamps are standard.

Ownership Costs (Projected)

Cost Area	5 Year Cost	Rating
Depreciation	$11,994	●
Financing ($357/month)	$4,195	
Insurance	$8,265	◉
State Fees	$858	
Fuel (Hwy 28 City 20)	$3,097	◉
Maintenance	$2,612	○
Repairs	$720	○

Warranty/Maintenance Info

Major Tune-Up (100K mile int.)	$212	○
Minor Tune-Up (30K mile int.)	$99	○
Brake Service	$215	○
Overall Warranty	3 yr/36k	○
Drivetrain Warranty	3 yr/36k	○
Rust Warranty	6 yr/100k	○
Maintenance Warranty	N/A	
Roadside Assistance	3 yr/36k	

Ownership Costs By Year (Projected)

$2,000 $4,000 $6,000 $8,000 $10,000 $12,000

■ 1999 ■ 2000 ■ 2001 ■ 2002 □ 2003

Resale Value

1999	2000	2001	2002	2003
$17,373	$15,261	$13,357	$11,458	$9,572

Cumulative Costs

	1999	2000	2001	2002	2003
Annual	$8,041	$5,739	$5,580	$6,327	$6,054
Total	$8,041	$13,780	$19,360	$25,687	$31,741

Projected Costs (5yr)

Relative	This Car
$30,667	$31,741
Cost/Mile 44¢	Cost/Mile 45¢

Ownership Cost Value
● Worse Than Average

---

* Includes shaded options

** Other purchase requirements apply

*** Price includes other options

 Poor
 Worse Than Average
 Average
 Better Than Average
 Excellent
 Insufficient Information

Refer to *Section 3: Annotated Vehicle Charts* for an explanation of these charts.

151

Pontiac Grand Am SE
4 Door Sedan

Compact

 2.4L 150 hp Gas Fuel Inject.　 4 Cylinder In-Line　Automatic 4 Speed　2 Wheel Front　Dual Airbags Std

Purchase Price

Car Item	Dealer Cost	List
Base Price	**$14,704**	**$16,070**
Anti-Lock Brakes	Std	Std
Manual Transmission	N/A	N/A
Optional Engine	N/A	N/A
Air Conditioning	Std	Std
Power Steering	Std	Std
Cruise Control	$209	$235
Power Windows	N/A	N/A
AM/FM Stereo Cassette	$174	$195
Steering Wheel, Tilt	Std	Std
1SA Package	N/C	N/C
*Options Price	**$174**	**$195**
*Total Price	**$14,878**	**$16,265**
Target Price	$15,664	
Destination Charge	$525	
Avg. Tax & Fees	$910	
Total Target $	**$17,099**	
Average Dealer Option Cost:	*89%*	
12 Month Price Increase:	*4%*	

The 1999 Grand Am SE sedan has been completely redesigned. The exterior now sports cat's-eye headlamps, a longer wheelbase and rear cornering lamps. The SE also includes safety features such as an enhanced traction system, front fog lamps, daytime running lamps and a rear window defroster. Standard interior amenities include power door locks, a tilt steering wheel and air conditioning. A rear spoiler, a keyless remote entry system and an AM/FM stereo with CD are available as optional equipment.

Ownership Costs (Projected)

Cost Area	5 Year Cost	Rating
Depreciation	$8,545	◔
Financing ($283/month)	$3,327	
Insurance	$7,463	●
State Fees	$685	
Fuel (Hwy 30 City 22)	$2,855	◕
Maintenance	$2,459	○
Repairs	$720	◔

Warranty/Maintenance Info

Major Tune-Up (100K mile int.)	$160	○
Minor Tune-Up (30K mile int.)	$76	○
Brake Service	$197	◔
Overall Warranty	3 yr/36k	●
Drivetrain Warranty	3 yr/36k	●
Rust Warranty	6 yr/100k	◔
Maintenance Warranty	N/A	
Roadside Assistance	3 yr/36k	

Ownership Costs By Year (Projected)

Legend: 1999, 2000, 2001, 2002, 2003

Resale Value

1999	2000	2001	2002	2003
$14,630	$12,972	$11,508	$10,033	$8,554

Cumulative Costs

	1999	2000	2001	2002	2003
Annual	$5,778	$4,801	$4,692	$5,413	$5,370
Total	$5,778	$10,579	$15,271	$20,684	$26,054

Projected Costs (5yr)

Relative	This Car
$26,698	$26,054
Cost/Mile 38¢	Cost/Mile 37¢

Ownership Cost Value
○ Better Than Average

Pontiac Grand Am SE 1
4 Door Sedan

Compact

 2.4L 150 hp Gas Fuel Inject.　 4 Cylinder In-Line　Automatic 4 Speed　2 Wheel Front　Dual Airbags Std

Base Model Shown

Purchase Price

Car Item	Dealer Cost	List
Base Price	**$15,985**	**$17,470**
Anti-Lock Brakes	Std	Std
Manual Transmission	N/A	N/A
3.4L 170 hp Gas	$530	$595
Air Conditioning	Std	Std
Power Steering	Std	Std
Cruise Control	Std	Std
Power Windows	Std	Std
AM/FM Stereo Cassette	Std	Std
Steering Wheel, Tilt	Std	Std
1SB Package	N/C	N/C
*Options Price	**$0**	**$0**
*Total Price	**$15,985**	**$17,470**
Target Price	$16,851	
Destination Charge	$525	
Avg. Tax & Fees	$975	
Total Target $	**$18,351**	
Average Dealer Option Cost:	*89%*	
12 Month Price Increase:	*None*	

The 1999 Grand Am SE1 sedan sports a redesigned interior and exterior. The all-new optional 3.4L V6 engine produces more horsepower than the previous 3.1L engine with nearly the fuel economy. Rear cornering lamps, dual power exterior mirrors, daytime running lamps and battery rundown protection are standard safety features. Options on the SE1 sedan include a power glass moonroof, a rear spoiler, a keyless remote entry system and a CD player.

Ownership Costs (Projected)

Cost Area	5 Year Cost	Rating
Depreciation	$9,166	○
Financing ($304/month)	$3,569	
Insurance	$7,463	●
State Fees	$733	
Fuel (Hwy 30 City 22)	$2,855	◕
Maintenance	$2,459	○
Repairs	$720	○

Warranty/Maintenance Info

Major Tune-Up (100K mile int.)	$160	○
Minor Tune-Up (30K mile int.)	$76	○
Brake Service	$197	○
Overall Warranty	3 yr/36k	●
Drivetrain Warranty	3 yr/36k	●
Rust Warranty	6 yr/100k	○
Maintenance Warranty	N/A	
Roadside Assistance	3 yr/36k	

Ownership Costs By Year (Projected)

Legend: 1999, 2000, 2001, 2002, 2003

Resale Value

1999	2000	2001	2002	2003
$15,669	$13,898	$12,329	$10,756	$9,185

Cumulative Costs

	1999	2000	2001	2002	2003
Annual	$6,085	$4,992	$4,857	$5,551	$5,480
Total	$6,085	$11,077	$15,934	$21,485	$26,965

Projected Costs (5yr)

Relative	This Car
$27,764	$26,965
Cost/Mile 40¢	Cost/Mile 39¢

Ownership Cost Value
○ Better Than Average

Pontiac Grand Am SE 2
4 Door Sedan

Compact

| 3.4L 170 hp Gas Fuel Inject. | 6 Cylinder "V" | Automatic 4 Speed | 2 Wheel Front | Dual Airbags Std |

Base Model Shown

Purchase Price

Car Item	Dealer Cost	List
Base Price	**$17,358**	**$18,970**
Anti-Lock Brakes	Std	Std
Manual Transmission	N/A	N/A
2.4L 150 hp Gas	($530)	($595)
Air Conditioning	Std	Std
Power Steering	Std	Std
Cruise Control	Std	Std
Power Windows	Std	Std
AM/FM Stereo CD	Std	Std
Steering Wheel, Tilt	Std	Std
1SC Package	N/C	N/C
*Options Price	**($530)**	**($595)**
*Total Price	**$16,828**	**$18,375**
Target Price	$17,717	
Destination Charge	$525	
Avg. Tax & Fees	$1,023	
Total Target $	**$19,265**	
Average Dealer Option Cost:	**89%**	
12 Month Price Increase:	N/A	

The 1999 Grand Am SE2 sedan sports a complete redesign of the interior and exterior and features a new 3.4L engine with 170 hp. Standard equipment on the SE2 sedan includes power windows, 16 inch multi-spoke aluminum wheels, an AM/FM stereo with CD, a high-performance speaker system and a keyless remote entry system. The SE2 also features the Sport Interior Group, which includes a leather-wrapped steering wheel, cargo net, driver's lumbar support and map/reading lights.

Ownership Costs (Projected)

Cost Area	5 Year Cost	Rating
Depreciation	$9,607	O
Financing ($319/month)	$3,749	
Insurance	$7,463	O
State Fees	$768	
Fuel (Hwy 30 City 22)	$2,855	O
Maintenance	$2,570	O
Repairs	$720	O

Warranty/Maintenance Info

Major Tune-Up (100K mile int.)	$160	O
Minor Tune-Up (30K mile int.)	$76	O
Brake Service	$197	O
Overall Warranty	3 yr/36k	O
Drivetrain Warranty	3 yr/36k	O
Rust Warranty	6 yr/100k	O
Maintenance Warranty	N/A	
Roadside Assistance	3 yr/36k	

Ownership Costs By Year (Projected)

$2,000 $4,000 $6,000 $8,000 $10,000

■ 1999
■ 2000
■ 2001
□ 2002
□ 2003

Resale Value

1999	2000	2001	2002	2003
$16,449	$14,594	$12,946	$11,298	$9,658

Cumulative Costs

	1999	2000	2001	2002	2003
Annual	$6,289	$5,133	$4,980	$5,767	$5,563
Total	$6,289	$11,422	$16,402	$22,169	$27,732

Projected Costs (5yr)

Relative	This Car
$28,601	$27,732
Cost/Mile 41¢	Cost/Mile 40¢

Ownership Cost Value

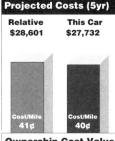

Excellent

Pontiac Grand Am GT
4 Door Sedan

Compact

| 3.4L 175 hp Gas Fuel Inject. | 6 Cylinder "V" | Automatic 4 Speed | 2 Wheel Front | Dual Airbags Std |

Purchase Price

Car Item	Dealer Cost	List
Base Price	**$17,815**	**$19,470**
Anti-Lock Brakes	Std	Std
Manual Transmission	N/A	N/A
Optional Engine	N/A	N/A
Air Conditioning	Std	Std
Power Steering	Std	Std
Cruise Control	Std	Std
Power Windows	Std	Std
AM/FM Stereo Cassette	Std	Std
Steering Wheel, Tilt	Std	Std
1SA Package	N/C	N/C
*Options Price	**$0**	**$0**
*Total Price	**$17,815**	**$19,470**
Target Price	$18,815	
Destination Charge	$525	
Avg. Tax & Fees	$1,083	
Total Target $	**$20,423**	
Average Dealer Option Cost:	**89%**	
12 Month Price Increase:	12%	

The 1999 Grand Am GT sedan sports a complete redesign of its interior and exterior and includes four-wheel disc brakes and an upgraded 3.4L engine with 175 hp and 205 lb-ft of torque. Additional improvements include a wider front fascia, a larger air dam opening and a redesigned grille for improved airflow. The GT sedan also features the Sport Interior Group, which includes a leather-wrapped steering wheel, cargo net, manual driver's lumbar support and map/reading lights.

Ownership Costs (Projected)

Cost Area	5 Year Cost	Rating
Depreciation	$10,998	O
Financing ($339/month)	$3,973	
Insurance	$7,837	O
State Fees	$813	
Fuel (Hwy 28 City 20)	$3,097	◉
Maintenance	$2,612	O
Repairs	$720	O

Warranty/Maintenance Info

Major Tune-Up (100K mile int.)	$212	O
Minor Tune-Up (30K mile int.)	$99	O
Brake Service	$215	O
Overall Warranty	3 yr/36k	O
Drivetrain Warranty	3 yr/36k	O
Rust Warranty	6 yr/100k	O
Maintenance Warranty	N/A	
Roadside Assistance	3 yr/36k	

Ownership Costs By Year (Projected)

$2,000 $4,000 $6,000 $8,000 $10,000 $12,000

■ 1999
■ 2000
■ 2001
□ 2002
□ 2003

Resale Value

1999	2000	2001	2002	2003
$16,949	$14,906	$13,072	$11,243	$9,425

Cumulative Costs

	1999	2000	2001	2002	2003
Annual	$7,153	$5,515	$5,370	$6,133	$5,879
Total	$7,153	$12,668	$18,038	$24,171	$30,050

Projected Costs (5yr)

Relative	This Car
$29,608	$30,050
Cost/Mile 42¢	Cost/Mile 43¢

Ownership Cost Value

Average

---

* Includes shaded options

** Other purchase requirements apply

*** Price includes other options

 Poor   Worse Than Average   Average   Better Than Average   Excellent   Insufficient Information

153

Refer to *Section 3: Annotated Vehicle Charts* for an explanation of these charts.

Pontiac Grand Am GT 1
4 Door Sedan

3.4L 175 hp Gas Fuel Inject.	6 Cylinder "V"	Automatic 4 Speed	2 Wheel Front	Dual Airbags Std

Compact

Base Model Shown

Purchase Price

Car Item	Dealer Cost	List
Base Price	**$19,188**	**$20,970**
Anti-Lock Brakes	Std	Std
Manual Transmission	N/A	N/A
Optional Engine	N/A	N/A
Air Conditioning	Std	Std
Power Steering	Std	Std
Cruise Control	Std	Std
Power Windows	Std	Std
AM/FM Stereo CD	Std	Std
Steering Wheel, Tilt	Std	Std
1SB Package	N/C	N/C
***Options Price**	$0	$0
***Total Price**	**$19,188**	**$20,970**
Target Price	$20,240	
Destination Charge	$525	
Avg. Tax & Fees	$1,162	
Total Target $	**$21,927**	
Average Dealer Option Cost:	89%	
12 Month Price Increase:	N/A	

The Grand Am GT1 sedan has been redesigned for 1999 with a longer wheelbase and a wider stance. Exterior changes include a wider front fascia, a larger air dam opening and a redesigned grille for improved airflow. The 3.4L engine also boasts an increase in output, now generating 175 hp and 205 lb-ft of torque. Safety enhancements include automatic daytime running lamps, steering wheel radio controls and the addition of four wheel antilock disc brakes.

Ownership Costs (Projected)

Cost Area	5 Year Cost	Rating
Depreciation	$12,311	●
Financing ($363/month)	$4,267	
Insurance	$7,837	◐
State Fees	$872	
Fuel (Hwy 28 City 20)	$3,097	●
Maintenance	$2,612	◐
Repairs	$720	◐

Warranty/Maintenance Info

Major Tune-Up (100K mile int.)	$212	◐
Minor Tune-Up (30K mile int.)	$99	◐
Brake Service	$215	◐
Overall Warranty	3 yr/36k	◐
Drivetrain Warranty	3 yr/36k	◐
Rust Warranty	6 yr/100k	◐
Maintenance Warranty	N/A	
Roadside Assistance	3 yr/36k	

Ownership Costs By Year (Projected)

$2,000 $4,000 $6,000 $8,000 $10,000 $12,000 $14,000

■ 1999
■ 2000
■ 2001
■ 2002
□ 2003

Resale Value

1999	2000	2001	2002	2003
$17,824	$15,596	$13,585	$11,590	$9,616

Cumulative Costs

	1999	2000	2001	2002	2003
Annual	$7,897	$5,794	$5,620	$6,347	$6,058
Total	$7,897	$13,691	$19,311	$25,658	$31,716

Projected Costs (5yr)

Relative	This Car
$31,059	$31,716
Cost/Mile 44¢	Cost/Mile 45¢

Ownership Cost Value

◐

Average

Pontiac Grand Prix GT
2 Door Coupe

3.8L 200 hp Gas Fuel Inject.	6 Cylinder "V"	Automatic 4 Speed	2 Wheel Front	Dual Airbags Std

Midsize

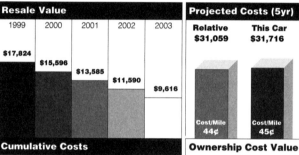

Purchase Price

Car Item	Dealer Cost	List
Base Price	**$19,210**	**$20,995**
Anti-Lock Brakes	Std	Std
Manual Transmission	N/A	N/A
Optional Engine	N/A	N/A
Air Conditioning	Std	Std
Power Steering	Std	Std
Cruise Control	Std	Std
Power Windows	Std	Std
AM/FM Stereo Cassette	Std	Std
Steering Wheel, Tilt	Std	Std
1SA Package	N/C	N/C
***Options Price**	$0	$0
***Total Price**	**$19,210**	**$20,995**
Target Price	$20,317	
Destination Charge	$560	
Avg. Tax & Fees	$1,168	
Total Target $	**$22,045**	
Average Dealer Option Cost:	89%	
12 Month Price Increase:	3%	

The Grand Prix GT coupe is now available with an optional customized Bose eight speaker premium sound system. It is designed to match the acoustical environment of the GT's interior, resulting in a balanced delivery of sound anywhere in the vehicle. Dark Bronzemist Metallic and Medium Gulf Blue Metallic have been added to the exterior color schemes. Automatic dual-zone climate control, a power sliding moonroof, keyless remote entry system and leather seating are optional equipment.

Ownership Costs (Projected)

Cost Area	5 Year Cost	Rating
Depreciation	$10,092	○
Financing ($365/month)	$4,288	
Insurance	$7,463	◐
State Fees	$875	
Fuel (Hwy 30 City 19)	$3,070	◐
Maintenance	$3,142	◐
Repairs	$895	◐

Warranty/Maintenance Info

Major Tune-Up (100K mile int.)	$243	◐
Minor Tune-Up (30K mile int.)	$124	◐
Brake Service	$242	◐
Overall Warranty	3 yr/36k	◐
Drivetrain Warranty	3 yr/36k	◐
Rust Warranty	6 yr/100k	○
Maintenance Warranty	N/A	
Roadside Assistance	3 yr/36k	

Ownership Costs By Year (Projected)

$2,000 $4,000 $6,000 $8,000 $10,000 $12,000

■ 1999
■ 2000
■ 2001
■ 2002
□ 2003

Resale Value

1999	2000	2001	2002	2003
$20,017	$17,773	$15,827	$13,854	$11,953

Cumulative Costs

	1999	2000	2001	2002	2003
Annual	$5,753	$5,739	$5,552	$5,777	$7,004
Total	$5,753	$11,492	$17,044	$22,821	$29,825

Projected Costs (5yr)

Relative	This Car
$30,714	$29,825
Cost/Mile 44¢	Cost/Mile 43¢

Ownership Cost Value

○

Better Than Average

Pontiac Grand Prix GTP
2 Door Coupe

Midsize

GT Model Shown

- 3.8L 240 hp Suprchrged Fuel Inject.
- 6 Cylinder "V"
- Automatic 4 Speed
- 2 Wheel Front
- Dual Airbags Std

Purchase Price

Car Item	Dealer Cost	List
Base Price	**$21,740**	**$23,760**
Anti-Lock Brakes	Std	Std
Manual Transmission	N/A	N/A
Optional Engine	N/A	N/A
Air Conditioning	Std	Std
Power Steering	Std	Std
Cruise Control	Std	Std
Power Windows	Std	Std
AM/FM Stereo CD	Std	Std
Steering Wheel, Tilt	Std	Std
1SA Package	$467	***$525
***Options Price**	$467	$525
***Total Price**	**$22,207**	**$24,285**
Target Price	$23,421	
Destination Charge	$560	
Avg. Tax & Fees	$1,340	
Total Target $	**$25,321**	
Average Dealer Option Cost:	**89%**	
12 Month Price Increase:	N/A	

Ownership Costs (Projected)

Cost Area	5 Year Cost	Rating
Depreciation	$12,129	◐
Financing ($420/month)	$4,926	
Insurance (Performance)	$9,007	◐
State Fees	$1,007	
Fuel (Hwy 28 City 18 -Prem.)	$3,871	◉
Maintenance	$3,186	◐
Repairs	$1,056	●

Warranty/Maintenance Info

Major Tune-Up (100K mile int.)	$243	◐
Minor Tune-Up (30K mile int.)	$124	◐
Brake Service	$242	◐
Overall Warranty	3 yr/36k	◐
Drivetrain Warranty	3 yr/36k	◐
Rust Warranty	6 yr/100k	○
Maintenance Warranty	N/A	
Roadside Assistance	3 yr/36k	

Ownership Costs By Year (Projected)

$2,000 $4,000 $6,000 $8,000 $10,000 $12,000 $14,000

- 1999
- 2000
- 2001
- 2002
- 2003

Resale Value

1999	2000	2001	2002	2003
$22,415	$19,853	$17,607	$15,354	$13,192

Cumulative Costs

	1999	2000	2001	2002	2003
Annual	$7,328	$6,721	$6,502	$6,706	$7,925
Total	$7,328	$14,049	$20,551	$27,257	$35,182

Projected Costs (5yr)

Relative	This Car
$34,471	$35,182
Cost/Mile 49¢	Cost/Mile 50¢

Ownership Cost Value

○ Average

The 1999 Grand Prix GTP coupe is the performance version of the model line, featuring a supercharged 3.8L 3800 Series II V6 with 240 hp and 280 lb-ft of torque. The GTP coupe comes fully equipped including power windows and locks, remote keyless entry, steering wheel-mounted radio controls and dual-zone climate control. For more stability, Grand Prix's Enhanced Traction System engages automatically when wheel spin is detected in either forward or reverse.

Pontiac Grand Prix SE
4 Door Sedan

Midsize

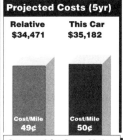

GT Model Shown

- 3.1L 160 hp Gas Fuel Inject.
- 6 Cylinder "V"
- Automatic 4 Speed
- 2 Wheel Front
- Dual Airbags Std

Purchase Price

Car Item	Dealer Cost	List
Base Price	**$17,765**	**$19,415**
Anti-Lock Brakes	Std	Std
Manual Transmission	N/A	N/A
3.8L 200 hp Gas	$369	**$415
Air Conditioning	Std	Std
Power Steering	Std	Std
Cruise Control	$209	$235
Power Windows	Std	Std
AM/FM Stereo Cassette	Pkg	Pkg
Steering Wheel, Tilt	Std	Std
1SA Package	N/C	N/C
***Options Price**	$209	$235
***Total Price**	**$17,974**	**$19,650**
Target Price	$18,983	
Destination Charge	$560	
Avg. Tax & Fees	$1,094	
Total Target $	**$20,637**	
Average Dealer Option Cost:	**89%**	
12 Month Price Increase:	3%	

Ownership Costs (Projected)

Cost Area	5 Year Cost	Rating
Depreciation	$9,390	○
Financing ($342/month)	$4,014	
Insurance	$7,140	○
State Fees	$821	
Fuel (Hwy 29 City 20)	$3,041	○
Maintenance	$3,110	○
Repairs	$895	○

Warranty/Maintenance Info

Major Tune-Up (100K mile int.)	$216	○
Minor Tune-Up (30K mile int.)	$124	○
Brake Service	$242	○
Overall Warranty	3 yr/36k	○
Drivetrain Warranty	3 yr/36k	○
Rust Warranty	6 yr/100k	○
Maintenance Warranty	N/A	
Roadside Assistance	3 yr/36k	

Ownership Costs By Year (Projected)

$2,000 $4,000 $6,000 $8,000 $10,000

- 1999
- 2000
- 2001
- 2002
- 2003

Resale Value

1999	2000	2001	2002	2003
$19,255	$17,025	$15,092	$13,135	$11,247

Cumulative Costs

	1999	2000	2001	2002	2003
Annual	$4,933	$5,568	$5,402	$5,618	$6,890
Total	$4,933	$10,501	$15,903	$21,521	$28,411

Projected Costs (5yr)

Relative	This Car
$29,431	$28,411
Cost/Mile 42¢	Cost/Mile 41¢

Ownership Cost Value

○ Better Than Average

The Grand Prix SE sedan is now available with the OnStar Communication System, which provides roadside assistance, travel route support and emergency services through a hands-free phone, advanced vehicle electronics and the Global Positioning System. Two new exterior colors are Dark Bronzemist Metallic and Medium Gulf Blue Metallic. To provide security on slippery surfaces, the SE is equipped with Pontiac's Enhanced Traction System, which automatically engages when wheel spin is detected.

---

* Includes shaded options
** Other purchase requirements apply
*** Price includes other options

 Poor Worse Than Average Average Better Than Average Excellent Insufficient Information

155

Refer to *Section 3: Annotated Vehicle Charts* for an explanation of these charts.

©1999 by IntelliChoice, Inc. (408) 866-1400 http://www.intellichoice.com All Rights Reserved. Reproduction Prohibited.

Pontiac Grand Prix GT
4 Door Sedan

Midsize

3.8L 200 hp Gas Fuel Inject.	6 Cylinder "V"
Automatic 4 Speed	2 Wheel Front
Dual Airbags Std	

Purchase Price

Car Item	Dealer Cost	List
Base Price	**$19,348**	**$21,145**
Anti-Lock Brakes	Std	Std
Manual Transmission	N/A	N/A
Optional Engine	N/A	N/A
Air Conditioning	Std	Std
Power Steering	Std	Std
Cruise Control	Std	Std
Power Windows	Std	Std
AM/FM Stereo Cassette	Std	Std
Steering Wheel, Tilt	Std	Std
1SA Package	N/C	N/C
*Options Price	$0	$0
*Total Price	$19,348	$21,145
Target Price	$20,465	
Destination Charge	$560	
Avg. Tax & Fees	$1,176	
Total Target $	**$22,201**	
Average Dealer Option Cost:	89%	
12 Month Price Increase:	2%	

The Grand Prix GT sedan is now available with the OnStar Communication System, which provides roadside assistance, travel route support and emergency services through a hands-free phone, advanced vehicle electronics and the Global Positioning System. The optional Bose eight speaker premium sound system has been designed to match the acoustical environment of the interior, resulting in a balanced delivery of sound anywhere in the vehicle. Additional options include leather seats and a moonroof.

Ownership Costs (Projected)

Cost Area	5 Year Cost	Rating
Depreciation	$10,013	◔
Financing ($368/month)	$4,319	
Insurance	$7,140	◔
State Fees	$881	
Fuel (Hwy 30 City 19)	$3,070	○
Maintenance	$3,142	○
Repairs	$895	○

Warranty/Maintenance Info

Major Tune-Up (100K mile int.)	$243	○
Minor Tune-Up (30K mile int.)	$124	○
Brake Service	$242	○
Overall Warranty	3 yr/36k	○
Drivetrain Warranty	3 yr/36k	○
Rust Warranty	6 yr/100k	○
Maintenance Warranty	N/A	
Roadside Assistance	3 yr/36k	

Ownership Costs By Year (Projected)

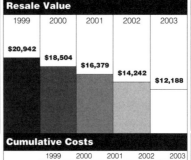

Legend: 1999, 2000, 2001, 2002, 2003

Resale Value

1999	2000	2001	2002	2003
$20,942	$18,504	$16,379	$14,242	$12,188

Cumulative Costs

	1999	2000	2001	2002	2003
Annual	$4,934	$5,879	$5,675	$5,880	$7,092
Total	$4,934	$10,813	$16,488	$22,368	$29,460

Projected Costs (5yr)

Relative	This Car
$30,867	$29,460
Cost/Mile 44¢	Cost/Mile 42¢

Ownership Cost Value

○ Excellent

Pontiac Grand Prix GTP
4 Door Sedan

Midsize

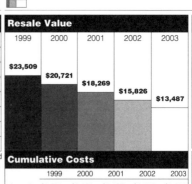

GT Model Shown

3.8L 240 hp Suprchrged Fuel Inject.	6 Cylinder "V"
Automatic 4 Speed	2 Wheel Front
Dual Airbags Std	

Purchase Price

Car Item	Dealer Cost	List
Base Price	**$21,878**	**$23,910**
Anti-Lock Brakes	Std	Std
Manual Transmission	N/A	N/A
Optional Engine	N/A	N/A
Air Conditioning	Std	Std
Power Steering	Std	Std
Cruise Control	Std	Std
Power Windows	Std	Std
AM/FM Stereo CD	Std	Std
Steering Wheel, Tilt	Std	Std
1SA Package	$494	***$555
*Options Price	$494	$555
*Total Price	$22,372	$24,465
Target Price	$23,598	
Destination Charge	$560	
Avg. Tax & Fees	$1,350	
Total Target $	**$25,508**	
Average Dealer Option Cost:	89%	
12 Month Price Increase:	N/A	

The 1999 Grand Prix GTP sedan features a customized Bose eight speaker premium sound system designed to match the acoustical environment of the GTP's interior, resulting in a balanced delivery of sound anywhere in the vehicle. The GTP is equipped with a supercharged 3.8L 3800 Series II V6 with 240 hp and 280 lb-ft of torque. The GTP sedan comes fully equipped including power windows and locks, remote keyless entry, steering wheel-mounted radio controls and dual-zone climate control.

Ownership Costs (Projected)

Cost Area	5 Year Cost	Rating
Depreciation	$12,021	◔
Financing ($423/month)	$4,962	
Insurance (Performance)	$8,610	◔
State Fees	$1,013	
Fuel (Hwy 28 City 18 -Prem.)	$3,871	◉
Maintenance	$3,186	○
Repairs	$1,056	●

Warranty/Maintenance Info

Major Tune-Up (100K mile int.)	$243	○
Minor Tune-Up (30K mile int.)	$124	○
Brake Service	$242	○
Overall Warranty	3 yr/36k	○
Drivetrain Warranty	3 yr/36k	○
Rust Warranty	6 yr/100k	○
Maintenance Warranty	N/A	
Roadside Assistance	3 yr/36k	

Ownership Costs By Year (Projected)

Legend: 1999, 2000, 2001, 2002, 2003

Resale Value

1999	2000	2001	2002	2003
$23,509	$20,721	$18,269	$15,826	$13,487

Cumulative Costs

	1999	2000	2001	2002	2003
Annual	$6,359	$6,880	$6,637	$6,820	$8,022
Total	$6,359	$13,239	$19,876	$26,696	$34,718

Projected Costs (5yr)

Relative	This Car
$34,704	$34,718
Cost/Mile 50¢	Cost/Mile 50¢

Ownership Cost Value

○ Average

Pontiac Sunfire SE
2 Door Coupe

2.2L 115 hp Gas Fuel Inject.

4 Cylinder In-Line

Manual 5 Speed

2 Wheel Front

Depowered Dual Airbags Std

Purchase Price

Car Item	Dealer Cost	List
Base Price	**$11,789**	**$12,745**
Anti-Lock Brakes	Std	Std
Manual 5 Speed	($721)	($810)
2.4L 150 hp Gas	N/C	**N/C
Air Conditioning	$739	$830
Power Steering	Std	Std
Cruise Control	Pkg	Pkg
Power Windows	Pkg	Pkg
AM/FM Stereo Cassette	($89)	($100)
Steering Wheel, Tilt	Pkg	Pkg
Rear Defroster	$160	$180
***Options Price**	**$89**	**$100**
***Total Price**	**$11,878**	**$12,845**
Target Price		$12,336
Destination Charge		$510
Avg. Tax & Fees		$725
Total Target $		**$13,571**
Average Dealer Option Cost:		*89%*
12 Month Price Increase:		2%

For 1999, Fern Green Metallic is a new exterior color available on the Sunfire SE coupe. All 1999 Sunfire models come standard with the PASSlock II security system, which disables the powertrain if any attempt is made to start the vehicle without the proper key. Antilock brakes, battery rundown protection, daytime running lamps and fade-out interior lights are also standard on the SE coupe. Remote keyless entry and steering wheel radio controls are among the available options.

Ownership Costs (Projected)

Cost Area	5 Year Cost	Rating
Depreciation	$6,999	◐
Financing ($225/month)	$2,640	
Insurance	$8,045	●
State Fees	$547	
Fuel (Hwy 34 City 24)	$2,566	◐
Maintenance	$2,290	○
Repairs	$610	◐

Warranty/Maintenance Info

Major Tune-Up (100K mile int.)	$243	○
Minor Tune-Up (30K mile int.)	$70	○
Brake Service	$197	○
Overall Warranty	3 yr/36k	◐
Drivetrain Warranty	3 yr/36k	◐
Rust Warranty	6 yr/100k	○
Maintenance Warranty	N/A	
Roadside Assistance	3 yr/36k	

Ownership Costs By Year (Projected)

$2,000 $4,000 $6,000 $8,000 $10,000

■ 1999
■ 2000
■ 2001
■ 2002
□ 2003

Resale Value

1999	2000	2001	2002	2003
$11,928	$10,479	$9,204	$7,898	$6,572

Projected Costs (5yr)

Relative $23,258	This Car $23,697
Cost/Mile 33¢	Cost/Mile 34¢

Cumulative Costs

	1999	2000	2001	2002	2003
Annual	$4,741	$4,428	$4,275	$5,292	$4,961
Total	$4,741	$9,169	$13,444	$18,736	$23,697

Ownership Cost Value

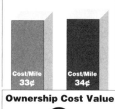

Average

Pontiac Sunfire GT
2 Door Coupe

2.4L 150 hp Gas Fuel Inject.

4 Cylinder In-Line

Manual 5 Speed

2 Wheel Front

Depowered Dual Airbags Std

Purchase Price

Car Item	Dealer Cost	List
Base Price	**$14,564**	**$15,745**
Anti-Lock Brakes	Std	Std
Manual 5 Speed	($721)	($810)
Optional Engine	N/A	N/A
Air Conditioning	Std	Std
Power Steering	Std	Std
Cruise Control	Pkg	Pkg
Power Windows	Pkg	Pkg
AM/FM Stereo CD	Std	Std
Steering Wheel, Tilt	Std	Std
Rear Defroster	Std	Std
***Options Price**	**($721)**	**($810)**
***Total Price**	**$13,843**	**$14,935**
Target Price		$14,404
Destination Charge		$510
Avg. Tax & Fees		$838
Total Target $		**$15,752**
Average Dealer Option Cost:		*89%*
12 Month Price Increase:		2%

A 2.4L twin-cam engine with a five speed manual transmission continues to be the standard powertrain for the 1999 Sunfire GT coupe. A four speed automatic overdrive transmission is optional. All Sunfire models are covered by Pontiac's roadside assistance program, which provides a toll-free 24 hour emergency service number. The roadside assistance program is standard and is good for three years or 36,000 miles, whichever comes first. Fern Green Metallic is a new color available this year.

Ownership Costs (Projected)

Cost Area	5 Year Cost	Rating
Depreciation	$8,602	●
Financing ($261/month)	$3,064	
Insurance	$8,500	●
State Fees	$631	
Fuel (Hwy 33 City 23)	$2,660	◐
Maintenance	$2,448	○
Repairs	$610	◐

Warranty/Maintenance Info

Major Tune-Up (100K mile int.)	$209	○
Minor Tune-Up (30K mile int.)	$70	○
Brake Service	$197	○
Overall Warranty	3 yr/36k	◐
Drivetrain Warranty	3 yr/36k	◐
Rust Warranty	6 yr/100k	○
Maintenance Warranty	N/A	
Roadside Assistance	3 yr/36k	

Ownership Costs By Year (Projected)

$2,000 $4,000 $6,000 $8,000 $10,000

■ 1999
■ 2000
■ 2001
■ 2002
□ 2003

Resale Value

1999	2000	2001	2002	2003
$13,621	$11,887	$10,332	$8,750	$7,150

Projected Costs (5yr)

Relative $25,345	This Car $26,515
Cost/Mile 36¢	Cost/Mile 38¢

Cumulative Costs

	1999	2000	2001	2002	2003
Annual	$5,499	$4,958	$4,771	$5,902	$5,385
Total	$5,499	$10,457	$15,228	$21,130	$26,515

Ownership Cost Value

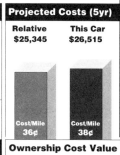

Average

---

* Includes shaded options

** Other purchase requirements apply

*** Price includes other options

● Poor   ◉ Worse Than Average   ◐ Average   ○ Better Than Average   ○ Excellent   ⊖ Insufficient Information

Refer to *Section 3: Annotated Vehicle Charts* for an explanation of these charts.

Pontiac Sunfire GT
2 Door Convertible

2.2L 115 hp Gas Fuel Inject.

4 Cylinder In-Line

PR|ND321 Automatic 4 Speed

2 Wheel Front

Depowered Dual Airbags Std

Subcompact

Purchase Price

Car Item	Dealer Cost	List
Base Price	**$19,559**	**$21,145**
Anti-Lock Brakes	Std	Std
Manual 5 Speed	($721)	**($810)
2.4L 150 hp Gas	Pkg	Pkg
Air Conditioning	Std	Std
Power Steering	Std	Std
Cruise Control	Std	Std
Power Windows	Pkg	Pkg
AM/FM Stereo CD	Std	Std
Steering Wheel, Tilt	Std	Std
Rear Defroster	Std	Std
*Options Price	$0	$0
*Total Price	**$19,559**	**$21,145**
Target Price	$20,235	
Destination Charge	$510	
Avg. Tax & Fees	$1,164	
Total Target $	**$21,909**	
Average Dealer Option Cost:	*89%*	
12 Month Price Increase:	*N/A*	

The Sunfire GT convertible is an all-new model for 1999. It replaces last year's SE convertible. The Sunfire GT convertible features a unique front fascia with round directional signals, a unique rear fascia, dual exhaust outlets and a rear decklid spoiler. The Sunfire GT convertible comes standard with a four speed automatic overdrive transmission and is available with a five speed manual transmission. Steering wheel radio controls and a remote keyless entry system are also available.

Ownership Costs (Projected)

Cost Area	5 Year Cost	Rating
Depreciation	$11,728	●
Financing ($363/month)	$4,262	
Insurance	$9,365	●
State Fees	$880	
Fuel (Hwy 31 City 23)	$2,748	○
Maintenance	$2,355	○
Repairs	$610	○

Warranty/Maintenance Info

Major Tune-Up (100K mile int.)	$243	○
Minor Tune-Up (30K mile int.)	$70	○
Brake Service	$197	○
Overall Warranty	3 yr/36k	○
Drivetrain Warranty	3 yr/36k	○
Rust Warranty	6 yr/100k	○
Maintenance Warranty	N/A	
Roadside Assistance	3 yr/36k	

Ownership Costs By Year (Projected)

$2,000 $4,000 $6,000 $8,000 $10,000 $12,000

1999 / 2000 / 2001 / 2002 / 2003

Resale Value

1999	2000	2001	2002	2003
$19,287	$16,833	$14,600	$12,378	$10,181

Cumulative Costs

	1999	2000	2001	2002	2003
Annual	$6,640	$6,250	$5,934	$6,851	$6,273
Total	$6,640	$12,890	$18,824	$25,675	$31,948

Projected Costs (5yr)

Relative	This Car
$31,702	$31,948
Cost/Mile 45¢	Cost/Mile 46¢

Ownership Cost Value

○
Average

Pontiac Sunfire SE
4 Door Sedan

2.2L 115 hp Gas Fuel Inject.

4 Cylinder In-Line

1 3 5 / 2 4 R Manual 5 Speed

2 Wheel Front

Depowered Dual Airbags Std

Subcompact

2 Door Coupe Model Shown

Purchase Price

Car Item	Dealer Cost	List
Base Price	**$11,789**	**$12,745**
Anti-Lock Brakes	Std	Std
Automatic 3 Speed	$534	$600
2.4L 150 hp Gas	Pkg	Pkg
Air Conditioning	$739	$830
Power Steering	Std	Std
Cruise Control	Pkg	Pkg
Power Windows	Pkg	Pkg
AM/FM Stereo Cassette	($89)	($100)
Steering Wheel, Tilt	Pkg	Pkg
Rear Defroster	$160	$180
*Options Price	$1,344	$1,510
*Total Price	**$13,133**	**$14,255**
Target Price	$13,647	
Destination Charge	$510	
Avg. Tax & Fees	$798	
Total Target $	**$14,955**	
Average Dealer Option Cost:	*89%*	
12 Month Price Increase:	*2%*	

Changes for the 1999 Sunfire SE sedan include one new exterior color, Fern Green Metallic. Several components have been changed on the optional 2.4L twin-cam engine, including new fuel injectors, exhaust manifolds, fuel injection rails and catalytic converter. Dual front second generation airbags, antilock brakes, rear seat ventilation ducts and PASSlock theft deterrent system are all standard on every Sunfire model. Battery rundown protection and fade-out interior lights are also standard.

Ownership Costs (Projected)

Cost Area	5 Year Cost	Rating
Depreciation	$7,563	○
Financing ($248/month)	$2,910	
Insurance	$7,294	◉
State Fees	$604	
Fuel (Hwy 29 City 23)	$2,847	◉
Maintenance	$2,290	○
Repairs	$610	○

Warranty/Maintenance Info

Major Tune-Up (100K mile int.)	$243	○
Minor Tune-Up (30K mile int.)	$70	○
Brake Service	$197	○
Overall Warranty	3 yr/36k	○
Drivetrain Warranty	3 yr/36k	○
Rust Warranty	6 yr/100k	○
Maintenance Warranty	N/A	
Roadside Assistance	3 yr/36k	

Ownership Costs By Year (Projected)

$2,000 $4,000 $6,000 $8,000

1999 / 2000 / 2001 / 2002 / 2003

Resale Value

1999	2000	2001	2002	2003
$13,410	$11,784	$10,340	$8,873	$7,392

Cumulative Costs

	1999	2000	2001	2002	2003
Annual	$4,658	$4,601	$4,417	$5,402	$5,040
Total	$4,658	$9,259	$13,676	$19,078	$24,118

Projected Costs (5yr)

Relative	This Car
$24,585	$24,118
Cost/Mile 35¢	Cost/Mile 34¢

Ownership Cost Value

○
Better Than Average

158

Porsche 911 Carrera
2 Door Coupe

 3.4L 296 hp Gas Fuel Inject.　 6 Cylinder Opposing　135R 246 Manual 6 Speed　 2 Wheel Rear　Dual Front/Side Airbags Std

Purchase Price

Car Item	Dealer Cost	List
Base Price	**$54,621**	**$65,030**
Anti-Lock Brakes	Std	Std
Automatic 5 Speed	$2,874	$3,420
Optional Engine	N/A	N/A
Auto Climate Control	Std	Std
Power Steering	Std	Std
Cruise Control	Std	Std
Power Windows	Std	Std
AM/FM Stereo Cassette	Std	Std
Steering Wheel, Tilt	N/A	N/A
Rear Defroster	Std	Std
*Options Price	$0	$0
*Total Price	**$54,621**	**$65,030**
Target Price	$63,452	
Destination Charge	$765	
Avg. Tax & Fees	$3,561	
Luxury Tax	$1,693	
Total Target $	**$69,471**	
12 Month Price Increase:	2%	

Ownership Costs (Projected)

Cost Area	5 Year Cost	Rating
Depreciation	$22,629	◐
Financing ($1,152/month)	$13,514	
Insurance (Performance)	$14,809	◉
State Fees	$2,645	
Fuel (Hwy 25 City 17 -Prem.)	$4,216	○
Maintenance		⊖
Repairs	$2,184	◉

Warranty/Maintenance Info

Major Tune-Up (60K mile int.)		⊖
Minor Tune-Up (30K mile int.)		⊖
Brake Service		⊖
Overall Warranty	2 yr/unlim. mi	◉
Drivetrain Warranty	2 yr/unlim. mi	◉
Rust Warranty	10 yr/unlim. mi	○
Maintenance Warranty	N/A	
Roadside Assistance	2 yr/unlim. mi	

Ownership Costs By Year (Projected)

$5,000　$10,000　$15,000　$20,000　$25,000

Legend: 1999, 2000, 2001, 2002, 2003

Insufficient Maintenance Information

Resale Value

1999	2000	2001	2002	2003
$64,764	$59,833	$55,343	$51,046	$46,842

Projected Costs (5yr)

Insufficient Information

Cumulative Costs

	1999	2000	2001	2002	2003
Annual	*Insufficient Information*				
Total	*Insufficient Information*				

Ownership Cost Value

⊖ Insufficient Information

The 911 Carrera is all-new for 1999. The exterior is longer, wider and sleeker than before, but it is still easily distinguished as a 911. For the first time in the history of 911, the engine is not air-cooled. The new 911 Carrera retains its rear engine/rear wheel drive layout, but the new 3.4L multi-valve engine is water-cooled. The 911 Carrera was developed concurrently with the Boxster to maximize production efficiencies and keep costs down.

Porsche 911 Carrera Cabriolet
2 Door Convertible

 3.4L 296 hp Gas Fuel Inject.　 6 Cylinder Opposing　 135R 246 Manual 6 Speed　 2 Wheel Rear　 Dual Front/Side Airbags Std

Purchase Price

Car Item	Dealer Cost	List
Base Price	**$64,523**	**$74,460**
Anti-Lock Brakes	Std	Std
Automatic 5 Speed	$2,874	$3,420
Optional Engine	N/A	N/A
Auto Climate Control	Std	Std
Power Steering	Std	Std
Cruise Control	Std	Std
Power Windows	Std	Std
AM/FM Stereo Cassette	Std	Std
Steering Wheel, Tilt	N/A	N/A
Rear Defroster	Std	Std
*Options Price	$0	$0
*Total Price	**$64,523**	**$74,460**
Target Price	$72,822	
Destination Charge	$765	
Avg. Tax & Fees	$4,076	
Luxury Tax	$2,255	
Total Target $	**$79,918**	
12 Month Price Increase:	2%	

Ownership Costs (Projected)

Cost Area	5 Year Cost	Rating
Depreciation	$28,571	○
Financing ($1,325/month)	$15,548	
Insurance (Performance)	$15,531	◉
State Fees	$3,022	
Fuel (Hwy 25 City 17 -Prem.)	$4,216	○
Maintenance		⊖
Repairs	$2,184	◉

Warranty/Maintenance Info

Major Tune-Up (60K mile int.)		⊖
Minor Tune-Up (30K mile int.)		⊖
Brake Service		⊖
Overall Warranty	2 yr/unlim. mi	◉
Drivetrain Warranty	2 yr/unlim. mi	◉
Rust Warranty	10 yr/unlim. mi	○
Maintenance Warranty	N/A	
Roadside Assistance	2 yr/unlim. mi	

Ownership Costs By Year (Projected)

$5,000　$10,000　$15,000　$20,000　$25,000　$30,000

Legend: 1999, 2000, 2001, 2002, 2003

Insufficient Maintenance Information

Resale Value

1999	2000	2001	2002	2003
$72,922	$67,009	$61,579	$56,395	$51,347

Projected Costs (5yr)

Insufficient Information

Cumulative Costs

	1999	2000	2001	2002	2003
Annual	*Insufficient Information*				
Total	*Insufficient Information*				

Ownership Cost Value

⊖ Insufficient Information

The all-new 1999 Cabriolet comes standard with an aluminum hard top and a cloth power-operated soft top. When the soft top is down, a hard body panel boot covers it. The Cabriolet weighs 165 pounds more than the coupe primarily because of the folding top mechanism. The folding top is very compact and does not impede on rear seat room. A unique safety feature of the Cabriolet are two spring-loaded hoops that pop up behind the rear seat whenever sensors predict a potential rollover situation.

● Poor　◉ Worse Than Average　◐ Average　○ Better Than Average　○ Excellent　⊖ Insufficient Information

Refer to *Section 3: Annotated Vehicle Charts* for an explanation of these charts.

Porsche Boxster
2 Door Convertible

Sport

 2.5L 201 hp Gas Fuel Inject.
 6 Cylinder Opposing
 Manual 5 Speed
 2 Wheel Rear
 Dual Front/Side Airbags Std

Purchase Price

Car Item	Dealer Cost	List
Base Price	**$35,895**	**$41,000**
Anti-Lock Brakes	Std	Std
Automatic 5 Speed	$2,657	$3,213
Optional Engine	N/A	N/A
Auto Climate Control	Std	Std
Power Steering	Std	Std
Cruise Control	$477	$561
Power Windows	Std	Std
AM/FM Stereo Cassette	Std	Std
Steering Wheel, Scope	Std	Std
Rear Defroster	Grp	Grp
***Options Price**	**$477**	**$561**
***Total Price**	**$36,372**	**$41,561**
Target Price	$42,375	
Destination Charge	$765	
Avg. Tax & Fees	$2,377	
Luxury Tax	$428	
Total Target $	**$45,945**	
12 Month Price Increase:	None	

For 1999, the Boxster returns with minimal changes to the interior and exterior. The Boxster is available with an optional child seat that automatically deactivates the passenger airbag. A wind deflector, GPS navigation system and upgraded trip computer are some of the options available. Standard features include partial leather bucket seats, automatic climate control, power windows, central locking and a power folding top. An optional hard top is available.

Ownership Costs (Projected)

Cost Area	5 Year Cost	Rating
Depreciation		⊖
Financing ($762/month)	$8,939	
Insurance (Performance)	$15,394	◉
State Fees	$1,706	
Fuel (Hwy 26 City 19 -Prem.)	$3,914	○
Maintenance		⊖
Repairs	$1,926	◉

Warranty/Maintenance Info

Major Tune-Up (60K mile int.)		⊖
Minor Tune-Up (30K mile int.)		⊖
Brake Service		⊖
Overall Warranty	2 yr/unlim. mi	◉
Drivetrain Warranty	2 yr/unlim. mi	◉
Rust Warranty	10 yr/unlim. mi	○
Maintenance Warranty	N/A	
Roadside Assistance	2 yr/unlim. mi	

Ownership Costs By Year (Projected)

$5,000 $10,000 $15,000 $20,000

Insufficient Depreciation Information

■ 1999
■ 2000
■ 2001
■ 2002
□ 2003

Insufficient Maintenance Information

Resale Value

Insufficient Information

Projected Costs (5yr)

Insufficient Information

Cumulative Costs

	1999	2000	2001	2002	2003
Annual	Insufficient Information				
Total	Insufficient Information				

Ownership Cost Value

⊖

Insufficient Information

Saab 9-3
2 Door Hatchback

Near Luxury

 2.0L 185 hp Turbo Gas Fuel Inject.
 4 Cylinder In-Line
 Manual 5 Speed
 2 Wheel Front
Dual Front/Side Airbags Std (Depowered)

Purchase Price

Car Item	Dealer Cost	List
Base Price	**$24,126**	**$25,500**
Anti-Lock Brakes	Std	Std
Automatic 4 Speed	$955	$1,110
Optional Engine	N/A	N/A
Air Conditioning	Std	Std
Power Steering	Std	Std
Cruise Control	Std	Std
Power Windows	Std	Std
AM/FM Stereo Cassette	Std	Std
Steering Wheel, Scope	Std	Std
Rear Defroster	Std	Std
***Options Price**	**$955**	**$1,110**
***Total Price**	**$25,081**	**$26,610**
Target Price	$25,898	
Destination Charge	$550	
Avg. Tax & Fees	$1,475	
Total Target $	**$27,923**	
Average Dealer Option Cost:	86%	
12 Month Price Increase:	4%	

The three-door 9-3 comes with the Saab Active Head Restraint system for the front seats, an electrostatic cabin air filter, a stereo with anti-theft lockout code and heat absorbent tinted glass. Other standard features include auto-off headlamps, a theft deterrent system and headlamp washers and wipers. Antilock brakes and daytime running lamps are also standard. Some of the available options include a power sunroof, Leather Package, heated front seats and mica paint.

Ownership Costs (Projected)

Cost Area	5 Year Cost	Rating
Depreciation	$12,559	○
Financing ($463/month)	$5,431	
Insurance	$8,093	○
State Fees	$1,099	
Fuel (Hwy 25 City 19)	$3,368	○
Maintenance		⊖
Repairs	$1,451	◉

Warranty/Maintenance Info

Major Tune-Up (60K mile int.)		⊖
Minor Tune-Up (30K mile int.)		⊖
Brake Service		⊖
Overall Warranty	4 yr/50k	○
Drivetrain Warranty	4 yr/50k	○
Rust Warranty	6 yr/unlim. mi	○
Maintenance Warranty	1 yr/8k	◉
Roadside Assistance	4 yr/50k	

Ownership Costs By Year (Projected)

$2,000 $4,000 $6,000 $8,000 $10,000 $12,000 $14,000

■ 1999
■ 2000
■ 2001
■ 2002
□ 2003

Insufficient Maintenance Information

Resale Value

1999	2000	2001	2002	2003
$26,786	$23,639	$20,840	$18,108	$15,364

Projected Costs (5yr)

Insufficient Information

Cumulative Costs

	1999	2000	2001	2002	2003
Annual	Insufficient Information				
Total	Insufficient Information				

Ownership Cost Value

⊖

Insufficient Information

160

 Poor
 Worse Than Average
 Average
 Better Than Average
○ Excellent
⊖ Insufficient Information

Refer to *Section 3: Annotated Vehicle Charts* for an explanation of these charts.

Saab 9-3
4 Door Hatchback

2.0L 185 hp Turbo Gas Fuel Inject.	4 Cylinder In-Line	Manual 5 Speed	2 Wheel Front	Dual Front/Side Airbags Std

Purchase Price

Car Item	Dealer Cost	List
Base Price	$24,230	$26,000
Anti-Lock Brakes	Std	Std
Automatic 4 Speed	$955	$1,110
Optional Engine	N/A	N/A
Air Conditioning	Std	Std
Power Steering	Std	Std
Cruise Control	Std	Std
Power Windows	Std	Std
AM/FM Stereo Cassette	Std	Std
Steering Wheel, Scope	Std	Std
Rear Defroster	Std	Std
*Options Price	$955	$1,110
*Total Price	$25,185	$27,110
Target Price	$26,048	
Destination Charge	$550	
Avg. Tax & Fees	$1,487	
Total Target $	$28,085	
Average Dealer Option Cost:	86%	
12 Month Price Increase:	None	

Ownership Costs (Projected)

Cost Area	5 Year Cost	Rating
Depreciation	$13,171	◐
Financing ($466/month)	$5,464	
Insurance	$8,093	○
State Fees	$1,120	
Fuel (Hwy 25 City 19)	$3,368	○
Maintenance		⊖
Repairs	$1,451	◐

Warranty/Maintenance Info

Major Tune-Up (60K mile int.)		⊖
Minor Tune-Up (30K mile int.)		⊖
Brake Service		⊖
Overall Warranty	4 yr/50k	○
Drivetrain Warranty	4 yr/50k	○
Rust Warranty	6 yr/unlim. mi	○
Maintenance Warranty	1 yr/8k	○
Roadside Assistance	4 yr/50k	

Ownership Costs By Year (Projected)

$2,000 $4,000 $6,000 $8,000 $10,000 $12,000 $14,000

- 1999
- 2000
- 2001
- 2002
- 2003

Insufficient Maintenance Information

Resale Value

1999	2000	2001	2002	2003
$25,793	$22,791	$20,128	$17,529	$14,914

Cumulative Costs

	1999	2000	2001	2002	2003
Annual	Insufficient Information				
Total	Insufficient Information				

Projected Costs (5yr)

Insufficient Information

Ownership Cost Value

⊖

Insufficient Information

The five-door 9-3 is equipped with child-proof rear door locks, a rear window defogger, carpeted floor mats, a fold-down rear seat and electrostatic cabin air filter. Other standard features include antilock brakes, the Saab Active Head Restraint system for the front seats and a stereo with anti-theft lockout code. Side guidance reversing lights are also standard. An integrated child seat, power glass sunroof and Leather Package are some of the options available this year.

Saab 9-3 SE
4 Door Hatchback

2.0L 185 hp Turbo Gas Fuel Inject.	4 Cylinder In-Line	Manual 5 Speed	2 Wheel Front	Dual Front/Side Airbags Std

Purchase Price

Car Item	Dealer Cost	List
Base Price	$29,795	$31,500
Anti-Lock Brakes	Std	Std
Automatic 4 Speed	$955	$1,110
Optional Engine	N/A	N/A
Auto Climate Control	Std	Std
Power Steering	Std	Std
Cruise Control	Std	Std
Power Windows	Std	Std
AM/FM Stereo Cassette	Std	Std
Steering Wheel, Scope	Std	Std
Rear Defroster	Std	Std
*Options Price	$955	$1,110
*Total Price	$30,750	$32,610
Target Price	$31,856	
Destination Charge	$550	
Avg. Tax & Fees	$1,803	
Total Target $	$34,209	
Average Dealer Option Cost:	86%	
12 Month Price Increase:	None	

Ownership Costs (Projected)

Cost Area	5 Year Cost	Rating
Depreciation	$17,374	◐
Financing ($567/month)	$6,655	
Insurance	$8,865	○
State Fees	$1,339	
Fuel (Hwy 24 City 19)	$3,443	◐
Maintenance		⊖
Repairs	$1,451	◐

Warranty/Maintenance Info

Major Tune-Up (60K mile int.)		⊖
Minor Tune-Up (30K mile int.)		⊖
Brake Service		⊖
Overall Warranty	4 yr/50k	○
Drivetrain Warranty	4 yr/50k	○
Rust Warranty	6 yr/unlim. mi	○
Maintenance Warranty	1 yr/8k	○
Roadside Assistance	4 yr/50k	

Ownership Costs By Year (Projected)

$5,000 $10,000 $15,000 $20,000

- 1999
- 2000
- 2001
- 2002
- 2003

Insufficient Maintenance Information

Resale Value

1999	2000	2001	2002	2003
$29,932	$26,332	$23,102	$19,961	$16,835

Cumulative Costs

	1999	2000	2001	2002	2003
Annual	Insufficient Information				
Total	Insufficient Information				

Projected Costs (5yr)

Insufficient Information

Ownership Cost Value

⊖

Insufficient Information

The 9-3 SE five-door comes equipped with daytime running lamps, the Saab Active Head restraint system for the front seats, an electrostatic cabin air filter and antilock brakes. The SE also features a walnut-trimmed instrument panel, leather seats and a leather-wrapped steering wheel and shift knob. Side guidance reversing lights and heated rear view mirrors are also standard. Some of the available options include heated front and rear seats, a CD player and mica paint.

---

* Includes shaded options

** Other purchase requirements apply

*** Price includes other options

 Poor   Worse Than Average   Average   Better Than Average   ○ Excellent   ⊖ Insufficient Information

Refer to *Section 3: Annotated Vehicle Charts* for an explanation of these charts.

Saab 9-3
2 Door Convertible

Near Luxury

2.0L 185 hp Turbo Gas Fuel Inject.	4 Cylinder In-Line
Manual 5 Speed	2 Wheel Front
Dual Front/Side Airbags Std	

Purchase Price

Car Item	Dealer Cost	List
Base Price	**$34,895**	**$36,500**
Anti-Lock Brakes	Std	Std
Automatic 4 Speed	$955	$1,110
Optional Engine	N/A	N/A
Air Conditioning	Std	Std
Power Steering	Std	Std
Cruise Control	Std	Std
Power Windows	Std	Std
AM/FM Stereo Cassette	Std	Std
Steering Wheel, Scope	Std	Std
Rear Defroster	Std	Std
***Options Price**	$955	$1,110
***Total Price**	**$35,850**	**$37,610**
Target Price	$36,906	
Destination Charge	$550	
Avg. Tax & Fees	$2,081	
Luxury Tax	$87	
Total Target $	**$39,624**	
12 Month Price Increase:	None	

The 9-3 convertible is manufactured in Uusikaupunki, Finland. Front and rear fog lamps, the Saab Active Head Restraint system for the front seats, an electrostatic cabin air filter and a stereo with anti-theft lockout code are standard features. In addition, the 9-3 convertible has leather seats, a leather-wrapped shift knob, a theft deterrent system and a power convertible top. Heated front seats, a CD player and mica paint are among the available options.

Ownership Costs (Projected)

Cost Area	5 Year Cost	Rating
Depreciation	$19,213	◒
Financing ($657/month)	$7,708	
Insurance	$9,524	◒
State Fees	$1,539	
Fuel (Hwy 25 City 19)	$3,368	◒
Maintenance		⊖
Repairs	$1,451	◉

Warranty/Maintenance Info

Major Tune-Up (60K mile int.)		⊖
Minor Tune-Up (30K mile int.)		⊖
Brake Service		⊖
Overall Warranty	4 yr/50k	○
Drivetrain Warranty	4 yr/50k	○
Rust Warranty	6 yr/unlim. mi	○
Maintenance Warranty	1 yr/8k	◒
Roadside Assistance	4 yr/50k	

Ownership Costs By Year (Projected)

$5,000	$10,000	$15,000	$20,000

- 1999
- 2000
- 2001
- 2002
- 2003

Insufficient Maintenance Information

Resale Value

1999	2000	2001	2002	2003
$36,347	$32,005	$28,054	$24,217	$20,411

Cumulative Costs

	1999	2000	2001	2002	2003
Annual	*Insufficient Information*				
Total	*Insufficient Information*				

Projected Costs (5yr)

Insufficient Information

Ownership Cost Value

⊖

Insufficient Information

Saab 9-3 SE
2 Door Convertible

Near Luxury

2.0L 185 hp Turbo Gas Fuel Inject.	4 Cylinder In-Line
Manual 5 Speed	2 Wheel Front
Dual Front/Side Airbags Std	

Purchase Price

Car Item	Dealer Cost	List
Base Price	**$39,845**	**$41,500**
Anti-Lock Brakes	Std	Std
Automatic 4 Speed	$955	$1,110
Optional Engine	N/A	N/A
Auto Climate Control	Std	Std
Power Steering	Std	Std
Cruise Control	Std	Std
Power Windows	Std	Std
AM/FM Stereo Cassette	Std	Std
Steering Wheel, Scope	Std	Std
Rear Defroster	Std	Std
***Options Price**	$955	$1,110
***Total Price**	**$40,800**	**$42,610**
Target Price	$41,886	
Destination Charge	$550	
Avg. Tax & Fees	$2,355	
Luxury Tax	$386	
Total Target $	**$45,177**	
12 Month Price Increase:	None	

The 9-3 SE convertible is manufactured in Uusikaupunki, Finland. Standard features include the Saab Active Head Restraint system for the front seats, an electrostatic cabin air filter, stereo with anti-theft lockout code and a power convertible top. A walnut-trimmed instrument panel, dual power-adjustable front seats, leather seating and automatic climate control are additional standard features. Heated front seats, a CD player and mica paint are among the available options.

Ownership Costs (Projected)

Cost Area	5 Year Cost	Rating
Depreciation	$22,551	◒
Financing ($749/month)	$8,789	
Insurance	$9,911	◒
State Fees	$1,739	
Fuel (Hwy 24 City 19)	$3,443	◉
Maintenance		⊖
Repairs	$1,451	◉

Warranty/Maintenance Info

Major Tune-Up (60K mile int.)		⊖
Minor Tune-Up (30K mile int.)		⊖
Brake Service		⊖
Overall Warranty	4 yr/50k	○
Drivetrain Warranty	4 yr/50k	○
Rust Warranty	6 yr/unlim. mi	○
Maintenance Warranty	1 yr/8k	◒
Roadside Assistance	4 yr/50k	

Ownership Costs By Year (Projected)

$5,000	$10,000	$15,000	$20,000	$25,000

- 1999
- 2000
- 2001
- 2002
- 2003

Insufficient Maintenance Information

Resale Value

1999	2000	2001	2002	2003
$40,366	$35,547	$31,136	$26,856	$22,626

Cumulative Costs

	1999	2000	2001	2002	2003
Annual	*Insufficient Information*				
Total	*Insufficient Information*				

Projected Costs (5yr)

Insufficient Information

Ownership Cost Value

⊖

Insufficient Information

162

* Includes shaded options
** Other purchase requirements apply
*** Price includes other options

 Poor
 Worse Than Average
 Average
Better Than Average
○ Excellent
⊖ Insufficient Information

Refer to *Section 3: Annotated Vehicle Charts* for an explanation of these charts.

Saab 9-5
4 Door Sedan

Near Luxury

| 2.3L 170 hp Turbo Gas Fuel Inject. | 4 Cylinder In-Line | Manual 5 Speed | 2 Wheel Front | Dual Front/Side Airbags Std |

Purchase Price

Car Item	Dealer Cost	List
Base Price	**$27,895**	**$29,995**
Anti-Lock Brakes	Std	Std
Automatic 4 Speed	$955	$1,110
Optional Engine	N/A	N/A
Auto Climate Control	Std	Std
Power Steering	Std	Std
Cruise Control	Std	Std
Power Windows	Std	Std
AM/FM Stereo Cass/CD	Std	Std
Steering Wheel, Tilt	Std	Std
Rear Defroster	Std	Std
*Options Price	$955	$1,110
*Total Price	$28,850	$31,105
Target Price	$29,908	
Destination Charge	$575	
Avg. Tax & Fees	$1,702	
Total Target $	**$32,185**	
Average Dealer Option Cost:	86%	
12 Month Price Increase:	N/A	

Ownership Costs (Projected)

Cost Area	5 Year Cost	Rating
Depreciation	$14,531	○
Financing ($533/month)	$6,262	
Insurance	$8,865	○
State Fees	$1,280	
Fuel (Hwy 27 City 18)	$3,322	○
Maintenance		⊖
Repairs	$1,491	●

Warranty/Maintenance Info

Major Tune-Up (60K mile int.)		⊖
Minor Tune-Up (30K mile int.)		⊖
Brake Service		⊖
Overall Warranty	4 yr/50k	○
Drivetrain Warranty	4 yr/50k	○
Rust Warranty	6 yr/unlim. mi	○
Maintenance Warranty	1 yr/8k	○
Roadside Assistance	4 yr/50k	

Ownership Costs By Year (Projected)

$5,000 $10,000 $15,000

1999
2000
2001
2002
2003

Insufficient Maintenance Information

Resale Value

1999	2000	2001	2002	2003
$30,582	$27,042	$23,860	$20,759	$17,654

Cumulative Costs

	1999	2000	2001	2002	2003
Annual	*Insufficient Information*				
Total	*Insufficient Information*				

Projected Costs (5yr)

Insufficient Information

Ownership Cost Value

⊖ Insufficient Information

The 9-5 sedan is a new vehicle for 1999. Dual front power-adjustable seats, a walnut-trimmed instrument panel and the Saab Active Head Restraint system for the front seats and are some of the 9-5's standard features. Safety features include side airbags, daytime running lamps and an engine-immobilizing theft deterrent system. Heated front and rear seats as well as ventilated front leather seats are optional. A power sunroof and an automatic transmission are also available.

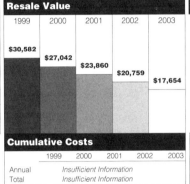

Saab 9-5 SE
4 Door Sedan

Near Luxury

| 2.3L 170 hp Turbo Gas Fuel Inject. | 4 Cylinder In-Line | Manual 5 Speed | 2 Wheel Front | Dual Front/Side Airbags Std |

Purchase Price

Car Item	Dealer Cost	List
Base Price	**$30,906**	**$33,495**
Anti-Lock Brakes	Std	Std
Automatic 4 Speed	$955	$1,110
Optional Engine	N/A	N/A
Auto Climate Control	Std	Std
Power Steering	Std	Std
Cruise Control	Std	Std
Power Windows	Std	Std
AM/FM Stereo Cass/CD	Std	Std
Steering Wheel, Tilt	Std	Std
Rear Defroster	Std	Std
*Options Price	$955	$1,110
*Total Price	$31,861	$34,605
Target Price	$33,114	
Destination Charge	$575	
Avg. Tax & Fees	$1,881	
Total Target $	**$35,570**	
Average Dealer Option Cost:	86%	
12 Month Price Increase:	N/A	

Ownership Costs (Projected)

Cost Area	5 Year Cost	Rating
Depreciation	$17,185	○
Financing ($590/month)	$6,920	
Insurance	$8,865	○
State Fees	$1,420	
Fuel (Hwy 26 City 19)	$3,299	○
Maintenance		⊖
Repairs	$1,491	●

Warranty/Maintenance Info

Major Tune-Up (60K mile int.)		⊖
Minor Tune-Up (30K mile int.)		⊖
Brake Service		⊖
Overall Warranty	4 yr/50k	○
Drivetrain Warranty	4 yr/50k	○
Rust Warranty	6 yr/unlim. mi	○
Maintenance Warranty	1 yr/8k	○
Roadside Assistance	4 yr/50k	

Ownership Costs By Year (Projected)

$5,000 $10,000 $15,000 $20,000

1999
2000
2001
2002
2003

Insufficient Maintenance Information

Resale Value

1999	2000	2001	2002	2003
$33,235	$29,171	$25,492	$21,925	$18,385

Cumulative Costs

	1999	2000	2001	2002	2003
Annual	*Insufficient Information*				
Total	*Insufficient Information*				

Projected Costs (5yr)

Insufficient Information

Ownership Cost Value

⊖ Insufficient Information

The 9-5 SE sedan is a new vehicle for 1999. Standard luxury amenities include leather bucket seats, dual-zone automatic climate control and a power glass sunroof. A traction control system, walnut-trimmed instrument panel and Harman/Kardon AM/FM stereo with cassette and CD are also standard. Safety features include side airbags, daytime running lamps and engine-immobilizing theft deterrent system. Heated front and rear seats as well as an integrated child booster seat are available.

---

* Includes shaded options
** Other purchase requirements apply
*** Price includes other options

 Poor   Worse Than Average   Average ○ Better Than Average ○ Excellent   Insufficient Information

163

Refer to *Section 3: Annotated Vehicle Charts* for an explanation of these charts.

Saab 9-5 V6
4 Door Sedan

Near Luxury

 3.0L 200 hp Turbo Gas Fuel Inject.　 6 Cylinder "V"　 PRND321 Automatic 4 Speed　 2 Wheel Front　 Depowered Dual Front/Side Airbags Std

Purchase Price

Car Item	Dealer Cost	List
Base Price	**$31,661**	**$33,750**
Anti-Lock Brakes	Std	Std
Manual Transmission	N/A	N/A
Optional Engine	N/A	N/A
Auto Climate Control	Std	Std
Power Steering	Std	Std
Cruise Control	Std	Std
Power Windows	Std	Std
AM/FM Stereo Cass/CD	Std	Std
Steering Wheel, Tilt	Std	Std
Rear Defroster	Std	Std
*Options Price	$0	$0
*Total Price	**$31,661**	**$33,750**
Target Price	$32,854	
Destination Charge	$550	
Avg. Tax & Fees	$1,859	
Total Target $	**$35,263**	
Average Dealer Option Cost:	86%	
12 Month Price Increase:	N/A	

The 9-5 V6 sedan was available in early 1998, but discontinued in August of 1998. Dual-zone automatic climate control, a walnut-trimmed instrument panel and dual power-adjustable front seats are some of the standard features. Safety features include side airbags, daytime running lamps, the Saab Active Head Restraint system for the front seats and engine-immobilizing theft deterrent system. Heated front and rear seats, ventilated front leather seats and a power sunroof are optional.

Ownership Costs (Projected)

Cost Area	5 Year Cost	Rating
Depreciation	$17,681	◐
Financing ($584/month)	$6,859	
Insurance	$9,524	◐
State Fees	$1,385	
Fuel (Hwy 26 City 18)	$3,387	◐
Maintenance		⊖
Repairs	$1,491	●

Warranty/Maintenance Info

Major Tune-Up (60K mile int.)		⊖
Minor Tune-Up (30K mile int.)		⊖
Brake Service		⊖
Overall Warranty	4 yr/50k	◐
Drivetrain Warranty	4 yr/50k	◐
Rust Warranty	6 yr/unlim. mi	◐
Maintenance Warranty	1 yr/8k	◐
Roadside Assistance	4 yr/50k	

Ownership Costs By Year (Projected)

Scale: $5,000 $10,000 $15,000 $20,000

Legend: 1999, 2000, 2001, 2002, 2003

Insufficient Maintenance Information

Resale Value

1999	2000	2001	2002	2003
$30,142	$26,696	$23,610	$20,599	$17,582

Cumulative Costs

	1999	2000	2001	2002	2003
Annual	*Insufficient Information*				
Total	*Insufficient Information*				

Projected Costs (5yr)

Insufficient Information

Ownership Cost Value

⊖ Insufficient Information

Saab 9-5 SE V6
4 Door Sedan

Near Luxury

 3.0L 200 hp Turbo Gas Fuel Inject.　 6 Cylinder "V"　 PRND321 Automatic 4 Speed　 2 Wheel Front　 Depowered Dual Front/Side Airbags Std

Base Model Shown

Purchase Price

Car Item	Dealer Cost	List
Base Price	**$34,574**	**$37,250**
Anti-Lock Brakes	Std	Std
Manual Transmission	N/A	N/A
Optional Engine	N/A	N/A
Auto Climate Control	Std	Std
Power Steering	Std	Std
Cruise Control	Std	Std
Power Windows	Std	Std
AM/FM Stereo Cass/CD	Std	Std
Steering Wheel, Tilt	Std	Std
Rear Defroster	Std	Std
*Options Price	$0	$0
*Total Price	**$34,574**	**$37,250**
Target Price	$35,979	
Destination Charge	$575	
Avg. Tax & Fees	$2,036	
Luxury Tax	$33	
Total Target $	**$38,623**	
12 Month Price Increase:	None	

The top of the line 9-5 SE V6 sedan is a new vehicle for 1999. The SE model adds a power sunroof, classic leather upholstery and power front seats with driver's side memory control to the list of standard equipment. Safety features include side airbags, daytime running lamps, the Saab Active Head Restraint system for the front seats and engine-immobilizing theft deterrent system. A unique option available on all 9-5 models are ventilated front seats with adjustable fan speed.

Ownership Costs (Projected)

Cost Area	5 Year Cost	Rating
Depreciation	$20,031	◉
Financing ($640/month)	$7,514	
Insurance	$9,911	◐
State Fees	$1,526	
Fuel (Hwy 26 City 18)	$3,387	◐
Maintenance		⊖
Repairs	$1,491	●

Warranty/Maintenance Info

Major Tune-Up (60K mile int.)		⊖
Minor Tune-Up (30K mile int.)		⊖
Brake Service		⊖
Overall Warranty	4 yr/50k	◐
Drivetrain Warranty	4 yr/50k	◐
Rust Warranty	6 yr/unlim. mi	◐
Maintenance Warranty	1 yr/8k	◐
Roadside Assistance	4 yr/50k	

Ownership Costs By Year (Projected)

Scale: $5,000 $10,000 $15,000 $20,000 $25,000

Legend: 1999, 2000, 2001, 2002, 2003

Insufficient Maintenance Information

Resale Value

1999	2000	2001	2002	2003
$32,703	$28,842	$25,356	$21,967	$18,592

Cumulative Costs

	1999	2000	2001	2002	2003
Annual	*Insufficient Information*				
Total	*Insufficient Information*				

Projected Costs (5yr)

Insufficient Information

Ownership Cost Value

⊖ Insufficient Information

164

* Includes shaded options
** Other purchase requirements apply
*** Price includes other options

● Poor	◉ Worse Than Average	◐ Average	◔ Better Than Average	○ Excellent	⊖ Insufficient Information

Refer to *Section 3: Annotated Vehicle Charts* for an explanation of these charts.

Saturn SC1
2 Door Coupe

Subcompact

1.9L 100 hp Gas Fuel Inject.	4 Cylinder In-Line	Manual 5 Speed	2 Wheel Front	Dual Airbags Std

Purchase Price

Car Item	Dealer Cost	List
Base Price	**$10,392**	**$11,945**
Anti-Lock Brakes	$605	$695
Automatic 4 Speed	$748	$860
Optional Engine	N/A	N/A
Air Conditioning	$835	$960
Power Steering	N/A	N/A
Cruise Control	$252	$290
Power Windows	Pkg	Pkg
AM/FM Stereo Cassette	$226	$260
Steering Wheel, Tilt	Std	Std
Rear Defroster	Std	Std
***Options Price**	**$1,061**	**$1,220**
***Total Price**	**$11,453**	**$13,165**
Target Price	$13,165	
Destination Charge	$440	
Avg. Tax & Fees	$761	
Total Target $	**$14,366**	
Average Dealer Option Cost:	**87%**	
12 Month Price Increase:	None	

Ownership Costs (Projected)

Cost Area	5 Year Cost	Rating
Depreciation	$6,364	○
Financing ($238/month)	$2,794	
Insurance	$7,294	◉
State Fees	$557	
Fuel (Hwy 40 City 29)	$2,152	○
Maintenance	$1,557	○
Repairs	$715	○

Ownership Costs By Year (Projected)

Scale: $2,000 — $4,000 — $6,000 — $8,000

Legend: 1999, 2000, 2001, 2002, 2003

Warranty/Maintenance Info

Major Tune-Up (100K mile int.)	$270	○
Minor Tune-Up (30K mile int.)	$79	○
Brake Service	$251	○
Overall Warranty	3 yr/36k	○
Drivetrain Warranty	3 yr/36k	○
Rust Warranty	6 yr/100k	○
Maintenance Warranty	N/A	
Roadside Assistance	3 yr/36k	

Resale Value

1999	2000	2001	2002	2003
$12,766	$11,485	$10,364	$9,200	$8,002

Cumulative Costs

	1999	2000	2001	2002	2003
Annual	$4,528	$4,076	$3,955	$4,361	$4,513
Total	$4,528	$8,604	$12,559	$16,920	$21,433

Projected Costs (5yr)

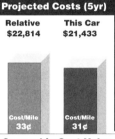

Relative $22,814	This Car $21,433
Cost/Mile 33¢	Cost/Mile 31¢

Ownership Cost Value

○ Excellent

The SC1 continues into the new model year boasting numerous engineering enhancements. Most notable are significant reductions in noise/vibration/harshness characteristics of the 1.9L engine. These changes help to provide a smoother and a quieter ride. Improved seatbelt latch plates and a new green exterior color round out the changes. Popular options include a power sunroof, air conditioning and a four wheel antilock braking system with an integrated all-speed traction control system.

Saturn SC1
3 Door Coupe

Subcompact

SC2 Model Shown

1.9L 100 hp Gas Fuel Inject.	4 Cylinder In-Line	Manual 5 Speed	2 Wheel Front	Dual Airbags Std

Purchase Price

Car Item	Dealer Cost	List
Base Price	**$10,827**	**$12,445**
Anti-Lock Brakes	$605	$695
Automatic 4 Speed	$748	$860
Optional Engine	N/A	N/A
Air Conditioning	$835	$960
Power Steering	N/A	N/A
Cruise Control	$252	$290
Power Windows	Pkg	Pkg
AM/FM Stereo Cassette	$226	$260
Steering Wheel, Tilt	Std	Std
Rear Defroster	Std	Std
***Options Price**	**$1,061**	**$1,220**
***Total Price**	**$11,888**	**$13,665**
Target Price	$13,665	
Destination Charge	$440	
Avg. Tax & Fees	$789	
Total Target $	**$14,894**	
Average Dealer Option Cost:	**87%**	
12 Month Price Increase:	1%	

Ownership Costs (Projected)

Cost Area	5 Year Cost	Rating
Depreciation	$6,576	○
Financing ($247/month)	$2,896	
Insurance	$7,294	◉
State Fees	$578	
Fuel (Hwy 40 City 29)	$2,152	○
Maintenance	$1,576	○
Repairs	$715	○

Ownership Costs By Year (Projected)

Scale: $2,000 — $4,000 — $6,000 — $8,000

Legend: 1999, 2000, 2001, 2002, 2003

Warranty/Maintenance Info

Major Tune-Up (100K mile int.)	$270	○
Minor Tune-Up (30K mile int.)	$88	○
Brake Service	$251	○
Overall Warranty	3 yr/36k	○
Drivetrain Warranty	3 yr/36k	○
Rust Warranty	6 yr/100k	○
Maintenance Warranty	N/A	
Roadside Assistance	3 yr/36k	

Resale Value

1999	2000	2001	2002	2003
$13,165	$11,860	$10,717	$9,534	$8,318

Cumulative Costs

	1999	2000	2001	2002	2003
Annual	$4,697	$4,133	$4,011	$4,397	$4,549
Total	$4,697	$8,830	$12,841	$17,238	$21,787

Projected Costs (5yr)

Relative $23,269	This Car $21,787
Cost/Mile 33¢	Cost/Mile 31¢

Ownership Cost Value

○ Excellent

The SC1 three-door coupe will begin production in November of 1998, replacing the SC1 two-door coupe. The SC1 three-door coupe is the world's first three-door coupe. Unprecedented convenience is achieved by opening both driver's side doors, allowing unobstructed access to the interior. For safety, the front door must be opened first. Several engine improvements this year help provide a smoother and quieter ride. All Saturns continue to use dent-resistant polymer bodyside panels.

---

* Includes shaded options
** Other purchase requirements apply
*** Price includes other options

● Poor	◉ Worse Than Average	◐ Average	○ Better Than Average	○ Excellent	⊖ Insufficient Information

165

Refer to *Section 3: Annotated Vehicle Charts* for an explanation of these charts.

Saturn SC2
2 Door Coupe

Subcompact

1.9L 124 hp Gas Fuel Inject.

4 Cylinder In-Line

Manual 5 Speed

2 Wheel Front

Dual Airbags Std

Purchase Price

Car Item	Dealer Cost	List
Base Price	**$12,619**	**$14,505**
Anti-Lock Brakes	$605	$695
Automatic 4 Speed	$748	$860
Optional Engine	N/A	N/A
Air Conditioning	Std	Std
Power Steering	Std	Std
Cruise Control	$252	$290
Power Windows	Pkg	Pkg
AM/FM Stereo Cassette	$226	$260
Steering Wheel, Tilt	Std	Std
Rear Defroster	Std	Std
*Options Price	$226	$260
*Total Price	**$12,845**	**$14,765**
Target Price	$14,765	
Destination Charge	$440	
Avg. Tax & Fees	$849	
Total Target $	**$16,054**	
Average Dealer Option Cost:	87%	
12 Month Price Increase:	4%	

Ownership Costs (Projected)

Cost Area	5 Year Cost	Rating
Depreciation	$7,326	◐
Financing ($266/month)	$3,123	◐
Insurance	$7,463	◉
State Fees	$621	
Fuel (Hwy 38 City 27)	$2,288	◐
Maintenance	$1,579	○
Repairs	$715	◐

Warranty/Maintenance Info

Major Tune-Up (100K mile int.)	$281	◐
Minor Tune-Up (30K mile int.)	$79	◐
Brake Service	$251	◐
Overall Warranty	3 yr/36k	◐
Drivetrain Warranty	3 yr/36k	◐
Rust Warranty	6 yr/100k	◐
Maintenance Warranty	N/A	
Roadside Assistance	3 yr/36k	

Ownership Costs By Year (Projected)

Legend: 1999, 2000, 2001, 2002, 2003

Resale Value

1999	2000	2001	2002	2003
$14,309	$12,809	$11,479	$10,116	$8,728

Cumulative Costs

	1999	2000	2001	2002	2003
Annual	$4,860	$4,459	$4,306	$4,698	$4,792
Total	$4,860	$9,319	$13,625	$18,323	$23,115

Projected Costs (5yr)

Relative $24,279	This Car $23,115
Cost/Mile 35¢	Cost/Mile 33¢

Ownership Cost Value

○ Better Than Average

The SC2's sporty intentions are met by a standard DOHC engine and a touring suspension system. Engine improvements this year include an eight-counterweight crankshaft (versus the usual four), new aluminum pistons and a revised timing chain (versus a more typical timing belt), resulting in reduced noise/vibration/harshness characteristics. As an added benefit of these changes, EPA fuel economy improves as well. Other changes include new seat fabrics and a new green exterior color.

Saturn SC2
3 Door Coupe

Subcompact

1.9L 124 hp Gas Fuel Inject.

4 Cylinder In-Line

Manual 5 Speed

2 Wheel Front

Dual Airbags Std

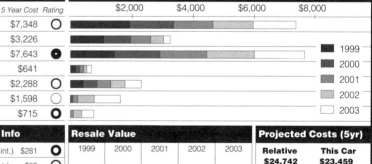

Purchase Price

Car Item	Dealer Cost	List
Base Price	**$13,054**	**$15,005**
Anti-Lock Brakes	$605	$695
Automatic 4 Speed	$748	$860
Optional Engine	N/A	N/A
Air Conditioning	Std	Std
Power Steering	Std	Std
Cruise Control	$252	$290
Power Windows	Pkg	Pkg
AM/FM Stereo Cassette	$226	$260
Steering Wheel, Tilt	Std	Std
Rear Defroster	Std	Std
*Options Price	$226	$260
*Total Price	**$13,280**	**$15,265**
Target Price	$15,265	
Destination Charge	$440	
Avg. Tax & Fees	$877	
Total Target $	**$16,582**	
Average Dealer Option Cost:	87%	
12 Month Price Increase:	8%	

Ownership Costs (Projected)

Cost Area	5 Year Cost	Rating
Depreciation	$7,348	○
Financing ($275/month)	$3,226	◐
Insurance	$7,643	◉
State Fees	$641	
Fuel (Hwy 38 City 27)	$2,288	○
Maintenance	$1,598	○
Repairs	$715	○

Warranty/Maintenance Info

Major Tune-Up (100K mile int.)	$281	○
Minor Tune-Up (30K mile int.)	$88	○
Brake Service	$251	○
Overall Warranty	3 yr/36k	○
Drivetrain Warranty	3 yr/36k	○
Rust Warranty	6 yr/100k	○
Maintenance Warranty	N/A	
Roadside Assistance	3 yr/36k	

Ownership Costs By Year (Projected)

Legend: 1999, 2000, 2001, 2002, 2003

Resale Value

1999	2000	2001	2002	2003
$14,633	$13,182	$11,901	$10,581	$9,234

Cumulative Costs

	1999	2000	2001	2002	2003
Annual	$5,138	$4,478	$4,327	$4,709	$4,807
Total	$5,138	$9,616	$13,943	$18,652	$23,459

Projected Costs (5yr)

Relative $24,742	This Car $23,459
Cost/Mile 35¢	Cost/Mile 34¢

Ownership Cost Value

○ Better Than Average

The SC2 three-door coupe arrives for 1999 as a new model. The three-door coupe will begin production in November of 1998 and will replace the two-door coupe. Heralded as the first coupe with three doors, the Saturn SC2 provides a unique level of convenience and style. The third door is located on the driver's side and for safety requires the main door to be opened first. Refinements to the engine provide a quieter ride by means of redesigned connecting rods, crankshaft, and pistons.

166

* Includes shaded options
** Other purchase requirements apply
*** Price includes other options

 ● Poor
 ◉ Worse Than Average
 ◐ Average
 ○ Better Than Average
 ○ Excellent
⊖ Insufficient Information

Refer to *Section 3: Annotated Vehicle Charts* for an explanation of these charts.

©1999 by IntelliChoice, Inc. (408) 866-1400 http://www.intellichoice.com All Rights Reserved. Reproduction Prohibited.

Saturn SL
4 Door Sedan

Compact

 1.9L 100 hp Gas Fuel Inject.   4 Cylinder In-Line   Manual 5 Speed   2 Wheel Front   Dual Airbags Std

Purchase Price

Car Item	Dealer Cost	List
Base Price	**$9,218**	**$10,595**
Anti-Lock Brakes	$605	$695
Automatic Transmission	N/A	N/A
Optional Engine	N/A	N/A
Air Conditioning	$835	$960
Power Steering	N/A	N/A
Cruise Control	N/A	N/A
Power Windows	N/A	N/A
AM/FM Stereo Cassette	$252	$290
Steering Wheel, Tilt	Std	Std
Rear Defroster	Std	Std
*Options Price	$1,087	$1,250
*Total Price	**$10,305**	**$11,845**
Target Price	$11,845	
Destination Charge	$440	
Avg. Tax & Fees	$689	
Total Target $	**$12,974**	
Average Dealer Option Cost:	87%	
12 Month Price Increase:	None	

The SL arrives this new model year featuring numerous key enhancements. Most noticeable are significant reductions in noise/vibration/harshness characteristics. Other changes include a new exterior color (Dark Blue), an improved shoulder belt height adjustment feature, improved seat belt latch location and improved EPA fuel economy. The SL continues as the value leader of the Saturn line with limited options such as an antilock braking system and floor mats.

Ownership Costs (Projected)

Cost Area	5 Year Cost	Rating
Depreciation	$5,628	◒
Financing ($215/month)	$2,523	
Insurance	$6,723	◒
State Fees	$505	
Fuel (Hwy 40 City 29)	$2,152	○
Maintenance	$1,557	○
Repairs	$715	○

Warranty/Maintenance Info

Major Tune-Up (100K mile int.)	$270	●
Minor Tune-Up (30K mile int.)	$79	○
Brake Service	$251	●
Overall Warranty	3 yr/36k	○
Drivetrain Warranty	3 yr/36k	○
Rust Warranty	6 yr/100k	○
Maintenance Warranty	N/A	
Roadside Assistance	3 yr/36k	

Ownership Costs By Year (Projected)

$2,000 $4,000 $6,000 $8,000

■ 1999
■ 2000
■ 2001
□ 2002
□ 2003

Resale Value

1999	2000	2001	2002	2003
$11,618	$10,470	$9,476	$8,431	$7,346

Cumulative Costs

	1999	2000	2001	2002	2003
Annual	$4,070	$3,746	$3,647	$4,081	$4,259
Total	$4,070	$7,816	$11,463	$15,544	$19,803

Projected Costs (5yr)

Relative	This Car
$22,692	$19,803
Cost/Mile 32¢	Cost/Mile 28¢

Ownership Cost Value

○ Excellent

Saturn SL1
4 Door Sedan

Compact

 1.9L 100 hp Gas Fuel Inject. 4 Cylinder In-Line   Manual 5 Speed   2 Wheel Front Dual Airbags Std

Purchase Price

Car Item	Dealer Cost	List
Base Price	**$9,827**	**$11,295**
Anti-Lock Brakes	$605	$695
Automatic 4 Speed	$748	$860
Optional Engine	N/A	N/A
Air Conditioning	$835	$960
Power Steering	Std	Std
Cruise Control	$252	$290
Power Windows	Pkg	Pkg
AM/FM Stereo Cassette	$226	$260
Steering Wheel, Tilt	Std	Std
Rear Defroster	Std	Std
*Options Price	$1,809	$2,080
*Total Price	**$11,636**	**$13,375**
Target Price	$13,375	
Destination Charge	$440	
Avg. Tax & Fees	$773	
Total Target $	**$14,588**	
Average Dealer Option Cost:	87%	
12 Month Price Increase:	None	

For 1999 the SL1 sedan benefits from engineering improvements to its 1.9L engine, resulting in a quieter ride and improved EPA fuel economy. Power steering, intermittent wipers and daytime running lamps are standard; individually tailored full cloth seats compliment the interior. Expanded luxury options include a power sunroof, power windows and power door locks, and an electronically-controlled overdrive automatic transmission that boasts more than 30 patents.

Ownership Costs (Projected)

Cost Area	5 Year Cost	Rating
Depreciation	$6,157	○
Financing ($242/month)	$2,838	
Insurance	$6,723	◒
State Fees	$566	
Fuel (Hwy 37 City 27)	$2,319	○
Maintenance	$1,557	○
Repairs	$715	○

Warranty/Maintenance Info

Major Tune-Up (100K mile int.)	$270	●
Minor Tune-Up (30K mile int.)	$79	○
Brake Service	$251	●
Overall Warranty	3 yr/36k	○
Drivetrain Warranty	3 yr/36k	○
Rust Warranty	6 yr/100k	○
Maintenance Warranty	N/A	
Roadside Assistance	3 yr/36k	

Ownership Costs By Year (Projected)

$2,000 $4,000 $6,000 $8,000

■ 1999
■ 2000
■ 2001
□ 2002
□ 2003

Resale Value

1999	2000	2001	2002	2003
$13,215	$11,931	$10,805	$9,636	$8,431

Cumulative Costs

	1999	2000	2001	2002	2003
Annual	$4,241	$4,014	$3,891	$4,291	$4,438
Total	$4,241	$8,255	$12,146	$16,437	$20,875

Projected Costs (5yr)

Relative	This Car
$23,792	$20,875
Cost/Mile 34¢	Cost/Mile 30¢

Ownership Cost Value

○ Excellent

---

* Includes shaded options
** Other purchase requirements apply
*** Price includes other options

● Poor ◉ Worse Than Average ◒ Average ○ Better Than Average ○ Excellent ⊖ Insufficient Information

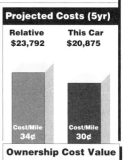

Refer to Section 3: Annotated Vehicle Charts for an explanation of these charts.

Saturn SL2
4 Door Sedan

Compact

1.9L 124 hp Gas Fuel Inject.	4 Cylinder In-Line	Manual 5 Speed	2 Wheel Front	Dual Airbags Std

Purchase Price

Car Item	Dealer Cost	List
Base Price	**$11,097**	**$12,755**
Anti-Lock Brakes	$605	$695
Automatic 4 Speed	$748	$860
Optional Engine	N/A	N/A
Air Conditioning	Std	Std
Power Steering	Std	Std
Cruise Control	$252	$290
Power Windows	Pkg	Pkg
AM/FM Stereo Cassette	$226	$260
Steering Wheel, Tilt	Std	Std
Rear Defroster	Std	Std
*Options Price	$974	$1,120
*Total Price	**$12,071**	**$13,875**
Target Price	$13,875	
Destination Charge	$440	
Avg. Tax & Fees	$800	
Total Target $	**$15,115**	
Average Dealer Option Cost:	**87%**	
12 Month Price Increase:	2%	

The SL2 differentiates itself by offering a standard DOHC engine with increased horsepower and a touring suspension system. Engine improvements include an eight-counterweight crankshaft (versus the usual four), new aluminum pistons and a revised timing chain (versus a more typical timing belt). The result is reduced noise/vibration/harshness characteristics and increased EPA fuel economy. Sporting appeal is met with options such as aluminum wheels, leather seating surfaces and a rear spoiler.

Ownership Costs (Projected)

Cost Area	5 Year Cost	Rating
Depreciation	$6,348	◔
Financing ($251/month)	$2,940	
Insurance	$6,852	◉
State Fees	$586	
Fuel (Hwy 35 City 25)	$2,477	◔
Maintenance	$1,570	◔
Repairs	$715	◔

Warranty/Maintenance Info

Major Tune-Up (100K mile int.)	$281	◉
Minor Tune-Up (30K mile int.)	$79	◔
Brake Service	$251	◉
Overall Warranty	3 yr/36k	◔
Drivetrain Warranty	3 yr/36k	◔
Rust Warranty	6 yr/100k	◔
Maintenance Warranty	N/A	
Roadside Assistance	3 yr/36k	

Ownership Costs By Year (Projected)

$2,000 $4,000 $6,000 $8,000

Legend: 1999, 2000, 2001, 2002, 2003

Resale Value

1999	2000	2001	2002	2003
$13,877	$12,503	$11,293	$10,046	$8,767

Cumulative Costs

	1999	2000	2001	2002	2003
Annual	$4,201	$4,193	$4,057	$4,457	$4,580
Total	$4,201	$8,394	$12,451	$16,908	$21,488

Projected Costs (5yr)

Relative $24,163	This Car $21,488
Cost/Mile 35¢	Cost/Mile 31¢

Ownership Cost Value
◯ Excellent

Saturn SW1
4 Door Wagon

Small Wagon

1.9L 100 hp Gas Fuel Inject.	4 Cylinder In-Line	Manual 5 Speed	2 Wheel Front	Dual Airbags Std

Purchase Price

Car Item	Dealer Cost	List
Base Price	**$10,697**	**$12,295**
Anti-Lock Brakes	$605	$695
Automatic 4 Speed	$748	$860
Optional Engine	N/A	N/A
Air Conditioning	$835	$960
Power Steering	Std	Std
Cruise Control	$252	$290
Power Windows	Pkg	Pkg
AM/FM Stereo Cassette	$226	$260
Steering Wheel, Tilt	Std	Std
Rear Defroster	Std	Std
*Options Price	$1,809	$2,080
*Total Price	**$12,506**	**$14,375**
Target Price	$14,375	
Destination Charge	$440	
Avg. Tax & Fees	$828	
Total Target $	**$15,643**	
Average Dealer Option Cost:	**87%**	
12 Month Price Increase:	None	

The SW1 is positioned as the value priced wagon of the Saturn line. Major changes to the 1.9L engine this year include an eight-counterweight crankshaft (versus the usual four), new aluminum pistons and a revised timing chain (versus a more typical timing belt), resulting in reduced noise/vibration/harshness characteristics. As an added benefit of these enhancements, EPA fuel economy improves as well. A new green exterior color is introduced and the front seatbelts receive comfort enhancements.

Ownership Costs (Projected)

Cost Area	5 Year Cost	Rating
Depreciation	$6,419	◔
Financing ($259/month)	$3,042	
Insurance	$6,852	◉
State Fees	$606	
Fuel (Hwy 35 City 26)	$2,431	◔
Maintenance	$1,557	◔
Repairs	$715	◔

Warranty/Maintenance Info

Major Tune-Up (100K mile int.)	$270	◔
Minor Tune-Up (30K mile int.)	$79	◔
Brake Service	$251	◔
Overall Warranty	3 yr/36k	◔
Drivetrain Warranty	3 yr/36k	◔
Rust Warranty	6 yr/100k	◔
Maintenance Warranty	N/A	
Roadside Assistance	3 yr/36k	

Ownership Costs By Year (Projected)

$2,000 $4,000 $6,000 $8,000

Legend: 1999, 2000, 2001, 2002, 2003

Resale Value

1999	2000	2001	2002	2003
$14,414	$13,008	$11,774	$10,510	$9,224

Cumulative Costs

	1999	2000	2001	2002	2003
Annual	$4,223	$4,248	$4,097	$4,468	$4,586
Total	$4,223	$8,471	$12,568	$17,036	$21,622

Projected Costs (5yr)

Relative $25,197	This Car $21,622
Cost/Mile 36¢	Cost/Mile 31¢

Ownership Cost Value
◯ Excellent

168

* Includes shaded options
** Other purchase requirements apply
*** Price includes other options

 ● Poor   ◉ Worse Than Average   ◐ Average   ◔ Better Than Average   ◯ Excellent ⊖ Insufficient Information

Refer to *Section 3: Annotated Vehicle Charts* for an explanation of these charts.

Saturn SW2
4 Door Wagon

Small Wagon

1.9L 124 hp Gas Fuel Inject.	4 Cylinder In-Line	Manual 5 Speed	2 Wheel Front	Depowered Dual Airbags Std

Purchase Price

Car Item	Dealer Cost	List
Base Price	**$12,402**	**$14,255**
Anti-Lock Brakes	$605	$695
Automatic 4 Speed	$748	$860
Optional Engine	N/A	N/A
Air Conditioning	Std	Std
Power Steering	Std	Std
Cruise Control	$252	$290
Power Windows	Pkg	Pkg
AM/FM Stereo Cassette	$226	$260
Steering Wheel, Tilt	Std	Std
Rear Defroster	Std	Std
***Options Price**	**$974**	**$1,120**
***Total Price**	**$13,376**	**$15,375**
Target Price	$15,375	
Destination Charge	$440	
Avg. Tax & Fees	$883	
Total Target $	**$16,698**	
Average Dealer Option Cost:	87%	
12 Month Price Increase:	7%	

The SW2 offers a unique blend of utility benefits and performance sedan flair all in one. A cargo volume of 24.9 cubic feet is achieved with the rear seat up, and 58.2 with the seats folded down, while a DOHC engine and touring suspension system make for a more exciting ride. For additional safety, a four wheel antilock braking system with traction control is optional. Changes this year include noise/vibration/harshness improvements, revised seatbelt latching and a new green exterior color.

Ownership Costs (Projected)

Cost Area	5 Year Cost	Rating
Depreciation	$7,350	◐
Financing ($277/month)	$3,248	
Insurance	$6,990	◐
State Fees	$646	
Fuel (Hwy 35 City 25)	$2,477	○
Maintenance	$1,570	○
Repairs	$715	○

Warranty/Maintenance Info

Major Tune-Up (100K mile int.)	$281	●
Minor Tune-Up (30K mile int.)	$79	○
Brake Service	$251	○
Overall Warranty	3 yr/36k	○
Drivetrain Warranty	3 yr/36k	○
Rust Warranty	6 yr/100k	○
Maintenance Warranty	N/A	
Roadside Assistance	3 yr/36k	

Ownership Costs By Year (Projected)

1999, 2000, 2001, 2002, 2003

Resale Value

1999	2000	2001	2002	2003
$15,381	$13,755	$12,308	$10,836	$9,348

Projected Costs (5yr)

Relative	This Car
$25,982	$22,996
Cost/Mile 37¢	Cost/Mile 33¢

Cumulative Costs

	1999	2000	2001	2002	2003
Annual	$4,425	$4,570	$4,397	$4,762	$4,842
Total	$4,425	$8,995	$13,392	$18,154	$22,996

Ownership Cost Value

○ Excellent

Subaru Impreza L AWD
2 Door Coupe

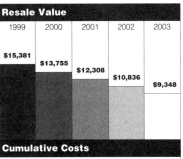
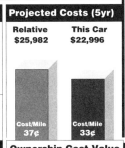

Subcompact

2.5 RS Shown

2.2L 142 hp Gas Fuel Inject.	4 Cylinder Opposing	Manual 5 Speed	4 Wheel Full-Time	Dual Airbags Std

Purchase Price

Car Item	Dealer Cost	List
Base Price	**$14,604**	**$15,895**
Anti-Lock Brakes	N/A	N/A
Automatic 4 Speed	$725	$800
Optional Engine	N/A	N/A
Air Conditioning	Std	Std
Power Steering	Std	Std
Cruise Control	$232	$357
Power Windows	Std	Std
AM/FM Stereo Cassette	Std	Std
Steering Wheel, Tilt	Std	Std
Rear Defroster	Std	Std
***Options Price**	**$0**	**$0**
***Total Price**	**$14,604**	**$15,895**
Target Price	$15,325	
Destination Charge	$495	
Avg. Tax & Fees	$889	
Total Target $	**$16,709**	
Average Dealer Option Cost:	75%	
12 Month Price Increase:	None	

For 1999 the Impreza L coupe's engine receives more horsepower and torque. The coupe is equipped with standard air conditioning, power door locks and power windows. Standard exterior features include a front air dam, rear spoiler and dual power side view mirrors. Safety features include a rear defroster and side-impact door beams. A keyless entry system and security system upgrade are optional. The optional Gauge Pack includes a compass, outside temperature gauge and a barometer/altimeter.

Ownership Costs (Projected)

Cost Area	5 Year Cost	Rating
Depreciation	$8,711	○
Financing ($277/month)	$3,251	
Insurance	$8,265	●
State Fees	$669	
Fuel (Hwy 29 City 22)	$2,906	◐
Maintenance	$4,418	●
Repairs	$791	◐

Warranty/Maintenance Info

Major Tune-Up (60K mile int.)	$233	○
Minor Tune-Up (30K mile int.)	$102	○
Brake Service	$231	○
Overall Warranty	3 yr/36k	○
Drivetrain Warranty	5 yr/60k	◐
Rust Warranty	5 yr/unlim. mi	○
Maintenance Warranty	N/A	
Roadside Assistance	N/A	

Ownership Costs By Year (Projected)

1999, 2000, 2001, 2002, 2003

Resale Value

1999	2000	2001	2002	2003
$13,845	$12,268	$10,868	$9,443	$7,998

Projected Costs (5yr)

Relative	This Car
$26,166	$29,011
Cost/Mile 37¢	Cost/Mile 41¢

Cumulative Costs

	1999	2000	2001	2002	2003
Annual	$6,307	$4,864	$5,315	$6,064	$6,461
Total	$6,307	$11,171	$16,486	$22,550	$29,011

Ownership Cost Value

● Poor

 Poor
 Worse Than Average
 Average
Better Than Average
○ Excellent
⊖ Insufficient Information

169

Refer to *Section 3: Annotated Vehicle Charts* for an explanation of these charts.

Subaru Impreza 2.5 RS AWD
2 Door Coupe

Subcompact

2.5L 165 hp Gas Fuel Inject.	4 Cylinder Opposing	Manual 5 Speed	4 Wheel Full-Time	Dual Airbags Std

Purchase Price

Car Item	Dealer Cost	List
Base Price	**$17,596**	**$19,195**
Anti-Lock Brakes	Std	Std
Automatic 4 Speed	$725	$800
Optional Engine	N/A	N/A
Air Conditioning	Std	Std
Power Steering	Std	Std
Cruise Control	$232	$357
Power Windows	Std	Std
AM/FM Stereo Cassette	Std	Std
Steering Wheel, Tilt	Std	Std
Rear Defroster	Std	Std
*Options Price	$0	$0
*Total Price	$17,596	$19,195
Target Price	$18,619	
Destination Charge	$495	
Avg. Tax & Fees	$1,070	
Total Target $	**$20,184**	
Average Dealer Option Cost:	75%	
12 Month Price Increase:	None	

For 1999, the Impreza 2.5 RS coupe features a redesigned 2.5L 165 hp engine with increased torque. Exterior features include special ground effects, hood scoop, oversized rear spoiler and power sunroof. Standard equipment includes a sport-tuned suspension, 16 inch alloy wheels and a custom tailpipe cover. Standard safety features include antilock brakes, projector beam fog lamps and a rear defroster. An optional automatic transmission, CD player, subwoofer and amplifier are also available.

Ownership Costs (Projected)

Cost Area	5 Year Cost	Rating
Depreciation	$9,904	◎
Financing ($335/month)	$3,926	
Insurance	$9,083	●
State Fees	$801	
Fuel (Hwy 29 City 22)	$2,906	◉
Maintenance	$4,560	●
Repairs	$791	◉

Warranty/Maintenance Info

Major Tune-Up (60K mile int.)	$233	○
Minor Tune-Up (30K mile int.)	$102	○
Brake Service	$216	○
Overall Warranty	3 yr/36k	○
Drivetrain Warranty	5 yr/60k	◯
Rust Warranty	5 yr/unlim. mi	◯
Maintenance Warranty	N/A	
Roadside Assistance	N/A	

Ownership Costs By Year (Projected)

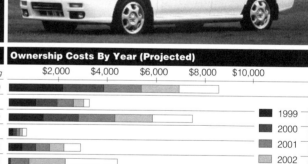

1999, 2000, 2001, 2002, 2003

Resale Value

1999	2000	2001	2002	2003
$16,717	$14,965	$13,409	$11,844	$10,280

Cumulative Costs

	1999	2000	2001	2002	2003
Annual	$7,328	$5,414	$5,802	$6,525	$6,902
Total	$7,328	$12,742	$18,544	$25,069	$31,971

Projected Costs (5yr)

Relative $29,470	This Car $31,971
Cost/Mile 42¢	Cost/Mile 46¢

Ownership Cost Value

Worse Than Average

Subaru Impreza L AWD
4 Door Sedan

Subcompact

   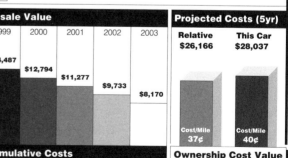

2.2L 142 hp Gas Fuel Inject.	4 Cylinder Opposing	Manual 5 Speed	4 Wheel Full-Time	Dual Airbags Std

Purchase Price

Car Item	Dealer Cost	List
Base Price	**$14,604**	**$15,895**
Anti-Lock Brakes	N/A	N/A
Automatic 4 Speed	$725	$800
Optional Engine	N/A	N/A
Air Conditioning	Std	Std
Power Steering	Std	Std
Cruise Control	$232	$357
Power Windows	Std	Std
AM/FM Stereo Cassette	Std	Std
Steering Wheel, Tilt	Std	Std
Rear Defroster	Std	Std
*Options Price	$0	$0
*Total Price	$14,604	$15,895
Target Price	$15,325	
Destination Charge	$495	
Avg. Tax & Fees	$889	
Total Target $	**$16,709**	
Average Dealer Option Cost:	74%	
12 Month Price Increase:	None	

For 1999 the Impreza L sedan's engine receives more horsepower and torque. Standard features include air conditioning, power door locks and power windows. Additional standard features include cup holders and an 80 watt AM/FM stereo with cassette. The optional Gauge Pack includes an outside temperature gauge, compass and a barometer/altimeter display. Additional options include cruise control, a CD player, security upgrade kit, rear spoiler, fog lamps and hood deflector.

Ownership Costs (Projected)

Cost Area	5 Year Cost	Rating
Depreciation	$8,539	○
Financing ($277/month)	$3,251	
Insurance	$7,463	○
State Fees	$669	
Fuel (Hwy 29 City 22)	$2,906	◉
Maintenance	$4,418	●
Repairs	$791	◉

Warranty/Maintenance Info

Major Tune-Up (60K mile int.)	$233	○
Minor Tune-Up (30K mile int.)	$102	○
Brake Service	$231	○
Overall Warranty	3 yr/36k	○
Drivetrain Warranty	5 yr/60k	◯
Rust Warranty	5 yr/unlim. mi	○
Maintenance Warranty	N/A	
Roadside Assistance	N/A	

Ownership Costs By Year (Projected)

1999, 2000, 2001, 2002, 2003

Resale Value

1999	2000	2001	2002	2003
$14,487	$12,794	$11,277	$9,733	$8,170

Cumulative Costs

	1999	2000	2001	2002	2003
Annual	$5,512	$4,823	$5,272	$6,019	$6,411
Total	$5,512	$10,335	$15,607	$21,626	$28,037

Projected Costs (5yr)

Relative $26,166	This Car $28,037
Cost/Mile 37¢	Cost/Mile 40¢

Ownership Cost Value

Worse Than Average

Poor	Worse Than Average	Average	Better Than Average	◯ Excellent	⊖ Insufficient Information

Refer to *Section 3: Annotated Vehicle Charts* for an explanation of these charts.

Subaru Impreza L AWD
4 Door Wagon

2.2L 142 hp Gas Fuel Inject.	4 Cylinder Opposing	Manual 5 Speed	4 Wheel Full-Time	Dual Airbags Std

Purchase Price

Car Item	Dealer Cost	List
Base Price	**$14,967**	**$16,295**
Anti-Lock Brakes	N/A	N/A
Automatic 4 Speed	$725	$800
Optional Engine	N/A	N/A
Air Conditioning	Std	Std
Power Steering	Std	Std
Cruise Control	$232	$357
Power Windows	Std	Std
AM/FM Stereo Cassette	Std	Std
Steering Wheel, Tilt	Std	Std
Rear Defroster	Std	Std
***Options Price**	**$725**	**$800**
***Total Price**	**$15,692**	**$17,095**
Target Price	$16,476	
Destination Charge	$495	
Avg. Tax & Fees	$953	
Total Target $	**$17,924**	
Average Dealer Option Cost:	**73%**	
12 Month Price Increase:	None	

For 1999 the Impreza L wagon's engine receives more horsepower and torque. Standard equipment includes a rear window wiper and washer, rear defroster and air conditioning. Power door locks, dual power mirrors and power windows with driver's side express down are also standard. Optional equipment includes a luggage rack, rear cargo tray and rear cargo net. The wagon is also available with a rear spoiler and custom tailpipe cover, along with an optional CD player, subwoofer and amplifier.

Ownership Costs (Projected)

Cost Area	5 Year Cost	Rating
Depreciation	$8,640	◑
Financing ($297/month)	$3,486	
Insurance	$7,643	◑
State Fees	$717	
Fuel (Hwy 29 City 23)	$2,847	◉
Maintenance	$4,418	●
Repairs	$791	◑

Warranty/Maintenance Info

Major Tune-Up (60K mile int.)	$233	◑
Minor Tune-Up (30K mile int.)	$102	◑
Brake Service	$231	◑
Overall Warranty	3 yr/36k	◑
Drivetrain Warranty	5 yr/60k	○
Rust Warranty	5 yr/unlim. mi	○
Maintenance Warranty	N/A	
Roadside Assistance	N/A	

Ownership Costs By Year (Projected)

$2,000 $4,000 $6,000 $8,000 $10,000

■ 1999
■ 2000
▨ 2001
▨ 2002
□ 2003

Resale Value

1999	2000	2001	2002	2003
$16,270	$14,394	$12,706	$10,998	$9,284

Cumulative Costs

	1999	2000	2001	2002	2003
Annual	$5,059	$5,104	$5,526	$6,246	$6,607
Total	$5,059	$10,163	$15,689	$21,935	$28,542

Projected Costs (5yr)

Relative $28,054	This Car $28,542
Cost/Mile 40¢	Cost/Mile 41¢

Ownership Cost Value

○ Better Than Average

Subaru Impreza Outback AWD
4 Door Wagon

2.2L 142 hp Gas Fuel Inject.	4 Cylinder Opposing	Manual 5 Speed	4 Wheel Full-Time	Dual Airbags Std

Purchase Price

Car Item	Dealer Cost	List
Base Price	**$16,501**	**$17,995**
Anti-Lock Brakes	Std	Std
Automatic 4 Speed	$725	$800
Optional Engine	N/A	N/A
Air Conditioning	Std	Std
Power Steering	Std	Std
Cruise Control	$232	$357
Power Windows	Std	Std
AM/FM Stereo Cassette	Std	Std
Steering Wheel, Tilt	Std	Std
Rear Defroster	Std	Std
***Options Price**	**$725**	**$800**
***Total Price**	**$17,226**	**$18,795**
Target Price	$18,163	
Destination Charge	$495	
Avg. Tax & Fees	$1,046	
Total Target $	**$19,704**	
Average Dealer Option Cost:	**74%**	
12 Month Price Increase:	None	

The 1999 Impreza Outback wagon features two-tone paint, a luggage rack and rear bumper cover, as well as an improved engine with increased horsepower and torque. Air conditioning, power door locks and power windows are also standard. Optional equipment includes a ski rack, bike attachment and kayak carrier. The optional Gauge Pack includes a compass, outside temperature gauge and a barometer/altimeter. Safety features include a rear defroster and rear window wiper and washer.

Ownership Costs (Projected)

Cost Area	5 Year Cost	Rating
Depreciation	$9,408	◑
Financing ($327/month)	$3,833	
Insurance	$7,837	◑
State Fees	$785	
Fuel (Hwy 29 City 23)	$2,847	◉
Maintenance	$4,782	●
Repairs	$791	◑

Warranty/Maintenance Info

Major Tune-Up (60K mile int.)	$233	◑
Minor Tune-Up (30K mile int.)	$102	◑
Brake Service	$231	◑
Overall Warranty	3 yr/36k	◑
Drivetrain Warranty	5 yr/60k	○
Rust Warranty	5 yr/unlim. mi	○
Maintenance Warranty	N/A	
Roadside Assistance	N/A	

Ownership Costs By Year (Projected)

$2,000 $4,000 $6,000 $8,000 $10,000

■ 1999
■ 2000
▨ 2001
▨ 2002
□ 2003

Resale Value

1999	2000	2001	2002	2003
$17,212	$15,351	$13,678	$11,991	$10,296

Cumulative Costs

	1999	2000	2001	2002	2003
Annual	$6,069	$5,238	$5,634	$6,687	$6,655
Total	$6,069	$11,307	$16,941	$23,628	$30,283

Projected Costs (5yr)

Relative $29,414	This Car $30,283
Cost/Mile 42¢	Cost/Mile 43¢

Ownership Cost Value

○ Average

---

* Includes shaded options

** Other purchase requirements apply

*** Price includes other options

● Poor ◉ Worse Than Average ◑ Average ○ Better Than Average ○ Excellent ⊖ Insufficient Information

171

Refer to *Section 3: Annotated Vehicle Charts* for an explanation of these charts.

Subaru Legacy L AWD
4 Door Sedan

Compact

2.2L 142 hp Gas Fuel Inject.	4 Cylinder Opposing
Manual 5 Speed	4 Wheel Full-Time
Dual Airbags Std	

2.5 GT Shown

Purchase Price

Car Item	Dealer Cost	List
Base Price	**$17,470**	**$19,195**
Anti-Lock Brakes	Std	Std
Automatic 4 Speed	$722	$800
Optional Engine	N/A	N/A
Air Conditioning	Std	Std
Power Steering	Std	Std
Cruise Control	Std	Std
Power Windows	Std	Std
AM/FM Stereo Cassette	Std	Std
Steering Wheel, Tilt	Std	Std
Rear Defroster	Std	Std
***Options Price**	$722	$800
***Total Price**	**$18,192**	**$19,995**
Target Price	$19,030	
Destination Charge	$495	
Avg. Tax & Fees	$1,097	
Total Target $	**$20,622**	
Average Dealer Option Cost:	77%	
12 Month Price Increase:	None	

Ownership Costs (Projected)

Cost Area	5 Year Cost	Rating
Depreciation	$10,206	◐
Financing ($342/month)	$4,012	
Insurance	$7,643	◐
State Fees	$832	
Fuel (Hwy 29 City 22)	$2,906	◐
Maintenance	$4,432	●
Repairs	$810	◐

Warranty/Maintenance Info

Major Tune-Up (60K mile int.)	$229	◐
Minor Tune-Up (30K mile int.)	$102	◐
Brake Service	$216	◐
Overall Warranty	3 yr/36k	◐
Drivetrain Warranty	5 yr/60k	○
Rust Warranty	5 yr/unlim. mi	◐
Maintenance Warranty	N/A	
Roadside Assistance	N/A	

For 1999, the Legacy L sedan continues with a few changes from last year's model, including an increase in the 2.2L engine's horsepower and torque. Standard features include air conditioning, cruise control, power windows and dual power side mirrors. Also included is a 60/40 split folding rear seat and front and rear stabilizer bars. Options include keyless remote entry system, woodgrain trim and door-mounted tweeters for improved sound quality. A rear differential protector is also available.

Ownership Costs By Year (Projected)

$2,000 $4,000 $6,000 $8,000 $10,000 $12,000

- 1999
- 2000
- 2001
- 2002
- 2003

Resale Value

1999	2000	2001	2002	2003
$17,258	$15,413	$13,758	$12,089	$10,416

Cumulative Costs

	1999	2000	2001	2002	2003
Annual	$6,987	$5,256	$5,639	$6,178	$6,781
Total	$6,987	$12,243	$17,882	$24,060	$30,841

Projected Costs (5yr)

Relative	This Car
$30,001	$30,841
Cost/Mile 43¢	Cost/Mile 44¢

Ownership Cost Value

◐ Average

Subaru Legacy 2.5 GT AWD
4 Door Sedan

Compact

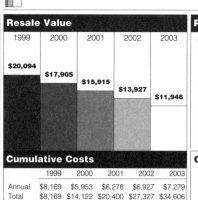

2.5L 165 hp Gas Fuel Inject.	4 Cylinder Opposing
Manual 5 Speed	4 Wheel Full-Time
Dual Airbags Std	

Purchase Price

Car Item	Dealer Cost	List
Base Price	**$20,681**	**$22,795**
Anti-Lock Brakes	Std	Std
Automatic 4 Speed	$722	$800
Optional Engine	N/A	N/A
Air Conditioning	Std	Std
Power Steering	Std	Std
Cruise Control	Std	Std
Power Windows	Std	Std
AM/FM Stereo Cassette	Std	Std
Steering Wheel, Tilt	Std	Std
Rear Defroster	Std	Std
***Options Price**	$722	$800
***Total Price**	**$21,403**	**$23,595**
Target Price	$22,459	
Destination Charge	$495	
Avg. Tax & Fees	$1,287	
Total Target $	**$24,241**	
Average Dealer Option Cost:	76%	
12 Month Price Increase:	None	

Ownership Costs (Projected)

Cost Area	5 Year Cost	Rating
Depreciation	$12,295	◉
Financing ($402/month)	$4,716	
Insurance	$8,045	◐
State Fees	$978	
Fuel (Hwy 26 City 21)	$3,150	●
Maintenance	$4,612	●
Repairs	$810	◐

Warranty/Maintenance Info

Major Tune-Up (60K mile int.)	$229	◐
Minor Tune-Up (30K mile int.)	$102	◐
Brake Service	$216	◐
Overall Warranty	3 yr/36k	◐
Drivetrain Warranty	5 yr/60k	○
Rust Warranty	5 yr/unlim. mi	◐
Maintenance Warranty	N/A	
Roadside Assistance	N/A	

Standard features for the 1999 Legacy 2.5 GT sedan include woodgrain trim, a leather-wrapped steering wheel and shift knob, air conditioning, a power moonroof and front fog lamps. Exterior features include body-colored extended side skirts, front and rear under spoilers, a hood scoop and rear deck lid spoiler. Additional standard features include cruise control, antilock brakes, illuminated visor mirrors and a custom tailpipe. Options include an automatic transmission and CD changer.

Ownership Costs By Year (Projected)

$2,000 $4,000 $6,000 $8,000 $10,000 $12,000 $14,000

- 1999
- 2000
- 2001
- 2002
- 2003

Resale Value

1999	2000	2001	2002	2003
$20,094	$17,905	$15,915	$13,927	$11,946

Cumulative Costs

	1999	2000	2001	2002	2003
Annual	$8,169	$5,953	$6,278	$6,927	$7,279
Total	$8,169	$14,122	$20,400	$27,327	$34,606

Projected Costs (5yr)

Relative	This Car
$33,521	$34,606
Cost/Mile 48¢	Cost/Mile 49¢

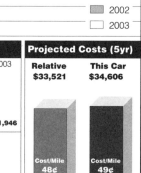

Ownership Cost Value

◉ Worse Than Average

---

* Includes shaded options
** Other purchase requirements apply
*** Price includes other options

 ● Poor
 ◉ Worse Than Average
 ◐ Average
 ◑ Better Than Average
 ○ Excellent
⊖ Insufficient Information

Refer to *Section 3: Annotated Vehicle Charts* for an explanation of these charts.

Subaru Legacy Sport Utility Sedan
4 Door Sedan

Compact

| 2.5L 165 hp Gas Fuel Inject. | 4 Cylinder Opposing | Automatic 4 Speed | 4 Wheel Full-Time | Dual Airbags Std |

Limited Model Shown

Purchase Price

Car Item	Dealer Cost	List
Base Price	**$20,990**	**$23,395**
Anti-Lock Brakes	Std	Std
Manual Transmission	N/A	N/A
Optional Engine	N/A	N/A
Air Conditioning	Std	Std
Power Steering	Std	Std
Cruise Control	Std	Std
Power Windows	Std	Std
AM/FM Stereo Cassette	Std	Std
Steering Wheel, Tilt	Std	Std
Rear Defroster	Std	Std
*Options Price	$0	$0
***Total Price**	**$20,990**	**$23,395**
Target Price	$22,069	
Destination Charge	$495	
Avg. Tax & Fees	$1,267	
Total Target $	**$23,831**	
Average Dealer Option Cost:	71%	
12 Month Price Increase:	N/A	

Ownership Costs (Projected)

Cost Area	5 Year Cost	Rating
Depreciation	$11,795	◐
Financing ($395/month)	$4,636	
Insurance	$8,265	◐
State Fees	$968	
Fuel (Hwy 26 City 21)	$3,150	●
Maintenance	$4,796	●
Repairs	$810	◐

Warranty/Maintenance Info

Major Tune-Up (60K mile int.)	$229	◐
Minor Tune-Up (30K mile int.)	$102	◐
Brake Service	$216	◐
Overall Warranty	3 yr/36k	◐
Drivetrain Warranty	5 yr/60k	○
Rust Warranty	5 yr/unlim. mi	○
Maintenance Warranty	N/A	
Roadside Assistance	N/A	

For 1999, the 30th Anniversary Legacy Sport Utility Sedan is introduced as a new model and includes a raised suspension, cruise control, alloy wheels and front fog lamps. Also included are a four speed automatic transmission, keyless remote entry system and an AM/FM/weatherband/cassette stereo. Additional features include a height-adjustable driver's seat, dark tinted glass, windshield wiper de-icers and map lights. Options include a CD changer and rear differential protector.

Ownership Costs By Year (Projected)

$2,000 $4,000 $6,000 $8,000 $10,000 $12,000

■ 1999
■ 2000
■ 2001
□ 2002
□ 2003

Resale Value

1999	2000	2001	2002	2003
$19,909	$17,790	$15,870	$13,950	$12,036

Cumulative Costs

	1999	2000	2001	2002	2003
Annual	$7,957	$5,902	$6,377	$6,781	$7,403
Total	$7,957	$13,859	$20,236	$27,017	$34,420

Projected Costs (5yr)

Relative	This Car
$33,051	**$34,420**
Cost/Mile 47¢	Cost/Mile 49¢

Ownership Cost Value

Worse Than Average

Subaru Legacy 2.5 GT Limited AWD
4 Door Sedan

Compact

| 2.5L 165 hp Gas Fuel Inject. | 4 Cylinder Opposing | Manual 5 Speed | 4 Wheel Full-Time | Dual Airbags Std |

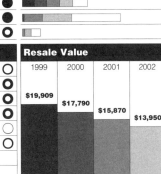

Base Model Shown

Purchase Price

Car Item	Dealer Cost	List
Base Price	**$21,841**	**$24,095**
Anti-Lock Brakes	Std	Std
Automatic 4 Speed	$722	$800
Optional Engine	N/A	N/A
Air Conditioning	Std	Std
Power Steering	Std	Std
Cruise Control	Std	Std
Power Windows	Std	Std
AM/FM Stereo Cass/CD	Std	Std
Steering Wheel, Tilt	Std	Std
Rear Defroster	Std	Std
*Options Price	$722	$800
***Total Price**	**$22,563**	**$24,895**
Target Price	$23,701	
Destination Charge	$495	
Avg. Tax & Fees	$1,356	
Total Target $	**$25,552**	
Average Dealer Option Cost:	77%	
12 Month Price Increase:	None	

Ownership Costs (Projected)

Cost Area	5 Year Cost	Rating
Depreciation	$13,416	●
Financing ($424/month)	$4,970	
Insurance	$8,045	◐
State Fees	$1,029	
Fuel (Hwy 26 City 21)	$3,150	●
Maintenance	$4,501	●
Repairs	$810	◐

Warranty/Maintenance Info

Major Tune-Up (60K mile int.)	$229	◐
Minor Tune-Up (30K mile int.)	$102	◐
Brake Service	$216	◐
Overall Warranty	3 yr/36k	◐
Drivetrain Warranty	5 yr/60k	○
Rust Warranty	5 yr/unlim. mi	○
Maintenance Warranty	N/A	
Roadside Assistance	N/A	

For 1999, the Legacy 2.5 GT Limited sedan continues mostly unchanged from last year. Standard features include body-colored ground effects, deep tinted glass, a leather interior and an 80 watt AM/FM/cassette sound system with CD and weatherband. Also included are power windows and door locks, air conditioning, simulated woodgrain trim and a keyless remote entry system. Options include a CD changer, rear cup holders, dual power outlets and a rear differential protector.

Ownership Costs By Year (Projected)

$2,000 $4,000 $6,000 $8,000 $10,000 $12,000 $14,000

■ 1999
■ 2000
■ 2001
□ 2002
□ 2003

Resale Value

1999	2000	2001	2002	2003
$21,068	$18,667	$16,479	$14,299	$12,136

Cumulative Costs

	1999	2000	2001	2002	2003
Annual	$8,606	$6,247	$6,538	$7,050	$7,480
Total	$8,606	$14,853	$21,391	$28,441	$35,921

Projected Costs (5yr)

Relative	This Car
$34,871	**$35,921**
Cost/Mile 50¢	Cost/Mile 51¢

Ownership Cost Value

Average

---

* Includes shaded options

** Other purchase requirements apply

*** Price includes other options

 Poor   Worse Than Average   Average ○ Better Than Average ○ Excellent ⊖ Insufficient Information

Refer to *Section 3: Annotated Vehicle Charts* for an explanation of these charts.

Subaru Legacy Sport Utility Sedan Limited
4 Door Sedan

Compact

2.5L 165 hp Gas Fuel Inject.	4 Cylinder Opposing	Automatic 4 Speed	4 Wheel Full-Time	Dual Airbags Std

Purchase Price

Car Item	Dealer Cost	List
Base Price	**$22,946**	**$25,595**
Anti-Lock Brakes	Std	Std
Manual Transmission	N/A	N/A
Optional Engine	N/A	N/A
Air Conditioning	Std	Std
Power Steering	Std	Std
Cruise Control	Std	Std
Power Windows	Std	Std
AM/FM Stereo Cass/CD	Std	Std
Steering Wheel, Tilt	Std	Std
Rear Defroster	Std	Std
***Options Price**	$0	$0
***Total Price**	**$22,946**	**$25,595**
Target Price	$24,167	
Destination Charge	$495	
Avg. Tax & Fees	$1,384	
Total Target $	**$26,046**	
Average Dealer Option Cost:	**71%**	
12 Month Price Increase:	N/A	

A new model for 1999, the 30th Anniversary Legacy Sport Utility Sedan Limited includes a raised suspension, a remote keyless entry system, a four speed automatic transmission and a six speaker AM/FM/weather band/cassette stereo with CD player. Additional features include a leather interior, gold accent alloy wheels, a power moonroof and woodgrain interior trim. Also included are air conditioning and power windows and door locks. Options include a CD changer and rear differential protector.

Ownership Costs (Projected)

Cost Area	5 Year Cost	Rating
Depreciation	$13,804	●
Financing ($432/month)	$5,067	
Insurance	$8,265	◉
State Fees	$1,058	
Fuel (Hwy 26 City 21)	$3,150	●
Maintenance	$4,727	●
Repairs	$810	◉

Warranty/Maintenance Info

Major Tune-Up (60K mile int.)	$229	◉
Minor Tune-Up (30K mile int.)	$102	◉
Brake Service	$216	◉
Overall Warranty	3 yr/36k	◉
Drivetrain Warranty	5 yr/60k	○
Rust Warranty	5 yr/unlim. mi	○
Maintenance Warranty	N/A	
Roadside Assistance	N/A	

Ownership Costs By Year (Projected)

$2,000 $4,000 $6,000 $8,000 $10,000 $12,000 $14,000

- 1999
- 2000
- 2001
- 2002
- 2003

Resale Value

1999	2000	2001	2002	2003
$21,473	$18,992	$16,728	$14,475	$12,242

Cumulative Costs

	1999	2000	2001	2002	2003
Annual	$8,776	$6,403	$6,828	$7,117	$7,757
Total	$8,776	$15,179	$22,007	$29,124	$36,881

Projected Costs (5yr)

Relative $35,325	This Car $36,881
Cost/Mile 50¢	Cost/Mile 53¢

Ownership Cost Value
◉ Worse Than Average

Subaru Legacy Brighton AWD
4 Door Wagon

Midsize Wagon

L Model Shown

2.2L 142 hp Gas Fuel Inject.	4 Cylinder Opposing	Manual 5 Speed	4 Wheel Full-Time	Dual Airbags Std

Purchase Price

Car Item	Dealer Cost	List
Base Price	**$15,957**	**$16,895**
Anti-Lock Brakes	N/A	N/A
Automatic 4 Speed	$722	$800
Optional Engine	N/A	N/A
Air Conditioning	Std	Std
Power Steering	Std	Std
Cruise Control	$218	$334
Power Windows	N/A	N/A
AM/FM Stereo Cassette	Std	Std
Steering Wheel, Tilt	Std	Std
Rear Defroster	Std	Std
***Options Price**	$940	$1,134
***Total Price**	**$16,897**	**$18,029**
Target Price	$17,374	
Destination Charge	$495	
Avg. Tax & Fees	$1,002	
Total Target $	**$18,871**	
Average Dealer Option Cost:	**71%**	
12 Month Price Increase:	None	

For 1999, the Legacy Brighton wagon is equipped with air conditioning, multi-reflector headlamps, an AM/FM stereo and a rear window wiper/washer, as well as a revised engine with increased horsepower and torque. Options include a CD changer, a leather-wrapped shift knob, cruise control, rear cup holders and dual power outlets. Also available are upgraded speakers, map/reading lamps, a rear differential protector and a wide selection of different luggage rack attachments.

Ownership Costs (Projected)

Cost Area	5 Year Cost	Rating
Depreciation	$7,796	○
Financing ($313/month)	$3,672	
Insurance	$7,294	◉
State Fees	$754	
Fuel (Hwy 29 City 22)	$2,906	○
Maintenance	$4,449	◉
Repairs	$810	○

Warranty/Maintenance Info

Major Tune-Up (60K mile int.)	$229	○
Minor Tune-Up (30K mile int.)	$102	○
Brake Service	$231	○
Overall Warranty	3 yr/36k	○
Drivetrain Warranty	5 yr/60k	○
Rust Warranty	5 yr/unlim. mi	○
Maintenance Warranty	N/A	
Roadside Assistance	N/A	

Ownership Costs By Year (Projected)

$2,000 $4,000 $6,000 $8,000

- 1999
- 2000
- 2001
- 2002
- 2003

Resale Value

1999	2000	2001	2002	2003
$17,807	$15,941	$14,341	$12,688	$11,075

Cumulative Costs

	1999	2000	2001	2002	2003
Annual	$4,485	$5,098	$5,428	$6,051	$6,619
Total	$4,485	$9,583	$15,011	$21,062	$27,681

Projected Costs (5yr)

Relative $28,108	This Car $27,681
Cost/Mile 40¢	Cost/Mile 40¢

Ownership Cost Value
○ Better Than Average

174

* Includes shaded options

** Other purchase requirements apply

*** Price includes other options

 ● Poor   ◉ Worse Than Average   ◉ Average   ○ Better Than Average   ○ Excellent   ⊖ Insufficient Information

Refer to *Section 3: Annotated Vehicle Charts* for an explanation of these charts.

Subaru Legacy L AWD
4 Door Wagon

Midsize Wagon

2.2L 142 hp Gas Fuel Inject.	4 Cylinder Opposing
Manual 5 Speed	4 Wheel Full-Time
Dual Airbags Std	

Purchase Price

Car Item	Dealer Cost	List
Base Price	**$18,097**	**$19,895**
Anti-Lock Brakes	Std	Std
Automatic 4 Speed	$722	$800
Optional Engine	N/A	N/A
Air Conditioning	Std	Std
Power Steering	Std	Std
Cruise Control	Std	Std
Power Windows	Std	Std
AM/FM Stereo Cassette	Std	Std
Steering Wheel, Tilt	Std	Std
Rear Defroster	Std	Std
*Options Price	$722	$800
*Total Price	**$18,819**	**$20,695**
Target Price	$19,697	
Destination Charge	$495	
Avg. Tax & Fees	$1,134	
Total Target $	**$21,326**	
Average Dealer Option Cost:	70%	
12 Month Price Increase:	None	

For 1999, the Legacy L wagon comes standard with cruise control, multi-reflector headlamps, interior map lights and a roof rack, as well as a revised engine with increased horsepower and torque. Also included are air conditioning, alloy wheels, rear headrests and a cargo area light. Options include a CD changer, leather-wrapped shift knob, woodgrain trim and carpeted floor mats. Also available are dual power outlets, a rear differential protector and a variety of luggage rack attachments.

Ownership Costs (Projected)

Cost Area	5 Year Cost	Rating
Depreciation	$10,192	◐
Financing ($353/month)	$4,149	
Insurance	$7,643	◐
State Fees	$861	
Fuel (Hwy 29 City 22)	$2,906	○
Maintenance	$4,432	◉
Repairs	$810	○

Warranty/Maintenance Info

Major Tune-Up (60K mile int.)	$229	○
Minor Tune-Up (30K mile int.)	$102	○
Brake Service	$216	○
Overall Warranty	3 yr/36k	◐
Drivetrain Warranty	5 yr/60k	○
Rust Warranty	5 yr/unlim. mi	○
Maintenance Warranty	N/A	
Roadside Assistance	N/A	

Ownership Costs By Year (Projected)

$2,000 $4,000 $6,000 $8,000 $10,000 $12,000

■ 1999
■ 2000
■ 2001
□ 2002
□ 2003

Resale Value

1999	2000	2001	2002	2003
$18,677	$16,609	$14,808	$12,949	$11,134

Cumulative Costs

	1999	2000	2001	2002	2003
Annual	$6,326	$5,523	$5,820	$6,391	$6,933
Total	$6,326	$11,849	$17,669	$24,060	$30,993

Projected Costs (5yr)

Relative	This Car
$30,867	$30,993
Cost/Mile 44¢	Cost/Mile 44¢

Ownership Cost Value

◐ Average

Subaru Legacy Outback AWD
4 Door Wagon

Midsize Wagon

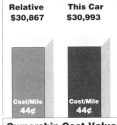

2.5L 165 hp Gas Fuel Inject.	4 Cylinder Opposing
Manual 5 Speed	4 Wheel Full-Time
Dual Airbags Std	

Purchase Price

Car Item	Dealer Cost	List
Base Price	**$20,408**	**$22,495**
Anti-Lock Brakes	Std	Std
Automatic 4 Speed	$722	$800
Optional Engine	N/A	N/A
Air Conditioning	Std	Std
Power Steering	Std	Std
Cruise Control	Std	Std
Power Windows	Std	Std
AM/FM Stereo Cassette	Std	Std
Steering Wheel, Tilt	Std	Std
Rear Defroster	Std	Std
*Options Price	$722	$800
*Total Price	**$21,130**	**$23,295**
Target Price	$22,289	
Destination Charge	$495	
Avg. Tax & Fees	$1,276	
Total Target $	**$24,060**	
Average Dealer Option Cost:	73%	
12 Month Price Increase:	None	

For 1999, the Legacy Outback includes air conditioning, raised heavy duty suspension, large diameter fog lamps with stone guards, alloy wheels and cruise control. Additional standard features include carpeted floor mats, splash guards, a trailer harness connector, map/reading lamps and a rear cargo tray. Available options include leather seats, woodgrain trim, hood deflector, engine underguard and rear window dust deflector. Also available are a rear cargo net and rear differential protector.

Ownership Costs (Projected)

Cost Area	5 Year Cost	Rating
Depreciation	$10,253	○
Financing ($399/month)	$4,679	
Insurance	$8,045	◐
State Fees	$965	
Fuel (Hwy 26 City 21)	$3,150	◐
Maintenance	$4,501	◉
Repairs	$810	○

Warranty/Maintenance Info

Major Tune-Up (60K mile int.)	$229	○
Minor Tune-Up (30K mile int.)	$102	○
Brake Service	$216	○
Overall Warranty	3 yr/36k	◐
Drivetrain Warranty	5 yr/60k	○
Rust Warranty	5 yr/unlim. mi	○
Maintenance Warranty	N/A	
Roadside Assistance	N/A	

Ownership Costs By Year (Projected)

$2,000 $4,000 $6,000 $8,000 $10,000 $12,000

■ 1999
■ 2000
■ 2001
□ 2002
□ 2003

Resale Value

1999	2000	2001	2002	2003
$21,792	$19,586	$17,665	$15,706	$13,807

Cumulative Costs

	1999	2000	2001	2002	2003
Annual	$6,275	$5,957	$6,198	$6,780	$7,193
Total	$6,275	$12,232	$18,430	$25,210	$32,403

Projected Costs (5yr)

Relative	This Car
$33,369	$32,403
Cost/Mile 48¢	Cost/Mile 46¢

Ownership Cost Value

○ Excellent

---

* Includes shaded options

** Other purchase requirements apply

*** Price includes other options

● Poor   ◐ Worse Than Average   ◑ Average   ○ Better Than Average   ○ Excellent   ⊖ Insufficient Information

175

Refer to *Section 3: Annotated Vehicle Charts* for an explanation of these charts.

©1999 by IntelliChoice, Inc. (408) 866-1400 http://www.intellichoice.com All Rights Reserved. Reproduction Prohibited.

Subaru Legacy 2.5 GT AWD
4 Door Wagon

2.5L 165 hp Gas Fuel Inject.	4 Cylinder Opposing	Manual 5 Speed	4 Wheel Full-Time	Dual Airbags Std

Midsize Wagon

L Model Shown

Purchase Price

Car Item	Dealer Cost	List
Base Price	**$21,308**	**$23,495**
Anti-Lock Brakes	Std	Std
Automatic 4 Speed	$722	$800
Optional Engine	N/A	N/A
Air Conditioning	Std	Std
Power Steering	Std	Std
Cruise Control	Std	Std
Power Windows	Std	Std
AM/FM Stereo Cassette	Std	Std
Steering Wheel, Tilt	Std	Std
Rear Defroster	Std	Std
*Options Price	$722	$800
*Total Price	**$22,030**	**$24,295**
Target Price	$23,130	
Destination Charge	$495	
Avg. Tax & Fees	$1,324	
Total Target $	**$24,949**	
Average Dealer Option Cost:	74%	
12 Month Price Increase:	None	

For 1999, the Legacy 2.5 GT wagon includes air conditioning, antilock brakes, a sport-tuned suspension, ground effects, rear spoiler and two-way power moonroof. Also standard are cruise control, fog lamps, a power antenna and simulated woodgrain interior. Options include leather seats, a keyless entry system, security system upgrade kit and a variety of different luggage rack attachments. Also available are a CD changer, amplifier, rear cup holders and dual power outlets.

Ownership Costs (Projected)

Cost Area	5 Year Cost	Rating
Depreciation	$12,295	◐
Financing ($414/month)	$4,854	
Insurance	$8,045	◐
State Fees	$1,005	
Fuel (Hwy 26 City 21)	$3,150	◐
Maintenance	$4,612	◉
Repairs	$810	○

Warranty/Maintenance Info

Major Tune-Up (60K mile int.)	$229	◐
Minor Tune-Up (30K mile int.)	$102	◐
Brake Service	$216	◐
Overall Warranty	3 yr/36k	◐
Drivetrain Warranty	5 yr/60k	○
Rust Warranty	5 yr/unlim. mi	◐
Maintenance Warranty	N/A	
Roadside Assistance	N/A	

Ownership Costs By Year (Projected)

$2,000 $4,000 $6,000 $8,000 $10,000 $12,000 $14,000

- 1999
- 2000
- 2001
- 2002
- 2003

Resale Value

1999	2000	2001	2002	2003
$21,243	$18,889	$16,819	$14,710	$12,654

Cumulative Costs

	1999	2000	2001	2002	2003
Annual	$7,782	$6,162	$6,391	$7,071	$7,365
Total	$7,782	$13,944	$20,335	$27,406	$34,771

Projected Costs (5yr)

Relative $34,103	This Car $34,771
Cost/Mile 49¢	Cost/Mile 50¢

Ownership Cost Value

◉ Worse Than Average

Subaru Legacy Outback Limited 30th Anniversary
4 Door Wagon

2.5L 165 hp Gas Fuel Inject.	4 Cylinder Opposing	Manual 5 Speed	4 Wheel Full-Time	Dual Airbags Std

Midsize Wagon

Purchase Price

Car Item	Dealer Cost	List
Base Price	**$22,295**	**$24,595**
Anti-Lock Brakes	Std	Std
Automatic 4 Speed	$722	$800
Optional Engine	N/A	N/A
Air Conditioning	Std	Std
Power Steering	Std	Std
Cruise Control	Std	Std
Power Windows	Std	Std
AM/FM Stereo Cass/CD	Std	Std
Steering Wheel, Tilt	Std	Std
Rear Defroster	Std	Std
*Options Price	$722	$800
*Total Price	**$23,017**	**$25,395**
Target Price	$24,325	
Destination Charge	$495	
Avg. Tax & Fees	$1,389	
Total Target $	**$26,209**	
Average Dealer Option Cost:	75%	
12 Month Price Increase:	None	

For 1999, the Legacy Outback Limited 30th Anniversary includes Sandstone colored lower body and wheel accents, a unique front grille, dual illuminated vanity mirrors and front seatback nets. Also included are variable intermittent windshield wipers, front door courtesy lights, a height-adjustable driver's seat, heated front seats and side mirrors, and map/reading lights. Options include a roof visor, front end full cover, rear spoiler and a variety of luggage rack attachments.

Ownership Costs (Projected)

Cost Area	5 Year Cost	Rating
Depreciation	$12,217	○
Financing ($434/month)	$5,098	
Insurance	$8,045	◐
State Fees	$1,048	
Fuel (Hwy 26 City 21)	$3,150	○
Maintenance	$4,501	◉
Repairs	$810	○

Warranty/Maintenance Info

Major Tune-Up (60K mile int.)	$229	○
Minor Tune-Up (30K mile int.)	$102	○
Brake Service	$216	○
Overall Warranty	3 yr/36k	◐
Drivetrain Warranty	5 yr/60k	○
Rust Warranty	5 yr/unlim. mi	○
Maintenance Warranty	N/A	
Roadside Assistance	N/A	

Ownership Costs By Year (Projected)

$2,000 $4,000 $6,000 $8,000 $10,000 $12,000 $14,000

- 1999
- 2000
- 2001
- 2002
- 2003

Resale Value

1999	2000	2001	2002	2003
$22,998	$20,518	$18,336	$16,128	$13,992

Cumulative Costs

	1999	2000	2001	2002	2003
Annual	$7,381	$6,365	$6,563	$7,098	$7,462
Total	$7,381	$13,746	$20,309	$27,407	$34,869

Projected Costs (5yr)

Relative $34,753	This Car $34,869
Cost/Mile 50¢	Cost/Mile 50¢

Ownership Cost Value

○ Average

176

* Includes shaded options
** Other purchase requirements apply
*** Price includes other options

● Poor	◉ Worse Than Average	◐ Average	○ Better Than Average	○ Excellent	⊖ Insufficient Information

Refer to *Section 3: Annotated Vehicle Charts* for an explanation of these charts.

Suzuki Esteem GL
4 Door Sedan

Subcompact

 1.6L 95 hp Gas Fuel Inject.
 4 Cylinder In-Line
 Manual 5 Speed
 2 Wheel Front
 Dual Airbags Std

Purchase Price

Car Item	Dealer Cost	List
Base Price	**$11,589**	**$12,199**
Anti-Lock Brakes	N/A	N/A
Automatic 4 Speed	$950	$1,000
Optional Engine	N/A	N/A
Air Conditioning	Std	Std
Power Steering	Std	Std
Cruise Control	N/A	N/A
Power Windows	N/A	N/A
AM/FM Stereo Cassette	Std	Std
Steering Wheel, Tilt	N/A	N/A
Rear Defroster	Std	Std
***Options Price**	**$0**	**$0**
***Total Price**	**$11,589**	**$12,199**
Target Price	$11,868	
Destination Charge	$430	
Avg. Tax & Fees	$692	
Total Target $	**$12,990**	
Average Dealer Option Cost:	**95%**	
12 Month Price Increase:	**2%**	

For 1999, the Esteem GL sedan's front sheet metal has been revised, and now features an all-new chrome grille and large multi-reflector headlamps. Standard features include daytime running lamps, fold-away dual outside mirrors, fold-down rear seat and remote fuel door and trunklid releases. A full front mask, hood protector and splash guards are accessories available to help preserve the Esteem's finish. Exterior optional accessories include aluminum alloy wheels, a roof rack and rear spoiler.

Ownership Costs (Projected)

Cost Area	5 Year Cost	Rating
Depreciation	$7,108	◐
Financing ($215/month)	$2,528	
Insurance	$7,837	●
State Fees	$518	
Fuel (Hwy 37 City 30)	$2,210	○
Maintenance	$3,760	●
Repairs	$610	○

Warranty/Maintenance Info

Major Tune-Up (60K mile int.)	$300	◐
Minor Tune-Up (30K mile int.)	$96	○
Brake Service	$241	○
Overall Warranty	3 yr/36k	○
Drivetrain Warranty	3 yr/36k	○
Rust Warranty	3 yr/unlim. mi	◐
Maintenance Warranty	N/A	
Roadside Assistance	N/A	

Ownership Costs By Year (Projected)

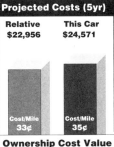

	$2,000	$4,000	$6,000	$8,000

- 1999
- 2000
- 2001
- 2002
- 2003

Resale Value

1999	2000	2001	2002	2003
$11,051	$9,681	$8,464	$7,194	$5,882

Cumulative Costs

	1999	2000	2001	2002	2003
Annual	$4,884	$4,203	$4,168	$5,389	$5,927
Total	$4,884	$9,087	$13,255	$18,644	$24,571

Projected Costs (5yr)

Relative $22,956	This Car $24,571
Cost/Mile 33¢	Cost/Mile 35¢

Ownership Cost Value

◉ Worse Than Average

Suzuki Esteem GLX
4 Door Sedan

Subcompact

 1.6L 95 hp Gas Fuel Inject.
 4 Cylinder In-Line
 Manual 5 Speed
 2 Wheel Front
 Dual Airbags Std

GL Model Shown

Purchase Price

Car Item	Dealer Cost	List
Base Price	**$12,634**	**$13,299**
Anti-Lock Brakes	Pkg	Pkg
Automatic 4 Speed	$950	$1,000
Optional Engine	N/A	N/A
Air Conditioning	Std	Std
Power Steering	Std	Std
Cruise Control	Pkg	Pkg
Power Windows	Std	Std
AM/FM Stereo Cassette	Std	Std
Steering Wheel, Tilt	N/A	N/A
Rear Defroster	Std	Std
***Options Price**	**$0**	**$0**
***Total Price**	**$12,634**	**$13,299**
Target Price	$12,946	
Destination Charge	$430	
Avg. Tax & Fees	$752	
Total Target $	**$14,128**	
Average Dealer Option Cost:	**95%**	
12 Month Price Increase:	**2%**	

For 1999, the Esteem GLX sedan's front sheet metal has been revised, and now features an all-new chrome grille and large multi-reflector headlamps. Standard features include upgraded upholstery, mud guards, bodyside moldings, dual power mirrors, a tachometer, a keyless entry system and a split fold-down rear seat. Available accessories include a theft deterrent system and CD changer. The optional GLX Plus Option Package includes cruise control, a power sunroof and antilock brakes.

Ownership Costs (Projected)

Cost Area	5 Year Cost	Rating
Depreciation	$7,957	◐
Financing ($234/month)	$2,748	
Insurance	$7,837	●
State Fees	$562	
Fuel (Hwy 37 City 30)	$2,210	○
Maintenance	$3,782	●
Repairs	$610	○

Warranty/Maintenance Info

Major Tune-Up (60K mile int.)	$300	◐
Minor Tune-Up (30K mile int.)	$96	○
Brake Service	$241	○
Overall Warranty	3 yr/36k	○
Drivetrain Warranty	3 yr/36k	○
Rust Warranty	3 yr/unlim. mi	◐
Maintenance Warranty	N/A	
Roadside Assistance	N/A	

Ownership Costs By Year (Projected)

	$2,000	$4,000	$6,000	$8,000

- 1999
- 2000
- 2001
- 2002
- 2003

Resale Value

1999	2000	2001	2002	2003
$11,863	$10,354	$9,003	$7,605	$6,171

Cumulative Costs

	1999	2000	2001	2002	2003
Annual	$5,296	$4,413	$4,356	$5,576	$6,065
Total	$5,296	$9,709	$14,065	$19,641	$25,706

Projected Costs (5yr)

Relative $24,055	This Car $25,706
Cost/Mile 34¢	Cost/Mile 37¢

Ownership Cost Value

◉ Worse Than Average

---

* Includes shaded options
** Other purchase requirements apply
*** Price includes other options

● Poor	◐ Worse Than Average	◑ Average	○ Better Than Average	○ Excellent	⊖ Insufficient Information

177

Refer to *Section 3: Annotated Vehicle Charts* for an explanation of these charts.

Suzuki Esteem GL
4 Door Wagon

 1.6L 95 hp Gas Fuel Inject. | 4 Cylinder In-Line | 1 3 5 / 2 4 R Manual 5 Speed | 2 Wheel Front | Dual Airbags Std

Small Wagon

Purchase Price

Car Item	Dealer Cost	List
Base Price	**$12,064**	**$12,699**
Anti-Lock Brakes	N/A	N/A
Automatic 4 Speed	$950	$1,000
Optional Engine	N/A	N/A
Air Conditioning	Std	Std
Power Steering	Std	Std
Cruise Control	N/A	N/A
Power Windows	N/A	N/A
AM/FM Stereo Cassette	Std	Std
Steering Wheel, Tilt	N/A	N/A
Rear Defroster	Std	Std
***Options Price**	**$950**	**$1,000**
***Total Price**	**$13,014**	**$13,699**
Target Price	$13,331	
Destination Charge	$430	
Avg. Tax & Fees	$773	
Total Target $	**$14,534**	
Average Dealer Option Cost:	**95%**	
12 Month Price Increase:	2%	

For 1999, the Esteem GL wagon's front sheet metal has been revised, and it sports an all-new chrome grille and large multi-reflector headlamps. The wagon holds 61 cubic feet of cargo with the rear seat folded down and features compartment trays under the flat cargo floor. Standard equipment includes 14 inch wheels, air conditioning, daytime running lamps and a four speaker AM/FM stereo with cassette. Available accessories include aluminum alloy wheels and a CD player.

Ownership Costs (Projected)

Cost Area	5 Year Cost	Rating
Depreciation	$7,921	◐
Financing ($241/month)	$2,827	
Insurance	$8,045	●
State Fees	$578	
Fuel (Hwy 33 City 26)	$2,509	○
Maintenance	$3,743	◉
Repairs	$610	○

Warranty/Maintenance Info

Major Tune-Up (60K mile int.)	$300	◉
Minor Tune-Up (30K mile int.)	$96	○
Brake Service	$241	○
Overall Warranty	3 yr/36k	○
Drivetrain Warranty	3 yr/36k	○
Rust Warranty	3 yr/unlim. mi	◉
Maintenance Warranty	N/A	
Roadside Assistance	N/A	

Ownership Costs By Year (Projected)

Legend: 1999, 2000, 2001, 2002, 2003

Resale Value

1999	2000	2001	2002	2003
$12,324	$10,805	$9,448	$8,048	$6,613

Cumulative Costs

	1999	2000	2001	2002	2003
Annual	$5,368	$4,547	$4,483	$5,655	$6,180
Total	$5,368	$9,915	$14,398	$20,053	$26,233

Projected Costs (5yr)

Relative	This Car
$25,656	$26,233
Cost/Mile 37¢	Cost/Mile 37¢

Ownership Cost Value

○ Average

Suzuki Esteem GLX
4 Door Wagon

 1.6L 95 hp Gas Fuel Inject. | 4 Cylinder In-Line | 1 3 5 / 2 4 R Manual 5 Speed | 2 Wheel Front | Dual Airbags Std

Small Wagon

GL Model Shown

Purchase Price

Car Item	Dealer Cost	List
Base Price	**$13,109**	**$13,799**
Anti-Lock Brakes	Pkg	Pkg
Automatic 4 Speed	$950	$1,000
Optional Engine	N/A	N/A
Air Conditioning	Std	Std
Power Steering	Std	Std
Cruise Control	Pkg	Pkg
Power Windows	Std	Std
AM/FM Stereo Cassette	Std	Std
Steering Wheel, Tilt	N/A	N/A
Rear Defroster	Std	Std
***Options Price**	**$950**	**$1,000**
***Total Price**	**$14,059**	**$14,799**
Target Price	$14,410	
Destination Charge	$430	
Avg. Tax & Fees	$833	
Total Target $	**$15,673**	
Average Dealer Option Cost:	**95%**	
12 Month Price Increase:	1%	

For 1999, the Esteem GLX wagon's front sheet metal has been revised, and it sports an all-new chrome grille and large multi-reflector headlamps. Standard GLX features include a roof spoiler, tachometer and power door locks and mirrors. The GLX Plus Option Package includes cruise control, a power sunroof and antilock brakes. Optional two-tone paint is available with the Plus Option Package. In addition, the standard keyless entry system can be connected to a theft deterrent system.

Ownership Costs (Projected)

Cost Area	5 Year Cost	Rating
Depreciation	$8,789	◉
Financing ($260/month)	$3,049	
Insurance	$8,045	●
State Fees	$622	
Fuel (Hwy 33 City 26)	$2,509	○
Maintenance	$3,760	◉
Repairs	$610	○

Warranty/Maintenance Info

Major Tune-Up (60K mile int.)	$300	◉
Minor Tune-Up (30K mile int.)	$96	○
Brake Service	$241	○
Overall Warranty	3 yr/36k	○
Drivetrain Warranty	3 yr/36k	○
Rust Warranty	3 yr/unlim. mi	◉
Maintenance Warranty	N/A	
Roadside Assistance	N/A	

Ownership Costs By Year (Projected)

Legend: 1999, 2000, 2001, 2002, 2003

Resale Value

1999	2000	2001	2002	2003
$13,111	$11,458	$9,969	$8,441	$6,884

Cumulative Costs

	1999	2000	2001	2002	2003
Annual	$5,807	$4,752	$4,669	$5,837	$6,319
Total	$5,807	$10,559	$15,228	$21,065	$27,384

Projected Costs (5yr)

Relative	This Car
$26,595	$27,384
Cost/Mile 38¢	Cost/Mile 39¢

Ownership Cost Value

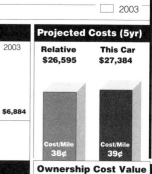

◉ Worse Than Average

178

* Includes shaded options
** Other purchase requirements apply
*** Price includes other options

● Poor | ◉ Worse Than Average | ○ Average | ○ Better Than Average | ○ Excellent | ⊖ Insufficient Information

Refer to *Section 3: Annotated Vehicle Charts* for an explanation of these charts.

Suzuki Swift
2 Door Hatchback

 1.3L 79 hp Gas Fuel Inject.
 4 Cylinder In-Line
 135 24R Manual 5 Speed
 2 Wheel Front
 Dual Airbags Std

Purchase Price

Car Item	Dealer Cost	List
Base Price	**$8,462**	**$9,099**
Anti-Lock Brakes	N/A	N/A
Automatic 3 Speed	$605	$650
Optional Engine	N/A	N/A
Air Conditioning	Dlr	Dlr
Power Steering	N/A	N/A
Cruise Control	N/A	N/A
Power Windows	N/A	N/A
AM/FM Stereo Cassette	Dlr	Dlr
Steering Wheel, Tilt	N/A	N/A
Rear Defroster	Std	Std
*Options Price	$0	$0
*Total Price	**$8,462**	**$9,099**
Target Price	$8,695	
Destination Charge	$380	
Avg. Tax & Fees	$516	
Total Target $	**$9,591**	
Average Dealer Option Cost:	93%	
12 Month Price Increase:	None	

The 1999 Swift offers numerous standard features including a four wheel independent suspension, fold-down rear seats, two-speed intermittent wipers and a removable rear cargo cover. It also comes equipped with safety features that include second generation dual airbags, side door impact beams, an electric rear window defogger and daytime running lamps. Options include an AM/FM stereo system and air conditioning. The Swift consistently ranks among the most fuel efficient cars in America.

Ownership Costs (Projected)

Cost Area	5 Year Cost	Rating
Depreciation	$5,152	◑
Financing ($159/month)	$1,866	
Insurance	$7,837	●
State Fees	$392	
Fuel (Hwy 43 City 39)	$1,811	○
Maintenance	$4,407	●
Repairs	$636	◑

Warranty/Maintenance Info

Major Tune-Up (60K mile int.)	$317	●
Minor Tune-Up (30K mile int.)	$95	◑
Brake Service	$271	●
Overall Warranty	3 yr/36k	◑
Drivetrain Warranty	3 yr/36k	◑
Rust Warranty	3 yr/unlim. mi	◑
Maintenance Warranty	N/A	
Roadside Assistance	N/A	

Ownership Costs By Year (Projected)

$2,000 $4,000 $6,000 $8,000

- 1999
- 2000
- 2001
- 2002
- 2003

Resale Value

1999	2000	2001	2002	2003
$8,713	$7,581	$6,592	$5,541	$4,439

Cumulative Costs

	1999	2000	2001	2002	2003
Annual	$3,491	$3,676	$3,700	$5,252	$5,982
Total	$3,491	$7,167	$10,867	$16,119	$22,101

Projected Costs (5yr)

Relative $19,752	This Car $22,101
Cost/Mile 28¢	Cost/Mile 32¢

Ownership Cost Value
● Poor

Toyota Avalon XL
4 Door Sedan

Large

 3.0L 200 hp Gas Fuel Inject.
 6 Cylinder "V"
 PRND321 Automatic 4 Speed
 2 Wheel Front
Dual Front/Side Airbags Std

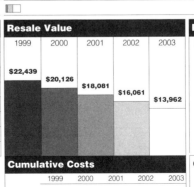

XLS Model Shown

Purchase Price

Car Item	Dealer Cost	List
Base Price	**$21,508**	**$24,568**
Anti-Lock Brakes	Std	Std
Manual Transmission	N/A	N/A
Optional Engine	N/A	N/A
Air Conditioning	Std	Std
Power Steering	Std	Std
Cruise Control	Std	Std
Power Windows	Std	Std
AM/FM Stereo Cassette	Std	Std
Steering Wheel, Tilt	Std	Std
Rear Defroster	Std	Std
*Options Price	$0	$0
*Total Price	**$21,508**	**$24,568**
Target Price	$23,207	
Destination Charge	$420	
Avg. Tax & Fees	$1,326	
Total Target $	**$24,953**	
Average Dealer Option Cost:	79%	
12 Month Price Increase:	1%	

The 1999 Avalon XL comes equipped with cruise control, power windows and door locks, air conditioning, variable intermittent wipers and automatic on/off headlamps. A four speaker deluxe AM/FM/cassette sound system with rear in-glass antenna is standard. Daytime running lamps, antilock brakes and heated outside mirrors are also standard, as are a heavy duty rear window defogger with timer, multi-adjustable front seats and solar energy absorbing glass.

Ownership Costs (Projected)

Cost Area	5 Year Cost	Rating
Depreciation	$10,991	○
Financing ($414/month)	$4,854	
Insurance	$8,045	○
State Fees	$1,013	
Fuel (Hwy 29 City 21)	$2,970	○
Maintenance	$3,855	●
Repairs	$625	○

Warranty/Maintenance Info

Major Tune-Up (60K mile int.)	$269	●
Minor Tune-Up (30K mile int.)	$179	●
Brake Service	$223	○
Overall Warranty	3 yr/36k	◑
Drivetrain Warranty	5 yr/60k	○
Rust Warranty	5 yr/unlim. mi	○
Maintenance Warranty	N/A	
Roadside Assistance	N/A	

Ownership Costs By Year (Projected)

$2,000 $4,000 $6,000 $8,000 $10,000 $12,000

- 1999
- 2000
- 2001
- 2002
- 2003

Resale Value

1999	2000	2001	2002	2003
$22,439	$20,126	$18,081	$16,061	$13,962

Cumulative Costs

	1999	2000	2001	2002	2003
Annual	$6,558	$6,091	$5,864	$7,116	$6,724
Total	$6,558	$12,649	$18,513	$25,629	$32,353

Projected Costs (5yr)

Relative $32,992	This Car $32,353
Cost/Mile 47¢	Cost/Mile 46¢

Ownership Cost Value
○ Better Than Average

Legend:
- ● Poor
- ◉ Worse Than Average
- ◑ Average
- ○ Better Than Average
- ○ Excellent
- ⊖ Insufficient Information

179

Refer to *Section 3: Annotated Vehicle Charts* for an explanation of these charts.

Toyota Avalon XLS
4 Door Sedan

Large

3.0L 200 hp Gas Fuel Inject.	6 Cylinder "V"	Automatic 4 Speed	2 Wheel Front	Dual Front/Side Airbags Std

Purchase Price

Car Item	Dealer Cost	List
Base Price	**$24,726**	**$28,578**
Anti-Lock Brakes	Std	Std
Manual Transmission	N/A	N/A
Optional Engine	N/A	N/A
Auto Climate Control	Std	Std
Power Steering	Std	Std
Cruise Control	Std	Std
Power Windows	Std	Std
AM/FM Stereo Cass/CD	Std	Std
Steering Wheel, Tilt	Std	Std
Rear Defroster	Std	Std
*Options Price	$0	$0
*Total Price	$24,726	$28,578
Target Price	$26,847	
Destination Charge	$420	
Avg. Tax & Fees	$1,530	
Total Target $	**$28,797**	
Average Dealer Option Cost:	78%	
12 Month Price Increase:	2%	

The 1999 Avalon XLS includes a premium AM/FM/cassette/CD audio system with seven speakers, a multi-function remote keyless entry system and anti-theft system with an engine immobilizer. Other standard features include dual power seats, simulated wood trim and an illuminated entry/exit fade-out system with battery rundown protection. Rear reading lights, automatic climate control and a leather-wrapped steering wheel are additional standard amenities.

Ownership Costs (Projected)

Cost Area	5 Year Cost	Rating
Depreciation	$13,144	◯
Financing ($477/month)	$5,602	
Insurance	$7,886	◯
State Fees	$1,173	
Fuel (Hwy 29 City 21)	$2,970	◯
Maintenance	$3,855	●
Repairs	$625	◯

Warranty/Maintenance Info

Major Tune-Up (60K mile int.)	$269	●
Minor Tune-Up (30K mile int.)	$179	◯
Brake Service	$223	◯
Overall Warranty	3 yr/36k	◐
Drivetrain Warranty	5 yr/60k	◯
Rust Warranty	5 yr/unlim. mi	◯
Maintenance Warranty	N/A	
Roadside Assistance	N/A	

Ownership Costs By Year (Projected)

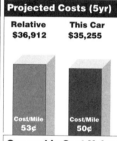

$2,000 $4,000 $6,000 $8,000 $10,000 $12,000 $14,000

Legend: 1999, 2000, 2001, 2002, 2003

Resale Value

1999	2000	2001	2002	2003
$25,723	$22,988	$20,537	$18,128	$15,653

Cumulative Costs

	1999	2000	2001	2002	2003
Annual	$7,381	$6,724	$6,425	$7,599	$7,126
Total	$7,381	$14,105	$20,530	$28,129	$35,255

Projected Costs (5yr)

Relative $36,912	This Car $35,255
Cost/Mile 53¢	Cost/Mile 50¢

Ownership Cost Value
◯ Excellent

Toyota Camry Solara SE
2 Door Coupe

Compact

2.2L 135 hp Gas Fuel Inject.	4 Cylinder In-Line	Manual 5 Speed	2 Wheel Front	Dual Airbags Std

Purchase Price

Car Item	Dealer Cost	List
Base Price	**$16,509**	**$18,638**
Anti-Lock Brakes	$473	**$550
Automatic 4 Speed	$709	$800
Optional Engine	N/A	N/A
Air Conditioning	Std	Std
Power Steering	Std	Std
Cruise Control	Std	Std
Power Windows	Std	Std
AM/FM Stereo Cassette	Std	Std
Steering Wheel, Tilt	Std	Std
Rear Defroster	N/A	N/A
*Options Price	$709	$800
*Total Price	$17,218	$19,438
Target Price	$18,425	
Destination Charge	$420	
Avg. Tax & Fees	$1,060	
Total Target $	**$19,905**	
Average Dealer Option Cost:	81%	
12 Month Price Increase:	N/A	

The Camry Solara SE is distinguished by its standard DOHC four cylinder engine, which produces 135 hp. The Solara shares its basic platform with the Camry sedan, with several key changes. Most notable are increased structural reinforcements, revised suspension components and steering system fine-tuning. The results are a more responsive ride and improved handling characteristics. Options include a power moonroof, side-impact airbags, four wheel antilock brakes and 15 inch aluminum wheels.

Ownership Costs (Projected)

Cost Area	5 Year Cost	Rating
Depreciation	$8,475	◯
Financing ($330/month)	$3,872	
Insurance	$8,265	◐
State Fees	$808	
Fuel (Hwy 30 City 23)	$2,796	◯
Maintenance	$3,652	●
Repairs	$515	◯

Warranty/Maintenance Info

Major Tune-Up (60K mile int.)	$268	●
Minor Tune-Up (30K mile int.)	$112	●
Brake Service	$195	◯
Overall Warranty	3 yr/36k	◐
Drivetrain Warranty	5 yr/60k	◯
Rust Warranty	5 yr/unlim. mi	◯
Maintenance Warranty	N/A	
Roadside Assistance	N/A	

Ownership Costs By Year (Projected)

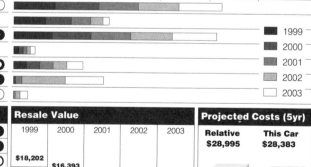

$2,000 $4,000 $6,000 $8,000 $10,000

Legend: 1999, 2000, 2001, 2002, 2003

Resale Value

1999	2000	2001	2002	2003
$18,202	$16,393	$14,764	$13,105	$11,430

Cumulative Costs

	1999	2000	2001	2002	2003
Annual	$5,371	$5,277	$5,126	$6,573	$6,036
Total	$5,371	$10,648	$15,774	$22,347	$28,383

Projected Costs (5yr)

Relative $28,995	This Car $28,383
Cost/Mile 41¢	Cost/Mile 41¢

Ownership Cost Value
◯ Better Than Average

180

* Includes shaded options
** Other purchase requirements apply
*** Price includes other options

 Poor   Worse Than Average   Average   Better Than Average Excellent ⊖ Insufficient Information

Refer to *Section 3: Annotated Vehicle Charts* for an explanation of these charts.

Toyota Camry Solara SE V6
2 Door Coupe

 3.0L 200 hp Gas Fuel Inject. 6 Cylinder "V" Manual 5 Speed 2 Wheel Front Dual Airbags Std

Compact

Purchase Price

Car Item	Dealer Cost	List
Base Price	**$18,768**	**$21,188**
Anti-Lock Brakes	Std	Std
Automatic 4 Speed	$709	$800
Optional Engine	N/A	N/A
Air Conditioning	Std	Std
Power Steering	Std	Std
Cruise Control	Std	Std
Power Windows	Std	Std
AM/FM Stereo Cassette	Std	Std
Steering Wheel, Tilt	Std	Std
Rear Defroster	N/A	N/A
***Options Price**	**$709**	**$800**
***Total Price**	**$19,477**	**$21,988**
Target Price	$20,896	
Destination Charge	$420	
Avg. Tax & Fees	$1,196	
Total Target $	**$22,512**	
Average Dealer Option Cost:	*81%*	
12 Month Price Increase:	N/A	

The Camry Solara SE V6 is based upon the familiar Camry sedan platform. In its conversion to a coupe, the platform underwent several key changes. To enhance ride and handling characteristics, structural changes and suspension refinements were implemented. Standard value-added features include four wheel disc antilock brakes and a six speaker cassette stereo. Optional on the SE V6 are sport upgrade packages that include a unique rear spoiler, 16 inch aluminum wheels and upgraded tires.

Ownership Costs (Projected)

Cost Area	5 Year Cost	Rating
Depreciation	$10,033	◐
Financing ($373/month)	$4,379	
Insurance	$8,500	◉
State Fees	$909	
Fuel (Hwy 28 City 20 -Midgrd)	$3,401	◉
Maintenance	$3,761	●
Repairs	$515	○

Warranty/Maintenance Info

Major Tune-Up (60K mile int.)	$259	◐
Minor Tune-Up (30K mile int.)	$154	●
Brake Service	$202	○
Overall Warranty	3 yr/36k	◐
Drivetrain Warranty	5 yr/60k	○
Rust Warranty	5 yr/unlim. mi	○
Maintenance Warranty	N/A	
Roadside Assistance	N/A	

Ownership Costs By Year (Projected)

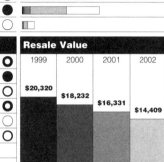

$2,000 $4,000 $6,000 $8,000 $10,000 $12,000

■ 1999
■ 2000
▨ 2001
▧ 2002
□ 2003

Resale Value

1999	2000	2001	2002	2003
$20,320	$18,232	$16,331	$14,409	$12,479

Cumulative Costs

	1999	2000	2001	2002	2003
Annual	$6,221	$5,889	$5,740	$7,104	$6,544
Total	$6,221	$12,110	$17,850	$24,954	$31,498

Projected Costs (5yr)

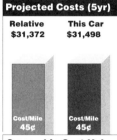

Relative	This Car
$31,372	**$31,498**
Cost/Mile 45¢	Cost/Mile 45¢

Ownership Cost Value

○ Average

Toyota Camry Solara SLE V6
2 Door Coupe

 3.0L 200 hp Gas Fuel Inject. 6 Cylinder "V" Automatic 4 Speed 2 Wheel Front Dual Airbags Std

Compact

Purchase Price

Car Item	Dealer Cost	List
Base Price	**$22,133**	**$24,988**
Anti-Lock Brakes	Std	Std
Manual Transmission	N/A	N/A
Optional Engine	N/A	N/A
Air Conditioning	Std	Std
Power Steering	Std	Std
Cruise Control	Std	Std
Power Windows	Std	Std
AM/FM Stereo Cass/CD	Std	Std
Steering Wheel, Tilt	Std	Std
Rear Defroster	N/A	N/A
***Options Price**	**$0**	**$0**
***Total Price**	**$22,133**	**$24,988**
Target Price	$23,837	
Destination Charge	$420	
Avg. Tax & Fees	$1,359	
Total Target $	**$25,616**	
Average Dealer Option Cost:	*81%*	
12 Month Price Increase:	N/A	

The Camry Solara SLE V6 features many upgrades as standard equipment. These include leather interior appointments, HomeLink universal transmitter, an auto-dimming rearview mirror and aluminum wheels. To further distinguish itself, the SLE features an automatic climate control system and a JBL audio system. This stereo boasts 200 watts of power driving eight speakers, and features both CD and cassette players. Among the limited options are a power moonroof and side-impact airbags.

Ownership Costs (Projected)

Cost Area	5 Year Cost	Rating
Depreciation	$12,044	○
Financing ($425/month)	$4,984	
Insurance	$8,313	◉
State Fees	$1,029	
Fuel (Hwy 28 City 20 -Midgrd)	$3,401	◉
Maintenance	$3,878	●
Repairs	$515	○

Warranty/Maintenance Info

Major Tune-Up (60K mile int.)	$259	○
Minor Tune-Up (30K mile int.)	$154	●
Brake Service	$202	○
Overall Warranty	3 yr/36k	○
Drivetrain Warranty	5 yr/60k	○
Rust Warranty	5 yr/unlim. mi	○
Maintenance Warranty	N/A	
Roadside Assistance	N/A	

Ownership Costs By Year (Projected)

$2,000 $4,000 $6,000 $8,000 $10,000 $12,000 $14,000

■ 1999
■ 2000
▨ 2001
▧ 2002
□ 2003

Resale Value

1999	2000	2001	2002	2003
$22,671	$20,250	$18,030	$15,801	$13,572

Cumulative Costs

	1999	2000	2001	2002	2003
Annual	$7,173	$6,379	$6,171	$7,473	$6,968
Total	$7,173	$13,552	$19,723	$27,196	$34,164

Projected Costs (5yr)

Relative	This Car
$34,366	**$34,164**
Cost/Mile 49¢	Cost/Mile 49¢

Ownership Cost Value

○ Average

---

* Includes shaded options

** Other purchase requirements apply

*** Price includes other options

● Poor ◉ Worse Than Average ○ Average ○ Better Than Average ○ Excellent ⊖ Insufficient Information

Refer to *Section 3: Annotated Vehicle Charts* for an explanation of these charts.

Toyota Camry CE
4 Door Sedan

Midsize

 2.2L 133 hp Gas Fuel Inject.
 4 Cylinder In-Line
 Manual 5 Speed
 2 Wheel Front
 Dual Airbags Std

Purchase Price

Car Item	Dealer Cost	List
Base Price	**$15,092**	**$17,038**
Anti-Lock Brakes	$521	$610
Automatic 4 Speed	$708	$800
Optional Engine	N/A	N/A
Air Conditioning	$804	$1,005
Power Steering	Std	Std
Cruise Control	$232	$290
Power Windows	Pkg	Pkg
AM/FM Stereo Cassette	Std	Std
Steering Wheel, Tilt	Std	Std
Rear Defroster	Std	Std
*Options Price	$2,265	$2,705
*Total Price	**$17,357**	**$19,743**
Target Price	$18,575	
Destination Charge	$420	
Avg. Tax & Fees	$1,070	
Total Target $	**$20,065**	
Average Dealer Option Cost:	78%	
12 Month Price Increase:	1%	

The Camry CE features standard interior amenities such as manually adjustable bucket seats, front and rear dual cup holders and an AM/FM stereo with cassette and diversity antenna. The optional Power Package includes color-keyed power mirrors and power windows and door locks. Additional optional equipment includes cruise control, air conditioning and a CD changer. Safety features available on the CE include antilock brakes, side-impact airbags and variable intermittent windshield wipers.

Ownership Costs (Projected)

Cost Area	5 Year Cost	Rating
Depreciation	$8,143	◔
Financing ($333/month)	$3,904	
Insurance	$7,643	○
State Fees	$819	
Fuel (Hwy 30 City 23)	$2,796	◔
Maintenance	$3,348	●
Repairs	$515	◔

Warranty/Maintenance Info

Major Tune-Up (60K mile int.)	$276	●
Minor Tune-Up (30K mile int.)	$112	○
Brake Service	$202	○
Overall Warranty	3 yr/36k	●
Drivetrain Warranty	5 yr/60k	○
Rust Warranty	5 yr/unlim. mi	○
Maintenance Warranty	N/A	
Roadside Assistance	N/A	

Ownership Costs By Year (Projected)

Legend: ■ 1999 ■ 2000 ■ 2001 ■ 2002 □ 2003

Resale Value

1999	2000	2001	2002	2003
$18,917	$16,998	$15,337	$13,614	$11,922

Cumulative Costs

	1999	2000	2001	2002	2003
Annual	$4,711	$5,276	$5,043	$6,247	$5,891
Total	$4,711	$9,987	$15,030	$21,277	$27,168

Projected Costs (5yr)

Relative	This Car
$28,848	$27,168
Cost/Mile 41¢	Cost/Mile 39¢

Ownership Cost Value

○ Excellent

Toyota Camry LE
4 Door Sedan

Midsize

 2.2L 133 hp Gas Fuel Inject.
 4 Cylinder In-Line
 Automatic 4 Speed
 2 Wheel Front
 Dual Airbags Std

Purchase Price

Car Item	Dealer Cost	List
Base Price	**$17,332**	**$19,798**
Anti-Lock Brakes	N/C	N/C
Manual Transmission	N/A	N/A
Optional Engine	N/A	N/A
Air Conditioning	Std	Std
Power Steering	Std	Std
Cruise Control	Std	Std
Power Windows	Std	Std
AM/FM Stereo Cassette	Std	Std
Steering Wheel, Tilt	Std	Std
Rear Defroster	Std	Std
*Options Price	$0	$0
*Total Price	**$17,332**	**$19,798**
Target Price	$18,613	
Destination Charge	$420	
Avg. Tax & Fees	$1,071	
Total Target $	**$20,104**	
Average Dealer Option Cost:	74%	
12 Month Price Increase:	None	

The Camry LE is available with optional features such as a power moonroof, aluminum wheels and an AM/FM stereo with cassette and CD player. Safety features on the LE include variable intermittent windshield wipers and optional side-impact airbags and antilock brakes. Standard interior features include air conditioning and power windows, door locks and mirrors. The optional Leather Package features leather bucket seats and a leather-wrapped shift knob and steering wheel.

Ownership Costs (Projected)

Cost Area	5 Year Cost	Rating
Depreciation	$9,087	◔
Financing ($333/month)	$3,911	
Insurance	$7,643	○
State Fees	$822	
Fuel (Hwy 30 City 23)	$2,796	◔
Maintenance	$3,478	◉
Repairs	$515	◔

Warranty/Maintenance Info

Major Tune-Up (60K mile int.)	$276	○
Minor Tune-Up (30K mile int.)	$112	○
Brake Service	$202	○
Overall Warranty	3 yr/36k	●
Drivetrain Warranty	5 yr/60k	○
Rust Warranty	5 yr/unlim. mi	○
Maintenance Warranty	N/A	
Roadside Assistance	N/A	

Ownership Costs By Year (Projected)

Legend: ■ 1999 ■ 2000 ■ 2001 ■ 2002 □ 2003

Resale Value

1999	2000	2001	2002	2003
$19,020	$16,850	$14,936	$12,960	$11,017

Cumulative Costs

	1999	2000	2001	2002	2003
Annual	$4,649	$5,530	$5,298	$6,502	$6,273
Total	$4,649	$10,179	$15,477	$21,979	$28,252

Projected Costs (5yr)

Relative	This Car
$28,825	$28,252
Cost/Mile 41¢	Cost/Mile 40¢

Ownership Cost Value

○ Better Than Average

182

* Includes shaded options
** Other purchase requirements apply
*** Price includes other options

 ● Poor
 ◉ Worse Than Average
 ◔ Average
 ○ Better Than Average
 ○ Excellent
⊖ Insufficient Information

Refer to *Section 3: Annotated Vehicle Charts* for an explanation of these charts.

Toyota Camry LE V6
4 Door Sedan

3.0L 194 hp Gas Fuel Inject.	6 Cylinder "V"	Manual 5 Speed	2 Wheel Front	Dual Airbags Std

Midsize

LE Base Model Shown

Purchase Price

Car Item	Dealer Cost	List
Base Price	**$19,163**	**$21,888**
Anti-Lock Brakes	Std	Std
Automatic 4 Speed	$699	$800
Optional Engine	N/A	N/A
Air Conditioning	Std	Std
Power Steering	Std	Std
Cruise Control	Std	Std
Power Windows	Std	Std
AM/FM Stereo Cassette	Std	Std
Steering Wheel, Tilt	Std	Std
Rear Defroster	Std	Std
*Options Price	$699	$800
*Total Price	**$19,862**	**$22,688**
Target Price	$21,374	
Destination Charge	$420	
Avg. Tax & Fees	$1,225	
Total Target $	**$23,019**	
Average Dealer Option Cost:	75%	
12 Month Price Increase:	None	

The Camry LE V6 is equipped with antilock brakes, intermittent windshield wipers and adjustable head restraints on outboard seating positions as standard safety features. The interior features luxury amenities such as air conditioning, cruise control and power windows and door locks. Traction control, a power moonroof and a power driver's seat are available as options. Additional optional equipment includes aluminum wheels, an AM/FM stereo with cassette and CD and a Leather Package.

Ownership Costs (Projected)

Cost Area	5 Year Cost	Rating
Depreciation	$10,472	◯
Financing ($382/month)	$4,479	
Insurance	$7,837	◯
State Fees	$938	
Fuel (Hwy 28 City 20)	$3,097	◯
Maintenance	$3,525	◉
Repairs	$515	◯

Warranty/Maintenance Info

Major Tune-Up (60K mile int.)	$257	◯
Minor Tune-Up (30K mile int.)	$154	●
Brake Service	$202	◯
Overall Warranty	3 yr/36k	◯
Drivetrain Warranty	5 yr/60k	◯
Rust Warranty	5 yr/unlim. mi	◯
Maintenance Warranty	N/A	
Roadside Assistance	N/A	

Ownership Costs By Year (Projected)

$2,000 $4,000 $6,000 $8,000 $10,000 $12,000

- 1999
- 2000
- 2001
- 2002
- 2003

Resale Value

1999	2000	2001	2002	2003
$21,414	$19,011	$16,877	$14,691	$12,547

Cumulative Costs

	1999	2000	2001	2002	2003
Annual	$5,490	$6,047	$5,807	$7,032	$6,487
Total	$5,490	$11,537	$17,344	$24,376	$30,863

Projected Costs (5yr)

Relative	This Car
$31,453	$30,863
Cost/Mile 45¢	Cost/Mile 44¢

Ownership Cost Value

◯ Better Than Average

Toyota Camry XLE
4 Door Sedan

2.2L 133 hp Gas Fuel Inject.	4 Cylinder In-Line	Automatic 4 Speed	2 Wheel Front	Dual Airbags Std

Midsize

Purchase Price

Car Item	Dealer Cost	List
Base Price	**$19,923**	**$22,758**
Anti-Lock Brakes	Std	Std
Manual Transmission	N/A	N/A
Optional Engine	N/A	N/A
Air Conditioning	Std	Std
Power Steering	Std	Std
Cruise Control	Std	Std
Power Windows	Std	Std
AM/FM Stereo CD	Std	Std
Steering Wheel, Tilt	Std	Std
Rear Defroster	Std	Std
*Options Price	$0	$0
*Total Price	**$19,923**	**$22,758**
Target Price	$21,459	
Destination Charge	$420	
Avg. Tax & Fees	$1,230	
Total Target $	**$23,109**	
Average Dealer Option Cost:	79%	
12 Month Price Increase:	1%	

The Camry XLE features the Leather Power Seat Package, which includes leather seating surfaces, a power driver's seat with lumbar support and a leather-wrapped steering wheel. The interior features standard luxury amenities such as cruise control, a theft deterrent system and dual power seats with illuminated visor vanity mirrors for both driver and passenger. Options on the XLE include a power moonroof, a rear spoiler and an AM/FM stereo with cassette and CD player.

Ownership Costs (Projected)

Cost Area	5 Year Cost	Rating
Depreciation	$11,277	◯
Financing ($383/month)	$4,496	
Insurance	$7,506	◯
State Fees	$940	
Fuel (Hwy 30 City 23)	$2,796	◯
Maintenance	$3,478	◉
Repairs	$515	◯

Warranty/Maintenance Info

Major Tune-Up (60K mile int.)	$276	◯
Minor Tune-Up (30K mile int.)	$112	◯
Brake Service	$202	◯
Overall Warranty	3 yr/36k	◯
Drivetrain Warranty	5 yr/60k	◯
Rust Warranty	5 yr/unlim. mi	◯
Maintenance Warranty	N/A	
Roadside Assistance	N/A	

Ownership Costs By Year (Projected)

$2,000 $4,000 $6,000 $8,000 $10,000 $12,000

- 1999
- 2000
- 2001
- 2002
- 2003

Resale Value

1999	2000	2001	2002	2003
$21,043	$18,551	$16,330	$14,059	$11,832

Cumulative Costs

	1999	2000	2001	2002	2003
Annual	$5,834	$6,014	$5,721	$6,865	$6,574
Total	$5,834	$11,848	$17,569	$24,434	$31,008

Projected Costs (5yr)

Relative	This Car
$31,525	$31,008
Cost/Mile 45¢	Cost/Mile 44¢

Ownership Cost Value

◯ Better Than Average

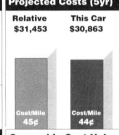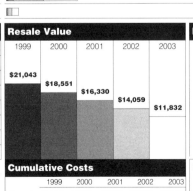

---

* Includes shaded options

** Other purchase requirements apply

*** Price includes other options

● Poor	◉ Worse Than Average	◯ Average	◯ Better Than Average	◯ Excellent	⊖ Insufficient Information

183

Refer to *Section 3: Annotated Vehicle Charts* for an explanation of these charts.

Toyota Camry XLE V6
4 Door Sedan

Midsize

 3.0L 194 hp Gas Fuel Inject. | 6 Cylinder "V" | PRND321 Automatic 4 Speed | 2 Wheel Front | Dual Airbags Std

Base Model Shown

Purchase Price

Car Item	Dealer Cost	List
Base Price	**$21,884**	**$24,998**
Anti-Lock Brakes	Std	Std
Manual Transmission	N/A	N/A
Optional Engine	N/A	N/A
Air Conditioning	Std	Std
Power Steering	Std	Std
Cruise Control	Std	Std
Power Windows	Std	Std
AM/FM Stereo CD	Std	Std
Steering Wheel, Tilt	Std	Std
Rear Defroster	Std	Std
*Options Price	$0	$0
*Total Price	**$21,884**	**$24,998**
Target Price	$23,623	
Destination Charge	$420	
Avg. Tax & Fees	$1,349	
Total Target $	**$25,392**	
Average Dealer Option Cost:	78%	
12 Month Price Increase:	1%	

The Camry XLE V6 is equipped with aluminum wheels, a theft deterrent system and power windows and door locks as standard equipment. The Leather Power Seat Package includes leather seating surfaces, a power driver's seat with lumbar support and a leather-wrapped steering wheel. Safety features on the XLE include traction control and side-impact airbags for the front passengers. Daytime running lamps, antilock brakes and variable intermittent windshield wipers are also standard.

Ownership Costs (Projected)

Cost Area	5 Year Cost	Rating
Depreciation	$12,473	◐
Financing ($421/month)	$4,940	
Insurance	$7,688	◐
State Fees	$1,030	
Fuel (Hwy 28 City 20)	$3,097	◐
Maintenance	$3,655	◉
Repairs	$515	○

Warranty/Maintenance Info

Major Tune-Up (60K mile int.)	$257	◐
Minor Tune-Up (30K mile int.)	$154	●
Brake Service	$202	◐
Overall Warranty	3 yr/36k	◐
Drivetrain Warranty	5 yr/60k	○
Rust Warranty	5 yr/unlim. mi	◐
Maintenance Warranty	N/A	
Roadside Assistance	N/A	

Ownership Costs By Year (Projected)

$2,000 $4,000 $6,000 $8,000 $10,000 $12,000 $14,000

■ 1999
■ 2000
■ 2001
■ 2002
□ 2003

Resale Value

1999	2000	2001	2002	2003
$22,748	$20,092	$17,716	$15,292	$12,919

Cumulative Costs

	1999	2000	2001	2002	2003
Annual	$6,680	$6,420	$6,132	$7,315	$6,851
Total	$6,680	$13,100	$19,232	$26,547	$33,398

Projected Costs (5yr)

Relative	This Car
$34,022	$33,398
Cost/Mile 49¢	Cost/Mile 48¢

Ownership Cost Value

○ Better Than Average

Toyota Celica GT
2 Door Liftback

Subcompact

 2.2L 130 hp Gas Fuel Inject. | 4 Cylinder In-Line | 1 3 5 / 2 4 R Manual 5 Speed | 2 Wheel Front | Dual Airbags Std

Purchase Price

Car Item	Dealer Cost	List
Base Price	**$18,875**	**$21,330**
Anti-Lock Brakes	Pkg	Pkg
Automatic 4 Speed	$705	$800
Optional Engine	N/A	N/A
Air Conditioning	Std	Std
Power Steering	Std	Std
Cruise Control	Std	Std
Power Windows	Std	Std
AM/FM Stereo CD	Std	Std
Steering Wheel, Tilt	Std	Std
Rear Defroster	Std	Std
*Options Price	$0	$0
*Total Price	**$18,875**	**$21,330**
Target Price	$20,257	
Destination Charge	$420	
Avg. Tax & Fees	$1,161	
Total Target $	**$21,838**	
Average Dealer Option Cost:	80%	
12 Month Price Increase:	4%	

For 1999, the Celica liftback model has no major changes. Standard features include a premium AM/FM/CD system with six speakers, power windows and door locks, cruise control and a rear spoiler. An engine cooler comes standard with the five speed manual transmission. Available options include alloy wheels and a power moonroof. The optional Liftback Upgrade Package includes Michelin P205/55R15 performance tires, 15 inch alloy wheels, antilock brakes and a sport-tuned suspension.

Ownership Costs (Projected)

Cost Area	5 Year Cost	Rating
Depreciation	$8,419	○
Financing ($362/month)	$4,249	
Insurance	$9,083	◉
State Fees	$884	
Fuel (Hwy 28 City 22)	$2,962	●
Maintenance	$3,600	●
Repairs	$515	○

Warranty/Maintenance Info

Major Tune-Up (60K mile int.)	$281	◐
Minor Tune-Up (30K mile int.)	$131	●
Brake Service	$146	○
Overall Warranty	3 yr/36k	◐
Drivetrain Warranty	5 yr/60k	○
Rust Warranty	5 yr/unlim. mi	◐
Maintenance Warranty	N/A	
Roadside Assistance	N/A	

Ownership Costs By Year (Projected)

$2,000 $4,000 $6,000 $8,000 $10,000

■ 1999
■ 2000
■ 2001
■ 2002
□ 2003

Resale Value

1999	2000	2001	2002	2003
$20,335	$18,469	$16,795	$15,107	$13,419

Cumulative Costs

	1999	2000	2001	2002	2003
Annual	$5,506	$5,648	$5,487	$6,767	$6,304
Total	$5,506	$11,154	$16,641	$23,408	$29,712

Projected Costs (5yr)

Relative	This Car
$30,918	$29,712
Cost/Mile 44¢	Cost/Mile 42¢

Ownership Cost Value

○ Better Than Average

Toyota Celica GT
2 Door Convertible

Subcompact

2.2L 130 hp Gas Fuel Inject.	4 Cylinder In-Line	Manual 5 Speed	2 Wheel Front	Dual Airbags Std

Purchase Price

Car Item	Dealer Cost	List
Base Price	**$22,089**	**$24,899**
Anti-Lock Brakes	Pkg	Pkg
Automatic 4 Speed	$701	$800
Optional Engine	N/A	N/A
Air Conditioning	Std	Std
Power Steering	Std	Std
Cruise Control	Std	Std
Power Windows	Std	Std
AM/FM Stereo Cass/CD	Std	Std
Steering Wheel, Tilt	Std	Std
Rear Defroster	Std	Std
***Options Price**	**$0**	**$0**
***Total Price**	**$22,089**	**$24,899**
Target Price	$23,780	
Destination Charge	$420	
Avg. Tax & Fees	$1,355	
Total Target $	**$25,555**	
Average Dealer Option Cost:	**80%**	
12 Month Price Increase:	1%	

The Celica convertible has all the same standard features as the liftback model. In addition, the convertible includes a premium AM/FM/cassette/CD sound system with eight speakers, fog lamps, power rear-quarter windows and 15 inch aluminum alloy wheels. The convertible's unibody is reinforced for extra rigidity. The power convertible top mechanism is electro-mechanical, and the top itself is made of cloth. The top also incorporates an electric defogger for its rear glass window.

Ownership Costs (Projected)

Cost Area	5 Year Cost	Rating
Depreciation	$9,431	◯
Financing ($424/month)	$4,970	
Insurance	$9,775	◉
State Fees	$1,026	
Fuel (Hwy 28 City 22)	$2,962	●
Maintenance	$3,600	●
Repairs	$515	◯

Warranty/Maintenance Info

Major Tune-Up (60K mile int.)	$281	◉
Minor Tune-Up (30K mile int.)	$131	●
Brake Service	$146	◯
Overall Warranty	3 yr/36k	◉
Drivetrain Warranty	5 yr/60k	◯
Rust Warranty	5 yr/unlim. mi	◯
Maintenance Warranty	N/A	
Roadside Assistance	N/A	

Ownership Costs By Year (Projected)

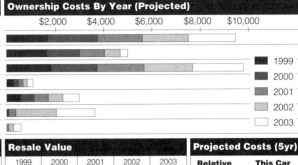

1999 / 2000 / 2001 / 2002 / 2003

Resale Value

1999	2000	2001	2002	2003
$23,836	$21,757	$19,881	$17,999	$16,124

Cumulative Costs

	1999	2000	2001	2002	2003
Annual	$6,134	$6,227	$6,005	$7,222	$6,691
Total	$6,134	$12,361	$18,366	$25,588	$32,279

Projected Costs (5yr)

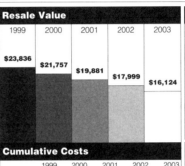

Relative $34,653	This Car $32,279
Cost/Mile 50¢	Cost/Mile 46¢

Ownership Cost Value

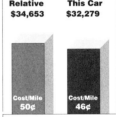

◯ Excellent

Toyota Corolla VE
4 Door Sedan

Compact

LE Model Shown

1.8L 120 hp Gas Fuel Inject.	4 Cylinder In-Line	Manual 5 Speed	2 Wheel Front	Dual Airbags Std

Purchase Price °

Car Item	Dealer Cost	List
Base Price	**$11,137**	**$12,218**
Anti-Lock Brakes	$473	$550
Automatic 3 Speed	$455	$500
Optional Engine	N/A	N/A
Air Conditioning	$760	$950
Power Steering	Std	Std
Cruise Control	N/A	N/A
Power Windows	N/A	N/A
AM/FM Stereo Cassette	$158	$210
Steering Wheel, Tilt	N/A	N/A
Rear Defroster	$156	$195
***Options Price**	**$1,529**	**$1,855**
***Total Price**	**$12,666**	**$14,073**
Target Price	$13,424	
Destination Charge	$420	
Avg. Tax & Fees	$781	
Total Target $	**$14,625**	
Average Dealer Option Cost:	**79%**	
12 Month Price Increase:	3%	

Built exclusively in North America, the Corolla VE returns for the 1999 model year with few changes to its interior and exterior. Several safety features are standard including daytime running lamps, dual airbags, child safety locks, seatbelt pretensioners and front and rear crumple zones. Automatic on/off headlamps, tinted glass and power steering are standard. Side-impact airbags and antilock brakes are offered as available options. Air conditioning is also optional.

Ownership Costs (Projected)

Cost Area	5 Year Cost	Rating
Depreciation	$6,401	◯
Financing ($242/month)	$2,845	
Insurance	$7,463	◉
State Fees	$592	
Fuel (Hwy 33 City 28)	$2,427	◯
Maintenance	$3,254	◉
Repairs	$481	◯

Warranty/Maintenance Info

Major Tune-Up (60K mile int.)	$261	◉
Minor Tune-Up (30K mile int.)	$131	●
Brake Service	$202	◯
Overall Warranty	3 yr/36k	◉
Drivetrain Warranty	5 yr/60k	◯
Rust Warranty	5 yr/unlim. mi	◯
Maintenance Warranty	N/A	
Roadside Assistance	N/A	

Ownership Costs By Year (Projected)

1999 / 2000 / 2001 / 2002 / 2003

Resale Value

1999	2000	2001	2002	2003
$13,155	$11,842	$10,682	$9,474	$8,224

Cumulative Costs

	1999	2000	2001	2002	2003
Annual	$4,513	$4,222	$4,185	$5,460	$5,083
Total	$4,513	$8,735	$12,920	$18,380	$23,463

Projected Costs (5yr)

Relative $24,680	This Car $23,463
Cost/Mile 35¢	Cost/Mile 34¢

Ownership Cost Value

◯ Excellent

Toyota Corolla CE
4 Door Sedan

Compact

1.8L 120 hp Gas Fuel Inject.	4 Cylinder In-Line	Manual 5 Speed	2 Wheel Front	Dual Airbags Std

LE Model Shown

Purchase Price

Car Item	Dealer Cost	List
Base Price	**$11,434**	**$12,908**
Anti-Lock Brakes	$473	$550
Automatic 4 Speed	$707	$800
Optional Engine	N/A	N/A
Air Conditioning	$760	$950
Power Steering	Std	Std
Cruise Control	$200	$250
Power Windows	Pkg	Pkg
AM/FM Stereo Cassette	Std	Std
Steering Wheel, Tilt	Std	Std
Rear Defroster	Std	Std
*Options Price	$1,467	$1,750
*Total Price	$12,901	$14,658
Target Price	$13,745	
Destination Charge	$420	
Avg. Tax & Fees	$801	
Total Target $	**$14,966**	
Average Dealer Option Cost:	76%	
12 Month Price Increase:	None	

For 1999, the Corolla CE returns with minimal changes. The Corolla is equipped with numerous standard features including a tilt steering wheel, intermittent wipers, a remote trunk release, covered center console storage and a deluxe AM/FM cassette radio with four speakers. Four wheel antilock brakes, side-impact airbags and a rear child restraint seat are offered as available options. Optional packages include a Value Package, a Touring Package and an All-Weather Guard Package.

Ownership Costs (Projected)

Cost Area	5 Year Cost	Rating
Depreciation	$6,580	◐
Financing ($248/month)	$2,911	
Insurance	$7,463	◉
State Fees	$617	
Fuel (Hwy 36 City 28)	$2,314	○
Maintenance	$3,254	◉
Repairs	$481	○

Warranty/Maintenance Info

Major Tune-Up (60K mile int.)	$261	◐
Minor Tune-Up (30K mile int.)	$131	●
Brake Service	$202	○
Overall Warranty	3 yr/36k	◐
Drivetrain Warranty	5 yr/60k	○
Rust Warranty	5 yr/unlim. mi	○
Maintenance Warranty	N/A	
Roadside Assistance	N/A	

Ownership Costs By Year (Projected)

■	1999			
■	2000			
■	2001			
▨	2002			
□	2003			

Resale Value

1999	2000	2001	2002	2003
$13,738	$12,312	$11,043	$9,732	$8,386

Cumulative Costs

	1999	2000	2001	2002	2003
Annual	$4,278	$4,337	$4,291	$5,553	$5,161
Total	$4,278	$8,615	$12,906	$18,459	$23,620

Projected Costs (5yr)

Relative $24,888	This Car $23,620
Cost/Mile 36¢	Cost/Mile 34¢

Ownership Cost Value

○ Excellent

Toyota Corolla LE
4 Door Sedan

Compact

1.8L 120 hp Gas Fuel Inject.	4 Cylinder In-Line	Manual 5 Speed	2 Wheel Front	Dual Airbags Std

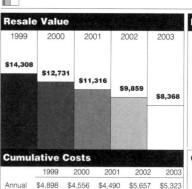

Purchase Price

Car Item	Dealer Cost	List
Base Price	**$13,168**	**$14,868**
Anti-Lock Brakes	$473	$550
Automatic 4 Speed	$709	$800
Optional Engine	N/A	N/A
Air Conditioning	Std	Std
Power Steering	Std	Std
Cruise Control	N/C	N/C
Power Windows	Std	Std
AM/FM Stereo Cassette	Std	Std
Steering Wheel, Tilt	Std	Std
Rear Defroster	Std	Std
*Options Price	$709	$800
*Total Price	$13,877	$15,668
Target Price	$14,794	
Destination Charge	$420	
Avg. Tax & Fees	$859	
Total Target $	**$16,073**	
Average Dealer Option Cost:	74%	
12 Month Price Increase:	None	

Equipped with several upper-level amenities, the Corolla LE returns with minimal changes to its interior and exterior. The LE features wider 185-series tires for added traction and stability. The LE also features power door locks, dual color-keyed power remote-controlled mirrors, protective color-keyed bodyside moldings and color-keyed door handles. For added safety, four wheel antilock brakes, a rear child safety seat and side-impact airbags are available options.

Ownership Costs (Projected)

Cost Area	5 Year Cost	Rating
Depreciation	$7,705	◐
Financing ($266/month)	$3,126	
Insurance	$7,463	◉
State Fees	$658	
Fuel (Hwy 36 City 28)	$2,314	○
Maintenance	$3,177	◐
Repairs	$481	○

Warranty/Maintenance Info

Major Tune-Up (60K mile int.)	$261	◐
Minor Tune-Up (30K mile int.)	$131	●
Brake Service	$202	○
Overall Warranty	3 yr/36k	◐
Drivetrain Warranty	5 yr/60k	○
Rust Warranty	5 yr/unlim. mi	○
Maintenance Warranty	N/A	
Roadside Assistance	N/A	

Ownership Costs By Year (Projected)

■	1999			
■	2000			
■	2001			
▨	2002			
□	2003			

Resale Value

1999	2000	2001	2002	2003
$14,308	$12,731	$11,316	$9,859	$8,368

Cumulative Costs

	1999	2000	2001	2002	2003
Annual	$4,898	$4,556	$4,490	$5,657	$5,323
Total	$4,898	$9,454	$13,944	$19,601	$24,924

Projected Costs (5yr)

Relative $25,766	This Car $24,924
Cost/Mile 37¢	Cost/Mile 36¢

Ownership Cost Value

○ Excellent

186

Refer to *Section 3: Annotated Vehicle Charts* for an explanation of these charts.

Volkswagen Beetle GL
2 Door Hatchback

Subcompact

 2.0L 115 hp Gas Fuel Inject.
 4 Cylinder In-Line
 Manual 5 Speed
 2 Wheel Front
 Dual Front/Side Airbags Std

Purchase Price

Car Item	Dealer Cost	List
Base Price	**$14,990**	**$15,900**
Anti-Lock Brakes	Std	Std
Automatic 4 Speed	$856	$875
Optional Engine	N/A	N/A
Air Conditioning	Std	Std
Power Steering	Std	Std
Cruise Control	N/A	N/A
Power Windows	Std	Std
AM/FM Stereo Cassette	Std	Std
Steering Wheel, Tilt	Std	Std
Rear Defroster	Std	Std
*Options Price	$0	$0
*Total Price	$14,990	$15,900
Target Price	$15,866	
Destination Charge	$525	
Avg. Tax & Fees	$915	
Total Target $	**$17,306**	
Average Dealer Option Cost:	98%	
12 Month Price Increase:	None	

The New Beetle GL bursts onto the new car scene as a newly designated trim level. Standard equipment includes four wheel antilock brakes, air conditioning with a pollen/odor filter, tilt/telescope steering wheel and an anti-theft alarm system. Optional equipment is limited to a four speed adaptive automatic transmission and California Emissions requirements. New items this year include an overhead storage console with a sunglasses holder, larger cup holders and an outside temperature gauge.

Ownership Costs (Projected)

Cost Area	5 Year Cost	Rating
Depreciation		⊖
Financing ($287/month)	$3,367	
Insurance	$7,643	◉
State Fees	$670	
Fuel (Hwy 31 City 24)	$2,692	○
Maintenance	$3,655	●
Repairs	$811	◉

Warranty/Maintenance Info

Major Tune-Up (60K mile int.)	$320	◉
Minor Tune-Up (30K mile int.)	$97	○
Brake Service	$245	○
Overall Warranty	2 yr/24k	◉
Drivetrain Warranty	10 yr/100k	○
Rust Warranty	6 yr/unlim. mi	○
Maintenance Warranty	2 yr/24k	○
Roadside Assistance	2 yr/unlim. mi	

Ownership Costs By Year (Projected)

Insufficient Depreciation Information

- 1999
- 2000
- 2001
- 2002
- 2003

Resale Value

Insufficient Information

Projected Costs (5yr)

Insufficient Information

Cumulative Costs

	1999	2000	2001	2002	2003
Annual	Insufficient Information				
Total	Insufficient Information				

Ownership Cost Value

⊖

Insufficient Information

Volkswagen Beetle GLS
2 Door Hatchback

Subcompact

GL Model Shown

 2.0L 115 hp Gas Fuel Inject.
4 Cylinder In-Line
 Manual 5 Speed
 2 Wheel Front
Dual Front/Side Airbags Std

Purchase Price

Car Item	Dealer Cost	List
Base Price	**$15,535**	**$16,850**
Anti-Lock Brakes	Std	Std
Automatic 4 Speed	$856	$875
1.9L 90 hp Trbo Dsl	$959	$1,050
Air Conditioning	Std	Std
Power Steering	Std	Std
Cruise Control	Std	Std
Power Windows	Std	Std
AM/FM Stereo Cassette	Std	Std
Steering Wheel, Tilt	Std	Std
Rear Defroster	Std	Std
*Options Price	$0	$0
*Total Price	$15,535	$16,850
Target Price	$16,654	
Destination Charge	$525	
Avg. Tax & Fees	$960	
Total Target $	**$18,139**	
Average Dealer Option Cost:	91%	
12 Month Price Increase:	N/A	

The New Beetle GLS bows this model year featuring a wide array of standard and optional equipment. In addition to standard power windows, cruise control and front fog lamps, popular options are now grouped into packages. The contents of these packages include a power sunroof, leather interior and alloy wheels. A 2.0L gas engine is standard, with a 1.9L turbodiesel continuing as an option. Enhanced sporting appeal will be met mid-year with the debut of a 1.8L turbo gas engine option.

Ownership Costs (Projected)

Cost Area	5 Year Cost	Rating
Depreciation		⊖
Financing ($301/month)	$3,528	
Insurance	$7,837	◉
State Fees	$708	
Fuel (Hwy 31 City 24)	$2,692	○
Maintenance	$3,655	●
Repairs	$811	●

Warranty/Maintenance Info

Major Tune-Up (60K mile int.)	$320	●
Minor Tune-Up (30K mile int.)	$97	○
Brake Service	$245	○
Overall Warranty	2 yr/24k	◉
Drivetrain Warranty	10 yr/100k	○
Rust Warranty	6 yr/unlim. mi	○
Maintenance Warranty	2 yr/24k	○
Roadside Assistance	2 yr/unlim. mi	

Ownership Costs By Year (Projected)

Insufficient Depreciation Information

- 1999
- 2000
- 2001
- 2002
- 2003

Resale Value

Insufficient Information

Projected Costs (5yr)

Insufficient Information

Cumulative Costs

	1999	2000	2001	2002	2003
Annual	Insufficient Information				
Total	Insufficient Information				

Ownership Cost Value

⊖

Insufficient Information

---

* Includes shaded options

** Other purchase requirements apply

*** Price includes other options

 Poor
 Worse Than Average
 Average
 Better Than Average
Excellent
⊖ Insufficient Information

187

Refer to *Section 3: Annotated Vehicle Charts* for an explanation of these charts.

Volkswagen Cabrio
2 Door Convertible

2.0L 115 hp Gas Fuel Inject.	4 Cylinder In-Line	Manual 5 Speed	2 Wheel Front	Dual Airbags Std

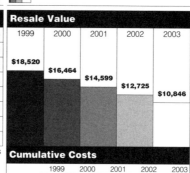

GLS Model Shown

Purchase Price

Car Item	Dealer Cost	List
Base Price	**$16,289**	**$17,975**
Anti-Lock Brakes	N/A	N/A
Automatic 4 Speed	$856	$875
Optional Engine	N/A	N/A
Air Conditioning	$750	$860
Power Steering	Std	Std
Cruise Control	Pkg	Pkg
Power Windows	Pkg	Pkg
AM/FM Stereo Cassette	Std	Std
Steering Wheel, Tilt	Std	Std
Rear Defroster	Std	Std
*Options Price	$750	$860
*Total Price	**$17,039**	**$18,835**
Target Price	$18,191	
Destination Charge	$500	
Avg. Tax & Fees	$1,047	
Total Target $	**$19,738**	
Average Dealer Option Cost:	90%	
12 Month Price Increase:	None	

Ownership Costs (Projected)

Cost Area	5 Year Cost	Rating
Depreciation	$8,892	◐
Financing ($327/month)	$3,840	
Insurance	$8,093	◉
State Fees	$786	
Fuel (Hwy 31 City 24)	$2,692	◐
Maintenance	$3,021	◐
Repairs	$811	◉

Warranty/Maintenance Info

Major Tune-Up (60K mile int.)	$329	◉
Minor Tune-Up (30K mile int.)	$116	◉
Brake Service	$285	◉
Overall Warranty	2 yr/24k	◉
Drivetrain Warranty	10 yr/100k	○
Rust Warranty	6 yr/unlim. mi	○
Maintenance Warranty	2 yr/24k	○
Roadside Assistance	2 yr/unlim. mi	

For 1999, the Cabrio returns with a restyled interior and exterior. Standard features on the GL include a glass rear window with defogger, an AM/FM cassette stereo, an anti-theft vehicle alarm system and power door locks. Safety features include daytime running lamps, a collapsible steering column, antilock brakes and optional heated power mirrors. The Cabrio GL includes a manual convertible vinyl top available in three colors: black, kiesel and white.

Ownership Costs By Year (Projected)

$2,000 $4,000 $6,000 $8,000 $10,000

■ 1999
■ 2000
■ 2001
■ 2002
□ 2003

Resale Value

1999	2000	2001	2002	2003
$18,520	$16,464	$14,599	$12,725	$10,846

Projected Costs (5yr)

Relative $28,846	This Car $28,135
Cost/Mile 41¢	Cost/Mile 40¢

Cumulative Costs

	1999	2000	2001	2002	2003
Annual	$4,787	$5,510	$5,456	$6,167	$6,215
Total	$4,787	$10,297	$15,753	$21,920	$28,135

Ownership Cost Value

○

Better Than Average

Volkswagen Cabrio GLS
2 Door Convertible

2.0L 115 hp Gas Fuel Inject.	4 Cylinder In-Line	Manual 5 Speed	2 Wheel Front	Dual Airbags Std

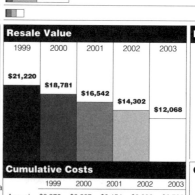

Purchase Price

Car Item	Dealer Cost	List
Base Price	**$20,240**	**$22,290**
Anti-Lock Brakes	Std	Std
Automatic 4 Speed	$856	$875
Optional Engine	N/A	N/A
Air Conditioning	Std	Std
Power Steering	Std	Std
Cruise Control	Std	Std
Power Windows	Std	Std
AM/FM Stereo Cassette	Std	Std
Steering Wheel, Tilt	Std	Std
Rear Defroster	Std	Std
*Options Price	$0	$0
*Total Price	**$20,240**	**$22,290**
Target Price	$21,575	
Destination Charge	$500	
Avg. Tax & Fees	$1,234	
Total Target $	**$23,309**	
Average Dealer Option Cost:	94%	
12 Month Price Increase:	None	

Ownership Costs (Projected)

Cost Area	5 Year Cost	Rating
Depreciation	$11,241	◐
Financing ($386/month)	$4,534	
Insurance	$8,865	◉
State Fees	$925	
Fuel (Hwy 31 City 24)	$2,692	◐
Maintenance	$3,021	◐
Repairs	$811	◉

Warranty/Maintenance Info

Major Tune-Up (60K mile int.)	$329	◉
Minor Tune-Up (30K mile int.)	$116	◉
Brake Service	$285	◉
Overall Warranty	2 yr/24k	◉
Drivetrain Warranty	10 yr/100k	○
Rust Warranty	6 yr/unlim. mi	○
Maintenance Warranty	2 yr/24k	○
Roadside Assistance	2 yr/unlim. mi	

The restyled 1999 Cabrio GLS includes many luxury amenities such as air conditioning, cruise control, leather seating and heated power mirrors. Safety features include daytime running lamps, a collapsible steering column, front fog lamps and optional side-impact airbags. Optional equipment for the GLS includes a four speed automatic transmission, metallic paint and an All-Weather Package. The standard electric power convertible cloth top is available in black, kiesel or white.

Ownership Costs By Year (Projected)

$2,000 $4,000 $6,000 $8,000 $10,000 $12,000

■ 1999
■ 2000
■ 2001
■ 2002
□ 2003

Resale Value

1999	2000	2001	2002	2003
$21,220	$18,781	$16,542	$14,302	$12,068

Projected Costs (5yr)

Relative $32,488	This Car $32,089
Cost/Mile 46¢	Cost/Mile 46¢

Cumulative Costs

	1999	2000	2001	2002	2003
Annual	$6,076	$6,267	$6,154	$6,806	$6,786
Total	$6,076	$12,343	$18,497	$25,303	$32,089

Ownership Cost Value

◐

Average

---

* Includes shaded options
** Other purchase requirements apply
*** Price includes other options

● Poor	◉ Worse Than Average	◐ Average	○ Better Than Average	○ Excellent	⊖ Insufficient Information

Refer to *Section 3: Annotated Vehicle Charts* for an explanation of these charts.

Volkswagen Golf GL
4 Door Hatchback

 2.0L 115 hp Gas Fuel Inject. | 4 Cylinder In-Line | Manual 5 Speed | 2 Wheel Front | Dual Airbags Std

Compact

GLS Model Shown

Purchase Price

Car Item	Dealer Cost	List
Base Price	**$12,455**	**$13,495**
Anti-Lock Brakes	$727	$775
Automatic 4 Speed	$856	$875
Optional Engine	N/A	N/A
Air Conditioning	$750	$860
Power Steering	Std	Std
Cruise Control	N/A	N/A
Power Windows	N/A	N/A
AM/FM Stereo Cassette	$423	$485
Steering Wheel, Tilt	N/A	N/A
Rear Defroster	Std	Std
*Options Price	$2,029	$2,220
*Total Price	$14,484	$15,715
Target Price	$15,227	
Destination Charge	$500	
Avg. Tax & Fees	$883	
Total Target $	**$16,610**	
Average Dealer Option Cost:	91%	
12 Month Price Increase:	None	

Ownership Costs (Projected)

Cost Area	5 Year Cost	Rating
Depreciation	$7,789	◯
Financing ($275/month)	$3,230	
Insurance	$7,688	◉
State Fees	$662	
Fuel (Hwy 28 City 22)	$2,962	◉
Maintenance	$3,048	◯
Repairs	$835	◉

Warranty/Maintenance Info

Major Tune-Up (60K mile int.)	$329	●
Minor Tune-Up (30K mile int.)	$116	◉
Brake Service	$285	●
Overall Warranty	2 yr/24k	◉
Drivetrain Warranty	10 yr/100k	◯
Rust Warranty	6 yr/unlim. mi	◯
Maintenance Warranty	2 yr/24k	◯
Roadside Assistance	2 yr/unlim. mi	

For 1999, the Golf GL is a carryover model from the 1998 model year. The GL is equipped with an anti-theft vehicle system for the doors, hood, trunklid and starter. Also standard is a central power locking system with two remote transmitters for the doors and trunk. Available options for the Golf GL include air conditioning, antilock brakes, a power glass sunroof with tilt feature and an AM/FM stereo with cassette. Front side airbags are also available as an option.

Ownership Costs By Year (Projected)

$2,000 — $4,000 — $6,000 — $8,000

■ 1999 ■ 2000 ■ 2001 ▨ 2002 ▢ 2003

Resale Value

1999	2000	2001	2002	2003
$14,478	$12,958	$11,609	$10,227	$8,821

Cumulative Costs

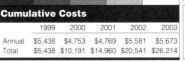

	1999	2000	2001	2002	2003
Annual	$5,438	$4,753	$4,769	$5,581	$5,673
Total	$5,438	$10,191	$14,960	$20,541	$26,214

Projected Costs (5yr)

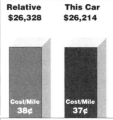

Relative	This Car
$26,328	$26,214
Cost/Mile 38¢	Cost/Mile 37¢

Ownership Cost Value

◯ Average

Volkswagen Golf Wolfsburg Edition
4 Door Hatchback

 2.0L 115 hp Gas Fuel Inject. | 4 Cylinder In-Line | Manual 5 Speed | 2 Wheel Front | Dual Airbags Std

Compact

GLS Model Shown

Purchase Price

Car Item	Dealer Cost	List
Base Price	**$14,298**	**$15,275**
Anti-Lock Brakes	$727	$775
Automatic 4 Speed	$856	$875
Optional Engine	N/A	N/A
Air Conditioning	Std	Std
Power Steering	Std	Std
Cruise Control	Std	Std
Power Windows	Std	Std
AM/FM Stereo Cassette	Std	Std
Steering Wheel, Tilt	N/A	N/A
Rear Defroster	Std	Std
*Options Price	$856	$875
*Total Price	$15,154	$16,150
Target Price	$15,769	
Destination Charge	$500	
Avg. Tax & Fees	$912	
Total Target $	**$17,181**	
Average Dealer Option Cost:	93%	
12 Month Price Increase:	None	

Ownership Costs (Projected)

Cost Area	5 Year Cost	Rating
Depreciation	$8,818	◯
Financing ($285/month)	$3,343	
Insurance	$7,688	◉
State Fees	$680	
Fuel (Hwy 28 City 22)	$2,962	◉
Maintenance	$3,048	◯
Repairs	$835	◉

Warranty/Maintenance Info

Major Tune-Up (60K mile int.)	$329	●
Minor Tune-Up (30K mile int.)	$116	◉
Brake Service	$285	●
Overall Warranty	2 yr/24k	◉
Drivetrain Warranty	10 yr/100k	◯
Rust Warranty	6 yr/unlim. mi	◯
Maintenance Warranty	2 yr/24k	◯
Roadside Assistance	2 yr/unlim. mi	

For 1999, the Golf Wolfsburg Edition comes with power windows, air conditioning and an AM/FM/cassette stereo sound system with CD changer controls. A central power locking system with two transmitters has a key-operated feature to open or close the windows, close the optional power sunroof and selectively unlock the driver or front passenger door. Safety features include daytime running lamps, fog lamps and dual front airbags. An automatic transmission is available.

Ownership Costs By Year (Projected)

$2,000 — $4,000 — $6,000 — $8,000 — $10,000

■ 1999 ■ 2000 ■ 2001 ▨ 2002 ▢ 2003

Resale Value

1999	2000	2001	2002	2003
$14,811	$13,086	$11,538	$9,959	$8,363

Cumulative Costs

	1999	2000	2001	2002	2003
Annual	$5,719	$4,993	$4,994	$5,796	$5,872
Total	$5,719	$10,712	$15,706	$21,502	$27,374

Projected Costs (5yr)

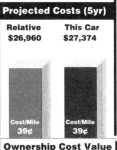

Relative	This Car
$26,960	$27,374
Cost/Mile 39¢	Cost/Mile 39¢

Ownership Cost Value

◯ Average

 Poor   Worse Than Average   Average ◯ Better Than Average ◯ Excellent ⊖ Insufficient Information

189

Refer to *Section 3: Annotated Vehicle Charts* for an explanation of these charts.

Volkswagen Golf GTI VR6
2 Door Hatchback

Compact

 2.8L 172 hp Gas Fuel Inject. | 6 Cylinder "V" | Manual 5 Speed | 2 Wheel Front | Dual Airbags Std

Purchase Price

Car Item	Dealer Cost	List
Base Price	**$18,678**	**$20,235**
Anti-Lock Brakes	Std	Std
Automatic Transmission	N/A	N/A
Optional Engine	N/A	N/A
Air Conditioning	Std	Std
Power Steering	Std	Std
Cruise Control	Std	Std
Power Windows	Std	Std
AM/FM Stereo Cassette	Std	Std
Steering Wheel, Tilt	Std	Std
Rear Defroster	Std	Std
*Options Price	$0	$0
*Total Price	$18,678	$20,235
Target Price	$19,661	
Destination Charge	$500	
Avg. Tax & Fees	$1,127	
Total Target $	**$21,288**	
Average Dealer Option Cost:	**90%**	
12 Month Price Increase:	None	

For 1999, the Golf GTI VR6 features a power glass sunroof with a tilt feature, white-faced instruments, seven spoke 15 inch alloy wheels and chrome-finished dual tailpipe extensions. The GTI also includes a multi-function trip computer, cruise control and power windows with express up/down and pinch protection. A 172 hp V6 engine, rear gas shock absorbers and a close-ratio five speed manual enhance the GTI's performance. Leather upholstery and a six disc CD changer are available options.

Ownership Costs (Projected)

Cost Area	5 Year Cost	Rating
Depreciation	$9,281	◯
Financing ($353/month)	$4,141	
Insurance	$8,556	◉
State Fees	$842	
Fuel (Hwy 26 City 19)	$3,299	●
Maintenance	$3,687	●
Repairs	$979	●

Warranty/Maintenance Info

Major Tune-Up (60K mile int.)	$354	●
Minor Tune-Up (30K mile int.)	$102	◯
Brake Service	$268	◉
Overall Warranty	2 yr/24k	◉
Drivetrain Warranty	10 yr/100k	◯
Rust Warranty	6 yr/unlim. mi	◯
Maintenance Warranty	2 yr/24k	◯
Roadside Assistance	2 yr/unlim. mi	

Ownership Costs By Year (Projected)

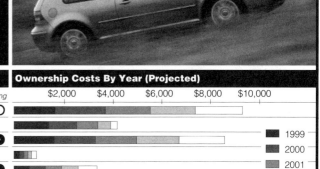

Legend: 1999, 2000, 2001, 2002, 2003

Resale Value

1999	2000	2001	2002	2003
$19,623	$17,568	$15,714	$13,856	$12,007

Cumulative Costs

	1999	2000	2001	2002	2003
Annual	$5,554	$5,846	$5,784	$6,776	$6,825
Total	$5,554	$11,400	$17,184	$23,960	$30,785

Projected Costs (5yr)

Relative	This Car
$30,513	$30,785
Cost/Mile 44¢	Cost/Mile 44¢

Ownership Cost Value

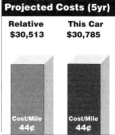

Average

Volkswagen Jetta GL
4 Door Sedan

Compact

 2.0L 115 hp Gas Fuel Inject. | 4 Cylinder In-Line | Manual 5 Speed | 2 Wheel Front | Dual Airbags Std

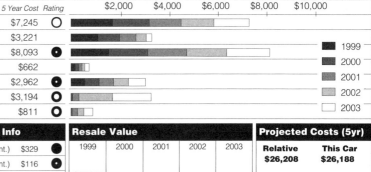

Purchase Price

Car Item	Dealer Cost	List
Base Price	**$13,500**	**$14,845**
Anti-Lock Brakes	$727	$775
Automatic 4 Speed	$856	$875
Optional Engine	N/A	N/A
Air Conditioning	$750	**$860
Power Steering	Std	Std
Cruise Control	$197	**$225
Power Windows	Std	Std
AM/FM Stereo Cassette	$423	**$485
Steering Wheel, Tilt	Std	Std
Rear Defroster	Std	Std
*Options Price	$856	$875
*Total Price	$14,356	$15,720
Target Price	$15,172	
Destination Charge	$500	
Avg. Tax & Fees	$880	
Total Target $	**$16,552**	
Average Dealer Option Cost:	**91%**	
12 Month Price Increase:	None	

The Jetta GL is equipped with many standard safety features, including open door warning reflectors, adjustable headrests, side-impact door beams, child safety locks and a theft deterrent system. The Jetta GL also includes daytime running lamps, emergency tensioning retractors for front safety belts and a rear child seat tether anchorage system. Heated side mirrors and a keyless entry system are also standard. Antilock brakes and driver and front passenger side airbags are optional.

Ownership Costs (Projected)

Cost Area	5 Year Cost	Rating
Depreciation	$7,245	◯
Financing ($274/month)	$3,221	
Insurance	$8,093	◉
State Fees	$662	
Fuel (Hwy 28 City 22)	$2,962	◉
Maintenance	$3,194	◯
Repairs	$811	◯

Warranty/Maintenance Info

Major Tune-Up (60K mile int.)	$329	●
Minor Tune-Up (30K mile int.)	$116	◉
Brake Service	$285	●
Overall Warranty	2 yr/24k	◉
Drivetrain Warranty	10 yr/100k	◯
Rust Warranty	6 yr/unlim. mi	◯
Maintenance Warranty	2 yr/24k	◯
Roadside Assistance	2 yr/unlim. mi	

Ownership Costs By Year (Projected)

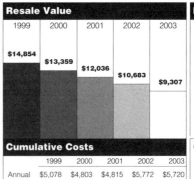

Legend: 1999, 2000, 2001, 2002, 2003

Resale Value

1999	2000	2001	2002	2003
$14,854	$13,359	$12,036	$10,683	$9,307

Cumulative Costs

	1999	2000	2001	2002	2003
Annual	$5,078	$4,803	$4,815	$5,772	$5,720
Total	$5,078	$9,881	$14,696	$20,468	$26,188

Projected Costs (5yr)

Relative	This Car
$26,208	$26,188
Cost/Mile 37¢	Cost/Mile 37¢

Ownership Cost Value

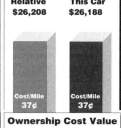

Average

190

* Includes shaded options
** Other purchase requirements apply
*** Price includes other options

● Poor	◉ Worse Than Average	◯ Average	◯ Better Than Average	◯ Excellent	⊖ Insufficient Information

Refer to *Section 3: Annotated Vehicle Charts* for an explanation of these charts.

Volkswagen Jetta TDI
4 Door Sedan

Compact

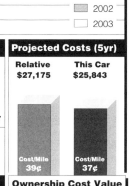 TD				
1.9L 90 hp Turbo Dsl Fuel Inject.	4 Cylinder In-Line	Manual 5 Speed	2 Wheel Front	Dual Airbags Std

Purchase Price

Car Item	Dealer Cost	List
Base Price	**$14,522**	**$15,770**
Anti-Lock Brakes	$727	$775
Automatic 4 Speed	$856	$875
Optional Engine	N/A	N/A
Air Conditioning	$750	**$860
Power Steering	Std	Std
Cruise Control	Std	Std
Power Windows	Pkg	Pkg
AM/FM Stereo Cassette	$423	**$485
Steering Wheel, Tilt	Std	Std
Rear Defroster	Std	Std
*Options Price	$856	$875
*Total Price	**$15,378**	**$16,645**
Target Price	$16,194	
Destination Charge	$500	
Avg. Tax & Fees	$935	
Total Target $	**$17,629**	
Average Dealer Option Cost:	91%	
12 Month Price Increase:	None	

The 1999 Jetta TDI features many of the same standard features as the GL, such as tilt steering, remote keyless entry and a theft deterrent system. Other standard items include cruise control, central locking, fold-down rear seats and intermittent wipers. With the Comfort Group option package, the TDI includes power windows, alloy wheels and power heated side mirrors. Optional equipment includes side-impact airbags, a power moonroof, a CD changer and air conditioning.

Ownership Costs (Projected)

Cost Area	5 Year Cost	Rating
Depreciation	$7,502	◯
Financing ($292/month)	$3,430	
Insurance	$8,093	◉
State Fees	$698	
Fuel (Hwy 47 City 38)	$1,741	◯
Maintenance	$3,198	◐
Repairs	$1,181	●

Warranty/Maintenance Info

Major Tune-Up (60K mile int.)	$219	◯
Minor Tune-Up (30K mile int.)	$76	◯
Brake Service	$285	●
Overall Warranty	2 yr/24k	◉
Drivetrain Warranty	10 yr/100k	◯
Rust Warranty	6 yr/unlim. mi	◯
Maintenance Warranty	2 yr/24k	◯
Roadside Assistance	2 yr/unlim. mi	

Ownership Costs By Year (Projected)

Legend: 1999, 2000, 2001, 2002, 2003

Resale Value

1999	2000	2001	2002	2003
$15,915	$14,347	$12,960	$11,551	$10,127

Cumulative Costs

	1999	2000	2001	2002	2003
Annual	$4,941	$4,740	$4,758	$5,742	$5,662
Total	$4,941	$9,681	$14,439	$20,181	$25,843

Projected Costs (5yr)

Relative $27,175	This Car $25,843
Cost/Mile 39¢	Cost/Mile 37¢

Ownership Cost Value

◯ Excellent

Volkswagen Jetta Wolfsburg Edition
4 Door Sedan

Compact

2.0L 115 hp Gas Fuel Inject.	4 Cylinder In-Line	Manual 5 Speed	2 Wheel Front	Dual Airbags Std

GLX Model Shown

Purchase Price

Car Item	Dealer Cost	List
Base Price	**$15,214**	**$16,500**
Anti-Lock Brakes	$727	$775
Automatic 4 Speed	$856	$875
Optional Engine	N/A	N/A
Air Conditioning	Std	Std
Power Steering	Std	Std
Cruise Control	Std	Std
Power Windows	Std	Std
AM/FM Stereo Cassette	Std	Std
Steering Wheel, Tilt	Std	Std
Rear Defroster	Std	Std
*Options Price	$856	$875
*Total Price	**$16,070**	**$17,375**
Target Price	$16,932	
Destination Charge	$500	
Avg. Tax & Fees	$976	
Total Target $	**$18,408**	
Average Dealer Option Cost:	93%	
12 Month Price Increase:	None	

The 1999 Jetta Wolfsburg Edition is equipped with several amenities including a leather-wrapped steering wheel, shift knob and handbrake, a CD changer, a luggage compartment cargo net, wheel locks and front sport seats. The Wolfsburg also includes special badging and a rear wing spoiler. The standard Power Package includes power windows, heated power mirrors and cruise control. Optional equipment includes an antilock braking system, side airbags, an automatic transmission and a power moonroof.

Ownership Costs (Projected)

Cost Area	5 Year Cost	Rating
Depreciation	$9,036	◯
Financing ($305/month)	$3,581	
Insurance	$8,093	◉
State Fees	$728	
Fuel (Hwy 28 City 22)	$2,962	◉
Maintenance	$3,194	◯
Repairs	$811	◯

Warranty/Maintenance Info

Major Tune-Up (60K mile int.)	$329	●
Minor Tune-Up (30K mile int.)	$116	◉
Brake Service	$285	●
Overall Warranty	2 yr/24k	◉
Drivetrain Warranty	10 yr/100k	◯
Rust Warranty	6 yr/unlim. mi	◯
Maintenance Warranty	2 yr/24k	◯
Roadside Assistance	2 yr/unlim. mi	

Ownership Costs By Year (Projected)

Legend: 1999, 2000, 2001, 2002, 2003

Resale Value

1999	2000	2001	2002	2003
$16,093	$14,294	$12,675	$11,030	$9,372

Cumulative Costs

	1999	2000	2001	2002	2003
Annual	$5,834	$5,222	$5,198	$6,122	$6,029
Total	$5,834	$11,056	$16,254	$22,376	$28,405

Projected Costs (5yr)

Relative $27,847	This Car $28,405
Cost/Mile 40¢	Cost/Mile 41¢

Ownership Cost Value

◯ Average

  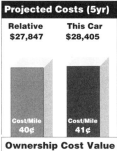

* Includes shaded options

** Other purchase requirements apply

*** Price includes other options

● Poor ◉ Worse Than Average ◯ Average ◯ Better Than Average ◯ Excellent ⊖ Insufficient Information

191

Refer to *Section 3: Annotated Vehicle Charts* for an explanation of these charts.

Volkswagen Jetta GLX
4 Door Sedan

 2.8L 172 hp Gas Fuel Inject.

 6 Cylinder "V"

 Manual 5 Speed

 2 Wheel Front

Dual Airbags Std

Purchase Price

Car Item	Dealer Cost	List
Base Price	$19,335	$20,955
Anti-Lock Brakes	Std	Std
Automatic 4 Speed	$856	$875
Optional Engine	N/A	N/A
Air Conditioning	Std	Std
Power Steering	Std	Std
Cruise Control	Std	Std
Power Windows	Std	Std
AM/FM Stereo Cassette	Std	Std
Steering Wheel, Tilt	Std	Std
Rear Defroster	Std	Std
*Options Price	$856	$875
*Total Price	$20,191	$21,830
Target Price		$21,206
Destination Charge		$500
Avg. Tax & Fees		$1,213
Total Target $		$22,919
Average Dealer Option Cost:		92%
12 Month Price Increase:		None

Ownership Costs (Projected)

Cost Area	5 Year Cost	Rating
Depreciation	$9,864	◐
Financing ($380/month)	$4,459	
Insurance	$8,865	●
State Fees	$906	
Fuel (Hwy 25 City 18)	$3,456	●
Maintenance	$3,787	●
Repairs	$955	●

Warranty/Maintenance Info

Major Tune-Up (60K mile int.)	$304	●
Minor Tune-Up (30K mile int.)	$121	◐
Brake Service	$268	◐
Overall Warranty	2 yr/24k	◐
Drivetrain Warranty	10 yr/100k	○
Rust Warranty	6 yr/unlim. mi	○
Maintenance Warranty	2 yr/24k	○
Roadside Assistance	2 yr/unlim. mi	

The 1999 Jetta GLX offers unique standard features including a multi-function trip computer (two programs, each featuring trip time, trip length, average trip speed, average trip fuel consumption, outside temperature and engine oil temperature), traction control and rear reading lights. A power moonroof and a folding rear center armrest are also standard. The GLX features a Bose music system with a Premium III AM/FM cassette stereo, amplifier, equalizer and ten speakers.

Ownership Costs By Year (Projected)

$2,000 $4,000 $6,000 $8,000 $10,000

■ 1999 ■ 2000 ■ 2001 ■ 2002 □ 2003

Resale Value

1999	2000	2001	2002	2003
$21,029	$18,879	$16,935	$14,991	$13,055

Cumulative Costs

	1999	2000	2001	2002	2003
Annual	$5,992	$6,113	$6,040	$7,254	$6,893
Total	$5,992	$12,105	$18,145	$25,399	$32,292

Projected Costs (5yr)

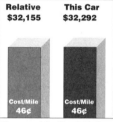

Relative	This Car
$32,155	$32,292
Cost/Mile 46¢	Cost/Mile 46¢

Ownership Cost Value

◐

Average

Volkswagen Jetta GL 1999.5
4 Door Sedan

 2.0L 115 hp Gas Fuel Inject.

 4 Cylinder In-Line

Manual 5 Speed

 2 Wheel Front

Dual Front/Side Airbags Std

Purchase Price

Car Item	Dealer Cost	List
Base Price	$15,059	$16,700
Anti-Lock Brakes	Std	Std
Automatic 4 Speed	$856	$875
Optional Engine	N/A	N/A
Air Conditioning	Std	Std
Power Steering	Std	Std
Cruise Control	N/A	N/A
Power Windows	N/A	N/A
AM/FM Stereo Cassette	Std	Std
Steering Wheel, Tilt	Std	Std
Rear Defroster	Std	Std
*Options Price	$856	$875
*Total Price	$15,915	$17,575
Target Price		$17,549
Destination Charge		$525
Avg. Tax & Fees		$1,007
Total Target $		$19,081
Average Dealer Option Cost:		98%
12 Month Price Increase:		N/A

Ownership Costs (Projected)

Cost Area	5 Year Cost	Rating
Depreciation	$7,888	○
Financing ($316/month)	$3,712	
Insurance	$7,688	◐
State Fees	$738	
Fuel (Hwy 28 City 22)	$2,962	◐
Maintenance	$3,193	○
Repairs	$811	○

Warranty/Maintenance Info

Major Tune-Up (60K mile int.)	$329	●
Minor Tune-Up (30K mile int.)	$116	◐
Brake Service	$268	◐
Overall Warranty	2 yr/24k	◐
Drivetrain Warranty	10 yr/100k	○
Rust Warranty	12 yr/unlim. mi	○
Maintenance Warranty	2 yr/24k	○
Roadside Assistance	2 yr/unlim. mi	

Completely redesigned inside and out, the new Jetta GL is introduced mid-year. The new Jetta GL is comprehensively equipped with air conditioning, dual front and side airbags, antilock brakes, a central locking system and daytime running lamps. A telescoping/height adjustable steering column, anti-theft alarm system, heated side mirrors and keyless entry system are also standard. The GL offers an automatic transmission, metallic paint and CD changer as options.

Ownership Costs By Year (Projected)

$2,000 $4,000 $6,000 $8,000

■ 1999 ■ 2000 ■ 2001 ■ 2002 □ 2003

Resale Value

1999	2000	2001	2002	2003
$17,144	$15,532	$14,102	$12,652	$11,193

Cumulative Costs

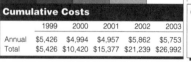

	1999	2000	2001	2002	2003
Annual	$5,426	$4,994	$4,957	$5,862	$5,753
Total	$5,426	$10,420	$15,377	$21,239	$26,992

Projected Costs (5yr)

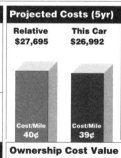

Relative	This Car
$27,695	$26,992
Cost/Mile 40¢	Cost/Mile 39¢

Ownership Cost Value

○

Better Than Average

---

 * Includes shaded options

** Other purchase requirements apply

*** Price includes other options

 Poor

 Worse Than Average

 Average

○ Better Than Average

○ Excellent

⊖ Insufficient Information

Refer to *Section 3: Annotated Vehicle Charts* for an explanation of these charts.

Volkswagen Jetta GLS 1999.5
4 Door Sedan

Compact

 2.0L 115 hp Gas Fuel Inject.
 4 Cylinder In-Line
 Manual 5 Speed
 2 Wheel Front
 Dual Front/Side Airbags Std

Purchase Price

Car Item	Dealer Cost	List
Base Price	**$15,907**	**$17,650**
Anti-Lock Brakes	Std	Std
Automatic 4 Speed	$856	$875
Optional Engine	N/A	N/A
Air Conditioning	Std	Std
Power Steering	Std	Std
Cruise Control	Std	Std
Power Windows	Std	Std
AM/FM Stereo Cassette	Std	Std
Steering Wheel, Tilt	Std	Std
Rear Defroster	Std	Std
*Options Price	$856	$875
*Total Price	**$16,763**	**$18,525**
Target Price	$18,517	
Destination Charge	$525	
Avg. Tax & Fees	$1,061	
Total Target $	**$20,103**	
Average Dealer Option Cost:	**91%**	
12 Month Price Increase:	N/A	

Completely redesigned inside and out, the new Jetta GLS is introduced mid-year. Standard upgrades for the GLS include cruise control, power windows with express up/down and pinch protection, power heated side mirrors and a center front armrest. To add extra comfort, two packages are now available: the Partial Leather Package and the Luxury Package (which includes a power sunroof and alloy wheels). An driver-adaptive automatic transmission is also optional.

Ownership Costs (Projected)

Cost Area	5 Year Cost	Rating
Depreciation	$8,271	◐
Financing ($333/month)	$3,911	
Insurance	$7,886	◉
State Fees	$774	
Fuel (Hwy 28 City 22)	$2,962	◉
Maintenance	$3,193	○
Repairs	$811	○

Warranty/Maintenance Info

Major Tune-Up (60K mile int.)	$329	●
Minor Tune-Up (30K mile int.)	$116	●
Brake Service	$268	●
Overall Warranty	2 yr/24k	●
Drivetrain Warranty	10 yr/100k	○
Rust Warranty	12 yr/unlim. mi	○
Maintenance Warranty	2 yr/24k	○
Roadside Assistance	2 yr/unlim. mi	

Ownership Costs By Year (Projected)

$2,000 $4,000 $6,000 $8,000 $10,000

■ 1999
■ 2000
■ 2001
■ 2002
□ 2003

Resale Value

1999	2000	2001	2002	2003
$18,666	$16,826	$15,172	$13,506	$11,832

Cumulative Costs

	1999	2000	2001	2002	2003
Annual	$5,040	$5,324	$5,268	$6,151	$6,025
Total	$5,040	$10,364	$15,632	$21,783	$27,808

Projected Costs (5yr)

Relative $28,535	This Car $27,808
Cost/Mile 41¢	Cost/Mile 40¢

Ownership Cost Value

○

Better Than Average

Volkswagen Jetta GL TDI 1999.5
4 Door Sedan

Compact

 1.9L 90 hp Turbo Dsl Fuel Inject.
 4 Cylinder In-Line
 Manual 5 Speed
 2 Wheel Front
Dual Front/Side Airbags Std

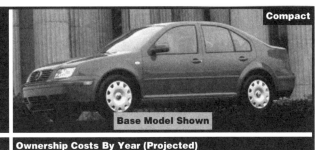

Base Model Shown

Purchase Price

Car Item	Dealer Cost	List
Base Price	**$16,581**	**$17,995**
Anti-Lock Brakes	Std	Std
Automatic 4 Speed	$856	$875
Optional Engine	N/A	N/A
Air Conditioning	Std	Std
Power Steering	Std	Std
Cruise Control	N/A	N/A
Power Windows	N/A	N/A
AM/FM Stereo Cassette	Std	Std
Steering Wheel, Tilt	Std	Std
Rear Defroster	Std	Std
*Options Price	$856	$875
*Total Price	**$17,437**	**$18,870**
Target Price	$18,885	
Destination Charge	$525	
Avg. Tax & Fees	$1,080	
Total Target $	**$20,490**	
Average Dealer Option Cost:	**98%**	
12 Month Price Increase:	N/A	

Completely redesigned inside and out, the new Jetta GL TDI is introduced mid-year. The new Jetta GL TDI includes air conditioning, engine braking control (EBC), dual front and side airbags, antilock brakes, a central locking system and daytime running lamps. A telescoping/height adjustable steering column, anti-theft alarm system, heated side mirrors and keyless entry system are also standard. The GL TDI offers an automatic transmission, metallic paint and CD changer as options.

Ownership Costs (Projected)

Cost Area	5 Year Cost	Rating
Depreciation	$8,383	○
Financing ($340/month)	$3,987	
Insurance	$7,886	◉
State Fees	$789	
Fuel (Hwy 45 City 34)	$1,931	○
Maintenance	$3,197	○
Repairs	$1,181	●

Warranty/Maintenance Info

Major Tune-Up (60K mile int.)	$219	○
Minor Tune-Up (30K mile int.)	$76	○
Brake Service	$268	●
Overall Warranty	2 yr/24k	●
Drivetrain Warranty	10 yr/100k	○
Rust Warranty	12 yr/unlim. mi	○
Maintenance Warranty	2 yr/24k	○
Roadside Assistance	2 yr/unlim. mi	

Ownership Costs By Year (Projected)

$2,000 $4,000 $6,000 $8,000 $10,000

■ 1999
■ 2000
■ 2001
■ 2002
□ 2003

Resale Value

1999	2000	2001	2002	2003
$18,526	$16,784	$15,234	$13,672	$12,107

Cumulative Costs

	1999	2000	2001	2002	2003
Annual	$5,399	$5,086	$5,050	$5,980	$5,839
Total	$5,399	$10,485	$15,535	$21,515	$27,354

Projected Costs (5yr)

Relative $29,219	This Car $27,354
Cost/Mile 42¢	Cost/Mile 39¢

Ownership Cost Value

○

Excellent

Volkswagen Jetta GLS TDI 1999.5
4 Door Sedan

Compact

 1.9L 90 hp Turbo Dsl Fuel Inject.   4 Cylinder In-Line   Manual 5 Speed   2 Wheel Front   Dual Front/Side Airbags Std

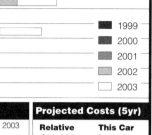

Purchase Price

Car Item	Dealer Cost	List
Base Price	**$17,225**	**$18,700**
Anti-Lock Brakes	Std	Std
Automatic 4 Speed	$856	$875
Optional Engine	N/A	N/A
Air Conditioning	Std	Std
Power Steering	Std	Std
Cruise Control	Std	Std
Power Windows	Std	Std
AM/FM Stereo Cassette	Std	Std
Steering Wheel, Tilt	Std	Std
Rear Defroster	Std	Std
*Options Price	$856	$875
*Total Price	**$18,081**	**$19,575**
Target Price	$19,604	
Destination Charge	$525	
Avg. Tax & Fees	$1,120	
Total Target $	**$21,249**	
Average Dealer Option Cost:	91%	
12 Month Price Increase:	N/A	

The completely-redesigned Jetta GLS TDI sports the same standard features as the 2.0L GLS. The mid-year GLS TDI also features engine braking control (EBC) as an aid in preventing skidding under slippery conditions. Standard features include cruise control, power windows with express up/down and pinch protection and power heated side mirrors. The optional Partial Leather Package includes a unique four spoke leather-wrapped steering wheel when ordered with the available automatic transmission.

Ownership Costs (Projected)

Cost Area	5 Year Cost	Rating
Depreciation	$8,493	◯
Financing ($352/month)	$4,133	
Insurance	$7,886	◉
State Fees	$818	
Fuel (Hwy 45 City 34)	$1,931	◯
Maintenance	$3,197	◯
Repairs	$1,181	●

Warranty/Maintenance Info

Major Tune-Up (60K mile int.)	$219	◯
Minor Tune-Up (30K mile int.)	$76	◯
Brake Service	$268	◉
Overall Warranty	2 yr/24k	◉
Drivetrain Warranty	10 yr/100k	◯
Rust Warranty	12 yr/unlim. mi	◯
Maintenance Warranty	2 yr/24k	◯
Roadside Assistance	2 yr/unlim. mi	

Ownership Costs By Year (Projected)

$2,000 $4,000 $6,000 $8,000 $10,000

Legend: 1999, 2000, 2001, 2002, 2003

Resale Value

1999	2000	2001	2002	2003
$19,089	$17,364	$15,834	$14,295	$12,756

Cumulative Costs

	1999	2000	2001	2002	2003
Annual	$5,652	$5,115	$5,066	$5,981	$5,825
Total	$5,652	$10,767	$15,833	$21,814	$27,639

Projected Costs (5yr)

Relative	This Car
$29,885	$27,639
Cost/Mile 43¢	Cost/Mile 39¢

Ownership Cost Value

◯ Excellent

Volkswagen Passat GLS
4 Door Sedan

Midsize

 1.8L 150 hp Turbo Gas Fuel Inject.   4 Cylinder In-Line   Manual 5 Speed   2 Wheel Front Dual Front/Side Airbags Std

Purchase Price

Car Item	Dealer Cost	List
Base Price	**$19,078**	**$21,200**
Anti-Lock Brakes	Std	Std
Automatic 5 Speed	$1,063	$1,075
Optional Engine	N/A	N/A
Air Conditioning	Std	Std
Power Steering	Std	Std
Cruise Control	Std	Std
Power Windows	Std	Std
AM/FM Stereo Cassette	Std	Std
St Whl, Power Scope/Tilt	Std	Std
Rear Defroster	Std	Std
*Options Price	$1,063	$1,075
*Total Price	**$20,141**	**$22,275**
Target Price	$21,634	
Destination Charge	$500	
Avg. Tax & Fees	$1,237	
Total Target $	**$23,371**	
Average Dealer Option Cost:	90%	
12 Month Price Increase:	2%	

The Passat GLS is powered by a 1.8L turbocharged four cylinder engine featuring Volkswagen's five valve per cylinder technology. Standard equipment for the GLS includes air conditioning, a premium AM/FM stereo with cassette, power windows and door locks, front passenger side-impact airbags and a Format velour interior. Optional equipment includes a power moonroof, a five speed automatic transmission with Tiptronic control, a leather interior and an All-Weather Package.

Ownership Costs (Projected)

Cost Area	5 Year Cost	Rating
Depreciation	$9,669	◯
Financing ($387/month)	$4,547	
Insurance	$7,886	◯
State Fees	$924	
Fuel (Hwy 31 City 21 -Prem.)	$3,406	◯
Maintenance	$3,967	●
Repairs	$1,020	●

Warranty/Maintenance Info

Major Tune-Up (60K mile int.)	$344	●
Minor Tune-Up (30K mile int.)	$108	◯
Brake Service	$304	●
Overall Warranty	2 yr/24k	◉
Drivetrain Warranty	10 yr/100k	◯
Rust Warranty	11 yr/unlim. mi	◯
Maintenance Warranty	2 yr/24k	◯
Roadside Assistance	2 yr/unlim. mi	

Ownership Costs By Year (Projected)

$2,000 $4,000 $6,000 $8,000 $10,000

Legend: 1999, 2000, 2001, 2002, 2003

Resale Value

1999	2000	2001	2002	2003
$21,141	$19,082	$17,303	$15,476	$13,702

Cumulative Costs

	1999	2000	2001	2002	2003
Annual	$6,171	$5,852	$5,712	$6,657	$7,027
Total	$6,171	$12,023	$17,735	$24,392	$31,419

Projected Costs (5yr)

Relative	This Car
$31,783	$31,419
Cost/Mile 45¢	Cost/Mile 45¢

Ownership Cost Value

◯ Average

---

* Includes shaded options
** Other purchase requirements apply
*** Price includes other options

 ● Poor ◉ Worse Than Average ◯ Average ◯ Better Than Average ◯ Excellent ⊖ Insufficient Information

Refer to *Section 3: Annotated Vehicle Charts* for an explanation of these charts.

Volkswagen Passat GLS V6
4 Door Sedan

Midsize

 2.8L 190 hp Gas Fuel Inject.
 6 Cylinder "V"
 Manual 5 Speed
 2 Wheel Front
 Dual Front/Side Airbags Std

Base Model Shown

Purchase Price

Car Item	Dealer Cost	List
Base Price	**$21,400**	**$23,800**
Anti-Lock Brakes	Std	Std
Automatic 5 Speed	$1,063	$1,075
Optional Engine	N/A	N/A
Air Conditioning	Std	Std
Power Steering	Std	Std
Cruise Control	Std	Std
Power Windows	Std	Std
AM/FM Stereo Cassette	Std	Std
St Whl, Power Scope/Tilt	Std	Std
Rear Defroster	Std	Std
***Options Price**	**$1,063**	**$1,075**
***Total Price**	**$22,463**	**$24,875**
Target Price	$24,204	
Destination Charge	$500	
Avg. Tax & Fees	$1,379	
Total Target $	**$26,083**	
Average Dealer Option Cost:	**90%**	
12 Month Price Increase:	3%	

The Passat GLS V6 features a 190 hp engine with variable valve timing and antilock brakes with integrated traction control. The GLS V6 features genuine interior wood trim, a Format velour interior and a premium AM/FM stereo with cassette. Optional equipment includes a five speed automatic transmission with Tiptronic control, a Leather Trim Package and an All-Weather Package, which includes heated front seats and heated windshield washer nozzles.

Ownership Costs (Projected)

Cost Area	5 Year Cost	Rating
Depreciation	$11,009	◐
Financing ($432/month)	$5,075	
Insurance	$8,093	◎
State Fees	$1,028	
Fuel (Hwy 29 City 18 -Prem.)	$3,806	◎
Maintenance	$4,252	●
Repairs	$1,020	●

Warranty/Maintenance Info

Major Tune-Up (60K mile int.)	$486	●
Minor Tune-Up (30K mile int.)	$133	◉
Brake Service	$304	●
Overall Warranty	2 yr/24k	◉
Drivetrain Warranty	10 yr/100k	○
Rust Warranty	11 yr/unlim. mi	○
Maintenance Warranty	2 yr/24k	○
Roadside Assistance	2 yr/unlim. mi	

Ownership Costs By Year (Projected)

$2,000 $4,000 $6,000 $8,000 $10,000 $12,000

- 1999
- 2000
- 2001
- 2002
- 2003

Resale Value

1999	2000	2001	2002	2003
$23,187	$20,942	$18,988	$16,999	$15,074

Cumulative Costs

	1999	2000	2001	2002	2003
Annual	$7,158	$6,341	$6,182	$7,074	$7,528
Total	$7,158	$13,499	$19,681	$26,755	$34,283

Projected Costs (5yr)

Relative	This Car
$34,834	**$34,283**
Cost/Mile **50¢**	Cost/Mile **49¢**

Ownership Cost Value

◎ Average

Volkswagen Passat GLS
4 Door Wagon

Midsize Wagon

 1.8L 150 hp Turbo Gas Fuel Inject.
 4 Cylinder In-Line
 Manual 5 Speed
 2 Wheel Front
Dual Front/Side Airbags Std

V6 Model Shown

Purchase Price

Car Item	Dealer Cost	List
Base Price	**$19,569**	**$21,750**
Anti-Lock Brakes	Std	Std
Automatic 5 Speed	$1,063	$1,075
Optional Engine	N/A	N/A
Air Conditioning	Std	Std
Power Steering	Std	Std
Cruise Control	Std	Std
Power Windows	Std	Std
AM/FM Stereo Cassette	Std	Std
St Whl, Power Scope/Tilt	Std	Std
Rear Defroster	Std	Std
***Options Price**	**$1,063**	**$1,075**
***Total Price**	**$20,632**	**$22,825**
Target Price	$22,176	
Destination Charge	$500	
Avg. Tax & Fees	$1,266	
Total Target $	**$23,942**	
Average Dealer Option Cost:	**90%**	
12 Month Price Increase:	2%	

The Passat GLS wagon is a carryover of last year's all-new model. A 150 hp 1.8L turbocharged engine featuring Volkswagen's five valve per cylinder design is standard. Heated side mirrors, auto unlock and lock for the central locking system and rear seat heat and air conditioning ducts are standard equipment. An All-Weather Package, Leather Trim Package and Luxury Package are available options. All exterior paint colors are carried over from last year.

Ownership Costs (Projected)

Cost Area	5 Year Cost	Rating
Depreciation	$9,999	○
Financing ($397/month)	$4,658	
Insurance	$7,886	◎
State Fees	$946	
Fuel (Hwy 31 City 21 -Prem.)	$3,406	○
Maintenance	$3,967	◎
Repairs	$1,020	◉

Warranty/Maintenance Info

Major Tune-Up (60K mile int.)	$344	●
Minor Tune-Up (30K mile int.)	$108	◎
Brake Service	$304	●
Overall Warranty	2 yr/24k	◉
Drivetrain Warranty	10 yr/100k	○
Rust Warranty	11 yr/unlim. mi	○
Maintenance Warranty	2 yr/24k	○
Roadside Assistance	2 yr/unlim. mi	

Ownership Costs By Year (Projected)

$2,000 $4,000 $6,000 $8,000 $10,000

- 1999
- 2000
- 2001
- 2002
- 2003

Resale Value

1999	2000	2001	2002	2003
$21,977	$19,772	$17,842	$15,865	$13,943

Cumulative Costs

	1999	2000	2001	2002	2003
Annual	$5,949	$6,034	$5,891	$6,825	$7,183
Total	$5,949	$11,983	$17,874	$24,699	$31,882

Projected Costs (5yr)

Relative	This Car
$32,905	**$31,882**
Cost/Mile **47¢**	Cost/Mile **46¢**

Ownership Cost Value

○ Excellent

---

* Includes shaded options

** Other purchase requirements apply

*** Price includes other options

● Poor   ◉ Worse Than Average   ◎ Average   ○ Better Than Average   ○ Excellent   ⊖ Insufficient Information

195

Refer to *Section 3: Annotated Vehicle Charts* for an explanation of these charts.

Volkswagen Passat GLS V6
4 Door Wagon

Midsize Wagon

 2.8L 190 hp Gas Fuel Inject.   6 Cylinder "V"   Manual 5 Speed   2 Wheel Front   Dual Front/Side Airbags Std

Purchase Price

Car Item	Dealer Cost	List
Base Price	**$21,892**	**$24,350**
Anti-Lock Brakes	Std	Std
Automatic 5 Speed	$1,063	$1,075
Optional Engine	N/A	N/A
Air Conditioning	Std	Std
Power Steering	Std	Std
Cruise Control	Std	Std
Power Windows	Std	Std
AM/FM Stereo Cassette	Std	Std
St Whl, Power Scope/Tilt	Std	Std
Rear Defroster	Std	Std
*Options Price	$1,063	$1,075
*Total Price	$22,955	$25,425
Target Price	$24,750	
Destination Charge	$500	
Avg. Tax & Fees	$1,408	
Total Target $	**$26,658**	
Average Dealer Option Cost:	**90%**	
12 Month Price Increase:	N/A	

The Passat GLS V6 wagon is a new addition to the 1999 Passat lineup. It features a 190 hp 30 valve engine and is optionally available with Volkswagen's Synchro all-wheel drive system. The GLS V6 wagon comes standard with a five speed manual transmission, and is available with a five speed driver-adaptive automatic transmission with Tiptronic control. Antilock brakes with integrated traction control and daytime running lamps are standard safety features.

Ownership Costs (Projected)

Cost Area	5 Year Cost	Rating
Depreciation	$11,343	◐
Financing ($442/month)	$5,187	
Insurance	$8,093	◐
State Fees	$1,049	
Fuel (Hwy 29 City 18 -Prem.)	$3,806	○
Maintenance	$4,252	○
Repairs	$1,020	●

Warranty/Maintenance Info

Major Tune-Up (60K mile int.)	$486	●
Minor Tune-Up (30K mile int.)	$133	●
Brake Service	$304	●
Overall Warranty	2 yr/24k	◉
Drivetrain Warranty	10 yr/100k	○
Rust Warranty	11 yr/unlim. mi	○
Maintenance Warranty	2 yr/24k	○
Roadside Assistance	2 yr/unlim. mi	

Ownership Costs By Year (Projected)

$2,000 $4,000 $6,000 $8,000 $10,000 $12,000

■ 1999
■ 2000
■ 2001
■ 2002
□ 2003

Resale Value

1999	2000	2001	2002	2003
$23,903	$21,542	$19,467	$17,358	$15,315

Cumulative Costs

	1999	2000	2001	2002	2003
Annual	$7,060	$6,493	$6,330	$7,211	$7,656
Total	$7,060	$13,553	$19,883	$27,094	$34,750

Projected Costs (5yr)

Relative $34,717	This Car $34,750
Cost/Mile 50¢	Cost/Mile 50¢

Ownership Cost Value

○ Better Than Average

Volvo C70
2 Door Coupe

Luxury

 2.4L 190 hp Turbo Gas Fuel Inject.   5 Cylinder In-Line  Automatic 4 Speed   2 Wheel Front Dual Front/Side Airbags Std

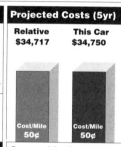

Purchase Price

Car Item	Dealer Cost	List
Base Price	**$33,145**	**$36,995**
Anti-Lock Brakes	Std	Std
Manual 5 Speed	N/C	N/C
2.3L 236 hp Turbo Gas	Pkg	Pkg
Auto Climate Control	Std	Std
Power Steering	Std	Std
Cruise Control	Std	Std
Power Windows	Std	Std
AM/FM Stereo Cass/CD	Std	Std
Steering Wheel, Tilt	Std	Std
Rear Defroster	Std	Std
*Options Price	$0	$0
*Total Price	$33,145	$36,995
Target Price	$35,325	
Destination Charge	$575	
Avg. Tax & Fees	$2,005	
Total Target $	**$37,905**	
Average Dealer Option Cost:	**78%**	
12 Month Price Increase:	None	

For 1999, the C70 coupe receives many engineering improvements and is now offered with a standard 2.4L light-pressure turbo engine and automatic transmission. A 236 hp high-pressure turbo engine, with a five speed manual or automatic transmission, is available. The C70 coupe comes standard with a power moonroof, AM/FM/CD changer stereo system, anti-theft system and dual-zone automatic climate control. Options include an electronic traction and stability control system (STC).

Ownership Costs (Projected)

Cost Area	5 Year Cost	Rating
Depreciation		⊖
Financing ($628/month)	$7,373	
Insurance	$9,911	○
State Fees	$1,516	
Fuel (Hwy 27 City 20 -Prem.)	$3,745	○
Maintenance	$3,643	●
Repairs	$1,115	○

Warranty/Maintenance Info

Major Tune-Up (60K mile int.)	$250	○
Minor Tune-Up (30K mile int.)	$138	○
Brake Service	$224	○
Overall Warranty	4 yr/50k	○
Drivetrain Warranty	4 yr/50k	○
Rust Warranty	8 yr/unlim. mi	○
Maintenance Warranty	N/A	
Roadside Assistance	4 yr/unlim. mi	

Ownership Costs By Year (Projected)

$2,000 $4,000 $6,000 $8,000 $10,000

Insufficient Depreciation Information

■ 1999
■ 2000
■ 2001
■ 2002
□ 2003

Resale Value

Insufficient

Information

Cumulative Costs

	1999	2000	2001	2002	2003
Annual	*Insufficient Information*				
Total	*Insufficient Information*				

Projected Costs (5yr)

Insufficient

Information

Ownership Cost Value

⊖ Insufficient Information

Volvo C70
2 Door Convertible

Luxury

 2.4L 190 hp Turbo Gas Fuel Inject.
 5 Cylinder In-Line
PRND321 Automatic 4 Speed
 2 Wheel Front
 Dual Front/Side Airbags Std

Purchase Price

Car Item	Dealer Cost	List
Base Price	**$38,895**	**$43,395**
Anti-Lock Brakes	Std	Std
Manual Transmission	N/A	N/A
Optional Engine	N/A	N/A
Auto Climate Control	Std	Std
Power Steering	Std	Std
Cruise Control	Std	Std
Power Windows	Std	Std
AM/FM Stereo Cass/CD	Std	Std
Steering Wheel, Tilt	Std	Std
Rear Defroster	Std	Std
*Options Price	$0	$0
*Total Price	**$38,895**	**$43,395**
Target Price	$41,655	
Destination Charge	$575	
Avg. Tax & Fees	$2,353	
Luxury Tax	$374	
Total Target $	**$44,957**	
12 Month Price Increase:	1%	

The 1999 C70 convertible continues on in its second year with numerous engineering enhancements. The C70 shares many components with the S70 sedan, and can accommodate four passengers. Standard features include side-impact airbags, eight-way power driver and passenger seats, daytime running lamps and 16 inch alloy wheels. Options include an electronic traction and stability control system (STC), 17 inch alloy wheels, heated front seats and a Dolby audio system with 14 speakers.

Ownership Costs (Projected)

Cost Area	5 Year Cost	Rating
Depreciation		⊖
Financing ($745/month)	$8,746	
Insurance	$10,297	◐
State Fees	$1,773	
Fuel (Hwy 27 City 20 -Prem.)	$3,745	○
Maintenance	$3,588	●
Repairs	$1,115	○

Warranty/Maintenance Info

Major Tune-Up (60K mile int.)	$250	○
Minor Tune-Up (30K mile int.)	$138	○
Brake Service	$224	○
Overall Warranty	4 yr/50k	○
Drivetrain Warranty	4 yr/50k	○
Rust Warranty	8 yr/unlim. mi	◔
Maintenance Warranty	N/A	
Roadside Assistance	4 yr/unlim. mi	

Ownership Costs By Year (Projected)

$2,000 $4,000 $6,000 $8,000 $10,000 $12,000

Insufficient Depreciation Information

■ 1999
■ 2000
■ 2001
■ 2002
□ 2003

Resale Value

Insufficient

Information

Projected Costs (5yr)

Insufficient

Information

Cumulative Costs

	1999	2000	2001	2002	2003
Annual		Insufficient Information			
Total		Insufficient Information			

Ownership Cost Value

⊖

Insufficient Information

Volvo S70
4 Door Sedan

Near Luxury

 2.4L 162 hp Gas Fuel Inject.
 5 Cylinder In-Line
135 24R Manual 5 Speed
 2 Wheel Front
Dual Front/Side Airbags Std

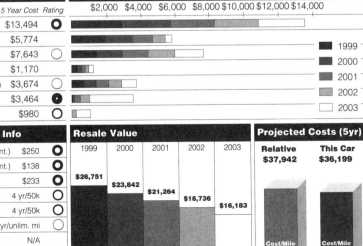

Purchase Price

Car Item	Dealer Cost	List
Base Price	**$25,159**	**$27,385**
Anti-Lock Brakes	Std	Std
Automatic 4 Speed	$975	$975
Optional Engine	N/A	N/A
Air Conditioning	Std	Std
Power Steering	Std	Std
Cruise Control	Std	Std
Power Windows	Std	Std
AM/FM Stereo Cassette	Std	Std
Steering Wheel, Tilt	Std	Std
Rear Defroster	Std	Std
*Options Price	$975	$975
*Total Price	**$26,134**	**$28,360**
Target Price	$27,535	
Destination Charge	$575	
Avg. Tax & Fees	$1,567	
Total Target $	**$29,677**	
Average Dealer Option Cost:	80%	
12 Month Price Increase:	1%	

The S70 sedan carries over into the 1999 model year with several engineering improvements. A new Special Value Package includes alloy wheels, automatic climate control, power driver's seat with memory, power sunroof and a trip computer. The standard remote entry and security system has a module that controls all locking and alarm functions. The system's wiring is completely integrated with the car and prevents the doors from locking when the key is in the ignition and in the off position.

Ownership Costs (Projected)

Cost Area	5 Year Cost	Rating
Depreciation	$13,494	○
Financing ($492/month)	$5,774	
Insurance	$7,643	◔
State Fees	$1,170	
Fuel (Hwy 28 City 20 -Prem.)	$3,674	○
Maintenance	$3,464	◐
Repairs	$980	○

Warranty/Maintenance Info

Major Tune-Up (60K mile int.)	$250	○
Minor Tune-Up (30K mile int.)	$138	○
Brake Service	$233	○
Overall Warranty	4 yr/50k	○
Drivetrain Warranty	4 yr/50k	○
Rust Warranty	8 yr/unlim. mi	◔
Maintenance Warranty	N/A	
Roadside Assistance	4 yr/unlim. mi	

Ownership Costs By Year (Projected)

$2,000 $4,000 $6,000 $8,000 $10,000 $12,000 $14,000

■ 1999
■ 2000
■ 2001
■ 2002
□ 2003

Resale Value

1999	2000	2001	2002	2003
$26,751	$23,842	$21,264	$18,736	$16,183

Projected Costs (5yr)

Relative	This Car
$37,942	$36,199
Cost/Mile 54¢	Cost/Mile 52¢

Cumulative Costs

	1999	2000	2001	2002	2003
Annual	$7,409	$7,065	$6,585	$6,608	$8,532
Total	$7,409	$14,474	$21,059	$27,667	$36,199

Ownership Cost Value

○

Excellent

---

* Includes shaded options

** Other purchase requirements apply

*** Price includes other options

 ● Poor
 ◑ Worse Than Average
○ Average
◔ Better Than Average
○ Excellent
⊖ Insufficient Information

197

Refer to *Section 3: Annotated Vehicle Charts* for an explanation of these charts.

Volvo S70 GLT
4 Door Sedan

 **Near Luxury**

 2.4L 190 hp Turbo Gas Fuel Inject.

 5 Cylinder In-Line

 Automatic 4 Speed

 2 Wheel Front

 Dual Front/Side Airbags Std

Purchase Price

Car Item	Dealer Cost	List
Base Price	**$29,256**	**$31,640**
Anti-Lock Brakes	Std	Std
Manual Transmission	N/A	N/A
Optional Engine	N/A	N/A
Auto Climate Control	Std	Std
Power Steering	Std	Std
Cruise Control	Std	Std
Power Windows	Std	Std
AM/FM Stereo Cassette	Std	Std
Steering Wheel, Tilt	Std	Std
Rear Defroster	Std	Std
***Options Price**	**$0**	**$0**
***Total Price**	**$29,256**	**$31,640**
Target Price	$30,824	
Destination Charge	$575	
Avg. Tax & Fees	$1,748	
Total Target $	**$33,147**	
Average Dealer Option Cost:	**80%**	
12 Month Price Increase:	None	

The S70 GLT sedan includes all the same features as the S70 base model. The GLT adds a 20 valve, 190 hp turbo intercooled engine with 199 lb-ft of torque. The engine is paired with a four speed automatic transmission. Automatic climate control, a power driver's seat with memory and a power sunroof are standard features, along with a dust/pollen filtration system and heated side mirrors. An anti-theft system, antilock brakes and a remote keyless entry system are also standard.

Ownership Costs (Projected)

Cost Area	5 Year Cost	Rating
Depreciation	$15,164	◐
Financing ($549/month)	$6,448	
Insurance	$7,506	○
State Fees	$1,302	
Fuel (Hwy 27 City 20 -Prem.)	$3,745	○
Maintenance	$3,602	◉
Repairs	$1,165	○

Warranty/Maintenance Info

Major Tune-Up (60K mile int.)	$250	○
Minor Tune-Up (30K mile int.)	$138	○
Brake Service	$233	○
Overall Warranty	4 yr/50k	○
Drivetrain Warranty	4 yr/50k	○
Rust Warranty	8 yr/unlim. mi	◯
Maintenance Warranty	N/A	
Roadside Assistance	4 yr/unlim. mi	

Ownership Costs By Year (Projected)

$5,000 $10,000 $15,000 $20,000

■ 1999
■ 2000
■ 2001
□ 2002
□ 2003

Resale Value

1999	2000	2001	2002	2003
$29,382	$26,250	$23,455	$20,729	$17,983

Cumulative Costs

	1999	2000	2001	2002	2003
Annual	$8,497	$7,492	$6,955	$7,091	$8,897
Total	$8,497	$15,989	$22,944	$30,035	$38,932

Projected Costs (5yr)

Relative	This Car
$40,025	$38,932
Cost/Mile 57¢	Cost/Mile 56¢

Ownership Cost Value

◯ Better Than Average

Volvo S70 T5
4 Door Sedan

 **Near Luxury**

 2.3L 236 hp Turbo Gas Fuel Inject.

5 Cylinder In-Line

 Manual 5 Speed

 2 Wheel Front

 Dual Front/Side Airbags Std

Purchase Price

Car Item	Dealer Cost	List
Base Price	**$30,292**	**$33,210**
Anti-Lock Brakes	Std	Std
Automatic 4 Speed	$975	$975
Optional Engine	N/A	N/A
Auto Climate Control	Std	Std
Power Steering	Std	Std
Cruise Control	Std	Std
Power Windows	Std	Std
AM/FM Stereo Cass/CD	Std	Std
Steering Wheel, Tilt	Std	Std
Rear Defroster	Std	Std
***Options Price**	**$975**	**$975**
***Total Price**	**$31,267**	**$34,185**
Target Price	$33,130	
Destination Charge	$575	
Avg. Tax & Fees	$1,878	
Total Target $	**$35,583**	
Average Dealer Option Cost:	**80%**	
12 Month Price Increase:	None	

The S70 T5 sedan has several engineering enhancements this year, including various improvements to the airbag systems. The T5 includes a 20 valve, 236 hp turbo intercooled engine with 243 lb-ft of torque. The engine is available with either a five speed manual or a four speed automatic transmission. The optional T5 Special Value Package upgrades include front fog lamps, a rear spoiler and leather bucket seats. The T5 comes standard with power driver and passenger seats.

Ownership Costs (Projected)

Cost Area	5 Year Cost	Rating
Depreciation	$15,832	○
Financing ($590/month)	$6,921	
Insurance (Performance)	$9,226	○
State Fees	$1,404	
Fuel (Hwy 27 City 20 -Prem.)	$3,745	○
Maintenance	$3,907	●
Repairs	$1,165	○

Warranty/Maintenance Info

Major Tune-Up (60K mile int.)	$250	○
Minor Tune-Up (30K mile int.)	$138	○
Brake Service	$233	○
Overall Warranty	4 yr/50k	○
Drivetrain Warranty	4 yr/50k	○
Rust Warranty	8 yr/unlim. mi	◯
Maintenance Warranty	N/A	
Roadside Assistance	4 yr/unlim. mi	

Ownership Costs By Year (Projected)

$5,000 $10,000 $15,000 $20,000

■ 1999
■ 2000
■ 2001
□ 2002
□ 2003

Resale Value

1999	2000	2001	2002	2003
$33,607	$29,823	$26,406	$23,075	$19,751

Cumulative Costs

	1999	2000	2001	2002	2003
Annual	$7,224	$8,632	$8,039	$8,431	$9,873
Total	$7,224	$15,856	$23,895	$32,326	$42,199

Projected Costs (5yr)

Relative	This Car
$41,739	$42,199
Cost/Mile 60¢	Cost/Mile 60¢

Ownership Cost Value

○ Average

198

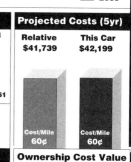

* Includes shaded options
** Other purchase requirements apply
*** Price includes other options

 ● Poor
 ◉ Worse Than Average
 ○ Average
 ◯ Better Than Average
 ◯ Excellent
 ⊖ Insufficient Information

Refer to *Section 3: Annotated Vehicle Charts* for an explanation of these charts.

Volvo S70 AWD
4 Door Sedan

Near Luxury

2.4L 190 hp Turbo Gas Fuel Inject.	5 Cylinder In-Line	Automatic 4 Speed	4 Wheel Full-Time	Dual Front/Side Airbags Std

Purchase Price

Car Item	Dealer Cost	List
Base Price	**$30,855**	**$33,520**
Anti-Lock Brakes	Std	Std
Manual Transmission	N/A	N/A
Optional Engine	N/A	N/A
Auto Climate Control	Std	Std
Power Steering	Std	Std
Cruise Control	Std	Std
Power Windows	Std	Std
AM/FM Stereo Cassette	Std	Std
Steering Wheel, Tilt	Std	Std
Rear Defroster	Std	Std
*Options Price	$0	$0
*Total Price	**$30,855**	**$33,520**
Target Price	$32,574	
Destination Charge	$575	
Avg. Tax & Fees	$1,846	
Total Target $	**$34,995**	
Average Dealer Option Cost:	**80%**	
12 Month Price Increase:	N/A	

New for the 1999 model year is the S70 AWD sedan. The S70 AWD is equipped with full-time all-wheel drive as well as traction control, headlamp wiper/washers and heated front seats. The full-time all-wheel drive system provides almost instantaneous traction selection. Other standard features include antilock brakes, keyless remote entry system, dual-zone automatic climate control and heated side mirrors. The optional AWD Special Value Package includes interior wood trim and leather bucket seats.

Ownership Costs (Projected)

Cost Area	5 Year Cost	Rating
Depreciation	$16,003	◐
Financing ($580/month)	$6,808	
Insurance	$7,837	○
State Fees	$1,378	
Fuel (Hwy 27 City 20 -Prem.)	$3,745	◐
Maintenance	$4,602	●
Repairs	$1,165	◐

Warranty/Maintenance Info

Major Tune-Up (60K mile int.)	$250	◐
Minor Tune-Up (30K mile int.)	$138	◐
Brake Service	$231	◐
Overall Warranty	4 yr/50k	◐
Drivetrain Warranty	4 yr/50k	◐
Rust Warranty	8 yr/unlim. mi	○
Maintenance Warranty	N/A	
Roadside Assistance	4 yr/unlim. mi	

Ownership Costs By Year (Projected)

$5,000 $10,000 $15,000 $20,000

■ 1999
■ 2000
■ 2001
□ 2002
□ 2003

Resale Value

1999	2000	2001	2002	2003
$32,869	$29,085	$25,665	$22,327	$18,992

Projected Costs (5yr)

Relative	This Car
$41,364	$41,538
Cost/Mile 59¢	Cost/Mile 59¢

Cumulative Costs

	1999	2000	2001	2002	2003
Annual	$7,062	$8,324	$7,737	$8,134	$10,281
Total	$7,062	$15,386	$23,123	$31,257	$41,538

Ownership Cost Value

◐ Average

Volvo S80 2.9
4 Door Sedan

Near Luxury

2.9L 201 hp Gas Fuel Inject.	6 Cylinder In-Line	Automatic 4 Speed	2 Wheel Front	Dual Front/Side Airbags Std

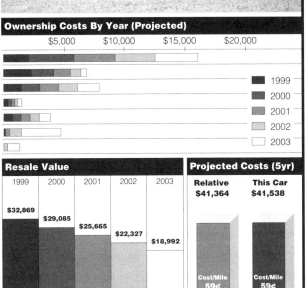

Purchase Price

Car Item	Dealer Cost	List
Base Price	**$32,520**	**$35,820**
Anti-Lock Brakes	Std	Std
Manual Transmission	N/A	N/A
Optional Engine	N/A	N/A
Auto Climate Control	Std	Std
Power Steering	Std	Std
Cruise Control	Std	Std
Power Windows	Std	Std
AM/FM Stereo Cass/CD	Std	Std
Steering Wheel, Tilt	Std	Std
Rear Defroster	Std	Std
*Options Price	$0	$0
*Total Price	**$32,520**	**$35,820**
Target Price	$34,679	
Destination Charge	$575	
Avg. Tax & Fees	$1,963	
Total Target $	**$37,217**	
Average Dealer Option Cost:	**80%**	
12 Month Price Increase:	4%	

For 1999, the S80 2.9 sedan is introduced. It is the first model built on the new large Volvo platform. The S80 2.9 has front wheel drive and sports a transverse-mounted inline six cylinder engine. Safety features include an airbag curtain for the front seats and Whiplash Protection System (WHIPS). Additional standard features include dual-zone climate control, stability and traction control (STC) and a theft deterrent system. Leather seating surfaces and a power moonroof are available.

Ownership Costs (Projected)

Cost Area	5 Year Cost	Rating
Depreciation	$16,159	○
Financing ($617/month)	$7,241	
Insurance	$9,775	○
State Fees	$1,469	
Fuel (Hwy 27 City 19 -Prem.)	$3,838	○
Maintenance	$5,322	●
Repairs	$980	○

Warranty/Maintenance Info

Major Tune-Up (60K mile int.)	$274	○
Minor Tune-Up (30K mile int.)	$221	●
Brake Service	$227	○
Overall Warranty	4 yr/50k	○
Drivetrain Warranty	4 yr/50k	○
Rust Warranty	8 yr/unlim. mi	○
Maintenance Warranty	N/A	
Roadside Assistance	4 yr/unlim. mi	

Ownership Costs By Year (Projected)

$5,000 $10,000 $15,000 $20,000

■ 1999
■ 2000
■ 2001
□ 2002
□ 2003

Resale Value

1999	2000	2001	2002	2003
$33,988	$30,424	$27,231	$24,138	$21,058

Projected Costs (5yr)

Relative	This Car
$42,954	$44,784
Cost/Mile 61¢	Cost/Mile 64¢

Cumulative Costs

	1999	2000	2001	2002	2003
Annual	$8,723	$8,641	$8,366	$8,090	$10,964
Total	$8,723	$17,364	$25,730	$33,820	$44,784

Ownership Cost Value

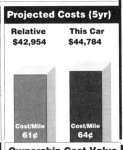

Worse Than Average

---

* Includes shaded options

** Other purchase requirements apply

*** Price includes other options

● Poor   ◑ Worse Than Average   ◐ Average   ◔ Better Than Average   ○ Excellent   ⊖ Insufficient Information

Refer to *Section 3: Annotated Vehicle Charts* for an explanation of these charts.

199

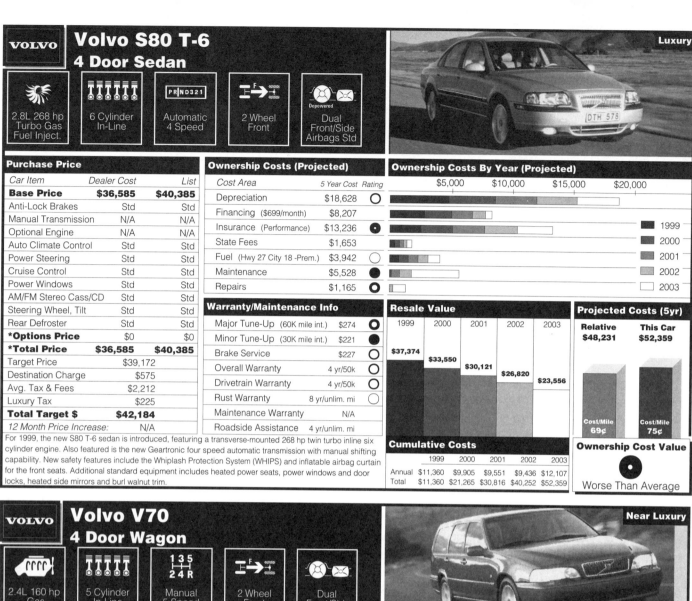

Volvo S80 T-6
4 Door Sedan
Luxury

2.8L 268 hp Turbo Gas Fuel Inject.	6 Cylinder In-Line
Automatic 4 Speed	2 Wheel Front
Dual Front/Side Airbags Std	

Purchase Price

Car Item	Dealer Cost	List
Base Price	**$36,585**	**$40,385**
Anti-Lock Brakes	Std	Std
Manual Transmission	N/A	N/A
Optional Engine	N/A	N/A
Auto Climate Control	Std	Std
Power Steering	Std	Std
Cruise Control	Std	Std
Power Windows	Std	Std
AM/FM Stereo Cass/CD	Std	Std
Steering Wheel, Tilt	Std	Std
Rear Defroster	Std	Std
*Options Price	$0	$0
*Total Price	**$36,585**	**$40,385**
Target Price	$39,172	
Destination Charge	$575	
Avg. Tax & Fees	$2,212	
Luxury Tax	$225	
Total Target $	**$42,184**	
12 Month Price Increase:	N/A	

Ownership Costs (Projected)

Cost Area	5 Year Cost	Rating
Depreciation	$18,628	◯
Financing ($699/month)	$8,207	
Insurance (Performance)	$13,236	◉
State Fees	$1,653	
Fuel (Hwy 27 City 18 -Prem.)	$3,942	◯
Maintenance	$5,528	●
Repairs	$1,165	◯

Warranty/Maintenance Info

Major Tune-Up (60K mile int.)	$274	◯
Minor Tune-Up (30K mile int.)	$221	●
Brake Service	$227	◯
Overall Warranty	4 yr/50k	◯
Drivetrain Warranty	4 yr/50k	◯
Rust Warranty	8 yr/unlim. mi	◯
Maintenance Warranty	N/A	
Roadside Assistance	4 yr/unlim. mi	

Ownership Costs By Year (Projected)

$5,000 — $10,000 — $15,000 — $20,000

■ 1999 ■ 2000 ■ 2001 ■ 2002 □ 2003

Resale Value

1999	2000	2001	2002	2003
$37,374	$33,550	$30,121	$26,820	$23,556

Cumulative Costs

	1999	2000	2001	2002	2003
Annual	$11,360	$9,905	$9,551	$9,436	$12,107
Total	$11,360	$21,265	$30,816	$40,252	$52,359

Projected Costs (5yr)

Relative	This Car
$48,231	$52,359
Cost/Mile 69¢	Cost/Mile 75¢

Ownership Cost Value
◉ Worse Than Average

For 1999, the new S80 T-6 sedan is introduced, featuring a transverse-mounted 268 hp twin turbo inline six cylinder engine. Also featured is the new Geartronic four speed automatic transmission with manual shifting capability. New safety features include the Whiplash Protection System (WHIPS) and inflatable airbag curtain for the front seats. Additional standard equipment includes heated power seats, power windows and door locks, heated side mirrors and burl walnut trim.

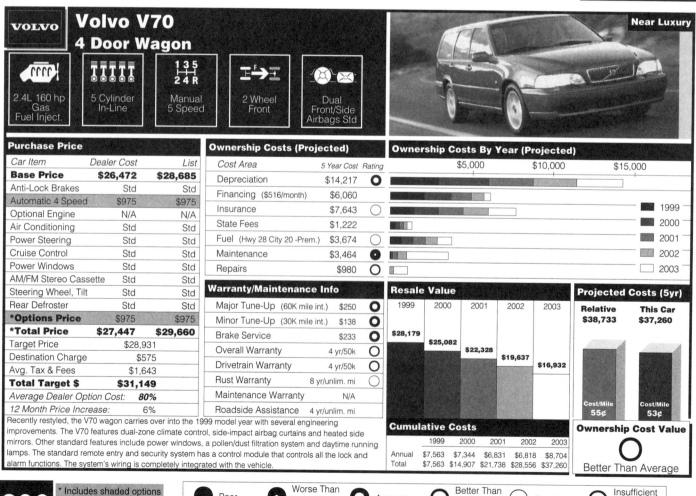

Volvo V70
4 Door Wagon
Near Luxury

2.4L 160 hp Gas Fuel Inject.	5 Cylinder In-Line
Manual 5 Speed	2 Wheel Front
Dual Front/Side Airbags Std	

Purchase Price

Car Item	Dealer Cost	List
Base Price	**$26,472**	**$28,685**
Anti-Lock Brakes	Std	Std
Automatic 4 Speed	$975	$975
Optional Engine	N/A	N/A
Air Conditioning	Std	Std
Power Steering	Std	Std
Cruise Control	Std	Std
Power Windows	Std	Std
AM/FM Stereo Cassette	Std	Std
Steering Wheel, Tilt	Std	Std
Rear Defroster	Std	Std
*Options Price	$975	$975
*Total Price	**$27,447**	**$29,660**
Target Price	$28,931	
Destination Charge	$575	
Avg. Tax & Fees	$1,643	
Total Target $	**$31,149**	
Average Dealer Option Cost:	**80%**	
12 Month Price Increase:	6%	

Ownership Costs (Projected)

Cost Area	5 Year Cost	Rating
Depreciation	$14,217	◯
Financing ($516/month)	$6,060	
Insurance	$7,643	◯
State Fees	$1,222	
Fuel (Hwy 28 City 20 -Prem.)	$3,674	◯
Maintenance	$3,464	◉
Repairs	$980	◯

Warranty/Maintenance Info

Major Tune-Up (60K mile int.)	$250	◯
Minor Tune-Up (30K mile int.)	$138	◯
Brake Service	$233	◯
Overall Warranty	4 yr/50k	◯
Drivetrain Warranty	4 yr/50k	◯
Rust Warranty	8 yr/unlim. mi	◯
Maintenance Warranty	N/A	
Roadside Assistance	4 yr/unlim. mi	

Ownership Costs By Year (Projected)

$5,000 — $10,000 — $15,000

■ 1999 ■ 2000 ■ 2001 ■ 2002 □ 2003

Resale Value

1999	2000	2001	2002	2003
$28,179	$25,082	$22,328	$19,637	$16,932

Cumulative Costs

	1999	2000	2001	2002	2003
Annual	$7,563	$7,344	$6,831	$6,818	$8,704
Total	$7,563	$14,907	$21,738	$28,556	$37,260

Projected Costs (5yr)

Relative	This Car
$38,733	$37,260
Cost/Mile 55¢	Cost/Mile 53¢

Ownership Cost Value
◯ Better Than Average

Recently restyled, the V70 wagon carries over into the 1999 model year with several engineering improvements. The V70 features dual-zone climate control, side-impact airbag curtains and heated side mirrors. Other standard features include power windows, a pollen/dust filtration system and daytime running lamps. The standard remote entry and security system has a control module that controls all the lock and alarm functions. The system's wiring is completely integrated with the vehicle.

Volvo V70 GLT
4 Door Wagon

 2.4L 190 hp Turbo Gas Fuel Inject. | 5 Cylinder In-Line | PR**ND**321 Automatic 4 Speed | 2 Wheel Front | Dual Front/Side Airbags Std

Near Luxury

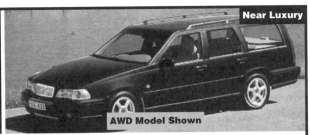

AWD Model Shown

Purchase Price

Car Item	Dealer Cost	List
Base Price	**$30,569**	**$32,940**
Anti-Lock Brakes	Std	Std
Manual Transmission	N/A	N/A
Optional Engine	N/A	N/A
Auto Climate Control	Std	Std
Power Steering	Std	Std
Cruise Control	Std	Std
Power Windows	Std	Std
AM/FM Stereo Cassette	Std	Std
Steering Wheel, Tilt	Std	Std
Rear Defroster	Std	Std
*Options Price	$0	$0
*Total Price	**$30,569**	**$32,940**
Target Price	$32,127	
Destination Charge	$575	
Avg. Tax & Fees	$1,820	
Total Target $	**$34,522**	
Average Dealer Option Cost:	**80%**	
12 Month Price Increase:	None	

Ownership Costs (Projected)

Cost Area	5 Year Cost	Rating
Depreciation	$15,680	◐
Financing ($572/month)	$6,717	
Insurance	$7,688	◔
State Fees	$1,354	
Fuel (Hwy 27 City 20 -Prem.)	$3,745	○
Maintenance	$3,594	⦿
Repairs	$1,165	○

Warranty/Maintenance Info

Major Tune-Up (60K mile int.)	$250	○
Minor Tune-Up (30K mile int.)	$138	○
Brake Service	$233	○
Overall Warranty	4 yr/50k	○
Drivetrain Warranty	4 yr/50k	○
Rust Warranty	8 yr/unlim. mi	○
Maintenance Warranty	N/A	
Roadside Assistance	4 yr/unlim. mi	

Ownership Costs By Year (Projected)

$5,000 $10,000 $15,000 $20,000

■ 1999
■ 2000
■ 2001
□ 2002
□ 2003

Resale Value

1999	2000	2001	2002	2003
$30,788	$27,503	$24,571	$21,709	$18,842

Cumulative Costs

	1999	2000	2001	2002	2003
Annual	$8,605	$7,766	$7,195	$7,300	$9,077
Total	$8,605	$16,371	$23,566	$30,866	$39,943

Projected Costs (5yr)

Relative	This Car
$41,111	$39,943
Cost/Mile 59¢	Cost/Mile 57¢

Ownership Cost Value
○ Better Than Average

Recently restyled, the V70 GLT wagon carries over into the 1999 model year with many engineering enhancements. An eight-way power driver's seat, automatic climate control and 15 inch alloy wheels are standard, as are power trunk and fuel door openers. There is a Special Value Package available on the GLT, which includes such features as leather seating surfaces, a power moonroof and burl walnut wood trim. The Cold Weather Package includes heated seats and headlamp wiper/washers.

Volvo V70 T5
4 Door Wagon

 2.3L 236 hp Turbo Gas Fuel Inject. | 5 Cylinder In-Line | 1 3 5 / 2 4 R Manual 5 Speed | 2 Wheel Front | Dual Front/Side Airbags Std

Near Luxury

XC AWD Model Shown

Purchase Price

Car Item	Dealer Cost	List
Base Price	**$31,605**	**$34,510**
Anti-Lock Brakes	Std	Std
Automatic 4 Speed	$975	$975
Optional Engine	N/A	N/A
Auto Climate Control	Std	Std
Power Steering	Std	Std
Cruise Control	Std	Std
Power Windows	Std	Std
AM/FM Stereo Cass/CD	Std	Std
Steering Wheel, Tilt	Std	Std
Rear Defroster	Std	Std
*Options Price	$975	$975
*Total Price	**$32,580**	**$35,485**
Target Price	$34,539	
Destination Charge	$575	
Avg. Tax & Fees	$1,954	
Total Target $	**$37,068**	
Average Dealer Option Cost:	**80%**	
12 Month Price Increase:	None	

Ownership Costs (Projected)

Cost Area	5 Year Cost	Rating
Depreciation	$16,409	○
Financing ($614/month)	$7,211	
Insurance (Performance)	$9,463	○
State Fees	$1,455	
Fuel (Hwy 27 City 20 -Prem.)	$3,745	○
Maintenance	$3,765	●
Repairs	$1,165	○

Warranty/Maintenance Info

Major Tune-Up (60K mile int.)	$250	○
Minor Tune-Up (30K mile int.)	$138	○
Brake Service	$233	○
Overall Warranty	4 yr/50k	○
Drivetrain Warranty	4 yr/50k	○
Rust Warranty	8 yr/unlim. mi	○
Maintenance Warranty	N/A	
Roadside Assistance	4 yr/unlim. mi	

Ownership Costs By Year (Projected)

$5,000 $10,000 $15,000 $20,000

■ 1999
■ 2000
■ 2001
□ 2002
□ 2003

Resale Value

1999	2000	2001	2002	2003
$34,559	$30,759	$27,327	$23,988	$20,659

Cumulative Costs

	1999	2000	2001	2002	2003
Annual	$7,912	$8,787	$8,171	$8,394	$9,949
Total	$7,912	$16,699	$24,870	$33,264	$43,213

Projected Costs (5yr)

Relative	This Car
$43,015	$43,213
Cost/Mile 61¢	Cost/Mile 62¢

Ownership Cost Value
○ Average

The V70 T5 wagon has several engineering enhancements this year, including various improvements to the airbag systems. The T5 includes a 20 valve, 236 hp turbo intercooled engine with 243 lb-ft of torque. The engine is available with either a five speed manual or four speed adaptive-shifting automatic transmission. Dual power front seats, a remote keyless entry system and automatic climate control are standard, as are an AM/FM/cassette/CD stereo system and trip computer.

● Poor ◐ Worse Than Average ◑ Average ○ Better Than Average ○ Excellent ⊖ Insufficient Information

Refer to *Section 3: Annotated Vehicle Charts* for an explanation of these charts.

Volvo V70 AWD
4 Door Wagon

Near Luxury

 2.4L 190 hp Turbo Gas Fuel Inject.
 5 Cylinder In-Line
 PRND321 Automatic 4 Speed
 4WD 4 Wheel Full-Time
 Dual Front/Side Airbags Std

Purchase Price

Car Item	Dealer Cost	List
Base Price	**$32,168**	**$34,820**
Anti-Lock Brakes	Std	Std
Manual Transmission	N/A	N/A
Optional Engine	N/A	N/A
Auto Climate Control	Std	Std
Power Steering	Std	Std
Cruise Control	Std	Std
Power Windows	Std	Std
AM/FM Stereo Cassette	Std	Std
Steering Wheel, Tilt	Std	Std
Rear Defroster	Std	Std
*Options Price	$0	$0
*Total Price	$32,168	$34,820
Target Price	$33,871	
Destination Charge	$575	
Avg. Tax & Fees	$1,917	
Total Target $	**$36,363**	
Average Dealer Option Cost:	80%	
12 Month Price Increase:	1%	

Ownership Costs (Projected)

Cost Area	5 Year Cost	Rating
Depreciation	$16,621	◎
Financing ($603/month)	$7,073	
Insurance	$7,886	○
State Fees	$1,429	
Fuel (Hwy 25 City 18 -Prem.)	$4,099	◉
Maintenance	$4,203	●
Repairs	$1,385	◎

Warranty/Maintenance Info

Major Tune-Up (60K mile int.)	$250	◎
Minor Tune-Up (30K mile int.)	$138	◎
Brake Service	$231	◎
Overall Warranty	4 yr/50k	○
Drivetrain Warranty	4 yr/50k	○
Rust Warranty	8 yr/unlim. mi	◔
Maintenance Warranty	N/A	
Roadside Assistance	4 yr/unlim. mi	

The V70 AWD wagon is fitted with a 190 hp five cylinder engine with a light-pressure turbocharger. It is available only with an adaptive-shifting automatic transmission. The full-time all-wheel drive system provides almost instantaneous traction selection. The V70 AWD rides on all-season tires mounted on five spoke alloy wheels. Velour upholstery and heated front seats are standard, along with a remote keyless entry/security system and heated power side mirrors.

Ownership Costs By Year (Projected)

Legend: 1999, 2000, 2001, 2002, 2003

Resale Value

1999	2000	2001	2002	2003
$33,043	$29,395	$26,111	$22,923	$19,742

Projected Costs (5yr)

Relative	This Car
$42,601	$42,696
Cost/Mile 61¢	Cost/Mile 61¢

Cumulative Costs

	1999	2000	2001	2002	2003
Annual	$8,436	$8,352	$7,744	$7,766	$10,398
Total	$8,436	$16,788	$24,532	$32,298	$42,696

Ownership Cost Value

◎ Average

Volvo V70 XC AWD
4 Door Wagon

Near Luxury

 2.4L 190 hp Turbo Gas Fuel Inject.
 5 Cylinder In-Line
 PRND321 Automatic 4 Speed
 4WD 4 Wheel Full-Time
 Dual Front/Side Airbags Std

Purchase Price

Car Item	Dealer Cost	List
Base Price	**$33,105**	**$35,995**
Anti-Lock Brakes	Std	Std
Manual Transmission	N/A	N/A
Optional Engine	N/A	N/A
Auto Climate Control	Std	Std
Power Steering	Std	Std
Cruise Control	Std	Std
Power Windows	Std	Std
AM/FM Stereo Cassette	Std	Std
Steering Wheel, Tilt	Std	Std
Rear Defroster	Std	Std
*Options Price	$0	$0
*Total Price	$33,105	$35,995
Target Price	$35,131	
Destination Charge	$575	
Avg. Tax & Fees	$1,986	
Total Target $	**$37,692**	
Average Dealer Option Cost:	80%	
12 Month Price Increase:	None	

Ownership Costs (Projected)

Cost Area	5 Year Cost	Rating
Depreciation	$17,212	◎
Financing ($625/month)	$7,333	
Insurance	$7,886	○
State Fees	$1,476	
Fuel (Hwy 25 City 18 -Prem.)	$4,099	◉
Maintenance	$4,259	●
Repairs	$1,385	◎

Warranty/Maintenance Info

Major Tune-Up (60K mile int.)	$250	◎
Minor Tune-Up (30K mile int.)	$138	◎
Brake Service	$231	◎
Overall Warranty	4 yr/50k	○
Drivetrain Warranty	4 yr/50k	○
Rust Warranty	8 yr/unlim. mi	◔
Maintenance Warranty	N/A	
Roadside Assistance	4 yr/unlim. mi	

The V70 XC AWD comes with a 190 hp five cylinder engine coupled with an adaptive-shifting automatic transmission. The XC sports 205/65R15 Continental Touring all-season tires, and has up to two more inches of ground clearance compared to other AWD V70s. It is equipped with leather/twill cloth interior upholstery. Standard equipment includes a power glass sunroof, electrically adjustable front driver and passenger seats with three memory settings and heated front seats and outside mirrors.

Ownership Costs By Year (Projected)

Legend: 1999, 2000, 2001, 2002, 2003

Resale Value

1999	2000	2001	2002	2003
$35,006	$31,045	$27,456	$23,961	$20,480

Projected Costs (5yr)

Relative	This Car
$43,560	$43,650
Cost/Mile 62¢	Cost/Mile 62¢

Cumulative Costs

	1999	2000	2001	2002	2003
Annual	$7,902	$8,747	$8,113	$8,171	$10,717
Total	$7,902	$16,649	$24,762	$32,933	$43,650

Ownership Cost Value

○ Average

202

* Includes shaded options
** Other purchase requirements apply
*** Price includes other options

 ● Poor
 ◉ Worse Than Average
 ◎ Average
 ○ Better Than Average
○ Excellent
⊖ Insufficient Information

Refer to Section 3: Annotated Vehicle Charts for an explanation of these charts.

Volvo V70 R AWD
4 Door Wagon

Near Luxury

- 2.3L 247 hp Turbo Gas Fuel Inject.
- 5 Cylinder In-Line
- PRND321 Automatic 4 Speed
- 4 Wheel Full-Time
- Dual Front/Side Airbags Std

Purchase Price

Car Item	Dealer Cost	List
Base Price	**$37,309**	**$41,395**
Anti-Lock Brakes	Std	Std
Manual Transmission	N/A	N/A
Optional Engine	N/A	N/A
Auto Climate Control	Std	Std
Power Steering	Std	Std
Cruise Control	Std	Std
Power Windows	Std	Std
AM/FM Stereo Cass/CD	Std	Std
Steering Wheel, Tilt	Std	Std
Rear Defroster	Std	Std
***Options Price**	**$0**	**$0**
***Total Price**	**$37,309**	**$41,395**
Target Price	$39,866	
Destination Charge	$575	
Avg. Tax & Fees	$2,253	
Luxury Tax	$266	
Total Target $	**$42,960**	
12 Month Price Increase:	1%	

The V70 R AWD wagon is equipped with a high-pressure turbocharged engine that produces 236 hp and 243 lb-ft of torque. It is fitted with high-performance Michelin 205/55R16 all-season tires on special 16 inch alloy wheels. Special interior treatment includes unique patterned alloy dash trim, diamond patterned seating surfaces and a 200 watt eight speaker audio system with an in-dash CD changer, AM/FM stereo and cassette. Other standard equipment includes a tilt and fold front passenger seat.

Ownership Costs (Projected)

Cost Area	5 Year Cost	Rating
Depreciation	$19,205	◐
Financing ($712/month)	$8,357	
Insurance (Performance)	$9,712	○
State Fees	$1,693	
Fuel (Hwy 25 City 18 -Prem.)	$4,099	◉
Maintenance	$4,383	●
Repairs	$1,385	○

Warranty/Maintenance Info

Major Tune-Up (60K mile int.)	$250	○
Minor Tune-Up (30K mile int.)	$138	○
Brake Service	$231	○
Overall Warranty	4 yr/50k	○
Drivetrain Warranty	4 yr/50k	○
Rust Warranty	8 yr/unlim. mi	○
Maintenance Warranty	N/A	
Roadside Assistance	4 yr/unlim. mi	

Ownership Costs By Year (Projected)

Scale: $5,000 $10,000 $15,000 $20,000

- ■ 1999
- ■ 2000
- ■ 2001
- ▨ 2002
- ☐ 2003

Resale Value

1999	2000	2001	2002	2003
$38,909	$34,758	$31,000	$27,358	$23,755

Cumulative Costs

	1999	2000	2001	2002	2003
Annual	$10,018	$9,624	$8,902	$8,987	$11,303
Total	$10,018	$19,642	$28,544	$37,531	$48,834

Projected Costs (5yr)

Relative	This Car
$48,642	$48,834
Cost/Mile 69¢	Cost/Mile 70¢

Ownership Cost Value

○ Average

203

SECTION SIX
Appendices

Appendix A

Financing Sources

When you consider a new car loan, it really pays to shop around and compare rates. (The same is also true for leasing!) Commercial banks, savings banks, credit unions, and even auto manufacturers offer a variety of loan terms for new cars. You probably know of a dozen or more local institutions willing to loan you money — but do you know which one has the lowest rate?

The chart below lists for each major metropolitan area the bank that has at one time offered the lowest rate among competitive banks in that area. Keep in mind, however, that rates change frequently, so there is no guarantee that the institution shown below currently offers the lowest rate in your area. While it is wise to consider the institutions listed here, make sure you also get price quotes from other financial institutions.

Average Interest rate, new auto loans (all terms): 8.46% 36 month: 8.36% 48 month: 8.43% 60 month: 8.56%

A Sample of Competitive New Auto Loans in Major Markets Around the Country

Based on a $15,000 loan

City	Institution	Recent rate	Term (months)
New York, NY	Independence Savings	7.50	48
Los Angeles, CA	National Bank Of California	7.95	48
Chicago, IL	First American Bank	7.45	60
Newark, NJ	Valley National Bank	7.49	60
Philadelphia, PA	Prime Bank	7.99	60
Detroit, MI	First State Bank	8.00	60
Washington, DC	Provident Bank of Maryland	7.25	60
Dallas, TX	First State Bank	7.50	60
San Francisco, CA	Bank of The Orient	8.00	60
Houston, TX	Preferred Bank	7.25	60
Miami, FL	Republic Bank	7.75	48
Boston, MA	East Cambridge Savings	7.50	60
Atlanta, GA	First Citizens Bank	7.90	60
San Diego, CA	Downey Savings	8.25	48
Minneapolis, MN	Northeast State Bank	7.50	48
St Louis, MO	UMB Bank	6.99	60
Baltimore, MD	Provident Bank of Maryland	6.99	60
Phoenix, AZ	National Bank of AZ	8.25	60
Tampa, FL	The Bank of Tampa	7.00	60
Seattle, WA	Seafirst Bank	8.24	60
Cleveland, OH	Fifth Third Bank	7.50	60
Denver, CO	Commercial Federal Bank	7.50	60
Milwaukee, WI	Bank One WI	7.75	48
Kansas City, MO	Bank Midwest	7.50	48
Portland, OR	Key Bank of Oregon	8.35	60
Norfolk, VA	First Coastal Bank	7.74	48
San Antonio, TX	Broadway National Bank	7.25	60
Indianapolis, IN	Bank One Indianapolis	7.75	60
New Orleans, LA	Metaire Bank & Trust	7.25	48
Charlotte, NC	Central Carolina Bank	7.25	48
Hartford, CT	American Savings Bank	7.75	48
Albequerque, NM	First State Bank	8.75	60
Salt Lake City, UT	Key Bank of Utah	8.35	48
Birmingham, AL	Colonial Bank	7.95	60
Las Vegas, NV	Citibank	8.00	60
Little Rock, AR	Regions Bank	7.75	60
Des Moines, IA	Mercantile Bank	8.35	48
Omaha, NE	First Fed Lincoln Bank	7.74	60
Providence, RI	Centreville Savings	7.50	48
Oklahoma City, OK	Bank of Oklahoma	8.50	60

Notes and sources: Loan rates from HSH Associates., 1200 Route 23 Butler N.J. 07405; WWW.HSH.COM 973-838-3330

Loan rates and averages are as of January 15, 1999, and are subject to change without notice.

Appendix B   Insurance Companies

Insurance is one of the largest of the seven ownership cost areas discussed throughout this book. If you live in a non-competitive insurance state (such as Massachusetts) then the rates are controlled by an insurance commission or rating bureau, and all insurers are required to charge the same premium. However, in all other states the rates are determined by each insurance company and may vary dramatically from one company to the next. Therefore, if you live in a competitive insurance state, it really pays to shop for the lowest rates.

The ten insurance companies listed below are the largest private passenger car insurers in the United States. To ensure that you are getting the most competitive rate, obtain quotes from several of the companies listed here, and compare them to smaller companies or independent agents. You can find a listing of insurance agents in your area by looking in the yellow pages under "Insurance." To help you make a side-by-side evaluation of different insurers, use the Insurance Comparison Worksheet on page 11A.

Although there are many differences between insurance companies, one thing you should seriously evaluate is the company's reputation when it comes to processing claims. Before you buy, it makes sense to check with a few local repair or body shops to find out which insurers have the best and the worst reputation. Also, you may want to check with the Council of Better Business Bureaus (Appendix D on page 120A).

The following is a listing of the top 10 auto insurers:

Allstate Insurance
2775 Sanders Road
Northbrook, IL 60062
(847) 402-5000

Farmers Insurance
4680 Wilshire Boulevard
Los Angeles, CA 90010
(213) 932-3200

Geico Corporation Insurance
One GEICO Plaza
Washington, D.C. 20076-001
(800) 841-1579

The Hartford
Hartford Plaza
690 Asylum Avenue
Hartford, CT 06115
(860) 547-5000

Progressive Insurance
6300 Wilson Mills Road
Mayfield Village, OH 44141-2182
(800) 888-7764

Liberty Mutual Insurance
175 Berkeley Street
Boston, MA 02117
(617) 357-9500

Nationwide Insurance
One Nationwide Plaza
Nationwide Enterprise
Columbus, OH 43215-2220
(800) 882-2822

State Farm Insurance
One State Farm Plaza
Bloomington, IL 61710
(309) 766-2311

Travelers Insurance
One Tower Square
Hartford, CT 06183
(800) 832 6842

USAA Insurance
USAA Building
9800 Fredericksburg Road
San Antonio, TX 78288
(800) 531-8100

Appendix C   Service Contract Locator

If you decide to purchase an Extended Service Contract, your choices may be limited. In most cases, the dealer will offer you a contract that is backed by the manufacturer. He may also offer a contract from an independent provider.

You probably won't choose a dealer based on the Extended Service Contract he sells. However, if you are considering an Extended Service Contract that is offered by a provider other than the manufacturer, you may wish to learn more about that company's reputation. One source for this information is the Council of Better Business Bureaus (Appendix D on page 120A). Also, you can directly contact the contract provider.

The following is a listing of the major independent Service Contract providers, and the insurance company that underwrites their policies:

GE Capital
Insurance Services Group
P.O. Box 140159
Denver, CO 80214-0159
(800) 521-4053

Backed by: Heritage Insurance
Other Info: In national service contract business approximately 10 years

Western General Insurance Co
16501 Ventura Blvd.
Suite 200
Encino, CA 91436
(818) 990-9590
(800) 242-9442

Backed by: Fireman's Fund/Western General Insurance Company
Other Info: In national service contract business approximately 9 years

JM&A Group
Fidelity Warranty Services
100 N.W. 12th Avenue
Deerfield Beach, FL 33442
(954) 429-2333

Backed by: Virginia Surety Company, Inc.
Other Info: In national service contract business approximately 21 years. Available in 45 states.

Resource Dealer Group
2550 West Golf Road, Suite 600
Rolling Meadows, IL 60008
(847) 357-2000

Backed by: Virginia Surety Company, Inc.
Other Info: In national service contract business approximately 22 years

Western National Warranty
Service Center
P.O. Box 2840
Scottsdale, AZ 85252-2840
(800) 345-0191

Backed by: Continental Insurance Company
Other Info: In national service contract business approximately 16 years

Appendix D Better Business Bureau Locations

Acquiring a new car usually involves many more business transactions than just the car deal! You will need insurance and financing, and may deal with an extended service contract administrator. After your purchase, you'll require the services of many more businesses , service stations, automobile clubs, car washes, and repair shops. The Council of Better Business Bureaus (BBB) can help satisfy your overall purchase and ownership experiences by providing related businesses services that are credible, honest, and deliver good value.

While it is still up to you to choose your service provider, the BBB does keep a log of complaints registered against businesses in your community. You can consult this log to help determine which businesses you'd rather not associate with. To refer you to the BBB office in your community, the following list of BBB Offices offer information and referrals for local and non-local business to help serve you.

UNITED STATES BUREAUS

ALABAMA

CENTRAL ALABAMA & WIREGRASS AREA
P.O. Box 55268
Birmingham, Al 35255-5268   Phone:(205) 558-2222
http://www.birmingham-al.bbb.org   Fax: (205) 558-2239

NORTHERN ALABAMA
P.O. Box 383
Huntsville, Al 35804-0383   Phone: (205) 533-1640
http://www.northalabama.bbb.org/   Fax: (205) 533-1177

SOUTHERN ALABAMA
100 North Royal Street
Mobile AL, 36602-3295   Phone: (334) 433-5494
http://www.mobile.bbb.org   Fax: (334) 438-3191

EAST ALABAMA, WEST GEORGIA
208 13th Street
Columbus, GA 31901   Phone: (706) 324-0712
http://www.columbus-ga.bbb.org   Fax: (706) 324-2181

ALASKA

BBB OF ALASKA, INC. (MAIN OFFICE)
2805 Bering Street, Suite 5
Anchorage, AK 99503-3819   Phone: (907)562-0704
http://www.alaska.bbb.org   Fax: (907) 562-4061

FAIRBANKS BRANCH
P.O. Box 74675
Fairbanks, AK 99707   Phone: (907) 451-0222
http://www.alaska.bbb.org   Fax: (907) 451-0228

KENAI BRANCH
P.O. Box 1229
Kenai, AK 99611   Phone: (907) 283-4880
http://www.kenai.net/bbbk   Fax: (907) 283-9486

ARIZONA

**CENTRAL, NORTHEAST, NORTHWEST,
& SOUTH WEST ARIZONA**
4428 North 12th Street
Phoenix, AZ 85014-4585   Phone: (602) 264-1721
http://www.phoenix.bbb.org   Fax: (602) 263-0997

**PIMA, COCHISE, SANTA CRUZ, GRAHAM
& GREENLEE COUNTIES**
3620 N. 1st Avenue, Suite 136
Tucson, AZ 85719   Phone: (520) 888-5353
http://www.tucson.bbb.org   Fax: (520) 888-6262

ARKANSAS

WEST TENNESSEE/NORTH MISSISSIPPI & EASTERN ARKANSAS
6525 Quail Hollow, Suite 410
Memphis, TN 38120   Phone: (901) 759-1300
http://www.memphis.bbb.org   Fax: (901) 757-2997

ARKANSAS
1415 South University
Little Rock, AR 72204-2605   Phone: (501) 664-7274
http://www.arkansas.bbb.org   Fax: (501) 664-0024

THE ARK-LA-TEX
3612 Youree Drive
Shreveport, LA 71105-2122   Phone: (318) 868-5146
http://www.shreveport.bbb.org Fax: (318) 861-6426

CALIFORNIA

KERN, INYO, KINGS AND SOUTH TULARE COUNTIES
705 Eighteenth Street
Bakersfield, CA 93301-4882   Phone: (805) 322-2074
http://www.bakersfield.bbb.org Fax: (805) 322-8318

CENTRAL CALIFORNIA
2519 W Shaw Suite 106
Fresno, CA 93711   Phone: (209) 222-8111
http://www.cencal.bbb.org   Fax: (209) 228-6518

OAKLAND/SAN FRANCISCO AREA & NORTHWEST COASTAL CALIFORNIA
510 16th Street, Suite 550
Oakland, CA 94612-1584   Phone: (510) 238-1000
http://www.oakland.bbb.org   Fax: (510) 238-1018

BBB OF SAN FRANCISCO (BRANCH OF OAKLAND)
114 Sansome Street, Suite 1108
San Francisco, CA 94104   Phone: (415) 243-9999
http://www.oakland.bbb.org   Fax: (415) 291-8172

NORTHERN NEVADA
991 Bible Way
Reno, NV 89502   Phone: (702) 322-0657
http://www.reno.bbb.org   Fax: (702) 322-8163

NORTH CENTRAL CALIFORNIA
400 S. Street
Sacramento, CA   Phone: (916) 443-6843
http://www.sacramento.bbb.org Fax: (916) 443-0376

LOS ANGELES, ORANGE, RIVERSIDE AND SAN BERNADINO COUNTIES
315 N. La Cadena
P.O. Box 970   Phone: (900) 225-5222
Colton, CA 90324-3052   (909) 426-0183
http://www.la.bbb.org   Fax: (909) 825-6246

ENCINO (BRANCH OF COLTON)
17609 Ventura Blvd., Suite LL03
Encino, CA 91316   Phone: (818) 386-5510
http://www.la.bbb.org   Fax: (818) 386-5513

CITY OF LOS ANGELES (BRANCH OF COLTON)
3727 West Sixth Street, Suite 607
Los Angeles, CA 90020   Phone: (900) 225-5222
http://www.la.bbb.org   (909) 426-0183

CITY OF TORRANCE (BRANCH OF COLTON)
20280 S. Vermont Ave. , Suite 201
Torrance, CA 90502   Phone: (900) 225-5222
http://www.la.bbb.org   (909) 426-0813
                               Fax: (310) 771-1446

PLACENTIA (BRANCH OF COLTON)
550 W. Orangethorpe Ave.
Placentia CA 92870-6837   Phone: (714) 985-8922
http://www.la.bbb.org   Fax: (714) 985-8920

SAN DIEGO AND IMPERIAL COUNTIES
5050 Murphy Canyon, Suite 110
San Diego, CA 92123   Phone: (619) 496-2131
http://www.sandiego.bbb.org/   Fax: (619) 496-2141

SANTA CLARA VALLEY
2100 Forest Ave, Suite 110
San Jose CA 95128   Phone: (408) 278-7400
http://www.sanjose.bbb.org   Fax: (408) 278-7444

SAN MATEO COUNTY
510 Broadway, Suite 200
Millbrae, CA 94030-1966   Phone: (650) 552-9222
http://www.sanmateo.bbb.org   Fax: (650) 652-1748

TRI COUNTIES—SAN LUIS OBISPO, SANTA BARBARA, & VENTURA COUNTIES
P. O. Box 129
Santa Barbara, CA 93101   Phone: (805) 963-8657
http://www.santabarbara.bbb.org Fax: (805) 962-8557

MID COUNTIES
11 S. San Joaquin St., Suite 803
Stockton, CA 95202-3202   Phone: (209) 948-4880
http://www.stockton.bbb.org   Fax: (209) 465-6302

Appendix D *continued*

Better Business Bureau Locations

COLORADO

PIKE'S PEAK REGION
P.O. Box 7970
Colorado Springs, CO 80933-7970
http://www.coloradosprings.bbb.org/
Phone: (719) 636-1155
Fax: (719) 636-5078

SOUTHERN COLORADO
119 West 6th, Street Suite 203
Pueblo, CO 81003-3119
http://www.pueblo.bbb.org
Phone: (719) 542-6464
Fax: (719) 542-5229

MOUNTAIN STATES—NORTHERN COLORADO, EAST & CENTRAL WYOMING
1730 S. College Avenue Suite 303
Fort Collins, CO 80525-1073
http://www.rockymtn.bbb.org
Phone: (303) 484-1348
Fax: (303) 221-1239

DENVER-BOULDER METRO AREA
1780 S Bellaire, Suite 700
Denver, CO 80222-4350
http://www.denver.bbb.org/
Phone: (303) 758-2100
TDD: (303) 758-4786
Fax: (303) 758-8321

FOUR CORNERS & GRAND JUNCTION, COLORADO
308 North Locke
Farmington, NM 87401-5855
http://www.farmington.bbb.org
Phone: (505) 326-6501
Fax:(505) 326-3525

CONNECTICUT

PARKSIDE BUILDING
821 N. Main Street Ext
Wallingford, CT 06492-2420
http://www.connecticut.bbb.org
Phone: (203) 269-2700
Fax: (203) 269-3124

CENTRAL MASSACHUSETTS, NORTHEAST CONNECTICUT
32 Franklin Street
Worcester, MA 01608-1900
http://www.worcester.bbb.org
Phone: (508) 755-2548
Fax: (508) 754-4158

COLUMBIA

METROPOLITAN WASHINGTON
1012 14th Street N.W. 14th Floor
Washington, DC 20005-3410
http://www.dc.bbb.org
Phone: (202) 393-8000
Fax: (202) 393-1198

DELAWARE

DELAWARE
1010 Concord Avenue
Wilmington, DE 19802
http://www.wilmington.bbb.org
Phone: (302) 594-9200
Fax: (302) 594-1052

FLORIDA

NORTHEAST FLORIDA
7820 Arlington Expressway #147
Jacksonville, FL 32211
http://www.jacksonville.bbb.org
Phone: (904) 721-2288
Fax: (904) 721-7373

NORTHWEST FLORIDA
P.O. Box 1511
Pensacola, FL 32597-1511
http://www.pensacola.bbb.org
Phone: (904) 429-0002
Fax: (904) 429-0006

CENTRAL FLORIDA
151 Wymore Rd, Ste 100
Altamonte Springs FL 32714
http://www.orlando.bbb.org
Phone: (407) 621-3300
Fax: (407) 786-2625

BBB OF PORT ST. LUCIE, INC. (BRANCH OF W. PALM BEACH)
1950 Port St. Lucie Blvd., Suite 211
Port St. Lucie, FL 34952-5579
http://www.westpalm.bbb.org
Phone: (407) 878-2010
Fax: (407) 337-2083

FLORIDA

PALM BEACH, MARTIN, ST. LUCIE, OKEECHOBEE, INDIAN RIVER AND HIGHLAND COUNTIES
580 Village Blvd., Suite 340
West Palm Beach, FL 33409   Phone: (407) 686-2200
http://www.westpalm.bbb.org   Fax: (407) 686-2775

WEST FLORIDA
P.O. Box 7950
Clearwater, FL 34618-7950   Phone: (813) 535-5522
http://www.clearwater.bbb.org   Fax: (813) 530-5863

GEORGIA

BBB OF SOUTHWEST GEORGIA, INC.
101 1/2 S. Jackson, Suite #2
Albany, GA 31702-3241   Phone: (912) 883-0744
http://www.columbus-ga.bbb.org   Fax: (912) 438-8222

WEST GEORGIA, EAST ALABAMA
P.O. Box 2587
Columbus, GA 31902-2587   Phone: (706) 324-0712
http://www.columbus-ga.bbb.org   Fax: (706) 324-2181

METROPOLITAN ATLANTA
PO Box 2707
Atlanta GA 30301   Phone: (404) 688-4910
http://www.atlanta.bbb.org   Fax: (404) 688-8901

CENTRAL GEORGIA
277 Martin Luther King Blvd., Suite 102
Macon, GA 31201-3476   Phone: (912) 742-7999
http://www.macon.bbb.org   Fax: (912) 742-8191

NORTHEAST GEORGIA, SOUTHWEST SOUTH CAROLINA
310 7th Street
Augusta, GA 30901   Phone: (706) 722-1574
http://www.augusta-ga.bbb.org   Fax: (706) 724-0969

SOUTHEAST GEORGIA AND SOUTHEAST SOUTH CAROLINA
6606 Abercorn Street, Suite 108C
Savannah, GA 31405   Phone: (912) 354-7521
http://www.savannah.bbb.org   Fax: (912) 354-5068

SOUTHEAST TENNESSEE, NORTHWEST GEORGIA
1010 Market Street, Suite 200
Chattanooga, TN 37402-2614   Phone: (423) 266-6144
http://www.chattanooga.bbb.org   Fax: (423) 265-5744

HAWAII

HAWAII
First Hawaiian Tower
1132 Bishop Street, 15th Floor
Honolulu, HI 96813-2822   Phone: (808) 536-6956
http://www.hawaii.bbb.org   Fax: (808) 523-2335

IDAHO

EASTERN OREGON/SOUTHWEST IDAHO
4619 Emerald, Suite A2
Boise, ID 83706   Phone: (208) 342-4649
http://www.boise.bbb.org   Fax: (208) 342-5116

INLAND NORTHWEST
508 W. Sixth Avenue, Suite 401
Spokane, WA 99204-2730   Phone: (509) 455-4200
http://www.spokane.bbb.org   Fax: (509) 838-1079

EASTERN IDAHO AND WESTERN WYOMING
1575 South Boulevard
Idaho Falls, ID 83404-5926   Phone: (208) 523-9754
http://www.idahofalls.bbb.org   Fax: (208) 524-6190

ILLINOIS

TRI-STATE—SOUTHWEST INDIANA
4004 Morgan Ave., Suite 201
Evansville, IN 47715-2265   Phone: (812) 473-0202
http://www.evansville.bbb.org   Fax: (812) 473-3080

BRANCH OF CHICAGO
810 E. State Street, 3rd Floor
Rockford, IL 61104-1001   Phone: (900) 225-5222
http://www.chicago.bbb.org   Fax: (815) 963-0329

CHICAGO & NORTHERN ILLINOIS
330 N. Wabash Ave.
Chicago, IL 60611   Phone: (900) 225-5222
http://www.chicago.bbb.org   Fax: (312) 580-7849

BBB/QUAD CITIES
852 Middle Road, Suite 290
Bettendorf, IA 52722-4100   Phone: (319) 355-6344
http://www.desmoines.bbb.org   Fax: (319) 355-0306

Appendix D *continued*

Better Business Bureau Locations

ILLINOIS (continued)

CENTRAL ILLINOIS
3024 West Lake
Peoria, IL 61615-3770   Phone: (309) 688-3741
http://www.peoria.bbb.org   Fax: (309) 681-7290

EAST MISSOURI & SOUTH ILLINOIS
12 Sunnen Drive, Suite 121
St. Louis, MO 63143-1400   Phone: (314) 645-3300
http://www.stlouis.bbb.org   Fax: (314) 645-2666

INDIANA

SOUTHERN OHIO, NORTHERN KENTUCKY, &
SOUTHEASTERN INDIANA
898 Walnut Street
Cincinnati, OH 45202-2097   Phone: (513) 421-3015
http://www.cincinnati.bbb.org   Fax: (513) 621-0907

ELKHART & LAGRANGE COUNTIES
P.O. Box 405
Elkhart, IN 46515-0405   Phone: (219) 262-8996
http://www.elkhart.bbb.org   Fax: (219) 262-9884

BBB OF MICHIANA, INC. (BRANCH OF GARY)
207 Dixie Way North, Suite 130
South Bend, IN 46637-3360   Phone: (219) 277-9121
http://www.gary.bbb.org   Fax: (219) 273-6666

CENTRAL INDIANA
Victoria Centre
22 E. Washington Street, Suite 200
Indianapolis, IN 46204-3584   Phone:(317) 488-2222
http://www.indianapolis.bbb.org   Fax: (317) 488-2224

SOUTHERN INDIANA & WESTERN KENTUCKY
844 South 4th Street
Louisville, KY 40203-2186   Phone: (502) 583-6546
http://www.louisville.bbb.org   Fax: (502) 589-9940

TRI-STATE–SOUTHWEST INDIANA
4004 Morgan Avenue, Suite 201
Evansville, IN 47715-2265   Phone: (812) 473-0202
http://www.evansville.bbb.org   Fax: (812) 473-3080

NORTHEASTERN INDIANA
1203 Webster Street
Fort Wayne, IN 46802-3493   Phone: (219) 423-4433
http://www.fortwayne.bbb.org   Fax: (219) 423-3301

NORTHWEST INDIANA
6111 Harrison St., Suite 101
Merrillville, IN 46410   Phone: (219) 980-1511
http://www.gary.bbb.org   Fax: (219) 884-2123

IOWA

CENTRAL & EASTERN IOWA
505 5th Avenue, Suite 950
Des Moines, IA 50309-2375   Phone: (515) 243-8137
http://www.desmoines.bbb.org   Fax: (515) 243-2227

BBB/QUAD CITIES
852 Middle Road, Suite 290
Bettendorf, IA 52722-4100   Phone: (319) 355-6344
http://www.desmoines.bbb.org   (Fax): (319) 355-0306

NORTHERN NEBRASKA & SOUTHWEST IOWA
2237 N. 91st Court
Omaha, NE 68134-6022   Phone: (402) 391-7612
http://www.omaha.bbb.org   Fax: (402) 391-7535

29 COUNTIES IN SOUTH DAKOTA, IOWA AND
NEBRASKA
505 Sixth Street, Suite 417
Sioux City, IA 51101   Phone: (712) 252-4501
http://www.siouxcity.bbb.org   Fax: (712) 252-0285

KANSAS

GREATER KANSAS CITY
306 East 12th Street, Suite 1024
Kansas City, MO 64106-2418   Phone: (816) 421-7800
http://www.kansascity.bbb.org   Fax: (816) 472-5442

NORTHEAST KANSAS
501 Southeast Jefferson, Suite 24
Topeka, KS 66607-1190   Phone: (913) 232-0454
http://www.topeka.bbb.org   Fax: (913) 232-9677

KANSAS (EXCEPT FOR NORTHEAST)
328 Laura
Wichita, KS 67211   Phone: (316) 263-3146
http://www.wichita.bbb.org   Fax: (316) 263-3063

KENTUCKY

SOUTHERN OHIO, NORTHERN KENTUCKY &
SOUTHEASTERN INDIANA
898 Walnut Street
Cincinnati, OH 45202-2097   Phone: (513) 421-3015
http://www.cincinnati.bbb.org   Fax: (513) 621-0907

CENTRAL AND EASTERN KENTUCKY
410 West Vine Street, Suite 340
Lexington, KY 40507-1616   Phone: (606) 259-1008
http://www.lexington.bbb.org   Fax: (606) 259-1639

WESTERN KENTUCKY AND SOUTHERN INDIANA
844 South 4th Street
Louisville, KY 40203-2186   Phone: (502) 583-6546
http://www.louisville.bbb.org   Fax: (502) 589-9940

TRI-STATE–SOUTHWEST INDIANA
4004 Morgan Avenue, Suite 201
Evansville, IN 47715-2265   Phone: (812) 473-0202
http://www.evanville.bbb.org   Fax: (812) 473-3080

NASHVILLE/MIDDLE TENNESSEE
P. O. BOX 198436
Nashville, TN 37219-8436   Phone: (615) 242-4222
http://www.nashville.bbb.org   Fax: (615) 254-8356

LOUISIANA

CENTRAL LOUSIANA
1605 Murray Street, Suite 117
Alexandria, LA 71301-6875   Phone: (318) 473-4494
http://www.alexandria-la.bbb.org   Fax: (318) 473-8906

SOUTH CENTRAL LOUISIANA
2055 Wooddale Boulevard
Baton Rouge, LA 70806-1546   Phone: (504) 926-3010
http://www.batonrouge.bbb.org   Fax: (504) 924-8040

BBB/TRI PARISH AREA (BRANCH OF NEW
ORLEANS)
5953 West Park Ave., Suite 4005
Houma LA 70364   Phone: (504) 868-3456
http://www.neworleans.bbb.org   Fax: (504) 876-7664

SOUTHWEST LOUISIANA
P.O. Box 7314
Lake Charles, LA 70606-7314   Phone: (318) 478-6253
http://www.lakecharles.bbb.org   Fax: (318) 474-8981

ARCADIAN
100 Huggins Road
Lafayette, LA 70506   Phone: (318) 981-3497
http://www.lafayette.bbb.org   Fax: (318) 981-7559

NORTHEAST LOUISIANA
141 Desiard Street, Suite 808
Monroe, LA 71201-7380   Phone: (318) 387-4600
http://www.monroe.bbb.org   Fax: (318) 361-0461

GREATER NEW ORLEANS
1539 Jackson Avenue, Suite 400
New Orleans, LA 70130-5843   Phone: (504) 581-6222
http://www.neworleans.bbb.   Fax: (504) 524-9110

THE ARK-LA-TEX
3612 Youree Drive
Shreveport, LA 71105-2122   Phone: (318) 868-5146
http://www.shreveport.bbb.org   Fax: (318) 861-6426

MAINE

BBB OF MAINE, INC. (BRANCH OF BOSTON)
812 Stevens Avenue
Portland, ME 04103-2648   Phone: (207) 878-2715
http://www.bosbbb.org   Fax: (207) 797-5818

MARYLAND

GREATER MARYLAND
2100 Huntingdon Avenue
Baltimore, MD 21211-3215   Phone: (900) 225-5222
http://www.baltimore.bbb.org   Fax: (410) 347-3936

METROPOLITAN WASHINGTON
1012 14th Street N.W., 14th Floor
Washington, DC 20005-3410   Phone: (202) 393-8000
http://www.dc.bbb.org   Fax: (202) 393-1198

MASSACHUSETTS

EASTERN MASSACHUSETTS, VERMONT & MAINE
20 Park Plaza, Suite 820
Boston, MA 02166-4344   Phone: (617) 426-9000
http://www.bosbbb.org   (802 area code only) (800)4BBB-811
       Fax: (617) 426-7813

WESTERN MASSACHUSETTS
293 Bridge Street, Suite 320
Springfield, MA 01103-1402   Phone: (413) 734-3114
http://www.springfield-ma.bbb.org   Fax: (413) 734-2006

Appendix D *continued*

Better Business Bureau Locations

MASSACHUSETTS (continued)

CENTRAL MASSACHUSETTS, NORTHEAST CONNECTICUT
P.O. Box 16555
Worcester, MA 01601-6555
http://www.worcester.bbb.org

Phone: (508) 755-2548
Fax: (508) 754-4158

MICHIGAN

DETROIT & EASTERN MICHIGAN
30555 Southfield Road, Suite 200
Detroit, MI 48076-7751
http://www.detroit.bbb.org

Phone: (810) 644-9100
Fax: (810) 644-5026

BBB OF MICHIANA, INC.
207 Dixie Way North, Suite 130
South Bend, IN 46637-3360
http://www.gary.bbb.org

Phone: (219) 277-9121
Fax: (219) 273-6666

WESTERN MICHIGAN
40 Pearl N.W., Suite 354
Grand Rapids, MI 49503
http://www.grandrapids.bbb.org

Phone: (616) 774-8236
(from W. MI only) (800) 684-3222
Fax: (616) 774-2014

NORTHWEST OHIO & SOUTHEAST MICHIGAN
3103 Executive Parkway, Suite 200
Toledo, OH 43606-1310
http://www.toledo.bbb.org

Phone: (419) 531-3116
Fax: (419) 578-6001

MINNESOTA

MINNESOTA
2706 Gannon Road
St. Paul, MN 55116-2600
http://www.minnesota.bbb.org

Phone: (612) 699-1111
Fax: (612) 699-7665

MISSISSIPPI

MISSISSIPPI
P.O. Box 12745
Jackson, MS 39206
http://www.bbbmississippi.bbb.org

Phone: (601) 987-8282
Fax: (601) 987-8285

WEST TENNESSEE/NORTH MISSSISSIPPI & EASTERN ARKANSAS
6525 Quail Hollow, Suite 410
Memphis, TN 38120
http://www.memphis.bbb.org

Phone: (901) 759-1300
Fax: (901) 757-2997

MISSOURI

GREATER KANSAS CITY
306 East 12th Street, Suite 1024
Kansas City, MO 64106-2418
http://www.kansascity.bbb.org

Phone: (816) 421-7800
Fax: (816) 472-5442

EAST MISSOURI AND SOUTH ILLINOIS
12 Sunnen Drive, Suite 121
St. Louis, MO 63143-1400
http://www.stlouis.bbb.org

Phone: (314) 645-3300
Fax: (314) 645-2666

SOUTHWEST MISSOURI
205 Park Central East, Suite 509
Springfield, MO 65806-1326
http://www.springfield-mo.bbb.org

Phone: (417) 862-4222
Fax: (417) 869-5544

NEBRASKA

SOUTHERN NEBRASKA
3633 O Street, Suite 1
Lincoln, NE 68510-1670
http://www.lincoln.bbb.org

Phone: (402) 476-8855
Fax: (402) 476-8221

NORTHERN NEBRASKA & SOUTHWEST IOWA
2237 N. 91st Court
Omaha, NE 68134-6022
http://www.omaha.bbb.org

Phone: (402) 391-7612
Fax: (402) 391-7535

29 COUNTIES IN SOUTH DAKOTA, IOWA AND NEBRASKA
505 Sixth Street, Suite 417
Sioux City, IA 51101
http://www.siouxcity.bbb.org

Phone: (712) 252-4501
Fax: (712) 252-0285

NEVADA

SOUTHERN NEVADA
5595 Spring Mountain Road
Las Vegas, NV 89146   Phone: (702) 320-4500
http://www.lasvegas.bbb.org   Fax: (702) 320-4560

NORTHERN NEVADA
991 Bible Way
Reno, NV 89502   Phone: (702) 322-0657
http://www.reno.bbb.org   Fax: (702) 322-8163

NEW HAMPSHIRE

NEW HAMPSHIRE
410 South Main Street, Suite #3
Concord, NH 03301-3483   Phone: (603) 224-1991
http://www.concord.bbb.org   Fax: (603) 228-9035

NEW JERSEY

SOUTH JERSEY
16 Maple Avenue
Westmont, NJ 08108-0303   Phone: (609) 854-8467
http://www.westmont.bbb.org   Fax: (609) 854-1130

CENTRAL NEW JERSEY
1700 Whitehorse-Hamilton Square, Suite D-5
Trenton, NJ 08690-3596   Phone: (609) 588-0808
http://www.trenton.bbb.org   Fax: (609) 588-0546

OCEAN COUNTY BBB
1721 Route 37, East
Toms River, NJ 08753-8239   Phone: (908) 270-5577
http://www.westmont.bbb.org   Fax: (908) 270-8739

NORTHERN NEW JERSEY
400 Lanidex Plaza
Parsippany, NJ 07054-2797   Phone: (201) 581-1313
http://www.parsippany.bbb.org Fax: (201) 581-7022

NEW MEXICO

NEW MEXICO (EXCEPT FOR FOUR CORNERS AREA)
2625 Pennsylvania N.E., Suite 2050
Albuquerque, NM 87110-3657   Phone: (505) 346-0110
http://www.albuquerque.bbb.org Fax: (505) 346-0696

FOUR CORNERS AND GRAND JUNCTION, COLORADO
308 North Locke
Farmington, NM 87401-5855   Phone: (505) 326-6501
http://www.farmington.bbb.org Fax: (505) 327-7731

NEW YORK

CENTRAL NEW YORK, N. COUNTY AND S. TIER
401 N. Salina Street
Syracuse, NY 13203-2552   Phone: (900) 225-5222
http://www.syracuse.bbb.org   Fax: (315) 479-5754

LONG ISLAND BBB (BRANCH OF NEW YORK CITY)
266 Main Street
Farmingdale, NY 11735-9998   Phone: (516) 420-0766
http://www.newyork.bbb.org   (900) CALLBBB
                             Fax: (516) 420-1095

WESTERN NEW YORK AND THE CAPITAL DISTRICT
741 Delaware Avenue, Suite 100
Buffalo NY 14209   Phone: (900) 225-5222
http://www.buffalo.bbb.org   Fax: (716) 883-5349

METROPOLITAN NEW YORK, MID-HUDSON, & LONG ISLAND REGIONS
257 Park Avenue South
New York City, NY 10010-7384 Phone: (212) 533-6200
http:www.newyork.bbb.org   (900) CALLBBB
                             Fax: (212) 477-4912

THE MID-HUDSON BBB (BRANCH OF NEW YORK CITY)
30 Glenn Street
White Plains, NY 10603-3213 Phone: (914) 428-1233
http://www.newyork.bbb.org   Fax: (914) 428-6030

NORTH CAROLINA

ASHEVILLE/WESTERN NORTH CAROLINA
1200 BB&T Building
Asheville, NC 28801-3418   Phone: (704) 253-2392
http://www.asheville.bbb.org   Fax: 704-252-5039

CENTRAL NORTH CAROLINA
3608 West Friendly Avenue
Greensboro, NC 27410-4895   Phone: (910) 852-4240
http://www.greensboro.bbb.org Fax: (910) 852-7540

SOUTHERN PIEDMONT CAROLINAS
5200 Park Road, Suite 202
Charlotte, NC 28209-3650   Phone: (704) 527-0012
http://www.charlotte.bbb.org   Fax: (704) 525-7624

GREATER HAMPTON ROADS
3608 Tidewater Drive
Norfolk, VA 23509-1499   Phone: (804) 627-5651
http://www.norfolk.bbb.org   Fax: (757) 531-1388

Appendix D *continued*

Better Business Bureau Locations

NORTH CAROLINA (continued)

EASTERN NORTH CAROLINA
3125 Poplarwood Court, Suite 308
Raleigh, NC 27604-1080   Phone: (919) 872-9240
http://www.raleigh-durham.bbb.org   Fax: (919) 954-0622

NORTHWEST NORTH CAROLINA
500 West 5th Street, Suite 202
Winston-Salem, NC 27101-2728   Phone: (910) 725-8348
http://www.winstonsalem.bbb.org   Fax: (910) 777-3727

CATAWBA & LINCOLN COUNTIES (BRANCH OF CHARLOTTE)
P.O. Box 69
Sherrills Ford, NC 28673-0069   Phone: (704) 478-5622
http://www.charlotte.bbb.org   Fax: (704) 478-5622

COASTAL CAROLINA
1601 North Oak Street, Suite 403
Myrtle Beach, SC 29577-1601   Phone: (803) 626-6881
http://www.mb.bbb.org   Fax: (803) 626-7455

NORTH DAKOTA

SERVING MINNESOTA
2706 Gannon Road
St. Paul MN 55116-2600   Phone: (612) 699-1111
http://www.minnesota.bbb.org   Fax: (612) 699-7665

OHIO

SUMMIT, POTTAGE, MEDINA, WAYNE, ASHLAND, & RICHLAND COUNTIES
222 W. Market Street
Akron, OH 44303-2111   Phone: (330) 253-4590
http://www.akron.bbb.org   Fax: (330) 253-6249

CENTRAL OHIO
1335 Dublin Road #30-A
Columbus, OH 43215-1000   Phone: (614) 486-6336
http://www.columbus-oh.bbb.org   Fax: (614) 486-6631

CANTON REGIONAL/WEST VIRGINIA
P.O. Box 8017
Canton, OH 44711-8017   Phone: (216) 454-9401
http://www.canton.bbb.org   Fax: (216) 456-8957

DAYTON/MIAMI VALLEY
40 West Fourth Street, Suite 1250
Dayton, OH 45402-1828   Phone: (513) 222-5825
http://www.dayton.bbb.org   Fax: (513) 222-3338

SOUTHERN OHIO, NORTHERN KENTUCKY, & SOUTH EASTERN INDIANA
898 Walnut Street
Cincinnati, OH 45202-2097   Phone: (513) 421-3015
http://www.cincinnati.bbb.org   Fax: (513) 621-0907

WEST CENTRAL OHIO
P.O. Box 269
Lima, OH 45802-0269   Phone: (419) 223-7010
http://www.wcohio.bbb.org   Fax: (419) 229-2029

LORAIN, CUYAHOGA, GEAUGA, LAKE, & ASHTABULA COUNTIES
2217 East 9th Street, Suite 200
Cleveland, OH 44115-1299   Phone: (216) 241-7678
http://www.cleveland.bbb.org   Fax: (216) 861-6365

NORTHWEST OHIO & SOUTHEAST MICHIGAN
3103 Executive Parkway, Suite 200
Toledo, OH 43606-1310   Phone: (419) 531-3116
http://www.toledo.bbb.org   Fax: (419) 578-6001

COLUMBIANA, TRUMBULL, AND MAHONING COUNTIES
P.O. Box 1495
Youngstown, OH 44501   Phone: (216) 744-3111
http://www.youngstown.bbb.org   Fax: (330) 744-7336

OKLAHOMA

CENTRAL OKLAHOMA
17 South Dewey
Oklahoma City, OK 73102-2400   Phone: (405) 239-6081
http://www.oklahomacity.bbb.org   Fax: (405) 235-5891

EASTERN OKLAHOMA
6711 South Yale, Suite 230
Tulsa, OK 74136-3327   Phone: (918) 492-1266
http://www.tulsa.bbb.org   Fax: (918) 492-1276

OREGON

EASTERN OREGON/SOUTHWEST IDAHO
1333 West Jefferson
Boise, ID 83702-5320   Phone: (208) 342-4649
http://www.boise.bbb.org   Fax: (208) 342-5116

OREGON/SOUTHWEST WASHINGTON
333 S.W. Fifth Avenue, Suite 300
Portland, OR 97204   Phone: (503) 226-3981
http://www.portland.bbb.org   Fax: (503) 226-8200

PENNSYLVANIA (continued)

BRANCH OF PHILADELPHIA, CAPITAL DIVISION
29 East King Street, Suite 322
Lancaster, PA 17602-2852   Phone: (900) 225-5222
http://www.easternpa.bbb.org   Fax: (717) 291-3241

BRANCH OF PHILADELPHIA, LEHIGH VALLEY DIVI SION
528 North New Street
Bethlehem, PA 18018-5789   Phone: (610) 866-8780
http://www.easternpa.bbb.org   Fax: (610) 868-8668

EASTERN PENNSYLVANIA
1608 Walnut Street, Suite 600
Philadelphia, PA 19103   Phone: (900) 225-5222
http://www.easternpa.bbb.org   Fax: (215) 893-9312

WESTERN PENNSYLVANIA
300 Sixth Avenue, Suite 100-UL
Pittsburgh, PA 15222-2511   Phone: (412) 456-2700
http://www.pittsburgh.bbb.org   Fax: (412) 456-2739

NORTHEASTERN PENNSYLVANIA
P.O. Box 993
Scranton, PA 18501-0993   Phone: (717) 342-9129
http://www.scranton.bbb.org   Fax: (717) 342-1282

PUERTO RICO

PUERTO RICO
123 O'Neill St., Second Floor
1608 Bori Street
San Juan PR 00918   Phone: (809) 756-5400
http://www.sanjuan.bbb.org   Fax: (809) 758-0095

RHODE ISLAND

RHODE ISLAND
120 Lavan Street
Warwick, RI 02888-1071   Phone: (787) 785-1212
http://www.rhodeisland.bbb.org   Fax: (787) 785-3061

SOUTH CAROLINA

NORTHEAST GEORGIA, SOUTHWEST SOUTH CAROLINA
301 7th Street
Augusta, GA 30901   Phone: (706) 722-1574
http://www.augusta-ga.bbb.org   Fax: (706) 724-0969

SOUTHERN PIEDMONT CAROLINAS
5200 Park Road, Suite 202
Charlotte, NC 28209-3650   Phone: (704) 527-0012
http://www.charlotte.bbb.org   Fax: (704) 525-7624

SOUTHEAST GEORGIA AND SOUTHEAST SOUTH CARO-LINA
6606 Abercorn Street, Suite 108C
Savannah, GA 31405   Phone: (912) 354-7521
http://www.savannah.bbb.org   Fax: (912) 354-5068

CENTRAL SOUTH CAROLINA & CHARLESTON AREA
2330 Devine Street
Columbia, SC 29205   Phone: (803) 254-2525
http://www.columbia.bbb.org   Fax: (803) 779-3117

THE FOOTHILLS
307-B Falls Street
Greenville, SC 29601-2829   Phone: (803) 242-5052
http://www.greenville.bbb.org   Fax: (803) 271-9802

COASTAL CAROLINA
1601 North Oak Street, Suite 101
Myrtle Beach, SC 29577-1601   Phone: (803) 626-6881
http://www.mb.bbb.org   Fax: (803) 626-7455

SOUTH DAKOTA

29 COUNTIES IN SOUTH DAKOTA, IOWA AND NEBRASKA
505 Sixth Street Suite 417
Sioux City, IA 51101   Phone: (712) 252-4501
http://www.siouxcity.bbb.org   Fax: (712) 252-0285

Appendix D *continued*

Better Business Bureau Locations

TENNESSEE

SOUTHEAST TENNESSEE, NORTHWEST GEORGIA
1010 Market Street, Suite 200
Chattanooga, TN 37402-2614   Phone: (423) 266-6144
http://www.chattanooga.bbb.org   Fax: (423) 265-5744

GREATER EAST TENNESSEE
P.O. Box 10327
Knoxville, TN 37939-0327   Phone: (615) 522-2552
http://www.knoxville.bbb.org   Fax: (615) 637-8042

BBB OF GREATER EAST TENNESSEE, INC.
P.O. Box 1178 TCA
Blountville, TN 37617-1178   Phone: (423) 325-6616
http://www.knoxville.bbb.org   Fax: (423) 325-6620

WEST TENNESSEE/MEMPHIS
P.O. Box 17036
Memphis, TN 38187-0036   Phone: (901) 759-1300
http://www.memphis.bbb.org   Fax: (901) 757-2997

NASHVILLE/MIDDLE TENNESSEE
P.O. Box 198436
Nashville, TN 37219-8436   Phone: (615) 242-4222
http://www.nashville.bbb.org   Fax: (615) 242-8796

TEXAS

ABILENE AREA
3300 South 14th Street, Suite 307
Abilene, TX 79605-5052   Phone: (915) 691-1533
http://www.abilene.bbb.org   Fax: (915) 691-0309

26 COUNTIES OF THE TEXAS PANHANDLE
P.O. Box 1905
Amarillo, TX 79101-3408   Phone: (806) 379-6222
http://www.amarillo.bbb.org   Fax: (806) 379-8206

CENTRAL TEXAS
2101 S. IH 35, Suite 302
Austin, TX 78741-3854   Phone: (512) 445-2911
http://www.centraltx.bbb.org   Fax: (512) 445-2096

SOUTHEAST TEXAS
P.O. Box 2988
Beaumont, TX 77701-2988   Phone: (409) 835-5348
http://www.beaumont.bbb.org   Fax: (409) 838-6858

BRAZOS VALLEY AND DEEP EAST TEXAS
P.O. Box 3868
Bryan, TX 77805-3868   Phone: (409) 260-2222
http://www.bryan.bbb.org   Fax: (409) 846-0276

COASTAL BEND
216 Park Avenue
Corpus Christi, TX 78401   Phone: (512) 887-4949
http://www.corpuschristi.bbb.org   Fax: (512) 887-4931

METROPOLITAN DALLAS AND NORTHEAST TEXAS
2001 Bryan Street, Suite 850
Dallas, TX 75201-3093   Phone: (900) 225-5222
http://www.dallas.bbb.org   Fax: (214) 740-0321

EL PASO AREA
State National Plaza, Suite 1101
El Paso, TX 79901   Phone: (915) 577-0191
http://www.elpaso.bbb.org   Fax: (915) 577-0209

**TARRANT, JOHNSON, HOOD, WISE, PARKER, ERATH
& PALO PINTO COUNTIES**
1612 Summit Avenue, Suite 260
Fort Worth, TX 76102-5978   Phone: (817) 332-7585
http://www.fortworth.bbb.org   Fax: (817) 882-0566

METROPOLITAN HOUSTON
5225 Katy Freeway, Suite 500
Houston, TX 77007   Phone: (900) 225-5222
http://www.bbbhou.org   Fax: (713) 867-4947

SOUTH PLAINS
916 Main Street, Suite 800
Lubbock, TX 79401-3410   Phone: (806) 763-0459
http://www.lubbock.bbb.org   Fax: (806) 744-9748

PERMIAN BASIN
P.O. Box 60206
Midland, TX 79711   Phone: (915) 563-1880
http://www.midland.bbb.org   Fax: (915) 561-9435

SAN ANGELO AREA
P.O. Box 3366
San Angelo, TX 76902-3366   Phone: (915) 949-2989
http://www.sanangelo.bbb.org   Fax: (915) 949-3514

SOUTH CENTRAL AREA
1800 Northeast Loop 410, Suite 400
San Antonio, TX 78217-5296   Phone: (210) 828-9441
http://www.sanantonio.bbb.org   Fax: (210) 828-3101

THE ARK-LA-TEX
3612 Youree Drive
Shreveport, LA 71105-2122   Phone: (318) 868-5146
http://www.shreveport.bbb.org   Fax: (318) 861-6426

19 EAST TEXAS COUNTIES
P.O. Box 6652
Tyler, TX 75711-6652   Phone: (903) 581-5704
http://www.tyler.bbb.org   Fax: (903) 534-8644

HEART OF TEXAS
2210 Washington Ave.
Waco TX 76701-1019   Phone: (254) 755-7772
http://www.waco.bbb.org   Fax: (254) 755-7774

SOUTH TEXAS
P.O. Box 69
Weslaco, TX 78599-0069   Phone: (210) 968-3678
http://www.weslaco.bbb.org   Fax: (210) 968-7638

TEXAS (continued)

NORTH CENTRAL TEXAS
4245 Kemp Boulevard, Suite 900
Wichita Falls ,TX 76308-2830   Phone: (817) 691-1172
http://www.wichitafalls.bbb.org   Fax: (817) 691-1175

UTAH

UTAH
1588 South Main Street
Salt Lake City, UT 84115-5382   Phone: (801) 487-4656
http://www.saltlakecity.bbb.org   Fax: (801) 485-9397

VERMONT

EASTERN MASSACHUSETTS, VERMONT & MAINE
20 Park Plaza, Suite 820
Boston, MA 02166-4344   Phone: (617) 426-9000
http://www.bosbbb.org   (802 area only) (800)4BBB-811
          Fax: (617) 426-7813

VIRGINIA

METROPLOITAN WASHINGTON & NORTHERN VIRGINIA
1012 14th Street NW 9th Floor
Washington, DC 20005-3410   Phone: (202) 393-8000
http://www.dc.bbb.org   Fax: (202) 393-1198

CENTRAL VIRGINIA (BRANCH OF RICHMOND)
11903 Main Street
Fredricksburg, VA, 22408   Phone: (703) 373-9872
http://www.richmond.bbb.org   Fax: (703) 373-0097

GREATER HAMPTON ROADS
586 Virginian Drive
Norfolk, VA 23505   Phone: (757) 531-1300
http://www.norfolk.bbb.org   Fax: (757) 531-1388

CENTRAL VIRGINIA
701 East Franklin, Suite 712
Richmond, VA 23219-2332   Phone: (804) 648-0016
http://www.richmond.bbb.org   Fax: (804) 648-3115

WESTERN VIRGINIA
31 West Campbell Avenue
Roanoke, VA 24011-1301   Phone: (540) 342-3455
http://www.roanoke.bbb.org   Fax: (540) 345-2289

WASHINGTON

PORTLAND OREGON OFFICE
333 S.W. Fifth Avenue, Suite 300
Portland, OR 97204   Phone: (503) 226-3981
http://www.portland.bbb.org   Fax: (503) 226-8200

INLAND NORTHWEST
508 W. Sixth Avenue, Suite 401
Spokane, WA 992-2730   Phone: (509) 455-4200
http://www.spokane.bbb.org   Fax: (509) 838-1079

OREGON AND WESTERN WASHINGTON
4800 S. 188th Street, Suite 222
Sea Tac, WA 98188   Phone: (900) 225-4222
http://www.seatac.bbb.org   Fax: (206) 431-2211

CENTRAL WASHINGTON
32 N. 3rd St., Suite 410
P.O. Box 1584
Yakima, WA 98901   Phone: (509) 248-1326
http://www.yakima.bbb.org   Fax: (509) 248-8026

TRI-CITY BBB, INC.
101 North Union #105
Kennewick, WA 99336-3819   Phone: (509) 783-0892
http://www.yakima.bbb.org   Fax: (509) 783-2893

Appendix D *continued*   Better Business Bureau Locations

WEST VIRGINIA

CANTON REGIONAL/WEST VIRGINIA
1434 Cleveland Avenue N.W.
Canton, OH 44703   Phone: (216) 454-9401
http://www.canton.bbb.org   Fax: (216) 456-8957

WISCONSIN

WISCONSIN
740 North PlankingtonAve.   Phone: (414) 273-1600
Milwaukee, WI 53203-2478   Fax: (414) 224-0881
http://www.wisconsin.bbb.org

WYOMING

MOUNTAIN STATES—NORTHERN COLORADO,   **EASTERN IDAHO & WESTERN WYOMING**
EAST & CENTRAL WYOMING   1575 South Boulevard
1730 S. College Avenue Suite 303   Idaho Falls, ID 83404-5926   Phone: (208) 523-9754
Fort Collins, CO 80525-1073   Phone: (303) 484-1348   http://www.idahofalls.bbb.org   Fax: (208) 524-6190
http://www.fortcollins.bbb.org   Fax: (303) 221-1239

INTERNATIONAL BUREAUS

CANADIAN NATIONAL HEADQUARTERS

CANADIAN COUNCIL OF BETTER BUSINESS BUREAUS
Suite 368
7330 Fisher Street SE
Calgary, AB T2H 2H8

Phone: (403) 531-8686
Fax: (403) 531-8697

ALBERTA

BBB OF SOUTHERN ALBERTA, INC.
7330 Fisher Street, S.E. Suite 350
Calgary, AB T2H 2H8
http://www.calgary.bbb.org

Phone: (403) 531-8780
Fax: (403) 640-2514

BBB/CENTRAL & NORTHERN ALBERTA
514 Capital Place
9707 110th Street
Edmonton, AB T5K 2L9
http://www.edmonton.bbb.org

Phone: (403) 482-2341
Fax: (403) 482-1150

BRITISH COLUMBIA

BBB OF MAINLAND BRITISH COLUMBIA
788 Beatty Street Suite 404
Vancouver, BC V6B 2M1
http://www.bbbmbc.com
email: bbbmail@bbbmbc.com

Phone: (604) 682-2711
Fax: (604) 681-1544

BBB OF VANCOUVER ISLAND
201-1005 Langley Street
Victoria, BC V8W 1V7
http://www.bbbvanisland.org/bbb/

Phone: (604) 386-6348
Fax: (604) 386-2367

MANITOBA

BBB OF WINNIPEG & MANITOBA
301 - 365 Hargrave Street
Winnipeg, MB R3B 2K3
http://www.manitoba.bbb.org

Phone: (204) 943-1486
Fax: (204) 943-1489

NEWFOUNDLAND

BBB OF NEWFOUNDLAND/LABRADOR
P.O. Box 360, Topsail Road
St. John's, NF A1E 2B6
http://www.newfoundland.bbb.org

Phone: (709) 364-2222
Fax: (709) 364-2255

NOVA SCOTIA

BBB OF NOVA SCOTIA
1888 Brunswick Street, Suite 601
Halifax, NS B3J 3B8
http://www.bbbns.com/bbbns/

Phone: (902) 422-6581
Fax: (902) 429-6457

ONTARIO

BBB OF SOUTH CENTRAL ONTARIO
100 King Street, East
Hamilton, ON I8N 1A8
http://www.hamilton.bbb.org

Phone: (905) 526-1112
Fax: (905) 526-1225

BBB OF MID-WESTERN ONTARIO
354 Charles Street, East
Kitchener, ON N2G 4L5
http://www.kitchener.bbb.org

Phone: (519) 579-3080
Fax: (519) 570-0072

ONTARIO (continued)

BBB/WESTERN ONTARIO
200 Queens Avenue, Suite 616
P.O. Box 2153
London, OH N6A 4E3
http://www.london.bbb.org
Phone: (519) 673-3222
Fax: (519) 673-5966

BBB OF OTTAWA AND HULL
The Varette Building
130 Albert Street, Suite 603
Ottawa, ON K1P 5G4
http://www.ottawa.bbb.org
Phone: (613) 237-4856
Fax: (613) 237-4878

BBB ST. CATHARINES
101 King Street
St. Catharines, ON L2R 3H6
http://www.hamilton.bbb.org
Phone: (905) 687-6688
Fax: (905) 687-1971

BBB/METROPOLITAN TORONTO
One St. John's Road, Suite 501
Toronto, ON M6P 4C7
http://www.toronto.bbb.org
Phone: (416) 866-5744
Fax: (416) 766-1970

BBB OF WINDSOR & DISTRICT
500 Riverside Drive West
Windsor, ON N9A 5K6
http://www.wincom.net/wbbb/
Phone: (519) 258-7222
Fax: (519) 258-5905

QUEBEC

BBB OF MONTREAL
2055 Peel Street, Suite 460
Montreal, PQ H3A 1V4
http://www.montreal.bbb.org
Phone: (514) 286-9281
Fax: (514) 286-2658

SASKATCHEWAN

BBB OF SASKATCHEWAN
2080 Broad Street, #302
Regina, SA S4P 1Y3
http://www.saskatchewan.bbb.org
Phone: (306) 352-7601

Appendix E

Additional Options
(Not included in Vehicle Charts)

This appendix shows all cost options included in the evaluation of each vehicle that do not appear in the Purchase Price section of the vehicle charts. For an in-depth explanation of our option selection methodology, please refer to the Purchase Price (Feature Shading) page of the Annotated Charts Section on page 87A.

Page	Vehicle		Option Name	Cost	List
P57	Dodge Neon Competition	2 Dr Coupe	Competition Group	$1,914.00	$2,080.00
P58	Dodge Neon Competition	4 Dr Sedan	Competition Group	$1,895.00	$2,060.00
P69	Ford Taurus LX	4 Dr Sedan	Locks, Power Door	$245.00	$275.00
P87	Infinit G20	4 Dr Sedan	Leather and Convenience Package	$1,124.00	$1,500.00
P142	Oldsmobile Intrigue GL	4 Dr Sedan	Traction Control	$129.05	$145.00
P143	Plymouth Neon Competition	2 Dr Coupe	Competition Group	$1,914.00	$2,080.00
P144	Plymouth Neon Competition	4 Dr Sedan	Competition Group	$1,895.00	$2,060.00
P155	Pontiac Grand Prix GTP	2 Dr Coupe	GTP Option Group 1SB	$467.25	$525.00
P156	Pontiac Grand Prix GTP	4 Dr Sedan	GTP Option Group 1SB	$493.95	$555.00

Appendix F
Automobile Manufacturers

Acura
1919 Torrance Blvd., Torrance, CA 90501-2746 .... 1-800-TO-ACURA
http://www.acura.com

AM General (Hummer)
100 East Wayne St., Suite 300, South Bend, IN 46601 .... 1-800-REAL4WD
http://www.hummer.com

Audi of America, Inc.
3800 Hamlin Rd., Auburn Hills, MI 48326 .... 1-800-FOR-AUDI
http://www.audiusa.com

BMW of North America, Inc.
300 Chestnut Ridge Rd., Woodcliff Lake, NJ 07675 .... 1-800-334-4BMW
http://www.bmwusa.com

Buick Motor Division
General Motor Corp., 902 E. Hamilton Ave., Flint, MI 48550 .... 1-800-4A-BUICK
http://www.buick.com

Cadillac Motor Car Division
General Motors Corp., 30009 Van Dyke Ave., Warren MI 48090-9025 .... 1-800-333-4CAD
http://www.cadillac.com

Chevrolet Motor Division
General Motors Corp., P.O. Box 7047, Troy, MI 48007-7047 1-800-222-1020
http://www.chevrolet.com

Chrysler Corporation - Daimler Chrysler
1000 Chrysler Drive, Auburn Hills, MI 48326-2766 .... 1-800-4A-CHRYSLER
http://www.chryslercars.com

Daewoo Motor America, Inc.
1055 W. Victoria St., Compton, CA 902206 .... 1-877-GO-DAEWOO
http://www.daewoous.com

Dodge Division
Chrysler Corp., 1000 Chrysler Drive, Auburn Hills, MI 48326-2766 .... 1-800-4A-DODGE
http://www.4adodge.com

East European Imports, Inc.
3191 Coral Way, Suite 904, Miami, FL 33145 1-305-461-4070
http://www.ARO4X4.com

Ford Motor Division
300 Renaissance Center, P.O. Box 43360, Detroit, MI 48243 1-800-392-3673
http://www.ford.com

GMC Truck Division
P.O. Box 436008, Pontiac, MI 48342 .... 1-800-GMC-TRUCK
http://www.gm.com or http://www.gmc.com

Honda - American Honda Motor Co., Inc.
1919 Torrance Blvd., Torrance, CA 90501 .... 1-800-33-HONDA
http://www.honda.com

Hyundai Motor America
10550 Talbert Ave., P.O. Box 20850, Fountain Valley, CA 92728-0850
http://www.hyundaiUSA.com
1-800-826-CARS

Infiniti Division - Nissan Motor Corp. USA
P.O. Box 47038, Gardena, CA 90247 1-800-826-6500
http://www.infiniti-usa.com

Isuzu - American Isuzu Motors Corp.
2300 Pellissier Place, P.O. Box 995, Whittier, CA 90608-0995 1-800-726-2700
http://www.isuzu.com

Jaguar Cars, Inc.
555 Mac Arthur Blvd., Mahwah, NJ 07430-2327 .... 1-800-4JAGUAR
http://www.us.jaguar.com

Jeep Division
1000 Chrysler Drive, Auburn Hills, MI 48326 .... 1-800-JEEP-EAGL
http://www.jeepunpaved.com

Kia Motors of America
http://www.kia.com
P.O. Box 52410, Irvine, CA 92719-2410 .... 1-800-3334KIA

Laforza Automobiles, Inc.
http://www.laforza.com
2312 Vineyard Ave., Escondido, CA 92029 1-800-523-6792

Land Rover of North America Inc.
http://www.best4x4.landrover.com
4371 Parliament Place, Lanham, MD 20706 .... 1-800-FINE-4WD

Lexus
http://www.lexus.com
19001 S. Western Ave., Torrance, CA 90509 1-800-872-5398

Lincoln Division - Ford Motor Co.
http://www.lincolnvehicles.com
2099 S. State College Blvd. Suite620, Anaheim, CA 92806 1-800-446-8888

Mazda Motor of America, Inc.
http://www.mazdausa.com
7755 Irvine Center Drive, P.O. Box 19734 Irvine, CA 92718-9734 1-800-639-1000

Mercedes Benz of North America, Inc.
http://www.usa.mercedes-benz.com
One Mercedes Drive, Montvale, NJ 07645-0350 1-800-222-0100

Mercury Division - Ford Motor Co.
http://www.mercuryvehicles.com
2099 S. State College Blvd. Suite 620, Anaheim, CA 92806 1-800-392-3673

Mitsubishi Motor Sales of America, Inc.
http://www.mitsucars.com
6400 Katella Ave., Cypress, CA 90630 .... 1-800-55-MITSU

Nissan North America, Inc.
http://www.nissanmotors.com
P.O. Box 191, Gardena, CA 90247 .... 1-800-NISSAN-3

Oldsmobile Division
http://www.oldsmobile.com
General Motors Corp., 920 Townsend, P.O. Box 30095, Lansing, MI 48909 1-800-442-6537

Plymouth Division - Chrysler Corp.
http://www.plymouthcars.com
1000 Chrysler Drive, Auburn Hills, MI 48326-2766 .... 1-800-PLYMOUTH

Pontiac Motor Division
http://www.pontiac.com
General Motors Corp., P.O. Box 436008, Pontiac, MI 48343-6008 .... 1-800-2PONTIAC

Porsche Cars North America, Inc.
http://www.porsche-usa.com
980 Hammond Drive, Suite 1000, Atlanta, GA 30328 1-800-767-7243

Saab Cars, USA Inc.
http://www.saabusa.com
4405-A International Blvd., Norcross, GA 30091 .... 1-800-582-SAAB

Saturn Corp. - General Motors Corp.
http://www.saturncars.com
Highway 31 South, 100 Saturn Parkway, Spring Hills, TN 37174 1-800-522-5000

Subaru of America, Inc.
http://www.subaru.com
Subaru Plaza, P.O. Box 6000, Cherry Hill, NJ 08034-6000 .... 1-800-SUBARU-3

Suzuki - American Suzuki Motor Corp.
http://www.suzuki.com
3251 East Imperial Highway, Brea, CA 92621 1-800-934-0934

Toyota Motor Sales, USA Inc.
http://www.toyota.com
Dept. A-102, 19001 S. Western Ave., Torrance, CA 90509 .... 1-800-GO-TOYOTA

Volkswagen of America, Inc.
http://www.vw.com
3800 Hamlin Road, Auburn Hills, MI 48326 1-800-822-8987

Volvo of North America Corp.
http://www.volvocars.com
7 Volvo Drive, P.O. Box 914, Rockleigh, NJ 07647 1-800-458-1552

Appendix G   Money Factor Conversion Table

If you know the money factor of a lease, you can get an approximation of the interest rate with this table. The left column shows the money factor, the right column the interest rate.

If your money factor is not shown on this chart, you can approximate the interest rate by multiplying the money factor by 2,400.

Please note that the interest rate derived in this manner is NOT comparable to the APR on a loan, unless the capital cost used in the lease is comparable to your purchase price on a loan. Even with similar prices, the residual used in the lease can make the comparison of lease or loan difficult.

Money Factor	Approximate Interest Rate	Money Factor	Approximate Interest Rate	Money Factor	Approximate Interest Rate
.0005	1.20%	.0037	8.88%	.0069	16.56%
.0006	1.44%	.0038	9.12%	.0070	16.80%
.0007	1.68%	.0039	9.36%	.0071	17.04%
.0008	1.92%	.0040	9.60%	.0072	17.28%
.0009	2.16%	.0041	9.84%	.0073	17.52%
.0010	2.40%	.0042	10.08%	.0074	17.76%
.0011	2.64%	.0043	10.32%	.0075	17.90%
.0012	2.88%	.0044	10.56%	.0076	18.24%
.0013	3.12%	.0045	10.80%	.0077	18.48%
.0014	3.36%	.0046	11.04%	.0078	18.72%
.0015	3.60%	.0047	11.28%	.0079	18.96%
.0016	3.84%	.0048	11.52%	.0080	19.20%
.0017	4.08%	.0049	11.76%	.0081	19.44%
.0018	4.32%	.0040	11.90%	.0082	19.68%
.0019	4.56%	.0051	12.24%	.0083	19.92%
.0020	4.80%	.0052	12.48%	.0084	20.16%
.0021	5.04%	.0053	12.72%	.0085	20.40%
.0022	5.28%	.0054	12.96%	.0086	20.64%
.0023	5.52%	.0055	13.20%	.0087	20.88%
.0024	5.76%	.0056	13.44%	.0088	21.12%
.0025	5.90%	.0057	13.68%	.0089	21.36%
.0026	6.24%	.0058	13.92%	.0090	21.60%
.0027	6.48%	.0059	14.16%	.0091	21.84%
.0028	6.72%	.0060	14.40%	.0092	22.08%
.0029	6.96%	.0061	14.64%	.0093	22.32%
.0030	7.20%	.0062	14.88%	.0094	22.56%
.0031	7.44%	.0063	15.12%	.0095	22.80%
.0032	7.68%	.0064	15.36%	.0096	23.04%
.0033	7.92%	.0065	15.60%	.0097	23.28%
.0034	8.16%	.0066	15.84%	.0098	23.52%
.0035	8.40%	.0067	16.08%	.0099	23.76%
.0036	8.64%	.0068	16.32%	.0100	24.00%

Appendix H

Lease Interest Rates

While there are a number of differences between a lease and a loan, they are both similar transactions to a financial analyst. Both involve the exchange of a major asset (in this case, a car) between the "selling" party and the "using" party; both are for a fixed time period; both require periodic payments; and most importantly, both involve the use of an interest rate to set the periodic payment.

A loan's interest rate, or A.P.R. (Annual Percentage Rate) is the one and only true measure of the **cost** of a loan. With the APR, you can compare any number of loans on an apples-to-apples basis.

However, whereas lenders have strict disclosure requirements for automobile loans, lessors do not have the same stringent requirements to inform you of the interest rate being used to determine the monthly lease payments.

Same as with comparing APR between loans, the interest rate used to calculate the lease is the one true measure of the cost of a lease.

The following table will help you determine the interest rate in any lease transaction. You can use this table to help you compare different leases and/or compare a lease to a loan.

To use the tables, here are the things you need to know. The lessor should be able to provide you with this information.

- The acquisition price of the vehicle (Technically, since you're not purchasing the vehicle, the price is called the "capital cost" and is the price upon which the lease payments are based.)
- Any fees or "capital cost reduction" (down payment) required at the start of the lease
- The residual value percentage that is being used in the lease calculation, or the residual value in dollars.
- The length of the lease
- The monthly lease payment

1. Find the table that corresponds to the length of your lease (24 months-pages 140A-141A, 30 months-pages 142A-143A, 36 months-pages 144A-145A, 42 months-pages 146A-147A, 48 months-pages 148A-149A, 60 months-pages 150A-151A).
2. There are eight tables for each lease term. Locate the table where the "Acquisition Price" is closest to the purchase price of the vehicle.
3. Read across the top row "Residual Value," and find the percent figure that is closest to the percent used to calculate your lease, or the dollar figure closest to the residual value in dollars.
4. Trace down that column to the row corresponding to the monthly lease payment.
5. The figure at the intersection is an approximation of the interest rate of your lease.

You may find that the acquisition price of the vehicle you are considering is somewhere between the prices listed in these tables. (For example, the price of the vehicle is actually $22,500, which would be in between the $20,000 table and the $25,000 table.) If this is the case, ask the lessor to give you the lease payment as if the car cost $20,000 or $25,000, and then use the tables listed here.

Appendix H *continued*

Lease Interest Rates

See instructions on page 139A.

24 Month Lease

$10,000 – *Acquisition Price (net of down payment or capital cost reduction)*

Residual Value (S)	$8,200	$8,000	$7,800	$7,600	$7,400	$7,200	$7,000	$6,800	$6,400	$6,000	$5,600	$5,200	$4,800	$4,400
$120	5.98%	4.92%	3.85%	2.75%	1.62%	0.47%	N.A.	N.A.	N.A.	N.A.	N.A.	N.A.	N.A.	N.A.
$140	8.64%	7.62%	6.57%	5.40%	4.40%	3.28%	2.13%	0.96%	N.A.	N.A.	N.A.	N.A.	N.A.	N.A.
$160	11.32%	10.32%	9.20%	8.25%	7.19%	6.00%	4.98%	3.84%	1.48%	N.A.	N.A.	N.A.	N.A.	N.A.
$180	14.00%	13.03%	12.03%	11.02%	9.98%	8.92%	7.84%	6.73%	4.43%	2.02%	N.A.	N.A.	N.A.	N.A.
$190	15.35%	14.38%	13.40%	12.40%	11.38%	10.33%	9.27%	8.17%	5.91%	3.54%	1.04%	N.A.	N.A.	N.A.
$200	16.69%	15.74%	14.77%	13.79%	12.78%	11.75%	10.69%	9.62%	7.39%	5.05%	2.59%	N.A.	N.A.	N.A.
$225	20.06%	19.14%	18.21%	17.25%	16.28%	15.29%	14.27%	13.23%	11.09%	8.84%	6.48%	3.90%	1.37%	N.A.
$250	23.45%	22.56%	21.65%	20.73%	19.79%	18.83%	17.86%	16.86%	14.79%	12.63%	10.37%	7.99%	5.48%	2.82%
$275	26.84%	25.98%	25.11%	24.22%	23.31%	22.39%	21.45%	20.48%	18.40%	16.42%	14.25%	11.97%	9.57%	7.04%
$300	30.25%	29.42%	28.58%	27.72%	26.84%	25.95%	25.04%	24.12%	22.20%	20.21%	18.13%	15.94%	13.65%	11.23%
$325	33.67%	32.87%	32.05%	31.22%	30.38%	29.52%	28.65%	27.75%	25.92%	24.00%	22.00%	19.91%	17.72%	15.42%

$12,500 – *Acquisition Price (net of down payment or capital cost reduction)*

Residual Value (S)	$10,250	$10,000	$9,750	$9,500	$9,250	$9,000	$8,750	$8,500	$8,000	$7,500	$7,000	$6,500	$6,000	$5,500
$150	5.98%	4.92%	3.85%	2.75%	1.62%	0.47%	N.A.	N.A.	N.A.	N.A.	N.A.	N.A.	N.A.	N.A.
$175	8.64%	7.62%	6.57%	5.40%	4.40%	3.28%	2.13%	0.96%	N.A.	N.A.	N.A.	N.A.	N.A.	N.A.
$200	11.32%	10.32%	9.20%	8.25%	7.19%	6.00%	4.98%	3.84%	1.48%	N.A.	N.A.	N.A.	N.A.	N.A.
$225	14.00%	13.03%	12.03%	11.02%	9.98%	8.92%	7.84%	6.73%	4.43%	2.02%	N.A.	N.A.	N.A.	N.A.
$250	16.69%	15.74%	14.77%	13.79%	12.78%	11.75%	10.69%	9.62%	7.39%	5.05%	2.59%	0.00%	N.A.	N.A.
$275	19.39%	18.46%	17.52%	16.56%	15.58%	14.58%	13.56%	12.51%	10.35%	8.08%	5.70%	3.10%	0.55%	N.A.
$300	22.09%	21.19%	20.28%	19.34%	18.39%	17.41%	16.42%	15.41%	13.31%	11.12%	8.81%	6.39%	3.83%	1.13%
$325	24.80%	23.93%	23.04%	22.13%	21.20%	20.26%	19.29%	18.31%	16.27%	14.15%	11.92%	9.58%	7.11%	4.51%
$350	27.52%	26.67%	25.80%	24.92%	24.02%	23.10%	22.16%	21.21%	19.24%	17.18%	15.02%	12.76%	10.39%	7.88%
$375	30.25%	29.42%	28.58%	27.72%	26.84%	25.95%	25.04%	24.12%	22.20%	20.21%	18.13%	15.94%	13.65%	11.23%
$400	32.98%	32.18%	31.36%	30.52%	29.67%	28.81%	27.92%	27.03%	25.17%	23.24%	21.23%	19.12%	16.91%	14.58%

$15,000 – *Acquisition Price (net of down payment or capital cost reduction)*

Residual Value (S)	$12,300	$12,000	$11,700	$11,400	$11,100	$10,800	$10,500	$10,200	$9,600	$9,000	$8,400	$7,800	$7,200	$6,600
$175	5.53%	4.47%	3.39%	2.29%	1.16%	N.A.	N.A.	N.A.	N.A.	N.A.	N.A.	N.A.	N.A.	N.A.
$200	7.75%	6.72%	5.66%	4.58%	3.47%	2.34%	1.19%	0.00%	N.A.	N.A.	N.A.	N.A.	N.A.	N.A.
$225	9.98%	8.97%	7.93%	6.87%	5.79%	4.69%	3.56%	2.40%	N.A.	N.A.	N.A.	N.A.	N.A.	N.A.
$250	12.21%	11.22%	10.21%	9.17%	8.12%	7.04%	5.93%	4.80%	2.46%	N.A.	N.A.	N.A.	N.A.	N.A.
$280	14.80%	13.93%	12.95%	11.94%	10.91%	9.86%	8.79%	7.69%	5.42%	3.03%	0.52%	N.A.	N.A.	N.A.
$300	16.69%	15.74%	14.77%	13.79%	12.78%	11.75%	10.69%	9.62%	7.39%	5.05%	2.59%	N.A.	N.A.	N.A.
$325	18.94%	18.01%	17.06%	16.00%	15.11%	14.11%	13.08%	12.03%	9.86%	7.58%	5.19%	2.67%	0.00%	N.A.
$350	21.19%	20.28%	19.36%	18.41%	17.45%	16.47%	15.47%	14.44%	12.32%	10.10%	7.78%	5.33%	2.74%	N.A.
$400	25.71%	24.84%	23.96%	23.06%	22.14%	21.20%	20.25%	19.27%	17.26%	15.16%	12.95%	10.64%	8.21%	5.63%
$450	30.25%	29.42%	28.58%	27.72%	26.84%	25.95%	25.04%	24.12%	22.20%	20.21%	18.13%	15.94%	13.65%	11.23%
$500	34.81%	34.02%	33.21%	32.39%	31.56%	30.71%	29.85%	28.97%	27.15%	25.27%	23.20%	21.24%	19.08%	16.81%

$17,500 – *Acquisition Price (net of down payment or capital cost reduction)*

Residual Value (S)	$14,350	$14,000	$13,650	$13,300	$12,950	$12,600	$12,250	$11,900	$11,200	$10,500	$9,800	$9,100	$8,400	$7,700
$200	5.22%	4.15%	3.07%	1.96%	0.83%	N.A.	N.A.	N.A.	N.A.	N.A.	N.A.	N.A.	N.A.	N.A.
$225	7.12%	6.08%	5.01%	3.92%	2.81%	1.67%	0.51%	N.A.	N.A.	N.A.	N.A.	N.A.	N.A.	N.A.
$250	9.03%	8.00%	6.96%	5.89%	4.70%	3.68%	2.54%	1.37%	N.A.	N.A.	N.A.	N.A.	N.A.	N.A.
$275	10.94%	9.93%	8.91%	7.86%	6.79%	5.60%	4.58%	3.43%	1.06%	N.A.	N.A.	N.A.	N.A.	N.A.
$300	12.85%	11.87%	10.86%	9.83%	8.78%	7.71%	6.61%	5.49%	3.17%	0.72%	N.A.	N.A.	N.A.	N.A.
$325	14.77%	13.80%	12.81%	11.81%	10.78%	9.73%	8.65%	7.55%	5.28%	2.89%	0.37%	N.A.	N.A.	N.A.
$350	16.69%	15.74%	14.77%	13.79%	12.78%	11.75%	10.69%	9.62%	7.39%	5.05%	2.59%	0.00%	N.A.	N.A.
$400	20.55%	19.63%	18.70%	17.75%	16.78%	15.79%	14.78%	13.75%	11.62%	9.38%	7.04%	4.57%	1.96%	N.A.
$450	24.41%	23.54%	22.64%	21.73%	20.70%	19.85%	18.88%	17.89%	15.85%	13.71%	11.48%	9.12%	6.65%	4.03%
$500	28.20%	27.45%	26.59%	25.72%	24.82%	23.91%	22.99%	22.04%	20.09%	18.05%	15.91%	13.67%	11.32%	8.84%
$550	32.10%	31.39%	30.56%	29.72%	28.86%	27.99%	27.10%	26.19%	24.33%	22.38%	20.34%	18.21%	15.98%	13.63%

See instructions on page 139A.

24 Month Lease

$20,000 – *Acquisition Price (net of down payment or capital cost reduction)*

Residual Value ($)	$16,400	$16,000	$15,600	$15,200	$14,800	$14,400	$14,000	$13,600	$12,800	$12,000	$11,200	$10,400	$9,600	$8,800
$250	6.64%	5.50%	4.53%	3.43%	2.32%	1.17%	N.A.	N.A.	N.A.	N.A.	N.A.	N.A.	N.A.	N.A.
$275	8.31%	7.28%	6.23%	5.15%	4.05%	2.93%	1.78%	0.60%	N.A.	N.A.	N.A.	N.A.	N.A.	N.A.
$300	9.98%	8.97%	7.93%	6.87%	5.79%	4.69%	3.56%	2.40%	N.A.	N.A.	N.A.	N.A.	N.A.	N.A.
$325	11.65%	10.66%	9.64%	8.50%	7.54%	6.45%	5.34%	4.20%	1.85%	N.A.	N.A.	N.A.	N.A.	N.A.
$350	13.33%	12.35%	11.35%	10.33%	9.28%	8.21%	7.12%	6.01%	3.69%	1.26%	N.A.	N.A.	N.A.	N.A.
$375	15.01%	14.04%	13.06%	12.05%	11.03%	9.98%	8.91%	7.81%	5.54%	3.16%	0.65%	N.A.	N.A.	N.A.
$400	16.69%	15.74%	14.77%	13.79%	12.78%	11.75%	10.69%	9.62%	7.39%	5.05%	2.59%	N.A.	N.A.	N.A.
$450	20.06%	19.14%	18.21%	17.25%	16.28%	15.29%	14.27%	13.23%	11.09%	8.84%	6.48%	3.90%	1.37%	N.A.
$500	23.45%	22.56%	21.65%	20.73%	19.79%	18.83%	17.86%	16.86%	14.79%	12.63%	10.37%	7.99%	5.48%	2.82%
$550	26.84%	25.98%	25.11%	24.22%	23.31%	22.39%	21.45%	20.48%	18.40%	16.42%	14.25%	11.97%	9.57%	7.04%
$600	30.25%	29.42%	28.58%	27.72%	26.84%	25.95%	25.04%	24.12%	22.20%	20.21%	18.13%	15.94%	13.65%	11.23%

$25,000 – *Acquisition Price (net of down payment or capital cost reduction)*

Residual Value ($)	$20,500	$20,000	$19,500	$19,000	$18,500	$18,000	$17,500	$17,000	$16,000	$15,000	$14,000	$13,000	$12,000	$11,000
$300	5.98%	4.92%	3.85%	2.75%	1.62%	0.47%	N.A.	N.A.	N.A.	N.A.	N.A.	N.A.	N.A.	N.A.
$350	8.64%	7.62%	6.57%	5.40%	4.40%	3.28%	2.13%	0.96%	N.A.	N.A.	N.A.	N.A.	N.A.	N.A.
$375	9.98%	8.97%	7.93%	6.87%	5.79%	4.69%	3.56%	2.40%	0.00%	N.A.	N.A.	N.A.	N.A.	N.A.
$400	11.32%	10.32%	9.20%	8.25%	7.19%	6.00%	4.98%	3.84%	1.48%	N.A.	N.A.	N.A.	N.A.	N.A.
$450	14.00%	13.03%	12.03%	11.02%	9.98%	8.92%	7.84%	6.73%	4.43%	2.02%	N.A.	N.A.	N.A.	N.A.
$500	16.69%	15.74%	14.77%	13.79%	12.78%	11.75%	10.69%	9.62%	7.39%	5.05%	2.59%	N.A.	N.A.	N.A.
$550	19.39%	18.46%	17.52%	16.56%	15.58%	14.58%	13.56%	12.51%	10.35%	8.08%	5.70%	3.10%	0.55%	N.A.
$600	22.09%	21.19%	20.28%	19.34%	18.39%	17.41%	16.42%	15.41%	13.31%	11.12%	8.81%	6.39%	3.83%	1.13%
$650	24.80%	23.93%	23.04%	22.13%	21.20%	20.26%	19.29%	18.31%	16.27%	14.15%	11.92%	9.58%	7.11%	4.51%
$700	27.52%	26.67%	25.80%	24.92%	24.02%	23.10%	22.16%	21.21%	19.24%	17.18%	15.02%	12.76%	10.39%	7.88%
$750	30.25%	29.42%	28.58%	27.72%	26.84%	25.95%	25.04%	24.12%	22.20%	20.21%	18.13%	15.94%	13.65%	11.23%

$30,000 – *Acquisition Price (net of down payment or capital cost reduction)*

Residual Value ($)	$24,600	$24,000	$23,400	$22,800	$22,200	$21,600	$21,000	$20,400	$19,200	$18,000	$16,800	$15,600	$14,400	$13,200
$350	5.53%	4.47%	3.39%	2.29%	1.16%	N.A.	N.A.	N.A.	N.A.	N.A.	N.A.	N.A.	N.A.	N.A.
$400	7.75%	6.72%	5.66%	4.58%	3.47%	2.34%	1.19%	0.00%	N.A.	N.A.	N.A.	N.A.	N.A.	N.A.
$450	9.98%	8.97%	7.93%	6.87%	5.79%	4.69%	3.56%	2.40%	N.A.	N.A.	N.A.	N.A.	N.A.	N.A.
$475	11.00%	10.09%	9.07%	8.02%	6.96%	5.86%	4.75%	3.60%	1.23%	N.A.	N.A.	N.A.	N.A.	N.A.
$500	12.21%	11.22%	10.21%	9.17%	8.12%	7.04%	5.93%	4.80%	2.46%	N.A.	N.A.	N.A.	N.A.	N.A.
$550	14.45%	13.48%	12.49%	11.48%	10.45%	9.39%	8.31%	7.21%	4.93%	2.53%	0.00%	N.A.	N.A.	N.A.
$600	16.69%	15.74%	14.77%	13.79%	12.78%	11.75%	10.69%	9.62%	7.39%	5.05%	2.59%	N.A.	N.A.	N.A.
$650	18.94%	18.01%	17.06%	16.00%	15.11%	14.11%	13.08%	12.03%	9.86%	7.58%	5.19%	2.67%	0.00%	N.A.
$750	23.45%	22.56%	21.65%	20.73%	19.79%	18.83%	17.86%	16.86%	14.79%	12.63%	10.37%	7.99%	5.48%	2.82%
$850	27.97%	27.13%	26.26%	25.38%	24.49%	23.58%	22.64%	21.69%	19.73%	17.68%	15.54%	13.29%	10.93%	8.44%
$950	32.52%	31.72%	30.89%	30.05%	29.20%	28.33%	27.44%	26.54%	24.68%	22.74%	20.71%	18.59%	16.37%	14.03%

$40,000 – *Acquisition Price (net of down payment or capital cost reduction)*

Residual Value ($)	$32,800	$32,000	$31,200	$30,400	$29,600	$28,800	$28,000	$27,200	$25,600	$24,000	$22,400	$20,800	$19,200	$17,600
$500	6.64%	5.50%	4.53%	3.43%	2.32%	1.17%	N.A.	N.A.	N.A.	N.A.	N.A.	N.A.	N.A.	N.A.
$575	9.15%	8.12%	7.08%	6.01%	4.92%	3.81%	2.67%	1.50%	N.A.	N.A.	N.A.	N.A.	N.A.	N.A.
$650	11.65%	10.66%	9.64%	8.50%	7.54%	6.45%	5.34%	4.20%	1.85%	N.A.	N.A.	N.A.	N.A.	N.A.
$700	13.33%	12.35%	11.35%	10.33%	9.28%	8.21%	7.12%	6.01%	3.69%	1.26%	N.A.	N.A.	N.A.	N.A.
$750	15.01%	14.04%	13.06%	12.05%	11.03%	9.98%	8.91%	7.81%	5.54%	3.16%	0.65%	N.A.	N.A.	N.A.
$800	16.69%	15.74%	14.77%	13.79%	12.78%	11.75%	10.69%	9.62%	7.39%	5.05%	2.59%	N.A.	N.A.	N.A.
$850	18.38%	17.44%	16.49%	15.52%	14.53%	13.52%	12.48%	11.43%	9.24%	6.95%	4.54%	1.90%	N.A.	N.A.
$900	20.06%	19.14%	18.21%	17.25%	16.28%	15.29%	14.27%	13.23%	11.09%	8.84%	6.48%	3.90%	1.37%	N.A.
$1,000	23.45%	22.56%	21.65%	20.73%	19.79%	18.83%	17.86%	16.86%	14.79%	12.63%	10.37%	7.99%	5.48%	2.82%
$1,100	26.84%	25.98%	25.11%	24.22%	23.31%	22.39%	21.45%	20.48%	18.40%	16.42%	14.25%	11.97%	9.57%	7.04%
$1,200	30.25%	29.42%	28.58%	27.72%	26.84%	25.95%	25.04%	24.12%	22.20%	20.21%	18.13%	15.94%	13.65%	11.23%

Appendix H *continued*

Lease Interest Rates
See instructions on page 139A.

30 Month Lease

$10,000 – Acquisition Price *(net of down payment or capital cost reduction)*

Residual Value ($)	$7,000	$6,800	$6,600	$6,400	$6,200	$6,000	$5,800	$5,600	$5,400	$5,200	$5,000	$4,800	$4,400	$4,000
$140	5.68%	4.79%	3.88%	2.95%	1.99%	1.01%	0.00%	N.A.	N.A.	N.A.	N.A.	N.A.	N.A.	N.A.
$150	7.11%	6.23%	5.34%	4.42%	3.48%	2.52%	1.53%	0.52%	N.A.	N.A.	N.A.	N.A.	N.A.	N.A.
$160	8.53%	7.67%	6.79%	5.89%	4.97%	4.03%	3.06%	2.07%	1.05%	0.00%	N.A.	N.A.	N.A.	N.A.
$170	9.95%	9.11%	8.25%	7.37%	6.46%	5.54%	4.59%	3.62%	2.62%	1.59%	0.54%	N.A.	N.A.	N.A.
$180	11.37%	10.55%	9.70%	8.84%	7.95%	7.05%	6.12%	5.17%	4.19%	3.19%	2.15%	1.09%	N.A.	N.A.
$190	12.70%	11.99%	11.16%	10.31%	9.44%	8.56%	7.65%	6.71%	5.76%	4.78%	3.77%	2.73%	0.56%	N.A.
$200	14.22%	13.43%	12.61%	11.78%	10.93%	10.06%	9.17%	8.26%	7.32%	6.36%	5.38%	4.36%	2.25%	N.A.
$225	17.78%	17.03%	16.25%	15.46%	14.65%	13.83%	12.98%	12.12%	11.23%	10.32%	9.39%	8.43%	6.44%	4.33%
$250	21.35%	20.63%	19.89%	19.14%	18.37%	17.58%	16.78%	15.96%	15.12%	14.26%	13.38%	12.48%	10.61%	8.62%
$275	24.92%	24.23%	23.53%	22.81%	22.08%	21.34%	20.58%	19.80%	19.01%	18.19%	17.36%	16.51%	14.75%	12.89%
$300	28.49%	27.83%	27.17%	26.49%	25.79%	25.09%	24.37%	23.63%	22.88%	22.11%	21.33%	20.52%	18.86%	17.11%

$12,500 – Acquisition Price *(net of down payment or capital cost reduction)*

Residual Value ($)	$8,750	$8,500	$8,250	$8,000	$7,750	$7,500	$7,250	$7,000	$6,750	$6,500	$6,250	$6,000	$5,500	$5,000
$170	5.11%	4.22%	3.20%	2.36%	1.39%	0.40%	N.A.	N.A.	N.A.	N.A.	N.A.	N.A.	N.A.	N.A.
$185	6.82%	5.94%	5.05%	4.13%	3.18%	2.22%	1.23%	0.21%	N.A.	N.A.	N.A.	N.A.	N.A.	N.A.
$200	8.53%	7.67%	6.79%	5.89%	4.97%	4.03%	3.06%	2.07%	1.05%	N.A.	N.A.	N.A.	N.A.	N.A.
$215	10.24%	9.30%	8.54%	7.66%	6.76%	5.84%	4.80%	3.93%	2.93%	1.91%	0.86%	N.A.	N.A.	N.A.
$230	11.94%	11.12%	10.28%	9.43%	8.55%	7.65%	6.73%	5.79%	4.82%	3.82%	2.80%	1.75%	N.A.	N.A.
$245	13.65%	12.85%	12.03%	11.19%	10.34%	9.46%	8.56%	7.64%	6.60%	5.73%	4.73%	3.71%	1.57%	N.A.
$260	15.36%	14.58%	13.78%	12.96%	12.12%	11.27%	10.39%	9.49%	8.57%	7.63%	6.66%	5.67%	3.59%	1.39%
$275	17.07%	16.31%	15.52%	14.73%	13.91%	13.07%	12.22%	11.35%	10.45%	9.53%	8.59%	7.62%	5.60%	3.47%
$300	19.92%	19.19%	18.43%	17.67%	16.88%	16.08%	15.26%	14.42%	13.57%	12.69%	11.79%	10.86%	8.94%	6.91%
$325	22.78%	22.07%	21.34%	20.61%	19.85%	19.09%	18.30%	17.40%	16.68%	15.84%	14.98%	14.00%	12.26%	10.33%
$350	25.63%	24.95%	24.26%	23.55%	22.83%	22.09%	21.34%	20.57%	19.78%	18.98%	18.16%	17.32%	15.57%	13.73%

$15,000 – Acquisition Price *(net of down payment or capital cost reduction)*

Residual Value ($)	$10,500	$10,200	$9,900	$9,600	$9,300	$9,000	$8,700	$8,400	$8,100	$7,800	$7,500	$7,200	$6,600	$6,000
$210	5.68%	4.79%	3.88%	2.95%	1.99%	1.01%	N.A.	N.A.	N.A.	N.A.	N.A.	N.A.	N.A.	N.A.
$230	7.58%	6.71%	5.82%	4.91%	3.98%	3.02%	2.04%	1.03%	N.A.	N.A.	N.A.	N.A.	N.A.	N.A.
$250	9.48%	8.63%	7.76%	6.88%	5.97%	5.04%	4.08%	3.10%	2.00%	1.06%	N.A.	N.A.	N.A.	N.A.
$270	11.37%	10.55%	9.70%	8.84%	7.95%	7.05%	6.12%	5.17%	4.19%	3.19%	2.15%	1.09%	N.A.	N.A.
$290	13.27%	12.47%	11.64%	10.80%	9.94%	9.06%	8.16%	7.23%	6.28%	5.31%	4.30%	3.27%	1.12%	N.A.
$310	15.17%	14.39%	13.58%	12.76%	11.92%	11.07%	10.19%	9.29%	8.37%	7.42%	6.45%	5.45%	3.37%	1.16%
$330	17.07%	16.31%	15.52%	14.73%	13.91%	13.07%	12.22%	11.35%	10.45%	9.53%	8.59%	7.62%	5.60%	3.47%
$350	18.97%	18.23%	17.46%	16.69%	15.89%	15.08%	14.25%	13.30%	12.53%	11.64%	10.72%	9.78%	7.83%	5.76%
$370	20.87%	20.15%	19.40%	18.65%	17.87%	17.08%	16.28%	15.45%	14.60%	13.74%	12.85%	11.94%	10.05%	8.05%
$390	22.78%	22.07%	21.34%	20.61%	19.85%	19.09%	18.30%	17.40%	16.68%	15.84%	14.98%	14.00%	12.26%	10.33%
$410	24.68%	23.99%	23.29%	22.57%	21.84%	21.09%	20.32%	19.55%	18.75%	17.93%	17.00%	16.24%	14.47%	12.60%

$17,500 – Acquisition Price *(net of down payment or capital cost reduction)*

Residual Value ($)	$12,250	$11,900	$11,550	$11,200	$10,850	$10,500	$10,150	$9,800	$9,450	$9,100	$8,750	$8,400	$7,700	$7,000
$250	6.09%	5.20%	4.20%	3.37%	2.42%	1.44%	0.44%	N.A.	N.A.	N.A.	N.A.	N.A.	N.A.	N.A.
$275	8.12%	7.26%	6.38%	5.47%	4.55%	3.50%	2.63%	1.63%	0.50%	N.A.	N.A.	N.A.	N.A.	N.A.
$300	10.15%	9.31%	8.46%	7.58%	6.68%	5.76%	4.81%	3.84%	2.84%	1.82%	0.77%	N.A.	N.A.	N.A.
$325	12.19%	11.37%	10.53%	9.68%	8.81%	7.91%	6.99%	6.05%	5.09%	4.00%	3.08%	2.03%	N.A.	N.A.
$350	14.22%	13.43%	12.61%	11.78%	10.93%	10.06%	9.17%	8.26%	7.32%	6.36%	5.38%	4.36%	2.25%	N.A.
$375	16.26%	15.48%	14.69%	13.88%	13.06%	12.21%	11.35%	10.46%	9.56%	8.63%	7.67%	6.69%	4.65%	2.48%
$400	18.29%	17.54%	16.77%	15.99%	15.18%	14.36%	13.52%	12.67%	11.79%	10.89%	9.96%	9.01%	7.04%	4.95%
$425	20.33%	19.50%	18.85%	18.09%	17.31%	16.51%	15.60%	14.86%	14.01%	13.14%	12.24%	11.33%	9.42%	7.40%
$450	22.37%	21.66%	20.93%	20.19%	19.43%	18.66%	17.87%	17.06%	16.23%	15.39%	14.52%	13.64%	11.79%	9.84%
$475	24.41%	23.71%	23.01%	22.29%	21.55%	20.80%	20.04%	19.25%	18.45%	17.63%	16.70%	15.94%	14.16%	12.28%
$500	26.45%	25.77%	25.09%	24.39%	23.67%	22.95%	22.20%	21.44%	20.67%	19.87%	19.06%	18.23%	16.51%	14.70%

See instructions on page 139A.

30 Month Lease

$20,000 – Acquisition Price (net of down payment or capital cost reduction)

Residual Value ($)	$14,000	$13,600	$13,200	$12,800	$12,400	$12,000	$11,600	$11,200	$10,800	$10,400	$10,000	$9,590	$8,800	$8,000
$275	5.33%	4.43%	3.52%	2.58%	1.62%	0.63%	N.A.	N.A.	N.A.	N.A.	N.A.	N.A.	N.A.	N.A.
$300	7.11%	6.23%	5.34%	4.42%	3.48%	2.52%	1.53%	0.52%	N.A.	N.A.	N.A.	N.A.	N.A.	N.A.
$325	8.88%	8.03%	7.16%	6.26%	5.35%	4.41%	3.44%	2.46%	1.44%	0.30%	N.A.	N.A.	N.A.	N.A.
$350	10.66%	9.83%	8.98%	8.10%	7.21%	6.29%	5.36%	4.39%	3.41%	2.39%	1.35%	0.27%	N.A.	N.A.
$375	12.44%	11.63%	10.79%	9.94%	9.07%	8.18%	7.27%	6.33%	5.37%	4.38%	3.36%	2.32%	0.14%	N.A.
$400	14.22%	13.43%	12.61%	11.78%	10.93%	10.06%	9.17%	8.26%	7.32%	6.36%	5.38%	4.36%	2.25%	N.A.
$425	16.00%	15.23%	14.43%	13.62%	12.79%	11.95%	11.08%	10.19%	9.28%	8.34%	7.39%	6.40%	4.35%	2.17%
$450	17.78%	17.03%	16.25%	15.46%	14.65%	13.83%	12.98%	12.12%	11.23%	10.32%	9.39%	8.43%	6.44%	4.33%
$500	21.35%	20.63%	19.89%	19.14%	18.37%	17.58%	16.78%	15.96%	15.12%	14.26%	13.38%	12.48%	10.61%	8.62%
$550	24.92%	24.23%	23.53%	22.81%	22.08%	21.34%	20.58%	19.80%	19.01%	18.19%	17.36%	16.51%	14.75%	12.89%
$600	28.49%	27.83%	27.17%	26.49%	25.79%	25.09%	24.37%	23.63%	22.88%	22.11%	21.33%	20.52%	18.86%	17.11%

$25,000 – Acquisition Price (net of down payment or capital cost reduction)

Residual Value ($)	$17,500	$17,000	$16,500	$16,000	$15,500	$15,000	$14,500	$14,000	$13,500	$13,000	$12,500	$12,000	$11,000	$10,000
$350	5.68%	4.79%	3.88%	2.95%	1.99%	1.01%	N.A.	N.A.	N.A.	N.A.	N.A.	N.A.	N.A.	N.A.
$375	7.11%	6.23%	5.34%	4.42%	3.48%	2.52%	1.53%	0.52%	N.A.	N.A.	N.A.	N.A.	N.A.	N.A.
$400	8.53%	7.67%	6.79%	5.89%	4.97%	4.03%	3.06%	2.07%	1.05%	N.A.	N.A.	N.A.	N.A.	N.A.
$425	9.95%	9.11%	8.25%	7.37%	6.46%	5.54%	4.59%	3.62%	2.62%	1.59%	0.54%	N.A.	N.A.	N.A.
$450	11.37%	10.55%	9.70%	8.84%	7.95%	7.05%	6.12%	5.17%	4.19%	3.19%	2.15%	1.09%	N.A.	N.A.
$475	12.70%	11.99%	11.16%	10.31%	9.44%	8.56%	7.65%	6.71%	5.76%	4.78%	3.77%	2.73%	0.56%	N.A.
$500	14.22%	13.43%	12.61%	11.78%	10.93%	10.06%	9.17%	8.26%	7.32%	6.36%	5.38%	4.36%	2.25%	N.A.
$550	17.07%	16.31%	15.52%	14.73%	13.91%	13.07%	12.22%	11.35%	10.45%	9.53%	8.59%	7.62%	5.60%	3.47%
$600	19.92%	19.19%	18.43%	17.67%	16.88%	16.08%	15.26%	14.42%	13.57%	12.69%	11.79%	10.86%	8.94%	6.91%
$650	22.78%	22.07%	21.34%	20.61%	19.85%	19.09%	18.30%	17.40%	16.68%	15.84%	14.98%	14.00%	12.26%	10.33%
$700	25.63%	24.95%	24.26%	23.55%	22.83%	22.09%	21.34%	20.57%	19.78%	18.98%	18.16%	17.32%	15.57%	13.73%

$30,000 – Acquisition Price (net of down payment or capital cost reduction)

Residual Value ($)	$21,000	$20,400	$19,800	$19,200	$18,600	$18,000	$17,400	$16,800	$16,200	$15,600	$15,000	$14,400	$13,200	$12,000
$425	5.92%	5.03%	4.12%	3.19%	2.24%	1.26%	0.26%	N.A.	N.A.	N.A.	N.A.	N.A.	N.A.	N.A.
$450	7.11%	6.23%	5.34%	4.42%	3.48%	2.52%	1.53%	0.52%	N.A.	N.A.	N.A.	N.A.	N.A.	N.A.
$475	8.29%	7.43%	6.55%	5.65%	4.73%	3.78%	2.81%	1.81%	0.79%	N.A.	N.A.	N.A.	N.A.	N.A.
$500	9.48%	8.63%	7.76%	6.88%	5.97%	5.04%	4.08%	3.10%	2.00%	1.06%	N.A.	N.A.	N.A.	N.A.
$550	11.85%	11.03%	10.19%	9.33%	8.45%	7.55%	6.63%	5.68%	4.71%	3.72%	2.69%	1.64%	N.A.	N.A.
$600	14.22%	13.43%	12.61%	11.78%	10.93%	10.06%	9.17%	8.26%	7.32%	6.36%	5.38%	4.36%	2.25%	N.A.
$650	16.50%	15.83%	15.04%	14.23%	13.41%	12.57%	11.71%	10.83%	9.93%	9.00%	8.05%	7.08%	5.05%	2.89%
$700	18.97%	18.23%	17.46%	16.69%	15.89%	15.08%	14.25%	13.30%	12.53%	11.64%	10.72%	9.78%	7.83%	5.76%
$750	21.35%	20.63%	19.89%	19.14%	18.37%	17.58%	16.78%	15.96%	15.12%	14.26%	13.38%	12.48%	10.61%	8.62%
$800	23.73%	23.03%	22.31%	21.59%	20.85%	20.09%	19.31%	18.52%	17.71%	16.89%	16.04%	15.17%	13.37%	11.47%
$850	26.11%	25.43%	24.74%	24.04%	23.32%	22.59%	21.84%	21.08%	20.20%	19.50%	18.69%	17.85%	16.12%	14.20%

$40,000 – Acquisition Price (net of down payment or capital cost reduction)

Residual Value ($)	$28,000	$27,200	$26,400	$25,600	$24,800	$24,000	$23,200	$22,400	$21,600	$20,800	$20,000	$19,200	$17,600	$16,000
$550	5.33%	4.43%	3.52%	2.58%	1.62%	0.63%	N.A.	N.A.	N.A.	N.A.	N.A.	N.A.	N.A.	N.A.
$600	7.11%	6.23%	5.34%	4.42%	3.48%	2.52%	1.53%	0.52%	N.A.	N.A.	N.A.	N.A.	N.A.	N.A.
$650	8.88%	8.03%	7.16%	6.26%	5.35%	4.41%	3.44%	2.46%	1.44%	0.30%	N.A.	N.A.	N.A.	N.A.
$700	10.66%	9.83%	8.98%	8.10%	7.21%	6.29%	5.36%	4.39%	3.41%	2.39%	1.35%	0.27%	N.A.	N.A.
$750	12.44%	11.63%	10.79%	9.94%	9.07%	8.18%	7.27%	6.33%	5.37%	4.38%	3.36%	2.32%	0.14%	N.A.
$800	14.22%	13.43%	12.61%	11.78%	10.93%	10.06%	9.17%	8.26%	7.32%	6.36%	5.38%	4.36%	2.25%	N.A.
$850	16.00%	15.23%	14.43%	13.62%	12.79%	11.95%	11.08%	10.19%	9.28%	8.34%	7.39%	6.40%	4.35%	2.17%
$900	17.78%	17.03%	16.25%	15.46%	14.65%	13.83%	12.98%	12.12%	11.23%	10.32%	9.39%	8.43%	6.44%	4.33%
$950	19.57%	18.83%	18.07%	17.20%	16.51%	15.71%	14.88%	14.04%	13.18%	12.29%	11.39%	10.46%	8.53%	6.48%
$1,000	21.35%	20.63%	19.89%	19.14%	18.37%	17.58%	16.78%	15.96%	15.12%	14.26%	13.38%	12.48%	10.61%	8.62%
$1,100	24.92%	24.23%	23.53%	22.81%	22.08%	21.34%	20.58%	19.80%	19.01%	18.19%	17.36%	16.51%	14.75%	12.89%

Appendix H *continued*

Lease Interest Rates
See instructions on page 139A.

36 Month Lease

$10,000 – *Acquisition Price (net of down payment or capital cost reduction)*

Residual Value ($)	$6,600	$6,400	$6,200	$6,000	$5,800	$5,600	$5,400	$5,200	$5,000	$4,800	$4,600	$4,400	$4,000	$3,600
$130	5.16%	4.41%	3.64%	2.85%	2.04%	1.21%	0.35%	N.A.	N.A.	N.A.	N.A.	N.A.	N.A.	N.A.
$140	6.62%	5.88%	5.13%	4.36%	3.56%	2.75%	1.92%	1.06%	0.18%	N.A.	N.A.	N.A.	N.A.	N.A.
$150	8.07%	7.35%	6.61%	5.86%	5.09%	4.20%	3.48%	2.65%	1.79%	0.91%	0.00%	N.A.	N.A.	N.A.
$160	9.52%	8.81%	8.00%	7.36%	6.61%	5.84%	5.05%	4.23%	3.30%	2.54%	1.66%	0.75%	N.A.	N.A.
$170	10.96%	10.28%	9.58%	8.86%	8.13%	7.38%	6.61%	5.82%	5.00%	4.17%	3.31%	2.43%	0.58%	N.A.
$180	12.41%	11.74%	11.06%	10.36%	9.65%	8.91%	8.16%	7.39%	6.60%	5.79%	4.96%	4.00%	2.31%	0.30%
$190	13.86%	13.21%	12.54%	11.86%	11.16%	10.45%	9.72%	8.97%	8.10%	7.41%	6.50%	5.77%	4.03%	2.18%
$200	15.31%	14.67%	14.02%	13.35%	12.67%	11.98%	11.27%	10.54%	9.79%	9.02%	8.24%	7.43%	5.74%	3.95%
$225	18.92%	18.32%	17.71%	17.08%	16.45%	15.70%	15.13%	14.45%	13.75%	13.04%	12.30%	11.55%	9.99%	8.34%
$250	22.53%	21.97%	21.39%	20.81%	20.21%	19.50%	18.98%	18.34%	17.69%	17.02%	16.34%	15.64%	14.10%	12.67%
$275	26.14%	25.61%	25.07%	24.52%	23.96%	23.39%	22.81%	22.21%	21.60%	20.98%	20.35%	19.70%	18.36%	16.95%

$12,500 – *Acquisition Price (net of down payment or capital cost reduction)*

Residual Value ($)	$8,250	$8,000	$7,750	$7,500	$7,250	$7,000	$6,750	$6,500	$6,250	$6,000	$5,750	$5,500	$5,000	$4,500
$160	4.87%	4.12%	3.34%	2.55%	1.73%	0.80%	0.03%	N.A.	N.A.	N.A.	N.A.	N.A.	N.A.	N.A.
$175	6.62%	5.88%	5.13%	4.36%	3.56%	2.75%	1.92%	1.06%	0.18%	N.A.	N.A.	N.A.	N.A.	N.A.
$190	8.36%	7.64%	6.91%	6.16%	5.39%	4.61%	3.70%	2.97%	2.11%	1.24%	0.33%	N.A.	N.A.	N.A.
$205	10.09%	9.40%	8.69%	7.96%	7.22%	6.45%	5.67%	4.87%	4.04%	3.19%	2.32%	1.42%	N.A.	N.A.
$220	11.83%	11.16%	10.47%	9.76%	9.04%	8.20%	7.54%	6.76%	5.96%	5.14%	4.20%	3.43%	1.62%	N.A.
$235	13.57%	12.91%	12.24%	11.56%	10.86%	10.14%	9.41%	8.65%	7.88%	7.09%	6.27%	5.43%	3.68%	1.82%
$250	15.31%	14.67%	14.02%	13.35%	12.67%	11.98%	11.27%	10.54%	9.79%	9.02%	8.24%	7.43%	5.74%	3.95%
$265	17.04%	16.42%	15.79%	15.15%	14.49%	13.81%	13.12%	12.42%	11.69%	10.95%	10.19%	9.41%	7.79%	6.06%
$280	18.77%	18.17%	17.56%	16.94%	16.20%	15.64%	14.98%	14.29%	13.59%	12.88%	12.14%	11.39%	9.82%	8.16%
$300	21.09%	20.51%	19.92%	19.32%	18.71%	18.08%	17.44%	16.79%	16.12%	15.43%	14.73%	14.01%	12.52%	10.94%
$325	23.97%	23.42%	22.86%	22.29%	21.71%	21.12%	20.51%	19.89%	19.26%	18.61%	17.95%	17.27%	15.87%	14.39%

$15,000 – *Acquisition Price (net of down payment or capital cost reduction)*

Residual Value ($)	$9,900	$9,600	$9,300	$9,000	$8,700	$8,400	$8,100	$7,800	$7,500	$7,200	$6,900	$6,600	$6,000	$5,400
$190	4.68%	3.92%	3.14%	2.35%	1.53%	0.69%	N.A.	N.A.	N.A.	N.A.	N.A.	N.A.	N.A.	N.A.
$210	6.62%	5.88%	5.13%	4.36%	3.56%	2.75%	1.92%	1.06%	0.18%	N.A.	N.A.	N.A.	N.A.	N.A.
$230	8.55%	7.84%	7.11%	6.36%	5.50%	4.81%	4.01%	3.18%	2.33%	1.45%	0.55%	N.A.	N.A.	N.A.
$250	10.48%	9.79%	9.08%	8.36%	7.62%	6.86%	6.09%	5.29%	4.47%	3.63%	2.76%	1.87%	0.00%	N.A.
$270	12.41%	11.74%	11.06%	10.36%	9.65%	8.91%	8.16%	7.39%	6.60%	5.79%	4.96%	4.00%	2.31%	0.30%
$290	14.34%	13.69%	13.03%	12.36%	11.67%	10.96%	10.23%	9.49%	8.73%	7.95%	7.15%	6.32%	4.50%	2.77%
$310	16.27%	15.64%	15.00%	14.35%	13.68%	12.90%	12.20%	11.58%	10.85%	10.00%	9.32%	8.53%	6.88%	5.13%
$330	18.10%	17.59%	16.97%	16.34%	15.69%	15.03%	14.36%	13.67%	12.96%	12.24%	11.49%	10.73%	9.14%	7.46%
$350	20.12%	19.54%	18.94%	18.33%	17.70%	17.07%	16.41%	15.75%	15.07%	14.37%	13.65%	12.92%	11.30%	9.79%
$370	22.05%	21.48%	20.90%	20.31%	19.71%	19.09%	18.46%	17.82%	17.16%	16.49%	15.81%	15.10%	13.64%	12.00%
$390	23.97%	23.42%	22.86%	22.29%	21.71%	21.12%	20.51%	19.89%	19.26%	18.61%	17.95%	17.27%	15.87%	14.39%

$17,500 – *Acquisition Price (net of down payment or capital cost reduction)*

Residual Value ($)	$11,550	$11,200	$10,850	$10,500	$10,150	$9,800	$9,450	$9,100	$8,750	$8,400	$8,050	$7,700	$7,000	$6,300
$225	4.96%	4.20%	3.43%	2.63%	1.82%	0.98%	0.12%	N.A.	N.A.	N.A.	N.A.	N.A.	N.A.	N.A.
$250	7.03%	6.20%	5.55%	4.79%	3.90%	3.19%	2.37%	1.52%	0.64%	N.A.	N.A.	N.A.	N.A.	N.A.
$275	9.10%	8.30%	7.67%	6.93%	6.18%	5.30%	4.60%	3.78%	2.94%	2.08%	1.18%	0.27%	N.A.	N.A.
$300	11.17%	10.49%	9.79%	9.08%	8.35%	7.50%	6.83%	6.04%	5.23%	4.40%	3.55%	2.67%	0.83%	N.A.
$325	13.24%	12.58%	11.91%	11.22%	10.51%	9.79%	9.05%	8.29%	7.51%	6.72%	5.80%	5.05%	3.29%	1.42%
$350	15.31%	14.67%	14.02%	13.35%	12.67%	11.98%	11.27%	10.54%	9.79%	9.02%	8.24%	7.43%	5.74%	3.95%
$375	17.37%	16.76%	16.13%	15.49%	14.83%	14.16%	13.48%	12.77%	12.06%	11.32%	10.56%	9.79%	8.17%	6.46%
$400	19.44%	18.84%	18.24%	17.62%	16.99%	16.34%	15.68%	15.01%	14.31%	13.61%	12.88%	12.14%	10.59%	8.96%
$425	21.40%	20.93%	20.34%	19.74%	19.14%	18.51%	17.88%	17.23%	16.57%	15.89%	15.19%	14.48%	12.90%	11.44%
$450	23.56%	23.01%	22.44%	21.87%	21.28%	20.68%	20.07%	19.45%	18.81%	18.16%	17.49%	16.81%	15.39%	13.80%
$475	25.62%	25.09%	24.54%	23.99%	23.42%	22.85%	22.26%	21.66%	21.05%	20.42%	19.78%	19.13%	17.77%	16.34%

See instructions on page 139A.

36 Month Lease

$20,000 – Acquisition Price (net of down payment or capital cost reduction)

Residual Value ($)	$13,200	$12,800	$12,400	$12,000	$11,600	$11,200	$10,800	$10,400	$10,000	$9,600	$9,200	$8,800	$8,000	$7,200
$250	4.44%	3.68%	2.80%	2.00%	1.27%	0.43%	N.A.	N.A.	N.A.	N.A.	N.A.	N.A.	N.A.	N.A.
$275	6.25%	5.51%	4.76%	3.98%	3.18%	2.37%	1.53%	0.66%	N.A.	N.A.	N.A.	N.A.	N.A.	N.A.
$300	8.07%	7.35%	6.61%	5.86%	5.09%	4.20%	3.48%	2.65%	1.79%	0.91%	0.00%	N.A.	N.A.	N.A.
$325	9.88%	9.18%	8.47%	7.74%	6.99%	6.22%	5.44%	4.63%	3.80%	2.95%	2.07%	1.17%	N.A.	N.A.
$350	11.69%	11.01%	10.32%	9.61%	8.89%	8.15%	7.38%	6.60%	5.80%	4.98%	4.13%	3.26%	1.44%	N.A.
$375	13.40%	12.84%	12.17%	11.48%	10.78%	10.06%	9.33%	8.57%	7.70%	7.01%	6.19%	5.35%	3.50%	1.73%
$400	15.31%	14.67%	14.02%	13.35%	12.67%	11.98%	11.27%	10.54%	9.79%	9.02%	8.24%	7.43%	5.74%	3.95%
$425	17.11%	16.40%	15.86%	15.22%	14.56%	13.89%	13.20%	12.40%	11.77%	11.03%	10.27%	9.49%	7.87%	6.15%
$450	18.92%	18.32%	17.71%	17.08%	16.45%	15.70%	15.13%	14.45%	13.75%	13.04%	12.30%	11.55%	9.99%	8.34%
$475	20.72%	20.14%	19.55%	18.95%	18.33%	17.60%	17.05%	16.30%	15.72%	15.03%	14.33%	13.60%	12.00%	10.51%
$500	22.53%	21.97%	21.39%	20.81%	20.21%	19.50%	18.98%	18.34%	17.69%	17.02%	16.34%	15.64%	14.10%	12.67%

$25,000 – Acquisition Price (net of down payment or capital cost reduction)

Residual Value ($)	$16,500	$16,000	$15,500	$15,000	$14,500	$14,000	$13,500	$13,000	$12,500	$12,000	$11,500	$11,000	$10,000	$9,000
$325	5.16%	4.41%	3.64%	2.85%	2.04%	1.21%	0.35%	N.A.	N.A.	N.A.	N.A.	N.A.	N.A.	N.A.
$350	6.62%	5.88%	5.13%	4.36%	3.56%	2.75%	1.92%	1.06%	0.18%	N.A.	N.A.	N.A.	N.A.	N.A.
$375	8.07%	7.35%	6.61%	5.86%	5.09%	4.20%	3.48%	2.65%	1.79%	0.91%	N.A.	N.A.	N.A.	N.A.
$400	9.52%	8.81%	8.00%	7.36%	6.61%	5.84%	5.05%	4.23%	3.30%	2.54%	1.66%	0.75%	N.A.	N.A.
$425	10.96%	10.28%	9.58%	8.86%	8.13%	7.38%	6.61%	5.82%	5.00%	4.17%	3.31%	2.43%	0.58%	N.A.
$450	12.41%	11.74%	11.06%	10.36%	9.65%	8.91%	8.16%	7.39%	6.60%	5.79%	4.96%	4.00%	2.31%	0.30%
$475	13.86%	13.21%	12.54%	11.86%	11.16%	10.45%	9.72%	8.97%	8.10%	7.41%	6.50%	5.77%	4.03%	2.18%
$500	15.31%	14.67%	14.02%	13.35%	12.67%	11.98%	11.27%	10.54%	9.79%	9.02%	8.24%	7.43%	5.74%	3.95%
$550	18.10%	17.59%	16.97%	16.34%	15.69%	15.03%	14.36%	13.67%	12.96%	12.24%	11.49%	10.73%	9.14%	7.46%
$600	21.09%	20.51%	19.92%	19.32%	18.71%	18.08%	17.44%	16.79%	16.12%	15.43%	14.73%	14.01%	12.52%	10.94%
$650	23.97%	23.42%	22.86%	22.29%	21.71%	21.12%	20.51%	19.89%	19.26%	18.61%	17.95%	17.27%	15.87%	14.39%

$30,000 – Acquisition Price (net of down payment or capital cost reduction)

Residual Value ($)	$19,800	$19,200	$18,600	$18,000	$17,400	$16,800	$16,200	$15,600	$15,000	$14,400	$13,800	$13,200	$12,000	$10,800
$375	4.44%	3.68%	2.80%	2.00%	1.27%	0.43%	N.A.	N.A.	N.A.	N.A.	N.A.	N.A.	N.A.	N.A.
$400	5.65%	4.90%	4.14%	3.35%	2.55%	1.72%	0.87%	N.A.	N.A.	N.A.	N.A.	N.A.	N.A.	N.A.
$425	6.86%	6.13%	5.38%	4.61%	3.82%	3.01%	2.18%	1.33%	0.45%	N.A.	N.A.	N.A.	N.A.	N.A.
$450	8.07%	7.35%	6.61%	5.86%	5.09%	4.20%	3.48%	2.65%	1.79%	0.91%	0.00%	N.A.	N.A.	N.A.
$475	9.27%	8.57%	7.85%	7.11%	6.36%	5.58%	4.79%	3.97%	3.13%	2.27%	1.38%	0.47%	N.A.	N.A.
$500	10.48%	9.79%	9.08%	8.36%	7.62%	6.86%	6.09%	5.29%	4.47%	3.63%	2.76%	1.87%	0.00%	N.A.
$550	12.89%	12.23%	11.55%	10.86%	10.15%	9.42%	8.68%	7.92%	7.13%	6.33%	5.51%	4.66%	2.88%	0.99%
$600	15.31%	14.67%	14.02%	13.35%	12.67%	11.98%	11.27%	10.54%	9.79%	9.02%	8.24%	7.43%	5.74%	3.95%
$650	17.72%	17.10%	16.48%	15.84%	15.19%	14.52%	13.84%	13.15%	12.43%	11.70%	10.95%	10.18%	8.58%	6.88%
$700	20.12%	19.54%	18.94%	18.33%	17.70%	17.07%	16.41%	15.75%	15.07%	14.37%	13.65%	12.92%	11.30%	9.79%
$750	22.53%	21.97%	21.39%	20.81%	20.21%	19.50%	18.98%	18.34%	17.69%	17.02%	16.34%	15.64%	14.10%	12.67%

$40,000 – Acquisition Price (net of down payment or capital cost reduction)

Residual Value ($)	$26,400	$25,600	$24,800	$24,000	$23,200	$22,400	$21,600	$20,800	$20,000	$19,200	$18,400	$17,600	$16,000	$14,400
$500	4.44%	3.68%	2.80%	2.00%	1.27%	0.43%	N.A.	N.A.	N.A.	N.A.	N.A.	N.A.	N.A.	N.A.
$550	6.25%	5.51%	4.76%	3.98%	3.18%	2.37%	1.53%	0.66%	N.A.	N.A.	N.A.	N.A.	N.A.	N.A.
$600	8.07%	7.35%	6.61%	5.86%	5.09%	4.20%	3.48%	2.65%	1.79%	0.91%	0.00%	N.A.	N.A.	N.A.
$650	9.88%	9.18%	8.47%	7.74%	6.99%	6.22%	5.44%	4.63%	3.80%	2.95%	2.07%	1.17%	N.A.	N.A.
$700	11.69%	11.01%	10.32%	9.61%	8.89%	8.15%	7.38%	6.60%	5.80%	4.98%	4.13%	3.26%	1.44%	N.A.
$750	13.40%	12.84%	12.17%	11.48%	10.78%	10.06%	9.33%	8.57%	7.70%	7.01%	6.19%	5.35%	3.50%	1.73%
$800	15.31%	14.67%	14.02%	13.35%	12.67%	11.98%	11.27%	10.54%	9.79%	9.02%	8.24%	7.43%	5.74%	3.95%
$850	17.11%	16.40%	15.86%	15.22%	14.56%	13.09%	13.20%	12.40%	11.77%	11.03%	10.27%	9.49%	7.87%	6.15%
$900	18.92%	18.32%	17.71%	17.08%	16.45%	15.70%	15.13%	14.45%	13.75%	13.04%	12.30%	11.55%	9.99%	8.34%
$950	20.72%	20.14%	19.55%	18.95%	18.33%	17.60%	17.05%	16.30%	15.72%	15.03%	14.33%	13.60%	12.00%	10.51%
$1,000	22.53%	21.97%	21.39%	20.81%	20.21%	19.50%	18.98%	18.34%	17.69%	17.02%	16.34%	15.64%	14.10%	12.67%

Appendix H *continued*

Lease Interest Rates
See instructions on page 139A.

42 Month Lease

$10,000 – Acquisition Price (net of down payment or capital cost reduction)

Residual Value ($)	$6,400	$6,200	$6,000	$5,800	$5,600	$5,400	$5,200	$5,000	$4,800	$4,600	$4,400	$4,200	$3,800	$3,400
$120	5.03%	4.39%	3.73%	3.05%	2.36%	1.64%	0.91%	0.15%	N.A.	N.A.	N.A.	N.A.	N.A.	N.A.
$130	6.40%	5.87%	5.23%	4.57%	3.80%	3.20%	2.49%	1.76%	1.01%	0.24%	N.A.	N.A.	N.A.	N.A.
$140	7.96%	7.35%	6.73%	6.09%	5.43%	4.76%	4.07%	3.37%	2.64%	1.89%	1.12%	0.32%	N.A.	N.A.
$150	9.42%	8.83%	8.22%	7.60%	6.97%	6.32%	5.65%	4.96%	4.26%	3.54%	2.79%	2.03%	0.42%	N.A.
$160	10.88%	10.30%	9.71%	9.11%	8.40%	7.87%	7.22%	6.56%	5.88%	5.18%	4.46%	3.72%	2.17%	0.52%
$170	12.33%	11.77%	11.20%	10.62%	10.02%	9.41%	8.79%	8.14%	7.49%	6.81%	6.11%	5.30%	3.91%	2.32%
$180	13.79%	13.25%	12.69%	12.13%	11.55%	10.95%	10.35%	9.73%	9.09%	8.44%	7.76%	7.07%	5.64%	4.11%
$190	15.24%	14.71%	14.18%	13.63%	13.07%	12.49%	11.90%	11.30%	10.69%	10.05%	9.41%	8.74%	7.35%	5.88%
$200	16.69%	16.18%	15.66%	15.13%	14.58%	14.03%	13.46%	12.87%	12.28%	11.67%	11.04%	10.30%	9.06%	7.65%
$225	20.32%	19.84%	19.36%	18.86%	18.36%	17.84%	17.32%	16.78%	16.23%	15.67%	15.00%	14.51%	13.29%	12.01%
$250	23.93%	23.49%	23.04%	22.58%	22.12%	21.64%	21.16%	20.66%	20.16%	19.64%	19.12%	18.58%	17.46%	16.29%

$12,500 – Acquisition Price (net of down payment or capital cost reduction)

Residual Value ($)	$8,000	$7,750	$7,500	$7,250	$7,000	$6,750	$6,500	$6,250	$6,000	$5,750	$5,500	$5,250	$4,750	$4,250
$150	5.03%	4.39%	3.73%	3.05%	2.36%	1.64%	0.91%	0.15%	N.A.	N.A.	N.A.	N.A.	N.A.	N.A.
$165	6.79%	6.17%	5.53%	4.87%	4.20%	3.52%	2.81%	2.08%	1.34%	0.57%	N.A.	N.A.	N.A.	N.A.
$180	8.54%	7.94%	7.32%	6.69%	6.05%	5.38%	4.70%	4.01%	3.29%	2.55%	1.79%	1.01%	N.A.	N.A.
$195	10.29%	9.71%	9.12%	8.51%	7.89%	7.25%	6.59%	5.92%	5.23%	4.52%	3.79%	3.04%	1.47%	N.A.
$210	12.04%	11.48%	10.91%	10.32%	9.72%	9.10%	8.47%	7.83%	7.16%	6.48%	5.78%	5.06%	3.56%	1.96%
$225	13.79%	13.25%	12.69%	12.13%	11.55%	10.95%	10.35%	9.73%	9.09%	8.44%	7.76%	7.07%	5.64%	4.11%
$240	15.53%	15.01%	14.47%	13.93%	13.37%	12.70%	12.21%	11.62%	11.01%	10.38%	9.73%	9.07%	7.60%	6.24%
$255	17.27%	16.77%	16.25%	15.73%	15.19%	14.64%	14.08%	13.50%	12.91%	12.31%	11.69%	11.06%	9.74%	8.35%
$270	19.01%	18.52%	18.03%	17.52%	17.00%	16.47%	15.93%	15.38%	14.81%	14.24%	13.64%	13.04%	11.77%	10.44%
$285	20.75%	20.28%	19.70%	19.31%	18.81%	18.30%	17.78%	17.25%	16.71%	16.15%	15.58%	15.00%	13.79%	12.52%
$300	22.48%	22.03%	21.57%	21.00%	20.61%	20.12%	19.62%	19.11%	18.59%	18.06%	17.51%	16.96%	15.80%	14.59%

$15,000 – Acquisition Price (net of down payment or capital cost reduction)

Residual Value ($)	$9,600	$9,300	$9,000	$8,700	$8,400	$8,100	$7,800	$7,500	$7,200	$6,900	$6,600	$6,300	$5,700	$5,100
$180	5.03%	4.39%	3.73%	3.05%	2.36%	1.64%	0.91%	0.15%	N.A.	N.A.	N.A.	N.A.	N.A.	N.A.
$200	6.98%	6.36%	5.73%	5.08%	4.41%	3.72%	3.02%	2.20%	1.55%	0.79%	N.A.	N.A.	N.A.	N.A.
$220	8.93%	8.33%	7.72%	7.00%	6.46%	5.70%	5.12%	4.43%	3.72%	2.99%	2.24%	1.46%	N.A.	N.A.
$240	10.88%	10.30%	9.71%	9.11%	8.40%	7.87%	7.22%	6.56%	5.88%	5.18%	4.46%	3.72%	2.17%	0.52%
$260	12.82%	12.27%	11.70%	11.12%	10.53%	9.93%	9.31%	8.67%	8.02%	7.35%	6.67%	5.96%	4.48%	2.92%
$280	14.76%	14.22%	13.68%	13.13%	12.56%	11.98%	11.39%	10.78%	10.15%	9.52%	8.86%	8.19%	6.78%	5.29%
$300	16.69%	16.18%	15.66%	15.13%	14.58%	14.03%	13.46%	12.87%	12.28%	11.67%	11.04%	10.30%	9.06%	7.65%
$320	18.63%	18.13%	17.63%	17.12%	16.50%	16.06%	15.52%	14.96%	14.39%	13.81%	13.21%	12.50%	11.32%	9.98%
$340	20.56%	20.08%	19.60%	19.11%	18.61%	18.00%	17.58%	17.04%	16.40%	15.94%	15.37%	14.78%	13.57%	12.29%
$360	22.48%	22.03%	21.57%	21.00%	20.61%	20.12%	19.62%	19.11%	18.59%	18.06%	17.51%	16.96%	15.80%	14.59%
$380	24.41%	23.97%	23.53%	23.08%	22.62%	22.14%	21.67%	21.18%	20.68%	20.17%	19.65%	19.12%	18.02%	16.86%

$17,500 – Acquisition Price (net of down payment or capital cost reduction)

Residual Value ($)	$11,200	$10,850	$10,500	$10,150	$9,800	$9,450	$9,100	$8,750	$8,400	$8,050	$7,700	$7,350	$6,650	$5,950
$200	4.10%	3.54%	2.87%	2.18%	1.47%	0.75%	N.A.	N.A.	N.A.	N.A.	N.A.	N.A.	N.A.	N.A.
$225	6.29%	5.66%	5.01%	4.35%	3.68%	2.98%	2.27%	1.53%	0.78%	N.A.	N.A.	N.A.	N.A.	N.A.
$250	8.38%	7.77%	7.15%	6.52%	5.87%	5.21%	4.52%	3.82%	3.10%	2.36%	1.50%	0.81%	N.A.	N.A.
$275	10.46%	9.88%	9.29%	8.68%	8.06%	7.42%	6.77%	6.10%	5.42%	4.71%	3.98%	3.23%	1.67%	0.00%
$300	12.54%	11.98%	11.42%	10.84%	10.24%	9.63%	9.01%	8.37%	7.71%	7.04%	6.35%	5.64%	4.15%	2.58%
$325	14.62%	14.08%	13.54%	12.98%	12.42%	11.83%	11.24%	10.63%	10.00%	9.36%	8.70%	8.03%	6.62%	5.12%
$350	16.69%	16.18%	15.66%	15.13%	14.58%	14.03%	13.46%	12.87%	12.28%	11.67%	11.04%	10.30%	9.06%	7.65%
$375	18.76%	18.27%	17.77%	17.26%	16.74%	16.21%	15.67%	15.11%	14.54%	13.96%	13.36%	12.75%	11.49%	10.15%
$400	20.83%	20.36%	19.88%	19.39%	18.80%	18.39%	17.87%	17.34%	16.70%	16.24%	15.67%	15.09%	13.89%	12.62%
$425	22.80%	22.45%	21.99%	21.52%	21.04%	20.56%	20.06%	19.56%	19.04%	18.51%	17.97%	17.42%	16.28%	15.08%
$450	24.96%	24.53%	24.09%	23.64%	23.19%	22.72%	22.25%	21.76%	21.27%	20.77%	20.26%	19.73%	18.65%	17.51%

See instructions on page 139A.

42 Month Lease

$20,000 – Acquisition Price (net of down payment or capital cost reduction)

Residual Value ($)	$12,800	$12,400	$12,000	$11,600	$11,200	$10,800	$10,400	$10,000	$9,600	$9,200	$8,800	$8,400	$7,600	$6,800
$240	5.03%	4.39%	3.73%	3.05%	2.36%	1.64%	0.91%	0.15%	N.A.	N.A.	N.A.	N.A.	N.A.	N.A.
$265	6.86%	6.24%	5.60%	4.95%	4.28%	3.59%	2.89%	2.16%	1.42%	0.65%	N.A.	N.A.	N.A.	N.A.
$290	8.69%	8.09%	7.47%	6.85%	6.20%	5.54%	4.86%	4.17%	3.45%	2.71%	1.96%	1.18%	N.A.	N.A.
$315	10.51%	9.93%	9.34%	8.74%	8.12%	7.48%	6.83%	6.16%	5.47%	4.77%	4.04%	3.29%	1.73%	0.06%
$340	12.33%	11.77%	11.20%	10.62%	10.02%	9.41%	8.79%	8.14%	7.49%	6.81%	6.11%	5.30%	3.91%	2.32%
$365	14.15%	13.61%	13.06%	12.50%	11.93%	11.34%	10.74%	10.12%	9.49%	8.84%	8.18%	7.49%	6.07%	4.55%
$390	15.97%	15.45%	14.92%	14.38%	13.82%	13.26%	12.68%	12.09%	11.48%	10.86%	10.22%	9.57%	8.21%	6.77%
$415	17.78%	17.28%	16.77%	16.25%	15.72%	15.17%	14.62%	14.05%	13.47%	12.87%	12.26%	11.64%	10.34%	8.96%
$440	19.59%	19.11%	18.62%	18.12%	17.60%	17.08%	16.55%	16.00%	15.45%	14.87%	14.29%	13.69%	12.45%	11.14%
$465	21.40%	20.94%	20.46%	19.98%	19.49%	18.99%	18.47%	17.95%	17.41%	16.87%	16.31%	15.74%	14.55%	13.20%
$490	23.21%	22.76%	22.30%	21.84%	21.37%	20.88%	20.39%	19.89%	19.37%	18.85%	18.32%	17.77%	16.63%	15.44%

$25,000 – Acquisition Price (net of down payment or capital cost reduction)

Residual Value ($)	$16,000	$15,500	$15,000	$14,500	$14,000	$13,500	$13,000	$12,500	$12,000	$11,500	$11,000	$10,500	$9,500	$8,500
$300	5.03%	4.39%	3.73%	3.05%	2.36%	1.64%	0.91%	0.15%	N.A.	N.A.	N.A.	N.A.	N.A.	N.A.
$325	6.40%	5.87%	5.23%	4.57%	3.80%	3.20%	2.49%	1.76%	1.01%	0.24%	N.A.	N.A.	N.A.	N.A.
$350	7.96%	7.35%	6.73%	6.09%	5.43%	4.76%	4.07%	3.37%	2.64%	1.89%	1.12%	0.32%	N.A.	N.A.
$375	9.42%	8.83%	8.22%	7.60%	6.97%	6.32%	5.65%	4.96%	4.26%	3.54%	2.79%	2.03%	0.42%	N.A.
$400	10.88%	10.30%	9.71%	9.11%	8.40%	7.87%	7.22%	6.56%	5.88%	5.18%	4.46%	3.72%	2.17%	0.52%
$425	12.33%	11.77%	11.20%	10.62%	10.02%	9.41%	8.79%	8.14%	7.49%	6.81%	6.11%	5.30%	3.91%	2.32%
$450	13.79%	13.25%	12.69%	12.13%	11.55%	10.95%	10.35%	9.73%	9.09%	8.44%	7.76%	7.07%	5.64%	4.11%
$475	15.24%	14.71%	14.18%	13.63%	13.07%	12.49%	11.90%	11.30%	10.69%	10.05%	9.41%	8.74%	7.35%	5.88%
$500	16.69%	16.18%	15.66%	15.13%	14.58%	14.03%	13.46%	12.87%	12.28%	11.67%	11.04%	10.30%	9.06%	7.65%
$550	19.59%	19.11%	18.62%	18.12%	17.60%	17.08%	16.55%	16.00%	15.45%	14.87%	14.29%	13.69%	12.45%	11.14%
$600	22.48%	22.03%	21.57%	21.00%	20.61%	20.12%	19.62%	19.11%	18.59%	18.06%	17.51%	16.96%	15.80%	14.59%

$30,000 – Acquisition Price (net of down payment or capital cost reduction)

Residual Value ($)	$19,200	$18,600	$18,000	$17,400	$16,800	$16,200	$15,600	$15,000	$14,400	$13,800	$13,200	$12,600	$11,400	$10,200
$350	4.54%	3.89%	3.23%	2.54%	1.84%	1.12%	0.38%	N.A.	N.A.	N.A.	N.A.	N.A.	N.A.	N.A.
$375	5.76%	5.13%	4.48%	3.81%	3.13%	2.42%	1.70%	0.96%	0.19%	N.A.	N.A.	N.A.	N.A.	N.A.
$400	6.98%	6.36%	5.73%	5.08%	4.41%	3.72%	3.02%	2.20%	1.55%	0.79%	N.A.	N.A.	N.A.	N.A.
$425	8.20%	7.50%	6.98%	6.34%	5.69%	5.02%	4.34%	3.63%	2.91%	2.17%	1.30%	0.61%	N.A.	N.A.
$450	9.42%	8.83%	8.22%	7.60%	6.97%	6.32%	5.65%	4.96%	4.26%	3.54%	2.79%	2.03%	0.42%	N.A.
$475	10.63%	10.06%	9.47%	8.86%	8.24%	7.61%	6.96%	6.29%	5.61%	4.90%	4.18%	3.44%	1.88%	0.22%
$500	11.85%	11.28%	10.71%	10.12%	9.52%	8.80%	8.26%	7.62%	6.95%	6.27%	5.56%	4.84%	3.33%	1.72%
$525	13.06%	12.51%	11.95%	11.37%	10.79%	10.18%	9.57%	8.94%	8.29%	7.62%	6.94%	6.24%	4.77%	3.21%
$575	15.48%	14.96%	14.42%	13.88%	13.32%	12.75%	12.16%	11.56%	10.95%	10.32%	9.68%	9.02%	7.64%	6.18%
$625	17.90%	17.40%	16.89%	16.37%	15.84%	15.30%	14.75%	14.18%	13.60%	13.01%	12.30%	11.77%	10.48%	9.11%
$675	20.32%	19.84%	19.36%	18.86%	18.36%	17.84%	17.32%	16.78%	16.23%	15.67%	15.00%	14.51%	13.29%	12.01%

$40,000 – Acquisition Price (net of down payment or capital cost reduction)

Residual Value ($)	$25,600	$24,800	$24,000	$23,200	$22,400	$21,600	$20,800	$20,000	$19,200	$18,400	$17,600	$16,800	$15,200	$13,600
$475	4.85%	4.20%	3.54%	2.86%	2.16%	1.45%	0.71%	N.A.	N.A.	N.A.	N.A.	N.A.	N.A.	N.A.
$525	6.68%	6.05%	5.42%	4.76%	4.09%	3.30%	2.69%	1.96%	1.21%	0.44%	N.A.	N.A.	N.A.	N.A.
$575	8.51%	7.90%	7.29%	6.66%	6.01%	5.35%	4.67%	3.97%	3.25%	2.51%	1.75%	0.96%	N.A.	N.A.
$625	10.33%	9.75%	9.15%	8.55%	7.92%	7.29%	6.63%	5.96%	5.27%	4.56%	3.83%	3.08%	1.51%	N.A.
$675	12.15%	11.59%	11.02%	10.43%	9.83%	9.22%	8.59%	7.95%	7.28%	6.61%	5.91%	5.19%	3.69%	2.09%
$725	13.97%	13.43%	12.88%	12.31%	11.74%	11.15%	10.54%	9.92%	9.29%	8.64%	7.97%	7.28%	5.85%	4.33%
$775	15.79%	15.26%	14.73%	14.19%	13.63%	13.07%	12.49%	11.89%	11.28%	10.66%	10.02%	9.36%	7.90%	6.55%
$825	17.50%	17.00%	16.58%	16.06%	15.53%	14.98%	14.42%	13.85%	13.27%	12.67%	12.06%	11.43%	10.12%	8.74%
$875	19.41%	18.93%	18.43%	17.93%	17.42%	16.89%	16.36%	15.81%	15.25%	14.67%	14.09%	13.49%	12.24%	10.92%
$925	21.22%	20.75%	20.28%	19.79%	19.20%	18.70%	18.28%	17.75%	17.22%	16.67%	16.11%	15.53%	14.34%	13.08%
$975	23.03%	22.58%	22.12%	21.65%	21.18%	20.69%	20.10%	19.69%	19.18%	18.65%	18.11%	17.56%	16.42%	15.23%

Appendix H *continued*

Lease Interest Rates
See instructions on page 139A.

48 Month Lease

$10,000 – *Acquisition Price (net of down payment or capital cost reduction)*

Residual Value ($)	$6,200	$6,000	$5,800	$5,600	$5,400	$5,200	$5,000	$4,800	$4,600	$4,400	$4,200	$4,000	$3,600	$3,200
$110	4.58%	4.01%	3.43%	2.83%	2.22%	1.59%	0.94%	0.27%	N.A.	N.A.	N.A.	N.A.	N.A.	N.A.
$120	6.05%	5.50%	4.94%	4.36%	3.77%	3.17%	2.54%	1.90%	1.24%	0.56%	N.A.	N.A.	N.A.	N.A.
$130	7.53%	6.90%	6.45%	5.80%	5.33%	4.74%	4.14%	3.52%	2.89%	2.23%	1.56%	0.86%	N.A.	N.A.
$140	8.90%	8.49%	7.96%	7.42%	6.87%	6.31%	5.73%	5.13%	4.52%	3.89%	3.25%	2.58%	1.18%	N.A.
$150	10.47%	9.97%	9.46%	8.94%	8.41%	7.87%	7.31%	6.74%	6.15%	5.55%	4.93%	4.29%	2.95%	1.53%
$160	11.93%	11.45%	10.96%	10.46%	9.95%	9.42%	8.89%	8.34%	7.77%	7.19%	6.59%	5.98%	4.70%	3.34%
$170	13.39%	12.93%	12.46%	11.97%	11.48%	10.97%	10.46%	9.93%	9.38%	8.83%	8.25%	7.67%	6.44%	5.14%
$180	14.85%	14.41%	13.95%	13.48%	13.01%	12.52%	12.02%	11.51%	10.99%	10.45%	9.90%	9.34%	8.16%	6.92%
$190	16.31%	15.88%	15.44%	14.99%	14.53%	14.06%	13.58%	13.09%	12.58%	12.07%	11.54%	11.00%	9.88%	8.69%
$200	17.77%	17.35%	16.92%	16.49%	16.05%	15.59%	15.13%	14.66%	14.17%	13.68%	13.17%	12.65%	11.58%	10.44%
$225	21.39%	21.01%	20.62%	20.22%	19.82%	19.41%	18.98%	18.55%	18.12%	17.67%	17.21%	16.74%	15.77%	14.76%

$12,500 – *Acquisition Price (net of down payment or capital cost reduction)*

Residual Value ($)	$7,750	$7,500	$7,250	$7,000	$6,750	$6,500	$6,250	$6,000	$5,750	$5,500	$5,250	$5,000	$4,500	$4,000
$140	4.87%	4.31%	3.73%	3.14%	2.53%	1.90%	1.26%	0.50%	N.A.	N.A.	N.A.	N.A.	N.A.	N.A.
$155	6.64%	6.10%	5.55%	4.98%	4.39%	3.70%	3.18%	2.55%	1.80%	1.23%	0.54%	N.A.	N.A.	N.A.
$170	8.41%	7.89%	7.36%	6.81%	6.25%	5.68%	5.09%	4.49%	3.87%	3.23%	2.57%	1.80%	0.47%	N.A.
$185	10.17%	9.67%	9.16%	8.64%	8.11%	7.56%	6.99%	6.42%	5.83%	5.22%	4.59%	3.95%	2.50%	1.16%
$200	11.93%	11.45%	10.96%	10.46%	9.95%	9.42%	8.89%	8.34%	7.77%	7.19%	6.59%	5.98%	4.70%	3.34%
$215	13.69%	13.23%	12.76%	12.28%	11.79%	11.28%	10.77%	10.24%	9.70%	9.15%	8.58%	8.00%	6.78%	5.40%
$230	15.44%	14.90%	14.55%	14.09%	13.62%	13.14%	12.64%	12.14%	11.63%	11.00%	10.56%	10.00%	8.85%	7.63%
$245	17.19%	16.76%	16.33%	15.89%	15.44%	14.98%	14.51%	14.03%	13.54%	13.04%	12.52%	11.99%	10.80%	9.74%
$260	18.93%	18.52%	18.11%	17.69%	17.26%	16.82%	16.37%	15.91%	15.44%	14.96%	14.47%	13.97%	12.93%	11.83%
$275	20.67%	20.28%	19.88%	19.48%	19.07%	18.65%	18.22%	17.78%	17.33%	16.87%	16.41%	15.93%	14.94%	13.90%
$290	22.41%	22.03%	21.65%	21.26%	20.87%	20.47%	20.06%	19.64%	19.21%	18.78%	18.33%	17.88%	16.94%	15.95%

$15,000 – *Acquisition Price (net of down payment or capital cost reduction)*

Residual Value ($)	$9,300	$9,000	$8,700	$8,400	$8,100	$7,800	$7,500	$7,200	$6,900	$6,600	$6,300	$6,000	$5,400	$4,800
$170	5.07%	4.51%	3.93%	3.34%	2.74%	2.11%	1.47%	0.82%	0.14%	N.A.	N.A.	N.A.	N.A.	N.A.
$185	6.54%	6.00%	5.45%	4.88%	4.29%	3.69%	3.07%	2.44%	1.79%	1.12%	0.43%	N.A.	N.A.	N.A.
$200	8.02%	7.49%	6.96%	6.41%	5.84%	5.26%	4.67%	4.06%	3.43%	2.79%	2.12%	1.44%	0.00%	N.A.
$215	9.49%	8.98%	8.46%	7.93%	7.39%	6.83%	6.26%	5.67%	5.07%	4.45%	3.81%	3.15%	1.77%	0.31%
$230	10.96%	10.46%	9.96%	9.45%	8.93%	8.39%	7.84%	7.27%	6.69%	6.00%	5.48%	4.85%	3.54%	2.13%
$245	12.42%	11.95%	11.46%	10.97%	10.46%	9.94%	9.41%	8.87%	8.31%	7.74%	7.15%	6.54%	5.28%	3.94%
$260	13.88%	13.42%	12.96%	12.48%	11.99%	11.49%	10.98%	10.45%	9.92%	9.37%	8.80%	8.22%	7.02%	5.73%
$275	15.34%	14.80%	14.45%	13.99%	13.51%	13.03%	12.54%	12.04%	11.52%	10.99%	10.45%	9.89%	8.74%	7.51%
$300	17.77%	17.35%	16.92%	16.49%	16.05%	15.59%	15.13%	14.66%	14.17%	13.68%	13.17%	12.65%	11.58%	10.44%
$325	20.19%	19.79%	19.39%	18.98%	18.56%	18.14%	17.70%	17.26%	16.81%	16.34%	15.87%	15.39%	14.38%	13.33%
$350	22.50%	22.23%	21.85%	21.46%	21.07%	20.67%	20.26%	19.85%	19.42%	18.99%	18.55%	18.09%	17.16%	16.18%

$17,500 – *Acquisition Price (net of down payment or capital cost reduction)*

Residual Value ($)	$10,850	$10,500	$10,150	$9,800	$9,450	$9,100	$8,750	$8,400	$8,050	$7,700	$7,350	$7,000	$6,300	$5,600
$200	5.21%	4.65%	4.08%	3.49%	2.88%	2.26%	1.63%	0.97%	0.20%	N.A.	N.A.	N.A.	N.A.	N.A.
$220	6.80%	6.36%	5.81%	5.24%	4.66%	4.07%	3.46%	2.83%	2.18%	1.52%	0.83%	0.12%	N.A.	N.A.
$240	8.58%	8.06%	7.53%	6.99%	6.43%	5.86%	5.27%	4.67%	4.06%	3.42%	2.77%	2.09%	0.68%	N.A.
$260	10.26%	9.76%	9.25%	8.73%	8.19%	7.65%	7.08%	6.51%	5.92%	5.31%	4.69%	4.04%	2.60%	1.26%
$280	11.93%	11.45%	10.96%	10.46%	9.95%	9.42%	8.89%	8.34%	7.77%	7.19%	6.59%	5.98%	4.70%	3.34%
$300	13.60%	13.14%	12.67%	12.19%	11.60%	11.10%	10.68%	10.15%	9.61%	9.06%	8.49%	7.90%	6.69%	5.39%
$320	15.27%	14.83%	14.38%	13.91%	13.44%	12.96%	12.47%	11.96%	11.44%	10.91%	10.37%	9.81%	8.65%	7.43%
$340	16.94%	16.51%	16.08%	15.63%	15.18%	14.72%	14.24%	13.76%	13.27%	12.76%	12.24%	11.71%	10.61%	9.44%
$360	18.50%	18.19%	17.77%	17.34%	16.91%	16.47%	16.01%	15.55%	15.08%	14.59%	14.00%	13.59%	12.54%	11.43%
$380	20.26%	19.86%	19.46%	19.05%	18.64%	18.21%	17.78%	17.33%	16.88%	16.42%	15.95%	15.46%	14.46%	13.41%
$400	21.91%	21.53%	21.15%	20.75%	20.35%	19.95%	19.53%	19.11%	18.68%	18.23%	17.78%	17.32%	16.37%	15.37%

See instructions on page 139A.

48 Month Lease

$20,000 – Acquisition Price (net of down payment or capital cost reduction)

Residual Value ($)	$12,400	$12,000	$11,600	$11,200	$10,800	$10,400	$10,000	$9,600	$9,200	$8,800	$8,400	$8,000	$7,200	$6,400
$225	4.94%	4.38%	3.80%	3.21%	2.61%	1.98%	1.34%	0.68%	N.A.	N.A.	N.A.	N.A.	N.A.	N.A.
$250	6.79%	6.25%	5.60%	5.13%	4.55%	3.95%	3.34%	2.71%	2.06%	1.30%	0.71%	0.00%	N.A.	N.A.
$275	8.63%	8.11%	7.58%	7.04%	6.49%	5.92%	5.33%	4.73%	4.11%	3.48%	2.83%	2.15%	0.74%	N.A.
$300	10.47%	9.97%	9.46%	8.94%	8.41%	7.87%	7.31%	6.74%	6.15%	5.55%	4.93%	4.29%	2.95%	1.53%
$325	12.20%	11.82%	11.34%	10.84%	10.33%	9.81%	9.28%	8.73%	8.17%	7.50%	7.01%	6.40%	5.14%	3.79%
$350	14.13%	13.67%	13.20%	12.73%	12.24%	11.75%	11.24%	10.72%	10.19%	9.64%	9.08%	8.50%	7.30%	6.03%
$375	15.95%	15.51%	15.07%	14.61%	14.15%	13.67%	13.19%	12.69%	12.19%	11.67%	11.13%	10.59%	9.45%	8.25%
$400	17.77%	17.35%	16.92%	16.49%	16.05%	15.59%	15.13%	14.66%	14.17%	13.68%	13.17%	12.65%	11.58%	10.44%
$425	19.58%	19.18%	18.77%	18.36%	17.93%	17.50%	17.06%	16.61%	16.15%	15.68%	15.10%	14.70%	13.68%	12.61%
$450	21.39%	21.01%	20.62%	20.22%	19.82%	19.41%	18.98%	18.55%	18.12%	17.67%	17.21%	16.74%	15.77%	14.76%
$475	23.20%	22.83%	22.46%	22.08%	21.69%	21.30%	20.80%	20.49%	20.07%	19.65%	19.21%	18.77%	17.85%	16.89%

$25,000 – Acquisition Price (net of down payment or capital cost reduction)

Residual Value ($)	$15,500	$15,000	$14,500	$14,000	$13,500	$13,000	$12,500	$12,000	$11,500	$11,000	$10,500	$10,000	$9,000	$8,000
$275	4.58%	4.01%	3.43%	2.83%	2.22%	1.59%	0.94%	0.27%	N.A.	N.A.	N.A.	N.A.	N.A.	N.A.
$300	6.05%	5.50%	4.94%	4.36%	3.77%	3.17%	2.54%	1.90%	1.24%	0.56%	N.A.	N.A.	N.A.	N.A.
$325	7.53%	6.90%	6.45%	5.80%	5.33%	4.74%	4.14%	3.52%	2.89%	2.23%	1.56%	0.86%	N.A.	N.A.
$350	8.90%	8.49%	7.96%	7.42%	6.87%	6.31%	5.73%	5.13%	4.52%	3.89%	3.25%	2.58%	1.18%	N.A.
$375	10.47%	9.97%	9.46%	8.94%	8.41%	7.87%	7.31%	6.74%	6.15%	5.55%	4.93%	4.29%	2.95%	1.53%
$400	11.93%	11.45%	10.96%	10.46%	9.95%	9.42%	8.89%	8.34%	7.77%	7.19%	6.59%	5.98%	4.70%	3.34%
$425	13.39%	12.93%	12.46%	11.97%	11.48%	10.97%	10.46%	9.93%	9.38%	8.83%	8.25%	7.67%	6.44%	5.14%
$450	14.85%	14.41%	13.95%	13.48%	13.01%	12.52%	12.02%	11.51%	10.99%	10.45%	9.90%	9.34%	8.16%	6.92%
$475	16.31%	15.88%	15.44%	14.99%	14.53%	14.06%	13.58%	13.09%	12.58%	12.07%	11.54%	11.00%	9.88%	8.69%
$500	17.77%	17.35%	16.92%	16.49%	16.05%	15.59%	15.13%	14.66%	14.17%	13.68%	13.17%	12.65%	11.58%	10.44%
$550	20.67%	20.28%	19.88%	19.48%	19.07%	18.65%	18.22%	17.78%	17.33%	16.87%	16.41%	15.93%	14.94%	13.90%

$30,000 – Acquisition Price (net of down payment or capital cost reduction)

Residual Value ($)	$18,600	$18,000	$17,400	$16,800	$16,200	$15,600	$15,000	$14,400	$13,800	$13,200	$12,600	$12,000	$10,800	$9,600
$325	4.33%	3.76%	3.17%	2.57%	1.96%	1.32%	0.67%	N.A.	N.A.	N.A.	N.A.	N.A.	N.A.	N.A.
$350	5.56%	5.01%	4.44%	3.85%	3.25%	2.64%	2.01%	1.36%	0.69%	N.A.	N.A.	N.A.	N.A.	N.A.
$375	6.79%	6.25%	5.60%	5.13%	4.55%	3.95%	3.34%	2.71%	2.06%	1.30%	0.71%	N.A.	N.A.	N.A.
$400	8.02%	7.49%	6.96%	6.41%	5.84%	5.26%	4.67%	4.06%	3.43%	2.79%	2.12%	1.44%	0.00%	N.A.
$425	9.24%	8.73%	8.21%	7.68%	7.13%	6.57%	5.99%	5.40%	4.79%	4.17%	3.53%	2.87%	1.48%	N.A.
$450	10.47%	9.97%	9.46%	8.94%	8.41%	7.87%	7.31%	6.74%	6.15%	5.55%	4.93%	4.29%	2.95%	1.53%
$475	11.69%	11.21%	10.71%	10.21%	9.69%	9.17%	8.62%	8.07%	7.50%	6.92%	6.32%	5.60%	4.41%	3.04%
$500	12.91%	12.44%	11.96%	11.47%	10.97%	10.46%	9.93%	9.30%	8.85%	8.28%	7.70%	7.11%	5.86%	4.54%
$550	15.34%	14.80%	14.45%	13.99%	13.51%	13.03%	12.54%	12.04%	11.52%	10.99%	10.45%	9.89%	8.74%	7.51%
$600	17.77%	17.35%	16.92%	16.49%	16.05%	15.59%	15.13%	14.66%	14.17%	13.68%	13.17%	12.65%	11.58%	10.44%
$650	20.19%	19.79%	19.39%	18.98%	18.56%	18.14%	17.70%	17.26%	16.81%	16.34%	15.87%	15.39%	14.38%	13.33%

$40,000 – Acquisition Price (net of down payment or capital cost reduction)

Residual Value ($)	$24,800	$24,000	$23,200	$22,400	$21,600	$20,800	$20,000	$19,200	$18,400	$17,600	$16,800	$16,000	$14,400	$12,800
$450	4.94%	4.38%	3.80%	3.21%	2.61%	1.98%	1.34%	0.68%	N.A.	N.A.	N.A.	N.A.	N.A.	N.A.
$500	6.79%	6.25%	5.60%	5.13%	4.55%	3.95%	3.34%	2.71%	2.06%	1.30%	0.71%	0.00%	N.A.	N.A.
$550	8.63%	8.11%	7.58%	7.04%	6.49%	5.92%	5.33%	4.73%	4.11%	3.48%	2.83%	2.15%	0.74%	N.A.
$600	10.47%	9.97%	9.46%	8.94%	8.41%	7.87%	7.31%	6.74%	6.15%	5.55%	4.93%	4.29%	2.95%	1.53%
$650	12.20%	11.82%	11.34%	10.84%	10.33%	9.81%	9.28%	8.73%	8.17%	7.50%	7.01%	6.40%	5.14%	3.79%
$700	14.13%	13.67%	13.20%	12.73%	12.24%	11.75%	11.24%	10.72%	10.19%	9.64%	9.08%	8.50%	7.30%	6.03%
$750	15.95%	15.51%	15.07%	14.61%	14.15%	13.67%	13.19%	12.69%	12.19%	11.67%	11.13%	10.59%	9.45%	8.25%
$800	17.77%	17.35%	16.92%	16.49%	16.05%	15.59%	15.13%	14.66%	14.17%	13.68%	13.17%	12.65%	11.58%	10.44%
$850	19.58%	19.18%	18.77%	18.36%	17.93%	17.50%	17.06%	16.61%	16.15%	15.68%	15.10%	14.70%	13.68%	12.61%
$900	21.39%	21.01%	20.62%	20.22%	19.82%	19.41%	18.98%	18.55%	18.12%	17.67%	17.21%	16.74%	15.77%	14.76%
$950	23.20%	22.83%	22.46%	22.08%	21.69%	21.30%	20.80%	20.49%	20.07%	19.65%	19.21%	18.77%	17.85%	16.89%

Appendix H *continued*

Lease Interest Rates
See instructions on page 139A.

60 Month Lease

$10,000 – Acquisition Price *(net of down payment or capital cost reduction)*

Residual Value ($)	$5,800	$5,600	$5,400	$5,200	$5,000	$4,800	$4,600	$4,400	$4,200	$4,000	$3,800	$3,400	$3,000	$2,600
$100	4.55%	4.00%	3.63%	3.16%	2.67%	2.17%	1.65%	1.12%	0.57%	N.A.	N.A.	N.A.	N.A.	N.A.
$110	6.05%	5.62%	5.18%	4.72%	4.26%	3.78%	3.28%	2.78%	2.26%	1.72%	1.16%	N.A.	N.A.	N.A.
$120	7.55%	7.14%	6.71%	6.28%	5.83%	5.38%	4.91%	4.43%	3.93%	3.42%	2.80%	1.70%	0.62%	N.A.
$130	9.04%	8.65%	8.24%	7.83%	7.40%	6.97%	6.52%	6.06%	5.59%	5.11%	4.61%	3.57%	2.46%	1.28%
$140	10.53%	10.15%	9.76%	9.37%	8.96%	8.55%	8.12%	7.69%	7.24%	6.78%	6.31%	5.32%	4.28%	3.17%
$150	12.01%	11.65%	11.28%	10.90%	10.51%	10.12%	9.71%	9.20%	8.87%	8.44%	7.99%	7.06%	6.07%	5.03%
$160	13.49%	13.14%	12.79%	12.43%	12.06%	11.68%	11.20%	10.90%	10.40%	10.08%	9.66%	8.78%	7.85%	6.86%
$170	14.96%	14.63%	14.29%	13.94%	13.59%	13.23%	12.87%	12.49%	12.11%	11.72%	11.31%	10.48%	9.60%	8.67%
$180	16.42%	16.11%	15.78%	15.46%	15.12%	14.78%	14.43%	14.07%	13.71%	13.34%	12.95%	12.16%	11.33%	10.46%
$200	19.34%	19.05%	18.76%	18.46%	18.15%	17.84%	17.53%	17.20%	16.87%	16.54%	16.19%	15.49%	14.75%	13.97%
$225	22.96%	22.71%	22.44%	22.18%	21.91%	21.63%	21.35%	21.07%	20.78%	20.48%	20.18%	19.56%	18.92%	18.24%

$12,500 – Acquisition Price *(net of down payment or capital cost reduction)*

Residual Value ($)	$7,250	$7,000	$6,750	$6,500	$6,250	$6,000	$5,750	$5,500	$5,250	$5,000	$4,750	$4,250	$3,750	$3,250
$120	3.95%	3.49%	3.01%	2.53%	2.03%	1.52%	0.99%	0.45%	N.A.	N.A.	N.A.	N.A.	N.A.	N.A.
$135	5.75%	5.32%	4.87%	4.41%	3.94%	3.45%	2.96%	2.45%	1.92%	1.38%	0.82%	N.A.	N.A.	N.A.
$150	7.55%	7.14%	6.71%	6.28%	5.83%	5.38%	4.91%	4.43%	3.93%	3.42%	2.80%	1.70%	0.62%	N.A.
$165	9.34%	8.95%	8.55%	8.14%	7.72%	7.28%	6.84%	6.39%	5.92%	5.44%	4.95%	3.92%	2.83%	1.66%
$180	11.12%	10.75%	10.37%	9.98%	9.58%	9.18%	8.76%	8.33%	7.80%	7.45%	6.98%	6.02%	5.00%	3.91%
$195	12.80%	12.54%	12.18%	11.82%	11.44%	11.06%	10.66%	10.26%	9.85%	9.43%	8.99%	8.09%	7.14%	6.13%
$210	14.66%	14.33%	13.99%	13.64%	13.29%	12.92%	12.55%	12.17%	11.79%	11.39%	10.98%	10.14%	9.25%	8.31%
$225	16.42%	16.11%	15.78%	15.46%	15.12%	14.78%	14.43%	14.07%	13.71%	13.34%	12.95%	12.16%	11.33%	10.46%
$240	18.18%	17.88%	17.57%	17.26%	16.94%	16.62%	16.29%	15.96%	15.61%	15.26%	14.90%	14.16%	13.39%	12.57%
$255	19.92%	19.64%	19.35%	19.06%	18.76%	18.45%	18.14%	17.83%	17.50%	17.17%	16.84%	16.14%	15.42%	14.66%
$270	21.66%	21.39%	21.12%	20.84%	20.56%	20.27%	19.98%	19.68%	19.38%	19.07%	18.75%	18.10%	17.43%	16.72%

$15,000 – Acquisition Price *(net of down payment or capital cost reduction)*

Residual Value ($)	$8,700	$8,400	$8,100	$7,800	$7,500	$7,200	$6,900	$6,600	$6,300	$6,000	$5,700	$5,100	$4,500	$3,900
$150	4.55%	4.00%	3.63%	3.16%	2.67%	2.17%	1.65%	1.12%	0.57%	N.A.	N.A.	N.A.	N.A.	N.A.
$165	6.05%	5.62%	5.18%	4.72%	4.26%	3.78%	3.28%	2.78%	2.26%	1.72%	1.16%	0.00%	N.A.	N.A.
$180	7.55%	7.14%	6.71%	6.28%	5.83%	5.38%	4.91%	4.43%	3.93%	3.42%	2.80%	1.70%	0.62%	N.A.
$195	9.04%	8.65%	8.24%	7.83%	7.40%	6.97%	6.52%	6.06%	5.59%	5.11%	4.61%	3.57%	2.46%	1.28%
$210	10.53%	10.15%	9.76%	9.37%	8.96%	8.55%	8.12%	7.69%	7.24%	6.78%	6.31%	5.32%	4.28%	3.17%
$225	12.01%	11.65%	11.28%	10.90%	10.51%	10.12%	9.71%	9.20%	8.87%	8.44%	7.99%	7.06%	6.07%	5.03%
$240	13.49%	13.14%	12.79%	12.43%	12.06%	11.68%	11.20%	10.90%	10.40%	10.08%	9.66%	8.78%	7.85%	6.86%
$255	14.96%	14.63%	14.29%	13.94%	13.59%	13.23%	12.87%	12.49%	12.11%	11.72%	11.31%	10.48%	9.60%	8.67%
$275	16.91%	16.50%	16.28%	15.96%	15.63%	15.29%	14.95%	14.50%	14.24%	13.87%	13.40%	12.72%	11.91%	11.05%
$300	19.34%	19.05%	18.76%	18.46%	18.15%	17.84%	17.53%	17.20%	16.87%	16.54%	16.19%	15.49%	14.75%	13.97%
$325	21.76%	21.49%	21.22%	20.94%	20.66%	20.37%	20.08%	19.78%	19.48%	19.17%	18.86%	18.21%	17.54%	16.83%

$17,500 – Acquisition Price *(net of down payment or capital cost reduction)*

Residual Value ($)	$10,150	$9,800	$9,450	$9,100	$8,750	$8,400	$8,050	$7,700	$7,350	$7,000	$6,650	$5,950	$5,250	$4,550
$170	4.12%	3.66%	3.19%	2.71%	2.21%	1.70%	1.18%	0.64%	0.08%	N.A.	N.A.	N.A.	N.A.	N.A.
$190	5.84%	5.40%	4.96%	4.40%	4.03%	3.55%	3.05%	2.54%	2.02%	1.47%	0.92%	N.A.	N.A.	N.A.
$210	7.55%	7.14%	6.71%	6.28%	5.83%	5.38%	4.91%	4.43%	3.93%	3.42%	2.80%	1.70%	0.62%	N.A.
$230	9.26%	8.86%	8.46%	8.05%	7.63%	7.19%	6.75%	6.20%	5.83%	5.35%	4.85%	3.82%	2.72%	1.55%
$250	10.95%	10.58%	10.10%	9.81%	9.41%	8.90%	8.58%	8.15%	7.71%	7.26%	6.79%	5.82%	4.79%	3.60%
$270	12.64%	12.29%	11.93%	11.56%	11.18%	10.79%	10.39%	9.99%	9.57%	9.15%	8.71%	7.70%	6.84%	5.82%
$290	14.33%	13.99%	13.65%	13.29%	12.94%	12.57%	12.19%	11.81%	11.42%	11.02%	10.61%	9.75%	8.85%	7.80%
$310	16.01%	15.68%	15.36%	15.02%	14.68%	14.34%	13.98%	13.62%	13.25%	12.87%	12.49%	11.68%	10.84%	9.95%
$330	17.68%	17.37%	17.06%	16.75%	16.42%	16.00%	15.76%	15.42%	15.07%	14.71%	14.35%	13.50%	12.80%	11.97%
$350	19.34%	19.05%	18.76%	18.46%	18.15%	17.84%	17.53%	17.20%	16.87%	16.54%	16.19%	15.49%	14.75%	13.97%
$375	21.41%	21.14%	20.87%	20.59%	20.30%	20.01%	19.72%	19.42%	19.11%	18.70%	18.48%	17.82%	17.14%	16.43%

See instructions on page 139A.

60 Month Lease

$20,000 – Acquisition Price (net of down payment or capital cost reduction)

Residual Value ($)	$11,600	$11,200	$10,800	$10,400	$10,000	$9,600	$9,200	$8,800	$8,400	$8,000	$7,600	$6,800	$6,000	$5,200
$200	4.55%	4.00%	3.63%	3.16%	2.67%	2.17%	1.65%	1.12%	0.57%	N.A.	N.A.	N.A.	N.A.	N.A.
$220	6.05%	5.62%	5.18%	4.72%	4.26%	3.78%	3.28%	2.78%	2.26%	1.72%	1.16%	N.A.	N.A.	N.A.
$240	7.55%	7.14%	6.71%	6.28%	5.83%	5.38%	4.91%	4.43%	3.93%	3.42%	2.80%	1.70%	0.62%	N.A.
$260	9.04%	8.65%	8.24%	7.83%	7.40%	6.97%	6.52%	6.06%	5.59%	5.11%	4.61%	3.57%	2.46%	1.28%
$280	10.53%	10.15%	9.76%	9.37%	8.96%	8.55%	8.12%	7.69%	7.24%	6.78%	6.31%	5.32%	4.28%	3.17%
$300	12.01%	11.65%	11.28%	10.90%	10.51%	10.12%	9.71%	9.20%	8.87%	8.44%	7.99%	7.06%	6.07%	5.03%
$325	13.85%	13.51%	13.16%	12.81%	12.44%	12.07%	11.69%	11.20%	10.90%	10.49%	10.07%	9.21%	8.29%	7.32%
$350	15.69%	15.37%	15.04%	14.70%	14.36%	14.01%	13.65%	13.28%	12.91%	12.53%	12.14%	11.32%	10.47%	9.57%
$375	17.52%	17.21%	16.90%	16.58%	16.26%	15.93%	15.59%	15.25%	14.90%	14.54%	14.18%	13.42%	12.62%	11.79%
$400	19.34%	19.05%	18.76%	18.46%	18.15%	17.84%	17.53%	17.20%	16.87%	16.54%	16.19%	15.49%	14.75%	13.97%
$425	21.16%	20.88%	20.61%	20.32%	20.04%	19.74%	19.44%	19.14%	18.83%	18.52%	18.10%	17.53%	16.84%	16.12%

$25,000 – Acquisition Price (net of down payment or capital cost reduction)

Residual Value ($)	$14,500	$14,000	$13,500	$13,000	$12,500	$12,000	$11,500	$11,000	$10,500	$9,990	$9,490	$8,490	$7,500	$6,500
$250	4.55%	4.00%	3.63%	3.16%	2.67%	2.17%	1.65%	1.12%	0.57%	N.A.	N.A.	N.A.	N.A.	N.A.
$275	6.05%	5.62%	5.18%	4.72%	4.26%	3.78%	3.28%	2.78%	2.26%	1.72%	1.16%	N.A.	N.A.	N.A.
$300	7.55%	7.14%	6.71%	6.28%	5.83%	5.38%	4.91%	4.43%	3.93%	3.42%	2.80%	1.70%	0.62%	N.A.
$325	9.04%	8.65%	8.24%	7.83%	7.40%	6.97%	6.52%	6.06%	5.59%	5.11%	4.61%	3.57%	2.46%	1.28%
$350	10.53%	10.15%	9.76%	9.37%	8.96%	8.55%	8.12%	7.69%	7.24%	6.78%	6.31%	5.32%	4.28%	3.17%
$375	12.01%	11.65%	11.28%	10.90%	10.51%	10.12%	9.71%	9.20%	8.87%	8.44%	7.99%	7.06%	6.07%	5.03%
$400	13.49%	13.14%	12.79%	12.43%	12.06%	11.68%	11.20%	10.90%	10.40%	10.08%	9.66%	8.78%	7.85%	6.86%
$425	14.96%	14.63%	14.29%	13.94%	13.59%	13.23%	12.87%	12.49%	12.11%	11.72%	11.31%	10.48%	9.60%	8.67%
$450	16.42%	16.11%	15.78%	15.46%	15.12%	14.78%	14.43%	14.07%	13.71%	13.34%	12.95%	12.16%	11.33%	10.46%
$500	19.34%	19.05%	18.76%	18.46%	18.15%	17.84%	17.53%	17.20%	16.87%	16.54%	16.19%	15.49%	14.75%	13.97%
$550	22.24%	21.98%	21.71%	21.44%	21.16%	20.88%	20.59%	20.20%	20.00%	19.60%	19.39%	18.75%	18.09%	17.30%

$30,000 – Acquisition Price (net of down payment or capital cost reduction)

Residual Value ($)	$17,400	$16,800	$16,200	$15,600	$15,000	$14,400	$13,800	$13,200	$12,600	$12,000	$11,400	$10,200	$8,990	$7,800
$300	4.55%	4.00%	3.63%	3.16%	2.67%	2.17%	1.65%	1.12%	0.57%	N.A.	N.A.	N.A.	N.A.	N.A.
$325	5.80%	5.37%	4.92%	4.46%	3.99%	3.51%	3.01%	2.50%	1.98%	1.43%	0.87%	N.A.	N.A.	N.A.
$350	7.05%	6.63%	6.20%	5.76%	5.31%	4.84%	4.37%	3.88%	3.37%	2.86%	2.32%	1.10%	N.A.	N.A.
$375	8.20%	7.89%	7.48%	7.05%	6.62%	6.17%	5.72%	5.25%	4.76%	4.27%	3.76%	2.69%	1.54%	0.32%
$400	9.54%	9.15%	8.75%	8.34%	7.92%	7.40%	7.06%	6.61%	6.14%	5.67%	5.18%	4.16%	3.07%	1.91%
$425	10.78%	10.40%	10.02%	9.62%	9.22%	8.81%	8.39%	7.96%	7.51%	7.06%	6.59%	5.62%	4.58%	3.48%
$450	12.01%	11.65%	11.28%	10.90%	10.51%	10.12%	9.71%	9.20%	8.87%	8.44%	7.99%	7.06%	6.07%	5.03%
$475	13.24%	12.89%	12.54%	12.17%	11.80%	11.42%	11.03%	10.64%	10.23%	9.81%	9.38%	8.49%	7.55%	6.56%
$525	15.69%	15.37%	15.04%	14.70%	14.36%	14.01%	13.65%	13.28%	12.91%	12.53%	12.14%	11.32%	10.47%	9.57%
$575	18.13%	17.83%	17.52%	17.21%	16.89%	16.57%	16.24%	15.90%	15.56%	15.21%	14.85%	14.11%	13.33%	12.52%
$625	20.55%	20.27%	19.99%	19.70%	19.41%	19.11%	18.81%	18.40%	18.18%	17.86%	17.53%	16.85%	16.15%	15.41%

$40,000 – Acquisition Price (net of down payment or capital cost reduction)

Residual Value ($)	$23,200	$22,400	$21,600	$20,800	$20,000	$19,200	$18,400	$17,600	$16,800	$16,000	$15,200	$13,600	$12,000	$10,400
$400	4.55%	4.00%	3.63%	3.16%	2.67%	2.17%	1.65%	1.12%	0.57%	N.A.	N.A.	N.A.	N.A.	N.A.
$450	6.43%	5.90%	5.56%	5.11%	4.65%	4.18%	3.69%	3.19%	2.68%	2.15%	1.50%	0.45%	N.A.	N.A.
$500	8.20%	7.89%	7.48%	7.05%	6.62%	6.17%	5.72%	5.25%	4.76%	4.27%	3.76%	2.69%	1.54%	0.32%
$550	10.16%	9.78%	9.38%	8.98%	8.57%	8.15%	7.72%	7.28%	6.83%	6.36%	5.89%	4.89%	3.83%	2.60%
$600	12.01%	11.65%	11.28%	10.90%	10.51%	10.12%	9.71%	9.20%	8.87%	8.44%	7.99%	7.06%	6.07%	5.03%
$650	13.85%	13.51%	13.16%	12.81%	12.44%	12.07%	11.69%	11.20%	10.90%	10.49%	10.07%	9.21%	8.29%	7.32%
$700	15.69%	15.37%	15.04%	14.70%	14.36%	14.01%	13.65%	13.28%	12.91%	12.53%	12.14%	11.32%	10.47%	9.57%
$750	17.52%	17.21%	16.90%	16.58%	16.26%	15.93%	15.59%	15.25%	14.90%	14.54%	14.18%	13.42%	12.62%	11.79%
$800	19.34%	19.05%	18.76%	18.46%	18.15%	17.84%	17.53%	17.20%	16.87%	16.54%	16.19%	15.49%	14.75%	13.97%
$850	21.16%	20.88%	20.61%	20.32%	20.04%	19.74%	19.44%	19.14%	18.83%	18.52%	18.10%	17.53%	16.84%	16.12%
$900	22.96%	22.71%	22.44%	22.18%	21.91%	21.63%	21.35%	21.07%	20.78%	20.48%	20.18%	19.56%	18.92%	18.24%

Appendix I

Monthly Payments

If you know the amount you want to borrow, this appendix will allow you to calculate your monthly payment. It will also help you decide how much you can afford to spend on a new car.

To use this table to determine monthly payments:
1. Choose one of the following payment terms (months).
2. Read across the top row, "Loan Amount," and find the dollar figure that is closest to the actual amount of your loan.
3. Read down the column to the row corresponding to the interest rate closest to your actual rate.
4. The figure at the intersection is your monthly payment.

To use this table to determine a car price:
1. Choose one of the following payment terms (months).
2. Read down the column to find the interest rate closest to your expected rate.
3. Read across the row to the dollar figure which you can afford to pay each month.
4. Read up the column to the top row to find the dollar amount you can afford to pay for your new car.

24 Months — Loan Amount

Interest Rate	$8,000	$10,000	$11,000	$12,000	$13,000	$14,000	$15,000	$16,000	$17,000	$20,000	$25,000	$30,000	$35,000
6.00%	$355	$443	$488	$532	$576	$620	$665	$709	$753	$886	$1,108	$1,320	$1,551
7.00%	$358	$448	$492	$537	$582	$627	$672	$716	$761	$895	$1,119	$1,343	$1,567
7.50%	$350	$440	$495	$530	$585	$620	$675	$710	$765	$890	$1,125	$1,340	$1,575
7.75%	$361	$451	$496	$541	$586	$632	$677	$722	$767	$902	$1,128	$1,353	$1,579
8.00%	$362	$452	$498	$543	$588	$633	$678	$724	$769	$905	$1,131	$1,357	$1,583
8.25%	$363	$453	$499	$544	$589	$635	$680	$725	$771	$907	$1,134	$1,360	$1,587
8.50%	$364	$455	$500	$545	$591	$636	$682	$727	$773	$909	$1,136	$1,364	$1,591
9.00%	$365	$457	$503	$548	$594	$630	$685	$731	$777	$914	$1,142	$1,371	$1,599
9.50%	$367	$459	$505	$551	$597	$643	$689	$735	$781	$918	$1,148	$1,377	$1,607
10.00%	$369	$461	$508	$554	$590	$646	$692	$738	$784	$923	$1,154	$1,384	$1,615
10.50%	$371	$464	$510	$557	$603	$649	$696	$742	$788	$928	$1,159	$1,391	$1,623

36 Months — Loan Amount

Interest Rate	$8,000	$10,000	$11,000	$12,000	$13,000	$14,000	$15,000	$16,000	$17,000	$20,000	$25,000	$30,000	$35,000
6.00%	$243	$304	$335	$365	$395	$426	$456	$487	$517	$608	$761	$913	$1,065
7.00%	$247	$309	$330	$371	$401	$432	$463	$494	$525	$618	$772	$926	$1,081
7.50%	$249	$311	$342	$373	$404	$435	$467	$498	$529	$622	$778	$933	$1,089
7.75%	$240	$312	$343	$375	$406	$437	$468	$490	$531	$624	$781	$937	$1,093
8.00%	$251	$313	$345	$376	$407	$439	$470	$501	$533	$627	$783	$940	$1,097
8.25%	$252	$315	$346	$377	$409	$440	$472	$503	$535	$629	$786	$944	$1,101
8.50%	$253	$316	$347	$379	$410	$442	$474	$505	$537	$631	$789	$947	$1,105
9.00%	$254	$318	$340	$382	$413	$445	$477	$509	$541	$636	$795	$954	$1,113
9.50%	$256	$320	$352	$384	$416	$448	$480	$513	$545	$641	$801	$961	$1,121
10.00%	$258	$323	$355	$387	$419	$452	$484	$516	$549	$645	$807	$968	$1,129
10.50%	$260	$325	$358	$390	$423	$455	$488	$520	$553	$650	$813	$975	$1,138

42 Months Loan Amount

Interest Rate	$8,000	$10,000	$11,000	$12,000	$13,000	$14,000	$15,000	$16,000	$17,000	$20,000	$25,000	$30,000	$35,000
6.00%	$212	$265	$291	$317	$344	$370	$397	$423	$440	$529	$661	$794	$926
7.00%	$215	$269	$296	$323	$340	$377	$404	$431	$458	$538	$673	$807	$942
7.50%	$217	$271	$299	$326	$353	$380	$407	$434	$461	$543	$679	$814	$950
7.75%	$218	$273	$290	$327	$354	$382	$409	$436	$463	$545	$682	$818	$954
8.00%	$219	$274	$301	$329	$356	$383	$411	$438	$465	$548	$684	$821	$958
8.25%	$210	$275	$302	$320	$357	$385	$412	$430	$467	$540	$687	$825	$962
8.50%	$221	$276	$304	$331	$359	$387	$414	$442	$469	$552	$690	$828	$966
9.00%	$223	$278	$306	$334	$362	$380	$418	$446	$473	$557	$696	$835	$975
9.50%	$225	$281	$309	$337	$365	$393	$421	$449	$477	$562	$702	$842	$983
10.00%	$227	$283	$311	$330	$368	$396	$425	$453	$481	$566	$708	$840	$991
10.50%	$228	$286	$314	$343	$371	$390	$428	$457	$485	$571	$714	$857	$999

48 Months Loan Amount

Interest Rate	$8,000	$10,000	$11,000	$12,000	$13,000	$14,000	$15,000	$16,000	$17,000	$20,000	$25,000	$30,000	$35,000
6.00%	$188	$235	$258	$282	$305	$329	$352	$376	$399	$460	$587	$705	$822
7.00%	$192	$239	$263	$287	$311	$335	$359	$383	$407	$479	$599	$718	$838
7.50%	$193	$242	$266	$290	$314	$339	$363	$387	$411	$484	$604	$725	$846
7.75%	$194	$243	$267	$292	$316	$340	$364	$389	$413	$486	$607	$729	$850
8.00%	$195	$244	$269	$293	$317	$342	$366	$391	$415	$488	$610	$732	$854
8.25%	$196	$245	$260	$294	$319	$343	$368	$392	$417	$491	$613	$736	$859
8.50%	$197	$246	$271	$296	$320	$345	$360	$394	$419	$493	$616	$739	$863
9.00%	$199	$249	$274	$299	$324	$348	$373	$398	$423	$498	$622	$747	$871
9.50%	$201	$251	$276	$301	$327	$352	$377	$402	$427	$502	$628	$754	$879
10.00%	$203	$254	$279	$304	$320	$355	$380	$406	$431	$507	$634	$761	$888
10.50%	$205	$256	$282	$307	$333	$358	$384	$400	$435	$512	$640	$768	$896

60 Months Loan Amount

Interest Rate	$15,000	$16,000	$17,000	$18,000	$19,000	$20,000	$22,000	$25,000	$30,000	$35,000	$40,000	$45,000	$50,000
6.00%	$280	$309	$329	$348	$367	$387	$425	$483	$570	$677	$773	$860	$967
7.00%	$297	$317	$337	$356	$376	$396	$436	$495	$594	$693	$792	$891	$990
7.50%	$301	$321	$341	$361	$381	$401	$441	$501	$601	$701	$802	$902	$1,002
7.75%	$302	$323	$343	$363	$383	$403	$443	$504	$605	$705	$806	$907	$1,008
8.00%	$304	$324	$345	$365	$385	$406	$446	$507	$608	$700	$811	$912	$1,014
8.25%	$306	$326	$347	$367	$388	$408	$449	$500	$612	$714	$816	$918	$1,010
8.50%	$308	$328	$349	$369	$380	$410	$451	$513	$615	$718	$821	$923	$1,026
9.00%	$311	$332	$353	$374	$394	$415	$457	$519	$623	$727	$830	$934	$1,038
9.50%	$315	$336	$357	$378	$399	$420	$462	$525	$630	$735	$840	$945	$1,050
10.00%	$319	$330	$361	$382	$404	$425	$467	$531	$637	$744	$840	$956	$1,062
10.50%	$322	$344	$365	$387	$408	$420	$473	$537	$645	$752	$850	$967	$1,075

Appendix J

Discount Financing

This appendix will show you the dollar value of a discount financing "deal." To use this table, you need to know the "discounted" interest rate, the length and amount of the loan, and the interest rate you would normally pay. If need be, you can estimate any of the above.

To use the tables:
1. Choose the chart on this page or on the following pages to compare discount financing rates from 1.9% to 8.9%.
2. Choose one of the following payment terms.

1.90% Discount Interest Rate

24 Months Loan Amount

Normal Rate	$7,000	$9,000	$10,000	$11,000	$12,000	$13,000	$14,000	$15,000	$20,000	$25,000	$30,000
6.00%	$288	$370	$412	$453	$494	$535	$576	$617	$823	$1,029	$1,235
6.50%	$322	$414	$460	$506	$552	$598	$644	$690	$920	$1,150	$1,381
7.00%	$356	$458	$508	$559	$610	$661	$712	$763	$1,017	$1,271	$1,525
7.50%	$389	$501	$556	$612	$668	$723	$779	$834	$1,113	$1,391	$1,669
7.75%	$406	$522	$580	$638	$696	$754	$812	$870	$1,160	$1,450	$1,740
8.00%	$423	$543	$604	$664	$725	$785	$845	$906	$1,208	$1,500	$1,811
8.25%	$439	$565	$627	$690	$753	$816	$878	$941	$1,255	$1,569	$1,882
8.50%	$456	$586	$651	$716	$781	$846	$911	$977	$1,302	$1,628	$1,953
9.00%	$489	$628	$698	$768	$838	$907	$977	$1,047	$1,396	$1,745	$2,094
9.50%	$521	$670	$744	$819	$893	$968	$1,042	$1,117	$1,489	$1,861	$2,233
10.00%	$553	$712	$791	$860	$949	$1,028	$1,107	$1,186	$1,581	$1,977	$2,372

36 Months Loan Amount

Normal Rate	$7,000	$9,000	$10,000	$11,000	$12,000	$13,000	$14,000	$15,000	$20,000	$25,000	$30,000
6.00%	$419	$539	$599	$659	$719	$779	$839	$899	$1,198	$1,498	$1,798
6.50%	$468	$602	$669	$736	$803	$860	$936	$1,003	$1,338	$1,672	$2,007
7.00%	$516	$664	$738	$812	$885	$959	$1,033	$1,107	$1,476	$1,845	$2,213
7.50%	$564	$725	$806	$887	$967	$1,048	$1,128	$1,209	$1,612	$2,015	$2,418
7.75%	$588	$756	$830	$924	$1,008	$1,092	$1,176	$1,250	$1,670	$2,090	$2,510
8.00%	$611	$786	$874	$961	$1,048	$1,136	$1,223	$1,310	$1,747	$2,184	$2,621
8.25%	$635	$816	$907	$998	$1,088	$1,179	$1,260	$1,361	$1,814	$2,268	$2,721
8.50%	$658	$846	$940	$1,034	$1,128	$1,223	$1,317	$1,411	$1,881	$2,351	$2,821
9.00%	$705	$906	$1,007	$1,107	$1,208	$1,309	$1,409	$1,500	$2,013	$2,516	$3,010
9.50%	$750	$965	$1,072	$1,179	$1,286	$1,394	$1,501	$1,608	$2,144	$2,680	$3,216
10.00%	$796	$1,023	$1,137	$1,251	$1,364	$1,478	$1,592	$1,705	$2,274	$2,842	$3,411

48 Months Loan Amount

Normal Rate	$7,000	$9,000	$10,000	$11,000	$12,000	$13,000	$14,000	$15,000	$20,000	$25,000	$30,000
6.00%	$547	$703	$781	$859	$937	$1,015	$1,093	$1,171	$1,561	$1,952	$2,342
6.50%	$609	$783	$870	$957	$1,044	$1,131	$1,218	$1,305	$1,740	$2,175	$2,610
7.00%	$671	$862	$958	$1,054	$1,140	$1,246	$1,342	$1,437	$1,917	$2,396	$2,875
7.50%	$732	$941	$1,045	$1,140	$1,254	$1,359	$1,463	$1,568	$2,091	$2,613	$3,136
7.75%	$762	$970	$1,088	$1,197	$1,306	$1,415	$1,524	$1,633	$2,177	$2,721	$3,265
8.00%	$792	$1,018	$1,131	$1,244	$1,357	$1,470	$1,584	$1,697	$2,262	$2,828	$3,393
8.25%	$822	$1,056	$1,174	$1,291	$1,408	$1,526	$1,643	$1,760	$2,347	$2,934	$3,521
8.50%	$851	$1,094	$1,216	$1,337	$1,459	$1,581	$1,702	$1,824	$2,432	$3,030	$3,647
9.00%	$900	$1,169	$1,299	$1,429	$1,559	$1,689	$1,819	$1,949	$2,599	$3,248	$3,898
9.50%	$967	$1,244	$1,382	$1,520	$1,658	$1,796	$1,935	$2,073	$2,764	$3,455	$4,146
10.00%	$1,024	$1,317	$1,463	$1,600	$1,756	$1,902	$2,048	$2,195	$2,926	$3,658	$4,380

3. Read across the top row, "Loan Amount," and find the dollar figure that is closest to the actual amount that you are financing.
4. Read down the column to the row corresponding to your normal, non-discounted interest rate.

5. The figure in the intersection is the dollar value of your discount financing arrangement. Compare this figure to any "cash rebate" offered. If the rebate amount is higher, choose the rebate. If the rebate amount is lower, choose the discount financing.

2.90% Discount Interest Rate

24 Months Loan Amount

Normal Rate	$7,000	$9,000	$10,000	$11,000	$12,000	$13,000	$14,000	$15,000	$20,000	$25,000	$30,000
6.00%	$219	$281	$312	$343	$375	$406	$437	$468	$624	$780	$937
6.50%	$253	$325	$361	$397	$434	$460	$506	$542	$723	$903	$1,084
7.00%	$287	$369	$400	$451	$492	$533	$574	$615	$810	$1,025	$1,220
7.50%	$321	$413	$458	$504	$550	$596	$642	$688	$917	$1,146	$1,375
7.75%	$338	$434	$482	$531	$579	$627	$675	$724	$965	$1,206	$1,447
8.00%	$354	$456	$506	$557	$608	$658	$709	$750	$1,013	$1,266	$1,519
8.25%	$371	$477	$530	$583	$636	$689	$742	$795	$1,061	$1,326	$1,591
8.50%	$388	$499	$554	$600	$665	$720	$776	$831	$1,108	$1,385	$1,662
9.00%	$421	$541	$601	$662	$722	$782	$842	$902	$1,203	$1,504	$1,804
9.50%	$454	$584	$648	$713	$778	$843	$908	$973	$1,297	$1,621	$1,945
10.00%	$487	$626	$695	$765	$834	$904	$973	$1,043	$1,390	$1,738	$2,086

36 Months Loan Amount

Normal Rate	$7,000	$9,000	$10,000	$11,000	$12,000	$13,000	$14,000	$15,000	$20,000	$25,000	$30,000
6.00%	$319	$400	$455	$501	$546	$592	$637	$683	$910	$1,138	$1,366
6.50%	$368	$473	$526	$578	$631	$684	$736	$789	$1,052	$1,315	$1,578
7.00%	$417	$536	$596	$655	$715	$775	$834	$894	$1,192	$1,480	$1,788
7.50%	$466	$599	$665	$732	$798	$865	$931	$998	$1,330	$1,663	$1,995
7.75%	$480	$620	$690	$769	$839	$909	$979	$1,049	$1,399	$1,749	$2,099
8.00%	$514	$660	$734	$807	$880	$954	$1,027	$1,101	$1,467	$1,834	$2,201
8.25%	$537	$691	$768	$845	$921	$998	$1,075	$1,152	$1,535	$1,919	$2,303
8.50%	$561	$721	$802	$882	$962	$1,042	$1,122	$1,202	$1,603	$2,004	$2,405
9.00%	$608	$782	$869	$956	$1,042	$1,129	$1,216	$1,303	$1,737	$2,172	$2,606
9.50%	$655	$842	$935	$1,029	$1,122	$1,216	$1,309	$1,403	$1,870	$2,338	$2,806
10.00%	$701	$901	$1,001	$1,101	$1,201	$1,301	$1,401	$1,502	$2,002	$2,503	$3,003

36 Months Loan Amount

Normal Rate	$7,000	$9,000	$10,000	$11,000	$12,000	$13,000	$14,000	$15,000	$20,000	$25,000	$30,000
6.00%	$416	$535	$594	$653	$713	$772	$832	$891	$1,188	$1,485	$1,782
6.50%	$470	$617	$685	$754	$822	$891	$959	$1,028	$1,370	$1,713	$2,055
7.00%	$543	$698	$775	$853	$930	$1,008	$1,085	$1,163	$1,550	$1,938	$2,325
7.50%	$605	$777	$864	$950	$1,037	$1,123	$1,209	$1,296	$1,728	$2,150	$2,592
7.75%	$635	$817	$908	$999	$1,089	$1,180	$1,271	$1,362	$1,816	$2,260	$2,723
8.00%	$666	$856	$951	$1,047	$1,142	$1,237	$1,332	$1,427	$1,903	$2,379	$2,854
8.25%	$696	$895	$995	$1,094	$1,194	$1,293	$1,393	$1,492	$1,980	$2,487	$2,984
8.50%	$727	$934	$1,038	$1,142	$1,245	$1,349	$1,453	$1,557	$2,076	$2,595	$3,114
9.00%	$786	$1,011	$1,123	$1,235	$1,348	$1,460	$1,572	$1,685	$2,246	$2,808	$3,369
9.50%	$845	$1,087	$1,207	$1,328	$1,449	$1,569	$1,690	$1,811	$2,414	$3,018	$3,622
10.00%	$903	$1,161	$1,290	$1,419	$1,548	$1,677	$1,806	$1,935	$2,581	$3,226	$3,871

Appendix J *continued*

Discount Financing

This appendix will show you the dollar value of a discount financing "deal." To use this table, you need to know the "discounted" interest rate, the length and amount of the loan, and the interest rate you would normally pay. If need be, you can estimate any of the above.

To use the tables:
1. Choose the chart on this page or on the pages preceding or following to compare discount financing rates from 1.9% to 8.9%.
2. Choose one of the following payment terms.

3.90% Discount Interest Rate

24 Months Loan Amount

Normal Rate	$7,000	$9,000	$10,000	$11,000	$12,000	$13,000	$14,000	$15,000	$20,000	$25,000	$30,000
6.00%	$148	$191	$212	$233	$255	$276	$297	$318	$424	$530	$636
6.50%	$183	$236	$262	$288	$314	$340	$366	$393	$523	$654	$785
7.00%	$218	$270	$311	$342	$373	$404	$435	$466	$622	$777	$933
7.50%	$252	$324	$350	$396	$432	$468	$504	$530	$710	$890	$1,079
7.75%	$269	$346	$384	$423	$461	$499	$538	$576	$768	$960	$1,152
8.00%	$286	$368	$408	$449	$490	$531	$572	$613	$817	$1,021	$1,225
8.25%	$303	$389	$432	$476	$519	$562	$605	$649	$865	$1,081	$1,297
8.50%	$310	$411	$457	$502	$548	$594	$639	$685	$913	$1,141	$1,360
9.00%	$353	$454	$504	$555	$605	$656	$706	$757	$1,009	$1,261	$1,513
9.50%	$386	$497	$552	$607	$662	$717	$773	$828	$1,104	$1,370	$1,656
10.00%	$419	$539	$599	$659	$719	$779	$839	$899	$1,198	$1,498	$1,797

36 Months Loan Amount

Normal Rate	$7,000	$9,000	$10,000	$11,000	$12,000	$13,000	$14,000	$15,000	$20,000	$25,000	$30,000
6.00%	$217	$279	$300	$341	$372	$403	$434	$465	$610	$774	$929
6.50%	$267	$343	$382	$410	$458	$496	$534	$572	$763	$954	$1,145
7.00%	$317	$407	$453	$498	$543	$588	$634	$679	$905	$1,132	$1,358
7.50%	$366	$471	$523	$575	$628	$670	$732	$784	$1,046	$1,307	$1,569
7.75%	$390	$502	$558	$614	$669	$725	$781	$837	$1,116	$1,395	$1,674
8.00%	$415	$533	$593	$652	$711	$770	$820	$889	$1,185	$1,481	$1,778
8.25%	$439	$564	$627	$680	$753	$815	$878	$941	$1,254	$1,568	$1,881
8.50%	$463	$595	$661	$728	$794	$850	$926	$992	$1,323	$1,654	$1,984
9.00%	$511	$657	$720	$803	$876	$949	$1,021	$1,094	$1,459	$1,824	$2,189
9.50%	$558	$717	$797	$877	$957	$1,036	$1,116	$1,196	$1,594	$1,993	$2,391
10.00%	$605	$778	$864	$950	$1,037	$1,123	$1,200	$1,296	$1,728	$2,150	$2,592

48 Months Loan Amount

Normal Rate	$7,000	$9,000	$10,000	$11,000	$12,000	$13,000	$14,000	$15,000	$20,000	$25,000	$30,000
6.00%	$283	$364	$405	$445	$486	$526	$567	$607	$800	$1,012	$1,214
6.50%	$348	$448	$498	$548	$597	$647	$697	$747	$996	$1,245	$1,494
7.00%	$413	$531	$580	$649	$708	$767	$825	$884	$1,179	$1,474	$1,769
7.50%	$476	$612	$680	$748	$816	$884	$952	$1,020	$1,360	$1,700	$2,040
7.75%	$507	$652	$725	$797	$860	$942	$1,015	$1,087	$1,440	$1,812	$2,175
8.00%	$539	$693	$760	$846	$923	$1,000	$1,077	$1,154	$1,539	$1,924	$2,309
8.25%	$560	$732	$814	$895	$976	$1,058	$1,139	$1,221	$1,627	$2,034	$2,441
8.50%	$600	$772	$858	$943	$1,029	$1,115	$1,201	$1,286	$1,715	$2,144	$2,573
9.00%	$661	$850	$945	$1,039	$1,134	$1,228	$1,322	$1,417	$1,889	$2,362	$2,834
9.50%	$721	$927	$1,030	$1,133	$1,237	$1,330	$1,443	$1,546	$2,061	$2,576	$3,091
10.00%	$781	$1,004	$1,115	$1,227	$1,338	$1,440	$1,561	$1,673	$2,230	$2,788	$3,345

3. Read across the top row, "Loan Amount," and find the dollar figure that is closest to the actual amount that you are financing.
4. Read down the column to the row corresponding to your normal, non-discounted interest rate.

5. The figure in the intersection is the dollar value of your discount financing arrangement. Compare this figure to any "cash rebate" offered. If the rebate amount is higher, choose the rebate. If the rebate amount is lower, choose the discount financing.

4.90% Discount Interest Rate

24 Months Loan Amount

Normal Rate	$7,000	$9,000	$10,000	$11,000	$12,000	$13,000	$14,000	$15,000	$20,000	$25,000	$30,000
6.00%	$78	$100	$111	$123	$134	$145	$156	$167	$223	$279	$334
6.50%	$113	$145	$162	$178	$194	$210	$226	$242	$323	$404	$485
7.00%	$148	$190	$211	$232	$254	$275	$296	$317	$423	$528	$634
7.50%	$182	$235	$261	$287	$313	$339	$365	$391	$521	$652	$782
7.75%	$190	$257	$285	$314	$342	$371	$399	$428	$570	$713	$856
8.00%	$217	$279	$300	$341	$372	$403	$434	$465	$619	$774	$929
8.25%	$234	$301	$334	$367	$401	$434	$468	$501	$668	$835	$1,002
8.50%	$251	$323	$358	$394	$430	$466	$502	$538	$717	$896	$1,075
9.00%	$285	$366	$407	$447	$488	$529	$569	$610	$813	$1,017	$1,220
9.50%	$318	$409	$455	$500	$546	$591	$637	$682	$909	$1,137	$1,364
10.00%	$352	$452	$502	$553	$603	$653	$703	$754	$1,005	$1,256	$1,507

36 Months Loan Amount

Normal Rate	$7,000	$9,000	$10,000	$11,000	$12,000	$13,000	$14,000	$15,000	$20,000	$25,000	$30,000
6.00%	$114	$147	$163	$179	$196	$212	$228	$245	$326	$408	$489
6.50%	$165	$212	$236	$259	$283	$307	$330	$354	$472	$580	$708
7.00%	$216	$277	$308	$339	$360	$400	$431	$462	$616	$770	$924
7.50%	$266	$341	$379	$417	$455	$493	$531	$569	$759	$949	$1,138
7.75%	$290	$373	$415	$456	$498	$539	$581	$622	$820	$1,037	$1,244
8.00%	$315	$405	$450	$495	$540	$585	$630	$675	$900	$1,125	$1,350
8.25%	$330	$437	$485	$534	$582	$631	$679	$728	$970	$1,213	$1,455
8.50%	$364	$468	$520	$572	$624	$676	$728	$780	$1,040	$1,300	$1,560
9.00%	$412	$530	$589	$648	$707	$766	$825	$884	$1,178	$1,473	$1,768
9.50%	$460	$592	$658	$724	$789	$855	$921	$987	$1,315	$1,644	$1,973
10.00%	$508	$653	$726	$798	$871	$943	$1,016	$1,088	$1,451	$1,814	$2,177

48 Months Loan Amount

Normal Rate	$7,000	$9,000	$10,000	$11,000	$12,000	$13,000	$14,000	$15,000	$20,000	$25,000	$30,000
6.00%	$149	$192	$213	$235	$256	$277	$299	$310	$427	$533	$630
6.50%	$216	$277	$308	$339	$360	$401	$432	$462	$616	$771	$925
7.00%	$281	$362	$402	$442	$482	$522	$563	$603	$804	$1,005	$1,205
7.50%	$346	$445	$494	$544	$593	$642	$692	$741	$988	$1,235	$1,483
7.75%	$378	$486	$530	$594	$648	$702	$756	$800	$1,070	$1,340	$1,610
8.00%	$400	$527	$585	$644	$702	$761	$819	$878	$1,171	$1,463	$1,756
8.25%	$441	$567	$630	$693	$756	$810	$883	$946	$1,261	$1,576	$1,891
8.50%	$473	$608	$675	$743	$810	$878	$945	$1,013	$1,350	$1,688	$2,026
9.00%	$535	$688	$764	$840	$917	$993	$1,069	$1,146	$1,528	$1,900	$2,292
9.50%	$596	$766	$851	$937	$1,022	$1,107	$1,192	$1,277	$1,703	$2,129	$2,554
10.00%	$656	$844	$938	$1,032	$1,125	$1,219	$1,313	$1,407	$1,876	$2,345	$2,813

Appendix J *continued*

This appendix will show you the dollar value of a discount financing "deal." To use this table, you need to know the "discounted" interest rate, the length and amount of the loan, and the interest rate you would normally pay. If need be, you can estimate any of the above.

Discount Financing

To use the tables:
1. Choose the chart on this page or on the previous pages to compare discount financing rates from 1.9% to 8.9%.
2. Choose one of the following payment terms.

5.90% Discount Interest Rate

24 Months Loan Amount

Normal Rate	$7,000	$9,000	$10,000	$11,000	$12,000	$13,000	$14,000	$15,000	$20,000	$25,000	$30,000
7.00%	$78	$90	$111	$122	$133	$144	$155	$167	$222	$278	$333
7.25%	$95	$122	$136	$140	$163	$177	$190	$204	$272	$330	$408
7.50%	$113	$145	$161	$177	$193	$209	$225	$241	$322	$402	$483
7.75%	$120	$167	$186	$204	$223	$241	$250	$279	$371	$464	$557
8.00%	$147	$189	$210	$231	$253	$274	$295	$316	$421	$526	$631
8.25%	$165	$212	$235	$259	$282	$306	$329	$353	$470	$588	$705
8.50%	$182	$234	$250	$286	$312	$338	$363	$389	$519	$649	$779
9.00%	$216	$278	$308	$339	$370	$401	$432	$463	$617	$771	$925
9.50%	$240	$321	$357	$393	$428	$464	$490	$535	$714	$892	$1,071
10.00%	$284	$365	$405	$446	$486	$527	$567	$608	$810	$1,013	$1,215
10.50%	$317	$408	$453	$498	$544	$589	$634	$679	$906	$1,132	$1,359

36 Months Loan Amount

Normal Rate	$7,000	$9,000	$10,000	$11,000	$12,000	$13,000	$14,000	$15,000	$20,000	$25,000	$30,000
7.00%	$113	$146	$162	$178	$194	$211	$227	$243	$324	$405	$486
7.25%	$139	$179	$198	$218	$238	$258	$278	$298	$397	$496	$595
7.50%	$164	$211	$235	$258	$281	$305	$328	$352	$469	$586	$704
7.75%	$189	$243	$270	$298	$325	$352	$379	$406	$541	$676	$811
8.00%	$214	$276	$306	$337	$368	$398	$429	$459	$613	$766	$919
8.25%	$239	$308	$342	$376	$410	$444	$479	$513	$684	$855	$1,026
8.50%	$264	$330	$377	$415	$453	$490	$528	$566	$755	$943	$1,132
9.00%	$313	$403	$448	$492	$537	$582	$627	$671	$895	$1,119	$1,343
9.50%	$362	$465	$517	$569	$620	$672	$724	$776	$1,034	$1,293	$1,551
10.00%	$410	$527	$586	$644	$703	$762	$820	$879	$1,172	$1,465	$1,758
10.50%	$458	$589	$654	$719	$785	$850	$916	$981	$1,308	$1,635	$1,962

48 Months Loan Amount

Normal Rate	$7,000	$9,000	$10,000	$11,000	$12,000	$13,000	$14,000	$15,000	$20,000	$25,000	$30,000
7.00%	$148	$191	$212	$233	$254	$275	$296	$318	$423	$529	$635
7.25%	$181	$233	$259	$285	$311	$337	$363	$388	$518	$647	$777
7.50%	$214	$275	$306	$337	$367	$398	$428	$459	$612	$765	$918
7.75%	$247	$317	$353	$388	$423	$458	$494	$529	$705	$881	$1,058
8.00%	$279	$359	$399	$439	$479	$519	$558	$598	$798	$997	$1,197
8.25%	$311	$400	$445	$489	$534	$578	$623	$667	$880	$1,112	$1,335
8.50%	$343	$441	$491	$530	$589	$638	$687	$736	$981	$1,226	$1,472
9.00%	$407	$523	$581	$639	$697	$755	$813	$872	$1,162	$1,453	$1,743
9.50%	$469	$603	$670	$737	$804	$871	$938	$1,005	$1,341	$1,676	$2,011
10.00%	$531	$683	$758	$834	$910	$986	$1,062	$1,138	$1,517	$1,896	$2,275
10.50%	$592	$761	$845	$920	$1,014	$1,099	$1,183	$1,268	$1,691	$2,113	$2,536

3. Read across the top row, "Loan Amount," and find the dollar figure that is closest to the actual amount that you are financing.
4. Read down the column to the row corresponding to your normal, non-discounted interest rate.

5. The figure in the intersection is the dollar value of your discount financing arrangement. Compare this figure to any "cash rebate" offered. If the rebate amount is higher, choose the rebate. If the rebate amount is lower, choose the discount financing.

6.90% Discount Interest Rate

24 Months Loan Amount

Normal Rate	$7,000	$9,000	$10,000	$11,000	$12,000	$13,000	$14,000	$15,000	$20,000	$25,000	$30,000
7.00%	$7	$9	$10	$11	$12	$13	$14	$15	$20	$25	$30
7.25%	$25	$32	$35	$39	$42	$46	$40	$53	$71	$88	$106
7.50%	$42	$54	$61	$67	$73	$79	$85	$91	$121	$151	$182
7.75%	$50	$77	$86	$94	$103	$111	$110	$128	$171	$214	$257
8.00%	$77	$90	$111	$122	$133	$144	$155	$166	$221	$276	$332
8.25%	$95	$122	$135	$149	$163	$176	$180	$203	$271	$339	$406
8.50%	$112	$144	$160	$176	$192	$208	$224	$240	$320	$401	$481
9.00%	$147	$189	$200	$231	$252	$272	$293	$314	$419	$524	$629
9.50%	$181	$233	$259	$284	$310	$336	$362	$388	$517	$646	$776
10.00%	$215	$276	$307	$338	$369	$399	$430	$461	$614	$768	$922
10.50%	$249	$310	$356	$391	$427	$462	$498	$533	$711	$889	$1,067

36 Months Loan Amount

Normal Rate	$7,000	$9,000	$10,000	$11,000	$12,000	$13,000	$14,000	$15,000	$20,000	$25,000	$30,000
7.00%	$10	$13	$15	$16	$18	$19	$21	$22	$20	$37	$44
7.25%	$36	$47	$52	$57	$62	$67	$72	$78	$103	$129	$155
7.50%	$62	$70	$88	$97	$106	$115	$124	$133	$177	$221	$265
7.75%	$87	$112	$125	$137	$140	$162	$175	$187	$240	$312	$375
8.00%	$113	$145	$161	$177	$193	$209	$226	$242	$322	$403	$483
8.25%	$138	$178	$197	$217	$237	$256	$276	$296	$395	$493	$592
8.50%	$163	$200	$233	$257	$270	$303	$326	$340	$466	$583	$690
9.00%	$213	$274	$305	$335	$365	$396	$426	$457	$609	$761	$914
9.50%	$263	$338	$375	$413	$450	$488	$525	$563	$750	$938	$1,125
10.00%	$311	$400	$445	$489	$534	$578	$623	$667	$880	$1,112	$1,335
10.50%	$350	$463	$514	$566	$617	$668	$710	$771	$1,028	$1,285	$1,542

48 Months Loan Amount

Normal Rate	$7,000	$9,000	$10,000	$11,000	$12,000	$13,000	$14,000	$15,000	$20,000	$25,000	$30,000
7.00%	$14	$17	$19	$21	$23	$25	$27	$29	$39	$48	$58
7.25%	$47	$61	$68	$74	$81	$88	$95	$101	$135	$169	$203
7.50%	$81	$104	$115	$127	$138	$150	$162	$173	$231	$289	$346
7.75%	$114	$147	$163	$179	$196	$212	$228	$244	$326	$407	$489
8.00%	$147	$189	$210	$231	$252	$273	$294	$315	$420	$525	$630
8.25%	$170	$231	$257	$283	$308	$334	$350	$386	$514	$643	$771
8.50%	$213	$273	$304	$334	$364	$395	$425	$455	$607	$759	$911
9.00%	$277	$356	$396	$435	$475	$515	$554	$594	$792	$980	$1,188
9.50%	$341	$438	$487	$536	$584	$633	$682	$730	$974	$1,217	$1,461
10.00%	$404	$519	$577	$634	$692	$740	$807	$865	$1,153	$1,442	$1,730
10.50%	$466	$599	$665	$732	$798	$865	$931	$998	$1,331	$1,663	$1,996

Appendix J *continued*

This appendix will show you the dollar value of a discount financing "deal." To use this table, you need to know the "discounted" interest rate, the length and amount of the loan, and the interest rate you would normally pay. If need be, you can estimate any of the above.

Discount Financing

To use the tables:
1. Choose the chart on this page or on the previous pages to compare discount financing rates from 1.9% to 8.9%.
2. Choose one of the following payment terms.

7.90% Discount Interest Rate

24 Months Loan Amount

Normal Rate	$7,000	$9,000	$10,000	$11,000	$12,000	$13,000	$14,000	$15,000	$20,000	$25,000	$30,000
9.00%	$77	$99	$110	$121	$132	$143	$154	$165	$220	$275	$330
9.10%	$91	$117	$120	$143	$156	$169	$182	$195	$250	$325	$380
9.40%	$105	$135	$140	$165	$170	$195	$200	$225	$299	$374	$449
9.60%	$119	$153	$169	$186	$203	$220	$237	$254	$339	$424	$508
9.80%	$132	$170	$189	$208	$227	$246	$265	$284	$378	$473	$567
10.00%	$146	$188	$209	$220	$250	$271	$292	$313	$417	$522	$626
10.10%	$150	$205	$228	$251	$274	$297	$310	$342	$457	$571	$685
10.30%	$173	$223	$248	$273	$297	$322	$347	$372	$496	$610	$743
10.50%	$187	$241	$267	$294	$321	$347	$374	$401	$535	$668	$802
10.70%	$201	$258	$287	$315	$344	$373	$401	$420	$573	$717	$850
11.00%	$214	$275	$306	$337	$367	$398	$428	$459	$612	$765	$918

36 Months Loan Amount

Normal Rate	$7,000	$9,000	$10,000	$11,000	$12,000	$13,000	$14,000	$15,000	$20,000	$25,000	$30,000
9.00%	$112	$144	$160	$176	$192	$208	$224	$240	$320	$401	$481
9.10%	$132	$170	$189	$208	$227	$246	$265	$283	$378	$472	$567
9.40%	$152	$196	$218	$239	$261	$283	$305	$326	$435	$544	$653
9.60%	$172	$221	$246	$271	$295	$310	$345	$369	$492	$615	$738
9.80%	$192	$247	$274	$302	$329	$357	$384	$412	$549	$686	$823
10.00%	$212	$272	$303	$333	$363	$394	$424	$454	$606	$757	$908
10.10%	$232	$298	$331	$364	$397	$430	$463	$496	$662	$827	$993
10.30%	$251	$323	$359	$395	$431	$467	$503	$538	$718	$897	$1,077
10.50%	$271	$348	$387	$426	$464	$503	$542	$580	$774	$967	$1,161
10.70%	$290	$373	$415	$456	$498	$539	$581	$622	$829	$1,037	$1,244
11.00%	$300	$398	$442	$487	$531	$575	$619	$664	$885	$1,106	$1,327

48 Months Loan Amount

Normal Rate	$7,000	$9,000	$10,000	$11,000	$12,000	$13,000	$14,000	$15,000	$20,000	$25,000	$30,000
9.00%	$146	$188	$209	$229	$250	$271	$292	$313	$417	$521	$626
9.10%	$172	$221	$246	$270	$295	$310	$344	$369	$492	$615	$738
9.40%	$198	$255	$283	$311	$339	$368	$396	$424	$566	$707	$849
9.60%	$224	$288	$310	$352	$384	$416	$448	$470	$630	$799	$959
9.80%	$240	$321	$356	$392	$428	$463	$499	$535	$713	$891	$1,069
10.00%	$275	$354	$393	$432	$472	$511	$550	$589	$786	$982	$1,179
10.10%	$300	$386	$429	$472	$515	$558	$601	$644	$858	$1,073	$1,288
10.30%	$326	$419	$465	$512	$558	$605	$651	$698	$931	$1,163	$1,396
10.50%	$351	$451	$501	$551	$601	$652	$702	$752	$1,002	$1,253	$1,504
10.70%	$376	$483	$537	$591	$644	$698	$752	$805	$1,074	$1,342	$1,611
11.00%	$401	$515	$572	$620	$687	$744	$801	$859	$1,145	$1,431	$1,717

3. Read across the top row, "Loan Amount," and find the dollar figure that is closest to the actual amount that you are financing.
4. Read down the column to the row corresponding to your normal, non-discounted interest rate.

5. The figure in the intersection is the dollar value of your discount financing arrangement. Compare this figure to any "cash rebate" offered. If the rebate amount is higher, choose the rebate. If the rebate amount is lower, choose the discount financing.

8.90% Discount Interest Rate

24 Months Loan Amount

Normal Rate	$7,000	$9,000	$10,000	$11,000	$12,000	$13,000	$14,000	$15,000	$20,000	$25,000	$30,000
9.00%	$7	$9	$10	$11	$12	$13	$14	$15	$20	$25	$30
9.10%	$21	$27	$30	$33	$36	$39	$42	$45	$60	$75	$90
9.40%	$35	$45	$50	$55	$60	$65	$70	$75	$100	$125	$150
9.60%	$49	$63	$60	$77	$84	$91	$98	$105	$130	$175	$200
9.80%	$63	$81	$80	$99	$108	$117	$126	$135	$170	$225	$260
10.00%	$77	$99	$100	$121	$132	$143	$154	$164	$219	$274	$329
10.10%	$91	$116	$129	$142	$155	$168	$181	$194	$259	$324	$388
10.30%	$104	$134	$149	$164	$179	$194	$209	$224	$298	$373	$447
10.50%	$118	$152	$169	$186	$203	$219	$236	$253	$338	$422	$506
10.70%	$132	$160	$188	$207	$226	$245	$264	$283	$377	$471	$565
11.00%	$146	$187	$208	$229	$249	$270	$291	$312	$416	$510	$624

36 Months Loan Amount

Normal Rate	$7,000	$9,000	$10,000	$11,000	$12,000	$13,000	$14,000	$15,000	$20,000	$25,000	$30,000
9.00%	$10	$13	$15	$16	$18	$19	$20	$22	$29	$37	$44
9.10%	$31	$39	$44	$48	$53	$57	$61	$66	$88	$109	$131
9.40%	$51	$66	$73	$80	$87	$95	$102	$109	$146	$182	$219
9.60%	$71	$92	$102	$112	$122	$132	$142	$153	$204	$254	$305
9.80%	$91	$118	$131	$144	$157	$160	$183	$196	$261	$326	$392
10.00%	$112	$143	$159	$175	$191	$207	$223	$239	$319	$398	$478
10.10%	$132	$169	$188	$207	$225	$244	$263	$282	$376	$460	$564
10.30%	$151	$195	$216	$238	$250	$281	$303	$324	$433	$541	$649
10.50%	$171	$220	$245	$269	$294	$318	$343	$367	$489	$612	$734
10.70%	$191	$246	$273	$300	$327	$355	$382	$409	$546	$682	$819
11.00%	$211	$271	$301	$331	$361	$391	$421	$452	$602	$753	$903

48 Months Loan Amount

Normal Rate	$7,000	$9,000	$10,000	$11,000	$12,000	$13,000	$14,000	$15,000	$20,000	$25,000	$30,000
9.00%	$13	$17	$19	$21	$23	$25	$27	$29	$38	$48	$57
9.10%	$30	$51	$57	$63	$68	$74	$70	$86	$114	$143	$171
9.40%	$66	$85	$95	$104	$114	$123	$133	$142	$180	$237	$285
9.60%	$93	$119	$132	$146	$159	$172	$185	$199	$265	$331	$397
9.80%	$119	$153	$160	$187	$204	$221	$238	$255	$330	$425	$509
10.00%	$145	$186	$207	$228	$248	$269	$280	$310	$414	$517	$621
10.10%	$171	$210	$244	$268	$293	$317	$342	$366	$488	$600	$732
10.30%	$197	$253	$281	$309	$337	$365	$393	$421	$562	$702	$842
10.50%	$222	$286	$317	$349	$381	$413	$444	$476	$635	$793	$952
10.70%	$248	$318	$354	$389	$425	$450	$495	$531	$708	$884	$1,061
11.00%	$273	$351	$380	$429	$468	$507	$546	$585	$770	$975	$1,160

Index

Page	Vehicle	Manufacturer	Page	Vehicle	Manufacturer
99	626 LX (S, 4 dr)	Mazda	72	Accord EX (C, 2 dr)	Honda
99	626 LX V-6 (S, 4 dr)	Mazda	72	Accord LX V-6 (C, 2 dr)	Honda
100	626 ES (S, 4 dr)	Mazda	73	Accord EX V-6 (C, 2 dr)	Honda
100	626 ES V-6 (S, 4 dr)	Mazda	73	Accord DX (S, 4 dr)	Honda
159	911 Carrera (C, 2 dr)	Porsche	74	Accord LX (S, 4 dr)	Honda
159	911 Carrera Cabriolet (CN, 2 dr)	Porsche	74	Accord EX (S, 4 dr)	Honda
121	3000GT (C, 2 dr)	Mitsubishi	75	Accord LX V-6 (S, 4 dr)	Honda
121	3000GT SL (C, 2 dr)	Mitsubishi	75	Accord EX V-6 (S, 4 dr)	Honda
122	3000GT VR-4 (C, 4WD, 2 dr)	Mitsubishi	135	Alero GX (C, 2 dr)	Oldsmobile
12	318 ti (H, 2 dr)	BMW	135	Alero GL (C, 2 dr)	Oldsmobile
13	323 iS (C, 2 dr)	BMW	136	Alero GLS (C, 2 dr)	Oldsmobile
13	323 iC (CN, 2 dr)	BMW	136	Alero GX (S, 4 dr)	Oldsmobile
14	323 i (S, 4 dr)	BMW	137	Alero GL (S, 4 dr)	Oldsmobile
14	328 iS (C, 2 dr)	BMW	137	Alero GLS (S, 4 dr)	Oldsmobile
15	328 iC (CN, 2 dr)	BMW	130	Altima XE (S, 4 dr)	Nissan
15	328 i (S, 4 dr)	BMW	130	Altima GXE (S, 4 dr)	Nissan
16	M3 (CN, 2 dr)	BMW	131	Altima SE (S, 4 dr)	Nissan
16	M3 (C, 2 dr)	BMW	131	Altima GLE (S, 4 dr)	Nissan
17	528 i (S, 4 dr)	BMW	138	Aurora (S, 4 dr)	Oldsmobile
17	528 i T (W, 4 dr)	BMW	179	Avalon XL (S, 4 dr)	Toyota
18	540 i (S, 4 dr)	BMW	180	Avalon XLS (S, 4 dr)	Toyota
18	540 i T (W, 4 dr)	BMW	55	Avenger (C, 2 dr)	Dodge
19	740 i (S, 4 dr)	BMW	56	Avenger ES (C, 2 dr)	Dodge
19	740 iL (S, 4 dr)	BMW	187	Beetle GL (H, 2 dr)	Volkswagen
20	750 iL (S, 4 dr)	BMW	187	Beetle GLS (H, 2 dr)	Volkswagen
160	9-3 (H, 2 dr)	Saab	146	Bonneville SE (S, 4 dr)	Pontiac
161	9-3 (H, 4 dr)	Saab	146	Bonneville SSE (S, 4 dr)	Pontiac
161	9-3 SE (H, 4 dr)	Saab	160	Boxster (CN, 2 dr)	Porsche
162	9-3 (CN, 2 dr)	Saab	143	Breeze (S, 4 dr)	Plymouth
162	9-3 SE (CN, 2 dr)	Saab	104	C230 Kompressor (S, 4 dr)	Mercedes-Benz
163	9-5 (S, 4 dr)	Saab	104	C280 (S, 4 dr)	Mercedes-Benz
163	9-5 SE (S, 4 dr)	Saab	105	C43 (S, 4 dr)	Mercedes-Benz
164	9-5 V6 (S, 4 dr)	Saab	196	C70 (C, 2 dr)	Volvo
164	9-5 SE V6 (S, 4 dr)	Saab	197	C70 (CN, 2 dr)	Volvo
7	A4 1.8T (S, 4 dr)	Audi	188	Cabrio (CN, 2 dr)	Volkswagen
7	A4 1.8T Quattro (S, 4WD, 4 dr)	Audi	188	Cabrio GLS (CN, 2 dr)	Volkswagen
8	A4 2.8 (S, 4 dr)	Audi	31	Camaro (C, 2 dr)	Chevrolet
8	A4 2.8 Quattro (S, 4WD, 4 dr)	Audi	32	Camaro Z28 (C, 2 dr)	Chevrolet
9	A4 1.8T Avant Quattro (W, 4WD, 4 dr)	Audi	32	Camaro (CN, 2 dr)	Chevrolet
9	A4 2.8 Avant Quattro (W, 4WD, 4 dr)	Audi	33	Camaro Z28 (CN, 2 dr)	Chevrolet
10	A6 (S, 4 dr)	Audi	180	Camry Solara SE (C, 2 dr)	Toyota
10	A6 Quattro (S, 4WD, 4 dr)	Audi	181	Camry Solara SE V6 (C, 2 dr)	Toyota
11	A6 Avant (W, 4WD, 4 dr)	Audi	181	Camry Solara SLE V6 (C, 2 dr)	Toyota
11	A8 3.7 (S, 4 dr)	Audi	182	Camry CE (S, 4 dr)	Toyota
12	A8 4.2 Quattro (S, 4WD, 4 dr)	Audi	182	Camry LE (S, 4 dr)	Toyota
81	Accent L (H, 2 dr)	Hyundai	183	Camry LE V6 (S, 4 dr)	Toyota
82	Accent GS (H, 2 dr)	Hyundai	183	Camry XLE (S, 4 dr)	Toyota
82	Accent GL (S, 4 dr)	Hyundai	184	Camry XLE V6 (S, 4 dr)	Toyota
71	Accord LX (C, 2 dr)	Honda	27	Catera (S, 4 dr)	Cadillac

| H-Hatchback | C-Coupe | S-Sedan | CN-Convertible | 4WD-4-Wheel Drive | W-Wagons |

H-Hatchback	C-Coupe	S-Sedan	CN-Convertible	4WD-4-Wheel Drive	W-Wagons

H-Hatchback	C-Coupe	S-Sedan	CN-Convertible	4WD-4-Wheel Drive	W-Wagons

H-Hatchback   C-Coupe   S-Sedan   CN-Convertible   4WD-4-Wheel Drive   W-Wagons

Need More Facts? - All the Facts?

You need the IntelliChoice comprehensive vehicle report that helps you choose the right vehicle and also helps you negotiate the best price!

Just the Facts™

$14.⁹⁵ → $14.⁹⁵

(VISA, Mastercard, American Express, Discover)

Just-the-Facts is designed for the ready-to-buy car shopper. It provides pricing for all vehicles in a model line-up highlighting the differences among models. Its thoroughness and clarity make it one of the most popular vehicle reports in the United States.

General
▶ Complete model line (up to 6 vehicles) in a single report
▶ Attractive and easy-to-understand
▶ Updated daily
▶ Objective, accurate information from *unbiased* recognized source
▶ Graphically-based, easy-to-read design, and high-quality production
▶ Our computer database is updated DAILY, so pricing is always up-to-date

To order call: 1-800-227-2665

Delivery Choices	Shipping	Price	Delivery
	1st class mail	$14.95	Included
	Express Fax	$14.95 +	$3.00
	For other delivery options, please call		

CA residents add applicable state sales tax

Pricing
▶ Complete price breakdown, including factoy invoice, retail prices, fees, and luxuy and gas-guzzler taxes
▶ Rebates, incentives, discount financing
▶ Dealer Holdback
▶ Competitor model pricing

Ownership Costs Information
What a buyer can expect to pay over a five-year period in the following cost areas:
▶ Depreciation
▶ Fuel
▶ Insurance
▶ State Fees
▶ Financing
▶ Maintenance
▶ Repairs

Now available on the Web at:
www.intellichoice.com

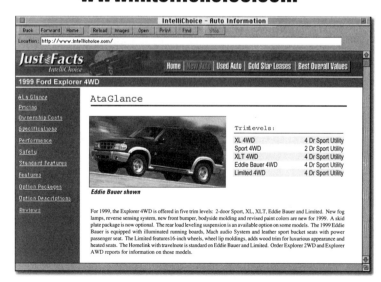

$4.⁹⁵* → $4.⁹⁵*

(VISA, Mastercard, American Express, Discover)

* Includes WindowSticker⁺™, IntelliChoice's powerful new auto configurator, an IntelliChoice exclusive.

Equipment
▶ All available standard and optional equipment

Consumer Information
▶ Safety features
▶ Child Safety features
▶ Performance data
▶ Safety record
▶ Government complaint and theft, collision, and injury indices
▶ Interior and exterior dimensions
▶ Interior and exterior color combinations
▶ Performance tests from *AutoWeek*™ magazine
▶ Reviews from *Automobile*™ magazine
▶ Warranty coverage
▶ Where vehicle is built

Just the Facts™ and WindowSticker⁺™ are a trademark of IntelliChoice, Inc.